classrooms around the world!

$97.05

"The textbook is clearly written and is easy to understand. Interpretation of marketing terms, graphs, images and illustrations make this textbook the first of its kind with respect to the quality in Russian marketing literature. The book is not only addressing students and faculty but also entrepreneurs and managers of the Russian companies."
—President of the Russian Marketing Association

"You can say all good things about the [Berkowitz et al] text…. I would like other textbooks to be like Marketing, first Polish edition. Why? Because it serves its primary purpose — it is easy and interesting to learn from."
—Student, Warsaw School of Economics

"…the Russian sales force is welcoming this new marketing edition [by Kerin et al]. This book will become a practical guide for operations of the marketing department of TZUM (Central Department Store of Moscow)."
—TZUM's General Director

"Good overall package with solid topic coverage and good integration."
—Radford University

MARKETING

CANADIAN 5th EDITION

Eric N. Berkowitz
University of Massachusetts

Frederick G. Crane
QMA Consulting Group Limited

Roger A. Kerin
Southern Methodist University

Steven W. Hartley
University of Denver

William Rudelius
University of St. Thomas

Contributor
Deborah L. Andrus
University of Calgary

McGraw-Hill Ryerson

Toronto   Montréal   Boston   Burr Ridge, IL   Dubuque, IA   Madison, WI   New York
San Francisco   St. Louis   Bangkok   Bogotá   Caracas   Kuala Lumpur   Lisbon   London
Madrid   Mexico City   Milan   New Delhi   Santiago   Seoul   Singapore   Sydney   Taipei

McGraw-Hill
Ryerson Limited

A Subsidiary of The McGraw·Hill Companies

Marketing
Fifth Canadian Edition

ISBN: 0-07-089833-2

3 4 5 6 7 8 9 10   TCP   0 9 8 7 6 5 4

Printed and bound in Canada.

Vice President and Editorial Director: Patrick Ferrier
Sponsoring Editor: James Buchanan
Developmental Editor: Lesley Mann, Sandra de Ruiter
Copy Editor: Kelli Howey
Production Coordinator: Jennifer Wilkie
Photo and Literary Permissions: Alison Derry, Permissions Plus
Marketing Manager: Kim Verhaeghe
Page Layout: Pronk&Associates
Cover Design: Dianna Little
Cover Image Credit: © Hiroyuki Ozaki/Photonica (background), © David Muir/Masterfile (globe); pda on back cover courtesy of Hewlett-Packard

Printer: Transcontinental Printing

National Library of Canada Cataloguing in Publication Data

Marketing / Eric N. Berkowitz ... [et al.]. – 5th Canadian ed.

Includes bibliographical references and index.
ISBN 0-07-089833-2

1. Marketing. 2. Marketing–Canada. I. Berkowitz, Eric N.

HF5415.M293   2002   658.8   C2002-904320-4

BRIEF CONTENTS

CONTENTS

Part 2   Understanding Buyers and Markets   116

Part 4   Satisfying Marketing Opportunities   266

10   DEVELOPING NEW PRODUCTS AND SERVICES   268

PREFACE

Dynamic . . . Exciting . . . Challenging . . . and Surprising! The 21st century is an extraordinary time for instructors, students, and managers to be involved in the field of marketing. Customer Relationship Management (CRM), virtual advertising, multichannel retailing, eCRM, cashless vending, everyday fair pricing, experience marketing, data mining, and brand equity are just a few of the many indications that marketing is racing into a new era. At the same time, many traditional elements of the discipline such as segmentation, new-product development, and pricing are growing in importance and use. The combination of the contemporary and the traditional elements of marketing create a truly exceptional topic to study and understand. We appreciate the opportunity to share our enthusiasm for the field with you and welcome you to your introduction to marketing!

The Fifth Canadian Edition of *Marketing* is the result of a detailed and rigorous development process designed to provide customer value in several ways. First, we continue to use the active-learning approach that has been the foundation of our previous editions. Second, we have incorporated many new examples, tools, and design elements that are consistent with the learning styles of today's students. Third, we have added, deleted, and modified topics and content based on our own expertise and the advice of many knowledgeable reviewers. Finally, we have invested in the most effective of the many evolving educational technologies. Overall, the Fifth Canadian Edition of *Marketing* represents our efforts to guarantee the high quality of previous editions and to continue our tradition of growth and improvement.

We are gratified by the growing interest in our approach to the study of marketing. Feedback from students and instructors continues to reinforce our pedagogical style. We hope that you will enjoy the text and your exploration of the knowledge, skills, and tools of the marketing discipline!

DISTINCTIVE FEATURES OF OUR APPROACH

The innovative pedagogical approach we developed through our own classroom experiences was introduced in the first edition in 1991. While each new edition has offered new content, cases, and examples to reflect changes in the marketing discipline and the marketplace, the distinctive features of our approach have remained as the foundation of the text and the supporting supplements. The features that you may recognize from previous editions and that are prominent in this edition include:

- An easy-to-read, high-involvement, interactive writing style that engages students through active learning techniques, timely and interesting examples, and challenging applications.
- A vivid and accurate description of businesses and marketing professionals— through cases, exercises, and testimonials—that allows students to "personalize" marketing and identify possible career interests and role models.
- The use of extended examples, involving people making marketing decisions, that students can easily relate to text concepts and that emphasize a decision-making orientation.
- Comprehensive and integrated coverage of traditional and contemporary scholarly concepts illustrated through relevant practitioner-related literature.
- A rigorous pedagogical framework based on the use of learning objectives, concept checks, key terms and concepts, chapter summaries, and supportive student supplements such as the Student CD-ROM and Study Guide.

- A package of support materials to accommodate a wide variety of instructor teaching styles and student learning styles.

Feedback from many of the instructors and students who have used our text and package in the past has encouraged us to build on these strengths as we developed the Fifth Canadian Edition of *Marketing*.

NEW AND REVISED CONTENT

- **The Role of the Internet and Technology in Marketing Today:** *Marketing*, Fifth Canadian Edition, recognizes that the Internet and other digital technologies provide us with powerful new tools that can greatly enhance communication and commerce. From cover to cover, *Marketing* integrates coverage of e-Commerce topics such as e-marketplaces, dynamic pricing, viral marketing, permission marketing, personalization, multichannel retailing, eCRM, collaborative filtering, file sharing and peer-to-peer communication, cyberservices, Internet appliances, interactive television, online secondary data sources, and virtual advertising.
- **New Chapter 21: Implementing Interactive and Multichannel Marketing:** This new chapter provides a framework for how to think about and implement marketing strategy in an Internet/Web-enabled marketspace. Emphasis is placed on interactive marketing practice and the growing application of multichannel marketing. Students will also find this chapter of interest because they will see how important it is for companies to forge collaborative channel relationships to improve their global market competitiveness.
- **Consumer Behaviour and Organizational Behaviour Chapters Earlier in Text:** In response to reviewer feedback the global markets chapter has been moved to follow the behaviour chapters allowing earlier coverage of these key chapters (now Chapters 5 and 6).
- **Increased Emphasis on Customer Value and Customer Relationship Management (CRM):** Chapter 1 presents an enhanced emphasis on customer value CRM, the role of brands and how they make firms accountable to consumers, new products, the breadth of marketing and how it is used by many types of organizations, and a complete update of Rollerblade's marketing program.
- **Updated Overview of the Marketing Environment:** Chapter 3 now includes a discussion of Napster's dramatic impact on the music industry; an introduction to current electronic business technologies including the Internet, the World Wide Web and e-Commerce; and the latest demographic and cultural trends affecting the Canadian marketplace.
- **Updated Consumer Behaviour Coverage:** Chapter 5 includes new examples related to the stages of the consumer-decision process; new discussions of customer satisfaction and retention and marketing strategies for high- and low-involvement products; and discussion of Canadian psychographic systems, including the Goldfarb segments and the Thirteen Tribes (Adams).
- **New Organizational Buying Coverage:** Chapter 6 features new sections on online buying in organizational markets, e-marketplaces, and online auctions.
- **Updated Global Markets Coverage:** Chapter 7 includes discussions of the emergence of a networked global marketspace, Canada's competitiveness in the global market, the influence of the World Trade Organization on the global rules of trade between nations, and important differences in the economic infrastructures of China, India, Eastern Europe, and the countries of the former Soviet Union.

- **Expanded Coverage of Marketing Research Technology:** Chapter 8 opens with an exciting example—the *Lord of the Rings* movie trilogy—and introduces up-to-date and comprehensive coverage of online databases and Internet resources. The chapter also includes new discussions of creative research techniques such as ethnographic research, the hiring of "cool hunters" to identify important cultural trends, and new coverage of Internet and fax survey techniques, data mining, and the impact of research on marketing actions.
- **Expanded Segmentation, Positioning, and Customization Material:** Chapter 9 includes coverage of the mass customization of shoes at Customatix.com, Apple's segmentation strategy, the chocolate milk positioning challenge, and updated coverage of product-market grids.
- **Updated Coverage of Brand Equity:** Chapter 11 now includes the Customer-based Brand Equity Pyramid, which helps explain the relationship between brand awareness and how consumers think and feel about a brand. This helps students understand how the added value of a brand name gives a product competitive and price advantage.
- **Updated Services Marketing Material:** Chapter 12 has been updated to include the Eight Ps of services marketing, a framework for managing services. The chapter also introduces the concept of experience marketing.
- **Updated Channels Coverage:** Chapter 15 includes new material and examples related to multiple channels of distribution, strategic alliances, vertical marketing, exclusive distribution, slotting allowances, and satisfying buyer requirements that show students how marketing channels are a necessity as a company builds sustainable market value.
- **Updated Supply Chain and Logistics Coverage:** Chapter 16 features current examples, such as "Dell Computer Corporation: A Responsive Supply Chain," and "Wal-Mart, Inc.: An Efficient Supply Chain," and current topics, such as "Information's Role in Supply Chain Responsiveness and Efficiency." Reverse logistics are used to explain the role of supply chains and logistics management in marketing and how a firm balances distribution costs against the need for effective customer service.
- **Updated Retailing Coverage:** Chapter 17 offers a new discussion of Tim Hortons, a successful retail marketer, updated coverage of the global expansion of many retailers and e-tailers, and popular retail formats such as franchising. In addition, the chapter provides coverage of important new technologies, including cashless vending systems and interactive television shopping, as well as new concepts, such as everyday low pricing and multichannel retailing.
- **Updated Advertising Coverage:** Chapter 19 now includes virtual advertising, interactive television, satellite radio, as well as Internet advertising. Up-to-date examples of the latest forms of promotion, including sweepstakes, product placement, and online coupons are also provided.
- Appendixes C and D have been moved to the Online Learning Centre (OLC) to allow for easy updates.

ORGANIZATION

The Fifth Canadian Edition of *Marketing* is divided into five parts. Part 1, "Initiating the Marketing Process," looks first at what marketing is and how it creates customer value and customer relationships (Chapter 1). Then Chapter 2 provides an overview of the strategic marketing process that occurs in an organization—which provides a framework for the text. Appendix A provides a sample marketing plan as a reference for students. Chapter 3 analyzes the five major environmental factors in our changing marketing environment, while Chapter 4 provides a framework for including ethical and social responsibility considerations in marketing decisions.

Part 2, "Understanding Buyers and Markets," first describes, in Chapter 5, how individual consumers reach buying decisions. Next, Chapter 6 looks at organizational buyers and how they make purchase decisions. And finally, in Chapter 7, the nature and scope of world trade and the influence of cultural differences on global marketing practices are explored.

In Part 3, "Targeting Marketing Opportunities," the marketing research function and how information about prospective consumers is linked to marketing strategy and decisions is discussed in Chapter 8. The process of segmenting and targeting markets and positioning products appears in Chapter 9.

Part 4, "Satisfying Marketing Opportunities," covers the Four Ps—the marketing mix elements. The product element is divided into the natural chronological sequence of first developing new products and services (Chapter 10) and then managing the existing products (Chapter 11) and services (Chapter 12). Pricing is covered in terms of underlying pricing analysis (Chapter 13), followed by actual price setting (Chapter 14), and Appendix B, Financial Aspects of Marketing. Three chapters address the place (distribution) aspects of marketing: Managing Marketing Channels and Wholesaling (Chapter 15), Integrating Supply Chain and Logistics Management (Chapter 16), and Retailing (Chapter 17). Retailing is a separate chapter because of its importance and interest as a career for many of today's students. Promotion is also covered in three chapters. Chapter 18 discusses integrated marketing communications and direct marketing, topics that have grown in importance in the marketing discipline recently. The primary forms of mass market communication—advertising, sales promotion, and public relations—are covered in Chapter 19. Personal selling and sales management is covered in Chapter 20.

Part 5, "Managing the Marketing Process," discusses issues and techniques related to interactive marketing technologies and the strategic marketing process. Chapter 21 describes how interactive technologies influence customer value and the customer experience through context, content, community, customization, connectivity, and commerce. Chapter 22 expands on Chapter 2 to describe specific techniques and issues related to blending the four marketing mix elements to plan, implement, and control marketing programs.

The book closes with a detailed glossary and three indexes (name, company/product, and subject).

ACKNOWLEDGMENTS

To ensure continuous improvement of our product, we have utilized an extensive review and development process for each of the past editions. Building on this history, the Fifth Canadian Edition development process included several phases of evaluation and a variety of stakeholder audiences. The first phase of the review process asked instructors to suggest improvements to the organization of the text and possible changes to the supplements. The second phase encompassed a more detailed analysis of each chapter of the book in terms of its effectiveness for instructors and students.

Reviewers who were vital in terms of helping us make improvements to this edition include:

May Aung
University of Guelph

Pat Brown
Kwantlen University College

Jennifer Daly-Cyr
Algonquin College

Gary Dover
Georgian College

Michael Hockenstein
Vanier College

Ashwin Joshi
York University

Rajesh Manchanda
University of Manitoba

Cindy McPherson
British Columbia Institute of Technology

Paul Myers
St. Clair College

Shelly Rinehart
University of New Brunswick

Janice Shearer
Mohawk College

The business community also provided substantial assistance by making available information that appears in the text and supplements—much of it for the first time in a college or university text. Thanks are due Alberta Health, Bell Mobility, Canadian Press, Canadian Tire, Clearly Canadian Beverage Corporation, Dairy Farmers of Canada, Federation des producteurs d'oeufs de consommation du Quebec, Four Seasons Hotel, Government of Canada, Grocery Gateway, Hard Rock Café-Montreal, Molson Breweries, and the Registered Nurses Association of Ontario.

Thanks to Debi Andrus of the University of Calgary for her contribution to the text, and Barry Potyondi, Context Inc., for his work on CBC video cases, Marcie Sayiner from Ipsos Reid and Dr. Jeff Rabin from Dundee Securities for their assistance in providing valuable proprietary information, as well as the following instructors who worked on the supplements that accompany the text: Gail Tibbo and Gerry Edwards of MarketProbe Market Analysts for their dedicated effort on the Study Guide, Beth Pett of Niagara College for her work on the Instructor's Manual, Rita Cossa, for the updated PowerPoint presentations, Janice Shearer for her work on the *i*ntegrator, Jo-Anne Chow of SAIT for all of the OLC work, and Marianne Marando of George Brown College for the updated Test Bank.

Finally, we acknowledge the professional efforts of the McGraw-Hill Ryerson Higher Education Group staff. Completion of our book and its many supplements required the attention and commitment of many editorial, production, marketing, and research personnel. Thanks to Lenore Gray and James Buchanan, Sponsoring Editors; Kelly Smyth, Marketing Manager; Kelly Dickson, Manager of Editorial Services; Lesley Mann and Sandra de Ruiter, Developmental Editors; Kelli Howey, Copyeditor; and Alison Derry, Permissions Plus, for her photo research.

I am responsible for the Canadianization of this text, so any questions or concerns about the book should be directed to me. I would like to thank my co-authors for their input, encouragement, and continued support.

I am dedicating this book to my beautiful wife, Doreen, whose love is unfailing; to Erinn, Jacquelyn, and Brenna, my scholar-athlete daughters who always make me proud; to my parents; to my best friend Ceilidh; and to God who continues to watch over me.

Frederick G. Crane

A STUDENT'S GUIDE TO MARKETING, 5/C/e

Marketing, 5/C/e offers an array of pedagogical features to help you learn and apply the concepts at hand.

Chapter-Opening Vignettes—Over 70% are new or revised!

Chapter-opening vignettes introduce you to the chapter concepts ahead, using a recognizable and interesting company example. For instance in Chapter 9, the authors use Heelys (a shoe with built-in wheels targeted at skateboard and inline skate enthusiasts) and the segmentation strategies of Reebok, Nike, New Balance, Vans, and others to grab your interest.

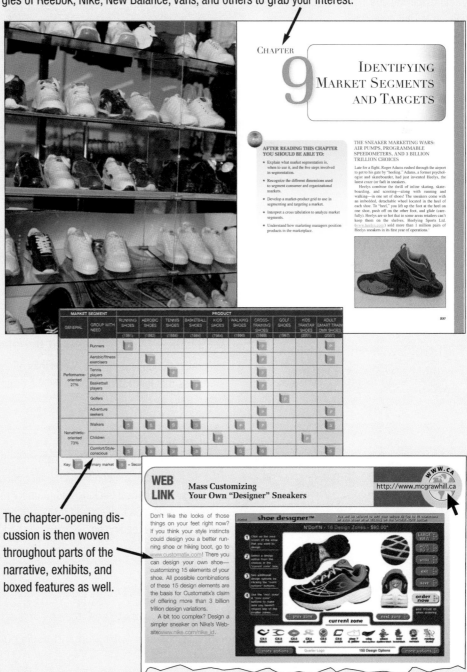

The chapter-opening discussion is then woven throughout parts of the narrative, exhibits, and boxed features as well.

MARKETING NEWSNET

The Multichannel Marketing Multiplier

Multichannel marketing is the blending of different communication and delivery channels that are mutually reinforcing in attracting, retaining, and building relationships with consumers who shop and buy in the traditional marketplace and marketspace. Industry analysts refer to the complementary role of different communication and delivery channels as an "influence effect."

Retailers that integrate and leverage their stores, catalogues, and Websites have seen a sizeable "lift" in yearly sales recorded from individual customers. Canadian Tire is a case in point. Customers who shop in two channels spend more money annually.

To build its multichannel operations and expand its contact list, Canadian Tire launched an online component to the "Big Spender Giveaway" contest in the fall of 2001. A total of $350 000 in merchandise and Canadian Tire money™ was given away to those entering either online or in-store. The online entrants were able to participate in an extra game: looking for the "Big Spender Briefcase" hidden in the site. This is considered one of the most popular online promotions in Canada, attracting 2.5 million visitors to Canadian Tire's Website.

Marketing NewsNet— *70% new or updated!*

This boxed feature provides exciting, current examples of marketing applications in action, organized around the following themes: Technology & E-Commerce, Customer Value, Global, and Cross Functional.

Ethics and Social Responsibility Alert—*Over 50% new or updated!*

These boxes increase your awareness and assessment of current topics of ethical and social concern.

http://www.mcgrawhill.ca

Web Link—*Over 70% new or updated!*

Integrated throughout the text, Web Links encourage you to explore digital strategies that innovative companies and organizations are employing online.

Concept Checks

Found at the end of each major chapter section, these checkpoints offer critical thinking and memory recall questions, helping you reflect on the text and test your comprehension of the material before reading on.

Concept Check

1. How does a product manager help manage a product's life cycle?
2. What does "creating new-use situations" mean in managing a product's life cycle?
3. Explain the difference between trading up and trading down in repositioning.

The Dairy Farmers of Canada conducted three types of marketing research in an effort to solve the decline in milk consumption problem. For details read the text.

Dairy Farmers of Canada
www.dairyfarmers.org

Website Addresses

The URLs of companies and organizations discussed in the text are easily located in the text margin—facilitating further exploration of these real-world examples.

Internet Exercises—*Over 70% new or updated!*

These end-of chapter exercises ask you to go online and think critically about a specific company's use of the Internet—helping you apply your knowledge of key chapter concepts, terms, and topics, as well as evaluate the success or failure of the company's efforts.

INTERNET EXERCISE

www.mcgrawhill.ca/college/berkowitz

As this chapter indicates, online retailing is now part of the Canadian retail landscape. Online retailing presents both opportunities and challenges for Canadian retailers. Go to the Retail Council of Canada Website (www.retailcouncil.org). Click on the E-commerce Overview Series: Retail Trade in Canada. Find "The Canadian Online Retailing Report" prepared by the Boston Consulting Group and the Retail Council of Canada. Read the report. From what you have gleaned from the report answer the following questions.

1 What factors are inhibiting the growth of online retailing in Canada?

2 How are current online retailers in Canada doing when it comes to their business performance?

VIDEO CASE 1–1 Rollerblade, Inc.: Rediscovering Growth

David Samuels, senior director for sports innovation at Rollerblade believes innovative technology—in the form of new and better skates—will continue to be key for Rollerblade to stay ahead of the competition. Rollerblade must also find ways to expand the market for in-line skates. "Our challenge is to provide new venues, new reasons for people to skate. There's a lot of growth for us to catch up on in terms of household penetration," says Samuels.

THE SITUATION TODAY

When Rollerblade was founded, it was the only manufacturer of in-line skates in the world. Today the industry has more than 30 competitors, many that sell lower-priced skates than Rollerblade through mass-merchandising chains. Some of the large sporting goods manufacturers, like Nike, that have not traditionally sold in-line skates are now looking for ways to grow and have entered the in-line skate market.

VIDEO CASE 3–1 Flyte Tyme Productions, Inc.: The Best Idea Wins!

"Terry was looking for a keyboard player to be in the band he was just starting," remembers Jimmy Jam of Flyte Tyme Productions, Inc. "I had sort of rebelled because I had first thought of myself as a drummer," says Jam. But after he listened and heard how good the drummer was, he told Terry, "I'll be the keyboard player."

The conversation took place a few weeks after Terry Lewis and Jimmy Jam met at a summer math program for gifted junior high school students, sponsored by a local university. The two came to prominence in the early 1980s as members of the funk band "The Time," which appeared as the opener on many of Prince's early tours. The pair still credit Prince for much of their tenacious work ethic and eclectic music[...] band, Terry and Jimmy sta[...] company—Flyte Tyme—cre[...] adapting the old one. Now i[...] have worked together for 20[...] Tyme Productions (www.fly[...] clients include Mary J. Bli[...] Carey, Janet Jackson, Micha[...] Usher, TLC, and many others[...]

These and other hits put Flyte Tyme in extraordinary company. Having produced 16 No. 1 singles on *Billboard's* pop chart, they are second only to the[...]

CBC VIDEO CASE 5–1 The Consumer on the Couch

To retailers, there is no more important question than "why do consumers buy?" Understanding the influences that affect purchasing behaviour can spell the difference between commercial success and failure.

Paco Underhill is a New York City–based "retail anthropologist" who has been retained by dozens of top-flight companies, including the Canadian Imperial Bank of Commerce, Burger King, and Calvin Klein, to determine what attracts customers to their locations, what makes them linger, and what makes them spend. His empirical findings, many of which are documented in his *Why We Buy: The Science of Shopping,* are based mainly on analysis of tens of thousands of hours of clandestine videotaping of shoppers in action. Underhill's studies have significantly expanded our understanding of the purchase decision process while raising important questions about the privacy rights of consumers.

SHAPE UP OR SHIP OUT

At las[...] and p[...] positi[...] more[...] more[...] sector[...]

READING THE RETAIL LANDSCAPE

Traditional market research on consumer behaviour has been done through analysis of barcodes scanned at the cash register and from direct surveys of shoppers conducted via telephone, one-on-one interviews, or focus groups. While the resulting data are valuable, rarely do they shed light on the discrepancy between what customers say about the process of making purchasing choices and what they actually do at the store. Consequently, Underhill and like-minded students of shopping are less concerned with what people buy than why they so often fail to buy.

To gain more understanding of shoppers, some retailers have turned to in-store customer surveillance. Using hidden cameras that videotape consumers as they approach, enter, and exit a store, and supplementing that evidence with surreptitious observations by in-store "trackers" who add a more qualitative dimension, retail anthropologists provide micro-level documentation of[...]

PART 1 CASE An Unpredictable Environment: Technology and Beyond

Technological innovation plays a large role in our daily lives. We are surrounded by the results of invention and innovation in products and services we use on a regular basis. Everything from our digital alarm clocks to our cell phones has been made available to us through the advances in technology. The influence of technological advances in the past decade has changed where we purchase products, the value of information in decision-making, and the ability to communicate anywhere, anytime. Technological advances in a variety of industries are changing both consumers and businesses. The quality of our lives has improved in a variety of ways—for example, we are able to eat meals cooked almost instantly in our microwaves. Technology, in its various forms, has touched every aspect of business as well as changed the ways in which products are created, manufactured, and purchased. And it isn't just technological advances that are shaping our lives in significant ways. Since 2000, a number of events have created new demands for businesses as economic, technological, and political changes have taken place in dramatic and often unexpected ways: a new currency, a dangerous downturn in the economy, plans by governments to deregulate[...] and new[...]

inevitable, creating the need for marketing managers to be relentless in understanding implications of changes in all aspects of the environment to identify opportunities and threats.

THE DOT-COM BUBBLE THAT BURST

Like no other technological innovation, the promise of providing more efficient, more cost-effective, and faster processes drove the dot-com fever to an incredibly high pitch. Venture capital was attracted to the potential of huge rewards for a winning application. *Fortune* magazine's cover story on March 20, 2000 was "Doing Business the Dot-Com Way."[2] The bubble burst on the dot-coms in April 2000, when the stock value of Internet pioneers took a dive.[3] At the end of 2000 Pets.com—one of the most famous Internet pioneers—was purchase by Petsmart: even Pets.com's creative advertising icon Sock Puppet could not save the company. Similarly, in February 2001 Petopia.com was acquired by Petco Animal Supplies Inc.[4] It seems that the online pet supply market isn't big enough for more then two or three players.

The dot-com crash was only the beginning of some hard times for companies in the information technology[...]

Video Case Studies

This end-of-chapter feature provides an up-close look at a company example—reinforcing the chapter content, while bringing the material to life! Rollerblade, Flyte Tyme, and Paco Underhill are just a few of the exciting video cases now available with the Fifth Canadian Edition.

Part-Ending Cases

At the end of each part of the text, a linked case examines technological innovation and its impact on the book-selling environment.

Appendix A: Creating an Effective Marketing Plan

Following Chapter 2, this sample marketing plan for Howlin' Coyote Chili provides you with an effective reference early on in the text.

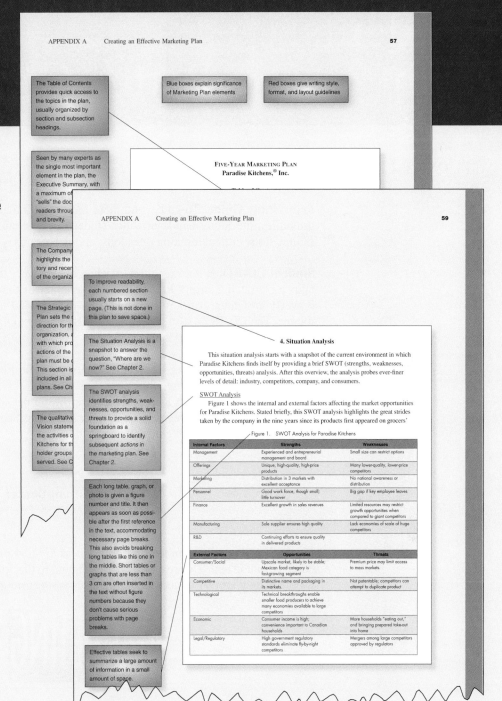

The Table of Contents provides quick access to the topics in the plan, usually organized by section and subsection headings.

Blue boxes explain significance of Marketing Plan elements

Red boxes give writing style, format, and layout guidelines

Seen by many experts as the single most important element in the plan, the Executive Summary, with a maximum of ... "sells" the doc... readers throu... and brevity.

The Company ... highlights the ... tory and recen... of the organiza...

The Strategic ... Plan sets the s... direction for th... organization, ... with which pro... actions of the ... plan must be c... This section is... included in all ... plans. See Ch...

The qualitative... Vision stateme... the activities o... Kitchens for th... holder groups ... served. See C...

FIVE-YEAR MARKETING PLAN
Paradise Kitchens,® Inc.

To improve readability, each numbered section usually starts on a new page. (This is not done in this plan to save space.)

The Situation Analysis is a snapshot to answer the question, "Where are we now?" See Chapter 2.

The SWOT analysis identifies strengths, weaknesses, opportunities, and threats to provide a solid foundation as a springboard to identify subsequent *actions* in the marketing plan. See Chapter 2.

Each long table, graph, or photo is given a figure number and title. It then appears as soon as possible after the first reference in the text, accommodating necessary page breaks. This also avoids breaking long tables like this one in the middle. Short tables or graphs that are less than 3 cm are often inserted in the text without figure numbers because they don't cause serious problems with page breaks.

Effective tables seek to summarize a large amount of information in a small amount of space.

4. Situation Analysis

This situation analysis starts with a snapshot of the current environment in which Paradise Kitchens finds itself by providing a brief SWOT (strengths, weaknesses, opportunities, threats) analysis. After this overview, the analysis probes ever-finer levels of detail: industry, competitors, company, and consumers.

SWOT Analysis
Figure 1 shows the internal and external factors affecting the market opportunities for Paradise Kitchens. Stated briefly, this SWOT analysis highlights the great strides taken by the company in the nine years since its products first appeared on grocers'

Figure 1.   SWOT Analysis for Paradise Kitchens

Internal Factors	Strengths	Weaknesses
Management	Experienced and entrepreneurial management and board	Small size can restrict options
Offerings	Unique, high-quality, high-price products	Many lower-quality, lower-price competitors
Marketing	Distribution in 3 markets with excellent acceptance	No national awareness or distribution
Personnel	Good work force, though small; little turnover	Big gap if key employee leaves
Finance	Excellent growth in sales revenues	Limited resources may restrict growth opportunities when compared to giant competitors
Manufacturing	Sole supplier ensures high quality	Lack economies of scale of huge competitors
R&D	Continuing efforts to ensure quality in delivered products	

External Factors	Opportunities	Threats
Consumer/Social	Upscale market, likely to be stable; Mexican food category is fast-growing segment	Premium price may limit access to mass markets
Competitive	Distinctive name and packaging in its markets	Not patentable; competitors can attempt to duplicate product
Technological	Technical breakthroughs enable smaller food producers to achieve many economies available to large competitors	
Economic	Consumer income is high; convenience important to Canadian households	More households "eating out," and bringing prepared take-out into home
Legal/Regulatory	High government regulatory standards eliminate fly-by-night competitors	Mergers among large competitors approved by regulators

Plus, when combined with the Marketing Planning Software on the enclosed Student CD-ROM, you can't lose when it comes to learning!

Students!
Want to Get Better Grades?

STUDENT LEARNING TOOLS

Print Study Guide: To go beyond mere memorization and actually apply marketing principles, the Study Guide provides students with chapter outlines for note-taking, sample tests, critical thinking questions, and flash cards.

Student CD-ROM: Packaged free-of-charge with every textbook, this CD-ROM contains a Narrated Concept Review for each chapter of the book. This study outline in PowerPoint features all key concepts from the text and narrated explanations of key figures. The CD-ROM also contains Self Assessment Quizzes with Feedback for each chapter, and Marketing Planning Software.

Student Online Learning Centre: Students can visit this rich book-specific Website to find interactive Learning Objectives, lots of self-study and quizzing resources, and the Berlow et al. Seventh Edition PowerWeb resources, including Daily News Feed, Weekly Case Updates, *Readings in Marketing*, PowerSearch research engine, Career Resources, Web Research guidance, and Study Tips.

Marketing **Magazine:** Students get free access to *Marketing* Magazine Archives with purchase of the text. This real-world complement to the 5th Canadian Edition is a great way to keep your course and classroom discussion current.

AN INSTRUCTOR'S GUIDE TO SUPPLEMENTS

With the greatly enhanced Fifth Canadian Edition package, you and your students are covered from the basic supplements to the latest in educational technologies. Check it out for yourself!

LECTURE PREPARATION TOOLS

Your **Integrated i-Learning Sales Specialist** is a McGraw-Hill Ryerson representative who has the experience, product knowledge, training, and support to help you assess and integrate any of the below-noted products, technology, and services into your course for optimum teaching and learning performance. Whether it's how to use our test bank software, helping your students improve their grades, or how to put your entire course online, your i-Learning Sales Specialist is there to help. Contact your local i-Learning Sales Specialist today to learn how to maximize all McGraw-Hill Ryerson resources!

Instructor's Manual: The thoroughly revised Instructor's Manual includes lecture notes; discussions of the Marketing NewsNet boxes, Web Link boxes, Ethics and Social Responsibility Alerts, and Internet Exercises; answers to the Applying Marketing Concepts and Applications questions; supplemental lecture notes; teaching suggestions; and detailed information about integrating other supplements into the course and classroom.

Instructor's CD-ROM: The CD-ROM includes the print and electronic supplements, so you have access to all of the supplements on one disk. It also contains the seventh edition Computest package.

Video Case and Appendix D Case Teaching Notes: This media resource guide includes teaching notes for the video cases and alternate cases.

New PowerPoint Lecture Presentation Assembly Guide: This printed guide contains a description of all of the individual multimedia assets from which you can construct a custom presentation. The assets are organized by chapter and by topic, and are contained on the CD-ROM packaged with the guide. This guide also includes instructions on how to import the video, audio, art, photos, and other files into new or existing PowerPoint presentations.

In-Class Activities Guide in the Instructor's Survival Kit: This resource provides you with detailed teaching notes, relevant handouts, props, and products for use in-class to illustrate marketing concepts and encourage student participation and collaboration.

Marketing Horizons: A monthly newsletter of current, real-world happenings in Canadian marketing! Created by an instructor, for instructors—we're doing the legwork for you!

Marketing **Magazine:** If you're looking for a topic for a group assignment or simply want your students to read an article about Canadian marketing, we're providing access to *Marketing* Magazine!

LECTURE PRESENTATION TOOLS

New and Revised **Video Case Studies:** A unique series of 22 contemporary marketing cases is available on cassette. Each video case corresponds with chapter-specific topics and an end-of-chapter case in the text. Selected new videos include Flyte Tyme, Nokia, Paco Underhill (from the CBC's *Marketplace* series), and Amazon.com, and substantially revised/updated videos, including Rollerblade, Palm Inc., and Reebok International.

New and Enhanced PowerPoint Presentation:
Featuring a high-quality photo and art program including figure slides, commercials, product shots, advertisements, marketing-in-practice shots, and video segments from the video package. The presentation is contained on CD-ROMs packaged with the new **PowerPoint Lecture Presentation Assembly Guide.**

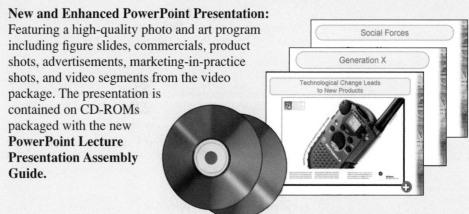

Instructor's Survival Kit (ISK): We understand how challenging it can be to engage a large class, that's why we're pleased to offer this kit to those instructors faced with the challenges of teaching to large class sections. The kit provides new ways to attract and retain the attention of students, for example:

- **In-Class Activities Guide** with learning objectives, transparency masters, appropriate handouts and templates, and detailed instructions for conducting the exercise.
- **In-Class Activities:** Popular activities from our past editions include brainstorming new advertising ideas for Breathe Right Strips, figuring out features of a better mousetrap, the Coke versus Pepsi taste test, and the "Ethics Quiz."
- **"Props":** To help implement the in-class activities and save instructor time, "props" such as labels for the original Magnetic Poetry Kit, Taro iMow Robotic Mower brochure, and Frito Lay's Cheetos Asteroids Go Snack canister.
- **Sample Products:** A number of new products are included in the survival kit, such as a Starbucks coffee packet and Starbucks card. Also, when appropriate, related ads are included in transparencies and PowerPoint.

Colour Acetates (U.S.): 200 four-colour overhead transparency acetates! 50% of these have been developed from information supplemental to the text and are accompanied by lecture notes to assist integration of this material into lectures.

ASSESSMENT TOOLS

Expanded 5000+ Question Test Bank: Dramatically expanded and improved, the test bank now contains 5000 questions categorized by topic, level of learning, and tied to learning objectives (definitional, conceptual, or application). The number of conceptual and application questions has been augmented with over 1000 additional questions.

Expanded Computerized Test Bank: This Computest is revised to contain all of the multiple-choice questions from the Test Bank, Web and Student CD-ROM Quizzes, Study Guide, and PowerWeb readings so you can include questions from these supplements in tests and quizzes. This allows you to reward students who go the extra mile and utilize these study aids. The Computest program allows you to select any of the questions, make changes if desired, or add new questions—and quickly print out a finished set customized to your course.

PageOut Quizzes with Instructor Gradebook: Assign quizzes in PageOut to give students incentive to read the text and prepare for class. Grades for each student will automatically post to your class gradebook.

Create a custom course Website with **PageOut**,
free with every McGraw-Hill Ryerson textbook.

To learn more, contact your McGraw-Hill Ryerson publisher's
representative or visit www.mhhe.com/solutions

Online Learning Centre and Student CD-ROM Quizzes: Helps to prepare students for taking tests: www.mcgrawhill.ca/college/berkowitz.

ONLINE TECHNOLOGY

Online Learning Centre with PowerWeb

This robust book-specific Website includes resources for both instructors and students. For the instructor, we offer downloadable supplement materials and continuous updates. Students have a 24/7 study centre to keep them up to date, to provide examples for application, and to prepare for a test. The Website also includes PowerWeb, featuring its online readings and daily newsfeed.

Instructor Centre

- **"Ask the Authors"**
- **Instructor's Manual**
- **PowerPoint:** Includes concept screens and art from the text and notes on other digital assets available in the PowerPoint Presentation Assembly Guide.
- **Content Updates and Current Events:** You can sign up for e-mail updates on material specific to the text and find postings of new articles—all accompanied with teaching notes and new PowerPoint slides as appropriate.
- **New Instructor's Survival Kit Items:** Twice during the school year, we will offer two new activities along with appropriate props and products for use in-class.
- **Appendix D:** Alternative cases.

Student Centre

Online Study Guide

How well do you understand the material? Are you ready for your next test? Work through the Multiple Choice and True/False questions for each chapter to get instant feedback with the auto-grading feature.

- **Marketing Workshop,** including:
  - Concept Application Exercise
  - Internet Application Exercises
  - Chapter Web Links
  - Self Quizzes

Career Section

This section will help you plan your career in marketing. With tips on how to market yourself successfully and an overview of the various career paths open to you, you'll be a step ahead of the competition.

Marketing Updates

Important articles related to marketing will be posted to help you stay on top of emerging trends in this dynamic field.

e-Services

McGraw-Hill Ryerson offers you a unique e-Services package upon an adoption of this textbook. This includes technical support, access to our educational technology conferences, and custom eCourses, to name just a few. Please speak to your i-Learning Sales Specialist for details.

PowerWeb

- **Daily News Feed:** Headlines with annotations from the leading periodicals and news sources—searchable by topic.
- **Weekly Case Updates:** Each week a new short case dealing with a company in the headlines is presented.
- *Readings in Marketing:* A collection of important articles selected by a team of marketing professors provides deeper topical study.
- **PowerSearch Current Journals and Periodicals:** Search engine powered by Northern Lights.
- **Career Resources**
- **Web Research**
- **Study Tips**

PowerWeb elements have been integrated into the Online Learning Centre to give students quicker access to additional online resources.

www.blackboard.com

Fully Compatible

You can use *Marketing*, Fifth Canadian Edition online material with any online platform—including Blackboard, WebCT, and eCollege—to expand the reach of your course and open up distance-learning options.

Create a course Website in no time!

PageOut

This unique point-and-click course Website tool enables you to create a high-quality course Website without knowing HTML coding. With PageOut you can post your syllabus online, assign McGraw-Hill Online Learning Centre or e-Book content, add links to important off-site resources, and maintain student results in the online gradebook.

1

INITIATING THE MARKETING PROCESS

Developing customer relationships and value. This is the essence of the marketing process described in Part 1. Chapter 1 introduces the marketing process by describing the actions of Rollerblade as it faces the challenges of finding strategies to build on the phenomenal success of the product that created an entirely new industry. Chapter 2 describes how organizations such as Bombardier utilize the strategic marketing process to compete effectively on a global scale. Following Chapter 2 is a sample marketing plan (Appendix A) that illustrates the outcome of the strategic marketing process and provides a reference for students to study and use. Chapter 3 scans the business environment and identifies important trends in the Canadian marketplace. The changes are described in terms of social, economic, technological, competitive, and regulatory forces. Finally, Chapter 4 provides a framework for including ethical and social responsibility considerations in marketing decisions.

DEVELOPING CUSTOMER RELATIONSHIPS AND VALUE THROUGH MARKETING

AFTER READING THIS CHAPTER YOU SHOULD BE ABLE TO:

- Define marketing and explain the importance of (1) discovering and (2) satisfying consumer needs and wants.

- Distinguish between marketing mix elements and environmental factors.

- Understand how organizations build strong customer relationships using current thinking about customer value and relationship marketing.

- Describe how today's market orientation era differs from prior eras oriented to production and selling.

- Understand the meaning of ethics and social responsibility and how they relate to the individual, organizations, and society.

- Know what is required for marketing to occur and how it creates customer value and utilities for consumers.

FUSION, CORE, AND LIGHTNING! PHYSICS 101?

Well . . . not quite!

This manufacturer has the classic marketing problem of any mind-bending company that has created an entire industry! What does it do for an encore? What does it do to innovate, to provide products that prospective buyers want . . . that build continuing, loyal customer relationships? A big part of the answer *is* fusion, core, and lightning or—more properly—Fusion™, Core™, and Lightning™. But that puts us ahead of the Rollerblade® story.

The Three-Centuries-Old Innovation   In the early 1700s a Dutch inventor trying to simulate ice skating in the summer created the first roller skates by attaching spools to his shoes. His in-line arrangement was the standard design until 1863, when the first skates with rollers set as two pairs appeared. This design became the standard, and in-line skates virtually disappeared from the market.

In 1980, two young hockey-playing brothers found an old pair of in-line skates while browsing through a sporting goods store. Working in their garage, they modified the design to add polyurethane wheels, a moulded boot shell, and a toe brake. They sold their product, which they dubbed "Rollerblade skates," out of the back of their truck to hockey players and skiers as a means of staying in shape during the summer. In the mid-1980s an entrepreneur bought the company from the brothers and then hired marketing executive Mary Horwath to figure out how to market Rollerblade skates.

Understanding the Consumer   "When I came here," remembers Horwath, "I knew there had to be a change." By focusing only on serious athletes who used in-line skates to train for other sports, Rollerblade had developed an image as a training product. Conversations with in-line skaters, however, convinced Horwath that using Rollerblade skates:

• Was incredible fun.
• Was a great aerobic workout and made the skater stronger and healthier.
• Was quite different from traditional roller skating, which was practised alone, mostly inside, and by young girls.
• Would have great appeal to people other than just off-season ice hockey skaters and skiers.

Horwath saw her task as changing the image in people's minds—or "repositioning"—Rollerblade skates to highlight the benefits people saw in in-line skating. Using what she called "guerilla marketing," Horwath used her tiny $280 000 annual marketing budget to gain national exposure for Rollerblade skates using inexpensive, nontraditional promotional methods such as "demo vans" loaded with skates that people could try for free.

What a Difference a Decade Makes   Fast-forward from the late 1980s to the early 21st century. The marketing problems of Rollerblade today are a far cry from those faced by Mary Horwath in the late 1980s. As shown in Figure 1–1,[1] she and the company succeeded in popularizing in-line skating—and actually succeeded in launching an entirely new industry, as evidenced by the 27.8 million in-line skaters in 1997 (the peak year). One measure of the success of in-line skating is that it appeared in the first Extreme Games competition in 1995. However, the flattening of participation in in-line skating in the late 1990s is a source of concern to Rollerblade.

FIGURE 1–1
Number of in-line skaters in North America. Where is the trend headed? For some answers, see the text.

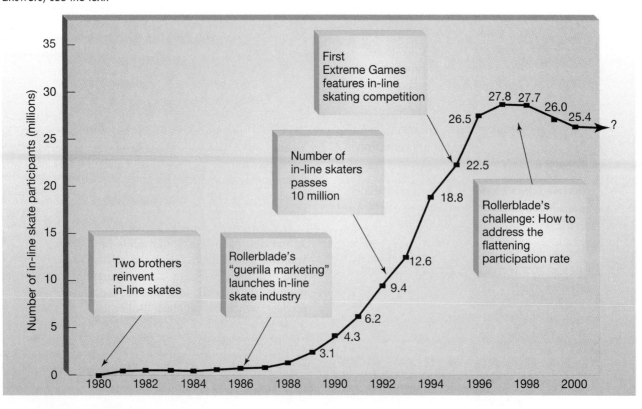

In addition to a decline in overall industry sales, Rollerblade also faces increased competition for skates. While Rollerblade currently has 35 percent of the annual industry sales, it faces off against 30 competitors, including Bauer Canada, which is a particularly strong brand in Canada.[2] Thus, Rollerblade's goal is to develop new skating products for current and new segments of buyers, forging strong, loyal customer relationships in the process. This is where breakthrough innovations on Rollerblade's in-line skates such as Fusion, Core, and Lightning come in. This situation presents a huge marketing lesson: Changing consumer tastes and changing competitive offerings require that organizations search continuously for ways to provide genuine value to customers, or the organizations will die. Thus, the future of organizations such as Rollerblade rely on the in-depth understanding of their customers' wants and needs and developing and marketing innovative products to satisfy them.

Rollerblade Skates, Marketing, and You   What marketing strategy is the Rollerblade marketing team using to try to rediscover the skyrocketing growth of in-line skating in the early 1990s shown in Figure 1–1? By the time you reach the end of this chapter, you will know some of the answers to this question.

One key to how well Rollerblade succeeds lies in the subject of this book: marketing. In this chapter and in the rest of the book we'll introduce you to many of the people, organizations, ideas, activities, and jobs in marketing that have spawned the products and services that have been towering successes, shattering failures, or something in between.

Marketing affects all individuals, all organizations, all industries, and all countries. This text seeks not only to teach you marketing concepts, but also to demonstrate marketing's many applications and how it affects our lives. This knowledge should make you a better consumer, help you in your career, and enable you to be a more informed citizen.

In this chapter and those that follow, you will feel the excitement of marketing. You will be introduced to the dynamic changes that will affect all of us in the future, and will also meet many men and women whose marketing creativity sometimes achieved brilliant, extraordinary results. And who knows? Somewhere in these pages you may find a career.

WHAT IS MARKETING?

Being a Marketing Expert: Good News–Bad News

In many respects you are a marketing expert already. But just to test your expertise, try the "marketing expert" questions in Figure 1–2. These questions—some of them easy, others mind-boggling—show the diverse problems marketing executives grapple with every day. You'll find the answers in the next few pages.

The Good News: You Already Have Marketing Experience   You are somewhat of an expert because you do many marketing activities every day. You already know many marketing terms, concepts, and principles. For example, would you sell more 43-inch Hitachi Big Screen HDTV monitors for $2500 or $999 each? The answer is $999, of course, so your experience in shopping for products—and maybe even selling them—already gives you great insights into the world of marketing. As a consumer, you've already been involved in thousands of marketing decisions—but mainly on the buying, not the marketing, side.

The Bad News: Surprises about the Obvious   Unfortunately, common sense doesn't always explain some marketing decisions and actions. An actress's saying that she often "rollerbladed" (question 1, Figure 1–2) sounds like great publicity,

FIGURE 1–2
The see-if-you're-really-a-
marketing-expert test

**ANSWER THE QUESTIONS BELOW. THE CORRECT ANSWERS ARE
GIVEN LATER IN THE CHAPTER.**

1. In a magazine article, a well-known actress said she often
   "rollerbladed" for fun and exercise. What was Rollerblade's reaction?
   (*a*) delighted, (*b*) upset, or (*c*) somewhere in between. Why?
2. The name is real so (*a*) what benefits might Kimberly-Clark (maker of
   Kleenex) provide consumers in its *Avert Virucidal Tissues* and (*b*)
   what things might kill this new product?
3. True or False: For the kids segment Rollerblade has a skate that
   expands as kids' feet grow.
4. Besides wool, to be socially responsible 3M puts what recycled
   material into its very successful Scotch-Brite™ Never Rust Wool
   Soap Pads? (*a*) aluminum cans, (*b*) steel-belted tires, (*c*) plastic
   bottles, (*d*) computer screens, (*e*) cardboard.

right? But Rollerblade was upset. Legally, Rollerblade is a registered trademark and, as a brand name, should be used only to identify that firm's products and services. With letters to offenders and advertisements like the one below, Rollerblade is trying to protect a precious asset: its brand identity.

Under trademark law, if consumers generally start using a brand name as the generic term to describe the product rather than the source of the product, then the company loses its exclusive rights to the name. "Rollerblade" skates would become "rollerblades"—just another English word to describe all kinds of in-line skates. That fate has already befallen some famous products such as linoleum, cellophane, escalator, yo-yo, corn flakes, and trampoline.[3]

Today, firms spend billions of dollars annually in promotion and court cases to protect the integrity of their brand names. As described in the Marketing NewsNet,

Rollerblade Inc. ran this ad to communicate a specific message. It's also part of a "reminder" letter sent to people who slip. What is the message? For the answer and why it is important, see the text.

Everyday, irregardless of his homework, Jeffrey went "rollerblading" because it was to nice to lay around with his nose in a english book.

*Of the seven errors in this headline, the use of "rollerblading" as a verb strikes
us as the most extreme. Rollerblade® is a brand name. It is, also, technically incorrect
to use "rollerblader" and "rollerblades" as nouns. Remember, the careful writer
skates on in-line skates known as Rollerblade® skates.*

© 1992 Rollerblade, Inc. Rollerblade and The Skate Logo are trademarks of Rollerblade, Inc.

MARKETING NEWSNET   The Challenge and Changing Role of Successful Brands

Brands are suddenly under major attack!

From the Critics

Criticism of Western brands runs something like this: In today's global economy, brands are a huge portion of a company's value and profits. So rather than simply sell products, companies are in the business of marketing aspirations, images, and lifestyles. The sad part of this is that the companies shift production to Third World countries where they pay poor wages and even exploit child labour. The "McDonaldsization of the globe" means that brands are so powerful that they make us all act alike and be alike—undermining our moral values.

From the Advocates

In contrast, *The Economist* magazine says "far from being instruments of oppression, [brands] make firms accountable to consumers." Brands started as a form of consumer protection, not consumer exploitation. Today brands not only simplify choices and guarantee a consistency of quality, but also, says *The Economist*, "they add fun and interest"—whether the example is Disney, Nokia, or Gap. As with Rollerblade's concern over "rollerblading," firms spend

millions of dollars to protect their brand names to ensure consumers get what they think they are buying.

Brands Today and Tomorrow

In today's competition carelessness or arrogance can devastate decades spent building a strong brand. Kellogg's, second among the world's top brands less than a decade earlier, in 2001 languished in 39th place according to Interbrand, a brand consultant. World Bank studies show that branded multinationals help developing economies by paying the best wages and offering the best working conditions. And for the future, firms may need to learn lessons from Nike, which revamped its supply chain after activists accused it of operating Third World sweatshops. Brands of the future may need to go beyond sending signals to consumers about quality and consistency of the product to encompass a good feeling about the company itself.

The Result

All kinds of products, organizations, and causes—from Nike and Sony to the Canadian Red Cross and Greenpeace—are fighting to preserve the integrity of their brand names.

some critics see brands as simply selling images and undermining moral values.[4] But, as discussed there and in Chapter 11, brands save consumers time and simplify their choices by assuring consistent quality. Further, the free market competition among high-quality brands ensures better product choices for consumers. Because legal and ethical issues such as the Rollerblade skates trademark problem are so central to many marketing decisions, they are addressed throughout the book.

Your common sense plus your in-depth study of the marketing concepts in the book will enable you to make better decisions and choices in the marketplace.

Marketing: Using Exchanges to Satisfy Needs

MARKETING
The process of planning and executing the conception, pricing, promotion, and distribution of ideas, goods, and services to create exchanges that satisfy individual and organizational objectives.

The American Marketing Association, representing marketing professionals, states that "**marketing** is the process of planning and executing the conception, pricing, promotion, and distribution of ideas, goods, and services to create exchanges that satisfy individual and organizational objectives."[5] Many people incorrectly believe that marketing is the same thing as advertising or personal selling; this definition shows marketing to be a far broader activity. Further, this definition stresses the importance of beneficial exchanges that satisfy the objectives of both those who buy and those who sell ideas, goods, and services—whether they be individuals or organizations.

To serve both buyers and sellers, marketing seeks (1) to discover the needs and wants of prospective customers and (2) to satisfy them. These prospective customers include both individuals buying for themselves and their households, and organizations that buy for their own use (such as manufacturers) or for resale (such as wholesalers and retailers). The key to achieving these two objectives is the idea of **exchange**, which is the trade of things of value between buyer and seller so that each is better off after the trade. This vital concept of exchange in marketing is covered below in more detail.

The Diverse Factors Influencing Marketing Activities

Although an organization's marketing activity focuses on assessing and satisfying consumer needs, countless other people, groups, and forces interact to shape the nature of its activities (Figure 1–3). Foremost is the organization itself, whose mission and objectives determine what business it is in and what goals it seeks. Within the organization, management is responsible for establishing these goals. The marketing department works closely with a network of other departments and employees to help provide the customer-satisfying products required for the organization to survive and prosper.

Figure 1–3 also shows the key people, groups, and forces outside the organization that influence marketing activities. The marketing department is responsible for facilitating relationships, partnerships, and alliances with the organization's customers, its shareholders (or often representatives of groups served by a nonprofit organization), its suppliers, and other organizations. Environmental forces such as social, technological, economic, competitive, and regulatory factors also shape an organization's marketing activities. Finally, an organization's marketing decisions are affected by and, in turn, often have an important impact on society as a whole.

The organization must strike a continual balance among the sometimes differing interests of these individuals and groups. For example, it is not possible to simultaneously provide the lowest-priced and highest-quality products to customers and pay the highest prices to suppliers, highest wages to employees, and maximum dividends to shareholders.

FIGURE 1–3
An organization's marketing department relates to many people, groups, and forces

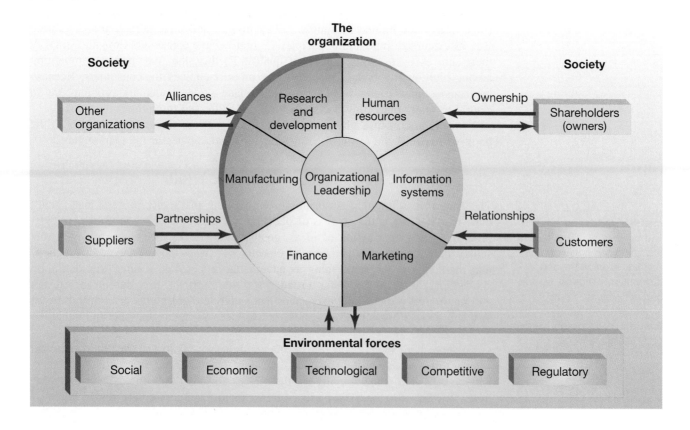

Requirements for Marketing to Occur

For marketing to occur, at least four factors are required: (1) two or more parties (individuals or organizations) with unsatisfied needs, (2) a desire and ability on their part to be satisfied, (3) a way for the parties to communicate, and (4) something to exchange.

Two or More Parties with Unsatisfied Needs   Suppose you've developed an unmet need—a desire for information about how computer and telecommunications are interacting to reshape the workplace—but you didn't yet know that *Computer-World* magazine existed. Also unknown to you was that several copies of *Computer-World* were sitting on the magazine rack at your nearest bookstore, waiting to be purchased. This is an example of two parties with unmet needs: you, with a need for technology-related information, and your bookstore owner, needing someone to buy a copy of *ComputerWorld*.

Desire and Ability to Satisfy These Needs   Both you and the bookstore owner want to satisfy these unmet needs. Furthermore, you have the money to buy the item and the time to get to the bookstore. The store's owner has not only the desire to sell *ComputerWorld* but also the ability to do so since it's stocked on the shelves.

A Way for the Parties to Communicate   The marketing transaction of buying a copy of *ComputerWorld* will never occur unless you know the product exists and its location. Similarly, the store owner won't stock the magazine unless there's a market of potential buyers nearby. When you receive a free sample in the mail or see the magazine on display in the bookstore, this communications barrier between you (the buyer) and your bookstore (the seller) is overcome.

Something to Exchange   Marketing occurs when the transaction takes place and both the buyer and seller exchange something of value. In this case, you exchange your money for the bookstore's magazine. Both you and the bookstore have gained something and also given up something, but you are both better off because you have each satisfied your unmet needs. You have the opportunity to read *ComputerWorld*, but you gave up some money; the store gave up the magazine but received money, which enables it to remain in business. This exchange process and, of course, the ethical and legal foundations of exchange are central to marketing.[6]

Concept Check

1. What is marketing?
2. Marketing focuses on _____ and _____ consumer needs.
3. What four factors are needed for marketing to occur?

HOW MARKETING DISCOVERS AND SATISFIES CONSUMER NEEDS

The importance of discovering and satisfying consumer needs is so critical to understanding marketing that we look at each of these two steps in detail next.

Discovering Consumer Needs

The first objective in marketing is discovering the needs of prospective consumers. Sound simple? Well, it's not. In the abstract discovering needs looks easy, but when you get down to the specifics of marketing problems crop up.

Yes, they're all for real! For these products, identify (1) what benefits the product provides buyers and (2) what "showstoppers" might kill the product in the marketplace. Answers are discussed in the text.

Kimberly-Clark's Avert
Virucidal tissues

Pfizer's Body Smarts
crunch bars and fruit chews

Toro's iMow
lawn mower

Samsung's 17-inch SyncMaster
flat-panel PC screen

The Challenge of Launching Winning New Products   New-product experts generally estimate that 80 to 94 percent of the over 25 000 new consumable products (food, beverage, health, beauty, and other household and pet products) introduced in North America annually "don't succeed in the long run." Robert M. McMath, who has studied over 40 000 of these new-product launches, has two key suggestions: (1) focus on what the customer benefit is and (2) learn from the past.[7]

The solution to preventing such product failures seems embarrassingly obvious. First, find out what consumers need and want. Second, produce what they need and want and don't produce what they don't need and want. This is far more difficult than it sounds. The four products shown above illustrate just how hard it is with today's competition to achieve new-product success, a topic covered in more detail in Chapter 10.

In terms of potential benefits to customers and possible showstoppers, let's look first at the two consumable products:

- *Kimberly-Clark's Avert Virucidal tissues.* Like the launch of Garlic Cake, the name confused consumers who couldn't quite understand what benefit a "virucidal" tissue provided. (It contained Vitamin C derivatives that were supposed to keep the germs from spreading when you blew into it.) Another problem: McMath observes that words that end in *cidal*—like homicidal or suicidal—don't put people in a buying mood. The clear showstoppers: Prospects were simply too confused and scared to risk their noses to Avert Virucidals (question 2, Figure 1–2).[8]
- *Pfizer's Body Smarts crunch bars and fruit chews.* Containing as much iron as a cup of spinach and as much fibre as a slice of bread, these chocolate and fruit-chew "nutraceuticals" let munchers indulge their sweet tooth believing they're getting solid nutrition, too. Launched in mid-2001 with a $70-million

ETHICS AND SOCIAL RESPONSIBILITY ALERT Junk Food Advertising

Between their second and twelfth birthdays, Canadian children will see 200 000 television commercials. About 80 percent of food commercials aired during Saturday morning kids' TV shows are for products of low nutritional value, or what some refer to as junk food. Spots for high-sugar products—for example, candy and cereals—form the majority of such ads. In many cases, the ads contain what some experts label "weasel words," or words and phrases that are meant to mislead children—such as "part of a complete breakfast."

Many health experts are concerned about the diets of young Canadians, suggesting that they eat too many foods with poor nutritional value. Furthermore, poor eating habits, including the high rate of consumption of junk food, have led to a steady increase in childhood obesity over the past 30 years. This increase in childhood obesity has many health experts concerned because they believe it will contribute to many diseases in decades to come, including higher rates of diabetes and cancer.

Nutritional experts suggest that because young children lack the decision-making ability to make wise food choices, something must be done to protect them from junk food advertising. But what? A complete ban on advertising junk food to children? Stricter regulations on what can be said and shown in such ads? Stronger parental involvement regarding food choices? There may not be a clear answer here. But this issue does reveal the possible ethical, social, or even legal aspects of marketing something as simple as a candy bar or box of cereal.

marketing campaign, the potential showstopper for Body Smarts is a carryover from bad past experiences: Good taste! If they're still on your candy counter when you read this, they probably taste good and are a winner.[9]

A bad buying decision with a consumable product may waste a dollar or two. But high-priced technical equipment involves a lot more thought during the buying process. So the revolutionary new lawn mower and computer monitor shown on page 12 still must demonstrate potential benefits to buyers:

- *Toro's iMow lawn mower.* Launched in 2001, this robot mower lets lazy or gadget-happy homeowners lie in their hammocks and watch their iMow cut their grass. The first step is to lay down a low-voltage perimeter wire to limit the cutting area. The potential time-saving benefit will confront the iMow's final exam question: Will it work as planned?[10]
- *Samsung's 17-inch SyncMaster 760TFT flat-panel PC screen.* The benefits compared to a bulky, heavy cathode-ray tube (CRT) computer monitor are that flat-panel screens save space and are easier to move. Introduced in fall 2001, the $790 SyncMaster faces both traditional CRTs and newly arriving flat-panel displays from competitors. Without quite the CRT's flexibility in pixel resolution, the flat-panel displays are leading-edge technology. But the potential show-stoppers: Are the price, quality, and timing right? Watch your computer store or Internet seller for the answer.[11]

Firms spend billions of dollars annually on marketing and technical research that significantly reduces—but doesn't eliminate—new-product failure.

Consumer Needs and Consumer Wants   Should marketing try to satisfy consumer needs or consumer wants? The answer is both! Heated debates rage over this question, depending on the definitions of needs and wants and the amount of freedom given to prospective customers to make their own buying decisions.

A *need* occurs when a person feels physiologically deprived of basic necessities such as food, clothing, and shelter. A *want* is a felt need that is shaped by a person's knowledge, culture, and personality. So if you feel hungry, you have developed a basic need and desire to eat something. Let's say you then want to eat an apple or a candy bar because, based on your past experience and personality, you know these will satisfy your hunger need. Effective marketing, in the form of creating an awareness of good products at convenient locations, can clearly shape a person's wants.

At issue is whether marketing persuades prospective customers to buy the "wrong" things—say, a candy bar rather than an apple to satisfy hunger pangs. Certainly, marketing tries to influence what we buy. A question then arises: at what point do we want the government and society to step in to protect consumers? Most consumers would say they want government to protect us from harmful drugs and unsafe cars, but from candy bars, cereals, and soft drinks? Read the Ethics and Social Responsibility Alert concerning the advertising of junk food directed at Canadian children.[12] What do you think about this issue? Sometimes there are no clear-cut answers when it comes to the issue of what should be marketed and how. In fact, there is continuing debate over what constitutes human *need* and *want* and whether somebody has the right to determine for someone else what is a need and what is a want. Because even psychologists and economists still argue about the exact meanings of need and want, we shall avoid the semantic arguments and use the terms interchangeably in the rest of the book.

As shown in Figure 1–4, discovering needs involves looking carefully at prospective customers, whether they are children buying M&M's candy, university students buying Rollerblade in-line skates, or firms buying Xerox photocopying machines. Principal activities of a firm's marketing department are to carefully scrutinize its consumers to understand what they need, to study industry trends, to examine competitors' products, and even to analyze the needs of a customer's customer.

MARKET

People with the desire and with the ability to buy a specific product.

What a Market Is   Potential consumers make up a **market**, which is (1) people (2) with the desire and (3) with the ability to buy a specific product. All markets ultimately are people. Even when we say a firm bought a Xerox copier, we mean one or several people in the firm decided to buy it. People who are aware of their unmet needs may have the desire to buy the product, but that alone isn't sufficient. People must also have the ability to buy, such as the authority, time, and money. People may even "buy" an idea that results in an action, such as having their blood pressure checked annually or turning down their thermostat to save energy.

Satisfying Consumer Needs

Marketing doesn't stop with the discovery of consumer needs. Because the organization obviously can't satisfy all consumer needs, it must concentrate its efforts on

FIGURE 1–4

Marketing's first task: discovering consumer needs

TARGET MARKET
One or more specific groups of potential consumers toward which an organization directs its marketing program.

certain needs of a specific group of potential consumers. This is the **target market** —one or more specific groups of potential consumers toward which an organization directs its marketing program.

The Four Ps: Controllable Marketing Mix Factors   Having selected the target market consumers, the firm must take steps to satisfy their needs. Someone in the organization's marketing department, often the marketing manager, must take action and develop a complete marketing program to reach consumers by using a combination of four tools, often called the four Ps—a useful shorthand reference to them first published by Professor E. Jerome McCarthy:[13]

- *Product.* A good, service, or idea to satisfy the consumer's needs.
- *Price.* What is exchanged for the product.
- *Promotion.* A means of communication between the seller and buyer.
- *Place.* A means of getting the product into the consumer's hands.

MARKETING MIX
The marketing manager's controllable factors; the marketing actions of product, price, promotion, and place that he or she can take to solve a marketing problem.

We'll define each of the four Ps more carefully later in the book, but for now it's important to remember that they are the elements of the marketing mix, or simply the **marketing mix**. These are the marketing manager's controllable factors, the marketing actions of product, price, promotion, and place that he or she can take to solve a marketing problem. The marketing mix elements are called controllable factors because they are under the control of the marketing department in an organization.

ENVIRONMENTAL FACTORS
The uncontrollable factors involving social, economic, technological, competitive, and regulatory forces.

The Uncontrollable, Environmental Factors   There are a host of factors largely beyond the control of the marketing department and its organization. These factors can be placed into five groups (as shown in Figure 1–3): social, economic, technological, competitive, and regulatory forces. Examples are what consumers themselves want and need, changing technology, the state of the economy in terms of whether it is expanding or contracting, actions that competitors take, and government restrictions. These are the **environmental factors** in a marketing decision, the uncontrollable factors involving social, economic, technological, competitive, and regulatory forces. These five forces may serve as accelerators or brakes on marketing, sometimes expanding an organization's marketing opportunities and other times restricting them. These five environmental factors are covered in Chapter 3.

Wal-Mart and Lands' End provide customer value using two very different approaches. For their strategies, see the text.

Wal-Mart
www.wal-mart.com

Lands' End Direct Merchants
www.landsend.com

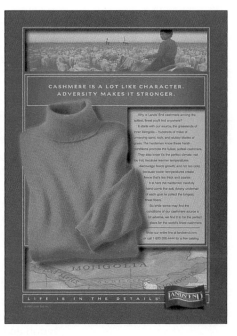

Traditionally, many marketing executives have treated these environmental factors as rigid, absolute constraints that are entirely outside their influence. However, recent studies and marketing successes have shown that a forward-looking, action-oriented firm can often affect some environmental factors, for example by achieving technological or competitive breakthroughs.

THE MARKETING PROGRAM: HOW CUSTOMER RELATIONSHIPS ARE BUILT

A firm's marketing program connects the firm to its customers. To clarify this link, we shall first discuss the critically important concepts of customer value, customer relationships, and relationship marketing, and then illustrate these concepts with the marketing program at Rollerblade.

Global Competition, Customer Value, and Customer Relationships

Intense competition in today's fast-paced domestic and global markets has caused massive restructuring in many Canadian industries and businesses. Canadian managers are seeking ways to achieve success in this new, more intense level of global competition.[14]

CUSTOMER VALUE
The unique combination of benefits received by targeted buyers that includes quality, price, convenience, on-time delivery, and both before-sale and after-sale service.

This has prompted many successful firms to focus on "customer value." That firms gain loyal customers by providing unique value is the essence of successful marketing. What is new, however, is a more careful attempt at understanding how a firm's customers perceive value. For our purposes, **customer value** is the unique combination of benefits received by targeted buyers that includes quality, price, convenience, on-time delivery, and both before-sale and after-sale service. As Chapter 5 points out, Canadian consumers are indeed becoming more "value conscious." Many Canadian companies are responding in various ways to this new consumer orientation.[15] But since research reveals that a firm cannot be "all things to all people," individual firms must find ways to build long-term customer relationships by providing unique value that they alone can deliver to targeted markets.[16] Accordingly, many successful firms have chosen to deliver outstanding customer value with one of three value strategies: best price, best product, or best service.

Companies such as Wal-Mart, Costco, and Dell Computer have all been successful offering consumers the best price. Other companies such as Nike, Starbucks, Microsoft Canada, and Johnson & Johnson claim to provide the best products on the market. Finally, companies such as Canadian Tire, Lands' End, and Amex Canada deliver value through exceptional service.

Relationship Marketing and the Marketing Program

Meaningful customer relationships are achieved by the firm's identifying creative ways to connect closely to its customers through the specific marketing mix actions implemented in its marketing program.

RELATIONSHIP MARKETING
Linking the organization to its individual customers, employees, suppliers, and other partners for their mutual long-term benefits.

Relationship Marketing: Easy to Understand   The hallmark of developing and maintaining effective customer relationships is today called **relationship marketing**, linking the organization to its individual customers, employees, suppliers, and other partners for their mutual long-term benefits. Note that these mutual long-term benefits between the organization and its customers require links to other vital stakeholders—including suppliers, employees, and "partners" such as wholesalers or retailers in a manufacturer's channel of distribution. In an ideal setting, relationship marketing involves a personal, ongoing relationship between the organization and an individual customer.

Relationship Marketing: Difficult to Implement   Huge manufacturers find this rigorous standard of relationship marketing difficult to achieve. Today's information technology, along with cutting-edge manufacturing and marketing processes, has led to tailoring goods or services to the tastes of individual customers in high volumes at a relatively low cost. Thus, you can place an Internet order for all the components of a Dell or Apple computer and have it delivered in four or five days—in a configuration tailored to your unique wants.

But there are other forces working against these kinds of personal relationships between company and customer. Researchers Fournier, Dobscha, and Mick observe that "the number of one-on-one relationships that companies ask consumers to maintain is untenable,"[17] as evidenced by the dozens of credit card and financing offers a typical consumer gets in a year. A decade ago you might have gone to a small store to buy a book or music record, being helped in your buying decision by a salesclerk or the store owner. With today's Internet purchases, you will probably have difficulty achieving the same personal, tender-loving-care connection that you once had with your own special book or music store.

The Marketing Program

MARKETING PROGRAM
A plan that integrates the marketing mix to provide a good, service, or idea to prospective buyers.

Effective relationship marketing strategies help marketing managers discover what prospective customers need. They must translate this information into some concepts for products the firm might develop (Figure 1–5). These concepts must then be converted into a tangible **marketing program**—a plan that integrates the marketing mix to provide a good, service, or idea to prospective buyers. These prospects then react to the offering favourably (by buying) or unfavourably (by not buying), and the process is repeated. As shown in Figure 1–5, in an effective organization this process is continuous: Consumer needs trigger product concepts that are translated into actual products that stimulate further discovery of consumer needs.

FIGURE 1–5
Marketing's second task: satisfying consumer needs

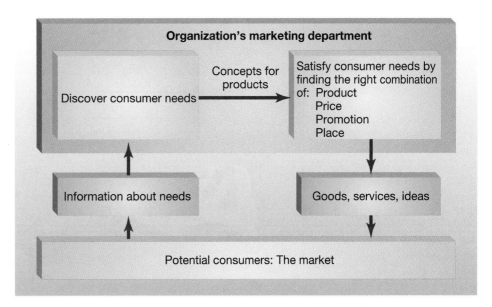

A Marketing Program for Rollerblade

To see some specifics of an actual marketing program, let's return to the earlier example of Rollerblade and its in-line skates. Looking at the in-line skating horizon, Rollerblade's long-run strategy is to focus on three areas: (1) expand the market, (2) use the company's strengths in technology, and (3) "stay ahead of the trends." These three areas are covered below.

Expanding the Market for Rollerblade Skates

In terms of expanding the market, one Rollerblade marketing manager comments, "Our challenges are to find new venues, new reasons for people to skate." The foundation on which to build marketing programs reaching these new settings rests on two key elements:

- Finding the right benefits—or competitive points of difference (discussed in detail in Chapter 10)—to stress in reaching potential buyers. Three key benefits and points of difference for customers underlie all of Rollerblade's marketing efforts: (1) fun, (2) fitness and health, and (3) excitement.
- Targeting key segments of prospective customers and satisfying them with the specific kinds of Rollerblade brands of skates that they want.

Today, while the fundamental customer benefits remain the same, Rollerblade is now trying to reach narrower, more focused segments of customers than in the past. Let's look at several of these market segments and the products that Rollerblade has developed to provide key benefits to satisfy their needs:[18]

- *Children segment.* Most parents can't afford to buy a new set of in-line skates each season as their children's feet grow. No problem now! With the Junior™ line, the skate "grows" in four extensions to provide a skate for four sizes of a child's feet (question 3, Figure 1–2).
- *Fitness segment.* Want a skate to get you to exercise, whether you're a beginner or intermediate skater? Then try a Core or Fusion skate that utilizes Rollerblade's key technologies.
- *Speed segment.* You're a really serious in-line skater? How about a five-wheeled Lightning or Road Runner™ that retails for up to $984?

Rollerblade's various product lines meet the needs of distinctly different segments of users.

* *Terrain/"aggressive" segment.* Like to skate down snowless ski hills in the summer? The Coyote™ fills the bill. Its pneumatic tires provide a full inch of shock absorption plus good traction on slick surfaces—an in-line skate for aggressive, all-terrain skating.

Rollerblade has more than 20 lines of skates targeted to different market segments. As illustrated in Figure 1–6 for the Junior and Core/Fusion brands, most Rollerblade brands require a slightly different marketing program to reach their targeted segments of potential customers.

Exploiting Strengths in Technology   In 1995 Rollerblade was sold to Nordica, an Italian ski company owned by the Benetton organization. This provided huge technology synergies for the two firms. Examples of exploiting tomorrow's technology—some with Nordica, some on Rollerblade's own—include:

* *CoolMax™.* A performance fabric used to keep a skater's feet dry, even with intense skating.
* *ABT®Lite.* A light, integral braking system that allows skaters to brake by sliding their foot forward, without compromising balance or performance.
* *Shock Eraser™.* A cushioning support system that absorbs vibrations while skating and improves overall performance.
* *Progressive Fit System™.* A series of liners and footbeds that bring fit and comfort to skaters of all abilities.

Rollerblade's stress on the technology is reflected in the more than 200 patents it holds on key elements of its in-line skate line.

FIGURE 1–6
Marketing programs for two of Rollerblade's skates, targeted at two distinctly different customer segments: fast-growing kids and fitness skaters

MARKETING PROGRAM ACTIVITY TO REACH:

MARKETING MIX ELEMENT	FAST-GROWING KIDS SEGMENT	FITNESS SEGMENT	RATIONALE FOR MARKETING PROGRAM ACTIVITY
Product	Offer the Junior, a skate for children that "extends" so that it changes four shoe sizes as the children grow	Offer the Core and Fusion skates for beginning and intermediate skaters simply wanting fun and exercise	Use new-product research and the latest technology to offer high-quality skates to satisfy the needs of key customer segments
Price	Price up to $99 a pair	Price up to $199 a pair	Set prices that provide genuine value to the customer segment that is targeted
Promotion	Use demo vans to introduce children to in-line skating and place ads in local newspapers	Feature Rollerblade in sports competitions and magazines like *Shape* and *Inline,* and local newspapers	Increase awareness of in-line skating to those new to the sport while offering specific skate designs for more advanced segments
Place	Distribute the Junior through sporting goods stores	Distribute the Core and Fusion lines through specialty and regular sporting goods stores	Make it easy for buyers in the segment to buy at an outlet that is convenient and where they feel comfortable

The Segway HT, with inventor Dean Kamen: competition for Rollerblade in special applications?

Staying Ahead of the Trends   Consumer tastes change—and quickly! This is the reason for Rollerblade's concerns that it stay ahead of trends in the marketplace.[19] The recent downturn in consumer participation in in-line skating shown in Figure 1–1 has sent up a red flag for Rollerblade executives. Competition is coming from directions in wheeled vehicles never anticipated even two or three years earlier. Rollerblade has always had to compete with skateboards and also mountain bikes used in both on-road and off-road cycling. But few in the in-line skate industry foresaw sales of millions of scooters in 2000, which cut heavily into skate sales. Nor did they foresee a million pairs of "Heelys"—a sneaker with an embedded, detachable wheel in the heel—flying off retail shelves in 2001 (see Chapter 9).

Now, another possible competitor: the Segway HT (human transporter)—initially known mysteriously as "It!" This may impact a minor business segment of in-line skate sales, skates sold to those using them for delivery purposes, as mentioned in the Internet Exercise at the end of the chapter.

Having created a new sport and an entirely new industry, Rollerblade must address these new, competitive challenges. In a free market system, success encourages competition and imitations. The Rollerblade Video Case at the end of the chapter lets us look at the marketing strategies that Rollerblade is developing for the 21st century.

Concept Check

1. An organization can't satisfy the needs of all consumers, so it must focus on one or more subgroups, which are its _____.

2. What are the four marketing mix elements that make up the organization's marketing program?

3. What are uncontrollable variables?

HOW MARKETING BECAME SO IMPORTANT

Marketing is a driving force in the modern global economy. To understand why this is so and some related ethical aspects, let us look at the (1) evolution of the market orientation, (2) ethics and social responsibility in marketing, and (3) breadth and depth of marketing activities.

Evolution of the Market Orientation

Many market-oriented manufacturing organizations have experienced four distinct stages in the life of their firms. We can use Pillsbury, now part of General Mills, and General Electric as examples.

Production Era   Goods were scarce in the early years in North America, so buyers were willing to accept virtually any goods that were produced and make do with them as best they could. The central notion was that products would sell themselves, so the major concern of business firms was production, not marketing. Robert Keith, a Pillsbury president, described his company at this stage: "We are professional flour millers.... Our basic function is to mill quality flour."[20] As shown in Figure 1–7, this production era generally continued through the 1920s.

FIGURE 1–7
Four different orientations in the history of North American business

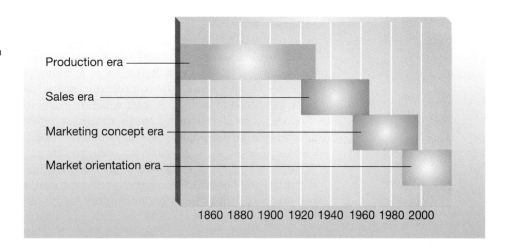

Production era

Sales era

Marketing concept era

Market orientation era

1860 1880 1900 1920 1940 1960 1980 2000

Sales Era   About that time, many firms discovered that they could produce more goods than their regular buyers could consume. Competition grew. The usual solution was to hire more salespeople to find new buyers. Pillsbury's philosophy at this stage was summed up simply by Keith: "We must hire salespersons to sell it [the flour] just as we hire accountants to keep our books." The role of the Pillsbury salesforce was simply to find consumers for the goods that the firm could produce best. This sales era continued into the 1950s for Pillsbury and into the 1960s for many other firms (see Figure 1–7).

Marketing Concept Era   In the 1960s, marketing became the motivating force among many firms. Then the policy became: "we are in the business of satisfying needs and wants of consumers." This is really a brief statement of what has come to be known as the **marketing concept**; the idea is that an organization should (1) strive to satisfy the needs of consumers (2) while also trying to achieve the organization's goals.

The statement of a firm's commitment to satisfying consumer wants and needs that probably launched the marketing concept appeared in a 1952 annual report of General Electric:[21] "The concept introduces . . . marketing . . . at the beginning rather than the end of the production cycle and integrates marketing into each phase of the business." This statement emphasizes that marketing ideas are fed into the production cycle from *after* an item is produced to *before* it is designed. Clearly the marketing concept is a focus on the consumer. Unfortunately, many companies found that actually implementing the concept was very difficult.

Market Orientation Era   Many of the implementation issues are now being addressed by the total quality management movement. Firms such as General Electric, Marriott, and Toyota have achieved great success by putting huge effort into implementing the marketing concept, giving their firms what has been called a *market orientation*. An organization that has a **market orientation** focuses its efforts on (1) continuously collecting information about customers' needs and competitors' capabilities, (2) sharing this information across departments, and (3) using the information to create customer value.[22]

An important outgrowth of this market orientation is the recent attention placed on **customer relationship management (CRM)**, the process of identifying prospective buyers, understanding them intimately, and developing favourable long-term perceptions of the organization and its offerings so that buyers will choose them in the marketplace.[23] It involves relationship-centric strategies to optimize the long-term value of an organization's selected customers. In short, it is all about getting, growing, and keeping customers. Or, in other words, managing the entire

MARKETING CONCEPT
The idea that an organization should (1) strive to satisfy the needs of consumers (2) while also trying to achieve the organization's goals.

MARKET ORIENTATION
Focusing organizational efforts on (1) continuously collecting information about customers' needs and competitors' capabilities, (2) sharing this information across departments, and (3) using the information to create customer value.

CUSTOMER RELATIONSHIP MANAGEMENT (CRM)
The process of identifying prospective buyers, understanding them intimately, and developing favourable long-term perceptions of the organization and its offerings so that buyers will choose them in the marketplace.

customer life cycle. The process requires the involvement and commitment of managers and employees throughout the organization and the growing application of information technology. CRM is not a technology per se, but technology is a key CRM enabler. In fact, with the advances in information technology and changes in customer buying behaviour—specifically, online buying—the scope of CRM has been broadened to include eCRM, which is discussed in Chapter 21.

Studies reveal that many North American firms have identified CRM as their number-one business initiative. Datamonitor studies predict that expenditures on CRM initiatives in North America will grow from $3.9 billion in 2000 to almost $12 billion by 2005. The Hudson's Bay Company, for example, has invested in CRM initiatives and has an awesome customer database that it uses to profile and segment customers as well as to monitor customer behaviour, loyalty, and value.[24]

Ethics and Social Responsibility: Balancing the Interests of Different Groups

As organizations have changed their orientation, society's expectations of marketers have also changed. Today, the standards of marketing practice have shifted from an emphasis on producers' interests to consumers' interests. In addition, organizations are increasingly encouraged to consider the social and environmental consequences of their actions for all parties. Guidelines for ethical and socially responsible behaviour can help managers balance consumer, organizational, and societal interests.

Ethics   Many marketing issues are not specifically addressed by existing laws and regulations. Should information about a firm's customers be sold to other organizations? Should advertising by professional service providers, such as accountants and attorneys, be restricted? Should consumers be on their own to assess the safety of a product? These questions raise difficult ethical issues. Many companies, industries, and professional associations have developed codes of ethics to assist managers.

Social Responsibility   While many ethical issues involve only the buyer and seller, others involve society as a whole. For example, suppose you change the oil in your old Chevy yourself and dump the used oil in a corner of your backyard. Is this just a transaction between you and the oil manufacturer? Not quite! The used oil may contaminate the soil, so society will bear a portion of the cost of your behaviour. This example illustrates the issue of social responsibility, the idea that organizations are accountable to a larger society. The well-being of society at large should also be recognized in an organization's marketing decisions. In fact, some marketing experts stress the **societal marketing concept**, the view that an organization should discover and satisfy the needs of its consumers in a way that also provides for society's well-being.[25] For example, Scotch-Brite Never Rust Wool Soap Pads from 3M—which are made from recycled plastic bottles—are more expensive than competitors (SOS and Brillo) but superior because they don't rust or scratch (question 4, Figure 1–2).

The societal marketing concept is directly related to **macromarketing**, which looks at the aggregate flow of a nation's goods and services to benefit society.[26] Macromarketing addresses broad issues such as whether marketing costs too much, whether advertising is wasteful, and what resource scarcities and pollution side effects result from the marketing system. While macromarketing issues are addressed briefly in this book, the book's main focus is on how an individual organization directs its marketing activities and allocates its resources to benefit its customers, or **micromarketing**. An overview of this approach appears in Chapter 2. Because of the importance of ethical and social responsibility issues in marketing today, Chapter 4 focuses on them; they are also touched on throughout the book.

SOCIETAL MARKETING CONCEPT
The view that an organization should discover and satisfy the needs of its consumers in a way that also provides for society's well-being.

MACROMARKETING
The study of the aggregate flow of a nation's goods and services to benefit society.

MICROMARKETING
How an individual organization directs its marketing activities and allocates its resources to benefit its customers.

The Breadth and Depth of Marketing

Marketing today affects every person and organization. To understand this, let's analyze (1) who markets, (2) what they market, (3) who buys and uses what is marketed, (4) who benefits from these marketing activities, and (5) how they benefit.

Who Markets?   Every organization markets! It is obvious that business firms involved in manufacturing (McCain Foods, General Motors of Canada, Ericsson Canada), retailing (Canadian Tire, Modrobes, The Bay), and providing services (Canadian Broadcasting Corporation, Air Canada, Via Rail, Vancouver Canucks, E*trade.ca) market their offerings. Today, many other types of marketing are also popular. Nonprofit organizations (Winnipeg Ballet, Canadian Red Cross, Canadian Museum of Civilization, Toronto Metro Zoo) also engage in marketing.[27] Your college or university, for example, probably has a marketing program to attract students, faculty members, and donations. Places (cities, provinces, countries) often use marketing efforts to attract tourists, conventions, or businesses. The province of Ontario, for example, has a marketing campaign designed to persuade businesses to locate there (www.ontariocanada.com). Organizations associated with special events or causes use marketing to inform and influence a target audience. These marketing activities range from government agencies encouraging AIDS prevention to professional organizations like the Registered Nurses Association of Ontario using marketing to recruit and retain nurses in Ontario. Finally, individuals such as politicians like Jean Chrétien often use marketing to gain attention and voter preference.

What Is Marketed?   Goods, services, and ideas are marketed. *Goods* are physical objects like Crest toothpaste, Nikon cameras, or Apple computers that satisfy consumer needs. *Services* are activities, deeds, or other basic intangibles such as airline trips on Zip airlines, financial advice from TD Waterhouse, or long-distance telephone calls offered by the Telus Group. *Ideas* are intangibles involving thoughts about actions or causes like donating to the Salvation Army or to the Trans Canada Trail project. Increasingly, goods and services in today's global marketplace are likely to cross national boundaries and involve transnational firms (Chapter 7).

As we mentioned earlier in the chapter, success in marketing involves finding out what consumers need and want and producing what they need and want. Many Canadian marketers are very creative in terms of following the process. Go to the accompanying Web Link to read the story of Modrobes, an upstart Ontario-based

Marketing is used by nonprofit organizations, causes, and places.

WEB LINK   The Modrobes Saga

http://www.mcgrawhill.ca

In this chapter we discuss how marketing is all about discovering and satisfying consumer needs. One upstart Canadian company found success in following that formula. Modrobes (pronounced *mode-robes*) is an entrepreneurial company that produces modern, functional sportswear clothing for hip young adults. It operates its own retail stores in Toronto, and has retail dealers all across Canada that carry the Modrobes clothing line. It also has a pretty cool Website where you can buy Modrobes clothing directly online. Visit www.modrobes.com and click on "The Saga" to read the story of founder Sal Debus and his

journey to make the company a reality. Examine why Debus began marketing his products. Sure, other marketers were already out there selling clothing—but not this particular type of clothing! For example, take note of his original "exam pants" and why they were invented. Maybe you have had the same problem as Debus did. Like him, perhaps you have sat through a four-hour exam and gotten, as Debus puts it, "a sore a__." What is your opinion about what he is marketing? Do his products appear to meet the needs of particular consumers in Canada? If so, why? If not, why not?

entrepreneurial venture. Find out just how the company determined what to market and how it went about marketing it.[28]

Who Buys and Uses What Is Marketed?   Both individuals and organizations buy and use goods and services that are marketed. **Ultimate consumers** are people—whether 80 years or 8 months old—who use the goods and services purchased for a household. In contrast, **organizational buyers** are units such as manufacturers, retailers, or government agencies that buy goods and services for their own use or for resale. Although the terms *consumers*, *buyers*, and *customers* are sometimes used for both ultimate consumers and organizations, there is no consistency on this. In this book, you will be able to tell from the example whether the buyers are ultimate consumers, organizations, or both.

Who Benefits?   In our free-enterprise society there are three specific groups that benefit from effective marketing: consumers who buy, organizations that sell, and society as a whole. True competition among products and services in the marketplace ensures that we as Canadian consumers can find value from the best products, the lowest prices, or exceptional service. Providing choices leads to consumer satisfaction and the quality of life that we have come to expect from our Canadian economic system.

Organizations that provide need-satisfying products combined with effective marketing programs—for example, McDonald's Restaurants of Canada, IBM Canada, and Microsoft Canada—have blossomed. But competition creates problems for ineffective competitors, such as eToys and the hundreds of other dot-com businesses that failed in the last few years.[29] Effective marketing actions result in rewards for organizations that serve customers and in thousands of marketing jobs for individuals all across the country.

Finally, effective marketing benefits society. It enhances competition, which in turn both improves the quality of products and services and lowers their prices. This makes countries more competitive in world markets and provides jobs and a higher standard of living for their citizens.

How Do Consumers Benefit?   Marketing creates **utility**, the benefits or customer value received by users of the product. This utility is the result of the marketing exchange process. There are four different utilities: form, place, time, and possession. The production of the good or service constitutes *form utility*. *Place utility* refers to having the offering available where consumers need it, whereas *time utility* means

Margin definitions

ULTIMATE CONSUMERS
People—whether 80 years or 8 months old—who use the goods and services purchased for a household.

ORGANIZATIONAL BUYERS
Those manufacturers, wholesalers, retailers, and government agencies that buy goods and services for their own use or for resale.

UTILITY
The benefits or customer value received by users of a product.

having it available when needed. *Possession utility* is getting the product to consumers so they can use it.

Thus, marketing provides consumers with place, time, and possession utilities by making the good or service available at the right place and right time for the right consumer. Although form utility usually arises in manufacturing activity and could be seen as outside the scope of marketing, an organization's marketing activities influence the product features and packaging. Marketing creates its utilities by bridging space (place utility) and hours (time utility) to provide products (form utility) for consumers to own and use (possession utility).

Concept Check

1. Like Pillsbury and General Electric, many firms have gone through four distinct orientations for their business: starting with the _____ era and ending with today's _____ era.

2. What are the two key characteristics of the marketing concept?

3. In this book the term *product* refers to what three things?

SUMMARY

1 Combining personal experience with more formal marketing knowledge will enable us to identify and solve important marketing problems.

2 Marketing is the process of planning and executing the conception, pricing, promotion, and distribution of ideas, goods, and services to create exchanges that satisfy individual and organizational objectives. This definition relates to two primary goals of marketing: (*a*) assessing the needs of consumers and (*b*) satisfying them.

3 For marketing to occur, it is necessary to have (*a*) two or more parties with unmet needs, (*b*) a desire and ability to satisfy them, (*c*) communication between the parties, and (*d*) something to exchange.

4 Because an organization doesn't have the resources to satisfy the needs of all consumers, it selects a target market of potential customers—a subset of the entire market—on which to focus its marketing program.

5 Four elements in a marketing program designed to satisfy customer needs are product, price, promotion, and place. These elements are called the marketing mix, the four Ps, or

the controllable variables because they are under the general control of the marketing department.

6 Environmental factors, also called uncontrollable variables, are largely beyond the organization's control. These include social, technological, economic, competitive, and regulatory forces.

7 Building on customer value and relationship marketing concepts, successful firms develop mutually beneficial long-term relationships with their customers.

8 In marketing terms, North American business history is divided into four periods: the production era, the sales era, the marketing concept era, and the current market orientation era.

9 Marketing managers must balance consumer, organizational, and societal interests. This involves issues of ethics and social responsibility.

10 Both profit-making and nonprofit organizations perform marketing activities. They market products, services, and ideas that benefit consumers, organizations, and countries. Marketing creates utilities that give benefits, or customer value, to users.

KEY TERMS AND CONCEPTS

customer relationship management (CRM) p. 21
customer value p. 16
environmental factors p. 15
exchange p. 10
macromarketing p. 22
market p. 14
market orientation p. 21
marketing p. 9
marketing concept p. 21

marketing mix p. 15
marketing program p. 17
micromarketing p. 22
organizational buyers p. 24
relationship marketing p. 16
societal marketing concept p. 22
target market p. 15
ultimate consumers p. 24
utility p. 24

INTERNET EXERCISE

www.mcgrawhill.ca/college/berkowitz

"It!" "Ginger!" "Jetson's scooter!" These were early names given the revolutionary Segway HT (human transporter), a technology shrouded in secrecy and mystery until it was launched with much fanfare in late 2001. Dean Kamen, the inventor of Segway HT, has also developed other high-tech innovations. The Segway HT relies on computers and gyroscopes to control its speed, balance, and direction. It weighs about 36 kg and can travel up to 24 km/h on a six-hour battery charge. A commercial version is expected to sell for U.S.$8000,

while the consumer version may sell for U.S.$3000 when it becomes available.

Go to www.segway.com and view both the consumer and business sections of the site.

1   What do you see as the advantages and disadvantages of the Segway HT?

2   For businesses, what applications could the Segway HT be used for?

3   Why would consumers want to purchase a Segway HT?

Want to get better grades, find tips on how to study more effectively, and stay up to date with happenings in the world of marketing? Visit the Online Learning Centre for practice tests, Study Smart software, and much more! www.mcgrawhill.ca/college/berkowitz

Interested in finding out what marketing looks like in the real world? *Marketing Magazine* is just a click away on your OLC! Visit www.mcgrawhill.ca/college/berkowitz

APPLYING MARKETING CONCEPTS AND PERSPECTIVES

1   What consumer wants (or benefits) are met by the following products or services? (*a*) Carnation Instant Breakfast, (*b*) Adidas running shoes, (*c*) Hertz Rent-A-Car, and (*d*) television home shopping programs.

2   Each of the four products, services, or programs in question 1 has substitutes. Respective examples are (*a*) a ham and egg breakfast, (*b*) regular tennis shoes, (*c*) taking a bus, and (*d*) a department store. What consumer benefits might these substitutes have in each case that some consumers might value more highly than those mentioned in question 1?

3   What are the characteristics (e.g., age, income, education) of the target-market customers for the following products or services? (*a*) *National Geographic* magazine, (*b*) *Wired* magazine, (*c*) Toronto Blue Jays baseball team, and (*d*) the Canadian Open tennis tournament.

4   A university in a metropolitan area wishes to increase its evening-school offerings of business-related courses such as marketing, accounting, finance, and management. Who are the target-market customers (students) for these courses?

5   What actions involving the four marketing mix elements might be used to reach the target market in question 4?

6   What environmental factors (uncontrollable variables) must the university in question 4 consider in designing its marketing program?

7   Polaroid introduced instant still photography, which proved to be a tremendous success. Yet Polavision, its instant movie system, was a total disaster. (*a*) What benefits does each provide to users? (*b*) What factors do you think contributed to Polavision's failure? (*c*) What research could have been undertaken that might have revealed Polavision's drawbacks?

8   Rollerblade is now trying to grow in-line skating globally. What are the advantages and disadvantages of trying to reach new global markets?

9   Does a firm have the right to "create" wants and try to persuade consumers to buy goods and services they didn't know about earlier? What are examples of "good" and "bad" want creation? Who should decide what is good and bad?

VIDEO CASE 1–1 Rollerblade, Inc.: Rediscovering Growth

David Samuels, senior director for sports innovation at Rollerblade believes innovative technology—in the form of new and better skates—will continue to be key for Rollerblade to stay ahead of the competition. Rollerblade must also find ways to expand the market for in-line skates. "Our challenge is to provide new venues, new reasons for people to skate. There's a lot of growth for us to catch up on in terms of household penetration," says Samuels.

THE SITUATION TODAY

When Rollerblade was founded, it was the only manufacturer of in-line skates in the world. Today the industry has more than 30 competitors, many that sell lower-priced skates than Rollerblade through mass-merchandising chains. Some of the large sporting goods manufacturers, like Nike, that have not traditionally sold in-line skates are now looking for ways to grow and have entered the in-line skate market.

In addition, both Rollerblade and other in-line skate manufacturers are facing increased competition from other wheeled sports. This includes everything from scooters and skateboards to on-road and off-road rides for mountain bikes. Even the Segway HT (see Internet Exercise) is a competitor in some situations. Further, as shown earlier in Figure 1–1, Samuels is concerned that the exploding growth of the in-line skate market seen in the early 1990s has turned to decline.

THE MARKETING PROGRAM

Expanding the market and continuing to be the leader in product innovation gives Rollerblade a strategic advantage in the marketplace. Yet it is a solid and creative marketing mix that will enable Rollerblade to pass these advantages along to the customer.

The product is the most important "P" in Rollerblade's marketing mix. This involves both innovative technologies and new skate designs. In terms of technologies, Rollerblade has pioneered the ABT and ABT Lite braking systems, more breathable fabrics, and vibration-absorbing cushioning systems. New skate designs include expandable skates for kids, the five-wheeled Lightning for speed skaters, the three-wheeled Coyote for off-road skaters, and specially designed skates to fit women's feet.

Rollerblade's promotional strategy continues to set it apart from the competitors, too. Its catalogues feature both its new technologies and new skate designs. The Rollerblade Website (www.rollerblade.com) is one of the most popular promotional tools with Rollerblade's loyal customers.

Since Rollerblade does not have the resources of an industry giant like Nike, it finds ways to communicate with customers that do not entail huge cash outlays. For example, Rollerblade provides information or product samples to media that, in turn, do in-line-skating features for articles or broadcast programs. It also develops promotional partnerships through sponsoring events and creating sweepstakes with other companies.

Finally, Rollerblade sponsors a competitive team of aggressive skaters and racers that competes around the world and regularly wins such events as ESPN's X-Games. It is creative and unorthodox approaches such as these that Samuels believes will keep Rollerblade ahead of the competition in the 21st century.

Rollerblade practises an across-the-board strategy when it comes to distribution and price. Samuels says, "Our distribution channels run the gamut. We are everywhere from the large mass market stores to specialty in-line dealers. Additionally, Rollerblade has chosen to hit every single price point possible. We have skates that are at the very high end, as well as skates as low as $79 under the Rollerblade brand. We also take a different brand name called Blade Runner and bring those products to the large mass markets of the world." Giving the lower-priced skates an alternate brand name allows Rollerblade to uphold its high-quality image in the marketplace while still providing an opportunity for beginners to test out the sport.

ISSUES FOR THE FUTURE

Some of the pressing issues in the future are global expansion, creating new segments of skaters, and expanding the product line. Currently, North America makes up only 50 percent of the marketplace worldwide. Rollerblade hopes to widen its global reach as the company continues to grow.

The youth segment should prove to be one of the most important segments in the future. "One of the biggest changes that's happened to us, and to the world really, is the power of youth. Kids who are anywhere from 10 to 12 years old on up into their twenties have been able to make a significant impact with so little money," explains Samuels. Rollerblade expects young people to continue to shape the recreational sports markets well into the future. Finally, Rollerblade has begun to offer products that are not in-line skates, such as accessories like helmets; wrist, elbow, and knee pads; skate bags; and skate tools. Rollerblade will continue to introduce products that respond to consumer needs and desires—constantly working to improve skate comfort, durability, and technologies.

Questions

1 What trends in environmental forces (social, economic, technological, competitive, and regulatory) identified in Figure 1–3 in the chapter (*a*) work for and (*b*) work against Rollerblade's potential growth in the 21st century?

2 What are the differences in marketing goals for Rollerblade (*a*) in 1986 when Rollerblade was launched and (*b*) today?

3 What are the (*a*) advantages and (*b*) disadvantages of having Rollerblade become part of the Benetton sport group? Refer to the text as well as the Video Case.

4 In searching for global markets to enter, (*a*) what are some criteria that Rollerblade should use to select countries to enter and (*b*) what three or four countries meet these criteria best and are the most likely candidates?

2

LINKING MARKETING AND CORPORATE STRATEGIES

AFTER READING THIS CHAPTER YOU SHOULD BE ABLE TO:

- Describe the three organizational levels of strategy and how they relate to each other and the marketing function.

- Understand why business definition, mission, culture, and goals are important in organizations.

- Describe how organizations set strategic directions by assessing where they are now and where they seek to be in the future.

- Understand the strategic marketing process and its three key phases: planning, implementation, and control.

- Explain how the marketing mix elements are blended into a cohesive marketing program.

- Describe how marketing control compares to actual results with planned objectives and acts on deviations from the plan.

BOMBARDIER—MOVING PEOPLE ON A GLOBAL SCALE

In 1942, J. Armand Bombardier founded a company in Quebec named L'Auto-Neige Bombardier Limitée to manufacture tracked vehicles for transportation on snow-covered terrain. In 1967 the company became Bombardier Inc. (www.bombardier.com), and its growth has been impressive! Today, Montreal-based Bombardier Inc. is a diversified manufacturing and service company with revenues of more than $21 billion. This Montreal-based firm is a world-leading manufacturer of business jets, regional aircraft, rail transportation equipment, and motorized recreational products. It is also a provider of financial services and asset management and employs more than 58 000 people in 12 countries in North America, Europe, and Asia. It is truly a global marketer, with more than 90 percent of its revenue generated outside Canada. We're sure many of you are familiar with some of Bombardier's branded products, such as Ski-Doo, Sea-Doo, Learjet, and Canadair.

But what makes Bombardier a Canadian success story? First, it has clearly defined the scope and nature of its business and the markets in which it competes (specifically, the fields of aerospace, rail transportation equipment, recreational products, and financial services). This provides the needed focus for the corporation. Next, it has established its basic mission: "to be the leader in all the markets in which it operates." This creates a unity of purpose and inspiration for the entire organization. Bombardier has also outlined clear goals or objectives for each of its business units or operating groups: "all Bombardier units must meet the needs of their customers and markets as well as reach and maintain world-class performance. They must also create added value in order to sustain their own growth and achieve a superior level of economic return to shareholders."

Bombardier Inc. also has a strong corporate culture that is focused on (1) being customer-oriented and keeping abreast of market trends to provide top-quality products and services at the best price–quality ratio, (2) continued innovation to constantly provide new products and services to its customers, (3) recognizing the importance of its employees to its corporate success, and (4) demonstrating respect for the environment and good corporate citizenship.

The company also believes in giving autonomy to its operating groups, with each group given the necessary authority to achieve a high level of performance consistent with the mission, code of ethics, policies, and internal governance of the corporation. All operating groups have a decentralized management structure to have the ability to act and react quickly to market trends and events and to stimulate entrepreneurship among employees. Coordination and transfer of know-how among operating groups is fostered and encouraged by the corporation.

All of these ingredients have created a company that is forward-thinking and market-oriented. And the company continues to find new ways to reach and serve its customers. For example, the Bombardier Recreational Products operating group recently launched its BombardierDirect program, an innovative e-commerce initiative that is designed to bring its dealers and consumers closer together. Bombardier-Direct is viewed by the company as a key element in its global marketing strategy and makes it possible for its dealer network to reach even more consumers by taking advantage of multichannel strategies to capture Internet and catalogue sales.[1]

Chapter 2 describes how organizations define their business, set their mission and overall direction, and link these activities to marketing strategies. Because of today's intense competition, firms must continuously revisit these tasks. In essence, this chapter describes how organizations like Bombardier Inc. try to implement the marketing concept to provide genuine value to their customers.

LEVELS OF STRATEGY IN ORGANIZATIONS

This chapter first distinguishes among different kinds of organizations and the various levels within them. It then compares strategies at three different levels in an organization, emphasizing the importance of activities at the functional level.

Today's Organizations: Kinds, Levels, and Teams

Large organizations today are extremely complex. All of us deal in some way with huge organizations every day, so it is useful to understand (1) the two basic kinds of organizations, (2) the levels that exist in them, and (3) the four building blocks that are vital to an organization's success.

PROFIT
The reward to a business firm for the risk it undertakes in offering a product for sale; the money left over after a firm's total expenses are subtracted from its total revenues.

Kinds of Organizations Today's organizations can be divided into business firms and nonprofit organizations. A *business firm* is a privately owned organization that serves its customers in order to earn a profit. Business firms must earn profits to survive. **Profit** is the reward to a business firm for the risk it undertakes in offering a product for sale: the money left over after a firm's total expenses are subtracted from its total revenues. In contrast to business firms, a *nonprofit organization* is a nongovernmental organization that serves its customers but does not have profit as an organizational goal. For simplicity in the rest of the book, however, the terms *firm*, *company*, *corporation*, and *organization* are used to cover both business and nonprofit operations.

Levels in Organizations and How Marketing Links to Them Whether explicit or implicit, organizations have a strategic direction. Marketing not only helps set this direction, but also must help implement it. Figure 2–1 summarizes the focus of this direction at each of the three levels in an organization.

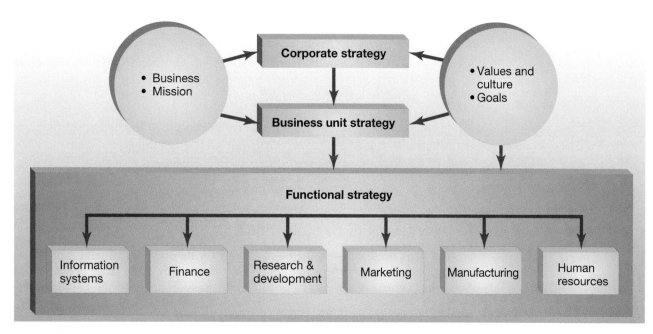

FIGURE 2–1
The three levels of strategy in organizations

CORPORATE LEVEL
Level at which top management directs overall strategy for the entire organization.

BUSINESS UNIT
An organization that markets a set of related products to a clearly defined group of customers.

BUSINESS UNIT LEVEL
Level at which business unit managers set the direction for their products and markets.

FUNCTIONAL LEVEL
Level at which groups of specialists actually create value for the organization.

The **corporate level** is where top management directs overall strategy for the entire organization. Multimarket, multiproduct firms such as Bombardier Inc. or Johnson & Johnson really manage a portfolio of businesses, often termed business units, operating groups, strategic business segments, or product-market units (PMUs).[2] This level creates value for the shareholders of the firm, as measured by stock performance and profitability.

The term **business unit** refers to an organization that markets a set of related products to a clearly defined group of customers. The **business unit level** is the level at which business unit managers set the direction for their products and markets to exploit value-creating opportunities. The strategic direction is more specific at the business level of an organization. For less complex firms with a single business focus, the corporate and business unit levels may merge.

Each business unit has marketing and other specialized activities (e.g., finance, research and development, or human resource management) at the **functional level**, which is where groups of specialists actually create value for the organization. The term *department* generally refers to these specialized functions, such as the marketing department or information systems department. At the functional level, the strategic direction becomes more specific and focused. So, just as there is a hierarchy of levels within organizations, there is also a hierarchy of strategic directions set by management at that level.

Because marketing's role is to look outward—to keep the organization focused on creating customer value—its activities tie to each of the three levels in Figure 2–1. In a large corporation with multiple business units, marketing may be called on to assess consumer trends and analyze marketing opportunities to aid in corporate strategic planning. At the business unit level, marketing may be asked to determine how to compete in given market segments or to develop customer service programs across all business units.

Where Things Happen: Functional Areas and Cross-Functional Teams   At the lowest level in Figure 2–1, marketing serves as part of a team of functional specialists. It is at this level where strategy formulation at higher levels turns into strategy implementation. In other words, marketing makes things happen! Customers are listened to, products are designed and produced, and customer needs are satisfied. The marketing department does not work alone, but works with all departments to deliver customer value and satisfaction.

CROSS-FUNCTIONAL TEAMS
A small number of people from different departments in an organization who are mutually accountable to a common set of performance goals.

In practice, new-product development and other activities in many organizations involve **cross-functional teams**, a small number of people from different departments in an organization who are mutually accountable to a common set of performance goals. Sometimes, very innovative firms develop cross-functional teams that consist of employees not only from different functional areas within the firm but also from its suppliers and customers.

Sometimes, cross-functional conflict can arise because other departments may see marketing's drive to implement the marketing concept and increase customer value as making their own jobs more difficult. The marketing department must make these other departments understand that without satisfied customers who buy the organization's product, there is no company and there are no jobs.

Strategy Issues in Organizations

Organizations need a *raison d'être*—a reason for their existence—and a direction. This is where their business definition, mission, culture, and goals converge. As shown in Figure 2–1, business definition and mission apply to the corporate and business unit levels, while culture and goals relate to all three levels.

Business Definition Organizations like Bombardier, the Canadian Red Cross, and your college or university exist for a purpose—to accomplish something for someone. At birth, most organizations have clear ideas about what "something" and "someone" mean. But as the organization grows over time, often its purpose grows fuzzy or unclear.

This is where the organization repeatedly asks some of the most difficult questions it ever faces: What is our business? Who are our customers? What offerings should we provide to give these customers value? One guideline in defining the organization's business: Try to understand the people served by the organization and the value they receive, which emphasizes the critical customer-driven focus that successful organizations possess.

Organizations must be careful not to define their businesses too narrowly or too broadly. If they do they may lose sight of who their customers are and how to best serve them.[3] With its focus on the customer, Disney does not view itself as being in the theme park or movie business, but rather in the business of creating entertainment, fun, and fantasy for customers. Similarly, Medtronic, a world leader in heart pacemakers, is *not* in the medical device business but *is* in the business of alleviating pain, restoring health, and extending life. Ottawa-based Corel Corporation, maker of software products including CorelDraw and WordPerfect, believes it is in business "to give customers boundless power to create. Anytime. Anywhere."

MISSION
A statement of the organization's scope.

Mission By properly defining its business, an organization can take steps to define its **mission**, a statement of the organization's scope that often identifies its customers, markets, products, technology, and values. Today, often used interchangeably with "vision," the "mission" statement frequently has an inspirational theme—something that can ignite the loyalty of employees and others with whom the organization comes in contact. Figure 2–2 provides the mission statement for a Holiday Inn in Burlington, Ontario. With this clearly defined mission, marketing activities at this Holiday Inn can be more focused and effective.

STAKEHOLDERS
Individuals or groups, either within or outside an organization, that relate to it in what it does and how well it performs.

Culture Organizations must connect not just with their employees but with all of their **stakeholders**, individuals or groups either within or outside an organization that relate to it in terms of what it does and how well it performs. Internal stakeholders include employees, officers, and board members. External stakeholders typically include customers, suppliers, distributors, governments, union, local communities, and the general public.[4]

FIGURE 2–2
Mission of the Holiday Inn
Burlington

The Holiday Inn Burlington is dedicated to providing quality hospitality product and service. Although we try to anticipate guest concerns before they arise, we understand that every customer is an individual who requires special attention. Therefore,

If a customer has a need or want, we fill it.

If a customer has a question, we find the answer.

If a customer has a concern, we resolve it.

If a customer is lost, we show them the way.

CULTURE
The set of values, ideas, and attitudes of a homogeneous group of people that are transmitted from one generation to the next.

GOALS or **OBJECTIVES**
Convert the mission into targeted levels of performance to be achieved.

MARKET SHARE
The ratio of sales revenue of the firm to the total sales revenue of all firms in the industry, including the firm itself.

Whether at the corporate, business, or functional level, a **culture** exists, which is a system of shared values, attitudes, and behaviours that distinguishes one organization from others. As you read in the chapter opener, Bombardier has a strong culture that focuses on delivering quality products and good value to customers, respecting and appreciating employees, protecting the natural environment, and being a good corporate citizen of the communities within which it operates.

Goals   **Goals** or **objectives** (the terms are used interchangeably in this textbook) convert the mission into targeted levels of performance to be achieved, often by a specific time. So these goals measure just how well a mission is being accomplished. As shown in Figure 2–1, goals exist at the corporate, business, and functional levels. All lower-level goals must contribute to achieving goals at the next, higher level. Firms can pursue several different types of goals:

- *Profit.* Classic economic theory assumes a firm seeks to maximize long-run profit, achieving as high a financial return on its investment as possible.
- *Sales revenue.* If profits are acceptable, a firm may elect to maintain or increase its sales level even though profitability may not be maximized. Canadian Tire's goal over the next five years is to increase top-line growth (sales) as well as improve its profitability.
- *Market share.* A firm may choose to maintain or increase its market share, sometimes at the expense of greater profits if industry status or prestige is at stake. **Market share** is the ratio of sales revenue of the firm to the total sales revenue of all firms in the industry, including the firm itself.
- *Unit sales.* Sales revenue may be deceiving because of the effects of inflation, so a firm may choose to maintain or increase the number of units it sells, such as cars, cases of breakfast cereal, or TV sets.
- *Quality.* A firm may target the highest quality products or services in its industry, as 3M does with its Six Sigma program (Chapter 10); Loblaws' goal is to offer customers high-quality food products and a quality shopping experience.
- *Customer satisfaction.* Customers are the reasons the organization exists, so their satisfaction is of vital importance. At Markham, Ontario–based IBM Canada, customer satisfaction is tracked just the same as financial revenue figures. At Maritime Life Assurance Company in Halifax, yearly bonuses paid to employees are based on customer satisfaction data.
- *Employee welfare.* A firm may recognize the critical importance of its employees by having an explicit goal stating its commitment to provide good employment opportunities and working conditions. Hewlett-Packard Canada owns a family resort that its employees can use; Merck Frosst offers daycare facilities to its employees, and BC Biomedical sponsors family events and activities annually.
- *Social responsibility.* A firm may seek to balance conflicting goals of consumers, employees, and shareholders to promote the overall welfare of all these groups, even at the expense of profits. Firms marketing on a global basis are often confronted with the notion of being "good global citizens." The Ethics and

ETHICS AND SOCIAL RESPONSIBILITY ALERT

The Global Dilemma: How to Achieve Sustainable Development

Corporate executives and world leaders are increasingly asked to address the issue of "sustainable development," a term that involves having each country find an ideal balance between protecting its environment and providing its citizens with the additional goods and services necessary to maintain and improve their standard of living.

Eastern Europe and the nations of the former Soviet Union provide an example. Tragically, poisoned air and dead rivers are the legacies of seven decades of communist rule.

With more than half of the households of many of these nations below the poverty level, should the immediate goal be a cleaner environment or more food, clothing, housing, and consumer goods? What should the heads of these governments do? What should Western nations do to help? What should Western firms trying to enter these new, growing markets do?

Should the environment or economic growth come first? What are the societal trade-offs?

Social Responsibility Alert deals with the concept of sustainable development, an issue relevant to global marketers.

Many Canadian private organizations that do not seek profits also exist. Examples include museums like the Montreal Museum for Fine Arts (www.mbam.qc.ca), symphony orchestras like the Edmonton Symphony Orchestra (www.edmonton symphony.com), hospitals like Saint Joseph's Hospital in Hamilton, Ontario (www.stjosham.on.ca), and research institutes like the Conference Board of Canada (www.conferenceboard.ca) and the Fraser Institute in Vancouver (www.fraser institute.ca). These organizations strive to serve consumers, members, or patrons with the greatest efficiency and the least cost.

Although technically not falling under the definition of "nonprofit organization," government agencies also perform marketing activities in trying to achieve their goal of serving the public good. For example, Industry Canada (www.ic.gc.ca) is a federal government department responsible for fostering a competitive, knowledge-based Canadian economy. The department works with Canadians in all parts of the country and throughout the economy to improve conditions for investment, improve Canada's innovation performance, increase Canada's share of global trade, and build a fair, efficient, and competitive marketplace. Some of their marketing initatives include promoting investment and trade, promoting tourism, and facilitating small business development.

Concept Check

1. What are the three levels in today's large organizations?

2. What is the difference between an organization's mission and its culture?

3. Give an example of a goal for a business and a goal for a nonprofit organization.

SETTING STRATEGIC DIRECTIONS

Setting strategic directions involves answering two other difficult questions: (1) Where are we now? and (2) Where do we want to go?

A Look Around: Where Are We Now?

Asking an organization where it is at the present time involves identifying its customers, competencies, and competitors. More detailed approaches of assessing "where are we now?" include both SWOT analysis (see Figure 2–7) and environmental scanning (Chapter 3), which may be done at each of the three levels in the organization.

Customers   A sound strategic direction is set by knowing in complete detail who an organization's customers and prospective customers are and the type of products and services (value) they are seeking. Moreover, where, how, and in what form they want this value delivered must also be known. Without such intimate knowledge, an organization's strategic direction may be misaligned and finite corporate resources wasted. In order to stay close to their customers and to understand their needs, every employee at R.C. Purdy's Chocolates of Vancouver (www.purdys.com) actually serves customers.

Competencies   "What do we do best?" asks about the organization's capabilities or competencies. **Competencies** are an organization's special capabilities, including the skills, technologies, and resources that distinguish it from other organizations. Exploiting these competencies can lead to organizational success.[5] Competencies should be distinctive enough to provide a **competitive advantage**, a unique strength relative to competitors that is often based on quality, time, cost, innovation, or customer intimacy.[6]

For example, if 3M has a goal of generating a specific portion of its sales from new products, it must have a supporting competency in research and development and new-product marketing. Canadian Tire believes one of its competitive advantages is its ability to stay close to the customer (customer intimacy). It is able to do so, in part, because of its strategic retail locations. In fact, 92 percent of the Canadian population lives within 15 minutes of a Canadian Tire store, and more than 40 percent of Canadian adults shop there every week. Once the customer is in the store, Canadian Tire associates attempt to provide outstanding customer service.

Another strategy is to develop a competency in producing high-quality products. **Quality** here means those features and characteristics of a product that influence its ability to satisfy customer needs. The Marketing NewsNet describes W. Edwards Deming's "quality chain," which has revolutionized global thinking about quality and is the foundation of many of today's quality initiatives.[7] Firms often try to improve quality through **benchmarking**—discovering how others do something better than your own firm so you can imitate or leapfrog the competition. Benchmarking can also involve studying operations in completely different businesses and applying this new knowledge to your own business.

Competitors   In today's globalized competitive world, in order to respond with their own strategies firms must continuously assess not only who the competitors are but also how they are changing. A brief look at Toronto-based Shoppers Drug Mart's situation provides a typical example of the complex array of competitors today's business firms face. Shoppers Drug Mart is a $5-billion retail powerhouse and owns one of Canada's premier brands (Life Brand). It has more than 860 franchised stores across Canada (including Quebec, where it operates under the Pharmaprix banner). Still, Shoppers, the long-standing industry leader with 17 percent of the market, faces a competitive squeeze play. On one flank there's the Edmonton-based Katz Group, which has suddenly emerged as a major competitor in the retail pharmacy market. Katz has 1500 Canadian drugstores under the Katz Group umbrella, including corporate-owned chains such as Rexall and Pharma Plus and independents operating under the Medicine Shoppe and IDA/Guardian banners. From seemingly out of nowhere, Katz vaulted into the number-two position behind Shoppers with sales of more than $4.3 billion.

On the other flank, the supermarkets—led by Loblaws and Safeway—and mass merchandisers such as Wal-Mart continue their charge into the pharmacy business, using loss-leader dispensing fees as a lure. The supermarkets and mass merchandisers

COMPETENCIES
An organization's special capabilities, including skills, technologies, and resources that distinguish it from other organizations.

COMPETITIVE ADVANTAGE
A unique strength relative to competitors, often based on quality, time, cost, innovation, or customer intimacy.

QUALITY
Those features and characteristics of a product that influence its ability to satisfy customer needs.

BENCHMARKING
Discovering how others do something better than your own firm so you can imitate or leapfrog competition.

MARKETING NEWSNET

Adding Customer Value through the Quality Chain Reaction

When W. Edwards Deming went to Japan in 1950 to help rebuild postwar Japan, he shared a very profound model with Japanese industry. This model helped launch the quality revolution that has contributed to dramatic global change in countless industries.

The model is shown below. It has become a mantra for the quality movement. Assuming an organization has an otherwise effective strategy and management structure in place, the model shows the additional benefits from improving the quality of products, services, and processes. The first benefit is a decrease in costs as a direct result of less waste. A consequence of less waste is greater process productivity. This allows lower prices, which combines with the improved

products and services to allow the organization to compete more effectively. The ultimate payoff is that the firm stays in business and provides jobs because it provides greater value to the customers.

The amount of benefit can be quantified by looking at the cost of poor quality. Experts claim that 10 percent to 20 percent of sales revenues are needed to cover the cost of poor quality in the form of production waste and rework, complaints and warranty costs, and defective products. Through well-designed marketing programs, marketers can help reduce the cost of poor quality and contribute directly to a firm's performance.

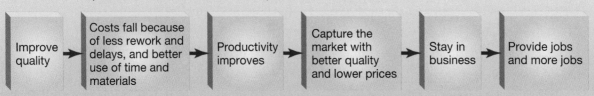

now collectively control about $8 billion of the $27-billion retail pharmacy market. In Ontario, which is by far Shoppers' strongest region, Loblaws now records drugstore-category sales of about $1.3 billion annually—up from $200 million a decade ago. In Quebec, Shoppers/Pharmaprix lags a distant third behind Jean Coutu Group Inc. This competitor has system-wide sales of $2 billion, making it the fourth-largest player in Canada—without any presence outside of Quebec.

"The biggest challenge that an organization like Shoppers faces," says David Dunne, a professor of marketing at the University of Toronto's Rotman School of Management, "is that their competition isn't what it used to be." And he is right! Given the strong direct and "intertype competition" (see Chapter 17) Shoppers faces, the company is embarking on new marketing intiatives including new outlets, stronger merchandising programs, and lower prices. Shoppers plans to sharply increase the "front-store" sales (paper products, health and beauty aids, etc.) by persuading its growing number of prescription-toting customers to pick up a few things on their way out. The marketing effort will include better promotion of private-label products and extra emphasis on marketing initiatives such as Shoppers' loyalty card. Glenn Murphy, Shoppers' new chairman and CEO, believes that the company can compete effectively in this new arena. If it cannot, the Katz Group might be willing to step in and acquire its major rival.[8]

Growth Strategies: Where Do We Want to Go?

Knowing where the organization is at present enables managers to set a direction for it and start to allocate resources to move there. Two techniques to aid in these decisions are (1) portfolio analysis and (2) market–product analysis.

The Portfolio of Businesses: BCG Analysis The Boston Consulting Group's (BCG) business portfolio analysis uses quantified performance measures and growth targets to analyze a firm's business units (in the BCG analysis called strategic business units, or SBUs) as though they were a collection of separate investments.[9]

FIGURE 2–3
Boston Consulting Group
growth-share matrix for a
strong, diversified firm
showing some strategic plans

Boston Consulting Group

www.bcg.com

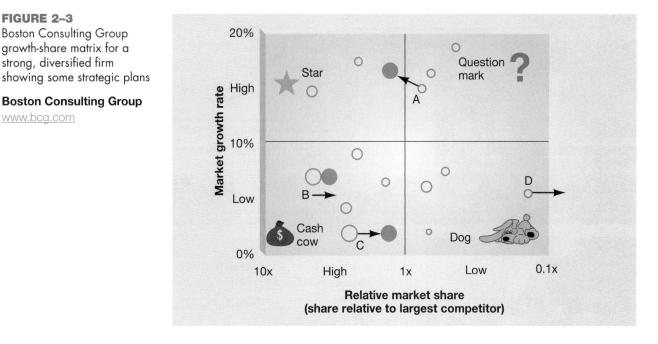

While used at the business unit level here, this BCG analysis has also been applied at the product line or individual product or brand level. The popularity of this kind of portfolio analysis is shown by the fact that more than 75 percent of the largest firms in North America have used it in some form. BCG, an internationally known management consulting firm, advises its clients to locate the position of its SBU on a growth-share matrix (Figure 2–3). The vertical axis is the market growth rate, which is the annual rate of growth of the specific market or industry in which a given SBU is competing. This axis in the figure runs from 0 to 20 percent, although in practice it might run even higher. The axis has arbitrarily been divided at 10 percent into high-growth and low-growth areas.

The horizontal axis is the *relative market share*, defined as the sales of the SBU divided by the sales of the largest firm in the industry. A relative market share of 10× (at the left end of the scale) means that the SBU has 10 times the share of its largest competitor, whereas a share of 0.1× (at the right end of the scale) means it has only 10 percent of the sales of its largest competitor. The scale is logarithmic and is arbitrarily divided into high and low relative market shares at a value of 1×.

BCG has given specific names and descriptions to the four resulting quadrants in its growth-share matrix based on the amount of cash they generate for or require from the firm:

- Cash cows (lower-left quadrant) are SBUs that typically generate large amounts of cash, far more than they can invest profitably in their own product line. They have a dominant share of a slow-growth market and provide cash to pay large amounts of company overhead and to invest in other SBUs.
- Stars (upper-left quadrant) are SBUs with a high share of high-growth markets that may not generate enough cash to support their own demanding needs for future growth. When their growth slows, they are likely to become cash cows.
- Question marks or problem children (upper-right quadrant) are SBUs with a low share of high-growth markets. They require large injections of cash just to maintain their market share, much less increase it. Their name implies management's dilemma for these SBUs: choosing the right ones to invest in and phasing out the rest.
- Dogs (lower-right quadrant) are SBUs with a low share of low-growth markets. Although they may generate enough cash to sustain themselves, they do not hold the promise of ever becoming real winners for the firm. Dropping SBUs

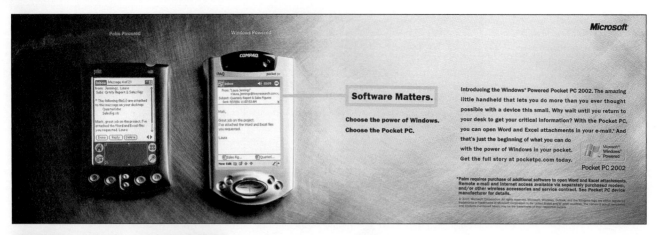

Strategies emerging from a business portfolio analysis: Microsoft "builds" its hand-held business while Procter & Gamble "divests" its Duncan Hines cake mix line to Aurora Foods.

in this quadrant from a business portfolio is generally advocated except when relationships with other SBUs, competitive considerations, or potential strategic alliances exist.

The 14 circles in Figure 2–3 show the current SBUs in a strong, diversified firm. The area of each circle is proportional to the corresponding SBU's annual sales revenue.

The portfolio in Figure 2–3 is a mixed one. On the favourable side, one-half of its SBUs are large and have high market shares; unfortunately, the other half are small with low market shares. Because most firms have limited influence on the market growth rate (the factor shown on the vertical axis), their main alternative in a growth-share matrix framework is to try to change the relative market share (the factor on the horizontal axis).

To accomplish this, management makes conscious decisions on what role each SBU should have in the future and either injects or removes cash from it. Four alternative strategies are available for each SBU. The firm can invest more in the SBU to *build* its share (SBU A in Figure 2–3). Or it can invest just enough to *hold* the SBU's share at about its current level (SBU B in the figure). Or it can *harvest* the SBU (SBU C in the figure), trying to milk its short-term cash flow even though it may lose share and become a dog in the longer run. Finally, the firm can *divest* the SBU (SBU D) by phasing it out or actually selling it to gain cash to invest in the remaining SBUs.

The primary strengths of business portfolio analysis include (1) forcing a firm to assess each of its SBUs in terms of its relative market share and industry market growth rate, which, in turn, (2) requires the firm to forecast which SBUs will be cash producers and cash users in the future. Weaknesses are that (1) it is often difficult to get the information needed to locate each SBU on the growth-share matrix, (2) there are other important factors missing from the analysis such as possible synergies among the SBUs when they use the same salesforce or research and development facilities, and (3) there are problems in motivating people in an SBU that has been labelled a dog or even a cash cow and is unlikely to get new resources from the firm to grow and provide opportunities for promotion.[10] In addition, planners have had difficulty incorporating competitive information into portfolio analysis, and formal experiments show the technique may not provide as effective an allocation of resources as more traditional methods of financial analysis.[11]

Market–Product Analysis   Firms can also view growth opportunities in terms of four combinations of (1) current and new markets and (2) current and new products, as shown in Figure 2–4.[12] As Rollerblade, Inc. attempts to increase sales revenue, it must consider all four of the alternative market–product strategies shown in Figure 2–4. For example, it can try to use a strategy of *market penetration*—increasing sales

FIGURE 2–4
Four market-product strategies: alternative ways to expand sales revenue for Rollerblade, Inc.

MARKETS	PRODUCTS	
	CURRENT	**NEW**
Current	**Market Penetration** Selling more in-line skates to Canadians	**Product Development** Selling a new product like the Fusion to Canadians
New	**Market Development** Selling in-line skates in Australia	**Diversification** Selling in-line skating accessories like helmets and clothing, or entering the bicycle business

of present products in existing markets, in this case by increasing sales of its present in-line skates to Canadian consumers. There is no change in either the product line or the market served, but increased sales are possible through actions such as better advertising, lower prices, or expanded distribution in retail outlets.

Market development, which for Rollerblade, Inc. means selling existing Rollerblade Inc. products to new markets, is a reasonable alternative. Australian and Western European consumers are good candidates as possible new markets.

An expansion strategy using *product development* involves selling a new product to existing markets. As you know from Chapter 1, Rollerblade, Inc. developed the Junior Line for the children's segment, the Core and Fusion skates for the fitness segment, and the Coyote for the aggressive, all-terrain skater—as well as the Bladerunner, a lower-priced skate for the value-conscious segment. One problem with a product development strategy is the possibility of *product cannibalism*—a new product gaining sales by stealing them from a firm's other products.

Diversification involves developing new products and selling them in new markets. This is potentially a high-risk strategy for most firms because the company has neither previous production experience nor marketing experience on which to draw. However, there are varying degrees of diversification. *Related diversification* occurs when new products and markets have something in common with existing operations. For example, Rollerblade, Inc. sells in-line skating accessories including helmets and clothing. *Unrelated diversification* means that the new products and markets have nothing in common with existing operations. In this case, Rollerblade, Inc. might diversify into a completely new area, such as the bicycle business. To check out Rollerblade, Inc.'s strategies, read the Web Link box.

WEB LINK

http://www.mcgrawhill.ca

Rollerblade, Inc., Market–Product Strategies

Rollerblade, Inc., has chosen to pursue multiple market–product strategies to achieve new sales growth. Go to its Website (www.rollerblade.com) and check out what the company's current strategies are and what its future plans are likely to be. What do you think about what you have uncovered there?

FIGURE 2–5
A combination of customer relationships, innovation, quality, and efficiency are the building blocks of an organization's success.

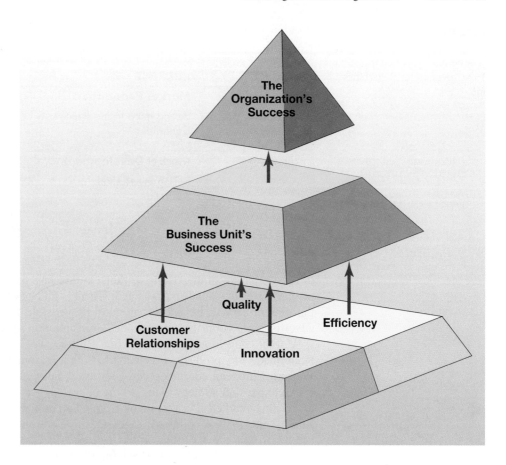

Building Blocks for an Organization's Success

Management theorists have attempted to identify key factors that are essential to a firm's success. One such structure appears in Figure 2–5, which identifies four critical factors: (1) customer relationships, to deliver genuine value for customers; (2) innovation, to create new and unique value; (3) quality, to ensure an excellence and consistency in what is sold; and (4) efficiency, to lower costs and, hence, the price paid by customers. Note that improving each of these factors at a particular time might cause other factors to decline. Thus, it is a continuing challenge for an organization to strike the right balance among these four "building blocks" that are the foundation of an organization's success.[13]

Lands' End provides an example of these building blocks. Its stores and Website (see photo) give a remarkable statement about its commitments to customer relationships and the quality of its products with these unconditional words:

GUARANTEED. PERIOD.®

Its Website points out that the Lands' End guarantee has always been an unconditional one and has read: "If you are not completely satisfied with any item you buy from us, at any time during your use of it, return it and we will refund your full purchase price." But to get the message across more clearly to its customers, it put it in the two-word guarantee above.

In terms of the innovation building block, Lands' End continuously improves its search engines to allow customers to use plain-language searches to find items more easily on its Website. And what about the efficiency block in Lands' End's arsenal? In 2000, Lands' End launched a new service, "My Personal Shopper," that guides Web shoppers and helps simplify their buying decisions. Its conversion rate with this? About 80 percent higher among those who used the Personal Shopper compared to those who used the nonpersonalized recommendations from its Website.[14]

Lands' End's unconditional guarantee for its products is part of its "success" strategy. Others are described in the text.

Concept Check

1. What are "competencies" and why are they important?

2. What is business portfolio analysis?

3. What are the four building blocks of an organization's success?

THE STRATEGIC MARKETING PROCESS

All approaches to planning try to find answers to these key questions:

1. Where are we now?
2. Where do we want to go?
3. How do we allocate our resources to get to where we want to go?
4. How do we convert our plans into actions?
5. How do our results compare with our plans, and do deviations require new plans and actions?

STRATEGIC MARKETING PROCESS
The approach whereby an organization allocates its marketing mix resources to reach its target markets.

MARKETING PLAN
A road map for the marketing activities of an organization for a specified future period of time, such as one year or five years.

This same approach is used in the **strategic marketing process**, whereby an organization allocates its marketing mix resources to reach its target markets. This process is divided into three phases: planning, implementation, and control (Figure 2–6).

The strategic marketing process is so central to the activities of most organizations that they formalize it as a **marketing plan**, which is a road map for an organization's marketing activities for a specified future period, such as one year or five years. Appendix A at the end of this chapter provides guidelines for writing a marketing plan and also presents a sample marketing plan for Paradise Kitchens,® Inc., a firm that produces and distributes a line of spicy chilies under the Howlin' Coyote® brand name. The sequence of activities that follows parallels the elements of the marketing plan that appears in Appendix A.

The following section gives an overview of the strategic marketing process that places Chapters 3 through 21 in perspective. In Chapter 22 we examine the strategic marketing process again in more depth.

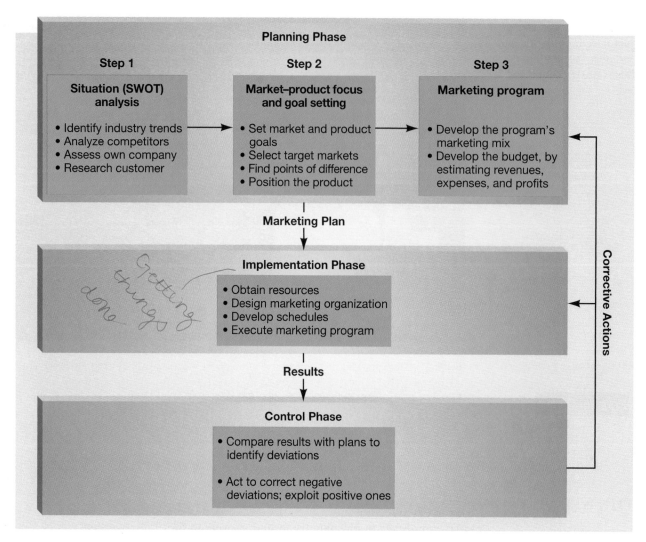

FIGURE 2–6
The strategic marketing
process

Strategic Marketing Process: The Planning Phase

As shown in Figure 2–6, the planning phase of the strategic marketing process consists of the three steps shown at the top of the figure: (1) situation analysis, (2) market–product focus and goal setting, and (3) the marketing program. Let's use the recent marketing planning experiences of several companies to look at each of these steps.

SITUATION ANALYSIS
Taking stock of where the firm or product has been recently, where it is now, and where it is headed in terms of the organization's plans and the external factors and trends affecting it.

SWOT ANALYSIS
An acronym describing an organization's appraisal of its internal strengths and weaknesses and its external opportunities and threats.

Step 1: Situation (SWOT) Analysis The essence of the **situation analysis** is taking stock of where the firm or product has been recently, where it is now, and where it is headed in light of the organization's plans and the external factors and trends affecting it. The situation analysis box in Figure 2–6 is the first of the three steps in the planning phase.

An effective shorthand summary of the situation analysis is a **SWOT analysis**, an acronym describing an organization's appraisal of its internal *s*trengths and *w*eaknesses and its external *o*pportunities and *t*hreats. Both the situation and SWOT analyses can be done at the level of the entire organization, the business unit, the product line, or the specific product. As an analysis moves from the level of the entire organization to the specific product, it, of course, becomes far more detailed. For small firms or those with basically a single product line, an analysis at the firm or product level is really the same thing.

Remember Rollerblade, Inc. from Chapter 1? Figure 2–7 shows what a SWOT analysis might look like for that firm. Note that the SWOT table shown has four

FIGURE 2–7
A SWOT analysis for
Rollerblade, Inc.

LOCATION OF FACTOR	TYPE OF FACTOR	
	FAVOURABLE	**UNFAVOURABLE**
Internal	**Strengths** • Industry leader • Innovative, in products and design • Strong brand awareness • Strong position in sporting goods and specialty outlets	**Weaknesses** • Premium-priced position puts off the "value-conscious" consumer • Limited distribution in mass merchandising outlets
External	**Opportunities** • Identify new market segments to serve • Promote a brand for the "value-conscious" consumer • Expand distribution globally • Expand accessories line	**Threats** • Fierce competition at both the premium and low end of market • Brand name may become a generic term for in-line skates

cells formed by the combination of internal and external factors (the rows) and favourable versus unfavourable factors (the columns) that summarize Rollerblade, Inc.'s strengths, weaknesses, opportunities, and threats.

A more in-depth SWOT analysis might use more detailed checklists of internal and external factors in the table. For example, internal factors might be broken down to include key elements such as products offered and the effectiveness of the functional areas such as sales or research and development (R&D) that affect marketing activities. Similarly, external factors are often formalized in the SWOT analysis by using the external or environmental factors affecting marketing activities, such as competition, consumer, or technological trends. An example of using these detailed breakdowns of internal and external factors appears in the Paradise Kitchens SWOT in Appendix A. For simplicity, Rollerblade, Inc.'s SWOT does not contain this level of detail.

A SWOT analysis helps a firm identify the strategy-related factors in these four cells that can have a major effect on the firm. However, all factors in such an analysis are not of equal value, so the ultimate goal is to identify the *critical* factors affecting the firm and then build on vital strengths, correct glaring weaknesses, exploit significant opportunities, and avoid disaster-laden threats. That is a big order. This ultimate goal is not simply to develop the SWOT analysis but to translate the results of the analysis into specific actions to help the firm grow and succeed.

Although the SWOT analysis is a shorthand look at the situation analysis, it is based on an exhaustive study of the four areas shown in Figure 2–6 that are the foundation on which the firm builds its marketing program:

- Identifying trends in the firm's industry.
- Analyzing the firm's competitors.
- Assessing the firm itself.
- Researching the firm's present and prospective customers.

Examples of more in-depth analysis in these four areas appear in the marketing plan in Appendix A and the chapters in this text that are cited in that plan.

MARKET SEGMENTATION
Aggregating prospective buyers into groups, or segments, that (1) have common needs and (2) will respond similarly to a marketing action.

Step 2: Market–Product Focus and Goal Setting   Finding a focus on what product offerings will be directed toward which customers (step 2 of the planning phase in Figure 2–6) is essential for developing an effective marketing program (step 3). This focus often comes from the firm's using **market segmentation**, which involves aggregating prospective buyers into groups, or segments, that (1) have common

A small business such as
Paradise Kitchens has a
carefully developed focus for
its marketing program.

needs and (2) will respond similarly to a marketing action. Ideally a firm can use market
segmentation to identify the segments on which it will focus its efforts—its target market
segments—and develop one or more marketing programs to reach them.

Goal setting here involves setting measurable marketing objectives to be achieved,
possibly for a specific market, a specific product or brand, or an entire marketing
program. As mentioned earlier, there is a hierarchy of goals and objectives flowing
from the corporate strategy set by top management on down to the levels of the
marketing managers.

We can illustrate steps 2 and 3 in the planning phase of the strategic marketing
process by using the Paradise Kitchens marketing plan from Appendix A. This firm
is trying to expand its line of Howlin' Coyote spicy chilies from 3 to 20 metropolitan
markets by 2003. Stated simply, the five-year marketing plan for Paradise Kitchens
specifies these step 2 activities:

- *Set marketing and product goals.* As mentioned later in Chapter 10, the chances
  of new-product success are increased by specifying both market and product
  goals. Paradise Kitchens will grow its present markets by expanding brands and
  flavours, adding 17 new metropolitan markets, entering the food-service market,
  and adding new products.
- *Select target markets.* Howlin' Coyote chilies will be targeted at one- to three-
  person households with annual incomes above $30 000 in which both adults are
  likely to work outside the home—adventurous consumers wanting premium-
  quality Mexican food products.
- *Find points of difference.* **Points of difference** are those characteristics of
  a product that make it superior to competitive substitutes. (Chapter 10 points
  out that this is the single most important factor in the success or failure of a
  new product.) For Howlin' Coyote chilies these are unique spicy taste; quality,
  convenience, and a range of flavours; and premium packaging.

POINTS OF DIFFERENCE
Those characteristics of a
product that make it superior
to competitive substitutes.

FIGURE 2–8
Elements of the marketing mix that compose a cohesive marketing program

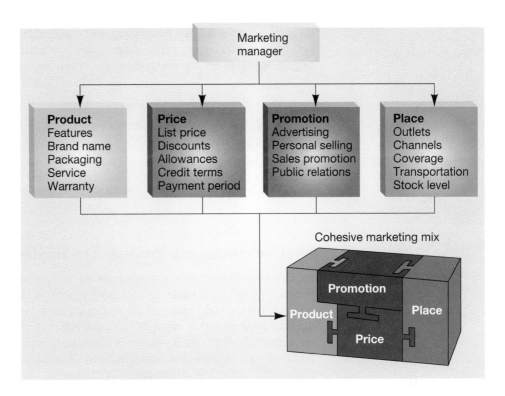

- *Position the product.* Howlin' Coyote chilies will be "positioned" in consumers' minds as "very high-quality, authentic Mexican tasting chilies that can be prepared easily and quickly."

Details in these four elements of step 2 provide a solid foundation to use in developing the marketing program—the next step in the planning phase of the strategic marketing process.

Step 3: Marketing Program   Activities in step 2 tell the marketing manager which customers to target and which customer needs the firm's product offerings can satisfy—the *who* and *what* aspects of the strategic marketing process. The *how* aspect, step 3 in the planning phase, involves developing the program's marketing mix and its budget.

Figure 2–8 shows components of each marketing mix element that are combined to provide a cohesive marketing program. For the five-year marketing plan of Paradise Kitchens, these marketing mix activities include the following:

- *Product strategy.* Offer a current line of five Howlin' Coyote chilies with proprietary flavouring, high-quality ingredients without preservatives, and distinctive packaging that communicates the brand's uniqueness.
- *Price strategy.* Price Howlin' Coyote chili at $2.99 for a 300-g package, comparable to other frozen offerings and higher than the canned and dried chili varieties.
- *Promotion strategy.* Feature in-store demonstrations to highlight the product's unique qualities, recipes using the brand to stimulate use, and various kinds of cents-off coupons to generate trial and repeat-purchase of the brand.
- *Place (distribution) strategy.* Use food distributors with current sales volumes, shifting to brokers as increased sales volumes justify them.

Putting this marketing program into effect requires that the firm commit time and money to it in the form of a budget. The budgeting process starts with a sales forecast based on estimates of units expected to be sold—probably by month, quarter, and year. Estimated expenses for the marketing mix activities comprising the marketing program are estimated and balanced against expected revenues to estimate the program's profitability. This budget is really the "sales" document presented to top management to gain approval for the budgeted resources to implement the marketing program.

Concept Check

1. What is the difference between a strength and an opportunity in a SWOT analysis?

2. What is market segmentation?

3. What are "points of difference" and why are they important?

Strategic Marketing Process: The Implementation Phase

As shown in Figure 2–6, the result of the tens or hundreds of hours spent in the planning phase of the strategic marketing process is the firm's marketing plan. Implementation, the second phase of the strategic marketing process, involves carrying out the marketing plan that emerges from the planning phase. If the firm cannot put the marketing plan into effect—in the implementation phase—the planning phase was a waste of time. Figure 2–6 also shows the four components of the implementation phase: (1) obtaining resources, (2) designing the marketing organization, (3) developing schedules, and (4) actually executing the marketing program designed in the planning phase. Kodak provides a case example.

Fortune magazine has called Kodak a "bureaucratic, wasteful, paternalistic, slow-moving, isolated, and beloved company,"[15] and one that requires the kind of restructuring IBM has gone through to compete in today's global marketplace. The first agent of change for Kodak's restructuring was George Fisher, its chief executive officer (CEO) in the late 1990s. His early decisions are classic management and marketing lessons in implementing and controlling the activities of a corporate giant.

Obtaining Resources   When George Fisher arrived at Kodak in the mid-1990s, he observed, "There are textbook types of things that are wrong with this company. Decisions are too slow. People don't take risks."[16] So he pushed some revolutionary decisions that seemed obvious to him:

- Focus on Kodak's core business: imaging.
- Serve customer needs better, and stress quality.
- Shorten product-development cycles.
- Encourage a more dynamic, risk-taking, fast-decision culture.

Fisher needed money to implement these ideas, however, so he obtained U.S.$8 billion by selling off divisions not related to Kodak's core imaging business.

Designing the Marketing Organization   A marketing program needs a marketing organization to implement it. This is especially true for firms such as Kodak that face constantly changing global markets. Figure 2–9 shows the organization chart of a typical manufacturing firm, giving some details of the marketing department's structure. Four managers of marketing activities are shown to report to the vice president of marketing: the managers of product planning, marketing research, sales, and advertising and promotion. Depending on the size of the organization, there may be several product planning managers—each responsible for a separate product line. Also, several regional sales managers and an international sales manager may report to the manager of sales. This marketing organization is responsible for converting marketing plans to reality.

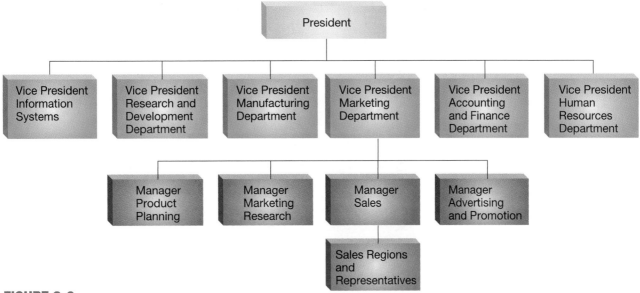

FIGURE 2–9
Organization of a typical manufacturing firm, showing a breakdown of the marketing department

Developing Schedules   In Fisher's late-1990s years Kodak's sales revenues declined or were flat (Figure 2–10), and in early 2000 Daniel Karp became Kodak's CEO. Karp immediately launched a two-pronged strategy: (1) move aggressively into digital camera and imaging technology while (2) improving Kodak's traditional cash cow film and film processing services. The focus—ugh!—on film comes about because 90 percent of customers are still happy using film cameras and Kodak's paper, chemicals, and technical savvy are needed to complete the picture and make great prints.[17] One key to effective implementation is setting deadlines, which are supported be detailed schedules. Karp set these deadlines for Kodak for 2001:

• Launch the mc3 digital camera line ($250–$350) targeted at 18- to 28-year-olds, which combines still camera, video camera, and MP3 player.
• Introduce a family (DX 3500, DX 3600) of EasyShare digital cameras ($400–$600) and docking stations ($80), facilitating easy uploading of photos to a computer and the Internet.
• Emphasize its Kodak.com Website (800 000 visits per month in 2001), which does everything from selling cameras to consumers to processing their film, arranging their photo albums, and letting them edit their images online.[18]

Executing the Marketing Program   Marketing plans are meaningless pieces of paper without effective execution of those plans. This effective execution requires attention to detail for both marketing strategies and marketing tactics. A **marketing strategy** is the means by which a marketing goal is to be achieved, usually characterized by a specified target market and a marketing program to reach it. Although the term *strategy* is often used loosely, it implies both the end sought (target market) and the means to achieve it (marketing program).

To implement a marketing program successfully, hundreds of detailed decisions are often required, such as writing ads or setting prices. These decisions, called **marketing tactics**, are detailed day-to-day operational decisions essential to the overall success of marketing strategies. Compared with marketing strategies, marketing tactics generally involve actions that must be taken right away. Here are examples of both kinds of decisions at Kodak:

• *Marketing strategy decision.* Kodak looked at the surprising success cameras targeted at 18- to 28-year-olds (the "Generation Y" or "Gen Y" consumers discussed in the next chapter) and teenagers: Nintendo's Game Boy digital camera and Polaroid's i-Zone instant camera. Kodak's strategy decision: Launch a new product targeted at Gen Y.

MARKETING STRATEGY
The means by which a marketing goal is to be achieved, usually characterized by a specified target market and a marketing program to reach it.

MARKETING TACTICS
The detailed day-to-day operational decisions essential to the overall success of marketing strategies.

FIGURE 2–10
Evaluation and control of
Kodak's marketing program

FIGURE 2–10
Evaluation and control of
Kodak's marketing program

- *Marketing tactics decision.* Concurrently, Kodak engineers were toying with the idea of hooking the computing power of digital cameras to digital MP3 music files. "We proposed the technology of the product," recalls engineer Clay Dunsmore, "but we didn't have a clear idea of who we would sell it to!" Kodak's tactics decision: Form a cross-functional team to work on the gadget—which became the mc3.[19]

Marketing strategies and marketing tactics shade into each other. Effective marketing program implementation requires excruciating concern for both.

Strategic Marketing Process: The Control Phase

The control phase of the strategic marketing process seeks to keep the marketing program moving in the direction set for it (see Figure 2–6). Accomplishing this requires the marketing manager (1) to compare the results of the marketing program with the goals in the written plans to identify deviations and (2) to act on these deviations—correcting negative deviations and exploiting positive ones.

Comparing Results with Plans to Identify Deviations   In late 2000, as Daniel Karp looked at the company's sales revenues from 1995 through 2000, he didn't like what he saw: the very flat trend, or AB in Figure 2–10. Extending the 1995–2000 trend to 2005 shows flat sales revenues: a totally unacceptable, no-growth strategy.

Kodak never achieved its late 1990s annual growth goal of 13 percent. Cutting this goal in half gives a more realistic target sales revenue line of BD from 2001 to 2005. This reveals a wedge-shaped shaded gap in the figure. Planners call this the *planning gap*, the difference between the projection of the path to reach a new goal (line BD) and the projection of the path of the results of a plan already in place (line BC).

The ultimate purpose of the firm's marketing program is to "fill in" this planning gap—in Kodak's case, to move its future sales revenue line from the no-growth line BC up to the challenging target of line BD. But poor performance can result in actual sales revenues being far less than the targeted levels. This is the essence of evaluation—comparing actual results with planned objectives.

Acting on Deviations   When evaluation shows that actual performance fails to meet expectations, managers need to take corrective actions. And when actual results are far better than the plan called for, creative managers find ways to exploit the situation. Two recent Kodak "midcourse corrections" for both positive and negative deviations from targets illustrate these management actions:

- *Exploiting a positive deviation.* Consumers like to take their film to Kodak mini-labs at retailers and get two sets of prints, but some also want to be able to edit their prints. So Kodak has strengthened its strategic partnerships with retailers like Wal-Mart and Kinko's to let the "second set of prints" be a CD-ROM that can be digitally edited.
- *Correcting a negative deviation.* Months of marketing research on digital camera users showed Kodak they wanted to get exact digital photos linked to PCs and the Internet with easy-to-use software, a problem with early designs. The fix: technical improvements leading to today's EasyShare camera-and-dock system.[20]

The strategic marketing process is discussed in greater detail again in Chapter 22.

Concept Check

1. What is the control phase of the strategic marketing process?

2. How do the objectives set for a marketing program in the planning phase relate to the control phase of the strategic marketing process?

SUMMARY

1   Today's large organizations, both business firms and non-profit organizations, are often divided into three levels: the corporate, business unit, and functional levels.

2   Marketing has a role in all three levels by keeping a focus on customers and finding ways to add genuine customer value. At the lowest level, marketing serves as part of a team of functional specialists whose day-to-day actions actually involve customers and create customer value.

3   Organizations exist for a purpose—to accomplish something for someone. To give organizations focus, they continuously assess their business, definition, mission, culture, and goals.

4   Setting strategic directions for an organization involves asking "Where are we now?" to assess the organization's customers, competencies, and competitors. It also involves asking "Where do we want to go?", which uses techniques like portfolio analysis and market–product analysis.

5   An organization's success rests on four building blocks: customer relationships, innovation, quality, and efficiency.

6   The strategic marketing process involves an organization allocating its marketing mix resources to reach its target markets using three phases: planning, implementation, and control.

7   The planning phase of the strategic marketing process has three steps, each with more specific elements: situation (SWOT) analysis, market–product focus and goal setting, and marketing program.

8   The implementation phase of the strategic marketing process has four key elements: obtaining resources, designing the marketing organization, developing schedules, and executing the marketing program.

9   The control phase of the strategic marketing process involves comparing results with the planned targets to identify deviations and taking actions to correct negative deviations and exploit positive ones.

KEY TERMS AND CONCEPTS

benchmarking p. 35
business unit p. 31
business unit level p. 31
competencies p. 35
competitive advantage p. 35
corporate level p. 31
cross-functional team p. 32
culture p. 33
functional level p. 31
goals p. 33
market segmentation p. 43
market share p. 33

marketing plan p. 41
marketing strategy p. 47
marketing tactics p. 47
mission p. 32
objectives p. 33
points of difference p. 44
profit p. 30
quality p. 35
situation analysis p. 42
stakeholders p. 32
strategic marketing process p. 41
SWOT analysis p. 42

INTERNET EXERCISE

www.mcgrawhill.ca/college/berkowitz

In April 2000, Unilever PLC, a multi-billion dollar, multinational consumer products conglomerate (Wisk, Vaseline, Lipton, etc.) based in Europe, "scooped up" Ben & Jerry's Homemade, Inc. for $326 million. Unilever added Ben & Jerry's to its portfolio of other famous ice cream brands, such as Breyers All Natural, Good-Humor, Klondike, and Popsicle, to increase its share of the ice cream market in North America. Co-founders Ben Cohen and Jerry Greenfield will remain with Ben & Jerry's to promote its brand of socially conscious capitalism as specified in its mission statement, even though some customers and other stakeholders thought the pair had sold out. Moreover, as a condition of the buyout, Unilever must continue to donate 7.5 percent of all pre-tax profits to the Ben & Jerry's Foundation and other organizations that engage in socially responsible activities.

Go to the Ben & Jerry's Website (www.benjerry.com/mission.html) and Unilever's Website (www.unilever.com/company/ourpurpose) to compare the mission statements that each firm has adopted. How are they similar? How are they different? Which mission statement do you believe will lead to "sustainable, profitable growth for the brand or businesses and the long-term creation of value for shareholders and employees" (from the *Introducing Unilever* promotional brochure)? Do you think that Unilever will continue to allow Ben & Jerry's to pursue the "social" aspect of its three-pronged mission, particularly during periods of economic difficulty when corporations typically reduce costs in an attempt to remain profitable? Also, since Ben & Jerry's cartoon ads no longer feature the images of its co-founders, do you think the brand will continue to retain its socially minded, counterculture image? Finally, how could a multinational firm like Unilever apply Ben & Jerry's business mission to its other brands or businesses?

Want to get better grades, find tips on how to study more effectively, and stay up to date with happenings in the world of marketing? Visit the Online Learning Centre for practice tests, Study Smart software, and much more! www.mcgrawhill.ca/college/berkowitz
Interested in finding out what marketing looks like in the real world? *Marketing Magazine* is just a click away on your OLC! Visit www.mcgrawhill.ca/college/berkowitz

APPLYING MARKETING CONCEPTS AND PERSPECTIVES

1 (*a*) Explain what a mission statement is. (*b*) Using Holiday Inn as an example from the chapter, explain how the mission statement gives a strategic direction to its organization. (*c*) Create a mission statement for your own career.

2 How might top management try to change the "culture" of its organization?

3 What competencies best describe (*a*) your college or university, (*b*) your favourite restaurant, and (*c*) the company that manufactures the computer you own or use most often?

4 Why does a product often start as a question mark and then move counterclockwise around BCG's growth-share matrix shown in Figure 2–3?

5 Many Canadian universities have traditionally offered an undergraduate degree in liberal arts (the product) to full-time 18- to 22-year-old students (the market). How might such a university use the four market–product expansion strategies shown in Figure 2–4 to compete in the 21st century?

6 What is the main result of each of the three phases of the strategic marketing process? (*a*) planning, (*b*) implementation, and (*c*) control.

7 Select one strength, one weakness, one opportunity, and one threat from the SWOT analysis for Rollerblade, Inc. shown in Figure 2–7, and suggest a specific possible action that the company might take to exploit or address each one.

8 The goal-setting step in the planning phase of the strategic marketing process sets quantified objectives for use in the control phase. What actions are suggested for a marketing manager if measured results are below objectives? Above objectives?

9 Read Appendix A, "A Sample Marketing Plan." Then write a 600-word executive summary for the marketing plan using the numbered headings shown in the plan.

VIDEO CASE 2–1 Specialized Bicycle Components, Inc.

The speaker leans forward with both intensity and pride in his voice. "We're in the business of creating a bike that delivers the customer their best possible ride," he explains. "When the customer sees our red 'S,' they say this is the company that understands the cyclist. It's a company of riders. The products they make are the rider's products." The speaker is Chris Murphy, director of marketing for Specialized Bicycle Components, Inc.—or just "Specialized" to serious riders.

THE COMPANY

Specialized was founded in 1974 by Mike Sinyard, a cycling enthusiast who sold his VW van for the $1500 startup capital. Sinyard started out importing hard-to-find "specialized" bike components, but the company began to produce its own bike parts by 1976. Specialized introduced the first major production mountain bike in the world in 1980, revolutionizing the bike industry, and since then has maintained a reputation as the technological leader in the bike and bike accessory market. In fact, since the company's founding, its formal mission statement has remained unchanged: "To give everyone the best ride of their life!"

You probably recognize the Stumpjumper and the Rockhopper, both made by Specialized, as two of the most popular mountain bikes today. The company continues to innovate, with its introduction of a European-style city bike, the Globe. It also sells road bikes and an extensive line of bike accessories, including helmets, water bottles, jerseys, and shoes. As Murphy says, "The customer is buying the ride from us, not just the bike."

The first professional mountain bike racing team was created by Specialized in 1983, and Ned Overland, the Team Specialized captain, became the first-ever world champion. Specialized also counts Overland as one of its design consultants. The company banks on the perception, and reality, that this race-proven technology trickles down to the entire line of Specialized bikes and products.

THE ENVIRONMENT

The bike market is driven by innovation and technology, and with the market becoming more crowded and competitive, the fight for the consumer is intense. Specialized divides the bike market into two categories: (1) the independent retailer, and (2) the end-user consumer. While its focus in designing the product is on the end-user consumer, it sells directly only to the retailer, and realizes that a strong relationship with the dealers is a key factor for success.

The end-user consumer is broken down into two target age groups: the 18- to 25-year-old college or university students and the 30- to 40-year-old professional "techies." To differentiate itself from the rest of the market, Specialized positions itself as the innovator in mountain bikes—its models are what the rest of the industry imitates.

Mountain bikes account for approximately two-thirds of total industry bike sales, with road bikes accounting for the other third. The sport of mountain biking experienced a huge surge from 1989 to 1993, but in the mid-1990s sales began to flatten. Does Murphy believe this trend will hurt Specialized? "We believe we will see growth in the next six or seven years as the entry level participants trade up—trade their lower end bikes for higher end bikes," he explains.

Specialized now has an extensive global distribution with subsidiaries in 25 countries in Asia, North America, South America, Europe, and Australia.

THE ISSUES

How can Specialized stay at the forefront of an industry that now includes more than 20 manufacturers? Strategic placement in the marketplace is one way. Specialized recently designed its own server, the World Ride Web, on the Internet (www.specialized.com/bikes/). The Website offers international mountain bike trail and road bike trail directories, e-mail access to Specialized engineers, a trail preservation network, and a dealer directory that connects users directly to dealer homepages, in addition to the standard product information. Specialized's new bike, the Globe, appeared on *Seinfeld* and was on display in Gap clothing stores. Specialized believes these nontraditional promotional strategies are helping to keep the Specialized name on the cutting edge and in front of the end-user consumer.

Targeting its other market segment, the dealers, Specialized launched a "Best Ride Tour." It loaded up trailers full of the new models and visited over 30 cities, enabling retailers and shop employees to test-ride the bikes they will be ordering for the coming year—"Ride Before You Buy."

To keep its technological edge, Specialized has also become involved in joint ventures, including one with DuPont that led to a more aerodynamic wheel. Specialized has also entered a distribution relationship with Grip-Shift, allowing the high-end gear manufacturer access to its extensive dealer network.

Specialized sponsors races, provides racer support teams, initiates mountain biking safety programs, and is involved in trail-access advocacy groups all over the world. But, as it was in Specialized's early years, Sinyard sees a commitment to top quality and design as the most important factor for future success: "Even though we've been around for 20 years, this company still feels like it has something to prove. I expect it will always be that way."

Questions

These questions focus on the three steps of the planning phase of the strategic marketing process.

1 Do a SWOT analysis for Specialized. Use Figure 2–7 in Chapter 2 and Figure 1 in Appendix A as guides. In assessing internal factors (strengths and weaknesses), use the material provided in the case. In assessing external factors (opportunities and threats), augment the case material with what you see happening in the bicycle industry.

2 As part of Step 2 of the planning phase, and using your SWOT analysis, select target markets that you might focus on for present and potential bikers.

3 As part of Step 3 of the planning phase and using your answers in questions 1 and 2 above, outline Specialized's marketing programs for the target market segments you chose.

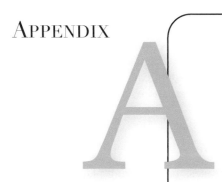

APPENDIX

CREATING AN EFFECTIVE MARKETING PLAN

"New ideas are a dime a dozen," observes Arthur R. Kydd, "and so are new products and new technologies." Kydd should know. As chief executive officer of St. Croix Venture Partners, he and his firm have provided the seed money and venture capital to launch more than 60 startup firms in the last 25 years. Today those firms have more than 5000 employees. Kydd elaborates:

> I get 200 to 300 marketing and business plans a year to look at, and St. Croix provides startup financing for only two or three. What sets a potentially successful idea, product, or technology apart from all the rest is markets and marketing. If you have a real product with a distinctive point of difference that satisfies the needs of customers, you may have a winner. And you get a real feel for this in a well-written marketing or business plan.[1]

This appendix (1) describes what marketing and business plans are—including their purposes and guidelines in writing effective plans, and (2) provides a sample marketing plan.

MARKETING PLANS

After explaining the meanings, purposes, and audiences of marketing plans and business plans, this section describes some writing guidelines for them and what external funders often look for in successful plans.

Marketing and Business Plans: Meanings, Purposes, and Audiences

A *marketing plan* is a road map for the marketing activities of an organization for a specified future period of time, such as one year or five years.[2] It is important to note that no single "generic" marketing plan applies to all organizations and all situations. Rather, the specific format for a marketing plan for an organization depends on the following:

- *The target audience and purpose.* Elements included in a particular marketing plan depend heavily on (1) who the audience is and (2) what its purpose is. A marketing plan for an internal audience seeks to point the direction for future marketing activities and is sent to all individuals in the organization who must implement the plan or who will be affected by it. If the plan is directed to an external audience, such as friends, banks, venture capitalists, or potential investors, for the purpose of raising capital, it has the additional function of being an important sales document. In this case it contains elements such as the strategic plan/focus, organization, structure, and biographies of key personnel that would rarely appear in an internal marketing plan. Also, the financial information is far more detailed when the plan is used to raise capital.

- *The kind and complexity of the organization.* A small neighbourhood restaurant has a somewhat different marketing plan than Nestlé, which serves international markets. The restaurant's plan would be relatively simple and directed at serving customers in a local market. In Nestlé's case, because there is a hierarchy of marketing plans, various levels of detail would be used, such as the entire organization, the business unit, or the product line.

- *The industry.* Both the restaurant serving a local market and Medtronic, selling heart pacemakers globally, analyze competition. Not only are their geographic thrusts far different, but the complexities of their offerings and, hence, the time periods likely to be covered by their plans also differ. A one-year marketing plan may be adequate for the restaurant, but Medtronic may need a five-year planning horizon because product-development cycles for complex, new medical devices may be three or four years.

In contrast to a marketing plan, a *business plan* is a road map for the entire organization for a specified future period of time, such as one year or five years.[3] A key difference between a marketing plan and a business plan is that the business plan contains details on the research and development (R&D)/operations/manufacturing activities of the organization. Even for a manufacturing business, the marketing plan is probably 60 or 70 percent of the entire business plan. For businesses like a small restaurant or auto repair shop, their marketing and business plans are virtually identical. The elements of a business plan typically targeted at internal and external audiences appear in the two right-hand columns in Figure A–1.

The Most-Asked Questions by Outside Audiences

Lenders and prospective investors reading a business or marketing plan that is used to seek new capital are probably the toughest audiences to satisfy. Their most-asked questions include the following:

1. Is the business or marketing idea valid?
2. Is there something unique or distinctive about the product or service that separates it from substitutes and competitors?
3. Is there a clear market for the product or service?
4. Are the financial projections realistic and healthy?
5. Are the key management and technical personnel capable, and do they have a track record in the industry in which they must compete?
6. Does the plan clearly describe how those providing capital will get their money back and make a profit?

Rhonda M. Abrams, author of *The Successful Business Plan*, observes that "within the first five minutes of reading your . . . plan, readers must perceive that the answers to these questions are favorable."[4] While her comments apply to plans seeking to raise capital, the first five questions just listed apply equally well to plans for internal audiences.

Writing and Style Suggestions

There are no magic one-size-fits-all guidelines for writing successful marketing and business plans. Still, the following writing and style guidelines generally apply:[5]

FIGURE A–1
Elements in typical marketing and business plans targeted at different audiences

Element of the Plan	Marketing Plan		Business Plan	
	For Internal Audience (to Direct Firm)	For External Audience (to Raise Capital)	For Internal Audience (to Direct Firm)	For External Audience (to Raise Capital)
1. Executive summary	✓	✓	✓	✓
2. Description of company		✓		✓
3. Strategic plan/focus		✓		✓
4. Situation analysis	✓	✓	✓	✓
5. Market-product focus	✓	✓	✓	✓
6. Marketing program strategy and tactics	✓	✓	✓	✓
7. R&D and operations program			✓	✓
8. Financial projections	✓	✓	✓	✓
9. Organization structure		✓		✓
10. Implementation plan	✓	✓	✓	✓
11. Evaluation and control	✓		✓	
Appendix A: Biographies of key personnel		✓		✓
Appendix B, etc.: Details on other topics	✓	✓	✓	✓

- Use a direct, professional writing style. Use appropriate business terms without jargon. Present and future tenses with active voice are generally better than past tense and passive voice.
- Be positive and specific to convey potential success. At the same time, avoid superlatives ("terrific," "wonderful,"). Specifics are better than glittering generalities. Use numbers for impact, justifying projections with reasonable quantitative assumptions where possible.
- Use bullet points for succinctness and emphasis. As with the list you are reading, bullets enable key points to be highlighted effectively and with great efficiency.
- Use "A-level" (the first level) and "B-level" (the second level) headings under the numbered section headings to help readers make easy transitions from one topic to another. This also forces the writer to organize the plan more carefully. Use these headings liberally, at least one every 200 to 300 words.
- Use visuals where appropriate. Photos, illustrations, graphs, and charts enable massive amounts of information to be presented succinctly.
- Shoot for a plan 15 to 35 pages in length, not including financial projections and appendixes. But an uncomplicated small business may require only 15 pages, while a high-technology startup may require more than 35 pages.
- Use care in layout, design, and presentation. Laser or ink-jet printers give a more professional look than do dot matrix printers or typewriters. Use 10- or 11-point type (you are now reading 10.5-point type) in the text. Use a serif type (with "feet," like that you are reading now) in the text because it is easier to read, and sans serif (without "feet") in graphs and charts. A bound report with a nice cover and clear title page adds professionalism.

These guidelines are used, where possible, in the sample marketing plan that follows.

SAMPLE FIVE-YEAR MARKETING PLAN FOR PARADISE KITCHENS, INC.

To help interpret the marketing plan for Paradise Kitchens,® Inc. that follows, we will describe the company and suggest some guidelines in interpreting the plan.

Background on Paradise Kitchens, Inc.

With a degree in chemical engineering, Randall F. Peters spent 15 years working for General Foods and Pillsbury with a number of diverse responsibilities: plant operations, R&D, restaurant operations, and new business development. His wife, Leah, with degrees in both molecular cellular biology and food science, held various Pillsbury executive positions in new-category development and packaged goods and restaurants R&D. In its startup years, the company survived on the savings of its co-founders, Randy and Leah. With their backgrounds they decided Randy should serve as president and CEO of Paradise Kitchens, and Leah should focus on R&D and corporate strategy. The first products entered distribution in 1990.

Interpreting the Marketing Plan

The marketing plan for Paradise Kitchens, Inc. that follows is based on an actual plan developed by the company.[6] To protect proprietary information the plan is assumed to have been written in 1998 and some details and data have been altered, but the basic logic of the plan has been preserved.

Notes in the margins next to the Paradise Kitchens plan fall into two categories:

1. *Substantive notes* are shaded blue and elaborate on the significance of an element in the marketing plan and are keyed to chapter references in this text.

2. *Writing style, format, and layout notes* are shaded red and explain the editorial or visual rationale for the element.

A closing word of encouragement! Writing an effective marketing plan is hard—but challenging and satisfying—work. However, dozens of the authors' students have used effective marketing plans they wrote for class in their interviewing portfolio to show prospective employers what they could do and to help them get their first job.

The Table of Contents provides quick access to the topics in the plan, usually organized by section and subsection headings.

Blue boxes explain significance of Marketing Plan elements

Red boxes give writing style, format, and layout guidelines

Seen by many experts as the single most important element in the plan, the Executive Summary, with a maximum of two pages, "sells" the documents to readers through its clarity and brevity.

The Company Description highlights the recent history and recent successes of the organization.

The Strategic Focus and Plan sets the strategic direction for the entire organization, a direction with which proposed actions of the marketing plan must be consistent. This section is not included in all marketing plans. See Chapter 2.

The qualitative Mission/ Vision statement focuses the activities of Paradise Kitchens for the stake-holder groups to be served. See Chapter 2.

FIVE-YEAR MARKETING PLAN
Paradise Kitchens,® Inc.

Table of Contents

1. Executive Summary

2. Company Description

Paradise Kitchens, Inc. was started in 1989 by cofounders Randall F. Peters and Leah E. Peters to develop and market Howlin' Coyote Chili, a unique line of single serve and microwaveable Mexican-style frozen chili products. The Howlin' Coyote line of chili was introduced into a single metropolitan market in 1990. The line was subsequently expanded to two new markets in 1992 and 1994.

To the Company's knowledge, Howlin' Coyote is the only premium-quality, authentic Mexican-style, frozen chili sold in grocery stores. Its high quality has gained fast, widespread acceptance in these markets. In fact, same-store sales doubled in the last year for which data are available. The Company believes the Howlin' Coyote brand can be extended to other categories of Mexican food products.

Paradise Kitchens believes its high-quality, high-price strategy has proven successful. This marketing plan outlines how the Company will extend its geographic coverage from 3 markets to 20 markets by the year 2003.

3. Strategic Focus and Plan

This section covers three aspects of corporate strategy that influence the marketing plan: (1) the mission/vision, (2) goals, and (3) core competence/sustainable competitive advantage of Paradise Kitchens.

Mission/Vision

The mission and vision of Paradise Kitchens is to market lines of high-quality Mexican food products at premium prices that satisfy consumers in this fast-growing food segment while providing challenging career opportunities for employees and above-average returns to shareholders.

The Goals section sets both the financial and non-financial targets—where possible in quantitative terms—against which the company's performance will be measured. See Chapter 2.

Lists use parallel construction to improve readability—in this case a series of infinitives starting with "To . . ."

Goals

For the coming five years Paradise Kitchens seeks to achieve the following goals:

- Nonfinancial goals
    1. To retain its present image as the highest-quality line of Mexican products in the food categories in which it competes.
    2. To enter 17 new metropolitan markets.
    3. To achieve national distribution in two convenience store or supermarket chains by 2002 and five by 2003.
    4. To add a new product line every third year.
    5. To be among the top three chili lines—regardless of packaging (frozen, canned) in one-third of the metro markets in which it competes by 2002 and two-thirds by 2003.
- Financial goals
    1. To obtain a real (inflation-adjusted) growth in earnings per share of 8 percent per year over time.
    2. To obtain a return on equity of at least 20 percent.
    3. To have a public stock offering by the year 2002.

In keeping with the goal of achieving national distribution through chains, Paradise Kitchens recently obtained distribution through a convenience store chain where it uses this point-of-purchase ad that adheres statically to the freezer case.

Core Competency and Sustainable Competitive Advantage

In terms of core competency, Paradise Kitchens seeks to achieve a unique ability (1) to provide distinctive, high-quality chilies and related products using Mexican recipes that appeal to and excite contemporary tastes for these products and (2) to deliver these products to the customer's table using effective manufacturing and distribution systems that maintain the Company's quality standards.

To translate these core competencies into a sustainable competitive advantage, the Company will work closely with key suppliers and distributors to build the relationships and alliances necessary to satisfy the high taste standards of our customers.

To improve readability, each numbered section usually starts on a new page. (This is not done in this plan to save space.)

The Situation Analysis is a snapshot to answer the question, "Where are we now?" See Chapter 2.

The SWOT analysis identifies strengths, weaknesses, opportunities, and threats to provide a solid foundation as a springboard to identify subsequent *actions* in the marketing plan. See Chapter 2.

Each long table, graph, or photo is given a figure number and title. It then appears as soon as possible after the first reference in the text, accommodating necessary page breaks. This also avoids breaking long tables like this one in the middle. Short tables or graphs that are less than 3 cm are often inserted in the text without figure numbers because they don't cause serious problems with page breaks.

Effective tables seek to summarize a large amount of information in a small amount of space.

4. Situation Analysis

This situation analysis starts with a snapshot of the current environment in which Paradise Kitchens finds itself by providing a brief SWOT (strengths, weaknesses, opportunities, threats) analysis. After this overview, the analysis probes ever-finer levels of detail: industry, competitors, company, and consumers.

SWOT Analysis

Figure 1 shows the internal and external factors affecting the market opportunities for Paradise Kitchens. Stated briefly, this SWOT analysis highlights the great strides taken by the company in the nine years since its products first appeared on grocers'

Figure 1.   SWOT Analysis for Paradise Kitchens

Internal Factors	Strengths	Weaknesses
Management	Experienced and entrepreneurial management and board	Small size can restrict options
Offerings	Unique, high-quality, high-price products	Many lower-quality, lower-price competitors
Marketing	Distribution in 3 markets with excellent acceptance	No national awareness or distribution
Personnel	Good work force, though small; little turnover	Big gap if key employee leaves
Finance	Excellent growth in sales revenues	Limited resources may restrict growth opportunities when compared to giant competitors
Manufacturing	Sole supplier ensures high quality	Lack economies of scale of huge competitors
R&D	Continuing efforts to ensure quality in delivered products	

External Factors	Opportunities	Threats
Consumer/Social	Upscale market, likely to be stable; Mexican food category is fast-growing segment	Premium price may limit access to mass markets.
Competitive	Distinctive name and packaging in its markets.	Not patentable; competitors can attempt to duplicate product
Technological	Technical breakthroughs enable smaller food producers to achieve many economies available to large competitors	
Economic	Consumer income is high; convenience important to Canadian households	More households "eating out," and bringing prepared take-out into home
Legal/Regulatory	High government regulatory standards eliminate fly-by-night competitors	Mergers among large competitors approved by regulators

The text discussion of Figure 1 (the SWOT analysis table) elaborates on its more important elements. This "walks" the reader through the information from the vantage of the plan's writer. (In terse plans this accompanying discussion is sometimes omitted, but is generally desirable to give the reader an understanding of what the company sees as the critical SWOT elements.)

The Industry Analysis section provides the backdrop for the subsequent, more detailed analysis of competition, the company, and the company's customers. Without an in-depth understanding of the industry, the remaining analysis may be misdirected. See Chapter 2.

Even though relatively brief, this in-depth treatment of the spicy and Mexican food industry demonstrates to the plan's readers the company's understanding of the industry in which it competes. It gives both external and internal readers confidence that the company thoroughly understands its own industry.

This summary of sales in the Mexican product category shows it is significant and provides a variety of future opportunities for Paradise Kitchens.

shelves. In the Company's favour internally are its strengths of an experienced management team and board of directors, excellent acceptance of its lines in the three metropolitan markets in which it competes, and a strong manufacturing and distribution system to serve these limited markets. Favorable external factors (opportunities) include the increasing appeal of Mexican foods, the strength of the upscale market for the Company's products, and food-processing technological breakthroughs that make is easier for smaller food producers to compete.

These favourable factors must be balanced against unfavourable ones, the main weakness is the limited size of Paradise Kitchens relative to its competitors in terms of the depth of the management team, available financial resources, and national awareness and distribution of product lines. Threats include the danger that the Company's premium prices may limit access to mass markets and competition from the "eating-out" and "take-out" markets.

<u>Industry Analysis: Trends in Spicy and Mexican Foods</u>

In the past 10 years, hot-spice consumption has doubled. Currently, Mexican food and ingredients are used in 46 percent of households. Burritos, enchiladas, and taco dinner kits, which had insignificant numbers in 1981, reached between 4 percent and 11 percent of households in 1996. By 1997, volume of Mexican dinner kits in Canada grew by 41 percent over 1996. Experts predict rapid growth in the Mexican food category and huge market potential.[7]

These trends reflect a generally more favourable attitude toward spicy foods. Total spice consumption increased 50 percent from 1983 to 1993, according to the Spice Trade Association. Retail sales of "spicy foods" were expected to top $1.8 Billion in 2000. The Mexican market includes the foods shown in Figure 2.

Figure 2. Some Foods Included in the Mexican Product Category

Item	Percentage of Sales	Sales in Millions
Salsa	39%	$624
Cheese/bean dips	13	208
Refried beans	9	144
Seasoning mix	8	128
Chilies	7	112
Taco shells	7	112
Dinner kits	5	80
Taco sauce	3	48
Enchilada sauce	2	32
Other	7	112
Total	100%	$1600

As with the Industry Analysis, the Competitors Analysis demonstrates that the company has a realistic understanding of who its major competitors are and what their marketing strategies are. Again, a realistic assessment gives confidence to both internal and external readers that subsequent marketing actions in the plan rest on a solid foundation. See Chapters 2, 3, 8, 9, and 21.

This page uses a block style and does *not* indent each paragraph, although an extra space separates each paragraph. Compare this page with page 62, which has indented paragraphs. Most readers find that indented paragraphs in marketing plans and long reports are easier to follow.

The Company Analysis provides details of the company's strengths and marketing strategies that will enable it to achieve the mission, vision, and goals identified earlier. See Chapters 2, 8, and 22.

Competitors in Mexican Market

The chili market represents $495 million in annual sales. The products fall primarily into two groups: canned chili (62 percent of sales) and dry chili (16 percent of sales). The remaining 22 percent of sales go to frozen chili products. Besides Howlin' Coyote, Stouffers and Marie Callender's offer frozen chilies as part of their broad line of frozen dinners and entrées. Major canned chili brands include Hormel, Wolf, Dennison, Stagg, Chili Man, and Castleberry's. Their retail prices range from $.99 to $1.79.

Bluntly put, the major disadvantage of the segment's dominant product, canned chili, is that it does not taste very good. A taste test described in the October 1990 issue of *Consumer Reports* magazine ranked 26 canned chili products "poor" to "fair" in overall sensory quality. The study concluded, "Chili doesn't have to be hot to be good. But really good chili, hot or mild, doesn't come out of a can."

Dry mix brands include such familiar spice brands as Lawry's, McCormick, French's, and Durkee, along with smaller offerings such as Wick Fowler's and Carroll Shelby's. Their retail prices range from $.99 to $1.99. The *Consumer Reports* study was more favourable about dry chili mixes, ranking them from "fair" to "very good." The magazine recommended, "If you want good chili, make it with fresh ingredients and one of the seasoning mixes we tested." A major drawback of dry mixes is that they require the preparers to add their own meat, beans, and tomatoes and take more preparation time than canned or frozen chilies.

The *Consumer Reports* study did not include the frozen chili entrées from Stouffer's or Marie Callender's (Howlin' Coyote was not yet on the market at the time of the test). However, it is fair to say that these products—consisting of ground beef, chili beans, and tomato sauce—are of average quality. Furthermore, they are not singled out for special marketing or promotional programs by their manufacturers. Marie Callender's retails for $3.09, and Stouffer's retails for $2.99.

Company Analysis

The husband-and-wife team that cofounded Paradise Kitchens, Inc. in 1989 has 44 years of experience between them in the food-processing business. Both have played key roles in the management of the Pillsbury Company. They are being advised by a highly seasoned group of business professionals, who have extensive understanding of the requirements for new-product development.

The higher-level "A heading" of Customer Analysis has a more dominant typeface and position than the lower-level "B heading" of Customer Characteristics. These headings introduce the reader to the sequence and level of topics covered. The organization of this textbook uses this kind of structure and headings.

Satisfying customers and providing genuine value to them is why organizations exist in a market economy. This section addresses the question of "Who are the customers for Paradise Kitchens's products?" See Chapters 5, 6, 7, 8, and 9.

Currently, Howlin' Coyote products compete in the chili and Mexican frozen entrée segments of the Mexican food market. While the chili obviously competes as a stand-alone product, its exceptional quality means it can complement such dishes as burritos, nachos, and enchiladas and can be readily used as a smothering sauce for pasta, rice, or potatoes. This flexibility of use is relatively rare in the prepared food marketplace.

The Company now uses a single outside producer with which it works closely to maintain the consistently high quality required in its products. The greater volume has increased production efficiencies, resulting in a steady decrease in the cost of goods sold.

Customer Analysis

In terms of customer analysis, this section describes (1) the characteristics of customers expected to buy Howlin' Coyote products and (2) health and nutrition concerns of consumers today.

Customer Characteristics. Demographically, chili products in general are purchased by consumers representing a broad range of socioeconomic backgrounds. Howlin' Coyote chili is purchased chiefly by consumers who have achieved higher levels of education and whose income is $30 000 and higher. These consumers represent 57 percent of canned and dry mix chili users.

The five Howlin' Coyote entrées offer a quick, tasty meal with high-quality ingredients.

The household buying Howlin' Coyote has one to three people in it. Among married couples, Howlin' Coyote is predominantly bought by households in which both spouses work. While women are a majority of the buyers, single men represent a significant segment. Anecdotally, Howlin' Coyote has heard from fathers of teenaged boys who say they keep a freezer stocked with the chili because the boys devour it.

Because the chili offers a quick way to make a tasty meal, the product's biggest users tend to be those most pressed for time. Howlin' Coyote's premium pricing also means that its purchasers are skewed toward the higher end of the income range. Buyers range in age from 25 to 55.

Health and Nutrition Concerns. Coverage of food issues in the media is often erratic and occasionally alarmist. Because consumers are concerned about their diets, studies from organizations of widely varying credibility frequently receive significant attention from the major news organizations. For instance, a study of fat levels of movie popcorn was reported in all the major media. Similarly, studies on the healthfulness of Mexican food have received prominent "play" in print and broadcast reports. The high caloric level of much Mexican food has been widely reported and often exaggerated.

Less certain is the link between these reports and consumer buying behaviour. Most indications are that while consumers are well-versed in dietary matters, they are not significantly changing their eating patterns. The experience of other food manufacturers is that consumers expect certain foods to be high in calories and are not drawn to those that claim to be low-calorie versions. Low-fat frozen pizza was a flop. Therefore, while Howlin' Coyote is already lower in calories, fat, and sodium than its competitors, those qualities are not being stressed in its promotions. Instead, in the space and time available for promotions, Howlin' Coyote's taste, convenience, and flexibility are stressed.

5. Market-Product Focus

This section describes the five-year marketing and product objectives for Paradise Kitchens and the target markets, points of difference, and positioning of its lines of Howlin' Coyote chilies.

<u>Marketing and Product Objectives</u>

Howlin' Coyote's marketing intent is to take full advantage of its brand potential while building a base from which other revenue sources can be

---

This section demonstrates the company's insights into a major trend that has a potentially large impact.

Size of headings should give a professional look to the report and not overwhelm the reader. These two headings are too large.

As noted in Chapter 10, the chances of success for a new product are significantly increased if objectives are set for the product itself and if target market segments are identified for it. This section makes these explicit for Paradise Kitchens. The objectives also serve as the planned targets against which marketing activities are measured in program implementation and control.

A heading should be spaced closer to the text that follows (and that it describes) than the preceding section to avoid confusion for the reader. This rule is *not* followed for the Target Markets heading, which now unfortunately appears to "float" between the preceding and following paragraphs.

This section identifies the specific niches or target markets toward which the company's products are directed. When appropriate and when space permits, this section often includes a market–product grid. See Chapter 9.

mined—both in and out of the retail grocery business. These are detailed in four areas below:

- Current markets. Current markets will be grown by expanding brand and flavour distribution at the retail level. In addition, same-store sales will be grown by increasing consumer awareness and repeat purchases. With this increase in same-store sales, the more desirable broker/warehouse distribution channel will become available, increasing efficiency and saving costs.

- New markets. By the end of Year 5, the chili and salsa business will be expanded to a total of 20 metropolitan areas. This will represent 72 percent of food store sales.

- Food service. Food service sales will include chili products and smothering sauces. Sales are expected to reach $693 000 by the end of Year 3 and $1.5 million by the end of Year 5.

- New products. Howlin' Coyote's brand presence will be expanded at the retail level through the addition of new products in the frozen-foods section. This will be accomplished through new product concept screening in Year 1 to identify new potential products. These products will be brought to market in Years 2 and 3. Additionally, the brand may be licensed in select categories.

Target Markets

The primary target market for Howlin' Coyote products is households with one to three people, where often both adults work, with individual income typically above $30 000 per year. These households contain more experienced, adventurous consumers of Mexican food and want premium-quality products.

To help buyers see the many different uses for Howlin' Coyote chili, recipes are printed even on the inside of the packages.

An organization cannot grow by offering only "me-too products." The greatest single factor in a new product's failure is the lack of significant "points of difference" that set it apart from competitors' substitutes. This section makes these points of difference explicit. See Chapter 10.

A positioning strategy helps communicate the company's unique points of difference of its products to prospective customers in a simple, clear way. This section describes this positioning. See Chapters 9 and 10.

Everything that has gone before in the marketing plan sets the stage for the marketing mix actions—the 4 Ps—covered in the marketing program. See Chapters 10 through 20.

This section describes in detail three key elements of the company's product strategy: the product line, its quality and how this is achieved, and its "cutting edge" packaging. See Chapters 10, 11, and 12.

<u>Points of Difference</u>

The "points of difference"—characteristics that make Howlin' Coyote chilies unique relative to competitors—fall into three important areas:

- Unique taste and convenience. No known competitor offers a high-quality, "authentic" frozen chili in a range of flavours. And no existing chili has the same combination of quick preparation and home-style taste.

- Taste trends. The consumer's palate is increasingly intrigued by hot spices, and Howlin' Coyote brands offer more "kick" than most other prepared chilies.

- Premium packaging. Howlin' Coyote's high-value packaging graphics convey the unique, high-quality product contained inside and the product's nontraditional positioning.

<u>Positioning</u>

In the past chili products have been either convenient or tasty, but not both. Howlin' Coyote pairs these two desirable characteristics to obtain a positioning in consumers' minds as very high-quality "authentic Mexican tasting" chilies that can be prepared easily and quickly.

6. Marketing Program

The four marketing mix elements of the Howlin' Coyote chili marketing program are detailed below. Note that "chile" is the vegetable and "chili" is the dish.

<u>Product Strategy</u>

After first summarizing the product line, the approach to product quality and packaging are covered.

Product Line. Howlin' Coyote chili, retailing for $2.99 for a 300 g serving, is available in five flavours. The five are:

- Green Chile Chili: braised extra-lean pork with fire-roasted green chiles, onions, tomato chunks, bold spices, and jalapeno peppers.

- Red Chile Chili: extra-lean cubed pork, deep-red acho chiles, and sweet onions.

- Beef and Black Bean Chili: lean braised beef with black beans, tomato chunks, and Howlin' Coyote's own blend of red chiles and authentic spicing.

> Using parallel structure, this bulleted list presents the product line efficiently and crisply.

- Chicken Chunk Chili: hearty chunks of tender chicken, fire-roasted green chiles, black beans, pinto beans, diced onions, and zesty spices.
- Mean Bean Chili: vegetarian, with nine distinctive bean varieties and fire-roasted green chiles, tomato chunks, onion, and a robust blend of spices and rich red chiles.

Unique Product Quality. The flavouring systems of the Howlin' Coyote chilies are proprietary. The products' tastiness is due to extra care lavished upon the ingredients during production. The ingredients used are of unusually high quality. Meats are low-fat cuts and are fresh, not frozen, to preserve cell structure and moistness. Chiles are fire-roasted for fresher taste, not the canned variety used by more mainstream products. Tomatoes and vegetables are select quality. No preservatives or artificial flavours are used.

Packaging. Reflecting the "cutting edge" marketing strategy of its producers, Howlin' Coyote bucks conventional wisdom in packaging. It avoids placing predictable photographs of the product on its containers. (Head to any grocer's freezer and you will be hard pressed to find a product that does not feature a heavily stylized photograph of the contents.) Instead, Howlin' Coyote's package communicates the product's out-of-the-ordinary positioning. This approach signals the product's nontraditional qualities: "adventurous" eating with minimal fuss—a frozen meal for people who do not normally enjoy frozen meals.

> A brief caption on photos and sample ads ties them to the text and highlights the reason for being included.

Howlin' Coyote's packages stand out in a supermarket's freezer case.

Price Strategy

> The Price Strategy section makes the company's price point very clear, along with its price position relative to potential substitutes. When appropriate and when space permits, this section might contain a break-even analysis. See Chapters 13 and 14.

Howlin' Coyote Chili is, at $2.99 for a 300 g package, priced comparably to the other frozen offerings and higher than the canned and dried chili varieties. However, the significant taste advantages it has over canned chilies and the convenience advantages over dried chilies justify this pricing strategy.

Elements of the Promotion Strategy are highlighted in terms of the three key promotional activities the company is emphasizing for its product line: in-store demonstrations, recipes featuring its Howlin' Coyote chilies, and cents-off coupons. For space reasons the company's online strategies are not shown in the plan. See Chapters 18, 19, 20 and 21.

Photos or sample ads can illustrate key points effectively, even if they are not in colour as they appear here.

<u>Promotion Strategy</u>

Key promotion programs feature in-store demonstrations, recipes, and cents-off coupons.

In-Store Demonstrations. In-store demonstrations will be conducted to give consumers a chance to try Howlin' Coyote products and learn about their unique qualities. Demos will be conducted regularly in all markets to increase awareness and trial purchases.

Recipes. Because the products' flexibility of use is a key selling point, recipes will be offered to consumers to stimulate use. The recipes will be given at all in-store demonstrations, on the back of packages, and through a mail-in recipe book offer. In addition, recipes will be included in coupons sent by direct mail or free-standing inserts. For new markets, recipes will be included on in-pack coupon inserts.

Cents-Off Coupons. To generate trial and repeat-purchase of Howlin' Coyote products, coupons will be distributed in four ways:

- In Sunday newspaper inserts. Inserts are highly read and will help generate awareness. Coupled with in-store demonstrations, this has been a very successful technique so far.

Sunday newspaper inserts encourage consumer trial and provide recipes to show how Howlin' Coyote chili can be used in summer meals.

Another bulleted list adds many details for the reader, including methods of gaining customer awareness, trial, and repeat purchases as Howlin' Coyote enters new metropolitan areas.

- In-pack coupons. Inside each box of Howlin' Coyote chili will be coupons for $1 off two more packages of the chili. These coupons will be included for the first three months the product is shipped to a new market. Doing so encourages repeat purchases by new users.
- Direct-mail chili coupons. Those households that fit the Howlin' Coyote demographics described above will be mailed coupons. This is likely to be an efficient promotion due to its greater audience selectivity.
- In-store demonstrations. Coupons will be passed out at in-store demonstrations to give an additional incentive to purchase.

The Place Strategy is described here in terms of both (1) the present method and (2) the new one to be used when the increased sales volume makes it feasible. See Chapters 15, 16, and 17.

Place (Distribution) Strategy

Howlin' Coyote is distributed in its present markets through a food distributor. The distributor buys the product, warehouses it, and then resells and delivers it to grocery retailers on a store-by-store basis. This is typical for products that have moderate sales—compared with, say, staples like milk or bread. As sales grow, we will shift to a more efficient system using a broker who sells the products to retail chains and grocery wholesalers.

All the marketing mix decisions covered in the just-described marketing program have both revenue and expense effects. These are summarized in this section of the marketing plan. See Appendix B.

7. Financial Data and Projections

Past Sales Revenues

Historically, Howlin' Coyote has had a steady increase in sales revenues since its introduction in 1990. In 1994, sales jumped spectacularly, due largely to new promotion strategies and the opportunities represented by the products' expansion to Western markets. The trend in sales revenues appears in Figure 3.

Note that this section contains no introductory overview sentence. While the sentence is not essential, many readers prefer to see it to avoid the abrupt start with Past Sales Revenues.

Figure 3.   Sales Revenues for Paradise Kitchens, Inc.

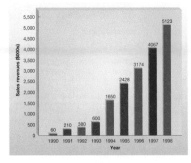

The graph shows the dramatic growth of sales revenue more clearly than data in a table would do.

<u>Five-Year Projections</u>

Five-year financial projections for Paradise Kitchens appear below:

				Projections			
		Actual	Year1	Year 2	Year 3	Year 4	Year 5
Financial Element	Units	1998	1999	2000	2001	2002	2003
Cases sold	1000	353	684	889	1 249	1 499	1 799
Net sales	$1000	5123	9913	12 884	18 111	21 733	26 080
Gross profit	$1000	2545	4820	6 527	8 831	10 597	12 717
Operating profit (loss)	$1000	339	985	2 906	2 805	3 366	4 039

These projections reflect the continuing growth in number of cases sold (with 8 packages of Howlin' Coyote chili per case) and increasing production and distribution economies of scale as sales volume increases.

8. Organization

Paradise Kitchens's present organization appears in Figure 4. It shows the four people reporting to the President. Below this level are both the full-time and part-time employees of the Company.

At present Paradise Kitchens operates with full-time employees in only essential positions. It now augments its full-time staff with key advisers, consultants, and subcontractors. As the firm grows, people with special expertise will be added to the staff.

Figure 4. The Paradise Kitchens Organization

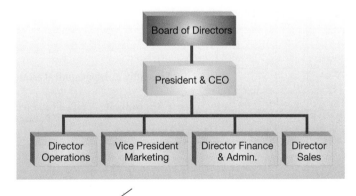

Because this table is very short, it is woven into the text, rather than given a figure number and title.

Because the plan proposes to enter 17 new metropolitan markets in the coming five years (for a total of 20), it is not possible to simply extrapolate the trend in Figure 3. Instead, management's judgment must be used. Methods of making sales forecasts—including the "lost horse" technique used here—are discussed in Chapter 8.

The Five-Year Financial Projections section starts with the judgment forecast of cases sold and the resulting net sales. Gross profit and then operating profit—critical for the company's survival—are projected and show the company passes break-even and becomes profitable in Year 2. An actual plan often contains many pages of computer-generated spreadsheet projections, usually shown in an appendix to the plan.

The Organization of Paradise Kitchens appears here. It reflects the bare-bones organizational structure of successful small businesses. Often a more elaborate marketing plan will show the new positions expected to be added as the firm grows. See Chapter 22.

The Implementation Plan shows how the company will turn plans into results. Gantt charts are often used to set deadlines and assign responsibilities for the many tactical marketing decisions needed to enter a new market. See Chapter 22.

9. Implementation Plan

Introducing Howlin' Coyote chilies to new metropolitan areas is a complex task and requires that creative promotional activities gain consumer awareness and initial trial among the target market households identified earlier. The anticipated rollout schedule to enter these metropolitan markets appears in Figure 5.

Figure 5.   Rollout Schedule to Enter New Markets

Year	New Markets Added	Cumulative Markets	Cumulative Percentage of U.S. Market
Today (1998)	2	5	16
Year 1 (1999)	3	8	21
Year 2 (2000)	4	12	29
Year 3 (2001)	2	14	37
Year 4 (2002)	3	17	55
Year 5 (2003)	3	20	72

The essence of Evaluation and Control is comparing actual sales with the targeted values set in the plan and taking appropriate actions. Note that the section briefly describes a contingency plan for alternative actions, depending on how successful the entry into a new market turns out to be. See Chapter 22.

10. Evaluation and Control

Monthly sales targets in cases have been set for Howlin' Coyote chili for each metropolitan area. Actual case sales will be compared with these targets and tactical marketing programs modified to reflect the unique sets of factors in each metropolitan area. The speed of the roll-out program will increase or decrease, depending on Paradise Kitchens's performance in the successive metropolitan markets it enters.

Various appendixes may appear at the end of the plan, depending on the purpose and audience for them. For example, résumés of key personnel or detailed financial spreadsheets often appear in appendixes. For space reasons these are not shown here.

Appendix A. Biographical Sketches of Key Personnel

Appendix B. Detailed Financial Projections

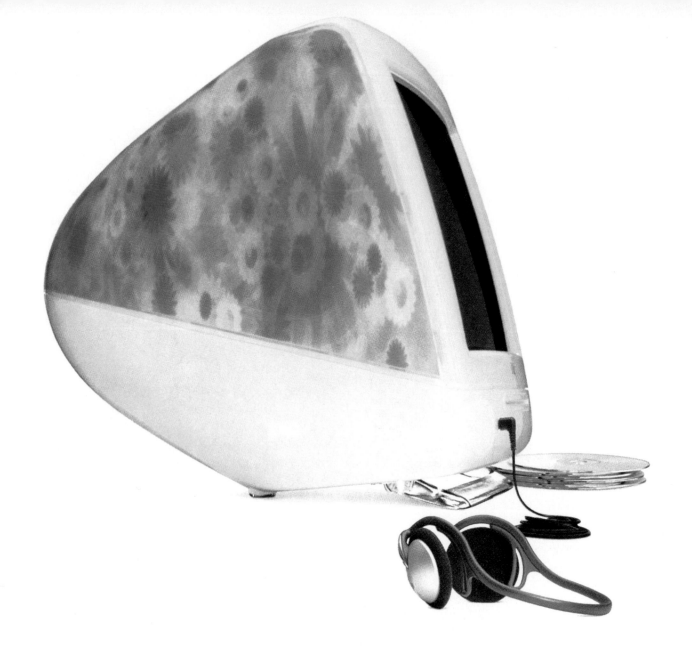

Rip. Mix. Burn.

The new iMac™ with iTunes + CD-RW. Take your favorite songs, put them in the order you want and burn a CD. After all, it's your music.

Think different.

CHAPTER

3

SCANNING THE MARKETING ENVIRONMENT

AFTER READING THIS CHAPTER YOU SHOULD BE ABLE TO:

- Understand how environmental scanning provides information about social, economic, technological, competitive, and regulatory forces.

- Explain how social forces such as demographics and culture and economic forces such as macroeconomic conditions and consumer income affect marketing.

- Describe how technological changes can affect marketing.

- Understand the forms of competition that exist in a market, key components of competition, and the impact of competition on corporate structures.

- Explain the major legislation that ensures competition and regulates the elements of the marketing mix.

HOW AN 18-YEAR-OLD CHANGED THE WORLD . . . WITH MUSIC!

Have you ever downloaded a song from the Internet? Createda collection of music hits on your computer? Burned a CD of your favourites? If you have, you may be one of 50 million users of Internet-based music file-sharing services like Napster. Napster creator Shawn Fanning was just 18 when he devised the software program that allowed computer users to share music files and, subsequently, changed almost everything about the music industry. Suddenly musicians, recording companies, retail stores, and consumers like you are part of a completely different music marketplace. How did this happen? The marketing environment changed!

First, consumer preferences changed. As one expert explains, the music industry "forces consumers to go to unpleasant stores to buy high-priced CDs, bundles bad songs along with good, encases its products in cheap plastic boxes that frequently break, then deliberately wraps the boxes in hard-to-open cellophane."[1] As a result music buyers started searching for a more customer-friendly distribution system.

Second, changes in technology facilitated the development of new products and services previously impossible to offer consumers. New computers with improved speed and storage capabilities were introduced. CD drives that could "burn" a customized CD became available. The Internet reached millions of computer users. And Shawn Fanning designed software that let almost anyone "share" a music file with anyone else on the Internet. In 2000, Internet piracy cost the recording industry lost sales of 1.3 percent worldwide and 5 percent in Canada.[2]

The creation of Napster and other file-sharing services like it has led to other changes in the marketing environment. Regulatory factors, for example, are influencing the activities of the services. The Recording Industry Association of America sued Napster and several other music-swapping services for copyright violations. In response, U.S. courts ruled that Napster must stop helping its users exchange copyrighted material. While many similar firms such as Bearshare and MusicCity continue to operate in their original form, Napster's future is in doubt. However, in the spring of 2002, two online music subscription services will be launched in Canada. PressPlay, a joint venture between Sony Corp and Vivendi Universal SA, will partner with Sympatico. Moontaxi Media Inc. will focus on jazz and classical music.[3]

Similarly, competitive factors have changed as music labels—EMI, Bertelsmann, and Warner Music—have created an online clearinghouse for their music, called MusicNet. Sony and Universal have created a joint venture called Duet, and MTV and Microsoft have announced their own licensing services. Consumers will also see a variety of new products designed to respond to file sharing. Intel's new Pentium processor campaign suggests that its product can "Give your whole music collection an upgrade," and Apple's new iMac is sold with iTunes software so users can "Rip. Mix. Burn!"[4]

Developments such as these are clearly changing the marketing environment. Anticipating and responding to changes often means the difference between marketing success and failure. This chapter describes how the marketing environment has changed in the past and how it is likely to change in the future.

ENVIRONMENTAL SCANNING IN THE NEW MILLENNIUM

Changes in the marketing environment are a source of opportunities and threats to be managed. The process of continually acquiring information on events occurring outside the organization to identify and interpret potential trends is called **environmental scanning**.

ENVIRONMENTAL SCANNING
The process of continually acquiring information on events occurring outside the organization to identify and interpret potential trends.

Tracking Environmental Trends

Environmental trends typically arise from five sources: social, economic, technological, competitive, and regulatory forces. As shown in Figure 3–1 and described later in this chapter, these forces affect the marketing activities of a firm in numerous ways.

To illustrate how environmental scanning is used, consider the following trend:[5]

Coffee industry marketers have observed that the percentage of adults who drink coffee has declined from 75 percent in 1962 to under 50 percent today. Age-specific analysis indicates that coffee consumption declined among all age groups, including 18- to 29-year-olds, despite the perception that young adults are leading a revival in coffee drinking.

What types of businesses are likely to be influenced by this trend? What future would you predict for coffee?

You may have concluded that this trend is likely to influence coffee manufacturers and supermarkets. If so, you are absolutely correct—manufacturers have responded by offering new flavours, and supermarkets have added coffee boutiques and gourmet brands such as Starbucks to try to reverse the trend.[6] Recently, Pepsi-Cola Canada introduced Starbucks Frappuccino in a glass bottle, with a focus on the markets in Ontario and Western Canada.[7] Predicting the future of coffee requires assumptions about the number of years the declining trend will continue and the rate of increase or decline in various age groups. Did you consider these issues in your analysis? Because experts make different assumptions, their forecasts

www.starbucks.com

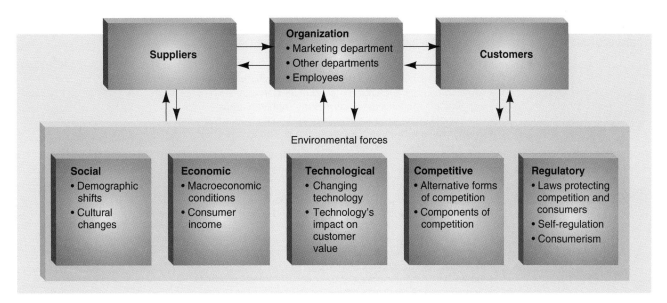

FIGURE 3–1
Environmental forces affecting
the organization, as well as its
suppliers and customers

range from a 30 percent decline to a 13 percent increase by 2005—a range that probably includes your forecast!

Environmental scanning also involves explaining trends. Why has coffee consumption been declining? One explanation is that consumers are switching from coffee to other beverages such as soft drinks, juices, or water. Another explanation is that preferences have shifted to better-tasting but more expensive types of coffee, and consumers have reduced their use to maintain the same level of expenditure. Identifying and interpreting trends, such as the decline in coffee consumption, and developing explanations, such as those offered in this paragraph, are essential to successful environmental scanning.

An Environmental Scan of Canada

What other trends might affect marketing in the future? A firm conducting an environmental scan of Canada might uncover key trends, such as those listed in Figure 3–2, for each of the five environmental factors.[8] Although the list of trends is far from complete, it reveals the breadth of an environmental scan—from population concentration in census metropolitan areas, to the growth of electronic commerce, to the emergence of "network corporations." These trends affect consumers and the businesses and nonprofit organizations that serve them. Trends such as these are covered as the five environmental forces are described in the following pages.

SOCIAL FORCES

SOCIAL FORCES
The demographic
characteristics of the
population and its values
in the environment.

The **social forces** of the environment include the demographic characteristics of the population and its values. Changes in these forces can have a dramatic impact on marketing strategy.

Demographics

DEMOGRAPHICS
Describing the population
according to selected
characteristics such as their
age, gender, ethnicity,
income, and occupation.

Demographics is the study of the characteristics of a human population. These characteristics include population size, population growth rate, gender, marital status, education, ethnicity, income, and so forth.

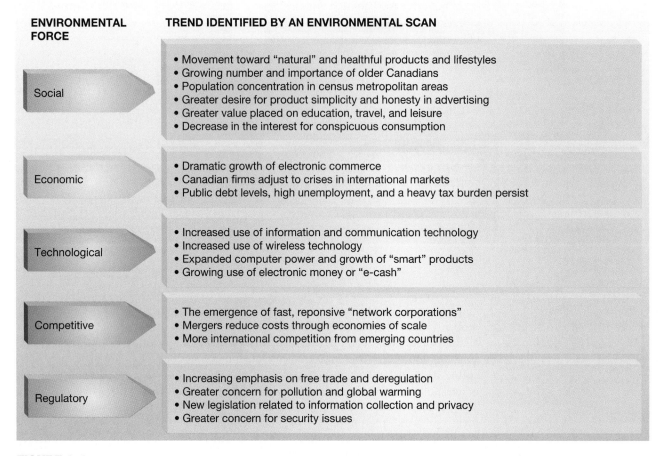

ENVIRONMENTAL FORCE	TREND IDENTIFIED BY AN ENVIRONMENTAL SCAN
Social	• Movement toward "natural" and healthful products and lifestyles • Growing number and importance of older Canadians • Population concentration in census metropolitan areas • Greater desire for product simplicity and honesty in advertising • Greater value placed on education, travel, and leisure • Decrease in the interest for conspicuous consumption
Economic	• Dramatic growth of electronic commerce • Canadian firms adjust to crises in international markets • Public debt levels, high unemployment, and a heavy tax burden persist
Technological	• Increased use of information and communication technology • Increased use of wireless technology • Expanded computer power and growth of "smart" products • Growing use of electronic money or "e-cash"
Competitive	• The emergence of fast, reponsive "network corporations" • Mergers reduce costs through economies of scale • More international competition from emerging countries
Regulatory	• Increasing emphasis on free trade and deregulation • Greater concern for pollution and global warming • New legislation related to information collection and privacy • Greater concern for security issues

FIGURE 3–2
An environmental scan of Canada

Population Size and Growth   The current population of Canada is 30 million, with a population growth rate of 4 percent since the 1996 Census.[9] The population is expected to be over 33 million by 2011.[10] The main source of growth in population comes from immigration, as there is a significant decrease in the natural growth rate (births and deaths).

Age Waves   Because age affects the needs, values, and purchasing habits of consumers, tracking consumers by age groupings is also part of an environmental scan. The size, habits, and relative purchasing power of various age groups is closely examined in an environmental scan.

Canadians are getting older. In 1999 the median age of the population was 35 years, which means 50 percent of the population was below that age but 50 percent was also above 35 years of age. The median age in Canada is projected to be over 40 years by 2011. The forecast age distribution of Canada's population for 2011 is shown in Figure 3–3.[11] As you can see, over 35 percent of the population will be over the age of 50 by that time. This is a significant demographic trend that indicates the greying of Canada.

MATURE HOUSEHOLDS
Households headed by people over 50 years old.

The over-50 age group—sometimes called the **mature household**—is a fast-growing age segment in Canada. In recent years, greater marketing attention has been focused on this market because people over 50 years of age control much of the *accumulated wealth* in this country—the value of net assets accumulated by households in the form of real property, financial securities, deposits, and pension assets. Many Canadian companies have responded aggressively to this important market by developing products and services specific to the mature market (such as retirement communities), using older celebrities in ads, and placing larger type on product labels.[12]

BABY BOOMERS
The generation of children born between 1946 and 1964.

A major reason for the greying of Canada is that the **baby boomers**—the generation of children born between 1946 and 1964—are growing older. As millions of boomers have aged, their participation in the workforce and their earnings have increased, making them an important consumer market. It has been estimated that this group accounts for the majority of the purchases in most consumer product and service categories. As the older boomers become part of the mature market, their buying behaviour is changing to reflect greater concern for their children's future and their own retirement. Even the younger boomers are showing greater concern about saving and financial planning.

As a group, boomers are shifting their focus from indulgence and luxury to quality and value.[13] Companies such as Club Med and Lee jeans are refocusing their strategies to a more mature boomer market. Club Med is trying to augment its singles image by promoting family vacations and facilities with child care in addition to vacations that cater to singles and couples, and Lee is responding to an aging baby boomer with loose-fitting jeans and advertising, "You're not a kid anymore."[14]

www.leejeans.com

FIGURE 3–3
The age distribution forecast for the Canadian population in 2011

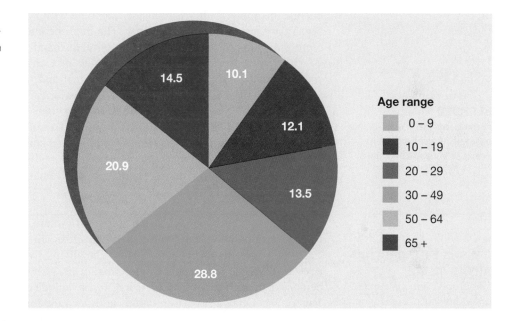

Age range
- 0 – 9
- 10 – 19
- 20 – 29
- 30 – 49
- 50 – 64
- 65 +

Which population groups are these advertisers trying to reach?

GENERATION X
The group of Canadians born between 1965 and 1976.

Generation X is the group of Canadians born between 1965 and 1976. Members of Generation X (Xers) represent about 15 percent of the Canadian population. It is a generation of consumers who are not prone to extravagance and are likely to pursue lifestyles and prefer products and services that are very different from those preferred by baby boomers. They are also likely to be more demanding consumers. Marketers are very much aware of this group of consumers and are interested in tracking this generation to identify the dominant consumption values of the 21st century.[15]

BABY BOOMLET
Canadians born after 1977; also described as Generation Y or the Net Generation.

The **baby boomlet** refers to Canadians born after 1977 and is also described as Generation Y, or the Net Generation. The boomlet generation already exerts influence on music, sports, computers, and video game purchases. Later in the 21st century, this group will influence markets, attitudes, and society much like the baby boomers do now and Generation X will do soon.[16]

The Canadian Family   The types of families in Canada are changing in both size and structure. The average family size in Canada is three persons. In 1971 one in three Canadian families consisted of the once-typical scenario of a husband working outside the home, with a wife inside the home with their children. Today, only one in seven families fall into this category. The dual-income family is the norm in Canada, representing approximately 64 percent of all husband-wife families.[17]

BLENDED FAMILY
Formed by the merging into a single household of two previously separated units.

About 50 percent of all first marriages in Canada end in divorce. Thus, the single-parent family is becoming more typical and, according to researchers, more acceptable to Canadian society.[18] But the majority of divorced people eventually remarry, giving rise to the **blended family**, one formed by the merging into a single household of two previously separated units. Today, many Canadians are finding themselves as a stepparent, stepchild, stepsibling, or some other member of a blended family—Hallmark Cards specially designs cards and verses for such blended families. Still, many people do not remarry, and single-parent families represent close to 19 percent of all family units in Canada.[19]

Population Shifts   Since the mid-1970s there has been a major shift in the Canadian population from rural to urban areas. In fact, more than 80 percent of Canadians are urban dwellers.[20] Most Canadians live in **census metropolitan areas** (CMAs), geographic labour market areas having a population of 100 000 persons or more. The top 27 CMAs in Canada include cities such as Toronto, Montreal, Vancouver, Ottawa, and Edmonton, and account for more than 64 percent of the Canadian population. With the concentration of the population in or near CMAs, marketers can reach large segments of the market efficiently and effectively. Some experts have predicted that by 2010 most Canadians will be located in seven or eight city-states and be within easy reach of most marketers.[21]

CENSUS METROPOLITAN AREAS (CMA)
Geographic labour market areas having a population of 100 000 persons or more.

Four major urban regions are emerging in Canada, representing 51 percent of the population with 15.3 million people living in these areas. These important regions are the Golden Horseshoe in Ontario (Oshawa, Toronto, Hamilton and St. Catharines–Niagara, Kitchener, Guelph, and Barrie); Montreal and adjacent regions (Salaberry-de-Valleyfield, Saint-Jean-sur-Richelieu, Saint-Hyacinthe, Sorel, Joliette, and Lachute); British Columbia's Lower Mainland and southern Vancouver Island; and the Calgary–Edmonton corridor.

REGIONAL MARKETING
Developing marketing plans to reflect specific area differences in taste preferences, perceived needs, or interests.

Regional Marketing   A recent trend within marketing focuses not only on the shifting of consumers geographically, such as the move from rural to urban areas, but also on the differences in their product preferences based on where they live. This concept has been referred to as **regional marketing**, which is developing marketing plans designed to reflect the specific area differences in taste preferences, perceived needs, or interests. Given the vastness of Canada, many marketers view the country as being composed of regions such as Atlantic Canada, Quebec, Ontario, Western Canada, and British Columbia. In Chapter 9, you will learn more about this approach to the market, referred to as *geographic segmentation*.

Because of differences in economics, topography, and natural resources, consumption patterns in the regions of Canada tend to differ. Some products and brands that sell successfully in one region do not do well in another. Strategies and tactics to sell them may also differ. Colgate-Palmolive found that marketing its Arctic Power cold water clothes detergent on an energy-savings dimension worked well in Quebec but not in the West, where cold-water washing was perceived to be easier on clothes. The company adjusted its marketing strategy accordingly.

Technology has aided marketers in understanding the variations in regional preferences. Computerized cash registers, for example, have allowed companies to coordinate and analyze sales data for geographic regions, determining what does and does not sell well in various regions. Pepsi-Cola can be a market leader in one region while Coca-Cola can be the leader in another. And, with advances in direct marketing approaches (Chapter 19), this focus on regional marketing allows for better targeting of ads and products. Still, the ability to market on a regional basis depends not only on the variance in regional preferences, but also on the sufficiency of size of the region and the cost of localized efforts. Often, regional or localized efforts can be more costly than one simple national effort. But, a better understanding of the geographic regions of Canada and any resultant differences in consumer preferences can lead to more successful marketing. For example, while Harvey's Restaurants sells the same products across Canada, it uses original French-language advertising for Quebec featuring Bernard Fortin, a high-profile and well-liked actor in Quebec. The uniqueness of the campaign has paid off for Harvey's. Sears Canada has featured celebrities on the covers of its catalogues. For the English catalogue, Michelle Wright graced the front, while Quebec pop singer Julie Masse appeared on the French version. And, finally, Pizza Hut Canada runs a Quebec-specific TV spot for a Quebec-specific product: a medium-size stuffed crust pizza.

Ethnic Diversity   While we often think of Canada as consisting of French and English Canadians, close to 3 out of 10 Canadians are of neither French nor British descent. While the majority of the non-British, non-French population are of European descent, there has been growth in other ethnic groups and visible minorities. Eighty different ethnic groups are represented in Canada.[22] In fact, close to 70 percent of all immigrants to Canada today are classified as visible minorities, primarily people from China, Southeast Asia, Africa, and India. Hong Kong Chinese and Southeast Asians are the fastest-growing ethnic groups in Canada, representing close to three percent of the Canadian population. Visible minorities are projected to represent close to 23 percent of the population by 2016.[23]

Much of the ethnic population can be found in major metropolitan areas such as Toronto, Vancouver, Montreal, Calgary, and Edmonton. Close to 20 percent of the populations in those areas register their native language as something other than English or French. Marketers have recognized the growing ethnic diversity in Canada. Many companies such as the Royal Bank and Bell Canada are putting "ethnic faces" in mainstream advertising. Many other companies such as Procter & Gamble and Ford Motors of Canada devote marketing efforts to cater specifically to these ethnic groups, which includes advertising in their language and providing personnel who speak their language. For example, the CIBC has an Aboriginal banking unit to develop better ways of serving the needs of their Aboriginal clients throughout Canada.[24]

Culture

CULTURE
The set of values, ideas, and attitudes of a homogeneous group of people that are transmitted from one generation to the next.

A second social force, **culture**, incorporates the set of values, ideas, and attitudes of a homogeneous group of people that are transmitted from one generation to the next. Culture includes both material and abstract elements, so monitoring cultural trends in Canada is difficult but important for effective marketing. We will deal with noteworthy cultural trends in Canada in this section. Cross-cultural analysis needed for successful global marketing is discussed in Chapter 7.

Ford and CIBC are companies
that recognize ethnic diversity
in Canada.

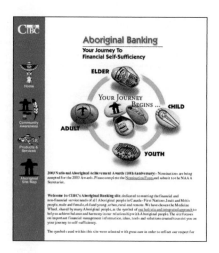

Changing Attitudes and Values   In recent years, Canadians have experienced some major attitudinal changes toward work, lifestyles, and consumption. There is a growing sense that the Puritan work ethic of "I live to work" may be redefined as "I work to live." Work is now more likely seen as a means to an end—recreation, leisure, and entertainment. Canadian consumers are placing more emphasis on quality of life as opposed to work, which has contributed to a growth in sales of products such as sports equipment, vacations, electronic entertainment equipment, and easily prepared foods.

At the same time, more women than ever are working outside the home; nationally, more than 65 percent of women do so. With more working women, the number of tasks to do is expanding while the time available to do them is shrinking. This phenomenon is often referred to as *time poverty*. So, even though more Canadians are working outside the home, these consumers are still concerned with quality of life. Therefore, they are demanding that marketers offer them greater convenience—such as express lanes at checkouts, longer store hours, drive-through windows, delivery services, and shopping electronically by the Internet. For example, Sobeys, Inc. of Nova Scotia offers time-pressed shoppers the convenience of one-stop shopping including groceries, in-store pharmacies, wellcentres, and banking services. The Hudson's Bay Company offers its customers the option of shopping in its retail stores or on the Internet via its online store, HBC.com. The Bay and Imperial Oil have even teamed up to allow customers to use The Bay and Zellers credit cards at Esso stations across Canada. In addition, Esso allows its customers to pay for their purchases with its electronic "Speedpass" payment system.[25]

There is greater concern for health and well being, as evidenced by the level of fitness activity and sports participation in Canada. Firms like Bauer Canada, Nike, and Reebok are profiting from this trend. Canadians are also more concerned about their diets, especially because of the link between diet and health. Growth in sales of low-fat or no-fat, cholesterol-free, and organic foods is evidence of this concern. For example, Loblaws' President's Choice Organics food line has shown real growth as consumers seek more natural and healthy foods. Consumers are also drinking healthier products including more bottled water and juices as opposed to traditional soft drinks. Clearly Canadian Beverages of Vancouver, a pioneer in the alternative beverage market, offers consumers an array of healthful drinks including its new Reebok Fitness Water, a product designed specifically for active adults.[26]

Health-conscious Canadians are also buying more health supplements and medical self-diagnostic kits. For example, sales of multivitamin and calcium supplements are soaring. Key players such as Centrum and Shoppers Drug Mart's Life brands have enjoyed significant growth. In fact, the market has attracted new entries such as Roots Canada, which now offers a new vitamin line through

Responding to consumer demand for value, Sobeys offers a value-based line of products that come with a low-price guarantee.

Boehringer Ingelheim of Burlington, Ontario.[27] Lifescan Canada of Burnaby, B.C., markets a variety of self-testing kits that can monitor cholesterol levels or test for colorectal cancer. The company suggests that well-educated and aging consumers are taking greater responsibility for their health, including self-diagnosis.

A change in consumption orientation is also apparent. Conspicuous consumption marked much of the past 20 years. Today, and for the foreseeable future, **value consciousness**—or the concern for obtaining the best quality, features, and performance of a product or service for a given price—will drive consumption behaviour. Innovative marketers have responded to this new orientation in numerous ways. Holiday Inn Worldwide has opened Holiday Express Hotels designed to offer comfortable accommodations with room rates lower than Holiday Inn's. Sobeys, Inc., one of Canada's top food retailers, now offers consumers its Smart Choice brand of products, which is a private-label, value-based line that comes with a low-price guarantee.[28] Even Canada's major banks are recognizing the value-consciousness trend and are offering consumers credit cards with lower interest rates and value-added enhancements such as frequent flyer programs and cash-back offers.[29]

VALUE CONSCIOUSNESS
The concern for obtaining the best quality, features, and performance of a product or service for a given price.

www.holidayinn.com

Concept Check

1. What is environmental scanning?

2. What is a census metropolitan area?

3. What are the marketing implications of blended families?

ECONOMIC FORCES

ECONOMY
The income, expenditures, and resources that affect the cost of running an organization or a household.

Another component of the environmental scan, the **economy**, pertains to the income, expenditures, and resources that affect the cost of running an organization or a household. We'll consider two aspects of these economic forces: a macroeconomic view of the marketplace and a microeconomic perspective of consumer income.

Macroeconomic Conditions

Of particular concern at the macroeconomic level is the inflationary or recessionary state of the nation's economy, whether actual or perceived, by consumers or businesses. In an inflationary economy, the cost to produce and buy products and services escalates as prices increase. From a marketing standpoint, if prices rise faster than consumer incomes, the number of items consumers can buy decreases.

Whereas inflation is a period of price increases, recession is a time of slow economic activity. Businesses decrease production, unemployment rises, and many consumers have less money to spend. The Canadian economy experienced recessions in the early 1970s, early 1980s, and early 1990s. The Canadian economy was relatively healthy in the late 1990s, but with the dot-com disappointments in 2000 the promise of the "new economy" evaporated, triggering an economic slowdown beginning in 2001.[30]

Assessing consumer expectations of an inflationary and recessionary economy is an important element of environmental scanning. Consumer spending, which accounts for two-thirds of Canadian economic activity, is affected by expectations of the future. Surveys of consumer expectations are tracked over time by researchers, who ask questions such as "Do you expect to be better or worse off financially a year from now?" Surveyors record the share of positive and negative responses to this question and related ones to develop an index, sometimes called a consumer confidence or consumer sentiment index. The higher the index, the more favourable are consumer expectations. Many firms evaluate such indexes in order to plan production levels. DaimlerChrysler, for example, uses such indexes to plan its automobile production levels in order to avoid overproducing cars during a recessionary economy.

Consumer Income

The microeconomic trends in terms of consumer income are also important issues for marketers. Having a product that meets the needs of consumers may be of little value if they are unable to purchase it. A consumer's ability to buy is related to income, which consists of gross, disposable, and discretionary components.

Gross Income   The total amount of money made in one year by a person, household, or family unit is referred to as **gross income**. Figure 3–4 shows the distribution of annual income among Canadian families.[31] Average gross family income in Canada is slightly over $57 000. But family income in Canada varies by province as well as by the education level and profession of the head(s) of the family. For example, the majority of families earning $75 000 or more are headed by university graduates.

GROSS INCOME
The total amount of money made in one year by a person, household, or family unit.

FIGURE 3–4
Income distribution of Canadian households

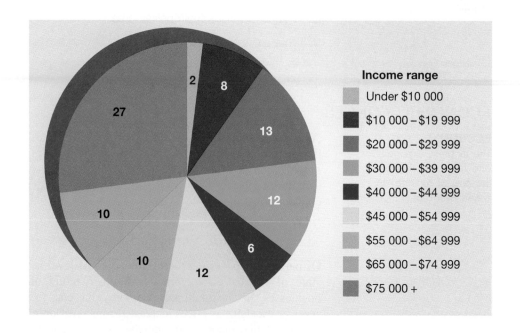

| Income range |
| Under $10 000 |
| $10 000 – $19 999 |
| $20 000 – $29 999 |
| $30 000 – $39 999 |
| $40 000 – $44 999 |
| $45 000 – $54 999 |
| $55 000 – $64 999 |
| $65 000 – $74 999 |
| $75 000 + |

As consumers' discretionary income increases, so does the enjoyment of pleasure travel.

Four Seasons Hotels
www.fourseasons.com

DISPOSABLE INCOME
The money a consumer has left after paying taxes to use for necessities such as food, shelter, and clothing.

Disposable Income The second income component, **disposable income**, is money a consumer has left after paying taxes to use for necessities such as food, shelter, and clothing. Thus, if taxes rise at a faster rate than does disposable income, consumers must economize. In recent years consumers' allocation of income has shifted. For example, the proportion of disposable income devoted to eating in the home has increased, while the proportion devoted to eating out has decreased. Two environmental factors account for this: the recession of the early 1990s caused people to cut back on expenses such as eating out, and many baby-boom households are in the midst of their child-raising years, causing increased spending on food at home.[32]

DISCRETIONARY INCOME
The money that remains after paying for taxes and necessities.

Discretionary Income The third component of income is **discretionary income**, the money that remains after paying for taxes and necessities. Discretionary income is used for luxury items such as vacations at a Four Seasons resort. An obvious problem in defining discretionary versus disposable income is determining what is a luxury and what is a necessity. Observation can be a way to make this determination—if a family has Royal Doulton china, Rolex watches, and Lexus automobiles, one could assume that they have, or had, discretionary income. Still, it is important to note that a product defined as a necessity by one individual may be viewed as a luxury by another. For example, some Canadians view a microwave oven as a necessity while others see it as a luxury item.

TECHNOLOGICAL FORCES

Our society is in a period of dramatic technological change. **Technology**, a major environmental force, refers to inventions or innovations from applied science or engineering research. Each new wave of technological innovation can replace existing products and companies. Do you recognize the items pictured below and what they may replace?

Technology of Tomorrow

Technological change is the result of research, so it is difficult to predict. Some of the most dramatic technological changes occurring now, however, include the following:

1. Advances in nanotechnology, the science of unimaginably small electronics, will lead to denser hard drives, smaller chips, and better medicine.
2. The convergence of personal computer and telephone technologies.
3. The Internet will become the communication backbone of information-intensive industries.
4. The emergence of biotechnology as a key component of the economy.

These trends in technology are already seen in today's marketplace. IBM has developed a 1-square-inch storage system that can record 400 gigabits of data. PDAs (personal digital assistants) such as Palm and Waterloo, Ontario–based Research in Motion's Blackberry offer computing capabilities and wireless messaging. Amgen Inc.'s new rheumatoid arthritis drug, Kineret, will assist arthritis sufferers. Other technologies such as satellite dishes, HDTV, and digital cameras are likely to replace or substitute for existing technologies such as cable, low-resolution TV, and film.[33]

Technology's Impact on Customer Value

Advances in technology are having important effects on marketing. First, the cost of technology is plummeting—causing the customer value assessment of technology-based products to focus on other dimensions such as quality, service, and relationships. When Computer Associates International introduced its software program Simply Money, it gave away the first million copies. Computer Associates reasoned that satisfied customers would later buy upgrades and related products. A similar approach is now used by many cellular telephone vendors, who charge little for the telephone if the purchase leads to a telephone service contract.[34]

Technological change leads to new products. What products might be replaced by these innovations?

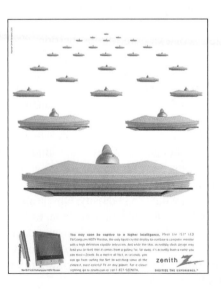

Technology also provides value through the development of new products. Oldsmobile now offers customers an auto-navigation system that uses satellite signals to help the driver reach any destination. Under development are radarlike collision avoidance systems that disengage cruise control, reduce the engine speed, and even apply the brakes.[35] Other new products likely to be available soon include a "smart ski" with an embedded microprocessor that will adjust the flexibility of the ski to snow conditions; injectable health monitors that will send glucose, oxygen, or other clinical information to a wristwatch-like monitor; and electronic books that will allow you to download any volume and view it on pages coated with electronic "ink" and embedded electrodes.[36]

Technology can also change existing products and the ways they are produced. Many companies are using technological developments to allow *recycling* products through the manufacturing cycle several times. The Packaging Association of Canada's *Reduction Report* estimates that since the 1970s, plastic trash bags have been made thinner by 50 percent and grocery bags by 66 percent.[37] In Squamish, B.C., Moore Enviro Systems Inc. now produces a shingle made of used tires called Moo Roof.[38] The roof comes with a 50-year warranty. Another approach is *precycling*—efforts by manufacturers to reduce waste by decreasing the amount of packaging they use. The development of new packaging materials, for example, has allowed DuPont to produce a collapsible pouch as an alternative to milk cartons in school lunch programs.[39]

Electronic Business Technologies

The transformative power of technology may be best illustrated by the rapid growth of the **marketspace**, an information- and communication-based electronic exchange environment mostly occupied by sophisticated computer and telecommunication technologies and digitized offerings. Any activity that uses some form of electronic communication in the inventory, exchange, advertisement, distribution, and payment of goods and services is often called **electronic commerce**. Although electronic commerce has existed through proprietary networks—such as those used to connect ATMs to your bank—for many years, in 1996 the World Wide Web burst onto the scene and started a new era of *electronic business*. Network technologies are now used for everything from filing expense reports, to monitoring daily sales, to sharing information with employees, to communicating instantly with suppliers.

The most widely visible application of electronic commerce exists in business-to-consumer interactive marketing, involving the Internet, the World Wide Web, and commercial online services. Many people view these three as being the same. They are not. The **Internet** is an integrated global network of computers that gives users access to information and documents. The **World Wide Web** is a part of the Internet that supports a retrieval system that formats information and documents into

MARKETSPACE
An information- and communication-based electronic exchange environment mostly occupied by sophisticated computer and telecommunication technologies and digitized offerings.

ELECTRONIC COMMERCE
Any activity that uses some form of electronic communication in the inventory, exchange, advertisement, distribution, and payment of goods and services.

INTERNET
An integrated global network of computers that gives users access to information and documents.

WORLD WIDE WEB
A part of the Internet that supports a retrieval system that formats information and documents into Web pages.

Examples of a recycling program by re Planet, a Norweigan-based company expanding into North America, and a precycling program by Lever.

COMMERCIAL ONLINE SERVICES
Companies that provide electronic information and marketing services to subscribers who are charged a monthly fee.

INTRANET
An Internet/Web-based network used within the boundaries of an organization.

Web pages. **Commercial online services** such as Sympatico offer electronic information and marketing services to subscribers who are charged a monthly fee. The combination of these technologies caused electronic commerce activity to skyrocket to more than $4 billion in 2000.[40]

Many companies have adapted Internet-based technology internally to support their electronic business strategies. An **intranet**, for example, is an Internet/Web-based network used within the boundaries of an organization. It is a private Internet that may or may not be connected to the public Internet. **Extranets**, which use Internet-based technologies, permit communication between a company and its supplier, distributors, and other partners (such as advertising agencies). The accompanying Marketing NewsNet describes how these technologies have transformed some companies into e-businesses![41]

COMPETITIVE FORCES

EXTRANET
A network that uses Internet-based technologies to permit communication between an organization and its suppliers, distributors, and other partners.

COMPETITION
The alternative firms that could provide a product to satisfy a specific market's needs.

Another component of the environmental scan is competition. **Competition** refers to the alternative firms that could provide a product to satisfy a specific market's needs. There are various forms of competition, and each company must consider its present and potential competitors in designing its marketing strategy.

Alternative Forms of Competition

Four basic forms of competition comprise a continuum: pure competition, monopolistic competition, oligopoly, and monopoly. Chapter 13 contains further discussions on pricing practices under these four forms of competition.

At one end of the continuum is *pure competition*, in which every company has a similar product. Companies that deal in commodities common to agribusiness (for example, wheat, rice, and other grains) often are in a pure competition position in which distribution (in the sense of shipping products) is important but other elements of marketing have little impact.

In the second point on the continuum, *monopolistic competition*, the many sellers compete with their products on a substitutable basis. For example, if the price of coffee rises too much, consumers may switch to tea. Coupons or frequent sales are marketing tactics often used in monopolistic competition.

MARKETING NEWSNET   The Net Worked!

Despite the recent failures of many dot-com businesses it is clear that the Internet is changing many industries. Because the Internet can dramatically reduce the cost of communication, information-intensive businesses such as financial services, entertainment, health care, education, government, and many others are benefiting substantially from the Net. Success stories include eBay, which offers online auctions; E-Cruiter.com Inc., which develops software for companies wanting to recruit online; Sears Canada, which has the largest Canadian online catalogue business; Canoe.ca, which is the largest information portal in Canada; and eharlequin.com, which sells romance e-books.

In addition, Net technologies are changing the way work is done within companies. For example, the Internet can increase the speed at which new-product ideas spread among employees, between companies, within economies, and across countries. At Procter & Gamble, a Web-based information-sharing network facilitates the collection and evaluation of new-product ideas from the company's 110 000 employees.

What's next? Some experts predict the World Wide Web will be bypassed by new Net technologies such as wireless services, peer-to-peer communication software, instant messaging, and machine-to-machine communication!

Oligopoly, a common industry structure, occurs when a few companies control the majority of industry sales. Because there are few sellers in an oligopolistic situation, price competition among firms is not desirable because it would lead to reduced revenue for all producers. Instead, nonprice competition is common, which means competing on other dimensions of the marketing mix such as product quality, distribution, and/or promotion. Canada is sometimes referred to by some economists as the "land of oligopoly" because it has several major industries that can be considered oligopolistic, including the airline industry and the banking industry.

The final point on the continuum, *monopoly*, occurs when only one firm sells the product or service. It has been common for producers of goods and services considered essential to a community: water, electricity, or telephone service. Typically, marketing plays a small role in a monopolistic setting because it is regulated by a provincial or the federal government. Government control usually seeks to ensure price protection for the buyer. Historically, there was no competition in the long-distance telephone business in Canada, but deregulation has given rise to new entrants such as MCI, AT&T Canada, Sprint, and Call-Net Enterprises. Bell Canada and the various provincial telephone companies across Canada now must compete in a different marketing environment, a monopolistic-competitive one. Marketing has now assumed a more important role at the traditional telephone companies. More recent deregulation of the communications industry has opened the local telephone services market in Canada. For a century, the telephone companies providing local service had a monopoly. This has now ended and local providers, long-distance carriers, and cable TV firms now compete in each other's markets.[42]

www.bell.ca

Components of Competition

In developing a marketing strategy, companies must consider the components that drive competition: entry, bargaining power of buyers and suppliers, existing rivalries, and substitution possibilities.[43] Scanning the environment requires a look at all of them. These relate to a firm's marketing mix decisions and may be used to create a barrier to entry, increase brand awareness, or intensify a fight for market share.

Entry   In considering the competition, a firm must assess the likelihood of new entrants. Additional producers increase industry capacity and tend to lower prices. A company scanning its environment must consider the possible **barriers to entry** for other firms, which are business practices or conditions that make it difficult for new firms to enter the market. Barriers to entry can be in the form of capital requirements, promotional expenditures, product identity, distribution access, or switching costs. The higher the expense of the barrier, the more likely it will deter new entrants. For example, IBM once created a switching cost barrier for organizations that considered Apple Computer equipment because IBM had a different programming language for its machines.

BARRIERS TO ENTRY
Business practices or conditions that make it difficult for new firms to enter the market.

Power of Buyers and Suppliers   A competitive analysis must consider the power of buyers and suppliers. Powerful buyers exist when they are few in number, there are low switching costs, or the product represents a significant share of the buyer's total costs. This last factor leads the buyer to exert significant pressure for price competition. A supplier gains power when the product is critical to the buyer and when it has built up the switching costs.

Existing Competitors and Substitutes   Competitive pressures among existing firms depend on the rate of industry growth. In slow-growth settings, competition is more heated for any possible gains in market share. High fixed costs also create competitive pressure for firms to fill production capacity. For example, many Canadian universities are increasing their advertising and public relations activities to fill classrooms, which represent a high fixed cost.

Startups, Entrepreneurs, and Small Business   Small and medium-sized enterprises contribute to the Canadian economy by providing job opportunities and economic growth. With the shift to a more global, knowledge-based economy, small and medium-sized enterprises (SMEs) in Canada are facing these challenges with an entrepreneurial spirit. There are 2.6 million SMEs in Canada contributing almost 45 percent of the GDP and responsible for 80 percent of new job creation. Currently SMEs dominate the information and communications technology sector in Canada, experiencing 10-percent annual growth since 1993.[44] This has happened in spite of the many failed dot-coms. The entrepreneurs of the country continue to invent and explore new markets, providing a valuable source of economic stimulation in light of the economic slowdown in 2001.

The New Look in Canadian Corporations

Competition has had two other important effects on Canadian corporations: (1) the use of the Internet as a way of doing business and (2) the restructuring of corporations.

Canadian corporations are rapidly changing the way they compete. For many managers the common practices that often ensured success in the past won't work any longer. The need to expand beyond the domestic markets, a general increase in the importance of intellectual capital, and the use of Internet technologies as competitive tools have all necessitated changes. Today's organization requires (1) constant change rather than stability, (2) networks rather than hierarchies, and (3) partnerships and alliances rather than self-sufficiency. Canadian corporations are adopting a new business model that consists of small business units, empowered workers with responsibility and accountability, and managers who "support" rather than control. Increases in productivity come by leveraging the creativity of individuals.

How will corporations facilitate these changes? One approach utilizes the Web as a management tool and leads to a model called the "network organization" or the "e-corporation." The Web gives everyone in the organization the ability to access and process information at any time and from any location. In addition, the Web allows employees to manage formal and informal networks of contractors, designers, manufacturers, and distributors. Software developer Ray Ozzie created Lotus Notes to help people quickly spread knowledge and information across organizations. It has been a huge success; more than 68 million users have purchased the product!

Another way Canadian companies are changing the way they compete is through restructuring. Although the process is known by various names—re-engineering, streamlining, or **restructuring**—the result is the same: striving for more efficient corporations that can compete globally. For many firms, restructuring means reducing duplicate efforts in multiple company locations, closing or changing unprofitable plants and offices, and often laying off hundreds or thousands of employees. For example, the Calgary-based conglomerate Canadian Pacific Ltd. recently restructured its company by breaking five business units into separate companies. Canadian Pacific, with interests in energy, railways, shipping, hotels, and coal, had been suffering from a "holding company discount" where the conglomerate's value was less than the value of the individual business units.[45] By creating five independent companies, each will have a greater ability to implement independent strategies and pursue growth opportunities. The five new companies are PanCanadian Energy Corp., Fairmont Hotels & Resorts Inc., Canadian Pacific Railway Co., CP Ships Holdings Inc., and Fording Inc.

Another approach to restructuring has been through mergers, acquisitions, and takeovers. The past few years have seen numerous well-publicized mega-mergers including DaimlerChrysler, BMW and Land Rover, and Ford and Volvo. Read the Web Link for a recent example from the Canadian coffee industry.[46]

RESTRUCTURING
Striving for more efficient corporations that can compete globally by reducing duplicate efforts in multiple company locations, closing or changing unprofitable plants and offices, and laying off employees.

WEB LINK   **Taking a Coffee Break**

http://www.mcgrawhill.ca

After a bitter fight, Toronto-based Cara Operations Limited has succeeded in taking over Second Cup following a valiant attempt by Michel Bergman to save the family stake of 24 percent in the company. Mississauga-based Cara, a food-service conglomerate, owned 39 percent of Second Cup and wanted to take the company public but needed the Bergman shares to do so. Cara Operations runs the

Harvey's and Swiss Chalet restaurant chains and also provides catering to airlines in Canada. This takeover will allow the company to continue to grow its complementary services.

At the time of writing, the takeover had just been completed. Visit Cara's Website at www.cara.com to see how Second Cup is managed by its new major stakeholder. What is your opinion of the takeover and the motivation behind it?

www.sunlife.com

Several years ago, the government blocked a major merger between the Bank of Montreal and the Royal Bank. However, the TD Bank and Canada Trust were allowed to merge. Now the insurance industry is experiencing similar changes, with Sun Life Financial buying both Clarica Life Insurance and Liberty Financial during one year. The oil and gas industry is changing as well, with Conoco buying Gulf Canada and Devon Energy buying Anderson Exploration.[47]

What is the explanation? In general, firms are striving for market dominance by ensuring control of distribution channels, access to markets, and cost reduction through economies of scale. Businesses are also discovering that information technology will allow effective management of large and complex organizations. Experts debate whether these mergers are good for the economy. While firms that dominate a market might command higher prices, they may also be vulnerable to faster, customer-focused entrepreneurs.

Concept Check

1. What is the difference between a consumer's disposable and discretionary income?

2. In pure competition there are _____ number of sellers.

3. What is a network organization?

REGULATORY FORCES

REGULATION
Restrictions the provincial and federal laws place on business with regard to the conduct of its activities.

For any organization, the marketing and broader business decisions are constrained, directed, and influenced by regulatory forces. **Regulation** consists of restrictions the provincial and federal laws place on business with respect to the conduct of its activities. Regulation exists to protect companies as well as consumers. Much of the regulation from the federal and provincial levels has been passed to ensure competition and fair business practices. For consumers, the focus of legislation is to protect them from unfair trade practices and ensure their safety.

Protecting Competition and Consumers

Legislation and regulations exist in Canada at all three levels of government—federal, provincial, and municipal—to protect and encourage a competitive environment, which is deemed desirable because it permits the consumer to determine which competitor will succeed and which will fail.

COMPETITION ACT
The key legislation designed
to protect competition and
consumers in Canada.

www.ic.gc.ca

The Competition Act   The key legislation designed to protect competition and consumers in Canada is the **Competition Act**, which replaced the Combines Investigation Act. The Combines legislation, in effect since 1923, has been found to be rather ineffectual. The Competition Act was introduced in two stages, in 1975 and 1986. The purpose of the Competition Act is:

> to maintain and encourage competition in Canada in order to promote the efficiency and adaptability of the Canadian economy, in order to expand opportunities for Canadian participation in world markets while at the same time recognizing the role of foreign competition in Canada, in order to ensure that small- and medium-sized enterprises have an equitable opportunity to participate in the Canadian economy and in order to provide consumers with competitive prices and product choices.[48]

In essence, the act is designed to protect and to balance the interests of competitors and consumers. The Bureau of Competition Policy, which is part of Industry Canada, is responsible for administering and enforcing the provisions of the act. The act contains both criminal and noncriminal provisions.

Criminal offences under Part VI of the act include conspiracy (e.g., price-fixing), bid-rigging, discriminatory and predatory pricing, price maintenance, and misleading or deceptive marketing practices such as double-ticketing or bait-and-switch selling.

Noncriminal reviewable matters under Part VIII of the act include mergers, abuse of dominant position, refusal to deal, consignment selling, exclusive dealing, tied selling, market restriction, and delivered pricing. The Director of the Bureau of Competition Policy refers these matters to the Competition Tribunal under noncriminal law standards. The tribunal was established when the act took effect and is governed by the Competition Tribunal Act. The tribunal adjudicates all reviewable matters under the act.

Industry Canada is responsible for most of the legislation affecting business practices in Canada. Figure 3–5 lists the more significant federal legislation that protects competition and consumers in Canada. Marketers must also be cognizant of the fact that, in addition to federal laws and regulations, there are many more at the provincial level. Many provinces have their own departments of consumer affairs in

FIGURE 3–5
Major federal legislation
designed to protect
competition and consumers

Bank Cost Borrowing Act	Hazardous Products Act
Bankruptcy Act	Income Tax Act
Bills of Exchange Act	Industrial Design Act
Board of Trade Act	Maple Products Industry Act
Broadcasting Act	Motor Vehicle Safety Act
Canada Agricultural Products Standards Act	Offical Languages Act
	Patent Act
Canada Cooperative Association Act	Personal Information and Electronic Documents Act
Canada Corporations Act	
Canada Dairy Products Act	Precious Metals Marketing Act
Canadian Human Rights Act	Privacy Act
Competition Act	Small Loans Act
Consumer Packaging and Labelling Act	Standards Council of Canada Act
Copyright Act	Textile Labelling Act
Criminal Code	The Interest Act
Department of Consumer and Corporate Affairs Act	Timber Marketing Act
	Trade-Marks Act
Electricity Inspection Act and Gas Inspection Act	True Labelling Act
	Weights and Measures Act
Fish Inspection Act	Winding-up Act
Food and Drugs Act	

order to administer any such legislation and regulations enacted on the provincial government level.

Unfortunately, the laws and regulations at the provincial level vary from province to province. A marketer may find it necessary to adapt some aspect of the marketing mix or some broader business practice depending on the province. For example, in Quebec there are specific laws dealing with store signage, packaging, and labelling. Additionally, advertising directed toward children is prohibited in Quebec. Many provinces, including Quebec, also have consumer protection acts and/or business or trade practices acts.

Self-Regulation

SELF-REGULATION
An alternative to government control where an industry attempts to police itself.

www.the-cma.org

The government has provided much legislation to create a competitive business climate and protect the consumer. An alternative to government control is **self-regulation**, where an industry attempts to police itself. The Canadian Broadcasting Association, whose members include major television networks and radio stations across the country, has a code of ethics that helps govern the conduct of its members in terms of protecting the consumer against deceptive trade practices such as misleading advertising. Similarly, the Advertising Standards Council, the self-regulatory arm of the Canadian Advertising Foundation, has established the Canadian Code of Advertising Standards for its members to follow. The members of this organization consist of major advertising agencies that are responsible for allocating the bulk of advertising dollars in Canada. The Canadian Radio-television and Telecommunications Commission, the federal agency responsible for licensing and regulating broadcasting in Canada, is in favour of greater industry self-regulation.

The Canadian Marketing Association, whose members represent 80 percent of direct-marketing sales in Canada, has mandated that its members comply with the consumer's right to privacy and honour consumers who request not to be contacted by telephone or mail for selling purposes. Critics argue that telemarketers in Canada demonstrate what is wrong with self-regulation efforts: noncompliance by members and enforcement (see the accompanying Ethics and Social Responsibility Alert).

Another well-known self-regulatory group is the Better Business Bureau (BBB). This organization is a voluntary alliance of companies whose goal is to help maintain fair business practices. Although the BBB has no legal power, it does try to use "moral suasion" to get members to comply with its regulations.

Consumerism

CONSUMERISM
A grassroots movement started in the 1960s to increase the influence, power, and rights of consumers in dealing with institutions.

Regulation by government and self-regulation by industry help in protecting the consumer in the marketplace. But the consumer can also play a direct and active role. **Consumerism** is a movement to increase the influence, power, and rights of consumers in dealing with institutions. Modern consumerism in Canada and the United States really began in the 1960s. U.S. President John F. Kennedy, in a speech entitled "Consumer Bill of Rights," outlined four basic consumer rights: (1) the right to safety, (2) the right to be informed, (3) the right to choose, and (4) the right to be heard. Although not passed as laws, these proclaimed rights serve as the basis for modern consumerism. Shortly after President Kennedy's Consumer Bill of Rights was unveiled in the United States, the Canadian government formed the Department of Consumer and Corporate Affairs, making it the agency responsible for protecting consumers and regulating corporate activities.

Canada also has many independent consumer organizations that advance the cause of consumerism. The Consumers Association of Canada (CAC) is the largest consumer group working on behalf of the Canadian consumer. The CAC serves as a channel for supplying consumers' views to government and industry, providing consumer information, and studying consumer problems and presenting recommended

ETHICS AND SOCIAL RESPONSIBILITY ALERT   All Is Not Right with Telemarketing

Telemarketing does not have a good image with most consumers. In fact, survey after survey shows that the majority of consumers asked believe telemarketing is an invasion of privacy, an offensive way to market, and a waste of the consumer's time. Why are many Canadians turned off by telemarketers? In some cases, there are telemarketers who engage in illegal and deceptive practices as well unethical behaviour. For example, take the case of a telemarketing company that phones consumers and tells them they have won prizes. The consumers are then asked to pay the shipping and handling costs for the prizes, the cost of which greatly exceeds the real costs of shipping and handling as well as the value of the prize.

In another case, consider telemarketing company representatives who lead consumers to believe they are volunteers requesting donations for a charity, but in fact are paid fundraisers who are working on commission. What about a telemarketer who uses a telemail program where

a consumer receives a direct-mail piece and is asked to phone a toll-free number for further information? Unknown to the consumer, the telemarketer uses an automatic number identification or caller ID intrusion system that identifies the incoming caller's number without their knowledge or consent. If the consumer does not buy the product or service initially, the company now has the consumer's telephone number and begins recalling the consumer in an attempt to sell them. The telemarketer also has an opportunity to capture and sell consumers' unlisted telephone numbers.

In many cases, there are telemarketers who are simply guilty of deception, legally; in other cases they engage in unethical, but perhaps not illegal, practices. This has tarnished the image of not only reputable telemarketers but also all other professional marketers. Do you have any personal experiences with a telemarketer who has engaged in an illegal or unethical practice? What can be done about these unethical telemarketers?

solutions to those problems. In addition to ensuring that the four original consumer rights are protected, the consumer movement of the 1990s also includes consumer demands for environmentally safe products and ethical and socially responsible business practices.

Concept Check

1. The _____ Act is the most important legislation designed to protect competition and consumers in Canada.

2. An alternative to legislation protecting competition and consumers is self-_____.

3. What is consumerism?

SUMMARY

1 The population in Canada is estimated at 30 million. The population is aging, and the number of traditional families as seen in the 1950s is diminishing. The dual-income family is now the norm in Canada and a blended family structure is becoming more common.

2 It is estimated that close to 80 percent of Canadians are urban dwellers, with most living in census metropolitan areas (CMAs). Regional marketing—developing marketing mixes designed to reflect specific geographic differences in taste preferences, perceived needs, or interests—is something Canadian marketers must consider.

3 Canada is becoming more ethnically diverse, including recent growth in the population of visible minorities.

4 Culture represents abstract values and material possessions. Values are changing toward work, quality of life, the roles of women and men, consumption, and personal security.

5 Disposable income is the number of dollars left after taxes. Discretionary income is the money consumers have after purchasing their necessities.

6 Technology increases customer value by reducing the cost of products, providing new products, and improving existing products. The most important new development for marketers may be advances in information technology that allow increasingly customized service.

7 Competition has had two major effects on Canadian corporations: (*a*) the use of the Internet as a way of doing business and (*b*) restructuring through mergers to improve efficiency.

8 For any organization, marketing and broader business decisions are constrained, directed, and influenced by regulatory forces. The most important legislation in Canada designed to protect competition and consumers is the Competition Act.

9 An alternative to government control is self-regulation, where an industry attempts to police itself. The effectiveness of self-regulation is coming under greater scrutiny.

10 The consumer can also play a direct and active role in influencing what happens in the marketplace. Consumerism is a movement to increase the influence, power, and rights of consumers in dealing with institutions. Modern consumers are demanding more environmentally safe products and ethical and socially responsible business practices.

KEY TERMS AND CONCEPTS

baby boomers p. 77
baby boomlet p. 78
barriers to entry p. 87
blended family p. 78
census metropolitan areas p. 78
commercial online services p. 86
competition p. 86
Competition Act p. 90
consumerism p. 91
culture p. 79
demographics p. 75
discretionary income p. 83
disposable income p. 82
economy p. 81
electronic commerce p. 85
environmental scanning p. 74

extranet p. 86
Generation X p. 78
gross income p. 82
Internet p. 85
intranet p. 86
marketspace p. 85
mature household p. 76
regional marketing p. 78
regulation p. 89
restructuring p. 88
self-regulation p. 91
social forces p. 75
technology p. 84
value consciousness p. 81
World Wide Web p. 85

INTERNET EXERCISE

www.mcgrawhill.ca/college/berkowitz

Many sources of information might be useful in an environmental scan. One particularly useful Website is Statistics Canada's site (www.statcan.ca). Statistics Canada is the source for Canadian statistics on Canadian population trends, consumer expenditures, and so on. Use this site to help answer the following questions:

1 What is the current (to the minute) population of Canada? What is the projected population of Canada in 2016?
2 How many people are aged 90 and over in Canada? (That's right, 90.)
3 How many lone-parent families are there in Canada?

Want to get better grades, find tips on how to study more effectively, and stay up to date with happenings in the world of marketing? Visit the Online Learning Centre for practice tests, Study Smart software, and much more! www.mcgrawhill.ca/college/berkowitz

Interested in finding out what marketing looks like in the real world? *Marketing Magazine* is just a click away on your OLC! Visit www.mcgrawhill.ca/college/berkowitz

APPLYING MARKETING CONCEPTS AND PERSPECTIVES

1 For many years Gerber has manufactured baby food in small, single-serving containers. In conducting an environmental scan, identify three trends or factors that might significantly affect this company's future business, and then propose how Gerber might respond to these changes.

2 Describe the new features you would add to an automobile designed for the mature household. In what magazines would you advertise to appeal to this target market?

3 New technologies are continuously improving and replacing existing products. Although technological change is often difficult to predict, suggest how the following companies and products might be affected by the Internet and digital technologies: (*a*) Kodak cameras and film, (*b*) Air Canada, and (*c*) the Museum of Art.

4 In recent years in the Canadian brewing industry, a couple of large firms that have historically had most of the beer sales

(Labatt and Molson) have faced competition from many small regional brands. In terms of the continuum of competition, how would you explain this change?

5 When the Canadian long-distance telephone industry became deregulated, how do you think the role of marketing changed? What elements of the marketing mix are more or less important since the deregulation?

6 The Johnson Company manufactures buttons and pins with slogans and designs. These pins are inexpensive to produce and are sold in retail outlets such as discount stores, hobby shops, and bookstores. Little equipment is needed for a new competitor to enter the market. What strategies should Johnson consider to create effective barriers to entry?

7 Today's consumer is more value-conscious. How could a retail home improvement centre sell the same products but still offer the consumer greater perceived value? What specific things could the retailer do?

VIDEO CASE 3–1   Flyte Tyme Productions, Inc.: The Best Idea Wins!

"Terry was looking for a keyboard player to be in the band he was just starting," remembers Jimmy Jam of Flyte Tyme Productions, Inc. "I had sort of rebelled because I had first thought of myself as a drummer," says Jam. But after he listened and heard how good the drummer was, he told Terry, "I'll be the keyboard player."

The conversation took place a few weeks after Terry Lewis and Jimmy Jam met at a summer math program for gifted junior high school students, sponsored by a local university. The two came to prominence in the early 1980s as members of the funk band "The Time," which appeared as the opener on many of Prince's early tours. The pair still credit Prince for much of their tenacious work ethic and eclectic musical tastes. After leaving the band, Terry and Jimmy started a music production company—Flyte Tyme—creating the new name by adapting the old one. Now in their early 40s, the two have worked together for 20 years, most of it in Flyte Tyme Productions (www.flytetyme.com), where their clients include Mary J. Blige, Boyz II Men, Mariah Carey, Janet Jackson, Michael Jackson, Patti LaBelle, Usher, TLC, and many others!

THE MUSIC

Sunglasses, fedoras, and sharp suits are Jam and Lewis's signature image, but—curiously—they have no signature sound. Instead, their approach is to tailor tunes for each artist. Janet Jackson's steamy bedroom ballads don't sound anything like Patti LaBelle's big Diane Warren ballads. They also work in a wide variety of music genres—from gospel (Yolanda Adams) and reggae (Shaggy) to jazz (Herb Alpert) and pop (Mariah Carey).

Flyte Tyme's successes are impressive. Recently they produced Usher's No. 1 pop hit "U Remind Me," which held the top spot on the charts for four weeks. They also produced Sting's Oscar-nominated song "My Funny Friend and Me" for the film *The Emperor's New Clothes*. And their work on Hikaru Utada's album helped it climb to the top of Japan's pop charts, selling 4 million copies in two weeks!

These and other hits put Flyte Tyme in extraordinary company. Having produced 16 No. 1 singles on *Billboard*'s pop chart, they are second only to the producer for the Beatles (with 23) and tied with the producer for Elvis Presley. Flyte Tyme has managed to stay at the top throughout the 1980s, '90s, and '00s, thanks in large part to Janet Jackson—nicknamed "The Franchise"—who accounts for 10 of their 16 No. 1 songs. Recently, they wrote and produced their fifth successive album for Janet Jackson, which set an industry record when "All For You" became the first single to be played by 100 percent of the pop, R & B, and rhythm radio stations reporting to trade publication *Radio & Records* in the first week after its release.

THE TEAM AND ITS FORMULA FOR SUCCESS

How have Jam and Lewis stayed at the top of the music game so long? Janet Jackson's answer: "There are no egos involved." Terry Lewis echoes this and says about his relationship with Jam: "He's the best partner a person could have. We've never had a contract—we've never had one argument in twenty-something years, not saying we don't disagree about things but our attitudes are the *best* idea wins. Not the right, not the wrong, but the *best*!"

"What we try to do is get everybody relaxed—check the egos at the door, that kind of thing. We find that we do it a lot more with new artists than with the older, more established artists," explains Jam. "Psychology is a big

part of producing. Some artists like to work right away, others like to play pool, have lunch, talk on the phone, then they mosey in and record," he says. "If you think of Janet Jackson or Mariah Carey—the people who you would think of as superstars—you would think that they would bring a superstar ego with them. But it's almost the opposite," says Jam. "New artists often come to Flyte Tyme with a feeling they have to prove something. And what happens is, you don't really get a natural performance," says Jam.

Another of Flyte Tyme's special strengths: adapting the music and lyrics to an artist's unique talents, not the other way around. Their interest in many types of music and their experience with many artists allow them to add new ideas to the creative process. Still, Flyte Tyme may work on several different versions based on its perceptions of what radio stations or MTV will play.

Jam and Lewis work on both the music and lyrics for many of their songs, but Jam leans slightly more toward the melodies and Lewis toward the vocals and lyrics. In fact, Lewis keeps "The Book of Titles," and any time someone says something clever or in an interesting way it goes into the book. "Music is the soundtrack of life," says Lewis. "The inspiration for words I just take from watching people, and life has a lot of verses in it."

MARKETING, DISTRIBUTION, COMPETITION

Selecting the best music ideas requires an instinct to find the right blend of art and business. The elements of the art include a huge respect for and understanding of the artists, an interest in a broad palette of musical sounds, and a good ear for melodies and vocals. The business components of their formula include understanding many of the factors—such as marketing, distribution, and competition—that influence their business.

Music artists walking in the door of Flyte Tyme receive an array of services: A studio facility with Jam, Lewis, and an experienced staff providing ideas, direction, and focus—"trying to get things out of them they didn't know they had in them," says Lewis. Flyte Tyme Records, the marketing arm, develops the artist's image, the marketing plan, advertising, and distribution—everything to get the record or CD on the rack to be sold. "If you have $100 000 to spend on promotion, you can do a nice music video and then you can spend a lot of time trying to get it played on MTV or BET or VH1 or any of the appropriate video channels," says Jam.

Or sometimes the music calls for a different strategy, Flyte Tyme's "groundhog approach." For example, in the early 1990s with one of its bands, Flyte Tyme piled the band in a Winnebago and hit college campuses.

Today Flyte Tyme creates a lot of that same groundhog buzz with its Website, where the music audience can learn about Flyte Tyme's artists and activities. Jam and Lewis note that Napster was a great tool in exposing music to the public. The delivery system—buying an album at a retail store, downloading music from the Internet, or burning a CD—doesn't affect the process of Flyte Tyme's making the music in its studio. But Lewis and Jam are concerned that the people who write the songs and the artists who deliver them get compensated fairly. "The record companies and everybody will eventually work it out," says Jam. "They have to because it's too valuable a commodity not to."

Questions

1 Based on the case information and what you know about today's music industry, conduct an environmental scan for Flyte Tyme to identify key trends. For each of the five environmental forces (social, economic, technological, competitive, and regulatory), identify trends likely to influence it in the near future.

2 Compared to many startup businesses—80 percent of which fail within five years—what reasons explain Flyte Tyme's continuing success?

3 What marketing factors and actions must Jimmy Jam and Terry Lewis consider in developing music for (*a*) a new, unknown artist and (*b*) an established artist like Janet Jackson?

4 What promotional and distribution strategies should Flyte Tyme use to get its music in front of prospective buyers?

SECOND-ROW SEATS STILL AVAILABLE.

CHAPTER

4

ETHICS AND SOCIAL RESPONSIBILITY IN MARKETING

AFTER READING THIS CHAPTER YOU SHOULD BE ABLE TO:

- Appreciate the nature and significance of ethics in marketing.

- Understand the differences between legal and ethical behaviour in marketing.

- Identify factors that influence ethical and unethical marketing decisions.

- Distinguish among the different concepts of ethics and social responsibility.

- Recognize the importance of ethical and socially responsible consumer behaviour.

AT MOLSON, THERE IS MORE BREWING THAN BEER

Why would a company spend millions of dollars to promote the responsible consumption of its products? Ask Molson (www.molson.com), one of Canada's largest brewers and a leader in the campaign for the responsible use of alcohol. Molson's "Don't Drink and Drive" program is a multi-million dollar national communications program that promotes the responsible use of, and attitude toward, alcohol and drinking. To promote the responsible-use message, Molson has implemented a number of programs ranging from television, print, and outdoor advertising to specific regional initiatives.

Within the brewing industry, Molson is a sponsor of cooperative programs that promote public awareness of responsible use and research on traffic safety. These programs, run by groups such as the Brewers Association of Canada, Brewers of Ontario, Brewers of Quebec, and the Brewer's Retail, complement the Molson Don't Drink and Drive message. Working in conjunction with a number of organizations and partners, Molson delivers educational programs about the responsible use of alcohol. Molson is also a founding sponsor of Taxiguy (Taxisvp in Quebec), which encourages taxicab transportation as an alternative to drinking and driving. A person need only call a toll-free number and a participating taxicab company will dispatch a car to pick up the caller.

Molson has a long-standing tradition of supporting the communities in which it operates—a tradition that dates back to the founder, John Molson, and his commitment to social responsibility and community involvement. For more than 200 years, making charitable donations and supporting community projects has been as much a part of the Molson tradition as making beer. The Molson

Donations Fund (MDF), the philanthropic arm of the corporation, is committed to supporting the charitable sector across Canada. Since it was created in 1973, its goal has been to raise awareness of important issues and make a difference in the communities where Molson's roots are deepest. MDF is present in four regions across Canada to help Molson keep in touch with specific community needs.

Local Heroes, a neighbourhood-based program, was introduced by Molson in 1998. It provides funding to help repair, revamp, or revitalize recreational facilities and is designed to encourage active lifestyles and foster community spirit. The program provides Molson employees the opportunity to connect with consumers at the grassroots level and work with people who play an active role in making their communities even better. Since its inception, Local Heroes has provided more than $2 million in funding, working with tens of thousands of volunteers from coast to coast.

Molson believes that taking responsibility for the products it sells is imperative. At the same time, the company is also involved in multifaceted efforts to support the communities in which it operates and to protect our natural environment. Molson has a long history of supporting countless charities and has founded some of Canada's major health, educational, and cultural institutions. Molson has also made protection of the environment a high priority. More than 96 percent of its bottles and 86 percent of its cans are returned to points of sale to be retrieved for reuse or recycling. Molson ensures that its breweries are environmentally efficient throughout all stages of the brewing process, and all its offices have recycling programs.[1]

This chapter focuses on ethics and social responsibility in marketing. You will see how some companies recognize that while ethically and socially responsible behaviour often comes with a price tag, the price for unethical and socially irresponsible behaviour is often much higher. In essence, in this marketplace companies *can* "do well by doing good."

NATURE AND SIGNIFICANCE OF MARKETING ETHICS

ETHICS
The moral principles and values that govern the actions and decisions of an individual or group.

Ethics are the moral principles and values that govern the actions and decisions of an individual or group.[2] Simply put, ethics serve as guidelines on how to act correctly and justly when faced with moral dilemmas. For marketing managers, ethics concern the application of moral principles and values to marketing decision making.

Ethical/Legal Framework in Marketing

A good starting point for understanding the nature and significance of ethics is the distinction between legality and ethicality of marketing decisions. Figure 4–1 helps you to visualize the relationship between laws and ethics.[3] While ethics deal with personal and moral principles and values, **laws** are society's values and standards that are enforceable in the courts.[4]

LAWS
Society's values and standards that are enforceable in the courts.

In general, what is illegal is also unethical. For example, deceptive advertising is illegal. It is also unethical, because it conflicts with the moral principles of honesty and fairness. But not all unethical conduct is illegal. For instance, price gouging is usually not illegal, but is often viewed as unethical. Marketing managers often find themselves in many situations where they must make judgments in defining ethical and legal boundaries. For some, the distinction between ethics and laws can sometimes lead to the rationalization that if a behaviour is within legal limits, then it is not really unethical. For example, a group of Canadian business students were surveyed and asked: "Is it okay to charge a higher price than normal when you know the customer really needs the product and will pay the higher price?" Almost 35 percent of the business students who took part in the survey responded "Yes."[5] How would you have answered this question?

FIGURE 4–1
Classifying marketing
decisions according to ethical
and legal relationships

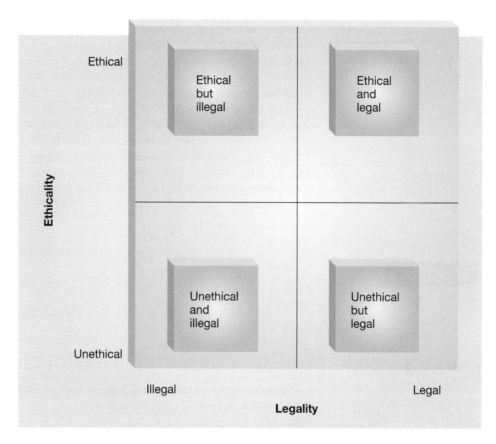

Now consider the following situations. After reading each, assign it to the cell in Figure 4–1 that you think best fits the situation along the ethical–legal continuum.

1. Several companies meet and agree to bid-rigging for sealed tendered government contract work. Bid-rigging is illegal under the *Competition Act* because it eliminates free and open competition.

2. A company uses a technique called "slugging," or selling under the guise of research. Once prospective customers agree to take part in the research, the salespeople switch to their sales pitch.

3. A real estate agent sells a high-rise condo unit to a customer, primarily because the customer loves the city view looking out the condo windows. The agent knows that in one year another high-rise will be built, effectively blocking the view so important to the customer. The agent decides not to tell that customer.

4. A company interviews a very qualified female for an industrial sales position. She is more qualified than any males who were interviewed. However, the company knows that some male purchasing agents prefer to deal with a male salesperson, so they hire a less qualified male applicant.

Do these situations fit neatly into Figure 4–1 as clearly defined ethical and legal or unethical and illegal? Some probably do not. As you read further in this chapter, you will be asked to consider other ethical dilemmas.

Current Perceptions of Ethical Behaviour

There has been much discussion about the possible deterioration of personal morality and ethical standards on a global scale. The news media offer well-publicized examples of personal dishonesty, hypocrisy, cheating, and greed. There also has been a public outcry about the ethical practices of businesspeople. In particular, there is widespread concern over unethical marketing practices such as price-fixing, bribery,

deceptive advertising, and unsafe products. Public opinion surveys as well as other research show that most adults believe the ethical standards of business have declined over the years.[6] The ethical conduct of Canadian companies is also under closer scrutiny. EthicScan Canada monitors the ethical performance of hundreds of Canadian companies and makes its findings available to the public.[7]

There are at least four possible reasons why the state of perceived ethical business conduct is at its present level. First, there is increased pressure on businesspeople to make decisions in a society characterized by diverse value systems.[8] Second, there is a growing tendency for business decisions to be judged publicly by groups with different values and interests. Third, the public's expectations regarding ethical business behaviour have increased. Finally, and most disturbing, ethical business conduct may have declined.

Concept Check

1. What are ethics?

2. What are laws?

UNDERSTANDING ETHICAL MARKETING BEHAVIOUR

Researchers have identified numerous factors that influence ethical marketing behaviour.[9] Figure 4–2 presents a framework that shows these factors and their relationships.

Societal Culture and Norms

As described in Chapter 3, *culture* refers to the set of values, ideas, and attitudes of a homogeneous group of people that are transmitted from one generation to the next. Culture also serves as a socializing force that dictates what is morally right and just. This means that moral standards are relative to particular societies. These standards often reflect the laws and regulations that affect social and economic behaviour, which can create moral dilemmas. For example, Levi Strauss decided to end much of its business dealings in China because of what the company called "pervasive human rights abuses." According to its vice president for corporate marketing: "There are wonderful commercial opportunities in China. But when ethical issues collide with commercial appeal, we try to ensure ethics as the trump card. For us, ethical issues precede all others."[10]

FIGURE 4–2
A framework for understanding ethical behaviour

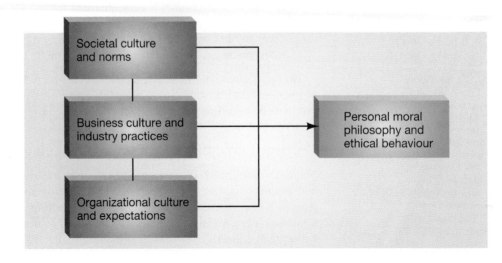

MARKETING NEWSNET   Global Business Software Piracy

By 2005, the Internet will link an estimated 1.17 billion Internet users worldwide. The many benefits of the Internet often overshadow its dark side: business software piracy. The explosive growth of the Internet is making piracy easy, because pirated copies of software can be distributed and downloaded quickly and globally with the click of a mouse. The Software & Information Industry Association (SIIA) and the Business Software Alliance (BSA) estimate that one in every three business software applications in use in the world is pirated. Piracy means lost jobs, wages, tax revenues, and a potential barrier to success for startup software companies around the globe.

It is estimated that the unauthorized copying of business software costs North American producers more than $12 billion in worldwide sales annually. Software piracy has become pandemic in many countries. According to SIIA/BSA estimates, 70 percent of the software in Eastern Europe is pirated, followed by rates of 60 percent and 59 percent in the Middle East and Africa and Latin America,

respectively. Countries with the highest piracy rates are Vietnam (98%), China (91%), Russia (89%), and Lebanon and Oman (88% each). For comparison, the piracy rate is 25 percent in the United States and 41 percent in Canada.

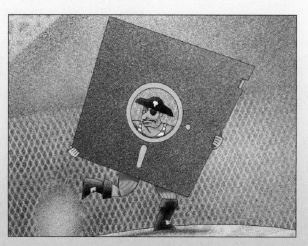

Actions that restrain trade, fix prices, deceive buyers, and result in unsafe products are considered morally wrong in Canada and other countries. However, different cultures view marketing practices differently. Consider the use of another's ideas, copyright, trademark, or patent. These are viewed as intellectual property and unauthorized use is illegal and unethical in Canada.

Outside Canada, however, is another story.[11] Unauthorized use of copyrights, trademarks, and patents is routine in countries such as China, Mexico, and Korea, and costs the authorized owners billions of dollars annually. In Korea, for instance, copying is partly rooted in its society's culture. According to international trade officials, many Koreans have the idea that the thoughts of one person should benefit all, and the Korean government rarely prosecutes infringements. Copyright infringement in the global business software industry is particularly widespread with the explosive growth of the Internet. Copies of software can be distributed and downloaded quickly and globally, with the click of a mouse. Read the accompanying Marketing NewsNet to find out where the unauthorized use of business software is most prevalent.[12]

Business Culture and Industry Practices

Societal culture provides a foundation for understanding moral and ethical behaviour in business activities. *Business cultures* "comprise the effective rules of the game, the boundaries between competitive and unethical behaviour, [and] the codes of conduct in business dealings."[13] Consumers have witnessed numerous instances where business cultures in the brokerage (insider trading), insurance (deceptive sales practices), and defence (bribery) industries went awry. Business culture affects ethical conduct both in the exchange relationship between sellers and buyers and in the competitive behaviour among sellers.

Ethics of Exchange   The exchange process is central to the marketing concept. Ethical exchanges between sellers and buyers should result in both parties being better off after a transaction.[14]

CAVEAT EMPTOR
The legal concept of "let the buyer beware" that was pervasive in Canadian business culture before the 1960s.

Prior to the 1960s, the legal concept of **caveat emptor**—let the buyer beware—was pervasive in Canadian business culture. The growth and strength of the consumer movement resulted in this concept becoming an unacceptable marketplace philosophy. A codification of ethics between buyers and sellers was established, with consumers recognizing their rights to safety, to be informed, to choose, and to be heard.

The right to safety manifests itself in industry and federal safety standards for most products sold in Canada. However, even the most vigilant efforts to ensure safe products cannot foresee every possibility. Mattel's experience with its Cabbage Patch Snacktime Kids doll is a case in point.[15] The doll was designed to "eat" plastic french fries, celery, and other tidbits by drawing them into its motorized mouth. Despite exhaustive laboratory and in-home testing, Mattel executives did not consider that a child's hair might become caught in the doll's mouth and cause harm. Unfortunately, this happened. Mattel immediately pulled the dolls from store shelves, refunded buyers, and discontinued the product.

The right to be informed means that marketers have an obligation to give consumers complete and accurate information about products and services. This right also applies to the solicitation of personal information over the Internet and its subsequent use by marketers.[16] For example, a recent survey of Websites indicated that 92 percent collect personal information such as consumer e-mail addresses, telephone numbers, shopping habits, and financial data. Yet only two-third of Websites inform consumers what is done with this information once obtained. Because consumers often assume that personal information is confidential, it was therefore understandable that subscribers to America Online (AOL) balked when AOL proposed giving member information to partners who could then telemarket to them. AOL backed down.

Relating to the right to choose, today many supermarket chains demand "slotting allowances" from manufacturers, in the form of cash rebates or free goods, to stock new products. This practice could limit the number of new products available to consumers and interfere with their right to choose. One critic of this practice remarked: "If we had had slotting allowances a few years ago, we might not have had granola, herbal tea, or yogurt."[17]

Finally, the right to be heard means that consumers should have access to company and/or public-policy makers regarding comments or complaints about products and services. Many Canadian companies have set up consumer service departments to deal with customer comments and complaints. In fact, it was consumer complaints about late-night and repeated calls by telemarketers that led to greater limitations on telemarketing practices.

Ethics of Competition   Business culture also affects ethical behaviour in competition. Two kinds of unethical behaviour are most common: (1) economic espionage and (2) bribery.

ECONOMIC ESPIONAGE
The clandestine collection of trade secrets or proprietary information about a company's competitors.

Economic espionage is the clandestine collection of trade secrets or proprietary information about a company's competitors. This practice is illegal and unethical and includes activities such as trespassing, theft, fraud, wire tapping, and searching a competitor's trash. Many Canadian and U.S. firms have uncovered espionage in some form, costing them billions of dollars a year.[18] This practice is most prevalent in high-technology industries such as electronics, specialty chemicals, industrial equipment, aerospace, and pharmaceuticals, where technical know-how and secrets separate industry leaders from followers.

But espionage can occur anywhere—the toy industry and even the ready-to-eat cookie industry! Procter & Gamble charged that competitors photographed its plants and production lines, stole a sample of its cookie dough, and infiltrated a confidential sales presentation to learn about its technology, recipe, and marketing plan. The competitors paid Procter & Gamble $120 million in damages after a lengthy dispute.[19]

The second form of unethical competitive behaviour is giving and receiving bribes and kickbacks. Bribes and kickbacks are often disguised as gifts, consultant fees, and favours. This practice is more common in business-to-business and government marketing than consumer marketing.

www.pg.com

WEB LINK   The Corruption Perceptions Index

The use of bribery as a means to win and retain business varies widely by country. Transparency International, based in Germany, periodically polls both employees of multinational firms and institutions and political analysts and ranks countries based on their perceived level of bribery to win or retain business. To obtain the most recent ranking, visit the Transparency International Website at www. transparency.org/cpi/index.html.

Scroll through the Corruption Perceptions Index to see where Canada stands in the worldwide rankings. How about our neighbours, the United States and Mexico? Any surprises? Which country listed in the most recent ranking has the highest ranking and which has the lowest ranking?

In general, bribery is most evident in industries experiencing intense competition and in countries in earlier stages of economic development. According to a recent study, 15 percent of all companies in industrialized countries have to pay bribes to win or retain business. Cameroon and Nigeria were the most likely countries to evidence bribery, while Denmark and Finland were the least likely.[20] Bribery on a worldwide scale is monitored by Transparency International. Visit its Website (described in the accompanying Web Link box) and view the most recent country rankings on this practice.

Organizational Culture and Expectations

A third influence on ethical practices is organizational culture. *Organizational culture* reflects the shared values, beliefs, and purpose of employees that affect individual and group behaviour. The culture of a company demonstrates itself in the dress ("We don't wear ties"), sayings ("The IBM Way"), and the manner of work (team efforts) of employees. Organizational culture is also apparent in the expectations for ethical behaviour present in formal codes of ethics and the ethical actions of top management and co-workers.

CODE OF ETHICS
A formal statement of ethical principles and rules of conduct.

www.nortelnetworks.com

Codes of Ethics   A **code of ethics** is a formal statement of ethical principles and rules of conduct. Research shows that 85 percent of Canadian companies surveyed had some sort of ethics code.[21] Ethics codes typically address issues such as contributions to government officials and political parties; relations with customers, competitors, and suppliers; conflicts of interest; and accurate recordkeeping. Nortel Networks provides ethical guidance to its employees through its *Living the Commitments* code, which all employees are to adhere to when conducting business on a worldwide basis. However, an ethics code is rarely enough to ensure ethical behaviour. One of the reasons for this is the lack of specificity of ethics codes. Ultimately, it is the employee who often judges whether a specific behaviour is really unethical. The American Marketing Association, representing Canadian and American marketing professionals, has addressed this issue by providing a detailed code of ethics, which all members agree to follow. This code is shown in Figure 4–3.

Ethical Behaviour of Management and Co-workers   A second reason for violating ethics codes rests in the perceived behaviour of top management and co-workers.[22] Observing peers and top management and gauging responses to unethical behaviour play an important role in individual actions. For example, what message do

CODE OF ETHICS

Members of the American Marketing Association (AMA) are committed to ethical professional conduct. They have joined together in subscribing to this Code of Ethics embracing the following topics:

Responsibilities of the Marketer

Marketers must accept responsibility for the consequence of their activities and make every effort to ensure that their decisions, recommendations, and actions function to identify, serve, and satisfy all relevant publics: customers, organizations, and society.

Marketers' professional conduct must be guided by:

1. The basic rule of professional ethics: not knowingly to do harm.
2. The adherence to all applicable laws and regulations.
3. The accurate representation of their education, training, and experience.
4. The active support, practice, and promotion of this Code of Ethics.

Honesty and Fairness

Marketers shall uphold and advance the integrity, honor, and dignity of the marketing profession by:

1. Being honest in serving consumers, clients, employees, suppliers, distributors, and the public.

2. Not knowingly participating in conflict of interest without prior notice to all parties involved.
3. Establishing equitable fee schedules including the payment or receipt of usual, customary, and/or legal compensation or marketing exchanges.

Rights and Duties of Parties in the Marketing Exchange Process

Participants in the marketing exchange process should be able to expect that:

1. Products and services offered are safe and fit for their intended uses.
2. Communications about offered products and services are not deceptive.
3. All parties intend to discharge their obligations, financial and otherwise, in good faith.
4. Appropriate internal methods exist for equitable adjustment and/or redress of grievances concerning purchases.

It is understood that the above would include, *but is not limited to,* the following responsibilities of the marketer:

In the area of product development and management

- Disclosure of all substantial risks associated with product or service usage.

FIGURE 4–3
American Marketing Association Code of Ethics

WHISTLEBLOWERS
Employees who report unethical or illegal actions of their employers.

MORAL IDEALISM
A personal moral philosophy that considers certain individual rights or duties as universal, regardless of the outcome.

UTILITARIANISM
A personal moral philosophy that focuses on the "greatest good for the greatest number" by assessing the costs and benefits of the consequences of ethical behaviour.

employees receive when they see personnel being rewarded for engaging in unethical troubling behaviour and see others punished for refusing to engage in unethical behaviour? Clearly, ethical dilemmas often bring personal and professional conflict. In many cases, **whistleblowers**, employees who report unethical or illegal actions of their employers, often face recrimination. Some firms, such as General Dynamics and Dun & Bradstreet, have appointed ethics officers who are responsible for safeguarding such individuals.[23]

Personal Moral Philosophy and Ethical Behaviour

Ultimately, ethical choices are based on the personal moral philosophy of the decision maker. Moral philosophy is learned through the process of socialization with friends and family and by formal education. It is also influenced by the societal, business, and organizational culture in which a person finds him- or herself. Moral philosophies are of two types: (1) moral idealism and (2) utilitarianism.[24]

Moral Idealism   **Moral idealism** is a personal philosophy that considers certain individual rights or duties as universal (e.g., right to freedom) regardless of the outcome. This philosophy is favoured by moral philosophers and consumer interest groups. This philosophy also applies to ethical duties such as informing the consumer about the safety hazards of a particular product or even conducting a large-scale recall of a deceptive product, regardless of cost, in order to uphold that consumer right to safety.

Utilitarianism   An alternative perspective on moral philosophy is **utilitarianism**, which is a personal moral philosophy that focuses on "the greatest good for the greatest number" by assessing the costs and benefits of the consequences of ethical behaviour.

FIGURE 4–3 *(CONCLUDED)*

- Identification of any product component substitution that might materially change the product or impact on the buyer's purchase decision.
- Identification of extra-cost added features.

In the area of promotions

- Avoidance of false and misleading advertising.
- Rejection of high-pressure manipulation, or misleading sales tactics.
- Avoidance of sales promotions that use deception or manipulation.

In the area of distribution

- Not manipulating the availability of a product for purpose of exploitation.
- Not using coercion in the marketing channel.
- Not exerting undue influence over the reseller's choice to handle the product.

In the area of pricing

- Not engaging in price fixing.
- Not practising predatory pricing.
- Disclosing the full price associated with any purchase.

In the area of marketing research

- Prohibiting selling or fund raising under the guise of conducting research.

- Maintaining research integrity by avoiding misrepresentation and omission of pertinent research data.
- Treating outside clients and suppliers fairly.

Organizational Relationships

Marketers should be aware of how their behaviour may influence or impact on the behaviour of others in organizational relationships. They should not demand, encourage, or apply coercion to obtain unethical behaviour in their relationships with others, such as employees, suppliers, or customers.

1. Apply confidentiality and anonymity in professional relationships with regard to privileged information.
2. Meet their obligations and responsiblities in contracts and mutual agreements in a timely manner.
3. Avoid taking the work of others, in whole or in part, and represent this work as their own or directly benefit from it without compensation or consent of the originator or owner.
4. Avoid manipulation to take advantage of situations to maximize personal welfare in a way that unfairly deprives or damages the organization or others.

Any AMA members found to be in violation of any provision of this Code of Ethics may have his or her Association membership suspended or revoked.

Source: Reprinted by permission of the American Marketing Association.

If the benefits exceed the costs, then the behaviour is ethical. If not, then the behaviour is unethical. This philosophy underlies the economic tenets of capitalism and, not surprisingly, is embraced by many business executives and students.[25]

Utilitarian reasoning was apparent in Nestlé Canada's original decision to add peanut product additives to some of the company's chocolate snacks. However some consumers, albeit only a small percentage of Canadians, are severely allergic to peanuts. Still, Nestlé was intent on pursuing this strategy until many Canadians protested the move. In the end, Nestlé decided to cancel the proposed practice and took out advertising in major newspapers to announce its decision. While the vast majority of Canadians may have enjoyed the newly formulated snacks, and certainly would not have been harmed by them, protestors believed that some consumers may have been harmed by this proposed practice. The views of the protestors prevailed in this case, even though Nestlé could have used the "greatest good for the greatest number" argument.[26]

An appreciation for the nature of ethics, coupled with a basic understanding of why unethical behaviour arises, alerts a person to when and how ethical issues exist in marketing decisions. Ultimately, ethical behaviour rests with the individual, but the consequences affect many.

Concept Check

1. What is caveat emptor?
2. What is a code of ethics?
3. What is meant by moral idealism?

UNDERSTANDING SOCIAL RESPONSIBILITY IN MARKETING

SOCIAL RESPONSIBILITY
The idea that organizations are part of a larger society and are accountable to that society for their actions.

As we saw in Chapter 1, the societal marketing concept stresses marketing's social responsibility by not only satisfying the needs of consumers but also providing for society's welfare. **Social responsibility** means that organizations are part of a larger society and are accountable to that society for their actions. Like ethics, agreement on the nature and scope of social responsibility is often difficult to come by, given the diversity of values present in different societal, business, and organizational cultures.[27]

Concepts of Social Responsibility

Figure 4–4 shows three concepts of social responsibility: (1) profit responsibility, (2) stakeholder responsibility, and (3) societal responsibility.

Profit Responsibility   *Profit responsibility* holds that companies have a simple duty—to maximize profits for their owners or shareholders. This view is expressed by Nobel Laureate Milton Friedman, who said, "There is one and only one social responsibility of business—to use its resources and engage in activities designed to increase its profits so long as it stays within the rules of the game, which is to say, engages in open and free competition without deception or fraud."[28] Genzyme, the maker of Ceredase, a drug that treats a genetic illness called Gaucher's disease that affects 20 000 people worldwide, has been criticized for apparently adopting this view in its pricing practices. A Genzyme spokesperson responded by saying that Ceredase profits are below industry standards and that the company freely gives the drug to patients without insurance.[29]

Stakeholder Responsibility   Frequent criticism of the profit view has led to a broader concept of social responsibility. *Stakeholder responsibility* focuses on the obligations an organization has to those who can effect achievement of its objectives.

FIGURE 4-4
Three concepts of social responsibility

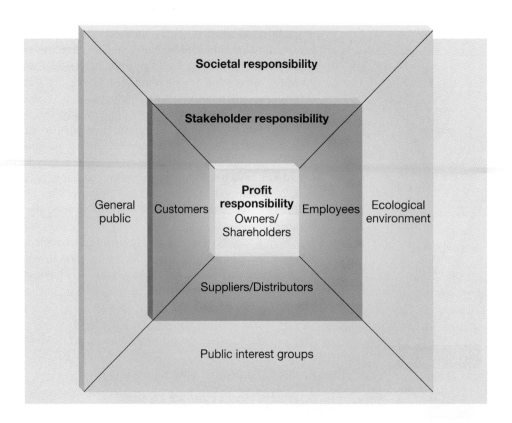

Which of the three concepts of social responsibility do you think Perrier applied when it learned of quality problems with its popular water? Read the text to learn how the company responded to this problem and its reasoning.

These constituencies include customers, employees, suppliers, and distributors. Source Perrier S.A., the supplier of Perrier bottled water, exercised this responsibility when it recalled 160 million bottles of water in 120 countries after traces of a toxic chemical were found in 13 bottles. The recall cost the company $35 million, and $40 million more was lost in sales. Even though the chemical level was not harmful to humans, Source Perrier's president believed he acted in the best interests of the firm's consumers, distributors, and employees by removing "the least doubt, as minimal as it might be, to weigh on the image of the quality and purity of our product"[30]

Societal Responsibility   An even broader concept of social responsibility has emerged in recent years. *Societal responsibility* refers to obligations that organizations have to the (1) preservation of the ecological environment and (2) general public. Concerns about the environment and public welfare are represented by interest and advocacy groups such as Greenpeace, an international environmental organization.

Chapter 3 detailed the growing importance of ecological issues in marketing. Companies have responded to this concern through what is termed **green marketing**—marketing efforts to produce, promote, and reclaim environmentally sensitive products. Green marketing takes many forms.[31] The Canadian aluminum industry recycles nearly two-thirds of all aluminum cans for reuse. The Food and Consumer Products Manufacturers of Canada (formerly GPMC) has a program known as the Grocery Industry Packaging Stewardship Initiative, which is designed to promote responsible waste and product recycling. Black Photo of Ontario has factored the environment into everything it does, from product conception to manufacturing, distribution, and sales. And Mercedes-Benz has designed its S-class sedans and 500/600 SEC luxury coupes to be entirely recyclable. These voluntary responses to environmental issues have been implemented with little or no additional cost to consumers.

A global undertaking to further green marketing efforts is the ISO 14000 initiative developed by the International Standards Organization (ISO) in Geneva, Switzerland. **ISO 14000** consists of worldwide standards for environmental quality and green marketing practices. These standards are embraced by over 80 countries, including Canada, members of the European Union, and most Pacific Rim countries.[32]

Socially responsible efforts on behalf of the general public are also becoming more common. A formal practice is **cause-related marketing** (CRM), which occurs when the charitable contributions of a firm are tied directly to the customer revenues produced through the promotion of one of its products.[33] This definition distinguishes CRM from a firm's standard charitable contributions, which are outright donations. For example, Procter & Gamble raises funds for the Special Olympics when consumers purchase selected company products, and MasterCard International linked usage of its card with fundraising for institutions that combat cancer, heart disease, child abuse, drug abuse, and muscular dystrophy. Avon Products, Inc. focuses on different issues in different countries: breast cancer in the United States, Canada, Philippines, Mexico, Venezuela, Malaysia, and Spain; programs for women who care for senior citizens in Japan; emotional and financial support for mothers in Germany; and AIDS in Thailand. CRM programs incorporate all three concepts of social responsibility by addressing public concerns, satisfying customer needs, and enhancing corporate sales and profits.[34]

GREEN MARKETING
Marketing efforts to produce, promote, and reclaim environmentally sensitive products.

ISO 14000
Worldwide standards for environmental quality and green marketing practices.

CAUSE-RELATED MARKETING
Occurs when the charitable contributions of a firm are tied directly to the customer revenues produced through the promotion of one of its products.

Marketing and social
responsibility programs are
often integrated, as is the case
with McDonald's. Its concern
for ill children is apparent in
the opening of another Ronald
McDonald House for children
and their families.

McDonald's
www.mcdonalds.com

The Social Audit

SOCIAL AUDIT
A systematic assessment of a
firm's objectives, strategies,
and performance in the
domain of social
responsibility.

Converting socially responsible ideas into actions involves careful planning and
monitoring of programs. Many companies develop, implement, and evaluate their
social responsibility efforts by means of a **social audit**, which is a systematic
assessment of a firm's objectives, strategies, and performance in the domain of social
responsibility. Frequently, marketing and social responsibility programs are integrated, as is the case with McDonald's. The company's concern for the needs of
families with children who are chronically or terminally ill was converted into
Ronald McDonald Houses around the world. These facilities, located near treatment
centres, enable families to stay together during a child's care. In this case, McDonald's
is contributing to the welfare of a portion of its target market.

A social audit consists of five steps:[35]

1. Recognition of a firm's social expectations and the rationale for engaging in
   social responsibility endeavours.
2. Identification of social responsibility causes or programs consistent with the
   company's mission.
3. Determination of organizational objectives and priorities for programs and
   activities it will undertake.
4. Specification of the type and amount of resources necessary to achieve social
   responsibility objectives.
5. Evaluation of social responsibility programs and activities undertaken and
   assessment of future involvement.

**SUSTAINABLE
DEVELOPMENT**
Conducting business in a
way that protects the natural
environment while making
economic progress.

Corporate attention to social audits will increase as companies seek to achieve
sustainable development and improve the quality of life in a global economy.[36]
Sustainable development involves conducting business in a way that protects
the natural environment while also making economic progress. Ecologically
responsible initiatives such as green marketing represent one such initiative.

Research initiatives related to working conditions at offshore manufacturing sites that produce goods for North American companies focus on quality-of-life issues. Public opinion surveys show that consumers are concerned about working conditions under which products are made in Asia and Latin America. Companies have responded by imposing closer supervision of offshore manufacturing activities. Reebok, for example, now monitors production of its sporting apparel and equipment to ensure that no child abuse occurs during the production of its products.[37]

Companies that demonstrate societal responsibility have been rewarded. Research has shown that these companies (1) benefit from favourable word-of-mouth among consumers and (2) typically outperform less responsible companies on financial performance.[38]

Turning the Table: Consumer Ethics and Social Responsibility

Consumers also have an obligation to act ethically and responsibly in the exchange process and in the use and disposition of products. Unfortunately, consumer behaviour is spotty on both counts.

Unethical practices of consumers are a serious concern to marketers.[39] These practices include filing warranty claims after the claim period, misredeeming coupons, making fraudulent returns of merchandise, providing inaccurate information on credit applications, tampering with utility meters, tapping cable TV lines, recording copyrighted music and videocassettes, and submitting phony insurance claims. The cost to marketers in lost sales revenue and prevention expenses is huge. For example, consumers who redeem coupons for unpurchased products or use coupons destined for other products cost manufacturers millions of dollars each year. The record industry alone loses millions of dollars annually due to illegal recording, and many VCR owners make illegal copies of videotapes, costing producers millions of dollars in lost revenue. Electrical utilities lose one to three percent of yearly revenues due to meter tampering.

Consumer purchase, use, and disposition of environmentally sensitive products relates to consumer social responsibility. Research indicates that consumers are generally sensitive to ecological issues.[40] However, research also shows that consumers (1) may be unwilling to sacrifice convenience and pay potentially higher prices to protect the environment and (2) lack the knowledge to make informed decisions dealing with the purchase, use, and disposition of products.[41]

For example, a Cap Gemini Ernst & Young/Maritz Automotive study showed that Canadians are indeed increasingly concerned about the environment. More than 80 percent of Canadians polled claimed that when purchasing a new car environmental concerns are a factor. The research even indicates that Canadian consumers might be willing to pay more for a greener car. However, they would do so only as long as the greater environmental friendliness doesn't come at the expense of performance and styling. Not surprisingly, sales of greener vehicles in Canada have been dismal. Canadians appear to be saying, "give us an alternative-fuel vehicle (a greener car) that is stylish and outperforms our current vehicles, otherwise forget it." With research results like this, automotive companies such as General Motors of Canada are not rushing to bring greener cars to market.[42]

Many marketers suggest that consumers must become aware of and increase their demand for environmentally sensitive products. For example, producers of environmentally certified lumber say the market for "green wood" is very small in Canada. Certified lumber comes from forest companies that use sustainable harvesting practices and produce wood products with the least environmental impact. J. D. Irving Co., a Canadian timber and energy conglomerate, has been pursuing certification of its forest lands. The company suggests that consumers should look for and demand wood products from certified forests. In doing so, consumers could end widespread clear-cutting, chemical spraying, and other destructive forestry practices. "Green

wood" products can be easily identified by a trademark product label: a green cross superimposed on a globe.[43]

Ultimately, marketers and consumers are accountable for ethical and socially responsible behaviour. The 21st century will prove to be a testing period for both.

Concept Check

1. What is meant by social responsibility?

2. Marketing efforts to produce, promote, and reclaim environmentally sensitive products are called _____.

3. What is a social audit?

SUMMARY

1 Ethics are the moral principles and values that govern the actions and decisions of an individual or group. Laws are society's values and standards that are enforceable in the courts. Operating according to the law does not necessarily mean that a practice is ethical.

2 Ethical behaviour of businesspeople has come under severe criticism by the public. There are four possible reasons for this criticism: (*a*) increased pressure on businesspeople to make decisions in a society characterized by diverse value systems, (*b*) a growing tendency to have business decisions judged publicly by groups with different values and interests, (*c*) an increase in the public's expectations for ethical behaviour, and (*d*) a possible decline in business ethics.

3 Numerous external factors influence ethical behaviour of businesspeople. These include the following: (*a*) societal culture and norms, (*b*) business culture and industry practices, and (*c*) organizational culture and expectations. Each factor

influences the opportunity to engage in ethical or unethical behaviour.

4 Ultimately, ethical choices are based on the personal moral philosophy of the decision maker. Two moral philosophies are most prominent: (*a*) moral idealism and (*b*) utilitarianism.

5 Social responsibility means that organizations are part of a larger society and are accountable to that society for their actions.

6 There are three concepts of social responsibility: (*a*) profit responsibility, (*b*) stakeholder responsibility, and (*c*) societal responsibility.

7 Growing interest in societal responsibility has resulted in systematic efforts to assess a firm's objectives, strategies, and performance in the domain of social responsibility. This practice is called a *social audit*.

8 Consumer ethics and social responsibility are as important as business ethics and social responsibility.

KEY TERMS AND CONCEPTS

cause-related marketing p. 107
caveat emptor p. 102
code of ethics p. 103
economic espionage p. 102
ethics p. 98
green marketing p. 107
ISO 14000 p. 107

laws p. 98
moral idealism p. 104
social audit p. 108
social responsibility p. 106
sustainable development p. 108
utilitarianism p. 104
whistleblowers p. 104

INTERNET EXERCISE

www.mcgrawhill.ca/college/berkowitz

The Canadian Centre for Ethics & Corporate Policy is a charitable, registered, independent ethics centre. It works with its own contributors and with other organizations involved in business ethics. The Centre is a volunteer-driven organization comprising corporations and individuals dedicated to developing and maintaining an ethical organizational culture. Visit its Website at www.ethicscentre.com and click on the newsletter icon.

Management Ethics is the Centre's bimonthly publication. Choose some topics from Chapter 4 pertaining to ethics or social responsibility that interest you, such as codes of ethics, ethical behaviour of management, sustainable development, and so on. Read some current and back issues of the newsletter. Update at least one example in the text related to your chosen topics.

Want to get better grades, find tips on how to study more effectively, and stay up to date with happenings in the world of marketing? Visit the Online Learning Centre for practice tests, Study Smart software, and much more! www.mcgrawhill.ca/college/berkowitz
Interested in finding out what marketing looks like in the real world? *Marketing Magazine* is just a click away on your OLC! Visit www.mcgrawhill.ca/college/berkowitz

APPLYING MARKETING CONCEPTS AND PERSPECTIVES

1 What concepts of moral philosophy and social responsibility are applicable to the practices of Molson described in the introduction to this chapter? Why?

2 Where would the following situations fit in Figure 4–1? (*a*) exaggerating the performance of a product to get a sale, and (*b*) selling a used automobile knowing it had a major mechanical problem and not telling the buyer.

3 A recent survey of Canadian business students asked, "Is calling your office pretending to be sick in order to take the day off ethical or unethical behaviour?" How would you respond to this question?

4 Compare and contrast moral idealism and utilitarianism as alternative personal moral philosophies.

5 How would you evaluate Milton Friedman's view of the social responsibility of a firm?

6 The text lists several unethical practices of consumers. Can you name others? Why do you think consumers engage in unethical conduct?

7 Cause-related marketing programs have become popular. Describe two such programs that you are familiar with.

VIDEO CASE 4–1 Pricing in the Pharmaceutical Industry

Canadians spend billions of dollars annually for prescription drugs to treat acute and chronic ailments. The pharmaceutical industry in Canada has often been criticized for its pricing practices. Many public health officials, government departments or agencies, and consumer advocacy groups argue that, in many cases, the industry is simply charging too much money for its products. Pharmaceutical company executives have responded to such criticism by citing large research and development costs, extensive testing requirements to obtain government approval to market the products, and marketplace uncertainties as valid reasons for the prices they charge for their drugs.

FAIR AND REASONABLE PRICING

A central issue in the debate concerning prescription drug pricing relates to what is a "fair and reasonable price." Critics of drug pricing spotlight instances where they believe the prices charged are excessive. For instance, drugs to treat ulcers sell in the range of $1300 to $1400 annually per patient. Drugs that control cholesterol cost $1015 to $1265 per year per patient. Persons suffering from high blood pressure pay almost $850 annually to treat this condition. People over the age of 65, many with fixed incomes, bear these costs. For example, 49 percent of the sales of high-blood-pressure medication are accounted for by the elderly.

Pharmaceutical firms counter critics' charges of excessive pricing using a variety of arguments. They note that the research and development cost of a new medication can be more than $150 million and span a decade of development and testing. Moreover, the risk is very high since most new drugs are never successfully commercialized. In addition, the pharmaceutical industry spends billions annually for marketing the newest drugs to doctors and consumers.

Debate over what is a "fair and reasonable" price for drugs typically focuses on economic versus societal factors, and the relative importance of a firm's stakeholders in setting prices. Often the final pricing decision depends on the individual judgment and moral sensitivity of the managers making the decision.

PROLIFE: PRICING ADL

Issues in the pricing of ADL, a treatment for Alzheimer's disease, which affects the elderly, were recently faced by Prolife, a small pharmaceutical company. A task force of company executives was considering the pricing strategy for ADL. Two points of view were expressed: (1) pursuing a high-price strategy designed to recoup the costs of the drug quickly and getting a jump on the competition and (2) pursuing a lower-price strategy to increase the drug's availability to victims of the disease.

Steve Vaughn, an assistant product manager at Prolife, was the principal proponent of a lower-price strategy. He argued that a less aggressive price strategy made sense even though it would take slightly longer to recoup the initial investment in ADL. Having a family member afflicted with Alzheimer's disease, Vaughn believed that the ability of victims and their families to pay for the drug should be considered when setting the price for ADL. He was overruled, however, by the task force members. Believing that his views deserved attention and action, and that "bottom-line" considerations did not negate his position, he lobbied other task force members and has considered expressing his opinion to senior executives at Prolife. He was cautioned by Bill Compton, a Prolife senior product manager and Vaughn's mentor, to reconsider his position, noting that Prolife is a business and that "rocking the boat" might not be an advantage to his career at Prolife.

Questions

1 Who are the primary stakeholders who must be considered when setting prices for prescription drugs?

2 How might the personal moral philosophies of moral idealism and utilitarianism be applied to prescription drug pricing in general and in the specific case of ADL?

3 How might the three concepts of social responsibility described in Chapter 4 be applied to prescription pricing in general and in the specific case of ADL?

4 If you were Steve Vaughn, what would you do in this situation?

PART 1 CASE **An Unpredictable Environment: Technology and Beyond**

Technological innovation plays a large role in our daily lives. We are surrounded by the results of invention and innovation in products and services we use on a regular basis. Everything from our digital alarm clocks to our cell phones has been made available to us through the advances in technology. The influence of technological advances in the past decade has changed where we purchase products, the value of information in decision-making, and the ability to communicate anywhere, anytime. Technological advances in a variety of industries are changing both consumers and businesses. The quality of our lives has been improved in a variety of ways—for example, we are able to eat meals cooked almost instantly in our microwaves. Technology, in its various forms, has touched every aspect of business as well as changed the ways in which products are created, manu-factured, and purchased. And it isn't just technological advances that are shaping our lives in significant ways. Since 2000, a number of events have created new demands for businesses as economic, technological, and political changes have taken place in dramatic and often unexpected ways: a new currency, a dangerous downturn in the economy, plans by governments to deregulate utilities, the collapse of several dot-coms, and a new focus in technology on wireless and "tiny." The events of September 11, 2001 have also caused major concern for governments and the public on issues relating to personal safety as well as national security.

In 1998, the business press and general news head-lines filled with stories of the dramatic influence the Internet would have in both consumer and business markets, creating an expectation of a major revolution.[1] Lives would be changed. Traditional business processes were attacked by young, aggressive innovators ready to transform businesses with the promise of new business models created around the Internet. The Internet did not deliver on its potential to transform lives and businesses, except for a lucky few who invested in the risky ventures and got out before they crashed. Uncertainties are

inevitable, creating the need for marketing managers to be relentless in understanding implications of changes in all aspects of the environment to identify opportunities and threats.

THE DOT-COM BUBBLE THAT BURST

Like no other technological innovation, the promise of providing more efficient, more cost-effective, and faster processes drove the dot-com fever to an incredibly high pitch. Venture capital was attracted to the potential of huge rewards for a winning application. *Fortune* magazine's cover story on March 20, 2000 was "Doing Business the Dot-Com Way."[2] The bubble burst on the dot-coms in April 2000, when the stock value of Internet pioneers took a dive.[3] At the end of 2000 Pets.com—one of the most famous Internet pioneers—was purchase by Petsmart: even Pets.com's creative advertising icon Sock Puppet could not save the company. Similarly, in February 2001 Petopia.com was acquired by Petco Animal Supplies Inc.[4] It seems that the online pet supply market isn't big enough for more then two or three players.

The dot-com crash was only the beginning of some hard times for companies in the information technology industries. After the growth in 1999 of PCs and related equipment due to Y2K, demand began to slip for PCs as well as certain portions of the telecommunications industry. Those betting on the success of the Internet to drive demand were caught having to restructure. Cisco, Lucent, Sprint, Yahoo, and even MTV Networks have laid off thousands in the hopes of recovering losses from 2000 and 2001.[5] Nortel Networks, Canada's largest telecommunications company, has begun the process of cutting another 20 000 jobs to focus on rebuilding the company after serious losses since 2000.[6]

An interesting development caused by the Internet is a new channel relationship called the C2C market—the consumer-to-consumer market. Companies like eBay help to facilitate Internet bargaining through auction sites. Napster, an innovative consumer-to-consumer

Website started by an 18-year-old, allowed people to download almost any song without paying. The copying of songs reduces revenue in the form of royalties for music publishers and songwriters. A multi-million dollar lawsuit by the recording industry was filed against Napster for allowing the unlicensed copying of songs. MP3.com was also sued by five record labels and settled with four of them to the tune of U.S.$20 million.[7] Napster was closed for most of 2001 by court order, finally settling with music publishers and songwriters for U.S.$26 million. In addition, when Napster eventually reopens—originally predicted to happen in the spring of 2002—it must also pay a percentage of the money it earns from subscription revenue.[8]

The Internet has created opportunities for some and disaster for others. Market forces took care of the over-valued dot-com companies, providing little or no value to consumers. A winner in the Internet gamble is eBay, which has remained profitable where others have failed.[9] Banks and investment institutions have also found that the Internet is helping them to build new business. The fee structure for services provided by the major Canadian banks is causing people to turn to banking online.[10] The Canadian Banking Association claims that 83 percent of 18- to 24-year-old Canadians are using online banking. The financial services industry is experiencing a major change as e-trading becomes more popular and more accepted across a wide range of socioeconomic groups.[11] Digital books, or e-books, were forecast to grow to 10 percent of all book sales by 2005; although the e-book devices are expensive and there have been some technical snags concerning copyright protection codes, there is still potential for this market to flourish.[12] The infrastructure is in place, and with proper planning and execution the promise of the Internet to deliver value to consumers through developing innovative applications may be more real.

THE NEW TECHNOLOGY OPPORTUNITIES

The buzz for a number of years in the business press was about the Internet. It is easy to forget that other advances in technology also create opportunities for companies. Wireless is the new buzz in information technology. Wireless technology is emerging as a new opportunity with its relatively speedy adoption by consumers and businesses. The benefits are obvious: "wireless" requires hardware to receive transmissions provided by a variety of technologies including infrared line of sight, cellular, microwave, satellite, and packet radio.[13] The wireless devices used to receive the transmission are wireless phones, personal digital assistants (PDAs), two-way pagers, and laptop computers; both PDAs and laptops use special modems to connect to the Web. Sierra Wireless, based in Richmond, B.C., is a major manufacturer of wireless modems used in PCs and PDAs.[14]

Connecting to the Internet requires one type of transmission technology. Providing the opportunity to develop products for short-range data connections between telecommunications, computing, automotive, and myriad consumer electronic devices requires a different standard. Uses for short-range transmission include connecting faxes, printers, and computers in an office, all without cumbersome wires. The possibilities for wireless connectivity within the home are also apparent. Manufacturers of the peripheral devices to be connected to a wireless network need to build to a specific standard allowing the devices to easily connect with each other and transmit data. The two standards currently battling for this market are Bluetooth and IEEE 802.11. The pioneer standard in this product category is 802.11, which is Ethernet-based and is widely used for connecting laptop and desktop computers.[15] Bluetooth, a wireless technology originally developed by Ericsson, uses low-power radio frequency to connect devices for file sharing and networking for distances up to 10 metres (33 feet).[16] These two short-range wireless standards are fighting to be *the* standard accepted by peripheral device manufacturers and, ultimately, the end user. Companies need to pay a licence to use the Ethernet standard; Bluetooth standards are free, provided the products are acceptable and certified by the Bluetooth Special Interest Group (SIG), an industry consortium managing its development and licensing.[17] The Bluetooth SIG was formed in 1998 with founders Ericsson, IBM, Intel, Nokia, and Toshiba. Today there are hundreds of companies involved in the initiative to develop products using one standard. It is too early to predict the ultimate industry standard. Regardless, this technological development will provide growth opportunities for a number of hardware manufacturers as businesses and consumers experience the benefits of wireless networking capabilities.

Wireless is providing opportunities to rejuvenate the sluggish peripheral and telecommunications industries, but another important technological development on the horizon is the "science of small." Nanotechnology is emerging as a science that involves creating objects on an atom-by-atom basis possibly used in microscopic machines.[18] The devices could be smaller than the width of a human hair. If this technology can deliver, amazing new materials and products could profoundly change our lives, particularly in the battle against some deadly diseases. A research unit in Texas has been experimenting with this technology by using it to destroy tumour cells without harming healthy cells.[19] This could mean the end of chemotherapy drugs as a choice in curing cancer. Other possibilities with this technology include performing intricate tasks involved in computer circuitry as well as providing an alternative way to clear clogged blood vessels. Applications for "small" will likely be found in unexpected places. As an example, General Motors is working with its partners to explore nanocomposite automotive applications.[20]

In Canada, the federal government selected the University of Alberta in Edmonton as the location of a government-funded National Research Centre facility with a mandate to focus on nanotechnology. The $60-million contribution for the Western Canadian lab is a commitment from the government indicating a priority in exploring ways in which this technology could change lives.[21]

ECONOMICS—UPS AND DOWNS: TO REGULATE OR NOT

After Y2K and the dot-com crash in 2000, the global economy began to slow down due in large part to the downturn in the telecommunications industry and reduced Internet infrastructure demand. These two industries had been driving the economic growth, particularly in North America.[22] Other international events have also influenced Canada's economic health. The European Monetary Union's euro became a reality in 1999; its value is closely monitored by economists and financial analysts to evaluate the effects of a new currency in the market. This event is considered monumental in terms of the international monetary system since the U.S. dollar displaced the sterling as the dominant currency.[23] The world economy now has a tripolar system based on the U.S. dollar, the euro, and the yen. The value of Canada's loonie took its worst beating ever in 2001, with a record low falling below U.S.60¢.[24] To give the Canadian economy a boost the Bank of Canada started dropping interest rates, and by the end of 2001 the bank rate was at 2.25 percent, the lowest rate since 1960.[25]

Coupled with slow economic growth have been the rising costs for oil and gas.[26] Deregulation in the energy industry has been taking place relatively slowly in Canada since the 1990s. Beginning with gas market deregulation, provincial governments such as Alberta and Ontario have also been working to deregulate the electricity industry. Alberta's electricity deregulation happened January 1, 2001, with Ontario planning deregulation for spring 2002. Ontario's plans were stopped after two unions took the government to court and Premier Ernie Eves agreed to retain government control of the utility, leaving open the possibility of a public offering of 49 percent.[27] Consumers in B.C., Saskatchewan, and Manitoba may be feeling happy that their provincial governments are not entering the electricity deregulation fray as yet. Although electricity deregulation in Australia and the U.K. caused a drop of 10 to 15 percent in electricity prices, in Alberta and California prices increased. Albertans are now paying five times the price for their electricity than before deregulation.[28] The role that the cost of energy and electricity plays in the overall economic health of Canada cannot be easily dismissed. There is, however, potential in this industry for using alternative technologies to generate power with cleaner, safer methods. Harnessing wind and solar power may develop into major industries reducing dependence on fossil-fuel alternatives.[29]

Canadian businesses face many uncertainties concerning their domestic and global markets. Marketing professionals can either be defeated by being unprepared, or face the future by looking for market opportunities presented by each unexpected event that provides challenges.

Discussion Questions

1. In your opinion, what relationship does a company's technology investment strategy have with its marketing strategy?

2. Can you identify specific uncontrollable, environmental factors that are the result of government intervention? Select an industry and relate how these factors are changing the industry.

3. Technological development provides marketing opportunities for companies. Discuss the implications to both businesses and consumers by referencing the new technological advances identified in this case.

4. Discuss ways in which companies could use marketing principles to identify opportunities during periods of economic slowdown.

UNDERSTANDING BUYERS AND MARKETS

CHAPTER 5
Consumer Behaviour

CHAPTER 6
Organizational Markets and Buyer Behaviour

CHAPTER 7
Reaching Global Markets

Using local and global perspectives to understand people as individual consumers and as members of companies that become organizational buyers is the focus of Part 2. Chapter 5 examines the actions buyers take in purchasing and using products, and explains how and why one product or brand is chosen over another. In Chapter 6 Gary Null, international business development director at Honeywell, helps illustrate how he and a worldwide team launched a new laser technology into a business-to-business market setting. Chapter 7 describes the nature and scope of world trade and examines the global marketing activities of companies such as Inniskillin, W.K. Buckley Ltd., IKEA, Nestlé, Coca-Cola, and CNS (makers of Breathe Right Strips). Together these chapters help marketing students understand individual, family, and organizational purchases in a variety of cultural environments.

The new Jag generation | the X-Type

all-wheel drive
manual transmission
automatic option
wood and leather interior
complimentary maintenance
24-hour roadside assistance

membership from: $29,950*
for a brochure, call 1-800-4JAGUAR

x-type.com

The art of performance | JAGUAR

The new Jag generation | the X-Type

all-wheel drive
manual transmission
automatic option
wood and leather interior
complimentary maintenance
24-hour roadside assistance

membership from: $29,950*
for a brochure, call 1-800-4JAGUAR

CHAPTER

5

CONSUMER BEHAVIOUR

AFTER READING THIS CHAPTER YOU SHOULD BE ABLE TO:

- Outline the stages in the consumer decision process.

- Distinguish among three variations of the consumer decision process: routine, limited, and extended problem solving.

- Explain how psychological influences affect consumer behaviour, particularly purchase decision processes.

- Identify major sociocultural influences on consumer behaviour and their effects on purchase decisions.

- Recognize how marketers can use knowledge of consumer behaviour to better understand and influence individual and family purchases.

SAVVY AUTOMAKERS KNOW THY CUSTOM(H)ER

Who will buy at least half of all new cars? Who already spends billions on new and used cars and trucks and automotive accessories? Who influences 80 percent of all automotive-buying decisions? Women—yes, women.

Women are a driving force in the Canadian automotive industry. Enlightened automakers have hired women design engineers and marketing executives to help them understand this valuable custom(h)er. What have they learned? First, women prefer "sporty" vehicles that are relatively inexpensive and fun to drive rather than "sports" cars, luxury cars, and full-sized trucks with bigger engines and higher price tags. Second, a vehicle's "feel" is important to women. Sleek exteriors and interior designs that fit the proportions of smaller drivers as well as opening ease for doors, trunks, and hoods are equally important.

Third, women approach car buying in a deliberate manner. They approach car buying, usage, and maintenance from a woman's point of view. They often visit auto-buying Websites to gather information and will shop an average of three dealerships before making a purchase decision. Fourth, while men and women look for the same car features, their priorities differ. Both sexes value dependability most, but more women consider it a higher priority. Women also rank low price, ease of maintenance, and safety higher than men. Men view horsepower and acceleration as being more important than do women. Finally, automakers have learned that 66 percent of women dislike the car-buying process.

Recognition of women as purchasers and influencers in car and truck buying has also altered the behaviour of dealers. Many dealers now use a one-price policy and have stopped negotiating a vehicle's price. Industry research indicates that 68 percent of new-car buyers dread the price negotiation process involved in buying a car, and women often refuse to do it at all![1]

CONSUMER BEHAVIOUR
The actions a person takes in purchasing and using products and services, including the mental and social processes that precede and follow these actions.

This chapter examines **consumer behaviour**, the actions a person takes in purchasing and using products and services, including the mental and social processes that precede and follow these actions. This chapter shows how the behavioural sciences help answer questions such as why people choose one product or brand over another, how they make these choices, and how companies use this knowledge to provide value to consumers.

CONSUMER PURCHASE DECISION PROCESS

PURCHASE DECISION PROCESS
The stages a buyer passes through in making choices about which products and services to buy.

Behind the visible act of making a purchase lies an important decision process that must be investigated. The stages a buyer passes through in making choices about which products and services to buy is the **purchase decision process**. This process has the five stages shown in Figure 5–1: (1) problem recognition, (2) information search, (3) alternatives evaluation, (4) purchase decision, and (5) postpurchase behaviour.

Problem Recognition: Perceiving a Need

Problem recognition, the initial step in the purchase decision, is perceiving a difference between a person's ideal and actual situations that is big enough to trigger a decision.[2] This can be as simple as finding an empty milk carton in the refrigerator; noting, as a first-year university student, that your high school clothes are not in the style that other students are wearing; or realizing that your laptop computer may not be working properly.

In marketing, advertisements or salespeople can activate a consumer's decision process by showing the shortcomings of competing (or currently owned) products. For instance, an advertisement for a compact disc (CD) player could stimulate problem recognition because it emphasizes the sound quality of new CD players over the one you may now own.

Information Search: Seeking Value

After recognizing a problem a consumer begins to search for information, the next stage in the purchase decision process. First, you may scan your memory for previous experiences with products or brands.[3] This action is called *internal search*. For frequently purchased products such as shampoo and conditioner, this may be enough. Or a consumer may undertake an *external search* for information.[4] This is especially needed when past experience or knowledge is insufficient, the risk of making a wrong purchase decision is high, and the cost of gathering information is low.

FIGURE 5–1
Purchase decision process

Brand	Model	Price	Headphones	Error correction	Bump immunity	Battery life (hours)	Controls
Sony	D-MJ95	$198	Very Good	Very Good	Excellent	26	Very Good
Sony	DSJ17CK	$245	Good	Very Good	Excellent	29	Excellent
Sony	DSJ01	$306	Good	Very Good	Excellent	33	Fair
Sony	DEJ611	$122	Good	Good	Excellent	26	Fair
Sony	DSJ15	$198	Good	Good	Excellent	25	Excellent
Panasonic	SL-SX280	$ 76	Good	Very Good	Very Good	23	Fair
Philips	AZ9213	$122	Good	Good	Very Good	17	Good
Philips	EXP103/17	$275	Good	Good	Very Good	8	Very Good
GPX	C394881	$ 92	Fair	Good	Fair	8	Good
Lenoxx Sound	CD-91	$ 84	Good	Fair	Fair	7	Fair

Rating: Excellent, Very Good, Good, Fair, Poor

FIGURE 5–2
Consumer Reports' evaluation of portable compact disc players (abridged). Prices in Canadian dollars.

Consumer Reports
www.consumerreports.org

The primary sources of external information are (1) *personal sources,* such as relatives and friends whom the consumer trusts; (2) *public sources,* including various product-rating organizations such as *Consumer Reports,* government agencies, and TV "consumer programs"; and (3) *marketer-dominated sources,* such as information from sellers that includes advertising, salespeople, and point-of-purchase displays in stores.

Suppose you consider buying a portable CD player. You will probably tap several of these information sources: friends and relatives, portable CD-player advertisements, and several stores carrying CD players (for demonstrations). You might study the comparative evaluation of portable CD players that appeared in *Consumer Reports,* published by a product-testing organization, a portion of which appears in Figure 5–2.[5]

Alternatives Evaluation: Assessing Value

The information search stage clarifies the problem for the consumer by (1) suggesting criteria to use for the purchase, (2) yielding brand names that might meet the criteria, and (3) developing consumer value perceptions. Based only on the information shown in Figure 5–2, what selection criteria would you use in buying a portable CD player? Would you use price, the quality of headphones, ease of using the controls, or some other combination of these and other criteria?

EVALUATIVE CRITERIA
Factors that represent both the objective attributes of a brand and the subjective ones a consumer uses to compare different products and brands.

For some of you, the information provided may be inadequate because it does not contain all the factors you might consider when evaluating portable CD players. These factors are a consumer's **evaluative criteria**, which represent both the objective attributes of a brand (such as the locate speed) and the subjective ones (such as prestige) you use to compare different products and brands.[6] Firms try to identify and capitalize on both types of criteria to create the best value for money sought by you and other consumers. These criteria are often displayed in advertisements.

EVOKED SET
The group of brands that a consumer would consider acceptable from among all the brands in the product class of which he or she is aware.

Consumers often have several criteria for evaluating brands. (Didn't you in the preceding exercise?) Knowing this, companies seek to identify the most important evaluative criteria that consumers use when judging brands. For example, among the evaluative criteria shown in the columns of Figure 5–2, suppose that you use three in considering brands of portable CD players: (1) a list price under $150, (2) error correction, and (3) controls. These criteria establish the brands in your **evoked set**—the group of brands that a consumer would consider acceptable from among all the brands in the product class of which he or she is aware.[7] Your three evaluative criteria result in two models in your evoked set. If these brands don't satisfy you, you can change your evaluation criteria to create a different evoked set of models.

Purchase Decision: Buying Value

Having examined the alternatives in the evoked set, you are almost ready to make a purchase decision. Two choices remain: (1) from whom to buy and (2) when to buy. For a product like a portable CD player, the information search process probably involved visiting retail stores, seeing different brands in catalogues, viewing portable CD-player promotions on a home shopping television channel, or visiting a seller's Web site. The choice of which seller to buy from will depend on such considerations as the terms of sale, your past experience buying from the seller, and the return policy. Often a purchase decision involves a simultaneous evaluation of both product attributes and seller characteristics. For example, you might choose the second-most preferred portable CD player brand at a store with a liberal refund and return policy versus the most preferred brand at a store with more conservative policies.

Deciding when to buy is frequently determined by a number of factors. For instance, you might buy sooner if one of your preferred brands is on sale or its manufacturer offers a rebate. Other factors such as the store atmosphere, pleasantness of the shopping experience, salesperson persuasiveness, time pressure, and financial circumstances could also affect whether a purchase decision is made or postponed.[8]

Use of the Internet to gather information, evaluate alternatives, and make buying decisions adds a technological dimension to the consumer purchase decision process.[9] Consumer benefits and costs associated with this technology and its marketing implications are detailed in Chapter 21.

Postpurchase Behaviour: Value in Consumption or Use

After buying a product, the consumer compares it with his or her expectations and is either satisfied or dissatisfied. If the consumer is dissatisfied, marketers must decide whether the product was deficient or consumer expectations too high. Product

deficiency may require a design change; if expectations are too high, perhaps the company's advertising or the salesperson oversold the product's features.

Sensitivity to a customer's consumption or use experience is extremely important in a consumer's value perception. For example, research on long-distance telephone services provided by MCI, Sprint, and AT&T indicates that satisfaction or dissatisfaction affects consumer value perceptions.[10] Studies show that satisfaction or dissatisfaction affects consumer communications and repeat-purchase behaviour. Satisfied buyers tell three other people about their experience. Dissatisfied buyers complain to nine people![11] Satisfied buyers also tend to buy from the same seller each time a purchase occasion arises. The financial impact of repeat-purchase behaviour

MARKETING NEWSNET

The Value of a Satisfied Customer

Customer satisfaction is an important focus of the marketing concept. But how much is a satisfied customer worth? This question has prompted firms to calculate the financial value of a satisfied customer over time. Esso estimates that a loyal customer will spend $500 annually for its branded gasoline, not including candy, snacks, oil, or repair services purchased at its gasoline stations. Kimberly-Clark reports that a loyal customer will buy 6.7 boxes of its Kleenex tissue each year and will spend $994 on facial tissues over 60 years, in today's dollars.

Sears Canada took its catalogue management systems seriously and with improvements discovered that providing loyal customers with a variety of shopping choices (multi-channels) has increased spending by 30 to 40 percent for those shoppers who want more than one way to purchase.

These calculations have focused marketer attention on customer satisfaction and retention. Ford Motor Company has set a target of increasing customer retention—the percentage of Ford owners whose next car is also a Ford—from 60 percent to 80 percent. Why? Ford executives say that each additional percentage point is worth a staggering $100 million in profits! This calculation is not unique to Ford. Research shows that a 5-percent improvement in customer retention can increase a company's profits by 70 to 80 percent.

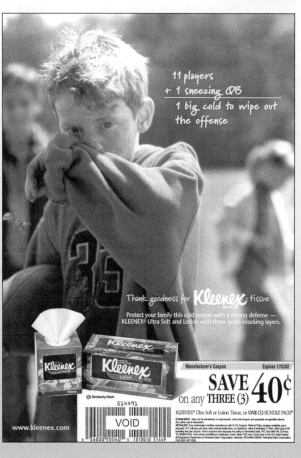

is significant, as described in the accompanying Marketing NewsNet.[12] For example, Ford Motor Company estimates that each time the company increases its number of repeat buyers by one percent, Ford increases its profit by $100 million. Accordingly, firms such as Nissan Canada, Johnson & Johnson, Coca-Cola, and British Airways focus attention on postpurchase behaviour to maximize customer satisfaction and retention.[13] These firms, among many others, now provide toll-free telephone numbers, offer liberal return and refund policies, and engage in staff training to handle complaints, answer questions, and record suggestions. Research has shown that such efforts produce positive postpurchase communications among consumers and contribute to relationship building between sellers and buyers.[14]

Often a consumer is faced with two or more highly attractive alternatives, such as a Panasonic or a Sony portable CD player. If you choose the Panasonic, you may think, "Should I have purchased the Sony?" This feeling of postpurchase psychological tension or anxiety is called **cognitive dissonance**. To alleviate it, consumers often attempt to applaud themselves for making the right choice. So after your purchase, you may seek information to confirm your choice by asking friends questions like, "Do you like my portable CD player?" or by reading ads of your chosen brand. You might even look for negative information about the brand you didn't buy and decide that Sony's error correction, which was rated "good" in Figure 5–2, was

www.att.com

www.nissancanada.com

COGNITIVE DISSONANCE
The feeling of postpurchase psychological tension or anxiety a consumer often experiences.

actually a deficiency. Firms often use ads or follow-up calls from salespeople in this postpurchase stage to try to convince buyers that they made the right decision. For many years, Buick ran an advertising campaign with the message, "Aren't you really glad you bought a Buick?"

Involvement and Problem-Solving Variations

INVOLVEMENT
The personal, social, and economic significance of the purchase to the consumer.

Sometimes consumers don't engage in the five-step purchase decision process. Instead, they skip or minimize one or more steps depending on the level of **involvement**, the personal, social, and economic significance of the purchase to the consumer.[15] High-involvement purchase occasions typically have at least one of three characteristics—the item to be purchased (1) is expensive, (2) can have serious personal consequences, or (3) could reflect on one's social image. For these occasions, consumers engage in extensive information search, consider many product attributes and brands, form attitudes, and participate in word-of-mouth communication. Low-involvement purchases, such as toothpaste and soap, barely involve most of us, whereas stereo systems and automobiles are very involving. Researchers have identified three general variations in the consumer purchase process based on consumer involvement and product knowledge. Figure 5–3 summarizes some of the important differences between the three problem-solving variations.[16]

Routine Problem Solving   For products such as toothpaste and milk, consumers recognize a problem, make a decision, and spend little effort seeking external information and evaluating alternatives. The purchase process for such items is virtually a habit and typifies low-involvement decision making. Routine problem solving is typically the case for low-priced, frequently purchased products. It is estimated that about 50 percent of all purchase occasions are of this kind.

Limited Problem Solving   In limited problem solving, consumers typically seek some information or rely on a friend to help them evaluate alternatives. In general, several brands might be evaluated using a moderate number of different attributes. You might use limited problem solving in choosing a toaster, a restaurant for dinner, and other purchase situations in which you have little time or effort to spend. Limited problem solving accounts for about 38 percent of purchase occasions.

Extended Problem Solving   In extended problem solving, each of the five stages of the consumer purchase decision process is used in the purchase, including considerable time and effort on external information search and in identifying and evaluating alternatives. Several brands are usually in the evoked set, and these are evaluated on many attributes. Extended problem solving exists in high-involvement purchase situations for items such as automobiles and financial investments in stocks and bonds. Firms marketing these products put significant effort into informing and educating these consumers. Twelve percent of purchase occasions fall into this category.

FIGURE 5–3
Comparison of problem-solving variations

	CONSUMER INVOLVEMENT		
	HIGH		LOW
CHARACTERISTICS OF PURCHASE DECISION PROCESS	**EXTENDED PROBLEM SOLVING**	**LIMITED PROBLEM SOLVING**	**ROUTINE PROBLEM SOLVING**
Number of brands examined	Many	Several	One
Number of sellers considered	Many	Several	Few
Number of product attributes evaluated	Many	Moderate	One
Number of external information sources used	Many	Few	None
Time spent searching	Considerable	Little	Minimal

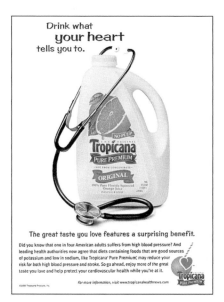

Drink what **your heart** tells you to.

Tropicana
PURE PREMIUM
ORIGINAL

The great taste you love features a surprising benefit.

Did you know that one in four American adults suffers from high blood pressure? And leading health authorities now agree that diets containing foods that are good sources of potassium and low in sodium, like Tropicana Pure Premium, may reduce your risk for both high blood pressure and stroke. So go ahead, enjoy more of the great taste you love and help protect your cardiovascular health while you're at it.

For more information, visit www.tropicanahealthnews.com

Involvement and Marketing Strategy   Low and high consumer involvement has important implications for marketing strategy. If a company markets a low-involvement product and its brand is a market leader, attention is placed on (1) maintaining product quality, (2) avoiding stock-out situations so that buyers don't substitute a competing brand, and (3) advertising messages that reinforce a consumer's knowledge or assure buyers they made the right choice. Market challengers have a different task. They must break buying habits and use free samples, coupons, and rebates to encourage trial of their brand. Advertising messages will focus on getting their brand into a consumer's evoked set. For example, Campbell's V-8 vegetable juice advertising message—"I could have had a V-8!"—was targeted at consumers who routinely purchased fruit juices and soft drinks. Challengers can also link their brand attributes with high-involvement issues. Tropicana does this by linking the natural attributes of orange juice with adult health concerns.

Marketers of high-involvement products recognize that their customers constantly seek and process information about objective and subjective brand attributes, form evaluative criteria, rate product attributes in various brands, and combine these ratings for an overall brand evaluation—like that described in the portable CD player purchase decision. Market leaders freely ply customers with product information through advertising and personal selling and create chat rooms on their company or brand Websites. Market challengers capitalize on this behaviour through comparative advertising that focuses on existing product attributes and often introduce novel evaluative criteria for judging competing brands. Increasingly, challengers benefit from Internet search engines such as MSN Search, Google, and Alta Vista that assist buyers of high-involvement products.

Situational Influences

Often the purchase situation will affect the purchase decision process. Five **situational influences** have an impact on your purchase decision process: (1) the purchase task, (2) social surroundings, (3) physical surroundings, (4) temporal effects, and (5) antecedent states.[17] The purchase task is the reason for engaging in the decision in the first place. Information searching and evaluating alternatives may differ depending on whether the purchase is a gift (which often involves social visibility) or for the buyer's own use. Social surroundings, including the other people present when a purchase decision is made, may also affect what is purchased. Physical surroundings such as decor, music, and crowding in retail stores may alter how purchase decisions are made. Temporal effects such as time of day or the amount of time available will influence where consumers have breakfast and lunch and what is ordered. Finally, antecedent states, which include the consumer's mood or the amount of cash on hand, can influence purchase behaviour and choice.

Figure 5–4 shows the many influences that affect the consumer purchase decision process. The decision to buy a product also involves important psychological and sociocultural influences, the two important topics discussed during the remainder of this chapter. Marketing mix influences are described in Chapters 10 through 20.

SITUATIONAL INFLUENCES
The purchase situation affects the purchase decision process through five situational influences: (1) the purchase task, (2) social surroundings, (3) physical surroundings, (4) temporal effects, and (5) antecedent states.

Concept Check

1. What is the first step in the consumer purchase decision process?

2. The brands a consumer considers buying out of the set of brands in a product class of which the consumer is aware are called the _____.

3. What is the term for postpurchase anxiety?

FIGURE 5–4
Influences on the
consumer purchase
decision process

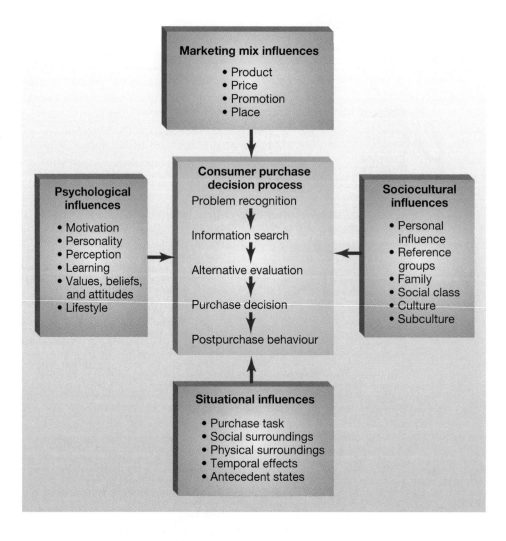

PSYCHOLOGICAL INFLUENCES ON CONSUMER BEHAVIOUR

Psychology helps marketers understand why and how consumers behave as they do. In particular, concepts such as motivation and personality; perception; learning; values, beliefs, and attitudes; and lifestyle are useful for interpreting buying processes and directing marketing efforts.

Motivation and Personality

Motivation and personality are two familiar psychological concepts that have specific meanings and marketing implications. They are both used frequently to describe why people do some things and not others.

MOTIVATION
The energizing force that causes behaviour that satisfies a need.

Motivation **Motivation** is the energizing force that causes behaviour that satisfies a need. Because consumer needs are the focus of the marketing concept, marketers try to arouse these needs.

An individual's needs are boundless. People possess physiological needs for basics such as water, sex, and food. They also have learned needs, including esteem, achievement, and affection. Psychologists point out that these needs are hierarchical; that is, once physiological needs are met, people seek to satisfy their learned needs. Figure 5–5 shows one need hierarchy and classification scheme that contains five need classes.[18] *Physiological needs* are basic to survival and must be satisfied first. A Burger King advertisement featuring a juicy hamburger attempts to activate the need for food. *Safety needs* involve self-preservation and physical well-being. Smoke

FIGURE 5–5
Hierarchy of needs

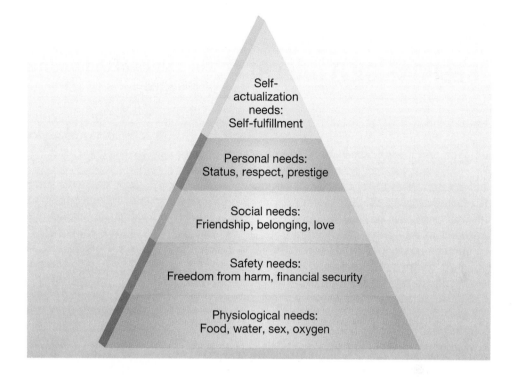

Self-
actualization
needs:
Self-fulfillment

Personal needs:
Status, respect, prestige

Social needs:
Friendship, belonging, love

Safety needs:
Freedom from harm, financial security

Physiological needs:
Food, water, sex, oxygen

detector and burglar alarm manufacturers focus on these needs. *Social needs* are concerned with love and friendship. Dating services and fragrance companies try to arouse these needs. *Personal needs* are represented by the need for achievement, status, prestige, and self-respect. The American Express Gold Card and Harry Rosen men's wear appeal to these needs. Sometimes firms try to arouse multiple needs to stimulate problem recognition. For example, Michelin combines security with parental love to promote tire replacement. *Self-actualization* needs involve personal fulfillment, such as completing your degree.

PERSONALITY
A person's consistent behaviours or responses to recurring situations.

Personality   **Personality** refers to a person's consistent behaviours or responses to recurring situations. Although numerous personality theories exist, most identify key traits—enduring characteristics within a person or in his or her relationships with others. Such traits include assertiveness, extroversion, compliance, dominance, and aggression, among others. Research suggests that compliant people prefer known brand names and use more mouthwash and toilet soaps. In contrast, aggressive types use razors, not electric shavers, apply more cologne and after-shave lotions, and purchase signature goods such as the Birks blue box, Yves St. Laurent, and Donna Karan as an indicator of status.[19] Cross-cultural analysis also suggests that residents of different countries have a **national character**, or a distinct set of personality characteristics common among people of a country or society.[20] For example, Canadians are more conservative and cautious about purchasing anything without examining it.[21]

NATIONAL CHARACTER
A distinct set of personality characteristics common among people of a country or society.

SELF-CONCEPT
The way people see themselves and the way they believe others see them.

These personality characteristics are often revealed in a person's **self-concept**, which is the way people see themselves and the way they believe others see them.[22] Marketers recognize that people have an actual self-concept and an ideal self-concept. The *actual self* refers to how people actually see themselves. The *ideal self* describes how people would like to see themselves. These two self "images" are reflected in the products and brands a person buys including automobiles, home appliances and furnishings, magazines, clothing, grooming and leisure products, and frequently, the stores a person shops. The importance of self-concept is summed up by a senior executive at Barnes & Noble: "People buy books for what the purchase says about them—their taste, their cultivation, their trendiness."[23]

ETHICS AND SOCIAL RESPONSIBILITY ALERT   The Ethics of Subliminal Messages

For almost 50 years, the topic of subliminal perception and the presence of subliminal messages embedded in commercial communications has sparked debate. To some, the concept of subliminal messages is a hoax. To others, the possibility of a person being influenced without their knowledge is either an exciting or frightening concept. Many experts suggest that the use of subliminal messages by marketers, effective or not, is deceptive and unethical.

But there are marketers who occasionally pursue opportunities to create these messages. For example, Time Warner Interactive's Endorfun, a CD-ROM puzzle game, has a music soundtrack with more than 100 subliminal messages meant to make players feel good about themselves, even if they can't solve the puzzle. One message says, "I am a winner." Puzzle players are informed that subliminal messages exist and instructions on how to turn off the soundtrack are provided.

Do you believe that attempts to implant subliminal messages are a deceptive practice and unethical, regardless of their intent?

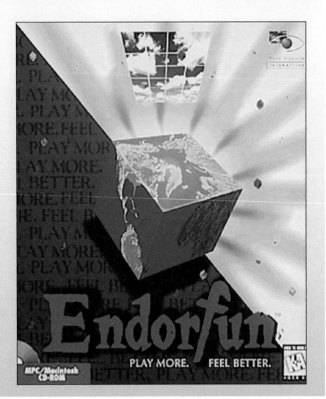

Perception

PERCEPTION
The process by which an individual selects, organizes, and interprets information to create a meaningful picture of the world.

One person sees a Cadillac as a mark of achievement; another sees it as ostentatious. This is the result of **perception**—the process by which an individual selects, organizes, and interprets information to create a meaningful picture of the world.

Selective Perception   Because the average consumer operates in a complex environment, the human brain attempts to organize and interpret information through a filtering process called *selective perception*. The four stages of selective perception are selective exposure, selective attention, selective comprehension, and selective retention. First, consumers are not exposed to all information or messages in the marketplace. In other words, there is *selective exposure*. For example, you may watch CTV, but not CBC television. In doing so, you do not expose yourself to any information broadcast on the CBC network. Because of selective exposure, marketers must work to determine where consumers are most likely to be exposed to information.

But even if a consumer is exposed to a message, either by accident or design, the consumer may not attend to that message. In general, with *selective attention*, the consumer will pay attention only to messages that are consistent with their attitudes and beliefs and will ignore those that are inconsistent. Consumers are also more likely to attend to messages when they are relevant or of interest to them. For example, a consumer is likely to pay attention to an ad about a product they just bought, or to an ad for a product they are interested in buying.

Selective comprehension involves interpreting information so that it is consistent with your attitudes and beliefs. A marketer's failure to understand this can have

Why does the Good Housekeeping seal for Clorox's new Fresh Step Crystals cat litter appear in the ad and why does Mary Kay, Inc. offer a free sample of its new Velocity brand fragrance through its Website? The answers appear in the text.

Clorox Fresh Step

www.freshstep.com

Mary Kay Velocity

www.mkvelocity.com

SUBLIMINAL PERCEPTION
Means that you see or hear messages without being aware of them.

PERCEIVED RISK
The anxieties felt because the consumer cannot anticipate the outcomes of a purchase but believes that there may be negative consequences.

disastrous results. For example, Toro introduced a small, lightweight snowblower called the Snow Pup. Even though the product worked, sales failed to meet expectations. Why? Toro later found out that consumers perceived the name to mean that Snow Pup was a toy or too light to do any serious snow removal. When the product was renamed "Snow Master," sales increased sharply.[24]

Selective retention means that consumers do not remember all the information they see, read, or hear, even minutes after exposure to it. This affects the internal and external information search stage of the purchase decision process. This is why furniture and automobile retailers often give consumers product brochures to take home after they leave the showroom.

Because perception plays such an important role in consumer behaviour, it is not surprising that the topic of subliminal perception is a popular item for discussion. **Subliminal perception** means that you see or hear messages without being aware of them. The presence and effect of subliminal perception on behaviour is a hotly debated issue, with more popular appeal than scientific support. Indeed, evidence suggests that such messages have limited effects on behaviour.[25] If these messages did influence behaviour, would their use be an ethical practice? (See the accompanying Ethics and Social Responsibility Alert.[26])

Perceived Risk   Perception plays a major role in the perceived risk in purchasing a product or service. **Perceived risk** represents the anxieties felt because the consumer cannot anticipate the outcomes of a purchase but believes that there may be negative consequences. Examples of possible negative consequences are the size of the financial outlay required to buy the product (Can I afford $200 for those skis?), the risk of physical harm (Is bungee jumping safe?), and the performance of the product (Will the hair colouring work?). A more abstract form is psychosocial (What will my friends say if I wear that sweater?). Perceived risk affects information search because the greater the perceived risk, the more extensive the external search phase is likely to be.

Recognizing the importance of perceived risk, companies develop strategies to reduce the consumer's risk and encourage purchases. These strategies and examples of firms using them include the following:

- Obtaining seals of approval: Canadian Standards Association (CSA) seal or the Good Housekeeping seal for Fresh Step Crystals cat litter.
- Securing endorsements from influential people: Athletes promoting milk consumption.
- Providing free trials of the product: sample packages of General Mills Cheerios Snack Mix or Mary Kay's Velocity fragrance.
- Giving extensive usage instructions: Clairol haircolouring.
- Providing warranties and guarantees: Cadillac's four-year, 80 000-kilometre, Gold Key bumper-to-bumper warranty.

Learning

Much consumer behaviour is learned. Consumers learn which sources to use for information about products and services, which evaluative criteria to use when assessing alternatives, and, more generally, how to make purchase decisions. **Learning** refers to those behaviours that result from (1) repeated experience and (2) thinking.

LEARNING
Those behaviours that result from (1) repeated experience and (2) thinking.

Behavioural Learning *Behavioural learning* is the process of developing automatic responses to a situation built up through repeated exposure to it. Four variables are central to how consumers learn from repeated experience: drive, cue, response, and reinforcement. A *drive* is a need that moves an individual to action. Drives, such as hunger, might be represented by motives. A *cue* is a stimulus or symbol perceived by consumers. A *response* is the action taken by a consumer to satisfy the drive, and a *reinforcement* is the reward. Being hungry (drive), a consumer sees a cue (a billboard), takes action (buys a hamburger), and receives a reward (it tastes great!).

Marketers use two concepts from behavioural learning theory. *Stimulus generalization* occurs when a response elicited by one stimulus (cue) is generalized to another stimulus. Using the same brand name for different products is an application of this concept, such as Tylenol Cold & Flu and Tylenol P.M. *Stimulus discrimination* refers to a person's ability to perceive differences in stimuli. Consumers' tendency to perceive all light beers as being alike led to Budweiser Light commercials that distinguished between many types of "lights" and Bud Light.

Cognitive Learning Consumers also learn through thinking, reasoning, and mental problem solving without direct experience. This type of learning, called *cognitive learning*, involves making connections between two or more ideas or simply observing the outcomes of others' behaviours and adjusting your own accordingly. Firms also influence this type of learning. Through repetition in advertising, messages such as "Advil is a headache remedy" attempt to link a brand (Advil) and an idea (headache remedy) by showing someone using the brand and finding relief.

Brand Loyalty Learning is also important because it relates to habit formation—the basis of routine problem solving. Furthermore, there is a close link between habits and **brand loyalty**, which is a favourable attitude toward and consistent purchase of a single brand over time. Brand loyalty results from the positive reinforcement of previous actions. So a consumer reduces risk and saves time by consistently purchasing the same brand of shampoo and has favourable results—healthy, shining hair. There is evidence of brand loyalty in many commonly purchased products in Canada and the global marketplace. However, the incidence of brand loyalty appears to be declining in North America, Mexico, European Union nations, and Japan.[27]

BRAND LOYALTY
A favourable attitude toward and consistent purchase of a single brand over time.

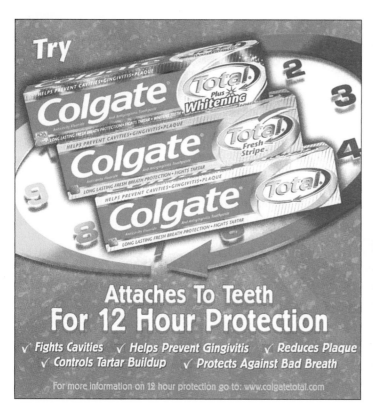

Attitudes toward Colgate toothpaste and Extra Strength Bayer Aspirin were successfully changed by these ads. How? Read the text to find out how marketers can change consumer attitudes toward products and brands.

Colgate-Palmolive
www.colgate.com

Bayer Corporation
www.bayer.ca

ATTITUDE
A learned predisposition to respond to an object or class of objects in a consistently favourable or unfavourable way.

BELIEFS
A consumer's subjective perception of how well a product or brand performs on different attributes; these are based on personal experience, advertising, and discussions with other people.

Values, Beliefs, and Attitudes

Values, beliefs, and attitudes play a central role in consumer decision making and related marketing actions.

Attitude Formation   An **attitude** is a "learned predisposition to respond to an object or class of objects in a consistently favourable or unfavourable way."[28] Attitudes are shaped by our values and beliefs, which are learned. Values vary by level of specificity. We speak of Canadian core values, including material well-being and humanitarianism. We also have personal values, such as thriftiness and ambition. Marketers are concerned with both, but focus mostly on personal values. Personal values affect attitudes by influencing the importance assigned to specific product attributes. Suppose thriftiness is one of your personal values. When you evaluate cars, fuel economy (a product attribute) becomes important. If you believe that a specific car has this attribute, you are likely to have a favourable attitude toward it.

Beliefs also play a part in attitude formation. **Beliefs** are a consumer's subjective perception of *how well* a product or brand performs on different attributes. Beliefs are based on personal experience, advertising, and discussions with other people. Beliefs about product attributes are important because, along with personal values, they create the favourable or unfavourable attitude the consumer has toward certain products and services.

Attitude Change   Marketers use three approaches to try to change consumer attitudes toward products and brands, as shown in the following examples.[29]

1. *Changing beliefs about the extent to which a brand has certain attributes.* To allay consumer concern that Aspirin use causes an upset stomach, Bayer Corporation successfully promoted the gentleness of its Extra Strength Bayer Plus Aspirin.
2. *Changing the perceived importance of attributes.* Pepsi-Cola made freshness an important product attribute when it stamped freshness dates on its cans.

Prior to doing so, few consumers considered cola freshness an issue. After Pepsi spent about $35 million on advertising and promotion, a consumer survey found that 61 percent of cola drinkers believed freshness dating was an important attribute![30]

3. *Adding new attributes to the product.* Colgate-Palmolive included a new antibacterial ingredient, tricloson, in its Colgate Total toothpaste and spent $140 million marketing the brand. The result? Colgate replaced Crest as the market leader for the first time in 25 years.[31]

Lifestyle

LIFESTYLE
A mode of living that is identified by how people spend their time and resources (activities), what they consider important in their environment (interests), and what they think of themselves and the world around them (opinions).

Lifestyle is a mode of living that is identified by how people spend their time and resources (activities), what they consider important in their environment (interests), and what they think of themselves and the world around them (opinions). The analysis of consumer lifestyles (also called *psychographics*) has produced many insights into consumers' behaviour. For example, lifestyle analysis has proven useful in segmenting and targeting consumers for new and existing products (see Chapter 8).

Lifestyle analysis typically focuses on identifying consumer profiles. Perhaps the best-known example of this type of analysis is the Values and Lifestyles (VALS) Program developed by SRI International.[32] The VALS Program has identified eight interconnected categories of adult lifestyles based on a person's self-orientation and resources. Self-orientation describes the patterns of attitudes and activities that help people reinforce their social self-image. Three patterns have been uncovered: they are oriented toward principles, status, and action. A person's resources encompass

FIGURE 5–6
The Goldfarb Segments

SEGMENT	PERCENTAGE OF POPULATION	CHARACTERISTICS
More traditional		
Structured	19%	Traditional value structure, religious, satisfied with life as it is; low risk; early followers in terms of product adoption.
Discontented	16%	Not likely to describe themselves as happy with their family life, friends, or work; like package deals and respond to feel-good messages.
Fearful	15%	Quiet, reserved, cautious, afraid; disapprove of biotechnology; and don't understand computers; don't want to be conspicuous in terms of behaviour or consumption.
Less Traditional		
Resentful	18%	Loners; want power and money; like expensive things; gamble; prepared to bend rules to suit themselves.
Assured	13%	Leading edge group; self-confident and self-oriented; optimistic; eager to try new experiences, new brands, new ideas; work hard and can also kick back and relax.
Floating Segment		
Caring	19%	Family is top priority; value relationships; strong work ethic; give back to society; do not buy things they cannot afford.

income, education, self-confidence, health, eagerness to buy, intelligence, and energy level. This dimension is a continuum ranging from minimal to abundant. While the VALS Program is the most widely known lifestyles or psychographics system in North America, it has been used only a few times in Canada for commercial marketing applications. Experts believe Canadian values differ from those of Americans, resulting in a few Canadian home-grown systems. The most comprehensive are the Goldfarb Segments and the Environics 13 social value tribes.

The Goldfarb Segments   The Goldfarb Segments were produced as a result of a large-scale sampling of adult Canadians and examining their responses to hundreds of questions concerning their activities, interests, and opinions. Six lifestyle or psychographic segments were identified and labelled as the Goldfarb Segments. Three of the segments are more traditional in their outlook, two are less traditional, and one segment floats somewhere in between. As you can see in Figure 5–6, the more traditional segments represent 50 percent of the population, the less traditional segments represent 31 percent, and the floating segment represents 19 percent of the population. Figure 5–6 also highlights selected lifestyle and behavioural characteristics of each segment.

The Thirteen Social Value Tribes

Since 1983, Environics has been tracking the values and attitudes of the Canadian population. Values and attitudes are tracked using a sociocultural map harmonizing demographics with values such as rejection of authority, destiny control, and pursuit of happiness.[33] Figure 5–7 shows the 13 tribes identified by Michael Adams of Environics, including estimates of the population represented by each tribe.[34] Understanding how values and attitudes change over time and can influence purchase choices directly affects marketing opportunities.

Concept Check

1. The problem with the Toro Snow Pup was an example of selective _____.

2. What three attitude-change approaches are most common?

3. What does *lifestyle* mean?

SOCIOCULTURAL INFLUENCES ON CONSUMER BEHAVIOUR

Sociocultural influences, which evolve from a consumer's formal and informal relationships with other people, also exert a significant impact on consumer behaviour. These involve personal influence, reference groups, the family, social class, culture, and subculture.

Personal Influence

A consumer's purchases are often influenced by the views, opinions, or behaviours of others. Two aspects of personal influence are important to marketing: opinion leadership and word-of-mouth activity.

Opinion Leadership   Individuals who exert direct or indirect social influence over others are called **opinion leaders**. Opinion leaders are more likely to be important for products that provide a form of self-expression. Automobiles, clothing, club membership, home audio and video equipment, and personal computers are products affected by opinion leaders, but appliances are not.[35] A study by *Popular Mechanics* magazine identified 18 million men who influence the purchases of some 85 million consumers for "do-it-yourself" products.[36]

OPINION LEADERS
Individuals who exert direct or indirect social influence over others.

www.popularmechanics.com

FIGURE 5–7
The thirteen social value tribes

CANADIAN TRIBES BASED ON SHARED VALUES

Tribes	Representation by Demographic Group	Representation by General Population
The Elders Born before the end of the Second World War		**25%**
Rational Traditionalists Typical profile of generation, risk-aversion, strong sense of right and wrong	46% Elders	12%
Extroverted Traditionalists Want to feel they belong, dread unforeseen events	29% Elders	7%
Cosmopolitan Modernists Keen concern of less fortunate, sociable, support progress and reform	25% Elders	6%
The Boomers Characterized by being busy, liberal, considering retirement		**40%**
Autonomous Rebels Defining boomer segment, inclination to question, personal destiny	27% Boomers	11%
Anxious Communitarians Status is important, "dress for success" group, will defer to authority	15% Boomers	6%
Connected Enthusiasts Reject consumerism, empathetic, experimental	15% Boomers	6%
Disengaged Darwinists Look for security, financial concerns, look for emotional experiences	43% Boomers	17%
Generation X Post-Boomers, most diverse segment, excitement and risk-taking		**35%**
Aimless Dependents Aimless, feel unconnected to institutions, like crowds	24% Gen X	8%
Thrill-seeking Materialists Value others' opinions, seek thrills	9% Gen X	3%
New Aquarians Most adaptable segment, early adopters, interested in spirituality	14% Gen X	5%
Autonomous Post-materialists Freedom is fundamental value, impatient with paternalism and hierarchy	25% Gen X	9%
Social Hedonists Party animals, looking for novelty, take chances, often bored	12% Gen X	4%
Security-seeking Ascetics Defer gratification, focused on financial success for family, conservative	16% Gen X	6%

Only a small percentage of adults are considered opinion leaders.[37] Identifying, reaching, and influencing opinion leaders is a major challenge for companies. Some firms use sports figures or celebrities as spokespersons to represent their products, such as Wayne Gretzky for Tylenol and Jaime Salé and David Pelletier for Cheerios, in the hope that they are opinion leaders. Others promote their products in media believed to reach opinion leaders. Still others use more direct approaches. For example, DaimlerChrysler recently invited influential community leaders and business executives to test-drive its Dodge Intrepid, Chrysler Concorde, and Eagle Vision models. Some 6000 accepted the offer, and 98 percent said they would recommend their tested car. DaimlerChrysler estimated that the number of favourable recommendations totalled 32 000.[38]

WORD OF MOUTH
People influencing each other during their face-to-face conversations.

Word of Mouth   People influencing each other during their face-to-face conversations is called **word of mouth**. Word of mouth is perhaps the most powerful information source for consumers because it typically involves friends viewed as trustworthy. A Canadian study found that 70 percent of those surveyed relied on word of mouth when selecting a bank; 95 percent said they used advice from friends when choosing a physician.[39]

The power of personal influence has prompted firms to promote positive and retard negative word of mouth.[40] For instance, "teaser" advertising campaigns are run in advance of new-product introductions to stimulate conversations. Other techniques such as advertising slogans, music, and humour also heighten positive word of mouth. On the other hand, rumours about Kmart (snake eggs in clothing), McDonald's (worms in hamburgers), and Corona Extra beer (contaminated beer) have resulted in negative word of mouth, none of which was based on fact. Overcoming or neutralizing negative word of mouth is difficult and costly. Firms have found that supplying factual information, providing toll-free numbers for consumers to call the company, and giving appropriate product demonstrations also have been helpful. Negative word of mouth is particularly challenging for global marketers, as described in the accompanying Marketing NewsNet.[41] The concept of word of mouth has been transferred to the Internet community with a Website, www.snopes2.com. This Website demonstrates the power of electronic word of mouth and urban legends for spreading information via the Internet.[42]

Firms use celebrities or sports figures as spokespersons to represent their products, such as Pierce Brosnan and Anna Kournikova for Omega, in the hope that they are opinion leaders.

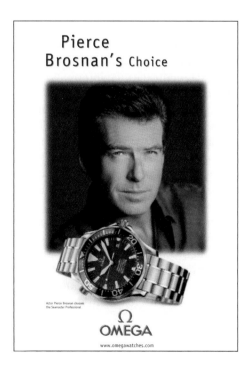

MARKETING NEWSNET

Psst, Have You Heard . . . ? The Legacy of Negative Word of Mouth in Global Marketing

Global marketers have learned painfully that word of mouth is a powerful information source in developing countries. Rumours that result in negative word of mouth are particularly common. For example, several food products in Indonesia, including some sold by Nestlé, were rumoured to contain pork, which is prohibited to the 160 million Muslim consumers in that country. Nestlé spent $350 000 in advertising to counteract the rumour. In Russia, Mars, Inc. had to confront the untrue claim that 200 000 Moscow children acquired diabetes from Snickers candy bars. Pabst Blue Ribbon beer was hit by a rumour in China that its beer was poisoned. Actually, a home-brewed beer had been poured into an empty Pabst bottle and resold.

Negative word of mouth has been shown to reduce the credibility of a company's advertising and consumers' intention to buy products. Its effect can be particularly damaging for companies that have recently entered a new country.

Reference Groups

REFERENCE GROUPS
People to whom an individual looks as a basis for self-appraisal or as a source of personal standards.

Reference groups are people to whom an individual looks as a basis for self-appraisal or as a source of personal standards. Reference groups affect consumer purchases because they influence the information, attitudes, and aspiration levels that help set a consumer's standards. For example, one of the first questions one asks others when planning to attend a social occasion is, "What are you going to wear?" Reference groups have an important influence on the purchase of luxury products but not of necessities—reference groups exert a strong influence on the brand chosen when its use or consumption is highly visible to others.[43]

Consumers have many reference groups, but three groups have clear marketing implications. A *membership group* is one to which a person actually belongs, including fraternities and sororities, social clubs, and the family. Such groups are easily identifiable and are targeted by firms selling insurance, insignia products, and charter vacations. An *aspiration group* is one that a person wishes to be a member of or wishes to be identified with, such as a professional society. Firms frequently rely on spokespeople or settings associated with their target market's aspiration group in their advertising. A *dissociative group* is one that a person wishes to maintain a distance from because of differences in values or behaviours.

Family Influence

Family influences on consumer behaviour result from three sources: consumer socialization, passage through the family life cycle, and decision making within the family or household.

Consumer Socialization   The process by which people acquire the skills, knowledge, and attitudes necessary to function as consumers is **consumer socialization**.[44] Children learn how to purchase (1) by interacting with adults in purchase situations and (2) through their own purchasing and product usage experiences. Research shows that children evidence brand preferences at age two, and these preferences often last a lifetime.[45] This knowledge has prompted Sony to introduce "My First Sony," a line of portable audio equipment for children; Time, Inc. to launch *Sports Illustrated for Kids*; Polaroid to develop the Cool Cam camcorder for children between ages 9 and 14; and Yahoo! and America Online to create special areas where young audiences can view their children's menu—Yahooligans! and Kids Only, respectively.

Family Life Cycle   Consumers act and purchase differently as they go through life. The **family life cycle** concept describes the distinct phases that a family progresses through from formation to retirement, each phase bringing with it identifiable purchasing behaviours.[46] Figure 5–8 illustrates the traditional progression as well as contemporary variations of the family life cycle. Young singles' buying preferences are for nondurable items, including prepared foods, clothing, personal care products, and entertainment. They represent a target market for recreational travel, automobile, and consumer electronics firms. Young married couples without children are typically more affluent than young singles because usually both spouses are employed. These couples exhibit preferences for furniture, housewares, and gift items for each other. Young marrieds with children are driven by the needs of their children. They make up a sizeable market for life insurance, various children's

CONSUMER SOCIALIZATION
The process by which people acquire the skills, knowledge, and attitudes necessary to function as consumers.

FAMILY LIFE CYCLE
The distinct phases that a family progresses through from formation to retirement, each phase bringing with it identifiable purchasing behaviours.

FIGURE 5–8
Modern family life cycle

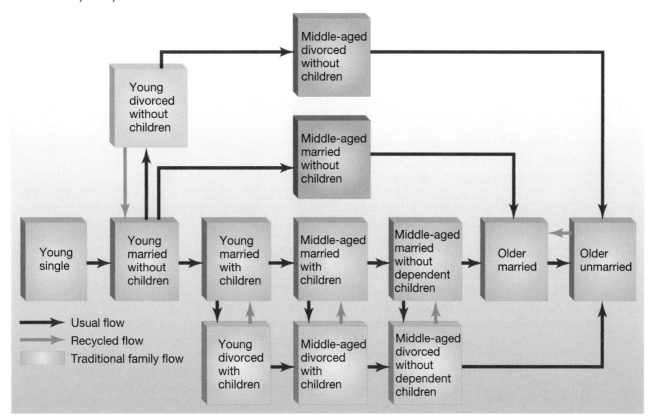

The Haggar Clothing Co. recognizes the important role women play in the choice of men's clothing. The company directs a large portion of its advertising toward women because they influence and purchase men's clothing.

Haggar Clothing Co.

www.haggar.com

products, and home furnishings. Single parents with children are the least financially secure of households with children. Their buying preferences are affected by a limited economic status and tend toward convenience foods, childcare services, and personal-care items.

Middle-aged married couples with children are typically better off financially than their younger counterparts. They are a significant market for leisure products and home improvement items and represent the fastest-growing family life cycle stage in the early 2000s. Middle-aged couples without children typically have a large amount of discretionary income. These couples buy better home furnishings, status automobiles, and financial services.

Persons in the last two phases—older married and older unmarried—make up a sizeable market for prescription drugs, medical services, vacation trips, and gifts for younger relatives. These consumers also represent one of the fastest-growing family life cycle stages in the early 2000s.

Family Decision Making   A third influence in the decision-making process occurs within the family. Two decision-making styles exist: spouse-dominant and joint decision making. With a joint decision-making style, most decisions are made by both husband and wife. Spouse-dominant decisions are those for which either the husband or the wife is responsible. Research indicates that wives tend to have the most say when purchasing groceries, children's toys, clothing, and medicines. Husbands tend to be more influential in home and car maintenance purchases. Joint decision making is common for cars, vacations, houses, home appliances and electronics, medical care, and long-distance telephone services. As a rule, joint decision making increases with the education of the spouses.[47]

Roles of individual family members in the purchase process are another element of family decision making. Five roles exist: (1) information gatherer, (2) influencer, (3) decision maker, (4) purchaser, and (5) user. Family members assume different roles for different products and services. This knowledge is important to firms.[48] For example, 89 percent of wives either influence or make outright purchases of men's clothing. Knowing this, Haggar Clothing, a menswear marketer, now advertises in women's magazines such as *Vanity Fair* and *Redbook*. Even though women are often the grocery decision maker, they are not necessarily the purchaser. More than 40 percent of all food-shopping dollars are spent by male customers. Increasingly, preteens and teenagers are the information gatherers, influencers, decision makers, and purchasers of products and services items for the family, given the prevalence of working parents and single-parent households. Children under 18 currently influence a variety of family purchase decisions.[49] This figure helps to explain why, for example, Nabisco, Johnson & Johnson, Apple Computer, Kellogg, P&G, and Oscar Mayer, among countless other companies, advertise in media that reach preteens and teens.

Social Class

SOCIAL CLASS
The relatively permanent, homogeneous divisions in a society into which people sharing similar values, lifestyles, interests, and behaviour can be grouped.

A more subtle influence on consumer behaviour than direct contact with others is the social class to which people belong. **Social class** may be defined as the relatively permanent, homogeneous divisions in a society into which people sharing similar values, interests, and behaviour can be grouped. A person's occupation, source of income (not level of income), and education determine his or her social class. Generally speaking, three major social class categories exist—upper, middle, and lower—with subcategories within each. This structure has been observed in Canada, the United States, Great Britain, Western Europe, and Latin America.[50]

To some degree, persons within social classes exhibit common attitudes, lifestyles, and buying behaviours. Compared with the middle classes, people in the lower classes have a more short-term time orientation, are more emotional than rational in their reasoning, think in concrete rather than abstract terms, and see fewer personal opportunities. Members of the upper classes focus on achievements and the future and think in abstract or symbolic terms.

Companies use social class as a basis for identifying and reaching particularly good prospects for their products and services. In general, people in the upper classes are targeted by companies for items such as financial investments, expensive cars, and evening wear. The middle classes represent a target market for home improvement centres, automobile parts stores, and personal hygiene products. Firms also recognize differences in media preferences among classes: lower and working classes prefer sports and scandal magazines, middle classes read fashion, romance, and celebrity (*People*) magazines, and upper classes tend to read literary, travel, and news magazines such as *Maclean's*.

Culture and Subculture

As described in Chapter 3, culture refers to the set of values, ideas, and attitudes that are accepted by a homogeneous group of people and transmitted to the next generation. This we often refer to as, say, Canadian culture, American culture, British culture, or Japanese culture. (Cultural underpinnings of Canadian buying patterns are described in Chapter 3, whereas Chapter 7 explores the role of culture in global marketing.)

SUBCULTURES
Subgroups within the larger, or national, culture with unique values, ideas, and attitudes.

Subgroups within the larger, or national, culture with unique values, ideas, and attitudes are referred to as **subcultures**. Subcultures can be identified by age (e.g., baby boomers vs. Generation X), geography (e.g., Western Canadian vs. Atlantic Canadian), and ethnicity. Here, we focus on ethnic subcultures.

An *ethnic subculture* is a segment of a larger society whose members are thought, by themselves and/or by others, to have a common origin and to participate in shared activities believed to be culturally significant.[51] Common traits such as customs, language, religion, and values hold ethnic subcultures together. Because of Canada's pluralistic tradition, ethnic groups do not necessarily join the cultural mainstream. Some people have referred to this concept as a *salad bowl* phenomenon, where a potpourri of people mix but do not blend. This allows for the maintenance of subcultural traditions and values.

French-Canadian Subculture   There are over seven million French-speaking Canadians in this country, about 25 percent of the population. The overwhelming majority of French Canadians live in Quebec. Research shows that French-speaking Quebecers do exhibit different consumption behaviour from the rest of Canadians.[52] French Quebecers link price to perceived value but will pass on a buy rather than

www.metro.ca

buy on credit. They are more willing to pay higher prices for convenience and premium brands, and they give more credence to advertising than the average Canadian. Metro-Richelieu Inc., a Quebec grocery store chain, says its research shows that 56 percent of Quebecers consult the grocery chain's weekly circulars.

But French Quebecers are cautious of new products and often postpone trial until the product has proven itself. They do exhibit brand loyalty but will switch for specials. They also prefer convenience and health food stores over food warehouses and local grocery stores. French Quebecers are less likely to buy grocery items on impulse and are increasingly calculating in their food purchases. Metro-Richelieu Inc. has responded by offering more discount coupons, weekly specials, and money-saving tips under one plan, called EconoMetro. Also, French Quebecers are more concerned with personal grooming and fashion, and more likely to shop in specialized clothing boutiques. Eaton's has shifted its advertising approach in Quebec in an attempt to appeal to Quebecers' heightened fashion sense while recognizing that department stores are not the most popular option for fashion in La Belle Province.

French Quebec has a higher percentage of wine and beer drinkers and more smokers. And, while Quebecers enjoy their beer, Molson says its research indicates that French Quebecers prefer a stronger beer. Accordingly, Molson launched O'Keefe 6.2 Brand (which contains 6.2 percent alcohol) exclusively for the Quebec market. There are fewer golfers, joggers, and gardeners, and the proportion of people who go to movies or entertain at home is also lower. There are, however, more cyclists, skiers, and live theatre fans.

French Quebecers are big buyers of lottery tickets and more likely to subscribe to book clubs, but they make fewer long-distance phone calls. They travel less, whether for business or pleasure. More French Quebec adults hold life insurance policies but they are less likely to have a credit card. They also tend to use credit unions (*caisses populaires*) more than banks.

Some argue that French Quebec can be characterized by a set of values that are traditional, consistent, and relatively static. But changes are evident. While values are still strong about family life, about having children in a marriage, and about giving them religious training, the use of birth control is on the rise and the marriage rate is below the national average.

Marketers must realize that certain products and other elements of the marketing mix may have to be modified in order to be successful in French Quebec. In addition to cultural differences, there are other issues that marketers must address. Commercial advertising to children is prohibited and greater restrictions exist for alcohol advertising. Provincial regulations also require that labels and packages must be both in French and English, while storefront signage must be in French, not English. Good investigation and analysis of this market is a requirement for all companies wishing to do business there.

Acadian Subculture Many Canadians assume that French Canadians are basically the same. Even though the majority of French-speaking Canadians reside in Quebec, another special group of French-speaking Canadians live outside of Quebec. These people are the Acadians, most of whom live in New Brunswick and are proud of their distinctive heritage. The Acadians are often referred to as the "forgotten French market."

Acadians are different from French Quebecers in many ways. In terms of consumption, Acadians are very fashion-oriented and tend to dine out more often than their French counterparts in Quebec. Acadians are also very price-conscious. They also prefer companies that speak to them in their language, which is slightly different than French Québécois.

Chinese-Canadian Subculture The Chinese-Canadian market currently represents over three percent of Canada's population, but it is one of the fastest-growing subcultures in Canada. This ethnic group is composed predominantly of immigrants from Hong Kong and Taiwan and is concentrated largely in Toronto and Vancouver.

Chinese Canadians have unique values. While most Canadians value straight-line thinking (logic), the Chinese value circular thinking (what goes around comes around). They value work, family, and education. They have different purchasing patterns and often perceive products differently from other Canadians. This group also appreciates companies that speak to them in their language. For example, many firms produce ads in Mandarin or Cantonese and run them in specialty publications such as the *Sing Tao*, a Toronto newspaper for Chinese readers.

The average Chinese Canadian has a higher income, is better educated, is less likely to be unemployed, and is significantly younger than the general Canadian population. Because of these characteristics, many firms see Chinese Canadians as a viable target market for a variety of products. For example, the Royal Bank sees them as good prospects for RSP and mutual fund products, while Cantel markets its cellular phones to this group.

Other Ethnic Subcultures   Many other ethnic Canadians can be found in large metropolitan centres or clustered in certain geographic areas. Kitchener-Waterloo has a large German Canadian population, Winnipeg is home to many Ukrainian Canadians, and Toronto has a large number of Italian Canadians. The emerging trend in Canada today is that 70 percent of all immigrants to this country are visible minorities. In addition to Asia, many new Canadians are coming from Africa, India, and Latin America.[53] Marketers must appreciate the fact that these new ethnic Canadians may carry with them distinctive social and cultural behaviour that will affect their buying patterns. Subcultural research and sensitivity can aid organizations in developing effective marketing strategies designed to appeal to these groups. For example, a common misconception is that ethnic Canadians have less spending power than Canadian-born people. However, studies show that arriving immigrants are bringing in large amounts of capital. This is particularly true of immigrants from Hong Kong, who have and continue to migrate here due to mainland China's takeover of Hong Kong. Moreover, it has been found that foreign-born Canadians earn more money, comparatively, than native-born Canadians.[54]

Concept Check

1. What are the two primary forms of personal influence?

2. Marketers are concerned with which types of reference groups?

3. What is an ethnic subculture?

SUMMARY

1 When a consumer buys a product, it is not an act but a process. There are five steps in the purchase decision process: problem recognition, information search, alternative evaluation, purchase decision, and postpurchase behaviour.

2 Consumers evaluate alternatives on the basis of attributes. Identifying which attributes are most important to consumers, along with understanding consumer beliefs about how a brand performs on those attributes, can make the difference between successful and unsuccessful products.

3 Consumer involvement with what is bought affects whether the purchase decision process involves routine, limited, or extended problem solving. Situational influences also affect the process.

4 Perception is important to marketers because of the selectivity of what a consumer sees or hears, comprehends, and retains.

5 Much of the behaviour that consumers exhibit is learned. Consumers learn from repeated experience and reasoning. Brand loyalty is a result of learning.

6 Attitudes are learned predispositions to respond to an object or class of objects in a consistently favourable or unfavourable way. Attitudes are based on a person's values and beliefs concerning the attributes of objects.

7 Lifestyle is a mode of living reflected in a person's activities, interests, and opinions of himself or herself and the world.

8 Personal influence takes two forms: opinion leadership and word-of-mouth activity. A specific type of personal influence exists in the form of reference groups.

9 Family influences on consumer behaviour result from three sources: consumer socialization, family life cycle, and decision making within the household.

10 Within Canada there are social classes and subcultures that affect a consumer's values and behaviour. Marketers must be sensitive to these sociocultural influences when developing a marketing mix.

KEY TERMS AND CONCEPTS

attitude p. 131
beliefs p. 131
brand loyalty p. 130
cognitive dissonance p. 123
consumer behaviour p. 120
consumer socialization p. 137
evaluative criteria p. 121
evoked set p. 122
family life cycle p. 137
involvement p. 124
learning p. 130
lifestyle p. 132
motivation p. 126

national character p. 127
opinion leaders p. 133
perceived risk p. 129
perception p. 128
personality p. 127
purchase decision process p. 120
reference groups p. 136
self-concept p. 127
situational influences p. 125
social class p. 139
subcultures p. 139
subliminal perception p. 129
word of mouth p. 135

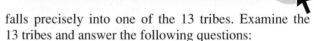

INTERNET EXERCISE   www.mcgrawhill.ca/college/berkowitz

A customer's consumption patterns and experience with products and services is related to his or her values and attitudes. Canadians are motivated less to part with their money for conspicuous consumption, but are increasingly interested in experiential consumption.

The Environics Website, www.environics.net (click through to the 3SC social values page), has a survey that can be filled out to determine your tribe. Not everyone

falls precisely into one of the 13 tribes. Examine the 13 tribes and answer the following questions:

1 What are the implications for financial institutions in terms of new services designed for the social hedonists?

2 Choose two tribes from different generational segments to compare and contrast how their social values influence the purchase of cars.

Want to get better grades, find tips on how to study more effectively, and stay up to date with happenings in the world of marketing? Visit the Online Learning Centre for practice tests, Study Smart software, and much more! www.mcgrawhill.ca/college/berkowitz

Interested in finding out what marketing looks like in the real world? *Marketing Magazine* is just a click away on your OLC! Visit www.mcgrawhill.ca/college/berkowitz

APPLYING MARKETING CONCEPTS AND PERSPECTIVES

1 Review Figure 5–2 in the text, which shows the CD-player attributes identified by *Consumer Reports*. Which attributes are important to you? What other attributes might you consider? Which brand would you prefer?

2 Suppose research at Apple Computer reveals that prospective buyers are anxious about buying computers for home use. What strategies might you recommend to the company to reduce consumer anxiety?

3 A Porsche salesperson was taking orders on new cars because he was unable to satisfy the demand with the limited number of cars in the showroom and lot. Several persons had backed out of the contract within two weeks of signing the order. What explanation can you give for this behaviour, and what remedies would you recommend?

4 Which social class would you associate with each of the following items or actions: (*a*) tennis club membership, (*b*) brass water sprinklers, (*c*) *True Romance* magazine, (*d*)

Maclean's magazine, (*e*) formally dressing for dinner frequently, and (*f*) being a member of a bowling team.

5 Assign one or more levels of the hierarchy of needs and the motives described in Figure 5–5 to the following products: (*a*) life insurance, (*b*) cosmetics, (*c*) *The Financial Post*, and (*d*) hamburgers.

6 With which stage in the family life cycle would the purchase of the following products and services be most closely identified: (*a*) bedroom furniture, (*b*) life insurance, (*c*) a Caribbean cruise, (*d*) a house mortgage, and (*e*) children's toys?

7 "The greater the perceived risk in a purchase situation, the more likely that cognitive dissonance will result." Does this statement have any basis given the discussion in the text? Why?

VIDEO CASE 5–1 The Consumer on the Couch

To retailers, there is no more important question than "why do consumers buy?" Understanding the influences that affect purchasing behaviour can spell the difference between commercial success and failure.

Paco Underhill is a New York City–based "retail anthropologist" who has been retained by dozens of top-flight companies, including the Canadian Imperial Bank of Commerce, Burger King, and Calvin Klein, to determine what attracts customers to their locations, what makes them linger, and what makes them spend. His empirical findings, many of which are documented in his *Why We Buy: The Science of Shopping,* are based mainly on analysis of tens of thousands of hours of clandestine videotaping of shoppers in action. Underhill's studies have significantly expanded our understanding of the purchase decision process while raising important questions about the privacy rights of consumers.

SHAPE UP OR SHIP OUT

At last count, the retail sector recorded sales of $277 billion and provided 12 percent of all jobs (about 1.75 million positions) in Canada. But while the sector has 100 percent more stores than it did 15 years ago, it has only 15 percent more customers. As participants in a key economic sector that is subject to tremendous domestic competition, Canadian retailers must do everything they can to understand consumer needs and motivations.

Their need for greater insight into consumer behaviour became critical in the mid-1990s, when international retailers began to vie for market share in Canada. Global competitors with deep pockets, such as Wal-Mart, Pottery Barn, and Payless ShoeSource, threatened the viability of many domestic firms. According to Underhill, Canada can expect even more competition from foreign retailers in the years ahead. Part of the problem, as he sees it, is that most Canadian outlets are "frumpy." By this, he means more than unattractive; he means that most are not designed with shoppers in mind. As he says in the *Venture* video, "If the 20th century was about marketers being leaders, the 21st century is about marketers being followers." Satisfying consumer expectations is the key to success at the cash register.

At the same time, Underhill is a stalwart fan of firms like Canadian Tire, which completely redesigned its hardware stores to curb the market penetration of big-box competitors such as Home Depot and Wal-Mart. Examples like this show clearly that domestic firms can compete successfully for the attention of increasingly fickle shoppers. And Underhill believes they must. "In the Canadian marketplace," he says, "retailers must shape up or go out of business."

READING THE RETAIL LANDSCAPE

Traditional market research on consumer behaviour has been done through analysis of barcodes scanned at the cash register and from direct surveys of shoppers conducted via telephone, one-on-one interviews, or focus groups. While the resulting data are valuable, rarely do they shed light on the discrepancy between what customers say about the process of making purchasing choices and what they actually do at the store. Consequently, Underhill and like-minded students of shopping are less concerned with what people buy than why they so often fail to buy.

To gain more understanding of shoppers, some retailers have turned to in-store customer surveillance. Using hidden cameras that videotape consumers as they approach, enter, and exit a store, and supplementing that evidence with surreptitious observations by in-store "trackers" who add a more qualitative dimension, retail anthropologists provide micro-level documentation of consumer behaviour. Nothing escapes their scrutiny. The result, when time-series data are compiled, is a telling view of a single store's failings as a shopping environment from the perspective of the customer. Retailers who have implemented changes based on such evidence attest that catering directly to the needs of their existing customer base has significantly improved their bottom line.

FOUR KEY OBSERVATIONS

A sharp turn to the right

Eighty percent of buying decisions are made on the shop floor, so the layout of the shop floor and the manner in which customers are lured onto it are crucial to raising sales volumes and profit levels. The fact that people will not read more than three or four words in a shop window, for example, implies that window displays must be primarily visual in content. And contrary to popular belief, the entry to a store is not the ideal location for a retailer's most desirable goods; rather, it is a commercially dead zone where customers orient themselves but almost never buy. Reserving the entry for a display that appeals to the senses and pulls uncommitted shoppers into the bowels of the store where they will spend is the best tactic.

But the real key to effective layout, says Underhill, is the tendency of almost all customers to enter a store and turn, immediately, to the right. That is the prime spot for snagging a customer's attention. In fact, Underhill has determined that sales can be increased as much as 15 percent merely by shifting the cash register from the right

visit us at www.mcgrawhill.ca/college/berkowitz

side of a store to the left. Once they have made that initial right turn, customers navigate the store in a counter-clockwise orbit. Articles placed strategically along that path are much more likely to be purchased.

Appealing to the senses

Underhill has found a strong, direct correlation between sensory stimulation and sales volume. The idea is akin to creating a bazaar-like atmosphere within the store: fill the air with a seductive scent, let customers sample some delicious food, place clothing so that it can be touched, and watch sales increase. Have a salesperson talk to the customer while they taste or touch the merchandise, and the odds of them buying increase by half again. Let them try on an article of clothing, and the odds get even better. In short, involving them directly with the product pays big dividends.

Women are a retailer's best friends

Seventy percent of shoppers are women, and women are believed to influence as much as 85 percent of all retail purchasing decisions. And if two women shop together, they will spend almost twice as much time in the store as a male–female couple. All of which is important in view of the strong relationship between the time spent shopping and the amount spent.

After observing shoppers for some 20 years, Underhill is adamant that women care much more than men about the shopping experience. Enhance a store's atmosphere according to the interests and concerns of the female shopper and the typical customer will stay longer and spend more. Generous, well-lit display spaces rank high on the list of vital enhancements, but pristine washrooms and garbage cans in fitting rooms matter too. Provide amenities for male companions and children, and the sales volume climbs even further. The Chapters-Indigo book chain, with its wide aisles, consistent lighting, clear signs, comfortable chairs, and aromatic coffee-house corner has been a particularly apt pupil when it comes to designing what Underhill defines as "female-friendly" retail space.

Butt-brushing

Culturally and socially, Western women are averse to anything that touches their posteriors. Video after video in the Underhill archives shows that females who inadvertently back into awkwardly placed display racks or narrowly spaced rows of shelving will leave a store immediately. And with them goes the potential sale. This is what he calls the "butt-brush factor," and it exemplifies the respect for unspoken customer sensitivities that every retailer must possess if they wish to succeed in business.

MEETING FUTURE CONSUMER NEEDS

Underhill says that change is good, but that constant change is better. He is referring not only to modifying today's retailing methods, but also to the importance of anticipating and addressing the needs of traditionally neglected customers and emerging markets. The first kind of change deals with tactical options, while the second is about choosing a long-term, strategic marketing direction. To assist companies in this, he has identified a number of key opportunities that lie ahead:
* the high-income seniors' market
* marketing to ethnic and minority groups
* addressing the needs of women who are buying non-traditional products (e.g., technology, automobiles, hardware)
* addressing the needs of men who are doing the family shopping and buying clothing

If retailers have what Underhill calls the "good manners" to identify and satisfy the different needs and expectations of these diverse groups, he is convinced they will profit.

Questions

1 Identify specific examples of Canadian retailers whose sales have been affected by international competitors. What behavioural factors can you cite to account for their success or failure?

2 If a single store offers a range of merchandise that appeals to various demographic groups, how can it hope to satisfy all their needs?

3 Corporate collection of customer data without permission has been controversial in the online retail world. How does that situation differ, if at all, from the methods typically employed by retail anthropologists like Paco Underhill?

4 What are the principal behavioural factors that need to be considered in addressing the rapidly growing seniors market? Discuss how a retailer selling goods or services via the Internet might use this information.

WDM INNOVATION Gbps
Gbps
Gbps WDM
Honeywell
OPTOELECTRONICS
RS232
FIBRE OPTIC MODEM
Honeywell
OPTOELECTRONICS
RS232
FIBRE OPTIC MODEM
Ser. No.

CHAPTER

6

ORGANIZATIONAL MARKETS AND BUYER BEHAVIOUR

AFTER READING THIS CHAPTER YOU SHOULD BE ABLE TO:

- Distinguish among industrial, reseller, and government markets.

- Recognize key characteristics of organizational buying that make it different from consumer buying.

- Understand how buying centres and buying situations influence organizational purchasing.

- Recognize the growing importance of online buying in industrial, reseller, and government markets.

LASER TECHNOLOGY IS BRIGHT AT HONEYWELL

Gary Null views light very differently from most people. He pictures a world where information is processed at the speed of light and electricity is converted to light with unprecedented efficiency.

As the International Business Development Director at Honeywell (www.honeywell.com), Micro Switch Division, Null shares responsibility for the global launch of Honeywell's newest innovation, the *V*ertical *C*avity *S*urface *E*mitting *L*aser, or VCSEL (pronounced "Vik-Sel"). VCSEL is emerging as the light source of choice for high-speed short-wavelength communication systems. Numerous other potential applications exist in computer networks and consumer, industrial, and office products.

Successful commercialization of this innovative laser technology depends on a coordinated worldwide team effort that draws on the talents of Micro Switch design and application engineers and marketing and sales professionals. Their efforts focus on demonstrating the performance, cost, and reliability advantages of the VCSEL over existing technology to a diverse set of organizational buyers around the world. It also requires knowing which people influence the purchasing decision; what factors they consider when choosing suppliers, technology, and products; and when, where, and how buying decisions are made in Asian, European, and Latin American business cultures.

Null believes Honeywell, Micro Switch Division, is poised to capture a significant share of the multi-billion dollar global market for laser technology and products. Ultimate success will depend on continued product development that creates customer value and effective marketing to an ever-increasing number of industrial buyers of laser technology in a worldwide marketplace.[1]

The challenge facing Null of marketing to organizations is often encountered by both small, startup corporations and large, well-established companies such as Honeywell. Important issues in marketing to organizations are examined in this chapter, which analyzes types of organizational buyers, key characteristics of organizational buying, and some typical buying decisions.

THE NATURE AND SIZE OF ORGANIZATIONAL MARKETS

BUSINESS MARKETING
The marketing of goods and services to commercial enterprises, governments, and other profit and not-for-profit organizations for use in the creation of goods and services that they then produce and market to other business customers as well as individuals and ultimate consumers.

Gary Null and Honeywell's Micro Switch Division engage in business marketing. **Business marketing** is the marketing of goods and services to commercial enterprises, government, and other profit and nonprofit organizations for use in the creation of goods and services that they then produce and market to other business customers, as well as individuals and ultimate consumers.[2] This is also sometimes referred to as business-to-business or B2B marketing. Because many Canadian business school graduates take jobs in firms that engage in business marketing, it is important to understand the fundamental characteristics of organizational buyers and their buying behaviour.

ORGANIZATIONAL BUYERS
Those manufacturers, wholesalers, retailers, and government agencies that buy goods and services for their own use or for resale.

Organizational buyers are those manufacturers, retailers, and government agencies that buy goods and services for their own use or for resale. For example, all these organizations buy computers and telephone services for their own use. However, manufacturers buy raw materials and parts that they reprocess into the finished goods they sell, whereas retailers resell goods they buy without reprocessing them. Organizational buyers include all the buyers in a nation except the ultimate consumers. These organizational buyers purchase and lease tremendous volumes of capital equipment, raw materials, manufactured parts, supplies, and business services. In fact, because they often buy raw materials and parts, process them, and sell the upgraded product several times before it is purchased by the final organizational buyer or ultimate consumer, the aggregate purchases of organizational buyers in a year are far greater than those of ultimate consumers.

Organizational buyers are divided into three markets: (1) industrial, (2) resellers, and (3) government markets.

Industrial Markets

INDUSTRIAL FIRM
An organizational buyer that in some way reprocesses a good or service it buys before selling it again to the next buyer.

There are thousands of firms in the industrial, or business, market in Canada. **Industrial firms** in some way reprocess a good or service they buy before selling it again to the next buyer. This is certainly true of a steel mill that converts iron ore into steel. It is also true (if you stretch your imagination) of a firm selling services, such as a bank that takes money from its depositors, reprocesses it, and "sells" it as loans to its commercial borrowers.

There has been a marked shift in the scope and nature of the industrial marketplace. Service industries are growing and currently make the greatest contribution to Canada's gross domestic product (GDP). Because of the importance of service firms, service marketing is discussed in detail in Chapter 12. Industrial firms and primary industries currently account for about 25 percent of Canada's GDP. Nevertheless, primary industries (e.g., farming, mining, fishing, and forestry) and the manufacturing sector are important components of Canada's economy. There are about 40 000 manufacturers in Canada whose estimated value of shipments are over $450 billion.[3]

Reseller Markets

RESELLER
A wholesaler or retailer that buys physical products and resells them again without any processing.

Wholesalers and retailers who buy physical products and resell them again without any reprocessing are **resellers**. Over 200 000 retailers and over 65 000 wholesalers are currently operating in Canada. Some of the largest retailers in Canada include The Hudson's Bay Co; Sears Canada, and Costco. Some major wholesalers are Cargill,

MedisHealth, and Federated Co-Operatives. These companies participate in B2B marketing. In Chapters 15 through 17 we see how manufacturers use wholesalers and retailers in their distribution ("place") strategies as channels through which their products reach ultimate consumers. In this chapter we look at resellers mainly as organizational buyers in terms of (1) how they make their own buying decisions and (2) which products they choose to carry.

Government Markets

GOVERNMENT UNITS
The federal, provincial, and local agencies that buy goods and services for the constituents they serve.

www.canada.gc.ca

Government units are the federal, provincial, and local agencies that buy goods and services for the constituents they serve. Their annual purchases vary in size from the billions of dollars for a federal department such as the Department of Defence to millions or thousands of dollars for a local university or school. The bulk of the buying at the federal government level is done by the Department of Supply and Services Canada. Most provincial governments have a government services department that does the buying on the provincial level. Hundreds of government departments, including agencies and Crown corporations such as CBC, VIA Rail, and the Royal Canadian Mint, must purchase goods and services to operate. The federal government is a large organizational consumer making total purchases of goods and services in excess of $180 billion annually.[4]

Global Organizational Markets

Industrial, reseller, and government markets also exist on a global scale. In fact, many of Canada's top exporters including Bombardier, Canadian Pacific, DuPont Canada, Maple Leaf Foods, and Pratt & Whitney focus on organizational customers, not ultimate consumers.

Most world trade involves manufacturers, resellers, and government agencies buying goods and services for their own use or for resale to others. The exchange relationships often involve numerous transactions spanning the globe. For example, Honeywell, Micro Switch Division sells its fibre-optic technology and products to manufacturers of data communication systems worldwide, through electronic component resellers in more than 20 countries, and directly to national governments in Europe and elsewhere. Europe's Airbus Industrie, the world's largest aircraft manufacturer, sells its passenger airplanes to Air Canada, which flies Canadian businesspeople to Asia. Ontario-based Inco, one of the world's largest nickel producers, is a global business participant marketing its products to customers around the world. In fact, it exports 90 percent of its products to global organizational markets.

www.inco.com

MEASURING DOMESTIC AND GLOBAL INDUSTRIAL, RESELLER, AND GOVERNMENT MARKETS

NORTH AMERICAN INDUSTRY CLASSIFICATION SYSTEM (NAICS)
Provides common industry definitions for Canada, Mexico, and the United States, which facilitate the measurement of economic activity in the three member countries of NAFTA.

The measurement of industrial, reseller, and government markets is an important first step for a firm interested in gauging the size of one, two, or all three of these markets in Canada and around the world. This task has been made easier with the **North American Industry Classification System (NAICS)**.[5] NAICS provides common industry definitions for Canada, Mexico, and the United States, which facilitate the measurement of economic activity in the three member countries of the North American Free Trade Agreement (NAFTA). NAICS replaced the Standard Industrial Classification (SIC) system, a version of which has been in place for more than 50 years in the three NAFTA member countries. The SIC neither permitted comparability across countries nor accurately measured new or emerging industries. Furthermore, NAICS is consistent with the International Standard Industrial Classification of All Economic Activities, published by the United Nations, to facilitate measurement of global economic activity.

Understanding Buyers and Markets PART TWO

The NAICS groups economic activity to permit studies of market share, demand for goods and services, import competition in domestic markets, and similar studies. NAICS designates industries with a numerical code in a defined structure. A six-digit coding system is used. The first two digits designate a sector of the economy, the third digit designates a subsector, and the fourth digit represents an industry group. The fifth digit designates a specific industry and is the most detailed level at which comparable data are available for Canada, Mexico, and the United States. The sixth digit designates individual country-level national industries. Figure 6–1 presents an abbreviated breakdown within the Information Industries Sector (code 51) to illustrate the classification scheme.

The NAICS permits a firm to find the NAICS codes of its present customers and then obtain NAICS-coded lists for similar firms. Also, it is possible to monitor NAICS categories to determine the growth in various sectors and industries to identify promising marketing opportunities. However, NAICS codes, like the earlier SIC codes, have important limitations. The NAICS assigns one code to each organization based on its major economic activity, so large firms that engage in many different activities are still given only one NAICS code. A second limitation is that five-digit national industry codes are not available for all three countries because the respective governments will not reveal data when too few organizations exist in a category. Despite these limitations, development of NAICS represents yet another effort toward economic integration in North America and the world.

Concept Check

1. What are the three main types of organizational buyers?

2. What is the North American Industry Classification System (NAICS)?

FIGURE 6–1
NAICS breakdown for information industries sector: NAICS code 51 (abbreviated)

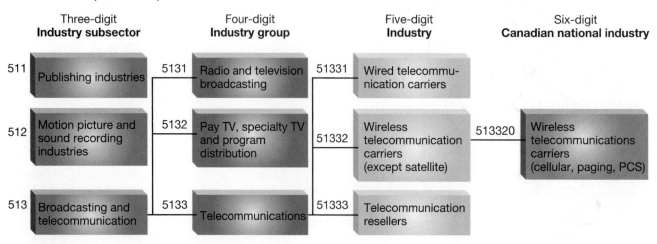

CHARACTERISTICS OF ORGANIZATIONAL BUYING

Organizations are different from individuals, so buying for an organization is different from buying for yourself or your family.[6] True, in both cases the objective in making the purchase is to solve the buyer's problem—to satisfy a need or want. But unique objectives and policies of an organization put special constraints on how it makes buying decisions. Understanding the characteristics of organizational buying is essential in designing effective marketing programs to reach these buyers.

Organizational buying behaviour is the decision-making process that organizations use to establish the need for products and services and identify, evaluate, and choose among alternative brands and suppliers. Key characteristics of organizational buying behaviour are listed in Figure 6–2 and discussed next.[7]

Demand Characteristics

Consumer demand for products and services is affected by their price and availability and by consumers' personal tastes and discretionary income. By comparison, industrial demand is derived. **Derived demand** means that the demand for industrial products and services is driven by, or derived from, demand for consumer products and services. For example, the demand for MacMillan Bloedel's pulp and paper products is based on consumer demand for newspapers, Domino's "keep warm" pizza-to-go boxes, Federal Express packages, and disposable diapers. Derived demand is often based on expectations of future consumer demand. For instance, Whirlpool purchases parts for its washers and dryers in anticipation of consumer demand, which is affected by the replacement cycle for these products and by consumer income.

As demand for air transportation grows, so too will the demand for aircraft. Read the accompanying Marketing NewsNet to see how Europe's Airbus Industrie intends to satisfy this demand with the construction of the largest airplane ever built.[8]

ORGANIZATIONAL BUYING BEHAVIOUR
The decision-making process that organizations use to establish the need for products and services and identify, evaluate, and choose among alternative brands and suppliers.

DERIVED DEMAND
Demand for industrial products and services driven by, or derived from, demand for consumer products and services.

FIGURE 6–2
Key characteristics of organizational buying behaviour

CHARACTERISTICS	DIMENSIONS
Market characteristics	• Demand for industrial products and services is derived. • Few customers typically exist, and their purchase orders are large.
Product or service characteristics	• Products or services are technical in nature and purchased on the basis of specifications. • There is a predominance of raw and semifinished goods purchased. • Heavy emphasis is placed on delivery time, technical assistance, postsale service, and financing assistance.
Buying process characteristics	• Technically qualified and professional buyers exist and follow established purchasing policies and procedures. • Buying objectives and criteria are typically spelled out, as are procedures for evaluating sellers and products (services). • Multiple buying influences exist, and multiple parties participate in purchase decisions. • Reciprocal arrangements exist, and negotiation between buyers and sellers is commonplace. • Online buying over the Internet is widespread.
Marketing mix characteristics	• Direct selling to organizational buyers is the rule, and physical distribution is very important. • Advertising and other forms of promotion are technical in nature. • Price is often negotiated, evaluated as part of broader seller and product (service) qualities, typically inelastic owing to derived demand, and frequently affected by trade and quantity discounts.

MARKETING NEWSNET

The Airbus A380 Superjumbo Jet Is About to Take Flight

Rapidly expanding demand for inter-continental passenger air traffic and the growth of the global airfreight industry bodes well for aircraft manufacturers. Europe's Airbus Industrie expects to transport future air travellers and cargo in the largest airplane ever built—its A380 superjumbo jet. Scheduled to begin service in 2006, the A380 features passenger models seating 555 to 800 people, spread over two full decks, and a freightliner model capable of delivering more than 150 000 kg of cargo. The A380 has a list price of about U.S.$220 million.

The demand for the A380 will depend on prospective buyers' expectation of future air transport traffic. If initial orders are an indication, the future is bright for superjumbo jet aircraft. Airbus has already taken orders for the A380 from buyers on five continents, including Singapore Airlines,

Qantas Airways, Virgin Atlantic Airways, Air France, Qatar Airways, and FedEx—which has 10 freightliners on order with an option to buy more.

Size of the Order or Purchase

The size of the purchase involved in organizational buying is typically much larger than that in consumer buying. The value of a single purchase made by an organization often runs into the thousands or millions of dollars. For example, Motorola was awarded an $88-million contract to install a cellular phone system in Brazil.[9] With so much money at stake, most organizations place constraints on their buyers in the form of purchasing policies or procedures. Buyers must often get competitive bids from at least three prospective suppliers when the order is above a specific amount, such as $5000. When the order is above an even higher amount, such as $50 000, it may require the review and approval of a vice president or even the president of the company. Knowing how the size of the order affects buying practices is important in determining who participates in the purchase decision and makes the final decision, and also the length of time required to arrive at a purchase agreement.

Number of Potential Buyers

Firms selling consumer products or services often try to reach thousands or millions of individuals or households. For example, your local supermarket or bank probably serves thousands of people, and Kelloggs Canada tries to reach more than 10 million Canadian households with its breakfast cereals and probably succeeds in selling to a third or half of these in any given year. In contrast, firms selling to organizations are often restricted to far fewer buyers. Bombardier can sell its business jets to a few thousand organizations throughout the world, and B. F. Goodrich sells its original equipment tires to fewer than 10 car manufacturers.

Organizational Buying Objectives

Organizations buy products and services for one main reason: to help them achieve their objectives. For business firms the buying objective is usually to increase profits through reducing costs or increasing revenues. 7-Eleven buys automated inventory systems to increase the number of products that can be sold through its convenience

Sylvania focuses on the organizational buyer's objective of reducing costs to improve profits.

Sylvania

www.sylvania.com

stores and to keep them fresh. Nissan Motor Company switched its advertising agency because it expects the new agency to devise a more effective ad campaign to help it sell more cars and increase revenues. To improve executive decision making, many firms buy advanced computer systems to process data. The objectives of nonprofit firms and government agencies are usually to meet the needs of the groups they serve. Thus, a hospital buys a high-technology diagnostic device to serve its patients better. Understanding buying objectives is a necessary first step in marketing to organizations. Recognizing the high costs of energy, Sylvania promotes to prospective buyers cost savings and increased profits made possible by its fluorescent and halogen lights.

Organizational Buying Criteria

ORGANIZATIONAL BUYING CRITERIA
The objective attributes of the supplier's products and services and the capabilities of the supplier itself.

In making a purchase the buying organization must weigh key buying criteria that apply to the potential supplier and what it wants to sell. **Organizational buying criteria** are the objective attributes of the supplier's products and services and the capabilities of the supplier itself. These criteria serve the same purpose as the evaluative criteria used by consumers and described in Chapter 5. Seven of the most commonly used criteria are (1) price, (2) ability to meet the quality specifications required for the item, (3) ability to meet required delivery schedules, (4) technical capability, (5) warranties and claim policies in the event of poor performance, (6) past performance on previous contracts, and (7) production facilities and capacity.[10] Suppliers that meet or exceed these criteria create customer value.

ISO 9000 STANDARDS
Registration and certification of a manufacturer's quality management and quality assurance system.

Organizational buyers who purchase products and services in a global marketplace often supplement their buying criteria with supplier ISO 9000 certification. **ISO 9000 standards**, developed by the International Standards Organization (ISO) in Geneva, Switzerland, refer to standards for registration and certification of a manufacturer's quality management and assurance system based on an on-site audit of practices and procedures. ISO certification is administered in Canada by SCC (Standards Council of Canada: www.scc.ca). Many Canadian companies that market globally have achieved this certification.[11]

REVERSE MARKETING
The deliberate effort by organizational buyers to build relationships that shape suppliers' products, services, and capabilities to fit a buyer's needs and those of its customers.

Many organizational buyers today are transforming their buying criteria into specific requirements that are communicated to prospective suppliers. This practice, called **reverse marketing**, involves the deliberate effort by organizational buyers to build relationships that shape suppliers' products, services, and capabilities to fit a buyer's needs and those of its customers.[12] For example, consider the case of Johnson Controls, Inc., the supplier of seats for DaimlerChrysler's small car, the Neon.[13] Johnson was able to meet DaimlerChrysler's cost target but not its safety, weight, and comfort requirements. After five 11-hour days, Johnson and the automaker's engineering and marketing staffs jointly worked out the technical details to satisfy performance requirements at a price acceptable to both parties. Ongoing reverse marketing efforts also exist. Harley-Davidson expects even its long-term suppliers to provide written plans of their efforts to improve quality, and it monitors the progress of these suppliers toward achieving these goals.

With many Canadian manufacturers using a "just-in-time" (JIT) inventory system that reduces the inventory of production parts to those to be used within hours or days, on-time delivery is becoming an even more important buying criterion and, in some instances, a requirement. Caterpillar trains its key suppliers at its Quality Institute in JIT inventory systems and conducts supplier seminars on how to diagnose, correct, and implement continuous quality improvement programs.[14] The just-in-time inventory system is discussed further in Chapter 16.

Buyer–Seller Relationships and Supply Partnerships

Another distinction between organizational and consumer buying behaviour lies in the nature of the relationship between organizational buyers and suppliers. Specifically, organizational buying is more likely to involve complex and lengthy negotiations concerning delivery schedules, price, technical specifications, warranties, and claim policies. These negotiations can last for more than a year. This was the case when a customer recently purchased a $49-million Cray Research T90 supercomputer that performs up to 60 million calculations per second.[15]

RECIPROCITY
An industrial buying practice in which two organizations agree to purchase each other's products and services.

www.strategis.ic.gc.ca

Reciprocal arrangements also exist in organizational buying. **Reciprocity** is an industrial buying practice in which two organizations agree to purchase each other's products and services. Industry Canada frowns on reciprocal buying because it restricts the normal operation of the free market. However, the practice exists and can limit the flexibility of organizational buyers in choosing alternative suppliers. Regardless of the legality of reciprocal buying, do you believe this practice is ethical? (See the accompanying Ethics and Social Responsibility Alert.)[16]

Long-term relationships are also prevalent.[17] As an example, International Truck and Engine Corporation (formerly Navistar) has a long-term relationship with Cummins, which sells engine technology to International for its heavy-duty trucks.[18]

SUPPLY PARTNERSHIP
A relationship that exists when a buyer and its supplier adopt mutually beneficial objectives, policies and procedures for the purpose of lowering the cost and/or increasing the value of products and services delivered to the ultimate consumers.

In some cases, buyer–seller relationships develop into supply partnerships.[19] A **supply partnership** exists when a buyer and its supplier adopt mutually beneficial objectives, policies, and procedures for the purpose of lowering the cost and/or increasing the value of products and services delivered to the ultimate consumer. Intel, the world's largest manufacturer of microprocessors and the "computer inside" most personal computers, is a case in point. Intel supports its suppliers by offering them quality management programs and by investing in supplier equipment that produces fewer product defects and boosts supplier productivity. Suppliers, in turn, provide Intel with consistent high-quality products at a lower cost for its customers, the makers of personal computers, and finally you, the ultimate customer. Retailers, too, are forging partnerships with their suppliers. Wal-Mart and Zellers have such a relationship with Procter & Gamble for ordering and replenishing P&G's products in their stores. By using computerized cash register scanning equipment and direct electronic linkages to P&G, these retailers can tell P&G what merchandise is needed, along with how much, when, and to which store to deliver it on a daily basis. Because supply partnerships also involve the physical distribution of goods, they are again discussed in Chapter 16 in the context of supply chains.

The Buying Centre: A Cross-Functional Group

For routine purchases with a small dollar value, a single buyer or purchasing manager often makes the purchase decision alone. In many instances, however, several people in the organization participate in the buying process. The individuals in this group, called a **buying centre**, share common goals, risks, and knowledge important to a purchase decision. For most large multistore chain resellers, such as Sears, 7-Eleven convenience stores, or Zellers, the buying centre is highly formalized and is called a *buying committee*. However, most industrial firms or government units use informal groups of people or call meetings to arrive at buying decisions.

> **BUYING CENTRE**
> The group of people in an organization who participate in the buying process and share common goals, risks, and knowledge important to a purchase decision.

The importance of the buying centre requires that a firm marketing to many industrial firms and government units understand the structure, technical and business functions represented, and behaviour of these groups. One researcher has suggested four questions to provide guidance in understanding the buying centre in these organizations:[20] Which individuals are in the buying centre for the product or service? What is the relative influence of each member of the group? What are the buying criteria of each member? How does each member of the group perceive our firm, our products and services, and our salespeople?

Answers to these questions are difficult to come by, particularly when dealing with industrial firms, resellers, and governments outside Canada.[21] For example, Canadian firms are often frustrated by the fact that Japanese buyers "ask a thousand questions" but give few answers, sometimes rely on third-party individuals to convey views on proposals, are prone to not "talk business," and often say yes to be courteous when they mean no. Firms in the global chemical industry recognize that production engineering personnel have a great deal of influence in Hungarian buying groups, while purchasing agents in the Canadian chemical industry have relatively more influence in buying decisions.

People in the Buying Centre   The composition of the buying centre in a given organization depends on the specific item being bought. Although a buyer or purchasing manager is almost always a member of the buying centre, individuals from other functional areas are included, depending on what is to be purchased. In buying a million-dollar machine tool, the president (because of the size of the purchase) and the production vice president or manager would probably be members. For key components to be incorporated in a final manufactured product, a cross-functional group of individuals from research and development (R&D), engineering, and quality control are likely to be added. For new word-processing equipment, experienced secretaries who will use the equipment would be members. Still, a major question in penetrating the buying centre is finding and reaching the people who will initiate, influence, and actually make the buying decision.

Roles in the Buying Centre   Researchers have identified five specific roles that an individual in a buying centre can play.[22] In some purchases the same person may perform two or more of these roles.

- *Users* are the people in the organization who actually use the product or service, such as a secretary who will use a new word processor.
- *Influencers* affect the buying decision, usually by helping define the specifications for what is bought. The information systems manager would be a key influencer in the purchase of a new mainframe computer.
- *Buyers* have formal authority and responsibility to select the supplier and negotiate the terms of the contract. The purchasing manager probably would perform this role in the purchase of a mainframe computer.
- *Deciders* have the formal or informal power to select or approve the supplier that receives the contract. Whereas in routine orders the decider is usually the buyer or purchasing manager, in important technical purchases it is more likely to be someone from R&D, engineering, or quality control. The decider for a key component being incorporated in a final manufactured product might be any of these three people.
- *Gatekeepers* control the flow of information in the buying centre. Purchasing personnel, technical experts, and secretaries can all keep salespeople or information from reaching people performing the other four roles.

Buying Situations and the Buying Centre   The number of people in the buying centre largely depends on the specific buying situation. Researchers who have studied organizational buying identify three types of buying situations, called **buy classes**. These buy classes vary from the routine reorder, or *straight rebuy*, to the completely new purchase, termed *new buy*. In between these extremes is the *modified rebuy*. Some examples will clarify the differences.[23]

BUY CLASSES
Three types of organizational buying situations: new buy, straight rebuy, and modified rebuy.

- *Straight rebuy.* Here the buyer or purchasing manager reorders an existing product or service from the list of acceptable suppliers, probably without even checking with users or influencers from the engineering, production, or quality control departments. Office supplies and maintenance services are usually obtained as straight rebuys.
- *Modified rebuy.* In this buying situation the users, influencers, or deciders in the buying centre want to change the product specifications, price, delivery schedule, or supplier. Although the item purchased is largely the same as with the straight rebuy, the changes usually necessitate enlarging the buying centre to include people outside the purchasing department.
- *New buy.* Here the organization is a first-time buyer of the product or service. This involves greater potential risks in the purchase, so the buying centre is enlarged to include all those who have a stake in the new buy. Procter & Gamble's recent purchase of a multi-million dollar fibre-optic network to link its corporate offices from Corning, Inc. represented a new buy.[24]

BUYING CENTRE DIMENSION	BUY-CLASS SITUATION	
	NEW BUY	STRAIGHT/MODIFIED REBUY
People involved	Many	Few
Decision time	Long	Short
Problem definition	Uncertain	Well-defined
Buying objective	Good solution	Low-price supplier
Suppliers considered	New/present	Present
Buying influence	Technical/operating personnel	Purchasing agent

FIGURE 6–3
How the buying situation affects buying centre behaviour

Figure 6–3 summarizes how buy classes affect buying centre tendencies in different ways.[25]

The marketing strategies of sellers facing each of these three buying situations can vary greatly because the importance of personnel from functional areas such as purchasing, engineering, production, and R&D often varies with (1) the type of buying situation and (2) the stage of the purchasing process.[26] If it is a new buy for the manufacturer, you should be prepared to act as a consultant to the buyer, work with technical personnel, and expect a long time for a buying decision to be reached. However, if the manufacturer has bought the component part from you before (a straight or modified rebuy), you might emphasize a competitive price and a reliable supply in meetings with the purchasing agent.

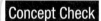
Concept Check

1. What one department is almost always represented by a person in the buying centre?

2. What are the three types of buying situations or buy classes?

CHARTING THE ORGANIZATIONAL BUYING PROCESS

Organizational buyers, like consumers, engage in a decision process when selecting products and services. As defined earlier in this chapter, organizational buying behaviour is the decision-making process that organizations use to establish the need for products and services and identify, evaluate, and choose among alternative brands and suppliers. There are important similarities and differences between the two decision-making processes. To better understand the nature of organizational buying behaviour, we first compare it with consumer buying behaviour and then describe an actual organizational purchase in detail.

Stages in the Organizational Buying Process

As shown in Figure 6–4 (and covered in Chapter 5), the five stages a student might use in buying a portable CD player also apply to organizational purchases. However, comparing the two right-hand columns in Figure 6–4 reveals some key differences. For example, when a portable CD player manufacturer buys earphones for its units from a supplier more individuals are involved, supplier capability becomes more important, and the postpurchase evaluation behaviour is more formalized.

The earphone-buying decision process is typical of the steps made by organizational buyers. Let's now examine in detail the decision-making process for a more complex product—machine vision systems.

STAGE IN THE BUYING DECISION PROCESS	CONSUMER PURCHASE: PORTABLE CD PLAYER FOR A STUDENT	ORGANIZATIONAL PURCHASE: EARPHONES FOR A PORTABLE CD PLAYER
Problem recognition	Student doesn't like the features of the portable CD player now owned and desires a new portable CD player.	Marketing research and sales departments observe that competitors are improving the earphones on their portable CD models. The firm decides to improve the earphones on its own new models, which will be purchased from an outside supplier.
Information search	Student uses past experience, that of friends, ads, the Internet, and *Consumer Reports* to collect information and uncover alternatives.	Design and production engineers draft specifications for earphones. The purchasing department identifies suppliers of portable CD player earphones.
Alternative evaluation	Alternative portable CD players are evaluated on the basis of important attributes desired in a portable CD player, and several stores are visited.	Purchasing and engineering personnel visit with suppliers and assess (1) facilities, (2) capacity, (3) quality control, and (4) financial status. They drop any suppliers not satisfactory on these factors.
Purchase decision	A specific brand of portable CD player is selected, the price is paid, and the student leaves the store.	They use (1) quality, (2) price, (3) delivery, and (4) technical capability as key buying criteria to select a supplier. Then they negotiate terms and award a contract.
Postpurchase behaviour	Student re-evaluates the purchase decision, may return the portable CD player to the store if it is unsatisfactory, and looks for supportive information to justify the purchase.	They evaluate suppliers using a formal vendor rating system and notify the supplier if earphones do not meet their quality standard. If the problem is not corrected, they drop the firm as a future supplier.

FIGURE 6–4

Comparing the stages in consumer and organizational purchases

Buying a Machine Vision System

Machine vision is widely regarded as one of the keys to the factory of the future. The chief elements of a machine vision system are its optics, light source, camera, video processor, and computer software. Vision systems are mainly used for product inspection. They are also becoming important as one of the chief elements in the information feedback loop of systems that control manufacturing processes. Vision systems, selling at around $5000, are mostly sold to original equipment manufacturers (OEMs) who incorporate them in still larger industrial automation systems that sell for $50 000 to $100 000.

Finding productive applications for machine vision involves the constant search for technology and designs that satisfy user needs. The buying process for machine vision components and assemblies is frequently a new buy because many machine vision systems contain elements that require some custom design. Let's track five purchasing stages that a company such as the Industrial Automation Division of Siemens, a large German industrial firm, would follow when purchasing components and assemblies for the machine vision systems it produces and installs.

Problem Recognition   Sales engineers constantly canvass industrial automation equipment users such as Ford Motor Company, Grumman Aircraft, and many Asian and European firms for leads on upcoming industrial automation projects. They also keep these firms current on Siemens' technology, products, and services. When a firm needing a machine vision capability identifies a project that would benefit from

MAKE–BUY DECISION
An evaluation of whether components and assemblies will be purchased from outside suppliers or built by the company itself.

www.siemens.com

VALUE ANALYSIS
A systematic appraisal of the design, quality, and performance of a product to reduce purchasing costs.

BIDDERS LIST
A list of firms believed to be qualified to supply a given item.

Siemens' expertise, company engineers typically work with the firm to determine the kind of system required to meet the customer's need.

After a contract is won, project personnel must often make a **make-buy decision**—an evaluation of whether components and assemblies will be purchased from outside suppliers or built by the company itself. (Siemens produces many components and assemblies.) When these items are to be purchased from outside suppliers, the company engages in a thorough supplier search and evaluation process.

Information Search   Companies such as Siemens employ a sophisticated process for identifying outside suppliers of components and assemblies. For standard items such as connectors, printed circuit boards, and components such as resistors and capacitors, the purchasing agent consults the company's purchasing databank, which contains information on hundreds of suppliers and thousands of products. All products in the databank have been prenegotiated as to price, quality, and delivery time, and many have been assessed using **value analysis**—a systematic appraisal of the design, quality, and performance of a product to reduce purchasing costs.

For one-of-a-kind components or assemblies such as new optics, cameras, and light sources, the company relies on its engineers to keep current on new developments in product technology. This information is often found in technical journals and industry magazines or at international trade shows where suppliers display their most recent innovations. In some instances, supplier representatives might be asked to make presentations to the buying centre at Siemens. Such a group often consists of a project engineer; several design, system, and manufacturing engineers; and a purchasing agent.

Alternative Evaluation   Three main buying criteria are used to select suppliers: price, performance, and delivery. Other important criteria include assurance that a supplier will not go out of business during the contractual period, assurance that the supplier will meet product quality and performance specifications, and service during the contractual period. Typically, two or three suppliers for each standard component and assembly are identified from a **bidders list**—a list of firms believed to be qualified to supply a given item. This list is generated from the company's purchasing databank as well as from engineering inputs. Specific items that are unique or one-of-a-kind may be obtained from a single supplier after careful evaluation by the buying centre.

Firms selected from the bidders list are sent a quotation request from the purchasing agent, describing the desired quantity, delivery date(s), and specifications of the components or assemblies. Suppliers are expected to respond within 30 days.

Purchase Decision   Unlike the short purchase stage in a consumer purchase, the period from supplier selection to order placement to product delivery can take several weeks or even months. Even after bids for components and assemblies are submitted, further negotiation concerning price, performance, and delivery terms is likely. Sometimes conditions related to warranties, indemnities, and payment schedules have to be agreed on. The purchase decision is further complicated by the fact that two or more suppliers of the same item might be awarded contracts. This practice can occur when large orders are requested. Furthermore, suppliers who are not chosen are informed why their bids were not selected.

Postpurchase Behaviour   As in the consumer purchase decision process, postpurchase evaluation occurs in the industrial purchase decision process, but it is formalized and often more sophisticated. All items purchased are examined in a formal product-acceptance process. The performance of the supplier is also monitored and recorded. Performance on past contracts determines a supplier's chances of being asked to bid on future purchases, and poor performance may result in a supplier's name being dropped from the bidders list.

The preceding example of an organizational purchase suggests four lessons for marketers to increase their chances of selling products and services to organizations.

The purchase of machine vision systems involves a lengthy organizational buying process.

Firms selling to organizations must (1) understand the organization's needs, (2) get on the right bidders list, (3) find the right people in the buying centre, and (4) provide value to the organizational buyer.

Concept Check

1. What is a make-buy decision?

2. What is a bidders list?

ONLINE BUYING IN ORGANIZATIONAL MARKETS

Organizational buying behaviour and business marketing continues to evolve with the application of Internet/Web technology. Organizations dwarf consumers in terms of both online transactions made and purchase volume.[27] In fact, organizational buyers account for about 80 percent of the total worldwide dollar value of all online transactions. It is projected that online organizational buyers around the world will purchase between \$6 trillion and \$7.5 trillion worth of products and services by 2005. Organizational buyers in the United States will account for about 60 percent of these purchases.

Prominence of Online Buying in Organizational Markets

Online buying in organizational markets is prominent for three major reasons.[28] First, organizational buyers depend heavily on timely supplier information that describes product availability, technical specifications, application uses, price, and delivery schedules. This information can be conveyed quickly via Internet/Web technology. Second, this technology has been shown to substantially reduce buyer order processing costs. At General Electric, online buying has cut the cost of a transaction from \$50 to \$100 per purchase to about \$5. Third, business marketers have found that Internet/Web technology can reduce marketing costs, particularly sales and advertising expense, and broaden their potential customer base for many types of products and services. For these reasons, online buying is popular in all three kinds of organizational markets. For example, airlines order more than \$400 million in spare parts from the Boeing Website each year. Customers of Provigo, a large Canadian food wholesaler, can buy online, while provincial and municipal governments across Canada also engage in online purchasing.

Online buying can assume many forms. Organizational buyers can purchase directly from suppliers. For instance, a buyer might acquire a dozen desktop photo-copiers from Xerox.ca. This same buyer might purchase office furniture and supplies through a reseller such as Staples at Staples.ca. Increasingly, organizational buyers and business marketers are using e-marketplaces and online auctions to purchase and sell products and services.

E-Marketplaces: Virtual Organizational Markets

E-MARKETPLACES
Online trading communities that bring together buyers and supplier organizations.

A significant development in organizational buying has been the creation and growth of online trading communities, called **e-marketplaces**, which bring together buyer and supplier organizations.[29] These online communities go by a variety of names, including *B2B exchanges* and *e-hubs*, and make possible the real-time exchange of information, money, products, and services. E-marketplaces will account for almost one-half of all online organizational purchases in 2005.

E-marketplaces can be independent trading communities or private exchanges.[30] Independent e-marketplaces typically focus on a specific product or service or serve a particular industry. They act as a neutral third party and provide an Internet/Web tech-nology trading platform and a centralized market that enables exchanges between buyers and sellers. Independent e-marketplaces charge a fee for their service and exist in settings that have one or more of the following features: (1) thousands of geographically dispersed buyers and sellers, (2) volatile prices caused by demand and supply fluctua-tions, (3) time sensitivity due to perishable offerings and changing technologies, and (4) easily comparable offerings among a variety of suppliers. Well-known independent e-marketplaces include e-Steel (steel products), PaperExchange (paper products), Plastic-Net (plastics), Altra Energy (electricity, natural gas, and crude oil), and MRO.com (maintenance, repair, and operating supplies). Small-business buyers and sellers in particular benefit from independent e-marketplaces. These e-marketplaces offer them an economical way to expand their customer base and reduce the cost of purchased products and services. Large companies tend to favour private exchanges that link them with their network of qualified suppliers and customers.[31]

Private exchanges focus on streamlining a company's purchase transactions with its suppliers and customers. Like independent e-marketplaces, they provide a technology trading platform and central marketplace for buyer–seller interactions. They are not a neutral third party, however, but represent the interests of their owners. For example, Worldwide Retail Exchange performs the buying function for its 11 members, including Target, Safeway, and Tesco, a large British supermarket chain. Rooster.com, formed by DuPont, Cargill, Inc., and Cenex Harvest States Cooperatives, sells pesticides and her-bicides to farmers.[32] The most ambitious e-marketplace yet devised is Covisint, which is expected to revolutionize the worldwide automotive industry. Owned principally by General Motors, Ford, and DaimlerChrysler, Covisint will be the world's largest B2B exchange when it is fully operational and is expected to process U.S.$750 billion in transactions annually. Learn about Covisint in the accompanying Web Link.[33]

Online Auctions in Organizational Markets

Online auctions have grown in popularity among organizational buyers and business marketers. Many e-marketplaces offer this service. Two general types of auctions are common: (1) a traditional auction, and (2) a reverse auction.[34] Figure 6–5 shows how buyer and seller participants and price behaviour differs by type of auction. Let's look at each auction type more closely to understand the implications of each for buyers and sellers.

TRADITIONAL AUCTION
A seller puts an item up for sale and would-be buyers are invited to bid in competition with each other.

In a **traditional auction** a seller puts an item up for sale and would-be buyers are invited to bid in competition with each other. As more would-be buyers become involved, there is an upward pressure on bid prices. Why? Bidding is sequential.

WEB LINK

Covisint: Building the World's Largest E-Marketplace

The origins of the Covisint name speak volumes about what will be the world's largest e-marketplace. Covisint, which gets its name from *Co*operation, *Vis*ion, and *Int*egration, will transform not only the automotive industry but also how large companies will do business with one another in the future.

Covisint is a global enterprise developed by automakers DaimlerChrysler, Ford Motor Company, General Motors, Nissan, and Renault along with technology partners Commerce One and Oracle. Visit Covisint at www.covisint.com. As you will see, online buying is an important functionality and is featured at the procurement link on the Covisint Website. What are the principal benefits to buyers and sellers made possible by Covisint? What other functions will Covisint provide buyers and sellers?

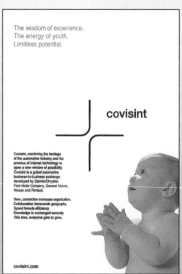

FIGURE 6–5
How buyer and seller participants and price behaviour differs by type of online auction.

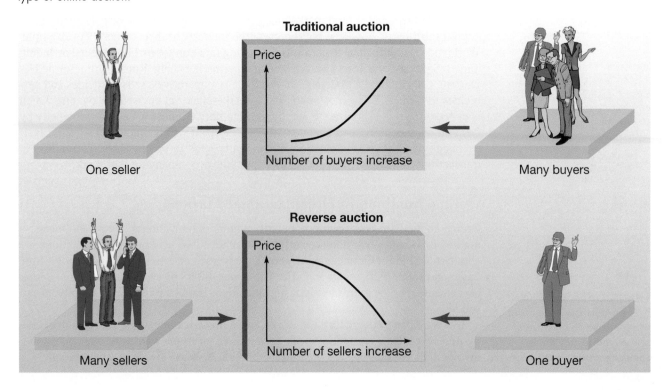

Prospective buyers observe the bids of others and decide whether to increase the bid price. The auction ends when a single bidder remains and "wins" the item with its highest price. Traditional auctions are frequently used to dispose of excess merchandise. For example, Dell Computer sells surplus, refurbished, or closeout computer merchandise at its Dellauction.com Website.

A reverse auction works in the opposite direction from a traditional auction. In a **reverse auction**, a buyer communicates a need for a product or service and would-be suppliers are invited to bid in competition with each other. As more would-be suppliers become involved, there is a downward pressure on bid prices for the buyer's business. Why? Like traditional auctions, bidding is sequential; prospective suppliers observe the bids of others and decide whether to decrease the bid price. The auction ends when a single bidder remains and "wins" the business with its lowest price. Reverse auctions benefit organizational buyers by reducing the cost of their purchases. As an example, General Electric's Global eXchange Services unit, which runs online reverse auctions for the company, claims it recently saved $780 million on the purchase of $6 billion worth of products and services.[35]

Clearly, buyers welcome the lower prices generated by reverse auctions. Some suppliers also favour reverse auctions because it gives them a chance to capture business that they might not have otherwise had due to a long-standing purchase relationship between the buyer and another supplier. On the other hand, suppliers argue that reverse auctions put too much emphasis on prices, discourage consideration of other important buying criteria, and threaten supply partnership opportunities.[36]

REVERSE AUCTION
A buyer communicates a need for a product or service and would-be suppliers are invited to bid in competition with each other.

Concept Check

1. What are e-marketplaces?

2. In general, which type of online auction creates upward pressure on bid prices and which type creates downward pressure on bid prices?

SUMMARY

1 Organizational buyers are divided into three different markets: industrial, reseller, and government.

2 Measuring industrial, reseller, and government markets is an important first step for firms interested in gauging the size of one, two, or all three markets. The North American Industry Classification System (NAICS) is a convenient starting point to begin this process.

3 Many aspects of organizational buying behaviour are different from consumer buying behaviour. Some key differences between the two include demand characteristics, size of the order or purchase, number of potential buyers, buying objectives, buying criteria, buyer–seller relationships and partnerships, and multiple buying influences within companies.

4 The buying centre concept is central to understanding organizational buying behaviour. Knowing who composes the buying centre and the roles they play in making purchase decisions is important in marketing to organizations. The buying centre usually includes a person from the purchasing department and possibly representatives from R&D, engineering, and production, depending on what is being purchased. These people can play one or more of five roles in a purchase decision: user, influencer, buyer, decider, or gatekeeper.

5 The three types of buying situations, or buy classes, are the straight rebuy, the modified rebuy, and the new buy. These form a scale ranging from a routine reorder to a totally new purchase.

6 The stages in an organizational buying decision are the same as those for consumer buying decisions: problem recognition, information search, alternative evaluation, purchase decision, and postpurchase behaviour. Examples of organizational purchases described are earphones by a portable CD manufacturer and machine vision technology components by an electronics manufacturer.

7 To market more effectively to organizations, a firm must try to understand the organization's needs, get on the right bidders list, reach the right people in the buying centre, and provide value to organizational buyers.

8 Online buying is prevalent in industrial, reseller, and government markets. E-marketplaces will account for almost one-half of all organizational purchases in 2005. Online auctions are also becoming commonplace.

KEY TERMS AND CONCEPTS

bidders list p. 159
business marketing p. 148
buy classes p. 156
buying centre p. 155
derived demand p. 151
e-marketplaces p. 161
government units p. 149
industrial firms p. 148
ISO 9000 standards p. 153
make-buy decision p. 159
North American Industry Classification System (NAICS) p. 149

organizational buyers p. 148
organizational buying behaviour p. 151
organizational buying criteria p. 153
reciprocity p. 154
resellers p. 148
reverse auction p. 163
reverse marketing p. 154
supply partnership p. 154
traditional auction p. 161
value analysis p. 159

INTERNET EXERCISE

www.mcgrawhill.ca/college/berkowitz

The North American Industry Classification System (NAICS) structures industrial sectors into their component industries. The NAICS can be accessed at www.statcan.ca/english/Subjects/Standard. A person only has to click NAICS codes to obtain industry breakdowns.

You have been hired by a large industrial firm as a market analyst. Your first assignment is to identify the kinds of companies and services that fall into the Utilities Sector (code 22) and make a presentation to senior management. Your immediate supervisor advises you that senior management would be interested in the following information:

1 How many three-, four-, five-, and six-digit industries exist in the Utilities Sector?

2 How is the sector structured? That is, how would you display this subsector using the framework shown in Figure 6–1?

Want to get better grades, find tips on how to study more effectively, and stay up to date with happenings in the world of marketing? Visit the Online Learning Centre for practice tests, Study Smart software, and much more! www.mcgrawhill.ca/college/berkowitz
Interested in finding out what marketing looks like in the real world? *Marketing Magazine* is just a click away on your OLC! Visit www.mcgrawhill.ca/college/berkowitz

APPLYING MARKETING CONCEPTS AND PERSPECTIVES

1 Describe the major differences among industrial firms, resellers, and government units in Canada.

2 Explain how the North American Industry Classification System (NAICS) might be helpful in understanding industrial, reseller, and government markets, and discuss the limitations inherent in this system.

3 List and discuss the key characteristics of organizational buying that make it different from consumer buying.

4 What is a buying centre? Describe the roles assumed by people in a buying centre and what useful questions should be raised to guide any analysis of the structure and behaviour of a buying centre.

5 Effective marketing is of increasing importance in today's competitive environment. How can firms more effectively market to organizations?

6 A firm that is marketing multi-million dollar wastewater treatment systems to cities has been unable to sell a new type of system. To date, the firm's marketing efforts have been directed to city purchasing departments to be included on approved bidders lists. Talks with city-employed personnel have indicated that the new system is very different from current systems and therefore city sanitary and sewer department engineers, directors of these two departments, and city council members are unfamiliar with the workings of the system. Consulting engineers, hired by cities to work on the engineering and design features of these systems and paid on a percentage of system cost, are also reluctant to favour the new system. (*a*) What roles do the various individuals play in the purchase process for a wastewater treatment system? (*b*) How could the firm improve the marketing effort behind the new system?

VIDEO CASE 6–1 Lands' End: Where Buyers Rule

Organizational buying is a part of the marketing effort that influences every aspect of business at Lands' End. As Senior Vice President of Operations Phil Schaecher explains, "When we talk about purchasing at Lands' End, most people think of the purchase of merchandise for resale, but we buy many other things aside from merchandise, everything from the simplest office supply to the most sophisticated piece of material-handling equipment." As a result, Lands' End has developed a sophisticated approach to organizational buying, which is one of the keys to its incredible success.

THE COMPANY

The company started by selling sailboat equipment, duffle bags, rainsuits, and sweaters from a basement location in Chicago's old tannery district. In its first catalogue, the company name was printed with a typing error—with the apostrophe in the wrong place—but the fledgling company couldn't afford to correct and reprint it. So, ever since the company name has been Lands' End—with a misplaced apostrophe!

When the company outgrew its Chicago location, founder Gary Comer relocated it to Dodgeville, Wisconsin, where he had fallen in love with the rolling hills and changing seasons. The original business ideas were simple: "Sell only things we believe in, ship every order the day it arrives, and unconditionally guarantee everything." Over time the company developed eight principles of doing business:

1. Never reduce the quality of a product to make it cheaper.
2. Price products fairly and honestly.
3. Accept any return for any reason.
4. Ship items in stock the day after the order is received.
5. What is best for the customer is best for Lands' End.
6. Place contracts with manufacturers who are cost-conscious and efficient.
7. Operate efficiently.
8. Keep overhead low.

These principles became the guidelines for the company's dedicated local employees and helped create extraordinary expectations from Lands' End customers.

Today, Lands' End is one of the world's largest direct merchants, with annual sales of traditionally styled clothing, luggage, and home products exceeding $1.4 billion. The products are offered through catalogues, the Internet, and retail stores. Last year, Lands' End distributed more than 260 million catalogues designed for specific segments, including *The Lands' End Catalog, Lands' End Men, Lands' End Women, Lands' End Kids, Lands' End for School, Lands' End Home,* and

Lands' End Corporate. In a typical day, catalogue shoppers place more than 40 000 telephone calls to the company. The Lands' End Website (www.landsend.com) also offers every Lands' End product and a wide variety of Internet shopping innovations such as a 3-D model customized to each customer (called My Virtual Model™); a "personal shopper," to suggest products that match the consumer's preferences; and a feature that allows customers to "chat" online directly with a customer service representative. Lands' End also operates 19 stores in the United States, the United Kingdom, and Japan.

The company's goal is to please customers with the highest levels of quality and service in the industry. Lands' End maintains the high quality of its products through several important activities. For example, the company works directly with mills and manufacturers to retain control of quality and design. "The biggest difference between Lands' End and some other retailers or catalogue businesses is that we actually design all the product here and we do all the specifications. Therefore, the manufacturer is building that product directly to our specs, we are not buying off of somebody else's line," explains Joan Mudget, Vice President of Quality Assurance. In addition, Lands' End tests its products for comfort and fit by paying real people (local residents and children) to "wear-test" and "fit-test" all types of garments.

Service has also become an important part of the Lands' End reputation. Customers expect prompt, professional service at every step—initiating the order, making selections, shipping, and follow-up (if necesary). Some of the ways Lands' End meets these expectations include offering the simplest guarantee in the industry—"Guaranteed. Period."—toll-free telephone lines open 24 hours a day, 364 days a year, continuous product training for telephone representatives, and 1 day shipping. Lands' End operators even send personal responses to all e-mail messages—approximately 230 000 per year!

ORGANIZATIONAL BUYING AT LANDS' END

The sixth Lands' End business principle (described above) is accomplished through the company's organizational buying process. First, its buyers specify fabric quality, construction, and sizing standards, which typically exceed industry standards, for current and potential Lands' End products. Then the buyers literally search around the world for the best possible source of fabrics and products. Once a potential supplier is identified, one of the company's 150 quality assurance personnel makes an information-gathering visit. The purpose of the visit is to understand the supplier's values, to assess four criteria (economic, quality, service, and vendor), and to determine if the Lands' End standards can be achieved.

Lands' End evaluations of potential suppliers lead to the selection of what the company hopes will become long-term partners. As Mudget explains, "When we're looking for new manufacturers we are looking for the long term. I think one of the most interesting things is we're not out there looking for new vendors every year to fill the same products." In fact, Lands' End believes that the term "supplier" does not adequately describe the importance the company places on the relationships. Lands' End suppliers are viewed as allies, supporters, associates, colleagues, and stakeholders in the future of the company. Once an alliance is formed the product specifications and the performance on those specifications are regularly evaluated.

Lands' End buyers face a variety of buying situations. Straight rebuys involve reordering an existing product—such as shipping boxes—without evaluating or changing specifications. Modified rebuys involve changing some aspect of a previously ordered product—such as the collar of a knit shirt—based on input from consumers, retailers, or other people involved in the purchase decision. Finally, new buys involve first-time purchases—such as Lands' End's addition of men's suits to its product line. The complexity of the process can vary with the type of purchase. Schaecher explains, "As you get more complicated in the purchase there are more things you look at to decide on a vendor."

FUTURE CHALLENGES FOR LANDS' END

Lands' End faces several challenges as it pursues improvements in its organizational buying process. First, new technologies offer opportunities for fast, efficient, and accurate communication with suppliers. Ed Smidebush, General Inventory Manager, describes a new system at Lands' End: "Our quick response system is a computerized system where we transmit electronically to our vendors each Sunday night, forecast information as well as stock positions and purchase order information so that on Monday morning this information will be incorporated directly into their manufacturing reports so that they can prioritize their production." Occasionally Lands' End must work with its suppliers to improve their technology and information system capabilities.

Another challenge for Lands' End is to anticipate changes in consumer interests. While it has many years of experience with retail consumers, preferences for colours, fabrics, and styles change frequently, requiring buyers to constantly monitor the marketplace. In addition, Lands' End's more recent offerings to corporate customers require constant attention "because business customers' wants and incentives, and the environment in which they're shopping, are very different from consumers at home," explains marketing manager Hilary Kleese.

Finally, Lands' End must anticipate the quantities of each of its products consumers are likely to order. To do this, historical information is used to develop forecasts. One of the best tests of their forecast accuracy is the holiday season, when Lands' End receives more than 100,000 calls each day. Having the right products available is important because, as every employee knows from Principle 4, every order must be shipped the day after it is received!

Questions

1 Who is likely to comprise the buying centre in the decision to select a new supplier for Lands' End? Which of the buying centre members are likely to play the roles of users, influencers, buyers, deciders, and gatekeepers?

2 Which stages of the organizational buying decision process does Lands' End follow when it selects a new supplier? What selection criteria do the company utilize in the process?

3 Describe purchases Lands' End buyers typically face in each of the three buying situations: straight rebuy, modified rebuy, new buy.

A MATCH MADE IN HEAVEN.

PRODUCED FROM GRAPES, NATURALLY FROZEN ON THE VINE DURING CANADA'S FRIGID WINTERS, INNISKILLIN VQA ICEWINE IS BLESSED WITH AN ENCHANTING AROMA, RICH GOLDEN COLOUR AND A VELVETY SMOOTH TASTE THAT LINGERS ON THE PALATE. DELICATELY COMPLEX WITH FLAVOURS OF APRICOT, LYCHEE, HONEY AND EXOTIC SPICES, IT TANTALIZES ON ITS OWN. EQUALLY IMPRESSIVE IS HOW WELL IT PAIRS WITH AND ENHANCES A DIVERSE RANGE OF EXTRAORDINARY DESSERTS. ONE SIP BECOMES A REVELATION AND ILLUSTRATES WHY INNISKILLIN ICEWINE RANKS AMONG THE WORLD'S FINEST WINES.

Inniskillin
ICEWINE

ONE OF THE WORLD'S
GREAT WINES

CHAPTER 7

REACHING GLOBAL MARKETS

AFTER READING THIS CHAPTER YOU SHOULD BE ABLE TO:

- Describe the nature and scope of world trade from a global perspective and its implications for Canada.

- Explain the effects of economic protectionism and the implications of economic integration for global marketing practices.

- Understand the importance of environmental factors (cultural, economic, and political) in shaping global marketing efforts.

- Describe alternative approaches firms use to enter and compete in global markets.

- Identify specific challenges marketers face when crafting worldwide marketing programs.

COMPETING IN THE GLOBAL MARKETPLACE

Canadian marketers cannot ignore the vast potential of global markets. Over 99 percent of the world's population lives outside of Canada, and collectively these potential customers possess tremendous purchasing power. Not only are global markets substantial, but many are also growing faster than comparable markets in Canada—a fact not lost on both large and small global-minded Canadian companies.

Successful Canadian marketers have responded to the challenges and opportunities in the global marketplace. They have satisfied the needs of a discriminating global consumer who increasingly purchases goods and services on the basis of value and quality. For example, Canada's Inniskillin Wines in Niagara-on-the-Lake (www.inniskillin.com) has achieved much success in European markets with its VQA Icewine. This is because the product is positioned as a unique, high-quality dessert beverage and is targeted toward an upscale and discerning European wine consumer who is often willing to pay $50 for a 375-mL bottle.[1]

Canadian marketers have also capitalized on the trend toward formal economic integration and free trade among nations throughout the world. For example, the North American Free Trade Agreement (NAFTA) has opened up the Mexican market for Canadian companies and many have found opportunities there in a variety of sectors including telecommunications and engineering services. Finally, Canadian marketers have leveraged the emergence of a networked global marketspace by offering goods and services to consumers anywhere at any time.

Pursuit of global markets by Canadian and foreign marketers ultimately results in world trade. The purpose of this chapter is to describe the nature and scope of world trade and to highlight challenges involved in global marketing.

DYNAMICS OF WORLD TRADE

The dollar value of world trade has more than doubled in the past decade and will exceed $11.5 trillion in 2005. Manufactured goods and commodities account for 75 percent of world trade. Service industries, including telecommunications, transportation, insurance, education, banking, and tourism, represent the other 25 percent of world trade.

World Trade Flows

All nations and regions of the world do not participate equally in world trade. World trade flows reflect interdependencies among industries, countries, and regions and manifest themselves in country, company, industry, and regional exports and imports.

Global Perspective   Figure 7–1 shows the estimated dollar value of exports and imports among North American countries, Western Europe, Asian/Pacific Rim countries, and the rest of the world, including intraregional (or intratrade) trade flows.[2] The United States, Western Europe, Canada, and Japan together account for two-thirds of world trade.[3]

Not all trade involves the exchange of money for goods or services. In a world where 70 percent of all countries do not have convertible currencies or where

FIGURE 7–1
Illustrative world trade flows (billions of dollars) for manufactured goods and commodities

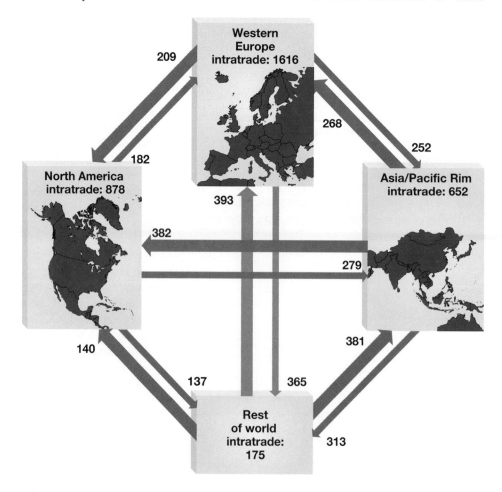

COUNTERTRADE
The practice of using barter rather than money for making international sales.

www.volvo.com

TRADE FEEDBACK EFFECT
A country's imports affect its exports and exports affect its imports.

GROSS DOMESTIC PRODUCT
The monetary value of all goods and services produced in a country during one year.

BALANCE OF TRADE
The difference between the monetary value of a nation's exports and imports.

www.inniskillin.com

www.bombardier.com

Team Canada Inc.
www.exportsource.ca

government-owned enterprises lack sufficient cash or credit for imports, other means of payment are used. An estimated 15 to 20 percent of world trade involves **countertrade**, the practice of using barter rather than money for making global sales.

Countertrade is popular with many Eastern European nations, Russia, and Asian countries. For example, the Malaysian government recently exchanged 20 000 tons of rice for an equivalent amount of Philippine corn. Volvo of North America delivered automobiles to the Siberian police force when Siberia had no cash to pay for them. It accepted payment in oil, which it then sold for cash to pay for media advertising.[4]

A global perspective on world trade views exports and imports as complementary economic flows: A country's imports affect its exports and exports affect its imports. Every nation's imports arise from the exports of other nations. As the exports of one country increase, its national output and income rise, which, in turn, leads to an increase in the demand for imports. This nation's greater demand for imports stimulates the exports of other countries. Increased demand for exports of other nations energizes their economic activity, resulting in higher national income, which stimulates their demand for imports. This phenomenon is called the **trade feedback effect** and is one argument for free trade among nations.

Canadian Perspective   Canada's **gross domestic product** (GDP), the monetary value of all goods and services produced in a country during one year, is valued at almost $1 trillion. Canada exports a significant percentage of the goods and services it produces. In fact, it exports almost 45 percent of GDP, making it an important trading nation.[5]

The difference between the monetary value of a nation's exports and imports is called the **balance of trade**. When a country's exports exceed its imports, it incurs a surplus in its balance of trade. When imports exceed exports, a deficit has occurred. Canada maintains an overall surplus in its balance of trade at this time.

Almost every Canadian is affected by Canada's trading activity. The effects vary from the products we buy (Samsung computers from Korea, Waterford crystal from Ireland, Lindemans wine from Australia) to those we sell (Moosehead beer to Sweden, Inniskillin ice wines to the EU, and Bombardier aircraft to Norway) and the additional jobs and improved standard of living that can result from world trade.

World trade flows to and from Canada reflect demand and supply interdependencies for goods and services among nations and industries. While Canada trades with dozens of other countries, the three largest importers of Canadian goods and services are the United States (accounting for over 80 percent), Japan, and the European Union (EU). These countries are also the top three exporters to Canada. The EU and Japan enjoy trade surpluses with our country, while the United States incurs a trade deficit.[6]

Trade is so important to Canada that it is one of the federal government's key priorities. It is so critical to the growth of the Canadian economy that the government established what it calls Team Canada Inc. (TCI), a network of more than 20 federal departments and agencies that work to help Canadian firms find new global markets and assist them in competing in those markets.

Competitive Advantage of Nations

As companies in many industries find themselves competing against foreign competitors at home and abroad, government policy makers around the world are increasingly asking why some companies and industries in a country succeed globally while others lose ground or fail. Michael Porter suggests a "diamond" to explain a nation's competitive advantage and why some industries and firms become world leaders.[7] He identified four key elements, which appear in Figure 7–2:

FIGURE 7–2
Porter's "diamond" of national competitive advantage

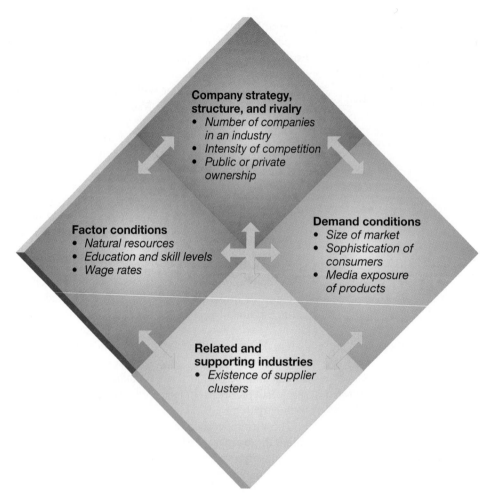

1. *Factor conditions.* These reflect a nation's ability to turn its natural resources, education, and infrastructure into a competitive advantage. Consider Holland, which exports 59 percent of the world's cut flowers. The Dutch lead the world in the cut-flower industry because of their research in flower cultivation, packaging, and shipping—not because of their weather.

2. *Demand conditions.* These include both the number and sophistication of domestic customers for an industry's product. Japan's sophisticated consumers demand quality in their TVs and radios, thereby making Japan's producers such as Sony, Sanyo, Matsushita, and Hitachi among the world leaders in the electronics industry.

3. *Related and supporting industries.* Firms and industries seeking leadership in global markets need clusters of world-class suppliers that accelerate innovation. The German leadership in scientific and industrial instrumentation relates directly to the cluster of supporting German precision engineering suppliers.

4. *Company strategy, structure, and rivalry.* These factors include the conditions governing the way a nation's businesses are organized and managed, along with the intensity of domestic competition. The Italian shoe industry has become a world leader because of intense domestic competition among firms such as MAB, Bruno Magli, and Rossimoda, which has made shoes for Christian Dior and Anne Klein Couture.

In Porter's study, case histories of firms in more than 100 industries were analyzed. While the strategies employed by the most successful global competitors were different in many respects, a common theme emerged—a firm that succeeds in global markets has first succeeded in intense domestic competition. Hence competitive advantage for global firms grows out of relentless, continuing improvement, innovation, and change.

Sony and Bruno Magli have succeeded in the global marketplace as well as in their domestic markets.

It is important to note, however, that it is not essential to be a giant company to gain benefits in global markets. Numerous small firms succeed in foreign niche markets or by utilizing unique products or positioning, licences, or technology. For example, Canadian icewines are achieving success in European markets because they are positioned as unique and costly dessert beverages for upscale consumers. In fact, Porter's study for the Canadian government on Canada's global competitiveness recommended, among other things, that Canadian firms should do more in terms of competing on the basis of unique products and services rather than with price-oriented commodities. He believes that by investing more in R&D, and enhancing domestic competition, Canadian firms will improve their global competitiveness.[8]

Concept Check

1. What is the trade feedback effect?

2. What variables influence why some companies and industries in a country succeed globally while others lose ground or fail?

EMERGENCE OF A BORDERLESS ECONOMIC WORLD

Four trends in the past decade have significantly affected world trade. One trend has been a gradual decline of economic protectionism exercised by individual countries. The second trend is apparent in the formal economic integration and free trade among nations. A third trend is evident in global competition among global companies for global consumers. The fourth trend is the emergence of a networked global marketspace.

Decline of Economic Protectionism

PROTECTIONISM
The practice of shielding one or more sectors of a country's economy from foreign competition through the use of tariffs or quotas.

Protectionism is the practice of shielding one or more sectors of a country's economy from foreign competition through the use of tariffs or quotas. The economic argument for protectionism is that it preserves jobs, protects a nation's political security, discourages economic dependency on other countries, and encourages the development of domestic industries. Read the accompanying Ethics and Social Responsibility Alert and ask yourself if protectionism has an ethical and social responsibility dimension.

Tariffs and quotas discourage world trade as depicted in Figure 7–3. **Tariffs**, which are a government tax on goods or services entering a country, primarily serve to raise prices on imports. For example, the average tariff on manufactured goods in industrialized countries is four percent.[9]

TARIFF
A government tax on goods or services entering a country primarily serving to raise prices on imports.

The effect of tariffs on world trade and consumer prices is substantial. Consider rice exports to Japan. Experts claims that if the Japanese rice market were opened to imports by lowering tariffs, lower prices would save Japanese consumers $8.4 billion annually. Similarly, tariffs imposed on bananas by Western European countries cost consumers $4.2 billion a year. Ecuador (the world's largest banana exporter), Mexico, Guatemala, and Honduras have negotiated a reduction in the levy by 2006.[10]

QUOTA
A restriction placed on the amount of a product allowed to enter or leave a country.

A **quota** is a restriction placed on the amount of a product allowed to enter or leave a country. Quotas can be mandated or voluntary and may be legislated or negotiated by governments. Import quotas seek to guarantee domestic industries access to a certain percentage of their domestic market. The best-known quota concerns the mandatory or voluntary limits of foreign automobile sales in many countries. Quotas imposed by European countries make European cars 25 percent more expensive than similar models in Japan, costing European customers $56 billion per year. Less visible quotas apply to the importation of produce and electronics. Ultimately, consumers usually pay higher prices because of quotas.[11]

Every country engages in some form of protectionism. However, protectionism has declined over the past 50 years due in large part to the *General Agreement on Tariffs and Trade (GATT)*. This international treaty was intended to limit trade barriers and promote world trade through the reduction of tariffs, which it did. However, GATT did not explicitly address non-tariff trade barriers, such as quotas and world trade in services, which often sparked heated trade disputes between nations.

FIGURE 7–3
How protectionism affects world trade

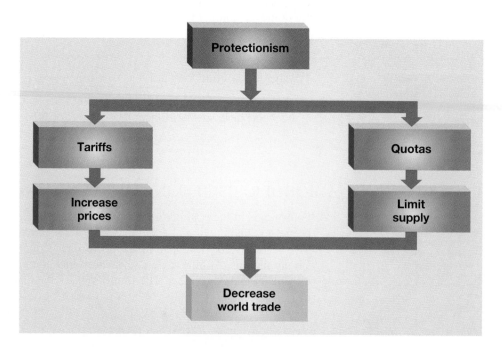

ETHICS AND SOCIAL RESPONSIBILITY ALERT

Global Ethics and Global Economics: The Case of Protectionism

World trade benefits from free and fair trade among nations. Nevertheless, governments of many countries continue to use tariffs and quotas to protect their various domestic industries. Why? Protectionism earns profits for domestic producers and tariff revenue for the government. There is a cost, however. For example, protectionist policies cost Japanese consumers billions annually. Canadian consumers also pay higher prices because of tariffs and other protective restrictions.

Sugar import quotas in the United States, automobile import quotas and banana import tariffs in many European countries, beer import tariffs in Canada, and rice import tariffs in Japan protect domestic industries but also interfere with world trade for these products. Regional trade agreements, such as those found in the provisions of the European Union and the North American Free Trade Agreement, may also pose a situation whereby member nations can obtain preferential treatment in quotas and tariffs whereas non-member nations cannot.

Protectionism, in its many forms, raises an interesting global ethical question. Is protectionism, no matter how applied, an ethical practice?

WORLD TRADE ORGANIZATION

A permanent institution that sets rules governing trade between its members through a panel of trade experts who (1) decide on trade disputes between members and (2) issue binding decisions.

World Trade Organization

www.wto.org

As a consequence, the major industrialized nations of the world formed the **World Trade Organization** (WTO) to address a broad array of world trade issues. There are over 140 WTO member countries, including Canada, which account for more than 90 percent of world trade. The WTO is a permanent institution that sets rules governing trade between its members through panels of trade experts who (1) decide on trade disputes between members and (2) issue binding decisions. The WTO reviews more than 200 disputes annually. For instance, the WTO denied Eastman Kodak's multi-million dollar damage claim that the Japanese government protected Fuji Photo from import competition. In another decision, the WTO allowed Britain, Ireland, and the European Union to reclassify U.S.-produced local area network (LAN) computer equipment as telecommunications gear. The new classification effectively doubled the import tariff on these U.S. goods.[12]

Rise of Economic Integration

In recent years a number of countries with similar economic goals have formed transnational trade groups or signed trade agreements for the purpose of promoting free trade among member nations and enhancing their individual economies. Two of the best-known examples are the European Union (or simply EU), and the North American Free Trade Agreement (NAFTA).

European Union

www.europa.eu.int

European Union   In 1993, 12 European countries effectively eliminated most of the barriers to the free flow of goods, services, capital, and labour across their borders. This event, after decades of negotiation, formed a single market composed of 375 million consumers. Original members of the European Union were Great Britain, Ireland, Denmark, Belgium, the Netherlands, Luxembourg, Germany, France, Italy, Greece, Portugal, and Spain. Austria, Finland, and Sweden joined the European Union in 1995, bringing its membership to 15 countries (see Figure 7–4). The Swiss have elected not to join the European Union.

The European Union creates abundant marketing opportunities because firms no longer find it necessary to market their products and services on a nation-by-nation basis. Rather, Pan-European marketing strategies are possible due to greater uniformity in product and packaging standards; fewer regulatory restrictions on transportation, advertising, and promotion imposed by countries; and removal of most tariffs that affect pricing practices.[13] For example, Colgate-Palmolive Company now markets its Colgate toothpaste with one formula and package across EU countries at one price.

FIGURE 7–4
The countries of the European Union in 2002.

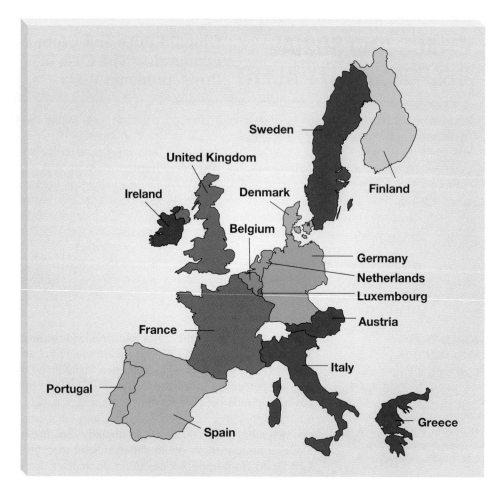

This practice was previously impossible because of different government regulations and tariffs. Europeanwide distribution from fewer locations is also feasible given open borders. French tire maker Michelin recently closed 180 of its European distribution centres and now uses just 20 to serve all EU countries. Pan-European marketing opportunities will benefit further given the issuance of the common currency, called the "euro."[14]

NAFTA

www.mac.doc.gov/nafta/

North American Free Trade Agreement   The North American Free Trade Agreement (NAFTA) became effective in 1994 and lifted many trade barriers between Canada, the United States, and Mexico. This agreement, when coupled with the 1988 U.S.–Canada Free Trade Agreement, established a North American trade arrangement similar to that of the European Union. The reduction of tariffs and other provisions of NAFTA promoted relatively free trade among Canada, the United States, and Mexico and created a marketplace with over 400 million consumers. Negotiations are under way to expand NAFTA to create a 34-country Free Trade Area of the Americas (FTAA) by 2005. This agreement would include Canada, the United States, Mexico, and Latin American and Caribbean countries.[15]

   NAFTA has stimulated trade flows among member nations as well as cross-border manufacturing and investment. For example, Whirlpool Corporation's Canadian subsidiary stopped making washing machines in Canada and moved that operation to Ohio. Whirlpool then shifted the production of household garbage compactors, kitchen ranges, and compact dryers to Canada. Ford invested $84 million in its Mexico City manufacturing plant to produce smaller cars and light trucks for global sales.

Other Free Trade Agreements   Other significant trade agreements include the Asia–Pacific Economic Cooperation (APEC) forum, which was established to promote economic integration around the Pacific Rim and to sustain economic growth. APEC currently has 21 members: Australia; Brunei Darussalam; Canada; Chile; People's Republic of China; Hong Kong; China; Indonesia; Japan; Republic of Korea; Malaysia; Mexico; New Zealand; Papua New Guinea; Peru; Republic of the Philippines; Russia; Singapore; Chinese Taipei; Thailand; USA; and Vietnam. APEC is a powerful trading group accounting for about half of the world's exports and imports. Another agreement is the ASEAN Free Trade Area (AFTA), established by the member nations of the Association of Southeast Asian Nations, which include Indonesia, Malaysia, Philippines, Singapore, Thailand, Brunei, Vietnam, Laos, Myanmar, and Cambodia.[16]

A New Reality: Global Competition among Global Companies for Global Consumers

The emergence of a largely borderless economic world has created a new reality for marketers of all shapes and sizes. Today, world trade is driven by global competition among global companies for global consumers.

GLOBAL COMPETITION
Exists when firms originate, produce, and market their products and services worldwide.

www.pepsico.com

STRATEGIC ALLIANCES
Agreements among two or more independent firms to cooperate for the purpose of achieving common goals.

www.nortelnetworks.com

Global Competition   **Global competition** exists when firms originate, produce, and market their products and services worldwide. The automobile, pharmaceutical, apparel, electronics, aerospace, and telecommunication fields represent well-known industries with sellers and buyers on every continent. Other industries that are increasingly global in scope include soft drinks, cosmetics, ready-to-eat cereals, snack chips, and retailing.

Global competition broadens the competitive landscape for marketers. The familiar "cola war" waged by Pepsi-Cola against Coca-Cola in Canada has been repeated around the world, including India, China, and Argentina. Procter & Gamble's Pampers and Kimberly-Clark's Huggies have taken their disposable diaper rivalry from Canada to Western Europe. Boeing and Europe's Airbus Industrie can be found vying for lucrative commercial aircraft contracts on virtually every continent.

Collaborative relationships also are becoming a common way to meet the demands of global competition. Global **strategic alliances** are agreements among two or more independent firms to cooperate for the purpose of achieving common goals such as a competitive advantage or customer value creation. For instance, several of the world's largest telecommunication equipment makers, including Ericsson (Sweden), Nortel (Canada), Siemens (Germany), and 3Com and Worldcom (two U.S. firms), have formed Juniper Networks, Inc., an alliance created to build devices to speed global Internet communications. General Mills and Nestlé of Switzerland created Cereal Partners Worldwide for the purpose of fine-tuning Nestlé's European cereal marketing and distributing General Mills cereals worldwide. This global alliance is expected to produce worldwide sales of more than $1.4 billion by 2005.[17] Another alliance you may be familiar with is Star Alliance, a global arrangement between more than a dozen major airlines including Air Canada, Air New Zealand, United, Lufthansa, and SAS (www.star-alliance.com).

Global Companies   Three types of companies populate and compete in the global marketplace: (1) international firms, (2) multinational firms, and (3) transnational firms.[18] All three employ people in different countries, and many have administrative, marketing, and manufacturing operations (often called divisions or subsidiaries) around the world. However, a firm's orientation toward and strategy for global markets and marketing defines the type of company it is or attempts to be.

An *international firm* engages in trade and marketing in different countries as an extension of the marketing strategy in its home country. Generally speaking, these firms market their existing products and services in other countries the same way

Pepsi-Cola is available in more than 190 countries.

MULTIDOMESTIC MARKETING STRATEGY
A multinational firm's offering as many different product variations, brand names, and advertising programs as countries in which it does business.

GLOBAL MARKETING STRATEGY
The practice of standardizing marketing activities when there are cultural similarities and adapting them when cultures differ.

www.gillette.com

GLOBAL CONSUMERS
Customer groups living in many countries or regions of the world who have similar needs or seek similar features and benefits from products or services.

www.ikea.com

they do in their home country. Avon, for example, successfully distributes its product line through direct selling in Asia, Europe, and South America, employing virtually the same marketing strategy used in North America.

A *multinational firm* views the world as consisting of unique parts and markets to each part differently. Multinationals use a **multidomestic marketing strategy**, which means that they have as many different product variations, brand names, and advertising programs as countries in which they do business. For example, Lever Europe—a division of Unilever—markets its fabric softener known as Snuggle in Canada in 10 different European countries under seven brand names, including Kuschelweich in Germany, Coccolino in Italy, and Mimosin in France. These products have different packages, different advertising programs, and occasionally different formulas.[19]

A *transnational firm* views the world as one market and emphasizes cultural similarities across countries or universal consumer needs and wants more than differences. Transnational marketers employ a **global marketing strategy**—the practice of standardizing marketing activities when there are cultural similarities and adapting them when cultures differ. This approach benefits marketers by allowing them to realize economies of scale from their production and marketing activities.

Global marketing strategies are popular among many business-to-business marketers such as Caterpillar and Komatsu (heavy construction equipment) and Texas Instruments, Intel, Hitachi, and Motorola (semiconductors). Consumer goods marketers such as Timex, Seiko, and Citizen (watches), Coca-Cola and Pepsi-Cola (cola soft drinks), Gillette (personal care products), L'Oréal (cosmetics) and McDonald's (fast foods) successfully execute this strategy.

Global Consumers   Global competition among global companies often focuses on the identification and pursuit of global consumers. **Global consumers** consist of customer groups living in many countries or regions of the world who have similar needs or seek similar features and benefits from products or services.[20] Evidence suggests the emergence of a global middle-income class, a youth market, and an elite segment, each consuming or using a common assortment of products and services regardless of geographic location. A variety of companies have capitalized on the global consumer. Whirlpool, Sony, and IKEA have benefited from the growing global middle-income-class desire for kitchen appliances, consumer electronics, and home

MARKETING NEWSNET

The Global Teenager: A Market of 500 Million Consumers with $100 Billion to spend

The "global teenager" market consists of 500 million 13- to 19-year-olds in Europe, North and South America, and industrialized nations of Asia who have experienced intense exposure to television (MTV broadcasts in more than 75 countries), movies, travel, the Internet, and global advertising by companies such as Benetton, Sony, Nike, and Coca-Cola. The similarities among teens in these countries are greater than their differences. For example, a global study of teenagers' rooms in 25 countries indicated it was difficult, if not impossible, to tell whether the rooms were in Vancouver, Mexico City, Tokyo, or Paris. Why? Teens buy a common gallery of products: Sony video games, Tommy Hilfiger apparel, Levi's blue jeans, Nike athletic shoes, Procter & Gamble Cover Girl makeup, and Clearasil facial medicine. Teenagers around the world appreciate fashion and music, and desire novelty and trendy designs and images.

furnishings, respectively. Levi's, Nike, Coca-Cola, and Benetton have tapped the global youth market, as described in the accompanying Marketing NewsNet.[21] DeBeers, Chanel, Gucci, and Rolls Royce successfully cater to the elite segment for luxury goods worldwide.

Emergence of a Networked Global Marketspace

The use of Internet/Web-based technology as a tool for exchanging goods, services, and information on a global scale is the fourth trend affecting world trade.[22] Some 785 million businesses, educational institutions, government agencies, and households worldwide are expected to have Internet access by 2005. The broad reach of this technology suggests that its potential for promoting world trade is huge. In fact, sales arising from electronic commerce are projected to represent 9 percent of world trade in 2005, up from about 1 percent in 2001.

The promise of a networked global marketspace is that it enables the exchange of goods, services, and information from companies *anywhere* to customers *anywhere*, at *any time* and at a lower cost. This promise has become a reality for buyers and sellers in industrialized countries that possess the telecommunications infrastructure necessary to support Internet/Web-based technology. In particular, companies engaged in business-to-business marketing have spurred the growth of global electronic commerce. Ninety percent of global electronic commerce revenue

Nestlé features multiple country and language Websites that customize content and communicate with consumers in their native tongue. The Website for Colombia shown here is an example.

arises from business-to-business transactions among a dozen countries in North America, Western Europe, and the Asia/Pacific Rim region. Industries that have benefited from this technology include industrial chemicals and controls; maintenance, repair, and operating supplies; computer and electronic equipment and components; aerospace parts; and agricultural and energy products. The United States, Canada, the United Kingdom, Germany, Sweden, Japan, and Taiwan are among the most active participants in worldwide business-to-business electronic commerce.

Marketers recognize that the networked global marketspace offers unprecedented access to prospective buyers on every continent. Companies that have successfully capitalized on this access manage multiple country and language Websites that customize content and communicate with consumers in their native tongue. Nestlé, the world's largest packaged food manufacturer, coffee roaster, and chocolate maker, is a case in point. The company operates 22 individual country Websites in 10 languages that span 5 continents. Amazon.com has Spanish-, Japanese-, French-, and German-language Websites.

Concept Check

1. What is protectionism?

2. The North American Free Trade Agreement was designed to promote free trade among which countries?

3. What is the difference between a multidomestic marketing strategy and a global marketing strategy?

A GLOBAL ENVIRONMENTAL SCAN

Global companies conduct continuing environmental scans of the five sets of environmental factors described earlier in Figure 3–1 (social, economic, technological, competitive, and regulatory forces). This section focuses on three kinds of uncontrollable environmental variables—cultural, economic, and political-regulatory variables—that affect global marketing practices in strikingly different ways than those in domestic markets.

CROSS-CULTURAL ANALYSIS
The study of similarities and differences among consumers in two or more nations or societies.

Cultural Diversity

Marketers must be sensitive to the cultural underpinnings of different societies if they are to initiate and consummate mutually beneficial exchange relationships with global consumers. A necessary step in this process is **cross-cultural analysis**, which involves the study of similarities and differences among consumers in two or more nations or societies.[23] A thorough cross-cultural analysis involves an understanding of and an appreciation for the values, customs, symbols, and language of other societies.

VALUES
Personally or socially preferable modes of conduct or states of existence that are enduring.

Values   A society's **values** represent personally or socially preferable modes of conduct or states of existence that are enduring. Understanding and working with these aspects of a society are important factors in successful global marketing. For example,

- McDonald's does not sell hamburgers in its restaurants in India because the cow is considered sacred by almost 85 percent of the population. Instead, McDonald's sells the McMaharajah: two all-mutton patties, special sauce, lettuce, cheese, pickles, onions on a sesame-seed bun.
- Germans have not been overly receptive to the use of credit cards such as Visa or MasterCard and instalment debt to purchase goods and services. Indeed, the German word for debt, *Schuld,* is the same as the German word for guilt.

These examples illustrate how cultural values can influence behaviour in different societies. Cultural values become apparent in the personal values of individuals that affect their attitudes and beliefs and the importance assigned to specific behaviours and attributes of goods and services. These personal values affect consumption-specific values, such as the use of instalment debt by Germans, and product-specific values, such as the importance assigned to credit card interest rates.

CUSTOMS
Norms and expectations about the way people do things in a specific country.

Customs   **Customs** are the norms and expectations about the way people do things in a specific country. Clearly customs can vary significantly from country to country. For example, 3M Company executives were perplexed when the company's Scotch-Brite floor-cleaning product initially produced lukewarm sales in the Philippines. When a Filipino employee explained that consumers there customarily clean floors by pushing coconut shells around with their feet, 3M changed the shape of the pad to a foot and sales soared! Some other customs are unusual to Canadians. Consider, for example, that in France men wear more than twice the number of cosmetics than women do and that Japanese women give Japanese men chocolates on Valentine's Day.

Customs also relate to nonverbal behaviour of individuals in different cultural settings.[24] For example, in many European countries it is considered impolite not to have both hands on the table in business meetings. A simple gesture in a commercial such as pointing a finger is perfectly acceptable in Western culture, but is perceived as an insult in Middle and Far Eastern countries. Direct eye contact is viewed positively in North and Latin America but negatively in Japan. Casual touching is also inappropriate in Japan, while men hold hands in Middle Eastern countries as a sign of friendship. Business executives in Japan like to hold their opinions, listen longer, and pause before responding in meetings. Sometimes the silence is misread by North American executives as their being nonresponsive.

CULTURAL SYMBOLS
Things that represent ideas and concepts.

SEMIOTICS
The field of study that examines the correspondence between symbols and their role in the assignment of meaning for people.

Cultural Symbols   **Cultural symbols** are things that represent ideas and concepts. Symbols or symbolism play an important role in cross-cultural analysis because different cultures ascribe different meanings to things. So important is the role of symbols that a field of study, called **semiotics**, has emerged that examines the correspondence between symbols and their role in the assignment of meaning for people. By adroitly using cultural symbols, global marketers can tie positive symbolism to their products and services to enhance their attractiveness to consumers. However, improper use of symbols can spell disaster. A culturally sensitive global marketer will know that[25]

- North Americans are superstitious about the number 13, and Japanese feel the same way about the number 4. *Shi,* the Japanese word for four, is also the word for death. Knowing this, Tiffany & Company sells its fine glassware and china in sets of five, not four, in Japan.

What cultural lesson did Coca-Cola executives learn when they used the Parthenon in a recent global advertising campaign?

• "Thumbs-up" is a positive sign in Canada. However, in Russia and Poland, this gesture has an offensive meaning when the palm of the hand is shown, as AT&T learned. The company reversed the gesture depicted in ads, showing the back of the hand, not the palm.

Cultural symbols evoke deep feelings. Consider how executives at Coca-Cola Company's Italian office learned this lesson. In a series of advertisements directed at Italian vacationers, the Eiffel Tower, the Empire State Building, and the Tower of Pisa were turned into the familiar Coca-Cola bottle. However, when the white marble columns in the Parthenon that crowns Athens' Acropolis were turned into Coca-Cola bottles, the Greeks were outraged. Greeks refer to the Acropolis as the "holy rock," and a government official said the Parthenon is an "international symbol of excellence" and that "whoever insults the Parthenon insults international culture." Coca-Cola apologized for the ad.[26]

Global markets are also sensitive to the fact that the "country of origin or manufacture" of products and services can symbolize superior or poor quality in some countries. For example, Russian consumers believe products made in Japan and Germany are superior in quality to products from North America and the United Kingdom. Japanese consumers believe Japanese products are superior to those made in Europe and North America.[27]

Language   Global marketers should know not only the native tongues of countries in which they market their products and services but also the nuances and idioms of a language. Even though about 100 official languages exist in the world, anthropologists estimate that at least 3000 different languages are spoken. There are 11 official languages spoken in the European Union, and Canada has two official languages (English and French). Seventeen major languages are spoken in India alone.

English, French, and Spanish are the principal languages used in global diplomacy and commerce. However, the best language to communicate with consumers is their own, as any seasoned global marketer will attest to. Unintended meanings of brand names and messages have ranged from the absurd to the obscene[28]:

- When the advertising agency responsible for launching Procter & Gamble's successful Pert shampoo in Canada realized that the name means "lost" in French, it substituted the brand name Pret, which means "ready."
- In Italy, Cadbury Schweppes, the world's third-largest soft drink manufacturer, realized that its Schweppes Tonic Water brand had to be renamed Schweppes Tonica because "il water" turned out to be the idiom for a bathroom.
- The Vicks brand name common in the United States is German slang for sexual intimacy; therefore, Vicks is called Wicks in Germany.

BACK TRANSLATION
Retranslating a word or phrase into the original language by a different interpreter to catch errors.

Experienced global marketers use **back translation**, where a translated word or phrase is retranslated into the original language by a different interpreter to catch errors.[29] For example, IBM's first Japanese translation of its "Solutions for a small planet" advertising message yielded "Answers that make people smaller." The error was caught and corrected. Nevertheless, unintended meanings still occur in the most

Do you see anything offensive in the logo design for a line of Nike athletic shoes? Read the text to understand the importance of language in global marketing.

unlikely situations. Just ask the logo designers for a line of Nike athletic shoes. The designers intended to portray "Air" with stylized flames on the shoe heel. Unfortunately, the logo inadvertently resembled the Arabic script for the word "Allah," the Arabic word for God. After receiving complaints from Muslim leaders, Nike apologized and withdrew the offending shoes from the market.

The use of language in global marketing is assuming greater importance in an increasingly networked and borderless economic world. For example, Oracle Corporation, a leading worldwide supplier of software, now markets its products by language groups instead of through 145 country-specific efforts. The French group markets to France, Belgium, Switzerland, and Canada. A Spanish-language group oversees Spain and Latin America. Eight other language groups—English, Japanese, Korean, Chinese, Portuguese, Italian, Dutch, and German—cover Oracle's top revenue-producing countries.

Cultural Ethnocentricity   The tendency for people to view their own values, customs, symbols, and language favourably is well known. However, the belief that aspects of one's culture are superior to another's is called *cultural ethnocentricity* and is a sure impediment to successful global marketing.

An outgrowth of cultural ethnocentricity exists in the purchase and use of goods and services produced outside of a country. Global marketers are acutely aware that certain groups within countries disfavour imported products, not on the basis of price, features, or performance, but purely because of their foreign origin. **Consumer ethnocentrism** is the tendency to believe that it is inappropriate, indeed immoral, to purchase foreign-made products.[30] Ethnocentric consumers believe that buying imported products is wrong because such purchases are unpatriotic, harm domestic industries, and cause domestic unemployment.[31]

CONSUMER ETHNOCENTRISM
The tendency to believe that it is inappropriate, indeed immoral, to purchase foreign-made products.

Economic Considerations

Global marketing is also affected by economic considerations. Therefore, a scan of the global marketplace should include (1) a comparative analysis of the economic development in different countries, (2) an assessment of the economic infrastructure in these countries, (3) measurement of consumer income in different countries, and (4) recognition of a country's currency exchange rates.

Stage of Economic Development   There are about 200 countries in the world today, each of which is at a slightly different point in terms of its stage of economic development. However, they can be classified into two major groupings that will help the global marketer better understand their needs:

- *Developed* countries have somewhat mixed economies. Private enterprise dominates, although they have substantial public sectors as well. Canada, the United States, Japan, and most of Western Europe can be considered developed.

- *Developing* countries are in the process of moving from an agricultural to an industrial economy. There are two subgroups within the developing category: (1) those that have already made the move including newly industrialized countries, or NICs, and (2) those that remain locked in a preindustrial economy. Countries such as Poland, Hungary, Israel, Venezuela, Singapore, and South Africa fall into the first group. In the second group are Pakistan, Sri Lanka, Tanzania, and Chad, where living standards are low and improvement will be slow.

A country's stage of economic development affects and is affected by other economic factors, as described next.

Economic Infrastructure   The *economic infrastructure*—a country's communications, transportation, financial, and distribution systems—is a critical consideration in determining whether to try to market to a country's consumers and organizations. Parts of the infrastructure that North Americans or Western Europeans take for granted can be huge problems elsewhere—not only in developing nations but even in countries of the former Soviet Union, Eastern Europe, the Indian sub-continent, and China, where such an infrastructure is assumed to be in place.[32] Consider, for instance, transportation and distribution systems in these countries. Two-lane roads that limit average speeds to 55 or 65 kilometres per hour are commonplace—and a nightmare for firms requiring prompt truck delivery. In China, the bicycle is the preferred mode of transportation. This is understandable because China has few navigable roads outside its major cities, where 80 percent of the population lives. In India, Coca-Cola uses large tricycles to distribute cases of Coke along narrow streets in many cities. Wholesale and retail institutions tend to be small, and a majority are operated by new owner-managers still learning the ways of a free market system. These conditions have prompted firms such as Danone, a French food company, to establish their own wholesale, retail, and delivery systems. Danone delivers its products to 700 shops in Russia and has set up 60 shops-in-shops, where it has its own retail sales associates and cash registers.[33]

The communication infrastructures in these countries also differ. This infrastructure includes communications systems and networks in use such as telephones, cable television, broadcast radio and television, computers, satellites, and wireless telephones. In general, the communication infrastructure in many developing countries is limited or antiquated compared with that of developed countries.

The Coca-Cola Company has made a huge financial investment in bottling and distribution facilities in Russia.

The Coca-Cola Company

www.thecoca-colacompany.com

Even the financial and legal systems can cause problems. Formal operating procedures among financial institutions and private properties did not exist under communism and are still limited. As a consequence, it is estimated that two-thirds of the commercial transactions in Russia involve non-monetary forms of payment.[34] The legal red tape involved in obtaining title to buildings and land for manufacturing, wholesaling, and retailing operations also has been a huge problem. Nevertheless, the Coca-Cola Company invested $750 million from 1991 through 1998 to build bottling and distribution facilities in Russia, Allied Lyons spent $30 million to build a plant to make Baskin-Robbins ice cream, and Mars recently opened a $200-million candy factory outside Moscow.[35]

Consumer Income and Purchasing Power A global marketer selling consumer goods must also consider what the average per-capita or household income is among a country's consumers and how the income is distributed to determine a nation's purchasing power. Per-capita income varies greatly between nations. Average yearly per-capita income in EU countries is $28 000 and is less than $250 in some developing countries such as Vietnam. A country's income distribution is important because it gives a more reliable picture of a country's purchasing power. Generally speaking, as the proportion of middle-income-class households in a country increases, the greater a nation's purchasing power tends to be. Figure 7–5 shows the worldwide disparity in the percentage distribution of households by level of purchasing power. In established market economies such as those in North America and Western Europe, 65 percent of households have an annual purchasing capability of $28 000 or more. In comparison, 75 percent of households in the developing countries of South Asia have an annual purchasing power of less than $7000.[36]

Seasoned global marketers recognize that people in developing countries often have government subsidies for food, housing, and health care that supplement their

FIGURE 7–5
How purchasing power differs around the world

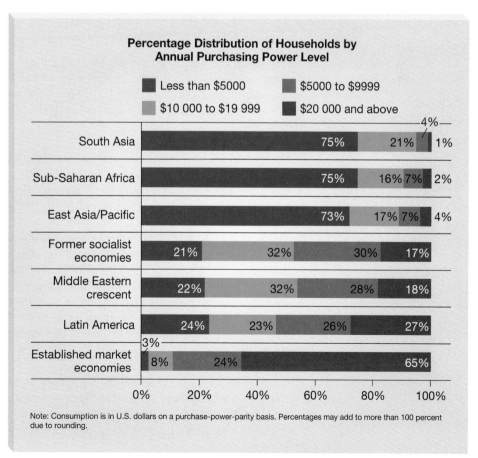

Note: Consumption is in U.S. dollars on a purchase-power-parity basis. Percentages may add to more than 100 percent due to rounding.

income. Accordingly, people with seemingly low incomes are actually promising customers for a variety of products. For example, a consumer in South Asia earning the equivalent of $350 per year can afford Gillette razors. When that consumer's income rises to $1400, a Sony television becomes affordable, and a new Volkswagen or Nissan can be bought with an annual income of $14 000. In developing countries of Eastern Europe, a $1400 annual income makes a refrigerator affordable, and $2800 brings an automatic washer within reach.

Income growth in developing countries of Asia, Latin America, and Central and Eastern Europe is expected to stimulate world trade well into the 21st century. The number of consumers in these countries earning the equivalent of $14 000 per year is expected to surpass the number of consumers in North America, Japan, and Western Europe combined by 2005.[37]

Currency Exchange Rates   Fluctuations in exchange rates among the world's currencies are of critical importance in global marketing. Such fluctuations affect everyone—from international tourists to global companies.

A **currency exchange rate** is the price of one country's currency expressed in terms of another country's currency, such as the Canadian dollar expressed in Japanese yen or Swiss francs. Failure to consider exchange rates when pricing products for global markets can have dire consequences.[38]

Exchange-rate fluctuations have a direct impact on the sales and profits made by global companies. When foreign currencies can buy more Canadian dollars, for example, Canadian products are less expensive for foreign customers. Short-term fluctuations, however, can have a significant effect on the profits of global companies. Hewlett-Packard gained nearly a half million dollars of additional profit through exchange rate fluctuation in one year. On the other hand, Honda lost over $400 million on its European operations due to currency swings in the Japanese yen compared with the euro and the British pound.[39]

Political-Regulatory Climate

The political and regulatory climate for marketing in a country or region of the world lies not only in identifying the current climate but also in determining how long a favourable or unfavourable climate will last. An assessment of a country or regional political-regulatory climate includes an analysis of its political stability and trade regulations.

Political Stability   Trade among nations or regions depends on political stability. Billions of dollars have been lost in the Middle East, the former Federal Republic of Yugoslavia, and Africa as a result of internal political strife and war. Losses such as these encourage careful selection of politically stable countries and regions of the world for trade.

Political stability in a country is affected by numerous factors, including a government's orientation toward foreign companies and trade with other countries. These factors combine to create a political climate that is favourable or unfavourable for marketing and financial investment in a country or region of the world. Marketing managers monitor political stability using a variety of measures and often track country risk ratings supplied by agencies such as the PRS Group. Visit the PRS Group Website shown in the accompanying Web Link and see the most recent political risk ratings for countries.

Trade Regulations   Countries have a variety of rules that govern business practices within their borders. These rules often serve as trade barriers.[40] For example, Japan has some 11 000 trade regulations. Japanese car safety rules effectively require all automobile replacement parts to be Japanese and not North American or European;

CURRENCY EXCHANGE RATE
The price of one country's currency expressed in terms of another country's currency.

WEB LINK — Checking a Country's Political Risk

http://www.mcgrawhill.ca

The political climate in every country is regularly changing. Governments can make new laws or enforce existing policies differently. Numerous consulting firms prepare political risk analyses that incorporate a variety of variables such as the risk of internal turmoil, external conflict, government restrictions on company operations, and tariff and nontariff trade barriers.

The PRS Group maintains multiple databases of country-specific information and projections, including country political risk ratings. These ratings can be accessed at

www.prsgroup.com. Click "Top Ranked Countries." What country has the most favourable business climate and the least favourable business climate?

public health rules make it illegal to sell Aspirin or cold medicine without a pharmacist present. The Malaysian government has advertising regulations stating that "advertisements must not project or promote an excessively aspirational lifestyle," Greece bans toy advertising, and Sweden outlaws all advertisements to children. And, until recently, the EU banned Canadian icewine from its markets because the icewine's alcohol content was beyond accepted levels.[41]

Trade regulations also appear in free trade agreements among countries. European Union nations abide by some 10 000 rules that specify how goods are to be made and marketed. For instance, the rules for a washing machine's electrical system are detailed on more than 100 typed pages. Regulations related to contacting consumers via telephone, fax, and e-mail without their prior consent also exist. The European Union's ISO 9000 quality standards, though not a trade regulation, have the same effect on business practice. These standards, described in Chapter 6, involve registration and certification of a manufacturer's quality management and quality assurance system. Many European companies require suppliers to be ISO 9000 certified as a condition of doing business with them. Certified companies have undergone an on-site audit that includes an inspection of its facilities to ensure that documented quality control procedures are in place and that all employees understand and follow them. More than 150 countries have adopted ISO 9000 standards, and 340 000 certificates have been issued worldwide.[42]

Concept Check

1. Semiotics involves the study of _____.

2. When foreign currencies can buy more Canadian dollars, are Canadian products more or less expensive for a foreign consumer?

GLOBAL MARKET-ENTRY STRATEGIES

Once a company has decided to enter the global marketplace, it must select a means of market entry. Four general options exist: (1) exporting, (2) licensing, (3) joint venture, and (4) direct investment.[43] As Figure 7–6 demonstrates, the amount of financial commitment, risk, marketing control, and profit potential increases as the firm moves from exporting to direct investment.

FIGURE 7–6
Alternative global market-entry strategies

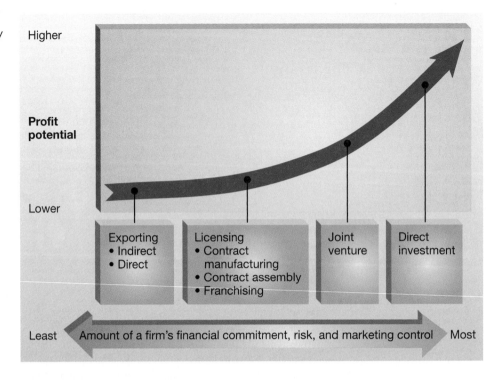

Higher

Profit potential

Lower

| Exporting • Indirect • Direct | Licensing • Contract manufacturing • Contract assembly • Franchising | Joint venture | Direct investment |

Least ← Amount of a firm's financial commitment, risk, and marketing control → Most

Exporting

EXPORTING
Producing goods in one country and selling them in another country.

Exporting is producing goods in one country and selling them in another country. This entry option allows a company to make the least number of changes in terms of its product, its organization, and even its corporate goals. Host countries usually do not like this practice because it provides less local employment than under alternative means of entry.

Indirect exporting is when a firm sells its domestically produced goods in a foreign country through an intermediary. It involves the least amount of commitment and risk but will probably return the least profit. This kind of exporting is ideal for the company that has no overseas contacts but wants to market abroad. The intermediary is often a broker or agent that has the marketing know-how and the resources necessary for the effort to succeed.

Harley-Davidson, Inc. exports about one fourth of its annual production of heavyweight motorcycles. The company is represented internationally by 577 independent dealers in 55 countries.

Harley-Davidson, Inc.
www.harley-davidson.com

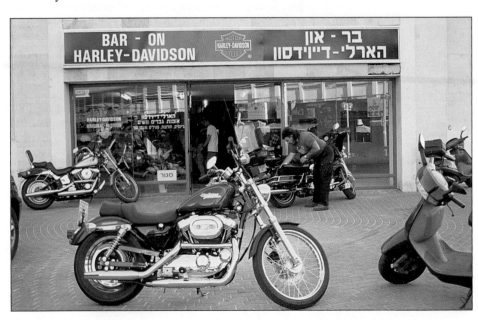

McDonald's uses franchising as a market-entry strategy and more than 60 percent of the company's sales came from foreign operations in 2001.

McDonald's

www.mcdonalds.com

Direct exporting occurs when a firm sells its domestically produced goods in a foreign country without intermediaries. Most companies become involved in direct exporting when they believe their volume of sales will be sufficiently large and easy to obtain that they do not require intermediaries. For example, the exporter may be approached by foreign buyers that are willing to contract for a large volume of purchases. Direct exporting involves more risk than indirect exporting for the company but also opens the door to increased profits.

W. K. Buckley Ltd. uses an indirect exporting strategy to market its cough remedy product (Buckley's Mixture) in the Australian market, and a direct exporting strategy for the United States market. Reif Estate Winery in Niagara-on-the-Lake and Andrés Wines of Grimsby, Ontario both engage in exporting their Canadian wines to the European Union as well as other foreign markets, where sales have grown significantly.[44]

Licensing

Under licensing, a company offers the right to a trademark, patent, trade secret, or other similarly valued items of intellectual property in return for a royalty or a fee. In international marketing, the advantages to the company granting the licence are low risk and a capital-free entry into a foreign country. The licensee gains information that allows it to start with a competitive advantage, and the foreign country gains employment by having the product manufactured locally. W. K. Buckley Ltd. used licensing for entering Holland. Similarly, Clearly Canadian Beverages of Vancouver used licensing to enter several markets, including the United States and Japan.

There are some serious drawbacks to this mode of entry, however. The licensor forgoes control of its product and reduces the potential profits gained from it. In addition, while the relationship lasts, the licensor may be creating its own competition. Some licensees are able to modify the product somehow and enter the market with product and marketing knowledge gained at the expense of the company that got them started. To offset this disadvantage, many companies strive to stay innovative so that the licensee remains dependent on them for improvements and successful operation. Finally, should the licensee prove to be a poor choice, the name or reputation of the company may be harmed.

Two variations of licensing, *contract manufacturing* and *contract assembly*, represent alternative ways to produce a product within the foreign country. With contract manufacturing, a Canadian company may contract with a foreign firm to manufacture products according to stated specifications. The product is then sold in the foreign country or exported back to Canada. With contract assembly, the Canadian company may contract with a foreign firm to assemble (not manufacture) parts and components that have been shipped to that country. In both cases, the advantage to the foreign country is the employment of its people, and the Canadian firm benefits from the lower wage rates in the foreign country.

A third variation of licensing is franchising. Franchising is one of the fastest-growing market-entry strategies. Franchises include soft-drink, motel, retailing, fast-food, and car rental operation and a variety of business services. McDonald's is a premier global franchiser: more than 70 percent of the company's stores are franchised, and over 60 percent of the company's sales come from foreign operations.[45]

Joint Venture

JOINT VENTURE
An arrangement in which a foreign company and a local firm invest together to create a local business, sharing ownership, control, and profits of the new company.

When a foreign country and a local firm invest together to create a local business, it is called a **joint venture**. These two companies share ownership, control, and profits of the new company. Investment may be made by having either of the companies buy shares in the other or by creating a third and separate entity. This was done by Caterpillar, Inc., the world's largest manufacturer of earth-moving and construction equipment. It recently created NEVAMASH with its joint-venture partner, Kirovsky Zvod, a large Russian manufacturer of heavy equipment.[46]

The advantages of this option are twofold. First, one company may not have the necessary financial, physical, or managerial resources to enter a foreign market alone. Ford and Volkswagen formed a joint venture to make four-wheel-drive vehicles in Portugal. Second, a government may require or strongly encourage a joint venture before it allows a foreign company to enter its market. This is the case in China. Today, more than 75 000 Chinese–foreign joint ventures operate in China, including W. K. Buckley Ltd. and its joint-venture partner.[47]

The disadvantages arise when the two companies disagree about policies or courses of action for their joint venture or when governmental bureaucracy bogs down the effort. For example, Canadian firms often prefer to reinvest earnings gained, whereas some foreign companies may want to spend those earnings. Or a Canadian firm may want to return profits earned to Canada, while the local firm or its government may oppose this—the problem now faced by many potential joint ventures in Eastern Europe, Russia, Latin America, and South Asia.

Direct Investment

DIRECT INVESTMENT
A domestic firm actually investing in and owning a foreign subsidiary or division.

www.hyundai.com

www.ey.com

The biggest commitment a company can make when entering the global market is **direct investment**, which entails a domestic firm actually investing in and owning a foreign subsidiary or division.[48] Examples of direct investment are Toyota's automobile plant in Ontario and Hyundai's plant in Quebec. Many Canadian-based companies are also switching to this mode of entry. Alcan Aluminium built a recycling plant in Worrington, England, and Ganong Brothers owns a plant that manufactures chocolates in Thailand.

For many firms, direct investment often follows one of the other three market-entry strategies.[49] For example, Ernst & Young, an international accounting and management consulting firm, entered Hungary first by establishing a joint venture with a local company. Ernst & Young later acquired the company, making it a subsidiary with headquarters in Budapest.

The advantages to direct investment include cost savings, better understanding of local market conditions, and fewer local restrictions. Firms entering foreign markets using direct investment believe that these advantages outweigh the financial commitments and risks involved.

Concept Check

1. What mode of entry could a company follow if it has no previous experience in global marketing?

2. How does licensing differ from a joint venture?

CRAFTING A WORLDWIDE MARKETING EFFORT

The choice of a market-entry strategy is a necessary first step for a marketer when joining the community of global companies. The next step involves the challenging task of designing, implementing, and controlling marketing programs worldwide.

Product and Promotion Strategies

Global companies have five strategies for matching products and their promotion efforts to global markets. As Figure 7–7 shows, the strategies focus on whether a company extends or adapts its product and promotion message for consumers in different countries.

A product may be sold globally in one of three ways: (1) in the same form as in its home market, (2) with some adaptations, or (3) as a totally new product[50]:

1. *Product extension.* Selling virtually the same product in other countries is a product extension strategy. It works well for products such as Coca-Cola, Gillette razors, Breathe Right nasal strips, Wrigley's gum, and Levi's jeans. However, it didn't work for Jell-O (a more solid gelatin was preferred to the powder in England) or Duncan Hines cakes (which were seen as too moist and crumbly to eat with tea in England).

2. *Product adaptation.* Changing a product in some way to make it more appropriate for a country's climate or consumer preferences is a product adaptation strategy. Gerber baby food comes in different varieties in different countries. Vegetable and Rabbit Meat is a favourite food in Poland. Freeze-Dried Sardines and Rice is popular in Japan. Maybelline's makeup is adapted in labs to local skin types and weather across the globe.

3. *Product invention.* Alternatively, companies can invent totally new products designed to satisfy common needs across countries. Black & Decker did this with its Snake Light Flexible Flashlight. Created to address a global need for portable lighting, the product became a best-seller in North America, Europe, Latin America, and Australia and is the most successful new product developed by Black & Decker.

www.blackanddecker.com

An identical promotion message is used for the product extension and product adaptation strategies around the world. Gillette uses the same global message for its men's toiletries: "Gillette, the Best a Man Can Get."

FIGURE 7–7
Five product and promotion strategies for global marketing

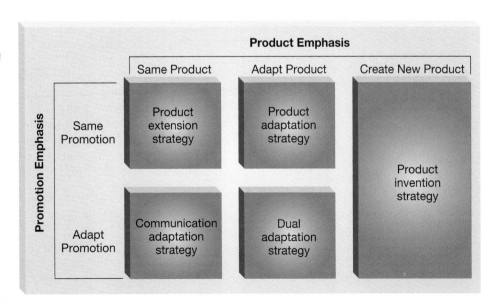

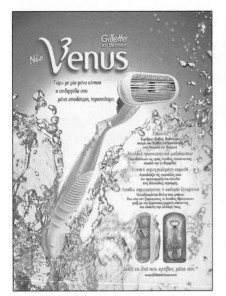
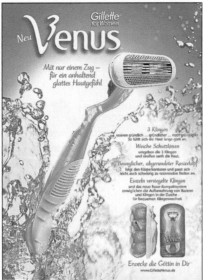
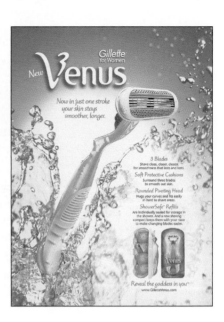

Gillette delivers the same global message whenever possible, as shown in the Gillette for Women Venus ads from Greece, Germany, and the United States.

The Gillette Company
www.gillette.com

Global companies may also adapt their promotion message. For instance, the same product may be sold in many countries but advertised differently. As an example, L'Oréal, a French health and beauty products marketer, introduced its Golden Beauty brand of sun care products through its Helena Rubenstein subsidiary in Western Europe with a communication adaptation strategy. Recognizing that cultural and buying motive differences related to skin care and tanning exist, Golden Beauty advertising features dark tanning for Northern Europeans, skin protection to avoid wrinkles among Latin Europeans, and beautiful skin for Europeans living along the Mediterranean Sea, even though the products are the same. Other companies use a dual adaptation strategy by modifying both their products and promotion messages. Nestlé does this with Nescafé coffee. Nescafé is marketed using different coffee blends and promotional campaigns to match consumer preferences in different countries. These examples illustrate a simple rule applied by global companies today: standardize product and promotion strategies whenever possible and adapt them whenever necessary. This is the art of global marketing.[51]

Distribution Strategy

Distribution is of critical importance in global marketing. The availability and quality of retailers and wholesalers as well as transportation, communication, and warehousing facilities are often determined by a country's stage of economic development. Figure 7–8 outlines the channel through which a product manufactured in one country must travel to reach its destination in another country. The first step involves the seller; its headquarters is the starting point and is responsible for the successful distribution to the ultimate consumer.

The next step is the channel between two nations, moving the product from one country to another. Intermediaries that can handle this responsibility include resident buyers in a foreign country, independent merchant wholesalers who buy and sell the product, or agents who bring buyers and sellers together.

FIGURE 7–8
Channels of distribution in global marketing

Once the product is in the foreign nation, that country's distribution channels take over.[52] These channels can be very long or surprisingly short, depending on the product line. In Japan, fresh fish go through three intermediaries before getting to a retail outlet. Conversely, shoes only go through one intermediary. In other cases, the channel does not even involve the host country. Procter & Gamble sells its soap door to door in the Philippines because there are no other alternatives in many parts of that country. The sophistication of a country's distribution channels increases as its economic infrastructure develops. Supermarkets facilitate selling products in many nations, but they are not popular or available in many others where culture and lack of refrigeration dictate shopping on a daily rather than a weekly basis. For example, when Coke and Pepsi entered China, both had to create direct-distribution channels, investing in trucks and refrigerator units for small retailers.

Pricing Strategy

Global companies also face many challenges in determining a pricing strategy as part of their worldwide marketing effort. Individual countries, even those with free trade agreements, may impose considerable competitive, political, and legal constraints on the pricing latitude of global companies. Of course, economic factors such as the costs of production, selling, and tariffs, plus transportation and storage costs also affect global pricing decisions.

DUMPING

When a firm sells a product in a foreign country below its domestic price or below its actual cost.

Pricing too low or too high can have dire consequences. When prices appear too low in one country, companies can be charged with dumping, a practice subject to severe penalties and fines. **Dumping** is when a firm sells a product in a foreign country below its domestic price or below its actual cost. This is often done to build a company's share of the market by pricing at a competitive level. Another reason is that the products being sold may be surplus or cannot be sold domestically and, therefore, are already a burden to the company. The firm may be glad to sell them at almost any price.

GREY MARKET

A situation where products are sold through unauthorized channels of distribution; also called *parallel importing*.

When companies price their products very high in some countries but competitively in others, they face a grey market problem. A **grey market**, also called *parallel importing*, is a situation where products are sold through unauthorized channels of distribution. A grey market comes about when individuals buy products in a lower-priced country from a manufacturer's authorized retailer, ship them to higher-priced countries, and then sell them below the manufacturer's suggested retail price through unauthorized retailers. Many well-known products have been sold through grey markets, including Olympus cameras, Seiko watches, IBM personal computers, and Mercedes-Benz cars.[53]

Concept Check

1. Products may be sold globally in three ways. What are they?
2. What is dumping?

SUMMARY

1 The dollar value of world trade has more than doubled in the past decade and will exceed $11.5 trillion in 2005. Manufactured goods and commodities account for 75 percent of world trade, while services account for 25 percent.

2 Not all world trade involves the exchange of money for goods or services. About 15–20 percent of world trade involves countertrade, the practice of using barter rather than money for making global sales.

3 A global perspective on world trade views exports and imports as complementary economic flows. A country's exports affect its imports and vice versa. This phenomenon is called the trade feedback effect.

4 Canada is a trading nation, exporting almost 45 percent of its gross domestic national product on an annual basis.

5 The reason some companies and some industries in a country succeed globally while others do not lies in their nation's competitive advantage. A nation's competitive advantage arises from specific conditions in a nation that foster success.

6 Four recent trends have significantly affected world trade: (*a*) a gradual decline of economic protectionism, (*b*) an increase in formal economic integration and free trade among nations, (*c*) global competition among global companies for global consumers, and (*d*) the emergence of a networked global marketspace.

7 Although global and domestic marketing are based on the same marketing principles, many underlying assumptions must be re-evaluated when a firm pursues global opportunities. A global environmental scan typically considers three kinds of uncontrollable environmental variables. These include cultural diversity, economic conditions, and political-regulatory climate.

8 Four global market-entry strategies are exporting, licensing, joint venture, and direct investment. The relative difficulty of global marketing, as well as the amount of financial commitment, risk, marketing control, and profit potential, increase in moving from exporting to direct investment.

9 Crafting a worldwide marketing effort involves designing, implementing, and controlling a marketing program that standardizes marketing mix elements when there are cultural similarities and adapting them when cultures differ.

KEY TERMS AND CONCEPTS

back translation p. 182
balance of trade p. 171
consumer ethnocentrism p. 183
countertrade p. 171
cross-cultural analysis p. 180
cultural symbols p. 181
currency exchange rate p. 186
customs p. 181
direct investment p. 190
dumping p. 193
exporting p. 188
global competition p. 177
global consumers p. 178

global marketing strategy p. 178
grey market p. 193
gross domestic product p. 171
joint venture p. 190
multidomestic marketing strategy p. 178
protectionism p. 174
quota p. 174
semiotics p. 181
strategic alliances p. 177
tariffs p. 174
trade feedback effect p. 171
values p. 181
World Trade Organization p. 175

INTERNET EXERCISE

www.mcgrawhill.ca/college/berkowitz

As you read in this chapter, Canada is a trading nation. Go to the Industry Canada Website at www.strategis. ic.gc.ca. Click on the "Trade, Investment" heading. Then click on the "Trade Strategies and Action Plan" heading. Finally, click on the "Information Technologies and Telecommunications" heading (ICT). Read this material. What are Canada's global priority markets for ICT products/services? What activities does the government plan to carry out to realize its strategies and objectives in those markets?

Want to get better grades, find tips on how to study more effectively, and stay up to date with happenings in the world of marketing? Visit the Online Learning Centre for practice tests, Study Smart software, and much more! www.mcgrawhill.ca/college/berkowitz

Interested in finding out what marketing looks like in the real world? *Marketing Magazine* is just a click away on your OLC! Visit www.mcgrawhill.ca/college/berkowitz

APPLYING MARKETING CONCEPTS AND PERSPECTIVES

1 What is meant by this statement: "Quotas are a hidden tax on consumers, whereas tariffs are a more obvious one"?

2 Is the trade feedback effect described in the text a long-run or short-run view on world trade flows? Explain your answer.

3 Since English is the official language in Australia, some Canadian global companies might select it as an easy market to enter. Others believe that this similarity in language could make it harder to successfully enter that market. Who's right? Why?

4 How successful would a television commercial in Japan be if it featured a husband surprising his wife in her dressing area on Valentine's Day with a small box of chocolates containing four candies? Why?

5 As a novice in global marketing, which alternative for global market-entry strategy would you be likely to start with? Why? What other alternatives do you have for a global market entry?

6 Coca-Cola is sold worldwide. In some countries, Coca-Cola owns the bottling facilities; in others, it has signed contracts with licensees or relies on joint ventures. When selecting a licensee in each country, what factors should Coca-Cola consider?

7 Now that China has taken back control of Hong Kong, what advice would you give to Canadian companies currently doing, or planning to do, business in Hong Kong?

VIDEO CASE 7–1 CNS, Inc., and 3M: Breathe Right Nasal Strip

"When we first began marketing this product, what was so gratifying, particularly as a physician, were the literally thousands of letters and phone calls we would receive talking about how much better people slept at night. Almost all the letters began with 'thank you, thank you, thank you!' Just three thank you's. It was, 'I haven't gotten a good night's sleep like this in 10 years.'"

What is Dr. Dan Cohen, CEO of CNS, Inc., talking about? It's Breathe Right® nasal strips, the innovative adhesive pad with a small spring inside that, when attached to the nose, pulls the nasal passages open and makes it easier to breathe. Since its introduction, Breathe Right strips have been coveted by athletes hoping to improve their performance through increased oxygen flow, snorers (and, more often, snorers' spouses) hoping for a sound night's sleep, and allergy and cold sufferers looking for relief for their stuffed noses.

HOW THIS WEIRD-LOOKING STRIP CAME ABOUT

The Breathe Right strip was invented by Bruce Johnson, who suffered from chronic nasal congestion. At times he would put straws or paper clips up his nose at night to keep his nasal passages open. After tinkering in his workshop for years, he came up with a prototype design for the Breathe Right strip. He brought the prototype to CNS, which was in the sleep disorders diagnostic equipment business at the time. Dr. Cohen knew instantly the market for the strips would be huge. After the products received government approval and became successful in the market, CNS divested its other interests and went to work marketing the strips full time.

Being a small company, CNS did not have the budget to launch a large-scale marketing campaign. But it got the break it needed when Jerry Rice, the wide receiver for the San Francisco 49ers, wore one of the strips on national TV when the 49ers won the 1995 Superbowl. The entire nation became aware of the product overnight, and demand for the strips increased dramatically. An indication of this national awareness was discussion on TV talk shows and even appearances of the strip in cartoons.

EVERYBODY HAS A NOSE: THE DECISION TO GO INTERNATIONAL

The problems that the Breathe Right strips solve—snoring, congestion—are not unique to the North American population. Also, with the media being so global today, people around the world were seeing athletes wearing the strip and wondering how they could get their noses on some. CNS decided to take Breathe Right international. But because it was still a relatively small company and had no experience in the global marketplace, it opted to take on a distribution partner that had extensive global outlets already in place as well as the ability to market the product abroad. 3M, makers of such products as Post-It™ notes and the leader in stick-to-skin products around the world, became the international distributor for Breathe Right strips.

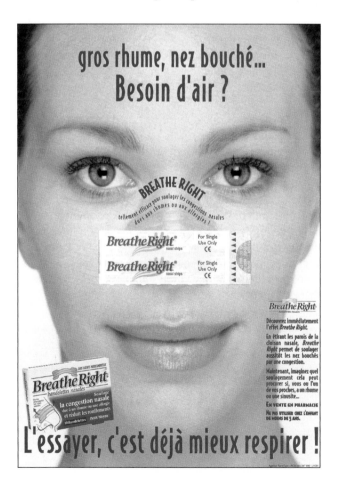

David Reynolds-Gooch, International Business Manager at 3M, explains that the strips fit in well with 3M's existing adhesive line of first-aid products and are sold in channels with which 3M has extensive leverage: pharmacies, hyper-markets, and food markets. 3M agreed to take control of all the marketing and communication responsibilities in addition to the distribution in return for a percentage of the sales revenue of the strips. The strips are "co-branded" in the international markets: The packages say both Breathe Right and 3M.

BREATHING RIGHT AROUND THE WORLD

3M introduced the Breathe Right strip in Japan, then it was rolled out in Europe, and now can be found in more than 40 countries from Australia to South America. 3M used a similar approach to that used by CNS in North America: Create awareness during the introduction phase through public relations—sports related and otherwise. "The first year we had incredible PR success," remembers Reynolds-Gooch. "We believe we got about $20 million worth of free TV, radio, and print time around the world." This was done through such tactics as having the South African rugby team wear the strips while it won the World Cup of rugby and having pulmonologists and breathing experts describe the benefits of the product on talk shows in Japan, Australia, Europe, and Latin America.

CNS quickly discovered some major differences in marketing the product here and abroad. For instance, as Gary Tschautscher, Vice President of International Marketing at CNS explains, "In the United States and Canada, we positioned and distributed the strips as part of the cough/cold category of products. As we rolled it out globally, suddenly we realized in some countries that section in the store doesn't even exist. So where do you position your product?" Additionally, says Reynolds-Gooch, "There really aren't many large drug chains or pharmacy chains. The stores are independent in most countries by law. So what that means is you have to go through multiple layers of distribution, and ultimately we were able to influence the pharmacists because of the other products 3M distributes in the stores." Finally, there is no couponing in most countries in the world. That vehicle for inducing trial of a new product is not available, and hence a lot more in-store sampling is needed.

BREATHE RIGHT IN THE TWENTY-FIRST CENTURY

Both CNS and 3M face some issues for the future as Breathe Right strips gain in popularity around the globe. While the athletic segment of the market gets most of the publicity, the snorers are the bulk of the market for the strips internationally. Reynolds-Gooch has identified creating heavy users—those who use the strip every night—as the most important marketing point for the future, ahead of people with seasonal colds or allergies. Also, many of the markets that have been identified as "hot" new markets throughout the business community may not be appropriate for the Breathe Right strips. For example, Latin America and Asia (especially China) are emerging markets with steadily increasing income levels and large populations, but the average age in these countries is under 30, and people under 30 typically do not have snoring problems with the frequency that older people do.

Questions

1 What are the advantages and disadvantages of CNS taking its Breathe Right strip into international markets?
2 What advantages does CNS gain by having 3M as its international licensing partner? What are the advantages for 3M?
3 What criteria might CNS and 3M use in selecting countries to enter? Using these criteria, which five or six countries would you enter?
4 Which market segment would you target in entering the international markets—snorers, athletes, people with chronic congestion and allergies, or a new segment?
5 Which marketing mix variables do you think CNS should concentrate on the most to succeed in a global arena? Why?

With the widespread acceptance of the Internet as an information and communication tool, together with the growing adoption of wireless technologies at home and in the office, understanding changing consumer attitudes is more important than ever for marketers. With the growing level of technology in our lives, attitudes about technology continue to change. Whether in business or at home, our dependence on technology affects our attitudes about our jobs as well as priorities in our lives. Attitudes depend on a number of variables including age, cultural attachment, and socioeconomic affiliation. Today's youth have grown up with technology and are more comfortable with computers and the Internet than are their parents. Understanding changes in attitudes of different groups within the population is key to understanding buying behaviour—whether it is within the consumer marketplace, the business-to-business marketplace, or the broader global marketplace.

Since the search for successful commercial Internet applications was set in motion, Amazon.com has been seen as a pioneer in e-commerce changing the way retailers and consumers develop relationships not only through traditional brick-and-mortar stores but also online. For a number of years now, Amazon.com has remained one of the top Websites for online shopping.[1] The hype originally generated by Amazon.com provided the opportunity for all businesses to evaluate their business practices and revisit critical aspects of their relationships with their suppliers and their customers. As one of the surviving pioneers of the dot-com frenzy, and as an example of a virtual company business model, Amazon.com has been successful in providing a level of convenient service and security to book, music, and video buyers—setting the stage for the next generation of Internet applications for both consumers and businesses. Experience with a variety of Websites and issues relating to security and privacy has influenced consumers' attitudes as they adjust their information search and buying behaviour on the Internet.

CONSUMERS AND THEIR BUYING PREFERENCES

According to a study by Ipsos-Reid, three-quarters of Canadians state that the Internet has affected their lives in a number of different ways including learning, communication, and education.[2] The Internet is changing the way in which consumers value the information and applications they seek online. At one time, banner advertising was a major revenue source for site owners and attracted the interest of online users. However, times have changed and now online users generally disregard Internet advertising.[3] Marketers, particularly Canadian companies wishing to develop online relationships with their customers, need to pay attention to these changing attitudes. In 1999, Canadian online shoppers spent more money at U.S. Websites than at Canadian sites.[4] A study done at that time by IBM Canada for the Retail Council of Canada discovered that Canadian online buyers spent 63 percent of their online money at U.S. sites. Studies done in 2001, however, show that in just a few years Canadians have changed their online buying preferences and now spend more money at Canadian sites. More Canadian sites are now available to consumers; this increased selection has resulted in Canadian e-retailers enjoying more business as 63 percent of Canadians now shop Canadian.[5] More good news for Canadian companies investing in e-commerce applications is that more than 50 percent of Canadians state that their favourite Website is based in Canada.[6]

American-based companies dominate the Internet. U.S. companies are now taking the time and investing the money to create Canadian sites, sometimes in both official languages, attempting to address the unique needs of Canadian consumers. Yahoo! Canada en français, launched in 2000, attracts more than 1.4 million Quebecers monthly.[7] Reasons for Canadians preferring Canadian sites may have more to do with economics than nationalism. With the Canadian dollar remaining weak against the U.S. dollar, purchases from U.S. sites can be costly when the exchange rates, shipping costs, and duties are tallied.

Canadians demonstrate very different behaviours using the Internet when compared with Americans. The top ten items purchased on the Internet by Canadians include banking services, downloadable computer software, books, music, tickets to events, clothing, air travel, and consumer electronics.[8] Almost two-thirds of Canadian Internet users have conducted some form of financial transaction online compared with 29 percent of U.S. Internet users.[9] As well, more Canadians invest online (15%) compared with only 10 percent of Americans investing online. Canadians appear to trust their banking institutions more than Americans—due to some extent to the structure of the banking industry in Canada, where national banks dominate the market; the United States has a more regional banking system. More than two-thirds of Canadian Internet users have shopped online, while 77 percent of Americans are likely to shop online. The lower numbers of Canadian online shoppers may be related to the fact that Canadian companies were slower to provide shopping opportunities online while American companies jumped into the fray much sooner.

The Internet continues to provide opportunities for companies that are prepared to invest in applications offering value to consumers. Another example of changing values and attitudes about online activity is highlighted in a study done by LIMRA, exploring perceptions of the need for financial planning.[10] The study compared two distinct groups within the population and looked at their financial needs. Not surprisingly, young upper-income couples without children showed little interest in risky investment products and were primarily interested in acccumulating wealth, balanced with the desire to spend today. These young couples are not necessarily interested in using the Internet to help them manage their money. In contrast, middle-income couples with children articulated an interest in insurance and are concerned about making ends meet and saving for their children's education. This group is older and understands the rewards of riskier investment options. This older group used the Internet to search for investment information, but still wanted a financial adviser when needed. The continual monitoring of attitudes and values as they relate to products and services that could potentially be sold online is becoming more important as more people use the Internet.

THE NEXT GENERATION AND THE NET

With the fast growth of Internet use over the past five years, there has been more attention given to individual groups using the Internet. A segment drawing attention to itself is the Net Generation. According to Don Tapscott (pictured), the Net Generation "refers to the generation of children who, in 1999, were between the ages of two and twenty-two."[11] This age group represents 30 percent of the population and will have a significant impact on society as they are important in terms of both numbers and values. This generation is used to digital media—they grew up with remote controls, video games, and computers with online access. A noteworthy difference between this young group of the population and previous generations is their relationship within the family. This is the first time in history that children have expertise within the family unit. A visit to the site www.growingupdigital.com will demonstrate this fact, as children and adults tell stories relaying examples of how children provide expert advice on technology to their parents.[12] This site was used in Don Tapscott's original research on the Net Generation and continues to be used to monitor changes in this unique population segment.

Parents may be concerned about the amount of time youngsters and teens spend online. Statistics Canada refutes the stereotype of young people on the Internet suffering from social isolation with a study that indicates teens aged 15 to 17 actually use the Internet to develop friendships.[13] The Internet is viewed by this age group as a means to stay in touch with family and friends. From his ongoing research on the Net Generation, Don Tapscott concludes that this generation is creating a culture of interaction. There are important values and attitudes developing within this generation including fierce independence, emotional and intellectual openness, inclusiveness, the need for immediacy, and the need to have free expression.

The Net Generation has been quick to create N-Gen communities, where "millions of children about the world are routinely gathering online to chat" instead of hanging around the mall or playing sports.[14] They have their own "netiquette" and will take action with those not conforming and showing respect.

As a purchasing group, youngsters and teens are currently not major online consumers.[15] As just discussed, youth use the Internet to gather information and communicate with friends. When they do purchase, the most popular items are music, clothing, books, toys, flowers, and some tickets.[16] A study of the global youth market (ages 12 to 24) and their Internet behaviour shows that American youth (43%) lead in terms of buying online while only 25 percent of Canadian youth are shopping online. The following table shows the penetration rate of youth online purchasing for the top five countries in the 16-country sample.

TOP FIVE COUNTRIES OF YOUTH ONLINE PURCHASING	
COUNTRY	**% OF YOUTH PURCHASING ONLINE**
United States	43%
Sweden	41%
Germany	33%
Canada	25%
Britain	22%

Source: Ipsos-Reid, "Young Americans First in Line at Virtual Till," Media Release, February 23, 2001 (www.angusreid.com).

THE BOOM OF THE VIRTUAL BUSINESS MARKET

The influence of the Internet reaches beyond the consumer market and into the business-to-business sector. Online purchasing has not only changed the attitudes and behaviours of various segments of the consumer market, it has also had serious implications for suppliers, manufacturers, and distributors with the supply chain. The promise of Internet applications and innovative business models collapsed to some degree with the crash of the dot-coms in the spring of 2000. Although some companies are revisiting their e-commerce strategic investments, there is one application that continues to be driving the online Internet marketplace: e-procurement. The buyer–seller relationship in the industrial marketplace continues to change as the use of technology takes away administrative tasks from salespeople and purchasing managers so that business problems can be tackled more strategically and effectively.[17]

In 1998, business-to-business online spending was estimated at $4.6 billion.[18] In a more recent report prepared by Forrester Research, by 2005 the online business trade is estimated to reach $272 billion.[19] In the Forrester report, titled "Canada's B2B Future," it was predicted that by the end of 2002, 82 percent of Canadian businesses would be using the Internet for business-to-business transactions. The e-marketplace for businesses can be categorized into three distinct models. These models include the procurement marketplace, the commodity marketplace, and the vertical sector marketplace.[20] The procurement marketplace includes those sites that act as brokers for horizontally connected companies looking for the power of aggregate purchases. Commodity marketplaces will be those sites such as Enbridge.com or Oilsphere.com where the purpose is to bring together oil and gas buyers and sellers. Vertical-

sector marketplaces are those spaces that bring specialized operations together for production planning and integrated supply chain schedules. These types of marketplaces will need to be more secure and involve a limited number of organizations. Whatever business models continue to evolve and survive in the Internet marketspace, the quest for efficiencies is the main driving force behind the development of business-to-business applications.

Before September 11, 2001, the airline industry was struggling to find ways and means to control its escalating costs and improve profitability. Aeroxchange is an Internet-based trading site that brings together 13 companies including Air Canada, Northwest Airlines, and FedEx to use their collective purchasing power in the airline industry to purchase aircraft parts and services.[21] The initiative was driven by Air Canada and went live in February 2001. It is a collaboration among a number of competitors, with the objective of managing costs more effectively as a group. In addition to the companies already mentioned, the project includes such companies as Cathay Pacific Airways, Japan Airlines, Lufthansa German Airlines, and KLM Royal Dutch Airlines. The airlines put aside their competitive differences to the tune of U.S.$50 million, with the hopes of re-engineering the supply chain to achieve cost savings through better vendor relationships for all involved. Oracle Corporation is the developer for this project, offering the group online auctioning, reverse auctioning, and contract and spot-buying in addition to supply chain planning tools to help suppliers automate inventory demand and product planning. Using technology in new ways makes these types of collaborations powerful in changing the nature of competition within industry.

Another example of companies looking to the Internet to save costs is Epost.ca, a bill delivery service. This service company is the outcome of a collaboration between Canada Post, Telus Corp., and the Bank of Montreal. The service was first announced in November 1999, but it took almost 18 months for the service to be fully operational.[22] Consumers can pay bills through links with their bank or by credit card. The revenue is currently being generated by charging the billing companies a service fee of 40 cents to send an invoice. This is a significant reduction in costs when compared with the cost of mailing a bill, which can range in price from 75 cents to $2. For this billing model to work, the consumers need to accept receiving their bills by e-mail; this is the barrier to adoption at the moment. Security concerns surrounding Internet transactions is an underlying reason for a relatively slow acceptance of online bill payment even though there are obvious benefits to bill payers in terms of time and expense. Epost.ca executives see this as a minor issue—they are counting on the association with the post office to mitigate these concerns.

BUYER BEWARE ON A MUCH LARGER SCALE

Security concerns related to Internet transactions are not to be treated lightly by anyone using the Internet to collect information and purchase online. The collection and dissemination of consumer information by marketers is a major concern, as is the possible abuse of credit card information. That is why legislation now exists in Canada to protect information collected through Internet transactions. The Personal Information Protection and Electronic Documents Act (Part 1, Bill C-6) became law January 1, 2001. This bill deals with sensitive forms of information—for example, health information—and contains important opt-out provisions.[23] The phrase "buyer beware" takes on a whole new meaning in the e-marketplace of today.

Discussion Questions

1 Discuss the principles of consumer buying behaviour and how they apply to the online shopper. Highlight similarities as well as differences between "click" shoppers and "brick" shoppers.

2 Based on what you know about consumers and what motivates them to make purchase choices, explain the high growth rates in online shopping and slower growth rates of other Internet applications such as online bill paying. Can you predict changes in attitudes and behaviours as more consumers experience online applications?

3 Why do you think business-to-business online transactions are predicted to generate considerably greater revenue opportunities than the consumer online shopping revenues? The case highlights some interesting applications for online business transactions. What additional opportunities do you believe exist for online business-to-business?

4 Do you believe that online shopping will replace traditional shopping? Why or why not? Support your answer with consumer behaviour theory.

PART

TARGETING
MARKETING
OPPORTUNITIES

CHAPTER 8
Turning Marketing Information into Action

CHAPTER 9
Identifying Market Segments and Targets

Part 3 focuses on targeting marketing opportunities. Chapter 8 describes how people with similar wants and needs become the target of marketing opportunities. This chapter details how information about prospective consumers is linked to marketing strategy and decisive actions, and how information technology improves the process. Chapter 9 describes how shoe manufacturing giants like Reebok and Nike, and upstarts like Heelys and Customatix, design shoes to satisfy different customers. In addition, this chapter covers the steps a firm uses in segmenting and targeting a market and then positioning its offering in the marketplace. The application of segmentation, targeting, and positioning is illustrated with Apple Computer's strategy for its hardware and software.

THE LORD OF THE RINGS
THE FELLOWSHIP OF THE RING

8 TURNING MARKETING INFORMATION INTO ACTION

AFTER READING THIS CHAPTER YOU SHOULD BE ABLE TO:

- Know what marketing research is and does.

- Explain the different types of marketing research.

- Understand the stages in the marketing research process.

- Know when and how to collect secondary data.

- Explain the use of surveys, experiments, and observation in marketing research.

- Identify ethical issues in the marketing research process.

- Understand how information technology enables information systems to be used that link massive amounts of marketing information to meaningful marketing actions.

- Recognize alternative methods to forecast sales and use the lost-horse and linear trend extrapolation methods to make a simple forecast.

TEST SCREENINGS: LISTENING TO CONSUMERS TO REDUCE MOVIE RISKS!

"Blockbuster" movies are essential for today's fiercely competitive world of filmmaking—examples being the *Lord of the Rings* trilogy (opposite page), *Shoeless Joe*, *Teenie Weenies*, and *3000!*

What's in a Movie Name? Can't remember those last three movies—even after scratching your head? Well, test screenings by the studios—a form of marketing research—found that moviegoers had problems with those titles, too. Here are the titles each of these three movies started with, where they wound up, and the reasons:

- *Shoeless Joe* became *Field of Dreams* because audiences thought Kevin Costner might be playing a homeless person.

- *Teenie Weenies* became *Honey, I Shrunk the Kids* when moviegoers could not relate the original title to what they saw in the movie.

- *3000* became *Pretty Woman* when audiences did not have a clue what the number meant. Hint: It was the payment Julia Roberts asked for to spend one week with Richard Gere.[1]

Filmmakers want movie titles that are concise, attention-getting, capture the essence of the film, and have no legal restrictions—basically the same factors that make a good brand name.

How Filmmakers Try to Reduce Risk   Is research on movie titles expensive? Very! But the greater expense is selecting a bad title that can kill a movie and cost the studio millions of dollars—not to mention the careers of producers and directors! So with today's films often costing more than $80 million to produce and market, movie studios use marketing research to reduce their risks.[2]

For test screenings, 300 to 400 prospective moviegoers are recruited to attend a "sneak preview" of a film before its release. After viewing the movie, the audience fills out an exhaustive survey to critique the title, plot, characters, music, and ending— as well as the marketing program (posters, trailers, etc.)—to identify improvements to make in the final edit of the movie. Director Ron Howard (*How the Grinch Stole Christmas, Apollo 13, Cocoon*) says "[While] the whole preview experience is no fun . . . you never want to be proven to be mistaken about anything.[3]

Without reading ahead, think about answers to these questions:

- Whom would you recruit for these test screenings?
- What questions would you ask audience members to help you in editing or modifying the title or parts of the film?

Virtually every major movie produced today uses test screenings to obtain the key reactions of consumers likely to be in the target market. Figure 8–1 summarizes some of the key questions that are used in these test screenings, both to select the people for the screenings and to obtain key reactions of those sitting in the screenings.

Here are some examples of changes to movies that have resulted from this kind of marketing research:

- *Making the plot move faster.* Disney cut a duet by Pocahontas and John Smith in *Pocahontas* because it got in the way of the action and confused test audiences.[4]
- *Reaching a market segment more effectively.* More action footage was added for Kevin Costner when preview screening showed young males were less enthusiastic about *The Bodyguard* than young females.[5]
- *Changing an ending. Fatal Attraction* had probably the most commercially successful "ending-switch" of all time. In its sneak previews, audiences liked everything but the ending, which had Alex (Glenn Close) committing suicide and managing to frame Dan (Michael Douglas) as her murderer by leaving his fingerprints on the knife she used. The studio shot $1.3 million of new scenes for the ending that regular audiences eventually saw.[6]

Sometimes studios get the pleasant news in test screenings that a movie or plot "works" with an audience. This was the case when James Cameron, writer-director of *Titanic*, sat in on the first test screening of his $200-million epic and watched the audience go wild, a huge relief after months of cost overruns and delayed premiers.[7]

New Line Cinema appears to have a hit on its hands with the *Lord of the Rings* trilogy. It cost the studio more than U.S.$300 million to produce and market! Its test screenings went very well, and the first instalment of the trilogy, *The Fellowship of the Ring*, was a box-office hit over the 2001 Christmas season. In fact, this movie alone helped Toronto-based Alliance Atlantis Communications Inc. post a 37-percent increase in fiscal third-quarter profit that year. New Line Cinema will release the next instalment, *The Two Towers*, for Christmas 2002, and the final instalment, *The Return of the King*, during Christmas 2003. Even though the first film in the trilogy was wildly successful, the studio faces the challenge of maintaining audience interest over the next two years.

Movie studios also use tracking studies, in which prospective moviegoers in the target audience are asked three key questions about an upcoming film release:[8]

- Are you aware of a particular film?
- Are you interested in seeing it?
- Would it be your first choice on a certain weekend?

POINT WHEN ASKED	KEY QUESTIONS	USE OF QUESTION(S)
Before the test screening	• How old are you? • How frequently do you pay to see movies? • What movies have you seen in the last three months?	Decide if person fits profile of target audience for movie. If yes, invite to test screening. If not, don't invite.
After the test screening	• What do you think of the title? What title would you suggest? • Were any characters too distasteful? Who? How? • Did any scenes offend you? Which ones? How? • How did you like the ending? If you didn't like it, how would you change it? • Would you recommend the movie to a friend?	Change movie title. Change aspects of some characters. Change scenes. Change or clarify ending. Overall indicator of liking of and/or satisfaction with movie.

FIGURE 8–1
Marketing research questions asked in test screenings of movies, and how they are used

Studios then use the data collected to forecast the movie's opening-weekend box office sales, or run last-minute ads to increase awareness and interest: the "buzz" or word-of-mouth for the film. In some cases, a studio may postpone or advance a film's release depending on the results for other movies scheduled for release at that time.

These examples show how marketing research is the link between marketing strategy and decisive decisions, the main topic of this chapter. Also, marketing research is often used to help a firm develop sales forecasts, the final topic in the chapter.

WHAT MARKETING RESEARCH IS AND DOES

MARKETING RESEARCH
The process of defining a marketing problem and opportunity, systematically collecting and analyzing information, and recommending actions to improve an organization's marketing activities.

Marketing research is the process of defining a marketing problem or opportunity, systematically collecting and analyzing information, and recommending actions to improve an organization's marketing activities.[9]

A Means of Reducing Risk and Uncertainty   Assessing the needs and wants of consumers and providing information to help design an organization's marketing program to satisfy them is the principal role that marketing research performs. This means that marketing research attempts to identify and define both marketing problems and opportunities and to generate and evaluate marketing actions. Although marketing research can provide few answers with complete assurance, it can reduce risk and uncertainty to increase the likelihood of the success of marketing decisions. It is a great help to the marketing managers who must make final decisions. Conducted properly, marketing research can solve most marketing-related problems that an executive might have. However, marketing research should not be designed to simply replace an executive's good sense, experience, or intuition but rather should be used in conjunction with those skills and as a way of taking out some of the guesswork in the marketing decision-making process.

TYPES OF MARKETING RESEARCH

To understand the variety of research activity, it is helpful to categorize different types of marketing research. Marketing research is often classified on the basis of either technique or function. Surveys, experiments, and observation are a few research techniques with which you may be familiar. However, categorizing research by its purpose or function shows how the nature of the marketing problem influences the choice of research techniques. The nature of the problem will determine whether the research is (1) exploratory, (2) descriptive, or (3) causal.

Exploratory Research

Exploratory research is preliminary research conducted to clarify the scope and nature of the marketing problem. It is generally carried out to provide the researcher with a better understanding of the dimensions of the problem. Exploratory research is often conducted with the expectation that subsequent and more conclusive research will follow. For example, the Dairy Farmers of Canada, an association representing dairy producers in the country, wanted to discover why milk consumption was declining in Canada.

They conducted a search of existing literature on milk consumption, talked to experts in the field, and even conducted preliminary interviews with consumers to get ideas about why consumers were drinking less milk. This exploratory research helped the association to crystallize the problem, and identify issues for more detailed follow-up research. We examine exploratory research as an integral component of the basic marketing research process later in the chapter.

www.milk.org

The Dairy Farmers of Canada conducted three types of marketing research in an effort to solve the decline in milk consumption problem. For details read the text.

Dairy Farmers of Canada

www.dairyfarmers.org

Fact: Milk is recommended for its many vital nutrients.

Descriptive Research

Descriptive research is research designed to describe basic characteristics of a given population or to profile particular marketing situations. Unlike exploratory research, with descriptive research the researcher has a general understanding of the marketing problem and is seeking conclusive data that answer the questions necessary to determine a particular course of action. Examples of descriptive research would include profiling product purchasers (e.g., the Canadian health food store shopper), describing the size and characteristics of markets (e.g., the Canadian pizza restaurant market), detailing product usage patterns (e.g., ATM usage by Canadian bank consumers), or outlining consumer attitudes toward particular brands (e.g., Canadian attitudes toward national, private, and generic brands).

Magazines, radio stations, and television stations almost always do descriptive research to identify the characteristics of their audiences in order to present it to prospective advertisers. As a follow-up to its exploratory research, the Dairy Farmers of Canada conducted descriptive research to determine the demographic characteristics of milk consumers, current usage patterns, and consumer attitudes toward milk consumption.

Causal Research

Causal research is research designed to identify cause-and-effect relationships among variables. In general, exploratory and descriptive research normally precede causal research. With causal research there is typically an expectation about the relationship to be explained, such as predicting the influence of a price change on product demand. In general, researchers attempt to establish that one event (e.g., a price change) will produce another event (e.g., a change in demand). Typical causal research studies examine the effect of advertising on sales; the relationship between price and perceived quality of a product; and the impact of a new package on product sales. When the Dairy Farmers of Canada conducted its descriptive research on milk consumers, it discovered that many believed milk was too fattening and too high in cholesterol. The association felt that these beliefs might be related to the overall decline in milk consumption in Canada. To test this assumption, the association ran a television advertising campaign to demonstrate that milk was a healthful product and essential to a person's diet. In its tracking studies, it found that the ad campaign did change consumer attitudes toward milk which, in turn, was causally related to a subsequent increase in milk consumption. We refer to causal research later in this chapter when we deal with experiments as a basic research technique.

Concept Check

1. What is marketing research?

2. What is the difference between exploratory, descriptive, and causal research?

THE MARKETING RESEARCH PROCESS

Marketing research should always be conducted based on the *scientific method*, a process of systematically collecting, organizing and analyzing data in an unbiased, objective manner. Marketing research must meet two basic principles of the scientific method—reliability and validity. *Reliability* refers to the ability to replicate research results under identical environmental conditions. In other words, if a research project were to be conducted for the second, third, or fourth time, the results should be the same. Marketers need to have reliable information to make effective decisions. If results of a study are not reliable, the research can do more harm than no research at all. *Validity* involves the notion of whether the research measured what was intended to be measured. In other words, does the research tell marketers what they needed to know? You should keep the concepts of reliability and validity in mind as we discuss the marketing research process.

Figure 8–2 outlines the basic marketing research process. The figure is perhaps an oversimplification of the process since marketing research does not always follow such a neat and ordered sequence of activities. However, all marketing research consists of four basic stages: (1) defining the problem, (2) determining the research design, (3) collecting and analyzing data, and (4) drawing conclusions and preparing a report.

In reviewing Figure 8–2 you can see that the researcher has a number of decisions and choices to make during the stages of the process. For example, the red boxes in Figure 8–2 indicate stages in the process where a choice of one or more techniques or methods must be made. The dotted line indicates the researcher's choice to bypass the exploratory research stage of the process.

FIGURE 8–2

The basic marketing research process

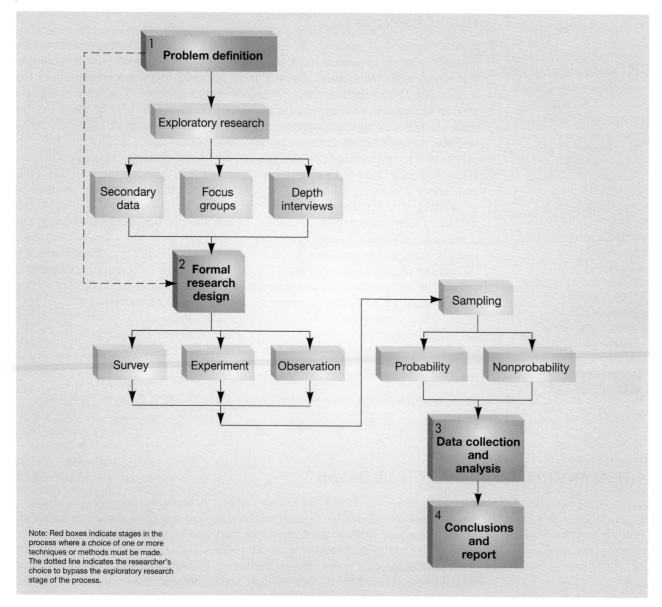

Note: Red boxes indicate stages in the process where a choice of one or more techniques or methods must be made. The dotted line indicates the researcher's choice to bypass the exploratory research stage of the process.

PROBLEM DEFINITION

www.oceanspray.com

The first step in the marketing research process is to properly define the scope and nature of the marketing problem to be investigated. In general, the term *problem* suggests that something has gone wrong. In reality, to the marketing researcher, the word *problem* may also mean something to explore or an opportunity to define, or a current marketing situation to monitor or evaluate. Sometimes the problem is obvious, but in other cases the problem may be more difficult to identify and define. In either case, the marketing researcher must fully understand and properly identify the problem at hand.

The marketing research process is often initiated by the marketing manager, who will approach the marketing researcher with a problem that requires information for decision making. For example, suppose you were the marketing manager for cranberry juice at Ocean Spray. You want to know if Asian consumers would buy cranberry juice when they have never heard of cranberries. You also have other problems. The word "cranberry" isn't part of any foreign language so you would have to find a name for it and its juice. Also, if you are going to take the product to Asia you have to find a way to encourage consumers there to try the new product.[10] The marketing researcher has to fully understand these problems. The researcher must also remember that the best place to begin a research project is at the end. In other words, the researcher must know what is to be accomplished through the research process. In this case, as the marketing manager what you really want to know is: Is there a market opportunity in Asia for cranberry juice? If so, how can it be exploited?

Proper problem definition is critical since research based on incorrect problem definition will be a waste of resources. Good marketing researchers adhere to the old adage "a problem well defined is a problem half-solved." If the research problem is clear, the chances of collecting the necessary information to solve the problem are increased.

Concept Check

1. What are reliability and validity?

2. What are the four basic stages in the marketing research process?

Exploratory Research

Your colleague, the marketing researcher at Ocean Spray, has to make a decision early on in the marketing research process. Should exploratory research be conducted in an attempt to help answer the question: Is there a market opportunity in Asia for cranberry juice? As we saw earlier in the chapter, exploratory research is preliminary research conducted to clarify the scope and nature of the marketing problem. In general, it is designed to provide the researcher with a better understanding of the dimensions of the problem and is often conducted with the expectation that subsequent and more conclusive research may follow.

Most researchers will usually conduct some basic exploratory research during the early stage of the research process. The extent of the exploratory research will depend on the magnitude of the problem as well as its complexity. If the researcher decides to conduct exploratory research, he or she has three basic techniques to choose from: (1) secondary data analysis, (2) focus groups, and (3) depth interviews.

Should Ocean Spray introduce
cranberry juice in Asia when
consumers there have never
heard of cranberries? See
the text.

Ocean Spray

SECONDARY DATA
Facts and figures that have
already been recorded
before the project at hand.

PRIMARY DATA
Facts and figures that
are newly collected for
the project.

www.statcan.ca

Secondary Data Exploratory research almost always involves the use of **secondary data** (or historical data)—data previously collected and assembled for some project other than the one at hand. **Primary data**, on the other hand, are data gathered and assembled specifically for the project at hand. As a rule, researchers gather secondary data before collecting primary data. In general, secondary data can be obtained more quickly and at a lower cost compared to primary data. However, there can be problems with secondary data. The required information may not exist, and if it does, it may not be current or particularly pertinent to the problem at hand. Still, most researchers agree that investigating secondary data sources can save researchers from "reinventing the wheel."

Researchers examine secondary data both inside and outside the organization. Internal secondary data include financial statements, research reports, customer letters, and customer lists. What did your colleague in marketing research at Ocean Spray discover during the secondary data search efforts? She was able to discover that Ocean Spray did attempt to introduce a bland cranberry juice in Japan—named "Cranby"—and it fizzled and was pulled off the market. As a marketing manager this information does provide some background, but you still have more questions than answers about the possible marketing opportunity in Asia.

Sources of external secondary data can be wide and varied. One key source, for example, is the federal government with data made available through Statistics Canada or local libraries. Statistics Canada completes the *Census of Canada* once every decade and updates certain census data every few years. The census provides detailed information on Canadian households. Statistics Canada also prepares annual or biannual reports including the *Family Expenditure Guide*, which gives a detailed breakdown of how families spend their money. These basic sources of information are used by manufacturers and retailers to identify characteristics and trends of ultimate consumers.

Statistics Canada produces many other census reports that are vital to business firms selling goods and services to organizations. Such reports include the *Census of Manufacturers*, which lists the number and size of manufacturing firms by industry group as well as other information including values of shipments and wages paid.

A marketing researcher can obtain from Statistics Canada their annual *Marketing Research Handbook* or the *Canada Year Book*, which includes a summary of key information often necessary to aid marketing decision making. Statistics Canada also has a database system known as CANSIM II (Canadian Socio-Economic Information Management System), which marketers can access directly in order to examine aggregate data.

In addition to government-supplied data, trade associations, universities, and business periodicals provide detailed data of value. For example, one business periodical, *Sales and Marketing Management*, publishes special issues each year that provide useful data for firms selling both consumer and industrial products. The most famous publication by *S&MM* is their *Annual Survey of Buying Power*. The *Financial Post* produces a publication called *Canadian Markets*, which provides demographic information and data on consumer spending power in provinces, cities, and towns across the country.

Companies such as MapInfo and ACNielsen offer both standard and customized information services to other firms on a subscription, or for-fee, basis. MapInfo can provide information on any geographic area of any size in Canada that highlights population, income, and retail expenditure trends in that area. Figure 8–3 shows some of the secondary data sources available to the marketer in Canada. There are also hundreds of useful online databanks and specialized data services such as Dow Jones, Dialog, and Infoglobe. The Web Link box provides examples.

New marketing data services have also emerged that offer *single-source data*, which is information provided by a single firm on household demographics and lifestyles, product purchases, media habits, and responses to sales promotions such as coupons and free samples. The principal advantage of single-source data is the ability of one service to collect, analyze, interrelate, and present all this information. For consumer product firms like Procter & Gamble, sales data from various channels are critical when allocating marketing resources among such channels. As a result, P&G uses single-source data providers, such as Information Resources' InfoScan and ACNielsen's ScanTrack, to collect product sales and coupon/free sample redemptions that have been scanned at the checkout counter from supermarket, drug, convenience, and mass merchandise retailers. Campbell Soup, maker of Swanson frozen dinners, used the information from a single-source data provider to shift its TV ad campaign from a serious to a light theme, which increased sales of Swanson dinners.

Getting back to our marketing researcher at Ocean Spray and the cranberry juice in Asia question, she discovers some external secondary data, specifically a study on Taiwan consumers that shows increased consumption of juice beverages. Still, the study is not specific to cranberry juice, and is about four years old. As marketing manager, you realize you still have a high degree of uncertainty about the possible marketing opportunity in Asia. So you ask your colleague in marketing research to continue the exploratory stage of the marketing process.

Focus Groups   A very popular exploratory research technique designed to obtain primary data is the use of focus groups. **Focus groups** are informal interview sessions in which 6 to 10 persons, relevant to the research project, are brought together in a room with a moderator to discuss topics surrounding the marketing research problem. The moderator poses questions and encourages the individuals to answer in their own words and to discuss the issues with each other. Often, the focus-group sessions are watched by observers through one-way mirrors and/or the sessions are videotaped. Of course, participants should be informed they are being observed and/or taped. Focus-group sessions often provide the marketer with valuable information for decision making or can uncover other issues that should be researched in a more quantitative fashion.

FOCUS GROUPS
An informal session of 6 to 10 past, present, or prospective customers in which a discussion leader, or moderator, asks their opinions about the firm's and its competitors' products.

SELECTED GUIDES, INDEXES, AND DIRECTORIES

Business Periodical Index
Canadian Almanac and Directory
Canadian Business Index
Canadian News Index
Canadian Periodical Index
Canadian Statistics Index
Canadian Trade Index
Directory of Associations in Canada
Fraser's Canadian Trade Directory
Predicasts Index
Scott's Directories
Standards Periodical Directory
Ulrich's International Periodicals Directory

SELECTED PERIODICALS AND NEWSPAPERS

Advertising Age
Adweek
American Demographics
Business Horizons
Canadian Business
Canadian Consumer
Forbes
Fortune
Harvard Business Review
Journal of Advertising
Journal of Advertising Research
Journal of Consumer Research
Journal of Marketing
Journal of Marketing Management
Journal of Marketing Research
Journal of Personal Selling and Sales Management
Journal of Retailing
Journal of Small Business
Marketing Magazine

Marketing & Media Decisions
Marketing News
Progressive Grocer
Sales and Marketing Management
The Globe and Mail
The Financial Post
The Financial Post Magazine
The Wall Street Journal

SELECTED STATISTICS CANADA PUBLICATIONS

Annual Retail Trade
Canadian Economic Observer
Canada Yearbook
Family Expenditure Guide
Market Research Handbook
Statistics Canada Catalogue

SELECTED TRADE SOURCES

ACNielsen
Conference Board of Canada
Dun & Bradstreet Canada
Financial Post Publishing
Find/SVP
Gale Research
MacLean Hunter Research Bureau
MapInfo Canada
Predicasts International
R. L. Polk

SELECTED DATABASES

CANSIM II (Statistics Canada)
Dialog
Dow Jones
Infoglobe
Infomart
The Source

FIGURE 8–3
Sources of secondary data

DEPTH INTERVIEWS
A detailed, individual interview with a person relevant to the research project.

Britain's Lewis Woolf Griptight, a manufacturer of infant and toddler products, conducted focus groups about possible brand names for their products before bringing a new product line to market. U.K. consumers turned thumbs down on using "Griptight" as a brand name for kids' products because they thought it sounded like "a carpet glue, a denture fixative, a kind of tire." So the firm called its product line by the name Kiddiwinks™—a British word for children.[11]

Depth Interviews   Another exploratory research technique used to obtain primary data involves the use of depth interviews. **Depth interviews** are detailed individual interviews with people relevant to the research project. The researcher questions the individual at length in a free-flowing conversational style in order to discover information that may help solve the marketing problem being investigated. Sometimes these interviews can take a few hours, and they are often recorded on audio- or videotape.

Hamburger Helper didn't fare too well with consumers when General Mills first introduced it. Initial instructions called for cooking a half pound of hamburger separately from the noodles, which were later mixed with the hamburger. Depth interviews revealed that consumers didn't think the recipe called for enough meat and that they didn't want the hassle of cooking in two different pots. So the Hamburger Helper product manager changed the recipe to call for a full pound of meat and to allow users to prepare it in one dish; this converted a potential failure into a success.

WEB LINK

Online Databases Useful in Marketing

http://www.mcgrawhill.ca

Information in online databases available through the Internet divide into two categories: (1) indexes to articles in publications, which are accessed through keyword searches, and (2) statistical and directory data on households, products, and companies.

Online databases of indexes, abstracts, and full-text information from journals and periodicals include:

- LexisNexis' Academic Universe, which gives full-text information from more than 5000 periodicals and publications. (www.lexis-nexis.com)
- ProQuest databases, which contain academic articles from more than 8000 management, marketing, and business periodicals and journals. (www.proquest.com)
- General BusinessFile ASAP from Information Access Company, which contains references, abstracts, and full-text articles from more than 1000 business and industry publications. (www.library.iacnet.com)

Statistical and directory information about households, products, and companies through online databases include:

- FIS online, which gives data on more than 28 000 companies that are traded on the NYSE, AMEX, and NASDAQ stock exchanges. (www.fisonline.com)
- Dow Jones Interactive from Dow Jones & Company (publisher of *The Wall Street Journal*), which provides up-to-the-minute business news; secondary research reports on companies, industries, and countries; and up to 25 years of historical pricing on thousands of securities. (www.dowjones.com)
- Statistics Canada, which provides census data and detailed information on Canadian households, as well as industrial and retail trade information. (www. statcan.ca)

Some of these sites are accessible only if a subscription fee has been paid by an organization. To check out these sites, access your college or university Website, click on the icon for your library, and then click on these or other useful databases to which your institution subscribes.

Researchers have also become creative in devising other exploratory research techniques. For example, finding "the next big thing" for consumers has become the obsession in many industries.[12] In order to unearth the next big thing, marketing researchers have developed some unusual techniques sometimes referred to as "fuzzy front-end" methods. These techniques are designed to identify elusive consumer tastes or trends far before typical consumers have recognized them themselves. For example, having consumers take a photo of themselves every time they snack resulted in General Mills' Homestyle "Pop Secret" popcorn, which delivers the real butter and bursts of salt in microwave popcorn consumers thought they could only get from the stovetop variety.[13]

Other unusual techniques are also being used to try to spot trends early. For example, Teenage Research Unlimited had teenagers complete a drawing to help discover what teenagers like, wear, listen to, and read.[14] Other companies hire "cool hunters," people with tastes far ahead of the curve, to identify the "next big things" likely to sweep popular culture. Wet Seal and Skechers use this method to anticipate teenage girls' fashion picks and footwear trends.[15]

Concept Check

1. What are secondary data?

2. What are focus groups?

FORMAL RESEARCH DESIGN

After identifying and clarifying the marketing problem, with or without exploratory research, the researcher must determine the basic framework for finding a solution to the problem. At the formal research design stage, the researcher produces a plan that outlines the method and procedures for collecting and analyzing the required information. The plan includes the objectives of the research; the sources of information to be used; the research methods (e.g., survey, experiment); the sampling plan; and the schedule and cost of the research.

In selecting basic research methods, the researcher must make decisions. In general, the objectives of the research, the available data sources, the nature of the information required, and timing and cost considerations will determine which research method will be chosen. The basic methods the researcher can choose for descriptive and causal research include: (1) survey, (2) experiment, and (3) observation.

Survey

SURVEY
A research technique used to generate data by asking people questions and recording their responses on a questionnaire.

The most common research method of generating new or primary data is the use of surveys. A **survey** is a research technique used to generate data by asking people questions and recording their responses on a questionnaire. Surveys can be conducted by mail, telephone, or personal interview. In choosing among the three alternatives, the marketing researcher has to make important trade-offs (as shown in Figure 8–4) to balance cost against the expected quality of the information obtained. The figure shows that personal interviews have a major advantage of enabling the interviewer to be flexible in asking probing questions or getting reactions to visual materials. In contrast, mail surveys usually have the lowest cost per completed survey of the three data collection procedures. Telephone surveys lie between the other two technologies in terms of flexibility and cost.

Sometimes marketers will survey over time the same sample of people, commonly known as a survey *panel*. A panel can consist of a sample of consumers, stores, or experts from which researchers can take a series of measurements. For example, a

FIGURE 8–4
Comparison of mail, telephone, and personal interview surveys

BASIS OF COMPARISON	MAIL SURVEYS	TELEPHONE SURVEYS	PERSONAL INTERVIEW SURVEYS
Cost per completed survey	Usually the least expensive, assuming adequate return rate	Moderately expensive, assuming reasonable completion rate	Most expensive, because of interviewer's time and travel expenses
Ability to probe and ask complex questions	Little, since self-administered format must be short and simple	Some, since interviewer can probe and elaborate on questions to a degree	Much, since interviewer can show visual materials, gain rapport, and probe
Opportunity for interviewer to bias results	None, since form is completed without interviewer	Some, because of voice inflection of interviewer	Significant, because of voice and facial expressions of interviewer
Anonymity given to respondent	Complete, since no signature is required	Some, because of telephone contact	Little, because of face-to-face contact

FIGURE 8–5
Typical problems in
wording questions

PROBLEM	SAMPLE QUESTION	EXPLANATION
Leading question	Why do you like Wendy's fresh meat hamburgers better than those of competitors?	Consumer is led to make statements favouring Wendy's hamburgers
Ambiguous question	Do you eat at fast-food restaurants regularly? ☐ Yes ☐ No	What is meant by word *regularly*—once a day, once a month, or what?
Unanswerable question	What was the occasion for your eating your first hamburger?	Who can remember the answer? Does it matter?
Two questions in one	Do you eat Wendy's hamburgers and chili? ☐ Yes ☐ No	How do you answer if you eat Wendy's hamburgers but not chili?
Nonexhaustive question	Where do you live? ☐ At home ☐ In dormitory	What do you check if you live in an apartment?
Non–mutually exclusive answers	What is your age? ☐ Under 20 ☐ 20–40 ☐ 40 and over	What answer does a 40-year-old check?

consumer's switch from one brand of breakfast cereal to another can be measured with panel data. The use of panels is becoming more popular with marketers as they attempt to obtain ongoing information about their constituents. Panel data are often incorporated into information systems, which are discussed later in the chapter.

When marketers decide to use surveys to ask questions, they assume that: (1) the right questions are being asked, (2) people will understand the questions being asked, (3) people know the answers to the questions, (4) people will answer the questions truthfully, and (5) the researchers themselves will understand the answers provided. Marketers must concern themselves not only with asking the right questions but also with how to properly word those questions. Proper phrasing of a question is vital in uncovering useful marketing information.

Figure 8–5 shows typical problems to guard against in wording questions to obtain meaningful answers from respondents. For example, in a question of whether you eat at fast-food restaurants regularly, the word regularly is ambiguous. Two people might answer "yes" to the question, but one might mean "once a day" while the other means "once or twice a year." Both answers appear as "yes" to the researcher who tabulates them, but they suggest that dramatically different marketing actions be directed to each of these two prospective consumers. Therefore, it is essential that marketing research questions be worded precisely so that all respondents interpret the same question similarly. Marketing researchers must also take great care not to use "leading" questions (wording questions in a way to ensure a particular response), which can lead to a very distorted picture of the respondents' actual feelings or opinions.

In Figure 8–6 we can see the number of different formats that questions can take in a survey instrument. The questions presented are taken from a Wendy's survey that assessed fast-food preferences among present and prospective consumers. Question 1 is an example of an *open-end question*, which the respondent can answer in his or her own words. In contrast, questions in which the respondent simply checks an answer are *closed-end* or *fixed alternative questions*. Question 2 is an example of the simplest fixed alternative question, a *dichotomous question* that allows only a "yes" or "no" answer. A fixed alternative question with three or more choices uses

FIGURE 8–6
Sample questions from
Wendy's survey

1 What things are most important to you when you decide to eat out and go to a restaurant?

_____

_____

_____

_____

_____

_____

2 Have you eaten fast-food restaurant food in the past month?
☐ Yes ☐ No

3 If you answered "yes" to Question 2, how often do you eat fast food?
☐ Once a week or more   ☐ Two or three times a month   ☐ Once a month or less

4 How important is it to you that a fast-food restaurant satisfy you on the following characteristics? Check the box that describes your feelings.

CHARACTERISTIC	VERY IMPORTANT	SOMEWHAT IMPORTANT	IMPORTANT	UNIMPORTANT	SOMEWHAT UNIMPORTANT	VERY UNIMPORTANT
Taste of food	☐	☐	☐	☐	☐	☐
Cleanliness	☐	☐	☐	☐	☐	☐
Price	☐	☐	☐	☐	☐	☐
Variety on menu	☐	☐	☐	☐	☐	☐

5 Check the space on the scale below that describes how you feel about Wendy's on the characteristics shown.

CHARACTERISTIC	CHECK THE SPACE DESCRIBING HOW WENDY'S IS		
Taste of food	Tasty	_ _ _ _ _ _ _ _ _	Not tasty
Cleanliness	Clean	_ _ _ _ _ _ _ _ _	Not clean
Price	Inexpensive	_ _ _ _ _ _ _ _ _	Expensive
Variety on menu	Broad	_ _ _ _ _ _ _ _ _	Narrow

a scale. Question 5 is an example of a question that uses a *semantic differential scale*, a nine-point scale in which the opposite ends have one- or two-word adjectives that have opposite meanings. For example, depending on how clean the respondent believes that Wendy's is, he or she would check the left-hand space on the scale, the right-hand space, or one of the seven intervening points. Question 6 uses a *Likert scale*, in which the respondent is asked to indicate the extent to which he or she agrees or disagrees with a statement.

The questionnaire in Figure 8–6 is an excerpt of a precisely worded survey that provides valuable information to the marketing researcher at Wendy's. Questions 1 to 8 inform him or her about the likes and dislikes in eating out, frequency of eating out at fast-food restaurants generally and at Wendy's specifically, and sources of information used in making decisions about fast-food restaurants. Question 9 gives details about the personal or household characteristics which can be used in trying to segment the fast-food market, a topic discussed in Chapter 9.

Surveys of distributors—retailers and wholesalers in the marketing channel—are also very important for manufacturers. A reason given for the success of many Japanese consumer products in Canada, such as Sony Walkmans and Toyota automobiles, is the stress that Japanese marketers place on obtaining accurate information from their distributors.

FIGURE 8–6
(concluded)

6 Check the box that describes your agreement or disagreement with the following statements.

STATEMENT	STRONGLY AGREE	AGREE	DON'T KNOW	DISAGREE	STRONGLY DISAGREE
Adults like to take their families to fast-food restaurants.	☐	☐	☐	☐	☐
Our children have a say in where the family eats.	☐	☐	☐	☐	☐

7 How important are each of the following information sources when you select a fast-food restaurant?

SOURCE OF INFORMATION	VERY IMPORTANT SOURCE	SOMEWHAT IMPORTANT SOURCE	NOT AN IMPORTANT SOURCE
Television	☐	☐	☐
Newspapers	☐	☐	☐
Radio	☐	☐	☐
Billboards	☐	☐	☐
Flyers	☐	☐	☐

8 In the past month, how often have you eaten at each of these three fast-food restaurants?

RESTAURANT	ONCE A WEEK OR MORE	TWO OR THREE TIMES A MONTH	ONCE A MONTH OR LESS
Burger King	☐	☐	☐
McDonald's	☐	☐	☐
Wendy's	☐	☐	☐

9 Please answer the following questions about you and your household.
  a Are you   ☐ Male   ☐ Female
  b Are you   ☐ Single   ☐ Married   ☐ Other (widowed, divorced)
  c How many children under age 18 live in your home?
      ☐ 0   ☐ 1   ☐ 2   ☐ 3 or more
  d What is your age?
      ☐ under 25   ☐ 25–44   ☐ 45 or over
  e What is your approximate total annual household income?
      ☐ Less than $15 000   ☐ $15 000–$49 999   ☐ $50 000 or more

www.labatt.com

Electronic technology has revolutionized the traditional concept of surveys. Today, respondents can walk up to a kiosk in a shopping centre, read questions off a screen, and key their answers into a computer on a touch screen. Labatt Breweries Ltd. uses an interactive kiosk in the shape of a beer can and rewards customers with coupons as a thank-you for completing an electronic survey.[16] Even fully automated systems exist for conducting surveys by telephone. An automated voice questions respondents over the telephone, who key their replies on a touch-tone telephone. The use of Internet survey tools and other research applications via the Web is also expanding rapidly.[17]

Experiment

EXPERIMENT
Obtaining data by manipulating factors under tightly controlled conditions to test cause and effect.

Another method that can be used by marketing researchers to generate primary data is the experiment. Marketing experiments offer the potential for establishing cause-and-effect relationships (causal research). An **experiment** involves the manipulation of an independent variable (cause) and the measurement of its effect on the dependent variable (effect) under controlled conditions.

In marketing experiments the independent variables are often one or more of the marketing mix variables, such as product features, price, or promotion used. An ideal dependent variable usually is a change in purchases of an individual, household, or entire organization. If actual purchases cannot be used as a dependent variable, factors that are believed to be highly related to purchases, such as preferences in a taste test or intentions to buy, are used.

A potential difficulty with experiments is that an extraneous (or outside) variable can distort the results of an experiment and affect the dependent variable.

Experiments can be conducted in the field or in a laboratory. In *field experiments*, the research is conducted in the real world such as in a store, bank, or on the street, wherever the behaviour being studied occurs naturally. Field experiments can be expensive but are a good way to determine people's reactions to changes in the elements of the marketing mix. Test marketing is probably the most common form of field experiments. Kraft Canada used test marketing before introducing its microwaveable, pre-baked cookie to the Canadian marketplace. And Toronto-based Grocery Gateway, Canada's first fully integrated Internet grocery retailer, used test marketing before successfully entering the online grocery business.[18] Remember your problem as marketing manager for cranberry juice at Ocean Spray? You wanted to know if Asian consumers would buy cranberry juice when they had never tasted cranberries? Perhaps your marketing research colleague might recommend taste tests in Asia to gauge consumers' responses to the product.

Because marketers cannot control all the conditions in the field, they sometimes turn to a laboratory setting. Laboratories are not the real world but do offer highly controlled environments. Unlike in the field, the marketer has control over all the factors that may play a role in impacting on the behaviour under investigation. For example, in a field experiment the marketer may wish to examine the impact of a price reduction on sales of a particular product. The competition, however, may see the price reduction and offer their own price deal, thus interfering with the

Successful test marketing led to Grocery Gateway's entry into the Internet-based retail grocery business.

Grocery Gateway
www.grocerygateway.com

possible results of the field experiment. This does not occur in a lab setting. Many companies are using laboratory settings where they can control conditions but can do so in a real-world fashion, such as simulated supermarkets or test stores. Here they can experiment with changes in aisle displays, packaging changes, or other variables that may affect buyer behaviour without the fear of other extraneous factors influencing the results.

Observation

OBSERVATION
Watching, either mechanically or in person, how people behave.

Another basic research method used to obtain primary data is observation. In general, **observation** involves watching, either mechanically or in person, how people behave. In some circumstances, the speed of events or the number of events being observed make mechanical or electronic observation more appropriate than personal observation. Retailers, for example, can use electronic cameras to count the number of customers entering or leaving a store.

A classic form of mechanical observation is ACNielsen's "people meter," which is a box attached to television sets, VCRs, cable boxes, and satellite dishes in selected households in Canada and the United States in order to determine the size of audiences watching television programs delivered by the networks. When a household member watches TV, he or she is supposed to push a button on a remote and push it again when viewing stops. The people meter is supposed to measure who in the household is watching what program on every TV set owned.

This information is used to calculate ratings for each TV program, which in turn is used to set advertising rates for such programs. But people meters have limitations—as with all observations collected mechanically. Critics don't believe the devices accurately measure who is watching a given TV program or what is actually watched. Moreover, people meters cannot measure large segments of the population that watch TV programs at parties, hotels, or sports bars. A new "passive, portable people meter" is now being tested by Nielsen and Arbitron, a service firm that also measures cable TV viewership as well as radio listenership. This device, which is the size of a pager, is carried by consumers and automatically detects inaudible codes in the programming of TV, cable, and radio broadcasters, both in-home and at outside venues. Each night, participants place the meter into a base station, which then transmits the data to Nielsen/Arbitron for analysis.

How do you do marketing research on things such as toothbrushes and fashion products for teenagers? For some creative answers, see the text.

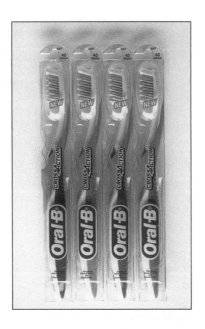

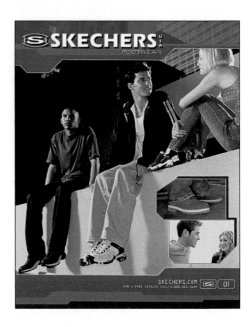

Nielsen also uses an electronic meter to record Internet user behaviour. These data are collected by tracking the actual mouse clicks made by users as they surf the Internet via a meter installed on their home or work computers. Nielsen has been able to identify the Websites that have the largest audiences, the top advertising banners viewed, the top Internet advertisers, and global Internet usage for selected countries.[19]

Watching consumers in person or by videotaping them are other observational approaches used to collect primary data. For example, Aurora Foods observes how consumers bake cakes in its Duncan Hines test kitchens to see if baking instructions on the cake box are understood and followed correctly. Fisher-Price uses it licensed nursery schools to observe how children use and abuse toys in order to develop better products. Gillette marketing researchers actually videotaped consumers brushing their teeth in their own bathrooms to see how they really brush—not just how they say they brush. The result: Gillette's new Oral-B CrossAction toothbrush that's supposed to do a better job![20]

ETHNOGRAPHIC RESEARCH
Observational approach to discover subtle emotional reactions as consumers encounter products in their "natural use environment."

A specialized observational approach is **ethnographic research**, in which anthropologists and other trained observers seek to discover subtle emotional reactions as consumers encounter products in their "natural use environment" such as in their home, car, or hotel. For example Best Western, a hotel chain, paid couples to videotape themselves as they spent three to seven days on a cross-country car trip. From this, Best Western found that women usually decided when to pull off the road and where to stay—the reverse of what was found during focus group research. The result: Best Western targets women more often with its promotional messages.[21] Read the accompanying Marketing NewsNet to see just how a new shower head came to market as a result of ethnographic research.[22]

Personal observation is both useful and flexible, but it can be costly and unreliable, especially when different observers report different conclusions in watching the same activities. Also, although observation can reveal what people do, it cannot determine why they do it, such as why they are buying or not buying a product. To determine why consumers behave as they do, marketing researchers must talk with consumers and record their responses. This is usually accomplished through the use of surveys.

Is There an Optimal Research Design?

In short, there is no optimal research design. A researcher may choose among a variety of alternative methods for solving a particular marketing problem. A good

MARKETING NEWSNET

The Naked Truth: Marketing Researchers Search for the Perfect Shower Head

As this chapter points out, a specialized observational research method is called *ethnographic research*. In short, researchers observe consumers interacting with products in their natural use environment. Before Moen Inc. put its new massaging shower head, the Revolution, on the market, it wanted to see what consumers thought about the new product design. But Moen didn't want to just give consumers the shower head and later ask them if they liked it or not. The company wanted to see the consumers actually using the product . . . in the shower. So it hired QualiData Research Inc. to do some observational research. Moen believed that people would not be able or willing to articulate what they really wanted in a shower head, or why they liked or didn't like the new shower head that Moen had developed. QualiData believed the only way to get real answers would be to watch people use the product in the shower. Obviously, not everyone would be willing to allow a stranger to observe or videotape them showering in the buff. So Moen and QualiData decided to enlist nudists as their volunteers. They wanted at least 20 people who varied in age and body type, and males and females of various ethnicities. For $250 each, the volunteers allowed the researchers to come into their homes. They answered the researchers' questions about their lifestyles while other team members installed a tiny video camera in the shower of each volunteer.

What truths did the videos reveal? Well, they showed that most people have only one hand free while they shower. And that most people close their eyes sporadically while showering. The videos also showed that often bathroom lighting did not penetrate the shower curtain. Because of these constraints, the people showering had a hard time fumbling around with massage settings. As a result of the research, the new Revolution massaging shower head has a peanut-shaped control dial below the water stream that allows consumers to constantly adjust the force and pulse of the water while providing coverage. The centre of the shower head spins and wobbles so that each stream of water twists and twirls, hence the name Revolution.

The Revolution appears to be a hit, selling out in many stores. Moen executives are not surprised, given the research effort to unearth consumer preferences. Oh—the cost of the shower head is about $60. Moen believes consumers will pay that price, given that it engineered the product exactly to consumer specifications!

marketing researcher understands that there is likely to be more than one way to tackle the problem. The ability to select the most appropriate research design develops with experience. Inexperienced researchers often embrace the survey method as the best design because they are most familiar with this method. More experienced researchers, on the other hand, recognize the value of other methods and can often put together creative research designs that can solve marketing problems more quickly and less expensively. Experienced researchers often note that proper definition of the marketing plays a central role in determining the most appropriate research design.

Sampling

Although sampling is an inherent component of the research design stage, it is a distinctive aspect of the research process. The researcher's sampling plan indicates who is to be sampled, how large a sample is needed, and how sampling units will be selected. Rarely does a research project involve a complete census of every person in the research population. This is because of the time and cost involved in conducting a census. Thus, sampling is used. **Sampling** is the process of gathering data from a subset of the total population rather than from all members (census) of that particular population. A *sample*, then, is a subset from a larger population.

SAMPLING
The process of selecting subsets from a population.

If proper statistical procedures are followed, a researcher does not need to select every member in a population, because a properly selected sample should be representative of the population as a whole. However, errors can and do occur in sampling and thus the reliability of the data obtained through sampling can sometimes become an issue. Thus, the first and most critical sampling question for researchers to ask is: Who is to be sampled?

Another key question concerns the sample size: How big should the sample be? As mentioned, it is usually unrealistic to expect a census of the research population be conducted. In general, larger samples are more precise than smaller ones, but proper sampling can allow a smaller subset of the total population to provide a reliable measure of the whole.

The final question in the sampling plan concerns how to select the sampling units. There are two basic sampling techniques: probability and nonprobability sampling. **Probability sampling** involves precise rules to select the sample such that each element of the population has a specific known chance of being selected. For example, if your university wants to know how last year's 1000 graduates are doing, it can put their names in a bowl and randomly select 100 names of graduates to contact. The chance of being selected—100/1000 or 0.10—is known in advance, and all graduates have an equal chance of being contacted. This procedure helps select a sample (100 graduates) that should be representative of the entire population (the 1000 graduates) and allows conclusions to be drawn about the entire population.

Nonprobability sampling involves the use of arbitrary judgment by the marketing researcher to select the sample so that the chance of selecting a particular element of the population is either unknown or zero. If your university decided to talk to 100 of last year's graduates but only those who lived closest to the university, many class members would be arbitrarily eliminated. This has introduced a bias, or possible lack of representativeness, which may make it dangerous to draw conclusions about the entire population of the graduating class. Nonprobability samples are often used when time and budgets are limited and are most often used for exploratory research purposes. In general, marketing researchers use data from such samples with caution.

PROBABILITY SAMPLING
Using precise rules to select the sample such that each element of the population has a specific known chance of being selected.

NONPROBABILITY SAMPLING
Using arbitrary judgments to select the sample so that the chance of selecting a particular element may be unknown or zero.

Concept Check

1. What is a survey?

2. Which research method offers the potential for establishing cause-and-effect relationship?

3. What is sampling?

DATA COLLECTION AND ANALYSIS

Once the research design has been formalized, the process of gathering or collecting data begins. Sometimes referred to as *fieldwork*, data collection at this stage of the research process includes all the activities that the researcher (and staff) undertakes, to obtain data from the identified sources or respondents. Since there are several research methods that could be used by the researcher, this means there may be multiple ways to collect the data. For example, with the survey method, data may be collected by telephone, mail, or personal interview.

However the data are collected, it is important to minimize errors in the process. Most research experts agree that the data collection stage of the research process is one of the major sources of error in marketing research. Some of the errors that occur are a result of a variety of problems ranging from failure to select the right respondents to incorrect recording of observations. Competent and well-trained researchers inside the organization or those employed by outside research companies can go a long way in ensuring proper data collection.

The next step for the marketing researcher is data analysis. Mark Twain once observed, "Collecting data is like collecting garbage. You've got to know what you're going to do with the stuff before you collect it." In essence, the marketing researcher must know *why* the data are being collected and *how* to analyze them effectively in order for the data to have any value in decision making.

The level of analysis conducted on the data depends on the nature of the research and the information needed to provide a solution to the marketing problem. For survey data, frequency analysis is completed—calculating the responses question by question. The researcher may then wish to identify patterns in the data or examine how data pertaining to some questions may relate to data obtained from asking other questions. Probably the most widely used technique for organizing and analyzing marketing data is cross-tabulation. This method is particularly useful for market segmentation analysis and is discussed in Chapter 9.

CONCLUSIONS AND REPORT

At this stage of the process, the marketing researcher, often in conjunction with marketing management, must review the analysis and ask: What does this information tell us? A critical aspect of the marketing researcher's job is to interpret the information and make conclusions with regard to managerial decision making. The researcher must prepare a report to communicate the research findings. Included in this report should be suggestions for actions that might be taken by the organization to solve the marketing problem.

The researcher must be careful not to overwhelm management with technical terminology. Rather, the report should highlight in a clear and concise manner the important results and conclusions. Ultimately, the marketing researcher and management must work closely together to ensure proper interpretation of the research results. In addition, management must make a commitment to act—to make decisions based on the research and their good judgment and knowledge of the situation. In other words, someone must "make something happen" to see that a solution to the marketing problems gets implemented. Failure to act on the research findings creates an appearance that the marketing research effort is of little value. Finally, once implemented, the proposed solution should be monitored to ensure intended results do occur.

ETHICAL ISSUES IN THE MARKETING RESEARCH PROCESS

Ethical issues can arise in marketing researchers' relationships with all parties involved in the research process, including respondents, the general public, their organizations, and/or their clients. Professional marketing researchers must make ethical decisions regarding the collecting, using, and reporting of research data. Examples of unethical behaviour include failure to report problems with research results because of incomplete data, reporting only favourable but not unfavourable results, using deception to collect information, and breaching the confidentiality of respondents and/or their personal data if anonymity or nondisclosure was guaranteed.[23] The Ethics and Social Responsibility Alert box shows a classic example of an ethical issue in marketing research, the incomplete reporting of data collected.[24] Also, many companies collect clickstream data on consumers when those consumers visit their Websites and sometimes use these data for marketing purposes without the knowledge and consent of the consumer.

Using formal statements on ethical policies and instituting rewards and punishments can help ensure that ethical behaviour is the norm in marketing research. For example, the Professional Marketing Research Society of Canada (PMRS) and the Canadian Association of Marketing Research Organizations (CAMRO) have codes of ethics or rules of conduct to which their members must adhere. However, unethical or inappropriate behaviour by individuals or organizations cannot be regulated away. As mentioned in Chapter 4, ethical behaviour rests with the individual but the consequences affect many.

www.camro.org

USING INFORMATION TECHNOLOGY TO TRIGGER MARKETING ACTIONS

INFORMATION TECHNOLOGY
Designing and managing computer and communication networks to provide a system to satisfy an organization's needs for data storage, processing, and access.

Today's marketing managers can be drowned in such an ocean of data that they need to adopt strategies for dealing with complex, changing views of the competition, the market, and the consumer. The Internet and the desktop PC power of today provide a gateway to exhaustive data sources that vary from well organized and correct to disorganized and incorrect. Current information about products, competitors, and customers is almost always accessed and analyzed by computer. So today, these activities fall under the broader term of **information technology**, which involves designing and managing computer and communications networks to provide a system to satisfy an organization's needs for data storage, processing, and access leading to effective marketing actions.

The Marketing Manager's View of Sales "Drivers"

There are many factors or "drivers" that influence the buying decisions of a household or organization and, hence, a company's sales. These factors or drivers include both the controllable marketing mix factors, like product and distribution, and uncontrollable factors like competition and the changing tastes of households or organizational buyers.

Understanding these drivers involves managing this ocean of data. Sometimes hundreds of thousands of bits of data are created each week. Sources feeding this database ocean range from internal data about sales and customers to external data from syndication services and TV ratings. The marketer's task is to convert this data ocean into useful information on which to base informed decisions. In practice, some marketing researchers distinguish "data" (the facts and figures) from "information" (the distilled facts and figures whose interpretation leads to actions).

Key Elements of an Information System

Figure 8–7 shows how marketing researchers and managers use information technology to frame questions that provide answers leading to marketing actions. At the bottom of Figure 8–7 the marketer queries the databases in the information system with marketing questions needing answers. These questions go through statistical models that analyze the relationships that exist among the data. The databases form the core, or "data warehouse," where the ocean of data is collected and stored. After the search of this data warehouse, the models select and link the pertinent data, often presenting them in tables and graphics for easy interpretation. Marketers can also use *sensitivity analysis* to query the database with "what if?" questions to determine how a hypothetical change in a driver like advertising can affect sales.

The Challenge in Mining Marketing Data

Making decisions from marketing information has many frustrations. Yet timely, useful facts and insights about the market and competition play a key role in shaping the marketing manager's expenditures on sales drivers. Many of these databases and models are very powerful, but major hurdles stand in the way of marketers getting both the answers they need and the resulting actions. Time is scarce and the information is incredibly complex. Seasoned professionals must organize and interpret information clearly, quickly, and simply to initiate timely marketing actions.

Data Mining: A New Approach to Searching the Data Ocean

Traditional marketing research typically involves developing a hypothesis about a driver and then collecting data: for example, increasing couponing (the driver) during spring will increase trial by first-time buyers (the result). Marketing researchers then try to collect information to attempt to verify the hypothesis.

DATA MINING
The extraction of hidden predictive information from large databases.

  In contrast, **data mining** is the extraction of hidden predictive information from large databases. Catalogue companies such as Sears Canada and Lands' End use data mining to find statistical links that suggest particular marketing actions. Data mining, in fact, often plays a critical role in a company's customer relationship management (CRM) efforts. Through data mining, a company can monitor customer behaviour and determine appropriate strategies based on that behaviour. For example, one catalogue company studies about 3500 variables over the lifetime of a customer's relations with the company and its catalogue. It found that customers who change residences are three times more likely to buy new tables and decorative products than other customers who do not change residences. So, the company actually created a catalogue geared to customers who have recently moved.

FIGURE 8–7
How marketing researchers and managers use information technology to turn information into action

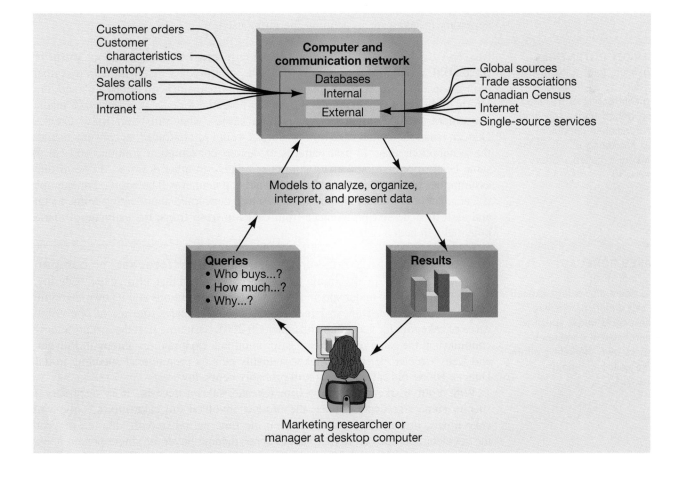

Some of these purchase patterns are common sense. Peanut butter and grape jelly purchases link and might suggest a joint promotion between Kraft peanut butter and Welch's grape jelly. Other patterns link seemingly unrelated purchases. Supermarkets mined checkout data scanners and discovered that men buying diapers in the evening sometimes buy a six-pack of beer as well. So, the supermarkets placed diapers and beer near each other. Placing potato chips between them increased sales on all three.

Still, the success in data mining ultimately depends on humans—the judgments of the marketing managers and researchers in how to select, analyze, and interpret the information.

Concept Check

    1. What does a marketing manager mean when she talks about a sales "driver"?

    2. How does data mining differ from traditional marketing research?

MARKET AND SALES FORECASTING

Forecasting or estimating the actual size of a market is often a key goal in a marketing research study. Good sales forecasts are important for a firm as it schedules production.[25] We will discuss (1) some basic forecasting terms, (2) two basic approaches to forecasting, and (3) specific sales forecasting techniques.

Basic Forecasting Terms

Unfortunately, there are no standard definitions for some forecasting concepts, so it's necessary to take care in defining the terms used.

MARKET POTENTIAL
Maximum total sales of a product by all firms to a segment during a specified time period under specified environmental conditions and marketing efforts of the firms (also called *industry potential*).

Market or Industry Potential   The term **market potential**, or **industry potential**, refers to the maximum total sales of a product by all firms to a segment during a specified time period under specified environmental conditions and marketing efforts of the firms. For example, the market potential for cake mix sales to Canadian consumers in 2005 might be two million cases—what Pillsbury, Betty Crocker, Duncan Hines, and other cake mix producers would sell to Canadian consumers under the assumptions that (1) past patterns of dessert consumption continue and (2) the same level of promotional effort continues relative to other desserts. If one of these assumptions proves false, the estimate of market potential will be wrong. For example, if Canadian consumers suddenly become more concerned about eating refined sugar and shift their dessert preferences from cakes to fresh fruits, the estimate of market potential will be too high.

SALES FORECAST
The maximum total sales of a product that a firm expects to sell during a specified time period under specified environmental conditions and its own marketing efforts (also called *company forecast*).

Sales or Company Forecast   The term **sales forecast**, or **company forecast**, refers to the maximum total sales of a product that a firm expects during a specified time period under specified environmental conditions and its own marketing efforts. For example, Duncan Hines might develop its sales forecast of one million cases of cake mix for Canadian consumers in 2005, assuming past dessert preferences continue and the same relative level of promotional expenditures among it, Pillsbury, and Betty Crocker. If Betty Crocker suddenly cuts its promotional spending in half, Duncan Hines' old sales forecast will probably be too low.

With both market potential estimates and sales forecasts, it is necessary to specify some significant details: the product involved (all cake mixes, only white cake mixes, or only Bundt cake mixes); the time period (month, quarter, or year); the segment (Canada, Western Canada, upper-income buyer, or single-person households); controllable marketing factors (price and level of promotional support);

uncontrollable factors (consumer tastes and actions of competitors); and the units of measurement (number of cases sold or total sales revenues).

Two Basic Approaches to Forecasting

A marketing manager rarely wants a single number for an annual forecast, such as 5000 units sold or $75 million in sales revenue. Rather the manager wants this total subdivided into elements the manager works with, such as sales by product line or sales by market segment. The two basic approaches to sales forecasting are (1) subdividing the total sales forecast (top-down forecast) or (2) building the total sales forecast by summing up the components (buildup forecast).

TOP-DOWN FORECAST
Subdividing an aggregate forecast into its principal components.

Top-down Forecast   A **top-down forecast** involves subdividing an aggregate forecast into its principal components. A shoe manufacturer can use a top-down forecast to estimate the percentage of total shoe sales in a province and develop province-by-province forecasts for shoe sales for the coming year. *Canadian Markets*, published by the *Financial Post* and *Sales and Marketing Management* magazine, are sources that are widely used for top-down forecasting information.

For example, as shown in Figure 8–8, the province of Ontario has 38.2 percent of the Canadian population, 40.7 percent of the personal income in Canada, and 37.8 percent of Canadian retail sales.[26] If the shoe manufacturers wanted to use a single factor related to expected shoe sales, it would choose the factor that has been closely related to shoe sales historically, in this case the percentage of Canadian retail sales found in Ontario. The top-down forecast would then be that 37.8 percent of the firm's sales would be made in the province of Ontario.

A single factor is rarely a true indicator of sales opportunity in a given market. So, sometimes multiple factors are considered when making forecasts. The Buying Power Index (BPI) developed by *Sales and Marketing Management* magazine gives weights of 0.2, 0.5, and 0.3, respectively, to the three previously mentioned factors, as follows.

$$
\begin{aligned}
\text{BPI} &= (0.2 \times \text{percentage of national population in area}) + (0.5 \times \text{percentage of national personal income in area}) + (0.3 \times \text{percentage of national retail sales in area}) \\
&= (0.2 \times 38.2) + (0.5 \times 40.7) + (0.3 \times 37.8) \\
&= 7.64 + 20.35 + 11.34 \\
&= 39.33 = 39.3\%
\end{aligned}
$$

Thus, the BPI forecasts that 39.3 percent of the firm's shoe sales will occur in Ontario, which is higher than if retail sales alone were used for the forecast. A marketer could also obtain data on retail sales and family expenditures from Statistics Canada and use this information to make sales forecasts.

FIGURE 8–8
Percentage of Canadian population, personal income, and retail sales in selected provinces, 2001

PROVINCES	POPULATION % OF CDN TOTAL	PERSONAL INCOME % OF CDN TOTAL	RETAIL SALES % OF CDN TOTAL
Newfoundland	1.7	1.2	1.7
Quebec	23.8	21.2	22.8
Ontario	38.2	40.7	37.8
British Columbia	13.2	12.1	13.1

FIGURE 8–9
Buildup approach to a
two-year sales forecast
for Boeing's aerospace
department

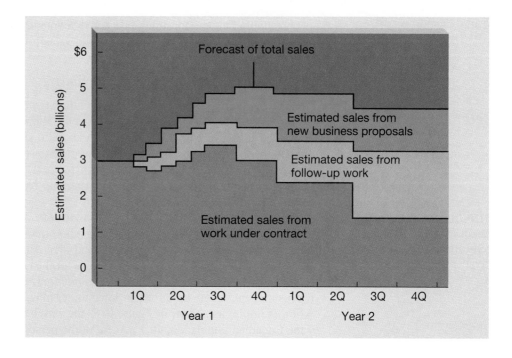

FIGURE 8–9
Buildup approach to a two-year sales forecast for Boeing's aerospace department

BUILDUP FORECAST
Summing the sales forecasts
of each of the components
to arrive at the total forecast.

DIRECT FORECAST
Estimating the value to
be forecast without any
intervening steps.

Buildup Forecast   A **buildup forecast** involves summing the sales forecasts of each of the components to arrive at the total forecast. It is a widely used method when there are identifiable components such as products, product lines, or market segments in the forecasting problem.

Figure 8–9 shows how Boeing's aerospace department uses the buildup approach to develop a sales forecast involving three broad categories of projects or products: (1) work currently under contract that can be forecast precisely, (2) follow-up work that is likely to result from current contracts, and (3) new business that results from Boeing's proposals for new business, which is difficult to forecast. Each of these three forecasts is the sum of a number of individual products or projects, which for simplicity are not shown. In turn, forecasts for each of the three kinds of business can be summed to give the total sales forecast for the entire department. Increasingly, with more detailed information available on all customers and segments in given markets, annual forecasting for Canadian firms has been transformed from a top-down forecast to a more buildup-oriented process.[27]

Specific Sales Forecasting Techniques

Three main sales forecasting techniques can be used in the top-down or buildup approaches. Ordered from least to most costly, these are (1) judgments of the decision maker, (2) surveys of knowledgeable groups, and (3) statistical methods.

Judgments of the Decision Maker   Probably 99.9 percent of all sales forecasts are judgments of the person who must act on the results of the forecast—the individual decision maker. An example is the forecasts of likely sales, and hence the quantity to order, for the 13 000 items stocked in a typical supermarket that must be forecast by the stock clerk or manager. A **direct forecast** involves estimating the value to be forecast without any intervening steps. Examples appear daily: How many litres of milk should I buy? How much time should I allow to drive to the game? How much money should I get out of the automated teller machine? Your mind may go through some intervening steps so quickly you're unaware of it.

So in estimating the amount of money to get from the automated teller machine, you probably made some intervening estimates (such as counting the cash in your pocket or the special events you need cash for) to obtain your direct estimate.

LOST-HORSE FORECAST
Starting with the last known value of the item being forecast, listing the factors that could affect the forecast, assessing whether they have a positive or negative impact, and making the final forecast.

Lost-horse forecasting does this in a more structured way. A **lost-horse forecast** involves starting with the last known value of the item being forecast, listing the factors that could affect the forecast, assessing whether they have a positive or negative impact, and making the final forecast. The technique gets its name from how you'd find a lost horse: go to where it was last seen, put yourself in its shoes, consider those factors that could affect where you might go (to the pond if you're thirsty, the hayfield if you're hungry, and so on), and go there. For example, a product manager for Wilson's tennis rackets in 2002 who needed to make a sales forecast through 2006 would start with the known value of 2002 sales and list the positive factors (more tennis courts, more TV publicity) and the negative ones (competition from other sports, high prices of graphite and ceramic racquets) to arrive at the final series of annual sales forecasts.

Surveys of Knowledgeable Groups   If you wonder what your firm's sales will be next year, ask people who are likely to know something about future sales. Four common groups that are surveyed to develop sales forecasts are prospective buyers, the firm's salesforce, its executives, and experts.

SURVEY OF BUYERS' INTENTIONS FORECAST
Asking prospective customers whether they are likely to buy the product during some future time period.

A **survey of buyers' intentions forecast** involves asking prospective customers whether they are likely to buy the product during some future time period. For industrial products with few prospective buyers this can be effective. There are only a few hundred customers in the entire world for Boeing's largest airplanes, so Boeing surveys them to develop its sales forecasts and production schedules.

SALESFORCE SURVEY FORECAST
Asking the firm's salespeople to estimate sales during a coming period.

A **salesforce survey forecast** involves asking the firm's salespeople to estimate sales during a coming period. Because these people are in contact with customers and are likely to know what customers like and dislike, there is logic to this approach. However, salespeople can be unreliable forecasters—painting too rosy a picture if they are enthusiastic about a new product and too grim a forecast if their sales quota is based on it.

JURY OF EXECUTIVE OPINION FORECAST
Asking knowledgeable executives inside the firm about likely sales during a coming period.

A **jury of executive opinion forecast** involves asking knowledgeable executives inside the firm—such as vice presidents of marketing, research and development, finance, and production—about likely sales during a coming period. Although this approach is fast and includes judgments from diverse functional areas, it can be biased by a dominant executive whose judgments are deferred to by the others. Also, how valuable are judgments from executives who rarely come in contact with customers—such as vice presidents of finance and production?

SURVEY OF EXPERTS FORECAST
Asking experts on a topic to make a judgment about some future event.

A **survey of experts forecast** involves asking experts on a topic to make a judgment about some future event. For example, 20 electronics and TV experts might

FIGURE 8–10
Linear trend extrapolation of sales revenues of Xerox, made at the start of 1999

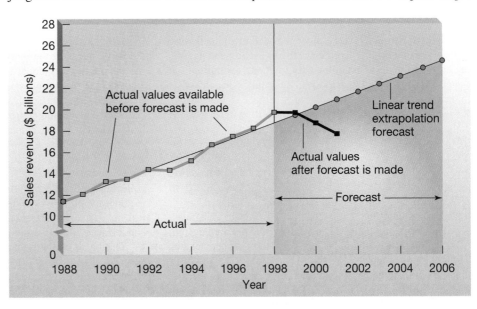

be asked when a 25-inch high-definition television (HDTV) set might sell to consumers for less than $500. One form of a survey of experts forecast is a *technological forecast*, which involves estimating when breakthroughs in basic science will occur. Such a technological forecast might help HDTV executives estimate when major cost reductions in key HDTV components might occur.

TREND EXTRAPOLATION
Extending a pattern observed in past data into the future.

www.xerox.com

Statistical Methods   The best-known statistical method of forecasting is **trend extrapolation**, which involves extending a pattern observed in past data into the future. When the pattern is described with a straight line, it is *linear trend extrapolation*. Suppose that in early 1999 you were a sales forecaster for the Xerox Corporation and had actual sales revenues running from 1988 to 1998 (Figure 8–10). Using linear trend extrapolation, you draw a line to fit the past data and project it into the future to give the forecast values shown for 1999 to 2006.

If in 2002 you want to compare your forecasts with actual results, you are in for a surprise—illustrating the strength and weakness of trend extrapolation. Trend extrapolation assumes that the underlying relationships in the past will continue into the future, which is the basis of the method's key strength: simplicity. If this assumption proves correct, you have an accurate forecast. However, if this proves wrong, the forecast is likely to be wrong. In this case your forecasts from 1999 through 2002 were too high, largely because of fierce competition in the photocopying industry.

In practice, marketing managers often use several of the forecasting techniques to estimate the size of markets important to them. Also, they often do three separate forecasts based on different sets of assumptions: (1) "best case" with optimistic assumptions, (2) "worst case" with pessimistic ones, and (3) "most likely case" with most reasonable assumptions.

Concept Check

1. What is the difference between the top-down and buildup approaches to forecasting sales?

2. How do you make a lost-horse forecast?

3. What is linear trend extrapolation?

SUMMARY

1   Marketing research is the process of defining a marketing problem or opportunity, systematically collecting and analyzing information, and recommending actions to improve an organization's marketing activities. Marketing research assists in decision making.

2   There are three basic types of marketing research: (1) exploratory research—preliminary research conducted to clarify the scope and nature of the marketing problem, (2) descriptive research—research designed to describe basic characteristics of a given population or to profile particular marketing situations, and (3) causal research—research designed to identify cause-and-effect relationships among variables.

3   All marketing research consists of four basic stages: (1) defining the problem, (2) determining the research design, (3) collecting and analyzing data, and (4) drawing conclusions and preparing a report.

4   The first stage of the marketing research process—problem definition—is critical since research based on incorrect problem definition will be a waste of resources.

5   If the researcher decides to conduct exploratory research in the early stages of the marketing research process, he or she has three basic techniques to choose from: (1) secondary data analysis, (2) focus groups, and (3) depth interviews.

6   Secondary data (or historical data) are data previously collected and assembled for some project other than the one at hand, whereas primary data are data gathered and assembled specifically for the project at hand.

7   At the formal research design stage, the researcher produces a plan that outlines the methods and procedures for collecting and analyzing the required information. The plan includes the objectives of the research; the sources of information to be used; the research methods; the sampling plan; and the schedule and cost of the research.

8   The basic methods the researcher can choose from for descriptive and causal research at the formal research design stage include (1) survey, (2) experiment, and (3) observation. A survey is a research technique used to generate data by asking people questions and recording their responses on a questionnaire. An experiment involves the manipulation of an independent variable (cause) and measuring its effect on the dependent variable (effect) under controlled conditions. Observation involves watching, either mechanically or in person, how people actually behave.

9 Sampling—the process of gathering data from a subset of the total population rather than from all members (census) of that particular population—is an inherent component of the research design stage. The researcher's sampling plan indicates who is to be sampled, how large a sample is needed, and how sampling units will be selected.

10 The third stage of the marketing research process is data collection and analysis. Sometimes referred to as fieldwork, data collection at this stage of the research process includes all the activities that the researcher (and staff) undertakes to obtain data from the identified sources or respondents. Once the data are collected, the marketing researcher must analyze and transform it into valuable information for decision making.

11 In the final stage of the process, the marketing researcher must take conclusions and prepare a research report. Included in this report should be suggestions for actions that might be taken by the organization that will solve the marketing problem.

12 Professional marketing researchers have to make ethical decisions in the collecting, using, and reporting of research.

13 Information technology enables massive amounts of marketing data to be stored, processed, and accessed. Databases can be queried using data mining to find statistical relationships between data that might be useful in taking marketing actions.

14 Two basic approaches to forecasting sales are the top-down and buildup methods. Three forecasting techniques are judgments of individuals, surveys of knowledgeable groups, and statistical methods.

KEY TERMS AND CONCEPTS

buildup forecast p. 230
data mining p. 227
depth interviews p. 214
direct forecast p. 230
ethnographic research p. 222
experiment p. 219
focus groups p. 213
information technology p. 226
jury of executive opinion forecast p. 231
lost-horse forecast p. 231
market or industry potential p. 228
marketing research p. 207
nonprobability sampling p. 224

observation p. 221
primary data p. 212
probability sampling p. 224
sales or company forecast p. 228
salesforce survey forecast p. 231
sampling p. 223
secondary data p. 212
survey p. 216
survey of buyers' intentions forecast p. 231
survey of experts forecast p. 231
top-down forecast p. 229
trend extrapolation p. 232

INTERNET EXERCISE

www.mcgrawhill.ca/college/berkowitz

WorldOpinion calls its Website "The World's Market Research Web Site." To check out the latest marketing research news, job opportunites, and details of more than 8500 research locations in 99 countries, go to www.worldopinion.com and do the following:

1 Click on the "News" banner on WorldOpinion's home page to read about the current news and issues facing the market research industry.

2 Under the "What's New" link, click on the link for the current monthly issue of *The Frame*, a set of online articles published by Survey Sampling, Inc.

3 Under the "Research resources" banner, click on the "Links to Major Researchers' Sites" link. Scroll down the Web page to obtain information on the following top market research firms:

a. Click on the "Gallup" link. Then under the "Special Features" banner, click on the "How Polls are Conducted" link to read about this topic. To view the results of recent polls, click on the "Poll Topics: A-Z" link on this page.

b. Click on the "Abt Associates, Inc." and "Market Facts, Inc." links or other marketing research firms of interest to identify job opportunities at these firms.

Want to get better grades, find tips on how to study more effectively, and stay up to date with happenings in the world of marketing? Visit the Online Learning Centre for practice tests, Study Smart software, and much more! www.mcgrawhill.ca/college/berkowitz
Interested in finding out what marketing looks like in the real world? *Marketing Magazine* is just a click away on your OLC! Visit www.mcgrawhill.ca/college/berkowitz

APPLYING MARKETING CONCEPTS AND PERSPECTIVES

1 Is it possible to make effective marketing decisions without marketing research?

2 Why is the problem definition stage of the marketing research process probably the most important stage?

3 You plan to open an ice-cream shop in your town. What type of exploratory research would you conduct to help determine its feasibility? You find the exploratory research doesn't answer all your questions. You decide to do a survey to determine whether you should open the shop. What kind of questions will you ask? Whom do you ask?

4 Suppose you are trying to determine the top three favourite department stores in your area. You show customers at a shopping mall a list of department stores and ask them to rank their three favourite stores from 1 to 3 (with 1 being the favourite). What problems can occur with the survey?

5 Your university bookstore wants to find out how students feel about the store's merchandise, prices, and customer service. What type of marketing research would you recommend to the store?

6 You are a marketing researcher observing what people do when selecting bread in a supermarket. You are behind a one-way mirror and none of the customers know they are being observed. During the course of the day, you observe several people shoplifting a smaller snack product near the bread section. You know personally two of the shoplifters you see. What are the ethical problems you face in this situation?

7 You plan to open a new rent-a-car business. You have drafted a survey you want to distribute to airline passengers. The survey will be left at the airports and respondents will mail the surveys back in a prepaid envelope. Some of the questions you plan to use are shown below. Use Figure 8–5 to (*a*) identify the problem with each question and (*b*) correct it. **Note:** Some questions may have more than one problem.

a. Do you own your own car or usually rent one? ____ Yes ____ No

b. What is your age? ____ 21–30 ____30–40 ____41–50 ____50+

c. How much did you spend on rental cars last year? ____$100 or less ____$101–$400 ____$401–$800 ____$800–$1000 ____$1000 or more

d. What is a good daily rental car rate? _____

8 Suppose you are to make a sales forecast using a top-down approach to estimate the percentage of a manufacturer's total Canadian sales going to each province. You plan to use only a single factor—percentage of Canadian population, percentage of personal income, or percentage of retail sales. Which of the three factors would you use if your sales forecast were for each of the following manufacturers, and why? (*a*) Sifto salt, (*b*) Christian Dior dresses, and (*c*) Columbia records.

9 Which of the following variables would linear trend extrapolation be more accurate for? (*a*) Annual population of Canada or (*b*) annual sales of cars produced in Canada by General Motors. Why?

CASE 8–1 Bookworms, Inc.

Late one August morning, Nancy Klein, co-owner of Bookworms, Inc., sat at her desk near the back wall of a cluttered office. With some irritation, she had just concluded that her nearby calculator could help no more. "What we still need," she thought to herself, "are estimates of demand and market share . . . but at least we have two weeks to get them."

Klein's office was located in the rear of Bookworms, Inc., an 1800-square-metre bookstore specializing in quality paperbacks. The store carries more than 10 000 titles and sold more than $520 000 worth of books last year. Titles were stocked in 18 categories, ranging from art, biography, and cooking to religion, sports, and travel.

Bookworms, Inc. was located in a small business district across the street from the boundary of Verdoon University (VU). VU currently enrolled about 12 000 undergraduate and graduate students majoring in the liberal arts, the sciences, and the professions. Despite national trends in enrollment, the VU admissions office had predicted that the number of entering students would grow at about one percent per year through the 1990s. The surrounding community, a city of about 350 000, was projected to grow at about twice that rate.

Bookworms, Inc. carried no texts, even though many of its customers were VU students. Both Klein and her partner, Susan Berman, felt that the VU bookstore had simply too firm a grip on the textbook market in terms of price, location, and reputation. Bookworms also caried no classical records, as of two months ago. Klein recalled with discomfort the $15 000 or so they had lost on the venture. "Another mistake like that and the bank will be running Bookworms," she thought. "And, despite what Susan thinks, the copy service could just be that final mistake."

The idea for a copy service had come from Susan Berman. She had seen the candy store next door to Bookworms (under the same roof) go out of business in July. She had immediately asked the building's owner, Ed Anderson, about the future of the 800-square-metre space. Upon learning it was available, she had met with Klein to discuss her idea for the copy service. She had spoken excitedly about the opportunity: "It can't help but make money. I could work there part-time and the rest of the time we could hire students. We could call it 'Copycats' and even use a sign with the same kind of letters we do in 'Bookworms.' I'm sure we could get Ed to knock the wall out between the two stores, if you think it would be a good idea. Probably we could rent most of the copying equipment, so there's not much risk."

Klein was not so sure. A conversation yesterday with Anderson had disclosed his desire for a five-year lease (with an option to renew) at $1000 per month. He had promised to hold the offer open for two weeks before attempting to lease the space to anyone else. Representatives from copying-equipment firms had estimated that charges would run between $200 and $2000 per month, depending on equipment, service, and whether the equipment was bought or leased. The copy service would also have other fixed costs in terms of utility expenses, interest, insurance, and the inventory (and perhaps equipment). Klein concluded that the service would begin to make a profit at about 20 000 copies per month under the best-case assumptions, and at about 60 000 copies per month under the worst-case assumptions.

Further informal investigation had identified two major competitors. One was the copy centre located in the Krismann Library on the west side of the campus, a kilometre away. The other was a private firm, Kinko's, located on the south side of the campus, also one kilometre away. Both offered service while you wait, on several machines. The library's price was about 1/2 cent per copy higher than Kinko's. Both offered collating, binding, colour copying, and other services, all on a seven-days-a-week schedule.

Actually, investigation had discovered that a third major "competitor" consisted of the VU departmental machines scattered throughout the campus. Most faculty and administrative copying was done on these machines, but students were allowed the use of some, at cost. In addition, at least 20 self-service machines could be found in the library and in nearby drugstores, grocery stores, and banks.

Moving aside a stack of books on her desk, Nancy Klein picked up the telephone and dialled her partner. When Berman answered, Klein asked, "Susan, have you any idea how many copies a student might make in a semester? I mean, according to my figure, we would break even somewhere between 20 000 and 60 000 copies per month. I don't know if this is half the market or what."

"You know, I have no idea," Berman answered. "I suppose when I was going to school I probably made 10 copies a month—for articles, class notes, old tests, and so on."

"Same here," Klein said. "But some graduate students must have done that many each week. You know, I think we ought to do some marketing research before we go much further on this. What do you think?"

"Sure. Only it can't take much more time or money. What do you have in mind, Nancy?"

"Well, we could easily interview our customers as they leave the store and ask them how many copies they've made in the past week or so. Of course, we'd have to make sure they were students."

"What about a telephone survey?" Berman asked. "That way we can have a random sample. We would still ask about the number of copies, but now we would know for sure they would be students."

"Or what about interviewing students in the union cafeteria? There's always a good-sized line there around noon, as I remember, and this might be even quicker."

"Boy, I just don't know. Why don't I come in this afternoon and we can talk about it some more?"

"Good idea," Klein responded. "Between the two of us, we should be able to come up with something."

Questions

1 What sources of information should Klein and Berman use?
2 How should Klein and Berman gather data?
3 What questions should they ask?
4 How should they sample?

9

IDENTIFYING MARKET SEGMENTS AND TARGETS

AFTER READING THIS CHAPTER YOU SHOULD BE ABLE TO:

- Explain what market segmentation is, when to use it, and the five steps involved in segmentation.

- Recognize the different dimensions used to segment consumer and organizational markets.

- Develop a market-product grid to use in segmenting and targeting a market.

- Interpret a cross tabulation to analyze market segments.

- Understand how marketing managers position products in the marketplace.

THE SNEAKER MARKETING WARS: AIR PUMPS, PROGRAMMABLE SPEEDOMETERS, AND 3 BILLION TRILLION CHOICES

Late for a flight, Roger Adams rushed through the airport to get to his gate by "heeling." Adams, a former psychologist and skateboarder, had just invented Heelys, the latest craze (or fad) in sneakers.

Heelys combine the thrill of inline skating, skateboarding, and scooting—along with running and walking—in one set of shoes! The sneakers come with an imbedded, detachable wheel located in the heel of each shoe. To "heel," you lift up the foot at the heel on one shoe, push off on the other foot, and glide (carefully). Heelys are so hot that in some areas retailers can't keep them on the shelves. Heelying Sports Ltd. (www.heelys.com) sold more than 1 million pairs of Heelys sneakers in its first year of operations.[1]

Finding the Segments   What do you need in the sneaker business to stand out from the pack when consumers are faced with hundreds of athletic shoe choices, often on sneaker "walls" like that shown in the opposite page? This is the multi-billion dollar question for manufacturers around the world. Today the global market for athletic footwear or sneakers exceeds U.S.$25 billion. Adams and Heelying Sports believe they've found a unique "niche" or market segment of buyers.

But all sneaker manufacturers continue to search for new market segments of consumers and ways to differentiate their products from the competition. This challenge applies to the giants, like Reebok and Nike, as well as to upstarts like Heelying and Customatix (www.customatix.com), which markets an Internet design-your-own-shoe service that it says offers more than 3 billion trillion combinations.

Competitive Trends   Changing consumer tastes and global competition have forced sneaker manufacturers to come up with new product technologies, advertising campaigns, and endorsement deals to develop and position their new and existing products for their target market segments. For example, Reebok signed a $40-million endorsement contract with Venus Williams for a signature line of tennis footwear and apparel and a multi-million dollar deal with Alan Iverson for a line of basketball shoes. Reebok also signed deals with both the NBA and NFL to be their exclusive team uniform providers and to offer branded apparel to fans. Some industry experts have identified some key trends for manufacturers to consider when planning for future battles in the sneaker wars:

- *Age segments.* Teenagers will represent close to one-quarter of total sales: they represent the largest segment of the market and are willing to spend more on sneakers than other segments.
- *Gender segments:* Both women and men are important segments but sales growth figures for women will be higher than those for men because they will buy more in total at higher average prices.
- *Kinds of sports.* Running, basketball, and cross-training shoes are and will be the top sellers.
- *Styles and use.* Most of the sales growth in sneakers will come from casual styles that have a strong fashion component. Almost three-fourths of all sneakers will be for casual wear rather than for sports or fitness purposes.

The strategies sneaker manufactures use to satisfy the needs of different customers illustrates successful market segmentation, the main topic of this chapter. The Marketing NewsNet box describes how firms from Reebok and Nike to Customatix have succeeded in using segmentation strategies to reach special groups of customers.[2]

After discussing why markets need to be segmented, this chapter covers the steps a firm uses in segmenting and targeting a market and then positioning its product offering in the marketplace.

WHY SEGMENT MARKETS?

www.reebok.com

MARKET SEGMENTATION
Aggregating prospective buyers into groups, or segments, that (1) have common needs and (2) will respond similarly to a marketing action.

A business firm segments its markets so it can respond more effectively to the wants of groups of prospective buyers and thus increase its sales and profits. Nonprofit organizations also segment the clients they serve in order to satisfy client needs more effectively while achieving the organization's goals. Let's use the dilemma of sneaker buyers finding their ideal Reebok shoes to describe (1) what market segmentation is and (2) when it is necessary to segment markets.

What Market Segmentation Means

People have different needs and wants, even though it would be easier for marketers if they didn't. **Market segmentation** involves aggregating prospective buyers

MARKETING NEWSNET   Sneaker Strategies: Who's Doing What

Microchips, air pumps and cushions, and wheels. Off-the-shelf vs. design-your-own with trillions of design combinations. As outlined below, these are just a few of the innovative technologies and strategies used by sneaker manufacturers to attract new consumers and differentiate their products from those offered by competitors.

Reebok

The 2001 Traxtar™ 2.0 line of kids' shoes not only features a computer chip and motion sensor to measure their running and jumping ability but also plays games and songs to motivate children. The adult version, called the Smart Train DMX, appeared in 2001 and has a microprocessor with a programmable speedometer, odometer, and calorie counter.

Nike

Originally launched in 1985, the 2001 "Michael-inspired" Air Jordan XVI basketball shoe incorporates the latest technologies for providing air cushioning in the heel and forefoot and for reducing painful turf toe. Recently, Nike introduced its Shox R4 running shoe that has the same air cushioning technology.

New Balance

Talk about boring: How about a marketing strategy that includes moderate prices, extra-wide shoe widths, more sizes, and links to podiatrists—all actions that target baby boomers who are most concerned with fit and comfort? To meet their needs, New Balance shoes incorporate shock absorbing (ABSORB®), foot rotation control (Rollbar® Stability System), and air cushioning (N-ergy S.C. System™) technologies.

Vans

Vans has targeted the rising wave of skateboard, snowboard, biking, and outdoor enthusiasts. To reach its targeted skateboard shoe market, Vans relies heavily on its endorsing athletes to design and market its signature lines and promote its skateboard events. Vans had a breakthrough when Foot Locker started selling its shoes in more than 1000 retail outlets.

Customatix

Customatix.com is a Website where you can completely design your own running or skateboarding shoes using up to 3 billion trillion combinations of colours, graphics, logos, and materials per shoe! Shoes are delivered within two weeks. Using the Shoe Designer™, you start by selecting either a blank shoe model or one of many predesigned versions. See the Web Link box later in the chapter to design your own shoe.

Whether you want off-the-shelf or personally designed sneakers, they're available.

MARKET SEGMENTS
The groups that result from the process of market segmentation; these groups ideally (1) have common needs and (2) will respond similarly to a marketing action.

PRODUCT DIFFERENTIATION
(1) A firm's using different marketing mix activities, such as product features and advertising, to help consumers perceive the product as being different and better than competing products. (2) A firm's selling two or more products with different features targeted to different market segments.

into groups that (1) have common needs and (2) will respond similarly to a marketing action. The groups that result from this process are **market segments**, a relatively homogeneous collection of prospective buyers.

The existence of different market segments has caused firms to use a marketing strategy of **product differentiation**, a strategy that has come to have two different but related meanings. In its broadest sense, product differentiation involves a firm's using different marketing mix activities, such as product features and advertising, to help consumers perceive the product as being different and better than competing products. The perceived differences may involve physical features or nonphysical ones, such as image or price.

In a narrower sense, product differentiation involves a firm's selling two or more products with different features targeted to different market segments. A firm can get into trouble when its different products blend together in consumers' minds and don't reach distinct market segments successfully. The Reebok example discussed below shows how the company is using both market segmentation and product differentiation strategies.

Segmentation: Linking Needs to Actions The definition of market segmentation first stresses the importance of aggregating—or grouping—people or organizations in a market according to the similarity of their needs and the benefits they are looking for in making a purchase. Second, such needs and benefits must be related to specific, tangible marketing actions the firm can take. These actions may

FIGURE 9–1
Market segmentation links
market needs to an
organization's marketing
program

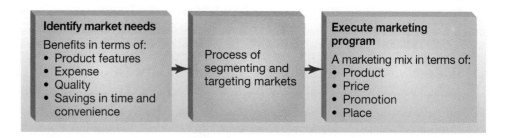

involve separate products or other aspects of the marketing mix such as price, advertising, or personal selling activities, or distribution strategies—the four Ps (product, price, promotion, place).

The process of segmenting a market and selecting specific segments as targets is the link between the various buyers' needs and the organization's marketing program (Figure 9–1). Market segmentation is only a means to an end: In an economist's terms, it relates supply (the organization's actions) to demand (customer needs). A basic test of the usefulness of the segmentation process is whether it leads to tangible marketing actions to increase sales and profitability.

How Reebok's Segmentation Strategy Developed   In 1979, Paul Fireman, who had dropped out of college to run his family's business, wandered through an international trade fair and saw Reebok's custom track shoes. He bought the North American licence from the British manufacturer and started producing top-of-the-line running shoes at about the time the running boom had peaked.

In a brilliant marketing decision, Fireman introduced the first soft-leather aerobic dance shoe—the Reebok "Freestyle"—in 1982. The flamboyant colours of these Reebok designer sneakers captured the attention of aerobic dance instructors and students alike. Figure 9–2 shows that Reebok has introduced a variety of shoes since 1982—from tennis and basketball shoes in 1984 to high-technology kids' and adult shoes in 2001. For simplicity, Figure 9–2 covers shoes only and does not show nonshoe lines—like Greg Norman apparel (1993), "fitness water" (2001), and a line of NFL/NBA/Olympics apparel (2001). These non-shoe lines have the advantage for Reebok of cutting across many of the segments shown in the rows.

A $3-billion-a-year sneaker business has a huge need to generate revenues from new opportunities. As a result, Reebok has expanded both the markets it targets and the products it develops to satisfy this need. For example, Reebok:[3]

* Developed a line of "DMX-enhanced" running shoes that its ads said were "the best running shoe in the history of the world" and which gave its users extra cushioning by distributing air through chambers in the shoe. Reebok plans to extend this technology to other shoe lines in 2001 and beyond.
* Launched its Traxtar™ line of children's shoes in 1999. In 2001, the Traxtar 2.0 line was launched. In late 2001, Reebok introduced the Smart Train DMX line of adult shoes, which incorporates the Traxtar microprocessor and DMX technologies.
* Relaunched its "The Pump" line of running and basketball shoes that allows users to manually inflate air sacs surrounding the foot to obtain a better fit by squeezing the "pump" located in the shoe's tongue.
* Launched notable marketing activities in 2000–2001, such as sponsoring several teams and athletes in the 2000 Summer Olympics and the CBS TV show *Survivor* (both Island and Outback series) and offering Reebok-branded merchandise.
* Operates over 200 Reebok, Rockport, Ralph Lauren, and Greg Norman stores in the United States that sell its respective branded footware, apparel, and accessories. It also sells its Reebok, Rockport, and Greg Norman products directly to consumers via the Internet.

MARKET SEGMENT		PRODUCT									
GENERAL	GROUP WITH NEED	RUNNING SHOES (1981)	AEROBIC SHOES (1982)	TENNIS SHOES (1984)	BASKETBALL SHOES (1984)	KIDS SHOES (1984)	WALKING SHOES (1986)	CROSS-TRAINING SHOES (1988)	GOLF SHOES (1997)	KIDS TRAXTAR SHOES (2001)	ADULT SMART TRAIN DMX SHOES (2001)
Performance-oriented 27%	Runners	P						P			P
	Aerobic/fitness exercisers		P					P			P
	Tennis players			P				P			
	Basketball players				P			P			
	Golfers								P		
	Adventure seekers							P			P
Nonathletic-oriented 73%	Walkers	S	S	S	S		P	P			S
	Children					P				P	
	Comfort/style-conscious	S	S	S	S		S	S			S

Key: P = Primary market   S = Secondary market

FIGURE 9–2
Market-product grid showing how different Reebok shoes reach segments of customers with different needs

MARKET-PRODUCT GRID
Framework to relate the segment of a market to products offered or potential marketing actions by the firm.

What segmentation strategy will Reebok use to take it further into the 21st century? Only Reebok knows, but it will certainly involve trying to differentiate its products more clearly from its global competitors and perhaps target new or retarget existing global consumers.

Using Market-Product Grids   A **market-product grid** is a framework to relate the segments of a market to products offered or potential marketing actions by the firm. The grid in Figure 9–2 shows different market segments of sneaker users as rows in the grid, whereas the columns show the different shoe product lines (or marketing actions) chosen by Reebok. Thus, each cell in a market-product grid can depict the estimated market size of a given product sold to a specific market segment.

The lightly shaded cells in Figure 9–2, labelled "P," represent Reebok's primary target market segment when it introduced each type of shoe. The dark shaded cells, labelled "S," represent the secondary target market segments that also bought these products. In some cases, Reebok discovered that large numbers of people in a segment not originally targeted for a particular shoe style bought it anyway. Thus, Reebok products are purchased by two types of segments: "performance-oriented" consumers (27 percent), who buy sneakers and apparel for athletic purposes; and "nonathletic-oriented" consumers (73 percent), who buy sneakers and apparel for comfort, style, price, or other nonathletic reasons. But as Figure 9–2 depicts, two segments of consumers in the "nonathletic-oriented" category, "comfort/style conscious" and "walker" (who may object to being referred to as "nonathletes"), bought running, aerobic, and cross-trainer shoes not initially targeted at their respective segments. When this trend became apparent to Reebok in 1986, it introduced its walking shoe line targeted directly at the walker segment.

Figure 9–2 also suggests one of the potential dangers faced by a firm that uses market segmentation: By subdividing an entire market into two or more segments, the firm runs the risk of diffusing its marketing efforts, thereby enabling competitors to attack these segments. To reach specific segments more effectively, Reebok uses "strategic business units," as discussed in Chapter 2, to focus its marketing efforts.[4]

Does Harry Potter appeal to only the kids' segment? See the text for the answer to this amazing publishing success.

When to Segment Markets

A business firm goes to the trouble and expense of segmenting its markets when this increases its sales revenue, profit, and return on investment. When its expenses more than offset the potentially increased revenues from segmentation, it should not attempt to segment its market. The specific situations that illustrate this point are the cases of (1) one product and multiple market segments, (2) multiple products and multiple market segments, and (3) "segments of one," or mass customization.

One Product and Multiple Market Segments When a firm produces only a single product or service and attempts to sell it to two or more market segments, it avoids the extra costs of developing and producing additional versions of the product, which often entail extremely high research, engineering, and manufacturing expenses. In this case, the incremental costs of taking the product into new product segments are typically those of a separate promotional campaign or a new channel of distribution. Although these expenses can be high, they are rarely as large as those for developing an entirely new product.

Movies, magazines, and books are single products frequently directed to two or more distinct market segments. Movie companies often run different TV commercials or magazine ads featuring different aspects of a newly released film (love, or drama, or spectacular scenery) that are targeted to different market segments. *Time* magazine now publishes more than 100 international editions, each targeted at its own geographic and demographic segments and each with its own mix of advertisements.

Author J.K. Rowling's *Harry Potter* book series has been a phenomenal success not only because of the fiction-writing wizardry but because of her publisher's creativity in marketing the books to pre-teen, teen, and adult segments of readers. Millions of Harry Potter books have been sold in North America and the books are often at the top of fiction best-seller lists for adults.[5] Although multiple TV commericals for movies and separate covers or advertisements for magazines or books are expensive, they are minor compared with the costs of producing an entirely new movie, magazine, or book for another market segment.

Multiple Products and Multiple Market Segments Reebok's different styles of shoes, each targeted at a different type of user, are an example of multiple products aimed at multiple markets. Similarly, Corel Corporation of Ottawa develops specific software tailored to distinctive segments such as home, business, government, and academic markets. Manufacturing these different products is clearly more expensive than producing one but seems worthwhile if it serves customers' needs better, doesn't reduce quality or increase price, and adds to the sales revenues and profits.

Marketing experts are increasingly stressing the need for what they call "two-tier marketing strategies" for the 21st century.[6] Affluent Canadians, about a fifth of the population in the country, have seen their incomes increase over the past two decades while middle-class and working-class Canadians have seen their incomes stagnate or even decline in terms of real buying power. The result is that many firms are now offering different products or services to high-end and low-end segments:

- Gap's Banana Republic chain sells blue jeans for $58, whereas its Old Navy stores sell a slightly different version for $22.
- General Motors' Saturn unit not only sells its no-haggling-on-price new cars but is aggressively marketing its "pre-owned" cars to reduce customer fears about buying a used car.
- The Walt Disney Company carefully markets two distinct Winnie-the-Poohs— such as the original line-drawn figures on fine china sold at upscale department stores and a cartoon-like Pooh on polyester bedsheets sold at Zellers and Wal-Mart—and these Poohs don't play together on the shelves of the same retailer.

www.disney.com

The lines between customer segments often blur, however, as shown by the Cadillacs and Mercedes in Wal-Mart and Costco parking lots.

Segments of One: Mass Customization   Canadian marketers are rediscovering today what their ancestors running the corner butcher shop or general store knew a century ago: Every customer is unique, has unique wants and needs, and desires special tender loving care from the seller—the essence of customer relationship management (CRM). Economies of scale in manufacturing and marketing during the past century made mass-produced goods so affordable that most customers were willing to compromise their individual tastes and settle for standardized products. Today's Internet ordering and flexible manufacturing and marketing processes have made possible *mass customization*, tailoring goods or services to the tastes of individual customers on a high-volume scale. The Web Link shows how mass customization lets you design your own personalized running shoe or hiking boot.

Mass customization is the next step beyond *build-to-order* (BTO), manufacturing a product only when there is an order from a customer. Dell Computer uses BTO systems that trim work-in-progress inventories and shorten delivery times to customers. Dell's three-day deliveries (see Chapter 16) are made possible by restricting its computer line to only a few basic modules and stocking a variety of each. This gives customers a good choice—Dell PCs being assembled in four minutes. Most Dell customization comes from spending 90 minutes loading the unique software each customer selects. But even this system falls a bit short of total mass customization with virtually unlimited specification of features by customers.[7]

SYNERGY
The increased customer value achieved through performing organizational functions more efficiently.

The Segmentation Trade-off: CRM vs Synergies   The key to successful product differentiation and market segmentation strategies is finding the ideal balance between satisfying a customer's individual wants and achieving organizational **synergy**, the increased customer value achieved through performing organizational functions more efficiently. The "increased customer value" can take many forms: more

WEB LINK

Mass Customizing Your Own "Designer" Sneakers

http://www.mcgrawhill.ca

Don't like the looks of those things on your feet right now? If you think your style instincts could design you a better running shoe or hiking boot, go to www.customatix.com! There you can design your own shoe—customizing 15 elements of your shoe. All possible combinations of these 15 design elements are the basis for Customatix's claim of offering more than 3 billion trillion design variations.

A bit too complex? Design a simpler sneaker on Nike's Website:www.nike.com/nike_id.

products, improved quality on existing products, lower prices, easier access to products through improved distribution, and so on. So the ultimate criterion for an organization's marketing success is that customers should be better off as a result of the increased synergies.

Customized perfumes from Procter & Gamble, customized jeans from Levi's, and customized employee uniforms from Lands' End are common today.[8] But are the customers of these firms really happy, given all the special technology? In spite of the critical importance of customer relationship management discussed in Chapter 1, a recent study found that two-thirds of such CRM projects fail. The essence of good customer relations is not the elegance of the latest technology but relentless attention to detail: good products, prompt service, and a dedicated staff willing to take an extra step to handle those special customer needs.[9]

Concept Check	**1.** Market segmentation involves aggregating prospective buyers into groups that have two key characteristics. What are they?
	2. What is product differentiation?
	3. The process of segmenting and targeting markets is a bridge between which two marketing activities?

STEPS IN SEGMENTING AND TARGETING MARKETS

The process of segmenting a market and then selecting and reaching the target segments is divided into the five steps discussed in this section, as shown in Figure 9–3. Segmenting a market is not a science—it requires large doses of common sense and managerial judgment.

Market segmentation and target markets can be abstract topics, so put on your entrepreneur's hat to experience the process. Suppose you own a Wendy's fast-food restaurant next to a large urban university that offers both day and evening classes. Your restaurant specializes in the Wendy's basics: hamburgers, french fries, Frosty milkshakes, and chili. Even though you are part of a chain and have some restrictions on menu and decor, you are free to set your hours of business and to undertake local advertising. How can market segmentation help?

www.wendys.com

Form Prospective Buyers into Segments

Grouping prospective buyers into meaningful segments involves meeting some specific criteria for segmentation and finding specific variables to segment the consumer or organizational market being analyzed.

FIGURE 9–3
The process of segmenting and targeting markets involves five key steps

Steps in segmenting and targeting markets

Identify market needs

- Form prospective buyers into segments
- Form products to be sold into groups
- Develop a market-product grid and estimate size of markets
- Select target markets
- Take marketing actions to reach target markets

Execute marketing program

Criteria to Use in Forming the Segments   A marketing manager should develop segments for a market that meet five principal criteria:

- *Potential for increased profit and ROI.* The best segmentation approach is the one that maximizes the opportunity for future profit and ROI. If this potential is maximized through no segmentation, don't segment. For non-profit organizations, the analogous criterion is the potential for serving client users more effectively.
- *Similarity of needs of potential buyers within a segment.* Potential buyers within a segment should be similar in terms of a marketing activity, such as product features sought or advertising media used.
- *Difference of needs of buyers among segments.* If the needs of the various segments aren't appreciably different, combine them into fewer segments. A different segment usually requires a different marketing action that, in turn, means greater costs. If increased revenues don't offset extra costs, combine segments and reduce the number of marketing actions.
- *Feasibility of a marketing action to reach a segment.* Reaching a segment requires a simple but effective marketing action. If no such action exists, don't segment.
- *Simplicity and cost of assigning potential buyers to segments.* A marketing manager must be able to put a market segmentation plan into effect. This means being able to recognize the characteristics of potential buyers and then assigning them to a segment without encountering excessive costs.

Ways to Segment Consumer Markets   Figure 9–4 shows the main dimensions used to segment Canadian consumer markets. These include geographic, demographic, psychographic, and behavioural segmentation.[10] By examining Figure 9–4, you can also see that a number of variables can be used within each dimension for segmentation purposes. What you should remember is that segmenting markets is not a pure science—it requires large doses of common sense and managerial judgment. A marketer may have to use several dimensions and multiple variables within each dimension to form proper market segments. Let's take a look at how some marketers might segment consumer markets using the information in Figure 9–4.

www.colgate-palmolive.com

- *Geographic Segmentation.* Using geographic segmentation, a marketer segments based on where consumers live. Geographic variables such as countries, regions, provinces, counties, cities, or even neighbourhoods could be used. Marketers often find that Canadians differ in terms of needs or preferences based on the region in which they live. This is a form of geographic segmentation. For example, Colgate-Palmolive markets Arctic Power, its cold-water detergent, on an energy-cost-saving dimension in Quebec, but as a clothes saver (cold-water washing is easier on clothes) in Western Canada.
- *Demographic Segmentation.* One of the most common ways to segment consumer markets is to use demographic segmentation, or segmenting a market based on population characteristics. This approach segments consumers according to variables such as age, gender, income, education, occupation, and so forth. Cyanamid Canada Inc. uses age as a segmentation variable, producing and marketing its vitamins to various age groups including children, young adults, and older Canadians. Centrum Select, for instance, is specifically designed for adults over 50. Trimark Investments of Ontario segments the financial services market by gender, targeting males and females with different products and different advertising campaigns. General Electric uses family size as a segmentation variable, targeting smaller families with compact microwaves and larger families with extra-large refrigerators. You should note, however, that a single demographic variable may not be sufficient in understanding and segmenting a given market. Thus, many marketers combine a number of

MAIN DIMENSIONS	VARIABLES	TYPICAL BREAKDOWNS
Geographic segmentation	Region	Atlantic, Quebec, Ontario, Prairies, British Columbia
	City or census metropolitan area (CMA) size	Under 5000; 5000–19 999; 20 000–49 000; 50 000–99 999; 100 000–249 000; 250 000–499 999; 500 000–999 000; 1 000 000–3 999 999; 4 000 000+
	Density	Urban; suburban; rural
	Climate	East; West
Demographic segmentation	Age	Infant; under 6; 6–11; 12–17; 18–24; 25–34; 35–49; 50–64; 65+
	Gender	Male; female
	Family size	1–2; 3–4; 5+
	Stage of family life cycle	Young single; young married, no children; young married, youngest child under 6; young married, youngest child 6 or older; older married, with children; older married, no children under 18; older single; other older married
	Income	Under $10 000; $10 000–19 999; $20 000–29 999; $30 000–39 999; $40 000–54 999; $55 000–74 999; $75 000+
	Occupation	Professional; managerial; clerical; sales; labourers; students; retired; housewives; unemployed
	Education	Grade school or less; some high school; high school graduate; some college; college graduate
	Race	White; Black; Asian; Native; other
	Home ownership	Own home; rent home
Psychographic segmentation	Personality	Gregarious; compulsive; extroverted; introverted
	Lifestyle (Goldfarb Segments)	Structured; discontented; fearful; assured; resentful; caring
Behavioural segmentation	Benefits sought	Quality; service; low price
	Usage rate	Light user; medium user; heavy user
	User status	Non-user; ex-user; prospect; first-time user; regular user
	Loyalty status	None, medium, strong

FIGURE 9–4

Segmentation variables and breakdowns for Canadian consumer markets

demographic variables that might clearly distinguish one segment from another. For example, cosmetics companies such as Clinique combine gender, income, and occupation in order to examine market segments for different lines of cosmetic products.

- *Psychographic Segmentation.* Marketers use psychographic segmentation when they segment markets according to personality or lifestyle. It has been found that people who share the same demographic characteristics can have very different psychographic profiles. As we saw in Chapter 5, personality traits have been linked to product preferences and brand choice. In addition, a person's lifestyle (his or her activities, interests, and opinions) also affects the types of products, and the particular brands of products that may be purchased. Remember the Goldfarb segments from Chapter 5? Members of the discontented segment like package deals when they buy because they do not want to make decisions.[11] On the other hand, those in the resentful segment like expensive brands and they don't worry about price.[12]

- *Behavioural Segmentation.* When marketers use consumers' behaviour with or toward a product to segment the market, they are using behavioural segmentation. A powerful form of behavioural segmentation is to divide the market according to the benefits consumers seek from a product category. Using *benefits sought*, the marketer examines the major benefits consumers look for in the product category, the kinds of consumers who look for each benefit, and

Wireless communications providers target young adults seeking specific benefits from wireless technology.

USAGE RATE
Quantity consumed or patronage—store visits—during a specific period; varies significantly among different customer groups.

80/20 RULE
A concept that suggests 80 percent of a firm's sales are obtained from 20 percent of its customers.

www.aircanada.ca

the major brands that deliver each benefit. For example, Telus Mobility and Bell Mobility both market their wireless communications products and services to young adults under 24 years of age who want text messaging "rather than talk" in order to ensure privacy. On the other hand, Rogers AT&T targets CEOs of large businesses who want to improve employee productivity through the use of wireless technology.[13]

Another behavioural segmentation variable often used by marketers is **usage rate**—quantity consumed or patronage during a specific period, which varies significantly among different customer groups. Air Canada, for example, focuses on usage rate for its frequent-flyer program, which is designed to encourage passengers to use its airline repeatedly. Usage rate is sometimes referred to in terms of the **80/20 rule**, a concept that suggests that 80 percent of a firm's sales are obtained from 20 percent of its customers. The percentages in the 80/20 rule are not really fixed; rather, the rule suggests that a small fraction of customers provide a large fraction of sales. For example, Air Canada pays special attention to the business travel segment that comprises only 20 percent of the airline seats but 40 percent of overall revenues.[14]

Research shows that the fast-food market can also be segmented into light, medium, or heavy users. For every $1.00 spent by a light user in a fast-food restaurant, each heavy user spends over $5.00.[15] This is the reason for the emphasis in almost all marketing strategies on effective ways to reach heavy users of products and services. Thus, as a Wendy's restaurant owner you want to keep the heavy-user segment constantly in mind. With advances in information technology, marketers are now able to conduct detailed segmentation studies. Some Canadian telecommunications companies, for example, can now segment based on more than 100 criteria, from calling patterns to promotional response.

Now, in determining one or two variables to segment the market for your Wendy's restaurant, very broadly we find two main markets: students and non-students. To segment the students, we could try a variety of demographic variables such as age, gender, year in school, or university major, or psychographic variables such as personality or lifestyle. But none of these variables really meets the five criteria listed previously—particularly the fourth criterion about leading to a feasible marketing action to reach the various segments. Four student segments that *do* meet these criteria include the following:

- Students living in dormitories (residence halls, fraternity houses).
- Students living near the university in apartments.
- Day commuter students living outside the area.
- Night commuter students living outside the area.

These segmentation variables are really a combination of where the student lives and the time he or she is on campus (and near your restaurant). For non-students who might be customers, similar variables might be used:

- Faculty and staff members at the university.
- People who live in the area but aren't connected with the university.
- People who work in the area but aren't connected with the university.

Ways to Segment Organizational Markets   Variables for segmenting organizational markets are shown in Figure 9–5. A product manager at Xerox responsible for its new network colour printer might use a number of these segmentation variables, as follows:

FIGURE 9–5
Dimensions used to segment Canadian organizational markets

MAIN DIMENSIONS	VARIABLES	TYPICAL BREAKDOWNS
Geographic segmentation	Region	Atlantic, Quebec, Ontario, Prairies, British Columbia
	Location	In CMA; not in CMA
Demographic segmentation	NAICS code	2-digit; 3-digit; 4-digit; 5-digit; 6-digit categories
	Number of Employees	1–19; 20–99; 100–249; 250+
	Annual Sales Volume	Less than $1 million; $1–10 million; $10–100 million; over $100 million
Behavioural segmentation	Benefits sought	Quality; customer service; low price
	Usage rate	Light user; medium user; heavy user
	User status	Non-user; ex-user; prospect; first-time user; regular user
	Loyalty status	None, medium, strong
	Purchase method	Centralized; decentralized; Individual; group
	Type of buy	New buy; modified rebuy; straight rebuy

What variables might Xerox use to segment the organizational markets for its answer to colour copying problems? For the possible answer and related marketing actions, see the text.

- *Geographic segmentation.* The product manager might segment based on region or actual location of the potential customer. Firms located in a census metropolitan area (CMA) might receive a personal sales call, whereas those outside the CMA might be contacted by phone.
- *Demographic segmentation.* Firms might be categorized by the North American Industry Classification System (NAICS). Manufacturers, for example, with global customers might have different printing needs than do retailers or lawyers serving local customers.
- *Behavioural segmentation.* The market might also be segmented based on benefits sought. Xerox may decide to focus on firms looking for quality product and good customer service as opposed to those looking for simply low prices. The product manager might also segment the market based on usage rate, recognizing that larger, more globally oriented firms are more likely to be heavy users.

Form Products to Be Sold into Groups

As important as grouping customers into segments is finding a means of grouping the products you're selling into meaningful categories. If the firm has only one product or service, this isn't a problem, but when it has dozens or hundreds, these must be grouped in some way so buyers can relate to them. This is why department stores and supermarkets are organized into product groups, with the departments or aisles containing related merchandise. Likewise, manufacturers have product lines that are the groupings they use in the catalogues sent to customers.

What are the groupings for your restaurant? It could be the item purchased, such as a Frosty, chili, hamburgers, and french fries, but this is where judgment—the qualitative aspect of marketing—comes in. Students really buy an eating experience, or a meal that satisfies a need at a particular time of day, so the product grouping can be defined by meal or time of day as breakfast, lunch, between-meal snack, dinner, and after-dinner snack. These groupings are more closely related to the way purchases are actually made and permit you to market the entire meal, not just your french fries or Frosties.

Develop a Market-Product Grid and Estimate Size of Markets

Developing a market-product grid means labelling the markets (or horizontal rows) and products (or vertical columns), as shown in Figure 9–6. In addition, the size of the market in each cell, or the market-product combination, must be estimated. For your restaurant this involves estimating the number of, or sales revenue obtained from, each kind of meal that can reasonably be expected to be sold to each market segment. This is a form of the usage rate analysis discussed earlier in the chapter.

The market sizes in Figure 9–6 may be simple "guesstimates" if you don't have time for formal marketing research (as discussed in Chapter 8). But even such crude estimates of the size of specific markets using a market-product grid are far better than the usual estimates of the entire market.

Select Target Markets

A firm must take care to choose its target market segments carefully. If it chooses too narrow a group of segments, it may fail to reach the volume of sales and profits it needs. If it selects too broad a group of segments, it may spread its marketing efforts so thin that the extra expenses more than offset the increased sales and profits.

Criteria to Use in Choosing the Target Segments   Two different kinds of criteria are present in the market segmentation process: (1) those to use in dividing the market into segments (discussed earlier) and (2) those to use in actually choosing the target segments. Even experienced marketing executives often confuse these two different sets of criteria. The five criteria to use in actually selecting the target segments apply to your Wendy's restaurant in this way:

- *Market size.* The estimated size of the market in the segment is an important factor in deciding whether it's worth going after. There is really no market for breakfasts among campus students (Figure 9–6), so why devote any marketing effort toward reaching a small or non-existent market?

FIGURE 9–6
Selecting a target market for your fast-food restaurant next to an urban university (target market is shaded)

MARKETS	PRODUCTS: MEALS: BREAK-FAST	LUNCH	BETWEEN-MEAL SNACK	DINNER	AFTER-DINNER SNACK
STUDENT					
Dormitory	0	1	3	0	3
Apartment	1	3	3	1	1
Day commuter	0	3	2	1	0
Night commuter	0	0	1	3	2
NON-STUDENT					
Faculty or staff	0	3	1	1	0
Live in area	0	1	2	2	1
Work in area	1	3	0	1	0

Key: 3 = Large market; 2 = Medium market; 1 = Small market; 0 = No market.

- *Expected growth.* Although the size of the market in a segment may be small now, perhaps it is growing significantly or is expected to grow in the future. For example, the segment using drive-through ordering is growing three times faster than the eat-inside segment. So having a fast-service drive-through facility may be critical for your restaurant's success.[16]
- *Competitive position.* Is there a lot of competition in the segment now or is there likely to be in the future? The less the competition, the more attractive the segment is. For example, if the university cafeterias announce a new policy of "no meals on weekends," this segment is suddenly more promising for your restaurant.
- *Cost of reaching the segment.* A segment that is inaccessible to a firm's marketing actions should not be pursued. For example, the few non-students who live in the area may not be economically reachable with ads in newspapers or other media. As a result, do not waste money trying to advertise to them.
- *Compatibility with the organization's objectives and resources.* If your restaurant doesn't have the cooking equipment to make breakfasts and has a policy against spending more money on restaurant equipment, then don't try to reach the breakfast segment.

As is often the case in marketing decisions, a particular segment may appear attractive according to some criteria and very unattractive according to others.

Choose the Segments Ultimately, a marketing executive has to use these criteria to choose the segments for special marketing efforts. As shown in Figure 9–6, let's assume you've written off the breakfast market for two reasons: too small market size and incompatibility with your objectives and resources. In terms of competitive position and cost of reaching the segment, you choose to focus on the four student segments and not the three non-student segments (although you're certainly not going to turn away business from the nonstudent segments). This combination of market-product segments—your target market—is shaded in Figure 9–6.

Take Marketing Actions to Reach Target Markets

The purpose of developing a market-product grid is to trigger marketing actions to increase revenues and profits. This means that someone must develop and execute an action plan.

How can Wendy's target different market segments like drive-through customers with different advertising programs? For the answer, see the text and Figure 9–7.

www.burgerking.com

Your Wendy's Segmentation Strategy With your Wendy's restaurant you've already reached one significant decision: There is a limited market for breakfast, so you won't open for business until 10:30 a.m. In fact, Wendy's first attempt at a breakfast menu was a disaster and was discontinued in 1986. Wendy's evaluates possible new menu items continuously, to compete not only with McDonald's and Burger King but also with a complex array of supermarkets, convenience stores, and gas stations that sell reheatable packaged foods as well as new "easy-lunch" products.

Another essential decision is where and what meals to advertise to reach specific market segments. An ad in the student newspaper could reach all the student segments, but you might consider this "shotgun approach" too expensive and want a more focused "rifle approach" to reach smaller segments. If you choose three segments for special actions (Figure 9–7), advertising actions to reach them might include:

- *Day commuters* (an entire market segment). Run ads inside commuter buses and put flyers under the windshield wipers of cars in parking lots used by day commuters. These ads and flyers promote all the meals at your restaurant to a single segment of students—a horizontal cut through the market-product grid.
- *Between-meals snacks* (directed to all four student markets). To promote eating during this downtime for your restaurant, offer "Ten percent off all purchases between 2:00 and 4:30 p.m. during the winter term." This ad promotes a single meal to all four student segments—a vertical cut through the market-product grid.
- *Dinners to night commuters.* The most focused of all three campaigns, this ad promotes a single meal to a single student segment. The campaign might consist of a windshield flyer offering a free Frosty with the coupon when the

FIGURE 9–7
Advertising actions to reach specific student segments

PRODUCTS: MEALS

MARKETS	LUNCH	BETWEEN-MEAL SNACK	DINNER	AFTER-DINNER SNACK
Dormitory students	1	3	0	3
Apartment students	3	3	1	1
Day commuter students	3	2	1	0
Night commuter students	0	1	3	2

Ads in buses; flyers under windshield wipers of cars in parking lots

Ad campaign: "Ten percent off all purchases between 2:00 and 4:30 P.M. during winter term"

Ad on flyer under windshield wipers of cars in night parking lots: "Free Frosty with this coupon when you buy a drive-through meal between 5:00 and 7:00 P.M."

Key: 3 = Large market; 2 = Medium market; 1 = Small market; 0 = No market.

person buys a drive-through meal between 5:00 and 7:00 P.M., which exploits efficiency in drive-through business.

Depending on how your advertising actions work, you can repeat, modify, or drop them and design new campaigns for other segments you feel warrant the effort. This example of advertising your Wendy's restaurant is just a small piece of a complete marketing program using all the elements of the marketing mix.

Apple's Ever-Changing Segmentation Strategy

Steve Jobs and Steve Wozniak didn't realize they were developing today's multi-billion dollar PC industry when they invented the Apple I in a garage on April Fool's Day, 1976. Hobbyists, the initial target market, were not interested in the product. However, when the Apple II was displayed at a computer trade show in 1977 consumers loved it and Apple Computer was born. Typical of young companies, Apple focused on its products and had little concern for its markets. When IBM—"Big Blue"—entered the PC market in 1981, Apple was forced to become a "real company," much to the chagrin of its creative young engineers who were likened to "Boy Scouts without adult supervision."

With the introduction of the IBM PC, Big Blue quickly dominated the fledgling market, having licensed the DOS operating system from Bill Gates of Microsoft. By 1983, Apple had lost significant market share. During the Super Bowl in 1984, Apple launched the Macintosh with an Orwellian TV ad that has been described as the best commercial ever. And while the new Macintosh initially sold well, sales fell off dramatically, eventually leading to the departure of Steve Jobs from Apple in 1985. Unfortunately, Apple continued to languish under new, changing leadership as it constantly altered its market-product strategies. By the end of 1996, Apple's losses mounted and it was time for a bold move: Bring back Steve Jobs.[17]

When Steve Jobs returned in 1997, he detailed his vision for a reincarnated Apple by describing a new market segmentation strategy that he called the "Apple Product Matrix." This strategy consisted of developing two general types of computers (desktops and portables) targeted at two general kinds of market segments (consumer and professional). He also announced the controversial "Think Different" advertising campaign, deleted several models from Apple's existing product line, and launched The Apple Store, in which Apple would sell its computers directly via the Internet or by telephone. In 1998, Apple re-targeted the consumer and educational markets by introducing the revolutionary new iMac, the greatest PC product launch in history.[18]

In 1999, Apple introduced the clamshell-looking iBook portable computer, based on the same innovative design principles as the iMac. In January 2001, Steve Jobs again changed the strategic direction of Apple. According to Jobs, the PC industry has now entered the third golden age of personal computing. The first era, which occurred from 1980 to 1994, featured the PC as an office productivity tool. Users bought PCs for their word processing, spreadsheet analysis, and desktop publishing, capabilities. The second era occurred from 1995 to 2000, when the PC became the primary access tool for the Internet. As PC sales slowed in 2000, experts began to ask "What's next?" They believed that a variety of small digital devices would replace personal computers. Steve Jobs says they're wrong and is betting the company on his conviction.

Jobs believes that the personal computer entered the Age of the Digital Lifestyle in 2001. In a keynote address, Jobs said that "the proliferation of digital devices— CD players, MP3 players, cell phones, handheld organizers (PDAs), digital cameras, digital camcorders, and more—will never have enough processing power and memory to stand alone." Jobs enthusiastically proclaimed "the Mac can become the digital hub of this new digital lifestyle by adding tremendous value to these devices"[19] Moreover, Jobs is convinced that "Apple is uniquely suited to do this because we are the last company in the [PC] business that has all these components [hardware, operating system, software applications, and accessories] under one roof." Apple is

What market segments for Apple's computers are represented by these products? The Marketing NewsNet and text discussion provide insights into Apple's market segmentation strategy.

Apple Computer

www.apple.com

betting that PC makers will not be willing to integrate their respective products into a cohesive "digital hub" that matches the simplicity of Apple's digital lifestyle strategy.[20]

Thus, Apple will no longer engage in a war for market share against the PC world dominated by Intel processors and Microsoft Windows operating systems. Instead, Jobs believes that Apple can thrive with a 5- to 10-percent share of the PC market, citing BMW's 2-percent share of the automotive market in its special niche. By repositioning Apple as the "digital hub" with "killer apps," such as iTunes, iMovie, iDVD, QuickTime, and so on, Jobs believes consumers can take full advantage of the new digital lifestyle era.

As in most segmentation situations, a single product does not fit into an exclusive market niche. Rather, there is overlap among products in the product line and also among the markets to which they are directed. But a market segmentation strategy enables Apple to offer different products to meet the needs of different market segments, as shown in the Marketing NewsNet box.[21]

What does Steve Jobs have in store for Apple in the near future? Here are some plans and successes to build on for 2002 and beyond:[22]

- Redesigning its iMac (which had sold over 6 million units by early 2002) and Power Mac G4 lines, which were both introduced in 1998.
- Adding more Apple retail stores, which were launched in May 2001, in the hopes of expanding its market share to 10 percent.
- Strengthening its relationship with the education market, which is Apple's largest target market segment, accounting for about 40 percent of its total sales.
- Developing new "killer apps," which include Mac OSX, a completely rewritten operating system that significantly reduces crashes; iTunes, which allows users to record CDs and play MP3 music; iMovie, which enables users to

MARKETING NEWSNET

Apple's Segmentation Strategy: Camp Runamok No Longer

"Camp Runamok" was the nickname given to Apple Computer in the early 1980s because the innovative company had no coherent series of product lines directed at identifiable market segments.

Today, Apple has targeted its various lines of Macintosh computers and software at specific market segments. Because the market–product grid shifts as a firm's strategy changes, the one shown below is based on Apple's market–product grid as of 2002. This market–product grid is a simplification because each "product grouping" consists of a line of Macintosh computers or software. Nevertheless, the grid suggests the following market segmentation strategy used by Apple, based on the Apple Product Matrix and digital lifestyle described in the text.

MARKETS		PRODUCTS							
		HARDWARE				SOFTWARE			
SECTOR	**SEGMENT**	Power Macintosh G4	PowerBook G4	iMac	iBook	iTunes	iMovies	iDVD	iPhoto
CONSUMER	Individuals			✓	✓	✓	✓	✓	✓
	Small/home office	✓	✓	✓	✓	✓	✓	✓	✓
	Students			✓	✓	✓	✓		✓
	Teachers	✓	✓	✓	✓				✓
PROFESSIONAL	Medium/large business	✓	✓	✓				✓	✓
	Creative	✓	✓			✓	✓	✓	✓
	College faculty	✓	✓	✓	✓			✓	✓
	College staff	✓	✓						✓

create and edit home movies recorded on digital media; iDVD, which allows users to create DVDs that can be played on their Mac or DVD player at home; and QuickTime, which enables Internet users to view/hear video, sound, animation, graphics, and music.

Stay tuned to see if Steve Jobs and these market-product strategies for his vision of the digital lifestyle era are on target. He's betting the company on it!

Concept Check

1. What are some of the variables used to segment consumer markets?

2. What are some criteria used to decide which segments to choose for targets?

3. Why is usage rate important in segmentation studies?

ANALYZING MARKET SEGMENTS USING CROSS TABULATIONS

To do a more precise market segmentation analysis of your Wendy's restaurant, suppose you survey fast-food patrons throughout the metropolitan area where your restaurant is located, using the questionnaire shown in Figure 8–6. You want to use this information as best you can to study the market's segments and develop your strategy. Probably the most widely used approach today in marketing is to develop and interpret cross tabulations of data obtained by questionnaires.

Developing Cross Tabulations

CROSS TABULATION
Method of presenting and relating data having two or more variables to analyze and discover relationships in the data.

A **cross tabulation**, or "cross tab," is a method of presenting and relating data having two or more variables. It is used to analyze and discover relationships in the data. Two important aspects of cross tabulations are deciding which of two variables to pair together to help understand the situation and forming the resulting cross tabulations.

Pairing the Questions   Marketers pair two questions to understand marketing relationships and to find effective marketing actions. The Wendy's questionnaire in Figure 8–6 gives many questions that might be paired to understand the fast-food business better and help reach a decision about marketing actions to increase revenues. For example, if you want to study your hypothesis that as the age of the head of household increases patronage of fast-food restaurants declines, you can cross tabulate questions 9d and 3.

Forming Cross Tabulations   Using the answers to question 3 as the column headings and the answers to question 9d as the row headings gives a cross tabulation, as shown in Figure 9–8, using the answers 586 respondents gave to both questions. The figure shows two forms of the cross tabulation:

- The raw data or answers to the specific questions are shown in Figure 9–8A. For example, this cross tab shows that 144 households whose head was 24 years or younger ate at fast-food restaurants once a week or more.
- Answers on a percentage basis, with the percentages running horizontally, are shown in Figure 9–8B. Of the 215 households headed by someone 24 years or younger, 67.0 percent ate at a fast-food restaurant at least once a week and only 8.8 percent ate there once a month or less.

Two other forms of cross tabulation using the raw data shown in Figure 9–8A are as described in problem 7 at the end of the chapter.

Interpreting Cross Tabulations

A careful analysis of Figure 9–8 shows that patronage of fast-food restaurants is related to the age of the head of the household. Note that as the age of the head of the household increases, fast-food restaurant patronage declines, as shown by the boxed percentages on the diagonal in Figure 9–8B. This means that if you want to reach the heavy-user segment, you should direct your marketing efforts to the segment that is 24 years old or younger.

As discussed earlier in the chapter, there are various ways to segment a consumer market besides according to age. For example, you could make subsequent cross tabulations to analyze patronage related to where students live and the meals they eat to obtain more precise information for the market-product grid in Figure 9–6.

Value of Cross Tabulations

Probably the most widely used technique for organizing and presenting marketing data, cross tabulations have some important advantages. The simple format permits direct interpretation and an easy means of communicating data to management. They have great flexibility and can be used to summarize experimental, observational, and questionnaire data. Also, cross tabulations may be easily generated by today's personal computers.

A. ABSOLUTE FREQUENCIES

| | FREQUENCY | | | |
AGE OF HEAD OF HOUSEHOLD (YEARS)	ONCE A WEEK OR MORE	2 OR 3 TIMES A MONTH	ONCE A MONTH OR LESS	TOTAL
24 or less	144	52	19	215
25 to 39	46	58	29	133
40 or over	82	69	87	238
Total	272	179	135	586

B. ROW PERCENTAGES: RUNNING PERCENTAGES HORIZONTALLY

| | FREQUENCY | | | |
AGE OF HEAD OF HOUSEHOLD (YEARS)	ONCE A WEEK OR MORE	2 OR 3 TIMES A MONTH	ONCE A MONTH OR LESS	TOTAL
24 or less	67.0%	24.2%	8.8%	100.0%
25 to 39	34.6	43.6	21.8	100.0
40 or over	34.4	29.0	36.6	100.0
Total	46.4%	30.6%	23.0%	100.0%

Cross tabulations also have some disadvantages. For example, they can be misleading if the percentages are based on too small a number of observations. Also, cross tabulations can hide some relations because each typically shows only two or three variables. Balancing both advantages and disadvantages, more marketing decisions are probably made using cross tabulations than any other method of analyzing data.

The ultimate value of cross tabulations to a marketing manager lies in obtaining a better understanding of the wants and needs of buyers and targeting key segments. This enables a marketing manager to "position" the offering in the minds of buyers, the topic discussed next.

POSITIONING THE PRODUCT

PRODUCT POSITIONING
The place an offering occupies in consumers' minds on important attributes relative to competitive offerings.

When a company offers a product commercially, a decision critical to its long-term success is how to position it in the market on introduction. **Product positioning** refers to the place an offering occupies in consumers' minds on important attributes relative to competitive offerings.

Two Approaches to Product Positioning

There are several approaches to positioning a new product in the market. Head-to-head positioning involves competing directly with competitors on similar product attributes in the same target market. Using this strategy, in the car-rental market Budget competes directly with Avis and Hertz.

Differentiation positioning involves seeking a less competitive, smaller market niche in which to locate a brand. SoyaWorld Inc. of Vancouver positions its soy beverage product, called So Good, to appeal to a small niche segment of the market that is looking for an alternative to cow's milk. Companies also follow a differentiation strategy among brands within their own product line to try to minimize cannibalization of a brand's sales or shares.

Product Positioning Using Perceptual Maps

A key to positioning a product effectively is the perceptions of consumers. In determining a brand's position and the preferences of consumers, companies obtain three types of data from consumers:

1. Evaluations of the important attributes for a product class.
2. Judgments of existing brands with the important attributes.
3. Ratings of an "ideal" brand's attributes.

PERCEPTUAL MAP
A means of displaying or graphing in two dimensions the location of products or brands in the minds of consumers.

From these data, it is possible to develop a **perceptual map**, a means of displaying or graphing in two dimensions the location of products or brands in the minds of consumers to enable a manager to see how consumers perceive competing products or brands and then take marketing actions.

GM's Positioning Nightmare Over the past three decades, General Motors faced a very difficult and costly positioning challenge. Consumers simply couldn't keep its brands straight in their own minds—they couldn't tell a Chevrolet from a Pontiac or an Oldsmobile from a Buick or Cadillac. In the 1990s, GM spent tens of millions of dollars trying to reposition its brands. **Repositioning** involves changing the place an offering occupies in a consumer's mind relative to competitive offerings. GM wanted to make Oldsmobile "the larger medium-priced brand" and Buick "the premium, near-luxury brand."[23] Unfortunately, GM was not successful with its repositioning efforts and, in 2001, it quietly announced the death of Oldsmobile—a major brand for the company for eight decades.

REPOSITIONING
Changing the place an offering occupies in a consumer's mind relative to competitive offerings.

Repositioning Chocolate Milk for Adults Figure 9–9 shows the positions that consumer beverages might occupy in the minds of adults. These positions may vary from one consumer to another, but for simplicity let's assume these are typical positions on the beverage perceptual maps of adults. Dairies, struggling to increase milk sales, hit on a wild idea: Try to reposition chocolate milk to the location of the star shown in the perceptual map in Figure 9–9. Their arguments are nutritionally powerful: for women chocolate milk provides calcium, critically important in the female diet. And dieters can get a more filling, nutritious beverage than a soft drink for about the same number of calories. The result: chocolate milk sales have increased dramatically, much of it due to adult consumption.[24]

FIGURE 9-9
Repositioning chocolate milk for adults

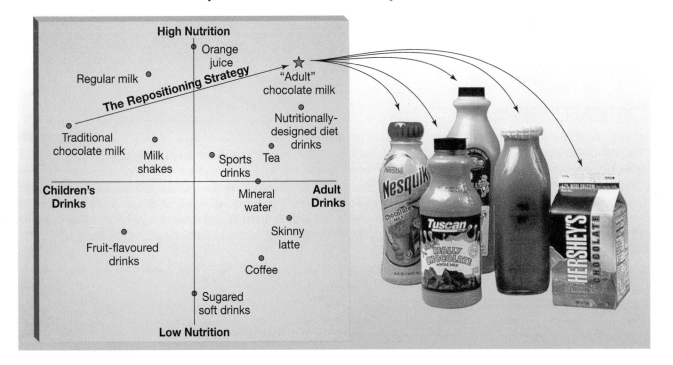

Concept Check

1. What is cross tabulation?

2. What are some advantages to cross tabulations?

3. Why do marketers use perceptual maps in product positioning decisions?

SUMMARY

1 Market segmentation is aggregating prospective buyers into groups that have common needs and will respond similarly to a marketing action.

2 A straightforward approach to segmenting, targeting, and reaching a market involves five steps: (*a*) form prospective buyers into segments by characteristics such as their needs, (*b*) form products to be sold into groups, (*c*) develop a market-product grid and estimate size of markets, (*d*) select target markets, and (*e*) take marketing actions to reach the target markets.

3 The main dimensions used to segment Canadian consumer markets include geographic, demographic, psychographic, and behavioural segmentation. A number of variables within each dimension can be used for segmentation purposes. For example, using demographic segmentation a marketer can use age, gender, education, or income as segmenting variables. Organizational markets can be segmented on geographic, demographic, and behavioural dimensions. Typical variables used to segment organizational markets include NAICS codes and size of firm.

4 Criteria used (*a*) to segment markets and (*b*) to choose target segments are related but different. The former includes

potential to increase profits, similarity of needs of buyers within a segment, difference of needs among segments, and feasibility of a resulting marketing action. The latter includes market size, expected growth, the competitive position of the firm's offering in the segment, and the cost of reaching the segment.

5 A market-product grid is a useful way to display what products can be directed at which market segments, but the grid must lead to marketing actions for the segmentation process to be worthwhile.

6 Cross tabulations are widely used today in market segmentation studies to identify the needs of various customer segments and the actions to reach them.

7 A company can position a product head-to-head against the competition or seek a differentiated position. A concern with positioning is often to avoid cannibalization of the existing product line. In positioning, a firm often uses consumer judgments in the form of perceptual maps to locate its product relative to competing ones.

KEY TERMS AND CONCEPTS

cross tabulation p. 255
80/20 rule p. 247
market segmentation p. 238
market segments p. 239
market-product grid p. 241
perceptual map p. 257

product differentiation p. 239
product positioning p. 256
repositioning p. 257
synergy p. 243
usage rate p. 247

INTERNET EXERCISE

www.mcgrawhill.ca/college/berkowitz

In its 25-year history, Apple Computer has initiated a series of creative market segmentation strategies, with new product lines targeted at specific market segments. For a continuing update of Apple's strategies, go to www.apple-history.com and click on the "Intro" and "History" menu options. As you read the narrative,

identify the new and remaining markets Apple has targeted with new and existing products, compared to those described in the text and the Marketing NewsNet box. Do you believe Apple will succeed in its quest to lead us into the digital lifestyle age of personal computing? Can it survive as a niche player? Why or why not?

Want to get better grades, find tips on how to study more effectively, and stay up to date with happenings in the world of marketing? Visit the Online Learning Centre for practice tests, Study Smart software, and much more! www.mcgrawhill.ca/college/berkowitz
Interested in finding out what marketing looks like in the real world? *Marketing Magazine* is just a click away on your OLC! Visit www.mcgrawhill.ca/college/berkowitz

APPLYING MARKETING CONCEPTS AND PERSPECTIVES

1 What variables might be used to segment these consumer markets? (*a*) lawn mowers, (*b*) frozen dinners, (*c*) dry breakfast cereals, and (*d*) soft drinks.

2 What variables might be used to segment these industrial markets? (*a*) industrial sweepers, (*b*) photocopiers, (*c*) computerized production control systems, and (*d*) car rental agencies.

3 In Figure 9–6 the dormitory market segment includes students living in university-owned residence halls. What market needs are common to these students that justify combining them into a single segment in studying the market for your Wendy's restaurant?

4 You may disagree with the estimates of market size given for the rows in the market-product grid in Figure 9–6. Estimate the market size, and give a brief justification for these market segments: (*a*) dormitory students, (*b*) day commuters, and (*c*) people who work in the area.

5 Suppose you want to increase revenues from your fast-food restaurant shown in Figure 9–7 even further. What advertising actions might you take to increase revenues from

(*a*) students, (*b*) dinners, and (*c*) after-dinner snacks from night commuters?

6 Look back at Figure 8–6. Which questions would you pair to form a cross tabulation to uncover the following relationships? (*a*) frequency of fast-food restaurant patronage and restaurant characteristics important to the customer, (*b*) age of the head of household and source of information used about fast-food restaurants, (*c*) frequency of patronage of Wendy's and source of information used about fast-food restaurants, or (*d*) how much children have to say about where the family eats and number of children in the household.

7 Look back at Figure 9–8A. (*a*) Run the percentages vertically and tell what they mean. (*b*) Express all numbers in the table as a percentage of the total number of people sampled (586) and tell what the percentages mean.

8 In Figure 9–8, (*a*) what might be other names for the three patronage levels shown in the columns? (*b*) Which is likely to be of special interest to Wendy's and why?

VIDEO CASE 9–1 Nokia: A Phone for Every Segment

"While practically everybody today is a potential mobile phone customer, everybody is simultaneously different in terms of usage, needs, lifestyles, and individual preferences," explains Nokia's Media Relations Manager, Keith Nowak. Understanding those differences requires that Nokia conduct ongoing research among different consumer groups throughout the world. The approach is reflected in the company's business strategy:

> We intend to exploit our leadership role by continuing to target and enter segments of the communications market that we believe will experience rapid growth or grow faster than the industry as a whole. . . .

In fact, Nowak believes that "to be successful in the mobile phone business of today and tomorrow, Nokia has to fully understand the fundamental nature and rationale of segmentation."

THE COMPANY

Nokia started in 1865, when a mining engineer built a wood-pulp mill in southern Finland to manufacture paper. Over the next century, the company diversified into industries ranging from paper to chemicals and rubber. In the

1960s, Nokia ventured into telecommunications by developing a digital telephone exchange switch. In the 1980s, Nokia developed the first "transportable" car mobile phone and the first "handportable" one. During the early 1990s, Nokia divested all of its non-telecommunications operations to focus on its telecommunications and mobile handset businesses.

Today, Nokia is the world leader in mobile communications. The company generates sales of more than $27 billion in a total of 130 countries and employs more than 60,000 people. Its simple mission: to "connect people."

The mission is accomplished by understanding consumer needs and providing offerings that meet or exceed those needs. Nokia believes that excellence in three areas—product design; services such as mobile Internet, messaging, and network security; and state-of-the-art technology—is the most important aspect of its offerings.

THE CELLULAR PHONE MARKET

In the 1980s, first-generation (1G) cell phones consisted of voice-only analog devices with limited range and features that were sold mainly in North America. In the 1990s, second-generation (2G) devices consisted of voice/data digital cell phones with higher data transfer rates, expanded range, and more features. Sales of these devices expanded to Europe and Asia. In the 21st century, Nokia and other companies are combining several digital technologies into third-generation (3G) communication devices that reach globally and feature the convergence of the cell phone, personal digital assistant (PDA), Internet services, and multimedia applications.

The global demand for cell phones has increased significantly over the years—from 284 million in 1999 to 410 million units in 2000 to 510 million units in 2001.

Producers of first- and second-generation cell phones used a geographic segmentation strategy as wireless communication networks were developed. Most started with the U.S. and then proceeded to Western Europe and Asia. However, each market grew at different rates. By 2001, Asia had the largest number of handsets—170 million units. Western Europe was a close second at 167 million units, followed by North America at 90 million units. Latin America had sales of 42 million units while the rest of the world had sales of 38 million units. In terms of market share, Nokia led all producers with 32 percent in 2000 and 35 percent in 2001. Motorola and Ericsson, the second and third share leaders respectively, each had less than 20 percent of the market in 2001.

The total number of worldwide wireless subscribers reached 1 billion in 2001 and is expected to increase to 2.3 billion by 2005. Demand should increase due to the growing demand by teens for high-speed handsets that will provide Internet and multimedia applications. According to the Cellular Telecommunications & Internet Association (CTIA), U.S. wireless subscribers spend an average of $45 per month on calls.

HOW NOKIA SEGMENTS ITS MARKETS

According to Debra Kennedy, Director of America's Brand Marketing at Nokia, "Different people have different usage needs. Some people want and need all of the latest and most advanced data-related features and functions, while others are happy with basic voice connectivity. Even people with similar usage needs often have differing lifestyles representing various value sets. For example, some people have an active lifestyle in which sports and fitness play an important role, while for others arts, fashion, and trends may be very important."

Based on its information about consumer usage, lifestyles, and individual preferences, Nokia currently defines six segments: "Basic" consumers who need voice connectivity and a durable style; "Expression" consumers who want to customize and personalize features; "Classic" consumers who prefer a traditional appearance

and Web browser function; "Fashion" consumers who want a very small phone as a fashion item; "Premium" consumers who are interested in all technological and service features; and "Communicator" consumers who want to combine all of their communication devices (e.g., telephone, pager, PDA).

NOKIA'S PRODUCT LINE

To meet the needs of these segments, Nokia has recently introduced several innovative products. For example, for the Communicator segment, Nokia's 7650 features a built-in digital camera, an enhanced user interface, large colour display, and multimedia messaging (MMS) functionality that allows users to combine audio, graphic, text, and imaging content in one message. Once the user has selected a picture, written text, and included an audio clip, a multimedia message can be sent directly to another multimedia messaging-capable terminal as well as to the recipient's e-mail address.

Nokia's 6340 phone allows Classic consumers to roam between various global networks; has a new wallet feature that stores the user's credit and debit card information for quick wireless Internet e-commerce transactions; supports voice-activated dialing, control of the user interface, and three minutes of voice memo recording; and includes a personal information manager (phone book and calendar).

To target the Basic segment, Nokia provides very easy-to-use, low-priced phones that are likely to be used primarily for voice communication. They are designed for consumers who are buying their first cell phone. "We want it to be a very easy choice for the consumer," explains Kennedy. Products designed for the Expression segment are still in the low price range but allow young adults to have fun while communicating with friends. Nokia recently introduced the 5210, a cell phone that offers a youthful and vibrant style with improved durability, for this group. Features include a removable shell, a built-in stopwatch, a thermometer, downloadable game packs, a personalized logo, and a personal information manager.

Nokia also designs phones for the Fashion segment—people who want a phone to "show off." The Nokia 8260 and 8390 products are in this category. They provide basic communication and other features but are not designed for heavy use. One of Nokia's television commercials for fashion phones showed two people sitting on a couch trying to talk to each other at a loud party—so they call each other on their phones! In addition, Nokia offers phones for the Premium segment—people who also want a distinctive and elegant design, but as a fine item to appreciate rather than to show off. The Nokia 8890, a phone with a chrome case and blue back light, was designed for this group. In addition, Nokia recently introduced the all-in-one 5510, which features an MP3 player that can store up to 2 hours of music, an FM radio, a messaging machine with full keyboard, a game platform with game controls for two hands and keys located on either side of the screen, and, of course, the cell phone.

THE FUTURE FOR NOKIA

A fast-growing segment for wireless mobile cell phones is the automobile. According to the ARC Group, the number of cars with "telematic" systems will increase from 1 million units to 56 million units by 2005. Ford, Nissan, and other automobile manufacturers have recently introduced systems in selected models. One reason for the expected popularity of these devices is their "hands-free, voice-activated" operation, which is designed to reduce cell-phone-related automobile accidents. The CTIA has recently developed a public service announcement (PSA) to curb this dangerous behaviour

and forestall legislation designed to eliminate cell phone use in the car entirely.

Nokia Executive Vice President Olli-Pekka Kallasvuo is so optimistic he recently commented that "our ambition should be extremely high," as the company has set its sights on capturing 50 percent of the worldwide mobile-phone market.

Questions

1 Why has segmentation been a successful marketing strategy for Nokia?

2 What customer characteristics were used by cellular phone manufacturers during the industry's early stages of growth? Which customer characteristics and segmentation variables are used by Nokia today?

3 Create a market-product grid for Nokia today. What potential new markets could you add to the grid?

PART 3 CASE   The Paradox of Book Readers: Tradition vs Technology

The Internet, with its ability to digitally transmit data, has touched every sector of the media and entertainment industry.[1] Technology takes on tradition like never before. Long-established markets are being transformed by technological innovation creating opportunities for growth in all aspects of the entertainment and leisure market. The changes to the information and communication industry structure have been so great that Statistics Canada has created a new industry category to monitor and understand the industry of information and cultural services.[2] This new "services industry" category includes publishers, libraries, motion picture and video producers, sound recorders, radio and television broadcasters, pay and specialty TV stations, telecommunications, and information services. These are the service sectors deemed to create and distribute products requiring copyright protection as well as those whose main purpose is to transform data into information. The service sectors specifically relating to the commercial production of entertainment-related material exclude telecommunication and information processing services. Publishing, motion picture and video production, sound recording, and radio and TV contribute almost $6 billion to the Canadian economy, representing just over 2 percent GDP.[3] There is competition for the entertainment dollar; within certain entertainment service sectors, there is more competition than others. In addition, due to the consolidation of the media industry over the past decade, companies like Alliance Atlantis, Sony, Indigo Books & Music, and Warner Brothers are looking for opportunities to either leverage their strategic business units or develop strategic alliances to generate profits.

TECHNOLOGY TRANSFORMS THE BOOK

Although all aspects of the entertainment industry are facing challenges due to technological innovation, the book publishing sector in particular has undergone incredible disruption over the past three to five years. This has been the result of the introduction of a new industry player, stimulated interest in fantasy books, industry restructuring due to mergers, and old-fashioned merchandising. The mature book retail industry is being transformed, yet it still provides a traditional form of entertainment: the enjoyment of reading a book. Technology has changed customer value perceptions in this market sector in two ways. First, Amazon.com has become the most recognizable virtual corporate brand because it created the digital bookshelf. The introduction of an alternative choice in purchasing a book stimulated interest in this mature retail category, proving that books are good business both for virtual sellers like Amazon.com as well as conventional brick-and-mortar stores. Amazon.com has been credited, to a large extent, for stimulating interest in book buying.

The interest in book buying and continued changes in the use of technology are creating a different type of book reader and purchaser. This addresses the second way in which technology is influencing the book buying market. Within the book buying market, there are specific audience segments that are well suited to using technology to increase interest in a specific genre. As well, with the continued media and entertainment industry convergence, book publishing and retailing fit well with other forms of entertainment production. The effects of television, video games, movies, and merchandising tie-ins are changing the industry for both the industry players and the consumers.[4]

The phenomenon of the Internet and its many applications for reaching a worldwide audience has created opportunities to apply market segmentation principles and interactive marketing promotions to a wide range of industries. Those companies in media and entertainment including newspaper and magazine publishers, broadcasters, and book publishers, together with advertising agencies, are exploring new ways to exploit the Internet to complement their existing product and service offerings opening new markets.[5]

With Amazon.com's entry into electronic book ordering in the mid-1990s there was increased activity in book publishing and retailing. After a brief surge in book buying in the late 1990s, the book retailing industry has been flat since 2000. In North America the total book publishing industry continued to remain flat in 2001, although in some book genres and product offerings growth was evident.[6] Hardcover books showed a marked decline in sales but paperbacks surged ahead, breaking another tradition within the book publishing market. Traditionally, books are launched in hardcover followed by a paperback version some time later. Now, paperback originals are being introduced with great success, particularly in certain segments like the young adult, self-help, and light reference books.[7] Whether a book is delivered as hardcover, paperback, or over the Internet, a critical aspect of success in book publishing is really the story and its appeal to the readers. Readers will ultimately decide how this industry will evolve.

READER TASTES AND INTERESTS DRIVE GENRES

Within the book business, publishers pay attention to specific *genres*, or mass market categories of books. The number of book genres changes over time, as does the influence specific genres have on overall book readership. The major genres in adult fiction include mystery/suspense, fantasy and science fiction, romance, the classics, and contemporary fiction. Then there are specific markets for books on business, self-help, spirituality and religion, cooking, gardening, renovation, and health. Another important sector in the book publishing market is educational publishing of textbooks and teaching materials for schools, professional development, universities, and colleges. A number of changes occurring within these genres and market sectors are changing both book publishing and retailing.

For example, mystery readers seem to be using the Internet more than fans of any other genre. "Mystery readers are generally very 'wired' and Internet savvy,"

says Kat Berman, director of online business for Penguin Putnam.[8] Mystery readers are an important segment of the book-reading public. They are considered heavy readers and tend to be very author-loyal. Mystery.com is an important place for mystery readers to gain more information about their favourite authors. The concept of reader involvement is part of book publishers creating demand for their authors' books. The extent to which this involvement will pay off for authors and publishers has yet to be determined. In 2000, Stephen King made an attempt at self-publishing on the Net. The book, *The Plant*, outsold all other e-books at the time with more than 120 000 downloads registered in the first week of release.[9] The plan was to charge a $1 fee per chapter, targeting a 75-percent download payment with one chapter released at a time. Unfortunately, Stephen King had only 46 percent paying for the chapters he published to the Net; the book is in hiatus. This initial experiment did not work as expected, but it's a start in using technology in a novel way.

One of the most significant mass market categories in book publishing and retailing is romance.[10] This genre is the largest in the non-fiction market, with more than 50 percent of the popular mass market category followed by mystery/detective/suspense holding a quarter of the market. Harlequin Enterprises Ltd., owned by Torstar Corporation, sells one out of every six mass market paperbacks in North America.[11] Harlequin's portfolio includes a number of romance series aiming at specific audience profiles. Red Dress Ink™, the newest series imprint, was launched in late 2001 to appeal to a younger audience of 18- to 34-year-old women quite different from the 47-year-old audience traditionally reading Harlequin romances. Harlequin is also working to integrate the Internet with its traditional paperback publishing and has created a Website that encourages online purchasing, reader involvement with the Harlequin community reading groups, online reads, and providing the opportunity for readers to meet their favourite authors.[12]

An interesting aspect for this genre is that it consists of a number of unique sub-categories. All companies publishing romance books are trying to broaden their audience by appealing to a variety of segments and interests such as historical romance, romantic erotica, and African-American romance (published by Arabesque/BET Books).[13] A new group in this genre is the Christian romance novel, appealing to the mostly female-driven Christian fiction market.[14] The young adult (YA) lines of books overlap every other genre of literature such as YA romance and YA fantasy and science fiction.[15] This young adult market is of interest to all publishers, as it is fast becoming the largest group in the population.

YOUNG ADULTS AND HARRY POTTER STIMULATE THE PUBLISHING INDUSTRY

Just who makes up the young adult book reading market? And why are they influencing the publishing industry in a such big way? The YA genre is not easy to define. Traditionally, the young adult was considered to be older teenagers, typically busy with school, sports, and each other—meaning that books were not high on the entertainment list. Some of the YA books crossed over into adult books and some were found in the children's section. In the 1980s the market changed: the young adult market took on a new dimension. For some reason the young adult segment changed from being older teenagers to younger teenagers wanting to be older. Younger teens, 12- to 14-year-olds, began changing the genre and the books available for reading.[16] Publishers are continually looking for ways to combine books with Websites, digital music, or electronic games to keep their audience engaged. The Net Generation is placing demands on the publishing industry as the Internet offers opportunities for teenagers to write and publish their own books as well as read them. Book discussion communities via the Internet are an interesting development in YA as schools and libraries encourage these teen reading groups.

Despite growth in the YA market, the publishing industry was unprepared for a boy wizard called Harry Potter. Harry was first introduced to young readers in 1997.[17] There was no indication that the boy and his story would capture the imagination of so many young people (and their parents!), ultimately creating a multi-million dollar industry around the series penned by Joanne Kathleen Rowling. The unprecedented success of this particular series of books flies in the face of the growth in video and digital games designed for the primary audience of Harry Potter. This digitally savvy generation also wants to read books. The primary audience for Harry Potter and its spin-off merchandise is

children 7 to 14 years old with parents 35 years and older.[18] This group was the primary target for Warner Brothers as they prepared for the movie opening of *Harry Potter and the Philosopher's Stone* in North America in November 2001. This preteen/young teen group overlaps the YA market, and it is unclear yet how this significant event will influence the YA market. The Harry Potter book series is encouraging an interest in books by a new generation.

The Harry Potter series, starting with *Harry Potter and the Philosopher's Stone*, has sold more than one million copies in Canada and 35 million copies worldwide.[19] The series is published by Bloomsbury Publishing in London; Raincoast Books in Vancouver is the publisher in Canada.[20] The fourth book in the series, *Harry Potter and the Goblet of Fire*, was released in July 2000 with a great deal of hype across Canada and the United States. There were weekend slumber parties at Chapters stores, and parents and children were lining up to purchase the first copies available.[21] Not only are Harry and his friends in the imaginary world of Hogwarts School of Witchcraft and Wizardry stimulating the book publishing and retailing business, they are also contributing to a much larger marketing opportunity for merchandising. Harry Potter Lego, Mattel's Harry Potter wands, and Harry Potter calendars, board games, and stationery are all spin-offs of the interest in the entertainment and marketing value of a successful character.[22] Warner Brothers created an official Harry Potter site (www.harrypotter.com) to connect Harry Potter fans and promote the movie's release. This site is interactive and designed to promote merchandise and encourage return visits. Harry Potter is connecting a group of young people across the country and around the world. There are more than 600 Harry Potter clubs registered at Yahoo Canada. In addition, Raincoast Publishing is taking interest in the Harry Potter experience to work with Simon Fraser University in creating The Canadian Book Camp for aspiring young writers aged 9 to 11 in the Vancouver area.[23] Reading appears to inspire writing in young people and merchandising for companies.

THE BATTLE OF THE BOOKS—THE BATTLE FOR THE ENTERTAINMENT DOLLAR

The entertainment industry in 2001 was taken by surprise when two books turned into major movies competed for the attention of holiday moviegoers. The fantasy and science fiction genre of the two blockbusters is not the only similarity in the battle for entertainment dollars. Both movies were adaptations of major best-selling books, one originally published in 1938, the other in 1997. Not only that, but each of these successful stories is a part of a series, with the promise of more movies and more merchandising.

Frodo Baggins, the main character in JRR Tolkien's *The Lord of the Rings* trilogy, competed with Harry Potter both in book stores and on the big screen in 2001. The estimate of the total Tolkien books sold since 1938 is 50 million.[24] *The Fellowship of the Ring*, Part One of the trilogy, sold 1.8 million in 2001; Part Two, *The Two Towers*, and Part Three, *The Return of the King*, have also picked up in sales, with 800 000 copies sold in 2001. Even *The Hobbit*, the prelude to the trilogy, experienced increased sales with 1.6 million sold in 2001. With the fifth Harry Potter book expected in 2002 and Warner Brothers wanting to capitalize on the success of the first Harry Potter movie, it is expected that Harry Potter and Frodo Baggins will be competing with each other for a few more years, both in bookstores and in movie theatres.

There may be some overlap in the two stories, and there is certainly interest in the special effects created by the producers of the movies, but there are two distinct markets for the two book series. The business of books continues to evolve, and whether it is through a paperback book, online, or in a movie theatre, good stories are still sought by a range of audiences worldwide.

Discussion Questions

1 Explain how you would segment the entertainment and leisure market. Does your description of the various segments apply for those shopping online? Why or why not?

2 Describe the important variables in segmenting book buyers. Compare these variables to variables used to segment television audiences.

3 Visit the site www.eharlequin.com. Based on what you see at the site, who is the target market? How does this Website use segmentation principles to encourage the purchase of any number of Harlequin product offerings?

4 In your opinion, what are the important segmentation variables for understanding the needs of online book purchasers? How would you use this knowledge to encourage online purchasing?

SATISFYING MARKETING OPPORTUNITIES

Part 4 covers the unique combination of products, price, place, and promotion that results in an offering for potential customers. How products and services are developed and managed is the focus of Chapters 10, 11, and 12. Pricing is covered in Chapters 13, 14, and Appendix B. Three chapters address the place (distribution) element with examples such as Avon's use of multiple marketing channels, Dell's responsive supply chain, Tim Hortons' retail strategy, and other current retail trends like multichannel retailing. Finally, three promotional chapters cover topics ranging from Disney's integrated marketing communications program, to "virtual advertisements" that don't really exist, to Xerox's efforts to increase market share by "selling the way customers want to buy."

"*I see. And how long have you had these feelings of inferiority to tape?*"

10

Developing New Products and Services

AFTER READING THIS CHAPTER YOU SHOULD BE ABLE TO:

- Understand the ways in which consumer and business goods can be classified and marketed.

- Explain the implications of alternative ways of viewing "newness" in new products.

- Analyze the factors contributing to a product's success or failure.

- Recognize and understand the purposes of each step of the new-product process.

3M: CONTINUOUS INNOVATION + GENUINE BENEFITS = SATISFIED CUSTOMERS

Ken Hart, Ph.D., Business Development Manager for 3M's VHB™ Tape, knows that "having a better mousetrap"—or in his case, an innovative industrial adhesive—isn't enough!

He knows that before any potential customers will buy it and use it, he must help them learn about the adhesive, understand its benefits, and think about ways to actually use it in their designs.[1] And every customer application differs a little bit from the last. Here's a quick take on the marketing issues he faced recently.

- *The product?* A revolutionary 3M VHB tape (for "very high bond") made with high-strength acrylic, pressure-sensitive adhesives that can make a continuous metal bond stronger than spot welds or rivets for applications such as on cargo trailers and highway signs.

- *The target market?* Mechanical engineers responsible for the designs of everything from trucks, airplanes, and cars to ceilings in buildings.

- *The special marketing task?* To get the target mechanical engineers to seriously consider the 3M VHB tape adhesive and actually use it in applications where decades of tradition make them normally specify welds, screws, or rivets in their designs.

Ken Hart and his marketing staff developed the tongue-in-cheek ad shown on the opposite page, which ran in design engineering magazines and confront an engineer's inertia in breaking free from traditional design solutions. The team's continuing challenge is to do marketing research on customer needs to develop an integrated marketing communications strategy (see Chapter 18) with advertising, public relations, and direct marketing to explain VHB's benefits to the design engineers. While 3M received the original patent two decades ago, continuous innovation requires upgrading the formula and mechanical delivery system for new applications.[2]

A brief look at some 3M products provides us with insights into how its new product research has enabled 3M to become a global leader in adhesives technology, leading to dozens of revolutionary 3M products, including:

- Post-it Notes®. The adhesive enables you to stick and unstick that note to your friend over and over again.
- Nexcare Tattoo™ Waterproof Bandages for kids. The bandage combines superior, waterproof wound protection with fun designs.
- Scotch™ Pop-up Tape. This is the latest version of the tape everyone uses to wrap gifts and mend well-worn pages in books.
- Latitude™ Transdermal Drug Delivery System. This uses drug-in-adhesive technology contained in a skin patch to deliver sustained doses of medications.

PRODUCT

A good, service, or idea consisting of a bundle of tangible and intangible attributes that satisfies consumers and is received in exchange for money or some other unit of value.

The essence of marketing is in developing products such as a new, technologically advanced adhesive to meet buyer needs. A **product** is a good, service, or idea consisting of a bundle of tangible and intangible attributes that satisfies consumers and is received in exchange for money or some other unit of value. Tangible attributes include physical characteristics such as colour or sweetness, and intangible attributes include becoming healthier or wealthier. Hence, a product includes the breakfast cereal you eat, the accountant who fills out your tax return, or the Canadian Red Cross, which provides you self-satisfaction when you donate your blood. In many instances we exchange money to obtain the product, whereas in other instances we exchange our time and other valuables, such as our blood.

The life of a company often depends on how it conceives, produces, and markets new products. This is the exact reason that 3M encourages its researchers to spend up to 15 percent of their time on new technologies and innovative product ideas of their own choosing—"scouting time," they call it. This strategy contributes to more than 500 3M patents a year.[3] Later we describe how 3M strives to "delight its customers" using cross-functional teams, "Six Sigma," and "lead user" initiatives.

In this chapter we discuss decisions involved in developing and marketing new products and services. Chapters 11 and 12 cover the process of managing existing products and services, respectively.

THE VARIATIONS OF PRODUCTS

A product varies in terms of whether it is a consumer or business good. For most organizations the product decision is not made in isolation because companies often offer a range of products. To better appreciate the product decision, let's first define some terms pertaining to products.

PRODUCT LINE

A group of products that are closely related because they satisfy a class of needs, are used together, are sold to the same customer group, are distributed through the same outlets, or fall within a given price range.

Product Line and Product Mix

A **product line** is a group of products that are closely related because they satisfy a class of needs, are used together, are sold to the same customer group, are distributed through the same type of outlets, or fall within a given price range.[4] Polaroid Canada has two major product lines consisting of cameras and film; Nike's product lines are shoes and clothing; the Toronto Hospital for Sick Children's product lines consist of inpatient hospital care, outpatient physician services, and medical research. Each product line has its own marketing strategy.

Nike's striking ads gain attention for its product lines of shoes and clothing.

Nike, Inc.

www.nike.com

Within each product line is the *product item*, a specific product as noted by a unique brand, size, or price. For example, Downy softener for clothes comes in 360-mL and 700-mL sizes; each size is considered a separate item and assigned a distinct ordering code, or *stock-keeping unit* (*SKU*).

PRODUCT MIX
The number of product lines offered by a company.

The third way to look at products is by the **product mix**, or the number of product lines offered by a company. Cray Research has a single product line consisting of supercomputers, which are sold mostly to governments and large businesses. Pillsbury Canada, however, has many product lines including Green Giant canned and frozen vegetables, Pillsbury refrigerated baked goods, Prima Pasta, Old El Paso Mexican foods, and Underwood meat spreads.

Classifying Products

Both the federal government and companies classify products, but for different purposes. The government's classification method helps it collect information on industrial activity. Companies classify products to help develop similar marketing strategies for the wide range of products offered. Two major ways to classify products are by type of user and degree of product tangibility.

CONSUMER GOODS
Products purchased by the ultimate consumer.

BUSINESS GOODS
Products that assist directly or indirectly in providing products for resale (also known as *B2B goods*, *industrial goods*, or *organizational goods*).

Type of User   A major type of product classification is based on the type of user. **Consumer goods** are products purchased by the ultimate consumer, whereas **business goods** (also called B2B goods, industrial goods, or organizational goods) are products that assist directly or indirectly in providing products for resale. In many instances the differences are distinct: Oil of Olay face moisturizer and Bass shoes are clearly consumer products, whereas Cray computers and high-tension steel springs are business goods used in producing other products or services.

There are difficulties, however, with this classification because some products can be considered both consumer and business items. A Compaq computer can be sold to consumers as a final product or to business firms for office use. Each classification results in different marketing actions. Viewed as a consumer product, the Compaq would be sold through computer stores or direct from its Website. As a business product, the Compaq might be sold by a salesperson offering discounts for multiple purchases. Classifying by the type of user focuses on the market and the user's purchase behaviour, which determine the marketing mix strategy.

Specialty goods like Raymond
Weil watches require distinct
marketing programs to reach
narrow target markets.

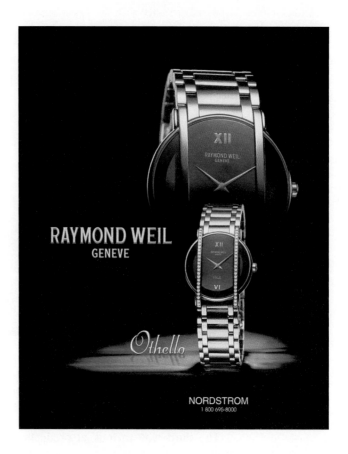

Degree of Tangibility   Classification by degree of tangibility divides products
into one of three categories. First is a *nondurable good*, an item consumed in one or a
few uses, such as food products and fuel. A *durable good* is one that usually lasts over
an extended number of uses, such as appliances, automobiles, and stereo equipment.
Services are defined as activities, deeds, or other basic tangibles offered for sale to
consumers in exchange for money or something else of value. According to this
classification, government data indicate that Canada has a service economy, the reason
for a separate chapter (Chapter 12) on the topic.

This classification method also provides direction for marketing actions.
Nondurable products such as Wrigley's gum are purchased frequently and at
relatively low cost. Advertising is important to remind consumers of the item's
existence, and wide distribution in retail outlets is essential. A consumer wanting
Wrigley's Spearmint Gum would most likely purchase another brand of spearmint
gum if Wrigley's were not available. Durable products, however, generally cost more
than nondurable goods and last longer, so consumers usually deliberate longer before
purchasing them. Therefore, personal selling is an important component in durable-
product marketing because it assists in answering consumer questions and concerns.

New Services Development   Developing new services, like a new airline
service or a new television show, is often difficult to observe step by step. Nevertheless,
service innovations do occur and can have a major impact on our lives. For example,
online banking and online brokerage firms have revolutionized the financial
services industry, while online travel agencies have changed the way we make travel
reservations.[5] And soon, interactive television will enable you to use your TV to view
500 channels, use the Internet, buy products, and download the latest movie.[6]

CLASSIFYING CONSUMER AND BUSINESS GOODS

CONVENIENCE GOODS
Items that the consumer purchases frequently and with a minimum of shopping effort.

SHOPPING GOODS
Items for which the consumer compares several alternatives on criteria such as price, quality, or style.

SPECIALTY GOODS
Items that a consumer makes a special effort to search out and buy.

UNSOUGHT GOODS
Items that the consumer either does not know about or knows about but does not initially want.

Because the buyer is the key to marketing, consumer and business product classifications are discussed in greater detail.

Classification of Consumer Goods

Convenience, shopping, specialty, and unsought products are the four types of consumer goods. They differ in terms of (1) effort the consumer expends on the decision, (2) attributes used in purchase, and (3) frequency of purchase. **Convenience goods** are items that the consumer purchases frequently, conveniently, and with a minimum of shopping effort. **Shopping goods** are items for which the consumer compares several alternatives on criteria, such as price, quality, or style. **Specialty goods** are items, such as Tiffany sterling silver, that a consumer makes a special effort to search out and buy. **Unsought goods** are items that the consumer either does not know about or knows about but does not initially want. Figure 10–1 shows how the classification of a consumer product into one of these four types results in different aspects of the marketing mix being stressed. Different degrees of brand loyalty and amounts of shopping effort are displayed by the consumer for a product in each of the four classes.

The manner in which a consumer good is classified depends on the individual. One person may view a camera as a shopping good and visit several stores before deciding on a brand, whereas a friend may view cameras as a specialty good and will only buy a Nikon.

FIGURE 10–1
Classification of consumer goods

TYPE OF CONSUMER GOOD

BASIS OF COMPARISON	CONVENIENCE	SHOPPING	SPECIALTY	UNSOUGHT
Product	Toothpaste, cake mix, hand soap, laundry detergent	Cameras, TVs, briefcases, clothing	Rolls Royce cars, Rolex watches	Burial insurance, thesaurus
Price	Relatively inexpensive	Fairly expensive	Usually very expensive	Varies
Place (distribution)	Widespread; many outlets	Large number of selective outlets	Very limited	Often limited
Promotion	Price, availability, and awareness stressed	Differentiation from competitors stressed	Uniqueness of brand and status stressed	Awareness is essential
Brand loyalty of consumers	Aware of brand, but will accept substitutes	Prefer specific brands, but will accept substitutes	Very brand loyal; will not accept substitutes	Will accept substitutes
Purchase behaviour of consumers	Frequent purchases; little time and effort spent shopping	Infrequent purchases; needs much comparison shopping time	Infrequent purchases; needs extensive search and decision time	Very infrequent purchases; some comparison shopping

Classification of Business Goods

A major characteristic of business goods is that their sales are often the result of *derived demand*; that is, sales of business goods frequently result (or are derived) from the sale of consumer goods. For example, if consumer demand for Ford cars (a consumer product) increases, the company may increase its demand for paint-spraying equipment (a business good). Business goods may be classified as production or support goods.

Production Goods

PRODUCTION GOODS
Items used in the manufacturing process that become part of the final product.

Production Goods   Items used in the manufacturing process that become part of the final product are **production goods**. These include raw materials such as grain or lumber, as well as component parts. For example, a company that manufactures door hinges used by GM in its car doors is producing a component part. As noted in Chapter 6, the marketing of production goods is based on factors such as price, quality, delivery, and service. Marketers of these products tend to sell directly to business users.

SUPPORT GOODS
Items used to assist in producing other goods and services.

Support Goods   The second class of business goods is **support goods**, which are items used to assist in producing other goods and services. Support goods include installations, accessory equipment, supplies, and services.

- *Installations* consist of buildings and fixed equipment. Because a significant amount of capital is required to purchase installations, the business buyer deals directly with construction companies and manufacturers through sales representatives. The pricing of installations is often by competitive bidding.
- *Accessory equipment* includes tools and office equipment and is usually purchased in small-order sizes by buyers. As a result, instead of dealing directly with buyers, sellers of business accessories use distributors to contact a large number of buyers.
- *Supplies* are similar to consumer convenience goods and consist of products such as stationery, paper clips, and brooms. These are purchased with little effort, using the straight rebuy decision sequence discussed in Chapter 6. Price and delivery are key factors considered by the buyers of supplies.
- *Services* are intangible activities to assist the business buyer. This category can include maintenance and repair services and advisory services such as tax or legal counsel where the seller's reputation is critical.

Concept Check

1. Explain the difference between product mix and product line.

2. What are the four main types of consumer goods?

3. To which type of good (business or consumer) does the term *derived demand* generally apply?

NEW PRODUCTS AND WHY THEY SUCCEED OR FAIL

New products are the lifeblood of a company and keep it growing, but the associated financial risks are large. Before discussing how new products reach the stage of commercialization when they are in the market, we'll begin by looking at *what* a new product is.

As you read the discussion about what "new" means in new-product development, think how it affects the marketing strategies of Sony and Microsoft in their new videogame launches.

Sony Corporation

www.sony.com

Microsoft Corporation

www.microsoft.com

What Is a New Product?

The term *new* is difficult to define. Is Sony's PlayStation 2 *new* when there was a PlayStation 1? Is Microsoft's Xbox *new* when Microsoft hasn't been a big player in video games before? What does *new* mean for new-product marketing? Newness from several points of view and some marketing implications of this newness are discussed below.

Newness Compared with Existing Products   If a product is functionally different from existing products, it can be defined as new. Sometimes this newness is revolutionary and creates a whole new industry, as in the case of the Apple II computer. We often think that newness in terms of more features or advanced technology is automatically better for everyone in the market. But simpler can be better for many potential customers, as described in the "less is more" Marketing NewsNet box. One surprise: Innovation research shows that firms using "disruptive innovation" and creating newness by simplifying the product are often *not* the industry leaders who sell the more sophisticated high-end products with more features.[7]

Newness in Legal Terms   Industry Canada, the federal government's department that regulates business practices, has determined that a product can be called "new" for only up to 12 months.

Newness from the Company's Perspective   Successful companies are starting to view newness and innovation in their products at three levels. At the lowest level, which usually involves the least risk, is a product line extension. This is an incremental improvement of an existing product for the company, such as Frosted Cheerios or Diet Cherry Coke or Gillette Venus for Women—extensions of the basic Cheerios or Diet Coke or men's Gillette Mach3 product lines, respectively. At the next level is a significant jump in the innovation or technology, such as Sony's leap from the micro tape recorder to the Walkman. The third level is true innovation, a truly revolutionary new product, like the first Apple computer in 1976. Effective new product programs in large firms deal at all three levels.

MARKETING NEWSNET

When Less Is More: How Reducing the Number of Features Can Open Up Huge Markets

New products! To invent them the natural thing is to add more features, new technologies, more glitz. Many new-product successes discussed in the chapter do just that.

But huge new markets can open up in moving the opposite direction by taking features away, simplifying the product, and doing a "worse job"—sometimes called "disruptive innovation." "Less is more" building design introduced in the 1930s revolutionized architecture. Here are some "less is more" new-product breakthroughs that revolutionized national or global markets:

1. *Canon's tabletop copiers*. Canon found it couldn't sell its little copiers to big companies, which were happy with the large Xerox machines. So Canon sold its little machines by the zillions to little companies with limited copying needs.
2. *Palm Computing's PalmPilot PDA*. Apple Computer's Newton personal digital assistant (PDA) seemed like a great idea, but users found it too complicated. Enter PalmPilot inventors Donna Dubinsky and Jeff Hawkins, who deleted features to achieve the market breakthrough.
3. *Intuit's QuickBooks accounting software*. Competitors offered complex accounting software containing every feature professional accountants might possibly want. Intuit then introduced QuickBooks, a smaller, cheaper program with less functionality that within two years won 70 percent of the huge market for small-business accounting software.
4. *Swatch watches*. In 1983 a slim plastic watch with only 51 components appeared on the global market. That simplicity—plus top quality, affordable price, and creative designs—is the reason that by 2001 more than 250 million Swatch watches had been sold.

Sometime much less is much, much more!

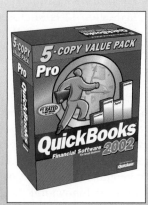

Newness from the Consumer's Perspective   A fourth way to define new products is in terms of their effects on consumption. This approach classifies new products according to the degree of learning required by the consumer, as shown in Figure 10–2.

With *continuous innovation*, no new behaviours must be learned. Samsung's wireless phone ad on the next page communicates a clear message: The phone is stylish and easy to use. Clearly, Samsung is marketing a user-friendly phone, but it is a continuous innovation not requiring new learned behaviours. Under these conditions, the beauty of this innovation is that effective marketing simply depends on generating awareness and having strong distribution in appropriate outlets, not completely re-educating customers.

With *dynamically continuous innovation*, only minor changes in behaviour are required for use. An example is built-in, fold-down child seats such as those available in DaimlerChrysler minivans. Built-in car seats for children require only minor bits of education and changes in behaviour, so the marketing strategy is to *educate* prospective buyers on their benefits, advantages, and proper use.

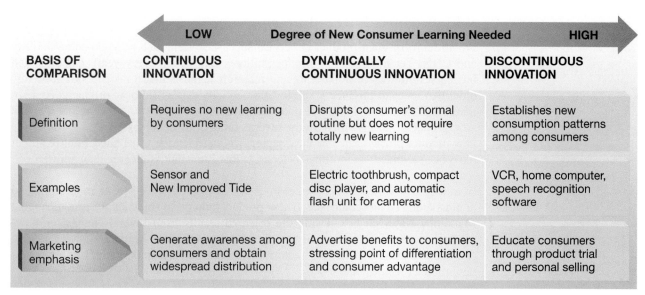

	LOW Degree of New Consumer Learning Needed HIGH		
BASIS OF COMPARISON	**CONTINUOUS INNOVATION**	**DYNAMICALLY CONTINUOUS INNOVATION**	**DISCONTINUOUS INNOVATION**
Definition	Requires no new learning by consumers	Disrupts consumer's normal routine but does not require totally new learning	Establishes new consumption patterns among consumers
Examples	Sensor and New Improved Tide	Electric toothbrush, compact disc player, and automatic flash unit for cameras	VCR, home computer, speech recognition software
Marketing emphasis	Generate awareness among consumers and obtain widespread distribution	Advertise benefits to consumers, stressing point of differentiation and consumer advantage	Educate consumers through product trial and personal selling

FIGURE 10–2

Consumption effects define newness

www.ibm.ca

A *discontinuous innovation* involves making the consumer learn entirely new consumption patterns in order to use the product. After decades of research, IBM introduced its ViaVoice speech recognition software. If you are using ViaVoice you are able to speak to your computer and watch your own words appear on your computer screen, and you can also open Windows programs with your voice. The risk that IBM faced in introducing this discontinuous innovation was that people had to learn new behaviours in producing word-processed memos and reports. Hence, marketing efforts for discontinuous innovations involve educating consumers on both the benefits and proper use of the innovative product—activities that can cost millions of dollars.

With Samsung's continuous-innovation cell phone, no new behaviours need to be learned.

Why Products Succeed or Fail

We all know of giant product or service success stories, such as Microsoft Windows and CNN. Yet thousands of product failures that occur every year cost Canadian businesses millions of dollars. Recent research suggests that it takes about 3000 raw unwritten ideas to produce a single commercially successful new product.[8] To learn marketing lessons and convert potential failures to successes, we can analyze why new products fail and then study several failures in detail. As we go through the new-product process later in the chapter, we can identify ways such failures might have been avoided—admitting, of course, that hindsight is clearer than foresight.

Marketing Reasons for New-Product Failures   Both marketing and nonmarketing factors contribute to new-product failures, as shown in the accompanying Marketing NewsNet box. Using the research results from several studies[9] on new-product success and failure and also those described in the Marketing NewsNet, we can identify critical marketing factors—sometimes overlapping—that often separate new-product winners and losers:

1. *Insignificant "point of difference."* Shown as the most important factor in the Marketing NewsNet box, a distinctive "point of difference" is essential for a new product to defeat competitive ones—through having superior characteristics that deliver unique benefits to the user. In the mid-1990s General Mills introduced "Fingos," a sweetened cereal flake about the size of a corn chip. Consumers were supposed to snack on them dry, but they didn't.[10] The point of difference was not important enough to get consumers to give up eating competing snacks such as popcorn, potato chips, or Cheerios from the box late at night.

2. *Incomplete market and product definition before product development starts.* Ideally, a new product needs a precise **protocol**, a statement that, before product development begins, identifies (1) a well-defined target market; (2) specific customers' needs, wants, and preferences; and (3) what the product will be and do. Without this precision, loads of money disappear as research and development (R&D) tries to design a vague product for a phantom market. This combines factors 2 and 5 in the Marketing NewsNet box. Apple Computer's hand-sized Newton computer, which intended to help keep the user organized, fizzled badly because no clear protocol existed.

PROTOCOL

A statement that, before product development begins, identifies (1) a well-defined target market; (2) specific customers' needs, wants, and preferences; and (3) what the product will be and do.

New-product success or failure? For the special problems these products face, see the text.

MARKETING NEWSNET

What Separates New-Product Winners and Losers

What makes some products winners and others losers? Knowing this answer is a key to a new-product strategy. R. G. Cooper and E. J. Kleinschmidt studied 203 new industrial products to find the answers shown below.

The researchers defined the "product success rate" of new products as the percentage of products that reached the company's own profitability criteria. Product "winners" are the best 20 percent of performers and "losers" are the

worst 20 percent. For example, for the first factor in the table below, 98 percent of the winners had a major point of difference compared with only 18 percent of the losers.

Note that the table below includes both marketing and nonmarketing factors. Most of the marketing factors tie directly to the reasons cited in the text for new-product failures that are taken from a number of research studies.

FACTOR AFFECTING PRODUCT SUCCESS RATE	PRODUCT "WINNERS" (BEST 20%)	PRODUCT "LOSERS" (WORST 20%)	% DIFFERENCE (WINNERS–LOSERS)
1. Point of difference, or uniquely superior product	98%	18%	80%
2. Well-defined product before actual development starts	85	26	59
3. Synergy, or fit, with firm's R&D and manufacturing capabilities	80	29	51
4. Quality of execution of technological activities	76	30	46
5. Quality of execution of activities before actual development starts	75	31	44
6. Synergy, or fit, with marketing mix activities	71	31	40
7. Quality of execution of marketing mix activities	71	32	39
8. Market attractiveness, ones with large markets and high growth	74	43	31

3. *Too little market attractiveness.* Shown as factor 8 in the Marketing NewsNet, market attractiveness refers to the ideal situation every new-product manager looks for: a large target market with high growth and real buyer need. But often, when looking for ideal market niches, the target market is too small and competitive to warrant the R&D, production, and marketing expenses necessary to reach it. In the early 1990s Kodak discontinued its Ultralife lithium battery. With its 10-year shelf life, the battery was touted as lasting twice as long as an alkaline battery. Yet the product was available only in the 9-volt size, which accounts for less than 10 percent of the batteries sold in North America.

4. *Poor execution of the marketing mix*: name, package, price, promotion, distribution. Coca-Cola thought its Minute Maid Squeeze-Fresh frozen orange juice concentrate in a squeeze bottle was a hit. The idea was that consumers could make one glass of juice at a time, and the concentrate stayed fresh in the refrigerator for more than a month. After two test markets, the product was finished. Consumers loved the idea, but the product was messy to use and the advertising and packaging didn't educate them effectively on how much concentrate to mix.

FIGURE 10–3
Why did these new products
fail?

As explained in detail in the text, new products often fail because of one or a combination of seven reasons. Look at the two products described below, and try to identify which reason explains why they failed in the marketplace.

- Kimberly-Clark's "Avert Virucidal" tissues that contained vitamin C derivatives scientifically designed to kill cold and flu germs when users sneezed, coughed, or blew their nose into them.

- OUT! International's Hey! There's A Monster In My Room spray that was designed to rid scary creatures from kids' rooms and had a bubble-gum fragrance.

Compare your insights with those in the text.

5. *Poor product quality on critical factors.* Overlapping somewhat with point 1, this factor stresses that problems on one or two critical factors can kill the product, even though the general quality is high. For example, the Japanese, like the British, drive on the left side of the road. Until 1996 North American carmakers sent Japan few right-drive cars—unlike German carmakers, who exported right-drive models in a number of their brands.[11]

6. *Bad timing.* The product is introduced too soon, too late, or at a time when consumer tastes are shifting dramatically. Bad timing gives new-product managers nightmares. IBM, for example, killed several laptop computer prototypes because competitors introduced better, more advanced machines to the marketplace before IBM could get there.

7. *No economical access to buyers.* Grocery products provide an example. Today's mega-supermarkets carry 30 000 different SKUs. With new food products introduced each day, the fight for shelf space is tremendous in terms of costs for advertising, distribution, and shelf space.[12] Because shelf space is judged in terms of sales per square foot, Thirsty Dog! (a zesty beef-flavoured, vitamin-enriched, mineral-loaded, lightly carbonated bottled water for your dog) must displace an existing product on the supermarket shelves, a difficult task with the precise measures of revenues per square foot these stores use.

A Look at Some Failures   Before reading further, study the product failures described in Figure 10-3, and try to identify which of the reasons is the most likely explanation for their failure. The two examples are discussed in greater detail below.

Kimberly-Clark's Avert Virucidal tissues lasted 10 months in a test market before being pulled from the shelves. People didn't believe the claims and were frightened by the name. So the tissue probably failed because of not having a clear point of difference, a bad name, and, hence, bad marketing mix execution—probably reasons #1 and #7 in the list in the text.

Out! International's "Hey! There's A Monster In My Room" spray was creative and cute when introduced in 1993. But the name probably kept the kids awake at night more than their fear of the monsters because it suggested the monster was still hiding in the room. Question: Wouldn't calling it the "Monster-Buster Spray" have licked the name problem? It looks like the spray was never really defined well in a protocol (reason #2) and definitely had poor name execution (reason #4).

Simple marketing research on consumers should have revealed the problems. Developing successful new products may sometimes involve luck, but more often it involves having a product that really meets a need and has significant points of difference over competitive products. The likelihood of success is improved by paying attention to the early steps of the new-product process described in the next section of the text.

1. From a consumer's viewpoint, what kind of innovation would an improved electric toothbrush be?

2. What does "insignificant point of difference" mean as a reason for new-product failure?

THE NEW-PRODUCT PROCESS

NEW-PRODUCT PROCESS
The sequence of activities a firm uses to identify business opportunities and convert them to a salable good or service.

Companies such as General Electric, Sony, and Procter & Gamble take a sequence of steps before their products are ready for market. Figure 10–4 shows the seven stages of the **new-product process**, the sequence of activities a firm uses to identify business opportunities and convert them to a saleable good or service. This sequence begins with new-product strategy development and ends with commercialization.

New-Product Strategy Development

NEW-PRODUCT STRATEGY DEVELOPMENT
Defining the role for a new product in terms of the firm's overall corporate objectives.

For companies, **new-product strategy development** involves defining the role for a new product in terms of the firm's overall corporate objectives. This step in the new-product process has been added by many companies recently to provide a needed focus for ideas and concepts developed in later stages.

Objectives of the Stage: Identify Markets and Strategic Roles   During this new-product strategy development stage the company uses the environmental scanning process described in Chapter 3 to identify trends that pose either opportunities or threats. Relevant company strengths and weaknesses are also identified. The outcome of new-product strategy development is not only new-product ideas but also identifying markets for which new products will be developed and strategic roles new products might serve—the vital protocol activity explained earlier in the discussion of the Marketing NewsNet on new-product winners and losers.

3M: Cross-Functional Teams, Six Sigma, and Lead Users   Key to 3M's success in new-product development is its use of *cross-functional teams*, a small number of people from different departments in an organization who are mutually accountable to a common set of performance goals. Today in 3M, teams are especially important in new-product development so that individuals from R&D, marketing, sales, manufacturing, and finance can simultaneously search together in a constructive environment for new product and market opportunities. In the past, 3M and other firms

FIGURE 10–4
Stages in the new-product process

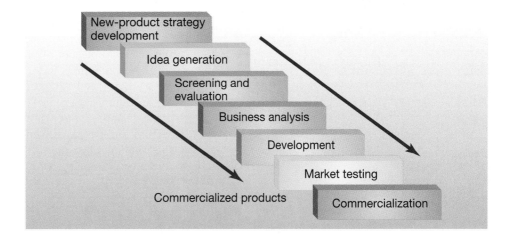

often utilized these department people in sequence—possibly resulting in R&D designing new products that the manufacturing department couldn't produce economically and that the marketing department couldn't sell.

Important today in 3M's cross-functional teams is **Six Sigma**, a means to "delight the customer" by achieving quality through a highly disciplined process to focus on developing and delivering near-perfect products and services. "Near perfect" here means being 99.9997 percent perfect, or allowing 3.4 defects per million products produced or transactions processed—getting as close as possible to "zero defects." Six Sigma's success lies in determining what variables impact the results, measuring them, and making decisions based on data, not gut feel.[13]

In the late-1990s, 3M became concerned that its new-product development too often involved making incremental improvements to existing lines. Innovation research shows that many revolutionary product breakthroughs are prototyped by "lead users"—*not* the manufacturers actually providing and selling the product. Lead users are companies, organizations, or individuals that have needs going far beyond normal user needs, so that they may have come up with innovations on their own. By putting cross-functional teams into contact with these lead users, the approach has resulted in several dozen new-product concepts for 3M.[14]

Idea Generation

Developing a pool of concepts as candidates for new products, or **idea generation**, must build on the previous stage's results. New-product ideas are generated by consumers, employees, basic R&D, and competitors.

SIX SIGMA
A means to "delight the customer" by achieving quality through a highly disciplined process to focus on developing and delivering near-perfect products and services.

IDEA GENERATION
Developing a pool of concepts as candidates for new products.

See the text for the unusual source on the new-product idea for Polaroid's i-Zone instant pocket camera.

i-Zone pocket camera and sticky film from Polaroid.

Customer and Supplier Suggestions   Companies often analyze consumer complaints or supplier ideas to discover new-product opportunities. Listening to growing concerns about cholesterol and fat in its food, McDonald's reformulated its shakes with a low-fat mixture and introduced a low-fat hamburger. Whirlpool, trying to reduce costs by cutting the number of different product platforms in half, got ideas on ways to standardize components.[15]

Employee and Co-worker Suggestions
Employees may be encouraged to suggest new product ideas through suggestion boxes or contests. The idea for General Mill's Nature Valley Granola Bars came when one of its marketing managers observed co-workers bringing granola to work in plastic bags. In 1997 a Polaroid employee in Tokyo saw a group of teenage girls crammed into a photo booth that took instant minipictures. Over objections from many company scientists, this idea became the $25 Polaroid i-Zone instant pocket camera, a top seller by early 2000, only four months after introduction. Its small photos are good enough for high schoolers, the original target market, as well as adults for whom fun, speed, convenience, and reasonable price are key buying criteria.[16]

MARKETING NEWSNET

The World's Consumer Electronics Champ: And Its Name Is . . . ?

The "battle for the living room" begins this company's 21st century. To win, it will have to keep linking its cool digital hardware technology, design, and entertainment content. With over $63 billion in global sales for 2000, it was voted one of the "most respected brands" and known—along with Coke, Nike, and MTV—as one of the four most creative companies in the world. Yet its army of product designers and engineers work in an "eel's bedroom." What is this firm, whose first product was a rice cooker launched shortly after its founding in 1946? Yes, it's Sony!

This Japan-based company with operations around the globe made the first transistor radio (1955) and television (1960), Walkman (1979), CD player (1982), and PlayStation video console (1995). And Sony innovation continues, from its DVD video player (1998), Clié hand-held PDA (2000), and flat-panel Organic Electroluminescence (OEL) monitors and TVs that are a little thicker than a credit card but have brighter images on the screen (2003).

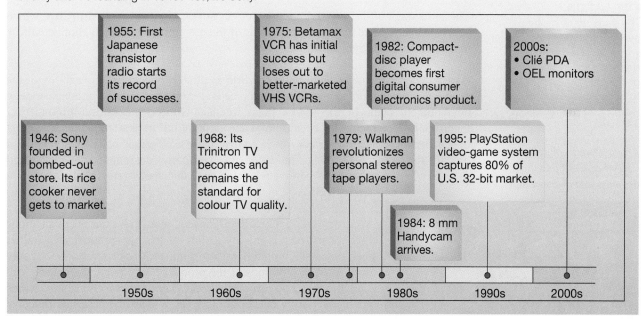

Research and Development Breakthroughs   Another source of new products is a firm's basic research, but the costs can be huge. As described in the Marketing NewsNet box,[17] Sony is the acknowledged world leader in new-product development in electronics. Its scientists and engineers produce an average of four new products each business day. Sony's research and development breakthroughs have led to innovative products, and its ability to manufacture and market those products has made it a legend in the electronics industry, popularizing VCRs, the Walkman, and—coming into your future?—flat-panel Organic Electroluminescence (OEL) monitors about the thickness of a credit card providing brighter images even on large, 30-inch screens.

Not all R&D labs have Sony's genius for moving electronic breakthroughs into the marketplace. Take Xerox Corporation's Palo Alto Research Center (PARC). In what may be the greatest electronic fumble of all time, by 1979 PARC had what's in your computer system now—graphical user interfaces, mice, windows and pull-down menus, laser printers, and distributed computing. Concerned with aggressive competition from Japan in its core photocopier business, Xerox didn't even bother to patent these breakthroughs. Apple Computer's Steven Jobs visited PARC in 1979, adapted many of the ideas for the Macintosh, and the rest is history.[18]

Professional R&D laboratories also provide new-product ideas. Labs at Arthur D. Little helped put the crunch in Cap'n Crunch cereal and the flavour in Carnation Instant Breakfast. As described in the Web Link, IDEO is a world-class new-product development firm, having designed more than 4000 of them. These range from the Apple mouse and Heartstream portable defibrillator to Crest's neat squeeze toothpaste dispenser and Nike's all-terrain sunglasses.

Competitive Products   New-product ideas can also be found by analyzing the competition. A six-person intelligence team from the Marriott Corporation spent six months travelling around and staying at economy hotels. The team assessed the competition's strengths and weaknesses on everything from the soundproof qualities of the rooms to the softness of the towels. Marriott then budgeted $700 million for a new economy hotel chain, Fairfield Inns.

SCREENING AND EVALUATION
The third stage of the new-product process, which involves internal and external evaluations of the new-product ideas to eliminate those that warrant no further effort.

A year's worth of consumer interviews went into the development of Sun Chips.

Screening and Evaluation

The third stage of the new-product process is **screening and evaluation**, which involves internal and external evaluations of the new-product ideas to eliminate those that warrant no further effort.

Internal Approach   Internally, the firm evaluates the technical feasibility of the proposal and whether the idea meets the objectives defined in the new-product strategy development step. In the 1990s Penn Racquet Sports, the largest producer of tennis balls, faced flat sales because of a decade-long lull in recreational tennis. What to do? Penn Racquet employees observed that many used tennis balls were given as a toy to the family dog. So in 1998 the company designed and introduced R. P. Fetchem—a dye-free "natural felt fetch toy" that looks remarkably like . . . a tennis ball![19]

External Approach   Concept tests are external evaluations that consist of preliminary testing of the new-product idea (rather than the actual product) with consumers. Concept tests usually rely on written descriptions of the product but may be augmented with sketches, mockups, or promotional literature. Several key questions are asked during concept testing: How does the customer perceive the product? Who would use it? How would it be used?

Frito-Lay spent a year interviewing 10 000 consumers about the concept of a multigrain snack chip. The company experimented with 50 different shapes before settling on a thin, rectangular chip with ridges and a slightly salty, nutty flavour. The product, Sun Chips, is highly successful.

Concept Check	**1.** What step in the new-product process has been added in recent years?
	2. What are four sources of new-product ideas?
	3. What is the difference between internal and external screening and evaluation approaches used by a firm in the new-product process?

Business Analysis

BUSINESS ANALYSIS
Involves specifying the features of the product and the marketing strategy needed to commercialize it and making necessary financial projections.

Business analysis involves specifying the features of the product and the marketing strategy needed to commercialize it and making necessary financial projections. This is the last checkpoint before significant capital is invested in creating a prototype of the product. Economic analysis, marketing strategy review, and legal examination of the proposed product are conducted at this stage. It is at this point that the product is analyzed relative to the firm's marketing and technological synergies, two criteria noted in the Marketing NewsNet shown earlier in the chapter.

The marketing strategy review studies the new-product idea in relation to the marketing program to support it. The proposed product is assessed to determine whether it will help or hurt sales of existing products. Likewise, the product is examined to assess whether it can be sold through existing channels or if new outlets will be needed. Profit projections involve estimating the number of units expected to be sold but also the costs of R&D, production, and marketing.

As an important aspect of the business analysis, the proposed new product is studied to determine whether it can be protected with a patent or copyright. An attractive new-product proposal is one in which the technology, product, or brand cannot easily be copied.

Development

DEVELOPMENT
Turning the idea on paper into a prototype.

Product ideas that survive the business analysis proceed to actual **development**, turning the idea on paper into a prototype. This results in a demonstrable, producible product in hand. Outsiders seldom understand the technical complexities of the development stage, which involves not only manufacturing the product but also performing laboratory and consumer tests to ensure that it meets the standards set. Design of the product becomes an important element.

Some new products can be so important and costly that the company is literally betting its very existence on success. And creative, out-of-the-box thinking can be critical. In the pharmaceutical industry no more than one out of every 5000 to 10 000 new compounds developed in the labs emerges as an approved drug.[20] Talking to a Merck colleague at a medical convention, Dr. Peppi Prosit discovered that the colleague's lab had made a breakthrough and developed a test to determine if a painkiller drug was less likely to cause the upset stomach that is a side effect of most pain and arthritis medicines. Moments later he saw a poster display from a Japanese researcher claiming to have developed just such a painkiller, but one not yet fit for humans. His challenge: Build a similar pain and arthritis drug for people that could pass Merck's new lab test.

Dr. Prosit's team cooked up hundreds of compounds costing tens of millions of dollars. The two best were sent to an oral surgeon who yanks the wisdom teeth of university students, hands them a pain pill, and puts them into a dorm attached to his clinic to measure their suffering. One of the two Merck compounds had outstanding "minimum-suffering results" among the students.

Merck's cross-functional team of marketing, manufacturing, and research people cut five weeks off the normal market-launch cycle for the drug—now branded

For how university students contributed their wisdom (teeth) to Merck's very successful Vioxx arthritis and pain drug, see the text.

"Vioxx." In a remarkable feat, Vioxx was stocked in 40 000 pharmacies within 11 days of receiving government approval to market the drug. The result: A spectacular success and continuing research to develop a better, second-generation Vioxx. Top management at Merck has said that if Vioxx had failed, Merck might have been forced to merge with another pharmaceutical firm.[21]

Merck's Vioxx drug prototype went through exhaustive lab and clinical tests to see if it met design criteria set for it if used the way it is intended. But safety tests are also critical for when the product isn't used as planned. To make sure seven-year-olds can't bite Barbie's head off and choke, Mattel clamps her foot in steel jaws in a test stand and then pulls on her head with a wire. Similarly, car manufacturers have done extensive safety tests by crashing their cars into concrete walls. As mentioned in the Ethics and Social Responsibility Alert box, consumer groups are increasingly concerned about what happens when a pickup truck or sport utility vehicle hits a small car when their bumpers don't line up.[22] Auto industry tests are identifying some feasible, but costly, solutions.

Mattel's laboratory testing subjects its toys and dolls, like Barbie here, to extreme tests to ensure quality and protect children.

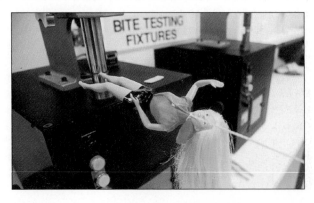

ETHICS AND SOCIAL RESPONSIBILITY ALERT

Sports Utilities versus Cars: Godzilla Meets a Chimp?

Make car wrecks safer. This sounds sort of stupid. But . . . the problem is death! The high and heavy pickups, vans, and sport utility vehicles (SUVs) are now involved in an increasing number of highway deaths. When one huge vehicle meets a bitty little car, the larger, higher one smashes the smaller one's passenger compartment, instead of going head-to-head at bumper level. The people in the cars, unfortunately, are more likely to be killed in such accidents.

The problem is also money. These mega-vehicles now account for a large percentage of Canadian automakers' sales and profits. Improving the smaller cars—with side air bags and steel supports—is cheaper than lowering the frame or adding a crumple zone for the frame of the bigger vehicle. Nothing is easy. And consumers love the power of

these hefty vehicles that are about 1000 kilograms heavier than a compact car.

But changes are on the way. Mercedes Benz has completely redesigned its M-class SUV. Mercedes engineers addressed the compatibility of their SUV with smaller cars so the Mercedes SUV frame and bumper is as much as 20 centimetres lower than its competitor's SUV models. This makes the bumpers of Mercedes SUVs and those of small cars more likely to meet in a crash, dramatically increasing the safety for small-car passengers.

Who should address the problem here? The federal government? The insurance companies? The vehicle manufacturers? Consumers?

Market Testing

MARKET TESTING
Exposing actual products to prospective consumers under realistic purchase conditions to see if they will buy.

The **market testing** stage of the new-product process involves exposing actual products to prospective consumers under realistic purchase conditions to see if they will buy. Often a product is developed, tested, refined, and then tested again to get consumer reactions through either test marketing or purchase laboratories.

Test Marketing   Test marketing involves offering a product for sale on a limited basis in a defined area. This test is done to determine whether consumers will actually buy the product and to try different ways of marketing it. Only about a third of the products test marketed do well enough to go on to the next phase. These market tests are usually conducted in cities that are viewed as being representative of Canadian consumers. Test marketing gives the company an indication of potential sales volume and market share. Market tests are also used to check other elements of the marketing mix besides the product itself such as price, level of advertising support, and distribution. Market tests are time consuming and expensive because production lines as well as promotion and sales programs must be set up. Costs can run to more than a million dollars. Market tests also reveal plans to competitors, sometimes enabling them to get a product into national distribution first. Competitors can also try to sabotage test markets. With such problems, some firms skip test markets completely or use simulated test markets.

Simulated Test Markets   Because of the time, cost, and confidentiality problems of test markets, consumer packaged goods companies often turn to *simulated* (or *laboratory*) *test markets* (*STM*), a technique that simulates a full-scale test market but in a limited fashion. STMs are often run in shopping malls, where consumers are questioned to identify who uses the product class being tested. Willing participants are questioned on usage, reasons for purchase, and important product attributes. Qualified persons are then shown TV commercials or print ads for the test product along with competitors' advertising and are given money to make a decision to buy or not buy a package of the product (or the competitors') from a real or simulated store environment. STMs are used early in the development process to screen new-product ideas and later in the process to make sales projections.

Commercializing a new french fry: For how Burger King's "audible crunches" confronted McDonald's fries, see the text.

COMMERCIALIZATION
Positioning and launching a new product in full-scale production and sales.

SLOTTING FEE
The payment a manufacturer makes to place a new item on a retailer's shelf.

FAILURE FEE
A penalty payment made by a manufacturer to compensate the retailer for sales its valuable shelf space never made.

When Test Markets Don't Work　Test marketing is a valuable step in the new-product process, but not all products can use it. Testing a service beyond the concept level is very difficult because the service is intangible and consumers can't see what they are buying. Similarly, test markets for expensive consumer products such as cars or VCRs or costly business products such as jet engines or computers are impractical. For these products consumer reactions to mockup designs or one-of-a-kind prototypes are all that is feasible. Carmakers test new style designs on "early adopters" (discussed in Chapter 11) who are more willing than the average customer to buy new designs or products.[23]

Commercialization

Finally, the product is brought to the point of **commercialization**—positioning and launching it in full-scale production and sales. Companies proceed very carefully at the commercialization stage because this is the most expensive stage for most new products, especially consumer products.

Burger King's French Fries: The Complexities of Commercialization　Burger King's "improved french fries" are an example of what can go wrong at the commercialization stage. In the fast-food industry, McDonald's french fries are the "gold standard" against which all other fries are measured. In 1996 Burger King decided to take on McDonald's fries and spent millions of R&D dollars developing a starch-coated fry designed to retain heat longer and "add crunch."

In Burger King's 19-page french fry specifications, one requirement astounded even veteran food scientists: Crispiness was to be determined "by an audible crunch that should be present for seven or more chews . . . loud enough to be apparent to the evaluator." A 100-person team set to work and developed the starch-coated fry that beat McDonald's fries in taste tests, 57 percent to 35 percent, with 8 percent no opinion. After "certifrying" 300 000 managers and employees on the new frying procedures, the fries were launched in early 1998 with a $70-million marketing budget. The launch turned to disaster. The reason: The new fry proved too complicated to get right day after day in Burger King restaurants, except under ideal conditions.[24]

By summer 2000 Burger King realized something had to be done. Solution: Launch a "new," coated fry in early 2001—not requiring "seven audible crunches." A commercialization-stage success? You be the judge.

The Risks and Uncertainties of the Commercialization Stage　As the Burger King french fries show, the job is far from over when the new product gets to the commercialization stage. If the firm moves quickly, sometimes a potential commercialization stage disaster can be averted, as with Coca-Cola's decision to reintroduce old Coke three months after New Coke was launched in 1985. In spite of brilliant technologies, the hundreds of dot-com failures in 2000 and 2001 show the difficulty of launching successful new products.

Grocery products pose special commercialization problems. Because shelf space is so limited, many supermarkets require a **slotting fee** for new products, a payment a manufacturer makes to place a new item on a retailer's shelf. This can run to several million dollars for a single product. But there's even another potential expense. If a new grocery product does not achieve a predetermined sales target, some retailers require a **failure fee**, a penalty payment by a manufacturer to compensate the retailer for sales its valuable shelf space never made. To minimize the financial risk of a new-product failure, many grocery product manufacturers use *regional rollouts*, introducing the product sequentially into

Effective cross-functional teams at Hewlett-Packard have reduced new-product development times significantly.

geographical areas of Canada to allow production levels and marketing activities to build up gradually.

Speed as a Factor in New-Product Success In recent years, companies have discovered that speed or "time to market" (TtM) is often vital in introducing a new product. Recent studies have shown that high-tech products coming to market on time are far more profitable than those arriving late. So some companies—such as Sony, Honda, AT&T, and Hewlett-Packard—have overlapped the sequence of stages described in this chapter. With this approach, termed *parallel development*, cross-functional team members who conduct the simultaneous development of both the product and the production process stay with the product from conception to production. This has enabled Hewlett-Packard to reduce the development time for computer printers from 54 months to 22. In software development, *fast prototyping* uses a "do it, try it, fix it" approach—encouraging continuing improvements even after the initial design.

Figure 10-5 identifies the purpose of each stage of the new-product process and the kinds of marketing information and methods used. The figure also suggests information that might help avoid some new-product failures. Although using the new-product process does not guarantee successful products, it does increase a firm's success rate.

FIGURE 10–5
Marketing information and methods used in the new-product process

STAGE OF PROCESS	PURPOSE OF STAGE	MARKETING INFORMATION AND METHODS USED
New-product strategy development	Identify new-product niches to reach in light of company objectives	Company objectives; assessment of firm's current strengths and weaknesses in terms of market and product
Idea generation	Develop concepts for possible products	Ideas from employees and co-workers, consumers, R&D, and competitors; methods of brainstorming and focus groups
Screening and evaluation	Separate good product ideas from bad ones inexpensively	Screening criteria, concept tests, and weighted point systems
Business analysis	Identify the product's features and its marketing strategy, and make financial projections	Product's key features, anticipated marketing mix strategy; economic, marketing, production, legal, and profitability analyses
Development	Create the prototype product, and test it in the laboratory and on consumers	Laboratory and consumer tests on product prototypes
Market testing	Test product and marketing strategy in the marketplace on a limited scale	Test markets, simulated test markets (STMs)
Commercialization	Position and offer product in the marketplace	Perceptual maps, product positioning, regional rollouts

Concept Check

1. How does the development stage of the new-product process involve testing the product inside and outside the firm?

2. What is a test market?

3. What is commercialization of a new product?

SUMMARY

1 A product is a good, service, or idea consisting of a bundle of tangible and intangible attributes that satisfies consumers and is received in exchange for money or some other unit of value. A company's product decisions involve the product item, product line, and range of its product mix.

2 Products can be classified by user and degree of tangibility. By user, the major distinctions are consumer or business goods. Consumer goods consist of convenience, shopping, and specialty products. Business goods are for either production or support. By degree of tangibility, products divide into nondurable goods, durable goods, and services.

3 There are several ways to define a new product, such as the degree of distinction from existing products, a time base specified by Industry Canada, a company perspective, or effect on a consumer's usage pattern.

4 In terms of its effect on a consumer's use of a product, a discontinuous innovation represents the greatest change and a continuous innovation the least. A dynamically continuous innovation is disruptive but not totally new.

5 The failure of a new product is usually attributable to one of seven marketing reasons: insignificant point of difference, incomplete market and product definition before product development begins, too little market attractiveness, poor execution of the marketing mix, poor product quality on

critical factors, bad timing, and no economical access to buyers.

6 The new-product process consists of seven stages. Objectives for new products are determined in the first stage, new-product strategy development; this is followed by idea generation, screening and evaluation, business analysis, development, market testing, and commercialization.

7 Ideas for new products come from several sources, including consumers, employees, R&D laboratories, and competitors.

8 Screening and evaluation can be done internally or externally.

9 Business analysis involves defining the features of the new product, a marketing strategy to introduce it, and a financial forecast.

10 Development involves not only producing a prototype product but also testing it in the lab and on consumers to see that it meets the standards set for it.

11 In market testing new products, companies often rely on market tests to see that consumers will actually buy the product when it's offered for sale and that other marketing mix factors are working. Products surviving this stage are commercialized—taken to market.

KEY TERMS AND CONCEPTS

business analysis p. 285
business goods p. 271
commercialization p. 288
consumer goods p. 271
convenience goods p. 273
development p. 285
failure fee p. 288
idea generation p. 282
market testing p. 287
new-product process p. 281
new-product strategy development p. 281
product p. 270

product line p. 270
product mix p. 270
production goods p. 274
protocol p. 278
screening and evaluation p. 284
shopping goods p. 273
Six Sigma p. 282
slotting fee p. 288
specialty goods p. 273
support goods p. 274
unsought goods p. 273

INTERNET EXERCISE

www.mcgrawhill.ca/college/berkowitz

Jalapeño soda? Aerosol mustard? Fingos? These are just three of the more than 65 000 products (both successes and failures) on the shelves of the NewProductWorks Showcase.

The Showcase includes food, beverages, health and beauty care, household, and pet products introduced from 1965 to the present. While you probably can't personally visit the company, you can visit its new Website (www.newproductworks.com). Study the "Hits and Misses" categories (www.newproductworks.com/product_poll/hm_index.html), such as "This Month's Picks," which are new products that have the potential

for success; "We Expect Them to Be Successes," which are those that probably will be commercial successes; "Jury Is Out," products whose future is in doubt; "Failures," which are recent products that have failed miserably; and "Favorite Failures," which are those that cause people to ask *What were they thinking*?" Study several of the failed products listed on the Website and try to identify the reasons discussed earlier in the chapter that may have led to their failure. Contrast these failed products with those that are deemed successes to learn why they became "sure-fire winners!"

Want to get better grades, find tips on how to study more effectively, and stay up to date with happenings in the world of marketing? Visit the Online Learning Centre for practice tests, Study Smart software, and much more! www.mcgrawhill.ca/college/berkowitz

Interested in finding out what marketing looks like in the real world? *Marketing Magazine* is just a click away on your OLC! Visit www.mcgrawhill.ca/college/berkowitz

APPLYING MARKETING CONCEPTS AND PERSPECTIVES

1 Products can be classified as either consumer or business goods. How would you classify the following products: (*a*) Johnson's baby shampoo, (*b*) a Black & Decker two-speed drill, and (*c*) an arc welder?

2 Are products such as Nature Valley Granola bars and Eddie Bauer hiking boots convenience, shopping, specialty, or unsought goods?

3 Based on your answer to problem 2, how would the marketing actions differ for each product and the classification to which you assigned it?

4 In terms of the behavioural effect on consumers, how would a portable computer, such as a Macintosh PowerBook or an IBM ThinkPad, be classified? In light of this classification, what actions would you suggest to the manufacturers of these products to increase their sales in the market?

5 Several alternative definitions were presented for a new product. How would a company's marketing strategy be affected if it used (*a*) the legal definition or (*b*) a behavioural definition?

6 What methods would you suggest to assess the potential commercial success for the following new products: (*a*) a new, improved ketchup, (*b*) a three-dimensional television system that took the company 10 years to develop, and (*c*) a new children's toy on which the company holds a patent?

7 Concept testing is an important step in the new-product process. Outline the concept tests for (*a*) an electrically powered car and (*b*) a new loan payment system for automobiles that is based on a variable rate of interest. What are the differences in developing concept tests for products as opposed to services?

VIDEO CASE 10–1 Palm Computing, Inc.

Developing new products often requires a complicated and challenging sequence of activities. "It's not as simple as taking what the customer wants and creating a product," says Joe Sipher, director—Wireless Products at Palm Computing Inc., a subsidiary of 3Com Corp. "If we did that, we would have ended up with something like Apple Computer's Newton, which was a failure because it incorporated too many features into the product." While this perspective seems counter-intuitive, it has proven highly successful for Palm computing, the market leader for personal digital assistants (PDAs).

THE COMPANY

The original PalmPilot inventors, Jeff Hawkins and Donna Dubinsky, started out developing personal computing connectivity and shorthand software for other PDA manufacturers in the spring of 1994. According to Dubinsky, "We started out as an applications software company. We worked with Casio, Sharp, Hewlett-Packard, Apple, and others—everybody who was working in the field at that time. But none of the platforms were compelling. Most people thought a PDA should be a smaller version of a laptop computer." Although Palm Computing was the leading software developer for these PDA entrants, sales were too low to keep the company running. "The reasons why early hand-held computers failed were because they had too many features, making them too big, too slow, too heavy, and too expensive," explains Andrea Butter, vice president of marketing.

Palm Computing managers saw a dismal future in being the leading applications provider for a nonexistent market. However, as Butter states, "We felt we knew what customers wanted to do in handheld computing and one day an investor challenged us and said, 'If you know how to do it, why don't you do it?'" They accepted the challenge and today Palm Computing is the market share leader in the PDA industry. To provide additional funding and technology for the PalmPilot, U.S. Robotics, a leading modem manufacturer, acquired Palm Computing in 1995, which in turn was acquired in 1997 by 3Com Corp, a leading manufacturer of information access products and network system solutions.

During 1998, Palm Computing sold 1.3 million units, and by 2000, Palm Computing's sales were expected to reach 1.8 million units in a total PDA market of 2.7 million units. In Canada, Palm currently holds more than 70 percent market share, followed by Handspring with 14 percent and Blackberry with 6 percent. According to experts, PDA growth will continue to be strong in Canada with as much as 75 percent of the Canadian population carrying a PDA by 2005.

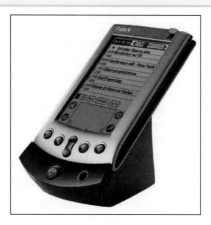

THE POSITIONING DILEMMA

Defining this type of product has been a challenge. These products have been referred to as information appliances, smart handheld computers, personal information managers, and personal digital assistants (PDA). Physically, these products have a thin, panel-like body (like the "communicator" from the original Star Trek series) measureing about 12 cm × 8 cm × 1 cm. They typically do not have keyboards or keypads; instead, they use a pen or stylus and handwriting recognition software to allow users to store addresses and telephone numbers, enter appointments on a calendar, make notes and to-do lists, and interface with personal computers to transfer e-mail and other data. Hawkins and Dubinsky viewed PDAs as digital replacements for paper-based systems, such as DayTimers, Rolodexes, and Post-it Notes.

PALM COMPUTING'S NEW-PRODUCT PROCESS

Hawkins used his own experience with the "GRiDPad," the first handheld computer developed in the mid-1980s, and "Graffiti," a shorthand-type of handwriting recognition software developed for other entrants in the PDA market, to design the original PalmPilot. Hawkins's R&D consisted of carrying a rectangular block of wood in his shirt pocket with "function buttons" glued to it. When people asked him if he was free for lunch, he would take out his "connected organizer," tap on a "button," and observe their reactions. Hawkins tried several variations before settling on a final design: the PalmPilot would have only four function buttons (calendar, addresses and phone numbers, to-do lists, and memos) because those were the most frequently used applications. In addition, Palm Computing conducted a survey among customers of Casio's "Zoomer" PDA. The most important finding was that 90 percent used a personal computer. As a result, the new PalmPilot would also include PC connectivity. Finally, the PalmPilot would be sold only in computer and office supply stores because their salespeople were perceived to have greater skills in selling technology-based products.

The original PalmPilot was launched in 1996 at Demo'96, a trade show whose attendees were technology opinion leaders. The PalmPilot was the "media darling of the show" and sales took off from there. The original PalmPilot has since been retired. The current PalmPilot Connected Organizer product line consists of the PalmPilot Professional ($149), the Palm III ($249), the Palm IIIx ($369), the Palm V ($449), and the Palm VII ($599). Each of these models has the same minimalist design as the original.

COMPETITION AND THE PDA MARKET

When Windows CE 1.0 came out in 1997, Dubinsky recalls, "We said 'Oh-oh, it's all over for us now.'" But it turned out that consumers weren't interested in devices that were positioned between PDAs and personal computers. In 1998, International Data Corp. reported that Windows CE devices held only a 15-percent market share, but may garner a 55-percent share by 2002. Hardware manufacturers, such as Hewlett-Packard, Casio, Philips, and so on, have partnered with Microsoft and are enthusiastic about newer versions of this OS software and other innovations in battery and memory technology that allow them to offer more features such as colour touchscreens for graphics, charts, and other presentations, slimmed down versions of Microsoft's popular Word and Excel programs, the familiar Windows-like interface, and Internet searching and paging via a PC card interface in their products. However, these products are stil pricy, sluggish, and consume more power than those from Palm Computing. At the low end of the market, companies such as Casio and Royal have introduced single-function PDA devices at $99 or less. Finally, Palm Computing faces competition from Web-based personal information managers (PIM), which perform identical functions as the PalmPilot. These organizers are stored at one's Internet service provider and accessed via browsers, such as Netscape or Internet Explorer, or portals, such as Yahoo! or America Online (AOL).

THE FUTURE OF PALM COMPUTING

Palm Computing has responded by introducing two new products: the Palm IIIx and Palm V. Both compete with Windows CE-based systems. Both products offer better screen contrast and faster processors, but no changes in the Palm OS, the "operating system" software that gives these PDAs their handwriting recognition, time management, database (address and telephone number), and note-taking functionality. The Palm IIIx offers twice the memory of previous models, while the Palm V has a sleeker, slimmer design, recessed buttons, and lithium instead of AAA batteries for 10 hours of life. Palm Computing also encouraged third-party software developers to extend the Palm OS's functionality to include e-mail, Internet search, expense recording, and even e-commerce applications. To further expand its share of the PDA market, Palm Computing has licensed its OS to other original equipment manufacturers (OEM) for their private-label brands, such as IBM's "WordPad" PDA and Qualcomm's "pdQ," a combination PDA organizer and cellular telephone. Finally, Palm Computing has encouraged others to develop accessories for the Palm Connected Organizer product line.

Palm Computing's Palm VII, introduced in mid-1999, could revolutionize the PDA marketplace. The Palm VII is targeted at the rapidly growing wireless and mobile market, which has an estimated potential market of 21 million subscribers by 2002. The $599 Palm VII is positioned between a two-way pager and a laptop computer with wireless Internet access, and is virtually identical to the Palm III except for the wireless antenna that connects users to the proprietary Palm.net "Web clipping" service. E-Trade, Ticketmaster, The Weather Channel, Yahoo!, and other Palm.net content partners optimized content for the memory and small screen of Palm VII. In addition, users can send and receive short e-mail messages through Palm.net's iMessenger service. Future Palm Computing PDAs may include full Internet Website access and e-mail messaging.

Questions

1   Which of the steps in the new-product process discussed in Chapter 10 did Palm Computing use to develop the PalmPilot? What activities did Palm Computing use in each step?

2   What are the characteristics of the PalmPilot target market?

3   What kinds of learning or behavioral changes were required by consumers who purchased the PalmPilot?

4   What are the key "points of difference" of the PalmPilot when compared to substitute products?

5   How would you rate the PalmPilot on the following reasons for success or failure: significant points of difference; size of market; product quality; market timing; and access to consumers?

MANAGING PRODUCTS AND BRANDS

AFTER READING THIS CHAPTER YOU SHOULD BE ABLE TO:

- Explain the product life cycle concept and relate a marketing strategy to each stage.

- Recognize the differences in product life cycles for various products and their implications for marketing decisions.

- Understand alternative approaches to managing a product's life cycle.

- Describe elements of brand personality and brand equity and the criteria used when selecting a good brand name.

- Explain the rationale for alternative branding strategies employed by companies.

- Understand the role of packaging, labelling, and warranties in the marketing of a product.

CLEARLY CANADIAN: THE ROAD TO GROWTH

Many industry experts credit Clearly Canadian Beverage Corporation of Vancouver with pioneering the alternative beverage industry. In 1988, Clearly Canadian (www.clearly.ca) began marketing its premium-priced, single-serve sparkling flavoured water to North American consumers. To date, the company has sold more than 2 billion bottles of Clearly Canadian. It is now focused on selling the next billion bottles. To achieve that goal, the company is following its pioneering spirit and innovating in order to stay current with consumers' needs and ahead of its competition.

Like Clearly Canadian itself, the alternative beverage market has grown dramatically over the past decade. The industry is currently valued at $10 billion. Clearly Canadian Sparkling Flavoured Water, the product that started the whole phenomenon, continues to be a market leader. But many products have also emerged to compete in this sector; industry players now range from small, entrepreneurial firms like Clearly Canadian to major beverage companies that use their marketing and distribution muscle to garner share of the alternative beverage market.

Despite the heavy competition and crowded store shelves, Clearly Canadian stays focused in terms of what it needs to do to manage its position in this category. According to Doug Mason, president and CEO of Clearly Canadian, experimentation and innovation are key success factors. Becoming a well-diversified beverage company is another. Toward that end, Clearly Canadian has added numerous products to its portfolio including O+2™, an oxygen-enhanced beverage for active adults; Battery, a drink that energizes and fuels the body; and Cascade Clear, a mountain spring water. In 2000, the company

also launched Tré Limone™, a sparkling lemon-ginger drink. Maintaining the product leadership of its flagship brand is also a priority. In 2001, the company rolled out its new-look sparkling flavoured water in a larger, more appealing package, and added a new diet line extension.

Its most recent innovation is Reebok Fitness Water. This new enhanced water beverage contains essential vitamins, minerals, and electrolytes and is designed to appeal to active, health-conscious consumers. Clearly Canadian is leading an aggressive brand-building program that is integrated into Reebok's overall brand-marketing activities. To continue down the road to growth, the company is also focused on maintaining good distribution and channel relationships and redoubling its efforts toward continuous cost-efficiency improvements.[1]

This chapter shows how the actions taken by Clearly Canadian Beverage Corporation are typical of those of successful marketers in managing products and brands in competitive marketing environments.

PRODUCT LIFE CYCLE

PRODUCT LIFE CYCLE
The stages a new product goes through in the marketplace: introduction, growth, maturity, and decline.

Products, like people, have been viewed as having a life cycle. The concept of the **product life cycle** describes the stages a new product goes through in the marketplace: introduction, growth, maturity, and decline (Figure 11–1).[2] There are two curves shown in this figure: total industry sales revenue and total industry profit, which represent the sum of sales revenue and profit of all firms producing the product. The reasons for the changes in each curve and the marketing decisions involved are discussed in the following pages.

Introduction Stage

The introduction stage of the product life cycle occurs when a product is first introduced to its intended target market. During this period sales grow slowly, and profit is minimal. The lack of profit is often the result of large investment costs in product development, such as the $1 billion spent by Gillette to develop and launch the MACH 3 razor shaving system. The marketing objective for the company at this stage is to create consumer awareness and stimulate *trial*—the initial purchase of a product by a consumer.

Companies often spend heavily on advertising and other promotion tools to build awareness among consumers in the introduction stage. For example, Gillette budgeted $300 million in advertising alone to introduce the MACH 3 razor to consumers.[3] These expenditures are often made to stimulate *primary demand*, or desire for the product class, rather than for a specific brand since there are few competitors with the same product. As more competitors introduce their own products and the product progresses along its life cycle, company attention is focused on creating *selective demand*, or demand for a specific brand.

Other marketing-mix variables also are important at this stage. Gaining distribution can be a challenge because channel intermediaries may be hesitant to carry a new product. Moreover, in this stage a company often restricts the number of variations of the product to ensure control of product quality. For example, Clearly Canadian Sparkling Water originally came in only one flavour. Gillette currently offers only a single version of the MACH 3 razor.

During introduction, pricing can be either high or low. A high initial price may be used as part of a *skimming* strategy to help the company recover the costs of development as well as capitalize on the price insensitivity of early buyers. 3M is a master of this strategy. According to a 3M manager, "We hit fast, price high, and get the heck out when the me-too products pour in."[4] High prices also tend to attract competitors more eager to enter the market because they see the opportunity for profit. To discourage competitive entry a company can price low, referred to as

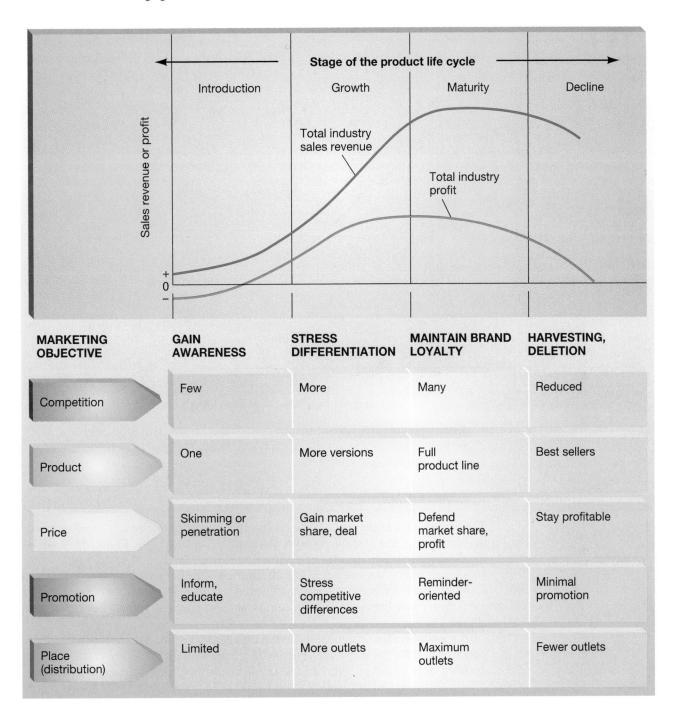

Stage of the product life cycle			
Introduction	Growth	Maturity	Decline

Total industry sales revenue

Total industry profit

Sales revenue or profit

+ 0 −

MARKETING OBJECTIVE	GAIN AWARENESS	STRESS DIFFERENTIATION	MAINTAIN BRAND LOYALTY	HARVESTING, DELETION
Competition	Few	More	Many	Reduced
Product	One	More versions	Full product line	Best sellers
Price	Skimming or penetration	Gain market share, deal	Defend market share, profit	Stay profitable
Promotion	Inform, educate	Stress competitive differences	Reminder-oriented	Minimal promotion
Place (distribution)	Limited	More outlets	Maximum outlets	Fewer outlets

FIGURE 11–1

How stages of the product life cycle relate to a firm's marketing objectives and marketing mix actions

penetration pricing. This pricing strategy also helps build unit volume, but a company must closely monitor costs. These and other pricing techniques are covered in depth in Chapter 14.

Figure 11–2 charts the stand-alone fax machine product life cycle for business use from the early 1970s through 2001.[5] As shown, sales grew slowly in the 1970s and early 1980s after Xerox pioneered the first lightweight portable fax machine that sent and received documents. Fax machines were originally sold direct to businesses through company salespeople and were premium priced. The average price for a fax machine in 1980 was $12 700. By today's standards, those fax machines were primitive. They contained mechanical parts, not electronic circuitry, and offered few of the features seen in today's models.

FIGURE 11–2
Product life cycle for the stand-alone fax machine for business use: 1970–2001

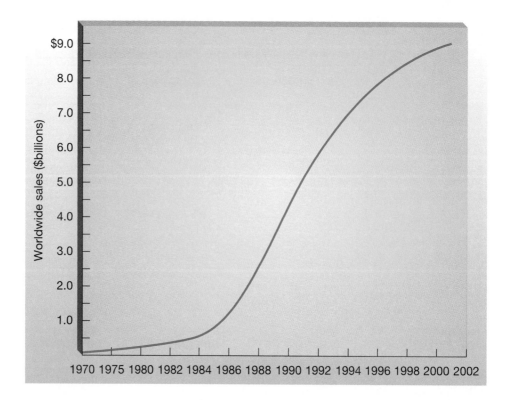

Several product classes are in the introductory stage of the product life cycle. These include high-definition television (HDTV) and "hybrid" (gasoline-and-electric-powered) automobiles.

Growth Stage

The second stage of the product life cycle, growth, is characterized by rapid increases in sales. It is in this stage that competitors appear. For example, Figure 11–2 shows the dramatic increase in sales of fax machines from 1986 to 1990. The number of companies selling fax machines was also increasing, from one in the early 1970s to four in the late 1970s to seven manufacturers in 1983, which sold nine brands. By 1990 there were some 25 manufacturers and 60 possible brands from which to choose.

The result of more competitors and more aggressive pricing is that profit usually peaks during the growth stage. For instance, the average price for a fax machine declined from $3300 in 1985 to $1500 in 1990. At this point the emphasis of advertising shifts to stimulating selective demand, in which product benefits are compared with those of competitors' offerings.

Product sales in the growth stage grow at an increasing rate because of new people trying or using the product and a growing proportion of *repeat purchasers*—people who tried the product, were satisfied, and bought again. As a product moves through the life cycle, the ratio of repeat to trial purchasers grows. Failure to achieve substantial repeat purchasers usually means an early death for a product. Alberto-Culver introduced Mr. Culver's Sparklers, which were solid air fresheners that looked like stained glass. The product moved quickly from the introduction to the growth stage, but then sales plummeted. The problem was there were almost no repeat purchasers because buyers treated the product like cheap window decorations, left them there, and didn't buy new ones. Durable fax machines meant that replacement purchases were rare; however, it was common for more than one machine to populate a business as their use became more widespread. In 1995, there was one fax machine for every eight people in a business.

Hybrid automobiles made by Honda are in the introductory stage of the product life cycle; DVD players produced by Toshiba are in the growth stage. Each product and company faces unique challenges based on its product life cycle stage.

Changes start to appear in the product during the growth stage. To help differentiate a company's brand from those of its competitors, an improved version or new features are added to the original design, and product proliferation occurs. Changes in fax machines included (1) models with built-in telephones; (2) models that used plain, rather than thermal, paper for copies; (3) models that integrated telex for electronic mail purposes; and (4) models that allowed for secure (confidential) transmissions. For Clearly Canadian, new flavours and package sizes were added during the growth stage.

In the growth stage it is important to gain as much distribution for the product as possible. In the retail store, for example, this often means that competing companies fight for display and shelf space. Expanded distribution in the fax industry is an example. In 1986, early in the growth stage, only 11 percent of office machine dealers carried this equipment. By the mid-1990s, more than 70 percent of these dealers carried fax equipment, distribution was expanded to other stores selling electronic equipment, and the fight continues for which brands will be displayed.

Numerous product classes or industries are in the growth stage of the product life cycle. Examples include DVD players and personal digital assistants (PDAs).

Maturity Stage

The third stage, maturity, is characterized by a slowing of total industry sales or product class revenue. Also, marginal competitors begin to leave the market. Most consumers who would buy the product are either repeat purchasers of the item or have tried and abandoned it. Sales increase at a decreasing rate in the maturity stage as fewer new buyers enter the market. Profit declines because there is fierce price competition among many sellers and the cost of gaining new buyers at this stage increases.

MARKETING NEWSNET

Will E-mail Spell Doom for the Familiar Fax?

Technological substitution often causes the decline stage in the product life cycle. Will the Internet and e-mail replace fax machines?

This question has caused heated debates. Even though sales of Internet host computers are in the growth stage of the product life cycle, fax machine sales continue to grow as well. Industry analysts estimate that there are more than one billion e-mail mailboxes worldwide. However, the growth of e-mail has not affected faxing because the two technologies do not directly compete for the same messaging applications.

E-mail is used for text messages and faxing is predominantly used for communicating formatted documents by business users. Fax usage is expected to increase through 2005, and sales of stand-alone fax machines are expected to increase as well. Internet technology may eventually replace facsimile technology, but not in the immediate future.

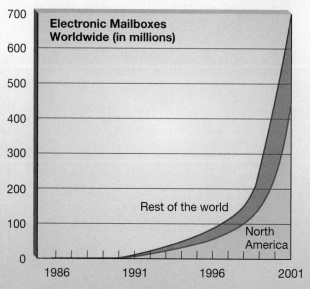

Marketing attention in the maturity stage is often directed toward holding market share through further product differentiation and finding new buyers. Gillette, for example, differentiated its MACH 3 razor through new product features specifically designed for women and then launched the Gillette Venus razor for women just as the MACH 3 razor entered its maturity stage. Fax machine manufacturers developed Internet-enabled models and introduced product features suitable for small and home businesses, which today represent a substantial portion of industry sales. Still, a major consideration in a company's strategy in this stage is to reduce overall marketing costs by improving promotional and distribution efficiency.

Stand-alone fax machines for business use approached the maturity stage in the late 1990s. By 2001, more than 80 percent of industry sales were captured by four producers (Brother, Canon, Panasonic, and Sharp), reflecting the departure of marginal competitors. Industry sales slowed in the late 1990s compared with triple-digit average annual dollar sales increases in the late 1980s. By early 2002, an estimated 100 million stand-alone fax machines for business were installed throughout the world.

Numerous product classes and industries are in the maturity stage of their product life cycle. These include carbonated soft drinks, automobiles, and TVs.

Decline Stage

The decline stage occurs when sales and profits begin to drop. Frequently, a product enters this stage not because of any wrong strategy on the part of the company but because of environmental changes. Technological innovation often precedes the decline stage as newer technologies replace older technologies. The word-processing capability of personal computers pushed typewriters into decline. Compact discs did the same to cassette tapes in the prerecorded music industry.

Will Internet technology and e-mail spell doom for fax machines? The accompanying Marketing NewsNet offers one perspective on this question.[6] Products in the decline stage tend to consume a disproportionate share of management time and financial resources relative to their potential future worth. A company will follow one of two strategies to handle a declining product: deletion or harvesting.

Deletion   Product *deletion*, or dropping the product from the company's product line, is the most drastic strategy. Because a residual core of consumers still consume or use a product even in the decline stage, product elimination decisions are not taken lightly. For example, Gillette continues to sell its Liquid Paper correction fluid for use in typewriters even in the era of word-processing equipment.

Harvesting   A second strategy, *harvesting*, occurs when a company retains the product but reduces marketing support costs. The product continues to be offered, but salespeople do not allocate time in selling nor are advertising dollars spent. The purpose of harvesting is to maintain the ability to meet customer requests. Coca-Cola, for instance, still sells Tab, its first diet cola, to a small group of die-hard fans. According to Coke's CEO, "It shows you care. We want to make sure those who want Tab, get Tab."[7]

Some Dimensions of the Product Life Cycle

Some important aspects of product life cycles are (1) their length, (2) the shape of their curves, and (3) how they vary with different levels of the products.

Length of the Product Life Cycle   There is no exact time that a product takes to move through its life cycle. As a rule, consumer products have shorter life cycles than business products. For example, many new consumer food products such as Frito-Lay's WOW brand potato chips move from the introduction stage to maturity in 18 months. The availability of mass communication vehicles informs consumers faster and shortens life cycles. Also, the rate of technological change tends to shorten product life cycles as new-product innovation replaces existing products.

The Shape of the Product Life Cycle   The product life-cycle curve shown in Figure 11–1 is the *generalized life cycle*, but not all products have the same shape to their curve. In fact, there are several different life-cycle curves, each type suggesting different marketing strategies. Figure 11–3 shows the shape of life-cycle curves for four different types of products: high learning, low learning, fashion, and fad products.

FIGURE 11–3
Alternative product life cycles

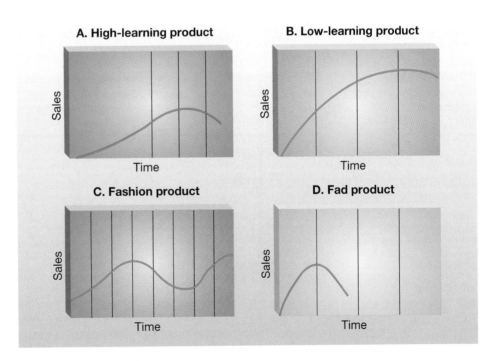

A. High-learning product

B. Low-learning product

C. Fashion product

D. Fad product

A *high-learning product* is one for which significant education of the customer is required and there is an extended introductory period (Figure 11–3A). Products such as home computers had this type of life-cycle curve because consumers have to understand the benefits of purchasing the product or be educated in a new way of performing a familiar task. Convection ovens, for example, necessitate that the consumer learn a new way of cooking and alter familiar recipes.

In contrast, for a *low-learning product* sales begin immediately because little learning is required by the consumer, and the benefits of purchase are readily understood (Figure 11–3B). This product often can be easily imitated by competitors, so the marketing strategy is to broaden distribution quickly. In this way, as competitors rapidly enter, most retail outlets already have the innovator's product. It is also important to have the manufacturing capacity to meet demand. A recent example of a successful low-learning product is Gillette's MACH 3 razor. Introduced in mid-1998, MACH 3 was projected to record $1 billion in sales before 2001.[8]

A *fashion product* (Figure 11–3C), such as hemline lengths on skirts or lapel widths on sports jackets, is introduced, declines, and then seems to return. Life cycles for fashion products most often appear in women's and men's clothing styles. The length of the cycles may be years or decades.

A *fad* experiences rapid sales on introduction and then an equally rapid decline (Figure 11–3D). These products are typically novelties and have a short life cycle. They include car tattoos, described as the first removable and reusable graphics for automobiles, and vinyl dresses, fleece bikinis, and an AstroTurf miniskirt.[9]

The Product Level: Class and Form   The product life shown in Figure 11–1 is a total industry or product class curve. Yet, in managing a product it is important to often distinguish among the multiple life cycles (class and form) that may exist. **Product class** refers to the entire product category or industry, such as video games shown in Figure 11–4.[10] **Product form** pertains to variations within the class. For video games, product form exists in the computing capability of game players such as 8-, 16- and 32/64- and the new 128-bit machines such as Sony's PlayStation 2, Nintendo's GameCube, and Microsoft's Xbox. Game consoles and software have a life cycle of their own and typically move from the introduction to maturity stage in five years.

The Life Cycle and Consumers   The life cycle of a product depends on sales to consumers. Not all consumers rush to buy a product in the introductory stage, and the shapes of the life-cycle curves indicate that most sales occur after the product has been on the market for some time. In essence, a product diffuses, or spreads, through the population, a concept called the *diffusion of innovation*.[11]

PRODUCT CLASS
The entire product category or industry.

PRODUCT FORM
Variations of a product within the product class.

FIGURE 11–4
Video game console and software life cycles by product class and product form

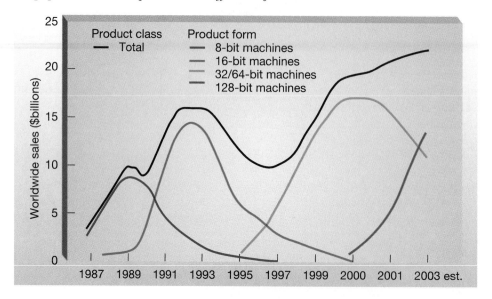

FIGURE 11–5
Five categories and profiles
of product adopters

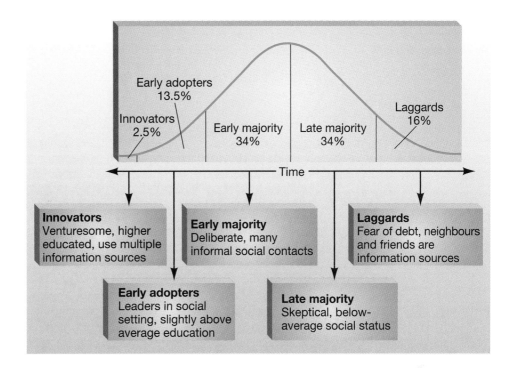

Some people are attracted to a product early, while others buy it only after they see their friends with the item. Figure 11–5 shows the consumer population divided into five categories of product adopters based on when they adopt a new product. Brief profiles accompany each category. For any product to be successful, it must be purchased by innovators and early adopters. This is why manufacturers of new pharmaceuticals try to gain adoption by leading hospitals, clinics, and physicians that are widely respected in the medical field. Once accepted by innovators and early adopters, the adoption of new products moves on to the early majority, late majority, and laggard categories.

Several factors affect whether a consumer will adopt a new product. Common reasons for resisting a product in the introduction stage are usage barriers (the product is not compatible with existing habits), value barriers (the product provides no incentive to change), risk barriers (physical, economic, or social), and psychological barriers (cultural differences or image).[12]

Companies attempt to overcome these barriers in numerous ways. They provide warranties, money-back guarantees, extensive usage instructions, demonstrations, and free samples to stimulate initial trial of new products. For example, software developers offer demonstrations downloaded from the Internet. Maybelline allows consumers to browse through the Cover Girl Color Match system on its Website to find out how certain makeup products will look. Free samples are one of the most popular means to gain consumer trial. For example, some Ontario winemakers from the Niagara region believe that sampling (via taste testing) is critical in order for a new wine product to be successful in a crowded and competitive Canadian market.[13]

www.maybelline.com

Concept Check

1. Advertising plays a major role in the _____ stage of the product life cycle, and _____ plays a major role in maturity.

2. How do high-learning and low-learning products differ?

3. What does the life cycle for a fashion product look like?

MANAGING THE PRODUCT LIFE CYCLE

An important task for a firm is to manage its products through the successive stages of their life cycles. This section discusses the role of the product manager, who is usually responsible for this, and analyzes three ways to manage a product through its life cycle: modifying the product, modifying the market, and repositioning the product.

Role of a Product Manager

The product manager (sometimes called *brand manager*) manages the marketing efforts for a close-knit family of products or brands.[14] Introduced by P&G in 1928, the product manager style of marketing organization is used by consumer goods firms such as General Mills and PepsiCo and by industrial firms such as Intel and Hewlett-Packard. Pillsbury Canada and General Motors of Canada also use product managers. All product managers are responsible for managing existing products through the stages of the life cycle, and some are also responsible for developing new products. Product managers' marketing responsibilities include developing and executing a marketing program for the product line described in an annual marketing plan and approving ad copy, media selection, and package design. The role of product managers in planning, implementing, and controlling marketing strategy is covered in depth in Chapter 21.

Modifying the Product

Product modification involves altering a product's characteristic, such as its quality, performance, or appearance, to try to increase and extend the product's sales. Wrinkle-free cotton slacks sold by Levi Strauss revitalized sales of men's casual pants and now account for 60 percent of the men's cotton pants product class sales. Heinz Canada modified its original red ketchup by adding a little food colouring to create new versions of ketchup called Blastin Green and Funky Purple. These product modifications have helped increase Heinz's share of the ketchup market. The new versions were designed specifically for Canadian kids, who consume more than half of the ketchup produced in Canada. Similarly, Pepsi has introduced a new blue, berry-flavoured variation of its cola called Pepsi Blue, while rival Coca-Cola has released a new vanilla version of its flagship cola beverage. Both product modifications are designed to appeal to the teenage male segment.[15]

New features, packages, or scents can be used to change a product's characteristics and give the sense of a revised product. Procter & Gamble revamped Pantene shampoo and conditioner with a new vitamin formula and relaunched the brand with a multi-million dollar advertising and promotion campaign. The result? Pantene, a brand first introduced in the 1940s, became the top-selling shampoo and conditioner in an industry with more than 1000 competitors.[16]

Modifying the Market

With **market modification** strategies, a company tries to find new customers, increase a product's use among existing customers, or create new-use situations.

Finding New Users   Produce companies have begun marketing and packaging prunes as "dried plums" for the purposes of attracting younger buyers. Sony has expanded its user base by developing PlayStation 2 video games specially designed for children under 13 years old.[17]

Increasing Use   Promoting more frequent usage has been a strategy of Campbell Soup Company. Since soup consumption rises in the winter and declines during the

www.pillsbury.com

PRODUCT MODIFICATION
Altering a product's characteristic, such as its quality, performance, or appearance, to try to increase and extend the product's sales.

Blastin Green Ketchup is a new product modification.

MARKET MODIFICATION
Strategy in which a company tries to find new customers, increase a product's use among existing customers, or create new-use situations.

summer, the company now advertises more heavily in warm months to encourage consumers to think of soup as more than a cold-weather food. Similarly, The Florida Orange Growers Association advocates drinking orange juice throughout the day rather than for breakfast only.

Creating New-Use Situations   Finding new uses for an existing product has been the strategy behind Woolite, a laundry soap. Originally intended for the hand washing of woollen fabric, Woolite now promotes itself for use with all fine clothing items. Mars, Inc. suggests a new-use situation when it markets its M&M's candy as a replacement for chocolate chips in baked goods.

Repositioning the Product

Often a company decides to reposition its product or product line in an attempt to bolster sales. *Product repositioning* is changing the place a product occupies in a consumer's mind relative to competitive products. A firm can reposition a product by changing one or more of the four marketing mix elements. Four factors that trigger a repositioning action are discussed next.

Reacting to a Competitor's Position   One reason to reposition a product is because a competitor's entrenched position is adversely affecting sales and market share. Procter & Gamble repositioned its venerable Ivory soap bar in response to the success of Lever 2000, sold by Lever Brothers. Lever 2000, a bar soap that moisturizes, deodorizes, and kills bacteria, eroded P&G's dominance of the bar soap market. P&G responded with its own triple-threat soap called New Ivory Ultra Safe Skin Care Soap. The problem? The new Ivory doesn't float![18]

Reaching a New Market   When Unilever introduced iced tea in Britain in the mid-1990s, sales were disappointing. British consumers viewed it as leftover hot tea, not suitable for drinking. The company made its tea carbonated and repositioned it as a cold soft drink to compete as a carbonated beverage and sales improved. New Balance, Inc. has repositioned its athletic shoes for aging baby boomers. Instead of competing head-on against Nike, Reebok, and Fila, the company offers an expansive range of widths tailored for an older consumer's higher weight and networks with podiatrists who use the wide models to insert foot-support devices.[19]

Catching a Rising Trend   Changing consumer trends can also lead to repositioning. Consumer interest in "functional foods" is an example.[20] These foods offer health and dietary benefits beyond nutrition. A number of products have capitalized on this trend. Quaker Oats now makes a government-approved claim that oatmeal, as part of a diet low in saturated fat and cholesterol, may reduce the risk of heart disease. Calcium-enriched products, such as Nutri-Grain bars and Uncle Ben's Calcium Plus rice, focus on healthy bone structure for children and adults. Clearly Canadian markets its Reebok Fitness Water as a vitamin and mineral enhanced beverage.

www.hbc.com

TRADING UP

Adding value to a product (or line) through additional features or higher-quality materials.

TRADING DOWN

Reducing the number of features, quality, or price.

Changing the Value Offered   In repositioning a product, a company can decide to change the value it offers buyers and trade up or down. **Trading up** involves adding value to the product (or line) through additional features or higher-quality materials. Michelin has done this with its "run-flat" tire, which can travel up to 70 kilometres after suffering total air loss. Dog food manufacturers, such as Ralston Purina, also have traded up by offering super premium foods based on "life-stage nutrition." Mass merchandisers, such as Sears Canada and The Bay, can trade up by adding a designer clothes section to their store.

  Trading down involves reducing the number of features, quality, or price. For example, airlines have added more seats, thus reducing leg room, and eliminated extras, such as snack service and food portions. Trading down often exists when

ETHICS AND SOCIAL RESPONSIBILITY ALERT
Consumer Economics of Downsizing: Get Less, Pay More

For more than 30 years, Starkist put 185 grams of tuna into its regular-sized can. Today, Starkist puts 175 grams of tuna into its can, but charges the same price. Frito-Lay (Doritos and Lay's snack chips), Procter & Gamble (Pampers and Luvs disposable diapers), Nestlé (Poland Spring and Calistoga bottled waters) have whittled away at package contents 5 to 10 percent while maintaining their products' package size, dimensions, and prices. Kimberly-Clark cut the retail price on its jumbo pack of Huggies diapers, but also reduced the number of diapers per pack from 48 to 42.

Consumer advocates charge that "downsizing" the content of packages while maintaining prices is a subtle and unannounced way of taking advantage of consumer buying habits. They also say downsizing is a price increase in disguise and deceptive, but legal. Manufacturers argue that this practice is a way of keeping prices from rising beyond psychological barriers for their products.

Is downsizing an unethical practice if manufacturers do not inform consumers that the package contents are less than they were previously?

DOWNSIZING
Reducing the content of packages without changing package size and maintaining or increasing the package price.

companies engage in **downsizing**—reducing the content of packages without changing package size and maintaining or increasing the package price. Firms have been criticized for this practice, as described in the accompanying Ethics and Social Responsibility Alert.[21]

Concept Check

1. How does a product manager help manage a product's life cycle?

2. What does "creating new-use situations" mean in managing a product's life cycle?

3. Explain the difference between trading up and trading down in repositioning.

BRANDING AND BRAND MANAGEMENT

BRANDING
Activity in which an organization uses a name, phrase, design, or symbols, or combination of these, to identify its products and distinguish them from those of competitors.

BRAND NAME
Any word, device (design, shape, sound, or colour), or combination of these used to distinguish a seller's goods or services.

TRADE NAME
A commercial, legal name under which a company does business.

TRADEMARK
Identifies that a firm has legally registered its brand name or trade name so the firm has its exclusive use.

A basic decision in marketing products is **branding**, in which an organization uses a name, phrase, design, symbols, or combination of these to identify its products and distinguish them from those of competitors. A **brand name** is any word, "device" (design, sound, shape, or colour), or combination of these used to distinguish a seller's goods or services. Some brand names can be spoken, such as Clearly Canadian or Rollerblade. Other brand names cannot be spoken, such as the rainbow-coloured apple (the *logotype* or *logo*) that Apple Computer puts on its machines and in its ads. A **trade name** is a commercial, legal name under which a company does business. The Campbell Soup Company is the trade name of that firm.

A **trademark** identifies that a firm has legally registered its brand name or trade name so the firm has its exclusive use, thereby preventing others from using it. In Canada, trademarks are registered under the Trade-marks Act with Industry Canada. A well-known trademark can help a company advertise its offerings to customers and develop their brand loyalty.

Because a good trademark can help sell a product, *product counterfeiting*, which involves low-cost copies of popular brands not manufactured by the original producer, has been a growing problem. Counterfeit products can steal sales from the original manufacturer or hurt the company's reputation.

Trademark protection is a significant issue in global marketing. For instance, the transformation of the Soviet Union into individual countries has meant that many firms, such as Xerox, had to reregister trademarks in each of the republics to prohibit misuse and generic use ("xeroxing") of their trademarks by competitors and consumers.

Can you describe the personality traits for these two brands? Not sure? Try visiting their Websites for more information.

got2b
www.got2b.com

Mambo
www.lizclaiborne.com/mambo

BRAND PERSONALITY
A set of human characteristics associated with a brand name.

BRAND EQUITY
The added value a given brand name gives to a product beyond the functional benefits provided.

Consumers may benefit most from branding. Recognizing competing products by distinct trademarks allows them to be more efficient shoppers. Consumers can recognize and avoid products with which they are dissatisfied, while becoming loyal to other, more satisfying brands. As discussed in Chapter 5, brand loyalty often eases consumers' decision making by eliminating the need for an external search. CanWest Global TV System uses a single brand, "Global," which it says makes it easier for viewers to identify the network's stations and to find the schedule they have.

Brand Personality and Brand Equity

Product managers recognize that brands offer more than product identification and a means to distinguish their products from competitors. Successful and established brands take on a **brand personality**, a set of human characteristics associated with a brand name.[22] Research shows that consumers often assign personality qualities to products—traditional, romantic, rugged, sophisticated, rebellious—and choose brands that are consistent with their own or desired self-image. Marketers can and do imbue a brand with a personality through advertising that depicts a certain user or usage situation and conveys certain emotions or feelings to be associated with the brand. For example, the personality traits associated with Coca-Cola are *real* and *cool*; with Pepsi, *young*, *exciting*, and *hip*; and with Dr. Pepper, *nonconforming*, *unique*, and *fun*.

Brand name importance to a company has led to a concept called **brand equity**, the added value a given brand name gives to a product beyond the functional benefits provided.[23] This value has two distinct advantages. First, brand equity provides a competitive advantage, such as the Sunkist label, which implies quality fruit, and the Disney name, which defines children's entertainment. A second advantage is that consumers are often willing to pay a higher price for a product with brand equity. Brand equity, in this instance, is represented by the premium a consumer will

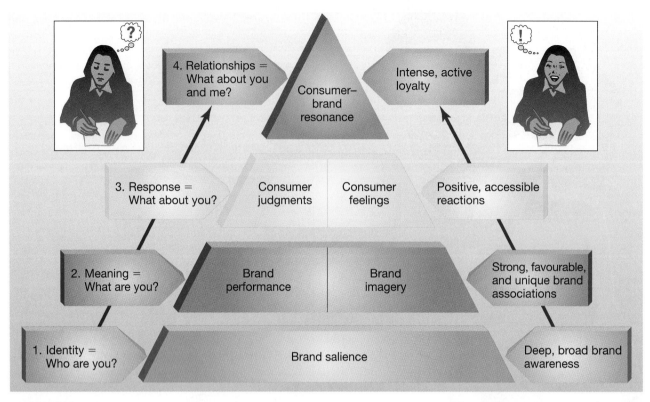

FIGURE 11–6
Customer-based brand equity pyramid

pay for one brand over another when the functional benefits provided are identical. Intel microchips, Bose audio systems, Duracell batteries, Microsoft computer software, and Louis Vuitton luggage all enjoy a price premium arising from brand equity.

Brand equity doesn't just happen. It is carefully crafted and nurtured by marketing programs that forge strong, favourable, and unique consumer associations and experiences with a brand. Brand equity resides in the minds of consumers and results from what they have learned, felt, seen, and heard about a brand over time. Marketers recognize that brand equity is not easily or quickly achieved. Rather, it arises from a sequential building process consisting of four steps (Figure 11–6).[24] The first step is to develop positive brand awareness and an association of the brand in consumers' minds with a product class or need to give the brand an identity. Gatorade and Kleenex have done this in the sports drink and facial tissue product classes, respectively. Next, a marketer must establish a brand's meaning in the minds of consumers. Meaning arises from what a brand stands for and has two dimensions: a functional, performance-related dimension and an abstract, imagery-related dimension. Nike has done this through continuous product development and improvement and its links to peak athletic performance in its integrated marketing communications program. The third step is to elicit the proper consumer responses to a brand's identity and meaning. Here attention is placed on how consumers think and feel about a brand. *Thinking* focuses on a brand's perceived quality, credibility, and superiority relative to other brands. *Feeling* relates to the consumer's emotional reaction to a brand. Michelin elicits both responses for its tires. Not only is Michelin thought of as a credible and superior-quality brand, but consumers also acknowledge a warm and secure feeling of safety, comfort, and self-assurance without worry or concern about the brand. The final and most difficult step is to create a consumer–brand resonance evident in an intense, active loyalty relationship between consumers and the brand. A deep psychological bond characterizes consumer–brand resonance and the personal identification consumers have with the brand. Examples of brands that have achieved this status include Harley-Davidson, Apple, and Coke.

Maple Leaf Sports & Entertainment Ltd. focuses on building bonds between fans and its sports teams.

LICENSING
A contractual agreement whereby a company allows another firm to use its brand name, patent, trade secret, or other property for a royalty or fee.

Ruffles and Chee-tos are available in Israel now, and more Frito-Lay snack items may follow. Entry into Israel was made possible through a licensing agreement with Elite Foods in Israel.

Elite Company
www.elite.co.il

Marketers of services also need to build their brand names and to create brand equity. Whether they market financial services or sports entertainment, the goal is the same. For example, Maple Leaf Sports & Entertainment Ltd. (MLS&E), which owns the Toronto Maple Leafs and the Toronto Raptors, markets its brand names diligently, focusing on building bonds between the fans and these sports teams. According to Tom Anselmi of MLS&E, "brand building is just as important in the business of sports as it is in selling laundry soap."[25]

Brand equity also provides a financial advantage for the brand owner. Successful, established names, such as Gillette, Nike, Gatorade, and Nokia, have an economic value in the sense that they are intangible assets. But unlike physical assets that depreciate with time and use, brands can appreciate in value when effectively managed. Conversely, brands can lose value as well when they are not managed properly.

Licensing

The value of brand equity is evident in the strategy of licensing. **Licensing** is a contractual agreement whereby a company allows another firm to use its brand name, patent, trade secret, or other property for a royalty or a fee. Licensing can be very profitable to a licensor and a licensee as annual worldwide retail sales of licensed products exceed $200 billion.[26] Playboy has earned more than $260 million licensing its name for merchandise ranging from shoes in North America to wallpaper in Europe and cooking classes in Brazil. Murjani has sold more than $500 million of clothing worldwide bearing the Coca-Cola logo. Disney earns about $300 million annually licensing its classic Disney characters such as Mickey Mouse and Winnie the Pooh to Mattel.

Licensing also assists companies in entering global markets with minimal risk. Frito-Lay licensed Elite Foods in Israel to produce and market Frito-Lay's Ruffles potato chips and Chee-tos cheese-flavoured corn puffs. These brands capture a significant percentage of the salty snack market in Israel.

Picking a Good Brand Name

We take brand names such as Dial, Sanyo, Porsche, and Adidas for granted, but it is often a difficult and expensive process to choose a good name. Companies will spend between $25 000 and $100 000 to identify and test a new brand name.[27] For instance, Intel spent $45 000 for the Pentium name given its family of microchips.[28] There are five criteria mentioned most often when selecting a good brand name.[29]

- The name should suggest the product benefits. For example, Accutron (watches), Easy Off (oven cleaner), Glass Plus (glass cleaner), Cling-Free (antistatic cloth for drying clothes), Powerbook (laptop computer), and Tidy Bowl (toilet bowl cleaner) all clearly describe the benefits of purchasing the product.
- The name should be memorable, distinctive, and positive. In the auto industry, when a competitor has a memorable name, others quickly imitate. When Ford named a car the Mustang, Pintos, Colts, and Broncos soon followed. The Thunderbird name led to the Phoenix, Eagle, Sunbird, and Firebird.
- The name should fit the company or product image. Sharp is a name that can apply to audio and video equipment. Excedrin, Anacin, and Nuprin are scientific-sounding names, good for an analgesic. However, naming a personal computer PCjr, as IBM did with its first computer for home use, neither fit the company nor the product. PCjr sounded like a toy and stalled IBM's initial entry into the home-use market.
- The name should have no legal or regulatory restrictions. Legal restrictions produce trademark infringement suits, and regulatory restrictions arise through improper use of words.[30] Increasingly, brand names need a corresponding address on the Internet. This further complicates name selection because millions of domain names are already registered.
- Finally, the name should be simple (such as Bold laundry detergent, Sure deodorant, and Bic pens) and should be emotional (such as Joy and Obsession perfumes). In the development of names for international use, having a non-meaningful brand name has been considered a benefit. A name such as Esso does not have any prior impressions or undesirable images among a diverse world population of different languages and cultures. The 7Up name is another matter. In Shanghai, China, the phrase means "death through drinking" in the local dialect, and sales have suffered as a result.[31]

Do you have an idea for a brand name? If you do, check to see if the name has been registered with Industry Canada's trademark division. Visit its Website, described in the accompanying Web Link.

WEB LINK

Have an Idea for a Brand or Trade Name? Check It Out!

http://www.mcgrawhill.ca

There are thousands of brand names or trade names already registered with Industry Canada and its trademark division. More and more are being registered every day.

An important step in choosing a brand or trade name is to determine whether the name has already been registered. Industry Canada offers a valuable service by allowing individuals and companies to quickly check to see if a name has been registered.

Do you have an idea for a brand or trade name for a new snack, software package, retail outlet, or service? Check to see if the name has been registered by visiting www.strategis.gc.ca. Then click on the trademark section under Industry Canada Services. You will be taken to the Canadian Intellectual Property Office section. Click on "trademark database." Enter your proposed brand name to find out if any person or organization has registered your chosen name.

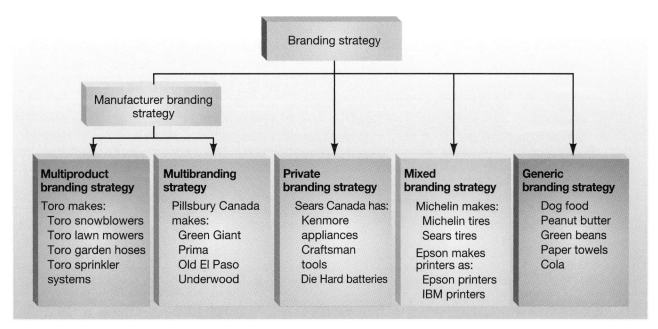

FIGURE 11–7
Alternative branding strategies

Branding Strategies

In deciding to brand a product, companies have several possible strategies, including manufacturer branding, private branding, or mixed branding approaches.

**MANUFACTURER
BRANDING**
The producer dictates the
brand name using either a
multiproduct or multibranding
approach.

**MULTIPRODUCT
BRANDING**
A company uses one name
for all products; also called
blanket or *family branding.*

Manufacturer Branding   With **manufacturer branding**, the producer dictates the brand name using either a multiproduct or multibrand approach. **Multiproduct branding** occurs when a company uses one name for all its products. This approach is often referred to as a *blanket* or *family* branding strategy (Figure 11–7).

There are several advantages to multiproduct branding. Capitalizing again on brand equity, consumers who have a good experience with the product will transfer this favourable attitude to other items in the product class with the same name. Therefore, this brand strategy makes possible *line extensions*, the practice of using a current brand name to enter a new market segment in its product class. Campbell Soup Company effectively employs a multiproduct branding strategy with soup line extensions. It offers regular Campbell soup, home-cooking style, and chunky varieties and more than 100 soup flavours. This strategy can also result in lower advertising and promotion costs because the same name is used on all products, thus raising the level of brand awareness. A risk with line extensions is that sales of an extension may come at the expense of other items in the company's product line. Therefore, line extensions work best when they provide incremental company revenue by taking sales away from competing brands or attracting new buyers.[32]

Some companies employ *subbranding*, which combines a family brand with a new brand. For example, ThinkPad is a subbrand to the IBM name.

A strong brand equity also allows for *brand extension*, the practice of using a current brand name to enter a completely different product class.[33] For instance, the equity in the Tylenol name as a trusted pain reliever allowed Johnson & Johnson to successfully extend this name to Tylenol Cold & Flu and Tylenol PM, a sleep aid. Fisher-Price, an established name in children's toys, was able to extend this name to children's shampoo and conditioners and baby bath and lotion products.

However, there is a risk with brand extensions. Too many uses for one brand name can dilute the meaning of a brand for consumers. Marketing experts claim this has happened to the Arm & Hammer brand given its use for toothpaste, laundry detergent, gum, cat litter, air freshener, carpet deodorizer, and anti-perspirant.[34]

www.johnsonjohnson.com

Black & Decker uses a multibranding strategy to reach different market segments. Black & Decker markets its line of tools for the do-it-yourselfer market with the Black & Decker name, but uses the DeWalt name for its professional tool line.

Black & Decker

www.blackanddecker.com

CO-BRANDING
The pairing of two brand names of two manufacturers on a single product.

MULTIBRANDING
A manufacturer's branding strategy giving each product a distinct name.

A recent variation on brand extensions is the practice of **co-branding**, the pairing of two brand names of two manufacturers on a single product.[35] Co-branding benefits firms by allowing them to enter new product classes, capitalize on an already established brand name in a product class, or reach new market segments. Second Cup of Toronto co-brands with Air Canada and Rogers Cantel Communications and AT&T Canada Inc. also co-brand, offering consumers seamless wireless telecommunications throughout North America.

An alternative manufacturer's branding strategy, **multibranding**, involves giving each product a distinct name. Multibranding is a useful strategy when each brand is intended for a different market segment. P&G makes Camay soap for those concerned with soft skin and Safeguard for those who want deodorant protection. Black & Decker markets its line of tools for the household do-it-yourselfer segment with the Black & Decker name, but uses the DeWalt name for its professional tool line. Disney uses the Miramax and Touchstone Pictures names for films directed at adults and its Disney name for children's films.

Multibranding strategies become more complex in the global marketplace. As an example, P&G uses multiple brand names for the same product when competing internationally. For instance, PertPlus shampoo is sold as Rejoice in Hong Kong, PertPlus in the Middle East, and Vidal Sassoon in the United Kingdom. However, international branding strategies do differ. In Japan, where corporate names are important, P&G markets the company's name prominently with the brand name of the product.

Compared with the multiproduct approach, promotional costs tend to be higher with multibranding. The company must generate awareness among consumers and retailers for each new brand name without the benefit of any previous impressions. The advantages of this approach are that each brand is unique to each market segment and there is no risk that a product failure will affect other products in the line. Nevertheless, some large multibrand firms have found that the complexity and cost of implementing this strategy can outweigh the benefits. For example, Unilever is currently pruning its brands from 1600 to 400 through product deletion and sales to other companies.[36]

The multibranding approach in Europe is slowly being replaced by **euro-branding**, the strategy of using the same brand name for the same product across all countries in the European Union. This strategy has many of the benefits linked with multi-product branding in addition to making Pan-European advertising and promotion programs possible.

EURO-BRANDING
The strategy of using the same brand name for the same product across all countries in the European Union.

Private Branding   A company uses **private branding**, often called *private labelling* or *reseller branding*, when it manufactures products but sells them under the brand name of a wholesaler or retailer. Radio Shack and Sears are large retailers that have their own brand names. Zellers also launched its Truly private brand hoping to foster the same customer loyalty as Loblaws' very successful President's Choice private brand. Other successful private brands in Canada include Sobeys' Smart Choice brand and Shoppers Drug Mart's Life brand.

Private branding is popular because it typically produces high profits for manufacturers and resellers. Consumers also buy these private brands with regularity.[37]

PRIVATE BRANDING
When a company manufactures products but sells them under the brand name of a wholesaler or retailer (often called *private labelling* or *reseller branding*).

Mixed Branding   A compromise between manufacturer and private branding is **mixed branding**, where a firm markets products under its own name and that of a reseller because the segment attracted to the reseller is different from its own market. Sanyo and Toshiba manufacture television sets for Sears as well as for themselves. This process is similar to Michelin's, which manufactures tires for Sears as well as under its own name. Kodak uses a mixed branding approach in Japan to increase its sales of 35-mm film. In addition to selling its Kodak brand, the company now makes "COOP" private-label film for the Japanese Consumer Cooperative Union, which is a group of 2500 stores. Priced significantly below its Kodak brand, the private label seeks to attract the price-sensitive Japanese consumer.[38]

MIXED BRANDING
A firm markets products under its own name and that of a reseller because the segment attracted by the reseller is different from its own market.

Generic Branding   An alternative branding approach is the **generic brand**, which is a no-brand product such as dog food, peanut butter, or green beans. There is no identification other than a description of the contents. The major appeal is that the price is up to one-third less than that of branded items. Generic brands account for less than one percent of total grocery sales. The limited appeal of generics has been attributed to the popularity of private brands and greater promotional efforts for manufacturer brand-name items. Consumers who use generics see these products as being as good as brand-name items, and, in light of what they expect, users of these products are relatively pleased with their purchases.

GENERIC BRAND
A no-name product with no identification other than a description of contents.

PACKAGING
Any container in which a product is offered for sale and on which label information is communicated.

PACKAGING AND LABELLING

The **packaging** component of a product refers to any container in which it is offered for sale and on which label information is communicated. A **label** is an integral part of the package and typically identifies the product or brand, who made it, where and when it was made, how it is to be used, and package contents and ingredients. To a great extent, the customer's first exposure to a product is the package and label and both are an expensive and important part of marketing strategy. For Pez Candy, Inc., the character-head-on-a-stick plastic container that dispenses a miniature brick candy is the central element of its marketing strategy, as described in the accompanying Marketing NewsNet.[39]

LABEL
An integral part of the package that typically identifies the product or brand, who made it, where and when it was made, how it is to be used, and package contents and ingredients.

MARKETING NEWSNET

Creating Customer Value through Packaging: Pez Heads Dispense More Than Candy

Customer value can assume numerous forms. For Pez Candy, Inc. (www.pez.com), customer value manifests itself in some 250 Pez character candy dispensers. Each 99-cent refillable dispenser ejects tasty candy tablets in a variety of flavours that delight preteens and teens alike.

Pez was formulated in 1927 by Austrian food mogul Edward Haas III and successfully sold in Europe as an adult breath mint. Pez, which comes from the German word for peppermint, *pfefferminz*, was originally packaged in a hygienic, headless plastic dispenser. Pez first appeared in North America in 1953 with a headless dispenser marketed to adults. After conducting extensive marketing research, Pez was repositioned with fruit flavours, repackaged with licensed character heads on top of the dispenser, and remarketed as a children's product in the mid-1950s. Since then, most top-level licensed characters and hundreds of other characters have become Pez heads. Consumers eat more than three billion Pez tablets annually, and company sales growth exceeds that of the candy industry as a whole.

The unique Pez package dispenses a "use experience" for its customers beyond the candy itself—namely, fun. And

fun translates into a 98-percent awareness level for Pez among teenagers and 89 percent among mothers with children. Pez has not advertised its product for years. With that kind of awareness, who needs advertising?

Creating Customer Value through Packaging and Labelling

Today's packaging costs Canadian companies billions of dollars, and an estimated 15 cents of every dollar spent by a consumer goes to packaging.[40] Despite the cost, packaging is essential because packages provide important benefits for the manufacturer, retailer, and ultimate consumer.

Communication Benefits   A major benefit of packaging is the label information on it conveyed to the consumer, such as directions on how to use the product and the composition of the product, which is needed to satisfy legal requirements of product disclosure. Other information consists of seals and symbols, either government-required or commercial seals of approval (such as the Good Housekeeping seal or the CSA seal). Packaging also can have brand equity benefits for a company. It has been shown that packaging can enhance brand recognition and facilitate the formation of strong, favourable, and unique brand associations.[41]

Functional Benefits   Packaging often plays an important functional role, such as convenience, protection, or storage. Quaker State changed its oil containers to eliminate the need for a separate spout, and Borden changed the shape of its Elmer's Wonder Bond adhesive to prevent clogging of the spout.

The convenience dimension of packaging is becoming increasingly important. Kraft Miracle Whip salad dressing and Heinz ketchup are sold in squeeze bottles, microwave popcorn has been a major market success, and Chicken of the Sea Tuna is now packaged in single-serving portions.

Consumer protection has become an important function of packaging, including the development of tamper-resistant containers. Today, companies commonly use safety seals or pop-tops that reveal previous opening. Nevertheless, no package is truly tamper resistant.

Can you name this soft drink brand?

Perceptual Benefits A third component of packaging and labelling is the perception created in the consumer's mind. Just Born Inc., a candy manufacturer of such brands as Jolly Joes and Mike and Ike Treats, discovered the importance of this component of packaging. For many years the brands were sold in old-fashioned black and white packages, but when the packaging was changed to four colour, with animated grape and cherry characters, sales increased 25 percent. Coca-Cola brought back its famous pale-green, contoured bottle to attract consumers who remember drinking soft drinks from glass bottles, not from aluminum cans and large plastic bottles. A worldwide sales increase of 8 percent was linked to the new-old bottle.[42]

Because labels list a product's source, brands competing in the global marketplace can benefit from "country of origin or manufacture" perceptions as described in Chapter 7. Consumers tend to have stereotypes about country–product pairings that they judge "best"—English tea, French perfume, Italian leather, and Japanese electronics—which can affect a brand's image.[43] Increasingly, Chinese firms are adopting the English language and Roman alphabet for their brands' labels. This is being done because of the perception in many Asian countries that "things Western are good," even if consumers do not understand the meaning of the English words![44]

A package can connote status, economy, and product quality. Procter & Gamble's Original Pringles, with its unique cylindrical packaging, offers uniform chips, minimal breakage, freshness, and better value for the money than flex-bag packages for chips.

In the past, the colour of packages was selected subjectively. For example, the famous Campbell's soup can was the inspiration of a company executive who liked Cornell University's red and white football uniforms. Today, there is greater recognition that colour affects consumers' perceptions.[45] Owens-Corning judged the pink colour of its fibre insulation to be so important that the colour was given trademark status by the courts.

Global Trends in Packaging

Two global trends in packaging originating in the mid-1990s will continue in the 21st century. One trend involves the environmental effects of packaging, the other focuses on packaging health and safety concerns.

The unique cylindrical packaging for Pringles provides both functional and perceptual benefits and serves as a major point of difference for the snack chip.

Pringles

www.pringles.com

Environmental Sensitivity Because of widespread worldwide concern about the growth of solid waste and the shortage of viable landfill sites, the amount, composition, and disposal of packaging material continues to receive much attention.[46] Recycling packaging material is a major thrust. Procter & Gamble now uses recycled cardboard in 70 percent of its paper packaging and is packaging Tide, Cheer, Era, and Dash detergents in jugs that contain 25 percent recycled plastic. Spic and Span liquid cleaner is packaged in 100-percent-recycled material. Other firms, such as the large U.K. retailer Sainsbury, emphasize the use of less packaging material. Sainsbury examines every product it sells to ensure that each uses only the minimum material necessary for shipping and display.

European countries have been trendsetters concerning packaging guidelines and environmental sensitivity. Many of these guidelines now exist in provisions governing trade to and within the European Union. In Germany, for instance, 80 percent of packaging material must be collected, and 80 percent of this amount must be recycled or reused to reduce solid waste in landfills. Canadian firms marketing in Europe have responded to these guidelines, and ultimately benefitted Canadian consumers.

Increasingly, firms are using life-cycle analysis (LCA) to examine the environmental effect of their packaging at every stage from raw material sources and production through distribution and disposal. A classic use of LCA was the decision by McDonald's to abandon the polystyrene clam-shells it used to package its hamburgers. LCA indicated that the environment would be better served if the amount of solid waste packaging were reduced than if the polystyrene shells were recycled. McDonald's elected to package its hamburgers in a light wrap made of paper and polyethylene and eliminate the polystyrene package altogether.

Health and Safety Concerns   A second trend involves the growing health and safety concerns of packaging materials. Today, a majority of North American and European consumers believe companies should make sure products and their packages are safe, regardless of the cost, and companies are responding to this view in numerous ways.[47] Most butane lighters sold today, such as those made by Bic, contain a child-resistant safety latch to prevent misuse and accidental fire. Childproof caps on pharmaceutical products and household cleaners and sealed lids on food packages are now common. New packaging technology and materials that extend a product's *shelf life* (the time a product can be stored) and prevent spoilage continue to be developed with special applications for less developed countries.

PRODUCT WARRANTY

WARRANTY
A statement indicating the liability of the manufacturer for product deficiencies.

A final component for product consideration is the **warranty**, which is a statement indicating the liability of the manufacturer for product deficiencies. There are various degrees of product warranties with different implications for manufacturers and customers.[48]

Some companies offer *express warranties*, which are written statements of liabilities. In recent years the government has required greater disclosure on express warranties to indicate whether the warranty is a limited-coverage or full-coverage alternative. A *limited-coverage warranty* specifically states the bounds of coverage and, more important, areas of noncoverage, whereas a *full warranty* has no limits of non-coverage. Cadillac is a company that boldly touts its warranty coverage. Also, in an effort to improve its image with Canadian consumers, Hyundai offers what it claims to be the best automobile warranty in the industry.

With greater frequency, manufacturers are being held to *implied warranties*, which assign responsibility for product deficiencies to the manufacturer. Studies show that warranties are important and affect a consumer's product evaluation. Brands that have limited warranties tend to receive less positive evaluations compared with full-warranty items.

Warranties are important in light of increasing product liability claims. In the early part of the 20th century the courts protected companies, but the trend now is toward "strict liability" rulings, where a manufacturer is liable for any product defect, whether it followed reasonable research standards or not. This issue is hotly contested by companies and consumer advocates.

Warranties represent much more to the buyer than just protection from negative consequences—they can hold a significant marketing advantage for the producer. Sears has built a strong reputation for its Craftsman tool line with a simple warranty: if you break a tool, it's replaced with no questions asked. Zippo has an equally simple guarantee: "If it ever fails, we'll fix it free."

Concept Check

1. How does a generic brand differ from a private brand?

2. Explain the role of packaging in terms of perception.

3. What is the difference between an expressed and an implied warranty?

SUMMARY

1 Products have a finite life cycle consisting of four stages: introduction, growth, maturity, and decline. The marketing objectives for each stage differ.

2 In the introductory stage the need is to establish primary demand, whereas the growth stage requires selective demand strategies. In the maturity stage the need is to maintain market share; the decline stage necessitates a deletion or harvesting strategy.

3 There are various shapes to the product life cycle. High-learning products have a long introductory period, and low-learning products rapidly enter the growth stage. There are also different curves for fashions and fads. Different product life-cycle curves can exist for the product class, product form, and brand.

4 In managing a product's life cycle, changes can be made in the product itself or in the target market. Product modification approaches include changes in quality, performance, or appearance. Market modification approaches entail increasing a product's use among existing customers, creating new-use situations, or finding new users.

5 Product repositioning can come about by reacting to a competitor's position, reaching a new market, capitalizing on a rising trend, or changing the value offered in a product.

6 Branding enables a firm to distinguish its product in the marketplace from those of its competitors. Successful and established brands take on a brand personality, a set of human characteristics associated with a brand name. A good brand name should suggest the product benefits, be memorable, fit the company or product image, be free of legal restrictions, and be simple and emotional. A good brand name is of such importance that it has led to a concept of brand equity, the added value a certain brand name gives to a product beyond the functional benefits provided.

7 Licensing of a brand name is being used by many companies. The company allows the name to be used without having to manufacture the product.

8 Manufacturers can follow one of three branding strategies: a manufacturer's brand, a reseller brand, or a mixed-brand approach. With a manufacturer's branding approach, the company can use the same brand name for all products in the line (multiproduct, or family, branding) or can give products different brands (multibranding).

9 A reseller, or private, brand is used when a firm manufactures a product but sells it under the brand name of a wholesaler or retailer. A generic brand is a product with no identification of manufacturer or reseller that is offered on the basis of price appeal.

10 Packaging and labelling provides communication, functional, and perceptual benefits. The two global emerging trends in packaging are greater concerns regarding the environmental impact and the health and safety of packaging materials.

11 The warranty, a statement of a manufacturer's liability for product deficiencies, is an important aspect of a manufacturer's product strategy.

KEY TERMS AND CONCEPTS

brand equity p. 307
brand name p. 306
brand personality p. 307
branding p. 306
co-branding p. 312
downsizing p. 306
euro-branding p. 313
generic brand p. 313
label p. 313
licensing p. 309
manufacturer branding p. 311
market modification p. 304
mixed branding p. 313

multibranding p. 312
multiproduct branding p. 311
packaging p. 313
private branding p. 313
product class p. 302
product form p. 302
product life cycle p. 296
product modification p. 304
trade name p. 306
trademark p. 306
trading down p. 305
trading up p. 305
warranty p. 317

INTERNET EXERCISE

www.mcgrawhill.ca/college/berkowitz

New Product News provides a central Internet location on the latest new products. It provides a forum for companies to present their most recent new products. New Product News is updated daily with company press releases from the entire world. Some 30 product categories with one or more new products are typically listed by New Product News each day. A company Website address link follows each new product description.

Visit the New Product News Website at www. newproductnews.com and go to "New items this week." Your assignment is outlined below:

1 Identify and describe how a new product listed promotes more frequent usage, creates a new-use situation, reaches a new market or new users, or changes the value offered to consumers.

2 Identify and describe a new product that is branded using a family branding strategy, a subbranding strategy, or a brand extension strategy.

Want to get better grades, find tips on how to study more effectively, and stay up to date with happenings in the world of marketing? Visit the Online Learning Centre for practice tests, Study Smart software, and much more! www.mcgrawhill.ca/college/berkowitz
Interested in finding out what marketing looks like in the real world? *Marketing Magazine* is just a click away on your OLC! Visit www.mcgrawhill.ca/college/berkowitz

APPLYING MARKETING CONCEPTS AND PERSPECTIVES

1 Listed here are three different products in various stages of the product life cycle. What marketing strategies would you suggest to these companies? (*a*) GTE cellular telephone company—growth stage, (*b*) Mountain Stream tap-water purifying systems—introductory stage, and (*c*) hand-held manual can openers—decline stage.

2 It has often been suggested that products are intentionally made to break down or wear out. Is this strategy a planned product modification approach?

3 The product manager of GE is reviewing the penetration of trash compactors in Canadian homes. After more than two decades in existence, this product is in relatively few homes. What problems can account for this poor acceptance? What is the shape of the trash compactor life cycle?

4 For several years Ferrari has been known as the manufacturer of expensive luxury automobiles. The company plans to attract the major segment of the car-buying market who purchase medium-priced automobiles. As Ferrari considers this trading-down strategy, what branding strategy would you recommend? What are the trade-offs to consider with your strategy?

5 The nature of product warranties has changed as the court system reassesses the meaning of warranties. How does the regulatory trend toward warranties affect product development?

VIDEO CASE 11–1 BMW: "Newness" and the Product Life Cycle

"We're fortunate right now at BMW in that all of our products are new and competitive," says Jim McDowell, vice president of marketing at BMW, as he explains BMW's product life cycle. "Now, how do you do that? You have to introduce new models over time. You have to logically plan out the introductions over time, so you're not changing a whole model range at the same time you're changing another model range."

BMW's strategy is to keep its products in the introduction and growth stages by periodically introducing new models in each of its product lines. In fact, BMW does not like to have any products in the maturity or decline stage of the product life cycle. Explains McDowell, "If a product is declining, we would prefer to withdraw it from the market, as opposed to having a strategy for dealing with the declining product. We're kind of a progressive, go get 'em company, and we don't think it does our brand image any good to have any declining products out there. So that's why we work so hard at managing the growth aspect."

BMW—THE COMPANY AND ITS PRODUCTS

BMW is one of the pre-eminent luxury car manufacturers in Europe, North America, and the world today. BMW produces several lines of cars, including the 3 series,

the 5 series, the 7 series, the Z line (driven by Pierce Brosnan as James Bond in *Goldeneye*), and the new X line, BMW's "sport activity" vehicle line. In addition, BMW is now selling Rovers, a British car line anchored by the internationally popular Land Rover sport utility vehicle, and will begin selling Rolls Royce vehicles in 2003. Sales of all the BMW, Rover, and Land Rover vehicles have been on the rise globally. High-profile image campaigns (such as the James Bond promotion) and the award-winning BMW Website (where users can design their own car) continue to increase the popularity of BMW's products.

PRODUCT LIFE CYCLE

BMW cars typically have a product life cycle of seven years. To keep products in the introductory and growth stages, BMW regularly introduces new models for each of its series to keep the entire series "new." For instance, with the 3 series, it will introduce the new sedan model one year, the new coupe the next year, then the convertible, then the station wagon, and then the sport hatchback. That's a new product introduction for five of the seven years of the product life cycle. McDowell explains, "So, even though we have seven-year life cycles, we constantly try and make the cars meaningfully different and new about every three years. And that involves adding features and other capabilities to the cars as well." How well does this strategy work? BMW often sees its best sales numbers in either the sixth or seventh year after the product introduction.

As global sales have increased, BMW has become aware of some international product-life-cycle differences. For example, it has discovered that some competitive products have life cycles that are shorter or longer than seven years. In Sweden and Britain automotive product life cycles are eight years, while in Japan they are typically only four years long.

BRANDING

"BMW is fortunate—we don't have too much of a dilemma as to what we're going to call our cars." McDowell is referring to BMW's trademark naming system that consists of the product line number and the motor type. For example, the designation "328" tells you the car is in the 3 series and the engine is 2.8 litres in size. BMW has found this naming system to be clear and logical and can be easily understood around the world. The Z and X series don't quite fit in with this system. BMW had a tradition of building experimental, open-air cars and calling them Z's, and hence when the prototype for the Z3 was built, BMW decided to continue with the Z name. For the sport activity vehicle, BMW also used a letter name—the X series—since the four-wheel-drive vehicle didn't fit with the sedan-oriented 3, 5, and 7 series. Other than the Z3 (the third in the Z series) and the X5 (named 5 to symbolize its mid-sized status within that series), the BMW branding strategy is quite simple, unlike the evocative names many car manufacturers choose to garner excitement for their new models.

MANAGING THE PRODUCT THROUGH THE WEB—THE WAVE OF THE FUTURE

One of the ways BMW is improving its product offerings even further is through its innovative Website (www.bmwusa.com). At the site, customers can learn about the particular models, e-mail questions, and request literature or test-drives from their local BMW dealership. What really sets BMW's Website apart from other car manufacturers, though, is the ability for customers to configure a car to their own specifications (interior choices, exterior choices, engine, packages, and options) and then transfer that information to their local dealer. As Carol Burrows, product communications manager for BMW, explains, "The BMW Website is an integrated part of the overall marketing strategy for BMW. The full range of products can be seen and interacted with online. We offer pricing options online. Customers can go to their local dealership via the Website to further discuss costs for purchase of a car. And it is a distribution channel for information that allows people access to the information 24 hours a day at their convenience."

Questions

1 Compare the product life cycle described by BMW for its cars to the product life cycle shown in Figure 11–1. How are they (*a*) similar and (*b*) dissimilar?

2 Based on BMW's typical product life cycle, what marketing strategies are appropriate for the 3 series? The X5?

3 Which of the three ways to manage the product life cycle does BMW utilize with its products—modifying the product, modifying the market, or repositioning the product?

4 How would you describe BMW's branding strategy (manufacturer branding, private branding, or mixed branding)? Why?

5 Go to the BMW Website (www.bmwusa.com) and design a car to your own specifications. How does this enable you as a customer to evaluate the product differently than would be otherwise possible?

12

MANAGING SERVICES

AFTER READING THIS CHAPTER YOU SHOULD BE ABLE TO:

- Describe four unique elements of services.

- Explain the services continuum.

- Understand the ways in which consumers purchase and evaluate services.

- Understand the important role of internal marketing in service organizations.

- Explain the special nature of the marketing mix for services, the Eight Ps of services marketing.

THE HARD ROCK CAFÉ KNOWS WHAT YOU WANT: AN EXCEPTIONAL EXPERIENCE!

Hard Rock Cafés "offer exciting nightlife, great food, and live entertainment," explains CEO and president Pete Beaudrault. In fact, the mission of Hard Rock Café International is "to spread the spirit of rock 'n' roll by delivering an exceptional entertainment and dining experience." If you've ever been to one of the cafés you'll probably agree—they are designed to emphasize the rock 'n' roll theme and provide a unique and distinctive experience for customers.

It all started more than 30 years ago when Eric Clapton gave the original Hard Rock Café in London his guitar to be displayed at his favourite table. Soon another guitar arrived from The Who's Pete Townshend, and ever since the restaurants have displayed memorabilia from rock's favourite musicians and bands including Elvis Presley, Jimi Hendrix, Aerosmith, The Red Hot Chili Peppers, Madonna, U2, Creed, and Matchbox Twenty. Today, there are more than 100 Hard Rock Cafés in 40 countries, including Canadian locations in Montreal and Toronto, and the music memorabilia collection is worth $32 million.

To add to the experience the company is using digital streaming to bring local musical performances to all of its locations. According to Scott Little, Hard Rock's strategic planner, "we'll use the Web to create a forum for up-and-coming artists and to bring national bands that play our large concert venues into the smaller locations." There is also an e-commerce aspect to the experience now as Hard Rock fans can use the Hard Rock Web page as an entertainment portal to listen to and purchase music, buy memorabilia through a special eBay auction service, and subscribe to digital music programming.[1]

The Hard Rock Café is one of many service organizations today competing for customers by offering enjoyable, memorable experiences rather than traditional service transactions. Walt Disney was one of the first to recognize the importance of sights, sounds, tastes, aromas, and textures to provide a unique experience when he created Disneyland. Chuck E. Cheese's uses a similar approach to sell birthday party experiences that include entertainment, food, music, and a fun environment. Companies that sell goods with a service element are also offering experiences. Nike, for example, offers fun activities and promotional events in its own store, Niketown, and Steinway provides a free concert including a pianist, invitations, and hors d'oeuvres in its customers' homes. These businesses are increasing the value of their offering to customers by engaging them in experiential elements of their service.

Some experts believe we are on the verge of a new economic era driven by an *experience economy*.[2] Coffee can be purchased as a commodity in a grocery store and brewed at home at a cost of about 10 cents per cup. Coffee can also be purchased from 7-Eleven, where consumers pay for the convenience of the service, for a cost of about 75 cents per cup. But most of us have often paid about $3 per cup at a Starbucks, where the look of the shop, the jazz music, and the baristas' knowledge of the beans creates a "coffee experience" that is still a good value. ESPN Zone, Home Depot, Planet Hollywood, and many other companies are responding to consumers' preferences for compelling experiences.

As the actions of the Hard Rock Café and the other examples above illustrate, the marketing of services is dynamic and challenging. In this chapter we discuss how services differ from traditional products (goods), how service consumers make purchase decisions, and the important aspects of developing and managing the marketing mix for services.

THE SERVICE ECONOMY

SERVICES
Intangible activities, benefits, or satisfactions that an organization provides to consumers in exchange for money or something else of value.

As defined in Chapter 1, **services** are activities, deeds, or other basic intangibles offered for sale to consumers in exchange for money or something else of value. One services-marketing expert suggests that services permeate every aspect of our lives.[3] We use transportation services like Via Rail (www.viarail.ca), Air Canada (www.aircanada.ca), and Thrifty car rental (www.thrifty.ca) when we travel. We use restaurant services like McDonald's (www.mcdonalds.com) to feed us and hotels like the Four Seasons (www.fourseasons.com) to put a roof over our heads when we are away from home. When we are at home, we rely on electricity providers like Ontario Power Generation (www.opg.com) to keep the lights on, and telephone services from Bell Canada (www.bell.ca) to keep in touch with family. We also use Sympatico (www.sympatico.ca) to keep us connected to the Net and Molly Maid (www.mollymaid.ca) to keep our house clean.

At work, we rely on Canada Post (www.canadapost.ca) to deliver our mail, and Purolator courier (www.purolator.com) to get our urgent documents to their destination overnight. And we use Servicemaster (www.servicemaster.ca) to keep our offices clean and Intercon Security services (www.interconsecurity.com) to keep them safe. Our employers use public relations firms like Edelman Public Relations (www.edelman.com) and advertising agencies like Cossette Communications (www.cossette.com) to maintain their corporate image, while we use the services of First Choice Haircutters (www.firstchoice.com) to maintain our personal appearance. We use colleges and universities to improve our minds, and online employment services like Workopolis (www.workopolis.com) to find us a better job. We use financial institutions like Scotiabank (www.scotiabank.com) to safeguard our money, and buy peace of mind with life insurance from Canada Life (www.canadalife.com). We use lawyers to draw up our wills, and E*Trade.ca to trade our stocks. In our leisure time we pop in to Blockbuster Video (www.blockbuster.ca) to rent a DVD, or stop by a Famous Players theatre (www.famousplayers.ca) to catch a flick.

We might even visit one of the casinos run by the Great Canadian Gaming Corporation (www.gcgaming.com).

We might use an online travel service like Travelocity (www.travelocity.ca) to book our well-deserved vacation and stay and ski at Whistler Resort, run by Intrawest Corporation (www.intrawest.com). While we're there, we might use our ING Direct card to pay for everything (www.ingdirect.ca). Of course, we always need to stay in touch, so the wireless telecommunications services provided by Rogers AT&T (www.rogers.com) come in handy. Since Whistler Resort doesn't allow dogs we had to use a boarding kennel or a personal pet watching service to care for our border collie. When we get home we realize the car needs an oil change so we drive to Mr. Lube (www.mrlube.com) to get it done. The washing machine also sounds a little funny, so we call the Maytag repair man. After a long day, we just might watch some digital cable (www.videotron.ca) and order in a pizza (www.pizzahut.ca). Because the television looks a little blurry, we decide that it is time to get rid of our eyeglasses and contact TLC Laser Eye Centres (www.tlcvision.com) to see if they might help. And, because we believe in future planning, we have already decided on the nursing home for our parents (www.extendicare.com) and even pre-purchased their funerals and burial plots. Services: from cradle to grave, we rely on them.

Services have become one of the most important components of the Canadian as well as world economy. The services sector now accounts for close to 60 percent of global gross national product, and with many service firms operating internationally exports of services are also increasing. In Canada, more than 60 cents out of every consumer dollar is spent on buying services. More than 7 out of 10 Canadians work in the service sector. In other words, more Canadians are doing things (performing services) than making things (producing goods). Experts predict that nearly all new employment in the future will be created by the service sector. They suggest that if current trends continue, almost all Canadians will be working in services by 2025.[4] Much of this employment is expected to be created by small service companies, particularly those offering personal, professional, and informational services. In fact, one of the fastest-growing segments of the Canadian services economy is information technology services, which includes computer training. And, of course, the Internet is now the new frontier for many newly emerging services such as online travel services, people locator services, and financial advisory services.

THE UNIQUENESS OF SERVICES

www.royalbank.com

FOUR I'S OF SERVICE
Four unique elements to services: intangibility, inconsistency, inseparability, and inventory.

As we noted in Chapter 10, when consumers buy products they are purchasing a bundle of tangible and intangible attributes that deliver value and satisfaction. In general, it is very difficult to define a pure good or a pure service. A pure good implies that the consumer obtains benefits from the good alone without any added value from service; conversely, a pure service assumes there is no "goods" element to the service that the customer receives. In reality, most services contain some goods element. For example, at McDonald's you receive a hamburger; at the Royal Bank you are provided with a bank statement. And most goods offer some service—even if it is only delivery. In fact, many goods-producing firms are adding service offerings as a way to differentiate their products from those of their competitors.

But there are certain commonalities between *services as products* that set them apart from tangible goods. The four unique elements to services are intangibility, inconsistency, inseparability, and inventory. These elements are sometimes referred to as the **four I's of services.**

Intangibility   Services are intangible; that is, they can't be held, touched, or seen before the purchase decision. In contrast, before purchasing a traditional product, a consumer can touch a box of laundry detergent, kick the tire of an automobile, or sample a new breakfast cereal. A major marketing need for services is to make them tangible or to show the benefits of using a service. American Express emphasizes

Why do many services emphasize their tangible benefits? The answer appears in the text.

Fairmont Hotels & Resorts

www.fairmont.com

the gifts available to cardholders through its Membership Rewards program; a leading insurance company says, "You're in Good Hands with Allstate"; Fairmont Hotels tells business travellers that they'll have the convenience of their offices away from their offices, including computer hook-ups and personal services.

Inconsistency Developing, pricing, promoting, and delivering services is challenging because the quality of a service is often inconsistent. Since services depend on the people who provide them, their quality varies with each person's capabilities and day-to-day job performance. Inconsistency is much more of a problem with services than it is with tangible goods. Tangible products can be good or bad in terms of quality, but with modern production lines the quality will at least be consistent. On the other hand, the Toronto Maple Leafs hockey team may look like potential Stanley Cup winners on one day, but lose by 10 goals the next day. Or a cello player with the Vancouver Symphony may not be feeling well and give a less-than-average performance. Whether the service involves tax assistance at Ernst & Young or guest relations at the Sheraton, organizations attempt to reduce inconsistency through standardization and training. Standardization through automation is becoming increasingly popular in many service industries including banking.

Inseparability A third difference between services and goods is inseparability. There are two dimensions to inseparability. The first is inseparability of production and consumption. Whereas goods are first produced, then sold, and then consumed, services are sold first, and then produced and consumed simultaneously. For example, you can buy a ticket at the Air Canada ticket office, then fly and consume in-flight service as it is being produced. The second dimension of inseparability is that, in most cases, the consumer cannot (and does not) separate the deliverer of the service from the service itself. For example, to receive an education, a person may attend a university. The quality of the education may be high, but if the student has difficulty interacting with instructors, finds counselling services poor, or does not receive adequate library or computer assistance, he or she may not be satisfied with the educational experience. In short, a student's evaluations of education will be influenced primarily by the perceptions of instructors, counsellors, librarians, and other people at the university responsible for delivering the education.

The amount of interaction between the consumer and the service deliverer or provider depends on the extent to which the consumer must be physically present

People often play an important role in delivering many services.

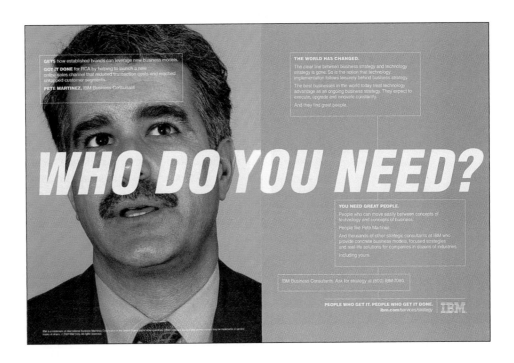

www.bmo.com

to receive the service. Some services such as golf lessons and medical diagnoses require the customer to participate in the delivery process. Other services, such as car repair or dry cleaning, that process tangible objects require less involvement from the customer. Finally, many services such as banking and insurance can now be delivered electronically, often requiring no face-to-face customer interaction, for example Bank of Montreal's Web-based banking service.

Inventory   Inventory of services is different from that of goods. Inventory problems exist with goods because many items are perishable and because there are costs associated with handling inventory. With services, inventory carrying costs are more subjective and are related to **idle production capacity**, which occurs when the service provider is available but there is no demand. The inventory cost of a service is the cost of paying the person used to provide the service along with any needed equipment. If a physician is paid to see patients but no one schedules an appointment, the fixed cost of the idle physician's salary is a high inventory carrying cost. In some service businesses, however, the provider of the service is on commission (the Merrill Lynch stockbroker) or is a part-time employee (a counterperson at McDonald's). In these businesses, inventory carrying costs can be significantly lower or nonexistent because the idle production capacity can be cut back by reducing hours or having no salary to pay because of the commission compensation system.

Figure 12–1 shows a scale of inventory carrying costs, represented on the high end by airlines and hospitals and on the low end by real estate agencies. The inventory carrying costs of airlines are high because of high-salaried pilots and very

IDLE PRODUCTION CAPACITY
When the service provider is available but there is no demand.

FIGURE 12–1
Inventory carrying costs of services

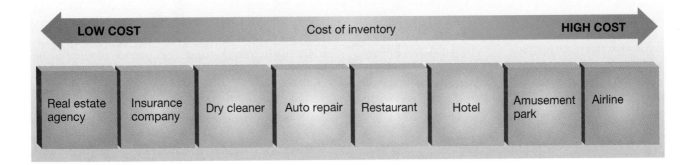

LOW COST	Cost of inventory	HIGH COST

| Real estate agency | Insurance company | Dry cleaner | Auto repair | Restaurant | Hotel | Amusement park | Airline |

expensive equipment. In contrast, real estate agencies have employees who work on commission and need little expensive equipment to conduct business. One reason why service providers must maintain production capacity is because of the importance of time to today's customers. People don't want to wait long for service.

The Service Continuum

The four I's differentiate services from goods in most cases, but as we mentioned earlier most products sold cannot be defined as pure goods or pure services. For example, does IBM Canada sell goods or services? While the company sells computers and software, a major component of its business is information technology services including consulting and training. Does Rogers Communications provide only goods when it publishes *Marketing* magazine, or does it consider itself a service because it presents up-to-date Canadian business information? As companies look at what they bring to the market, there is a range from the tangible to the intangible or good-dominant to service-dominant offerings referred to as the **service continuum** (Figure 12–2).

Teaching, nursing, and the theatre are intangible, service-dominant activities, and intangibility, inconsistency, inseparability, and inventory are major concerns in their marketing. Salt, neckties, and dog food are tangible goods, and the problems represented by the four I's are not relevant in their marketing. However, some businesses are a mix of intangible-service and tangible-good factors. A clothing tailor provides a service but also a good, the finished suit. How pleasant, courteous, and attentive the tailor is to the customer is an important component of the service, and how well the clothes fit is an important part of the product. As shown in Figure 12–2, a fast-food restaurant is about half tangible goods (the food) and half intangible services (courtesy, cleanliness, speed, convenience).

For many businesses today it is useful to distinguish between their core service and their supplementary services. A core service offering—such as a bank account, for example—also has supplementary services such as deposit assistance, parking or drive-through availability, ATMs, and monthly statements. Supplementary services often allow service providers to differentiate their offering from competitors, and they may add value for consumers. While there are many potential supplementary services, key categories of supplementary services include information delivery, consultation, order taking, billing procedures, and payment options.[5]

SERVICE CONTINUUM
A range from the tangible to the intangible or goods-dominant to service-dominant offerings available in the marketplace.

FIGURE 12–2
Service continuum

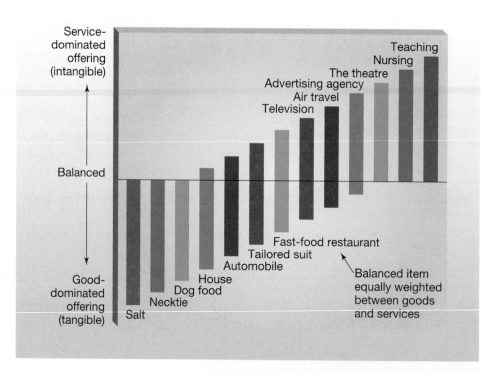

1. What are the four I's of services?

2. Would inventory carrying costs for an accounting firm employing chartered accountants be (a) high, (b) low, or (c) nonexistent?

3. To eliminate inconsistencies, organizations rely on _____ and _____.

HOW CONSUMERS PURCHASE SERVICES

Universities, hospitals, hotels, and lawyers are facing an increasingly competitive environment. Successful service organizations, like successful goods-producing firms, must understand how the consumer makes a purchase decision and a post-purchase evaluation. Service companies will be better able to position themselves effectively if they understand why a consumer chooses to use a particular sevice. Moreover, by understanding the consumer's postpurchase evaluation process, service companies can identify sources of customer satisfaction or dissatisfaction.

Purchasing a Service

Because of their intangible nature, it is generally more difficult for consumers to evaluate services before purchase than it is to evaluate goods (see Figure 12–3). Tangible goods such as clothes, jewellery and furniture have *search* qualities, such as colour, size, and style, which can be determined before purchase. But rarely can a consumer inspect, try out, or test a service in advance. This is because some services such as restaurants and child care have *experience* qualities, which can be discerned only after purchase or consumption. Other services provided by special-ized professionals such as medical diagnosis and legal services have *credence* qualities, or characteristics that the consumer may find impossible to evaluate even after purchase and consumption.[6]

The experience and credence qualities of services forces consumers to make a prepurchase examination of the service by assessing the tangible characteristics that are part of, or surround, the service.[7] In other words, consumers will evaluate what they cannot see by what they can see. For example, you might consider the actual appearance of the dentist's office, or its physical location, when making a judgment about the possible quality of dental services that might be supplied there.

FIGURE 12–3
Services are more difficult to evaluate than goods before a purchase

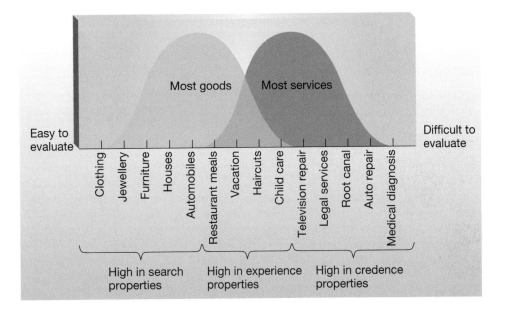

Many service organizations go to great lengths to ensure that the tangible aspects of the services convey the appropriate image and serve as surrogate indicators of the intangible service to be provided.

Service marketers recognize that because of the uncertainty created by experience and credence qualities, consumers turn to personal sources of information such as early adopters, opinion leaders, and reference group members during the purchase decision process. Accordingly, services marketers work to ensure customer satisfaction in order to ensure positive word-of-mouth referral.

Customer Contact Audit

CUSTOMER CONTACT AUDIT

A flowchart of the points of interaction between consumer and service provider.

To better understand the service purchasing process, service firms can develop a **customer contact audit**—a flowchart of the points of interaction between consumer and service provider.[8] These points of interaction are often referred to as *contact points* or *service encounter elements*. Constructing a customer contact audit is particularly important in high-contact services such as educational institutions, health care, and even automobile rental agencies. Figure 12–4 illustrates a customer contact audit for renting a car from Hertz. The interactions identified in a customer contact audit often serve as the basis for developing better services and delivering them more efficiently and effectively.

When a customer decides to rent a car he or she (1) contacts the rental company (see Figure 12–4). A customer service representative receives the information (2) and checks the availability of the car at the desired location. When a customer arrives at the rental site (3), the reservation system is again accessed, and the customer provides information regarding payment, address, and driver's licence (4). A car is assigned to the customer (5), who proceeds by bus to the car pickup (6). On return to the rental location (7), the car is parked and the customer checks in (8),

FIGURE 12–4

Customer contact in car rental (green shaded boxes indicate customer activity)

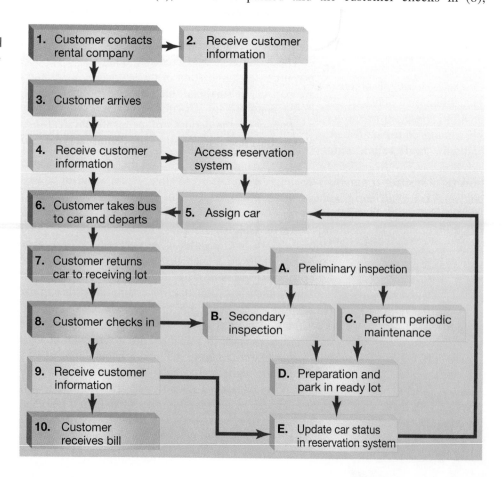

providing information on mileage, gas consumption, and damages (9). A bill is subsequently prepared (10).

Each of the steps numbered 1 to 10 is a customer contact point where the tangible aspects of Hertz service are seen by the customer. Figure 12–4, however, also shows a series of steps lettered A to E that involve two levels of inspections on the automobile. These steps are essential in providing a car that runs, but they are not points of customer interaction. To be successful, Hertz must create a competitive advantage in the sequence of interactions with the customer. In essence, Hertz must attempt to deliver the car in a seamless and timely manner, limiting the amount of time and effort required on the part of the customer. The customer contact audit is one tool that may help create that competitive advantage for Hertz or any other service firm.

Postpurchase Evaluation

Once a consumer tries a service, how is it evaluated? The primary method is by comparing expectations about the service offering with the actual experience a consumer has with the service.[9] Differences between a consumer's expectations and experience are often identified through **gap analysis**. This type of analysis asks consumers to assess their expectations and experiences on various dimensions of service quality. Expectations are influenced by word-of-mouth communications, personal needs, past experience, and marketing communications activities, while actual experiences are determined by the way an organization delivers the service.

GAP ANALYSIS
An evaluation tool that compares expectations about a service offering to the actual experience a consumer has with the service.

One popular instrument developed by researchers to measure service quality and to conduct gap analysis is called SERVQUAL.[10] Researchers measure consumers' expectations and their actual service experience using a multi-item instrument. Consumers are asked to rate the importance of various dimensions of service quality and to score the service in terms of their expectations and actual experience. SERVQUAL provides the services marketer with a consumer rating of service quality and an indication of where improvements can be made.

Researchers using SERVQUAL have found that consumers judge service quality along five key dimensions: tangibles, reliability, responsiveness, assurance, and empathy (see Figure 12–5).[11] However, the relative importance of these various dimensions of service quality has been found to vary by type of service.[12]

Service marketers must understand what dimensions consumers use in judging service quality, recognize the relative importance of each dimension, find out how they rate in terms of service quality, and take actions to deliver service quality that is consistent with consumer expectations. As a consumer, you play an important role in ensuring that service firms deliver service quality. However, as the Ethics and

---

ETHICS AND SOCIAL RESPONSIBILITY ALERT   The Consumer's Role in Improving Service Quality

Research has shown that many consumers are reluctant to provide feedback to service firms about the quality of their services. In fact, current studies show that only 5 to 10 percent of service customers offered direct feedback to service firms that might be important in improving service quality.

Most services marketers want to know if customers are happy or satisfied with the services provided, and many try a variety of methods (e.g., customer response or comment cards) to obtain or encourage answers regarding perceived service quality. However, most consumers do not take the time to respond, even if they are dissatisfied. Instead, consumers, if unhappy, will simply not return and will switch providers. Moreover, while they will not take the time to tell the organization about their dissatisfaction, they will take the time to tell their friends and co-workers.

The question is, why? If you have a problem with a service firm—whether it is inconvenient hours or rude employees—wouldn't it be better to tell the firm? Is it ethical for you to complain to your friends without informing the firm?

FIGURE 12–5
Dimensions of service quality

DIMENSION	DEFINITION	EXAMPLES OF QUESTIONS AIRLINE CUSTOMERS MIGHT ASK
Tangibles	Appearance of physical facilities, equipment, personnel, and communications materials.	Are the plane, the gate and baggage area clean?
Reliability	Ability to perform the promised service dependably and accurately.	Is my flight on time?
Responsiveness	Willingness to help customers and provide prompt service.	Are the flight attendants willing to answer my question?
Assurance	Respectful, considerate personnel who listen to customers and answer their questions.	Are the employees knowledgeable?
Empathy	Knowing the customer and understanding their needs. Approachable and available.	Do the employees know that I have special seating and meal requirements?

Social Responsibility Alert points out, sometimes consumers do not provide the feedback necessary to improve service quality.[13]

There are benefits to the customer and the service provider when service quality is improved. For the customer, improved service quality increases the likelihood that you will return to the same provider that offers the benefits of continuity of a single provider, customized service potential, reduced stress due to repetitive purchase process, and an absence of switching costs. For the service provider, retaining existing customers is much less costly than attracting new customers, and repeat customers are clearly more profitable over time.

Service firms see service quality as a basis for relationship marketing. And recent surveys have indicated that consumers concur. In fact, these same surveys indicate that many customers are intersted in being "relationship customers," provided, of course, that the relationship is balanced in terms of loyalty, benefits, and respect for privacy.[14]

Concept Check

1. What are the differences between search, experience, and credence qualities?

2. What is gap analysis?

3. An instrument or approach used to measure service quality is _____.

MANAGING THE MARKETING OF SERVICES: THE EIGHT Ps

Just as the unique aspects of services necessitate changes in the consumer's purchase process, the marketing management process requires special adaptation. As we have seen in earlier chapters, the traditional marketing mix is composed of the Four Ps: product, price, place, and promotion. Careful management of the Four Ps is important when marketing services. However, the distinctive nature of services requires that other additional variables be effectively managed by service marketers.

Logos create service identities

The concept of an expanded marketing mix for services has been adopted by many service-marketing organizations. In addition to the traditional Four Ps, the services marketing mix includes people, physical evidence, process, and productivity, or the Eight Ps.[15] Let's now discuss the special nature of the marketing mix for services.

Product (Service)

To a large extent, the concepts of the product component of the marketing mix discussed in Chapters 10 and 11 apply equally to Cheerios (a good) and to Royal Bank Visa (a service). Managers of goods and services must design the product concept, whether a good or a service, with the features and benefits desired by customers. An important aspect of the product concept is branding. Because services are intangible and, therefore, more difficult to describe, the brand name or identifying logo of the service organization is particularly important when a consumer makes a purchase decision. Therefore, service organizations such as banks, hotels, rental car companies, and restaurants rely on branding strategies in order to distinguish themselves in the minds of the consumers. Strong brand names and symbols are important for service marketers, not only for differentiation purposes but also for conveying an image of quality. A service firm with a well-established brand reputation will also find it easier to market new services than firms without such brand reputation.[16]

Take a look at the figures at the top of the page to determine how successful some companies have been in branding their services by name, logo, or symbol.

Price

In service industries, price is often referred to in many ways. Hospitals refer to *charges*; consultants, lawyers, physicians, and accountants to *fees*; airlines to *fares*; hotels to *rates*; and colleges and universities to *tuition*. Because of the intangible nature of services, price is often perceived by consumers as a possible indicator of the quality of the service. For example, would you be willing to risk a $10 dental surgery? Or a $50 divorce lawyer? In many cases, there may be few other available cues for the customer to judge a service, so price becomes very important as a quality indicator.[17]

Pricing of services also goes beyond the traditional tasks of setting the selling price. When customers buy services they consider non-monetary costs such as time as well as the mental and physical efforts required to consume the service. Therefore, service marketers must also try to minimize the non-monetary costs customers may bear in purchasing and using a service. Finally, as we will see later in this section, pricing also plays a role in balancing consumer demand for services.

Place (Distribution)

Place or distribution is a major factor in developing a service marketing strategy because of the inseparability of services from the producer. Rarely are intermediaries involved in the distribution of a service; the distribution site and the service

Price influences perceptions of services.

deliverer are the tangible components of the service. And, until recently, customers generally had to go to the service provider's physical location to purchase the service. Increased competition has forced many service firms to consider the value of convenient distribution and to find new ways of distributing services to demanding customers. Hairstyling chains, like First Choice Haircutters, legal firms, and accounting firms all use multiple locations for the distribution of services. Technology is also being used to deliver services beyond the provider's physical locations. For example, in the banking industry customers of participating banks using the Interac system can access any one of thousands of automated teller machines across Canada and need not visit their own specific bank branch. The availability of electronic distribution of services over the Internet also allows for global reach and coverage for a variety of services including travel services, banking, education, entertainment, and many other information-based services. With speed and convenience becoming increasingly important to customers when they select service providers, service firms can leverage the use of the Internet to deliver services on a 24/7 basis, in real time, on a global scale. In short, forward-looking firms no longer see face-to-face delivery of services as the only distribution option.[18]

Promotion

The value of promotion, especially advertising, for many services is to show consumers the benefits of purchasing the service. For example, advertising can be an effective way to demonstrate attributes such as availability, location, consistent quality, efficient and courteous service, and assurance of satisfaction.[19] While many service firms are using the Internet as an alternative distribution channel, they are also using it as an advertising or promotional medium. Many community colleges and universities, for example, have their own well-designed Websites to convey their messages to prospective students. Tourism marketers are also finding the Internet a valuable tool in reaching their prospective target markets. Use the Web Link to check out Nunavut Tourism's Website.

Public relations is an important promotional tool for service firms. It is particularly useful in conveying a proper image and in helping to support a firm's positioning strategy. Public relations tools such as event sponsorship or public-service activities are very popular among service companies. This is particularly true for professional service firms, which are often restricted in the use of advertising by their professional governing bodies.

WEB LINK   Nunavut's Tourism Initiative

http://www.mcgrawhill.ca

Canada's newest territory, Nunavut is trying to attract tourism to the northern region of our country. Go to their Website (www.nunavut.com). What do you think of the site? Given they are targeting adventure tourists and eco-tourists, are they providing enough information? Is the message and image they are trying to convey appropriate? Do you think the site would encourage tourists to visit Nunavut?

Personal selling also plays an important role in services marketing. It has been said that when a consumer buys a service, he or she is buying the person selling the service. Personal selling is valuable not only in attracting customers but also in retaining them. Increasingly, many service marketers are following the path set by packaged-goods firms; that is, they are developing integrated marketing communications plans.[20]

People

Many services depend on people for the creation and delivery of services. In such cases, the service employee will play a central role in attracting, building, and maintaining relationships with customers.[21] The nature of the interaction between employees and customers strongly influences the customer's perceptions of service quality. In short, customers will often judge the quality of service they receive based on the performances of the people providing the service. This aspect of services marketing has led to a concept called internal marketing.[22]

INTERNAL MARKETING
The notion that a service organization must focus on its employees, or internal market, before successful programs can be directed at customers.

Internal marketing is based on the notion that in order for a service organization to serve its customers well, it must care for and treat its employees like valued customers. In essence, it must focus on its employees (or its internal market) before successful marketing efforts can be directed at customers.[23] Internal marketing involves creating an organizational climate in general, and jobs in particular, that lead to the right service personnel performing the service in the right way. The organization must properly select, train, and motivate all its employees to work together to provide service quality and customer satisfaction. Research has shown that service organizations that want to be truly customer-oriented must be employee-oriented.[24] Finally, customer behaviour influences not only their own service outcomes, but also other customers. Whether at a hockey game or in a classroom, customers can influence the perceived quality of service by their actions. Therefore, the *people* element in services includes not only employees and the customer, but also other customers.

Physical Evidence

The appearance of the environment in which the service is delivered and where the firm and customer interact can influence the customer's perception of the service. The physical evidence of the service includes all the tangibles surrounding the service: the buildings, landscaping, vehicles, furnishings, signage, brochures, and equipment. Service firms need to manage physical evidence carefully and systematically in order to convey the proper impression of the service to the customer. This is sometimes referred to as *impression management*. With highly tangible services, physical evidence provides an opportunity for the firm to send consistent and strong messages about the nature of the service to be delivered.

Process

In services marketing, *process* refers to the actual procedures, mechanisms, and flow of activities by which the service is created and delivered. The actual creation and delivery steps that the customer experiences provide customers with evidence on which to judge the service. In services marketing, process involves not only "what" gets created, but also "how" it gets created. The customer contact audit discussed earlier in the chapter is relevant to understanding the service process discussed here. The customer contact audit—the flowchart of the points of interaction between customer and service provider—can serve as a basis for ensuring better service creation and delivery processes. Badly designed processes are likely to create unhappy customers, and poorly conceived operational processes can make it difficult for front-line employees to do their jobs well. Mr. Lube (www.mrlube.com) believes it has the right process in the vehicle oil change and fluid exchange service business. Customers don't need appointments, most stores are open seven days a week, and customers are in and out in 15 to 20 minutes. While the service is being performed customers can drink a coffee and read the newspaper.

Productivity

Most services have a limited capacity due to the inseparability of the service from the service provider and the perishable nature of the service. For example, a patient must be in the hospital at the same time as the surgeon to receive an appendectomy, and only one patient can be helped at that time. Similarly, no additional surgery can be conducted tomorrow because of an unused operating room or an available surgeon today—the service capacity is lost if it is not used. So, if service marketers have a relatively fixed capacity to produce a service, they must make that capacity as productive as possible without compromising service quality.[25] This is referred to as **capacity management**.

CAPACITY MANAGEMENT
Making service capacity as productive as possible without compromising service quality.

Service organizations must manage the availability of the offering so that (1) demand matches capacity over the duration of the demand cycle (e.g., one day, week, month, year) and (2) the organization's assets are used in ways that will maximize the return on investment.[26] Figure 12–6 shows how a hotel tries to manage its capacity during the high and low seasons. Differing price structures are assigned to each segment of consumers to help moderate or adjust demand for the service. Airline contracts fill a fixed number of rooms throughout the year. In the slow season, when more rooms are available, tour packages at appealing prices are used to attract groups or conventions, such as an offer for seven nights at a reduced price. Weekend packages are also offered to buyers. In high-demand season, groups are less desirable because more individual guests will be available and willing to pay higher prices. The use of **off-peak pricing**, which consists of charging different prices during different times of the day or days of the week to reflect variations in demand for the service, plays an important role in capacity management. For example, airlines offer discounts for weekend travel, movie theatres offer matinee pricing, and restaurants offer early-bird pricing in order to maintain the productivity of their service capacity.

OFF-PEAK PRICING
Charging different prices during different times of the day or days of the week to reflect variations in demand for the service.

SERVICES IN THE FUTURE

What can we expect from the services industry in the future? New and better services, of course, and an unprecedented variety of choices—changes that are being driven by deregulation, technology, and consumer interests.

Deregulation in telecommunications, financial services, utilities, professional services, and other service industries has led to a greater variety of services and, in

FIGURE 12-6

Managing capacity in a hotel

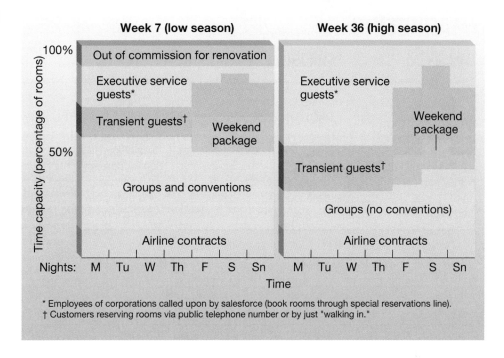

* Employees of corporations called upon by salesforce (book rooms through special reservations line).
† Customers reserving rooms via public telephone number or by just "walking in."

many cases, to a convergence of many of the suppliers of services. Many financial services suppliers, for example, have moved to a complete one-stop-shopping environment where consumers can obtain loans, credit cards, mortgages, and insurance all under one roof—or even completely online. Traditional manufacturers have also added service offerings. For example, General Electric is now in the financial services industry, offering consumer and commercial loans.

Technology is also changing the services marketing landscape. Internet-based banking and travel services have established themselves and now new "cyberservices" such as online photography Websites have emerged. It is now possible to obtain videos, movies, and even entire textbooks like this one electronically.[27] Educational institutions are offering courses and even entire degrees via Web-based learning sites. Readers of this text can interact with other students and communicate with their instructors on a dedicated Website. And one of the hottest new services on the Internet? Matchmaking! Yes, according to the experts there may soon be as many as 10 000 matchmaking services available online. The services are so popular in Japan that they are offered in i-mode, the technology that allows Web access from wireless phones.[28]

Other changes in services are being driven by changes in consumer interests. Experts suggest that "time will be the currency of the future." Consumers are searching for new services that reduce the time needed to go to the post office, bank, or supermarket or to prepare food, clean clothes, or maintain their homes. Consumers are placing increased demand on service companies, expecting greater choice, convenience, information, responsiveness, and access to service. Technology is playing a key role in satisfying those demands. Many banking customers, for example, prefer to visit their bank as little as possible and many are now doing more business by phone or over the Internet. Virtual banks such as ING are available to Canadian banking customers, who now have the choice of doing everything electronically or dealing with a real person at a traditional brick and mortar bank.

Finally, as we mentioned in the chapter opener, consumers will be looking to purchase "experiences," not just basic goods and services. Many services have become commoditized, or are seen by most consumers to be virtually identical. In that case, price often becomes the driver when making a service selection. But many

MARKETING NEWSNET

Marketing Experiences!

As we have discussed in this chapter, many services have become commoditized, or seen by most consumers to be virtually identical. In order for service firms to differentiate among themselves, many have turned to selling experiences and not just services per se. Service marketers believe that if they can customize a service for a customer, it can transform the service into an experience. Experts believe that services can be successfully transformed into experiences if (1) the service offering can be made memorable (it remains with the customer for a long time), (2) the customer is drawn into the offering such that they feel a real sensation (such as actually swimming with dolphins), and (3) highly skilled employees (actors) can dynamically personalize each experience for each customer.

Disney has long been recognized as offering experiences to its theme park visitors or guests. But now other services marketers are also in the experience business. For example, British Airways states "what we do is to go beyond the function (air passenger service) and compete on the basis of providing an experience. The aircraft and the flight is the stage for a distinctive en route experience." Experience-economy experts Pine and Gilmore suggest there are four types of experiences that marketers can offer customers: (1) entertainment, (2) educational, (3) esthetic, and (4) escapist. They suggest that service firms that can offer some or all of these experiences in the right combination will be successful experience marketers.

consumers want something more than just a commoditized service and are prepared to pay for it. If a service firm can customize a service, it turns it into an experience. For example, Pizza Hut can offer a customer more than a meal; it will host your child's birthday party and customize it the way you want it.[29] The Fairmont Southampton Princess Resort in Bermuda has plenty of competition on the tiny island. While prices for rooms at the Fairmont are competitive with other upscale resorts, it offers its guests a unique experience that the others do not: a chance to swim with dolphins. And customers are lining up to pay for that experience. The price? About $150 per person for 45 minutes! Read the accompanying Marketing NewsNet to see just how services marketers can create experiences, which are a distinct offering from services.[30]

The Fairmont Southampton Princess Resort markets more than a nice place to vacation: it creates and markets experiences, like swimming with dolphins.

Concept Check

1. Matching demand with capacity is the focus of _____ management.

2. What factors will influence future changes in services?

SUMMARY

1 Services are activities, deeds, or other basic intangibles offered for sale to consumers in exchange for money or something else of value. Services have become one of the most important components of the Canadian and world economy.

2 Services share four commonalities that set them apart from goods: intangibility, inconsistency, inseparability, and inventory.

3 Intangibility refers to the difficulty in communicating service benefits. Inconsistency refers to the difficulty of providing the same level of quality each time a service is purchased. Inseparability means that services are produced and consumed simultaneously and that consumers cannot separate the service deliverer from the service itself. Inventory costs for services are related to the cost of maintaining production capacity.

4 Many companies are not clearly service-based or goods-based organizations. As companies look at what they bring to the market, there is a range from the tangible to the intangible or goods-dominant to service-dominant offerings, referred to as the service continuum.

5 Consumers can evaluate goods by the search properties, but must evaluate services by their experience and credence properties.

6 A customer contact audit is a flowchart of the points of interaction between a service provider and its customers.

7 A gap analysis determines if consumers' expectations are different from their actual experiences. Gap analysis usually measures dimensions of service quality including tangibles, reliability, responsiveness, assurance, and empathy.

8 Internal marketing is based on the notion that in order for a service organization to serve its customers well, it must care for and treat its employees like valued customers. In short, it must focus on its employees, or internal market, before successful programs can be directed at customers.

9 Because services are intangible, branding a service is particularly important in order to differentiate the service and to convey an image of quality. The brand name or identifying logo helps "tangiblize" the service for the consumer.

10 The inseparability of production and consumption of services means capacity management is important in services marketing. Capacity management involves smoothing demand to meet capacity.

11 The intangible nature of services makes price an important cue to service quality.

12 Distribution is important as a tangible component of a service offering. Technology is allowing service firms to expand their distribution including the use of marketspace.

13 Promotion is important in services marketing in order to demonstrate to consumers the benefits of purchasing a service.

14 Three factors are driving changes in the service industry: deregulation, technology, and consumer interests.

KEY TERMS AND CONCEPTS

capacity management p. 336
customer contact audit p. 330
four I's of services p. 325
gap analysis p. 331
idle production capacity p. 327

internal marketing p. 335
off-peak pricing p. 336
service continuum p. 328
services p. 324

INTERNET EXERCISE

www.mcgrawhill.ca/college/berkowitz

The American Marketing Association provides a variety of useful services for anyone interested in the latest service-marketing concepts and strategies. Go to AMA's Website (www.ama.org) and click on "resources," "shared interest groups," and "services marketing" to review the information and services available. If you click on "publications," you can review articles from a variety of publications including *Marketing Health Services*. Investigate a services marketing topic that is of interest to you.

1 What publications are available regarding the topic you selected?

2 Describe two insights you obtained from the summaries of the publications.

Want to get better grades, find tips on how to study more effectively, and stay up to date with happenings in the world of marketing? Visit the Online Learning Centre for practice tests, Study Smart software, and much more! www.mcgrawhill.ca/college/berkowitz
Interested in finding out what marketing looks like in the real world? *Marketing Magazine* is just a click away on your OLC! Visit www.mcgrawhill.ca/college/berkowitz

APPLYING MARKETING CONCEPTS AND PERSPECTIVES

1 Explain how the four I's of services would apply to a branch office of the Royal Bank.

2 Idle production capacity may be related to inventory or capacity management. How would the pricing component of the marketing mix reduce idle production capacity for (*a*) a car wash, (*b*) a stage theatre group, and (*c*) a university?

3 What are the search, experience, and credence properties of an airline for the business traveller and pleasure traveller? What qualities are most important to each group?

4 This chapter showed that consumers judge service quality along five key dimensions: tangibles, reliability, responsiveness, assurance, and empathy. Indicate the one dimension that is most important to you in judging service quality of each of the following services: (*a*) physicians, (*b*) banking, (*c*) car rental companies, and (*d*) dry cleaning.

5 The text suggests that internal marketing is necessary before a successful marketing effort can be directed at consumers. Why is this particularly true for service organizations?

6 Outline the capacity management strategies that an airline must consider.

7 Draw the channel of distribution for the following services: (*a*) a restaurant, (*b*) a hospital, and (*c*) a hotel.

8 How does off-peak pricing influence demand for services?

9 In recent years, many service businesses have begun to provide their employees with uniforms. Explain the rationale behind this strategy in terms of the concepts discussed in this chapter.

10 Look at the service continuum in Figure 12–2. Explain how the following points in the continuum differ in terms of consistency: (*a*) salt, (*b*) automobile, (*c*) advertising agency, and (*d*) teaching.

CASE 12–1 National Hockey League

The National Hockey League (www.nhl.com) traces its beginnings to November 22, 1917, and as such is the second-oldest professional sports league of the four major team sports in North America. Only professional baseball predates it. Throughout its history, the NHL has been recognized for its ideas and innovations. For example, the NHL was the first major sports league to introduce a playoff system, which has been adopted by all other major sports.

However, historically the NHL and many of the team owners had a negative mindset toward marketing. Marketing was actually considered unseemly. The general approach was to simply open the doors of the arena and wait for customers to come. But with rising costs to operate the league, particularly player salaries, the NHL needed a bigger audience both at the games and on television. The league now fully embraces marketing—and it starts at the top. NHL Commissioner Gary Bettman, the former vice president of the NBA (National Basketball Association), leads the NHL's marketing effort.

In addition to trying to sell seats to fans at arenas and selling hockey to TV viewers, the league is also involved in product merchandising and product licensing. For example, it has an online store where fans can purchase official NHL merchandise. Fans can actually use their NHL MasterCard—complete with the logo of their favourite team—to purchase the merchandise. The league's highly interactive Website allows fans to log on to find the latest scores and player statistics, and the Website also offers NHL Broadband TV, NHL Game Radio, and an opportunity for fans to be directly involved in the NHL Fantasy Games programs. Corporate involvement and sponsorship is also a key priority with the league. Several teams have built new arenas and have

attracted major corporate sponsors to be associated with the new complexes. For example, General Motors Place is home to the Vancouver Canucks, the Molson Centre is home to the Montreal Canadiens, the Air Canada Centre is home to the Toronto Maple Leafs, and the Corel Centre is home to the Ottawa Senators.

The NHL has also penetrated the European television market, with ESPN broadcasting NHL games on prime-time Swedish TV. Europe is also a good market for the NHL's product merchandising and licensing programs. In an effort to improve the entertainment value of the game for television viewers, the league has worked to improve how games are televised, including adding more cameras (e.g., cameras in the nets) and a variety of different camera angles from which fans can view the game.

Recently, marketing professional hockey in the United States has been a major focus for the NHL. While Canada was the birthplace of hockey, the NHL believes it is the United States that offers the best opportunity to ensure the long-term prosperity of the league. The NHL believes that strong franchises in major U.S. cities will help sell the game to a larger and new generation of fans outside of Canada. In fact, strong fan support, media interest, and corporate sponsorship has led to an expansion of teams in the United States including teams owned by Disney (the Mighty Ducks in Anaheim) and Blockbuster Entertainment (the Florida Panthers in Miami).

In 2002 the league consisted of 30 teams, with only 6 Canadian franchises and 24 U.S.–based franchises. The league is divided into two major Conferences (Eastern and Western), each with three divisions (see Figure 1). The teams play a regular season schedule of more than 80 games. The top eight teams in each conference advance to the playoff rounds. The eventual winner of the playoffs takes home the Stanley Cup, the world's oldest professional sports trophy.

Still, while other major sports leagues command massive broadcasting fees, the NHL collects comparatively modest fees from the networks that carry its games, including CBC, ABC, and ESPN. The size of the NHL's product merchandising and product licensing program is also small compared to the other major-league sports. Most teams still generate more than 80 percent of their revenue at the gate. However, rising player salaries are putting a squeeze on many franchises. In order to pay for those high player salaries—some as high as $10 million per year—the teams basically need to fill the seats of their arenas every single game. To do so, the teams need to offer fans a quality entertainment product. If not, the fans may not return. The home teams do not necessarily have to win every game, but fans need to feel they have received real entertainment value for their price of admission. In addition, if the teams do not entertain the fans who are watching the games at home, viewership is likely to drop and so will the league's ability to charge reasonable fees for broadcast rights.

The NHL realizes it must aggressively market professional hockey. It believes it must put great players on the ice with great teams, and it must offer wholesome and fun entertainment. If it does not, customers will not continue to support and patronize professional hockey. And without fan support there will be no more *Hockey Night in Canada*—or anywhere else, for that matter.

FIGURE 1—NHL LEAGUE SETUP

EASTERN CONFERENCE	WESTERN CONFERENCE
Northeast Division	Central Division
Boston	Detroit
Toronto	Chicago
Ottawa	St. Louis
Montreal	Nashville
Buffalo	Columbus
Southeast Division	Northwest Division
Carolina	Colorado
Washington	Edmonton
Tampa Bay	Vancouver
Atlanta	Calgary
Florida	Minnesota
Atlantic Division	Pacific Division
Philadelphia	Los Angeles
NY Islanders	Dallas
NY Rangers	Phoenix
Pittsburgh	Anaheim

Questions

1   What is the "real product" that the NHL is marketing to prospective fans?

2   Who is the NHL competing with in terms of fan attendance?

3   How does marketing professional hockey differ from marketing a consumer product like breakfast cereal?

visit us at www.mcgrawhill.ca/college/berkowitz

BUILDING THE PRICE FOUNDATION

AFTER READING THIS CHAPTER YOU SHOULD BE ABLE TO:

- Identify the elements that make up a price.

- Recognize the constraints on a firm's pricing latitude and the objectives a firm has in setting prices.

- Explain what a demand curve is and how it affects a firm's total and marginal revenue.

- Recognize what price elasticity of demand means to a manager facing a pricing decision.

- Explain the role of costs in pricing decisions.

- Calculate a break-even point for various combinations of price, fixed cost, and unit variable cost.

HERE'S A PRICING PROBLEM FOR YOU!

Imagine you are part of the management team for Strait Crossing Bridge Ltd. (SCBL), a subsidiary company of Strait Crossing Development Inc. You know—the company that built the Confederation Bridge (www.confederationbridge.com), the bridge that joins Borden-Carleton, Prince Edward Island and Cape Jourimain, New Brunswick? Yeah, that one. It's 12.9 kilometres long and is the longest bridge over ice-covered waters in the world. And, it just cost you $1 billion to build it. Now you must determine what price to charge users who might want to cross it.

Well, you have many things to ponder. First, you must consider what it is that you are offering customers. You have a pretty good handle on that. Your bridge carries two lanes of traffic 24 hours a day, seven days a week, and it takes approximately 10 minutes to cross at normal travelling speed, which is 80 km/hour. So, compared to ferry service, which often involves a wait and a much longer travel time to cross, you believe consumers will want to use the bridge. But how many customers and how often are two key questions. In this case, things aren't so clear. You do know, however, that consumer demand for your product clearly affects the price that can be charged.

So, you hire a consulting firm that does some demand estimates for you. The problem is, you must consider the type of user for the bridge, or more specifically, the type of vehicle being driven across the bridge. Why? Because traffic volume is made up of a variety of different vehicles, from passenger cars and buses to recreational vehicles and motorcycles. Some vehicles, particularly heavy trucks, put more wear and tear on the bridge, and therefore you believe that these types of vehicles should pay more to use the bridge. So, now you try to crunch some numbers: traffic volume by type of vehicle.

But wait a minute. Before you can set prices to make some revenue projections, you must consult the federal government of Canada. The federal government, through its regulatory agency, Transport Canada, has the power to dictate the price you charge, or in this case, the toll users will pay. You are told that the base rate for tolls by vehicle type must be developed based on previous ferry-service revenue data plus the rate of inflation. With all this information, you must come up with a pricing strategy for the bridge—a pricing strategy that will cover your capital and operating costs as well as provide some long-run profits for the firm. Wow, it is a pricing problem![1]

Welcome to the fascinating—and intense—world of pricing, where myriad forces come together in the specific price prospective buyers are asked to pay. This chapter and Chapter 14 cover important factors used in setting prices. By the way, the toll rate for a passenger vehicle, round trip, is $37 and is collected on exiting PEI. If you are riding a motorcycle, it is a little cheaper at $14.75. But if you're driving a tractor trailer, you pay $52.75.

NATURE AND IMPORTANCE OF PRICE

The price paid for goods and services goes by many names. You pay *tuition* for your education, *rent* for an apartment, *interest* on a bank credit card, and a *premium* for car insurance. Your dentist or physician charges you a *fee*, a professional or social organization charges *dues*, and operators of the Confederation Bridge charge you a *fare* or a *toll* to use their bridge. In business, a consultant may require a *retainer* for services rendered, an executive is given a *salary*, a salesperson receives a *commission*, and a worker is paid a *wage*. Of course, what you pay for clothes or a haircut is termed a *price*.

What Is a Price?

PRICE
The money or other considerations (including other goods and services) exchanged for the ownership or use of a good or service.

BARTER
The practice of exchanging goods and services for other goods and services rather than for money.

These examples highlight the many varied ways that price plays a part in our daily lives. From a marketing viewpoint, **price** is the money or other considerations (including other goods and services) exchanged for the ownership or use of a good or service. For example, Shell Oil recently exchanged one million pest-control devices for sugar from a Caribbean country, and Wilkinson Sword exchanged some of its knives for advertising used to promote its razor blades. This practice of exchanging goods and services for other goods and services rather than for money is called **barter**. These transactions account for billions of dollars annually in domestic and international trade.

For most products and services money is exchanged, although the amount is not always the same as the list or quoted price because of the discounts, allowances, and extra fees shown in Figure 13–1. Suppose you decide to buy a Lamborghini Murciélago ("Bat") because its 6.2 litre, 571-horsepower engine moves you from 0 to 100 km/hr in 3.8 seconds. The list price is $300 000. As a vehicle rebate you receive $21 000 off the list price. You agree to pay half down and the other half when the car is delivered, which results in a financing fee of $3285. To ship the car from Italy you will pay a $5000 destination charge. You are given a trade-in allowance of $5000 for your 1996 Honda Civic DX, which is the *Kelley Blue Book* (www.kbb.com) value of your car.[2]

Applying the "price equation" (as shown in Figure 13–1) to your purchase, your price is:

Profit = List price − Incentives and allowances + Extra fees
      = $300 000 − ($21 000 + $5000) + ($3285 + $5000)
      = $282 285

Lamborghini Murciélago

Your monthly payment for a 6-month loan of $140 000 is $23 880.79. Are you still interested? Figure 13–1 illustrates how the price equation applies to a variety of different products and services.

Price as an Indicator of Value

From a consumer's standpoint, price is often used to indicate value when it is paired with the perceived benefits of a product or service. Specifically, **value** can be defined as the ratio of perceived benefits to price, or:[3]

$$\text{Value} = \frac{\text{Perceived benefits}}{\text{Price}}$$

This relationship shows that, for a given price, as perceived benefits increase value increases. Similarly, for a given price value decreases when perceived benefits decrease. Creative marketers engage in **value-pricing**, the practice of simultaneously increasing product and service benefits and maintaining or decreasing price.

VALUE
The ratio of perceived benefits to price.

VALUE-PRICING
The practice of simultaneously increasing service and product benefits and maintaining or decreasing price.

FIGURE 13–1
The price of four different purchases

PRICE EQUATION

ITEM PURCHASED	PRICE	= LIST PRICE	INCENTIVES AND – ALLOWANCES	+ EXTRA FEES
New car bought by an individual	Final price	= List price	– Rebate Cash discount Old car trade-in	+ Financing charges Special accessories Destination charges
Term in university bought by a student	Tuition	= Published tuition	– Scholarship Other financial aid Discounts for number of credits taken	+ Special activity fees
Bank loan obtained by a small business	Principal and interest	= Amount of loan sought	– Allowance for collateral	+ Premium for uncertain creditworthiness
Merchandise bought from a wholesaler by a retailer	Invoice price	= List price	– Quantity discount Cash discount Seasonal discount Functional or trade discount	+ Penalty for late payment

For some products, price influences the perception of overall quality and, ultimately, value to consumers.[4] For example, in a survey of home furnishing buyers, 84 percent agreed with the following statement: "The higher the price, the higher the quality." For computer software it has been shown that consumers believe a low price implies poor quality.[5]

Consumer value assessments are often comparative. Here value involves the judgment by a consumer of the worth and desirability of a product or service relative to substitutes that satisfy the same need. In this instance a "reference value" emerges, which involves comparing the costs and benefits of substitute items.[6] For example, Kohler recently introduced a walk-in bathtub that is safe for children and the elderly. Although priced higher than conventional step-in bathtubs, it has proven very successful because buyers place great "value" on the extra safety.

Price in the Marketing Mix

PROFIT EQUATION
Profit = Total revenue – Total cost, or Profit = (Unit price x Quantity sold) – Total cost.

Pricing is also a critical decision made by a marketing executive because price has a direct effect on a firm's profits. This is apparent from a firm's **profit equation**:

Profit = Total revenue – Total cost

or

Profit = (Unit price × Quantity sold) – Total cost

What makes this relationship even more important is that price affects the quantity sold, as illustrated with demand curves later in this chapter. Furthermore, since the quantity sold sometimes affects a firm's costs because of efficiency of production, price also indirectly affects costs. Thus, pricing decisions influence both total revenue and total cost, which makes pricing one of the most important decisions marketing executives face.

The importance of price in the marketing mix necessitates an understanding of six major steps involved in the process organizations go through in setting prices (Figure 13–2):

- Identify pricing constraints and objectives.
- Estimate demand and revenue.
- Determine cost, volume, and profit relationships.
- Select an approximate price level.

FIGURE 13–2
Steps in setting price

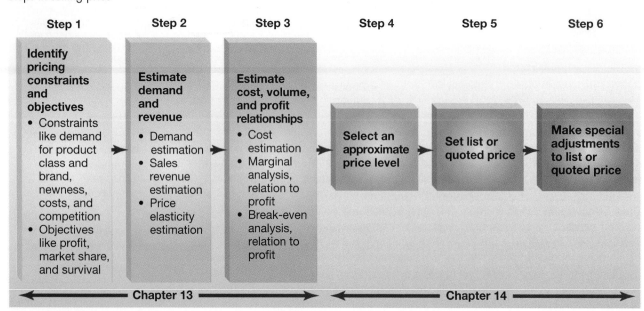

Step 1	Step 2	Step 3	Step 4	Step 5	Step 6
Identify pricing constraints and objectives • Constraints like demand for product class and brand, newness, costs, and competition • Objectives like profit, market share, and survival	**Estimate demand and revenue** • Demand estimation • Sales revenue estimation • Price elasticity estimation	**Estimate cost, volume, and profit relationships** • Cost estimation • Marginal analysis, relation to profit • Break-even analysis, relation to profit	**Select an approximate price level**	**Set list or quoted price**	**Make special adjustments to list or quoted price**

← Chapter 13 → ← Chapter 14 →

- Set list or quoted price.
- Make special adjustments to list or quoted price.

The first three steps are covered in this chapter and the last three in Chapter 14.

STEP 1: IDENTIFYING PRICING CONSTRAINTS AND OBJECTIVES

To define a problem, it is important to consider both the objectives and constraints that narrow the range of alternatives available to solve it. These same principles apply in solving a pricing problem. Let's first review the pricing constraints so that we can better understand the nature of pricing alternatives.

Identifying Pricing Constraints

PRICING CONSTRAINTS
Factors that limit the latitude of price a firm may set.

Factors that limit the latitude of prices a firm may set are **pricing constraints**. Consumer demand for the product clearly affects the price that can be charged. Other constraints on price vary from factors within the organization to competitive factors outside the organization. Legal and regulatory constraints on pricing are discussed in Chapter 14.

Demand for the Product Class, Product, and Brand   The number of potential buyers for the product class (such as cars), product (sports cars), and brand (Dodge Viper) clearly affects the price a seller can charge. So does whether the item is a luxury—like a Viper—or a necessity—like bread and a roof over your head. In fact, when a consumer is in urgent need of a particular necessity, a marketer may command a premium price. In this case, there may be ethical issues involved (see the accompanying Ethics and Social Responsibility Alert).[7] The nature of demand is discussed further later in this chapter.

Newness of the Product: Stage in the Product Life Cycle   The newer a product and the earlier it is in its life cycle, the higher the price that can usually be charged. Willing to spend up to $1000 for a new electronic book? The high initial price

---

ETHICS AND SOCIAL RESPONSIBILITY ALERT   Getting an Unfair Premium Price?

The drug Clozapine is one of the most significant advances in antipsychotic drugs in two decades. But few of the people who really need this drug get it since the drug costs about $9000 a year. Pharmaceutical companies have been accused of price-gouging with respect to this drug and other critical life-saving drugs, such as those used in AIDS treatment.

Some consumer advocates argue that many industries have a tendency to command premium prices for necessary products or services knowing that consumers usually have little choice but to pay them. Oil companies, for example, are often criticized for raising prices on home-heating oil during the cold Canadian winters. The oil companies argue it is simply a supply-and-demand issue. Many consumers, however, feel they are being gouged unfairly because oil companies realize the consumer has little choice but to pay the

price. Price-gouging claims are also levied against major airlines during peak travel periods. Individual companies are sometimes accused of price gouging during shortages. For example, during water shortages bottled water suppliers have sometimes increased the price of their product by two to three times its original price. University students often report paying high and unfair prices for off-campus housing when demand is high and supply is low.

The practice of commanding premium prices for luxuries and necessities appears to be gaining acceptability with marketers. A recent survey of Canadian MBA students found that 30 percent of them stated they would charge higher than normal prices if they believed the consumer would pay the higher price.

Is the use of premium pricing for necessities fair? Is it ethical? What should be done about this practice?

WEB LINK

Pricing 101: $5900 for a 1969 Used Hotwheels Volkswagen Van, or a Mint-Condition 1952 Mickey Mantle Topps Baseball Card for $121 000?

http://www.mcgrawhill.ca

Prices of "collectibles"—such as toys or old sneakers—are set by demand and supply forces discussed in this chapter. And for fads, the prices can fluctuate wildly. Some other recent collectibles prices, besides those mentioned above:

- Zip, a cat, Beanie Baby: $250 (if it has black paws).
- 1985 Nike Dunks, high-top, blue-and-black basketball shoes: $3200.
- Mint-in-package Star Wars "Empire Strikes Back" Han Solo figure: $350.

To get a feel for prices of some of these collectibles, visit www.ebay.com

Marathon runner Malcolm East now wishes he had done a little more research on sneaker prices. At his wife's insistence he threw out six pairs of old shoes—which he now thinks would have fetched $19 000!

Want in on the collectibles business? Think twice. The Zip Beanie Baby sold for $2250 in 1998, almost $2000 more than in 2001.

is possible because of patents and limited competition early in its product life cycle. By the time you read this, the price will probably be much lower.[8]

Sometimes—when nostalgia or fad factors come into play—prices may rise later in the product life cycle. As described in the Web Link box, collectibles such as a 1952 Mickey Mantle baseball card or old sneakers can experience skyrocketing prices.[9] Publishing competitive prices on the Internet for the same or similar brands of products has revolutionized the access to price comparisons for both collectors and buyers of more traditional products.

www.sony.com

Single Product versus a Product Line   When Sony introduced its CD player, not only was it unique and in the introductory stage of its product life cycle but also it was the *only* CD player Sony sold, so the firm had great latitude in setting a price. Now, with a wide range of Sony CD products and technologies, the price of individual models has to be consistent with the others based on features provided and meaningful price differentials that communicate value to consumers.

Cost of Producing and Marketing the Product   In the long run, a firm's price must cover all the costs of producing and marketing a product. If the price doesn't cover the cost the firm will fail, so in the long term a firm's costs set a floor under its price. The operators of the Confederation Bridge are clearly conscious of the fact that the total cost of providing their bridge service must not exceed total revenue, otherwise they cannot succeed.

Are these real "collectibles" or "trashables?" The text describes factors that affect a product's price. Check the Web Link box to see if those old Beanie Babies or Nikes in your attic have value!

www.sears.com

Cost of Changing Prices and Time Period They Apply   If Air Canada asks General Electric (GE) to provide spare jet engines to power the new Boeing 737 it just bought, GE can easily set a new price for the engines to reflect its latest information since only one buyer has to be informed. But if Sears Canada decides that sweater prices are too low in its winter catalogues after thousands of catalogues have been mailed to customers it has a big problem, so it must consider the cost of changing prices and the time period for which they apply in developing the price list for its catalogue items. A recent study of four supermarket chains found the average annual cost of these price changes was $148 241, which represents 0.70 percent of revenues and an astounding 35.2 percent of net margins.[10] In actual practice, research indicates that most firms change the price for their major products once a year.[11] On a Website, prices can change from minute to minute.

Type of Competitive Markets   The seller's price is constrained by the type of market in which it competes. Economists generally delineate four types of competitive markets: pure monopoly, oligopoly, monopolistic competition, and pure competition. Figure 13–3 shows that the type of competition dramatically influences the latitude of price competition and, in turn, the nature of product differentiation and extent of advertising. A firm must recognize the general type of competitive market it is in to understand the latitude of both its price and non-price strategies. For example, prices can be significantly affected by four competitive situations:

www.johnsonandjohnson.com

- *Pure monopoly.* In 1994 Johnson & Johnson (J&J) revolutionized the treatment of coronary heart diseases by introducing the "stent"—a tiny mesh tube "spring" that props clogged arteries open. Initially a monopolist, J&J stuck with its early $2235 price and achieved $1.4 billion in sales and 91-percent market share by the end of 1996. But its reluctance to give price reductions for large-volume purchases to hospitals antagonized them. When competitors introduced an improved stent at lower prices, J&J's market share plummeted to eight percent two years later.[12]
- *Oligopoly.* The few sellers of aluminum (Alcan, Alcoa) or mainframe computers try to avoid price competition because it can lead to disastrous price wars in which all lose money. Yet firms in such industries stay aware of a competitor's price cuts or increases and may follow suit. The products can be undifferentiated

FIGURE 13–3
Pricing, product, and advertising strategies available to firms in four types of competitive markets

TYPE OF COMPETITIVE MARKET

STRATEGIES AVAILABLE	PURE MONOPOLY (One seller who sets the price for a unique product)	OLIGOPOLY (Few sellers who are sensitive to each other's prices)	MONOPOLISTIC COMPETITION (Many sellers who compete on nonprice factors)	PURE COMPETITION (Many sellers who follow the market price for identical, commodity products)
Extent of price competition	None: sole seller sets price	Some: price leader or follower of competitors	Some: compete over range of prices	Almost none: market sets price
Extent of product differentiation	None: no other producers	Various: depends on industry	Some: differentiate products from competitors	None: products are identical
Extent of advertising	Little: purpose is to increase demand for product class	Some: purpose is to inform but avoid price competition	Much: purpose is to differentiate firm's products from competitors	Little: purpose is to inform prospects that seller's products are available

(aluminum) or differentiated (mainframe computers), and informative advertising that avoids head-to-head price competition is used.

- *Monopolistic competition.* Dozens of regional, private brands of peanut butter compete with national brands like Skippy and Jif. Both price competition (regional, private brands being lower than national brands) and non-price competition (product features and advertising) exist.
- *Pure competition.* Hundreds of local grain elevators sell corn whose price per bushel is set by the marketplace. Within strains, the corn is identical, so advertising only informs buyers that the seller's corn is available.

Competitors' Prices   A firm must know or anticipate what specific price its present and potential competitors are charging now or will charge. When the NutraSweet Company planned the market introduction of Simplesse® all-natural fat substitute, it had to consider the price of fat replacements already available as well as potential competitors, including Procter & Gamble's Olestra, Pfizer Inc.'s VeriLo, and the Stellar brand made by A. E. Staley Company.

Identifying Pricing Objectives

Expectations that specify the role of price in an organization's marketing and strategic plans are **pricing objectives**. To the extent possible, these organizational pricing objectives are also carried to lower levels in the organization, such as in setting objectives for marketing managers responsible for an individual brand. H. J. Heinz, for example, has specific pricing objectives for its Heinz ketchup brand that vary by country. Chapter 2 discussed six broad objectives that an organization may pursue, which tie in directly to the organization's pricing policies.

PRICING OBJECTIVES
Expectations that specify the role of price in an organization's marketing and strategic plans.

www.heinz.com

Profit   Three different objectives relate to a firm's profit, usually measured in terms of return on investment (ROI) or return on assets. One objective is *managing for long-run profits*, which is followed by many Japanese firms that are willing to forgo immediate profit in cars, TV sets, or computers to develop quality products that can penetrate competitive markets in the future. A *maximizing current profit* objective, such as during this quarter or year, is common in many firms because the targets can be set and performance measured quickly. Canadian firms are sometimes criticized for this short-run orientation. A *target return* objective involves a firm such as Irving Oil or Mohawk setting a goal (such as 20 percent) for pretax ROI. These three profit objectives have different implications for a firm's pricing objectives.

Another profit consideration for firms such as movie studios and manufacturers, discussed in more depth in Chapter 14, is to ensure that those firms in their channels of distribution make adequate profits. Without profits for these channel members, the movie studio or manufacturer is cut off from its customers. For example, Figure 13–4 shows where each dollar of your movie ticket goes. The 51 cents the movie studio gets must cover both its production expenses and its profit—a big order if it's the $100 million of expenses it took to produce *Pearl Harbor*. While the studio would like more than 51 cents of your dollar, it settles for this amount to make sure theatres and distributors are satisfied and willing to handle their movies. Still, with revenues close to $1 billion, the Canadian movie theatre industry has actually been raising ticket prices to increase its profitability.[13]

Theatre
19¢

Distributor
30¢

Movie
studio
51¢

10¢ = Theatre expenses
9¢ = Left for theatre
6¢ = Misc. expenses
24¢ = Left for distributor
20¢ = Advertising and publicity expenses
8¢ = Actors' share of gross
23¢ = Left for movie studio

FIGURE 13–4
Where each dollar of your movie ticket goes

Sales   Given that a firm's profit is high enough for it to remain in business, its objectives may be to increase sales revenue. The hope is that the increase in sales revenue will in turn lead to increases in market share and profit. Cutting price on one product in a firm's line may increase its sales revenue but reduce those of related products. Objectives related to sales revenue or unit sales have the advantage of being translated easily into meaningful targets for marketing managers responsible for a product line or brand—far more easily than with an ROI target, for example.

Market Share   Market share is the ratio of the firm's sales revenues or unit sales to those of the industry (competitors plus the firm itself). Companies often pursue a market share objective when industry sales are relatively flat or declining. The Molson and Labatt breweries have adopted this objective in the beer market while Pepsi-Cola Canada and Coca-Cola Canada battle for market share in the soft drink category.[14] But although increased market share is the primary goal of some firms, others see it as a means to an end: increasing sales and profits.

www.labatt.com

Unit Volume   Many firms use *unit volume*, the quantity produced or sold, as a pricing objective. These firms often sell multiple products at very different prices and are sensitive to matching production capacity with unit volume. Using unit volume as an objective, however, can sometimes be misleading from a profit standpoint. Volume can be increased by employing sales incentives (such as lowering prices, giving rebates, or offering lower interest rates). By doing this the company chooses to lower profits in the short run to quickly sell its product. This happened when Fiat offered $1600 rebates and zero-interest financing in Italy on its $10 000 Uno compact car.[15]

Survival   In some instances, profits, sales, and market share are less important objectives of the firm than mere survival. Continental Airlines has struggled to attract passengers with low fares, no-penalty advance-booking policies, and aggressive promotions to improve the firm's cash flow. This pricing objective has helped Continental to stay alive in the competitive airline industry.

Social Responsibility   A firm may forgo higher profit on sales and follow a pricing objective that recognizes its obligations to customers and society in general. Medtronics followed this pricing policy when it introduced the world's first heart pacemaker. Gerber supplies a specially formulated product free of charge to children who cannot tolerate foods based on cow's milk. Government agencies, which set many prices for services they offer, use social responsibility as a primary pricing objective.

Concept Check

1. What factors impact the list price to determine the final price?

2. How does the type of competitive market a firm is in affect its latitude in setting price?

STEP 2: ESTIMATING DEMAND AND REVENUE

Basic to setting a product's price is the extent of customer demand for it. Marketing executives must also translate this estimate of customer demand into estimates of revenues the firm expects to receive.

www.newsweek.com

DEMAND CURVE
The summation of points representing the maximum number of products consumers will buy at a given price.

DEMAND FACTORS
Factors that determine consumers' willingness and ability to pay for goods and services.

FIGURE 13-5
Illustrative demand curves for *Newsweek* magazine

Fundamentals of Estimating Demand

Newsweek decided to conduct a pricing experiment at newsstands in 11 cities.[16] In one city, newsstand buyers paid $2.25. In five cities, newsstand buyers paid the regular $2.00 price. In another city, the price was $1.50, and in four other cities it was only $1.00. By comparison, the regular newsstand price for *Time* was $1.95. Why did *Newsweek* conduct the experiment? According to a *Newsweek* executive, at that time, "We wanted to figure out what the demand curve for our magazine at the newsstand is." And you thought that demand curves only existed to confuse you on a test in basic economics!

The Demand Curve   A **demand curve** shows a maximum number of products consumers will buy at a given price. Demand curve D_1 in Figure 13–5 shows the newsstand demand for Newsweek under existing conditions. Note that as price falls, people buy more. But price is not the complete story in estimating demand. Economists stress three other key factors:

1. *Consumer tastes.* As we saw in Chapter 3, these depend on many factors such as demographics, culture, and technology. Because consumer tastes can change quickly, up-to-date marketing research is essential.
2. *Price and availability of other products.* As the price of close substitute products falls (the price of *Time*) and their availability increases, the demand for a product declines (the demand for *Newsweek*).
3. *Consumer income.* In general, as real consumer income (allowing for inflation) increases, demand for a product also increases.

The first of these two factors influences what consumers want to buy, and the third affects what they *can* buy. Along with price, these are often called **demand factors**, or factors that determine consumers' willingness and ability to pay for goods and services. As discussed earlier in Chapters 8 and 10, it is often very difficult to estimate demand for new products, especially because consumer likes and dislikes are often so difficult to read clearly. For example, Campbell Soup spent seven years and $75 million on a supersecret project to produce a line of Intelligent Quisine (IQ) food products. The company expected that its line of 41 breakfasts, lunches, dinners, and snacks would be the first foods "scientifically proven to lower

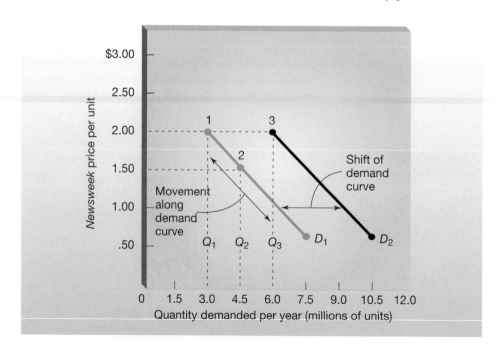

FIGURE 13–6
Fundamental revenue concepts

Total revenue (TR) is the total money received from the sale of a product. If:

TR = Total revenue
 P = Unit price of the product
 Q = Quantity of the product sold

then:

TR = P × Q

Average revenue (AR) is the average amount of money received for selling one unit of the product, or simply the price of that unit. Average revenue is the total revenue divided by the quantity sold:

$$AR = \frac{TR}{Q} = P$$

Marginal revenue (MR) is the change in total revenue obtained by selling one additional unit:

$$MR = \frac{\text{Change in TR}}{1 \text{ unit increase in Q}} = \frac{\Delta TR}{\Delta DQ} = \text{slope of TR curve}$$

high levels of cholesterol, blood sugar, and blood pressure."[17] After 15 months in a test market, Campbell Soup yanked the entire IQ line when it fell far short of expectations because customers found the line too pricey and lacking in variety.

Movement Along versus Shift of a Demand Curve   Demand curve D_1 in Figure 13–5 shows that as the price is lowered from $2 to $1.50, the quantity demanded increases from 3 million (Q_1) to 4.5 million ($Q2$) units per year. This is an example of a movement along a demand curve and assumes that other factors (consumer tastes, price and availability of substitutes, and consumer income) remain unchanged.

What if some of these factors change? For example, if advertising causes more people to want *Newsweek*, newsstand distribution is increased, and consumer incomes double, then the demand increases. This is shown in Figure 13–5 as a shift of the demand curve to the right, from D_1 to D_2. This increased demand means that more *Newsweek* magazines are wanted for a given price: At a price of $2, the demand is 6 million units per year (Q_3) on D^2 rather than 3 million units per year (Q_1) on D_1.

Fundamentals of Estimating Revenue

While economists may talk about "demand curves," marketing executives are more likely to speak in terms of "revenues generated." Demand curves lead directly to three related revenue concepts critical to pricing decisions: **total revenue**, **average revenue**, and **marginal revenue** (Figure 13–6).

Demand Curves and Revenue   Figure 13–7A again shows the demand curve for *Newsweek*, but it is now extended to intersect both the price and quantity axes. The demand curve shows that as price is changed, the quantity of *Newsweek* magazines sold increases. This relationship holds whether the price is increased from $2.50 to $3.00 on the demand curve or is reduced from $1 to $0 on the curve. In the former case the market demands no *Newsweek* magazines, whereas in the latter case nine million could be given away at $0 per unit.

It is likely that if *Newsweek* were given away, more than nine million would be demanded. This fact illustrates two important points. First, it can be dangerous to extend a demand curve beyond the range of prices for which it really applies. Second, most demand curves are rounded (or convex) to the origin, thereby avoiding an unrealistic picture of what demand looks like when a straight-line curve intersects either the price axis or the quantity axis.

TOTAL REVENUE
The total money received from the sale of a product.

AVERAGE REVENUE
The average amount of money received for selling one unit of a product.

MARGINAL REVENUE
The change in total revenue obtained by selling one additional unit.

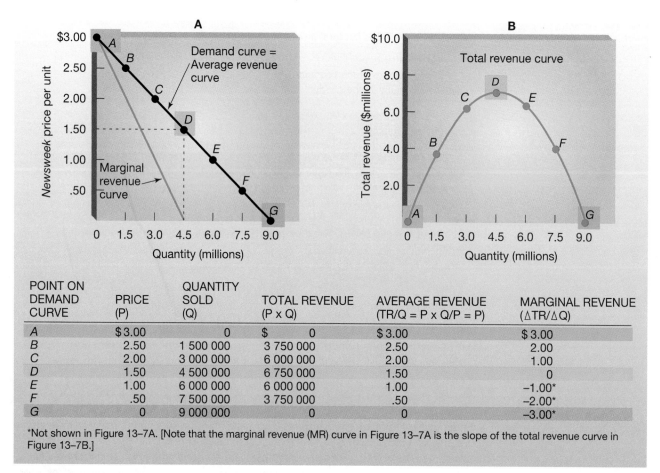

POINT ON DEMAND CURVE	PRICE (P)	QUANTITY SOLD (Q)	TOTAL REVENUE (P x Q)	AVERAGE REVENUE (TR/Q = P x Q/P = P)	MARGINAL REVENUE (ΔTR/ΔQ)
A	$3.00	0	$ 0	$ 3.00	$ 3.00
B	2.50	1 500 000	3 750 000	2.50	2.00
C	2.00	3 000 000	6 000 000	2.00	1.00
D	1.50	4 500 000	6 750 000	1.50	0
E	1.00	6 000 000	6 000 000	1.00	–1.00*
F	.50	7 500 000	3 750 000	.50	–2.00*
G	0	9 000 000	0	0	–3.00*

*Not shown in Figure 13–7A. [Note that the marginal revenue (MR) curve in Figure 13–7A is the slope of the total revenue curve in Figure 13–7B.]

FIGURE 13–7

How a downward-sloping demand curve affects total, average, and marginal revenue

Figure 13–7B shows the total revenue curve for *Newsweek* calculated from the demand curve shown in Figure 13–7A. The total revenue curve is developed by simply multiplying the unit price times the quantity for each of the points on the demand curve. Total revenue starts at $0 (point *A*), reaches a maximum of $6 750 000 at point *D*, and returns to $0 at point *G*. This shows that as price is reduced in the *A*-to-*D* segment of the curve, total revenues are increased. However, cutting price in the *D*-to-*G* segment results in a decline in total revenue.

Marginal revenue, which is the slope of the total revenue curve, is positive but decreasing when the price lies in the range from $3 to above $1.50 per unit. Below $1.50 per unit, though, marginal revenue is actually negative, so the extra quantity of magazines sold is more than offset by the decrease in the price per unit.

For any downward-sloping, straight-line demand curve, the marginal revenue curve always falls at a rate twice as fast as the demand curve. As shown in Figure 13–7A, the marginal revenue becomes $0 per unit at a quantity sold of 4.5 million units—the very point at which total revenue is maximum (see Figure 13–7A). A rational marketing manager would never operate in the region of the demand curve in which marginal revenue is negative. This means that in Figure 13–7A this manager would set prices only in the *A*-to-*D* segment of the demand curve. Also, when market share falls, the easy answer is to cut prices—often with devastating results: a 1-percent price cut in the food and drug industry results in a 24-percent decline in profits, other factors being equal.[18]

What price did *Newsweek* select after conducting its experiment? It kept the price at $2.00. However, through expanded newsstand distribution and more aggressive advertising, *Newsweek* was later able to shift its demand curve to the right and charge a price of $2.50 without affecting its newsstand volume.

PRICE ELASTICITY OF DEMAND
The percentage change in quantity demanded relative to a percentage change in price.

Price Elasticity of Demand   With a downward-sloping demand curve, we have been concerned with the responsiveness of demand to price changes. This can be conveniently measured by **price elasticity of demand**, or the percentage change in quantity demanded relative to a percentage change in price. Price elasticity of demand (E) is expressed as follows:

$$E = \frac{\text{Percentage change in quantity demanded}}{\text{Percentage change in price}}$$

Because quantity demanded usually decreases as price increases, price elasticity of demand is usually a negative number. However, for the sake of simplicity and by convention, elasticity figures are shown as positive numbers.

Price elasticity of demand assumes three forms: elastic demand, inelastic demand, and unitary demand elasticity. *Elastic demand* exists when a small percentage decrease in price produces a larger percentage increase in quantity demanded. Price elasticity is greater than 1 with elastic demand. *Inelastic demand* exists when a small percentage decrease in price produces a smaller percentage increase in quantity demanded. With inelastic demand, price elasticity is less than 1. *Unitary demand* exists when the percentage change in price is identical to the percentage change in quantity demanded. In this instance, price elasticity is equal to 1.

Price elasticity of demand is determined by a number of factors. First, the more substitutes a product or service has, the more likely it is to be price elastic. For example, butter has many possible substitutes in a meal and is price elastic, but gasoline has almost no substitutes and is price inelastic. Second, products and services considered to be necessities are price inelastic. For example, open-heart surgery is price inelastic, whereas airline tickets for a vacation are price elastic. Third, items that require a large cash outlay compared with a person's disposable income are price elastic. Accordingly, cars and yachts are price elastic; books and movie tickets tend to be price inelastic.

Price elasticity is important to marketing managers because of its relationship to total revenue. For example, with elastic demand, total revenue increases when price decreases, but decreases when price increases. With inelastic demand, total revenue increases when price increases and decreases when price decreases. Finally, with unitary demand total revenue is unaffected by a slight price change.

Because of this relationship between price elasticity and a firm's total revenue, it is important that marketing managers recognize that price elasticity of demand is not the same over all possible prices of a product. Figure 13–7B illustrates this point using the *Newsweek* demand curve shown in Figure 13–7A. As the price decreases from $2.50 to $2, total revenue increases, indicating an elastic demand. However, when the price decreases from $1 to 50 cents, total revenue declines, indicating an inelastic demand. Unitary demand elasticity exists at a price of $1.50.

Price Elasticities for Brands and Product Classes   Marketing executives also recognize that the price elasticity of demand is not always the same for product classes (such as stereo receivers) and brands within a product class (such as Sony and Marantz). For example, marketing experiments on brands of cola, coffee, and snack and specialty foods generally show elasticities of 1.5 to 2.5, indicating they are price elastic. By comparison, entire product classes of fruits and vegetables have elasticities of about 0.8—they are price inelastic.[19]

Recently, the price elasticity of demand for cigarettes has become a hotly debated public health issue and a matter of corporate ethics and social responsibility. Research generally shows that cigarettes are price inelastic.[20] However, price elasticity differs by the age of the smoker. Because 12- to 17-year-olds often have limited spending money, this group is very price elastic in its demand for cigarettes. As a result, many legislators recommend even higher taxes on cigarettes to increase their prices significantly, with the goal of reducing teenage smoking. Thus, price elasticity is not only a relevant concept for marketing managers, but it is also important for public policy affecting pricing practices.

1. What is the difference between a movement along and a shift of a demand curve?

2. What does it mean if a product has a price elasticity of demand that is greater than 1?

STEP 3: ESTIMATING COST, VOLUME, AND PROFIT RELATIONSHIPS

While revenues are the monies received by the firm from selling its products or services to customers, costs or expenses are the monies the firm pays out to its employees and suppliers. Marketing managers often use marginal analysis and break-even analysis to relate revenues and costs at various levels of units sold, topics covered in this section.

TOTAL COST
The total expense incurred by a firm in producing and marketing a product. Total cost is the sum of fixed cost and variable cost.

FIXED COST
The sum of expenses of the firm that are stable and do not change with the quantity of product that is produced and sold.

VARIABLE COST
The sum of the expenses of the firm that vary directly with the quantity of product that is produced and sold.

MARGINAL COST
The change in total cost that results from producing and marketing one additional unit.

The Importance of Controlling Costs

The profit equation described at the beginning of the chapter showed that Profit = Total revenue – Total cost. Therefore, understanding the role and behaviour of costs is critical for all marketing decisions, particularly pricing decisions. Four cost concepts are important in pricing decisions: **total cost**, **fixed cost**, **variable cost**, and **marginal cost** (Figure 13–8).

Many firms go bankrupt because their costs get out of control, causing their total costs to exceed their total revenues over an extended period of time. This is why sophisticated marketing managers make pricing decisions that balance both their revenues and costs. The Marketing NewsNet box describes how some dot-com companies have failed while others have succeeded with regard to balancing costs and revenues. [21]

Marginal Analysis and Profit Maximization

A basic idea in business, economics, and indeed everyday life is marginal analysis. In personal terms, marginal analysis means that people will continue to do something as long as the incremental return exceeds the incremental cost. This same idea

FIGURE 13–8
Fundamental cost concepts

Total cost (TC) is the total expense incurred by a firm in producing and marketing the product. Total cost is the sum of fixed cost and variable cost.

Fixed cost (FC) is the sum of the expenses of the firm that are stable and do not change with the quantity of product that is produced and sold. Examples of fixed costs are rent on the building, executive salaries, and insurance.

Variable cost (VC) is the sum of the expenses of the firm that vary directly with the quantity of product that is produced and sold. For example, as the quantity sold doubles, the variable cost doubles. Examples are the direct labour and direct materials used in producing the product and the sales commissions that are tied directly to the quantity sold. As mentioned above:

$$TC = FC + VC$$

Variable cost expressed on a per unit basis is called *unit variable cost* (UVC).

Marginal cost (MC) is the change in total cost that results from producing and marketing one additional unit:

$$MC = \frac{\text{Change in TC}}{1 \text{ unit increase in Q}} \quad \frac{\Delta TC}{\Delta Q} = \text{slope of TC curve}$$

MARKETING NEWSNET

Pricing Lessons from the Dot-coms: Understand Revenues and Costs

Price, revenue, fixed cost, variable cost. Boring topics from finance or economics? Not necessarily. These concepts are also critical to marketing success, as shown by lessons learned by successful dot-coms and by those that have failed. Over the past several months, hundreds of dot-com companies have gone out of business. Why? Many experts agree that some of the reasons for such failure include (1) setting prices too low to cover the huge fixed costs of inventory, warehousing, and order fulfillment, especially on low-margin goods like groceries; (2) spending too much on advertising and promotion; and (3) believing consumers would forgo shopping at traditional stores—a problem, for example, with a dot-com like Pets.com competing against a brick-and-mortar store like Petsmart.

On the other hand, other dot-com firms have been more successful, including travel operations. Why? Besides time and money savings for customers, the travel dot-coms have special strategies for success, including (1) reaching key customer segments who will actually pay higher prices for hotel rooms or airline tickets; (2) reaching customer segments like seniors or students whose last-minute flexibility enables them to reserve hotel rooms or airline seats that would otherwise go unsold; and (3) being able to conduct almost all operations electronically, without the warehousing and order fulfillment problems that other dot-com companies have experienced. In short, the dot-coms that overestimated their revenue streams and underestimated their costs of doing business were not able to sustain their operations—a tough lesson for their shareholders and their employees.

Why is Pets.com and its sock puppet only a memory? For the answers, see the text and the Marketing NewsNet box.

MARGINAL ANALYSIS
A continuing, concise trade-off of incremental costs against incremental revenues.

BREAK-EVEN ANALYSIS
A technique that analyzes the relationship between total revenue and total cost to determine profitability at various levels of output.

BREAK-EVEN POINT (BEP)
Quantity at which total revenue and total cost are equal and beyond which profit occurs.

holds true in marketing and pricing decisions. In this setting, **marginal analysis** means that as long as revenue received from the sale of an additional product (marginal revenue) is greater than the additional cost of production and selling it (marginal cost), a firm will expand its output of that product.[22]

Marginal analysis is central to the concept of maximizing profits. In Figure 13–9A, marginal revenue and marginal cost are graphed. Marginal cost starts out high at lower quantity levels, decreases to a minimum through production and marketing efficiencies, and then rises again due to the inefficiencies of overworked labour and equipment. Marginal revenue follows a downward slope. In Figure 13–9B, total cost and total revenue curves corresponding to the marginal cost and marginal revenue curves are graphed. Total cost initially rises as quantity increases but increases at the slowest rate at the quantity where marginal cost is lowest. The total revenue curve increases to a maximum and then starts to decline, as shown in Figure 13–9B.

The message of marginal analysis, then, is to operate up to the quantity and price level where marginal revenue equals marginal cost (MR = MC). Up to the output quantity at which MR = MC, each increase in total revenue resulting from selling one additional unit exceeds the increase in the total cost of producing and marketing that unit. Beyond the point at which MR = MC, however, the increase in total revenue from selling one more unit is less than the cost of producing and marketing that unit. At the quantity at which MR = MC, the total revenue curve lies farthest above the total cost curve, they are parallel, and profit is a maximum.

Break-Even Analysis

Marketing managers often employ a simpler approach for looking at cost, volume, and profit relationships, which is also based on the profit equation. **Break-even analysis** is a technique that analyzes the relationship between total revenue and total cost to determine profitability at various levels of output. The **break-even point** (BEP) is the quantity at which total revenue and total cost are equal and beyond which profit occurs. In terms of the definitions in Figure 13–8:

$$BEP_{Quantity} = \frac{Fixed\ cost}{Unit\ price - Unit\ variable\ cost}$$

FIGURE 13–9
Profit maximization pricing

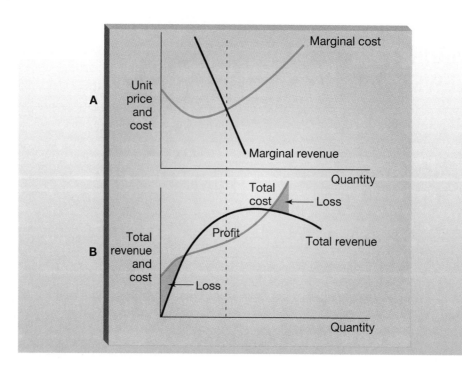

Calculating a Break-Even Point   Consider, for example, a corn farmer who wishes to identify how many bushels of corn he must sell to cover his fixed cost at a given price. Suppose the farmer had a fixed cost (FC) of $2000 (for real estate taxes, interest on a bank loan, and other fixed expenses) and a unit variable cost (UVC) of $1 per bushel (for labour, corn seed, herbicides, and pesticides). If the price (P) is $2 per bushel, his break-even quantity is 2000 bushels:

$$BEP_{Quantity} = \frac{FC}{P - UVC} = \frac{\$2000}{\$2 - \$1} = 2000 \text{ bushels}$$

The shaded row in Figure 13–10 shows that the break-even quantity at a price of $2 per bushel is 2000 bushels because, at this quantity, total revenue equals total cost. At less than 2000 bushels the farmer incurs a loss, and at more than 2000 bushels he makes a profit. Figure 13–11 shows a graphic presentation of the break-even analysis, called a **break-even chart**.

BREAK-EVEN CHART
A graphic presentation of the break-even analysis.

Applications of Break-Even Analysis   Because of its simplicity, break-even analysis is used extensively in marketing, most frequently to study the impact on profit of changes in price, fixed cost, and variable cost. The mechanics of break-even analysis are the basis of the widely used electronic spreadsheets offered by computer programs such as Microsoft Excel that permit managers to answer hypothetical "what if . . ." questions about the effect of changes in price and cost on their profit.

FIGURE 13–10
Calculating a break-even point

QUANTITY SOLD (Q)	PRICE PER BUSHEL (P)	TOTAL REVENUE (TR) (P × Q)	UNIT VARIABLE COST (UVC)	TOTAL VARIABLE COSTS (TVC) (UVC × Q)	FIXED COST (FC)	TOTAL COST (TC) (FC + VC)	PROFIT (TR – TC)
0	$2	$ 0	$1	$ 0	$2 000	$2 000	–$2 000
1 000	2	2 000	1	1 000	2 000	3 000	–1 000
2 000	2	4 000	1	2 000	2 000	4 000	0
3 000	2	6 000	1	3 000	2 000	5 000	1 000
4 000	2	8 000	1	4 000	2 000	6 000	2 000
5 000	2	10 000	1	5 000	2 000	7 000	3 000
6 000	2	12 000	1	6 000	2 000	8 000	4 000

FIGURE 13–11
Break-even analysis chart

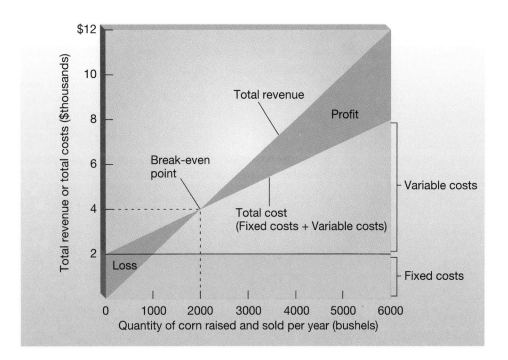

An example will show the power of break-even analysis. As described in Figure 13–12, if an electronic calculator manufacturer automates its production, thereby increasing fixed cost and reducing variable cost by substituting machines for workers, this increases the break-even point from 333 333 to 500 000 units per year.

But what about the impact of the higher level of fixed cost on profit? Remember, profit at any output quantity is given by:

Profit = Total revenue − Total cost
     = (P × Q) − [FC + (UVC × Q)]

So profit at 1 million units of sales before automation is:

Profit = (P × Q) − [FC + (UVC × Q)]
     = ($10 × 1 000 000) − [$1 000 000 + ($7 × 1 000 000)]
     = $10 000 000 − $8 000 000
     = $2 000 000

After automation, profit is:

Profit = (P × Q) − [FC + (UVC × Q)]
     = ($10 × 1 000 000) − [$4 000 000 + ($2 × 1 000 000)]
     = $10 000 000 − $6 000 000
     = $4 000 000

Automation, by adding to fixed cost, increases profit by $2 million at one million units of sales. Thus, as the quantity sold increases for the automated plant, the potential increase or leverage on profit is tremendous. This is why, with large production and sales volumes, automated plants for GM cars or Texas Instruments calculators produce large profits. Also, firms in other industries, such as airline, railway, and hotel and motel industries, that require a high fixed cost can reap large profits when they go even slightly beyond the break-even point.

FIGURE 13–12

The cost trade-off: fixed versus variable costs

Executives in virtually every mass-production industry—from locomotives and cars to electronic calculators and breakfast cereals—are searching for ways to increase quality and reduce production costs to remain competitive in world markets. Increasingly they are substituting robots, automation, and computer-controlled manufacturing systems for blue- and white-collar workers.

To understand the implications of this on the break-even point and profit, consider this example of an electronic calculator manufacturer:

BEFORE AUTOMATION			**AFTER AUTOMATION**		
P	=	$10 per unit	P	=	$10 per unit
FC	=	$1 000 000	FC	=	$4 000 000
UVC	=	$7 per unit	UVC	=	$2 per unit
$BEP_{Quantity}$	=	$\dfrac{FC}{P-UVC}$	$BEP_{Quantity}$	=	$\dfrac{FC}{P-UVC}$
	=	$\dfrac{\$1\,000\,000}{\$10-\$7}$		=	$\dfrac{\$4\,000\,000}{\$10-\$2}$
	=	333 333 units		=	500 000 units

The automation increases the fixed cost and increases the break-even quantity from 333 333 to 500 000 units per year. So if annual sales fall within this range, the calculator manufacturer will incur a loss with the automated plant, whereas it would have made a profit if it had not automated.

But what about its potential profit if it sells 1 million units a year? Look carefully at the two break-even charts below, and see the text to check your conclusions:

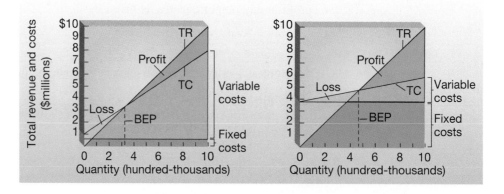

1. What is the difference between fixed cost and variable cost?

2. What is a break-even point?

SUMMARY

1 Price is the money or other considerations exchanged for the ownership or use of a product or service. Although price typically involves money, the amount exchanged is often different from the list or quoted price because of allowances and extra fees.

2 Consumers use price as an indicator of value when it is paired with the perceived benefits of a good or service. Sometimes price influences consumer perceptions of quality itself and at other times consumers make value assessments by comparing the costs and benefits of substitute items.

3 Pricing constraints such as demand, product newness, costs, competitors, other products sold by the firm, and the type of competitive market restrict a firm's pricing latitude.

4 Pricing objectives, which specify the role of price in a firm's marketing strategy, may include pricing for profit, sales revenue, market share, unit sales, survival, or some socially responsible price level.

5   A demand curve shows the maximum number of products consumers will buy at a given price and for a given set of (*a*) consumer tastes, (*b*) price and availability of other products, and (*c*) consumer income. When any of these change, there is a shift of the demand curve.

6   Important revenue concepts include total revenue, average revenue, and marginal revenue.

7   Price elasticity of demand measures the sensitivity of units sold to a change in price. When demand is elastic, a reduction

in price is more than offset by an increase in units sold, so that total revenue increases.

8   It is necessary to consider cost behaviour when making pricing decisions. Important cost concepts include total cost, variable cost, fixed cost, and marginal cost.

9   Break-even analysis shows the relationship between total revenue and total cost at various quantities of output for given conditions of price, fixed cost, and variable cost. The break-even point is where total revenue and total cost are equal.

KEY TERMS AND CONCEPTS

average revenue p. 353
barter p. 344
break-even analysis p. 357
break-even chart p. 358
break-even point p. 357
demand curve p. 352
demand factors p. 352
fixed cost p. 356
marginal analysis p. 357
marginal cost p. 356
marginal revenue p. 353

price p. 344
price elasticity of demand p. 355
pricing constraints p. 347
pricing objectives p. 350
profit equation p. 346
total cost p. 356
total revenue p. 353
value p. 345
value-pricing p. 345
variable cost p. 356

INTERNET EXERCISE   www.mcgrawhill.ca/college/berkowitz

Want to check out the options and prices on your next car? First, write down the features you want in a car. Then, check out these three Websites:

• General Motors: www.gmcanada.com
• Ford: www.fordcanada.com
• An independent car buying service: www.autobytel.ca

After you have printed the price quotes for the cars you desire from the above Web sites, call or visit a local dealer and get a quote for the cars with the same features. Compare the prices and experiences of buying a car from the Internet and the traditional car dealer. What are the similarities and differences, if any, in negotiating the list prices, rebates, trade-in allowances, financing, warranties, accessories (or option packages), destination charges, and so on for the cars you want?

Want to get better grades, find tips on how to study more effectively, and stay up to date with happenings in the world of marketing? Visit the Online Learning Centre for practice tests, Study Smart software, and much more! www.mcgrawhill.ca/college/berkowitz

Interested in finding out what marketing looks like in the real world? *Marketing Magazine* is just a click away on your OLC! Visit www.mcgrawhill.ca/college/berkowitz

APPLYING MARKETING CONCEPTS AND PERSPECTIVES

1   How would the price equation apply to the purchase price of (*a*) gasoline, (*b*) an airline ticket, and (*c*) a chequing account?

2   What would be your response to the statement, "Profit maximization is the only legitimate pricing objective for the firm"?

3   How is a downward-sloping demand curve related to total revenue and marginal revenue?

4   A marketing executive once said, "If the price elasticity of demand for your product is inelastic, then your price is probably too low." What is this executive saying in terms of the economic principles discussed in this chapter?

5   A marketing manager reduced the price on a brand of cereal by 10 percent and observed a 25-percent increase in quantity sold. The manager then thought that if the price were reduced by another 20 percent, a 50-percent increase in quantity sold would occur. What would be your response to the marketing manager's reasoning?

6   A student theatre group at a university has developed a demand schedule that shows the relationship between ticket prices and demand based on a student survey, as follows:

TICKET PRICE	NUMBER OF STUDENTS WHO WOULD BUY
$1	300
2	250
3	200
4	150
5	100

(a) Graph the demand curve and the total revenue curve based on these data. What ticket price might be set based on this analysis? (b) What other factors should be considered before the final price is set?

7 Touché Toiletries, Inc. has developed an addition to its Lizardman Cologne line tentatively branded Ode d'Toade Cologne. Unit variable costs are 45 cents for a 60-mL bottle, and heavy advertising expenditures in the first year would result in total fixed costs of $900 000. Ode d'Toade Cologne is priced at $7.50 for a 60-mL bottle. How many bottles of Ode d'Toade must be sold to break even?

8 Suppose that marketing executives for Touché Toiletries reduced the price to $6.50 for a 60-mL bottle of Ode d'Toade and the fixed costs were $1 100 000. Suppose further that the unit variable cost remained at 45 cents for a 60-mL bottle. (a) How many bottles must be sold to break even? (b) What dollar profit level would Ode d'Toade achieve if 200 000 bottles were sold?

9 Executives of Random Recordings, Inc. produced an album entitled *Sunshine/Moonshine* by the Starshine Sisters Band. The cost and price information was as follows:

Album cover	$ 1.00 per album
Songwriter's royalties	0.30 per album
Recording artists' royalties	0.70 per album
Direct material and labour costs to produce the album	1.00 per album
Fixed cost of producing an album (advertising, studio fee, etc.)	100 000.00
Selling price	7.00 per album

(a) Prepare a chart like that in Figure 13–11 showing total cost, fixed cost, and total revenue for album quantity sold levels starting at 10 000 albums through 100 000 albums at 10 000 album intervals; that is, 10 000, 20 000, 30 000, and so on. (b) What is the break-even point for the album?

VIDEO CASE 13–1 Washburn International, Inc.

"The relationship between musicians and their guitars is something really extraordinary—and is a fairly strange one," says Brady Breen in a carefully understated tone of voice. Breen has the experience to know. He's production manager of Washburn International (www.washburn.com), one of the most prestigious guitar manufacturers in the world. Washburn's instruments range from one-of-a-kind, custom-made acoustic and electric guitars and basses to less expensive, mass-produced ones.

THE COMPANY AND ITS HISTORY

The modern Washburn International started in 1977 when a small firm bought the century-old Washburn brand name and a small inventory of guitars, parts, and promotional supplies. At that time annual revenues of the company were $300 000 for the sale of about 2500 guitars. Washburn's first catalogue, appearing in 1978, told a frightening truth:

> Our designs are translated by Japan's most experienced craftsmen, assuring the consistent quality and craftmanship for which they are known.

At that time the North American guitar-making craft was at an all-time low. Guitars made by Japanese firms such as Ibane and Yamaha were in use by an increasing number of professionals.

Times have changed for Washburn. Today the company sells about 250 000 guitars a year. Annual sales exceed $50 million. All this resulted from Washburn's aggressive marketing strategies to develop product lines with different price points targeted at musicians in distinctly different market segments.

THE PRODUCTS AND MARKET SEGMENTS

Arguably the most trendsetting guitar developed by the modern Washburn company appeared in 1980. This was the Festival Series of cutaway, thin-bodied flattops, with built-in bridge pickups and controls, which went on to become the virtual standard for live performances. John Lodge of the Moody Blues endorsed the 12-string version—his gleaming white guitar appeared in both concerts and ads for years. In the time since the Festival Series appeared, countless rock and country stars have used these instruments including Bob Dylan, Dolly Parton, Greg Allman, John Jorgenson, and George Harrison.

Until 1991 all Washburn guitars were manufactured in Asia. That year Washburn started building its high-end guitars in North America. Today Washburn marketing executives divide its product line into four levels. From high-end to low-end, these are:

- One-of-a-kind, custom units.
- Batch-custom units.
- Mass-customized units.
- Mass-produced units.

The one-of-a-kind custom units are for the many stars that use Washburn instruments. The mass-produced units targeted at first-time buyers are still manufactured in Asian factories.

PRICING ISSUES

Setting prices for its various lines presents a continuing challenge for Washburn. Not only do the prices have to reflect the changing tastes of its various segments of musicians, but the prices must also be competitive with the prices set for guitars manufactured and marketed globally. In fact, Washburn and other well-known guitar manufacturers have a prestige-niche strategy. For Washburn this involves endorsements by internationally known musicians who play its instruments and lend their names to lines of Washburn signature guitars. This has the effect of reducing the price elasticity or price sensitivity for these guitars. Stars playing Washburn guitars like Nuno Bettencourt, David Gilmour of Pink Floyd, Joe Perry of Aerosmith, and Darryl Jones of the Rolling Stones have their own lines of signature guitars—the "batch-custom" units mentioned earlier.

Joe Baksha, Washburn's executive vice president, is responsible for reviewing and approving prices for the company's lines of guitars. Setting a sales target of 2000 units for a new line of guitars, he is considering a suggested retail price of $329 per unit for customers at one of the hundreds of retail outlets carrying the Washburn line. For planning purposes, Baksha estimates half of the final retail price will be the price Washburn nets when it sells its guitar to the wholesalers and dealers in its channel of distribution.

Looking at Washburn's financial data for its present North American plant, Baksha estimates that this line of guitars must bear these fixed costs:

Rent and taxes	= $12 000
Depreciation of equipment	= $ 4 000
Management and quality control program	= $20 000

In addition, he estimates the variable costs for each unit to be:

Direct materials =	$25/unit
Direct labour =	8 hours/unit @ $14/hour

Carefully kept production records at Washburn's North American plant make Baksha believe that these are reasonable estimates. He explains, "Before we begin a production run, we have a good feel for what our costs will be. The North American-built N-4, for example, simply costs more than one of our foreign-produced Mercury or Wing series electrics."

Caught in the global competition for guitar sales, Washburn searches for ways to reduce and control costs. After much agonizing, the company decided to move to Nashville, Tennessee. In this home of country music, Washburn expects to lower its manufacturing costs because there are many skilled workers in the region, and its fixed costs will be reduced by avoiding some of the expenses of having a big-city location. Specifically, Washburn projects that it will reduce its rent and taxes expense by 40 percent and the wage rate it pays by 15 percent in relocating from its current plant to Nashville.

Questions

1 What factors are most likely to affect the demand for the lines of Washburn guitars (*a*) bought by a first-time guitar buyer and (*b*) bought by a sophisticated musician who wants a signature model signed by David Gilmour or Joe Perry?

2 For Washburn what are examples of (*a*) shifting the demand curve to the right to get a higher price for a guitar line (movement *of* the demand curve) and (*b*) pricing decisions involving moving *along* a demand curve?

3 In Washburn's current plant what is the break-even point for the new line of guitars if the retail price is (*a*) $329, (*b*) $359, and (*c*) $299? Also, (*d*) if Washburn achieves the sales target of 2000 units at the $329 retail price, what will its profit be?

4 Assume that Washburn moves its production to Nashville and that the costs are reduced as projected in the case. Then, what will be the (*a*) new break-even point at a $329 retail price for this line of guitars and (*b*) the new profit if it sells 2000 units?

5 If for competitive reasons Washburn eventually has to move all its production back to Asia, (*a*) which specific costs might be lowered and (*b*) what additional costs might it expect to incur?

AA 4 PACK
NEW M3 Technology
DURACELL®
ULTRA
THE MOST POWERFUL DURACELL® BATTERY*
SIZE AA ALKALINE BATTERY
GUARANTEED FRESH THROUGH 2007
POWER CHECK™
A TESTER ON EVERY ALKALINE BATTERY
M3 Technology
MORE FUEL
MORE EFFICIENCY
MORE POWER
321781-01-00
DURACELL ULTRA
MAY EXPLODE OR LEAK.
MADE IN U.S.A.
DURACELL® POWERCHECK
Test at 70°F/21°C
Patented DURACELL INC. Bethel, CT 06801

CHAPTER

14

ARRIVING AT THE FINAL PRICE

AFTER READING THIS CHAPTER YOU SHOULD BE ABLE TO:

- Understand how to establish the initial "approximate price level" using demand-oriented, cost-oriented, profit-oriented, and competition-oriented approaches.

- Identify the major factors considered in deriving a final list or quoted price from the approximate price level.

- Describe adjustments made to the approximate price level based on geography, discounts, and allowances.

- Prepare basic financial analyses useful in evaluating alternative prices and arriving at the final sales price.

- Describe the principal laws and regulations affecting pricing practices.

DURACELL KNOWS THE VALUE OF PORTABLE POWER

How is value defined for an alkaline battery? Ask Duracell, the world's leading manufacturer and marketer of high-performance alkaline batteries.

As the global leader of the $8-billion alkaline battery category, Duracell pioneered the high-performance segment of alkaline batteries with the launch of Duracell Ultra, the most successful new battery ever introduced. Duracell Ultra was designed to meet the extraordinary power requirements of today's portable electronic devices. Duracell Ultra with M3 Technology AA alkaline batteries last up to 180 percent longer than ordinary alkaline batteries in digital cell phones; up to 140 percent longer in handheld personal computers; and up to 100 percent longer in camcorders. M3 Technology's patented and patent-pending advancements and design enhancements not only provide longer battery life, but also improve the performance of devices. For example, halogen flashlights shine brighter and camera flashes recycle faster with M3 Technology.

Product innovation that benefits the consumer is a critical ingredient in Duracell Ultra's marketing success. "M3 Technology is readily understood and appreciated by consumers because it answers their fundamental needs for portable power," says Duracell's senior vice president for business management and business development. "Moreover, consumers expect this type of advance from the leader in the category." Such innovation naturally translates into the price consumers are willing to pay. Duracell Ultra with M3 Technology is priced about 25 percent higher than Duracell alkaline batteries.[1]

The marketing success of Duracell Ultra illustrates the imaginative commercialization of new alkaline

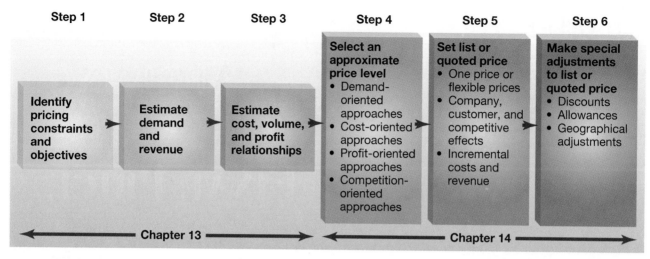

FIGURE 14–1
Steps in setting price

battery technology at a price point that creates value for the consumer. In addition to understanding consumer demand, cost, competition, and profit considerations played a role in Duracell's pricing decision (to be discussed later).

This chapter describes how companies select an approximate price level, highlights important considerations in setting a list or quoted price, and identifies various price adjustments that can be made to prices set by the firm—the last three steps an organization uses in setting price (Figure 14–1). In addition, an overview of important legal and regulatory aspects of pricing is provided.

STEP 4: SELECT AN APPROXIMATE PRICE LEVEL

A key to a marketing manager's setting a final price for a product is to find an "approximate price level" to use as a reasonable starting point. Four common approaches to helping find this approximate price level are (1) demand-oriented, (2) cost-oriented, (3) profit-oriented, and (4) competition-oriented approaches (Figure 14–2). Although these approaches are discussed separately below, some of them overlap, and an effective marketing manager will consider several in searching for an approximate price level.

Demand-Oriented Approaches

Demand-oriented approaches weigh factors underlying expected customer tastes and preferences more heavily than such factors as cost, profit, and competition when selecting a price level.

SKIMMING PRICING
The highest initial price that customers really desiring the product are willing to pay.

Skimming Pricing   A firm introducing a new or innovative product can use **skimming pricing**, setting the highest initial price that customers who really desire the product are willing to pay. These customers are not very price sensitive because they weigh the new product's price, quality, and ability to satisfy their needs against the same characteristics of substitutes. As the demand of these customers is satisfied, the firm lowers the price to attract another, more price-sensitive segment. Thus, skimming pricing gets its name from skimming successive layers of "cream," or customer segments, as prices are lowered in a series of steps.

Skimming pricing is an effective strategy when (1) enough prospective customers are willing to buy the product immediately at the high initial price to make these sales profitable, (2) the high initial price will not attract competitors, (3) lowering price has only a minor effect on increasing the sales volume and reducing the unit costs, and (4) customers interpret the high price as signifying high quality. These

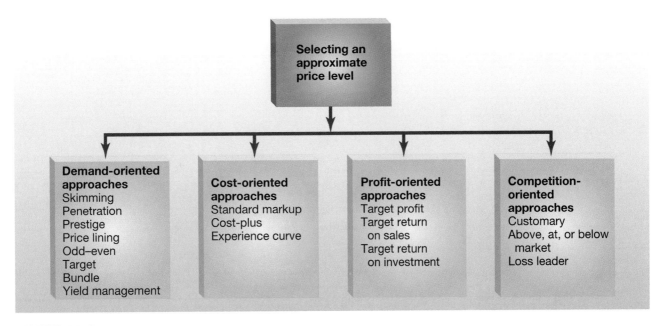

FIGURE 14–2
Four approaches for selecting
an approximate price level

four conditions are most likely to exist when the new product is protected by patents or copyrights or its uniqueness is understood and valued by customers. Duracell adopted a skimming strategy for the Duracell Ultra alkaline battery because many of these conditions applied.

Penetration Pricing   Setting a low initial price on a new product to appeal immediately to the mass market is **penetration pricing**, the exact opposite of skimming pricing. Nintendo consciously chose a penetration strategy when it introduced its GameCube video game console. GameCube was priced at substantially less than Microsoft's Xbox and Sony's PlayStation 2 consoles.[2]

The conditions favouring penetration pricing are the reverse of those supporting skimming pricing: (1) many segments of the market are price sensitive, (2) a low initial price discourages competitors from entering the market, and (3) unit production and marketing costs fall dramatically as production volumes increase. A firm using penetration pricing may (1) maintain the initial price for a time to gain profit lost from its low introductory level, or (2) lower the price further, counting on the new volume to generate the necessary profit.

In some situations penetration pricing may follow skimming pricing. A company might initially price a product high to attract price-insensitive consumers and recoup initial research and development costs and introductory promotional expenditures. Once this is done, penetration pricing is used to appeal to a broader segment of the population and increase market share.[3]

Prestige Pricing   As noted in Chapter 13, consumers may use price as a measure of the quality or prestige of an item so that as price is lowered beyond some point, demand for the item actually falls. **Prestige pricing** involves setting a high price so that quality- or status-conscious consumers will be attracted to the product and buy it (Figure 14–3A). The demand curve slopes downward and to the right between points A and B but turns back to the left between points B and C because demand is actually reduced between points B and C. From A to B buyers see the lowering of price as a bargain and buy more; from B to C they become dubious about the quality and prestige and buy less. A marketing manager's pricing strategy here is to stay above price P_0 (the initial price).

PENETRATION PRICING
Setting a low initial price on a new product to appeal immediately to the mass market.

www.nintendo.com

PRESTIGE PRICING
Setting a high price so that status-conscious consumers will be attracted to the product and buy it.

FIGURE 14–3
Demand curves for two
types of demand-oriented
approaches

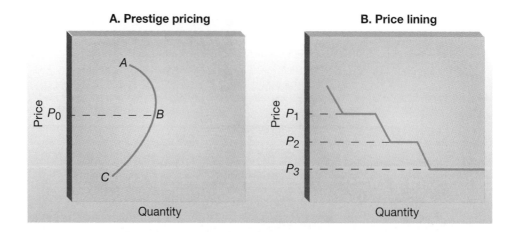

A. Prestige pricing

B. Price lining

Rolls-Royce cars, diamonds, perfumes, fine china, Swiss watches, and crystal have an element of prestige pricing in them and may sell worse at lower prices than at higher ones.[4] The recent success of Swiss watchmaker TAG Heuer is an example. The company raised the average price of its watches from $250 to $1000, and its sales volume increased sevenfold![5] Recently, Energizer learned that buyers of high-performance alkaline batteries tend to associate a lower price with lower quality. The accompanying Marketing NewsNet describes the pricing lesson learned by Energizer.[6]

PRICE LINING
Setting the price of a line
of products at a number of
different specific pricing
points.

Price Lining   Often a firm that is selling not just a single product but a line of products may price them at a number of different specific pricing points, which is called **price lining**. For example, a discount department store manager may price a line of women's dresses at $59, $79, and $99. As shown in Figure 14–3B, this assumes that

MARKETING NEWSNET

Energizer's Lesson in Price Perception: Value Lies in the Eye of the Beholder

Battery manufacturers are as tireless as a certain drum-thumping bunny in their efforts to create products that perform better, last longer, and, not incidentally, outsell the competition. The commercialization of new alkaline battery technology at a price that creates value for consumers is not always obvious or easy. Just ask the marketing executives at Energizer about their experience with pricing Energizer Advanced Formula and Energizer e[2] AA alkaline batteries.

When Duracell launched its high-performance Ultra brand AA alkaline battery with a 25-percent price premium over standard Duracell batteries, Energizer quickly countered with its own high-performance battery—Energizer Advanced Formula. Believing that consumers would not pay the premium price, Energizer priced its Advanced Formula brand at the same price as its standard AA alkaline battery, expecting to gain market share from Duracell. It didn't happen. Why not? According to industry analysts, consumers associated Energizer's low price with inferior quality in the high-performance segment. Instead of gaining market share, Energizer lost market share to Duracell and Rayovac, the number-three battery manufacturer.

Having learned its lesson, Energizer subsequently released its e[2] high-performance battery, this time priced 4 percent higher than Duracell Ultra and about 50 percent higher than Advanced Formula. The result? Energizer recovered lost sales and market share. The lesson learned? Value lies in the eye of the beholder.

demand is elastic at each of these price points but inelastic between these price points. In some instances all the items might be purchased for the same cost and then marked up at different percentages to achieve these price points based on colour, style, and expected demand. In other instances manufacturers design products for different price points, and retailers apply approximately the same markup percentages to achieve the three or four different price points offered to consumers. Sellers often feel that a limited number (such as three or four) of price points is preferable to 8 or 10 different ones, which may only confuse prospective buyers.[7]

www.sears.ca

ODD–EVEN PRICING
Setting prices a few dollars or cents under an even number, such as $19.95.

Odd–Even Pricing   Sears Canada offers a Craftsman radial saw for $499.99, the suggested retail price for a MACH 3 razor set (razor and two blades) is $6.99, and Dollarama sells greeting cards for 99 cents. Why not simply price these items at $500, $7, and $1, respectively? These firms are using **odd–even pricing**, which involves setting prices a few dollars or cents under an even number. The presumption is that consumers see the Sears radial saw as priced at "something over $400" rather than "about $500." In theory, demand increases if the price drops from $500 to $499.99. There is some evidence to suggest that this does happen. However, research suggests that overuse of odd-ending prices tends to mute its effect on demand.[8]

TARGET PRICING
Manufacturer deliberately adjusting the composition and features of a product to achieve the target price to consumers.

Target Pricing   Manufacturers will sometimes estimate the price that the ultimate consumer would be willing to pay for a product. They then work backward through markups taken by retailers and wholesalers to determine what price they can charge wholesalers for the product. This practice, called **target pricing**, results in the manufacturer deliberately adjusting the composition and features of a product to achieve the target price to consumers. Canon uses this practice for pricing its cameras, and Heinz adopted target pricing for its complete line of pet foods.

BUNDLE PRICING
The marketing of two or more products in a single "package" price.

Bundle Pricing   A frequently used demand-oriented pricing practice is **bundle pricing**—the marketing of two or more products in a single "package" price. For example, Air Canada offers vacation packages that include airfare, car rental, and lodging. Bundle pricing is based on the idea that consumers value the package more than the individual items. This is due to benefits received from not having to make separate purchases and enhanced satisfaction from one item given the presence of another. Moreover, bundle pricing often provides a lower total cost to buyers and lower marketing costs to sellers.[9] For example, Rogers AT&T offers an all-in-one wireless phone and service package that includes a Nokia phone and a calling plan for less than $20 a month.[10]

www.aircanada.ca

YIELD MANAGEMENT PRICING
The charging of different prices to maximize revenue for a set amount of capacity at any given time.

Yield Management Pricing   Have you noticed seats on your Air Canada flights are priced differently within economy class? What you observed is **yield management pricing**—the charging of different prices to maximize revenue for a set amount of capacity at any given time.[11] As described in Chapter 12, service businesses engage in capacity management, and an effective way to do this is by varying price by time, day, week, or season. Yield management pricing is a complex approach that continually matches demand and supply to customize the price for a service. Airlines, hotels, cruise ships, and car rental companies use it. The airline industry reports that yield management pricing produces hundreds of millions of dollars of revenue each year that might not ordinarily be produced using traditional pricing practices.[12]

Concept Check

1. What are the circumstances in pricing a new product that might support skimming or penetration pricing?

2. What is odd–even pricing?

Cost-Oriented Approaches

With cost-oriented approaches the price setter stresses the supply or cost side of the pricing problem, not the demand side. Price is set by looking at the production and marketing costs and then adding enough to cover direct expenses, overhead, and profit.

STANDARD MARKUP PRICING
Adding a fixed percentage to the cost of all items in a specific product class.

Standard Markup Pricing   Managers of supermarkets and other retail stores have such a large number of products that estimating the demand for each product as a means of setting price is impossible. Therefore, they use **standard markup pricing**, which entails adding a fixed percentage to the cost of all items in a specific product class. This percentage markup varies depending on the type of retail store (such as furniture, clothing, or grocery) and on the product involved. High-volume products usually have smaller markups than do low-volume products. Supermarkets such as Sobeys, Safeway, and Loblaws have different markups for staple items and discretionary items. The markup on staple items like sugar, flour, and dairy products varies from 10 percent to 23 percent, whereas markups on discretionary items like snack foods and candy range from 27 percent to 47 percent. These markups must cover all expenses of the store, pay for overhead costs, and contribute something to profits. For supermarkets, these markups, which may appear very large, result in only a one-percent profit on sales revenue if the store is operating efficiently. By comparison, consider the markups on snacks and beverages purchased at your local movie theatre. The markup on soft drinks is 87 percent, 65 percent on chocolate bars, and a whopping 90 percent on popcorn! An explanation of how to compute a markup, along with operating statement data and other ratios, is given in Appendix B following this chapter.

COST-PLUS PRICING
The practice of summing the total unit cost of providing a product or service and adding a specific amount to the cost to arrive at a price.

Cost-Plus Pricing   Many manufacturing, professional services, and construction firms use a variation of standard markup pricing. **Cost-plus pricing** involves summing the total unit cost of providing a product or service and adding a specific amount to the cost to arrive at a price. Cost-plus pricing generally assumes two forms. With *cost-plus percentage-of-cost pricing*, a fixed percentage is added to the total unit costs. This is often used to price one- or few-of-a-kind items, as when an architectural firm charges a percentage of the construction costs of, say, the multi-million dollar Air Canada Centre (home of the Toronto Maple Leafs). In buying highly technical, few-of-a-kind products such as hydro-electric power plants or space satellites, buyers—particularly government agencies—have found that general contractors are reluctant to specify a formal, fixed price for the procurement. Therefore, they use *cost-plus fixed-fee pricing*, which means that a supplier is reimbursed for all costs, regardless of what they turn out to be, but is allowed only a fixed fee as profit that is independent of the final cost of the project. For example, suppose that the Department of National Defence agreed to pay a manufacturer $1.2 billion as the cost of a new military satellite and agreed to a $100-million fee for providing the satellite. Even if the manufacturer's cost increased to $2 billion for the satellite, its fee would remain $100 million.

Cost-plus pricing is the most commonly used method to set prices for business products. But increasingly, this method is finding favour among business-to-business marketers in the service sector. For example, the rising cost of legal fees has prompted some law firms to adopt a cost-plus pricing approach. Rather than billing business clients on an hourly basis, lawyers and their clients agree on a fixed fee based on expected costs plus a profit for the law firm.[13] Many advertising agencies also use this approach. Here, the client agrees to pay the agency a fee based on the cost of its work plus some agreed-on profit, which is often a percentage of total cost.[14]

EXPERIENCE CURVE PRICING
A method of pricing based on the learning effect, which holds that the unit cost of many products and services declines by 10 percent to 30 percent each time a firm's experience at producing and selling them doubles.

Experience Curve Pricing   The method of **experience curve pricing** is based on the learning effect, which holds that the unit cost of many products and services declines by 10 percent to 30 percent each time a firm's experience at producing

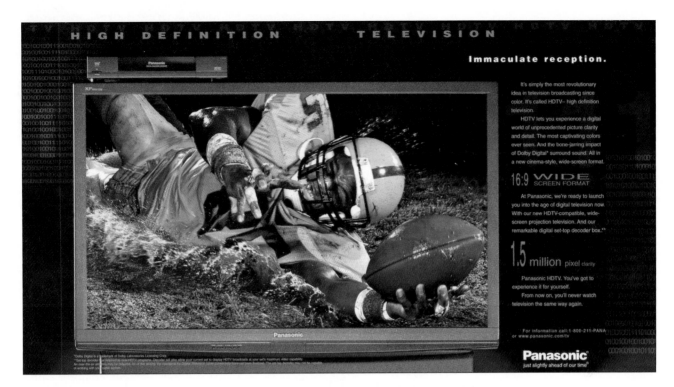

Panasonic expects to be a leader in the successful commercialization of HDTV.

Panasonic

www.panasonic.com

and selling them doubles.[15] This reduction is regular or predictable enough that the average cost per unit can be mathematically estimated. For example, if the firm estimates that costs will fall by 15 percent each time volume doubles, then the cost of the 100th unit produced and sold will be about 85 percent of the cost of the 50th unit, and the 200th unit will be 85 percent of the 100th unit. Therefore, if the cost of the 50th unit is $100, the 100th unit would cost $85, the 200th unit would be $72.25, and so on. Since prices often follow costs with experience curve pricing, a rapid decline in price is possible. Japanese firms in the electronics industry often adopt this pricing approach. This cost-oriented pricing approach complements the demand-oriented pricing strategy of skimming followed by penetration pricing. For example, CD player prices have decreased from $900 to less than $200, fax machine prices have declined from $1000 to under $300, and cellular telephones that once sold for $4000 are now priced below $99. Panasonic, Sony, Samsung, Zenith, and other television manufacturers will use experience curve pricing for HDTV sets. Consumers will benefit because prices will decline as cumulative sales volume grows.

Profit-Oriented Approaches

A price setter may choose to balance both revenues and costs to set price using profit-oriented approaches. These might involve either a target of a specific dollar volume of profit or express this target profit as a percentage of sales or investment.

Target Profit Pricing   A firm may set an annual target of a specific dollar volume of profit, which is called **target profit pricing**. Suppose a picture framing store owner wishes to use target profit pricing to establish a price for a typical framed picture and assumes the following:

TARGET PROFIT PRICING
Setting an annual target of a specific dollar volume of profit.

- Variable cost is a constant $22 per unit.
- Fixed cost is a constant $26 000.
- Demand is insensitive to price up to $60 per unit.
- A target profit of $7000 is sought at an annual volume of 1000 units (framed pictures).

The price can be calculated as follows:

Profit = Total revenue − Total cost

Profit = (P × Q) − [FC + (UVC × Q)]

$7000 = (P × 1000) − [$26 000 + ($22 × 1000)]

$7000 = 1000P − ($26 000 + $22 000)

1000P = $7000 + $48 000

P = $55

Note that a critical assumption is that this higher average price of a framed picture will not cause the demand to fall.

Target Return-on-Sales Pricing   A difficulty with target profit pricing is that although it is simple and the target involves only a specific dollar volume, there is no benchmark of sales or investment used to show how much of the firm's effort is needed to achieve the target. Firms such as supermarket chains often use **target return-on-sales pricing** to set typical prices that will give the firm a profit that is a specified percentage—say, one percent of the sales volume. Suppose the owner decides to use target return-on-sales pricing for the frame shop and makes the same first three assumptions shown previously. The owner now sets a target of 20-percent return on sales at an annual volume of 1250 units. This gives

$$\text{Target return on sales} = \frac{\text{Target profit}}{\text{Total revenue}}$$

$$20\% = \frac{TR - TC}{TR}$$

$$0.20 = \frac{P \times Q - [FC + (UVC - Q)]}{TR}$$

$$0.20 = \frac{P \times 1250 - [\$26\,000 + (\$22 \times 1250)]}{P \times 1250}$$

$$P = \$53.50$$

So at a price of $53.50 per unit and an annual quantity of 1250 frames,

TR = P × Q = $53.50 × 1250 = $66 875

TC = FC + (UVC × Q) = $26 000 + ($22 × 1250) = $53 500

Profit = TR − TC = $66 875 − $53 500 = $13 375

As a check,

$$\text{Target return on sales} = \frac{\text{Target profit}}{\text{Total revenue}} = \frac{\$13\,375}{\$66\,875} = 20\%$$

Target Return-on-Investment Pricing   Firms such as GM and many public utilities set annual return-on-investment (ROI) targets such as ROI of 20 percent. **Target return-on-investment pricing** is a method of setting prices to achieve this target.

Suppose the store owner sets a target ROI of 10 percent, which is twice that achieved the previous year. She considers raising the average price of a framed picture to $54 or $58—up from last year's average of $50. To do this, she might improve product quality by offering better frames and higher-quality matting, which will increase the cost but will probably offset the decreased revenue from the lower number of units that can be sold next year.

To manage this wide variety of assumptions, today's managers use computerized spreadsheets to project operating statements based on a diverse set of assumptions. Figure 14–4 shows the results of computerized spreadsheet simulation, with assumptions shown at the top and the projected results at the bottom. A previous year's

TARGET RETURN-ON-SALES PRICING
Setting a price to achieve a profit that is a specified percentage of the sales volume.

TARGET RETURN-ON-INVESTMENT PRICING
Setting a price to achieve a return-on-investment (ROI) target.

ASSUMPTIONS OR RESULTS	FINANCIAL ELEMENT	LAST YEAR	SIMULATION			
			A	**B**	**C**	**D**
ASSUMPTIONS	Price per unit (P)	$50	$54	$54	$58	$58
	Units sold (Q)	1 000	1 200	1 100	1 100	1 000
	Change in unit variable cost (UVC)	0%	+10%	+10%	+20%	+20%
	Unit variable cost	$22.00	$24.20	$24.20	$26.20	$26.40
	Total expenses	$8 000	Same	Same	Same	Same
	Owner's salary	$18 000	Same	Same	Same	Same
	Investment	$20 000	Same	Same	Same	Same
	Provincial and federal taxes	50%	Same	Same	Same	Same
SPREADSHEET SIMULATION	Net sales (P x Q)	$50 000	$64 800	$59 400	$63 800	$58 000
	Less: COGS (Q x UVC)	22 000	29 040	26 620	29 040	26 400
	Gross margin	$28 000	$35 760	$32 780	$34 760	$31 600
	Less: total expenses	8 000	8 000	8 000	8 000	8 000
	Less: owner's salary	18 000	18 000	18 000	18 000	18 000
	Net profit before taxes	$2 000	$9 760	$6 780	$8 760	$5 600
	Less: taxes	1 000	4 880	3 390	4 380	2 800
	Net profit after taxes	$1 000	$4 880	$3 390	$4 380	$2 800
	Investment	$20 000	$20 000	$20 000	$20 000	$20 000
	Return on investment	5.0%	24.4%	17.0%	21.9%	14.0%

FIGURE 14–4

Results of computer spreadsheet simulation to select price to achieve a target return on investment

operating statement results are shown in the column headed "Last Year," and the assumptions and spreadsheet results for four different sets of assumptions are shown in columns A, B, C, and D.

In choosing a price or another action using spreadsheet results, the decision maker must (1) study the results of the computer simulation projections and (2) assess the realism of the assumptions underlying each set of projections. For example, the store owner sees from the bottom row of Figure 14–4 that all four spreadsheet simulations exceed the after-tax target ROI of 10 percent. But, after more thought, she judges it to be more realistic to set an average price of $58 per unit, allow the unit variable cost to increase by 20 percent to account for more expensive framing and matting, and settle for the same unit sales as the 1000 units sold last year. She selects simulation D in this computerized spreadsheet approach to target ROI pricing and has a goal of 14 percent after-tax ROI. Of course, these same calculations can be done by hand, but this is far more time consuming.

Competition-Oriented Approaches

Rather than emphasize demand, cost, or profit factors, a price setter can stress what competitors (or "the market") are doing.

CUSTOMARY PRICING

A method of pricing based on tradition, a standardized channel of distribution, or other competitive factors.

Customary Pricing   For some products where tradition, a standardized channel of distribution, or other competitive factors dictate the price, **customary pricing** is used. Tradition prevails in the pricing of Swatch watches. The $40 customary price for the basic model has changed little in 10 years. Chocolate bars offered through standard vending machines have a customary price of 50 cents, and a significant departure from this price may result in a loss of sales for the manufacturer. Hershey typically has changed the amount of chocolate in its chocolate bars depending on the price of raw chocolate rather than vary its customary retail price so that it can continue selling through vending machines.

ABOVE-, AT-, OR BELOW-MARKET PRICING
Pricing based on market price.

Above-, At-, or Below-Market Pricing For most products it is difficult to identify a specific market price for a product or product class. Still, marketing managers often have a subjective feel for the competitor's price or market price. Using this benchmark, they then may deliberately choose a strategy of **above-, at-, or below-market pricing**.

Among watch manufacturers, Rolex takes pride in emphasizing that it makes one of the most expensive watches you can buy—a clear example of above-market pricing. Manufacturers of national brands of clothing such as Alfred Sung and Christian Dior and retailers such as Holt Renfrew deliberately set premium prices for their products.

Large mass-merchandise chains such as Sears Canada and The Bay generally use at-market pricing. These chains often establish the going market price in the minds of competitors. Similarly, Revlon generally prices its products "at market." These companies also provide a reference price for competitors that use above- and below-market pricing.

In contrast, a number of firms use a strategy of below-market pricing. Manufacturers of all generic products and retailers who offer their own private brands of products ranging from peanut butter to shampoo deliberately set prices for these products about 8 percent to 10 percent below the prices of nationally branded competitive products such as Skippy peanut butter, Vidal Sassoon shampoo, or Crest toothpaste. Below-market pricing also exists in business-to-business marketing. Hewlett-Packard, for instance, consciously priced its line of office personal computers below IBM to promote a value image among corporate buyers.[16]

Loss-Leader Pricing For a special promotion many retail stores deliberately sell a product below its customary price to attract attention to it. For example, supermarkets will often use produce or paper goods as loss leaders. The purpose of **loss-leader pricing** is not to increase sales of that particular produce but to attract customers in hopes they will buy other products as well, particularly discretionary items carrying large markups.[17]

LOSS-LEADER PRICING
Deliberately selling a product below its customary price to attract attention to it.

Concept Check

1. What is standard markup pricing?

2. What profit-based pricing approach should a manager use if he or she wants to reflect the percentage of the firm's resources used in obtaining the profit?

3. What is the purpose of loss-leader pricing when used by a retail firm?

STEP 5: SET THE LIST OR QUOTED PRICE

The first four steps in setting price covered in Chapter 13 and this chapter result in an approximate price level for the product that appears reasonable. But it still remains for the manager to set a specific list or quoted price in light of all relevant factors.

One-Price versus Flexible-Price Policy

ONE-PRICE POLICY
Setting one price for all buyers of a product or service. Also called *fixed pricing*.

A seller must decide whether to follow a one-price or flexible-price policy. A **one-price policy**, also called *fixed pricing*, is setting one price for all buyers of a product or service. For example, when you buy a Wilson Sting tennis racquet from a discount store, you are offered the product at a single price. You can buy it or not, but there is no variation in the price under the seller's one-price policy. Saturn Corporation uses this approach in its stores and features a "no haggle, one price" price for its

FLEXIBLE-PRICE POLICY
Setting different prices for products and services depending on individual buyers and purchase situations. Also called *dynamic pricing*.

cars. Some retailers, such as Dollar Stores, have married this policy with a below-market approach and sell everything in their stores for $1 or less![18]

In contrast, a **flexible-price policy**, also called *dynamic pricing*, involves setting different prices for products and services depending on individual buyers and purchase situations. A flexible-price policy gives sellers considerable discretion in setting the final price in light of demand, cost, and competitive factors. Yield-management pricing is a form of flexible pricing because prices vary by an individual buyer's purchase situation, company cost considerations, and competitive conditions.[19] Dell Computer Corporation recently adopted flexible pricing. It continually adjusts prices in response to changes in its own costs, competitive pressures, and demand from customers, from one segment of the personal computer market to another. "Our flexibility allows us to be [priced] different even within a day," says a Dell spokesperson.[20]

Most companies use a one-price policy. However, flexible pricing has grown in popularity because of increasingly sophisticated information technology. Today, many marketers have the ability to customize a price for an individual on the basis of his or her purchasing patterns, product preferences, and price sensitivity, all of which are stored in company data warehouses. Price customization is particularly prevalent for products and services bought online. Online marketers routinely adjust prices in response to purchase situations and past purchase behaviours of online buyers. Some online marketers monitor an online shopper's "clickstream"—the way that person navigates through its Website. If the visitor behaves like a price-sensitive shopper—perhaps by comparing many different products—that person may be offered a lower price. However, as noted at the end of this chapter, flexible pricing carried to the extreme could be considered price discrimination and is a practice prohibited under the Competition Act.[21]

Company, Customer, and Competitive Effects

As the final list or quoted price is set, the effects on the company, customers, and competitors must be assessed.

Company Effects   For a firm with more than one product, a decision on the price of a single product must consider the price of other items in its product line or related product lines in its product mix. Within a product line or mix there are usually some products that are substitutes for one another and some that complement each other. Frito-Lay recognizes that its tortilla chip product line consisting of Baked Tostitos, Tostitos, and Doritos brands are partial substitutes for one another and its bean and cheese chip dip line and salsa sauces complement the tortilla chip line.

PRODUCT-LINE PRICING
The setting of prices for all items in a product line.

A manager's challenge when marketing multiple products is **product-line pricing**, the setting of prices for all items in a product line. When setting prices, the manager seeks to cover the total cost and produce a profit for the complete line, not necessarily for each item. For example, the penetration price for Nintendo's GameCube video-game console was likely below its cost, but the price of its video games (complementary products) was set high enough to cover the loss and deliver a profit for the Nintendo product line.

Product-line pricing involves determining (1) the lowest priced product and price, (2) the highest priced product and price, and (3) price differentials for all other products in the line.[22] The lowest and highest priced items in the product line play important roles. The highest priced item is typically positioned as the premium item in quality and features. The lowest priced item is the traffic builder designed to capture the attention of the hesitant or first-time buyer. Price differentials between items in the line should make sense to customers and reflect differences in their perceived value of the products offered. Behavioural research also suggests that the price differentials should get larger as one moves up the product line.

Customer Effects   In setting price, retailers weigh factors heavily that satisfy the perceptions or expectations of ultimate consumers, such as the customary prices for a variety of consumer products. Retailers have found that they should not price their store brands 20 to 25 percent below manufacturers' brands. When they do, consumers often view the lower price as signalling lower quality and don't buy.[23] Manufacturers and wholesalers must choose prices that result in profit for resellers in the channel to gain their cooperation and support. Toro failed to do this on its lines of lawn mowers and snow throwers. It decided to augment its traditional hardware outlet distribution by also selling through big discounters such as Zellers and Wal-Mart. To do so, it set prices for the discounters substantially below those for its traditional hardware outlets. Many unhappy hardware stores abandoned Toro products in favour of mowers and snow throwers from other manufacturers.

Competitive Effects   A manager's pricing decision is immediately apparent to most competitors, who may retaliate with price changes of their own. Therefore, a manager who sets a final list or quoted price must anticipate potential price responses from competitors. Regardless of whether a firm is a price leader or follower, it wants to avoid cutthroat price wars in which no firm in the industry makes a satisfactory profit. A **price war** involves successive pricing by competitors to increase or maintain their unit sales or market share. For example, price wars in the airline industry

PRICE WAR
Successive price cutting by competitors to increase or maintain their unit sales or market share.

Frito-Lay recognizes that its tortilla chip products are partial substitutes for one another and its bean and cheese dips and salsa sauces complement tortilla chips. This knowledge is used for Frito-Lay product-line pricing.

Frito-Lay, Inc.
www.frito-lay.com

usually result in losses for all players. Similarly, in the residential long-distance telephone industry, even price reductions as little as one percent can have a significant effect in a highly competitve environment. In general, each time a competitor lowers its per-minute charge and is matched by the other players, revenues tend to tumble for everyone. In the Canadian brewery industry, a recent price war between Molson and Labatt trimmed millions off the bottom lines of both companies. Marketers are advised to consider price cutting only when one or more conditions exist: (1) the company has a cost or technological advantage over its competition, (2) primary demand for the product class will grow if prices are lowered, and (3) the price cut is confined to specific products or customers (as with airline tickets), and not across the board.[24]

Balancing Incremental Costs and Revenues

When a price is changed or new advertising or selling programs are planned, their effect on the quantity sold must be considered. This assessment, called *marginal analysis* (Chapter 13), involves a continuing, concise trade-off of incremental costs against incremental revenues.

Do marketing and business managers really use marginal analysis? Yes, they do, but they often don't use phrases such as *marginal revenue*, *marginal cost*, and *elasticity of demand*.

Think about these managerial questions:

- How many extra units do we have to sell to pay for that $1000 advertisement?
- How much savings on unit variable cost do we have to get to keep the break-even point the same if we invest in a $10 000 labour-saving machine?
- Should we hire three more salespeople or not?

All these questions are a form of marginal or incremental analysis, even though these exact words are not used.

Figure 14–5 shows the power—and some limitations—of marginal analysis applied to a marketing decision. Note that the frame store owner must either conclude that a simple advertising campaign will more than pay for itself in additional sales or not undertake the campaign. The decision could also have been made to increase the average price of a framed picture to cover the cost of the campaign, but the principle still applies: expected incremental revenues from pricing and other marketing actions must more than offset incremental costs.

FIGURE 14–5
The power of marginal analysis in real-world decisions

Suppose the owner of a picture framing store is considering buying a series of magazine ads to reach her upscale target market. The cost of the ads is $1000, the average price of a framed picture is $50, and the unit variable cost (materials plus labour) is $30.

This is a direct application of marginal analysis that an astute manager uses to estimate the incremental revenue or incremental number of units that must be obtained to at least cover the incremental cost. In this example, the number of extra picture frames that must be sold is obtained as follows:

$$\text{Incremental number of frames} = \frac{\text{Extra fixed cost}}{\text{Price} - \text{Unit variable cost}}$$

$$= \frac{\$1000 \text{ of advertising}}{\$50 - \$30}$$

$$= 50 \text{ frames}$$

So unless there are some other benefits of the ads, such as long-term goodwill, she should buy the ads only if she expects they will increase picture frame sales by at least 50 units.

The example in Figure 14–5 shows both the main advantage and difficulty of marginal analysis. The advantage is its common-sense usefulness, and the difficulty is obtaining the necessary data to make decisions. The owner can measure the cost quite easily, but the incremental revenue generated by the ads is difficult to measure. She could partly solve this problem by offering $2 off the purchase price with use of a coupon printed in the ad to see which sales resulted from the ad.

STEP 6: MAKE SPECIAL ADJUSTMENTS TO THE LIST OR QUOTED PRICE

When you pay 50 cents for a bag of M&Ms in a vending machine or receive a quoted price of $10 000 from a contractor to build a new kitchen, the pricing sequence ends with the last step just described: setting the list or quoted price. But when you are a manufacturer of M&M candies or gas grills and sell your product to dozens or hundreds of wholesalers and retailers in your channel of distribution, you may need to make a variety of special adjustments to the list or quoted price. Wholesalers also must adjust list or quoted prices they set for retailers. Three special adjustments to the list or quoted price are (1) discounts, (2) allowances, and (3) geographical adjustments (Figure 14–6).

Discounts

Discounts are reductions from list price that a seller gives a buyer as a reward for some activity of the buyer that is favourable to the seller. Four kinds of discounts are especially important in marketing strategy: (1) quantity, (2) seasonal, (3) trade (functional), and (4) cash discounts.[25]

Quantity Discounts

QUANTITY DISCOUNTS
Reductions in unit costs for a larger order.

Quantity Discounts   To encourage customers to buy larger quantities of a product, firms at all levels in the channel of distribution offer **quantity discounts**, which are reductions in unit costs for a larger order. For example, an instant photocopying service might set a price of 10 cents a copy for 1 to 25 copies, 9 cents a copy for 26 to 100, and 8 cents a copy for 101 or more. Because the photocopying service gets more of the buyer's business and has longer production runs that reduce its order-handling costs, it is willing to pass on some of the cost savings in the form of quantity discounts to the buyer.

FIGURE 14–6
Three special adjustments to list or quoted price

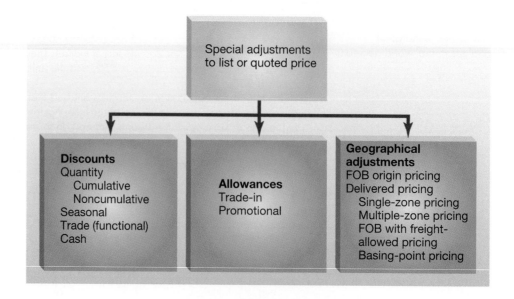

Special adjustments to list or quoted price

Discounts
Quantity
   Cumulative
   Noncumulative
Seasonal
Trade (functional)
Cash

Allowances
Trade-in
Promotional

Geographical adjustments
FOB origin pricing
Delivered pricing
   Single-zone pricing
   Multiple-zone pricing
   FOB with freight-allowed pricing
   Basing-point pricing

Toro uses seasonal discounts to stimulate consumer demand and smooth out seasonal manufacturing peaks and troughs.

The Toro Company
www.toro.com

Quantity discounts are of two general kinds: noncumulative and cumulative. *Noncumulative quantity discounts* are based on the size of an individual purchase order. They encourage large individual purchase orders, not a series of orders. This discount is used by Federal Express to encourage companies to ship a large number of packages at one time. *Cumulative quantity discounts* apply to the accumulation of purchases of a product over a given time period, typically a year. Cumulative quantity discounts encourage repeat buying by a single customer to a far greater degree than do noncumulative quantity discounts.

Seasonal Discounts   To encourage buyers to stock inventory earlier than their normal demand would require, manufacturers often use seasonal discounts. A firm such as Toro that manufactures lawn mowers and snow throwers offers seasonal discounts to encourage wholesalers and retailers to stock up on lawn mowers in January and February and on snow throwers in July and August—five or six months before the seasonal demand by ultimate consumers. This enables Toro to smooth out seasonal manufacturing peaks and troughs, thereby contributing to more efficient production. It also rewards wholesalers and retailers for the risk they accept in assuming increased inventory carrying costs and having supplies in stock at the time they are wanted by customers.

Trade (Functional) Discounts   To reward wholesalers and retailers for marketing functions they will perform in the future, a manufacturer often gives trade, or functional, discounts. These reductions off the list or base price are offered to resellers in the channel of distribution on the basis of (1) where they are in the channel and (2) the marketing activities they are expected to perform in the future.

Suppose a manufacturer quotes prices in the following form: list price—$100 less 30/10/5. The first number in the percentage sequence always refers to the retail end of the channel, and the last number always refers to the wholesaler or jobber closest to the manufacturer in the channel. The trade discounts are simply subtracted one at a time. This price quote shows that $100 is the manufacturer's suggested retail price; 30 percent of the suggested retail price is available to the retailer to cover

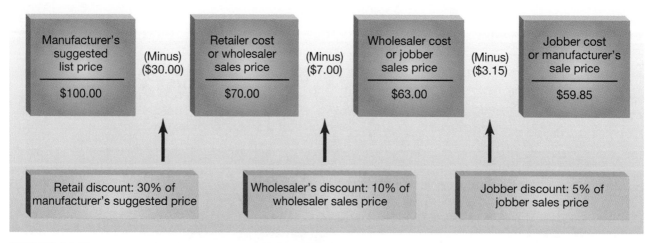

FIGURE 14–7
The structure of trade discounts

costs and provide a profit of $30 ($100 × 0.3 = $30); wholesalers closest to the retailer in the channel get 10 percent of their selling price ($70 × 0.1 = $7); and the final group of wholesalers in the channel (probably jobbers) that are closest to the manufacturer get 5 percent of their selling price ($63 × 0.05 = $3.15). Thus, starting with the manufacturer's retail price and subtracting the three trade discounts shows that the manufacturer's selling price to the wholesaler or jobber closest to it is $59.85 (Figure 14–7).

Traditional trade discounts have been established in various product lines such as hardware, food, and pharmaceutical items. Although the manufacturer may suggest the trade discounts shown in the example just cited, the sellers are free to alter the discount schedule depending on their competitive situation.

Cash Discounts   To encourage retailers to pay their bills quickly, manufacturers offer them cash discounts. Suppose a retailer receives a bill quoted at $1000, 2/10 net 30. This means that the bill for the product is $1000, but the retailer can take a 2 percent discount ($1000 × 0.02 = $20) if payment is made within 10 days and send a cheque for $980. If the payment cannot be made within 10 days, the total amount of $1000 is due within 30 days. It is usually understood by the buyer that an interest charge will be added after the first 30 days of free credit.

Naive buyers may think that the 2-percent discount offered is not substantial. What this means is that the buyer pays 2 percent on the total amount to be able to use that amount an extra 20 days—from day 11 to day 30. In a 360-day business year, this is an effective annual interest rate of 36 percent (2% × 360/20 = 36%). Because the effective interest rate is so high, firms that cannot take advantage of a 2/10 net 30 cash discount often try to borrow money from their local banks at rates far lower than the 36 percent they must pay by not taking advantage of the cash discount.

Retailers provide cash discounts to consumers as well to eliminate the cost of credit granted to consumers. These discounts take the form of discount-for-cash policies. Canadian Tire is famous for its discount-for-cash policy where consumers receive 3 percent off for cash purchases in the form of cash-bonus coupons that can be used against future purchases.

Allowances

Allowances—like discounts—are reductions from list or quoted prices to buyers for performing some activity.

Trade-in Allowances   A new-car dealer can offer a substantial reduction in the list price of that new Toyota Camry by offering you a trade-in allowance of $500 for your Chevrolet. A trade-in allowance is a price reduction given when a used product is part of the payment on a new product. Trade-ins are an effective way to lower the price a buyer has to pay without formally reducing the list price.

Promotional Allowances   Sellers in the channel of distribution can qualify for **promotional allowances** for undertaking certain advertising or selling activities to promote a product. Various types of allowances include an actual cash payment or an extra amount of "free goods" (as with a free case of pizzas to a retailer for every dozen cases purchased). Frequently, a portion of these savings is passed on to the consumer by retailers.

Some companies, such as Procter & Gamble, have chosen to reduce promotional allowances for retailers by using everyday low pricing. **Everyday low pricing** (EDLP) is the practice of replacing promotional allowances with lower manufacturer list prices. EDLP promises to reduce the average price to consumers while minimizing promotional allowances that cost manufacturers billions of dollars every year.

Geographical Adjustments

Geographical adjustments are made by manufacturers or even wholesalers to list or quoted prices to reflect the cost of transportation of the products from seller to buyer. The two general methods for quoting prices related to transportation costs are (1) FOB origin pricing and (2) uniform delivered pricing.

FOB Origin Pricing   FOB means "free on board" some vehicle at some location, which means the seller pays the cost of loading the product onto the vehicle that is used (such as a barge, railway car, or truck). **FOB origin pricing** usually involves the seller's naming the location of this loading as the seller's factory or warehouse (such as "FOB Toronto" or "FOB factory"). The title to the goods passes to the buyer at the point of loading, so the buyer becomes responsible for picking the specific mode of transportation, for all the transportation costs, and for subsequent handling of the product. Buyers farthest from the seller face the big disadvantage of paying the higher transportation costs.

Uniform Delivered Pricing   When a **uniform delivered pricing** method is used, the price the seller quotes includes all transportation costs. It is quoted in a contract as "FOB buyer's location," and the seller selects the mode of transportation, pays the freight charges, and is responsible for any damage that may occur because the seller retains title to the goods until delivered to the buyer. Although they go by various names, four kinds of delivered pricing methods are (1) single-zone pricing, (2) multiple-zone pricing, (3) FOB with freight-allowed pricing, and (4) basing-point pricing.

In *single-zone pricing* all buyers pay the same delivered price for the products, regardless of their distance from the seller. Canada Post, for example, charges the same price for a first-class stamp regardless of the distance the mail will travel across Canada. So although a store offering free delivery in a metropolitan area has lower transportation costs for goods shipped to customers nearer the store than for those shipped to distant ones, customers pay the same delivered price.

In *multiple-zone pricing* a firm divides its selling territory into geographic areas or zones. The delivered price to all buyers within any one zone is the same, but prices across zones vary depending on the transportation cost to the zone and the level of competition and demand within the zone. This system is also used in setting prices on long-distance phone calls. As another example of multiple-zone pricing, Sable Gas is being sold to Maritime and northeast natural gas customers at prices based on their proximity to the gas pipeline. The closer the customer is to the gas, the lower the price.

PROMOTIONAL ALLOWANCE
Cash payment or extra amount of "free goods" awarded sellers in the channel of distribution for undertaking certain advertising or selling activities to promote a product.

EVERYDAY LOW PRICING
The practice of replacing promotional allowances with lower manufacturer list prices.

FOB ORIGIN PRICING
A method of pricing where the title of goods passes to the buyer at the point of loading.

UNIFORM DELIVERED PRICING
The price the seller quotes includes all transportation costs.

Sable Offshore Energy Incorporated
www.soep.com

With *FOB with freight-allowed pricing*, also called *freight absorption pricing*, the price is quoted by the seller as "FOB plant—freight allowed." The buyer is allowed to deduct freight expenses from the list price of the goods, so the seller agrees to pay, or "absorbs," the transportation costs.

Basing-point pricing involves selecting one or more geographical locations (basing point) from which the list price for products plus freight expenses are charged to the buyer. For example, a company might designate Montreal as the basing point and charge all buyers a list price of $100 plus freight from Montreal to their location. Basing-point pricing methods have been used in the steel, cement, and lumber industries where freight expenses are a significant part of the total cost to the buyer and products are largely undifferentiated.

Legal and Regulatory Aspects of Pricing

Arriving at a final price is clearly a complex process. The task is further complicated by legal and regulatory restrictions. Chapter 3 described the regulatory environment of companies. Here we elaborate on the specific laws and regulations affecting pricing decisions. Five pricing practices have received the most scrutiny: (1) price fixing, (2) price discrimination, (3) deceptive pricing, (4) predatory pricing, and (5) delivered pricing.

PRICE FIXING
A conspiracy among firms to set prices for a product.

Price Fixing
A conspiracy among firms to set prices for a product is termed **price fixing**. Price fixing is illegal per se under the Competition Act (*per se* means in and of itself). When two or more competitors explicitly or implicitly set prices, this practice is called *horizontal price fixing*.

Vertical price fixing involves controlling agreements between independent buyers and sellers (a manufacturer and a retailer) whereby sellers are required not to sell products below a minimum retail price. This practice, called *resale price maintenance*, is also illegal under the provisions of the Competition Act.

It is important to recognize that a manufacturer's "suggested retail price" is not illegal per se. The issue of legality arises only when manufacturers enforce such a practice by coercion. Furthermore, there appears to be a movement toward a "rule of reason" in pricing cases. This rule holds that circumstances surrounding a practice must be considered before making a judgment about its legality. The "rule of reason" perspective is the direct opposite of the per se rule, which holds that a practice is illegal in and of itself.

PRICE DISCRIMINATION
The practice of charging different prices to different buyers for goods of like trade and quality.

Price Discrimination
The Competition Act prohibits **price discrimination**—the practice of charging different prices to different buyers for goods of like grade and quality. The Competition Act also covers promotional allowances. To legally offer promotional allowances to buyers, sellers must do so on a proportionally equal basis to all buyers distributing the seller's products. In general, this rule of reason is applied frequently in price discrimination cases and is often applied to cases involving flexible pricing policies of firms. It is not easy to prove price discrimination has actually taken place, especially when firms practise flexible-price policies.

Under the Competition Act, the legislation requires that there be a "practice" of price discrimination, implying more than one instance, or even two or three instances. However, some suggest that the use of flexible pricing may create the potentiality for some firms to engage in price discrimination. Even if the practice cannot be proved legally as price discrimination, there may be some ethical issues involved (see the Ethics and Social Responsibility Alert).[26]

Deceptive Pricing
Price deals that mislead consumers fall into the category of deceptive pricing. Deceptive pricing is outlawed by the Competition Act. The five most common deceptive pricing practices are described in Figure 14–8. Over the past few years, companies from Newfoundland to British Columbia have been found guilty

ETHICS AND SOCIAL RESPONSIBILITY ALERT — Flexible Pricing or Price Discrimination?

Many buyers dread the prospect of buying a new automobile. Why? They dread negotiating the price. Price bargaining, however, has a more serious side and demonstrates the potential pitfalls of flexible pricing: possible price discrimination based on ethnicity or gender. Research shows that some car dealers offer females higher prices on vehicles than males. Similarly, non-white buyers, male or female, may also be offered higher prices on cars than white buyers. This occurs despite the fact that all buyers used identical bargaining strategies when negotiating the price of a new car.

Even if the practice cannot be proved as systematic price discrimination, it raises an ethical question: should car dealers be allowed to charge higher prices to some buyers for the identical vehicle? Some car dealers argue that the price is largely determined based on how well the consumer negotiates. They add that some buyers are simply better at haggling than others.

However, there have been some indications that some dealers have taken advantage of newly arrived immigrants who do not understand the car-buying process, particularly the concept of price negotiation. Similarly, some females argue that after purchasing a new car, they discovered that they paid more than a male counterpart who had purchased an identical vehicle under similar terms and conditions.

Saturn Corporation has eliminated new-car price negotiating and offers a no-haggle, one-price policy. According to a Saturn executive, "People don't want to dicker on price, period, whether it's a house, suit of clothes, or a car. When you have to dicker, you feel uncomfortable because you always feel you paid too much." In certain instances, some consumers do. Many times, however, it tends to be female buyers and non-white purchasers. What is your feeling on this situation?

---

and fined for deceptive pricing practices. However, as you examine Figure 14–8, you should remember that it is often difficult for the government to police and enforce all these laws. So it is essential to rely on ethical standards of those making and publicizing pricing decisions. A frequently used promotional practice is to offer goods or services

FIGURE 14–8
Five most common deceptive pricing practices

DECEPTIVE PRACTICE	DESCRIPTION
Bait and switch	A deceptive practice exists when a firm offers a very low price on a product (the bait) to attract customers to a store. Once in the store, the customer is persuaded to purchase a higher-priced item (the switch) using a variety of tricks, including (1) downgrading the promoted item and (2) not having the item in stock or refusing to take orders for the item.
Bargains conditional on other purchases	This practice may exist when a buyer is offered "1-Cent Sales," "Buy 1, Get 1 Free," and "Get 2 for the Price of 1." Such pricing is legal only if the first items are sold at the regular price, not a price inflated for the offer. Substituting lower-quality items on either the first or second purchase is also considered deceptive.
Comparable value comparisons	Advertising such as "Retail Value $100.00, Our Price $85.00" is deceptive if a verified and substantial number of stores in the market area did not price the item at $100.
Comparisons with suggested prices	A claim that a price is below a manufacturer's suggested or list price may be deceptive if few or no sales occur at that price in a retailer's market area.
Former price comparisons	When a seller represents a price as reduced, the item must have been offered in good faith at a higher price for a substantial previous period. Setting a high price for the purpose of establishing a reference for a price reduction is deceptive.

WEB LINK

Free or Not So Free, According to the Canadian Competition Bureau

http://www.mcgrawhill.ca

The offer of "free" goods or services as a promotional device is often used to attract customers. However, the Competition Bureau recognizes that such offers must be made with care to avoid any possibility that consumers will be misled or deceived.

The Competition Bureau has a publication called "Misleading Advertising Guidelines," which deals with the issue of the use of "free" as a promotional device. In this guide, many examples of the use of free are discussed. In some cases, the use of the word free is acceptable, while in other cases it is considered deceptive. Go to www.strategis. ic.gc.ca/SSG.ct01299e.html#d and check out Section 52(1)(d)–C to get an idea about the use of the word free from the government agency charged with the responsibility of protecting consumers against deceptive pricing practices.

"free." Check the accompanying Web Link box to see what the federal government says about the word "free."

Predatory Pricing   Two types of predatory pricing are defined within the Competition Act. The first is called *geographic predatory pricing*. Sellers are prohibited from engaging in a policy of selling products or services in one region in Canada at a price lower than another region with the intent or effect of lessening competition or of eliminating a competitior.

The second type of predatory pricing offence is committed when a business engages in a policy of selling products or services at "unreasonably low" prices in an attempt to substantially lessen competition. In many cases, the very low prices are designed to drive competitiors out of business. Once competitors have been driven out, the firm raises its prices.

Delivered Pricing   Delivered pricing is the practice of refusing a customer delivery of an article on the same trade terms as other customers in the same location. It is a noncriminal offence, but the Competition Tribunal can prohibit suppliers from engaging in such a practice.

Concept Check

1. Why would a seller choose a flexible-price policy over a one-price policy?

2. If a firm wished to encourage repeat purchases by a buyer throughout a year, would a cumulative or noncumulative quantity discount be a better strategy?

3. Which pricing practices are covered by the Competition Act?

SUMMARY

1 Four general approaches of finding an approximate price level for a product or service are demand-oriented, cost-oriented, profit-oriented, and competition-oriented pricing.

2 Demand-oriented pricing approaches stress consumer demand and revenue implications of pricing and include eight types: skimming, penetration, prestige, price lining, odd–even, target, bundle, and yield management.

3 Cost-oriented pricing approaches emphasize the cost aspects of pricing and include three types: standard markup, cost-plus, and experience curve pricing.

4 Profit-oriented pricing approaches focus on a balance between revenues and costs to set a price and include three types: target profit, target return-on-sales, and target return-on-investment pricing.

5 Competition-oriented pricing approaches stress what competitors or the marketplace are doing and include three types: customary; above-, at-, or below-market; and loss-leader pricing.

6 Given an approximate price level for a product, a manager must set a list or quoted price by considering factors such as one-price versus a flexible-price policy; the effects of the proposed price on the company, customer, and competitors; and balancing incremental costs and revenues.

7 List or quoted price is often modified through discounts, allowances, and geographical adjustments.

8 Legal and regulatory issues in pricing focus on price fixing, price discrimination, deceptive pricing, predatory pricing, and delivered pricing.

KEY TERMS AND CONCEPTS

above-, at-, or below-market pricing p. 374
bundle pricing p. 369
cost-plus pricing p. 370
customary pricing p. 373
everyday low pricing p. 381
experience curve pricing p. 370
flexible-price policy p. 375
FOB origin pricing p. 381
loss-leader pricing p. 374
odd–even pricing p. 369
one-price policy p. 374
penetration pricing p. 367
prestige pricing p. 367
price discrimination p. 382

price fixing p. 382
price lining p. 368
price war p. 376
product-line pricing p. 375
promotional allowance p. 381
quantity discounts p. 378
skimming pricing p. 366
standard markup pricing p. 370
target pricing p. 369
target profit pricing p. 371
target return-on-investment pricing p. 372
target return-on-sales pricing p. 372
uniform delivered pricing p. 381
yield management pricing p. 369

INTERNET EXERCISE   www.mcgrawhill.ca/college/berkowitz

As you know, the Competition Bureau is responsible for administrating the Competition Act in Canada. As you read in this chapter, competition can be lessened and/or consumers can be harmed by unfair pricing practices. Visit the Competition Bureau's home page at http://www.strategis.ic.gc.ca/ssg/ct01250e.html

Go to the media room section on the site. Then click on News Releases.
1 What are the types of pricing violations involving Canadian and international companies reported on the site?
2 What types of penalties were imposed?
3 What is your opinion regarding these pricing violations?

Want to get better grades, find tips on how to study more effectively, and stay up to date with happenings in the world of marketing? Visit the Online Learning Centre for practice tests, Study Smart software, and much more! www.mcgrawhill.ca/college/berkowitz
Interested in finding out what marketing looks like in the real world? *Marketing Magazine* is just a click away on your OLC! Visit www.mcgrawhill.ca/college/berkowitz

APPLYING MARKETING CONCEPTS AND PERSPECTIVES

1 Under what conditions would a camera manufacturer adopt a skimming price approach for a new product? A penetration approach?

2 What are some similarities and differences between skimming pricing, prestige pricing, and above-market pricing?

3 A producer of microwave ovens has adopted an experience curve pricing approach for its new model. The firm believes it can reduce the cost of producing the model by 20 percent each time volume doubles. The cost to produce the first unit was $1000. What would be the approximate cost of the 4096th unit?

4 The Hesper Corporation is a leading manufacturer of high-quality upholstered sofas. Current plans call for an increase of $600 000 in the advertising budget. If the firm sells its sofas for

an average price of $850 and the unit variable costs are $550, then what dollar sales increase will be necessary to cover the additional advertising?

5 Suppose executives estimate that the unit variable cost for their VCR is $100, the fixed cost related to the product is $10 million annually, and the target volume for next year is 100 000 recorders. What sales price will be necessary to achieve a target profit of $1 million?

6 A manufacturer of motor oil has a trade discount policy whereby the manufacturer's suggested retail price is $30 per case with the terms of 40/20/10. The manufacturer sells its products through jobbers, who sell to wholesalers, who sell to gasoline stations. What will the manufacturer's sale price be?

7 What are the effective annual interest rates for the following cash discount terms? (*a*) 1/10 net 30, (*b*) 2/10 net 30, and (*c*) 2/10 net 60.

8 Suppose a manufacturer of exercise equipment sets a suggested price to the consumer of $395 for a particular piece of equipment to be competitive with similar equipment. The manufacturer sells its equipment to a sporting goods wholesaler who receives a 25-percent markup and a retailer who receives a 50-percent markup. What demand-oriented pricing approach is being used, and at what price will the manufacturer sell the equipment to the wholesaler?

VIDEO CASE 14–1 My Own Meals

"The kids generally like the fast-food meals. I tend to not like them because I try to stay away from the high fat," says Angela Harmon, mother of three young girls. "I have to have something that is nutritious and fast," remarks Mary Champlain, mother of two. Comments like these and her own experiences led Mary Anne Jackson to conclude that there was an opportunity to provide parents with better children's food options. As Mary explains, "being a busy working mother, I knew that there was a need for this type of product in the marketplace."

THE IDEA

Mary's insight about the marketplace was supported by several socioeconomic trends. For example:

- More than 65 percent of working mothers now have school-age children, the highest percentage ever.
- About 90 percent of children under the age of 7 eat at McDonald's at least 4 times per month.
- More than 90 percent of homes in Canada now have microwave ovens.
- Women already represent almost half of the total workforce.

With this evidence, some food industry experience and business education, and a lot of entrepreneurial spirit, Mary Anne Jackson set out to satisfy the need for nutritious, convenient children's meals. Her idea: develop a line of healthy, microwaveable meals for children 2 to 10 years old.

THE COMPANY

Jackson started by founding a company, My Own Meals, Inc., with a line of five healthy microwaveable meals. The meals were offered in shelf-stable "retort" packages, which are like flexible cans. This created a whole new category of prepared foods, and raised more than a few eyebrows among the major food companies. Jackson observed that "The need for children's meals was not being addressed in the past, and I think this was because most major food companies are run by men." Eventually, however, the big companies challenged My Own Meals with their own entries into the new category. The competition reinforced Jackson's efforts. "Having competitors come into the marketplace justified the existence of the category," she explains.

The product line was developed using a lot of marketing research—hundreds of busy mothers provided input about product quality, usage rates, and price. The results indicated that customers would serve their children high-quality meals between three and four times each month and that they would be willing to pay approximately $2.30 for each meal.

THE ISSUE: SETTING RETAIL PRICES

"We were trying to decide if we were priced appropriately and competitively for the marketplace, and we decided that we would look at the price elasticity for our product line," observes Jackson. "We found that the closer we came to $3.00 a unit, the lower the volume was, and overall we were losing revenues and profits."

To arrive at final retail prices for her company's products Jackson considered factors related to demand, cost, profit, and competition. For example, because lower-quality brands had entered the market, My Own Meals needed a retail price that reflected the superior quality of its products. "We're premium priced because we're a higher quality product than any of our competitors. If we weren't, our quality image would be lowered to the image that they have," explains Jackson. At some stores, however, prices approached $3.00 and consumer demand decreased.

To estimate the prices consumers would see on their shelves, Jackson needed to estimate the cost of producing the meals and add My Own Meals' markup. Then she determined the markup that each of the distribution channels—retail grocery stores, mass merchants, daycare centres, and military commissaries—would add to reach the retail price. The grocery stores were very concerned about profitability and used a concept called *direct product profitability* (DPP) to determine prices and shelf space. "They want to know how much money they make on each square foot of the shelf dedicated to each product line. I had to do a DPP analysis to show them why they were making more on our products for our space than the competition," remarks Jackson. Finally, she considered competitors' prices, which were:

- Looney Toons (Tyson) $2.49
- Kid Cuisine (Banquet) $1.89
- Kid's Kitchen (Hormel) $1.19

Jackson knew that it was important to consider all of these factors in her pricing decisions. The price would influence the interest of consumers and retailers, the reactions of competitors, and ultimately the success of My Own Meals!

Questions

1 In what ways are the demand factors of (*a*) consumer tastes, (*b*) price and availability of substitute products, and (*c*) consumer income important in influencing consumer demand for My Own Meals products?

2 How can (*a*) demand-oriented, (*b*) cost-based, (*c*) profit-oriented, and (*d*) competition-based approaches be used to help My Own Meals arrive at an approximate price level?

3 Why might the retail price of My Own Meals' products be different in grocery stores, mass merchants, daycare centres, and cafeterias?

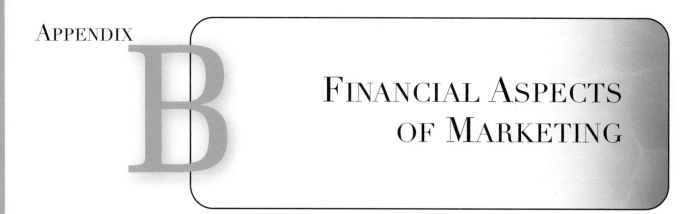

FINANCIAL ASPECTS
OF MARKETING

Basic concepts from accounting and finance provide valuable tools for marketing executives. This appendix describes an actual company's use of accounting and financial concepts and illustrates how they assist the owner in making marketing decisions.

THE CAPLOW COMPANY

An accomplished artist and calligrapher, Jane Westerlund, decided to apply some of her experience to the picture framing business. She bought an existing retail frame store, The Caplow Company, from a friend who owned the business and wanted to retire. She avoided the do-it-yourself end of the framing business and chose three kinds of business activities: (1) cutting the frame, mats, and glass for customers who brought in their own pictures or prints to be framed; (2) selling prints and posters that she had purchased from wholesalers; and (3) restoring high-quality frames and paintings.

To understand how accounting, finance, and marketing relate to each other, let's analyze (1) the operating statement for her frame shop, (2) some general ratios of interest that are derived from the operating statement, and (3) some ratios that pertain specifically to her pricing decisions.

The Operating Statement

The operating statement (also called an *income statement* or *profit-and-loss statement*) summarizes the profitability of a business firm for a specific time period, usually a month, quarter, or year. The title of the operating statement for The Caplow Company shows it is for a one-year period (Figure B–1). The purpose of an operating statement is to show the profit of the firm and the revenues and expenses that led to that profit. This information tells the owner or manager what has happened in the past and suggests actions to improve future profitability.

The left side of Figure B–1 shows that there are three key elements to all operating statements: (1) sales of the

firm's goods and services, (2) costs incurred in making and selling the goods and services, and (3) profit or loss, which is the difference between sales and costs.

Sales Elements The sales element of Figure B–1 has four terms that need explanation:

- *Gross sales* are the total amount billed to customers. Dissatisfied customers or errors may reduce the gross sales through returns or allowances.
- *Returns* occur when a customer gives the item purchased back to the seller, who either refunds the purchase price or allows the customer a credit on subsequent purchases. In any event, the seller now owns the item again.
- *Allowances* are given when a customer is dissatisfied with the item purchased and the seller reduces the original purchase price. Unlike returns, in the case of allowances the buyer owns the item.
- *Net sales* are simply gross sales minus returns and allowances.

The operating statement for The Caplow Company shows that

Gross sales	$80 500
Less: Returns and allowances	500
Net sales	$80 000

The low level of returns and allowances shows the shop generally has done a good job in satisfying customers, which is essential in building the repeat business necessary for success.

Cost Elements The *cost of goods sold* is the total cost of the products sold during the period. This item varies according to the kind of business. A retail store purchases finished goods and resells them to customers without reworking them in any way. In contrast, a manufacturing firm combines raw and semifinished materials and parts, uses labour and overhead to rework these into finished goods, and then sells them to customers. All these activities are reflected in the cost of goods sold item on a manufacturer's operating statement. Note that

FIGURE B–1
Examples of an operating
statement

THE CAPLOW COMPANY

**Operating Statement
For the Year Ending December 31, 2003**

Sales	Gross sales			$80 500
	Less: Returns and allowances			500
	Net sales			$80 000
Costs	Cost of goods sold:			
	Beginning inventory at cost		$ 6 000	
	Purchases at billed cost	$21 000		
	Less: Purchase discounts	300		
	Purchases at net cost	20 700		
	Plus freight-in	100		
	Net cost of delivered purchases		20 800	
	Direct labour (framing)		14 200	
	Cost of goods available for sale		41 000	
	Less: Ending inventory at cost		5 000	
	Cost of goods sold			36 000
	Gross margin (gross profit)			$44 000
	Expenses:			
	Selling expenses:			
	Sales salaries	2 000		
	Advertising expense	3 000		
	Total selling expense		5 000	
	Administrative expenses:			
	Owner's salary	18 000		
	Bookkeeper's salary	1 200		
	Office supplies	300		
	Total administrative expense		19 500	
	General expenses:			
	Depreciation expense	1 000		
	Interest expense	500		
	Rent expense	2 100		
	Utility expenses (heat, electricity)	3 000		
	Repairs and maintenance	2 300		
	Insurance	2 000		
	Canada Pension Plan	2 200		
	Total general expense		13 100	
	Total expenses			37 600
Profit or loss	Profit before taxes			$ 6 400

the frame shop has some features of a pure retailer (prints and posters it buys that are resold without alteration) and a pure manufacturer (assembling the raw materials of moulding, matting, and glass to form a completed frame).

Some terms that relate to cost of goods sold need clarification:

- *Inventory* is the physical material that is purchased from suppliers, may or may not be reworked, and is available for sale to customers. In the frame shop inventory includes moulding, matting, glass, prints, and posters.
- *Purchase discounts* are reductions in the original billed price for reasons such as prompt payment of the bill or the quantity bought.
- *Direct labour* is the cost of the labour used in producing the finished product. For the frame shop this is the cost of producing the completed frames from the moulding, matting, and glass.
- *Gross margin (gross profit)* is the money remaining to manage the business, sell the products or services, and give some profit. Gross margin is net sales minus cost of goods sold.

The two right-hand columns in Figure B–1 between "Net sales" and "Gross margin" calculate the cost of goods sold:

Net sales		$80 000
Cost of goods sold		
Beginning inventory at cost	$ 6 000	
Net cost of delivered purchases	20 800	
Direct labour (framing)	14 200	
Cost of goods available for sale	41 000	
Less: ending inventory at cost	5 000	
Cost of goods sold		36 000
Gross margin (gross profit)		$44 000

This section considers the beginning and ending inventories, the net cost of purchases delivered during the year, and the cost of the direct labour going into making the frames. Subtracting the $36 000 cost of goods sold from the $80 000 net sales gives the $44 000 gross margin.

Three major categories of expenses are shown in Figure B–1 below the gross margin:

- *Selling expenses* are the costs of selling the product or service produced by the firm. For the Caplow Company there are two such selling expenses: sales salaries of part-time employees waiting on customers and the advertising expense of simple newspaper ads and direct-mail ads sent to customers.

- *Administrative expenses* are the costs of managing the business, and, for The Caplow Company, include three expenses: the owner's salary, a part-time bookkeeper's salary, and office supplies expense.

- *General expenses* are miscellaneous costs not covered elsewhere; for the frame shop these include seven items: depreciation expense (on her equipment), interest expense, rent expense, utility expense, repair and maintenance expense, insurance expense, and employment insurance and Canada Pension plan.

As shown in Figure B–1, selling, administrative, and general expenses total $37 600 for the Caplow Company.

Profit Element   What the company has earned, the *profit before taxes*, is found by subtracting cost of goods sold and expenses from net sales. For the Caplow Company, Figure B–1 shows that profit before taxes is $6400.

General Operating Ratios to Analyze Operations

Looking only at the elements of Caplow's operating statement that extend to the right column highlights the firm's performance on some important dimensions. Using operating ratios such as *expense-to-sales ratios* for expressing basic expense or profit elements as a percentage of net sales gives further insights:

ELEMENT IN OPERATING STATEMENT	DOLLAR VALUE	PERCENTAGE OF NET SALES
Gross sales	$80 500	
Less: Returns and allowances	500	
Net sales	80 000	100%
Less: Cost of goods sold	36 000	45
Gross margin	44 000	55
Less: Total expenses	37 600	47
Profit (or loss) before taxes	$ 6 400	8%

Westerlund can use this information to compare her firm's performance from one time period to the next. To do so, it is especially important that she keep the same definitions for each element of her operating statement, also a significant factor in using the electronic spreadsheets discussed in Chapter 14. Performance comparisons between periods are more difficult if she changes definitions for the accounting elements in the operating statement.

She can use either the dollar values or the operating ratios (the value of the element of the operating statement divided by net sales) to analyze the firm's performance. However, the operating ratios are more valuable than the dollar values for two reasons: (1) the simplicity of working with percentages rather than dollars and (2) the availability of operating ratios of typical firms in the same industry, which are published by Dun & Bradstreet and trade associations. Thus, Westerlund can compare her firm's performance not only with that of *other* frame shops but also with that of *small* frame shops that have annual net sales, for example, of under $100 000. In this way she can identify where her operations are better or worse than other similar firms. For example, if trade association data showed a typical frame shop of her size had a ratio of cost of goods sold to net sales of 37 percent, compared with her 45 percent, she might consider steps to reduce this cost through purchase discounts, reducing inbound freight charges, finding lower-cost suppliers, and so on.

Ratios to Use in Setting and Evaluating Price

Using the Caplow Company as an example, we can study four ratios that relate closely to setting a price: (1) markup, (2) markdown, (3) stockturns, and (4) return on investment. These terms are defined in Figure B–2 and explained below.

Markup   Both markup and gross margin refer to the amount added to the cost of goods sold to arrive at the selling price, and they may be expressed either in dollar or percentage terms. However, the term *markup* is more commonly used in setting retail prices. Suppose the average price Westerlund charges for a framed picture is $80. Then in terms of the first two definitions in Figure B–2 and the earlier information from the operating statement,

FIGURE B–2

How to calculate selling price, markup, markdown, stockturn, and return on investment

NAME OF FINANCIAL ELEMENT OR RATIO	WHAT IT MEASURES	EQUATION
Selling price ($)	Price customer sees	Cost of goods sold (COGS) + Markup
Markup ($)	Dollars added to COGS to arrive at selling price	Selling price – COGS
Markup on selling price (%)	Relates markup to selling price	$\frac{\text{Markup}}{\text{Selling price}} \times 100 = \frac{\text{Selling price} - \text{COGS}}{\text{Selling price}} \times 100$
Markup on cost (%)	Relates markup to cost	$\frac{\text{Markup}}{\text{COGS}} \times 100 = \frac{\text{Selling price} - \text{COGS}}{\text{COGS}} \times 100$
Markdown (%)	Ability of firm to sell its products at initial selling price	$\frac{\text{Markdowns}}{\text{Net Sales}} \times 100$
Stockturn rate	Ability of firm to move its inventory quickly	$\frac{\text{COGS}}{\text{Average inventory at cost}}$ or $\frac{\text{Net sales}}{\text{Average inventory at selling price}}$
Return on investment (%)	Profit performance of firm compared with money invested in it	$\frac{\text{Net profit after taxes}}{\text{Investment}} \times 100$

ELEMENT OF PRICE	DOLLAR VALUE
Cost of goods sold	$36
Markup (or gross margin)	44
Selling price	$80

The third definition in Figure B–2 gives the percentage markup on selling price:

$$\text{Markup on selling price (\%)} = \frac{\text{Markup}}{\text{Selling price}} \times 100$$

$$= \frac{44}{80} \times 100 = 55\%$$

And the percentage markup on cost is obtained as follows:

$$\text{Markup on cost (\%)} = \frac{\text{Markup}}{\text{Cost of goods sold}} \times 100$$

$$= \frac{44}{36} \times 100 = 122.2\%$$

Inexperienced retail clerks sometimes fail to distinguish between the two definitions of markup, which (as the preceding calculations show) can represent a tremendous difference, so it is essential to know whether the base is cost or selling price. Marketers generally use selling price as the base for talking about "markups" unless they specifically state that they are using cost as a base.

Retailers and wholesalers that rely heavily on markup pricing (discussed in Chapter 15) often use standardized tables that convert markup on selling price to markup on cost, and vice versa. The two equations below show how to convert one to the other:

$$\text{Markup on selling price (\%)} = \frac{\text{Markup on cost (\%)}}{100\% + \text{Markup on cost (\%)}}$$

$$\text{Markup on cost (\%)} = \frac{\text{Markup on selling price (\%)}}{100\% - \text{Markup on selling price (\%)}}$$

Using the data from the Caplow Company gives

$$\text{Markup on selling price (\%)} = \frac{\text{Markup on cost (\%)}}{100\% + \text{Markup on cost (\%)}} \times 100$$

$$= \frac{122.2}{100 + 122.2} \times 100 = 55\%$$

$$\text{Markup on cost (\%)} = \frac{\text{Markup on selling price (\%)}}{100\% - \text{Markup on selling price (\%)}} \times 100$$

$$= \frac{55}{100 - 55} \times 100 = 122.2\%$$

The use of an incorrect markup base is shown in Westerlund's business. A markup of 122.2 percent on her cost of goods sold for a typical frame she sells gives 122.2% × $36 = $44 of markup. Added to the $36 cost of goods sold, this gives her a selling price of $80 for the framed picture. However, a new clerk working for her who erroneously priced the framed picture at 55 percent of cost of goods sold set the final price at $55.80 ($36 of cost of goods sold plus 55% × $36 = $19.80). The error, if repeated, can be disastrous: frames would be accidentally sold at $55.80, or $24.20 below the intended selling price of $80.

Markdown   A markdown is a reduction in a retail price that is necessary if the item will not sell at the full selling price to which it has been marked up. The item might not sell for a variety of reasons: the selling price was set too high or the item is out of style or has become soiled or damaged. The seller "takes a markdown" by lowering the price to sell it, thereby converting it to cash to buy future inventory that will sell faster.

The markdown percentage cannot be calculated directly from the operating statement. As shown in the fifth item of Figure B–2, the numerator of the markdown percentage is the total dollar markdowns. Markdowns are reductions in the prices of goods that are purchased by customers. The denominator is net sales.

Suppose the Caplow Company had a total of $700 in markdowns on the prints and posters that are stocked and available for sale. Since the frames are custom made for individual customers, there is little reason for a markdown there. Caplow's markdown percentage is then

$$\text{Markdown}(\%) = \frac{\text{Markdowns}}{\text{Net sales}} \times 100$$
$$= \frac{\$700}{\$80\,000} \times 100$$
$$= 0.875\%$$

Other kinds of retailers often have markdown ratios several times this amount. For example, women's dress stores have markdowns of about 25 percent, and menswear stores have markdowns of about 2 percent.

Stockturn Rate   A business firm is anxious to have its inventory move quickly, or "turn over." Stockturn rate, or simply stockturns, measures this inventory movement. For a retailer a slow stockturn rate may show it is buying merchandise customers don't want, so this is a critical measure of performance. When a firm sells only a single product, one convenient way to measure stockturn rate is simply to divide its cost of goods sold by average inventory at cost. The sixth item in Figure B–2 shows how to calculate stockturn rate using information in the following operating statement:

$$\text{Stockturn rate} = \frac{\text{Cost of goods sold}}{\text{Average inventory at cost}}$$

The dollar amount of average inventory at cost is calculated by adding the beginning and ending inventories for the year and dividing by 2 to get the average. From Caplow's operating statement, we have

$$\text{Stockturn rate} = \frac{\text{Cost of goods sold}}{\text{Average inventory at cost}}$$
$$= \frac{\text{Cost of goods sold}}{\frac{\text{Beginning inventory} + \text{Ending inventory}}{2}}$$
$$= \frac{\$36\,000}{\frac{\$6000 + \$5000}{2}}$$
$$= \frac{\$36\,000}{\$5500}$$
$$= 6.5 \text{ stockturns per year}$$

What is considered a "good stockturn" varies by the kind of industry. For example, supermarkets have limited shelf space for thousands of new products from manufacturers each year, so they watch stockturn carefully by product line. The stockturn rate in supermarkets for breakfast foods is about 17 times per year, for pet food about 22 times, and for paper products about 25 times per year.

Return on Investment   A better measure of the performance of a firm than the amount of profit it makes in a year is its ROI, which is the ratio of net income to the investment used to earn that net income. To calculate ROI, it is necessary to subtract income taxes from profit before taxes to obtain net income, then divide this figure by the investment that can be found on a firm's balance sheet (another accounting statement that shows the firm's assets, liabilities, and net worth). While financial and accounting experts have many definitions for "investment," an often-used definition is "total assets."

For our purposes, let's assume that Westerlund has total assets (investment) of $20 000 in The Caplow Company, which covers inventory, store fixtures, and framing equipment. If she pays $1000 in income taxes, her store's net income is $5400, so her ROI is given by the seventh item in Figure B–2:

$$\text{Return on investment} = \text{Net income/investment} \times 100$$
$$= \$5400/\$20\,000 \times 100$$
$$= 27\%$$

Jane Westerlund (left) and an
assistant assess the restoration
of a gold frame for reguilding.

If Westerlund wants to improve her ROI next year, the strategies she might take
are found in this alternative equation for ROI:

ROI = Net sales/investment × Net income/net sales
    = Investment turnover × Profit margin

This equation suggests that the Caplow Company's ROI can be improved by raising turnover or increasing profit margin. Increasing stockturns will accomplish the
former, whereas lowering cost of goods sold to net sales will cause the latter.

beComing
AVON CENTER.

beCo

beComing
luminous

AVON
CAMPAIGN 24

Breathe
new life
into your
skin
ANEW
PURE O₂

PURE O₂
oxygenating
youth complex
complexe
jeunesse
oxygénant
SPF/FPS 15 UVA/UVB

OXYGENATING
YOUTH
COMPLEX
SPF 15

Try now, pay later. FREE gift with purchase.
details inside

AVON
the company for women

Location: http://www.avon.ca/flash2/eng

What's R

AVON
the company for women

kiss goodbye to breast cancer

Help us KISS GOODBYE to Breast Cancer!
Send a Virtual Kiss! For every Kiss you send,
we'll donate 10¢ to Breast Cancer Research

About Avon Canada

Personal Skin Care Guide

How to Buy Avon Products

Become a Sales Dealer

Careers at Avon Canada

Commitment to Women

Hot Beauty Tips

How you
can become a
Sales Dealer

CLICK HERE

Visit our

CHAPTER

15

MANAGING MARKETING CHANNELS AND WHOLESALING

AFTER READING THIS CHAPTER YOU SHOULD BE ABLE TO:

- Explain what is meant by a marketing channel of distribution and why intermediaries are needed.

- Recognize differences between marketing channels for consumer and industrial products and services in domestic and global markets.

- Describe the types and functions of firms that perform wholesaling activities.

- Distinguish among traditional marketing channels, electronic marketing channels, and different types of vertical marketing systems.

- Describe factors considered by marketing executives when selecting and managing a marketing channel, including channel conflict and legal restrictions.

AVON'S MAKEOVER IS MORE THAN COSMETIC

Avon Products, Inc. is in the midst of its own makeover. As the world's leading direct seller of cosmetic and related items to women in 139 countries, Avon has begun calling on new customers, in new ways, with new products.

Avon's makeover represents a significant departure from its traditional manner of doing business. For more than 115 years, the company successfully marketed its products through an extensive network of independent representatives, which today number 3.4 million worldwide. However, Avon's marketing research indicated that 59 percent of women who don't buy Avon products would if they were more accessible. The message to Avon's senior management was clear: Give busy women a choice in how they do their buying—through an Avon representative, in a store, or online. According to Andrea Jung, Avon's chief executive officer, "While direct selling will always be our principal sales channel, expanding access to new customers will help accelerate top-line [sales] growth."

The goal of expanded access to new customers has materialized in novel ways. Avon earmarked $60 million to build a Website (avon.com) focused around the company's representatives and catalogue. Company-operated kiosks have also been opened. In late 2001, Avon introduced a shop-within-a-store format in selected JCPenney stores. These shops feature beComing, Avon's new brand of makeup, skin care, fragrance, and other personal care items, which are not sold by Avon representatives or in Avon kiosks. The stores are "not without risk, but with great opportunity," says Jung. "It's a giant step."

Is the Avon makeover achieving its goal? In a word, yes. "We've learned that at retail, we attract new customers, not the same people that our representatives are serving directly," said Debora Coffey, an Avon spokeswoman.[1]

This chapter focuses on marketing channels of distribution and why they are an important component in the marketing mix. It then shows how such channels benefit consumers and the sequence of firms that make up a marketing channel. Finally, it describes factors that influence the choice and management of marketing channels, including channel conflict and legal restrictions.

NATURE AND IMPORTANCE OF MARKETING CHANNELS

Reaching prospective buyers, either directly or indirectly, is a prerequisite for successful marketing. At the same time, buyers benefit from distribution systems used by firms.

Defining Marketing Channels of Distribution

You see the results of distribution every day. You may have purchased Lay's Potato Chips at the 7-Eleven store, a book through Chapters.Indigo.ca, and Levi's jeans at Sears. Each of these items was brought to you by a marketing channel of distribution, or simply a **marketing channel**, which consists of individuals and firms involved in the process of making a product or service available for use or consumption by consumers or industrial users.

MARKETING CHANNEL
Individuals and firms involved in the process of making a product or service available for use or consumption by consumers or industrial users.

Marketing channels can be compared with a pipeline through which water flows from a source to terminus. Marketing channels make possible the flow of goods from a producer, through intermediaries, to a buyer. Intermediaries go by various names (Figure 15–1) and perform various functions.[2] Some intermediaries actually purchase items from the seller, store them, and resell them to buyers. For example, Sunshine Biscuits produces cookies and sells them to food wholesalers. The wholesalers then sell the cookies to supermarkets and grocery stores, which, in turn, sell them to consumers. Other intermediaries such as brokers and agents represent sellers but do

FIGURE 15–1
Terms used for marketing intermediaries

TERM	DESCRIPTION
Intermediary	Any intermediary between manufacturer and end-user markets
Agent or broker	Any intermediary with legal authority to act on behalf of the manufacturer
Wholesaler	An intermediary who sells to other intermediaries, usually to retailers; usually applies to consumer markets
Retailer	An intermediary who sells to consumers
Distributor	An imprecise term, usually used to describe intermediaries who perform a variety of distribution functions, including selling, maintaining inventories, extending credit, and so on; a more common term in business markets but may also be used to refer to wholesalers
Dealer	An even more imprecise term that can mean the same as distributor, retailer, wholesaler, and so forth

www.century21.com

not actually take title to products—their role is to bring a seller and buyer together. Century 21 real estate agents are examples of this type of intermediary. The importance of intermediaries is made even clearer when we consider the functions they perform and the value they create for buyers.

Value Created by Intermediaries

Few consumers appreciate the value created by intermediaries; however, producers recognize that intermediaries make selling goods and services more efficient because they minimize the number of sales contacts necessary to reach a target market. Figure 15–2 shows a simple example of how this comes about in the digital camera industry. Without a retail intermediary (such as Future Shop), Kodak, Sony, Panasonic, and Hewlett-Packard would each have to make four contacts to reach the four buyers shown who are in the target market. However, each producer has to make only one contact when Future Shop acts as an intermediary. Equally important from a macromarketing perspective, the total number of industry transactions is reduced from 16 to 8, which reduces producer cost and hence benefits the consumer.

Functions Performed by Intermediaries   Intermediaries make possible the flow of products from producers to buyers by performing three basic functions (Figure 15–3). Most prominently, intermediaries perform a transactional function that involves buying, selling, and risk taking because they stock merchandise in anticipation of sales. Intermediaries perform a logistical function evident in the gathering, storing, and dispersing of products (see Chapter 16 on supply chain and logistics management). Finally, intermediaries perform facilitating functions, which assist producers in making goods and services more attractive to buyers.

All three groups of functions must be performed in a marketing channel, even though each channel member may not participate in all three. Channel members often negotiate about which specific functions they will perform. Sometimes disagreements result, and a breakdown in relationships among channel members occurs. This happened recently when PepsiCo's bottler in Venezuela switched to Coca-Cola. Because all marketing channel functions had to be performed, PepsiCo either had to set up its own bottling operation to perform the marketing channel functions or find another bottler, which it did.[3]

FIGURE 15–2
How intermediaries minimize transactions

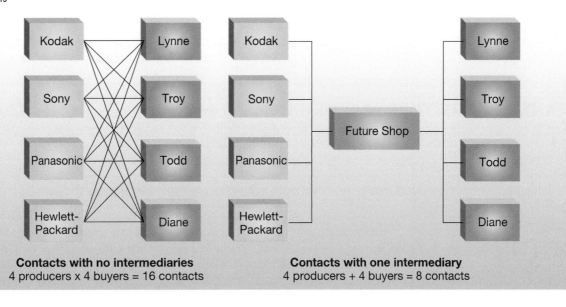

Contacts with no intermediaries
4 producers x 4 buyers = 16 contacts

Contacts with one intermediary
4 producers + 4 buyers = 8 contacts

TYPE OF FUNCTION	ACTIVITIES RELATED TO FUNCTION
Transactional function	• *Buying*: Purchasing products for resale or as an agent for supply of a product • *Selling*: Contacting potential customers, promoting products, and soliciting orders • *Risk taking*: Assuming business risks in the ownership of inventory that can become obsolete or deteriorate
Logistical function	• *Assorting*: Creating product assortments from several sources to serve customers • *Storing*: Assembling and protecting products at a convenient location to offer better customer service • *Sorting*: Purchasing in large quantities and breaking into smaller amounts desired by customers • *Transporting*: Physically moving a product to customers
Facilitating function	• *Financing*: Extending credit to customers • *Grading*: Inspecting, testing, or judging products, and assigning them quality grades • *Marketing information and research*: Providing information to customers and suppliers, including competitive conditions and trends

FIGURE 15–3
Marketing channel functions performed by intermediaries

Consumer Benefits from Intermediaries   Consumers also benefit from intermediaries. Having the goods and services you want, when you want them, where you want them, and in the form you want them is the ideal result of marketing channels. In more specific terms, marketing channels help create value for consumers through the four utilities described in Chapter 1: time, place, form, and possession. *Time utility* refers to having a product or service when you want it. For example, FedEx provides next-morning delivery. *Place utility* means having a product or service available where consumers want it, such as having an Esso gas station located on a long stretch of lonely highway. *Form utility* involves enhancing a product or service to make it more appealing to buyers. For example, Compaq Computer delivers unfinished PCs to dealers, which then add memory, chips, modems, and other parts, based on consumer specifications. *Possession utility* entails efforts by intermediaries to help buyers take possession of a product or service, such as having airline tickets delivered by a travel agency.

1. What is meant by a marketing channel?

2. What are the three basic functions performed by intermediaries?

CHANNEL STRUCTURE AND ORGANIZATION

A product can take many routes on its journey from a producer to buyers, and marketers search for the most efficient route from the many alternatives available.

Marketing Channels for Consumer Goods and Services

Figure 15–4 shows the four most common marketing channels for consumer goods and services. It also shows the number of levels in each marketing channel, as evidenced by the number of intermediaries between a producer and ultimate buyers. As the number of intermediaries between a producer and buyer increases, the channel is viewed as increasing in length. Thus the producer → wholesaler → retailer → consumer channel is longer than the producer → consumer channel.

FIGURE 15–4
Common marketing channels for consumer goods and services

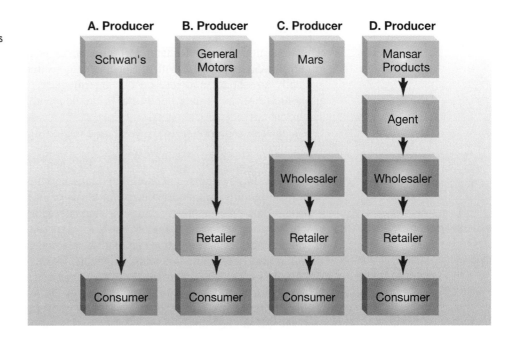

DIRECT CHANNEL
A marketing channel where a producer and ultimate consumer deal directly with each other.

Channel A represents a **direct channel** because a producer and ultimate consumers deal directly with each other. Many products and services are distributed this way. A number of insurance companies sell their financial services using a direct channel and branch sales offices, and World Book Educational Products sells its encyclopedias direct to consumers. Schwan's Sales Enterprises markets a full line of frozen foods using door-to-door salespeople who sell from refrigerated trucks. Because there are no intermediaries with a direct channel, the producer must perform all channel functions.

INDIRECT CHANNEL
A marketing channel where intermediaries are inserted between the producer and consumers and perform numerous channel functions.

The remaining three channel forms are considered **indirect channels** because intermediaries are inserted between the producer and consumers and perform numerous channel functions. Channel B, with a retailer added, is most common when a retailer is large and can buy in large quantities from a producer or when the cost of inventory makes it too expensive to use a wholesaler. Manufacturers such as General Motors, Ford, and DaimlerChrysler use this channel, and a local car dealer acts as a retailer. Why is there no wholesaler? So many variations exist in the product that it would be impossible for a wholesaler to stock all the models required to satisfy buyers; in addition, the cost of maintaining an inventory would be too high. However, large retailers such as Sears Canada, 7-Eleven, and The Bay buy in sufficient quantities to make it cost-effective for a producer to deal with only a retail intermediary.

Adding a wholesaler in Channel C is most common for low-cost, low-unit-value items that are frequently purchased by consumers, such as candy, confectionary items, and magazines. For example, Mars sells its line of candies to wholesalers in case quantities; then they can break down (sort) the cases so that individual retailers can order in boxes or much smaller quantities.

Channel D, the most indirect channel, is employed when there are many small manufacturers and many small retailers and an agent is used to help coordinate a large supply of the product. Mansar Products, Ltd. is a Belgian producer of specialty jewellery that uses agents to sell to wholesalers, which then sell to many small retailers.

Marketing Channels for Business Goods and Services

The four most common channels for business goods and services are shown in Figure 15–5. In contrast with channels for consumer products, business channels typically are shorter and rely on one intermediary or none at all because business users are fewer in number, tend to be more concentrated geographically, and buy in larger quantities (see Chapter 6).

Channel A, represented by IBM's large, mainframe computer business, is a direct channel. Firms using this channel maintain their own salesforce and perform all channel functions. This channel is employed when buyers are large and well defined, the sales effort requires extensive negotiations, and the products are of high unit value and require hands-on expertise in terms of installation or use.

INDUSTRIAL DISTRIBUTOR
Performs a variety of marketing channel functions, including selling, stocking, delivering a full product assortment, and financing.

Channels B, C, and D are indirect channels with one or more intermediaries to reach industrial users. In Channel B an **industrial distributor** performs a variety of marketing channel functions, including selling, stocking, and delivering a full product assortment and financing. In many ways, industrial distributors are like wholesalers in consumer channels. Caterpillar relies on industrial distributors to sell its construction and mining equipment in almost 200 countries. In addition to selling, Caterpillar distributors stock 40 000 to 50 000 parts and service equipment using highly trained technicians.[4]

Channel C introduces a second intermediary, an *agent*, who serves primarily as the independent selling arm of producers and represents a producer to industrial users. For example, Stake Fastener Company, a producer of industrial fasteners, has an agent call on industrial users rather than employing its own salesforce.

Channel D is the longest channel and includes both agents and distributors. For instance, Culligan, a producer of water treatment equipment, uses agents to call on distributors, who sell to industrial users.

Electronic Marketing Channels

These common marketing channels for consumer and business goods and services are not the only routes to the marketplace. Advances in electronic commerce have opened new avenues for reaching buyers and creating customer value.

ELECTRONIC MARKETING CHANNELS
Employ the Internet to make goods and services available for consumption or use by consumers or business buyers.

Interactive electronic technology has made possible **electronic marketing channels** that employ the Internet to make goods and services available for consumption or use by consumers or business buyers. A unique feature of these channels is that they combine electronic and traditional intermediaries to create time, place, form, and possession utility for buyers.[5]

FIGURE 15–5
Common marketing channels for business goods and services

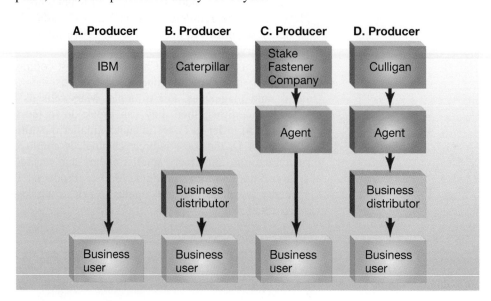

FIGURE 15–6
Representative electronic marketing channels

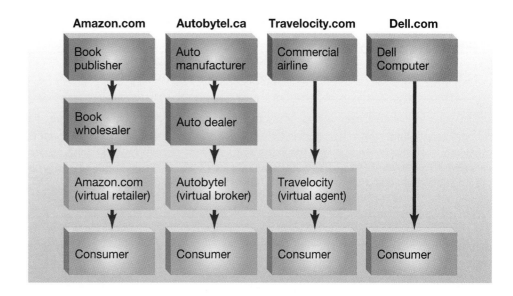

Figure 15–6 shows the electronic marketing channels for books (Amazon.com), automobiles (Autobytel.ca), reservation services (Travelocity.com), and personal computers (Dell.com). Are you surprised that they look a lot like common marketing channels? An important reason for the similarity resides in channel functions detailed in Figure 15–3. Electronic intermediaries can and do perform transactional and facilitating functions effectively and at a relatively lower cost than traditional intermediaries because of efficiencies made possible by information technology. However, electronic intermediaries are incapable of performing elements of the logistical function, particularly for products such as books and automobiles. This function remains with traditional intermediaries or with the producer, as evident with Dell Computer Corporation and its direct channel. In fact, the inability of many electronic intermediaries to master the logistical function in a cost-effective manner contributed to their demise in the "dot-com crash" of 2001.

Many services can be distributed through electronic marketing channels, such as travel reservation marketed by Travelocity.com, financial securities by Schwab.com, and insurance by MetLife.com. Software too can be marketed this way. However, many other services such as health care and auto repair still involve traditional intermediaries.

Direct Marketing Channels

DIRECT MARKETING CHANNELS
Allow consumers to buy products by interacting with various advertising media without a face-to-face meeting with a salesperson.

Many firms also use direct marketing channels to reach buyers. **Direct marketing channels** allow consumers to buy products by interacting with various advertising media without a face-to-face meeting with a salesperson. Direct marketing includes mail-order selling, direct-mail sales, catalogue sales, telemarketing, interactive media, and televised home shopping.[6]

Some firms sell products almost entirely through direct marketing channels. These firms include L.L. Bean (apparel), Sharper Image (expensive gifts and novelties), and Egghead.com (personal computers). Manufacturers such as Nestlé and Sunkist, in addition to using traditional channels composed of wholesalers and retailers, employ direct marketing through catalogues and telemarketing to reach more buyers. At the same time, retailers such as Sears Canada use direct marketing techniques to augment conventional store merchandising activities. Some experts believe that direct marketing accounts for 20 percent of all retail transactions in North America and 10 percent of retail transactions in Europe. Direct marketing is covered in greater depth in Chapter 18.

MARKETING NEWSNET

Nestlé and General Mills: Cereal Partners Worldwide

Can you say Nestlé Cheerios *miel amandes*? Millions of French start their day with this European equivalent of General Mills' Honey Nut Cheerios, made possible by Cereal Partners Worldwide (CPW). CPW is the food industry's first strategic alliance designed to be a global business; it joined the cereal manufacturing and marketing capability of General Mills with the worldwide distribution clout of Nestlé.

From its headquarters near Lake Geneva, Switzerland, CPW first launched General Mills cereals under the Nestlé label in France, the United Kingdom, Spain, and Portugal in 1991. Today, CPW competes in 70 markets worldwide and soon expects to achieve its goal of $1.4 billion in profitable sales.

The General Mills–Nestlé strategic alliance is also likely to increase the ready-to-eat worldwide market share of these

companies, which are already rated as the two best-managed firms in the world. CPW is on track to reach its goal of a 20-percent worldwide share.

Multiple Channels and Strategic Alliances

DUAL DISTRIBUTION
An arrangement by which a firm reaches buyers by employing two or more different types of channels for the same basic product.

www.hallmark.com

STRATEGIC CHANNEL ALLIANCES
A practice whereby one firm's marketing channel is used to sell another firm's products.

www.generalmills.com

In some situations producers use **dual distribution**, an arrangement whereby a firm reaches different buyers by employing two or more different types of channels for the same basic product. For example, GE sells its large appliances directly to home and apartment builders but uses retail stores to sell to consumers. In some instances, firms use multiple channels when a multibrand strategy is employed (see Chapter 11). This is done to minimize cannibalization of the firm's family brand and differentiate the channels. For example, Hallmark sells its Hallmark greeting cards through Hallmark stores and select department stores, and its Ambassador brand of cards through discount and drugstore chains. Avon Products sells the Avon brand through its independent representatives, its Website, and kiosks in shopping malls, but markets the beComing brand through its JCPenney shop-within-a-store, as described in the chapter-opening example.

A recent innovation in marketing channels is the use of **strategic channel alliances**, whereby one firm's marketing channel is used to sell another firm's products.[7] An alliance between Kraft Foods and Starbucks is a case in point. Kraft distributes Starbucks coffee in supermarkets. Strategic alliances are popular in global marketing, where the creation of marketing channel relationships is expensive and time-consuming. For example, General Motors distributes the Swedish Saab through its Saturn dealers in Canada. General Mills and Nestlé have an extensive alliance that spans 70 international markets. Read the accompanying Marketing NewsNet so you won't be surprised when you are served Nestlé (not General Mills) Cheerios in Europe, South America, and parts of Asia.[8]

A Closer Look at Channel Intermediaries

Channel structures for consumer and industrial products assume various forms based on the number and type of intermediaries. Knowledge of the roles played by these intermediaries is important for understanding how channels operate in practice.

The terms *wholesaler*, *agent*, and *retailer* have been used in a general fashion consistent with the meanings given in Figure 15–1. However, on closer inspection, a variety of specific types of intermediaries emerges. These intermediaries engage in wholesaling activities—those activities involved in selling products and services to those who are buying for the purposes of resale or business use. Intermediaries engaged in retailing activities are discussed in detail in Chapter 17. Figure 15–7 describes the functions performed by major types of independent wholesalers.[9]

MERCHANT WHOLESALERS
Independently owned firms that take title to the merchandise they handle.

Merchant Wholesalers **Merchant wholesalers** are independently owned firms that take title to the merchandise they handle. They go by various names, including industrial distributor (described earlier). About 83 percent of the firms engaged in wholesaling activities are merchant wholesalers.

Merchant wholesalers are classified as either full-service or limited-service wholesalers, depending on the number of functions performed. Two major types of full-service wholesalers exist. *General merchandise* (or *full-line*) *wholesalers* carry a broad assortment of merchandise and perform all channel functions. This type of wholesaler is most prevalent in the hardware, drug, and clothing industries. However, these wholesalers do not maintain much depth of assortment within specific product lines. *Specialty merchandise* (or *limited-line*) *wholesalers* offer a relatively narrow range of products but have an extensive assortment within the product lines carried. They perform all channel functions and are found in the health foods, automotive parts, and seafood industries.

FIGURE 15–7
Functions performed by independent wholesaler types

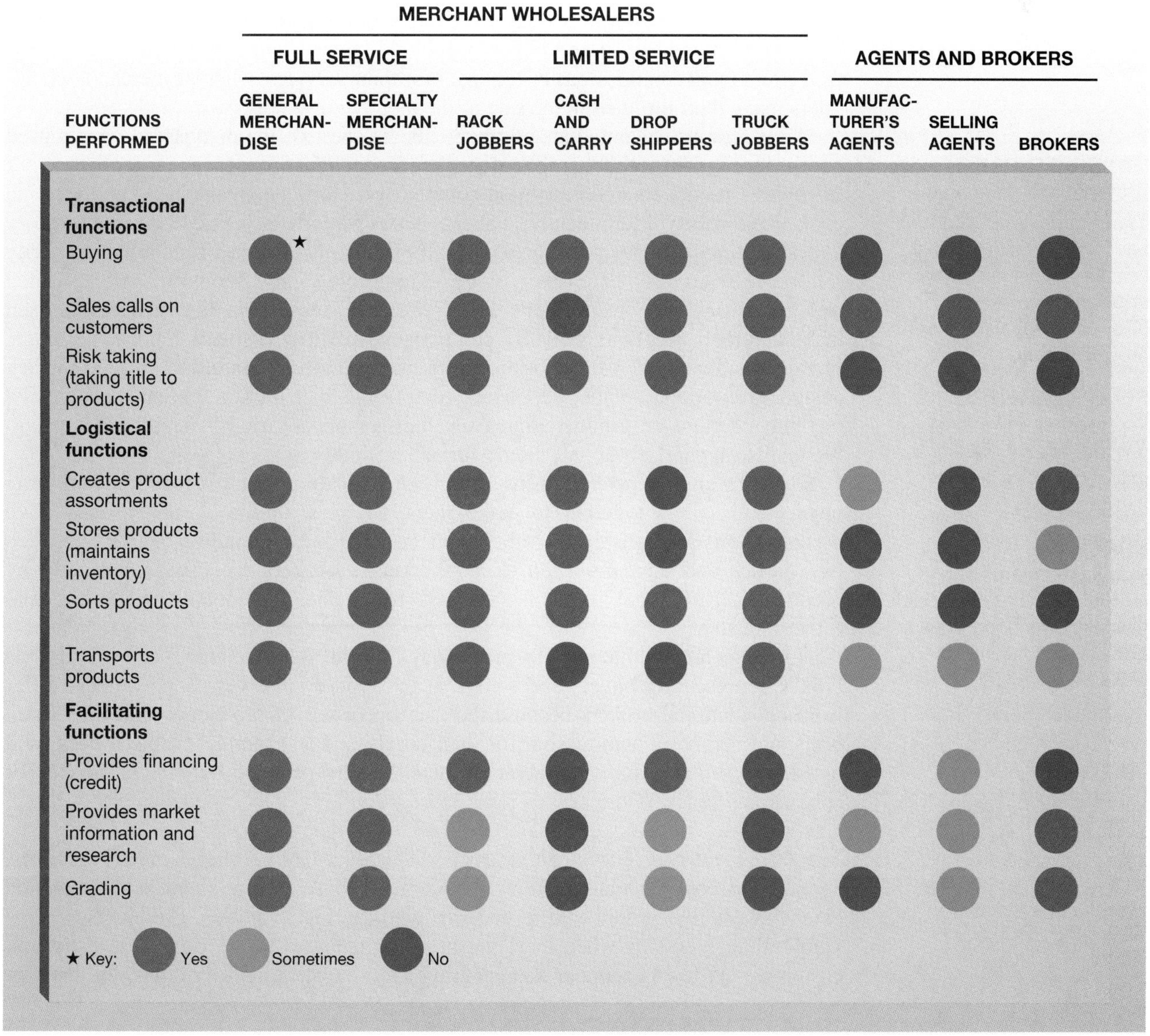

MERCHANT WHOLESALERS

FUNCTIONS PERFORMED	FULL SERVICE		LIMITED SERVICE				AGENTS AND BROKERS		
	GENERAL MERCHAN-DISE	SPECIALTY MERCHAN-DISE	RACK JOBBERS	CASH AND CARRY	DROP SHIPPERS	TRUCK JOBBERS	MANUFAC-TURER'S AGENTS	SELLING AGENTS	BROKERS

★ Key: ● Yes ● Sometimes ● No

Four major types of limited-service wholesalers exist. *Rack jobbers* furnish the racks or shelves that display merchandise in retail stores, perform all channel functions, and sell on consignment to retailers, which means they retain the title to the products displayed and bill retailers only for the merchandise sold. Familiar products such as hosiery, toys, housewares, and health and beauty aids are sold by rack jobbers. *Cash and carry wholesalers* take title to merchandise but sell only to buyers who call on them, pay cash for merchandise, and furnish their own transportation for merchandise. They carry a limited product assortment and do not make deliveries, extend credit, or supply market information. This wholesaler is common in electric supplies, office supplies, hardware products, and groceries. *Drop shippers*, or *desk jobbers*, are wholesalers who own the merchandise they sell but do not physically handle, stock, or deliver it. They simply solicit orders from retailers and other wholesalers and have the merchandise shipped directly from a producer to a buyer. Drop shippers are used for bulky products such as coal, lumber, and chemicals, which are sold in extremely large quantities. *Truck jobbers* are small wholesalers who have a small warehouse from which they stock their trucks for distribution to retailers. They usually handle limited assortments of fast-moving or perishable items that are sold for cash directly from trucks in their original packages. Truck jobbers handle products such as bakery items, dairy products, and meat.

Agents and Brokers

Unlike merchant wholesalers, agents and brokers do not take title to merchandise and typically provide fewer channel functions. They make their profit from commissions or fees paid for their services, whereas merchant wholesalers make their profit from the sale of the merchandise they own.

Manufacturer's agents and selling agents are the two major types of agents used by producers. **Manufacturer's agents**, or *manufacturer's representatives*, work for several producers and carry non-competitive, complementary merchandise in an exclusive territory. Manufacturer's agents act as a producer's sales arm in a territory and are principally responsible for the transactional channel functions, primarily selling. They are used extensively in the automotive supply, footwear, and fabricated steel industries. However, Swank Jewelry and Japanese computer firms have used manufacturer's agents as well. By comparison, **selling agents** represent a single producer and are responsible for the entire marketing function of that producer. They design promotional plans, set prices, determine distribution policies, and make recommendations on product strategy. Selling agents are used by small producers in the textile, apparel, food, and home furnishing industries.

Brokers are independent firms or individuals whose principal function is to bring buyers and sellers together to make sales. Brokers, unlike agents, usually have no continuous relationship with the buyer or seller but negotiate a contract between two parties and then move on to another task. Brokers are used extensively by producers of seasonal products (such as fruits and vegetables) and in the real estate industry.

A unique broker that acts in many ways like a manufacturer's agent is a food broker, representing buyers and sellers in the grocery industry. Food brokers differ from conventional brokers because they act on behalf of producers on a permanent basis and receive a commission for their services. For example, Nabisco uses food brokers to sell its candies, margarine, and Planters peanuts, but it sells its line of cookies and crackers directly to retail stores.

Manufacturer's Branches and Offices

Unlike merchant wholesalers, agents, and brokers, manufacturer's branches and sales offices are wholly owned extensions of the producer that perform wholesaling activities. Producers assume wholesaling functions when there are no intermediaries to perform these activities, customers are few in number and geographically concentrated, or orders are large or

MANUFACTURER'S AGENTS
Work for several producers and carry noncompetitive, complementary merchandise in an exclusive territory; also called *manufacturer's representatives.*

SELLING AGENTS
Represent a single producer and are responsible for the entire marketing function of that producer.

BROKERS
Independent firms or individuals whose principal function is to bring buyers and sellers together to make sales.

require significant attention. A *manufacturer's branch office* carries a producer's inventory and performs the functions of a full-service wholesaler. A *manufacturer's sales office* does not carry inventory, typically performs only a sales function, and serves as an alternative to agents and brokers.

Vertical Marketing Systems and Channel Partnerships

The traditional marketing channels described so far represent a loosely knit network of independent producers and intermediaries brought together to distribute goods and services. However, new channel arrangements have emerged for the purpose of improving efficiency in performing channel functions and achieving greater marketing effectiveness. These new arrangements are called vertical marketing systems and channel partnerships. **Vertical marketing systems** are professionally managed and centrally coordinated marketing channels designed to achieve channel economies and maximum marketing impact.[10] Figure 15–8 depicts the major types of vertical marketing systems: corporate, contractual, and administered.

Corporate Systems   The combination of successive stages of production and distribution under a single ownership is a *corporate vertical marketing system*. For example, a producer might own the intermediary at the next level down in the channel. This practice, called *forward integration*, is exemplified by Irving Oil, which refines gasoline and also operates retail gasoline stations. Other examples of forward integration include Goodyear, Singer, Sherwin Williams, and the building materials division of Boise Cascade. Alternatively, a retailer might own a manufacturing operation, a practice called *backward integration*. For example, Safeway supermarkets operate their own bakeries. Companies seeking to reduce distribution costs and gain greater control over supply sources or resale of their products pursue forward and backward integration. However, both types of integration increase a company's capital investment and fixed costs. For this reason, many companies favour contractual vertical marketing systems to achieve channel efficiencies and marketing effectiveness.

VERTICAL MARKETING SYSTEMS
Professionally managed and centrally coordinated marketing channels designed to achieve channel economies and maximum marketing impact.

FIGURE 15–8
Types of vertical marketing systems

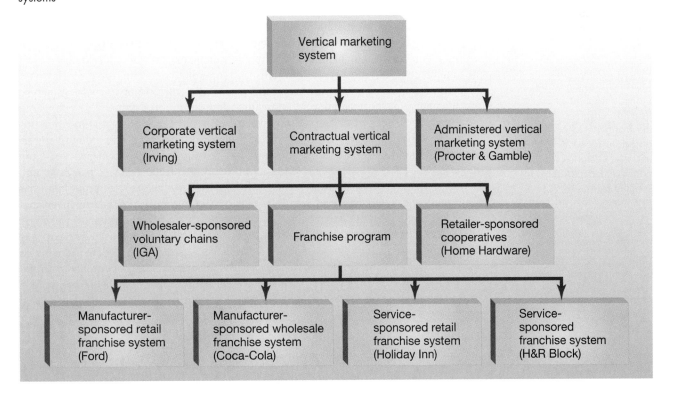

Sherwin-Williams and Ace Hardware represent two different types of vertical marketing systems.

Sherwin-Williams

www.sherwin-williams.com

Ace Hardware

www.acehardware.com

Contractual Systems   Under a *contractual vertical marketing system*, independent production and distribution firms integrate their efforts on a contractual basis to obtain greater functional economies and marketing impact than they could achieve alone. Contractual systems are the most popular among the three types of vertical marketing systems. They account for about 40 percent of all retail sales.

Three variations of contractual systems exist. *Wholesaler-sponsored voluntary chains* involve a wholesaler that develops a contractual relationship with small, independent retailers to standardize and coordinate buying practices, merchandising programs, and inventory management efforts. With the organization of a large number of independent retailers, economies of scale and volume discounts can be achieved to compete with chain stores. IGA stores represent wholesaler-sponsored voluntary chains. *Retailer-sponsored cooperatives* exist when small, independent retailers form an organization that operates a wholesale facility cooperatively. Member retailers then concentrate their buying power through the wholesaler and plan collaborative promotional and pricing activities. Home Hardware is an example of a retailer-sponsored cooperative.

The most visible variation of contractual systems is **franchising**, a contractual arrangement between a parent company (a franchisor) and an individual or firm (a franchisee) that allows the franchise to operate a certain type of business under an established name and according to specific rules. Four types of franchise arrangements are most popular. Manufacturer-sponsored retail franchise systems are prominent in the automobile industry, where a manufacturer such as Ford licenses dealers to sell its cars subject to various sales and service conditions. Manufacturer-sponsored wholesale systems are evident in the soft-drink industry, where Pepsi-Cola licenses wholesalers (bottlers) who purchase concentrate from Pepsi-Cola and then carbonate, bottle, promote, and distribute its products to supermarkets and restaurants. Service-sponsored retail franchise systems are provided by firms that have designed a unique approach for performing a service and wish to profit by selling the franchise to others. Holiday Inn, Avis, and McDonald's represent this franchising approach. Service-sponsored franchise systems exist when franchisors license individuals or firms to dispense a service under a trade name and specific guidelines. An example is H&R Block tax services. Service-sponsored franchise arrangements are the fastest-growing type of franchise. Franchising is discussed further in Chapter 17.

FRANCHISING

Contractual arrangement between a parent company (a franchisor) and an individual or firm (a franchisee) that allows the franchise to operate a certain type of business under an established name and according to specific rules.

Administered Systems   In comparison, *administered vertical marketing systems* achieve coordination at successive stages of production and distribution by the size and influence of one channel member rather than through ownership. Procter &

Gamble, given its broad product assortment ranging from disposable diapers to detergents, is able to obtain cooperation from supermarkets in displaying, promoting, and pricing its products. Wal-Mart can obtain cooperation from manufacturers in terms of product specifications, price levels, and promotional support, given its position as the world's largest retailer.

CHANNEL PARTNERSHIP
Agreements and procedures among channel members for ordering and physically distributing a producer's product through the channel to the ultimate consumer.

Channel Partnerships   Increasingly, channel members are forging channel partnerships akin to supply partnerships described in Chapter 6. A **channel partnership** consists of agreements and procedures among channel members for ordering and physically distributing a producer's products through the channel to the ultimate consumer.[11] A central feature of channel partnerships is the collaborative use of information and communication technology to better serve customers and reduce the time and cost of performing channel functions.

The partnership Levi Strauss & Company has with Modell's Sporting Goods is a case in point.[12] By using point-of-sale scanning equipment and direct electronic linkage to Levi Strauss, Modell's can instantaneously inform Levi Strauss what styles and sizes of jeans are needed, create purchase orders, and convey shipping instructions without any human involvement. The result? The costs of performing transaction, logistic, and facilitating functions are substantially reduced, and the customer is virtually assured of having his or her preferred 501 Levi jeans in stock. The role of information and communication technology in supply chain and logistics management is discussed further in Chapter 16.

Concept Check

1. What is the difference between a direct and an indirect channel?

2. Why are channels for industrial products typically shorter than channels for consumer products?

3. What is the principal distinction between a corporate vertical marketing system and an administered vertical marketing system?

CHANNEL CHOICE AND MANAGEMENT

Marketing channels not only link a producer to its buyers but also provide the means through which a firm implements various elements of its marketing strategy. Therefore, choosing a marketing channel is a critical decision.

Factors Affecting Channel Choice and Management

The final choice of a marketing channel by a producer depends on a number of factors that often interact with each other.

Environmental Factors   The changing environment described in Chapter 3 has an important effect on the choice and management of a marketing channel. For example, the Fuller Brush Company, a name synonymous with door-to-door selling, now uses catalogues and telemarketing to reach customers. Rising employment among women, resulting in fewer being at home during working hours, prompted this action. Advances in the technology of growing, transporting, and storing perishable cut flowers has allowed many retailers such as Calgary's Kensington Florist to eliminate flower wholesalers and buy direct from flower growers. Additionally, the Internet has created new marketing channel opportunities for online marketing of flowers as well as consumer electronics, books, and music and video products.

Kensington Florist
www.kensingtonflorist.com

Consumer Factors   Consumer characteristics have a direct bearing on the choice and management of a marketing channel. Determining which channel is most appropriate is based on answers to fundamental questions such as: Who are potential customers? Where do they buy? When do they buy? How do they buy? What do they buy? These answers also indicate the type of intermediary best suited to reaching target buyers. For example, Ricoh Company, Ltd. studied the serious (as opposed to recreational) camera user and concluded that a change in marketing channels was necessary. The company terminated its contract with a wholesaler who sold to mass merchandise stores and began using manufacturer's agents who sold to photo specialty stores. These stores agreed to stock and display Ricoh's full line and promote it prominently. Sales volume tripled within 18 months. Recognizing that car buyers now comparison shop on the Internet, automakers now have their own Websites to provide price and model information.

Product Factors   In general, highly sophisticated products such as large, scientific computers, unstandardized products such as custom-built machinery, and products of high unit value are distributed directly to buyers. Unsophisticated, standardized products with low unit value, such as table salt, are typically distributed through indirect channels. A product's stage in the life cycle also affects marketing channels. This was shown in the description of the fax machine product life cycle in Chapter 11.

Company Factors   A firm's financial, human, or technological capabilities affect channel choice. For example, firms that are unable to employ a salesforce might use manufacturer's agents or selling agents to reach wholesalers or buyers. If a firm has multiple products for a particular target market, it might use a direct channel, whereas firms with a limited product line might use intermediaries of various types to reach buyers.

Company factors also apply to intermediaries. For example, personal computer hardware and software producers wishing to reach business users might look to value-added resellers such as Future Shop, which has its own salesforce and service staff that calls on businesses.

www.futureshop.com

Channel Design Considerations

Recognizing that numerous routes to buyers exist and also recognizing the factors just described, marketing executives typically consider three questions when choosing a marketing channel and intermediaries:

1. Which channel and intermediaries will provide the best coverage of the target market?
2. Which channel and intermediaries will best satisfy the buying requirements of the target market?
3. Which channel and intermediaries will be the most profitable?

Target Market Coverage   Achieving the best coverage of the target market requires attention to the density and type of intermediaries to be used at the retail level of distribution. Three degrees of distribution density exist: intensive, exclusive, and selective. **Intensive distribution** means that a firm tries to place its products and services in as many outlets as possible. Intensive distribution is usually chosen for convenience products or services; for instance, candy, fast food, newspapers, and soft drinks. Increasingly, medical services are distributed in this fashion. Cash—yes, cash—is also distributed intensively by Visa. Visit Visa's Website described in the Web Link to locate the nearest Visa automated teller machine.

Exclusive distribution is the extreme opposite of intensive distribution because only one retail outlet in a specified geographical area carries the firm's product. Exclusive distribution is typically chosen for specialty products or services;

INTENSIVE DISTRIBUTION
A firm tries to place its products or services in as many outlets as possible.

EXCLUSIVE DISTRIBUTION
Only one retail outlet in a specific geographical area carries the firm's products.

for example, automobiles, some women's fragrances, men's suits, and yachts. Sometimes retailers sign exclusive distribution agreements with manufacturers. Gucci, one of the world's leading luxury goods companies, uses exclusive distribution.[13] Sometimes retailers sign exclusive distribution agreements with manufacturers and suppliers. For instance, Radio Shack sells only Compaq personal computers in its stores.[14]

SELECTIVE DISTRIBUTION
A firm selects a few retail outlets in a specific geographical area to carry its products.

Selective distribution lies between these two extremes and means that a firm selects a few retail outlets in a specific geographical area to carry its products. Selective distribution weds some of the market coverage benefits of intensive distribution to the control over resale evident with exclusive distribution. For this reason, selective distribution is the most common form of distribution intensity and is usually associated with shopping goods or services such as Rolex watches and Ping golf clubs.

Satisfying Buyer Requirements   A second consideration in channel design is gaining access to channels and intermediaries that satisfy at least some of the interests buyers might want fulfilled when they purchase a firm's products or services. These interests fall into four categories: (1) information, (2) convenience, (3) variety, and (4) attendant services.

Information is an important requirement when buyers have limited knowledge or desire specific data about a product or service. Properly chosen intermediaries communicate with buyers through in-store displays, demonstrations, and personal selling. Personal computer manufacturers such as Gateway and Apple Computer have opened their own retail outlets staffed with highly trained personnel to inform buyers how their products can better meet each customer's needs.[15]

Convenience has multiple meanings for buyers, such as proximity or driving time to a retail outlet. For example, 7-Eleven stores with outlets nationwide satisfy this interest for buyers, and candy and snack food firms benefit by gaining display space in these stores. For other consumers, convenience means a minimum of time and hassle. Jiffy Lube and Mr. Lube, which promise to change engine oil and filters quickly, appeal to this aspect of convenience. For those who shop on the Internet, convenience means that Websites must be easy to locate and navigate, and image downloads must be fast. A commonly held view among Website developers is the "eight-second rule": consumers will abandon their efforts to enter or navigate a Website if download time exceeds eight seconds.[16]

WEB LINK

**Need Cash Fast?
Check the Visa ATM Locator**

http://www.mcgrawhill.ca

Short of cash? Visa offers a valuable Web resource in its ATM Locator, which can be accessed at www.visa.com. Visa has some 750 000 automated teller machines in 120 countries. One is probably in your neighbourhood, wherever that is in the world! To find the nearest Visa ATM, follow the easy ATM Locator directions and request a site map. You'll be in the money in no time. Here's the map for McGraw-Hill Higher Education's neighbourhood.

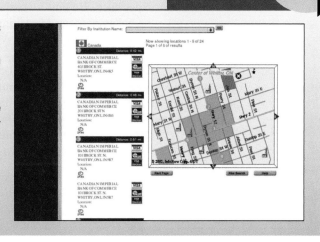

MARKETING NEWSNET

Apple Computer, Inc.: Think Different, Shop Different

Think Different. Apple Computer's catchy advertising conveys the company's spirit. Apple ignited the personal computer revolution in the 1970s with the Apple II, reinvented the personal computer in the 1980s with the Macintosh, and captured the imagination of personal computer buyers worldwide with the introduction of the Apple iMac—a design and technological breakthrough.

Now Apple invites buyers to *Shop Different* at its new Apple Stores, which seek to satisfy the buying requirements of today's PC purchaser. At each Apple Store, knowledgeable salespeople demonstrate Macs® running innovative applications like iTunes for burning custom CDs and iMovie™ for making home videos, as well as Mac® OSX, Apple's new operating system. All of the Macs are connected to the Internet. Several Macs are connected to digital lifestyle products that complement the Mac experience, such as digital cameras, digital camcorders, MP3 players, and handheld organizers. The stores carry more than 300 third-party software titles for creative professionals, students, educators, and consumers and maintain inventory for every Apple and third-party product to ensure immediate fulfillment of buyer requests. If a buyer has a question about specific applications, he or she can visit the "Genius Bar," staffed by Apple-trained personnel, for the answer.

Interested in visiting an Apple store? Log on to the company's Website at www.apple.com to take a virtual tour or find a location near you.

Variety reflects buyers' interest in having numerous competing and complementary items from which to choose. Variety is evident in both the breadth and depth of products and brands carried by intermediaries, which enhances their attraction to buyers. Thus, manufacturers of pet food and supplies seek distribution through pet superstores such as Petco and Petsmart, which offer a wide array of pet products.

Attendant services provided by intermediaries are an important buying requirement for products such as large household appliances that require delivery, installation, and credit. Therefore, Whirlpool seeks dealers that provide such services.

Steven P. Jobs, Apple Computer's CEO, is one person who believes that computer retailers have failed to satisfy the buying requirements of today's consumer. Believing that "Buying a car is no longer the worst purchasing experience. Buying a computer is No. 1," he launched Apple Stores in 2001. Read the accompanying Marketing NewsNet to see how Apple Stores intend to satisfy the information, convenience, variety, and service interests of consumers.[17]

Profitability   The third consideration in designing a channel is profitability, which is determined by the margins earned (revenues minus cost) for each channel member and for the channel as a whole. Channel cost is the critical dimension of profitability. These costs include distribution, advertising, and selling expenses associated with different types of marketing channels. The extent to which channel members share these costs determines the margins received by each member and by the channel as a whole.

For the answer to how Schick became a razor and blade market share leader in Japan, read the text.

Warner Lambert Company
www.warner-lambert.com

CHANNEL CONFLICT
Arises when one channel member believes another channel member is engaged in behaviour that prevents it from achieving its goals.

DISINTERMEDIATION
Channel conflict that arises when a channel member bypasses another member and sells or buys products direct.

Global Dimensions of Marketing Channels

Marketing channels around the world reflect traditions, customs, geography, and the economic history of individual countries and societies. Even so, the basic marketing channel functions must be performed. But differences do exist and are illustrated by highlighting marketing channels in Japan—the world's second-largest economy.

Intermediaries outside Western Europe and North America tend to be small, numerous, and often owner-operated. Japanese marketing channels tend to include many intermediaries based on tradition and lack of storage space. As many as five intermediaries are involved in the distribution of soap in Japan compared with one or two in North America.

Understanding marketing channels in global markets is often a prerequisite to successful marketing. For example, Gillette attempted to sell its razors and blades through company salespeople in Japan as it does in North America, thus eliminating wholesalers traditionally involved in marketing toiletries. Warner-Lambert Company sold its Schick razors and blades through the traditional Japanese channel involving wholesalers. The result? Schick achieved a commanding lead over Gillette in the Japanese razor and blade market.[18]

Channel relationships also must be considered. In Japan, the distribution *keiretsu* (translated as "alignments") bonds producers and intermediaries together.[19] The bond, through vertical integration and social and economic ties, ensures that each channel member benefits from the distribution alignment. The dominant member of the distribution *keiretsu*, which is typically a producer, has considerable influence over channel member behaviour, including which competing products are sold by other channel members. Well-known Japanese companies such as Matsushita (electronics), Nissan and Toyota (automotive products), Nippon Gakki (musical instruments), and Kirin (and other brewers and distillers) employ the distribution *keiretsu* extensively. Shiseido and Kanebo, for instance, influence the distribution of cosmetics through Japanese department stores.

Channel Relationships: Conflict, Cooperation, and Law

Unfortunately, because channels consist of independent individuals and firms, there is always potential for disagreements concerning who performs which channel functions, how profits are allocated, which products and services will be provided by whom, and who makes critical channel-related decisions. These channel conflicts necessitate measures for dealing with them. Sometimes they result in legal action.

Conflict in Marketing Channels **Channel conflict** arises when one channel member believes another channel member is engaged in behaviour that prevents it from achieving its goals. Two types of conflict occur in marketing channels: vertical conflict and horizontal conflict.[20]

Vertical conflict occurs between different levels in a marketing channel; for example, between a manufacturer and a wholesaler or retailer or between a wholesaler and a retailer. Three sources of vertical conflict are most common. First, conflict arises when a channel member bypasses another member and sells or buys products direct, a practice called **disintermediation**. This conflict emerged when Jenn-Air, a producer of kitchen appliances, decided to terminate its distributors and sell direct to retailers. Second, disagreements over how profit margins are distributed among channel members produce conflict. This happened when Compaq Computer Corporation and one of its dealers disagreed over how price discounts were applied in the sale of Compaq's products. Compaq Computer stopped selling to the dealer for 13 months until the issue was resolved. A third conflict situation arises when manufacturers believe wholesalers or retailers are not giving their products adequate attention. For example, H. J. Heinz Company found itself in a conflict situation with its supermarkets in Great Britain when the supermarkets promoted and displayed private brands at the expense of Heinz brands.

Horizontal conflict occurs between intermediaries at the same level in a marketing channel, such as between two or more retailers (Zellers and Wal-Mart) or two or more wholesalers that handle the same manufacturer's brands. Two sources of horizontal conflict are common. First, horizontal conflict arises when a manufacturer increases its distribution coverage in a geographical area. For example, a franchised Cadillac dealer might complain to General Motors that another franchised Cadillac dealer has located too close to its dealership. Second, dual distribution causes conflict when different types of retailers carry the same brands. For instance, the launch of Elizabeth Taylor's Black Pearls fragrance by Elizabeth Arden was put on hold when some upscale department store chains refused to stock the item once they learned that mass merchants would also carry the brand. Elizabeth Arden subsequently introduced the brand only through department stores.[21]

Cooperation in Marketing Channels

Conflict can have destructive effects on the workings of a marketing channel, so it is necessary to secure cooperation among channel members. One means is through a **channel captain**, a channel member that coordinates, directs, and supports other channel members. Channel captains can be producers, wholesalers, or retailers. P&G assumes this role because it has a strong consumer following in brands such as Crest, Tide, and Pampers. Therefore, it can set policies or terms that supermarkets will follow. Wal-Mart and Home Depot are retail channel captains because of their strong consumer image, number of outlets, and purchasing volume.

A firm becomes a channel captain because it is typically the channel member with the ability to influence the behaviour of other members.[22] Influence can take four forms. First, economic influence arises from the ability of a firm to reward other members given its strong financial position or customer franchise. Microsoft Corporation and Toys "Я" Us have such influence. Expertise is a second source of influence over other channel members. Third, identification with a particular channel member may also create influence for that channel member. For instance, retailers may compete to carry the Ralph Lauren line, or clothing manufacturers may compete to be carried by Eaton's or the Bay. In both instances the desire to be associated with a channel member gives that firm influence over others. Finally, influence can arise from the legitimate right of one channel member to direct the behaviour of other members. This situation would occur under contractual vertical marketing systems where a franchisor could legitimately direct how a franchisee behaves. Other means for securing cooperation in marketing channels rest in the different variations of vertical marketing systems.

Channel influence can be used to gain concessions from other channel members. For instance, some large supermarket chains expect manufacturers to pay allowances, in the form of cash or free goods, to stock and display their products. Some manufacturers call these allowances "extortion," as described in the Ethics and Social Responsibility Alert.[23]

Legal Considerations

Conflict in marketing channels is typically resolved through negotiation or the exercise of influence by channel members. Sometimes conflict produces legal action. Therefore, knowledge of legal restrictions affecting channel strategies and practices is important. Some restrictions were described in Chapter 14, namely vertical price-fixing and price discrimination. However, other legal considerations unique to marketing channels warrant attention.

In general, suppliers have the right to choose the intermediaries who carry or represent their products. However, suppliers can run into legal difficulty over *refusing to deal* with customers who can meet the usual trade terms offered by the supplier. The Competition Act looks seriously at cases where a supplier withholds or withdraws products from a customer if such behaviour will adversely affect the customer.

CHANNEL CAPTAIN
A marketing channel member that coordinates, directs, and supports other channel members; may be a producer, wholesaler, or retailer.

ETHICS AND SOCIAL RESPONSIBILITY ALERT   The Ethics of Slotting Allowances

Have you ever wondered why your favourite cookies are no longer to be found at your local supermarket? Or why that delicious tortilla chip you like to serve at parties is missing from the shelf and replaced by another brand?

Blame it on slotting allowances. Some large supermarket chains demand slotting allowances from food manufacturers, paid in the form of money or free goods, to stock and display products. These allowances can run up to $25 000 per item for a supermarket chain. Not surprisingly, slotting allowances have been labelled "ransom," "extortional

allowances," and "commercial bribery" by manufacturers, because they already pay supermarkets "trade dollars" to promote and discount their products. Small food manufacturers, in particular, view slotting allowances as an economic barrier to distribution for their products. Supermarket operators see these allowances as a reasonable cost of handling business for manufacturers.

Is the practice of charging slotting allowances unethical behaviour?

Dual distribution is a situation where a manufacturer distributes through its own vertically integrated channel in direct competition with wholesalers and retailers that also sell its products. If the manufacturer's behaviour is viewed as an attempt to unduly lessen competition by eliminating wholesalers or retailers, then such action may violate the Competition Act and would be examined by the Competition Bureau.

Vertical integration is viewed in a similar light. Like dual distribution, it is not illegal, but the practice could be subject to legal action if such integration were designed to eliminate or lessen competition unduly.

Exclusive dealing and tied selling are prohibited under the Competition Act if they are found to unduly lessen competition or create monopolies. *Exclusive dealing* exists when a supplier requires channel members to sell only its products or restricts distributors from selling directly competitive products. *Tied selling* occurs when a supplier requires a distributor purchasing some products to buy others from the supplier. These arrangements often arise in franchising. Tied selling would be investigated by the Competition Bureau if the tied products could be purchased at fair market value from other suppliers at desired standards of the franchisor and if the arrangements were seen as restricting competition. Full-line forcing is a special kind of tied selling. This is a supplier's requiring that a channel member carry its full line of products to sell a specific item in the supplier's line.

Resale or market restrictions refer to a supplier's attempt to stipulate to whom distributors may resell the supplier's products and in what specific geographical areas or territories they may be sold. These practices could be subject to review under the Competition Act if such restrictions were deemed to be restraining or lessening competition.

Concept Check

1. What are the three degrees of distribution density?

2. What are the three questions marketing executives consider when choosing a marketing channel and intermediaries?

3. What is meant by "exclusive dealing"?

SUMMARY

1 A marketing channel consists of individuals and firms involved in the process of making a product or service available for use by consumers or business users.

2 Intermediaries make possible the flow of products and services from producers to buyers by performing transactional, logistical, and facilitating functions. At the same time, intermediaries create time, place, form, and possession utility.

3 Channel structure describes the route taken by products and services from producers to buyers. Direct channels represent the shortest route because producers interact directly with buyers. Indirect channels include intermediaries between producers and buyers.

4 In general, marketing channels for consumer products and services contain more intermediaries than do channels for business products and services. In some situations, producers use Internet, direct marketing, multiple channels, and strategic channel alliances to reach buyers.

5 Numerous types of wholesalers can exist within a marketing channel. The principal distinction between the various types of wholesalers lies in whether they take title to the items they sell and the channel functions they perform.

6 Vertical marketing systems are channels designed to achieve channel function economies and marketing impact. A vertical marketing system may be one of three types: corporate, administered, or contractual.

7 Marketing managers consider environmental, consumer, product, and company factors when choosing and managing marketing channels.

8 Channel design considerations are based on the target market coverage sought by producers, the buyer requirements to be satisfied, and the profitability of the channel. Target market coverage comes about through one of three levels of distribution density: intensive, exclusive, and selective distribution. Buyer requirements are evident in the amount of information, convenience, variety, and service sought by consumers. Profitability relates to the margins obtained by each channel member and the channel as a whole.

9 Marketing channels in the global marketplace reflect traditions, customs, geography, and the economic history of individual countries and societies. These factors influence channel structure and relationships among channel members.

10 Conflicts in marketing channels are inevitable. Vertical conflict occurs between different levels in a channel. Horizontal conflict occurs between intermediaries at the same level in the channel.

11 Legal issues in the management of marketing channels typically arise from six practices: refusal to deal, dual distribution, vertical integration, exclusive dealing, tied selling, and resale or market restrictions.

KEY TERMS AND CONCEPTS

brokers p. 406
channel captain p. 414
channel conflict p. 413
channel partnership p. 409
direct channel p. 401
direct marketing channels p. 403
disintermediation p. 413
dual distribution p. 404
electronic marketing channels p. 402
exclusive distribution p. 410
franchising p. 408

indirect channel p. 401
industrial distributor p. 402
intensive distribution p. 410
manufacturer's agents p. 406
marketing channel p. 398
merchant wholesalers p. 405
selective distribution p. 411
selling agents p. 406
strategic channel alliances p. 404
vertical marketing systems p. 407

INTERNET EXERCISE

www.mcgrawhill.ca/college/berkowitz

Franchising is a large and growing industry. For many individuals, franchising offers an opportunity to operate one's own business.

The Internet provides a number of Websites that feature franchising opportunities. The International Franchise Association (www.franchise.org) features an extensive array of information, including answers to questions about franchising. The Canadian Franchise

Association (www.cfa.ca) shows franchise opportunities for the aspiring franchisee.

1 Visit www.cfa.ca. What are some of the more interesting franchise opportunities available to Canadians?

2 Visit the International Franchise Association Website, and go to Frequently Asked Questions about Franchising. What are the current trends in franchising?

Want to get better grades, find tips on how to study more effectively, and stay up to date with happenings in the world of marketing? Visit the Online Learning Centre for practice tests, Study Smart software, and much more! www.mcgrawhill.ca/college/berkowitz
Interested in finding out what marketing looks like in the real world? *Marketing Magazine* is just a click away on your OLC! Visit www.mcgrawhill.ca/college/berkowitz

APPLYING MARKETING CONCEPTS AND PERSPECTIVES

1 A distributor for Celanese Chemical Company stores large quantities of chemicals, blends these chemicals to satisfy requests of customers, and delivers the blends to a customer's warehouse within 24 hours of receiving an order. What utilities does this distributor provide?

2 Suppose the president of a carpet manufacturing firm has asked you to look into the possibility of bypassing the firm's wholesalers (who sell to carpet, department, and furniture stores) and selling direct to these stores. What caution would you voice on this matter, and what type of information would you gather before making this decision?

3 What type of channel conflict is likely to be caused by dual distribution, and what type of conflict can be reduced by direct distribution? Why?

4 How does the channel captain idea differ among corporate, administered, and contractual vertical marketing systems with particular reference to the use of the different forms of influence available to firms?

5 Comment on this statement: "The only distinction among merchant wholesalers and agents and brokers is that merchant wholesalers take title to the products they sell."

6 How do specialty, shopping, and convenience goods generally relate to intensive, selective, and exclusive distribution? Give a brand name that is an example of each goods–distribution matchup.

VIDEO CASE 15–1 Creston Vineyards

Larry Rosenbloom's customers include individuals, retail stores, restaurants, and hotels. Because of the many types and large numbers of customers, distribution is as important as production at Creston Vineyards. As Larry explains, "We need distributors in our business . . . as most other [businesses] do, to get the product to the end user, to the consumer."

THE COMPANY

In 1980, Stephanie and Larry Rosenbloom purchased an abandoned ranch and started Creston Vineyards. Because it takes several years for vines to grow and produce grapes, Creston did not sell its first wine until 1982. Today, the 220-hectare ranch has 70 hectares of planted vineyards and produces over 55 000 cases of eight varieties of wines. The production facilities include a 1650-square-metre winery and 15 square metres of laboratory and office space.

Since 1982 Creston wines have won over 500 awards in wine-tasting events and competitions.

THE INDUSTRY AND DISTRIBUTION CHANNELS

The wine industry is undergoing several very interesting changes. First, sales have increased in recent years after a general decline since 1984. The decline was attributed to changing consumer demographics, shifting buying habits, and concerns about the economy. At least some of the recent interest in wine is related to the press reports suggesting the possible health benefits of red wine. A second change is the significant increase in the price of wine due to a low supply of good international wines and changing exchange rates, and an infestation of vine-eating insects (phylloxera). Finally, many wine producers are trying to change the image of wine from a beverage only for special occasions and gourmet foods to a beverage for any occasion.

The industry also faces several distribution challenges. The large number of wine producers and the variety of consumers requires a sophisticated system of distribution channels. By combining different types of intermediaries, the industry is able to meet the requirements of many customers. In addition, because the sale of wine is regulated, the use of multiple distribution channels facilitates the sale of wine in many locations.

One of the most common channels of distribution involves a distributor buying wine directly from the vineyard and reselling it to retail stores and restaurants within a geographic area. Some distributors, however, may not need quantities large enough to warrant purchasing directly from the vineyard. They usually purchase several brands at the same time from a warehouse. A broker may facilitate sales by providing information to distributors, training the distributor's salesforce, and even assisting in sales calls to retailers. John Drady, 1 of 12 brokers for Creston Vineyards, explains: "It's very important that we translate our knowledge and our selling skills to the distributor's salespeople so they can, in turn, go out and [sell] more readily on their own."

Other channels are also used by Creston. For example, in some markets Creston can sell directly to some large retailers. Another channel of distribution is through wine clubs that provide club members with information about wines and an average of six wines per year. The popularity of wine clubs has been increasing and they now account for 15 percent of Creston's sales. The newest type of distribution channel is through online services. Creston now has a site on the World Wide Web (www.wines.com) that provides information about its wines and allows orders to be shipped directly to consumers. Customers will also find greetings from Alex Trebek, the Canadian-born game-show host, who is the owner of Creston Vineyards.

THE ISSUES

In an industry with thousands of products and hundreds of producers, Creston is relatively new and small. Selecting and managing its distribution channels to best meet the needs of many constituents is a key task.

Providing marketing assistance, product information, and appropriate assortment, transportation, storage, and credit are just a few of the functions the warehouse, brokers, distributors, and retailers may provide as the product moves from the vineyard to the end user.

Creston also faces a situation where new, and possibly more efficient, channels are becoming available. Direct sales, wine clubs, and online services have generated substantial sales for Creston. Other channels, or new variations of existing channels, may also be available in the future. Overall, Creston must continue to utilize distribution channels to provide value to customers ranging from large retailers to hotels and restaurants to individuals.

Questions

1 What functions must be performed by intermediaries in the wine industry?
2 What intermediaries and distribution channels are currently used by Creston Vineyards?
3 How do different channels of distribution reach different segments? Are there any segments Creston does not reach with its current channels?

Supply Chain:
Managing Logistics
For the 21st Century

CHAPTER

16

INTEGRATING SUPPLY CHAIN AND LOGISTICS MANAGEMENT

AFTER READING THIS CHAPTER YOU SHOULD BE ABLE TO:

- Explain what supply chain and logistics management are and how they relate to marketing strategy.

- Understand the distinction between supply chain responsiveness and efficiency.

- Explain how managers trade off different "logistics costs" relative to customer service in order to make a supply chain decision.

- Recognize how customer service in logistics decisions contributes to customer value and successful marketing programs.

- Describe the key logistics functions of transportation, warehousing and materials handling, order processing, and inventory management and the role of third-party logistics providers.

SNAP! CRACK! POP! EVEN WORLD-CLASS COMPANIES CAN FEEL THE BULLWHIP'S STING

Bad things can happen to great companies. Just ask Boeing, Hewlett-Packard, Bristol-Myers Squibb, Nike, and Procter & Gamble. Each of these industry leaders has experienced the bullwhip's sting at one time or another for one or more of their products.

What is the bullwhip, and why does its sting hurt so much? Companies define the bullwhip as too much or too little inventory to satisfy customer needs, missed production schedules, and ineffective transportation or delivery caused by miscommunication among material suppliers, manufacturers, and resellers of consumer and industrial goods. Its sting is poor customer service and lost revenue and profit opportunities.

Suppliers, manufacturers, and resellers know that to get a handle on the bullwhip, attention needs to focus on the technology and coordinated activities that make possible the physical flow and transformation of goods from the raw materials stage to the final consumer or industrial user. They also recognize that accurate, timely, and shared information can soften the bullwhip's sting, thereby benefiting customers and companies alike.[1]

Welcome to the world of supply chain and logistics management. The essence of the problem is simple: It makes no sense to have brilliant marketing programs to sell world-class products if the products aren't available at the right time, at the right place, and in the right form and condition that customers want them. It's finding the continuing solutions through time that's always the problem. This chapter describes the role of supply chains and logistics management in marketing and how a firm balances distribution costs against the need for effective customer service.

SIGNIFICANCE OF SUPPLY CHAIN AND LOGISTICS MANAGEMENT

We often use the term *physical distribution* but rarely consider its significance in marketing. Canadian companies spend billions of dollars transporting raw materials and finished goods each year, billions of dollars more on material handling, warehousing, storage, and holding inventory, and billions more on managing the distribution process, including the cost of information technology. Worldwide, these activities cost companies hundreds of billions of dollars annually.[2] In this section, we highlight contemporary perspectives on physical distribution, including supply chains and logistics, and describe the linkage between supply chain management and marketing strategy.

Relating Marketing Channels, Logistics, and Supply Chain Management

A marketing channel relies on logistics to actually make products available to consumers and business users—a point emphasized in the previous chapter. **Logistics** involves those activities that focus on getting the right amount of the right products to the right place at the right time at the lowest possible cost. The performance of these activities is **logistics management**, the practice of organizing the *cost-effective flow* of raw materials, in-process inventory, finished goods, and related information from point of origin to point of consumption to satisfy *customer requirements*.[3]

Three elements of this definition deserve emphasis. First, logistics deals with decisions needed to move a product from the source of raw materials to consumption, or the *flow* of the product. Second, those decisions have to be made in a *cost-effective* manner. While it is important to drive down logistics costs, there is a limit— the third point of emphasis. A firm needs to drive down logistics costs as long as it can deliver expected *customer service*, which means satisfying customer requirements. The role of management is to see that customer needs are satisfied in the most cost-effective manner. When properly done, the results can be spectacular. Procter & Gamble is a case in point. Beginning in the early 1990s, the company set out to meet the needs of consumers more effectively by collaborating and partnering with its suppliers and retailers to ensure that the right products reached store shelves at the right time and at a lower cost. The effort was judged a success when, during an 18-month period in the late 1990s, P&G's retail customers recorded a $65-million savings in logistics costs while customer service increased.[4]

The Procter & Gamble experience is not an isolated incident. Today, logistics management is embedded in a broader view of physical distribution, consistent with the emphasis on supply and channel partnering described in Chapters 6 and 15. Companies now recognize that getting the right items needed for consumption or production to the right place at the right time in the right condition at the right cost is often beyond their individual capabilities and control. Instead, collaboration, coordination, and information sharing among manufacturers, suppliers, and distributors are necessary to create a seamless flow of goods and services to customers. This perspective is represented in the concept of a supply chain and the practise of supply chain management.

A **supply chain** is a sequence of firms that perform activities required to create and deliver a good or service to consumers or industrial users.[5] It differs from a marketing channel in terms of membership. A supply chain includes suppliers who provide raw material inputs to a manufacturer as well as the wholesalers and retailers who deliver finished goods to you. The management process is also different. **Supply chain management** is the integration and organization of information and logistics activities *across firms* in a supply chain for the purpose of creating and delivering goods and services that provide value to consumers. The relationship among marketing channels, logistics management, and supply chain management is

Margin definitions

LOGISTICS
Those activities that focus on getting the right amount of the right products to the right place at the right time at the lowest possible cost.

LOGISTICS MANAGEMENT
The practice of organizing the cost-effective flow of raw materials, in-process inventory, finished goods, and related information from point of origin to point of consumption to satisfy customer requirements.

SUPPLY CHAIN
A sequence of firms that perform activities required to create and deliver a good or service to consumers or industrial users.

SUPPLY CHAIN MANAGEMENT
The integration and organization of information and logistics activities across firms in a supply chain for the purpose of creating and delivering goods and services that provide value to customers.

FIGURE 16–1
Relating marketing channels,
logistics management, and
supply chain management

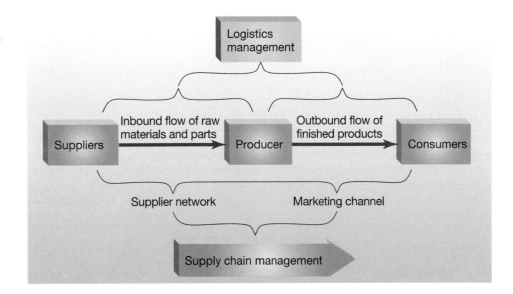

shown in Figure 16–1. An important feature of supply chain management is its application of sophisticated information technology, which allows companies to share and operate systems for order processing, transportation scheduling, and inventory and facility management.

Sourcing, Assembling, and Delivering a New Car: The Automotive Supply Chain

All companies are members of one or more supply chains. A supply chain is essentially a sequence of linked suppliers and customers in which every customer is, in turn, a supplier to another customer until a finished product reaches the final consumer. Even the simplified supply chain diagram for car makers shown in Figure 16–2 illustrates how complex a supply chain can be.[6] A car maker's supplier network includes thousands of firms that provide the 5000 or so parts in a typical automobile. They provide items ranging from raw materials such as steel and rubber to components, including transmissions, tires, brakes, and seats, to complex subassemblies and assemblies evident in chassis and suspension systems that make for a smooth, stable ride. Coordinating and scheduling material and component flows for their assembly into actual automobiles by car makers is heavily dependent on logistical activities, including transportation, order processing, inventory control, materials handling, and information technology. A central link is the car maker supply chain manager, who is responsible for translating customer requirements into actual orders and arranging for delivery dates and financial arrangements for automobile dealers. This is not an easy task given different consumer preferences and the amount consumers are willing to pay. To appreciate the challenge facing supply chain

FIGURE 16–2
The automotive supply chain

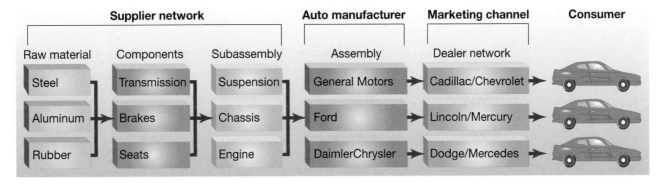

managers, visit the Saturn Website described in the accompanying Web Link, and assemble your own car based on your preferences and price point.

Logistical aspects of the automobile marketing channel are also an integral part of the supply chain. Major responsibilities include transportation, which involves the selection and oversight of external carriers (trucking, airline, railroad, and shipping companies) for cars and parts to dealers, the operation of distribution centres, the management of finished goods inventories, and order processing for sales. Supply chain managers also play an important role in the marketing channel. They work with extensive car dealer networks to ensure that the right mix of automobiles are delivered to different locations. In addition, they make sure that spare and service parts are available so that dealers can meet the car maintenance and repair needs of consumers. All of this is done with the help of information technology that links the entire automotive supply chain. What does all of this cost? It is estimated that logistics costs represent 25 to 30 percent of the retail price of a typical new car.

Supply Chain Management and Marketing Strategy

The automotive supply chain illustration shows how information and logistics activities are integrated and organized across firms to create and deliver a car for you. What's missing from this illustration is the linkage between a specific company's supply chain and its marketing strategy. Just as companies have different marketing strategies, they also manage supply chains differently. More specifically, the goals to be achieved by a firm's marketing strategy determine whether its supply chain needs to be more responsive or efficient in meeting customer requirements.

Aligning a Supply Chain with Marketing Strategy There are a variety of supply chain configurations, each which is designated to perform a different task well. Marketers today recognize that the choice of a supply chain follows from a clearly defined marketing strategy and involves three steps[7]:

1. *Understand the customer.* To understand the customer, a company must identify the needs of the customer segment being served. These needs, such as a desire for a low price or convenience of purchase, help a company define the relative importance of efficiency and responsiveness in meeting customer requirements.

2. *Understand the supply chain.* Second, a company must understand what a supply chain is designed to do well. Supply chains range from those that emphasize being responsive to customer requirements and demand to those that emphasize efficiency with a goal of supplying products at the lowest possible delivered cost.

3. *Harmonize the supply chain with the marketing strategy.* Finally, a company needs to ensure that what the supply chain is capable of doing well is consistent with the targeted customer's needs and its marketing strategy. If a mismatch exists between what the supply chain does particularly well and a company's marketing strategy, the company will either need to redesign the supply chain to support the marketing strategy or change the marketing strategy. The bottom line is that a poorly designed supply chain can do serious damage to an otherwise brilliant marketing strategy. Read the accompanying Marketing NewsNet to learn how Nike's supply chain hampered the marketing of its popular Air Force Ones basketball shoe.[8]

How are these steps applied and how are efficiency and responsive considerations built into a supply chain? Let's briefly look at how two market leaders—Dell Computer Corporation and Wal-Mart, Inc.—have harmonized their supply chain and marketing strategy.

Dell Computer Corporation: A Responsive Supply Chain   The Dell marketing strategy targets customers who wish to have the most up-to-date personal computer equipment customized to their needs. These customers are also willing to (1) wait to have their customized personal computer delivered in a few days, rather than picking out a model at a retail store, and (2) pay a reasonable, though not the lowest, price in the marketplace. Given Dell's customer segment, the company has the option of adopting an efficient or responsive supply chain. An efficient supply chain may use inexpensive but slower modes of transportation, emphasize economics of scale in its production process by reducing the variety of PC configurations offered, and limit its assembly and inventory storage facilities to a single location. If Dell opted only for efficiency in its supply chain, it would be difficult if not impossible to satisfy its target customer's desire for rapid delivery and a wide variety of customizable products. Dell instead has opted for a responsive supply chain. It relies on more expensive express transportation for receipt of components from suppliers and delivery of finished products to customers. The company achieves product variety and manufacturing

---

MARKETING NEWSNET

Nike: The Swoosh Supply Chain Stumbles

Ever innovative, Nike, the world's leading athletic shoe maker, recently invested $400 million to streamline the way it produces, ships, and delivers shoes to retailers. The investment was intended to help Nike better match store supply with consumer demand, and avoid having warehouses full of shoes that had gone out of style, while boosting sales of trendier models. The multi-million dollar investment, principally in supply chain management information technology, was intended to build more responsiveness into Nike's supply chain. The goal was to advance the company's well-earned reputation for delivering the right athletic shoes at the right time, price, and quantity to satisfy the fashion and functional needs of its customers.

The result? It didn't happen. So what went wrong? Using the new information technology, Nike mistakenly sent double orders to its factories, resulting in an oversupply of many slow-selling shoes, a Nike spokeswoman said. Meanwhile, production of its hot-selling items, like the Air Force Ones basketball shoe, did not keep pace with demand. To offset shipping delays for its popular shoes, Nike had to transport them by plane at $4 to $8 a pair, compared with about 75 cents a pair by boat, according to an industry analyst. Company profitability suffered because of this supply-chain stumble, and Nike's stock price dropped.

World-class marketers Dell Computer and Wal-Mart emphasize responsiveness and efficiency in their supply chains.

efficiency by designing common platforms across several products and using common components. Dell operates manufacturing facilities in various countries to ensure rapid delivery. Moreover, Dell has invested heavily in information technology to link itself with suppliers and customers.

Wal-Mart, Inc.: An Efficient Supply Chain   Now let's consider Wal-Mart. Wal-Mart's marketing strategy is to be a reliable, lower-price retailer for a wide variety of mass-consumption consumer goods. This strategy favours an efficient supply chain designed to deliver products to consumers at the lowest possible cost. Efficiency is achieved in a variety of ways. For instance, Wal-Mart keeps relatively low inventory levels, and most inventory is stocked in stores available for sale, not in warehouses gathering dust. The low inventory arises from Wal-Mart's innovative use of **crossdocking**—a practice that involves unloading products from suppliers, sorting products for individual stores, and quickly reloading products onto trucks for a particular store. No warehousing or storing of products occurs, except for a few hours or at most a day. Crossdocking allows Wal-Mart to operate only a small number of distribution centres to service its vast network of Wal-Mart stores, Supercentres, and Sam's Clubs, which contributes to efficiency. On the other hand, the company runs its own fleet of trucks to service its stores. This does increase cost and investment, but the benefits in terms of responsiveness justify the cost in Wal-Mart's case. Wal-Mart has invested significantly more than its competitors in information technology to operate its supply chain. The company feeds information about customer requirements and demand from its stores back to its suppliers, which manufacture only what is being demanded. This large investment has improved the efficiency of Wal-Mart's supply chain and made it responsive to customer needs.

Three lessons can be learned from these two examples. First, there is no one best supply chain for every company. Second, the best supply chain is the one that is consistent with the needs of the customer segment being served and complements a company's marketing strategy. And finally, supply chain managers are often called upon to make trade-offs between efficiency and responsiveness on various elements of a company's supply chain.

CROSSDOCKING
The practice of unloading products from suppliers, sorting products for individual stores, and quickly reloading products onto trucks for a particular store.

Concept Check

1. What is the principal difference between a marketing channel and a supply chain?

2. The choice of a supply chain involves what three steps?

INFORMATION AND LOGISTICS MANAGEMENT OBJECTIVE IN A SUPPLY CHAIN

The objective of information and logistics management in a supply chain is to minimize logistics costs while delivering maximum customer service. The Dell

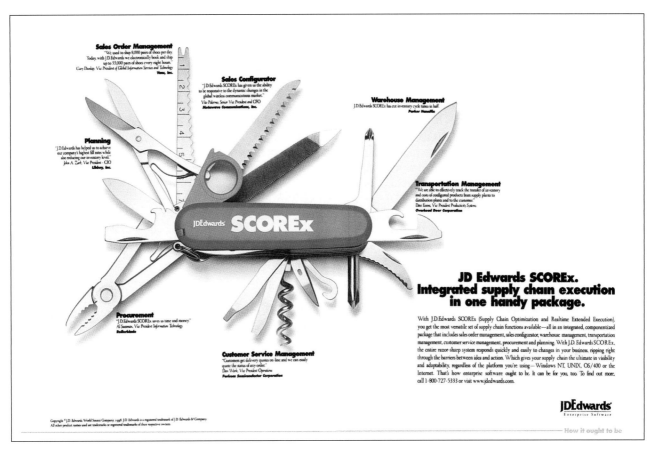

JD Edwards & Company is an internationally recognized supply chain management consulting firm.

JD Edwards & Company

www.jdedwards.com

Computer and Wal-Mart examples highlight how two market leaders have realized this objective by different means. An important similarity between these two companies is that both use information to leverage logistics activities, reduce logistics costs, and improve customer service.

Information's Role in Supply Chain Responsiveness and Efficiency

Information consists of data and analysis regarding inventory, transportation, distribution facilities, and customers throughout the supply chain.[9] Continuing advances in information technology make it possible to track logistics activities and customer service variables and manage them for efficiency and responsiveness. For example, information on customer demand patterns allows pharmaceutical companies such as Eli Lilly and Smithkline Beecham to produce and stock drugs in anticipation of customer needs. This improves supply chain responsiveness because customers will find the drugs when and where they want them. Demand information improves supply chain efficiency because pharmaceutical firms are better able to forecast customer needs and produce, transport, and store the required amount of inventory.

A variety of technologies are used to transmit and manage information in a supply chain. **Electronic data interchanges (EDI)** combine proprietary computer and telecommunication technologies to exchange electronic invoices, payments, and information between suppliers, manufacturers, and retailers. When linked with store scanning equipment and systems, EDI provides a seamless electronic link from a retail checkout counter to suppliers and manufacturers. Wal-Mart and Procter & Gamble actually pioneered the use of EDI. EDI is commonly used in the retail, apparel, transportation, pharmaceutical, grocery, health care, and insurance industries, as well as by local, provincial, and federal government agencies. About

ELECTRONIC DATA INTERCHANGE (EDI) Combines proprietary computer and telecommunication technologies to exchange electronic invoices, payments, and information among suppliers, manufacturers, and retailers.

95 percent of the companies listed in the *Fortune 1000* use EDI, as do most of the Canadian companies listed in the *Financial Post 500*. At Hewlett-Packard, for example, one million EDI transactions are made every month.

EXTRANET
An Internet/Web-based network that permits secure business-to-business communication between a manufacturer and its suppliers, distributors, and sometimes other partners.

Another technology is the **Extranet**, which is an Internet/Web-based network that permits secure business-to-business communication between a manufacturer and its suppliers, distributors, and sometimes other partners (such as advertising agencies). Extranets are less expensive and more flexible to operate than EDI because of their connection to the public Internet. This technology is prominent in private electronic exchanges described in Chapter 6. For example, WhirlpoolWebWorld.com allows Whirlpool to fulfill retailer orders quickly and inexpensively and better match appliance demand and supply.

Whereas EDI and Extranets transmit information, other technologies help manage information in a supply chain. Enterprise resource planning (ERP) technology and supply chain management software track logistics cost and customer service variables, both of which are described next.

Total Logistics Cost Concept

TOTAL LOGISTICS COST
Expenses associated with transportation, materials handling and warehousing, inventory, stockouts, order processing, and return goods handling.

For our purposes **total logistics cost** includes expenses associated with transportation, materials handling and warehousing, inventory, stockouts (being out of inventory), order processing, and return goods handling.[10] Note that many of these costs are interrelated, so changes in one will impact the others. For example, as the firm attempts to minimize its transportation costs by shipping in larger quantities, it will also experience an increase in inventory levels. Larger inventory levels will not only increase inventory costs but should also reduce stockouts. It is important, therefore, to study the impact on all of the logistics decision areas when considering a change.

Figure 16–3 provides a graphic example. An oft-used supply chain strategy is for a firm to have a number of warehouses, which receive shipments in large quantities and then redistribute smaller shipments to local customers. As the number of warehouses increases, inventory costs rise and transportation costs fall. That is, more inventory is warehoused, but it is transported in volume closer to customers. The net effect is to minimize the total costs of logistics shown in Figure 16–3 by having 10 warehouses. This means the total cost curve is minimized at a point where neither of the two individual cost elements is at a minimum but the overall system is.

Studying its total logistics cost has had revolutionary consequences for National Semiconductor, which produces computer chips. In two years it cut its standard delivery time 47 percent, reduced distribution costs 2.5 percent, and increased sales 34 percent by shutting down six warehouses around the world and air-freighting its microchips from its huge distribution centre in Singapore. It does this even though it has six factories worldwide. National also discovered that a lot of its chips were actually profit-losers, and it cut the number of products it sells by 45 percent, thereby simplifying logistics and increasing profits.[11]

FIGURE 16–3
How total logistics cost varies with number of warehouses used

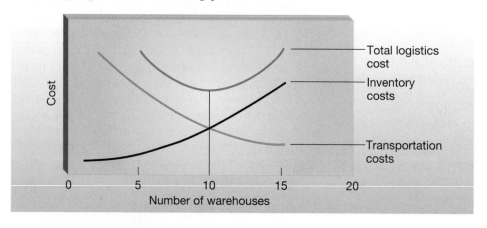

FIGURE 16–4
Supply chain managers balance total logistics cost factors against customer service factors

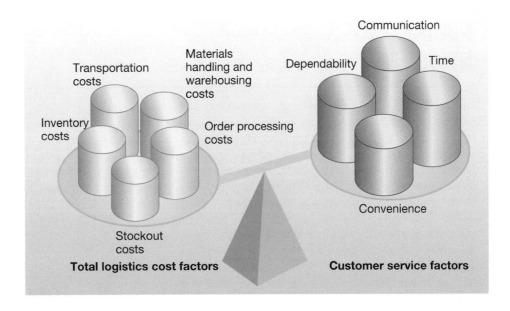

Customer Service Concept

If a supply chain is a *flow*, the end of it—or *output*—is the service delivered to customers. However, service can be expensive. One firm found that to increase on-time delivery from a 95-percent rate to a 100-percent rate tripled total logistics costs. Higher levels of service require tactics such as more inventory to reduce stockouts, more expensive transportation to improve speed and lessen damage, and double or triple checking of orders to ensure correctness. A firm's goal should be to provide adequate customer service while controlling logistics costs. Customer service is now seen not merely as an expense but as a means to increase customer satisfaction and sales. For example, a 3M survey about customer service among 18 000 European customers in 16 countries revealed surprising agreement in all countries about the importance of customer service. Respondents stressed factors such as condition of product delivered, on-time delivery, quick delivery after order placement, and effective handling of problems.[12]

Within the context of a supply chain, **customer service** is the ability of logistics management to satisfy users in terms of time, dependability, communication, and convenience. As suggested by Figure 16–4, a supply chain manager's key task is to balance these four customer service factors against total logistics cost factors.

Time   In a supply chain setting, time refers to **lead time** for an item, which means the lag from ordering an item until it is received and ready for use or sale. This is also referred to as *order cycle time* or *replenishment time* and may be more important to retailers or wholesalers than consumers. The various elements that make up the typical order cycle include recognition of the need to order, order transmittal, order processing, documentation, and transportation. A current emphasis in supply chain management is to reduce lead time so that the inventory levels of customers may be minimized. Another emphasis is to make the process of reordering and receiving products as simple as possible, often through electronic data and inventory systems called **quick response** and **efficient consumer response** delivery systems.[13] These inventory management systems are designed to reduce the retailer's lead time for receiving merchandise, thereby lowering a retailer's inventory investment, improving customer service levels, and reducing logistics expense (see the accompanying Marketing NewsNet).[14] The order processing portion of lead time will be discussed later in this chapter.

CUSTOMER SERVICE
The ability of logistics management to satisfy users in terms of time, dependability, communication, and convenience.

LEAD TIME
Lag from ordering an item until it is received and ready for use or sale. Also called *order cycle time* or *replenishment time.*

QUICK RESPONSE/EFFICIENT CONSUMER RESPONSE
An inventory management system designed to reduce the retailer's lead time, thereby lowering its inventory investment, improving customer service levels, and reducing logistics expense.

MARKETING NEWSNET

For Fashion and Food Merchandising, Haste Is as Important as Taste

Fashion and food have a lot in common. Both depend a lot on taste and both require timely merchandising. By its nature, fashion dictates that suppliers and retailers be able to adjust to new styles, colours, and different seasons. Fashion retailers need to identify what's hot so it can be ordered quickly and what's not to avoid markdowns. Many fashion retailers have employed a *quick response* delivery system for fashion merchandise since the mid 1990s. They use point-of-sale scanner systems to record each day's sales. When stock falls below a minimum level, the system automatically generates a replenishment order. Vendors of fashion merchandise, such as Donna Karan (DKNY), receive an electronic order, which is processed within 48 hours.

Food marketers and retailers use the term *efficient consumer response* to describe their replenishment systems. All major food companies, including General Mills, Del Monte,

Heinz, Nestlé, and Kraft, and many supermarket chains such as Loblaws, Safeway, and A&P, rely on electronic replenishment systems to minimize stockouts of popular items and overstocks of slow-moving items. Lowered retailer inventories and efficient logistics practices save Canadian grocery shoppers money on the food they purchase.

Dependability   Dependability is the consistency of replenishment. This is important to all firms in a supply chain and to consumers. It can be broken into three elements: consistent lead time, safe delivery, and complete delivery. Consistent service allows planning (such as appropriate inventory levels), whereas inconsistencies create surprises. Intermediaries may be willing to accept longer lead times if they know about them in advance and can thus make plans. While surprise delays may shut down a production line, early deliveries will be almost as troublesome because of the problems of storing the extra inventory. Dependability is essential for the just-in-time inventory strategies discussed at the end of the chapter.

Communication   Communication is a two-way link between buyer and seller that helps in monitoring service and anticipating future needs. Status reports on orders are a typical example of improved communication between buyer and seller. The increased communication capability of transportation carriers has enhanced the accuracy of such tracing information and improved the ability of buyers to schedule shipments. Note, however, that such information is still reactive and is not a substitute for consistent on-time deliveries. Therefore, some firms have partnered with firms specializing in logistics in an effort to institutionalize a more proactive flow of useful information that, in turn, improves on-time deliveries. Hewlett-Packard (HP), a high-tech computer printer manufacturer, recently turned its inbound raw materials over to a logistics firm. HP lets this firm manage the warehousing and coordinate parts delivery so that HP can focus on its printer business. In the process, HP estimates it has cut its warehouse operating costs by about 10 percent.[15]

Convenience   The concept of convenience for a supply chain manager means that there should be a minimum of effort on the part of the buyer in doing business with the seller. Is it easy for the customer to order? Are the products available from many outlets? Does the buyer have to buy huge quantities of the product? Will the seller arrange all necessary details, such as transportation? The seller must concentrate on removing unnecessary barriers to customer convenience. This customer service factor has promoted the use of vendor-managed inventory practices discussed later in the chapter.

Customer Service Standards

Firms that operate effective supply chains usually develop a set of written customer service standards. These serve as objectives and provide a benchmark against which results can be measured for control purposes. In developing these standards, information is collected on customers' needs. It is also necessary to know what competitors offer as well as the willingness of customers to pay a bit more for better service. After these and similar questions are answered, realistic standards are set and an ongoing monitoring program is established. The examples below suggest that customer service standards will differ by type of firm.

TYPE OF FIRM	CUSTOMER SERVICE STANDARD
Wholesaler	At least 98% of orders filled accurately
Manufacturer	Order cycle time of no more than 5 days
Retailer	Returns accepted within 30 days
Airline	At least 90% of arrivals on time
Trucking	A maximum of 5% loss and damage per year
Restaurant	Lunch served within 5 minutes of order

Concept Check

1. The objective of information and logistics management in a supply chain is to _____.

2. How does consumer demand information increase supply chain responsiveness and efficiency?

3. What is the relationship between the number of warehouses a company operates, its inventory costs, and its transportation costs?

KEY LOGISTICS FUNCTIONS IN A SUPPLY CHAIN

THIRD-PARTY LOGISTICS PROVIDERS
Firms that perform most or all of the logistics functions that manufacturers, suppliers, and distributors would normally perform themselves.

The four key logistic functions in a supply chain include (1) transportation, (2) warehousing and materials handling, (3) order processing, and (4) inventory management. These functions have become so complex and interrelated that many companies have outsourced them to third-party logistics providers. **Third-party logistics providers** are firms that perform most or all of the logistics functions that manufacturers, suppliers, and distributors would normally perform themselves.[16] Today, many of Canada's top manufacturers outsource one or more logistics functions, at least on a limited basis. UPS Logistics, FedEx, Roadway Logistics, Emery Worldwide, Global Logistics, and Penske are just a few of the companies that specialize in handling logistics functions for their clients. For example, UPS Logistics manages Compaq Computer Corporation's transportation carriers, service parts inventory, field stocking, central warehousing and distribution, returned goods handling, and order fulfillment. UPS Logistics also provides similar services for other computer manufacturers, including Dell Computer Corporation.[17] The four major logistics functions and the involvement of third-party logistics providers are described in detail next.

Transportation

Transportation provides the movement of goods necessary in a supply chain. There are five basic modes of transportation: railroads, motor carriers, air carriers, pipelines, and water carriers, and modal combinations involving two or more modes, such as highway trailers on a rail flatcar.

FedEx and Emery Worldwide are two third-party logistics providers that perform most or all of the logistics functions that manufacturers, suppliers, and distributors would normally perform.

FedEx

All transportation modes can be evaluated on six basic service criteria:

- *Cost.* Charges for transportation.
- *Time.* Speed of transit.
- *Capability.* What can be realistically carried with this mode.
- *Dependability.* Reliability of service regarding time, loss, and damage.
- *Accessibility.* Convenience of the mode's routes (such as pipeline availability).
- *Frequency.* Scheduling.

Figure 16–5 summarizes service advantages and disadvantages of five of the modes of transportation available.[18]

Railroads   Railroads carry heavy, bulky items over long distances. Of the commodities tracked by the rail industry, coal, farm products, chemicals, and nonmetallic minerals represent the bulk of the total tonnage. Railroads can carry larger shipments than trucks (in terms of total weight per vehicle), but their routes are less extensive. Service innovations include unit trains and intermodal service. A *unit train* is dedicated to one commodity (often coal), using permanently coupled cars that run a continuous loop from a single origin to a single destination and back. Even though the train returns empty, the process captures enough operating efficiencies to make it one of the lowest-cost transportation alternatives available. Unit trains keep to a specific schedule so that the customers can plan on reliable delivery and usually carry products that can be loaded and unloaded quickly and automatically.

INTERMODAL TRANSPORTATION
Combining different transportation modes to get the best features of each.

Railroads also apply the unit train concept to **intermodal transportation**, which involves combining different transportation modes to get the best features of each. The result is a service that attracts high-valued freight, which would normally go by truck. The most popular combination is truck–rail, called *piggyback* or *trailer on flatcar (TOFC)*. The other popular use of an intermodal combination is associated with export/import traffic and uses containers in place of trailers. These containers can be loaded on ships, trains, and truck trailers, so in terms of the on-land segment

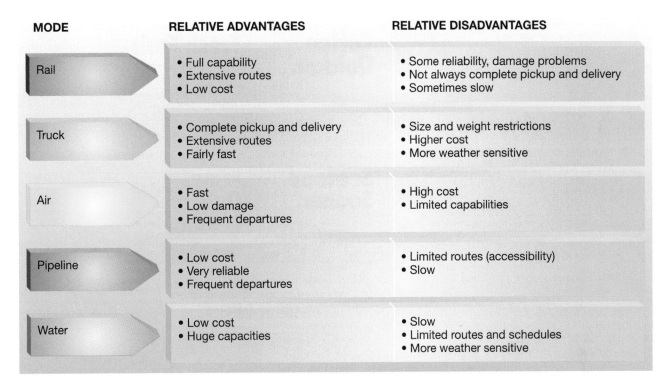

MODE	RELATIVE ADVANTAGES	RELATIVE DISADVANTAGES
Rail	• Full capability • Extensive routes • Low cost	• Some reliability, damage problems • Not always complete pickup and delivery • Sometimes slow
Truck	• Complete pickup and delivery • Extensive routes • Fairly fast	• Size and weight restrictions • Higher cost • More weather sensitive
Air	• Fast • Low damage • Frequent departures	• High cost • Limited capabilities
Pipeline	• Low cost • Very reliable • Frequent departures	• Limited routes (accessibility) • Slow
Water	• Low cost • Huge capacities	• Slow • Limited routes and schedules • More weather sensitive

FIGURE 16–5
Advantages and
disadvantages of five
modes of transportation

of international shipments, a container is handled the same way as a trailer. Containers are used in world trade because they use less space on ocean-going vessels.

Motor Carriers   In contrast to the railroad industry, the for-hire motor carrier industry is composed of many small firms, including many independent truckers and firms that own their own trucks for transporting their own products.

The greatest advantage of motor carriers is the complete door-to-door service. Trucks can go almost anywhere there is a road, and with the design of specialized equipment they can carry most commodities. Their physical limitations are size and weight restrictions enforced by provincial governments. Trucks have the reputation for maintaining a better record than rail for loss and damage and providing faster, more reliable service, especially for shorter distances. As a result, trucks carry higher-valued goods that are time-sensitive and expensive to carry in inventory. The trade-off is that truck rates are substantially higher than rail rates.

Air Carriers and Express Companies   Air freight is costly, but its speed may create savings in lower inventory. The items that can be carried are limited by space constraints and are usually valuable, time-sensitive, and lightweight, such as perishable flowers, clothing, and electronic parts. Specialized firms provide ground support in terms of collecting shipments and delivering them to the air terminal. When air freight is handled by major airlines—such as Air Canada—it is often carried as cargo using the excess luggage space of scheduled passenger flights.

FREIGHT FORWARDERS
Firms that accumulate small
shipments into larger lots and
then hire a carrier to move
them, usually at reduced
rates.

Freight Forwarders   **Freight forwarders**, already mentioned a number of times, are firms that accumulate small shipments into larger lots and then hire a carrier to move them, usually at reduced rates. Recall that transportation companies provide rate incentives for larger quantities. Forwarders collect many small shipments consigned to a common destination and pay the carrier the lower rate based on larger volume, so they often convert shipments that are less-than-truckload (LTL) into full truckloads, thereby receiving better shipping rates. The rates charged by the forwarder to the individual shippers, in turn, are somewhat less than the small-quantity rate, and the difference is the forwarder's margin. In general, the shipment receives improved service at lower cost.

Export/import shippers such as Maersk Line use containers to move a wide variety of products, including perishable ones.

Maersk Line

www.maerskline.com

Air freight forwarders are an example of specialization in one transportation mode. In some cases, airlines will subcontract excess space to *air freight forwarders* or *express companies*, which are firms that market air express services to the general public. Where markets are large enough, major airlines have responded with pure air freight service between specific airports—often involving international destinations.

Warehousing and Materials Handling

Warehouses may be classified in one of two ways: (1) storage warehouses and (2) distribution centres. In *storage warehouses* the goods are intended to come to rest for some period of time, as in the aging of products or in storing household goods. *Distribution centres*, on the other hand, are designed to facilitate the timely movement of goods and represent a very important part of a supply chain. They represent the second most significant cost in a supply chain after transportation.

Distribution centres not only allow firms to hold their stock in decentralized locations but also are used to facilitate sorting and consolidating products from different plants or different suppliers. Some physical transformation can also take place in distribution centres such as mixing or blending different ingredients, labelling, and repackaging. Paint companies such as Sherwin-Williams and Benjamin Moore use distribution centres for this purpose. In addition, distribution centres may serve as manufacturer sales offices, described in Chapter 15, and order processing centres.

MATERIALS HANDLING

Moving goods over short distances into, within, and out of warehouses and manufacturing plants.

Materials handling, which involves moving goods over short distances into, within, and out of warehouses and manufacturing plants, is a key part of warehouse operations. The two major problems with this activity are high labour costs and high rates of loss and damage. Every time an item is handled, there is a chance for loss or damage. Common materials handling equipment includes forklifts, cranes, and conveyors. Today, materials handling in warehouses is automated by using computers and robots to reduce the cost of holding, moving, and recording inventories.

Materials handling through automation is now common in distribution centres.

Order Processing

There are several stages in the processing of an order, and a failure at any one of them can cause a problem with the customer. The process starts with transmitting the order by a variety of means such as the Internet, an Extranet, or electronic data interchange (EDI). This is followed by entering the order in the appropriate databases and sending the information to those who need it. For example, a regional warehouse is notified to prepare an order. After checking inventory, a new quantity may need to be reordered from the production line, or purchasing may be requested to reorder from a vendor. If the item is currently out of stock, a "backorder" is created, and the whole process of keeping track of a small part of the original order must be managed. In addition, credit may have to be checked for some customers, all documentation for the order must be prepared, transportation must be arranged, and an order confirmation must be sent. Order processing systems are evaluated in terms of speed and accuracy.

Electronic order processing has replaced manual processing for most large companies.[19] For example, IBM soon expects to be doing business electronically with all of its suppliers, either on the Internet or through EDI. Kiwi Brands, the marketer of Kiwi shoe polish, Endust, and Behold, receives 75 percent of its retailers' purchase orders via EDI. The company has also implemented financial EDI, sending invoices to retailers and receiving payment order/remittance advice documents and electronic funds transfer (EFT) payments. Shippers as well are linked to the system, allowing Kiwi to receive shipment status messages electronically.

Inventory Management

Inventory management is one of the primary responsibilities of the supply chain manager. The major problem is maintaining the delicate balance between too little and too much. Too little inventory may result in poor service, stockouts, brand switching, and loss of market share; too much leads to higher costs because of the money tied up in inventory and the chance that it may become obsolete. Remember the sting of the bullwhip described at the beginning of the chapter?

The key to Saturn's JIT system: a Ryder truck driver downloads a key-shaped floppy disk from an onboard computer to get delivery instructions.

Ryder System, Inc.

www.ryder.com

Reasons for Inventory   Traditionally, carrying inventory has been justified on several grounds: (1) to offer a buffer against variations in supply and demand, often caused by uncertainty in forecasting demand; (2) to provide better service for those customers who wish to be served on demand; (3) to promote production efficiencies; (4) to provide a hedge against price increases by suppliers; (5) to promote purchasing and transportation discounts; and (6) to protect the firm from contingencies such as strikes and shortages. However, companies today view inventory as something to be moved, not stored, and more of a liability than an asset. The traditional justification for inventory has resulted in excessive inventories that have proven costly to maintain. Consider the North American automobile industry. Despite efforts to streamline its supply chain, industry analysts estimate that more than $230 billion worth of excess inventory piles up annually in the form of unused raw materials, parts waiting to be delivered, and vehicles sitting on dealers' lots.[20]

Inventory Costs   Specific inventory costs are often hard to detect because they are difficult to measure and occur in many different parts of the firm. A classification of inventory costs includes the following:

- *Capital costs.* The opportunity costs resulting from tying up funds in inventory instead of using them in other, more profitable investments; these are related to interest rates.
- *Inventory service costs.* Items such as insurance and taxes that are present in many provinces.
- *Storage costs.* Warehousing space and materials handling.
- *Risk costs.* Possible loss, damage, pilferage, perishability, and obsolescence.

Storage costs, risk costs, and some service costs vary according to the characteristics of the items inventoried. For example, perishable products or highly seasonal items have higher risk costs than a commodity-type product such as lumber. Capital costs are always present and are proportional to the *values* of the item and prevailing interest rates. The costs of carrying inventory vary with the particular circumstances but quite easily could range from 10 to 35 percent for different firms.

Supply Chain Inventory Strategies   Conventional wisdom a decade ago was that a firm should protect itself against uncertainty by maintaining a reserve inventory at each of its production and stocking points. This has been described as a "just-in-case" philosophy of inventory management and led to unnecessarily high levels of inventory. In contrast is the **just-in-time (JIT) concept**, which is an inventory supply system that operates with very low inventories and requires fast, on-time delivery. When parts are needed for production, they arrive from suppliers "just in time," which means neither before nor after they are needed. Note that JIT is used in situations where demand forecasting is reliable, such as when supplying an automobile production line, and is not suitable for inventories that are to be stored over significant periods of time.

JUST-IN-TIME (JIT) CONCEPT

An inventory supply system that operates with very low inventories and requires fast, on-time delivery.

ETHICS AND SOCIAL RESPONSIBILITY ALERT

Reverse Logistics and Green Marketing Go Together at Estée Lauder Companies, Inc.

Retailing industry research firms and trade groups report that North American consumers return billions of dollars in merchandise to retailers each year. Until recently, returned merchandise was often disposed of in solid waste landfills.

Estée Lauder Companies, Inc. used to dump about $60 million worth of its products into landfills each year, destroying more than one-third of its name-brand cosmetics returned by retailers. That changed recently when Estée Lauder developed a sophisticated reverse logistics system that cut the volume of destroyed products in half. During the system's first year of operation, the company was able to evaluate 24 percent more returned products, redistribute 150 percent more of its returns, and save $475 000 in labour costs. Estée Lauder still destroyed 27 percent of returned products because their shelf life had expired, but that was down from 37 percent the previous year. The company

expects to reduce its disposal rate to 15 percent as the reverse logistics system becomes even more efficient. The net effect of Estée Lauder's initiative has been a reduction in costs and a cleaner environment.

Saturn uses a sophisticated JIT system. A central computerized system directs trucks to deliver pre-inspected parts at specific times 21 hours a day, six days a week to one of the plant's 56 receiving docks. Incredibly, the JIT system must coordinate Saturn's suppliers, many of whom are located hundreds of kilometres from the Saturn facility. Does the JIT system work for Saturn? The answer is a resounding yes. The Saturn production line has been shut down only once—for 18 minutes!—because the right part was not delivered at the right place and time.

Ryder Integrated Logistics is charged with making Saturn's JIT system work smoothly. Ryder long-haul trucks and their drivers are the most expensive part of the system. The key—very literally—to this JIT system is a computer disk in the form of a plastic key that drivers plug into an on-truck computer. The computer screen then tells the driver where to go, the route to use, and how much time to spend getting there.[21]

Electronic data interchange and electronic messaging technology coupled with the constant pressure for faster response time in replenishing inventory have also changed the way suppliers and customers do business in a supply chain. The approach, called **vendor-managed inventory** (VMI), is an inventory-management system whereby the *supplier* determines the product amount and assortment a customer (such as a retailer) needs and automatically delivers the appropriate items.[22]

Campbell Soup's system illustrates how VMI works.[23] Campbell first establishes EDI links with retailers. Every morning, retailers electronically inform the company of their demand for all Campbell products and the inventory levels in their distribution centres. Campbell uses that information to forecast future demand and determine which products need replenishment based on upper and lower inventory limits established with each retailer. Trucks leave the Campbell shipping plant that afternoon and arrive at the retailer's distribution centres with the required replenishments the same day.

VENDOR-MANAGED INVENTORY

An inventory management system whereby the supplier determines the product amount and assortment a customer (such as a retailer) needs and automatically delivers the appropriate items.

Closing the Loop: Reverse Logistics

REVERSE LOGISTICS
A process of reclaiming recyclable and reusable materials, returns, and reworks from the point of consumption or use for repair, remanufacturing, redistribution, or disposal.

The flow of goods in a supply chain does not end with the consumer or industrial user. Companies today recognize that a supply chain can work in reverse.[24] **Reverse logistics** is a process of reclaiming recyclable and reusable materials, returns, and reworks from the point of consumption or use for repair, remanufacturing, redistribution, or disposal. The effect of reverse logistics can be seen in the reduced waste in landfills and lowered operating costs for companies. The Ethics and Social Responsibility Alert on page 437 describes the successful reverse logistics initiative at Estée Lauder Companies, Inc.[25]

Companies such as Eastman Kodak (reusable cameras), Hewlett-Packard (printer toner cartridges returned for filling), and Xerox and IBM (remanufacturing and recycling equipment parts) have implemented acclaimed reverse logistics programs.[26] Other firms have enlisted third-party logistics providers to handle this process along with other supply chain functions. GNB Technologies, Inc., a manufacturer of lead-acid batteries for automobiles and boats, has outsourced much of its supply chain activity to UPS Logistics.[27] The company contracts with UPS to manage its shipments between plants, distribution centres, recycling centres, and retailers. This includes movement of both new batteries and used products destined for recycling and covers both truck and railroad shipments. This partnership along with the initiatives of other battery makers has paid economic and ecological dividends. By recycling 90 percent of the lead from used batteries, manufacturers have kept the demand for new lead in check, thereby holding down costs to consumers. Also, solid waste management costs and the environmental impact of lead in landfills is reduced.

Concept Check

1. What are the basic trade-offs among the modes of transportation?

2. What types of inventory should use storage warehouses and which type should use distribution centres?

3. What are the strengths and weaknesses of a just-in-time system?

SUMMARY

1 Logistics involves those activities that focus on getting the right amount of the right products to the right place at the right time at the lowest possible cost. Logistics management includes the coordination of the flows of both inbound and outbound goods, an emphasis on making these flows cost-effective, and customer service.

2 A supply chain is a sequence of firms that perform activities required to create and deliver a good or service to consumers or industrial users. Supply chain management is the integration and organization of information and logistics across firms for the purpose of creating value for consumers.

3 The goals to be achieved by a firm's marketing strategy determine whether its supply chain needs to be more responsive or efficient in meeting customer requirements. Marketers today recognize that the choice of a supply chain involves three steps: (*a*) understand the customer, (*b*) understand the supply chain, and (*c*) harmonize the supply chain with the marketing strategy.

4 The objective of information and logistics management in a supply chain is to minimize logistics costs while delivering maximum customer service. Information can leverage logistics activities, reduce total logistics costs, and improve customer service.

5 Minimizing total logistics cost is irrelevant without specifying an acceptable customer service level that must be maintained. Although key customer service factors depend on the situation, important elements of the customer service program are likely to be time-related dependability, communications, and convenience.

6 Four key logistics functions in a supply chain include (*a*) transportation, (*b*) warehousing and material handling, (*c*) order processing, and (*d*) inventory management. Third-party logistics perform most or all of the logistics functions that manufacturers, suppliers, and distributors would normally perform themselves.

7 The modes of transportation (e.g., railroads, motor carriers, air carriers, and trucks) offer shippers different service benefits. Better service often costs more, although it should result in savings in other areas of the logistics system.

8 The function of warehousing and material handling in a supply chain is to facilitate storage and movement of goods. Distribution centres provide flexibility and facilitate sorting and consolidating products from different plants or different suppliers.

9 Inventory management and order processing go hand in hand in a supply chain. Both functions have benefited from information technology. Two popular supply chain inventory

management practices are just-in-time and vendor-managed inventory management systems.

10 Reverse logistics closes the loop in a supply chain. Reverse logistics is the process of reclaiming recyclable and reusable materials, returns, and reworks from the point of consumption or use for repair, remanufacturing, redistribution, or disposal.

KEY TERMS AND CONCEPTS

crossdocking p. 426
customer service p. 429
electronic data interchange (EDI) p. 427
Extranet p. 428
freight forwarders p. 433
intermodal transportation p. 432
just-in-time (JIT) concept p. 436
lead time p. 429
logistics p. 422

logistics management p. 422
materials handling p. 434
quick response/efficient consumer response p. 429
reverse logistics p. 438
supply chain p. 422
supply chain management p. 422
third-party logistics providers p. 431
total logistics cost p. 428
vendor-managed inventory p. 437

INTERNET EXERCISE

www.mcgrawhill.ca/college/berkowitz

The bullwhip effect is a common problem in supply chains. The bullwhip's significance is evident in the attention afforded it in the QuickMBA. QuickMBA's purpose is to offer a concise discussion on important issues facing today's manager.

The Quick MBA, at www.quickmba.com/ops/scm, which also gives an overview of supply chain manage-

ment, provides insights into the bullwhip effect. Visit QuickMBA at the address given to learn more about the bullwhip effect and answer the following questions:

1. What are the principal contributors to the bullwhip effect?
2. How have companies reduced the sting of the bullwhip?

Want to get better grades, find tips on how to study more effectively, and stay up to date with happenings in the world of marketing? Visit the Online Learning Centre for practice tests, Study Smart software, and much more! www.mcgrawhill.ca/college/berkowitz

Interested in finding out what marketing looks like in the real world? *Marketing Magazine* is just a click away on your OLC! Visit www.mcgrawhill.ca/college/berkowitz

APPLYING MARKETING CONCEPTS AND PERSPECTIVES

1 List several companies to which logistical activities might be unimportant. Also list several whose focus is on only the inbound or outbound side.

2 What are some types of businesses in which order processing may be among the paramount success factors?

3 What behavioural problems might arise to negate the logistics concept within the firm?

4 List the customer service factors that would be vital to buyers in the following types of companies: (*a*) manufacturing, (*b*) retailing, (*c*) hospitals, and (*d*) construction.

5 Name some cases when extremely high service levels (e.g., 99 percent) would be warranted.

6 Name the mode of transportation that would be the best for the following products: (*a*) farm machinery, (*b*) cut flowers, (*c*) frozen meat, and (*d*) coal.

7 The auto industry is a heavy user of the just-in-time concept. Why? What other industries would be good candidates for its application? What do they have in common?

8 Look again at Figure 16–3. Explain why as the number of warehouses increases, (*a*) inventory costs rise and (*b*) transportation costs fall.

VIDEO CASE 16–1   Amazon: Delivering the Goods . . . Millions of Times Each Day!

"The new economy means that the balance of power has shifted toward the consumer," explains Jeff Bezos, CEO of Amazon.com, Inc. The global online retailer is a pioneer of fast, convenient, low-cost virtual shopping that has attracted millions of consumers. Of course, while Amazon has changed the way many people shop, the company still faces the traditional and daunting task of creating a seamless flow of deliveries to its customers—often millions of times each day!

THE COMPANY

Bezos started Amazon.com with a simple idea: to use the Internet to transform book buying into the fastest, easiest, and most enjoyable shopping experience possible. The company was incorporated in 1994 and opened its virtual doors in July 1995. At the forefront of a huge growth of dot-com businesses, Amazon pursued a get-big-fast business strategy. Sales grew rapidly and Amazon began adding products and services other than books. In fact, Amazon soon set its goal on being the world's most customer-centric company, where customers can find and discover anything they might want to buy online!

Today Amazon claims to have the "Earth's Biggest Selection™" of products and services, including books, CDs, videos, toys and games, electronics, kitchenware, computers, free electronic greeting cards, and auctions. Other services allow customers to:

- search for books, music, and videos with any word from the title or any part of the artist's name,
- browse hundreds of product categories, and
- receive personalized recommendations, based on past purchases, through e-mail or when they log on.

These products and services have attracted millions of people in more than 220 countries and made Amazon.com, along with its international sites in the United Kingdom, Germany, Japan, and France, the leading online retailer.

Despite its incredible success with consumers and continuing growth in sales to more than $3 billion annually, Amazon.com found it difficult to be profitable. Many industry observers questioned the viability of online retailing and Amazon's business model. Then, Amazon shocked many people by announcing its first profit in the fourth quarter of 2001. There are a variety of explanations for the turnaround. Generally, Bezos suggests that "efficiencies allow for lower prices, spurring sales growth across the board, which can be handled by existing facilities without much additional cost." More specifically, the facilities Bezos is referring to are the elements of its supply chain—which are one of the most complex and expensive aspects of the company's business.

SUPPLY CHAIN AND LOGISTICS MANAGEMENT AT AMAZON.COM

What happens after an order is submitted on Amazon's Website but before it arrives at the customer's door? A lot! Amazon.com maintains seven huge distribution, or "fulfillment," centres, where it keeps inventory of more than 2.7 million products. This is one of the key differences between Amazon.com and some of its competitors—it actually stocks products. So Amazon must manage the flow of products from its suppliers to its distribution centres and the flow of customer orders from the distribution centres to individuals' homes or offices.

The process begins with the suppliers. "Amazon's goal is to collaborate with our suppliers to increase efficiencies and improve inventory turnover," explains Jim Miller, vice president of supply chain at Amazon.com. "We want to bring to suppliers the kind of interactive relationship that has inspired customers to shop with us," he adds. For example, Amazon is using software to more accurately forecast purchasing patterns by region, which allows it to give its suppliers better information about delivery dates and volumes. Prior to the development of this software, 12 percent of incoming inventory was sent to the wrong location, leading to lost time and delayed orders. Now only 4 percent of the incoming inventory is mishandled.

At the same time, Amazon has been improving the part of the process that sorts the products into the individual orders. Jeffrey Wilke, Amazon's senior vice president of operations, says, "We spent the whole year really focused on increasing productivity." Again, technology has been essential. "The speed at which telecommunications networks allow us to pass information back and forth has enabled us to do the real-time work that we keep talking about. In the past it would have taken too long to get this many items through a system," explains Wilke. Once the order is in the system, computers ensure that all items are included in the box before it is taped and labelled. A network of trucks and regional postal hubs then conclude the process with delivery of the order.

The success of Amazon's logistics and supply chain management activities may be most evident during the year-end holiday shopping season. Amazon received orders for 37.9 million items between November 9 and December 21, including orders for 450 000 Harry Potter books and products and orders for 36 000 items placed just before the holiday delivery deadline. Well over 99 percent of the orders were shipped and delivered on time!

visit us at www.mcgrawhill.ca/college/berkowitz

AMAZON'S CHALLENGES

Despite all of Amazon's recent improvements, logistics experts estimate that the company's distribution centres are operating at approximately 40 percent of their capacity. This situation suggests that Amazon must reduce its capacity or increase its sales.

Several sales growth options are possible. First, Amazon can continue to pursue growth through sales of books, CDs, and videos. Expanded lists of books, music, and movies from throughout the world and convenient selection services may appeal to current and potential customers. Second, Amazon can continue its expansion into new product and service categories. This approach would prevent Amazon from becoming a niche merchant of books, music, and movies, and position it as an online department store. Finally, Amazon can pursue a strategy of providing access to its existing operations to other retailers. For example, Amazon took over the Toys "Я" Us Website, adding it as a store on Amazon's site. Borders, Expedia, and Circuit City have begun similar partnerships.

Amazon.com has come a long way toward proving that online retailing can work. As the company strives to maintain profitability and continue its growth, its future success is likely to depend on the success of its logistics and supply chain management activities!

Questions

1 How do Amazon.com's logistics and supply chain management activities help the company create value for its customers?

2 What systems did Amazon develop to improve the flow of products from suppliers to Amazon distribution centres? What systems improved the flow of orders from the distribution centres to customers?

3 Why will logistics and supply chain management play an important role in the future success of Amazon.com?

17

RETAILING

AFTER READING THIS CHAPTER YOU SHOULD BE ABLE TO:

- Identify retailers in terms of the utilities they provide.

- Explain the alternative ways to classify retail outlets.

- Understand the many methods of nonstore retailing.

- Classify retailers in terms of the retail positioning matrix.

- Develop retailing mix strategies over the life cycle of a retail store.

TIM HORTONS . . . "ALWAYS FRESH" AND "A FRIEND ALONG THE WAY"

Tim Hortons (www.timhortons.com) is the largest coffee and fresh-baked-goods restaurant chain in Canada. Founded in 1964 by former hockey great Tim Horton, this retail company is considered a Canadian cultural icon. And, indeed, Tim Hortons is a friend along the way. Busy consumers can find an outlet in over 2000 locations all across Canada. Tim Hortons' "Always fresh" promise has struck a resonant chord with Canadians. The chain has a 60-percent market share of the coffee and fresh-baked-goods segment. And despite all the talk about American retailers invading Canada, Tim Hortons has actually expanded into the United States, opening more than 120 units to date while still maintaining a firm grip on its market here in Canada.

Tim Hortons is a Canadian retail success story. The company employs more than 42 000 people in its franchised units. It also maintains major distribution centres and a fleet of trucks. The company has achieved sales in excess of $1.3 billion, with average store sales estimated at over $1.35 million. In a key strategic move, the company merged with Wendy's in 1995 and is considered a growth business for Wendy's International, Inc.

The key objective of the employees who work in the restaurants is to deliver what Canadians know as the Tim Hortons experience. According to Paul House, company president and chief operating officer, this means "everything from our front counter staff greeting customers with a friendly hello, to our premium blend coffee served in a china mug, to our sandwiches made on fresh buns served with a hot bowl of soup." Most Tim Hortons restaurants are open 24 hours a day and bake fresh products twice a day. The chain features standard stores that are about 3000 square feet with full-production baking kitchens. These stores supply non-standard units that do not have a kitchen, ranging from 500-square-foot locations in hospitals and universities to kiosks in airports to convenient double-drive-through units. This flexibility in terms of store concept allows the company to fit an outlet almost anywhere while maintaining quality, convenience, and access. In doing so, the company is able to penetrate markets aggressively and to continue the growth of its franchise chain system. Oh, and in case you are interested, the franchise costs are between $360 000 and $395 000 plus working capital. Of course, as a franchisee you have to supply the land and the building as well.[1]

RETAILING
All activities involved in selling, renting, and providing goods and services to ultimate consumers for personal, family, or household use.

Tim Hortons is just one example of many dynamic and exciting retailers you may encounter today. This chapter examines the concept of **retailing**, which includes all activities involved in selling, renting, and providing goods and services to ultimate consumers for personal, family, or household. We will look at the critical role of retailing in the marketplace and the challenging decisions retailers face as they strive to create value for their customers. In the channel of distribution, retailing is where the customer meets the product. It is through retailing that exchange (a central aspect of marketing) occurs.

THE VALUE OF RETAILING

Retailing is an important marketing activity. Not only do producers and consumers meet through retailing actions, but retailing also creates customer value and has a significant impact on the economy. To consumers, the value of retailing is in the form of utilities provided. Retailing's economic value is represented by the people employed in retailing as well as by the total amount of money exchanged in retail sales.

Consumer Utilities Offered by Retailing

The utilities provided by retailers create value for consumers. Time, place, possession, and form utilities are offered by most retailers in varying degrees, but one utility is often emphasized more than others. Look at Figure 17–1 to see how well you can match the retailer with the utility being emphasized in the description.

Providing ATMs and phone or online banking, as the Royal Bank does, puts the bank's products and services close to the consumer, providing place utility. By providing financing or leasing and taking used cars as trade-ins, Saturn makes the purchase easier and provides possession utility. Form utility—production or alteration of a product—is offered by Levi Strauss & Co. as it creates "Original Spin" jeans to meet each customer's specifications. Finding toy shelves stocked in May is the time utility dreamed about by every child (and many parents) who enters Toys "Я" Us. Many retailers offer a combination of the four basic utilities. Some supermarkets, for example, offer convenient locations (place utility) and are open 24 hours (time utility). In addition, consumers may seek additional utilities such as entertainment, recreation, or information.[2]

The Global Economic Impact of Retailing

Retailing is important to the Canadian and global economies. Retail sales in Canada are expected to surpass $300 billion in 2002.[3] The retail sector also employs over 1.5 million people in Canada, or more than 10 percent of the total employed labour force. Just three major retail categories—automotive, food stores, and furniture stores—represent more than 67 percent of total retail trade in Canada (see Figure 17–2).[4]

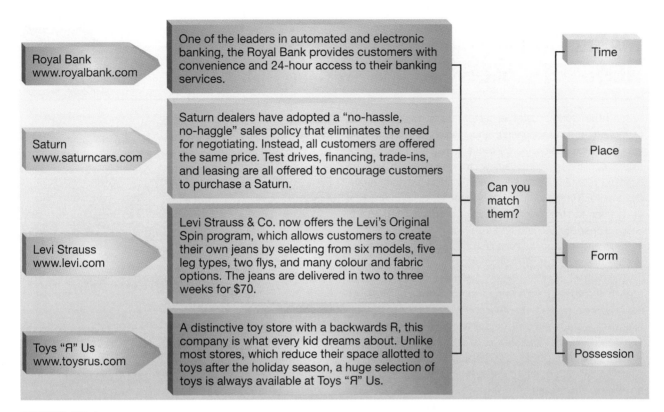

FIGURE 17–1
Which company best
represents which utilities?

FIGURE 17–2
Retail sales ($billions), by type
of business

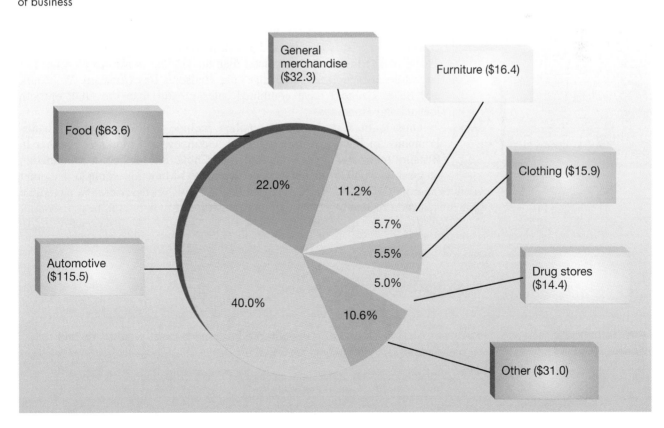

MARKETING NEWSNET   Bricks *and* Clicks Are Going Global

Around the world, customer tastes are converging, trade restrictions are disappearing, and retailers are responding with global expansion. Convenience store giant 7-Eleven, for example, plans to open one new store each month over the next five years—in Denmark alone! Swedish furniture manufacturer IKEA plans to open five new stores in North America each year for the next 10 years. Office product retailer Staples opened 189 new stores outside of the United States in 2000 and 160 new stores in 2001. And Italy's Benetton already has stores in 120 countries!

The biggest global expansion, however, may be in e-tailer growth. Companies such as Amazon.com, Yahoo! and eBay are rapidly expanding into other countries. Amazon.com, for example, has opened a site and distribution centre in Britain and has a French headquarters in development. Yahoo! is Europe's largest portal with twice as many visitors as Germany's T-Online, and online broker E*Trade has opened an office in Stockholm.

Why are retailers and e-tailers expanding? One reason is that local market growth rates are slowing, so merchants are looking for new places to invest. As Wal-Mart's CFO John B.

Menzer explains, "someday the (domestic market) will slow down, and international will be the growth vehicle for the company." A second reason is that these companies want to benefit from strong brand names and create global brands!

The magnitude of retail sales is hard to imagine. Some of Canada's top retailers, for example, have annual sales revenues that surpass the gross domestic product of several nation-states. For example, Canada's top three grocery store rivals (Loblaws, Sobeys, and A&P) have combined sales in excess of $35 billion, a sum greater than the GDP of North Korea; Canada's largest department store companies (The Hudson's Bay Company, Wal-Mart, and Sears Canada) have combined sales greater than the GDP of both Iceland and Honduras.

Outside of Canada, large retailers include Daiei in Japan, Pinault-Printemps in France, Karstadtquelle in Germany, and Marks & Spencer in Britain.[5] In emerging economies such as China and Mexico, a combination of local and global retailers are evolving. Wal-Mart, for example, has joint ventures in both China and Korea. The Marketing NewsNet describes the incredible global expansion of major retailers around the world.[6]

Concept Check

1. When Levi Strauss makes jeans cut to a customer's exact preferences and measurements, what utility is provided?

2. Two measures of the importance of retailing in the global economy are _____ and _____.

Classifying Retail Outlets

For manufacturers, consumers, and the economy, retailing is an important component of marketing that has several variations. Because of the large number of alternative forms of retailing, it is easier to understand the differences among retail institutions by recognizing that outlets can be classified in several ways. First, **form of ownership** distinguishes retail outlets based on whether individuals, corporate chains, or contractual systems own the outlet. Second, **level of service** is used to describe the degree of service provided to the customer. Finally, the type of **merchandise line** describes how many different types of products a store carries and in what assortment. A more in-depth discussion of the alternative types of outlets follows.

Form of Ownership

Independent Retailer   One of the most common forms of retail ownership is the independent business, owned by an individual. The independent retailer accounts for over 60 percent of total retail trade in Canada. Small retailers tend to dominate in bakeries, sporting goods, jewellery, and gift stores. They are also popular retailers of auto supplies, books, paint, flowers, and women's accessories. The advantage of this form of ownership for the owner is that he or she can be his or her own boss. For customers, the independent store can offer convenience, quality, personal service, and lifestyle compatibility.[7]

Corporate Chain   A second form of ownership, the corporate chain, involves multiple outlets under common ownership. If you've ever shopped at The Bay, Zellers, or Loblaws, you've shopped at a chain outlet.

In a chain operation, centralization in decision making and purchasing is common. Chain stores have advantages in dealing with manufacturers, particularly as the size of the chain grows. A large chain can bargain with a manufacturer to obtain good service or volume discounts on orders. The buying power of chains allows them to offer consumers competitive prices on merchandise. Wal-Mart's large volume makes it a strong negotiator with manufacturers of most products. Consumers also benefit in dealing with chains because there are multiple outlets with similar merchandise and consistent management policies.

Retailing has become a high-tech business for many large chains. Wal-Mart, for example, has developed a sophisticated inventory management and cost-control system that allows rapid price changes for each product in every store. Although the technology requires a substantial investment, it is a necessary competitive tool today—a lesson illustrated by Mexico's largest drugstore chain. When Wal-Mart and other discounters opened stores in Mexico, Farmacias Benavides used its state-of-the-art computer system to match prices on popular pharmaceutical products that were also available in the new competitors' stores.[8]

Contractual System   Contractual systems involve independently owned stores that band together to act like a chain. The three kinds described in Chapter 15 are retailer-sponsored cooperatives, wholesaler-sponsored voluntary chains, and franchises. One retailer-sponsored cooperative is Guardian Drugs, which consists of neighbourhood pharmacies that all agree to buy their products from the same wholesaler. In this way, members can take advantage of volume discounts commonly available to chains and also give the impression of being a large chain, which may be viewed more favourably by some consumers. Wholesaler-sponsored voluntary chains such as Ace Hardware and Independent Grocers' Alliance (IGA) try to achieve similar benefits.

As noted in Chapter 15, in a franchise system an individual or firm (the franchisee) contracts with a parent company (the franchisor) to set up a business or retail

FORM OF OWNERSHIP
Distinguishes retail outlets based on whether individuals, corporate chains, or contractual systems own the outlet.

LEVEL OF SERVICE
The degree of service provided to the customer by self-, limited-, and full-service retailers.

MERCHANDISE LINE
How many different types of products a store carries and in what assortment.

www.acehardware.com

outlet. Tim Hortons, McDonald's, Holiday Inn, Radio Shack, Merry Maids, and Blockbuster Video all offer franchising opportunities. The franchisor usually assists in selecting the store location, setting up the store, advertising, and training personnel. In addition, in "business format" franchising the franchisor provides step-by-step procedures for the major aspects of the business and guidelines for the most likely decisions a franchisee will confront. The franchisee pays a one-time franchise fee and an annual royalty, usually tied to the store's sales.

Although franchises might be seen as a relatively new phenomenon, this ownership approach has been used with gas stations since the early 1900s.[9] Franchising is attractive because it provides an opportunity for people to enter a well-known, established business where managerial advice is provided. Also, the franchise fee may be less than the cost of setting up an independent business. What is one of the fastest growing franchises around? Recently, it has been 7-Eleven, which now has 21 000 locations domestically and internationally.[10]

Franchise fees paid to the franchisor can range from $10 000 for a Subway franchise to $45 000 for a McDonald's restaurant franchise. When the fees are combined with other costs such as real estate and equipment, however, the total investment can be much higher. Figure 17–3 shows the top five franchises in North America, as rated by *Entrepreneur* magazine, based on factors such as size, financial strength, stability, years in business, and costs. By selling franchises, an organization reduces the cost of expansion but loses some control. A good franchisor, however, will maintain strong control of the outlets in terms of delivery and presentation of merchandise and try to enhance recognition of the franchise name. Canadian entrepreneurs have plenty of franchise opportunities, from automotive care to wine making. You can check it out at the Canadian Franchise Association Website (www.cfa.ca).[11]

Level of Service

Even though most customers perceive little variation in retail outlets by form of ownership, differences among retailers are more obvious in terms of level of service. In some department stores very few services are provided. Some warehouse grocery stores have customers bag the food themselves. Other retail outlets, such as Holt Renfrew, provide a wide range of customer services from gift wrapping to wardrobe consultation.

FIGURE 17–3
The top five franchises in North America

Self-Service Self-service is at the extreme end of the level of service continuum because the customer performs many functions and little is provided by the outlet. Home building supply outlets and gas stations are often self-service. Warehouse stores, usually in buildings several times larger than a conventional store, are self-service with

FRANCHISE	TYPE OF BUSINESS	TOTAL STARTUP COSTS	NUMBER OF FRANCHISES
Subway	Sandwich restaurant	$63 000–175 000	15 200
Mail Boxes Etc.	Postal services	$126 000–196 000	4400
McDonald's	Fast-food restaurant	$478 000–1 400 000	21 000
Jiffy Lube	Automobile fluid service	$174 000–194 000	1700
Taco Bell	Fast-food restaurant	$236 000–515 000	4500

all nonessential customer services eliminated. Several new forms of self-service include Federal Express' placement of hundreds of self-service package shipping stations in retail stores such as Staples and self-service scanning systems for self-checkouts at department stores and grocery stores.[12]

Limited Service   Limited-service outlets provide some services, such as credit and merchandise return, but not others, such as custom-made clothes. General merchandise stores such as Wal-Mart and Zellers are usually considered limited-service outlets. Customers are responsible for most shopping activities, although salespeople are available in departments such as consumer electronics, jewellery, and lawn and garden.

Full-Service   Full-service retailers, which include most specialty stores and some department stores, provide many services to their customers. Services can include more salespeople on the floor or delivering purchases to customers' homes. Often this full-service strategy is a competitive advantage for such stores.[13]

Merchandise Line

DEPTH OF PRODUCT LINE
The store carries a large assortment of each item.

BREADTH OF PRODUCT LINE
The variety of different items a store carries.

Retail outlets also vary by their merchandise lines, the key distinction being the breadth and depth of the items offered to customers (Figure 17–4). **Depth of product line** means that the store carries a large assortment of each item, such as a shoe store that offers running shoes, dress shoes, and children's shoes. **Breadth of product line** refers to the variety of different items a store carries.

Depth of Line   Stores that carry a considerable assortment (depth) of a related line of items are limited-line stores. Black's photography stores carry considerable depth in photography equipment. Stores that carry tremendous depth in one primary line of merchandise are single-line stores. Victoria's Secret carries great depth in women's lingerie. Both limited- and single-line stores are often referred to as *specialty outlets*.

Specialty discount outlets focus on one type of product, such as electronics, business supplies, or books, at very competitive prices. These outlets are referred to in the trade as *category killers* because they often dominate the market. Toys "Я" Us, for example, controls a significant share of the toy market, while Staples holds a large share in the office supply category.[14]

SCRAMBLED MERCHANDISING
Offering several unrelated product lines in a single retail store.

HYPERMARKET
A large store (more than 200 000 square feet) offering a mix of 40 percent food products and 60 percent general merchandise.

Breadth of Line   Stores that carry a broad product line, with limited depth, are referred to as *general merchandise stores*. For example, large department stores carry a wide range of different types of products but not unusual sizes. The breadth and depth of merchandise lines are important decisions for a retailer. Traditionally, outlets carried related lines of goods. Today, however, **scrambled merchandising**, offering several unrelated product lines in a single store, is common. The modern drugstore carries food, camera equipment, magazines, paper products, toys, small hardware items, and pharmaceuticals. Supermarkets rent video tapes, develop film, and sell flowers.

A form of scrambled merchandising, the **hypermarket**, has been successful in Europe since the late 1960s. These hypermarkets are large stores (more than 200 000 square feet) offering a mix of 40 percent food products and 60 percent general merchandise. Prices are typically 5 to 20 percent below discount stores. The general concept behind the stores is simple: Offer consumers everything in a single outlet, eliminating the need to stop at more than one location.

Despite their success in Europe, hypermarkets have not been popular in North America. Many consumers are uncomfortable with the huge size of these stores. In addition, the competitive environment is tough: warehouse stores beat hypermarkets on price, category killers beat them on selection, and discounters beat them on location.[15]

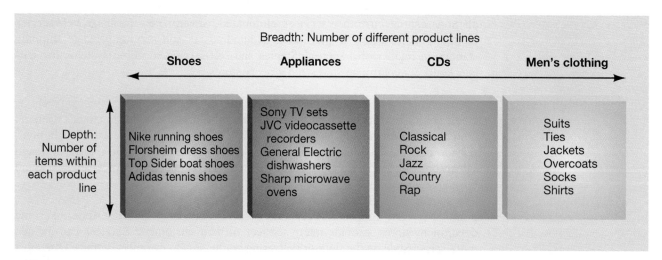

Breadth: Number of different product lines

| Shoes | Appliances | CDs | Men's clothing |

Depth: Number of items within each product line

Nike running shoes
Florsheim dress shoes
Top Sider boat shoes
Adidas tennis shoes

Sony TV sets
JVC videocassette recorders
General Electric dishwashers
Sharp microwave ovens

Classical
Rock
Jazz
Country
Rap

Suits
Ties
Jackets
Overcoats
Socks
Shirts

FIGURE 17–4
Breadth versus depth of merchandise lines

Searching for a better concept, some retailers are trying new stores, called *supercentres*, that combine a typical general merchandise store with a full-size grocery outlet. Loblaws, one of Canada's top retail grocery chains, has introduced its supercentre concept. One of its new stores, McCowan Market in Markham, Ontario, is 115 000 square feet. Along with the familiar Photolab and President's Choice Financial kiosks are an expanded housewares selection and new sections for office supplies, undergarments, cosmetics, and electronics. Much of this innovative concept has emerged through testing at the chain's Real Canadian Superstores in British Columbia, which feature 40 percent general merchandise. Loblaws continues to fine-tune the breadth and depth of its non-food offering. The goal is to offer Canadian consumers a whole new shopping experience all under one roof. But Loblaws may soon be joined in the supercentre category by Wal-Mart. It currently operates more than 900 supercentres in the United States and has plans to operate supercentres in Canada. The size of their supercentres is currently between 100 000 and 200 000 square feet.[16]

INTERTYPE COMPETITION
Competition between very dissimilar types of retail outlets.

Scrambled merchandising is convenient for consumers because it eliminates the number of stops required in a shopping trip. However, for the retailer this merchandising policy means there is competition between very dissimilar types of retail outlets, or **intertype competition**. A local bakery may compete with a department store, discount outlet, or even a local gas station. Scrambled merchandising and intertype competition make it more difficult to be a retailer. As you recall from Chapter 2, many Canadian retailers, including Shoppers Drug Mart, are attempting to deal with this new competitive arena.

Concept Check

1. Centralized decision making and purchasing are an advantage of _____ ownership.

2. What are some examples of new forms of self-service retailers?

3. Would a shop for big men's clothes carrying pants in sizes 40 to 60 have a broad or deep product line?

NONSTORE RETAILING

Most of the retailing examples discussed earlier in the chapter, such as corporate chains, department stores, and limited- and single-line specialty stores, involve store retailing. Many retailing activities today, however, are not limited to sales in a store. Nonstore retailing occurs outside a retail outlet through activities that involve

varying levels of customer and retailer involvement. Figure 17–5 shows six forms of nonstore retailing: automatic vending, direct mail and catalogues, television home shopping, online retailing, telemarketing, and direct selling.

Automatic Vending

Nonstore retailing includes vending machines, which make it possible to serve customers when and where stores cannot. Maintenance and operating costs are high, so product prices in vending machines tend to be higher than those in stores. Typically, small convenience products are available in vending machines. In fact, most of the machines in use in Canada are soft-drink machines.

In Japan, however, products available in vending machines include dried squid, hair tonic, boxers, green tea, CDs, books, clothing, and even music downloaded from a satellite transmission system. Sanyo Electric recently introduced a fully automated convenience store.[17] Improved technology will soon make vending machines even easier to use by reducing the need for cash. In Europe, for example, Marconi Online Systems has installed 6000 vending machines that allow consumers to pay for products using a wireless phone. Similarly, the world's largest vending machine company, Canteen Vending Services, is testing a cashless system called FreedomPay, which allows consumers to wave a small wand in front of a sensor to make a purchase. Another improvement in vending machines—the use of wireless technology to notify retailers when their machines are empty—is one reason automatic merchandising sales are expected to increase in the future.[18]

Direct Mail and Catalogues

Direct mail and catalogue retailing is attractive because it eliminates the cost of a store and clerks. In addition, it improves marketing efficiency through segmentation and targeting and creates customer value by providing a fast and convenient means

FIGURE 17–5
Forms of nonstore retailing

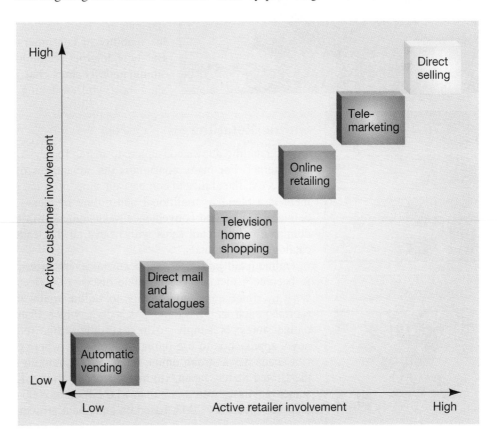

of making a purchase. Canadians have been increasing the amount they spend on direct mail catalogue merchandise. Internationally, spending is also increasing.[19] Direct marketers, for example, offer rural Japanese farmers outdoor gear at discount prices through direct mail campaigns—and deliver within 72 hours![20]

As consumers' direct mail and catalogue purchases have increased, the number of direct mailings and number of catalogues as well as the number of products sold has increased. A typical household now receives dozens of catalogues per year. The competition, combined with higher paper and postal costs, however, has caused direct retailers to focus on proven customers rather than "prospects." A successful approach now used by many catalogue retailers is to send specialty catalogues to market niches identified in their databases. L.L. Bean, a longstanding catalogue retailer, has developed an individual catalogue for fly fishing enthusiasts.[21]

Creative forms of catalogue retailing are also being developed. Hallmark, for example, offers cards for businesses in its colourful 32-page "Business Expressions" catalogue. Victoria's Secret mails as many as 45 catalogues a year to its customers to generate mail-order and 800-number business and to increase traffic in its 900 stores. Many catalogue retailers such as Sharper Image now accept telephone orders, mail orders, and e-mail orders![22]

Television Home Shopping

Television home shopping is possible when consumers watch a shopping channel on which products are displayed; orders are then placed over the telephone or on the Internet. Two popular programs, the Canadian Home Shopping Network and QVC, reach millions of Canadian households. Because these programs have traditionally attracted women over 35, other programs such as MTV Network's "House of Style," with host Molly Sims, are designed to attract a younger audience. A limitation of TV shopping has been the lack of buyer–seller interaction and the inability of consumers to control the items they see. But new Internet technologies now allow consumers to simultaneously shop, chat, and interact with their favourite show host while watching TV.[23]

Online Retailing

Online retailing allows consumers to search for, evaluate, and order products through the Internet. For many consumers the advantages of this form of retailing are the 24/7 access, the ability to comparison shop, in-home privacy, and variety. In Canada, there is a blend of traditional and online retailers—"bricks and clicks"—who are delivering value and convenience to customers. But currently, multichannel retailers dominate online retail sales with nearly all the leaders having brick-and-mortar or catalogue backgrounds.

Online retail purchases can occur in several ways. First, consumers can pay dues to become a member of an online discount service; use a shopping "bot" such as www.mysimon.com; go directly to online malls or online shopping directories (portals) such as www.retailcanada.com, which features more than 5000 Canadian online stores; or simply go to a specific online retailer's individual site. Another novel approach is to use online auction sites where consumers can bid on products.

Canada has a strong online retail market, ranking among the top five along with the United States, Japan, Germany, and the United Kingdom. Canadian online consumer purchases were more than $3.6 billion in 2000, but are expected to reach more than $15 billion by 2003, based on an annual growth rate of more than 70 percent.[24]

Internet cafés provide access
to the Web.

Still, Canada compares poorly to the United States with respect to the percentage of leading traditional retailers that are selling online. Canadians can purchase online from only 15 of the top 50 Canadian retailers (30 percent), compared to 28 of the top 50 U.S. retailers (56 percent).[25] Also, there are few entirely pure-play online retailers with established strong consumer brands in Canada. Bid.com, Grocery Gateway, and a few others are building consumer brands. But the number and strength of these brands pale in comparison to U.S. brands such as Amazon and Priceline. However, Canadian online retailers are outperforming their U.S. counterparts on several key drivers including customer acquisition cost, order conversion, and customer loyalty. Several U.S.–based companies, including eBay, E*Trade, Schwab, and Travelocity, have also launched Canadian-specific sites as a way to capture more Canadian consumers.[26]

Online retailers are trying to improve the online retailing experience by adding experiential or interactive activities to their Websites. The Web Link describes how an apparel store uses "virtual models" to involve consumers in the purchase process and help with product selection.[27] Other changes that are occurring to improve online retailing are the growing availability of high-speed digital telephone lines and cable connections that run 50 to 100 times faster than typical telephone lines. In addition, the merger of television home shopping and online retailing is also possible through TV-based Web platforms such as WebTV, AOLTV, and UltimateTV, which use an "Internet appliance" attached to a television to connect to the Internet.[28] In fact, owning a television or a computer now isn't even a necessity for online retailing. More than 4000 "Internet cafés" in 148 countries provide guests with access to computer stations linked to the Internet.[29]

Telemarketing

TELEMARKETING
Using the telephone to
interact with and sell directly
to consumers.

Another form of nonstore retailing, called **telemarketing**, involves using the telephone to interact with and sell directly to consumers. Compared to direct mail, telemarketing is often viewed as a more efficient means of targeting consumers, although the two techniques are often used together. For example, Information Management Network sends direct mail to millions on its mailing lists each year to generate responses from people who are then contacted by telemarketers. At Ryder Consumer Truck Rental, well-trained agents talk to 15 prospective customers each hour, while a staff of 24 at Lens Express makes 100 000 calls each month. Telemarketing has grown in popularity as companies search for ways to cut costs but still provide convenient access to their customers.[30]

As the use of telemarketing has grown, consumer privacy has become a topic of discussion among consumers, the federal and provincial governments, and businesses. Issues such as industry standards, ethical guidelines, and new privacy laws are evolving to provide a balance between the varying perspectives.[31]

Direct Selling

Direct selling, sometimes called door-to-door retailing, involves direct sales of goods and services to consumers through personal interactions and demonstrations in their

home or office. A variety of companies, including familiar names such as Fuller Brush, Avon, World Book, and Mary Kay Cosmetics, have created a multi-billion-dollar industry by providing consumers with personalized service and convenience. In Canada, however, sales have been declining as retail chains such as Wal-Mart begin to carry similar products at discount prices and as the increasing number of dual-career households reduces the number of potential buyers at home.

In response to the changes, many direct-selling retailers are expanding into other markets. Avon, for example, already has 3.0 million sales representatives in 137 countries including Mexico, Poland, Argentina, and China.[32] Similarly, other retailers such as Amway, Herbalife, and Electrolux are rapidly expanding. More than 70 percent of Amway's $7 billion in sales now comes from outside North America, and sales in Japan alone exceed sales in North America.[33] Direct selling is likely to continue to grow in markets where the lack of effective distribution channels increases the importance of door-to-door convenience and where the lack of consumer knowledge about products and brands will increase the need for a person-to-person approach.[34]

Concept Check

1. Successful catalogue retailers often send _____ catalogues to _____ markets identified in their databases.

2. How are retailers increasing consumer interest and involvement in online retailing?

3. Where are direct selling retail sales growing? Why?

RETAILING STRATEGY

This section identifies how a retail store positions itself and describes specific actions it can take to develop a retailing strategy.

Positioning a Retail Store

The classification alternatives presented in the previous sections help determine one store's position relative to its competitors.

Retail Positioning Matrix   The **retail positioning matrix** was developed by the MAC Group, Inc., a management consulting firm.[35] This matrix positions retail outlets on two dimensions: breadth of product line and value added. As defined previously, breadth of product line is the range of products sold through each outlet. The second dimension, *value added*, includes elements such as location (as with 7-Eleven stores), product reliability (as with Holiday Inn or McDonald's), or prestige (as with Birks).

The retail positioning matrix in Figure 17–6 shows four possible positions. An organization can be successful in any position, but unique strategies are required within each quadrant. Consider the four stores shown in the matrix:

www.birks.com

1. The Bay has high value added and a broad product line. Retailers in this quadrant pay great attention to store design and product lines. Merchandise often has a high margin of profit and is of high quality. The stores in this position typically provide high levels of service.
2. Zellers has low value added and a broad line. Zellers and similar firms typically trade a lower price for increased volume in sales. Retailers in this position focus on price with low service levels and an image of being a place for good buys.
3. Birks has high value added and a narrow line. Retailers of this type typically sell a very restricted range of products that are of high status quality. Customers are also provided with high levels of service.
4. Payless ShoeSource has low value added and a narrow line. Such retailers are specialty mass merchandisers. Payless, for example, carries attractively priced shoes for the entire family. These outlets appeal to value-conscious consumers.[36] Economies of scale are achieved through centralized advertising, merchandising, buying, and distribution. Stores are usually the same in design, layout, and merchandise; hence, they are often referred to as "cookie-cutter" stores.

FIGURE 17–6
Retail positioning matrix

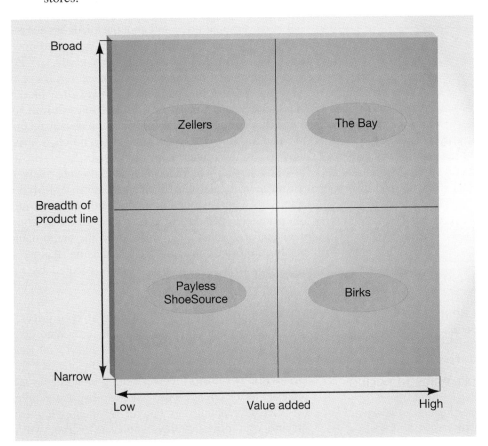

Keys to Positioning   To successfully position a store, it must have an identity that has some advantages over the competitors yet is recognized by consumers. A company can have outlets in several positions on the matrix, but this approach is usually done with different store names. The Hudson's Bay Company, for example, owns The Bay department stores (with high value added and a broad line) and Zellers stores (low value added and a broad line). Shifting from one box in the retail positioning matrix to another is also possible, but all elements of retailing strategy must be re-examined.[37]

Retailing Mix

In developing retailing strategy, managers work with the **retailing mix**, which includes the (1) goods and services, (2) physical distribution, and (3) communications tactics chosen by a store (Figure 17–7).[38] Decisions relating to the mix focus on the consumer. Each of the areas shown is important, but we will cover only three basic areas: (1) pricing, (2) store location, and (3) image and atmosphere. The communications and promotion components are discussed in Chapter 19 on advertising and Chapter 20 on personal selling.

Retail Pricing   In setting prices for merchandise, retailers must decide on the markup, markdown, and timing for markdowns. As mentioned in the appendix to Chapter 14 (Appendix B), the *markup* refers to how much should be added to the cost the retailer paid for a product to reach the final selling price. Retailers decide on the *original markup*, but by the time the product is sold, they end up with a *maintained markup*. The original markup is the difference between retailer cost and initial selling price. When products do not sell as quickly as anticipated, their price is reduced. The difference between the final selling price and retailer cost is the maintained markup, which is also called the *gross margin*.

Discounting a product, or taking a *markdown*, occurs when the product does not sell at the original price and an adjustment is necessary. Often new models or styles force the price of existing models to be marked down. Discounts may also be used to increase demand for complementary products.[39] For example, retailers might take a markdown on stereos to increase sales of CDs or reduce the price of cake mix to generate frosting purchases. The *timing* of a markdown can be important. Many retailers take a markdown as soon as sales fall off to free up valuable selling space and cash. However, other stores delay markdowns to discourage bargain hunters and maintain an image of quality. There is no clear answer, but retailers must consider how the timing might affect future sales.

Although most retailers plan markdowns, many retailers use price discounts as part of their regular merchandising policy. Wal-Mart and Home Depot, for example, emphasize consistently low prices and eliminate most markdowns with a strategy often called *everyday low pricing*.[40] Because consumers often use price as an indicator of product quality, however, the brand name of the product and the image of the store become important decision factors in these situations.[41] Another strategy, *everyday fair pricing*, is advocated by retailers that may not offer the lowest price but try to create value for customers through service and the total buying experience.[42]

A special issue for retailers trying to keep prices low is **shrinkage**, or theft of merchandise by customers and employees. Who do you think steals more? For the answer, see the accompanying Ethics and Social Responsibility Alert.[43]

Off-price retailing is a retail pricing practice that has become quite common. **Off-price retailing** involves selling brand-name merchandise at lower than regular prices. The difference between the off-price retailer and a discount store is that off-price merchandise is bought by the retailer from manufacturers with excess inventory at prices below wholesale prices, while the discounter buys at full

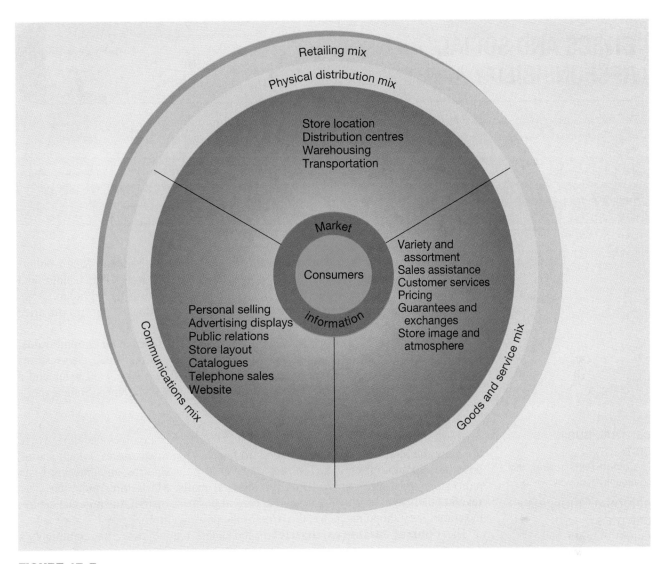

FIGURE 17–7
The retailing mix

wholesale price (but takes less of a markup than do traditional department stores). Because of this difference in the way merchandise is purchased by the retailer, selection at an off-price retailer is unpredictable, and searching for bargains has become a popular activity for many consumers. Savings to the consumer at off-price retailers are reported as high as 70 percent off the prices of a traditional department store.[44]

There are several variations of off-price retailing. One is the warehouse club. These large stores (more than 100 000 square feet) began as rather stark outlets with no elaborate displays, customer service, or home delivery. They require an annual membership fee (usually $25) for the privilege of shopping there. While a typical Zellers stocks 100 000 items, warehouse clubs carry about 3500 items and usually stock just one brand name of appliance or food product. Service is minimal, and customers usually must pay by cash or cheque. However, the extremely competitive pricing of merchandise makes warehouse clubs attractive. Some major warehouse clubs you may be familiar with include Wal-Mart's Sam's Club, BJ's Wholesale Club, and Price/Costco. Sales of these off-price retailers have grown dramatically over the past decade.[45]

A second variation is the outlet store. Factory outlets, such as Van Heusen Factory Store, Bass Shoe Outlet, and Oneida Factory Store, offer products for 25 to 30 percent off the suggested retail price. Manufacturers use the stores to clear excess

www.costco.com

merchandise and to reach consumers who focus on value shopping. Retail outlets such as Brooks Brothers Outlet Store allow retailers to sell excess merchandise and still maintain an image of offering merchandise at full price in their primary store. Some experts expect the next trend to combine the various types of off-price retailers in "value-retail centres."[46]

A third variation of off-price retailing is offered by single-price, or extreme value, retailers such as Family Dollar, Dollar General, and Dollar Tree. These stores average about 6000 square feet in size and attract customers who want value and a "corner store" environment rather than a large supercentre experience. Some experts predict extraordinary growth of these types of retailers.[47]

CENTRAL BUSINESS DISTRICT
The oldest retail setting, the community's downtown area.

REGIONAL SHOPPING CENTRES
Consist of 50 to 150 stores that typically attract customers who live within an 8- to 16-km range, often containing two or three anchor stores.

COMMUNITY SHOPPING CENTRE
A retail location that typically has one primary store (usually a department store branch) and 20 to 40 smaller outlets, serving a population of consumers who are within a 10- to 20-minute drive.

STRIP LOCATION
A cluster of stores serving people who live within a 5- to 10-minute drive.

POWER CENTRE
A huge shopping strip with multiple anchor (or national) stores, a convenient location, and a supermarket.

Store Location A second aspect of the retailing mix involves deciding where to locate the store and how many stores to have. Department stores, which started downtown in most cities, have followed customers to the suburbs, and in recent years more stores have been opened in large regional malls. Most stores today are near several others in one of five settings: the central business district, the regional centre, the community shopping centre, the strip, or the power centre.

The **central business district** is the oldest retail setting, the community's downtown area. Until the regional outflow to suburbs, it was the major shopping area, but the suburban population has grown at the expense of the downtown shopping area.

Regional shopping centres consist of 50 to 150 stores that typically attract customers who live or work within an 8- to 16-km range. These large shopping areas often contain two or three *anchor stores*, which are well-known national or regional stores such as Sears and The Bay. The largest variation of a regional centre is the West Edmonton Mall in Alberta. The shopping centre is a conglomerate of 600 stores, six amusement centres, 110 restaurants, and a 355-room Fantasyland hotel.[48]

A more limited approach to retail location is the **community shopping centre**, which typically has one primary store (usually a department store branch) and often about 20 to 40 smaller outlets. Generally, these centres serve a population of consumers who are within a 10- to 20-minute drive.

Not every suburban store is located in a shopping mall. Many neighbourhoods have clusters of stores, referred to as a **strip location**, to serve people who are within a 5- to 10-minute drive. Gas station, hardware, laundry, grocery, and pharmacy outlets are commonly found in a strip location. Unlike the larger shopping centres, the composition of these stores is usually unplanned. A variation of the strip shopping location is called the **power centre**, which is a huge shopping strip with multiple anchor (or national) stores. Power centres are seen as having the convenient location found in many strip centres and the additional power of national stores. These large strips often have two to five anchor stores and often contain a supermarket, which brings the shopper to the power centre on a weekly basis.[49]

Several new types of retail locations include carts, kiosks (including electronic kiosks) and wall units. These forms of retailing have been popular in airports and mall common areas because they provide consumers with easy access and also provide rental income for the property owner. Retailers benefit from the relatively low cost compared with a regular store.

Retail Image and Atmosphere   Deciding on the image of a retail outlet is an important retailing mix factor that has been widely recognized and studied since the late 1950s. Pierre Martineau described image as "the way in which the store is defined in the shopper's mind," partly by its functional qualities and partly by an aura of psychological attributes.[50] In this definition, *functional* refers to mix elements such as price ranges, store layouts, and breadth and depth of merchandise lines. The psychological attributes are the intangibles such as a sense of belonging, excitement, style, or warmth. Image has been found to include impressions of the corporation that operates the store, the category or type of store, the product categories in the store, the brands in each category, merchandise and service quality, and the marketing activities of the store.[51]

Closely related to the concept of image is the store's atmosphere or ambiance. Many retailers believe that sales are affected by layout, colour, lighting, and music in the store as well as by how crowded it is. In addition, the physical surroundings that influence customers may affect the store's employees.[52] In creating the right image and atmosphere, a retail store tries to identify its target audience and what the target audience seeks from the buying experience so the store will fortify the beliefs and the emotional reactions buyers are seeking.[53] Sears Canada, for example, has attempted to shift from its appliance and tool image with advertising that speaks to all members of a family, emphasizing a broad range of brand-name merchandise and one-stop shopping convenience. The recent acquisition of Lands' End will now provide Sears with a better image for upscale casual apparel, which had been a weakness for it in the past.[54]

Concept Check

1. What are the two dimensions of the retail positioning matrix?

2. How does original markup differ from maintained markup?

3. A huge shopping strip with multiple anchor stores is a _____ centre.

THE CHANGING NATURE OF RETAILING

Retailing is the most dynamic aspect of a channel of distribution. Stores such as factory outlets show that new retailers are always entering the market, searching for a new position that will attract customers. The reason for this continual change is explained by two concepts: the wheel of retailing and the retail life cycle.

The Wheel of Retailing

WHEEL OF RETAILING
A concept that describes how new retail outlets enter the market as low-status, low-margin stores and gradually add embellishments that raise their prices, and status. They now face a new low-status, low-margin operator, and the cycle starts to repeat itself.

The **wheel of retailing** describes how new forms of retail outlets enter the market.[55] Usually they enter as low-status, low-margin stores such as a drive-in hamburger stand with no indoor seating and a limited menu (Figure 17–8, box 1). Gradually these outlets add fixtures and more embellishments to their stores (in-store seating, plants, and chicken sandwiches as well as hamburgers) to increase the attractiveness for customers. With these additions, prices and status rise (box 2). As time passes, these outlets add still more services and their prices and status increase even further (box 3). These retail outlets now face some new form of retail outlet that again appears as a low-status, low-margin operator (box 4), and the wheel of retailing turns as the cycle starts to repeat itself.

FIGURE 17–8
The wheel of retailing

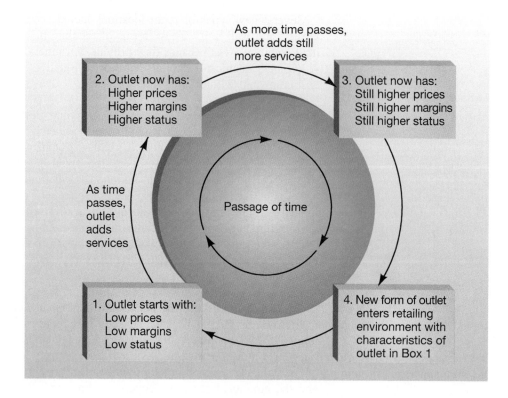

As more time passes, outlet adds still more services

2. Outlet now has:
Higher prices
Higher margins
Higher status

3. Outlet now has:
Still higher prices
Still higher margins
Still higher status

As time passes, outlet adds services

Passage of time

1. Outlet starts with:
Low prices
Low margins
Low status

4. New form of outlet enters retailing environment with characteristics of outlet in Box 1

In the 1950s, McDonald's and Burger King had very limited menus of hamburgers and french fries. Most stores had no inside seating for customers. Over time, the wheel of retailing for fast-food restaurants has turned. These chains have changed by altering their stores and expanding their menus. Today, McDonald's is testing new products such as Sourdough Supreme Burgers and Strawberry Cheesecake, new formats such as its gourmet coffee and dessert outlet called McCafe in Montreal, and new decor options such as a 50s-style store. The changes are leaving room for new forms of outlets that offer only the basics—burgers, fries, and cola, a drive-through window, and no inside seating.[56] For still others, the wheel has come full circle. Taco Bell is now opening small, limited-offering outlets in gas stations, discount stores, or "wherever a burrito and a mouth might possibly intersect."[57]

Discount stores were a major new retailing form in the 1960s and priced their products below those of department stores. As prices in discount stores rose, in the 1980s they found themselves overpriced compared with a new form of retail outlet—the warehouse retailer. Today, off-price retailers and factory outlets are offering prices even lower than warehouses!

The Retail Life Cycle

RETAIL LIFE CYCLE
The process of growth and decline that retail outlets, like products, experience.

The process of growth and decline that retail outlets, like products, experience is described by the **retail life cycle**.[58] Figure 17–9 shows the retail life cycle and the position of various current forms of retail outlets on it. *Early growth* is the stage of emergence of a retail outlet, with a sharp departure from existing competition. Market share rises gradually, although profits may be low because of startup costs. In the next stage, *accelerated development*, both market share and profit achieve their greatest growth rates. Usually multiple outlets are established as companies focus on the distribution element of the retailing mix. In this stage some later competitors may enter. Wendy's, for example, appeared on the hamburger chain scene almost 20 years after McDonald's had begun operation. The key goal for the retailer in this stage is to establish a dominant position in the fight for market share.

The battle for market share is usually fought before the *maturity* phase, and some competitors drop out of the market. New retail forms enter in the maturity phase,

FIGURE 17–9
The retail life cycle

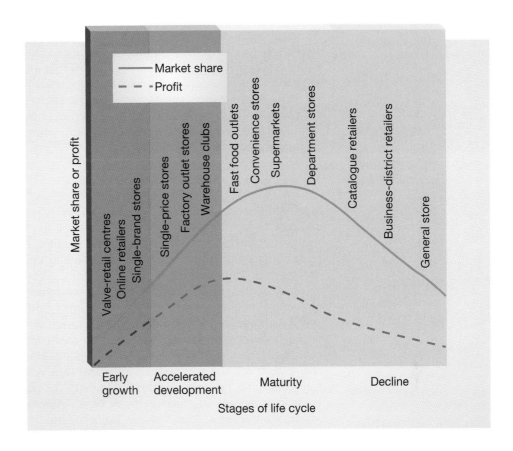

stores try to maintain their market share, and price discounting occurs. For example, when McDonald's introduced its Extra Value Meal, a discounted package of burger, fries, and drink, Wendy's followed with its 99¢ Value Menu.

The challenge facing retailers is to delay entering the *decline* stage, in which market share and profit fall rapidly. Specialty apparel retailers, such as The Gap, Limited, Benetton, and Ann Taylor, have noticed a decline in market share after a decade of growth. To prevent further decline, these retailers will need to find ways of discouraging their customers from moving to low-margin, mass-volume outlets or high-price, high-service boutiques.[59]

FUTURE CHANGES IN RETAILING

Three exciting trends in retailing—the growth of multichannel retailing, the increasing impact of technology, and the dramatic changes in the way we shop—are likely to lead to many changes for retailers and consumers in the future.

Multichannel Retailing

The retailing formats described previously in this chapter represent an exciting menu of choices for creating customer value in the marketplace. Each format allows retailers to offer unique benefits and meet particular needs of various customer groups. While each format has many successful applications, retailers in the future are likely to combine many of the formats to offer a broader spectrum of benefits and experiences. These **multichannel retailers** will utilize and integrate a combination of traditional store formats and nonstore formats such as catalogues, television, electronic kiosks, and online retailing. For example, Canadian Tire markets via its retail stores, catalogues, and online, while Chapters offers customers both traditional retail stores as well as online shopping.

Integrated channels can make shopping simpler and more convenient. A consumer can research choices online or in a catalogue and then make a purchase online, over

MULTICHANNEL RETAILERS

Utilize and integrate a combination of traditional store formats and nonstore formats such as catalogues, television, and online retailing.

the telephone, or at the closest store. In addition, the use of multiple channels allows retailers to reach a broader profile of customers. While online retailing may cannibalize catalogue business to some degree, a Web transaction costs about half as much to process as a catalogue order. Multichannel retailers also benefit from the synergy of sharing information among the different channel operations. Online retailers, for example, have recognized that the Internet is more of a transactional medium than a relationship-building medium and are working to find ways to complement traditional customer interactions.[60]

The Impact of Technology

One of the most significant changes retailers may face in the future is the way consumers pay for purchases. Today, one of the most convenient and popular methods of payment is a credit card. But credit cards themselves are likely to be replaced by smart cards, which look the same as credit cards but store information on computer chips instead of magnetic strips. They hold information about bank accounts and available funds, and contain customer purchase information such as airline seat preferences and clothing sizes. Smart cards are already popular in Europe and Asia. Benefits for consumers include faster service—a smart card transaction is much faster than having a cheque or credit card approved—and they are a convenient method of paying for small-dollar-amount transactions. Merchants will also benefit because they will save the five to seven percent usually paid to credit card companies or lost in handling. Currently the absence of processing equipment is slowing the use of smart cards in North America. But recent investments by several companies such as Visa are likely to help.

Changing Shopping Behaviour

In recent years consumers have become precision shoppers. The number of stores consumers visit and the number of times they visit those stores each month is declining. Shoppers are demanding convenient hours and locations, outstanding service and selection, and reasonable prices from retailers. As a result, familiar forms of retailers such as supermarkets, travel agencies, car dealerships, and hardware stores are likely to change or be replaced by new types of retailers. For example, local car dealers and neighbourhood hardware stores will be challenged by what are referred to as "big-box" retailers. Car Canada Group, for example, is considered a big-box car dealer that offers over 400 reconditioned vehicles, warranties, financing, and fast transaction times. Big-box home improvement centres are also experiencing growth. Some retail experts suggest that consumers like these types of retailers because they are often fast, focused, and flexible.

Another response to the changes in consumers' preferences is a form of co-branding where two retailers share a location. For example, McDonald's has developed partnerships with Wal-Mart that will lead to thousands of satellite outlets in the retail stores. Starbucks Coffee Co. has opened cafés in conjunction with Chapters bookstores. And KFC, which attracts a strong dinner crowd, now also includes Taco Bell, which is stronger in the lunch market, at 800 of its stores. Retailers hope that consumers will appreciate the convenience of the new locations.[61]

www.chapters.ca

Concept Check

1. According to the wheel of retailing, when a new retail form appears how would you characterize its image?

2. Market share is usually fought out before the _____ stage of the retail life cycle

3. What is a smart card?

SUMMARY

1 Retailing provides customer value in the form of various utilities: time, place, possession, and form. Economically, retailing is important in terms of the people employed and money exchanged in retail sales.

2 Retailing outlets can be classified along several dimensions: the form of ownership, level of service, or merchandise line.

3 There are several forms of ownership: independent, chain, retailer-sponsored cooperative, wholesaler-sponsored chain, or franchise.

4 Stores vary in the level of service they provide. Three levels are self-service, limited service, or full service.

5 Retail outlets vary in terms of the breadth and depth of their merchandise lines. Breadth refers to the number of different items carried, and depth refers to the assortment of each item offered.

6 Nonstore retailing includes automatic vending, direct mail and catalogues, television home shopping, online retailing, telemarketing, and direct selling.

7 A retail store positions itself on two dimensions: breadth of product line and value added, which includes elements such as location, product reliability, and prestige.

8 Retailing strategy is based on the retailing mix, consisting of goods and services, physical distribution, and communication tactics.

9 In retail pricing, retailers must decide on the markup, markdown, and timing for the markdown. Off-price retailers offer brand-name merchandise at lower than regular prices. This retailing form includes warehouse clubs, outlet stores, and single-price retailers.

10 Retail store location is an important retail mix decision. The common alternatives are the central business district, a regional shopping centre, a community shopping centre, or a strip location. A variation of the strip location is the power centre, which is a strip location with multiple national anchor stores and a supermarket.

11 Retail image and atmosphere help retailers create the appropriate buying experience for their target market.

12 New retailing forms are explained by the wheel of retailing. Stores enter as low-status, low-margin outlets. Over time, they add services and raise margins, which allows a new form of low-status, low-margin retailing outlet to enter.

13 Like products, retail outlets have a life cycle consisting of four stages: early growth, accelerated development, maturity, and decline.

14 Multichannel retailing and technology will change the way consumers shop and pay for purchases in the future. Smart cards may lead to a cashless society.

KEY TERMS AND CONCEPTS

breadth of product line p. 449
central business district p. 458
community shopping centre p. 458
depth of product line p. 449
form of ownership p. 447
hypermarket p. 449
intertype competition p. 450
level of service p. 447
merchandise line p. 447
multichannel retailers p. 461
off-price retailing p. 456

power centre p. 458
regional shopping centres p. 458
retail life cycle p. 460
retail positioning matrix p. 455
retailing p. 444
retailing mix p. 456
scrambled merchandising p. 449
shrinkage p. 456
strip location p. 458
telemarketing p. 453
wheel of retailing p. 459

INTERNET EXERCISE

www.mcgrawhill.ca/college/berkowitz

As this chapter indicates, online retailing is now part of the Canadian retail landscape. Online retailing presents both opportunities and challenges for Canadian retailers. Go to the Retail Council of Canada Website (www.retailcouncil.org). Click on the E-commerce Overview Series: Retail Trade in Canada. Find "The Canadian Online Retailing Report" prepared by the Boston Consulting Group and the Retail Council of Canada. Read the report. From what you have gleaned from the report answer the following questions.

1 What factors are inhibiting the growth of online retailing in Canada?

2 How are current online retailers in Canada doing when it comes to their business performance?

Want to get better grades, find tips on how to study more effectively, and stay up to date with happenings in the world of marketing? Visit the Online Learning Centre for practice tests, Study Smart software, and much more! www.mcgrawhill.ca/college/berkowitz

Interested in finding out what marketing looks like in the real world? *Marketing Magazine* is just a click away on your OLC! Visit www.mcgrawhill.ca/college/berkowitz

APPLYING MARKETING CONCEPTS AND PERSPECTIVES

1   Discuss the impact of the growing number of dual-income households on (*a*) nonstore retailing and (*b*) the retail mix.

2   How does value added affect a store's competitive position?

3   In retail pricing, retailers often have a maintained markup. Explain how this maintained markup differs from original markup and why it is so important.

4   What are the similarities and differences between the product and retail life cycles?

5   How would you classify Zellers in terms of its position on the wheel of retailing versus that of an off-price retailer?

6   Develop a chart to highlight the role of each of the three main elements of the retailing mix across the four stages of the retail life cycle.

7   In Figure 17–6 Payless was placed on the retail positioning matrix. What strategies should Payless follow to move itself into the same position as Birks?

8   Breadth and depth are two important components in distinguishing among types of retailers. Discuss the breadth and depth implications of the following retailers discussed in this chapter: (*a*) Levi Strauss, (*b*) Wal-Mart, (*c*) L.L. Bean, and (*d*) Future Shop.

9   According to the wheel of retailing and the retail life cycle, what will happen to factory outlet stores?

10   The text discusses the development of online retailing. How does the development of this retailing form agree with the implications of the retail life cycle?

CASE 17–1   IKEA

IKEA began as a mail-order firm in Sweden in the 1940s. Today it is one of the world's largest retail home furnishings chains with more than 150 outlets in 28 countries and sales of U.S.$10 billion. IKEA has 24 stores in North America, 9 in Canada and 15 in the United States. Sales in these outlets totalled more than $1.7 billion in 2001.

THE IKEA CONCEPT

Founded by Swedish catalogue king Ingvar Kamprad, IKEA is an acronym for his name and hometown, Elmtaryd Agunnaryd. IKEA is guided by a corporate philosophy spelled out in Kamprad's "Testament of a Furniture Retailer." The basic philosophy can be summed up as "form, function, price = attractive, useful and affordable furniture." Specifically, IKEA's promise is "to offer a wide range of home furnishing items of good design and function, at prices so low, that the majority of people can afford to buy them." The corporate values of thrift, inventiveness, informality, and hard work are deeply rooted in the company.

Instead of traditional stores, IKEA stores are a combination of gallery and warehouse. Sales staff on the floor are kept to a minimum. Products are displayed in rooms that are fully furnished, allowing consumers to visualize how they would look in a home setting. Products are stored in flat cartons, which the consumer picks up and takes home for final assembly. In essence, IKEA's consumers are really "prosumers" (half producers, half consumers) since they assume responsibility for assembly of the products. The consumers are also active players in the distribution process since they must transport the products to their homes.

While the key to the IKEA concept is self-service and self-assembly, IKEA does offer its customers some services. For example, home delivery is available in most stores at an extra charge. If delivery is not available, IKEA will refer customers to a delivery service company in the area. IKEA will even rent out automobile roof racks to customers to transport their purchases home. Many IKEA stores offer a home decoration service if customers wish to furnish an entire room or home, and most also offer a kitchen planning service. Using computer simulations, trained kitchen planners work with the customer to plan and choose the right kitchen. IKEA's products are easy to assemble and require no skills or tools. But if customers desire, IKEA will refer them to assembly companies that will come to the customer's home to assemble the products.

There are about 12 000 products in the total IKEA product range. Each store carries a selection of products depending on store size. The core products are the same worldwide. IKEA contracts more than 2000 suppliers in over 60 countries to manufacture its products. The manufacturers ship the components to large warehouses or distribution centres which, in turn, supply the various stores. The suppliers must provide well-designed and high-quality products that are distinctively Scandinavian. They must also be able to provide the product at a low price and ensure continuity of supply.

IKEA's key promotion vehicle is its catalogue. More than 110 million copies of its catalogue are distributed in 34 languages. The company also uses attention-getting and often provocative advertising designed to generate additional word-of-mouth publicity. For example, the company was the first to feature gay consumers in mainstream TV ads. The company also uses quirky and humorous ad appeals to reach customers. And, of course, IKEA also has its own Website to communicate with its customers (www.ikea.com). Consumers can browse the online catalogue or use the printed catalogue to make product selections and place on order over the Internet. IKEA will then deliver the product to your door in one to three weeks.

The primary target market of IKEA is young (if not in age, at least in thought), educated, liberal-minded professionals who are not overly concerned with status symbols. This target market is similar across countries and regions where IKEA is located. However, because of changing demographics, especially the aging of the population in many countries, IKEA is attempting to broaden its target market to include the "older customer." IKEA also offers a line of business furnishings for the commercial market segment.

IKEA takes a managed-growth perspective in terms of retail expansion. Globally, only a few new stores are planned for each year.

Questions

1 Outline IKEA's basic marketing mix.
2 Why do you think IKEA has been successful in a highly competitive retail furnishings market?
3 From the consumer's perspective, what makes IKEA's approach to retailing an attractive alternative to traditional furniture shopping?

18

INTEGRATED MARKETING COMMUNICATIONS AND DIRECT MARKETING

AFTER READING THIS CHAPTER YOU SHOULD BE ABLE TO:

- Explain the communication process and its elements.

- Understand the promotional mix and the uniqueness of each component.

- Select the promotional approach appropriate to a product's life-cycle stage and characteristics.

- Differentiate between the advantages of push and pull strategies.

- Appreciate the value of an integrated marketing communications approach.

- Understand the value of direct marketing for consumers and sellers

INTEGRATED MARKETING COMMUNICATIONS MAKE MAGIC AT DISNEY!

How are you at remembering birthdays? Well even if you are usually forgetful, Disney is using its expertise at integrating many forms of communication to help you remember—and celebrate—the 100th anniversary of the company's founder, Walt Disney. The plan calls for a $250-million budget during a 15-month campaign, which includes advertising, partnerships with other companies, direct marketing, Internet promotions, and many other ways of getting the message to Disney fans.

The TV advertising includes four versions targeted at families, children, parents, and grandparents. The partnerships include agreements with McDonald's, Coca-Cola, American Express, Kellogg, and Hallmark Cards to run joint promotions. Direct marketing activities include special offers mailed to many of the 31 million households in Disney's database. The Website, DisneyWorld.com, provides information about the events associated with the celebration and allows consumers to make reservations and travel plans. The campaign also includes an anthem—"Then the dream began to grow and come alive, Touching every one of us, lighting up the skies"—and an in-park promotion called "100 Years of Magic!"

Disney applies a similar integrated approach to the marketing of all of its products, services, and events. Other promotional activities include advertising on Radio Disney, sponsorship of documentaries on the ABC television network, Internet-linked kiosks to allow potential customers to check for location and availability of products at its stores, and contests and giveaways. Another component of Disney's promotion plan is a membership program called Disney Club, which currently has 300 000 members who pay $39.95 annually to receive unique merchandise offers, VIP treatment at special events, and discounts. More than 4000 members of the club, for example, were invited to preview Disney's new Adventure theme park at half price before it opened to the public. To promote the release of its movie *Atlantis: The Lost Empire*, Disney gave away 13 million copies of a CD-based interactive game. Disney stores use in-store promotion that complements the online offering and the Disney catalogues.

Disney also uses "cross-media" deals, co-branding agreements, and joint ventures. A deal with Toys "Я" Us, for example, includes a $30-million multimedia plan for magazine, newspaper, movie, radio, and television promotion. Ads will appear on Disney Kids Network and Toon Disney cable network and in a newspaper supplement reaching 50 million homes. The co-branding agreements include Minute Maid's 18-variety line of Disney Xtreme Coolers and Kellogg's lines of Disney-based cereals, toaster pastries, and waffles. Cereals tied to the movie *Monsters, Inc.*, for example, scream when opened! And Disney created a joint venture with Oriental Land to create and promote its newest theme park, the marine-themed DisneySea in Tokyo.[1]

All of the many types of promotion used by Disney are becoming an important part of marketing. Applications of the techniques demonstrate the importance of creativity in communicating with potential customers. In addition, to ensure that a consistent message is delivered through all promotional activities, a process that integrates marketing communications is a necessity.

Promotion represents the fourth element in the marketing mix. The promotional element comprises a mix of tools available for the marketer called the *promotional mix*, which consists of advertising, personal selling, sales promotion, public relations, and direct marketing. All of these elements can be used to (1) inform prospective buyers about the benefits of the product, (2) persuade them to try it, and (3) remind them later about the benefits they enjoyed by using the product. This chapter first gives an overview of the communication process and the promotional elements used in marketing and then discusses direct marketing. Chapter 19 covers advertising, sales promotion, and public relations, and Chapter 20 discusses personal selling.

THE COMMUNICATION PROCESS

COMMUNICATION
The process of conveying a message to others, which requires six elements: a source, a message, a channel of communication, a receiver, and the processes of encoding and decoding.

SOURCE
A company or person who has information to convey.

MESSAGE
The information sent by a source to a receiver in the communication process.

CHANNEL OF COMMUNICATION
The means of conveying a message to a receiver.

Communication is the process of conveying a message to others and requires six elements: a source, a message, a channel of communication, a receiver, and the processes of encoding and decoding[2] (Figure 18–1). The **source** may be a company or person who has information to convey. The information sent by a source, such as a description of a new wireless telephone, forms the **message**. The message is conveyed by means of a **channel of communication** such as a salesperson, advertising media, or public relations tools. Consumers who read, hear, or see the message are the **receivers**.

Encoding and Decoding

RECEIVERS
Consumers who read, hear, or see the message sent by a source in the communication process.

ENCODING
The process of having the sender transform an abstract idea into a set of symbols.

DECODING
The process of having the receiver take a set of symbols, the message, and transform them back to an abstract idea.

Encoding and decoding are essential to communication. **Encoding** is the process of having the sender transform an abstract idea into a set of symbols. **Decoding** is the reverse, or the process of having the receiver take a set of symbols, the message, and transform them back to an abstract idea. Look at the accompanying automobile advertisement: Who is the source, and what is the message?

FIGURE 18–1
The communication process

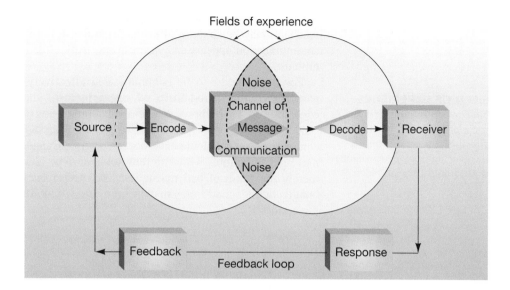

Decoding is performed by the receivers according to their own frame of reference: their attitudes, values, and beliefs.[3] In the ad, Mercedes-Benz is the source and the message is this advertisement, which appeared in a magazine (the channel). How would you interpret (decode) this advertisement? The picture and text in the advertisement show that the source's intention is to generate interest in a vehicle with "the big engine that could"—a statement the source believes will appeal to the readers of the magazine.

The process of communication is not always a successful one. Errors in communication can happen in several ways. The source may not adequately transform the abstract idea into an effective set of symbols, a properly encoded message may be sent through the wrong channel and never make it to the receiver, the receiver may

A source and a message.

Mercedes-Benz
www.mercedes-benz.ca

The big engine that could.

Once upon a time, there was the Mercedes-Benz SLK Roadster. Then we added a 215-horsepower, V-6 engine, creating another SLK – the 320. Its sporty six-speed transmission does zero to sixty in a hair-raising 6.6 seconds. And with a stylish leather and wood interior, you'll arrive at your destination quickly, and in total luxury as well. Now that's a happy ending. To learn more, call 1-800-FOR-MERCEDES or visit us at MBUSA.com. **The SLK 320**

Mercedes-Benz

FIELD OF EXPERIENCE
Similar understanding and knowledge; to communicate effectively, a sender and a receiver must have a mutually shared field of experience.

not properly transform the set of symbols into the correct abstract idea, or finally, feedback may be so delayed or distorted that it is of no use to the sender. Although communication appears easy to perform, truly effective communication can be very difficult.

For the message to be communicated effectively, the sender and receiver must have a mutually shared **field of experience**—similar understanding and knowledge. Figure 18–1 shows two circles representing the fields of experience of the sender and receiver, which overlap in the message. Some of the better-known communication problems have occurred when Canadian companies have taken their messages to cultures with different fields of experience. Many misinterpretations are merely the result of bad translations. For example, KFC made a mistake when its "finger-lickin' good" slogan was translated into Mandarin Chinese as "eat your fingers off"![4]

Feedback

RESPONSE
The impact the message had on the receiver's knowledge, attitudes, or behaviours.

FEEDBACK
The communication flow from receiver back to the sender that helps the sender know whether the message was decoded and understood as intended.

Figure 18–1 shows a line labelled *feedback loop*, which consists of a response and feedback. A **response** is the impact the message had on the receiver's knowledge, attitudes, or behaviours. **Feedback** is the sender's interpretation of the response and indicates whether the message was decoded and understood as intended. Chapter 19 reviews approaches called *pretesting* that ensure that messages are decoded properly.

Noise

NOISE
Extraneous factors that can work against effective communication by distorting a message or the feedback received.

Noise includes extraneous factors that can work against effective communication by distorting a message or the feedback received (Figure 18–1). Noise can be a simple error, such as a printing mistake that affects the meaning of a newspaper advertisement, or using words or pictures that fail to communicate the message clearly. Noise can also occur when a salesperson's message is misunderstood by a prospective buyer, such as when a salesperson's accent, use of slang terms, or communication style make hearing and understanding the message difficult.

Concept Check

1. What are the six elements required for communication to occur?

2. A difficulty for Canadian companies advertising in foreign markets is that the audience does not share the same _____.

3. A misprint in a newspaper ad is an example of _____.

THE PROMOTIONAL ELEMENTS

To communicate with consumers, a company can use one or more of five promotional alternatives: advertising, personal selling, public relations, sales promotion, and direct marketing. Figure 18–2 summarizes the distinctions among these five elements. Three of these elements—advertising, sales promotion, and public relations—are often said to use *mass selling* because they are used with groups of prospective buyers. In contrast, personal selling uses *customized interaction* between a seller and a prospective buyer. Personal selling activities include face-to-face, telephone, and interactive electronic communication. Direct marketing also uses messages customized for specific customers.

PROMOTIONAL ELEMENT	MASS VERSUS CUSTOMIZED	PAYMENT	STRENGTHS	WEAKNESSES
Advertising	Mass	Fees paid for space or time	• Efficient means for reaching large numbers of people	• High absolute costs • Difficult to receive good feedback
Personal selling	Customized	Fees paid to salespeople as either salaries or commissions	• Immediate feedback • Very persuasive • Can select audience • Can give complex information	• Extremely expensive per exposure • Messages may differ between salespeople
Public relations	Mass	No direct payment to media	• Often most credible source in the consumer's mind	• Difficult to get media cooperation
Sales promotion	Mass	Wide range of fees paid, depending on promotion selected	• Effective at changing behaviour in short run • Very flexible	• Easily abused • Can lead to promotion wars • Easily duplicated
Direct marketing	Customized	Cost of communication through mail, telephone, or computer	• Messages can be prepared quickly • Facilitates relationship with customer	• Declining customer response • Database management is expensive

FIGURE 18–2
The promotional mix

ADVERTISING
Any paid form of nonpersonal communication about an organization, good, service, or idea by an identified sponsor.

An attention-getting advertisement.

Advertising

Advertising is any paid form of nonpersonal communication about an organization, good, service, or idea by an identified sponsor. The *paid* aspect of this definition is important because the space for the advertising message normally must be bought. An occasional exception is the public service announcement, where the advertising time or space is donated. A full-page, four-colour ad in *Canadian Living* magazine, for example, costs over $25 000, and over $12 000 in *L'Actualité*. The *nonpersonal* component of advertising is also important. Advertising involves mass media (such as TV, radio, and magazines), which are nonpersonal and do not have an immediate feedback loop as does personal selling. So before the message is sent, marketing research plays a valuable role; for example, it determines that the target market will actually see the medium chosen, and that the message will be understood.

There are several advantages to a firm using advertising in its promotional mix. It can be attention-getting—as with this Altoids ad—and also can communicate specific product benefits to prospective buyers. By paying for the advertising space, a company can control *what* it wants to say and, to some extent, to *whom* the message is sent. If an electronics company wants university students to receive its message about CD players, advertising space is purchased in a campus newspaper. Advertising also allows the company to decide *when* to send its message (which includes how often). The non-personal aspect of advertising also has its advantages. Once the message is created, the same message is sent to all receivers in a market segment. If the message is properly pretested, the company can trust that the same message will be decoded by all receivers in the market segment.

Advertising has some disadvantages. As shown in Figure 18–2 and discussed in depth in Chapter 19, the costs to produce and place a message are significant, and the lack of direct feedback makes it difficult to know how well the message was received.

Personal Selling

The second major promotional alternative is **personal selling**, defined as the two-way flow of communication between a buyer and seller, designed to influence a person's or group's purchase decision. Unlike advertising, personal selling is usually face-to-face communication between the sender and receiver (although telephone and electronic sales are growing). Why do companies use personal selling?

There are important advantages to personal selling, as summarized in Figure 18–2. A salesperson can control to *whom* the presentation is made. Although some control is available in advertising by choosing the medium, some people may read the campus newspaper, for example, who are not in the target audience for CD players. For the CD-player manufacturer, those readers outside the target audience are *wasted coverage*. Wasted coverage can be reduced with personal selling. The personal component of selling has another advantage over advertising in that the seller can see or hear the potential buyer's reaction to the message. If the feedback is unfavourable, the salesperson can modify the message.

The flexibility of personal selling can also be a disadvantage. Different salespeople can change the message so that no consistent communication is given to all customers. The high cost of personal selling is probably its major disadvantage. On a cost-per-contact basis, it is generally the most expensive of the five promotional elements.

Public Relations

Public relations is a form of communication management that seeks to influence the feelings, opinions, or beliefs held by customers, prospective customers, shareholders, suppliers, employees, and other publics about a company and its products or services.[5] Many tools such as special events, lobbying efforts, annual reports, and image management may be used by a public relations department, although publicity often plays the most important role. **Publicity** is a nonpersonal, indirectly paid presentation of an organization, good, or service. It can take the form of a news story, editorial, or product announcement. A difference between publicity and both advertising and personal selling is the "indirectly paid" dimension. With publicity a company does not pay for space in a mass medium (such as television or radio) but attempts to get the medium to run a favourable story on the company. In this sense there is an indirect payment for publicity in that a company must support a public relations staff.

An advantage of publicity is credibility. When you read a favourable story about a company's product (such as a glowing restaurant review), there is a tendency to believe it. Travellers throughout the world have relied on Arthur Frommer's guides such as *Ireland from $60 a Day*. These books outline out-of-the-way, inexpensive restaurants, hotels, inns, and bed-and-breakfast rooms, giving invaluable publicity to these establishments. Such businesses do not (nor can they) buy a mention in the guides, which in recent years have sold millions of copies.

PERSONAL SELLING
The two-way flow of communication between a buyer and seller, often in a face-to-face encounter, designed to influence a person's or group's purchase decision.

PUBLIC RELATIONS
A form of communication management that seeks to influence the feelings, opinions, or beliefs held by customers, prospective customers, shareholders, suppliers, employees, and other publics about a company and its products or services.

PUBLICITY
A nonpersonal, indirectly paid presentation of an organization, good, or service.

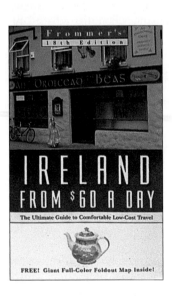

The disadvantages of publicity relate to the lack of the user's control over it. A company can invite a news team to preview its innovative exercise equipment and hope for a favourable mention on the 6 P.M. newscasts. But without buying advertising time, there is no guarantee of any mention of the new equipment or that it will be aired when the target audience is watching. The company representative who calls the station and asks for a replay of the story may be told, "Sorry, it's only news once." With publicity there is little control over what is said, to whom, or when. As a result, publicity is rarely the main component of a promotional campaign.

Sales Promotion

SALES PROMOTION
A short-term inducement of value offered to arouse interest in buying a good or service.

A fourth promotional element is **sales promotion**, a short-term inducement of value offered to arouse interest in buying a good or service. Used in conjunction with advertising or personal selling, sales promotions are offered to intermediaries as well as to ultimate consumers. Coupons, rebates, samples, and sweepstakes are just a few examples of sales promotions discussed later in this chapter.

The advantage of sales promotion is that the short-term nature of these programs (such as a coupon or sweepstakes with an expiration date) often stimulates sales for their duration. Offering value to the consumer in terms of a cents-off coupon or rebate may increase store traffic from consumers who are not store-loyal.[6]

Sales promotions cannot be the sole basis for a campaign because gains are often temporary and sales drop off when the deal ends.[7] Advertising support is needed to convert the customer who tried the product because of a sales promotion into a long-term buyer.[8] If sales promotions are conducted continuously, they lose their effectiveness. Customers begin to delay purchase until a coupon is offered, or they question the product's value. Some aspects of sales promotions also are regulated by the federal government. These issues are reviewed in detail later in Chapter 19.

Direct Marketing

DIRECT MARKETING
Promotional element that uses direct communication with consumers to generate a response in the form of an order, a request for further information, or a visit to a retail outlet.

Another promotional alternative, **direct marketing**, uses direct communication with consumers to generate a response in the form of an order, a request for further information, or a visit to a retail outlet.[9] The communication can take many forms including face-to-face selling, direct mail, catalogues, telephone solicitations, direct response advertising (on television and radio and in print), and online marketing. Like personal selling, direct marketing often consists of interactive communication. It also has the advantage of being customized to match the needs of specific target markets. Messages can be developed and adapted quickly to facilitate one-to-one relationships with customers.

While direct marketing has been one of the fastest-growing forms of promotion, it has several disadvantages. First, most forms of direct marketing require a comprehensive and up-to-date database with information about the target market. Developing and maintaining the database can be expensive and time-consuming. In addition, growing concern about privacy has led to a decline in response rates among some customer groups. Companies with successful direct marketing programs are sensitive to these issues and often use a combination of direct marketing alternatives together, or direct marketing combined with other promotional tools, to increase value for customers.

Concept Check

1. Explain the difference between advertising and publicity when both appear on television.

2. Which promotional element should be offered only on a short-term basis?

3. Cost per contact is high with the _____ element of the promotional mix.

INTEGRATED MARKETING COMMUNICATIONS—DEVELOPING THE PROMOTIONAL MIX

PROMOTIONAL MIX
The combination of one or more of the promotional elements a firm uses to communicate with consumers. The promotional elements include advertising, personal selling, sales promotion, public relations, and direct marketing.

A firm's **promotional mix** is the combination of one or more of the promotional elements it chooses to use. In putting together the promotional mix, a marketer must consider several issues. First, the balance of the elements must be determined. Should advertising be emphasized more than personal selling? Should a promotional rebate be offered? Would public relations activities be effective? Several factors affect such decisions: the target audience for the promotion,[10] the stage of the product's life cycle, characteristics of the product, decision stage of the buyer, and even the channel of distribution. Second, because the various promotional elements are often the responsibility of different departments, coordinating a consistent promotional effort is necessary. A promotional planning process designed to ensure integrated marketing communications can facilitate this goal.

The Target Audience

Promotional programs are directed to the ultimate consumer, to an intermediary (retailer, wholesaler, or industrial distributor), or to both. Promotional programs directed to buyers of consumer products often use mass media because the number of potential buyers is large. Personal selling is used at the place of purchase, generally the retail store. Direct marketing may be used to encourage first-time or repeat purchases. Combinations of many media alternatives are a necessity for some target audiences today. The Marketing NewsNet describes how Generation Y consumers give media only partial attention but can be reached through integrated programs.[11]

Advertising directed to industrial buyers is used selectively in trade publications, such as *Fence Industry* magazine for buyers of fencing material. Because industrial buyers often have specialized needs or technical questions, personal selling is particularly important. The salesperson can provide information and the necessary support after sales.

MARKETING NEWSNET

Communicating with Gen Y... 29.8 Hours per Day!

Recent research indicates that consumers have created 29.8-hour days by using more than one communication medium at the same time—a behaviour often called "multi-tasking." Generation Y seems to be particularly adept at this new phenomenon. For example, it would not be unusual for a university student to log on to the Internet while listening to the radio *and* checking out Web addresses in a magazine! One reason is that media are pervasive—the average student may be exposed to 5000 messages each day—but another reason is the desire to be informed and to "keep in touch." As a result, this group of consumers probably doesn't give its full attention to any single message. Instead, it uses continuous partial attention to scan the media.

Marketers can still communicate with Gen Y by using a variety of promotional tools—from advertising to packaging to word-of-mouth communication—with an integrated message. Which media work particularly well with Gen Y? The most popular television channel is MTV. The most popular magazines are *Sports Illustrated* and *Seventeen*. Favourite

Websites include anything with content related to their interests: celebrities, music, sports, and video games. Another tactic growing in popularity is viral, or "buzz" marketing. Volkswagen, for example, holds on-campus contests to see how many people can fit into a Volkswagen Beetle (the current record is 26). The participants and the observers end up experiencing and talking about the product for at least part of their 29-hour day!

Intermediaries are often the focus of promotional efforts. As with industrial buyers, personal selling is the major promotional ingredient. The salespeople assist intermediaries in making a profit by coordinating promotional campaigns sponsored by the manufacturer and by providing marketing advice and expertise. Intermediaries' questions often pertain to the allowed markup, merchandising support, and return policies.

The Product Life Cycle

www.purina.com

All products have a product life cycle (see Chapter 11), and the composition of the promotional mix changes over the four life-cycle stages, as shown for Purina Puppy Chow in Figure 18–3.

Introduction Stage   Informing consumers in an effort to increase their level of awareness is the primary promotional objective in the introduction stage of the product life cycle. In general, all the promotional mix elements are used at this time, although the use of specific mix elements during any stage depends on the product and situation. News releases about Purina's new nutritional product are sent to veterinary magazines, trial samples are sent to registered dog owners, advertisements are placed in *Dog World* magazine, and the salesforce begins to approach supermarkets to get orders. Advertising is particularly important as a means of reaching as many people as possible to build up awareness and interest. Publicity may even begin slightly before the product is commercially available.

Growth Stage   The primary promotional objective of the growth stage is to persuade the consumer to buy the product—Purina Puppy Chow—rather than substitutes, so the marketing manager seeks to gain brand preference and solidify distribution. Sales promotion assumes less importance in this stage, and publicity is not a factor because it depends on novelty of the product. The primary promotional element is advertising, which stresses brand differences. Personal selling is used to solidify the channel of distribution. For consumer products such as puppy food, the salesforce calls on wholesalers and retailers in hopes of increasing inventory levels and gaining shelf space. For industrial products, the salesforce often tries to get contractual arrangements to be the sole source of supply for the buyer.

FIGURE 18–3
Promotional tools used over the product life cycle of Purina Puppy Chow

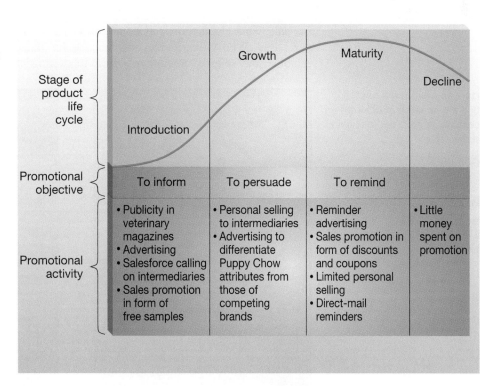

Purina Puppy Chow: a product in the maturity stage of its life cycle.

Maturity Stage In the maturity stage the need is to maintain existing buyers, and advertising's role is to remind buyers of the product's existence. Sales promotion, in the form of discounts and coupons offered to both ultimate consumers and intermediaries, is important in maintaining loyal buyers. In a test of one mature consumer product, it was found that 80 percent of the product's sales at this stage resulted from sales promotions.[12] For the past four years Purina has sponsored the Incredible Dog Challenge, which is now covered by ESPN.[13] Direct marketing actions such as direct mail are used to maintain involvement with existing customers and to encourage repeat purchases. Price cuts and discounts can also significantly increase a mature brand's sales. The salesforce at this stage seeks to satisfy intermediaries. An unsatisfied customer who switches brands is hard to replace.

Decline Stage The decline stage of the product life cycle is usually a period of phaseout for the product, and little money is spent in the promotional mix.

Product Characteristics

The proper blend of elements in the promotional mix also depends on the type of product. Three specific characteristics should be considered: complexity, risk, and ancillary services. *Complexity* refers to the technical sophistication of the product and hence the amount of understanding required to use it. It's hard to provide much information in a one-page magazine ad or 30-second television ad, so the more complex the product, the greater the emphasis on personal selling. Gulfstream asks potential customers to call their senior vice president in its ads. No information is provided for simple products such as Heinz ketchup.

A second element is the degree of *risk* represented by the product's purchase. Risk for the buyer can be assessed in terms of financial risk, social risk, and physical risk. A private jet, for example, might represent all three risks—it is expensive, employees and customers may see and evaluate the purchase, and safety and reliability are important. Although advertising helps, the greater the risk, the greater the need for personal selling. Consumers are unlikely to associate any of these risks with, say, cereal.

The level of *ancillary services* required by a product also affects the promotional strategy. Ancillary services pertain to the degree of service or support required after the sale. This characteristic is common to many industrial products and consumer purchases. Who will provide maintenance for the plane? Advertising's role is to establish the seller's reputation. Direct marketing can be used to describe how a

How do Gulfstream aircraft and Heinz ketchup differ on complexity, risk, and ancillary services?

Gulfstream
www.gulfstreamvsp.com

Heinz
www.heinz.com

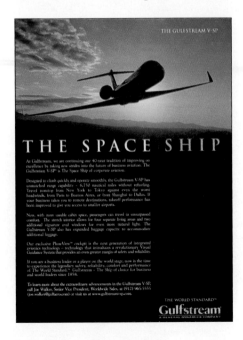

product or service can be customized to individual needs. However, personal selling is essential to build buyer confidence and provide evidence of customer service.

Stages of the Buying Decision

Knowing the customer's stage of decision making can also affect the promotional mix. Figure 18–4 shows how the importance of the promotional elements varies with the three stages in a consumer's purchase decision.

Prepurchase Stage   In the prepurchase stage advertising is more helpful than personal selling because advertising informs the potential customer of the existence of the product and the seller. Sales promotion in the form of free samples also can play an important role to gain low-risk trial. When the salesperson calls on the customer after heavy advertising, there is some recognition of what the salesperson represents. This is particularly important in industrial settings in which sampling of the product is usually not possible.

Purchase Stage   At the purchase stage the importance of personal selling is highest, whereas the impact of advertising is lowest. Sales promotion in the form of coupons, deals, point-of-purchase displays, and rebates can be very helpful in encouraging demand. In this stage, although advertising is not an active influence on the purchase, it is the means of delivering the coupons, deals, and rebates that are often important.

Postpurchase Stage   In the postpurchase stage the salesperson is still important. In fact, the more personal contact after the sale, the more the buyer is satisfied. Advertising is also important to assure the buyer that the right purchase was made. Advertising and personal selling help reduce the buyer's postpurchase anxiety.[14] Sales promotion in the form of coupons and direct marketing reminders can help encourage repeat purchases from satisfied first-time users. Public relations plays a small role in the postpurchase stage.

Channel Strategies

Chapter 15 discussed the channel flow from producer to intermediaries to consumer. Achieving control of the channel is often difficult for the manufacturer, and promotional strategies can assist in moving a product through the channel of distribution. This is where a manufacturer has to make an important decision about whether to use a push strategy, a pull strategy, or both in its channel of distribution.[15]

FIGURE 18–4
How the importance of promotional elements varies during the consumer's purchase decision

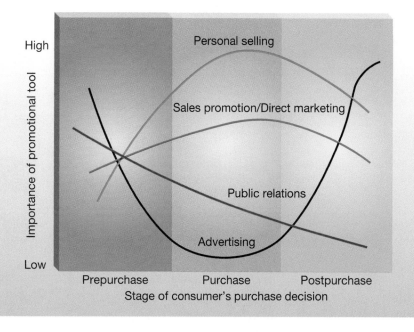

PUSH STRATEGY
Directing the promotional mix to channel members to gain their cooperation in ordering and stocking a product.

www.pepsico.com

PULL STRATEGY
Directing the promotional mix at ultimate consumers to encourage them to ask the retailer for the product.

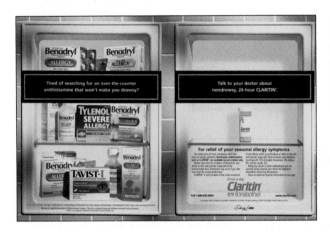

Push Strategy   Figure 18–5A shows how a manufacturer uses a **push strategy**, directing the promotional mix to channel members to gain their cooperation in ordering and stocking the product. In this approach, personal selling and sales promotions play major roles. Salespeople call on wholesalers to encourage orders and provide sales assistance. Sales promotions, such as case discount allowances (20 percent off the regular case price), are offered to stimulate demand. By pushing the product through the channel, the goal is to get channel members to push it to their customers.

Canadian firms such as Pepsi-Cola Canada and Clearly Canadian Beverages spend a significant amount of their marketing resources on maintaining their relationships with their distributors and, through them, with retailers. In general, Canadian consumer goods firms are allocating greater percentages of their promotional budgets toward intermediaries. In some cases, as much as 60 percent of the promotional budget is being allocated to personal selling and sales promotions designed to reach intermediaries, while 40 percent is spent on promotional activities directed toward ultimate consumers.[16]

Pull Strategy   In some instances manufacturers face resistance from channel members who do not want to order a new product or increase inventory levels of an existing brand. As shown in Figure 18–5B, a manufacturer may then elect to implement a **pull strategy** by directing its promotional mix at ultimate consumers to encourage them to ask the retailer for the product. Seeing demand from ultimate consumers, retailers order the product from wholesalers and thus the item is pulled through the intermediaries. Pharmaceutical companies, for example, have typically used marketing programs consisting of personal selling and free samples directed only to doctors.[17] They now also spend millions annually to advertise prescription drugs directly to consumers. The strategy is designed to encourage consumers to ask their physicians for a specific drug by name—pulling it through the channel. Successful advertising strategies, such as Claritin's "Talk to your doctor…" campaign, can have dramatic effects on the sales of a product.[18]

FIGURE 18–5
A comparison of push and pull promotional strategies

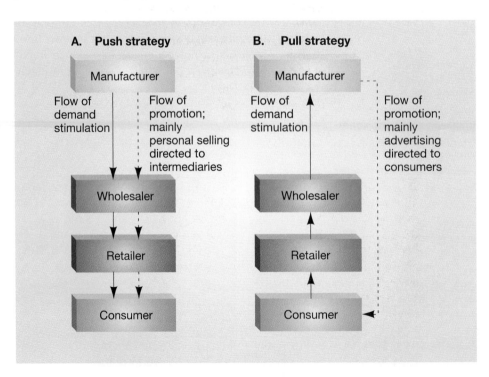

Integrated Marketing Communications

In the past the promotional elements were regarded as separate functions handled by experts in separate departments. The salesforce designed and managed its activities independently of the advertising department, and sales promotion and public relations were often the responsibility of outside agencies or specialists. The result was often an overall communication effort that was uncoordinated and, in some cases, inconsistent. Today the concept of designing marketing communications programs that coordinate all promotional activities—advertising, personal selling, sales promotion, public relations, and direct marketing—to provide a consistent message across all audiences and to maximize the promotional budget is referred to as **integrated marketing communications** (IMC).

The key to developing successful IMC programs is to create a process that facilitates their design and use. A tool used to evaluate a company's current process is the IMC audit. The audit analyzes the internal communication network of the company, identifies key audiences, evaluates customer databases, assesses messages in recent ads, public relations releases, packaging, video news releases, signage, sales promotion pieces, and direct mail, and determines managers' knowledge of IMC.[19] While many organizations are interested in improving their IMC process, a recent survey suggests that fewer than one-third have been successful at implementing IMC. The reasons include lack of expertise, lack of budget, and lack of management approval.[20]

Once the IMC process is implemented, most organizations want to assess its benefits. The tendency is to try to determine which element of promotion "works" better. In an integrated program, however, media advertising might be used to build awareness, sales promotion to generate an inquiry, direct mail to provide additional information to individual prospects, and a personal sales call to complete the transaction. The tools are used for different reasons, and their combined use creates a synergy that should be the focus of the assessment.[21] Another level of integration is necessary when firms have international promotion programs. The accompanying Web Link box describes Disney's effort to integrate its programs in 20 countries![22]

INTEGRATED MARKETING COMMUNICATIONS
The concept of designing marketing communications programs that coordinate all promotional activities—advertising, personal selling, sales promotion, public relations, and direct marketing—to provide a consistent message across all audiences and to maximize the promotional budget.

Concept Check

1. For consumer products, why is advertising emphasized more than personal selling?

2. Explain the differences between a push strategy and a pull strategy.

3. Integrated marketing communications programs provide a _____ message across all audiences.

DEVELOPING THE PROMOTION PROGRAM

Because media costs are high, promotion decisions must be made carefully, using a systematic approach. Paralleling the planning, implementation, and control steps described in the strategic marketing process (Chapter 2), the promotion decision process is divided into (1) developing, (2) executing, and (3) evaluating the promotion program (Figure 18–6). Development of the promotion program focuses on the four *W*s:

- *Who* is the target audience?
- *What* are (1) the promotion objectives, (2) the amounts of money that can be budgeted for the promotion program, and (3) the kinds of promotion to use?
- *Where* should the promotion be run?
- *When* should the promotion be run?

Identifying the Target Audience

The first decision in developing the promotion program is identifying the *target audience*, the group of prospective buyers toward which a promotion program is directed. To the extent that time and money permit, the target audience for the promotion program is the target market for the firm's product, which is identified from marketing research and market segmentation studies. The more a firm knows about its target audience's profile—including their lifestyle, attitudes, and values—the easier it is to develop a promotion program. If a firm wanted to reach you with television and magazine ads, for example, it would need to know what TV shows you watch and what magazines you read.

Specifying Promotion Objectives

After the target audience is identified, a decision must be reached on what the promotion should accomplish. Consumers can be said to respond in terms of a **hierarchy of effects**, which is the sequence of stages a prospective buyer goes through from initial awareness of a product to eventual action (either trial or adoption of the product).[23]

HIERARCHY OF EFFECTS
The sequence of stages a prospective buyer goes through from initial awareness of a product to eventual action (either trial or adoption of the product). The stages include awareness, interest, evaluation, trial, and adoption.

- *Awareness*. The consumer's ability to recognize and remember the product or brand name.
- *Interest*. An increase in the consumer's desire to learn about some of the features of the product or brand.
- *Evaluation*. The consumer's appraisal of the product or brand on important attributes.
- *Trial*. The consumer's actual first purchase and use of the product or brand.
- *Adoption*. Through a favourable experience on the first trial, the consumer's repeated purchase and use of the product or brand.

FIGURE 18–6
The promotion decision process

| Planning
**Developing the
promotion program**
• Identify the target
   audience
• Specify the objectives
• Set the budget
• Select the right
   promotional elements
• Design the promotion
• Schedule the promotion | Implementation
**Executing the
promotion program**
• Pretest the promotion
• Carry out the
   promotion | Control
**Evaluating the
promotion program**
• Post-test the promotion
• Make needed changes |

Corrective actions   Corrective actions

For a totally new product the sequence applies to the entire product category, but for a new brand competing in an established product category it applies to the brand itself. These steps can serve as guidelines for developing promotion objectives.

Although sometimes an objective for a promotion program involves several steps in the hierarchy of effects, it often focuses on a single stage. Regardless of what the specific objective might be, from building awareness to increasing repeat purchases,[24] promotion objectives should possess three important qualities. They should (1) be designed for a well-defined target audience, (2) be measurable, and (3) cover a specified time period.

Setting the Promotion Budget

After setting the promotion objectives, a company must decide on how much to spend. The promotion expenditures needed to reach millions of Canadian households are enormous. Canadian companies spent over $9 billion in 2001 on advertising and, by some estimates, double that amount on sales promotion and direct marketing to reach these households.[25] Some companies such as McDonald's Canada, Procter & Gamble, General Motors of Canada, and the Royal Bank spend hundreds of millions of dollars each year.

Determining the ideal amount for the budget is difficult because there is no precise way to measure the exact results of spending promotion dollars. However, several methods are used to set the promotion budget.[26]

www.royalbank.com

PERCENTAGE OF SALES BUDGETING
Allocating funds to advertising as a percentage of past or anticipated sales, in terms of either dollars or units sold.

Percentage of Sales   In the **percentage of sales budgeting** approach, funds are allocated to promotion as a percentage of past or anticipated sales, in terms of either dollars or units sold. A common budgeting method,[27] this approach is often stated in terms such as, "Our promotion budget for this year is three percent of last year's gross sales." The advantage of this approach is obvious: it's simple and provides a financial safeguard by tying the promotion budget to sales. However, there is a major fallacy in this approach, which implies that sales cause promotion. Using this method, a company may reduce its promotion budget because of a downturn in past sales or an anticipated downturn in future sales—situations where it may need promotion the most.

COMPETITIVE PARITY BUDGETING
Matching the competitors' absolute level of spending or the proportion per point of market share.

Competitive Parity   A second common approach, **competitive parity budgeting**, is matching the competitor's absolute level of spending or the proportion per point of market share. This approach has also been referred to as *matching competitors* or *share of market*. It is important to consider the competition in budgeting.[28] Consumer responses to promotion are affected by competing promotional activities, so if a competitor runs 30 radio ads each week, it may be difficult for a firm to get its message across with only five messages.[29] The competitor's budget level, however, should not be the only determinant in setting a company's budget. The competition might have very different promotional objectives, which require a different level of promotion expenditures.

ALL-YOU-CAN-AFFORD BUDGETING
Allocating funds to promotion only after all other budget items are covered.

All You Can Afford   Common to many small businesses is **all-you-can-afford budgeting**, in which money is allocated to promotion only after all other budget items are covered. As one company executive said in reference to this budgeting process, "Why, it's simple. First, I go upstairs to the controller and ask how much they can afford to give us this year. She says a million and a half. Later, the boss comes to me and asks how much we should spend, and I say 'Oh, about a million and a half.' Then we have our promotion appropriation."[30]

Fiscally conservative, this approach has little else to offer. Using this budgeting philosophy, a company acts as though it doesn't know anything about a promotion–sales relationship or what its promotion objectives are.

FIGURE 18–7
The objective and task
approach

> **OBJECTIVE**
>
> To increase awareness among university students for a new video game. Awareness at the end of one semester should be 20 percent of all students from the existing 0 percent today.
>
> | TASKS | COSTS |
> | --- | --- |
> | Advertisements once a week for a semester in 500 university papers | $280 000 |
> | Direct-mail samples to student leaders on 500 university campuses | 50 000 |
> | Sponsor a national contest for video-game players | 100 000 |
> | Total budget | $430 000 |

OBJECTIVE AND TASK BUDGETING

A budgeting approach whereby the company (1) determines its promotion objectives, (2) outlines the tasks to accomplish these objectives, and (3) determines the promotion cost of performing these tasks.

Objective and Task   The best approach to budgeting is **objective and task budgeting**, whereby the company (1) determines its promotion objectives, (2) outlines the tasks to accomplish these objectives, and (3) determines the promotion cost of performing these tasks.[31]

This method takes into account what the company wants to accomplish and requires that the objectives be specified.[32] Strengths of the other budgeting methods are integrated into this approach because each previous method's strength is tied to the objectives. For example, if the costs are beyond what the company can afford, objectives are reworked and the tasks revised. The difficulty with this method is the judgment required to determine the tasks needed to accomplish objectives. Would two or four insertions in *Time* magazine be needed to achieve a specific awareness level? Figure 18–7 shows a sample media plan with objectives, tasks, and budget outlined. The total amount to be budgeted is $430 000. If the company can afford only $300 000, the objectives must be reworked, tasks redefined, and the total budget recalculated.

Selecting the Right Promotional Tools

Once a budget has been determined, the combination of the five basic IMC tools—advertising, personal selling, sales promotion, public relations, and direct marketing—can be specified. While many factors provide direction for selection of the appropriate mix, the large number of possible combinations of the promotional tools means that many combinations can achieve the same objective. Therefore, an analytical approach and experience are particularly important in this step of the promotion decision process. The specific mix can vary from a simple program using a single tool to a comprehensive program using all forms of promotion. The Olympics have become a very visible example of a comprehensive integrated communication program. Because the Games are repeated every two years, the promotion is almost continuous. Included in the program are advertising campaigns, personal selling efforts by the Olympic committee and organizers, sales promotion activities such as product tie-ins and sponsorships, public relations programs managed by the host cities, and direct marketing efforts targeted at a variety of audiences including governments, organizations, firms, athletes, and individuals.[33] At this stage, it is also important to assess the relative importance of the various tools. While it may be desirable to utilize and integrate several forms of promotion, one may deserve emphasis. The Olympics, for example, place exceptional importance on public relations and publicity.

www.olympics.com

Designing the Promotion

The central element of a promotion program is the promotion itself. Advertising consists of advertising copy and the artwork that the target audience is intended to see or hear. Personal selling efforts depend on the characteristics and skills of the salesperson. Sales promotion activities consist of the specific details of inducements such as coupons, samples, and sweepstakes. Public relations efforts are readily seen in tangible elements such as news releases, and direct marketing actions depend on written, verbal, and electronic forms of delivery. The design of the promotion will play a primary role in determining the message that is communicated to the audience. This design activity is frequently viewed as the step requiring the most creativity. In addition, successful designs are often the result of insight regarding consumers' interests and purchasing behaviour. All of the promotion tools have many design alternatives. Advertising, for example, can utilize fear, humour, or other emotions in its appeal. Similarly, direct marketing can be designed for varying levels of personal or customized appeals. One of the challenges of IMC is to design each promotional activity to communicate the same message.

Scheduling the Promotion

Once the design of each of the promotional program elements is complete, it is important to determine the most effective timing of their use. The promotion schedule describes the order in which each promotional tool is introduced and the frequency of its use during the campaign. New Line Cinema, for example, developed one of the longest promotion schedules on record for its *Lord of the Rings* movie trilogy. To generate interest in the first movie months before its release, a movie "trailer" was shown on the television season premier of *Angel*. Stickers and other products were then released to stores, followed by a global marketing program at Burger King's 10 000 restaurants.[34] Overall, the scheduling of the various promotions was designed to generate interest, bring consumers into theatres, and then encourage additional purchases after seeing the movie. Several factors such as seasonality and competitive promotion activity can also influence the promotion schedule. Businesses such as ski resorts, airlines, and professional sports teams are likely to reduce their promotional activity during the "off" season. Similarly, restaurants, retail stores, and health clubs are likely to increase their promotional activity when new competitors enter the market.

EXECUTING AND EVALUATING THE PROMOTION PROGRAM

As shown earlier in Figure 18–6, the ideal execution of a promotion program involves pretesting each design before it is actually used to allow for changes and modifications that improve its effectiveness. Similarly, post-tests are recommended to evaluate the impact of each promotion and the contribution of the promotion toward achieving the program objectives. The most sophisticated pretest and post-test procedures have been developed for advertising and are discussed in Chapter 19. Testing procedures for sales promotion and direct marketing efforts currently focus on comparisons of different designs or responses of different segments. To fully benefit from IMC programs, companies must create and maintain a test-result database that allows comparisons of the relative impact of the promotional tools, and their execution options, in varying situations. Information from the database will allow informed design and execution decisions and provide support for IMC activities during internal reviews by financial or administrative personnel. The Montreal Expos baseball team, for example, developed a database of information relating attendance to its integrated campaign using special events, merchandise sales, and a loyalty program.

Carrying out the promotion program can be expensive and time-consuming. One researcher estimates that "an organization with sales less than $10 million can successfully implement an IMC program in one year, one with sales between $200 million and $500 million will need about three years, and one with sales between $2 billion and $5 billion will need five years." To facilitate the transition there are approximately 200 integrated marketing communications agencies in operation in North America. In addition, some of the largest advertising agencies are adopting approaches that embrace "total communications solutions." J. Walter Thompson, for example, now has a Total Solutions Group that is responsible for designing integrated programs such as the "Shadows" diamond campaign for De Beers. The campaign appears in 23 countries on television, in print, and in other media and is supported by an extensive range of public relations, point-of-sale, and educational materials. While most agencies still have departments dedicated to promotion, direct marketing, and other specialties, the trend today is clearly toward a long-term perspective in which all forms of promotion are integrated.[35]

Concept Check

1. What are the characteristics of good promotion objectives?

2. What are the weaknesses of the percentage of sales budgeting approach?

3. How have advertising agencies changed to facilitate the use of IMC programs?

DIRECT MARKETING

Direct marketing has many forms and utilizes a variety of media. Several forms of direct marketing—direct mail and catalogues, television, telemarketing, and direct selling—were discussed as methods of nonstore retailing in Chapter 17. In addition, although advertising is discussed in Chapter 19, a form of advertising—direct response advertising—is often an important part of direct marketing. Finally, interactive or online marketing is discussed in detail in Chapter 21. In this section the growth of direct marketing, its value, and key global, technological, and ethical issues are discussed.

The Growth of Direct Marketing

The increasing interest in customer relationship management is reflected in the dramatic growth of direct marketing. The ability to customize communication efforts and create one-to-one interactions is appealing to most marketers, particularly those with IMC programs. While direct marketing methods are not new, the ability to design and use them has increased with the availability of databases. In recent years direct marketing growth—in terms of spending, revenue generated, and employment—has outpaced total economic growth. Direct marketing revenues of about 14 billion in 2001 are expected to grow at a double-digit rate through 2005.[36]

Columbia House is one example of the kinds of companies fuelling the growth in direct marketing. You may have received the company's letters in the mail offering 12 free music CDs if you agree to buy five additional CDs over the next two years. In the past, the CDs were automatically delivered unless the customer told the company not to send them. Today, customers decide when to order. Columbia House also has similar offers for DVDs, videos, and television shows. With more than 16 million club members, Columbia House is the largest direct marketer of entertainment products. Because one of its largest markets is university and college students, its business typically surges about 30 percent in August when students return to campus![37]

Another component of the growth in direct marketing is the increasing popularity of the newest direct marketing channel—the Internet. Continued growth in the number of consumers with Internet access and the number of businesses with Websites and electronic commerce offerings is likely to contribute to the future growth of direct marketing. In fact, online sales in Canada are expected to increase from an estimated $6 billion in 2001 to over $15 billion by 2003.

DIRECT ORDERS
The result of direct marketing offers that contain all the information necessary for a prospective buyer to make a decision to purchase and complete the transaction.

LEAD GENERATION
The result of a direct marketing offer designed to generate interest in a product or a service, and a request for additional information.

TRAFFIC GENERATION
The outcome of a direct marketing offer designed to motivate people to visit a business.

The Value of Direct Marketing

One of the most visible indicators of the value of direct marketing for consumers is the level of use of various forms of direct marketing. For example, about half of the Canadian population has ordered merchandise or services by phone or mail; millions have purchased items from a television offer; millions spend hours accessing online services; and about 20 percent of adults purchase from a catalogue each year. Consumers report many benefits, including the following: they don't have to go to a store, they can usually shop 24 hours a day, buying direct saves time, they avoid hassles with salespeople, they can save money, it's fun and entertaining, and direct marketing offers more privacy than in-store shopping. Many consumers also believe that direct marketing provides excellent customer service.[38] Toll-free telephone numbers, customer service representatives with access to information regarding purchasing preferences, overnight delivery services, and unconditional guarantees all help create value for direct marketing customers. At landsend.com, when customers need assistance they can click a "help" icon and a sales rep will take control of their browser until the correct product is found. "It's like we were walking down the aisle in a store" says one customer.[39]

The value of direct marketing for sellers can be described in terms of the responses it generates.[40] **Direct orders** are the result of offers that contain all the information necessary for a prospective buyer to make a decision to purchase and complete the transaction. Club Med, for example, uses direct e-mail offers to sell "last-minute specials" to people in its database. The messages, which are sent mid-week, describe rooms and air transportation available at a 30 to 40 percent discount if the customer can make the decision to travel on such short notice.[41] **Lead generation** is the result of an offer designed to generate interest in a product or service and a request for additional information. America Online used a contest with its direct advertising and used a direct mail trial offer to generate interest in its latest release.[42] Finally, **traffic generation** is the outcome of an offer designed to motivate people to visit a business. Mitsubishi recently mailed a sweepstakes offer to one million prospective buyers to encourage them to visit a Mitsubishi dealer and test drive the new Galant. The names of prospects who took test drives were entered in the sweepstakes, which included a Galant, a trip to Hawaii, and large-screen TVs as prizes.[43]

Technological, Global, and Ethical Issues in Direct Marketing

The information technology and databases described in Chapter 8 are key elements in any direct marketing program. Databases are the result of organizations' efforts to collect demographic, media, and consumption profiles of customers so that direct marketing tools—such as catalogues—can be directed at specific customers.[44]

While most companies try to keep records of their customers' past purchases, many other types of data are needed to use direct marketing to develop one-to-one relationships with customers. Data, however, have little value by themselves. To translate data into information, the data must be unbiased, timely, pertinent, accessible, and organized in a way that helps the marketing manager make decisions that lead to direct marketing actions. Some data, such as lifestyles, media use, and consumption behaviour, must be collected from the consumers. Other types of data can be collected from the businesses where purchases are made. Today, technology such as optical scanners helps collect data with as little intrusion on the customer as possible. Safeway supermarkets, for example, use scanners to read bar codes and track customers' purchases in its database.

Technology may also prove to be important in the global growth of direct marketing. Compared with Canada and the United States, other countries' direct marketing systems are undeveloped. The mail and telephone systems in many countries are likely to improve, however, creating many new direct marketing opportunities. Developments in international marketing research and database management will also facilitate global growth. In Argentina, for example, mail service is very slow,

ETHICS AND SOCIAL RESPONSIBILITY ALERT

How Do You Like Your E-Mail? "Opt-out" or "Opt-in" Are Your Choices

Billions of e-mail messages are sent each day around the globe. Many of those messages are direct marketing messages, some in the form of very personalized offers from various companies to specific individuals. Marketers believe that e-mail messages that offer one-to-one conversations with each prospective consumer can be effective. The average cost per e-mail message is also attractive: less than $0.1 compared to $.75 to $2.00 for direct mail and $1 to $3 for telemarketing.

But consumers have complained that they are inundated with unsolicited messages—knowm as *spam*—and ignore them, while marketers believe that better management of e-mail campaigns will improve the value of e-mail advertising for customers. Two general approaches to managing e-mail are the "opt-out" versus the "opt-in" systems. The opt-out system allows recipients to decline future messages after the first contact. The opt-in system requires advertisers to obtain e-mail addresses from registration questions on Websites, business-reply cards, and even entry forms from contests or sweepstakes. Research indicates that about 77 percent of unsolicited e-mails are deleted without being read, while only 2 percent of the e-mails received with consumer permission are deleted.

The European Union's Committee for Citizens' Freedoms and Rights recently stated it favoured the opt-out system. However, opt-in systems are still prevalent around the globe. The Canadian Marketing Association (CMA) www.the-cma.org offers consumers a Web-based e-mail preference service that allows Canadian consumers and businesses to register to have their e-mail addresses removed from the marketing lists of companies. Consumers can register at www.e-mps.org, where e-mail addresses are added to an "opt-out" list and companies can no longer contact those consumers. However, the service does not apply to opt-in lists, which are currently used by many companies. What is your opinion on opt-out versus opt-in systems? Which one do you prefer and why?

---

telephone service is poor, and response to some forms of direct marketing such as coupons is negligible. The country is the first, however, to fully deregulate its postal service and expects rapid improvement from the private company, Correo Argentino. In Mexico direct marketing activities are more advanced. Pond's recently mailed 20 000 direct mail offers within Mexico and was surprised by a 33-percent response.[45] Another issue for global marketers is payment. Because fewer consumers have credit cards, alternatives such as C.O.D. and bank deposits are needed.

Global and domestic direct marketers both face challenging and ethical issues today. Of course there has been considerable attention given to some annoying direct marketing activities such as telephone solicitations during dinner and evening hours. Recent concerns about privacy, however, have led to various attempts to provide guidelines that balance consumer and business interests. The European Union passed a consumer privacy law, called the Data Protection Directive, and the Canadian government established The Office of the Privacy Commissioner of Canada as well as the Personal Information Protection and Electronic Documents Act (www.privcom.qc.ca) as a way of protecting the privacy of Canadians. Industry associations including the Canadian Marketing Association (www.the-CMA.org) have also developed guidelines for their members with regard to consumer privacy.[46] The issue of e-mail advertising has also received increased attention from consumers and marketers. The accompanying Ethics and Social Responsibility Alert discusses the issue of e-mail advertising and options for controlling this most recent form of direct marketing communication.[47]

Concept Check

1. The ability to design and use direct marketing programs has increased with the availability of _____ and _____.

2. What are the three types of responses generated by direct marketing activities?

SUMMARY

1 Communication is the process of conveying a message to others and requires a source, a message, a channel of communication, a receiver, and the processes of encoding and decoding.

2 For effective communication to occur, the sender and receiver must have a shared field of experience. The receiver's response provides feedback to the sender and helps determine whether decoding has occurred or noise has distorted the message.

3 The promotional elements consist of advertising, personal selling, sales promotion, public relations, and direct marketing. These tools vary according to whether they are personal; can be identified with a sponsor; and can be controlled with regard to whom, when, where, and how often the message is sent.

4 In selecting the appropriate promotional mix, marketers must consider the target audience, the stage of the product's life cycle, characteristics of the product, decision stage of the buyer, and the channel of distribution.

5 The target for promotional programs can be the ultimate consumer, an intermediary, or both. Ultimate consumer programs rely more on advertising, whereas personal selling is more important in reaching industrial buyers and intermediaries.

6 The emphasis on the promotional tools varies with a product's life cycle. In introduction, awareness is important. During growth, creating brand preference is essential. Advertising is more important in the former stage and personal selling in the latter. Sales promotion helps maintain buyers in the maturity stage.

7 The appropriate promotional mix depends on the complexity of the product, the degree of risk associated with its purchase, and the need for ancillary services.

8 In the prepurchase stage of a customer's purchase decision, advertising and public relations are emphasized; at the purchase stage personal selling, sales promotion, and direct marketing are most important; and during the postpurchase stage advertising, personal selling, and sales promotion are used to reduce postpurchase anxiety.

9 When a push strategy is used, personal selling and sales promotions directed to intermediaries play major roles. In a pull strategy, advertising and sales promotions directed to ultimate consumers are important.

10 Integrated marketing communications programs coordinate all promotional activities to provide a consistent message across all audiences and to maximize the promotion budget.

11 The promotion decision process involves developing, executing, and evaluating the promotion program. Developing the promotion program focuses on determining who is the target audience, what to say, where the message should be said, and when to say it.

12 Setting promotion objectives is based on the hierarchy of effects. Objectives should be measurable, have a specified time period, and state the target audience.

13 Budgeting methods often used are percentage of sales, competitive parity, and the all-you-can-afford approaches. The best budgeting approach is based on the objectives set and tasks required.

14 Selecting, designing, and scheduling promotional elements requires experience and creativity because of the large number of possible combinations of the promotion mix.

15 Direct marketing offers consumers convenience, entertainment, privacy, time savings, low prices, and customer service. Sellers benefit from direct orders, lead generation, and traffic generation.

16 Global opportunities for direct marketing will increase as mail and telephone systems improve worldwide. Consumers' concerns about privacy will be a key issue for direct marketers in the future.

KEY TERMS AND CONCEPTS

advertising p. 471
all-you-can-afford budgeting p. 481
channel of communication p. 468
communication p. 468
competitive parity budgeting p. 481
decoding p. 468
direct marketing p. 473
direct orders p. 485
encoding p. 468
feedback p. 470
field of experience p. 470
hierarchy of effects p. 480
integrated marketing communications p. 479
lead generation p. 485
message p. 468

noise p. 470
objective and task budgeting p. 482
percentage of sales budgeting p. 481
personal selling p. 472
promotional mix p. 474
public relations p. 472
publicity p. 472
pull strategy p. 478
push strategy p. 478
receivers p. 468
response p. 470
sales promotion p. 473
source p. 468
traffic generation p. 485

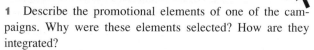

Several large advertising agencies have described shifts in their philosophies to include IMC approaches to communication. In many cases the outcome has been campaigns that utilize a combination of the five promotional elements. Go to J. Walter Thompson's Website at www.jwt.com and review its integrated campaigns.

1 Describe the promotional elements of one of the campaigns. Why were these elements selected? How are they integrated?

2 How would you evaluate the effectiveness of each of the promotional elements used? How would you evaluate the effectiveness of the entire campaign?

Want to get better grades, find tips on how to study more effectively, and stay up to date with happenings in the world of marketing? Visit the Online Learning Centre for practice tests, Study Smart software, and much more! www.mcgrawhill.ca/college/berkowitz
Interested in finding out what marketing looks like in the real world? *Marketing Magazine* is just a click away on your OLC! Visit www.mcgrawhill.ca/college/berkowitz

APPLYING MARKETING CONCEPTS AND PERSPECTIVES

1 After listening to a recent sales presentation, Mary Smith signed up for membership at the local health club. On arriving at the facility, she learned there was an additional fee for racquetball court rentals. "I don't remember that in the sales talk; I thought they said all facilities were included with the membership fee," complained Mary. Describe the problem in terms of the communication process.

2 Develop a matrix to compare the five elements of the promotional mix on three criteria—to *whom* you deliver the message, *what* you say, and *when* you say it.

3 Explain how the promotional tools used by an airline would differ if the target audience were (*a*) consumers who travel for pleasure and (*b*) corporate travel departments that select the airlines to be used by company employees.

4 Suppose you introduced a new consumer food product and invested heavily both in national advertising (pull strategy) and in training and motivating your field salesforce to sell the product to food stores (push strategy). What kinds of feedback would you receive from both the advertising and your salesforce? How could you increase both the quality and quantity of each?

5 Fisher-Price Company, long known as a manufacturer of children's toys, has introduced a line of clothing for children. Outline a promotional plan to get this product introduced in the marketplace.

6 Many insurance companies sell health insurance plans to companies. In these companies the employees pick the plan, but the set of offered plans is determined by the company. Recently Blue Cross–Blue Shield, a health insurance company, ran a television ad stating, "If your employer doesn't offer you Blue Cross–Blue Shield coverage, ask why." Explain the promotional strategy behind the advertisement.

7 Identify the sales promotion tools that might be useful for (*a*) Tastee Yogurt—a new brand introduction, (*b*) 3M self-sticking Post-it notes, and (*c*) Wrigley's Spearmint Gum.

8 Design an integrated marketing communications program—using each of the five promotional elements—for Music Boulevard, an online music store.

9 BMW recently introduced its first sport-utility vehicle, the X5, to compete with other popular SUV vehicles such as the Mercedes-Benz M-class and Jeep Grand Cherokee. Design a direct marketing program to generate (*a*) leads, (*b*) traffic in dealerships, and (*c*) direct orders.

10 Develop a privacy policy for database managers that provides a balance of consumer and seller perspectives. How would you encourage voluntary compliance with your policy? What methods of enforcement would you recommend?

VIDEO CASE 18–1 AIRWALK, INC.

"To effectively communicate with the youth audience," observes Sharon Lee, "it is important to earn their respect by knowing what they think and how they think. You must stay one step ahead of them by constantly studying what they are reading, doing, listening to, playing, and watching."

Sharon Lee speaks from experience. She is an account director at Lambesis, the advertising agency whose integrated marketing communications (IMC) program launched Airwalk shoes into the stratosphere. Lee's job is to be the key link between Airwalk and Lambesis. Her special insights into the youth market have helped make Airwalk's recent success possible. But it wasn't always so easy.

EARLY DAYS: THE STRUGGLE

George Yohn founded the company in 1986—searching for a piece of the fast-growing athletic shoe craze headed by Nike and Reebok. His first efforts marketing an aerobic shoe hit the wall, so he had to find a new product and marketing strategy. Then one of his designers found a sport that other sneaker manufacturers hadn't yet discovered: skateboarding. Yohn watched skateboarders drag their feet to turn and brake, so he developed a special athletic shoe that had extra layers of leather, more rubber in the sole, and double stitching to add longer life. Watching skateboarders do a popular trick of popping the board into the air, he named his new company "Airwalk."

The colourful skateboard shoes almost jumped off the surf and skate shops stocking them, so Airwalk moved into other freestyle segments like snowboarding and BMX and mountain bike riding. Airwalk sales hit $20 million in 1990, but an anti-snowboarding movement soon closed many slopes to snowboarders and sales fell $8 million in 1992.

REPOSITIONING AIRWALK: TARGETING MAINSTREAM YOUTH

At this point Yohn got his great insight: if basketball shoes aren't worn just by basketball players, why should skateboarding shoes be worn just by skateboarders? This gave Yohn his new challenge in 1992: reposition Airwalk to bring its hotdogger image to mainstream youth who were looking for stylish shoes but weren't into skateboarding.

While this repositioning looked great on paper, making it actually happen was a big, big order! Although Airwalk was well known among action-sport enthusiasts, the brand name was almost unknown among mainstream youth. It was at this point that Airwalk introduced its active/casual line of sneakers targeted at these youth, mainly teens.

RESEARCH: FINDING WHAT'S COOL!

Looking back on the early 1990s, it's now possible to find some key elements that have led to Airwalk's success today. One example is the huge effort it puts into "trend spotting" research, discussed earlier in Chapter 8. Dee Gordon, a nationally known expert in trend spotting, is on the staff of Lambesis. She authors the *L Report*, published quarterly by Lambesis, which surveys 18 000 trendsetter and mainstream respondents from ages 14 to 30 and touches on every aspect of their lives. Gordon's research gives other Lambesis employees like Sharon Lee and its clients in-depth insights into what the trendsetters and cool kids are thinking, doing, and buying.

Dee Gordon also studies trends around the world as a foundation for global marketing strategies developed by Lambesis clients.

MAKING IT HAPPEN: THE IMC STRATEGY

Airwalk and Lambesis recognized that much of Nike's and Reebok's success is that they recognize their business is no longer simply about selling shoes—it's about creating a cool image for their shoes. Mastering the marketing of the hard-to-define concept known as "cool" was the task that Airwalk dropped in the lap of Lambesis when Airwalk launched its first active/casual footwear line, targeted at the youth market.

The special challenge for Lambesis was to expand the market for Airwalk shoes by reaching the new, broader cool segments for its shoes without diluting their image among the existing core segments. Chad Farmer, the creative director at Lambesis who is charged with coming up with ideas for Airwalk ads, saw an opportunity to position Airwalk to the youth market as the harbinger of style in casual footwear. At the same time, Airwalk's integrated marketing communications program must retain its shoes' reputation for quality and durability while featuring their original designs and colours.

Chad Farmer's IMC program illustrates the diversity of media and strategies available to creative agencies and clients trying to break through the media clutter. This clutter is reflected in today's youth often seeing about 3000 advertising messages in a typical day. Airwalk's TV commercials and print ads are alive with humour, irreverence, and unrestrained attitude. In many of the 14 countries where Airwalks are sold, youth steal its outdoor posters to hang in their rooms. Airwalk's Website (www.airwalk.com) not only displays its latest line of shoes, but also provides graphics, animation, and recent TV commercials that can be downloaded.

Airwalk's IMC strategy doesn't stop with conventional media. Airwalk team "riders" include the best competitive skateboarders, snowboarders, mountain bike riders, and surfers who represent the company in major competitions globally. Bands and musicians such as the Beastie Boys, Green Day, Pearl Jam, and R.E.M. wear Airwalks—gaining great visibility for the brand. Lambesis gets product placement everywhere from movies and music videos to skateboard/BMX camps and fashion magazine photos.

What has resulted from all of this? In the mid-1990s, sales increased 400 percent in a single year. Today's sales are more than $300 million. And Teen Research Unlimited, a marketing research group, reports that Airwalk is among the top 20 percent of "coolest" brands and still climbing.

Questions

1   What were Airwalk's promotional objectives when it decided to target mainstream youth with its line of shoes in its IMC program?

2   Airwalk has developed what it calls a "tripod" strategy to stress three simple one-word concepts to communicate to the youth it targets and to stress in its IMC program. From reading the case and from what you know about the youth market, what might these be?

3   Describe how Airwalk and Lambesis might use the following media or promotional elements in their IMC strategy to target the notoriously difficult-to-reach target market of youth: (*a*) TV, (*b*) billboards, (*c*) product placements in movies, (*d*) special events, and (*e*) Website. Explain your answers.

4   As Airwalk sells its shoes around the world, it has chosen to use a *global* marketing strategy, as defined in Chapter 7. (*a*) What are the advantages and disadvantages for Airwalk of this strategy? (*b*) For example, how might Airwalk take advantage of this strategy in print ads?

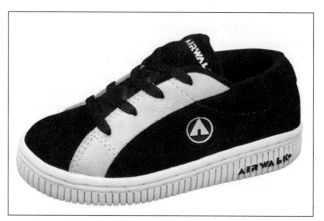

ADVERTISING, SALES PROMOTION, AND PUBLIC RELATIONS

AFTER READING THIS CHAPTER YOU SHOULD BE ABLE TO:

- Explain the differences between product advertising and institutional advertising and the variations within each type.

- Understand the steps used to develop, execute, and evaluate an advertising program.

- Explain the advantages and disadvantages of alternative advertising media.

- Understand the strengths and weaknesses of consumer-oriented and trade-oriented sales promotions.

- Recognize public relations as an important form of communication.

WHAT'S THE FUTURE OF ADVERTISING? THE ANSWER IS PERSONAL!

Have you ever seen an advertisement for a product you probably would never buy? Maybe you saw a cat food ad, but you own three dogs! Or the program you like keeps running milk ads, but you are allergic to dairy products. Well, several new technologies hope to change the world of advertising so that what you see will better match your personal interests. Virtual advertising, personal video recorders, and interactive television are all contributing to the change, and some experts predict that in the future your TV will select commercials targeted specifically for you!

Virtual advertising, for example, uses a patented computer system that digitally inserts ads into sporting events and other broadcasts—not as a traditional 15, 30, or 60-second advertising message, but as a visual part of the program. On ESPN's coverage of baseball games, for example, television viewers see ads that appear to be on the backstop behind home plate that are invisible to fans at the game. Television broadcasts of soccer games show a Coca-Cola logo on the field, even though the players see only green grass!

Personal video recorders (PVRs), such as the units offered by Ultimate TV and TiVo, enable viewers to basically program their own personal network. Just specify the programs you want, and by updating its programming guide through a telephone connection the PVR records all the shows from any channel at any time for the entire season. In addition, by monitoring your recording preferences and using your answers to PVR set-up questions the technology will also record programs that it "thinks" you will like. New versions of the personalization software will soon allow advertisers to insert ads that are specific to the viewer of that television. So if parents typically watch a different television than their children, the ads on the two TVs are likely to be different even if the same program is tuned in!

Finally, interactive television will bring consumers interactive advertising. Eventually, viewers will be able to access information on any product or service seen during a program—a piece of art on Frasier's wall, clothing worn by any of the Friends, or a vehicle driven by a someone on the set of *CSI*. Using their remotes, interested viewers could click on a jacket worn by Chandler or Rachel to reach a menu of additional personalized information—photos of the jacket in the viewer's colour preferences and sizes, reminders of how the jacket would fit with other wardrobe items purchased recently, a list of nearby stores currently carrying the jacket, or online order and payment options. This approach provides instant information requested by the consumer—perhaps the ultimate in personalized advertising![1]

ADVERTISING
Any paid form of nonpersonal communication about an organization, good, service, or idea by an identified sponsor.

Virtual advertising, personal video recorders, and interactive advertising are just a few of the many exciting changes taking place in the field of advertising today. Chapter 18 described **advertising** as any *paid* form of *nonpersonal* communication about an organization, good, service, or idea by an identified sponsor. This chapter describes alternative types of advertisements, the advertising decision process, sales promotion, and public relations.

TYPES OF ADVERTISEMENTS

PRODUCT ADVERTISEMENTS
Advertisements that focus on selling a good or service and take three forms: (1) pioneering (or informational), (2) competitive (or persuasive), and (3) reminder.

As you look through any magazine or watch television, listen to the radio, or browse the Internet, the number of advertisements you see or hear may give you the impression that they have few similarities. Advertisements are prepared for different purposes, but they basically consist of two types: product and institutional. These two types of ads can also be classified on the basis of whether they are intended to get the consumer to take immediate action (*direct-response advertising*) or to influence future purchase or actions (*delayed-response advertising*).

Product Advertisements

Advertisements serve varying purposes. Which ad would be considered (1) pioneering, (2) competitive, and which is used as (3) a reminder?

Focused on selling a good or service, **product advertisements** take three forms: (1) pioneering (or informational), (2) competitive (or persuasive), and (3) reminder. Look at the ads below by Jeep, Xerox, and FTD, and determine the type and objective of each ad.

Dial soap uses reinforcement ads to encourage consumers to keep using the product.

Used in the introductory stage of the life cycle, *pioneering* advertisements tell people what a product is, what it can do, and where it can be found. The key objective of a pioneering advertisement (such as the ad for Jeep's new Liberty) is to inform the target market. Informative ads have been found to be interesting, convincing, and effective.[2]

Advertising that promotes a specific brand's features and benefits is *competitive*. The objective of these messages is to persuade the target market to select the firm's brand rather than that of a competitor. An increasingly common form of competitive advertising is comparative advertising, which shows one brand's strengths relative to those of competitors.[3] The Xerox ad, for example, highlights the competitive advantage of Xerox over its primary competitor Hewlett-Packard. Studies indicate that comparative ads attract more attention and increase the perceived quality of the advertiser's brand.[4] Firms that use comparative advertising need market research to provide legal support for their claims.[5]

Reminder advertising is used to reinforce previous knowledge of a product. The FTD ad shown reminds consumers about the association between its product and a special event—in this case, Valentine's Day. Reminder advertising is good for products that have achieved a well-recognized position and are in the mature phase of their product life cycle. Another type of reminder ad, *reinforcement*, is used to assure current users they made the right choice. One example: "Aren't you glad you use Dial? Don't you wish everybody did?"

Institutional Advertisements

INSTITUTIONAL ADVERTISEMENTS
Advertisements designed to build goodwill or an image for an organization, rather than promote a specific good or service.

www.ibm.com

The objective of **institutional advertisements** is to build goodwill or an image for an organization, rather than promote a specific good or service. Institutional advertising has been used by companies such as the Royal Bank, Pfizer, and IBM Canada to build confidence in the company name.[6] Often this form of advertising is used to support the public relations plan or counter adverse publicity. Four alternative forms of institutional advertisements are often used:

1. *Advocacy* advertisements state the position of a company on an issue. For example, Molson's "Take Care" ads encourage the responsible use of alcohol.
2. *Pioneering institutional* advertisements, like the pioneering ads for products discussed earlier, are used for announcement about what a company is, what it can do, or where it is located. Recent Bayer ads stating "We cure more headaches than you think" are intended to inform consumers that the company produces many products in addition to Aspirin.
3. *Competitive institutional* advertisements promote the advantages of one product class over another and are used in markets where different product classes compete for the same buyers. The Steel Alliance, for example, made up of major North American steel producers including Stelco, Dofasco, and Ipsco,

spend millions on advertising promoting steel's advantages over alternative products like wood, plastic, and aluminum.

4. *Reminder institutional* advertisements, like the product form, simply bring the company's name to the attention of the target market again.

As mentioned earlier, advertising can also be classified as either direct-response advertising or delayed-response advertising. *Direct-response advertising* seeks to motivate the customer to take immediate action, such as a television ad asking you to phone a toll-free telephone number and place an order right now. *Delayed-response advertising*, on the other hand, presents images and/or information designed to influence the consumer in the near future when making purchases or taking other actions. Direct marketers (Chapters 17, 19, 21) often rely on direct-response advertising as part of their direct marketing efforts. However, even traditional marketers are also using this form of advertising as they attempt to obtain an immediate return on their advertising dollar and measured response in terms of advertising effectiveness.

Concept Check

1. What is the difference between pioneering and competitive ads?

2. What is the purpose of an institutional advertisement?

3. What is direct-response advertising?

DEVELOPING THE ADVERTISING PROGRAM

The promotion decision process described in Chapter 18 can be applied to each of the promotional elements. Advertising, for example, can be managed by following the three steps (developing, executing, and evaluating) of the process.

Identifying the Target Audience

To develop an effective advertising program advertisers must identify the target audience. All aspects of an advertising program are likely to be influenced by the characteristics of the prospective consumer. Understanding the lifestyles, attitudes, and demographics of the target market is essential. Mary Quinlan, vice chairman of the MacManus Group advertising agency, suggests that when women are the target it is important that the ad content reflects that women "like to see other women who are diverse, confident, and naturally beautiful," and that "women respond to emotional truth and real-life experience."[7] Similarly, the placement of ads depends on the audience. When Hummer, the biggest and most expensive sport-utility vehicle in the market, began its $3-million campaign targeted at "rugged individualists" with incomes above $200 000, it selected *Wired, Spin, Red Herring, Business Week, Skiing*, and *Cigar Aficionado* to carry the ads.[8] Even scheduling can depend on the audience. Claritin, the nation's most prescribed allergy medication, schedules its use of brochures, in-store displays, coupons, and advertising to correspond to the allergy season, which varies by geographic region.[9] To eliminate possible bias that might result from subjective judgements about some population segments, advertising program decisions should be based on market research about the target audience.[10]

Specifying Advertising Objectives

The guidelines for setting promotion objectives described in Chapter 18 also apply to setting advertising objectives. This step helps advertisers with other choices in the promotion decision process such as selecting media and evaluating a campaign.

Advertising with an objective of creating awareness, for example, would be better matched with a magazine than a directory such as the Yellow Pages.[11] Similarly, an advertiser looking to induce consumers to trial or to take other direct action like visit a store location would use a direct-response form of advertising like direct mail. The Canadian Advertising Foundation believes that establishing advertising objectives is so important that it established the CASSIE Awards, where advertisers are recognized for achieving ad campaign objectives. Experts believe that factors such as product category, brand, and consumer involvement in the purchase decision may change the importance—and, possibly, the sequence—of the stages of the hierarchy of effects. Snickers, for example, knew that its consumers were unlikely to engage in elaborate information processing when it designed a recent campaign. The result was ads with simple humorous messages rather than extensive factual information.

Setting the Advertising Budget

The methods used to set the overall promotion budget as outlined in Chapter 18 can be used to establish a specific advertising budget. As with the promotional or IMC budget, the best approach to setting the ad budget is the objective and task approach. There are numerous advertising options available to the advertiser and most of the alternatives require substantial financial commitments. A formal budgeting process that involves matching the target audience to the available advertising options, evaluating the ability of those options to achieve specified objectives, and weighing the relative costs of the advertising options is definitely a requirement for effective advertising.

Designing the Advertisement

An advertising message usually focuses on the key benefits of the product that are important to a prospective buyer in making trial and adoption decisions. The message depends on the general form or appeal used in the ad and the actual words included in the ad.

Message Content   Most advertising messages are made up of both informational and persuasional elements. These two elements, in fact, are so intertwined that it is sometimes difficult to tell them apart. For example, basic information contained in many ads such as the product name, benefits, features, and price is presented in a way that tries to attract attention and encourage purchase. On the other hand, even the most persuasive advertisements must contain at least some basic information to be successful.

Information and persuasive content can be combined in the form of an appeal to provide a basic reason for the consumer to act. Although the marketer can use many different types of appeals, common advertising appeals include fear appeals,[12] sex appeals, and humorous appeals.

Fear appeals suggest to the consumer that he or she can avoid some negative experience through the purchase and use of a product or through a change in behaviour. Insurance companies often try to show the negative effects of premature death on the relatives of those who don't carry enough life or mortgage insurance. Food producers encourage the purchase of low-fat, high-fibre products as a means of reducing cholesterol levels and the possibility of a heart attack.[13] When using fear appeals, the advertiser must be sure that the appeal is strong enough to get the audience's attention and concern, but not so strong that it will lead them to "tune out" the message. The accompanying Marketing NewsNet suggests some guidelines for developing an ad with a fear appeal.[14]

In contrast, *sex appeals* suggest to the audience that the product will increase the attractiveness of the user. Sex appeals can be found in almost any product category, from automobiles to toothpaste. Unfortunately, many commercials that use sex

Molson's "pet beaver" commerical uses humour to appeal to Canadian beer drinkers. What makes humorous ads successful? What are their possible drawbacks? See the text for answers.

Molson

www.iam.ca

appeals are successful only at gaining the attention of the audience; they have little impact on how consumers think, feel, or act. Some advertising experts even argue that such appeals get in the way of successful communication by distracting the audience from the purpose of the ad.

Humorous appeals imply either directly or more subtly that the product is more fun or exciting than competitors' offerings. As with fear and sex appeals, the use of humour is widespread in advertising and can be found in many product categories. In fact, if you flip through the winners' book for the recent Marketing Awards hosted by *Marketing* magazine, you will come face to face with the fact that the use of humour is sweeping the ad world. No product sector appears immune. The Breast Cancer Society of Canada even used humour in its ads encouraging women to do regular breast exams, and its TV spot was the gold winner in the public-service category.[15] Molson also has people laughing with its series of "I Am Canadian" spots, featuring characters like Joe the Patriot and the pet beaver whose Canadian owner unleashes him on mocking Americans. Unfortunately for the advertiser, humour tends to wear out quickly, eventually boring the consumer. Another problem with humorous appeals is that their effectiveness may vary across cultures.[16]

MARKETING NEWSNET

Designing Ads That Deal with Negative Issues

Have you ever developed anxiety over a message you've received from an advertisement? If your answer is yes, chances are that your reaction was the result of what advertisers call a *fear appeal*. Examples you may be familiar with include fire or smoke detector ads that depict a family home burning, political candidate endorsements that warn against the rise of other unpopular ideologies, or social cause ads warning of the serious consequences of drug use, alcoholism, or unsafe sex. This approach is based on three steps—the creation of a fearful situation by giving the audience information about the severity of the threat and the probability of its occurrence, describing the effectiveness of a solution or coping response, and suggesting how the solution can be implemented.

How individuals react to fear appeals, though, varies significantly with their prior knowledge and experience. Indeed, the varying levels of anxiety that result from the ads suggest several ethical concerns for the psychological well-being of consumers. Therefore, advertisers need to consider four guidelines when developing their ads:

1. Whenever possible, use low or moderate (rather than high) levels of fear.
2. Offer more than one alternative as a solution.
3. Avoid deceptive implications (e.g., that a product will completely eliminate a fearful condition).
4. Pretest each ad to ensure a balance between the message and the level of anxiety.

Creating the Actual Message   The "creative people" in an advertising agency—copywriters and art directors—have the responsibility to turn appeals and features such as quality, style, dependability, economy, and service into attention-getting, believable advertisements. Translating the creative ideas into an actual advertisement is a complex process. Designing quality artwork, layout, and production for the advertisements is also often costly and time-consuming. High-quality TV commercials typically cost more than $200 000 to produce a 30-second ad. High-visibility integrated ad campaigns can even be more expensive. For example, Sony Canada's ad campaign to support the launch of its MD Walkman involved TV spots, print ads, and wild, creative posters. More frequently Canadians also are seeing sports heroes or rock stars appearing in ads as advertisers turn to "celebrity spokespeople" as a way to increase the visibility of their ads. To judge for yourself the quality of some recent Canadian advertising, see the accompanying Web Link.[17]

Concept Check

1. What are the three common advertising appeals?

2. Who is responsible for turning appeals and product features into attention-getting advertising?

Selecting the Right Media

Every advertiser must decide where to place its advertisements. The alternatives are the *advertising media*, the means by which the message is communicated to the

FIGURE 19–1
Canadian advertising expenditures by medium, as a percentage of total ad spending

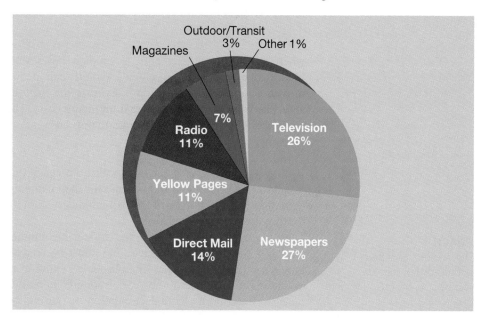

The use of celebrity spokespersons is popular in Canadian advertising.

target audience. Newspapers, magazines, radio, and TV are examples of advertising media. This "media selection" decision is related to the target audience, type of product, nature of the message, campaign objectives, available budget, and the costs of the alternative media. Figure 19–1 shows the distribution of the more than $9 billion spent on advertising in Canada among the many media alternatives.[18] Some of Canada's leading advertisers include General Motors of Canada, Sears Canada, BCE (Bell Canada Enterprises), the Government of Canada, Procter & Gamble, Rogers Communications, The Hudson's Bay Co., and Ford Motor Co. of Canada.

Choosing a Medium and a Vehicle within That Medium

In deciding where to place advertisements, a company has several media to choose from and a number of alternatives, or vehicles, within each medium. Often advertisers use a mix of media forms and vehicles to maximize the exposure of the message to the target audience while at the same time minimizing costs. These two conflicting goals of (1) maximizing exposure and (2) minimizing costs are of central importance to media planning.

Basic Terms

Media buyers speak a language of their own, so every advertiser involved in selecting the right media for their campaigns must be familiar with some common terms used in the advertising industry. Figure 19–2 shows the most common terms used in media decisions.

Because advertisers try to maximize the number of individuals in the target market exposed to the message, they must be concerned with reach. **Reach** is the number of different people or households exposed to an advertisement. The exact definition of reach sometimes varies among alternative media. Newspapers often use reach to describe their total circulation or the number of different households that

REACH
The number of different people or households exposed to an advertisement.

FIGURE 19–2
The language of the media buyer

TERM	WHAT IT MEANS
Reach	The number of different people or households exposed to an advertisement.
Rating	The percentage of households in a market that are tuned to a particular TV show or radio station.
Frequency	The average number of times an individual is exposed to an advertisement.
Gross rating points (GRPs)	Reach (expressed as a percentage of the total market) multiplied by frequency.
Cost per thousand (CPM)	The cost of advertising divided by the number of thousands of individuals or households who are exposed.

RATING
The percentage of households in a market that are tuned to a particular TV show or radio station.

FREQUENCY
The average number of times a person in the target audience is exposed to a message or advertisement.

GROSS RATING POINTS (GRPs)
A reference number for advertisers, created by multiplying reach (expressed as a percentage of the total market) by frequency.

COST PER THOUSAND (CPM)
The cost of reaching 1000 individuals or households with an advertising message in a given medium.

buy the paper. Television and radio stations, in contrast, describe their reach using the term **rating**—the percentage of households in a market that are tuned to a particular TV show or radio station. In general, advertisers try to maximize reach in their target market at the lowest cost.

Although reach is important, advertisers are also interested in exposing their target audience to a message more than once. This is because consumers often do not pay close attention to advertising messages, some of which contain large amounts of relatively complex information. When advertisers want to reach the same audience more than once, they are concerned with **frequency**, the average number of times a person in the target audience is exposed to a message or advertisement. Like reach, greater frequency is generally viewed as desirable.[19] Studies also indicate that with repeated exposure to advertisements consumers respond more favourably to new brand extensions.[20]

When reach (expressed as a percentage of the total market) is multiplied by frequency, an advertiser will obtain a commonly used reference number called **gross rating points** (GRPs). To obtain the appropriate number of GRPs to achieve an advertising campaign's objectives, the media planner must balance reach and frequency. The balance will also be influenced by cost. **Cost per thousand** (CPM) refers to the cost of reaching 1000 individuals or households with the advertising message in a given medium (*M* is the Roman numeral for 1000).

Different Media Alternatives

Figure 19–3[21] summarizes the advantages and disadvantages of the important advertising media, which are described in more detail below.

Television   Television is a valuable medium because it communicates with sight, sound, and motion. Print advertisements alone could never give you the sense of a sports car cornering at high speed or communicate Ford's excitement about its new Mustang. In addition, network television is the only medium that can reach 99 percent of the homes in Canada.[22]

Television's major disadvantage is cost: the average price of a prime-time 30-second spot on a Canadian national network can be $30 000.[23] Because of these high charges, many advertisers have reduced the length of their commercials from 30 seconds to 15 seconds. This practice, referred to as *splitting 30s*, reduces costs but severely restricts the amount of information and emotion that can be conveyed. Research indicates, however, that two different versions of a 15-second commercial, run back-to-back, will increase recall over long intervals.[24]

Another problem with television is the likelihood of *wasted coverage*—having people outside the market for the product see the advertisement. In recent years the cost and wasted-coverage problems of TV have been reduced through the introduction

MEDIUM	ADVANTAGES	DISADVANTAGES
Television	Reaches extremely large audience; uses picture, print, sound, and motion for effect; can target specific audiences.	High cost to prepare and run ads; short exposure time and perishable message; difficult to convey complex information.
Radio	Low cost; can target specific audiences; ads can be placed quickly; can use sound, humour, and intimacy effectively.	No visual element; short exposure time and perishable message; difficult to convey complex information.
Magazines	Can target specific audiences; high-quality colour; long life of ad; ads can be clipped and saved; can convey complex information.	Long time needed to place ad; relatively high cost; competes for attention with other magazine features.
Newspapers	Excellent coverage of local markets; ads can be placed and changed quickly; ads can be saved; quick consumer response; low cost.	Ads compete for attention with other newspaper features; short life span; poor or no colour.
Internet	Video and audio capabilities; animation can capture attention; ads can be interactive and link to advertiser.	Animation and interactivity require large files and more time to "load." Effectiveness is still uncertain.
Outdoor	Low cost; local market focus; high visibility; opportunity for repeat exposures.	Message must be short and simple; low selectivity of audience; criticized as a traffic hazard.
Direct mail	Best for targeting specific audiences; very flexible; ad can be saved; measurable.	Relatively high cost; audience often see it as "junk mail."

FIGURE 19–3
Advantages and disadvantages of major advertising media

www.muchmusic.com

INFOMERCIALS
Program-length (30-minute) advertisements that take an educational approach to communication with potential customers.

of cable and direct broadcast (satellite) channels. Advertising time is often less expensive on cable and direct broadcast channels than on the major networks. There are currently many channel options—such as TSN, Much Music, HGTV, Canadian Learning, and CNN—that reach very narrowly defined audiences. Other forms of television are changing television advertising also. Pay-per-view movie services and PVRs, for example, offer the potential of commerical-free viewing.

Another popular form of television advertising is the infomercial. **Infomercials** are program-length (30-minute) advertisements that take an educational approach to communication with potential customers. Volvo, Club Med, General Motors, Mattel, Revlon, and many other companies are using infomercials as a means of providing information that is relevant, useful, and entertaining to prospective customers. In many cases, marketers are using infomericals for direct-response purposes, asking customers to order products and/or to request further information during the airing.

Radio   There are over 900 radio stations in Canada.[25] The major advantage of radio is that it is a segmented medium. There are jazz stations, classic music stations, all-talk shows, and hard rock stations, all listened to by different market segments. The average university or college student is a surprisingly heavy radio listener and spends more time during the day listening to radio than watching network television—2.2 hours versus 1.6 hours. Thus, advertisers with university and college students as their target market must consider radio.

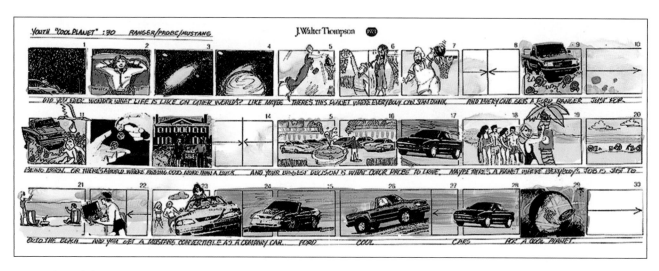

TV storyboards lead to commercials, which communicate with sight, sound, and motion.

The disadvantage of radio is that it has limited use for products that must be seen. Another problem is the ease with which consumers can tune out a commercial by switching stations. Radio is also a medium that competes for people's attention as they do other activities such as driving, working, or relaxing. Peak radio listening time, for example, is during the drive times (6 to 10 A.M. and 4 to 7 P.M.).

Finally, radio, like television, is also considered a passive medium. To overcome the passive nature of the medium, Pepsi-Cola Canada recently launched its "interactive radio" advertising campaign to support its Pepsi Taste Challenge. The announcer instructs listeners to turn their speaker balance control to the right if they prefer Pepsi, and to the left if they prefer Coke. The right speaker plays a message that begins "Congratulations. You picked Pepsi . . ." while the left says, "Hey we're sorry to hear that . . .." If you don't want to play along, you'll hear both messages simultaneously. Pepsi-Cola says this is the first such interactive radio campaign in Canada.[26]

Magazines   Magazines have become a very specialized medium. There are about 500 consumer magazines in Canada.[27] The marketing advantage of this medium is the great number of special-interest publications that appeal to narrowly defined segments. Runners read *Runner's World*, sailors buy *Sail*, gardeners subscribe to *Gardening Life*, and children peruse *Sports Illustrated for kids*. Each magazine's readers often represent a unique profile. Take the *Rolling Stone* reader, who tends to travel, backpack, and ski more than most people—so a manufacturer of ski equipment that places an ad in *Rolling Stone* knows it is reaching the desired target audience. In addition to the distinct audience profiles of magazines, good colour production is an advantage that allows magazines to create strong images.

The cost of advertising in national magazines is a disadvantage, but many national publications publish regional and even metro editions, which reduce the absolute cost and wasted coverage. In addition to cost, a limitation to magazines is their infrequency. At best, magazines are printed on a weekly basis, with many specialized publications appearing only monthly or less often.

Newspapers   Newspapers are an important local medium with excellent reach potential. Because of the daily publication of most papers, they allow advertisements to focus on specific current events, such as a "24-hour sale." Local retailers often use newspapers as their sole advertising medium.

Newspapers are rarely saved by the purchaser, however, so companies are generally limited to ads that call for an immediate customer response (although customers can clip and save ads they want). Companies also cannot depend on newspapers for colour reproduction as good as that in most magazines.

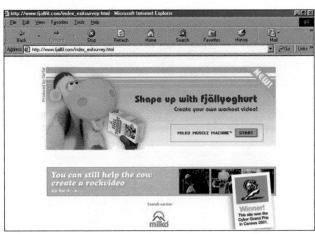

Internet advertising must engage and entertain the viewer.

www.globeandmail.ca

National advertising campaigns rarely include this medium except in conjunction with local distributors of their products. In these instances both parties often share the advertising costs using a cooperative advertising program, which is described later in this chapter. Another exception is the use of newspapers such as *The Globe and Mail*, which has national distribution.

In an effort to deliver timely news coverage, many newspapers are delivering online and this is opening up new advertising potential for such newspapers.

Direct Mail   Direct mail advertising is often considered the cornerstone of many direct marketers' (Chapter 17, Chapter 18) efforts to reach consumers. But any advertiser looking for good audience selectivity can find direct mail advertising effective. Also, direct mail advertising allows the marketer to provide more information to the customer than is possible on a television or radio spot. In many cases, direct mail advertising is being used in conjunction with other media, particularly broadcast, in order to create integrated marketing communications. The mass media are used to create awareness while direct mail advertising is used to build a relationship and facilitate a purchase.

One disadvantage of direct mail advertising is its rising costs due to postal cost increases. Another limitation is that people often view direct mail advertising as junk, and are reluctant to open such mail. One novel approach to overcome that problem is the use of *self-mailers*. Many Canadian advertisers are sending out these simple white envelopes to their consumers. Bereft of any promotional messaging, the white envelopes are more likely to be opened by the consumer. The increased use of robust databases is also improving the advertiser's ability to send mail only to well-defined targets with appealing offers, and thus increasing the chances of consumer response.[28]

Internet   The Internet represents a relatively new medium for advertisers, although it has already attracted a wide variety of industries. Online advertising is similar to print advertising in that it offers a visual message. It has additional advantages, however, because it can also use the audio and video capabilities of the Internet. Sound and movement may simply attract more attention from viewers, or they may provide an element of entertainment to the message. Online advertising also has the unique feature of being interactive. Called *rich media*, these interactive ads have drop-down menus, built-in games, or search engines to engage viewers. While online advertising is relatively small compared to other traditional media, it offers an opportunity to reach younger consumers who have developed a preference for online communication.[29]

There are a variety of online advertising options. The most common—banner ads—represent approximately 50 percent of online ad expenditures, although their effectiveness has declined to a current "click-through" rate of .3 percent. IBM used a banner ad with the question "What's on your mind?" to engage viewers by encouraging them to view a larger ad, and then click through to IBM's Website. Other forms of online advertising include skyscrapers, pop-ups, interstitials, and minisites, which use streaming video and audio, and are becoming similar to television advertising. Many advertisers are also adding entertainment elements. The online advertising grand prize winner of the Cannes International Advertising Festival, for example, was a Website for Milko milk where visitors could create their own work-out video! Online advertising also includes e-mail marketing (discussed in Chapter 18). Lee Jeans sent 200 000 e-mail messages to young men, who forwarded the message to an average of six friends each. The messages directed consumers to an online game, and ultimately to stores where secret codes for prizes were printed on price tags![30]

One disadvantage of online advertising is that because the medium is new, technical and administrative standards for the various formats are still evolving. This situation makes it difficult for advertisers to run national online campaigns across multiple sites. The Internet Advertising Bureau of Canada (www.IABCanada.com) provides some guidance for online advertising standards and makes recommendations for new formats. Another disadvantage of online advertising is the difficulty of measuring impact. Online advertising lags behind radio, TV, and print in offering advertisers proof of effectiveness. To address this issue several companies are testing methods of tracking where viewers go on their computer in the days and weeks after seeing an ad. Nielsen's rating service, for example, measures actual click-by-click behaviour through meters installed on the computers of 225 000 individuals in 26 countries both at home and at work (see www.nielsen-netratings.com for recent ratings). Another suggestion being tested by Volvo and Unilever is "permission-based" advertising where viewers agree to watch a commercial online in exchange for points, samples, or access to premium content, and advertisers pay only for completed views![31] Internet advertising is discussed further in Chapter 21 in the context of interactive marketing.

A catchy billboard ad for eggs.

Outdoor A very effective medium for reminding consumers about your product is outdoor advertising. The most common form of outdoor advertising, called *billboards*, often results in good reach and frequency and has been shown to increase purchase rates.[32] The visibility of this medium is good supplemental reinforcement for well-known products, and it is a relatively low-cost, flexible alternative. A company can buy space just in the desired geographical market. A disadvantage to billboards, however, is that no opportunity exists for lengthy advertising copy. Also, a good billboard site depends on traffic patterns and sight lines. In many areas environmental laws have limited the use of this medium.

If you have ever lived in a metropolitan area, chances are you might have seen another form of outdoor advertising, transit advertising. This medium includes messages on the interior and exterior of buses, subway cars, and taxis. As use of mass transit grows, transit advertising may become increasingly important. Selectivity is available to advertisers, who can buy space by neighbourhood or bus route. For example, Shoppers Drug Mart of Toronto used two Toronto Transit Commission buses wrapped with Life labels and slogans and selected Toronto-area bus routes with possible high-traffic morning and evening rush hours. One disadvantage to this medium is that the heavy travel times, when the audiences are the largest, are not conducive to reading advertising copy. People are standing shoulder to shoulder on the subway, hoping not to miss their stop, and little attention is paid to the advertising.

Captivate TV Network offers "TV in Elevators."

Other Media   As traditional media have become more expensive and cluttered, advertisers have been attracted to a variety of nontraditional advertising options, called *place-based media*. Messages are placed in locations that attract a specific target audience such as airports, doctors' offices, health clubs, theatres (where ads are played on the screen before the movies are shown), even bathrooms of bars, restaurants, and nightclubs![33] You have probably also seen advertising on video screens on gas pumps, ATMs, and in elevators!

Selection Criteria   Choosing between these alternative media is difficult and depends on several factors. First, knowing the media habits of the target audience is essential to deciding among the alternatives. Second, occasionally product attributes necessitate that certain media be used. For example, if colour is a major aspect of product appeal, radio is excluded. Newspapers allow advertising for quick actions to confront competitors, and magazines are more appropriate for complicated messages because the reader can spend more time reading the message. The final factor in selecting a medium is cost. When possible, alternative media are compared using a common denominator that reflects both reach and cost—a measure such as CPM.

Scheduling the Advertising

There is no correct schedule to advertise a product, but three factors must be considered. First is the issue of *buyer turnover*, which is how often new buyers enter the market to buy the product. The higher the buyer turnover, the greater the amount of advertising required. A second issue in scheduling is the *purchase frequency*; the more frequently the product is purchased, the less repetition is required. Finally, companies must consider the *forgetting rate*, the speed with which buyers forget the brand if advertising is not seen.

Setting schedules requires an understanding of how the market behaves. Most companies tend to follow one of three basic approaches:

1. *Continuous (steady) schedule.* When seasonal factors are unimportant, advertising is run at a continuous or steady schedule throughout the year.
2. *Flighting (intermittent) schedule.* Periods of advertising are scheduled between periods of no advertising to reflect seasonal demand.
3. *Pulse (burst) schedule.* A flighting schedule is combined with a continuous schedule because of increases in demand, heavy periods of promotion, or introduction of a new product.

For example, products such as dry breakfast cereals have a stable demand throughout the year and would typically use a continuous schedule of advertising. In contrast, products such as snow skis and suntan lotions have seasonal demands and receive flighting-schedule advertising during the seasonal demand period. Some products such as toys or automobiles require pulse-schedule advertising to facilitate sales throughout the year and during special periods of increased demand (such as holidays or new car introductions). Some evidence suggests that pulsing schedules are superior to other advertising strategies.[34] In addition, recent findings indicate that the effectiveness of a particular ad "wears out" quickly and, therefore, many alternative forms of an advertisement may be more effective.[35]

Concept Check

1. You see the same ad in *Time* and *Maclean's* magazines and on billboards and TV. Is this an example of reach or frequency?

2. Why has the Internet become a popular advertising medium?

3. What factors must be considered when choosing among alternative media?

EXECUTING THE ADVERTISING PROGRAM

Executing the advertising program involves pretesting the advertising copy and actually carrying out the advertising program. An advertiser once remarked, "I know half my advertising is wasted, but I don't know what half." By evaluating advertising efforts marketers can try to ensure that their advertising expenditures are not wasted.[36] Evaluation is done usually at two separate times: before and after the advertisements are run in the actual campaign. Several methods used in the evaluation process at the stages of idea formulation and copy development are discussed below. Post-testing methods are reviewed in the section on evaluation.

Pretesting the Advertising

To determine whether the advertisement communicates the intended message or to select among alternative versions of the advertisement, **pretests** are conducted before the advertisements are placed in any medium.

PRETESTS
Tests conducted before an advertisement is placed to determine whether it communicates the intended message or to select among alternative versions of an advertisement.

Portfolio Tests   Portfolio tests are used to test copy alternatives. The test ad is placed in a portfolio with several other ads and stories, and consumers are asked to read through the portfolio. Afterward, subjects are asked for their impressions of the ads on several evaluative scales, such as from "very informative" to "not very informative."

Jury Tests   Jury tests involve showing the ad copy to a panel of consumers and having them rate how they liked it, how much it drew their attention, and how attractive they thought it was. This approach is similar to the portfolio test in that consumer reactions are obtained. However, unlike the portfolio test, a test advertisement is not hidden within other ads.

Theatre Tests   Theatre testing is the most sophisticated form of pretesting. Consumers are invited to view new television shows or movies in which test commercials are also shown. Viewers register their feelings about the advertisements either on handheld electronic recording devices used during the viewing or on questionnaires afterward.

www.FCB.ca

Carrying Out the Advertising Program

The responsibility for actually carrying out the advertising program can be handled in one of three ways, as shown in Figure 19–4. The **full-service agency** provides the most complete range of services, including market research, media selection, copy development, artwork, and production. Agencies that assist a client by both developing and placing advertisements have traditionally charged a commission of 15 percent of media costs. Some of Canada's leading full-service ad agencies include FCB Canada, Cossette Communications, Vickers & Benson, Grey Canada, and Young & Rubicam. As corporations have introduced integrated marketing approaches, however, most (70%) advertisers have switched from paying commissions to incentives or fees based on performance. Brad Brinegar, CEO of advertising agency Leo Burnett, suggests that "a lot of value we offer is in strategic thinking, and how to pay for that is very different from traditional media spending." The most common performance criteria used are sales, brand and ad awareness, market share, and copy test results. Procter & Gamble's switch to sales-based incentives actually turned out better for its agency than media commissions would have. Global marketing director Bob Wehling explains: "P&G's goal in changing compensation wasn't to cut costs, the goal was to increase sales and support agencies in developing more comprehensive marketing plans that focus less exclusively on TV advertising and more on a broad array of reaching consumers."[37]

FULL-SERVICE AGENCY
An advertising agency providing the most complete range of services, including market research, media selection, copy development, artwork, and production.

www.cossette.com

FIGURE 19–4
Alternative structures of
advertising agencies used
to carry out the advertising
program

TYPE OF AGENCY	SERVICES PROVIDED
Full-service agency	Does research, selects media, develops copy, and produces artwork; also coordinates integrated companies with all marketing efforts
Limited-service specialty agency	Specializes in one aspect of creative process; usually provides creative production work; buys previously unpurchased media space
In-house agency	Provides range of services, depending on company needs

LIMITED-SERVICE AGENCY
Specializes in one aspect of
the advertising process such
as providing creative services
to develop the advertising
copy or buying previously
unpurchased media space.

Limited-service agencies specialize in one aspect of the advertising process such as providing creative services to develop the advertising copy or buying previously unpurchased media space. Limited-service agencies that deal in creative work are compensated by a contractual agreement for the services performed. Finally, **in-house agencies** made up of the company's own advertising staff may provide full services or a limited range of services.

EVALUATING THE ADVERTISING PROGRAM

IN-HOUSE AGENCY
A company's own advertising
staff, which may provide full
services or a limited range
of services.

The advertising decision process does not stop with executing the advertising program. The advertisements must be post-tested to determine whether they are achieving their intended objectives, and results may indicate that changes must be made in the advertising program.

Post-testing the Advertising

POST-TESTS
Tests conducted after an
advertisement has been
shown to the target audience
to determine whether it has
accomplished its intended
purpose.

An advertisement may go through **post-tests** after it has been shown to the target audience to determine whether it accomplished its intended purpose. Five approaches common in post-testing are discussed here.[38]

Aided Recall (Recognition-Readership)   After being shown an ad, respondents are asked whether their previous exposure to it was through reading, viewing, or listening. The Starch test shown in the accompanying photo uses aided recall to determine the percentage (1) who remember seeing a specific magazine ad (*noted*), (2) who saw or read any part of the ad identifying the product or brand (*seen-associated*), and (3) who read at least half of the ad (*read most*). Elements of the ad are then tagged with the results, as shown in the picture.

Starch scores an
advertisement.

Unaided Recall   A question such as, "What ads do you remember seeing yesterday?" is asked of respondents without any prompting to determine whether they saw or heard advertising messages.

Attitude Tests   Respondents are asked questions to measure changes in their attitudes after an advertising campaign, such as whether they have a more favourable attitude toward the product advertised.[39]

Inquiry Tests   Additional product information, product samples, or premiums are offered to an ad's readers or viewers. Ads generating the most inquiries are presumed to be the most effective.

Sales Tests   Sales tests involve studies such as controlled experiments (e.g., using radio ads in one market and newspaper ads in another and comparing the results) and consumer purchase tests (measuring retail sales that result from a given advertising campaign). The most sophisticated experimental methods today allow a manufacturer, a distributor, or an advertising agency to manipulate an advertising variable (such as schedule or copy) through cable systems and observe subsequent sales effects by monitoring data collected from checkout scanners in supermarkets.[40]

Making Needed Changes

Results of post-testing the advertising copy are used to reach decisions about changes in the advertising program. If the post-test results show that an advertisement is doing poorly in terms of awareness or cost efficiency, it may be dropped and other ads run in its place in the future. Sometimes, advertisers drop their ads as a result of complaints they receive. Advertising Standards Canada (ASC), for example, indicates consumer complaints against Canadian ads have reached a record high and many companies drop the offending ads to save face with their consumers.[41] On the other hand, sometimes an advertisement may be so successful it is run repeatedly or used as the basis of a larger advertising program, as with Colgate's "White on White" laundry detergent commercials now used in 30 countries.

Concept Check

1. Explain the difference between pretesting and post-testing advertising copy.

2. What is the difference between aided and unaided recall post-tests?

SALES PROMOTION

The Importance of Sales Promotion

At one time, sales promotion was considered by many to be a supplemental ingredient of the promotional mix. But more recently the use of sales promotion has increased, and so has its perceived importance to marketers. In fact, in Canada, more money is now spent on sales promotion than on advertising.[42]

There are several reasons for the growth in importance of sales promotion. For one, many marketers are looking for measurable results from their promotional efforts. Sales promotion is viewed as an effective tool in this regard. Second, consumers and the trade (e.g., retailers) have become more value-conscious and thus more responsive to sales promotion activities. Third, some suggest that the use of sales promotion has grown because it has become contagious. In short, many marketers are simply responding to the increased use of sales promotion by competitors. Finally, the availability of information technology such as computerized scanning equipment has also served as a stimulus for the growth of sales promotion.

While sales promotion techniques have grown in use and in stature, they are rarely used in isolation or as a stand-alone promotional tool. With the trend toward integrated marketing communications, sales promotion techniques are used more commonly in conjunction with other promotional activities. However, the selection and integration of the many sales promotion techniques requires a good understanding of the relative advantages and disadvantages of each kind of sales promotion.

CONSUMER-ORIENTED SALES PROMOTIONS
Sales tools used to support a company's advertising and personal selling efforts directed to ultimate consumers; examples include coupons, sweepstakes, and samples.

Consumer-Oriented Sales Promotions

Directed to ultimate consumers, **consumer-oriented sales promotions**, or simply consumer promotions, are sales tools used to support a company's advertising and personal selling efforts. The alternative consumer-oriented sales promotion tools include coupons, deals, premiums, contests, sweepstakes, samples, continuity programs, point-of-purchase displays, rebates, and product placement (see Figure 19–5).

Coupons   Coupons are typically printed certificates that give the bearer a saving or a stated price reduction when they purchase a specific product. Coupons can be used to stimulate demand for mature products, or promote the early trial of a new brand.

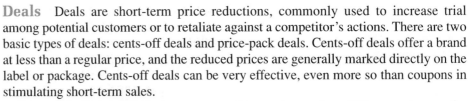

Billions of direct-to-consumer coupons are distributed annually in Canada. Canadians redeem millions of these coupons resulting in savings of over $100 million on products as a result of using coupons.[43]

Studies show that when coupons are used, a company's market share does increase during the period immediately after they are distributed.[44] There are indications, however, that couponing can reduce gross revenues by lowering the price paid by already-loyal consumers.[45] Therefore, manufacturers and retailers are particularly interested in coupon programs directed at potential first-time buyers. One means of focusing on these potential buyers is through electronic in-store coupon machines that match coupons to your most recent purchases.

Deals   Deals are short-term price reductions, commonly used to increase trial among potential customers or to retaliate against a competitor's actions. There are two basic types of deals: cents-off deals and price-pack deals. Cents-off deals offer a brand at less than a regular price, and the reduced prices are generally marked directly on the label or package. Cents-off deals can be very effective, even more so than coupons in stimulating short-term sales.

Price-pack deals offer consumers something extra, such as "20 percent more for the same price," or "Two packages for the price of one." Price-pack deals can be very effective in retaliating against or pre-empting a competitor's actions. For example, if a rival manufacturer introduces a new cake mix, the company could respond with the price-pack deal (e.g., 2 for 1), building up the stock on the kitchen shelves of cake mix buyers and making the competitor's introduction more difficult. Marketers must be careful, however, of overusing deals. If consumers expect a deal they may delay a purchase until the deal occurs. Moreover, frequent deals may erode the perceived value of the brand to the consumer.

Premiums   Premiums are items offered free or at a significant savings as incentives to buy a product. A premium offered at below its normal price is known as *self-liquidating* because the cost charged to the consumers covers the cost of the item. For example, McDonald's used a free premium in a promotional partnership with Disney/Pixar during the release of the movie *Monsters, Inc.*; collectable toys that portrayed movie characters were given away free with the purchase of a Happy Meal. Offering premiums at no cost or at low cost encourages customers to return frequently or to use more of the product. However, the company must be careful that the consumer doesn't just buy the premium.

Contests   In the fourth sales promotion shown in Figure 19–5, the contest, consumers apply their analytical or creative thinking to try to win a prize. Most often a consumer submits an entry to be judged by a panel. Many companies use contests not only to increase consumer purchases, but also to obtain the names and addresses of consumers for use in database marketing purposes. Gillette's Cavalcade of Sports 25-week hockey pool contest awarded a $1-million cash prize to each week's winner. If you like contests, you can even enter online now at Websites such as www.playhere.com!

Sweepstakes   A sweepstakes requires participants to submit some kind of entry form but are purely games of chance requiring no analytical or creative effort by the consumer. *Reader's Digest* and Publisher's Clearing House are two of the

KIND OF SALES PROMOTION	OBJECTIVES	ADVANTAGES	DISADVANTAGES
Coupons	Stimulate demand	Encourage retailer support	Consumers delay purchases
Deals	Increase trial; retaliate against competitor's actions	Reduce consumer risk	Consumers delay purchases; reduce perceived product value
Premiums	Build goodwill	Consumers like free or reduced-price merchandise	Consumers buy for premium, not product
Contests	Increase consumer purchases; build business inventory	Encourage consumer involvement with product	Require creative or analytical thinking
Sweepstakes	Encourage present customers to buy more; minimize brand switching	Get customer to use product and store more often	Sales drop after sweepstakes
Samples	Encourage new-product trial	Low risk for consumer	High cost for company
Continuity programs	Encourage repeat purchases	Help create loyalty	High cost for company
Point-of-purchase displays	Increase product trial; provide in-store support for other promotions	Provide good product visibility	Hard to get retailer to allocate high-traffic space
Rebates	Encourage customers to purchase; stop sales decline	Effective at stimulating demand	Easily copied; steal sales from future; reduce perceived product value
Product placement	Introduce new products; demonstrate product use	Positive message in a noncommercial setting	Little control over presentation of product

FIGURE 19–5
Sales promotion alternatives

better-known sweepstakes. Canada has federal and provincial regulations covering sweepstakes, contests, and games regarding fairness, to ensure that the chance of winning is represented honestly and to guarantee that the prizes are awarded.

Samples Another common consumer sales promotion is sampling, or offering the product free or at a greatly reduced price. Often used for new products, sampling puts the product in the consumer's hands: a trial size is generally offered that is smaller than the regular package size. If consumers like the sample, it is hoped they will remember and buy the product. Kimberly-Clark used sampling to promote its UltraTrim diapers. It undertook a personally addressed sample mailing to 235 000 Canadian households using a database of mothers provided by Welcome Wagon. The sampling program was backed by TV advertising developed specifically for the Canadian market, as well as newspaper and magazine ads with coupons. Shoppers Drug Mart of Toronto handed out 18 000 samples of Life brand health & beauty products on Toronto Transit Commission buses, while EMI Music Canada is offering customers a free CD sampler featuring new Canadian bands.

Continuity Programs   Continuity programs, sometimes referred to as loyalty programs, are a sales promotion tool used to encourage and reward repeat purchases by acknowledging each purchase made by a consumer and offering a premium as purchases accumulate. The most popular continuity programs today are frequent-flyer and frequent traveller programs used by airlines, hotels, and car rental companies to reward loyal customers. Some programs are free while others require the customer to pay an annual membership fee. Chapters Inc. offers a continuity program that provides

discounts and gift certificates to loyal customers. The Royal Bank just recently launched a new loyalty program called "Ultimix" which gives its Visa cardholders the opportunity to gain points to redeem for gifts and to also win prizes instantly. But perhaps the most famous and most successful loyalty program in Canada is the Canadian Tire money program. Now, in addition to receiving your Canadian Tire money at the checkout when you make your purchases, you can also collect "virtual" money through the use of a Canadian Tire credit card, and even through the use of the company's Website.[46]

Point-of-Purchase Displays   In a store aisle, you often encounter a sales promotion called a point-of-purchase display. These product displays take the form of

advertising signs, which sometimes actually hold or display the product, and are often located in high-traffic areas near the cash register or the end of an aisle. The accompanying picture shows a point-of-purchase display for Nabisco's annual Back-to-School program. The display is designed to maximize the consumer's attention to lunch-box and after-school snacks and to provide storage for the products.

Some studies estimate that two-thirds of a consumer's buying decisions are made in the store. This means that grocery product manufacturers want to get their message to you at the instant you are next to their brand in your supermarket aisle—perhaps through a point-of-purchase display. At many supermarkets this may be done through Actmedia's in-store marketing network. Supermarket shopping cart displays, video screens in the aisles, and audio messages remind shoppers about products they might consider buying. The advantage of these methods of promotion is that they do not rely on consumers' ability to remember the message for long periods of time. Other in-store promotions such as interactive kiosks are also becoming popular.

Rebates   Another consumer sales promotion in Figure 19–5, the cash rebate, offers the return of money based on proof of purchase. This tool has been used heavily by car manufacturers facing increased competition. When the rebate is offered on lower-priced items, the time and trouble of mailing in a proof-of-purchase to get the rebate cheque means that many buyers—attracted by the rebate offer—never take advantage of it. However, this "slippage" is less likely to occur with frequent users of rebate promotions.

PRODUCT PLACEMENT
Using a brand-name product in a movie, television show, video, or a commercial for another product.

Product Placement   A final consumer promotion, **product placement**, involves the use of a brand-name product in a movie, television show, video, or commercial for another product. It was Steven Spielberg's placement of Hershey's Reese's Pieces in *E.T.* that first brought a lot of interest to the candy. Similarly, when Tom Cruise wore Bausch and Lomb's Ray-Ban sunglasses in *Risky Business* and its Aviator sunglasses in *Top Gun*, sales skyrocketed from 100 000 pairs to 7 million pairs in five years. More recently, you might remember seeing participants in the television show *Survivor* eating Doritos and drinking Mountain Dew, actors in the movie *Bandits* driving a Chrysler PT Cruiser, or women in the cast of *Ally McBeal* wearing BeBe

Can you identify these product placements?

TRADE-ORIENTED SALES PROMOTIONS
Sales tools used to support a company's advertising and personal selling efforts directed to wholesalers, distributors, or retailers. Three common approaches are allowances and discounts, cooperative advertising, and salesforce training.

clothing. And after driving a BMW in his last three movies, James Bond is driving Aston Martin's new V12 Vanquish once again (the only car he drove in the first 16 Bond movies). Another form of product placement uses new digital technology, which can make "virtual" placements in any existing program. Reruns of *Seinfeld*, for example, could insert a Pepsi on a desktop, a Lexus parked on the street, or a box of Tide on Jerry's countertop![47]

Companies are usually eager to gain exposure for their products, and the studios believe that product placements add authenticity to the film or program. The studios receive fees—Warner Bros. reportedly charged America Online between $3 million and $6 million for using its e-mail service in the movie *You've Got Mail*—in exchange for the onscreen exposure. How are product placements arranged? Many companies simply send brochures and catalogues to the studio resource departments; others are approached by agents who review scripts to find promising scenes where a product might be used.[48]

Trade-Oriented Sales Promotions

Trade-oriented sales promotions, or simply trade promotions, are sales tools used to support a company's advertising and personal selling directed to wholesalers, retailers, or distributors. Some of the sales promotions just reviewed are used for this purpose, but there are three other common approaches targeted uniquely to these intermediaries: (1) allowances and discounts, (2) cooperative advertising, and (3) training of distributors' salesforces.

Allowances and Discounts   Trade promotions often focus on maintaining or increasing inventory levels in the channel of distribution. An effective method for encouraging such increased purchases by intermediaries is the use of allowances and discounts. However, overuse of these "price reductions" can lead to retailers changing their ordering patterns in the expectation of such offerings. Although there are many variations that manufacturers can use with discounts and allowances, three common approaches include the merchandise allowance, the case allowance, and the finance allowance.[49]

Reimbursing a retailer for extra in-store support or special featuring of the brand is a *merchandise allowance*. Performance contracts between the manufacturer and trade member usually specify the activity to be performed, such as a picture of the product in a newspaper with a coupon good at only one store. The merchandise allowance then consists of a percentage deduction from the list case price ordered during the promotional period. Allowances are not paid by the manufacturer until it sees proof of performance (such as a copy of the ad placed by the retailer in the local newspaper).

A second common trade promotion, a *case allowance*, is a discount on each case ordered during a specific time period. These allowances are usually deducted from the invoice. A variation of the case allowance is the "free goods" approach, whereby retailers receive some amount of the product free based on the amount ordered, such as one case free for every 10 cases ordered.[50]

A final trade promotion, the *finance allowance*, involves paying retailers for financing costs or financial losses associated with consumer sales promotions. This trade promotion is regularly used and has several variations. One type is the floor stock protection program—manufacturers give retailers a case allowance price for products in their warehouse, which prevents shelf stock from running down during the promotional period. Also common are freight allowances, which compensate retailers that transport orders from the manufacturer's warehouse.

Cooperative Advertising   Resellers often perform the important function of promoting the manufacturer's products at the local level. One common sales promotional activity is to encourage both better quality and greater quantity in the local

COOPERATIVE ADVERTISING
Advertising programs by which a manufacturer pays a percentage of the retailer's local advertising expense for advertising the manufacturer's products.

advertising efforts of resellers through **cooperative advertising**. These are programs by which a manufacturer pays a percentage of the retailer's local advertising expense for advertising the manufacturer's products.

Usually the manufacturer pays a percentage, often 50 percent, of the cost of advertising up to a certain dollar limit, which is based on the amount of the purchases the retailer makes of the manufacturer's products. In addition to paying for the advertising, the manufacturer often furnishes the retailer with a selection of different ad executions, sometimes suited for several different media. A manufacturer may provide, for example, several different print layouts as well as a few broadcast ads for the retailer to adapt and use.[51]

Training of Distributors' Salesforces One of the many functions the intermediaries perform is customer contact and selling for the producers they represent. Both retailers and wholesalers employ and manage their own sales personnel. A manufacturer's success often rests on the ability of the reseller's salesforce to represent its products.

Thus, it is in the best interest of the manufacturer to help train the reseller's salesforce. Because the reseller's salesforce is often less sophisticated and knowledgeable about the products than the manufacturer might like, training can increase their sales performance. Training activities include producing manuals and brochures to educate the reseller's salesforce. The salesforce then uses these aids in selling situations. Other activities include national sales meetings sponsored by the manufacturer and field visits to the reseller's location to inform and motivate the salesperson to sell the products. Manufacturers also develop incentive and recognition programs to motivate reseller's salespeople to sell their products.

Concept Check

1. Which sales promotional tool is most common for new products?

2. What's the difference between a coupon and a deal?

3. Which trade promotion is used on an ongoing basis?

PUBLIC RELATIONS

As noted in Chapter 18, public relations is a form of communication management that seeks to influence the image of an organization and its products and services. Public relations efforts may utilize a variety of tools and may be directed at many distinct audiences. While public relations personnel usually focus on communicating positive aspects of the business, they may also be called on to minimize the negative impact of a problem or crisis. Firestone, for example, recalled millions of tires after receiving complaints from consumers about product safety. Debates with Ford about the tire failures created a difficult situation for the Firestone public relations department.[52]

Public Relations Tools

In developing a public relations campaign, several tools and tactics are available to the marketer. The most frequently used public relations tool is publicity, which we defined in Chapter 18 as a nonpersonal, indirectly paid presentation of an organization, good, or service. Publicity usually takes the form of a *news release*, consisting of an announcement regarding changes in the company, or the product line.

The objective of a news release is to inform a newspaper, radio station, or other medium of an idea for a story. A study found that more than 40 percent of all free mentions of a brand name occur during news programs.[53] A second common publicity

ETHICS AND SOCIAL RESPONSIBILITY ALERT

Public Relations: What Should We Believe?

Many organizations realize that most consumers view public relations, particularly news-oriented publicity, as more credible than advertising per se. As such, many organizations have turned to well-managed public relations programs in order to influence the perceptions that relevant publics have toward them or their causes. Many organizations disseminate information that will cast them only in the best possible light or to ensure that their view on a particular issue is conveyed to the public. However, there is a growing concern about the public relations battle being waged between PETA (People for the Ethical Treatment of Animals) and the Canadian Cattlemen's Association. PETA is using a public relations campaign to persuade men to stop eating meat. Their message: eating meat causes impotence. But doctors claim that while there may be some truth in the claim, it's only a small part of the story. The Canadian Cattlemen's Association, which represents beef producers, dismisses PETA's claims as "ludicrous." This campaign by PETA follows on the heels of another campaign titled "Jesus Was a Vegetarian," that encourages Christians to give up meat.

What are the dangers when organizations with conflicting views on an issue market their positions via public relations activities? What roles do the media have in this situation?

www.redcross.ca

tool is the *news conference*. Representatives of the media are invited to an informational meeting, and advance materials regarding the content are sent. This tool is often used when negative publicity—as in the cases of the Tylenol poisonings and the Audi 5000 acceleration problem—requires a company response.[54]

Nonprofit organizations rely heavily on publicity to spread their messages. PSAs (*public service announcements*), where free space or time is donated by the media, is a common use of publicity for these organizations. The Canadian Red Cross, for example, depends on PSAs on radio and television to announce their needs.

A growing area of public relations involves the creation, or support, and publicizing of *special events* such as company-sponsored seminars, conferences, sports competitions, entertainment events, or other celebrations. The goal of events sponsorship is to create a forum to disseminate company information or to create brand identification to members of the target audience. College sports events such as the CIAU hockey and football championships are sponsored by Coca-Cola and General Motors, while AT&T Canada is the official sponsor of the Calgary Stampede and the Canadian Senior Golf Championship. DaimlerChrysler, Petro-Canada and others sponsor the development of the Trans Canada Trail.[55]

Another public relations tool is for the organization to engage in *public-service activities* such as establishing or supporting community-based initiatives that benefit the well-being of society. For example, Ciba-Geigy Canada sponsors Health & Welfare Canada's Quit 4 Life Program, which encourages teens to quit smoking.

Finally, the development of *collateral materials* such as annual reports, brochures, newsletters, or video presentations about the company and its products are also basic public relations tools. These materials provide information to target publics and often generate publicity.

Good public relations activities should be planned and made part of an organization's integrated marketing communications effort. However, public relations activities must be used wisely and in an ethical and socially responsible manner (see the accompanying Ethics and Social Responsibility Alert).[56]

Concept Check

1. What is a news release?

2. A growing area of public relations is _____ .

SUMMARY

1 Advertising may be classified as either product or institutional. Product advertising can take three forms: pioneering, competitive, or reminder. Institutional ads are one of these three or advocacy.

2 The promotion decision process described in Chapter 18 can be applied to each of the promotional elements such as advertising.

3 Copywriters and art directors have the responsibility of identifying the key benefits of a product and communicating them to the target audience with attention-getting advertising. Common appeals include fear, sex, and humour.

4 In selecting the right medium, there are distinct trade-offs among television, radio, magazines, newspapers, direct mail, Internet, outdoor, and other media. The decision is based on media habits of the target audience, product characteristics, message requirements, and media costs.

5 In determining advertising schedules, a balance must be made between reach and frequency. Scheduling must take into account buyer turnover, purchase frequency, and the rate at which consumers forget.

6 Advertising is evaluated before and after the ad is run. Pretesting can be done with portfolio, jury, or theatre tests. Post-testing is done on the basis of aided recall, unaided recall, attitude tests, inquiry tests, and sales tests.

7 To execute an advertising program, companies can use several types of advertising agencies. These firms can provide a full range of services or specialize in creative or placement activities. Some firms use their own in-house agency.

8 More money is spent on sales promotion than on advertising. Selecting sales promotions requires a good understanding of the advantages and disadvantages of each option.

9 There is a wide range of consumer-oriented sales promotions: coupons, deals, premiums, contests, sweepstakes, samples, continuity programs, point-of-purchase displays, rebates, and product placements.

10 Trade-oriented promotions consist of allowances and discounts, cooperative advertising, and training of distributors' salesforces. These are used at all levels of the channel.

11 The most frequently used public relations tool is publicity—a nonpersonal, indirectly paid presentation of an organization, good, or service conducted through new releases, news conferences, or public service announcements.

12 Efforts to improve the value of promotion include emphasizing long-term relationships and increasing self-regulation.

KEY TERMS AND CONCEPTS

advertising p. 494
cooperative advertising p. 514
cost per thousand p. 501
customer-oriented sales promotions p. 509
frequency p. 501
full-service agency p. 507
gross rating points p. 501
infomericals p. 502
in-house agency p. 508

institutional advertisements p. 495
limited-service agencies p. 508
post-tests p. 508
pretests p. 507
product advertisements p. 494
product placement p. 512
rating p. 501
reach p. 500
trade-oriented sales promotions p. 513

INTERNET EXERCISE

www.mcgrawhill.ca/college/berkowitz

Most Websites accept some form of advertising. If you were to advise your college or university to advertise on the Web, what three Websites would you recommend? You can use the information at www.adhome.com to help make your recommendation.

1 What is the monthly rate for a full banner ad at each of the Websites?
2 Describe the profile of the audience for each of the Websites.
3 Calculate the CPM for each Website.

WEB SITE	MONTHLY RATE	AUDIENCE PROFILE	CPM
1.			
2.			
3.			

Want to get better grades, find tips on how to study more effectively, and stay up to date with happenings in the world of marketing? Visit the Online Learning Centre for practice tests, Study Smart software, and much more! www.mcgrawhill.ca/college/berkowitz
Interested in finding out what marketing looks like in the real world? *Marketing Magazine* is just a click away on your OLC! Visit www.mcgrawhill.ca/college/berkowitz

APPLYING MARKETING CONCEPTS AND PERSPECTIVES

1 How does competitive product advertising differ from competitive institutional advertising?

2 Suppose you are the advertising manager for a new line of children's fragrances. Which form of media would you use for this new product?

3 You have recently been promoted to be director of advertising for the Timkin Tool Company. In your first meeting with Mr. Timkin, he says, "Advertising is a waste! We've been advertising for six months now and sales haven't increased. Tell me why we should continue." Give your answer to Mr. Timkin.

4 A large life insurance company has decided to switch from using a strong fear appeal to a humorous approach. What are the strengths and weaknesses of such a change in message strategy?

5 Some national advertisers have found that they can have more impact with their advertising by running a large number of ads for a period and then running no ads at all for a period. Why might such a flighting schedule be more effective than a steady schedule?

6 Which medium has the lowest cost per thousand?

MEDIUM	COST	AUDIENCE
TV show	$5000	25 000
Magazine	2200	6000
Newspaper	4800	7200
FM radio	420	1600

7 Each year managers at Bausch and Lomb evaluate the many advertising media alternatives available to them as they develop their advertising program for contact lenses. What advantages and disadvantages of each alternative should they consider? Which media would you recommend to them?

8 What are two advantages and two disadvantages of the advertising post-tests described in the chapter?

9 The Royal Bank is interested in consumer-oriented sales promotions that would encourage senior citizens to direct-deposit their Canada pension cheques with the bank. Evaluate the sales promotion options, and recommend two of them to the bank.

VIDEO CASE 19–1 Lysol

L&F is a North American business unit of the Kodak Corporation. An important brand for L&F is the Lysol product line. Most Canadian consumers are familiar with Lysol Spray, but L&F wants to increase sales of not only the spray product, but also the entire line of Lysol products. It is attempting to develop a strategy in Canada in order to market more of the entire line of Lysol products.

Lysol, primarily the spray, has a long brand heritage in Canada. The disinfectant benefit of the product is very distinctive. In the early 1990s, Lysol spray had 44 percent household penetration in Canada, but the other Lysol products—Lysol Basin, Tub & Tile Cleaner; Lysol Toilet Bowl Cleaner; and Lysol Liquid (All-Purpose) Cleaner—had much lower penetration. With little existing synergy between the products within the line, L&F wanted to bring these disparate products together. In doing so, L&F could achieve economies of scale in terms of marketing expenses. The company believed that by combining the marketing budgets for the four separate products, it could achieve a greater impact on the market. It was believed that one way to link the products together was through the unifying benefit of disinfection.

L&F wanted to achieve a greater market penetration with all four products. However, the overall household cleaning product category was not growing and in some areas was actually declining. Some industry people felt that one reason for this was that many households were cleaning less. They also felt that the recession was impacting on sales in the category. Therefore, new growth for Lysol would have to come at the expense of existing competitors.

While all competitors were using advertising and couponing, the intensity of the battle was at the shelf level. Competitive firms were literally battling it out for shelf space in order to capture market share. This meant that trade sales promotions were being used extensively, often in the form of price discounting. L&F felt it shouldn't get more involved in trade discounts because of the squeeze it put on margins. It did believe, however, that limited use of consumer coupons should be part of its overall consumer-focused marketing communications activity.

L&F believed that the Lysol brand probably had a rather tired personality. The company wanted to give it a 1990s contemporary, interesting, and even provocative image. The problem was that to most consumers, household cleaning products were really an uninteresting category. As such, building consumer awareness of the entire line would not be possible without increasing the level of consumer involvement. The question was how to create interest or involvement with the product line. A way had to be found to demonstrate the line and to have consumers pay attention.

L&F knew that timing would be important. For example, interest in the category would be highest just before or during traditional spring cleaning time in Canada, which ran between late February and early May. Interest would also be high again in late fall or early winter. But if the product line itself could not be made interesting or more involving, even good timing wouldn't help.

L&F had to determine an appropriate creative message for the consumer, select an appropriate communications medium, and consider other ways to build sales and market share for the line.

Questions

1   What would be the most appropriate advertising medium for L&F to use in order to communicate with its market?

2   What would be a creative way to build consumer involvement with the product line? What would be the specific message and execution?

3   Besides the specific advertising medium you recommended to L&F in question 1, what other promotional activities would you recommend to build sales and market share for the Lysol line?

4   What type of advertising schedule would you recommend L&F use during the year?

20

PERSONAL SELLING AND SALES MANAGEMENT

AFTER READING THIS CHAPTER YOU SHOULD BE ABLE TO:

- Recognize different types of personal selling.

- Describe the stages in the personal selling process.

- Specify the functions and tasks in the sales management process.

- Determine whether a firm should use manufacturer's representatives or a company salesforce and the number of people needed in a company's salesforce.

- Understand how firms recruit, select, train, motivate, compensate, and evaluate salespeople.

- Describe recent applications of salesforce automation and customer relationship management.

SELLING THE WAY CUSTOMERS WANT TO BUY

Anne Mulcahy has a tough assignment. As the newly named president and chief executive officer at Xerox, she is in the midst of successfully implementing one of the greatest feats in the annals of business history—restoring Xerox's legendary marketing and financial vitality. "As CEO of Xerox, I am ready and privileged to lead a team of dedicated employees who are as sharply focused and committed as I am in the successful turnaround of our company, transforming it to the realities of the digital age and putting Xerox back on a growth trajectory," said Mulcahy (shown on the opposite page).

Mulcahy is ideally suited to the task. She began her 25-year Xerox career as a field sales representative and assumed increasingly responsible management and executive positions. These included chief staff officer, president of Xerox's General Markets Operations, and most recently, president and chief operating officer of Xerox. As CEO, Mulcahy has to muster the knowledge and experience gained from this varied background. Not surprisingly, her sales background has played a pivotal role.

"We will win back market share one customer at a time, one sale at a time," Mulcahy says. "We'll do that by providing greater value than our competitors — and that means selling the way customers want to buy." She adds that Xerox must offer a broad range of products and services at competitive prices through direct, indirect, Web and telephone sales, and customer support. Her approach to sales, coupled with her considerable management experience, has already borne fruit as Xerox positions itself in the 21st century.[1]

This chapter examines the scope and significance of personal selling and sales management in marketing. It first highlights the many forms of personal selling and outlines the selling process. Sales management functions are then described, including recent advances in salesforce automation and customer relationship management (CRM).

SCOPE AND SIGNIFICANCE OF PERSONAL SELLING AND SALES MANAGEMENT

Chapter 18 described personal selling and management of the sales effort as being part of the firm's promotional mix. Although it is important to recognize that personal selling is a useful vehicle for communicating with present and potential buyers, it is much more. Take a moment to answer the questions in the personal selling and sales management quiz in Figure 20–1. As you read on, compare your answers with those in the text.

Nature of Personal Selling and Sales Management

PERSONAL SELLING
The two-way flow of communication between a buyer and seller, often in a face-to-face encounter, designed to influence a person's or group's purchase decision.

Personal selling involves the two-way flow of communication between a buyer and seller, often in a face-to-face encounter, designed to influence a person's or group's purchase decision. However, with advances in telecommunications, personal selling also takes place over the telephone, through video teleconferencing, and through Internet/Web-enabled links between buyers and sellers.

Personal selling remains a highly human-intensive activity despite the use of technology. Accordingly, the people involved must be managed. **Sales management** involves planning the selling program and implementing and controlling the personal selling effort of the firm. The tasks involved in managing personal selling include setting objectives; organizing the salesforce; recruiting, selecting, training, and compensating salespeople; and evaluating the performance of individual salespeople.

SALES MANAGEMENT
Planning the selling program and implementing and controlling the personal selling effort of the firm.

Pervasiveness of Selling

"Everyone lives by selling something," wrote author Robert Louis Stevenson a century ago. His observation still holds true today. In Canada, more than one million people are employed in sales positions.[2] Included in this number are manufacturing sales personnel, real estate brokers, stockbrokers, and salesclerks who work in retail stores. In reality, however, virtually every occupation that involves customer contact has an element of personal selling. For example, lawyers, accountants, bankers, and company personnel recruiters perform sales-related activities, whether or not they acknowledge it.

FIGURE 20–1
Personal selling and sales management quiz

1. About how much does it cost for a field sales representative to make a single personal sales call? (check one)

   $100 _____ $175 _____ $250 _____
   $150 _____ $200 _____ $300 _____

2. "A salesperson's job is finished when a sale is made." True or false? (circle one)

              True   False

3. About what percentage of companies include customer satisfaction as a measure of salesperson performance? (check one)

   10% _____   30% _____   50% _____
   20% _____   40% _____   60% _____

Could this be a salesperson in the operating room? Read the text to find why Medtronic salespeople visit hospital operating rooms.

Medtronic

www.medtronic.com

Many executives in major companies, like Anne Mulcahy at Xerox, have held sales positions at some time in their careers. Selling often serves as a stepping-stone to top management, as well as being a careeer path in itself.

Personal Selling in Marketing

Personal selling serves three major roles in a firm's overall marketing effort. First, salespeople are the critical link between the firm and its customers. This role requires that salespeople match company interests with customer needs to satisfy both parties in the exchange process. Second, salespeople *are* the company in a consumer's eyes. They represent what a company is or attempts to be and are often the only personal contact a customer has with the company. For example, the "look" projected by Gucci salespeople is an important factor in communicating the style of the company's apparel line. Third, personal selling may play a dominant role in a firm's marketing program. This situation typically arises when a firm uses a push marketing strategy, described in Chapter 18. Avon, for example, pays almost 40 percent of its total sales dollars for selling expenses. Pharmaceutical firms and office and educational equipment manufacturers also rely heavily on personal selling in the marketing of their products.

Creating Customer Value through Salespeople: Relationship and Partnership Selling

As the critical link between the firm and its customers, salespeople can create customer value in many ways. For instance, by being close to the customer, salespeople can identify creative solutions to customer problems. Salespeople at Medtronic, Inc., the world leader in the heart pacemaker market, are in the operating room for more than 90 percent of the procedures performed with their product, and are on call, wearing pagers, 24 hours a day. "It reflects the willingness to be there in every situation, just in case a problem arises—even though nine times out of ten the procedure goes just fine," notes a satisfied customer.[3] Salespeople can create value by easing the customer buying process. This happened at AMP, Inc., a producer of electrical products. Salespeople and customers had a difficult time getting product specifications and performance data on AMP's 70 000 products quickly and accurately. The company now records all information on CD-ROMs that can be scanned instantly by salespeople and customers. Customer value is also created by salespeople who follow through after the sale. At Jefferson Smurfit Corporation, a multi-billion dollar supplier of packaging products, one of its salespeople juggled production from three of the company's plants to satisfy an unexpected demand for boxes from General Electric. This person's action led to the company being given GE's "Distinguished Supplier Award."

RELATIONSHIP SELLING
The practice of building ties to customers based on a salesperson's attention and commitment to customer needs over time.

www.merckfrosst.com

Customer value creation is made possible by **relationship selling**, the practice of building ties to customers based on a salesperson's attention and commitment to customer needs over time. Relationship selling involves mutual respect and trust among buyers and sellers. It focuses on creating long-term customers, not a one-time sale.[4] A survey of senior sales executives revealed that 96 percent consider "building long-term relationships with customers" to be the most important activity affecting sales performance. Companies such as Merck Frosst Canada, IBM Canada, National Bank, Bell Canada, and Kraft Canada have made relationship building a core focus of their sales effort.[5]

PARTNERSHIP SELLING
The practice whereby buyers and sellers combine their expertise and resources to create customized solutions; commit to joint planning; and share customer, competitive, and company information for their mutual benefit, and ultimately the customer. Sometimes called *enterprise selling*.

Some companies have taken relationship selling a step further and forged partnerships between buyer and seller organizations. With **partnership selling**, sometimes called *enterprise selling*, buyers and sellers combine their expertise and resources to create customized solutions; commit to joint planning; and share customer, competitive, and company information for their mutual benefit, and ultimately the customer.[6] As an approach to sales, partnership selling relies on cross-functional business specialists who apply their knowledge and expertise to achieve higher productivity, lower cost, and greater customer value. Partnership selling complements supplier and channel partnering described in Chapters 6, 15, and 16. This practice is embraced by companies such as IBM Canada, 3M, DuPont, and Honeywell, which have established partnerships with customers such as Air Canada, Ford, and McDonald's.[7]

Relationship and partnership selling represent another dimension of customer relationship management (CRM). Both emphasize the importance of learning about customer needs and wants and tailoring solutions to customer problems as a means to create customer value.

Concept Check

1. What is personal selling?

2. What is involved in sales management?

THE MANY FORMS OF PERSONAL SELLING

Personal selling assumes many forms based on the amount of selling done and the amount of creativity required to perform the sales task. Broadly speaking, three types of personal selling exist: order taking, order getting, and sales support activities. While some firms use only one of these types of personal selling, others use a combination of all three.

Order Taking

ORDER TAKER
Processes routine orders or reorders for products that were already sold by the company.

Typically, an **order taker** processes routine orders or reorders for products that were already sold by the company. The primary responsibility of order takers is to preserve an ongoing relationship with existing customers and maintain sales. Two types of order takers exist. *Outside order takers* visit customers and replenish inventory stocks of resellers, such as retailers or wholesalers. For example, Frito-Lay salespeople call on supermarkets, neighbourhood grocery stores, and other

A Frito-Lay salesperson takes inventory of snacks for the store manager to sign. In this situation, the manager will make a straight rebuy decision.

Frito-Lay, Inc.
www.fritolay.com

establishments to ensure that the company's line of snack products is in adequate supply. In addition, outside order takers often provide assistance in arranging displays. *Inside order takers*, also called *order* or *salesclerks*, typically answer simple questions, take orders, and complete transactions with customers. Many retail clerks are inside order takers. Inside order takers are often employed by companies that use *inbound telemarketing*, the use of toll-free telephone numbers that customers can call to obtain information about products or services and make purchases. In industrial settings, order taking arises in straight rebuy situations. Order takers generally do little selling in a conventional sense and engage in only modest problem solving with customers. They often represent products that have few options, such as confectionary items, magazine subscriptions, and highly standardized industrial products. Inbound telemarketing is also an essential selling activity for more "customer service" driven firms, such as Dell Computer. Order takers in such firms undergo extensive training so that they can better assist callers with their purchase decisions.

Order Getting

ORDER GETTER
A salesperson who sells in a conventional sense and identifies prospective customers, provides customers with information, persuades customers to buy, closes sales, and follows up on customers' use of a product or service.

An **order getter** sells in a conventional sense and identifies prospective customers, provides customers with information, persuades customers to buy, closes sales, and follows up on customers' use of a product or service. Like order takers, order getters can be inside (an automobile salesperson) or outside (a Xerox salesperson). Order getting involves a high degree of creativity and customer empathy and is typically required for selling complex or technical products with many options, so considerable product knowledge and sales training are necessary. In modified-rebuy or new-buy purchase situations in industrial selling, an order getter acts as a problem solver who identifies how a particular product may satisfy a customer's need. Similarly, in the purchase of a service, such as insurance, a Metropolitan Life insurance agent can provide a mix of plans to satisfy a buyer's needs depending on income, stage of the family's life cycle, and investment objectives.

Order getting is not a 40-hour-per-week job. Industry research indicates that outside order getters, or field service representatives, work about 48 hours per week. As shown in Figure 20–2, 54 percent of their time is spent selling and another 13 percent is devoted to customer service calls. The remainder of their work is occupied by getting to customers and performing numerous administrative tasks.[8]

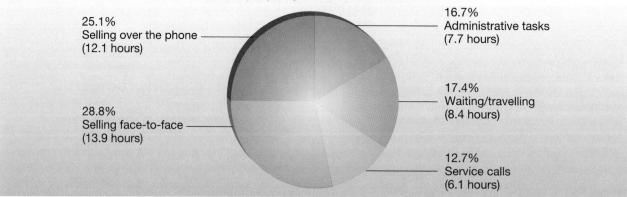

How salespeople spend their time each week

25.1%
Selling over the phone
(12.1 hours)

16.7%
Administrative tasks
(7.7 hours)

17.4%
Waiting/travelling
(8.4 hours)

28.8%
Selling face-to-face
(13.9 hours)

12.7%
Service calls
(6.1 hours)

FIGURE 20–2
How outside order-getting salespeople spend their time each week

Order getting by outside salespeople is also expensive. It is estimated that the average cost of a single field sales call is almost $170, factoring in salespeople compensation, benefits, and travel and entertainment expenses.[9] (What amount did you check for question 1 in Figure 20–1?) This cost illustrates why outbound telemarketing is so popular today. *Outbound telemarketing* is the practice of using the telephone rather than personal visits to contact customers. A significantly lower cost per sales call (in the range of $20 to $25) and little or no field expense accounts for its widespread appeal. Accordingly, outbound telemarketing has grown significantly over the past decade.[10]

Customer Sales Support Personnel

MISSIONARY SALESPEOPLE
Sales support personnel who do not directly solicit orders but rather concentrate on performing promotional activities and introducing new products.

Customer sales support personnel augment the selling effort of order getters by performing a variety of services. For example, **missionary salespeople** do not directly solicit orders but rather concentrate on performing promotional activities and introducing new products. They are used extensively in the pharmaceutical industry, where they persuade physicians to prescribe a firm's product. Actual sales are made through wholesalers or directly to pharmacists who fill prescriptions. A **sales engineer** is a salesperson who specializes in identifying, analyzing, and solving customer problems and brings know-how and technical expertise to the selling situation but often does not actually sell products and services. Sales engineers are popular in selling industrial products such as chemicals and heavy equipment.

SALES ENGINEER
A salesperson who specializes in identifying, analyzing, and solving customer problems and who brings know-how and technical expertise to the selling situations, but does not actually sell goods and services.

In many situations firms engage in cross-functional **team selling**, the practice of using an entire team of professionals in selling to and servicing major customers.[11] Team selling is used when specialized knowledge is needed to satisfy the different interests of individuals in a customer's buying centre. For example, a selling team might consist of a salesperson, a sales engineer, a service representative, and a financial executive, each of whom would deal with a counterpart in the customer's firm. Selling teams have grown in popularity due to partnering and take different forms. In *conference selling*, a salesperson and other company resource people meet with buyers to discuss problems and opportunities. In *seminar selling*, a company team conducts an educational program for a customer's technical staff, describing state-of-the-art developments. IBM and Xerox pioneered cross-functional team selling in working with prospective buyers. Other firms have embraced this practice and created and sustained value for their customers, as described in the accompanying Marketing NewsNet.[12]

TEAM SELLING
Using an entire team of professionals in selling to and servicing major customers.

Concept Check

1. What is the principal difference between an order taker and an order getter?

2. What is team selling?

MARKETING NEWSNET

Creating and Sustaining Customer Value through Cross-Functional Team Selling

The day of the lone salesperson calling on a customer is rapidly becoming history. Many companies today are using cross-functional teams of professionals to work with customers to improve relationships, find better ways of doing things, and, of course, create and sustain value for their customers.

Xerox and IBM pioneered cross-functional team selling, but other firms were quick to follow as they spotted the potential to create and sustain value for their customers. Recognizing that corn growers needed a herbicide they could apply less often, a DuPont team of chemists, sales and marketing executives, and regulatory specialists created just the right product that recorded sales of $80 million in its first year. Procter & Gamble uses teams of marketing, sales, advertising, computer systems, and distribution personnel to work with its major retailers, such as Wal-Mart, to identify ways to develop, promote, and deliver products. Pitney Bowes, Inc., which produces sophisticated computer systems that weigh, rate, and track packages for firms such as UPS and Federal Express, also uses sales teams to meet customer needs. These teams consist of sales personnel, "carrier management specialists," and engineering and administrative executives who continually find ways to

improve the technology of shipping goods across town and around the world.

Efforts to create and sustain customer value through cross-functional team selling have become a necessity as customers seek greater value for their money. According to the vice president for procurement of a Fortune 500 company, "Today, it's not just getting the best price but getting the best value—and there are a lot of pieces to value."

THE PERSONAL SELLING PROCESS: BUILDING RELATIONSHIPS

PERSONAL SELLING PROCESS
Sales activities occurring before and after the sale itself, consisting of six stages: (1) prospecting, (2) preapproach, (3) approach, (4) presentation, (5) close, and (6) follow-up.

Selling, and particularly order getting, is a complicated activity that involves building buyer–seller relationships. Although the salesperson–customer interaction is essential to personal selling, much of a salesperson's work occurs before this meeting and continues after the sale itself. The **personal selling process** consists of six stages: (1) prospecting, (2) preapproach, (3) approach, (4) presentation, (5) close, and (6) follow-up (Figure 20–3).

Prospecting

Personal selling begins with *prospecting*—the search for and qualification of potential customers.[13] For some products that are one-time purchases, such as encyclopedias, continual prospecting is necessary to maintain sales. There are three types of prospects. A *lead* is the name of a person who may be a possible customer. A *prospect* is a customer who wants or needs the product. If an individual wants the product, can afford to buy it, and is the decision maker, this individual is a *qualified prospect*.

Leads and prospects are generated using several sources. For example, advertising may contain a coupon or a toll-free number to generate leads. Some companies use exhibits at trade shows, professional meetings, and conferences to generate leads or prospects. Staffed by salespeople, these exhibits are used to attract the attention of prospective buyers and disseminate information. Others use lists and directories. Another approach for generating leads is through *cold canvassing* in person or by

FIGURE 20–3
Stages and objectives of the
personal selling process

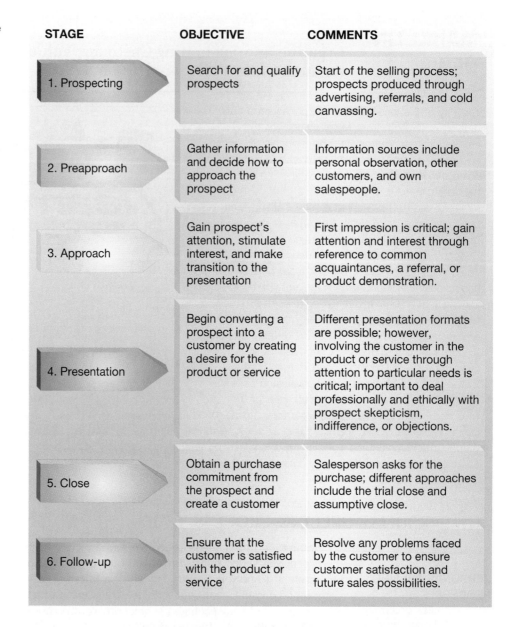

STAGE	OBJECTIVE	COMMENTS
1. Prospecting	Search for and qualify prospects	Start of the selling process; prospects produced through advertising, referrals, and cold canvassing.
2. Preapproach	Gather information and decide how to approach the prospect	Information sources include personal observation, other customers, and own salespeople.
3. Approach	Gain prospect's attention, stimulate interest, and make transition to the presentation	First impression is critical; gain attention and interest through reference to common acquaintances, a referral, or product demonstration.
4. Presentation	Begin converting a prospect into a customer by creating a desire for the product or service	Different presentation formats are possible; however, involving the customer in the product or service through attention to particular needs is critical; important to deal professionally and ethically with prospect skepticism, indifference, or objections.
5. Close	Obtain a purchase commitment from the prospect and create a customer	Salesperson asks for the purchase; different approaches include the trial close and assumptive close.
6. Follow-up	Ensure that the customer is satisfied with the product or service	Resolve any problems faced by the customer to ensure customer satisfaction and future sales possibilities.

telephone. This approach simply means that a salesperson may open a directory, pick a name, and visit or call that individual or business. Although the refusal rate is high with cold canvassing, this approach can be successful. For example, 41 brokers at a major brokerage firm identified 18 004 prospects, qualified 1208 of them, made 659 sales presentations, and opened 40 new accounts in four working days.[14] However, cold canvassing is frowned upon in most Asian and Latin American societies. Personal visits, based on referrals, are expected.[15]

Cold canvassing is also often criticized by Canadian consumers. Many consumers see cold canvassing as an intrusion to their privacy, and many find it simply distasteful.[16] Many trade associations have codes of ethics for dealing with this issue such as adhering to consumers' "do not call," "do not mail," or "do not visit" requests. The Canadian government has also attempted to more closely regulate cold canvassing with the Canadian Radio-television and Telecommunications Commission requiring telemarketers to inform consumers that they have the right to say no to such solicitations.[17]

Trade shows are a popular source for leads and prospects.

Preapproach

Once a salesperson has identified a qualified prospect, preparation for the sale begins with the preapproach. The *preapproach* stage involves obtaining further information on the prospect and deciding on the best method of approach. Knowing how the prospect prefers to be approached, and what the prospect is looking for in a product or service, is essential regardless of cultural setting. For example, a Merrill Lynch stockbroker will need information on a prospect's discretionary income, investment objectives, and preference for discussing brokerage services over the telephone or in person. For industrial product companies such as Texas Instruments, the preapproach involves identifying the buying role of a prospect (for example, influencer or decision maker), important buying criteria, and the prospect's receptivity to a formal or informal presentation. Identifying the best time to contact a prospect is also important. For example, insurance companies have discovered the best times to call on people in different occupations: dentists before 9:30 A.M., lawyers between 11:00 A.M. and 2:00 P.M., and university professors between 7:00 and 8:00 P.M.

This stage is very important in global selling where customs dictate appropriate protocol. In many South American countries, for example, buyers expect salespeople to be punctual for appointments. However, prospective buyers are routinely 30 minutes late. South Americans take negotiating seriously and prefer straightforward presentations, but a hard-sell approach will not work.[18]

Successful salespeople recognize that the preapproach stage should never be shortchanged. Their experience coupled with research on customer complaints indicates that failure to learn as much as possible about the prospect is unprofessional and the ruin of a sales call.[19]

Approach

The *approach* stage involves the initial meeting between the salesperson and prospect, where the objectives are to gain the prospect's attention, stimulate interest, and build the foundation for the sales presentation itself and the basis for a working relationship. The first impression is critical at this stage, and it is common for salespeople to begin the conversation with a reference to common acquaintances, a referral, or even the product or service itself. Which tactic is used will depend on the information obtained in the prospecting and preapproach stages.

The approach stage is very important in international settings. In many societies outside Canada, considerable time is devoted to non-business talk designed to estab-

lish a rapport between buyers and sellers. For instance, it is common for two or three meetings to occur before business matters are discussed in the Middle East and Asia. Gestures are also very important. The initial meeting between a salesperson and a prospect in Canada customarily begins with a firm handshake. Handshakes also apply in France, but they are gentle, not firm. Forget the handshake in Japan. A bow is appropriate. What about business cards? Business cards should be printed in English on one side and the language of the prospective customer on the other. Knowledgeable Canadian salespeople know that their business cards should be handed to Asian customers using both hands, with the name facing the receiver. In Asia, anything involving names demands respect.[20]

Presentation

The *presentation* is at the core of the order-getting selling process, and its objective is to convert a prospect into a customer by creating a desire for the product or service. Three major presentation formats exist: (1) stimulus-response format, (2) formula selling format, and (3) need-satisfaction format.

STIMULUS-RESPONSE PRESENTATION

A selling format that assumes the prospect will buy if given the appropriate stimulus by a salesperson.

Stimulus-Response Format   The **stimulus-response presentation** format assumes that, given the appropriate stimulus by a salesperson, the prospect will buy. With this format the salesperson tries one appeal after another, hoping to "hit the right button." A counter clerk at McDonald's is using this approach when he or she asks whether you'd like an order of french fries or a dessert with your meal. The counter clerk is engaging in what is called *suggestive selling*. Although useful in this setting, the stimulus-response format is not always appropriate, and for many products a more formalized format is necessary.

FORMULA SELLING PRESENTATION

Providing information in an accurate, thorough, and step-by-step manner to inform the prospect.

Formula Selling Format   A more formalized presentation, the **formula selling presentation** format, is based on the view that a presentation consists of information that must be provided in an accurate, thorough, and step-by-step manner to inform the prospect. A popular version of this format is the *canned sales presentation*, which is a memorized, standardized message conveyed to every prospect. Used frequently by firms in telephone and door-to-door selling of consumer products (for example, Hoover vacuum cleaners), this approach treats every prospect the same, regardless of differences in needs or preference for certain kinds of information. Canned sales presentations can be advantageous when the differences between prospects are unknown or with novice salespeople who are less knowledgeable about the product and selling process than experienced salespeople. Although it guarantees a thorough presentation, it often lacks flexibility and spontaneity and, more important, does not provide for feedback from the prospective buyer—a critical component in the communication process and the start of a relationship.

NEED-SATISFACTION PRESENTATION
A selling format that emphasizes probing and listening by the salesperson to identify needs and interests of prospective buyers.

Need-Satisfaction Format   The stimulus-response and formula selling formats share a common characteristic: the salesperson dominates the conversation. By comparison, the **need-satisfaction presentation** format emphasizes probing and listening by the salesperson to identify needs and interests of prospective buyers. Once these are identified, the salesperson tailors the presentation to the prospect and highlights product benefits that may be valued by the prospect. The need-satisfaction format, which emphasizes problem solving, is the most consistent with the marketing concept and relationship building. Two selling styles are associated with this format. **Adaptive selling** involves adjusting the presentation to fit the selling situation, such as knowing when to offer solutions and when to ask for more information.[21] Sales research and practice show that knowledge of the customer and sales situation are key ingredients for adaptive selling. Many consumer service firms such as brokerage and insurance firms like ING Canada and consumer product firms like Gillette effectively apply this selling style. **Consultative selling** focuses on problem identification, where the salesperson serves as an expert on problem recognition and resolution.[22] With consultative selling, problem solution options are not simply a matter of choosing from an array of existing products or services. Rather, novel solutions often arise thereby creating unique value for the customer. Consultative selling is prominent in business-to-business marketing. IBM Canada is often recognized for its consultative selling style.[23]

ADAPTIVE SELLING
A need-satisfaction sales presentation that involves adjusting the presentation to fit the selling situation.

CONSULTATIVE SELLING
Focuses on problem definition, where the salesperson serves as an expert on problem recognition and resolution.

Handling Objections   A critical concern in the presentation stage is handling objections. *Objections* are excuses for not making a purchase commitment or decision. Some objections are valid and are based on the characteristics of the product or service or price. However, many objections reflect prospect skepticism or indifference. Whether valid or not, experienced salespeople know that objections do not put an end to the presentation. Rather, techniques can be used to deal with objections in a courteous, ethical, and professional manner. The following six techniques are the most common:[24]

1. *Acknowledge and convert the objection.* This technique involves using the objection as a reason for buying. For example, a prospect might say, "The price is too high." The reply: "Yes, the price is high because we use the finest materials. Let me show you . . . ."
2. *Postpone.* The postpone technique is used when the objection will be dealt with later in the presentation: "I'm going to address that point shortly. I think my answer would make better sense then."
3. *Agree and neutralize.* Here a salesperson agrees with the objection, then shows that it is unimportant. A salesperson would say, "That's true and others have said the same. However, they concluded that issue was outweighed by the other benefits."
4. *Accept the objection.* Sometimes the objection is valid. Let the prospect express such views, probe for the reason behind it, and attempt to stimulate further discussion on the objection.
5. *Denial.* When a prospect's objection is based on misinformation and clearly untrue, it is wise to meet the objection head on with a firm denial.
6. *Ignore the objection.* This technique is used when it appears that the objection is a stalling mechanism or is clearly not important to the prospect.

Each of these techniques requires a calm, professional interaction with the prospect and is most effective when objections are anticipated in the preapproach stage. Handling objections is a skill requiring a sense of timing, appreciation for the prospect's state of mind, and adeptness in communication. Objections also should be handled ethically. Lying or misrepresenting product or service features are grossly unethical practices.

MARKETING NEWSNET   The Subtlety of Saying Yes in East Asia

The economies of East Asia—spanning from Japan to Indonesia—closely rival the North American and EU economics. The marketing opportunities in East Asia are great, but effective selling in these countries requires a keen cultural ear. Seasoned global marketers know that in many Asian societies it is impolite to say *no*, and *yes* has multiple meanings.

Yes in Asian societies can have at least four meanings. It can mean that listeners are simply acknowledging that a speaker is talking to them even though they don't understand what is being said, or it can mean that a speaker's words are understood, but not that they are agreed with. A third meaning of *yes* conveys that a presentation is understood, but other people must be consulted

before any commitment is possible. Finally, *yes* can also mean that a proposal is understood and accepted. However, experienced negotiators also note that this *yes* is subject to change if the situation is changed.

This example illustrates why savvy salespeople are sensitive to cultural underpinnings when engaged in cross-cultural sales negotiations.

Close

The *closing* stage in the selling process involves obtaining a purchase commitment from the prospect. This stage is the most important and the most difficult because the salesperson must determine when the prospect is ready to buy. Telltale signals indicating a readiness to buy include body language (prospect re-examines the product or contract closely), statements ("This equipment should reduce our maintenance costs"), and questions ("When could we expect delivery?"). The close itself can take several forms. Three closing techniques are used when a salesperson believes a buyer is about ready to make a purchase: (1) trial close, (2) assumptive close, and (3) urgency close. A *trial close* involves asking the prospect to make a decision on some aspect of the purchase: "Would you prefer the blue or grey model?" An *assumptive close* entails asking the prospect to consider choices concerning delivery, warranty, or financing terms under the assumption that a sale has been finalized. An *urgency close* is used to commit the prospect quickly by making reference to the timeliness of the purchase: "The low-interest financing ends next week," or, "That is the last model we have in stock." Of course, these statements should be used only if they accurately reflect the situation; otherwise, such claims would be unethical. When a prospect is clearly ready to buy, the final close is used, and a salesperson asks for the order.

Knowing when the prospect is ready to buy becomes even more difficult in cross-cultural buyer–seller negotiations where societal customs and language play a large role. Read the accompanying Marketing NewsNet to understand the multiple meanings of *yes* in Japan and other societies in East Asia.[25]

Follow-Up

The selling process does not end with the closing of a sale; rather, professional selling requires customer follow-up. One marketing authority equated the follow-up with courtship and marriage,[26] by observing ". . . the sale merely consummates the courtship. Then the marriage begins. How good the marriage is depends on how well the relationship is managed." The *follow-up stage* includes making certain the customer's purchase has been properly delivered and installed and difficulties experienced with the use of the item are addressed. Attention to this stage of the selling process solidifies the buyer–seller relationship. Moreover, research shows that the cost and effort to obtain repeat sales from a satisfied customer is roughly half of that necessary to gain a sale from a new customer.[27] In short, today's satisfied customers become tomorrow's qualified prospects or referrals. (What was your answer to question 2 in the quiz?)

Concept Check

1. What are the six stages in the personal selling process?

2. What is the distinction between a lead and a qualified prospect?

3. Which presentation format is most consistent with the marketing concept? Why?

THE SALES MANAGEMENT PROCESS

Selling must be managed if it is going to contribute to a firm's overall objectives. Although firms differ in the specifics of how salespeople and the selling effort are managed, the sales management process is similar across firms. Sales management consists of three interrelated functions: (1) sales plan formulation, (2) sales plan implementation, and (3) evaluation and control of the salesforce (Figure 20–4).

Sales Plan Formulation

Formulating the sales plan is the most basic of the three sales management functions. According to the vice president of the Harris Corporation, a global communications company, "If a company hopes to implement its marketing strategy, it really needs a detailed sales planning process."[28] The **sales plan** is a statement describing what is to be achieved and where and how the selling effort of salespeople is to be deployed. Formulating the sales plan involves three tasks: (1) setting objectives, (2) organizing the salesforce, and (3) developing account management policies.

SALES PLAN

A statement describing what is to be achieved and where and how the selling effort of salespeople is to be deployed.

Setting Objectives   Setting objectives is central to sales management because this task specifies what is to be achieved. In practice, objectives are set for the total salesforce and for each salesperson. Selling objectives can be output related and focus on dollar or unit sales volume, number of new customers added, and profit. Alternatively, they can be input related and emphasize the number of sales calls and selling expenses. Output- and input-related objectives are used for the salesforce as a whole and for each salesperson. A third type of objective that is behaviourally related is typically specific for each salesperson and includes his or her product knowledge, customer service, and selling and communication skills. Increasingly, firms are also emphasizing knowledge of competition as an objective since salespeople are calling on customers and should see what competitors are doing.[29] But should salespeople

FIGURE 20–4
The sales management process

ETHICS AND SOCIAL RESPONSIBILITY ALERT
The Ethics of Asking Customers about Competitors

Salespeople are a valuable source of information about what is happening in the marketplace. By working closely with customers and asking good questions, salespeople often have first-hand knowledge of customer problems and wants. They also are able to spot the activities of competitors. However, should salespeople explicitly ask customers about competitor strategies such as pricing practices, product development efforts, and trade and promotion programs?

Gaining knowledge about competitors by asking customers for information is a ticklish ethical issue. Research indicates that 25 percent of North American salespeople engaged in business-to-business selling consider this practice unethical, and their companies have explicit guidelines for this practice. It is also noteworthy that Japanese salespeople consider this practice to be more unethical than do salespeople in North America.

Do you believe that asking customers about competitor practices is unethical? Why or why not?

explicitly ask their customers for information about competitors? Read the accompanying Ethics and Social Responsibility Alert to see how salespeople view this practice.[30]

Whatever objectives are set, they should be precise and measurable and specify the time period over which they are to be achieved. Once established, these objectives serve as performance standards for the evaluation of the salesforce—the third function of sales management.

Organizing the Salesforce   Establishing a selling organization is the second task in formulating the sales plan. Three questions are related to organization. First, should the company use its own salesforce, or should it use independent agents such as manufacturer's representatives? Second, if the decision is made to employ company salespeople, then should they be organized according to geography, customer type, or product or service? Third, how many company salespeople should be employed?

The decision to use company salespeople or independent agents is made infrequently. However, recently Coca-Cola's Food Division replaced its salesforce with independent agents (food brokers). The Optoelectronics Division of Honeywell, Inc. has switched back and forth between agents and its own salesforce over the last 25 years and now uses both. The decision is based on an analysis of economic and behavioural factors. An economic analysis examines the costs of using both types of salespeople and is a form of break-even analysis.

Consider a situation in which independent agents would receive a five-percent commission on sales, and company salespeople would receive a three-percent commission, salaries, and benefits. In addition, with company salespeople, sales administration costs would be incurred for a total fixed cost of $500 000 per year. At what sales level would independent or company salespeople be less costly? This question can be answered by setting the costs of the two options equal to each other and solving for the sales level amount, as shown in the following equation:

$$\underbrace{\frac{\text{Total cost of company salespeople}}{0.03(X) + \$500,000}} = \underbrace{\frac{\text{Total cost of independent agents}}{0.05(X)}}$$

where X = sales volume. Solving for X, sales volume equals $25 million, indicating that below $25 million in sales independent agents would be cheaper, but above $25 million a company salesforce would be cheaper. This relationship is shown in Figure 20–5.

Economics alone does not answer this question, however. A behavioural analysis is also necessary and should focus on issues related to the control, flexibility, effort, and availability of independent and company salespeople.[31] An individual firm must weigh the pros and cons of the economic and behavioural considerations before making this decision.

FIGURE 20–5
Break-even chart for comparing independent agents and a company salesforce

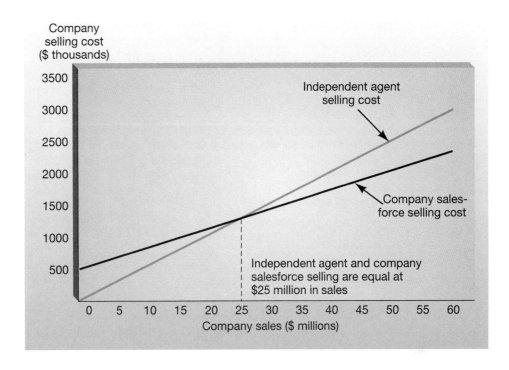

If a company elects to employ its own salespeople, then it must choose an organizational structure based on (1) geography, (2) customer, or (3) product (Figure 20–6). A geographical structure is the simplest organization, where Canada, or indeed the globe, is first divided into regions and each region is divided into districts or territories. Salespeople are assigned to each district with defined geographical boundaries and call on all customers and represent all products sold by the company. The principal advantage of this structure is that it can minimize travel time, expenses, and duplication of selling effort. However, if a firm's products or customers require specialized knowledge, then a geographical structure is not suitable.

When different types of buyers have different needs, a customer sales organizational structure is used. In practice this means that a different salesforce calls on each separate type of buyer or marketing channel. For example, Kodak recently switched from a geographical to a marketing channel structure with different sales teams serving specific retail channels: mass merchandisers, photo specialty outlets, and food and drug stores. The rationale for this approach is that more effective, specialized customer support and knowledge are provided to buyers. However, this structure often leads to higher administrative costs and some duplication of selling effort, because two separate salesforces are used to represent the same products.

MAJOR ACCOUNT MANAGEMENT
The practice of using team selling to focus on important customers so as to build mutually beneficial, long-term, cooperative relationships. Also called *key account management*.

A variation of the customer organizational structure is **major account management**, or *key account management*, the practice of using team selling to focus on important customers so as to build mutually beneficial, long-term, cooperative relationships.[32] Major account management involves teams of sales, service, and often technical personnel who work with purchasing, manufacturing, engineering, logistics, and financial executives in customer organizations. This approach, which often assigns company personnel to a customer account, results in "customer specialists" who can provide exceptional service. Procter & Gamble uses this approach with Wal-Mart, as does Black & Decker with Home Depot.

When specific knowledge is required to sell certain types of products, then a product sales organization is used. For example, a steel manufacturer has a salesforce that sells drilling pipe to oil companies and another that sells specialty steel products to manufacturers. The primary advantage of this structure is that salespeople can develop expertise with technical characteristics, applications, and selling methods associated

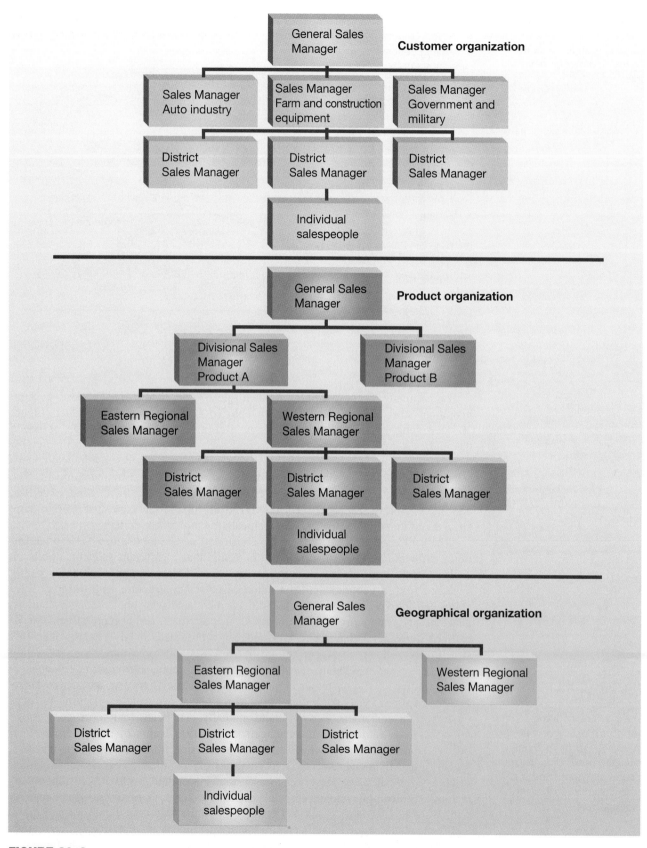

FIGURE 20–6
Organizing the salesforce
by customer, product,
and geography

with a particular product or family of products. However, this structure also produces high administrative costs and duplication of selling effort because two company salespeople may call on the same customer.

In short, there is no one best sales organization for all companies in all situations. Rather, the organization of the salesforce should reflect the marketing strategy of the firm. Each year about 10 percent of firms change their sales organizations to implement new marketing strategies.

The third question related to salesforce organization involves determining the size of the salesforce. For example, why does Frito-Lay have about 17 500 salespeople who call on supermarkets, grocery stores, and other establishments to sell snack foods? The answer lies in the number of accounts (customers) served, the frequency of calls on accounts, the length of an average call, and the amount of time a salesperson can devote to selling.

A common approach for determining the size of a salesforce is the **workload method**. This formula-based method integrates the number of customers served, call frequency, call length, and available selling time to arrive at a figure for the salesforce size. For example, Frito-Lay needs about 17 500 salespeople according to the following workload method formula:

$$NS = \frac{NC \times CF \times CL}{AST}$$

where:

NS = Number of salespeople

NC = Number of customers

CF = Call frequency necessary to service a customer each year

CL = Length of an average call

AST = Average amount of selling time available per year

Frito-Lay sells its products to 350 000 supermarkets, grocery stores, and other establishments. Salespeople should call on these accounts at least once a week, or 52 times a year. The average sales call lasts an average of 81 minutes (1.35 hour). An average salesperson works 2000 hours a year (50 weeks × 40 hours a week), but 12 hours a week are devoted to non-selling activities such as travel and administration, leaving 1400 hours a year. Using these guidelines, Frito-Lay would need

$$NS = \frac{350\ 000 \times 52 \times 1.35}{1400} = 17\ 550 \text{ salespeople}$$

The value of this formula is apparent in its flexibility; a change in any one of the variables will affect the number of salespeople needed. Changes are determined, in part, by the firm's account management policies.

Developing Account Management Policies
The third task in formulating a sales plan involves developing **account management policies** specifying whom salespeople should contact, what kinds of selling and customer service activities should be engaged in, and how these activities should be carried out. These policies might state which individuals in a buying organization should be contacted, the amount of sales and service effort that different customers should receive, and the kinds of information salespeople should collect before or during a sales call.

An example of an account management policy in Figure 20–7 shows how different accounts or customers can be grouped according to level of opportunity and the firm's competitive sales position.[33] When specific account names are placed in each cell, salespeople clearly see which accounts should be contacted, with what level of selling and service activity, and how to deal with them. Accounts in cells 1 and 2 might have high frequencies of personal sales calls and increased time spent on a call. Cell 3 accounts will have lower call frequencies, and cell 4 accounts might be contacted through telemarketing or direct mail rather than in person.[34]

www.fritolay.com

WORKLOAD METHOD
A formula-based method for determining the size of a salesforce that integrates the number of customers served, call frequency, call length, and available selling time to arrive at a salesforce size.

ACCOUNT MANAGEMENT POLICIES
Policies that specify whom salespeople should contact, what kinds of selling and customer service activities should be engaged in, and how these activities should be carried out.

Competitive position of sales organization

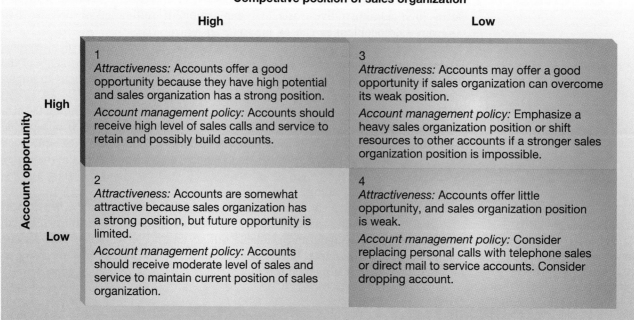

	High	**Low**
High	**1** *Attractiveness:* Accounts offer a good opportunity because they have high potential and sales organization has a strong position. *Account management policy:* Accounts should receive high level of sales calls and service to retain and possibly build accounts.	**3** *Attractiveness:* Accounts may offer a good opportunity if sales organization can overcome its weak position. *Account management policy:* Emphasize a heavy sales organization position or shift resources to other accounts if a stronger sales organization position is impossible.
Low	**2** *Attractiveness:* Accounts are somewhat attractive because sales organization has a strong position, but future opportunity is limited. *Account management policy:* Accounts should receive moderate level of sales and service to maintain current position of sales organization.	**4** *Attractiveness:* Accounts offer little opportunity, and sales organization position is weak. *Account management policy:* Consider replacing personal calls with telephone sales or direct mail to service accounts. Consider dropping account.

(left axis label: Account opportunity)

FIGURE 20–7
Account management
policy grid

Sales Plan Implementation

The sales plan is put into practice through the tasks associated with sales plan implementation. Whereas sales plan formulation focuses on "doing the right things," implementation emphasizes "doing things right." The three major tasks involved in implementing a sales plan are (1) salesforce recruitment and selection, (2) salesforce training, and (3) salesforce motivation and compensation.

Salesforce Recruitment and Selection   Effective recruitment and selection of salespeople is one of the most crucial tasks of sales management. It entails finding people who match the type of sales position required by a firm. Recruitment and selection practices would differ greatly between order-taking and order-getting sales positions, given the differences in the demands of these two jobs. Therefore, recruitment and selection begin with a carefully crafted job analysis and job description followed by a statement of job qualifications.[35]

A *job analysis* is a study of a particular sales position, including how the job is to be performed and the tasks that make up the job. Information from a job analysis is used to write a *job description*, a written document that describes job relationships and requirements that characterize each sales position. It explains (1) to whom a salesperson reports, (2) how a salesperson interacts with other company personnel, (3) the customers to be called on, (4) the specific activities to be carried out, (5) the physical and mental demands of the job, and (6) the types of products and services to be sold. The job description is then translated into a statement of job qualifications, including the aptitudes, knowledge, skills, and a variety of behavioural characteristics considered necessary to perform the job successfully. Qualifications for order-getting sales positions often mirror the expectations of buyers: (1) imagination and problem-solving ability, (2) honesty, (3) intimate product knowledge, and (4) attentiveness reflected in responsiveness to buyer needs and customer loyalty and follow-up.[36] Firms use a variety of methods for evaluating prospective salespeople. Personal interviews, reference checks, and background information provided on application forms are the most frequently used methods.

WEB LINK   What Is Your Emotional Intelligence?

http://www.mcgrawhill.ca

A person's success at work depends on many talents, including intelligence and technical skills. Recent research indicates that an individual's emotional intelligence is also important, if not more important! Emotional intelligence (E-IQ) has five dimensions: (1) self-motivation skills; (2) self-awareness, or knowing one's own emotions; (3) the ability to manage one's emotions and impulses; (4) empathy, or the ability to sense how others are feeling; and (5) social skills, or the ability to handle the emotions of other people.

What is your E-IQ? Visit the Website at www.utne.com. Answer the questions to learn what your E-IQ quotient is and obtain additional insights.

EMOTIONAL INTELLIGENCE
The ability to understand one's own emotions and the emotions of people with whom one interacts on a daily basis.

www.can.ibm.com

Successful selling also requires a high degree of emotional intelligence. **Emotional intelligence** is the ability to understand one's own emotions and the emotions of people with whom one interacts on a daily basis. These qualities are important for adaptive selling and may spell the difference between effective and ineffective order-getting salespeople.[37] Are you interested in what your emotional intelligence might be? Read the accompanying Web Link and test yourself.

The search for qualified salespeople has produced an increasingly diverse salesforce in Canada. Women now represent half of all professional salespeople, and minority representation is growing.[38]

Salesforce Training   Whereas recruitment and selection of salespeople is a one-time event, salesforce training is an ongoing process that affects both new and seasoned salespeople. Sales training covers much more than selling practices. For example, IBM Global Services salespeople, who sell consulting and various information technology services, take at least two weeks of in-class and Web-based training on both consultative selling and the technical aspects of business.[39]

On-the-job training is the most popular type of training, followed by individual instruction taught by experienced salespeople. Formal classes and seminars taught by sales trainers are also popular.

Salesforce Motivation and Compensation   A sales plan cannot be successfully implemented without motivated salespeople. Research on salesperson motivation suggests that (1) a clear job description, (2) effective sales management practices, (3) a personal need for achievement, and (4) proper compensation, incentives, or rewards will produce a motivated salesperson.[40]

The importance of compensation as a motivating factor means that close attention must be given to how salespeople are financially rewarded for their efforts. Salespeople are paid using one of three plans: (1) straight salary, (2) straight commission, or (3) a combination of salary and commission. Under a *straight salary compensation plan* a salesperson is paid a fixed fee per week, month, or year. With a *straight commission compensation plan* a salesperson's earnings are directly tied to the sales or profit generated. For example, an insurance agent might receive a 2-percent commission of $2000 for selling a $100 000 life insurance policy. A *combination compensation plan* contains a specified salary plus a commission on sales or profit generated.

Each compensation plan has its advantages and disadvantages. A straight salary plan is easy to administer and gives management a large measure of control over how salespeople allocate their efforts. However, it provides little incentive to expand sales volume. This plan is used when salespeople engage in many non-selling activities, such as account servicing. A straight commission plan provides the maximum amount of selling incentive but can detract salespeople from providing customer service. This plan is common when non-selling activities are minimal. Combination plans are most preferred by salespeople and attempt to build on the advantages of salary and commission plans while reducing potential shortcomings of each.[41] Today, 63 percent of companies use combination plans, 17 percent use straight salary, and 20 percent rely solely on commissions.

Non-monetary rewards are also given to salespeople for meeting or exceeding

Mary Kay Cosmetics recognizes a top salesperson at its annual sales meeting.

Mary Kay Cosmetics, Inc.

www.marykay.com

objectives. These rewards include trips, honour societies, distinguished salesperson awards, and letters of commendation. Some unconventional rewards include the new pink Cadillacs and Pontiacs, fur coats, and jewellery given by Mary Kay Cosmetics to outstanding salepeople. Mary Kay, with 10 000 cars, has the largest fleet of General Motors cars in the world![42]

Effective recruitment, selection, training, motivation, and compensation programs combine to create a productive salesforce. Ineffective practices often lead to costly salesforce turnover. Canadian and American firms experience an annual 11.6 percent turnover rate, which means that more than 1 of every 10 salespeople are replaced each year.[43] The expense of replacing and training a new salesperson, including the cost of lost sales, can be high. Moreover, new recruits are often less productive than established salespeople.

Salesforce Evaluation and Control

The final function in the sales management process involves evaluating and controlling the salesforce. It is at this point that salespeople are assessed as to whether sales objectives were met and account management policies were followed. Both quantitative and behavioural measures are used to tap different selling dimensions.[44]

Quantitative Assessments   Quantitative assessments, called quotas, are based on input- and output-related objectives set forth in the sales plan. Input-related measures focus on the actual activities performed by salespeople such as those involving sales calls, selling expenses, and account management policies. The number of sales calls made, selling expense related to sales made, and the number of reports submitted to superiors are frequently used input measures.

Output measures focus on the results obtained and include sales produced, accounts generated, profit achieved, and orders produced compared with calls made. Dollar sales volume, last year/current year sales ratio, the number of new accounts, and sales of specific products are frequently used measures when evaluating salesperson output.

Behavioural Evaluation   Behavioural measures are also used to evaluate salespeople. These include assessments of a salesperson's attitude, attention to customers, product knowledge, selling and communication skills, appearance, and professional demeanour. Even though these assessments are sometimes subjective, they are frequently considered, and, in fact, inevitable, in salesperson evaluation. Moreover, these factors are often important determinants of quantitative outcomes.

Toshiba America Medical System salespeople have found computer technology to be an effective sales tool and training device.

Toshiba America Medical Systems

www.toshiba.com

 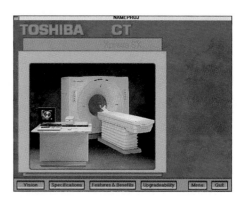

Almost 60 percent of companies now include customer satisfaction as a behavioural measure of salesperson performance.[45] (What percentage did you check for question 3 in Figure 20–1?) IBM Canada has been the most aggressive in using this behavioural measure. Forty percent of an IBM salesperson's evaluation is linked to customer satisfaction; the remaining 60 percent is linked to profits achieved. Eastman Chemical Company surveys its customers with eight versions of its customer satisfaction questionnaire printed in nine languages. Some 25 performance items are studied, including on-time and correct delivery, product quality, pricing practice, and sharing of market information. The survey is managed by the salesforce, and salespeople review the results with customers. Eastman salespeople know that "the second most important thing they have to do is get their customer satisfaction surveys out to and back from customers," says Eastman's sales training director. "Number one, of course, is getting orders."[46]

Salesforce Automation and Customer Relationship Management

Personal selling and sales management are undergoing a technological revolution with the integration of salesforce automation into customer relationship management (CRM) processes. In fact, the convergence of computer, information, communication, and Internet/Web technologies has transformed the sales function in many companies and made the promise of CRM a reality. Computer software packages by PeopleSoft, Siebel, and Oracle enable the salespeople to manage customer data and track customer needs. **Salesforce automation** (SFA) is the use of these technologies to make the sales function more effective and efficient. SFA applies to a wide range of activities, including each stage in the personal selling process and management of the salesforce itself.

SALESFORCE AUTOMATION
The use of technology to make the sales function more effective and efficient.

Salesforce automation represents both an opportunity and a challenge for companies. Examples of SFA applications include computer hardware and software for account analysis, time management, order processing and follow-up, sales presentations, proposal generation, and product and sales training. But, applications are not free. It is estimated that companies worldwide spent $2.6 billion for SFA software alone in 2001 and will spend over $4 billion in 2004. In addition, companies are investing two to three times these amounts for SFA salesforce training and technology integration services.[47]

Salesforce Computerization   Computer technology has become an integral part of field selling through innovations such as laptop, notebook, palmtop, pad, and tablet computers. For example, salespeople for Godiva Chocolates use their laptop computers to process orders, plan time allocations, forecast sales, and communicate with Godiva personnel and customers. While in a department store candy buyer's office, such as Neiman Marcus, a salesperson can calculate the order cost (and discount), transmit the order, and obtain a delivery date within minutes from Godiva's order processing department.[48]

Computer and communication technologies have made it possible for Compaq Computer salespeople to work out of their homes.

Compaq Computer Corporation

www.compaq.com

Toshiba America Medical System salespeople now use laptop computers with built-in CD-ROM capabilities to provide interactive presentations for their computerized tomography (CT) and magnetic resonance imaging (MRI) scanners. In it the customer sees elaborate three-dimensional animations, high-resolution scans, and video clips of the company's products in operation as well as narrated testimonials from satisfied customers. Toshiba has found this application to be effective both for sales presentations and for training its salespeople.[49]

Salesforce Communication   Technology also has changed the way salespeople communicate with customers, other salespeople and sales support personnel, and management. Facsimile, electronic mail, and voice mail are three common communication technologies used by salespeople today. Wireless phone technology, which now allows salespeople to exchange data as well as voice transmissions, is equally popular. Whether travelling or in a customer's office, these technologies provide information at the salesperson's fingertips to answer customer questions and solve problems.

Advances in communication and computer technologies have made possible the mobile and home sales office. Some salespeople now equip minivans with a fully functional desk, swivel chair, light, computer, printer, fax machine, wireless phone, and satellite dish. If a prospect can't see the salesperson right away, he or she can go outside to work in the mobile office until the prospect is available.[50] Home offices are now common. Compaq Computer Corporation is a case in point. The company recently shifted its salesforce into home offices, closed three regional sales offices, and saved $10 million in staff salaries and office rent. A fully equipped home office for each salesperson costs the company about $8000 and includes a laptop computer, fax/copier, cellular phone, two phone lines, and office furniture.[51]

Perhaps the greatest impact on salesforce communication is the application of Internet/Web-based technology. Today, salespeople are using their company's intranet for a variety of purposes. At EDS, a professional services firm, salespeople access its intranet to download client material, marketing content, account information, technical papers, and competitive profiles. In addition, EDS offers 7000 training classes that salespeople can take anytime, anywhere.[52]

Salesforce automation is clearly changing how selling is done and how salespeople are managed. Its numerous applications promise to boost selling productivity, improve customer relationships, and decrease selling cost. As applications increase, SFA has the potential to transform selling and sales management in the 21st century.

Concept Check

1. What are the three types of selling objectives?

2. What three factors are used to structure sales organizations?

3. How does emotional intelligence tie to adaptive selling?

SUMMARY

1 Personal selling involves the two-way flow of communication between a buyer and a seller, often in a face-to-face encounter, designed to influence a person's or group's purchase decision. Sales management involves planning the sales program and implementing and controlling the personal selling effort of the firm.

2 Personal selling is pervasive since virtually every occupation that involves customer contact has an element of selling attached to it.

3 Personal selling plays a major role in a firm's marketing effort. Salespeople occupy a boundary position between buyers and sellers; they *are* the company to many buyers and account for a major cost of marketing in a variety of industries; and they can create value for customers.

4 Three types of personal selling exist: order-taking, order-getting, and sales support activities. Each type differs from the others in terms of actual selling done and the amount of creativity required to perform the job.

5 The personal selling process, particularly for order getters, is a complex activity involving six stages: (1) prospecting, (2) preapproach, (3) approach, (4) presentation, (5) close, and (6) follow-up.

6 The sales management process consists of three interrelated functions: (1) sales plan formulation, (2) sales plan implementation, and (3) evaluation of the salesforce.

7 A sales plan is a statement describing what is to be achieved and where and how the selling effort of salespeople is to be deployed. Sales planning involves setting objectives, organizing the salesforce, and developing account management policies.

8 Effective salesforce recruitment and selection efforts, sales training that emphasizes selling skills and product knowledge, and motivation and compensation practices are necessary to successfully implement a sales plan.

9 Salespeople are evaluated using quantitative and behavioural measures that are linked to selling objectives and account management policies.

10 Salesforce automation involves the use of technology designed to make the sales function more effective and efficient. It applies to a wide range of activities, including each stage in the personal selling process and management of the salesforce itself.

KEY TERMS AND CONCEPTS

account management policies p. 537
adaptive selling p. 531
consultative selling p. 531
emotional intelligence p. 539
formula selling presentation p. 530
major account management p. 535
missionary salespeople p. 526
need-satisfaction presentation p. 531
order getter p. 525
order taker p. 524
partnership selling p. 524

personal selling p. 522
personal selling process p. 527
relationship selling p. 524
sales engineer p. 526
sales management p. 522
sales plan p. 533
salesforce automation p. 541
stimulus-response presentation p. 530
team selling p. 526
workload method p. 537

INTERNET EXERCISE

www.mcgrawhill.ca/college/berkowitz

A unique resource for the latest developments in personal selling and sales management is the Sales Marketing Network (SMN) at www.info-now.com. SMN provides highly readable reports on a variety of topics including many discussed in this chapter, such as telemarketing, motivation, sales training, and sales management. These reports contain concise overviews, definitions, statistics, and reviews of critical issues. They also include references to additional information and links to related material elsewhere on the SMN site. Registration (at no cost) is required to view some of the reports.

Visit the SMN site and do the following:

1 Select a chapter topic, and update the statistics for, say, sales training costs or the popularity of different salesforce incentives.

2 Select a topic covered in the chapter such as telemarketing, and summarize the critical issues identified for this practice.

Want to get better grades, find tips on how to study more effectively, and stay up to date with happenings in the world of marketing? Visit the Online Learning Centre for practice tests, Study Smart software, and much more! www.mcgrawhill.ca/college/berkowitz
Interested in finding out what marketing looks like in the real world? *Marketing Magazine* is just a click away on your OLC! Visit www.mcgrawhill.ca/college/berkowitz

APPLYING MARKETING CONCEPTS AND PERSPECTIVES

1 Jane Dawson is a new sales representative for the Charles Schwab brokerage firm. In searching for clients, Jane purchased a mailing list of subscribers to *The Financial Post* and called them all regarding their interest in discount brokerage services. She asked if they have any stocks and if they have a regular broker. Those people without a regular broker were asked their investment needs. Two days later Dawson called back with investment advice and asked if they would like to open an account. Identify each of Jane Dawson's actions in terms of the steps of selling.

2 For the first 50 years of business the Johnson Carpet Company produced carpets for residential use. The salesforce was structured geographically. In the past five years a large percentage of carpet sales has been to industrial users, hospitals, schools, and architects. The company also has broadened its product line to include area rugs, Oriental carpets, and wall-to-wall carpeting. Is the present salesforce structure appropriate, or would you recommend an alternative?

3 Where would you place each of the following sales jobs on the order-taker/order-getter continuum shown below? (*a*) Tim Hortons counter clerk, (*b*) automobile insurance salesperson, (*c*) IBM computer salesperson, (*d*) life insurance salesperson, and (*e*) shoe salesperson.

Order taker   Order getter

4 Listed here are two different firms. Which compensation plan would you recommend for each firm, and what reasons would you give for your recommendations? (*a*) A newly formed company that sells lawn care equipment on a door-to-door basis directly to consumers; and (*b*) the Nabisco Company, which sells heavily advertised products in supermarkets by having the salesforce call on these stores and arrange shelves, set up displays, and make presentations to store buying committees.

5 The TDK tape company services 1000 audio stores throughout Canada. Each store is called on 12 times a year, and the average sales call lasts 30 minutes. Assuming a salesperson works 40 hours a week, 50 weeks a year, and devotes 75 percent of the time to actual selling, how many salespeople does TDK need?

6 A furniture manufacturer is currently using manufacturer's representatives to sell its line of living room furniture. These representatives receive an 8-percent commission. The company is considering hiring its own salespeople and has estimated that the fixed cost of managing and paying their salaries would be $1 million annually. The salespeople would also receive a 4-percent commission on sales. The company has sales of $25 million, and sales are expected to grow by 15 percent next year. Would you recommend that the company switch to its own salesforce? Why or why not?

7 Suppose someone said to you, "The only real measure of a salesperson is the amount of sales produced." How might you respond?

VIDEO CASE 20–1 Reebok International Ltd.

"I think face-to-face selling is the most important and exciting part of this whole job. It's not writing the sales reports. It's not analyzing trends and forecasting. It's the two hours that you have to try to sell the buyer your products in a way that's profitable for both you and the retailer," relates Robert McMahon, key account sales representative. McMahon's job encompasses myriad activities, from supervising other sales representatives to attending companywide computer training sessions to monitoring competitors' activities. But it's the actual selling that is most appealing to McMahon. "That's the challenging, stimulating part of the job. Selling to the buyer is a different challenge every day. Every sales call, as well as you may have preplanned it, can change based on shifts and trends in the market. So you need to be able

to react to those changes and really think on your feet in front of the buyer."

REEBOK—HOT ON NIKE'S HEELS IN THE ATHLETIC SHOE AND APPAREL MARKET

Reebok is the second largest athletic shoe manufacturer behind the market leader, Nike. In addition to its athletic shoes, Reebok also sells Rockport, Greg Norman Collection, and Ralph Lauren Footwear shoes. The Reebok sporting goods line remains the flagship brand, though, and distinguishes itself on the market through the DMX cushioning technology in its footwear. Reebok concentrates its resources on getting its footwear and sporting goods gear into a diversified mix of distribution channels such as athletic footwear specialty stores, department stores, and large sporting goods stores. Reebok is unique in that it emphasizes relationships with the retailers as an integral part of its marketing strategy. As an employee at MVP Sports, one of Reebok's major retailers, puts it, "Reebok is the only company that comes in on a regular basis and gives us information. Nike comes in once in a great while. New Balance comes in every six months. Saucony has come in twice. That's been it. Reebok comes in every month to update us on new information and new products. They tell us about the technology so we can tell the customers." Says Laurie Sipples, "vector" representative for Reebok, "There's a partnership that exists between Reebok and an account like MVP Sports that sets us apart. That relationship is a great asset that Reebok has because the retailer feels more in touch with us than other brands."

THE SELLING PROCESS AT REEBOK

Selling at Reebok includes three elements—building trust between the salesperson and the retailer, providing enough information to the retailer for them to be successful selling Reebok products, and, finally, supporting the retailer after the sale. Sean Neville, senior vice president and general manager of Reebok North America, explains, "Our goal is not to sell to the retailer, our goal is ultimately to sell to the consumer, and so we use the retailer as a partner. The salespeople are always keeping their eyes open and thinking like the retailer and selling to the consumer."

Reebok sells in teams that consist of the account representatives, who do the actual selling to the retailer, and the "vector" representatives, who spend their time in the stores training the store salespeople and reporting trends back to the account manager. The selling teams are organized geographically so that the salespeople live and work in the area they are selling in. This allows the sales team to understand the consumer intuitively. Neville explains, "If you have someone from one city fly to another and try to tell someone on the streets of that city what's happening from a trends standpoint and what products to purchase, it's very difficult."

Reebok Unlimited
ARE YOU FEELING IT?

In this sport, accomplishments are measured in hundredths of a second, fractions of an inch, and sometimes, over a century.

In 1895, our founder, Joe Foster, invented the running spike. It changed track and field, and we've been innovating ever since. In the 1999 Reebok track and field collection, you'll find shoes that will help you make the most of your efforts, whatever your event. With 101 years of innovation, they'll give you every advantage you need to accomplish your personal best.

Pro Triple Jump   3D Road Racer   Pro Sprint   Pro Javelin   Pro Distance   Pro Glide   Pro High Jump   Pro Long Jump/ Pole Vault

www.reebok.com © 1999 Reebok International Ltd. All Rights Reserved. REEBOK, DMX and the Vector Logo (/) are registered trademarks of Reebok.

On average, Reebok salespeople spend 70 percent of their time preparing for a sale and 30 percent of their time actually selling. The sales process at Reebok typically follows the six steps of the personal selling process identified in Figure 20–3: (1) Reebok identifies the outlets it would like to carry its athletic gear; (2) the salesforce prepares for the a presentation by familiarizing themselves with the store and its customers; (3) a Reebok representative approaches the prospect and suggests a meeting and presentation; (4) as the presentation begins, the salesperson summarizes relevant market conditions and consumer trends to demonstrate Reebok's commitment to a partnership with the retailer, states what s/he hopes to get out of the sales meeting, explains how the products work, and reinforces the benefits of Reebok products; (5) the salesperson engages in an action close (gets a signed document or a firm confirmation of the sale); and (6) later, various members of the salesforce frequently visit the retailer to provide assistance and monitor consumer preferences.

THE SALES MANAGEMENT PROCESS AT REEBOK

The sales teams at Reebok are organized based on Reebok's three major distribution channels: athletic specialty stores, sporting goods stores, and department stores. The smaller stores have sales teams assigned to them based on geographical location. The salesforce is then further broken down into footwear and apparel teams. The salesforce is primarily organized by distribution channel because this is most responsive to customer needs and wants. The salesforce is compensated on both a short-term and a long-term basis. In the short term, salespeople are paid based on sales results and profits for the current quarter as well as forecasting. In the long term, salespeople are compensated based on their teamwork and teambuilding efforts. As Neville explains,

"Money is typically fourth or fifth on the list of pure motivation. Number one is recognition for a job well done. And that drives people to succeed." Management at Reebok is constantly providing feedback to the salesforce acknowledging their success, not just during annual reviews, and Neville feels this is the key to the high level of motivation, energy, and excitement that exists in the salesforce at Reebok.

WHAT'S NEW ON THE HORIZON FOR THE SALESFORCE AT REEBOK?

Reebok has recently issued laptop computers to its entire salesforce, which enable the salespeople to check inventories in the warehouses, make sure orders are being shipped on time, and even enter orders while they're out in the field. Reebok is also focusing more on relationship selling. McMahon describes his relationship with a major buyer as, "one of trust and respect. It's gotten to the point now where we're good friends. We go to a lot of sporting events together, which I think really helps." Another recent innovation is for the salesforce to incentivize the store's sales clerks. For instance, whoever sells the most pairs of Reebok shoes in a month will get tickets to a concert or a football game.

Questions

1 How does Reebok create customer value for its major accounts through relationship selling?

2 How does Reebok utilize team selling to provide the highest level of customer value possible to its major accounts?

3 Is Reebok's salesforce organized based on geography, customer, or product?

4 What are some ways Reebok's selling processes are changing due to technical advancements?

PART 4 CASE   Transforming Book Retailing

Amazon.com went online in 1994 and became the pioneer virtual bookseller—creating a rollercoaster ride for book readers, publishers, and retailers. At the time no one could have predicted the extent to which consumers would change their purchasing patterns or the dramatic changes that would take place within the marketing channel. Amazon.com caused a ripple effect by injecting a breath of fresh air into a staid, predictable channel of distribution. The innovative alternative to the traditional book shopping experience originally increased sales for publishers, distributors, and retailers. By the end of 2000, however, after the dot-com crash and with few virtual companies showing a profit, the revenues in the book industry remained flat. Increased pressure on publishers to provide choices for consumers in the form of different purchase options either in-store or online eroded profits as executives made aggressive investments in both new stores and online systems, extending resources beyond the market's potential.

Added to that, some online publishers are providing the option of e-books, taking a run at the traditional paper publishers. Napster-like technology now exists allowing users to download entire copies of pirated books, causing major concern in the publishing industry.[1] Peer-to-peer networks are appearing and there are now a number of pirated science fiction novels and computer manuals available online. Chapters and Indigo Music and Books clashed as they fought for the Canadian book reader, and with the 2001 downturn in the economy the stage is set for dramatic changes yet to come. Together, these events combine to create an environment contributing to the transformation in the book publishing industry as companies and consumers adapt to technological changes.

HOW THE TRANSFORMATION BEGAN

Amazon.com reinvented the retail game on a number of fronts, but specifically book retailing changed forever. This does not mean the end of the story for brick-and-mortar companies—quite the contrary. Those companies understanding how to add value to the consumer by integrating both in-store and online experiences are winning the customer. Amazon.com can claim the honour of being a pioneer and creating interest in e-commerce and book retailing even though long-term profitability is not a given for Amazon.com. Pioneer companies do not always survive in the long term. There is evidence that late movers in a market can outsell pioneers in a product category if they are innovative.[2] This means that although Amazon.com was first to market with its form

of online purchasing, it has taken on traditional book retailers with strong brand names in a number of different markets around the world. The traditional booksellers may have entered the online purchasing environment late, but that doesn't mean they aren't adapting and fighting to survive. Canadian book retailers like Chapters and Indigo have leveraged their brands, giving Canadian companies a strong chance of holding back the advances of Amazon.com in Canada.[3]

Amazon.com changed the perception of book buying, book publishing, and book retailing—replacing the image of dusty bookshelves and old book jackets with a modern one-click experience. Shopping on the Net versus shopping in person gives consumers different experiences and meets different needs. Buying a book online is a fast, convenient way to browse titles, topics, and authors at any time of the day or night. It cannot provide the experience of picking up a book and reading it while sipping a mocha latte, which can be done in a Chapters or Indigo store. The different environments created by each superstore encourage buyers to take their time to find the perfect book or selection of music instead of hurtling through cyberspace. Amazon.com made significant inroads in capturing a share of the Canadian online buying market due in part to the fact that Americans have embraced the opportunity to purchase online faster than Canadians have. Canadians are interested in buying Canadian items online but, until recently, were restricted in their choices. This happened because Canadian retailers were slow to recognize that American online retailers could actually present a threat to their business. This reason, together with the lack of capital to support the development of the technology, has caused Canadian retailers to move cautiously with the development of online purchasing opportunities for Canadians.[4]

CANADIAN RETAILERS PROTECT THEIR TURF

While battling each other, two Canadian book retailers also took on Amazon.com to limit its opportunity to grow its presence in the Canadian marketplace. Toronto-based Chapters Inc. is one of these companies and began its journey into the cyberspace battlefield in 1998 with the launch of its first Website, www.chaptersglobe.com. A second Website, www.chapters.ca, was introduced in April 1999. Chapters claimed to appeal to two different market segments; two sites would prove to be too much for one company. Chapters believed it could offer something different compared to its largest cyberspace competitor, Amazon.com, by offering book buyers something special. Chapters.ca contained author talks

and book reviews and included a variety of product lines such as videos, CDs, DVDs, and software. How is this different from Amazon.com? Canadian book readers and audiophiles can do business in Canadian currency, a bonus given the difference between the U.S. and Canadian dollar. Through focus groups, Chapters found that Canadian book readers were different than Americans. Canadians are attracted to book-reading events, creating differentiation compared to Amazon.com. As well, Canadians are more protective of their privacy than American Internet users, creating an opportunity for Chapters to provide options for their customer base, including giving Internet shoppers the option of declining cookies (customized electronic identifiers) sent to their hard drive. An online customer is also given a choice to opt in or opt out of targeted direct e-mails or special offers.

Chapters was once the largest book retailer in Canada, with 59 superstores and 305 traditional stores in almost every region of the country under the banner names Coles, SmithBooks/LibraireSmith, Classic Bookstores, and The Book Company. Chapters also managed the McGill University bookstore, wanting it to be a flagship for its campus bookstore division.[5] Even before online retailing, Chapters was creating a store inventory management system (SIMS) and a state-of-the-art

distribution facility to provide cost savings and efficiencies in managing book titles and other related merchandise requiring careful management to keep inventory costs under control. Chapters originally spent $1.5 million to go online, with a portion of that money going to support the development of the logistics infrastructure to handle Internet orders.[6] The distribution centre, just outside of Toronto in Brampton, Ontario, was considered crucial to the future success of Chapters through efficient warehousing and distribution. Having new book titles in stores across the country when people are ready to buy is one part of the distribution challenge. With online purchasing, there is a different challenge in managing consumer expectations of availability, pricing, packaging, and delivery. Where distribution of merchandise to stores across the country can be done in large batches, Internet distribution is done one or two items at a time. Chapters was determined to compete with Amazon.com using technology and building a loyal Canadian customer base.

Indigo Books & Music Café was the second contender seeking a share of the book retailing market. Indigo opened its storefront doors in 1996 and, after successfully capturing interest from book readers, went online in late 1998. Heather Reisman, Indigo's president and CEO, recognized from the beginning that online retailing was going to be important. "For us, it was just an issue of timing and pacing; we had to get our core physical business and our infrastructure going."[7] The president of Indigo believes the people attracted to her stores are those who are "passionate about books and words on paper."[8]

Both Chapters and Indigo created their superstores to include a growing number of amenities. Chapters' stores have Starbucks coffee shops, whereas Indigo has a coffee bar with a café feel. Reisman created a unique boutique feel in Indigo stores. The ambiance pays! Research showed that a Chapters customer will linger for 62 to 75 minutes per visit, which is five times the amount spent in a traditional bookstore like SmithBooks or Coles. The average amount spent per transaction in a Chapters store is $20, almost twice the average transaction of $11 to $12 spent at a mall store.[9] The battle between Chapters and Indigo not only stimulated revenue in the book retailing market, it rejuvenated the Canadian publishing industry at the same time.

The early 1990s were bleak for Canadian book publishers. Being a small market, it is difficult in Canada to profitably publish even well known Canadian authors.[10] David Kent, president of Random House Canada, attributes some of the woes of the Canadian book publishing industry to Canada's small market size, but points out that Canada is "like a mouse living next door to an elephant."[11] Canadian publishers, unlike our southern neighbours, have had difficulty staying profitable due to distribution challenges as the result of tremendous distances and scattered population pockets across the country. The United States does not have this problem, which is why it is the largest and most profitable book market in the world. Online book buying, combined with two ambitious major Canadian book retailers, has created demand for Canadian literature. This is good for authors and publishers. With demand for new Canadian fiction increasing, says Anna Porter of Key Porter, "American titles seem very expensive now and people seem to be buying more Canadian-produced books as a result."[12] Canadian storefront and online book retailers can offer something that even Amazon.com cannot—Canadian book titles from Canadian publishers in Canadian dollars.

As any retailer understands, there are cycles in businesses and particularly in businesses with an entertainment focus. It has been important to Chapters, Indigo, and Amazon.com to pay attention to well-designed, customer-centred Websites. That is not the only investment needed to be competitive in this new channel. Distribution is important in delivering the right product to the right customer. As Chapters and Indigo adapted to meet Amazon.com's challenge in the market-space, the two Canadian big-box bookstores fought each other for dominance in the Canadian book business, creating drama and a tragic end for one as two companies become one.

THE UNENDING DRAMA—WHEN TWO BECAME ONE

As both Chapters and Indigo aggressively pursued the Canadian book reader, music listener, and video viewer both in-store and online, the limited market size capped profitability creating intense pressure in the Canadian book retail market. After five years of rapid growth for Chapters, the executives at the big-box bookstore realized too late that it expanded too quickly.[13] Chapters posted a record $84.5-million loss for fiscal 2001, blaming the situation on the restructuring of the Pegasus distribution centre, Chapters Online, too many marginal stores, and slow-moving inventory.[14] The chain lost $14.7 million to inventory shrinkage alone. Two Websites and a massive investment in the distribution system as mentioned earlier did not pay off for Chapters. The loss made Chapters a target for a takeover. Future Shop tried to purchase the book chain, but was outmaneuvered by Heather Reisman and her husband Gerry Schwartz. Using Trilogy, their investment company, they successfully took over Chapters Inc. in February 2001 for $121.5 million.[15]

Merging Chapters Inc. and Indigo Books & Music creates an enormous presence in the book retailing industry. In April of 2001, the federal Competition Bureau agreed to the merger with a number of stipulations and a code of conduct dictating rules for discounts, payment cycles, and returns.[16] This code is in force for five years and requires scaling back book returns, speeding up payments to publishers, and reducing fees charged to publishers for displaying books.[17] In addition, under the merger agreement Chapters-Indigo needs to offer for sale a book distribution centre, certain online assets, up to three of Chapters' store brand names, 13 superstores, and 10 mall stores across Canada. Chapters will not be allowed to operate more than one store per shopping mall.

The Canadian drama unfolding in our bookstores continues. Chapters-Indigo is having trouble meeting the deadline for selling its properties. Indigo Books & Music Inc. reported improved operating results even though Indigo and Chapters Inc. are individually showing losses for the last quarter of 2001.[18] Chapters-Indigo Online revenue declined 46 percent in late 2001 due to both the decline in purchasing behaviour post–September 11 as well as the aggressive moves of Amazon.com, which was lowering prices, cutting costs, and adding products.[19] Amazon.com now has four times more Canadian visitors than Chapters-Indigo online. The future of book retailing in Canada continues to be uncertain for retailers as well as publishers.

CANADIAN PUBLISHERS UNDER INCREASED PRESSURE

Canadian publishers are facing uncertainty due to the major changes happening at the retail level. In addition, there are other uncertainties relating to technological developments that could prove to seriously undermine the publishing industry in Canada. E-publishing and the e-book are waiting on the horizon. Anne McDermid, an agent in the industry, says "publishers are waiting for stores, stores are waiting for customers and customers aren't exactly breaking down the door."[20] The option to download chapters and books exists at some publishers' Websites (see www.eharlequin.com), one form of electronic publishing. The reader may simply print the work or read it from a computer screen. However, it is difficult to read a book this way by a pool or in the bathtub. "The electronic book is either an idea whose time has come, or a cybernightmare that only a nerd could love."[21] The challenge for e-books is the device. A book reader device needs to have a screen large enough to make it easy to read yet small enough to resemble a book. There are a number of reader devices currently on the market, but the adoption of these devices is relatively slow.[22] None of the Rocket eBook, The SoftBook Reader, or RCA's Ebook have really captured the imagination of book readers.[23] Although the publishing industry is concerned about the impact this technology will have on its future, it appears that it will be some time yet before book readers will trade in their books for electronic devices.

Discussion Questions

1 From what you know about the Canadian book publishing industry, identify the following as either consumer or business products/services: (*a*) McGraw-Hill Publishing; (*b*) software for order tracking; (*c*) Indigo's card and gift section. Discuss the rationale for your classification choices.

2 Demonstrate your understanding of distribution channels by drawing a diagram of the relationships among the companies as discussed in the case. Draw the channel to the end consumer. What does your diagram tell you about the nature of this industry?

3 Discuss implications of the merger of Chapters and Indigo in terms of channel relationships and power. How does this relate to the code of conduct imposed on Indigo by the Competition Bureau?

4 Discuss the major pricing issues for Canadian book retailers when competing with American companies like Amazon.com. In this case, what role does price play in this market?

5 If you were the new product development manager for Indigo Books & Music Café, what would you recommend to Heather Reisman as the next addition to the product portfolio? Why?

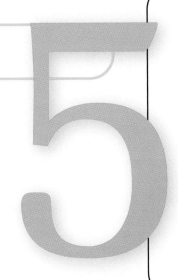

MANAGING THE MARKETING PROCESS

Part 5 discusses issues and techniques related to interactive marketing technologies and the planning, implementation, and control phases of the strategic marketing process. Chapter 21 describes how the evolution of a new exchange environment has led to a new marketing mantra: "Anytime, Anywhere, Any way!" The chapter also illustrates how interactive technologies influence customer value and the customer experience through context, content, community, customization, communication, connectivity, and commerce. Chapter 22 explains how marketing executives search for competitive advantage and allocate the firm's marketing resources to maximize the effects of marketing efforts. Frameworks for improving marketing planning, guidelines for creating an effective marketing plan, and alternatives for organizing a marketing department are also discussed.

21

IMPLEMENTING INTERACTIVE AND MULTICHANNEL MARKETING

AFTER READING THIS CHAPTER YOU SHOULD BE ABLE TO:

- Understand what interactive marketing is and how it creates customer value, customer relationships, and customer experiences in the new marketplace.

- Identify online consumers, their profiles, and their purchasing behaviours.

- Recognize why certain types of products and services are particularly suited for interactive marketing.

- Distinguish between multiple channels and multichannel marketing in reaching online customers.

- Understand the differences between transactional Websites and promotional Websites in multichannel marketing.

ANYTIME, ANYWHERE, ANY WAY: THE NEW MARKETING MANTRA

What a difference a year (or three) makes. Just yesterday it seems, the Internet and the World Wide Web's promise of immediacy and interactivity was hailed as a compelling new technology that would revolutionize marketing and forever change how consumers shop and purchase products and services. It's clear that Internet/Web technology has altered consumer behaviour and marketing practice, but not in quite the manner pundits prognosticated.

Internet/Web technology has empowered consumers to seek information, evaluate alternatives, and make purchase decisions on their own terms and conditions. At the same time, this technology has challenged marketers to deliver to consumers *more* (selection, service, quality, enjoyment, convenience, and information) *for less* (money, time, effort). In short, the initial promise of immediacy and interactivity quickly transformed itself into a "straight A" customer value standard and marketing mantra: Anytime, Anywhere, Any way!

Today, consumers expect to shop and buy their favourite products and services anytime, anywhere, and anyway without constraints. Marketers have responded by engaging in interactive and multichannel marketing. This chapter describes how companies design and implement marketing programs that capitalize on the unique value-creation capabilities of Internet/Web technology. We begin by explaining how this technology can create customer value, build customer relationships, and produce customer experiences in novel ways. Next, we describe how consumer behaviour and marketing practice are affected by Internet/Web technology. Finally, we show how marketers integrate and leverage their communication and delivery channels using Internet/Web technology.[1]

CREATING CUSTOMER VALUE, RELATIONSHIPS, AND EXPERIENCES IN THE NEW MARKETSPACE

Consumers and companies populate two market environments today. One is the traditional marketplace. Here buyers and sellers engage in face-to-face exchange relationships in a material environment characterized by physical facilities (stores and offices) and mostly tangible objects. The other is the marketspace, an Internet/Web-enabled digital environment characterized by "face-to-screen" exchange relationships and electronic images and offerings.

The existence of two market environments has been a boon for consumers. Today, consumers can shop for and purchase a wide variety of products and services in either market environment. Actually, many consumers now browse and buy in both market environments and more are expected to do so in the future as access to and familiarity with Internet/Web technology grows.[2] As an illustration, Figure 21–1 shows the 6-year growth trend in Internet/Web users and estimated online retail sales in Canada.[3] The value of Canada's retail online revenue is not exact as a variety of organizations, including Statistics Canada, The Retail Council of Canada and various consulting companies attempt to estimate the size and growth of purchasing online. What is certain is that more Canadians are purchasing online as more Canadian retailers provide the opportunity to use the Internet for more than simply an information tool.[4]

Marketing in two market environments poses significant challenges for companies. Companies with origins in the traditional marketplace, such as Procter & Gamble, Canadian Tire, and General Motors, are challenged to define the nature and scope of their marketspace presence. These companies need to determine the role of Internet/Web technology in attracting, retaining, and building consumer relationships to improve their competitive positions in the traditional marketplace while achieving a marketspace presence. Consider Toys "Я" Us, a leading toy retailer in the traditional marketplace. It has formed an alliance with Amazon.com to create a marketspace presence—Toysrus.com. Toys "Я" Us leverages its toy merchandising know-how and immense store network with Amazon's knowledge and experience with Internet/Web technology. The result? Toys "Я" Us now has a presence in two market environments. On the other hand, companies with marketspace origins, including Amazon.com, eBay, and E*Trade, are challenged to continually refine, broaden, and deepen their marketspace presence, and consider what role, if any, the traditional marketplace will play in their future. Gateway Computer is a good example.[5] This direct marketer and marketspace pioneer also operates a network of

FIGURE 21–1

The 6-year trend in Internet revenue and activity in Canada

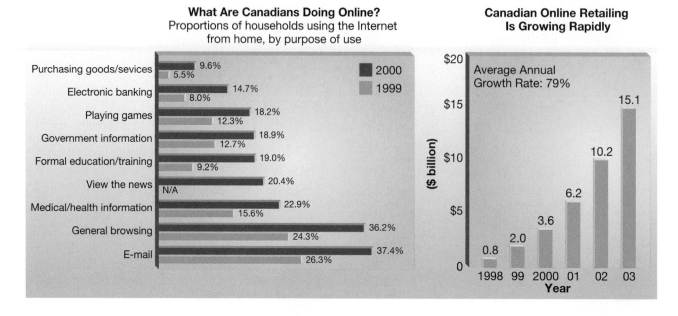

Gateway Country showrooms for personal computer buyers who prefer browsing in a store, physically handling the merchandise, and talking face-to-face with a salesperson. A company's success in achieving a meaningful marketspace presence hinges largely on designing and executing a marketing program that capitalizes on the unique customer value-creation capabilities of Internet/Web technology.

Customer Value Creation in Marketspace

Despite the widespread interest in marketspace, its economic significance remains small compared with the traditional marketplace. Electronic commerce is expected to represent less than 20 percent of Canadian consumer and business goods and services expenditures in 2006, and less than 9 percent of global expenditures.[6] Why then has the new marketspace captured the eye and imagination of marketers?

Marketers believe that the possibilities for customer value creation are greater in marketspace than in the traditional marketplace. Recall from Chapter 1 that marketing creates time, place, form, and possession utilities for customers, thereby providing value. In marketspace, the provision of direct, on-demand information is possible from marketers *anywhere* to customers *anywhere at any time*. Why? Operating hours and geographical constraints do not exist in marketspace. For example, Recreational Equipment (www.rei.com), an outdoor gear marketer, reports that 35 percent of its orders are placed between 10:00 P.M. and 7:00 A.M., long after and before retail stores are open for business. This isn't surprising. About 58 percent of Internet/Web users prefer to shop and buy in their night clothes or pajamas![7] Similarly, a Canadian consumer from Saskatchewan can access Marks & Spencer (www.marks-and-spencer.co.uk), the well-known British department store, to shop for clothing as easily as a person living near London's Piccadilly Square. Possession utility—getting a product or service to consumers so they can own or use it—is accelerated. Airline, car rental, and lodging electronic reservation systems such as Orbitz (www.orbitz.com) allow comparison shopping for the lowest fares, rents, and rates and almost immediate access to and confirmation of travel arrangements and accommodations.

The greatest marketspace opportunity for marketers, however, lies in its potential for creating form utility. Interactive two-way Internet/Web-enabled communication capabilities in marketspace invite consumers to tell marketers exactly what their

Orbitz offers consumers the most low-cost airfares and flight options on the Web as well as rental cars, lodging, cruises, vacation packages, and other travel deals.

Orbitz

www.orbitz.com

requirements are, making customization of a product or service to fit the buyer's exact needs possible. For instance, KraftCanada.ca encourages customers to try recipes and even provides help for creating meals with ingredients provided in real time. KraftCanada.ca will keep track of your recipes in My Recipe Box.

Interactivity, Individuality, and Customer Relationships in Marketspace

Marketers also benefit from two unique capabilities of Internet/Web technology that promote and sustain customer relationships. One is *interactivity*; the other is *individuality*.[8] Both capabilities are important building blocks for buyer-seller relationships. For these relationships to occur, companies need to interact with their customers by listening and responding to their needs. Marketers must also treat customers as individuals and empower them to (1) influence the timing and extent of the buyer-seller interaction and (2) have a say in the kind of products and services they buy, the information they receive, and in some cases, the prices they pay. In doing so, companies are transforming their customer relationship management (CRM) efforts into **eCRM**—a Web-centric, personalized approach to managing customer relationships electronically.

An integral component of eCRM is interactive marketing. **Interactive marketing** involves two-way buyer–seller electronic communication in a computer-mediated environment in which the buyer controls the kind and amount of information received from the seller. Interactive marketing today is characterized by sophisticated choiceboard and personalization systems that transform information supplied by customers into customized responses to their individual needs.

Choiceboards   A **choiceboard** is an interactive, Internet/Web-enabled system that allows individual customers to design their own products and services by answering a few questions and choosing from a menu of product or service attributes (or components), prices, and delivery options.[9] Customers today can design their own computers with Dell Computer's online configurator, create their own athletic shoe at Niketown.com, assemble their own investment portfolios with Schwab's mutual fund evaluator, and even mix their own cereal ingredients at General Mills's experimental MyCereal.com Website. Because choiceboards collect precise information about the preferences and behaviour of individual buyers, a company becomes more knowledgeable about the customer and better able to anticipate and fulfill that customer's needs. Read the accompanying Marketing NewsNet to learn how Reflect.com uses choiceboard technology to create made-to-order cosmetics and other personal care items for women.[10]

Most choiceboards are essentially transaction devices. However, companies such as Dell Computer have expanded the functionality of choiceboards using collaborative filtering technology. **Collaborative filtering** is a process that automatically groups people with similar buying intentions, preferences, and behaviours and predicts future purchases.[11] For example, say two people who have never met buy a few of the same CDs over time. Collaborative filtering software is programmed to reason that these two buyers might have similar musical tastes: If one buyer likes a particular CD, then the other will like it as well. The outcome? Collaborative filtering gives marketers the ability to make a dead-on sales recommendation to a buyer in real time!

Choiceboards and collaborative filtering represent two important capabilities of Internet/Web technology and have changed the way companies operate today. According to an electronic commerce manager at IBM, "The business model of the past was make and sell. Now instead of make and sell, it's sense and respond."[12]

---

eCRM
A Web-centric, personalized approach to managing customer relationships electronically.

INTERACTIVE MARKETING
Two-way buyer–seller electronic communication in a computer-mediated environment in which the buyer controls the kind and amount of information received from the seller.

CHOICEBOARD
An interactive, Internet/Web-enabled system that allows individual customers to design their own products and services by answering a few questions and choosing from a menu of product or service attributes (or components), prices, and delivery options.

COLLABORATIVE FILTERING
A process that automatically groups people with similar buying intentions, preferences, and behaviours and predicts future purchases.

MARKETING NEWSNET

Reflect.com: Creating Customized Cosmetics

"We're learning that customization is powerful," says Ginger Kent, CEO of Reflect.com (www.reflect.com), based in San Francisco. Reflect.com is the first online marketer that allows users to create their own cosmetics—everything from skin and body care items to hair care, colour cosmetics, fragrances, and accessories. The company lets customers tailor their own products by suggesting beauty ingredients they like most. "It's an incredibly powerful idea—like a throwback to the 1800s and how apothecaries mixed formulas for people," notes Kent.

Reflect.com is targeted to women who crave individualized products. In fact, no Reflect product exists before it is created by the consumer. Over a million "customizations" have been done for online shoppers and the incidence of new users continues to grow. Today, Reflect.com is considered the second most visited beauty Website. Contrary to other beauty Websites that have failed, Kent says confidently: "Our business model has a high profit margin, and also includes repeat customers." What's more, almost 90 percent of customers recommend the site to others.

PERSONALIZATION
The consumer-initiated practice of generating content on a marketer's Website that is custom tailored to an individual's specific needs and preferences.

PERMISSION MARKETING
The solicitation of a consumer's consent (called "opt-in") to receive e-mail and advertising based on personal data supplied by the consumer.

Personalization   Choiceboards and collaborative filtering are marketer-initiated efforts to provide customized responses to the needs of individual buyers. Personalization systems are typically buyer-initiated efforts. **Personalization** is the consumer-initiated practice of generating content on a marketer's Website that is custom tailored to an individual's specific needs and preferences. For example, Yahoo! (www.yahoo.ca) allows users to create personalized MyYahoo pages. Users can add or delete a variety of types of information from their personal pages, including specific stock quotes, weather conditions in any city in the world, and local television schedules. In turn, Yahoo! can use the buyer profile data entered when users register at the site to tailor e-mail messages, advertising, and content to the individual—and even post a birthday greeting on the user's special day!

An aspect of personalization is a buyer's willingness to have tailored communications brought to his or her attention. Obtaining this approval is called **permission marketing**—the solicitation of a consumer's consent (called "opt-in") to receive e-mail and advertising based on personal data supplied by the consumer. Permission marketing is a proven vehicle for building and maintaining customer relationships, provided it is properly used. Companies that successfully employ permission marketing adhere to three rules.[13] First, they make sure "opt-in" customers receive only information that is relevant and meaningful to them. Second, their customers are given the option of "opting out" or changing the kind, amount, or timing of information sent to them. Finally, their customers are assured that their name or buyer profile data will not be sold or shared with others. This assurance is important because 83 percent of non-online shoppers have expressed concern about the privacy of their personal information.[14] See Chapter 18 for more on opt-in and opt-out marketing.

Canadian companies are exploring the opportunities associated with permission-based, outbound e-mail campaigns. Le Chateau's Website is used to contact their loyal clientele on a regular basis. The Website (www.lechateau.ca) has been designed to encourage online customers into their stores. The company has collected more than 20 000 addresses and uses them to create monthly product promotions and contest giveaways.[15]

Creating an Online Customer Experience

A continuing challenge for companies is the design and execution of marketing programs that capitalize on the unique and evolving customer value-creation capabilities of Internet/Web technology. Companies now realize that simply applying Internet/Web technology to create time, place, form, and possession utility

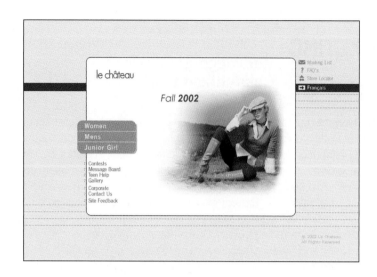

is not enough to claim a meaningful marketspace presence. Today, the quality of the customer experience produced by a company is the standard by which a meaningful marketspace presence is measured.

CUSTOMER EXPERIENCE
The sum total of interactions that a customer has with a company's Website.

From an interactive marketing perspective, **customer experience** is defined as the sum total of the interactions that a customer has with a company's Website, from the initial look at a home page through the entire purchase decision process.[16] Companies produce a customer experience through seven Website design elements. These elements are context, content, community, customization, communication, connection, and commerce, each of which is summarized in Figure 21–2.[17] A closer look at these elements illustrates how each contributes to customer experience.

FIGURE 21–2
Website design elements that drive customer experience

Context refers to a Website's aesthetic appeal and functional look and feel reflected in site layout and design. A functionally oriented Website focuses largely on the company's offering, be it products, services, or information. For instance,

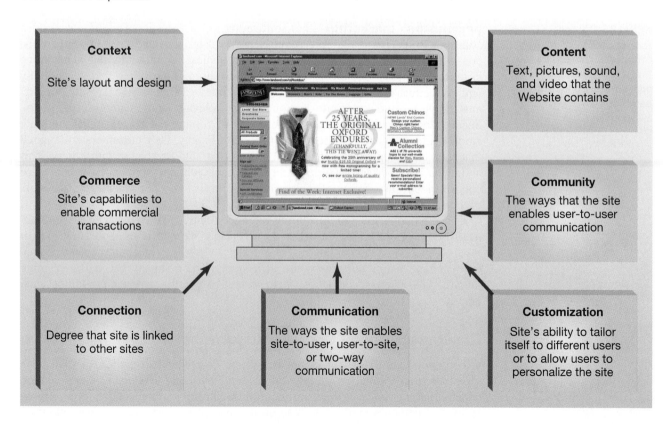

travel Websites tend to be functionally oriented with an emphasis on destinations, scheduling, and prices. In contrast, the Le Château Website is a more aesthetically oriented site with its focus on fashion products. As these examples suggest, context attempts to convey the core consumer benefit provided by the company's offering(s). *Content* includes all digital information included on a Website, including the presentation form—text, video, audio, and graphics. Content quality and presentation along with context dimensions combine to engage a Website visitor and provide a platform for the five remaining design elements.

Website *customization* is the ability of a site to modify itself to—or be modified by—each individual user. This design element is prominent in Websites that offer personalized content, such as My eBay and MyYahoo. The *connection* element in Website design is the network of formal linkages between a company's site and other sites. These links are embedded in the Website; appear as highlighted words, a picture, or graphic; and allow a user to effortlessly visit other sites with a mouse click. Connection is a major design element for informational Websites such as Canoe.ca. For example, users can access shop.canoe.ca to purchase a range of products, including a direct link to SportChek.

Communication refers to the dialogue that unfolds between the Website and its users. Consumers—particularly those who have registered at a site—now expect that communication be interactive and individualized in real time much like a personal conversation. In fact, some Websites now enable a user to talk directly with a customer representative while shopping the site. For example, two-thirds of the sales through Dell Computer's Website involve human sales representatives. In addition, an increasing number of company Websites encourage user-to-user communications hosted by the company to create virtual communities, or simply, *community*. This design element is growing in popularity because it has been shown to enhance customer experience and build favourable buyer–seller relationships. Examples of communities range from the Fifty-Plus Community sponsored by the Canadian Association of the Fifty Plus (www.50plus.com) to the Harley Owners Group (H.O.G) sponsored by Harley-Davidson (www.harley-davidson.com).

Harley-Davidson pays close attention to creating a favourable customer experience at its Website.

Harley-Davidson
www.harley-davidson.com

The seventh design element is *commerce*—the Website's ability to conduct sales transactions for products and services. Online transactions are quick and simple in well-designed Websites. Amazon.com has mastered this design element with "one-click shopping," a patented feature that allows users to place and order products with a single mouse click.

All Websites do not include all design elements. Although every Website has context and content, they differ in the use of the remaining five elements. Why? Websites have different purposes. For example, only Websites that emphasize the actual sale of products and services include the commerce element. Websites that are used primarily for advertising and promotion purposes emphasize the communication element. The difference between these two types of Websites is discussed later in the chapter.

Concept Check

1. The greatest marketspace opportunity for marketers lies in the creation of what kind of utility?

2. The consumer-initiated practice of generating content on a marketer's Website that is custom tailored to an individual's specific needs and preferences is called _____.

3. Companies produce a customer experience through what seven Website design elements?

ONLINE CONSUMER BEHAVIOUR AND MARKETING PRACTICE IN MARKETSPACE

Who are online consumers, and what do they buy? Why do they choose to shop and purchase products and services in the new marketspace rather than or in addition to the traditional marketplace? Answers to these questions have a direct bearing on marketspace marketing practices.

The Online Consumer

Online consumers are given many labels—cybershoppers, Netizens, and e-shoppers—suggesting they are a homogeneous segment of the population. They are not, but as a group they do differ demographically from the general population.

Profiling the Online Consumer   Online consumers differ from the general population in one important respect. They own or have access to a computer or an Internet/Web-enabled device, such as a wireless cellular telephone. Approximately 60 percent of Canadian households have a computer in their home with Internet/Web access, although access is often possible at work or school. Figure 21–3 shows the growth of Internet access at home.[18]

Online consumers are the subsegment of all Internet/Web users who employ this technology to research products and services and make purchases. Research indicates that about 80 percent of all adult Internet/Web users have sought online product or service information at one time or another.[19] For example, some 70 percent of prospective travellers have researched travel information online, even though fewer than 25 percent have actually made online travel reservations. Over 40 percent have researched automobiles before making a purchase, but only 8 percent of users actually bought a vehicle online.[20] About two-thirds of adult Internet/Web users have actually purchased a product or service online at one time or another.[21]

ONLINE CONSUMERS
The subsegment of all Internet/Web users who employ this technology to research products and services and make purchases.

FIGURE 21–3
Profiles of Canadian
online users

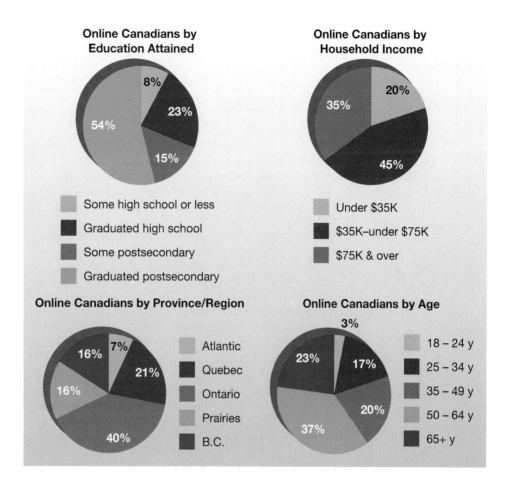

**Online Canadians by
Education Attained**

8%
23%
54%
15%

▢ Some high school or less

■ Graduated high school

▢ Some postsecondary

▢ Graduated postsecondary

**Online Canadians by
Household Income**

20%
35%
45%

▢ Under $35K

■ $35K–under $75K

▢ $75K & over

Online Canadians by Province/Region

16% 7%
21%
16%
40%

▢ Atlantic

■ Quebec

▢ Ontario

▢ Prairies

■ B.C.

Online Canadians by Age

3%
23%   17%
20%
37%

▢ 18 – 24 y

■ 25 – 34 y

▢ 35 – 49 y

▢ 50 – 64 y

■ 65+ y

As a group, online consumers, like Internet/Web users, are evenly split between men and women, and tend to be better educated, younger, and more affluent than the general Canadian population, which makes them an attractive market. Even though online shopping and buying is growing in popularity, a small percentage of online consumers still account for a disproportionate share of online retail sales.

Online Consumer Lifestyle Segmentation   Not all Internet/Web users use the technology the same way, nor are they likely to be exclusive online consumers. Numerous marketing research firms have studied the lifestyles and shopping and spending habits of online consumers. A recurrent insight is that online consumers are diverse and represent different kinds of people seeking different kinds of online experiences. As an illustration, Harris Interactive, a large research firm, has identified six distinct online consumer lifestyle segments.[22]

The largest online consumer lifestyle segment, called *click-and-mortar*, consists of female homemakers who tend to browse retailer Websites but actually buy products in traditional retail outlets. They make up 23 percent of online consumers and represent an important segment for multichannel retailers that also feature catalogue and store operations, such as J. Crew and JCPenney. Twenty percent of online consumers are *hunter-gatherers*—married baby boomers with children at home who use the Internet like a consumer magazine to compare products and prices. They can be found visiting comparison shopping Websites such as Dealcatcher.com and Mysimon.com on a regular basis. Nineteen percent of online consumers are *brand loyalists* who regularly visit their favourite bookmarked Websites and spend the most money online. They are better-educated and more-affluent Internet/Web users who effortlessly navigate familiar and trusted Websites and enjoy the online browsing and buying experience. Next there are *time-sensitive materialists* who regard the Internet as a convenience tool for buying music, books, and computer software and electronics. They account for 17 percent of online consumers and can be found visiting Amazon.com, Dell.com, Sony.com, and BMG.com. The *hooked, online, and single* segment consists of young, affluent, and single online consumers who bank, play games, and spend more time online than any other segment as documented in the accompanying Web Link. They make up 16 percent of online consumers, enjoy auction Websites such as eBay, and visit game Websites like iWon.com, ea.com, and games.yahoo.com. Five percent of online consumers are the *ebivalent newbies*—newcomers to the Internet who rarely spend money online, but seek product information. Do any of these segments describe your online lifestyle and spending habits?

What Online Consumers Buy

Much still needs to be learned about online consumer purchase behaviour in the new marketspace. While research has documented the most frequently purchased products and services bought online, marketers also need to know why these items are popular and why consumers prefer to shop and buy in the new marketspace.

Six general product and service categories appear to be particularly suited for electronic commerce.[23] One category consists of items for which product information is an important part of the purchase decision, but prepurchase trial is not necessarily critical. Items such as computers, computer accessories, and consumer electronics sold by Dell.com and Egghead.com fall into this category. So do books, which accounts for the sales growth of Amazon.com and Chapters-Indigo (www.chapters.indigo.com). Both booksellers publish short reviews of new books that visitors to their Websites can read before making a purchase decision. According to an authority on electronic commerce, "You've read the reviews, you want it, you don't need to try it on."[24] A second category includes items for which audio or video demonstration is important. This category consists of CDs and videos sold by Columbiahouse.com, CDnow.com, and HMV.com. The third category contains items that can be delivered digitally, including computer software, travel reservations and confirmations, brokerage services, and electronic ticketing. Popular Websites for these items include Travelocity.ca, Ticketmaster.ca, and Schwab.com.

Unique items, such as collectibles, specialty goods, and foods and gifts, represent a fourth category. Collectible auction houses (www.auctions-on-line.com) and (www.eworldauction.com), and flower and gift marketer 1-800-Flowers (www.1800flowers.com) sell these products. A fifth category includes items that are regularly purchased and where convenience is very important. Many consumer-packaged goods, such as grocery products, fall into this category, which has benefited Peapod.com and Netgrocer.com, two online grocers. A final category of

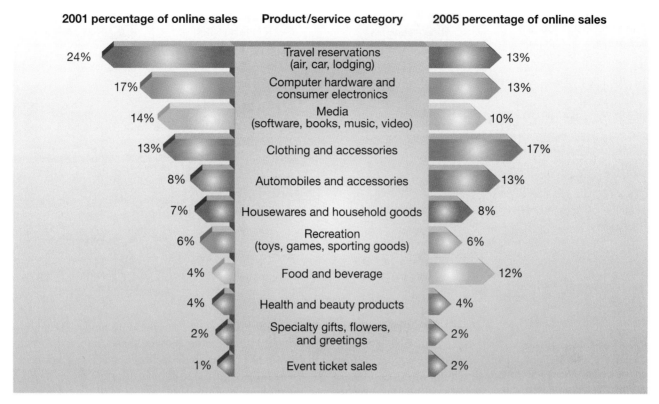

2001 percentage of online sales	Product/service category	2005 percentage of online sales
24%	Travel reservations (air, car, lodging)	13%
17%	Computer hardware and consumer electronics	13%
14%	Media (software, books, music, video)	10%
13%	Clothing and accessories	17%
8%	Automobiles and accessories	13%
7%	Housewares and household goods	8%
6%	Recreation (toys, games, sporting goods)	6%
4%	Food and beverage	12%
4%	Health and beauty products	4%
2%	Specialty gifts, flowers, and greetings	2%
1%	Event ticket sales	2%

FIGURE 21–4

Online consumer sales by product/service category: 2001 and 2005

items consists of highly standardized products and services for which information about price is important. Certain kinds of insurance (auto and homeowners), home improvement products, casual apparel, and toys comprise this category. These categories dominate online consumer shopping today and for the foreseeable future, as shown in Figure 21–4.[25]

Several trends have created opportunities for Canadian shoppers to purchase online. Experienced online purchasers continue to use the Internet for their shopping convenience and over the past few years has increased along with the number of Canadian e-retailers providing availability and selection. The number of Canadian adults who have purchased online exceeds 5 million, almost 25 percent of the population. Canadians are purchasing more from Canadian sites and the major purchases are banking services, computer software, books, music, tickets to events, and consumer electronics.[26]

Why Consumers Shop and Buy Online

Marketers emphasize the customer value-creation possibilities, the importance of interactivity, individuality and relationship building, and producing customer experience in the new marketspace. However, consumers typically refer to six reasons why they shop and buy online: convenience, choice, customization, communication, cost, and control (Figure 21–5).

Convenience   Online shopping and buying is *convenient*. Consumers can visit Zellers at www.zellers.ca/zellers to scan and order from among thousands of displayed products without fighting traffic, finding a parking space, walking through long aisles, and standing in store checkout lines. Alternatively, online consumers can use **bots**, electronic shopping agents or robots that comb Websites, to compare prices and product or service features. In either instance an online consumer has never ventured from his or her computer monitor. However, for convenience to remain a source of customer value creation, Websites must be easy to locate and navigate, and image

BOTS

Electronic shopping agents or robots that comb Websites to compare prices and product or service features.

FIGURE 21–5
Why consumers shop and
buy online

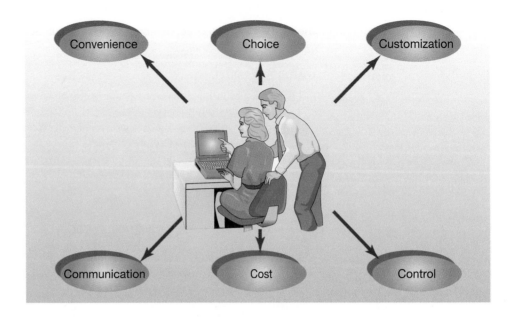

EIGHT-SECOND RULE
Customers will abandon their
efforts to enter and navigate
a Website if download time
exceeds eight seconds.

downloads must be fast. As mentioned in Chapter 15, a commonly held view among online marketers is the **eight-second rule**: Customers will abandon their efforts to enter and navigate a Website if download time exceeds eight seconds.[27] Furthermore, the more clicks and pauses between clicks required to access information or make a purchase, the more likely it is a customer will exit a Website.

Choice   *Choice* is a second reason why consumers shop and buy online and has two dimensions. First, choice exists in the product or service selection offered to consumers. Buyers desiring selection can avail themselves of numerous Websites for almost anything they want. For instance, online buyers of consumer electronics can shop individual manufacturers such as Bose (www.bose.com) or Sony (www.sony.com), or visit iqvc.com, a general merchant, that offers more than 100 000 products. Choice assistance is the second dimension. Here, the interactive capabilities of Internet/Web-enabled technologies invite customers to engage in an electronic dialogue with marketers for the purpose of making informed choices. Lands' End (www.landsend.com) provides choice assistance with its "My Virtual Model" apparel service. Men and women submit their body shape, skin colour, hair style, height, weight, and other attributes. The model then "tries on" outfits identified by the customer. Like any good salesperson, the service recommends flattering outfits for purchase.

Customization   Even with a broad selection and choice assistance, some customers prefer one-of-a-kind items that fit their specific needs. *Customization* arises from Internet/Web-enabled capabilities that make possible a highly interactive and individualized information and exchange environment for shoppers and buyers. Remember the earlier Le Château, Nike, Schwab, Dell Computer, and General Mills examples? To varying degrees, online consumers also benefit from **customerization**—the growing practice of customizing not only a product or service, but also personalizing the marketing and overall shopping and buying interaction for each customer.[28] Customerization seeks to do more than offer consumers the right product, at the right time, at the right price. It combines choice-board and personalization systems to expand the exchange environment beyond a transaction and makes shopping and buying an enjoyable, personal experience.

CUSTOMERIZATION
The growing practice of
customizing not only a
product or service but also
personalizing the marketing
and overall shopping and
buying interaction for each
customer.

Communication   Online consumers particularly welcome the *communication* capabilities of Internet/Web-enabled technologies. This communication can take three forms: (1) marketer-to-consumer e-mail notification, (2) consumer-to-marketer buying and service requests, and (3) consumer-to-consumer chat rooms and instant messaging.[29] This communication capability is evidenced in the fact that more than 4 trillion e-mail messages are sent annually worldwide.[30]

Communication has proven to be a double-edged sword for online consumers. On the one hand, the interactive communication capabilities of Internet/Web-enabled technologies increase consumer convenience, reduce information search costs, and make choice assistance and customization possible. Communication also promotes the development of company-hosted and independent **Web communities**— Websites that allow people to congregate online and exchange views on topics of common interest. For instance, iVillage.com, the Women's Network, is a web community for women and includes topics such as career management, personal finances, parenting, relationships, beauty, and health. On the other hand, communication can take the form of electronic junk mail or unsolicited e-mail, called **spam**. The prevalence of spam has prompted some online services such as Hotmail to institute policies and procedures to prevent spammers from spamming their subscribers.

Internet/Web-enabled communication capabilities also make possible *buzz*, a popular term for word-of-mouth behaviour in marketspace. Chapter 5 described the importance of word of mouth in consumer behaviour. Internet/Web technology has magnified its significance. In marketspace, the scope and speed of word of mouth has increased fourfold on average because of consumer chat rooms, instant messaging, and product and service review Websites such as epinions.com and consumerreview.com.[31] Buzz is particularly influential for toys, cars, sporting goods, motion pictures, apparel, consumer electronics, pharmaceuticals, health and beauty products, and health care services. Some marketers have capitalized on this phenomenon by creating buzz through viral marketing.

Viral marketing is an Internet/Web-enabled promotional strategy that encourages individuals to forward marketer-initiated messages to others via e-mail.[32] There are three approaches to viral marketing. Marketers can embed a message in the product or service so that customers hardly realize they are passing it along. The classic example is Hotmail, which was one of the first companies to provide free, Web-based e-mail. Each outgoing e-mail message has the tagline: Get Your Private, Free Email from MSN Hotmail at http://www.hotmail.com. Today, Hotmail has some 80 million users! Marketers can also make the Website content so compelling that viewers want to share it with others. De Beers has done this at www.adiamondisforever.com, where users can design their own rings and show them to others. One out of five Website visitors e-mail their ring design to friends and relatives who visit the site. Similarly, eBay reports that more than half its visitors were referred by other visitors. Finally, marketers can offer incentives (discounts, sweepstakes, or free merchandise) for referrals. Procter & Gamble did this for its Physique shampoo. People who referred 10 friends to the shampoo's Website (www.physique.com) received a free travel-sized styling spray and were entered in a sweepstakes to win a year's supply of the shampoo. The response? The promotion generated 2 million referrals and made Physique the most successful new shampoo launched by Procter & Gamble.

Cost   Consumer *cost* is a fifth reason for online shopping and buying. Research indicates that many popular items bought online can be purchased at the same price or cheaper than in retail stores.[33] Although 75 percent of Internet customers indicate low prices as an important factor for online purchases, only 8 percent are "bargain hunters."[34] Lower prices also result from Internet/Web-enabled software that permits **dynamic pricing**, the practice of changing prices for products and services in real time in response to supply and demand conditions. As described in Chapter 14, dynamic pricing is a form of flexible pricing and can often result in lower prices. It is typically used for pricing time-sensitive items like airline seats, scarce items found at

---

WEB COMMUNITIES
Websites that allow people to congregate online and exchange views on topics of common interest.

SPAM
Electronic junk mail or unsolicited e-mail.

VIRAL MARKETING
An Internet/Web-enabled promotional strategy that encourages users to forward marketer-initiated messages to others via e-mail.

DYNAMIC PRICING
The practice of changing prices for products and services in real time in response to supply and demand conditions.

De Beers effectively applied viral marketing in the launch of its custom ring Website.

De Beers

www.adiamondisforever.com

art or collectible auctions, and out-of-date items such as last year's models of computer equipment and accessories. A consumer's cost of external information search, including time spent and often the hassle of shopping, is also reduced. Greater shopping convenience and lower external search costs are two major reasons for the popularity of online shopping and buying among women, and particularly for those who work outside the home.

Control The sixth reason consumers prefer to buy online is the *control* it gives them over their shopping and purchase decision process. Online shoppers and buyers are empowered consumers. They deftly use Internet/Web technology to seek information, evaluate alternatives, and make purchase decisions on their own time, terms, and conditions. Nearly 80 percent of online consumers regularly engage **portals** and "search engines," which are electronic gateways to the World Wide Web that supply a broad array of news and entertainment, information resources, and shopping services.[35] Well-known portals include Yahoo.ca, Sympatico.ca, and Canoe.ca. To evaluate alternatives, consumers visit comparison shopping Websites such as comparenet.com and price.com or employ bots such as Yahoo! Shopping and Excite's Product Finder, which provide product descriptions and prices for a wide variety of brands and models. The result of these activities is a more informed consumer and discerning shopper. In the words of one marketing consultant, "In the marketspace, the customer is in charge."[36]

Even though consumers have many reasons for shopping and buying online, a segment of Internet/Web users refrain from making purchases for privacy and security reasons, as described in the accompanying Ethics and Social Responsibility Alert.[37] These consumers are concerned about a rarely mentioned seventh "C"— cookies. **Cookies** are computer files that a marketer can upload onto the computer of an online shopper who visits the marketer's Website. Cookies allow the marketer's Website to record a user's visit, track visits to other Websites, and store and retrieve this information in the future. Cookies also contain information provided by visitors, such as expressed product preferences, personal data, and financial information, including credit card numbers. Clearly, cookies make possible customized and personalized content for online shoppers. The controversy surrounding cookies is summed up by an authority on the technology: "At best a cookie makes for a user-friendly Web world: like a doorman or salesclerk who knows who you are. At worst, cookies represent a potential loss of privacy."[38]

PORTALS

Electronic gateways to the World Wide Web that supply a broad array of news and entertainment, information resources, and shopping services.

COOKIES

Computer files that a marketer can upload onto the computer of an online shopper who visits the marketer's Website.

ETHICS AND SOCIAL RESPONSIBILITY ALERT
Sweet and Sour Cookies in the New Marketspace

Privacy and security are two key reasons consumers are leery of online shopping. An Angus Reid report (www.angusreid.ca) shows that Canadians are concerned about giving out personal and credit card information online, and very concerned about someone being able to track where they go as they travel online.

The privacy and security concerns of online consumers are related to the "cookies" described in the text and how those cookies can be used or misused. The Canadian Marketing Association (CMA) introduced new regulations regarding online marketing by its members. Consumers must be informed if information is being collected on them when they visit Websites, and how this information will be used. Consumers must also be able to opt out from having such information collected or transferred for marketing purposes. The CMA says members who break these regulations face public censure or expulsion from the CMA.

The Personal Information Protection and Electronic Documents Act (Part 1, Bill C-6) became law January 1, 2001. This bill deals with sensitive forms of information, such as health information, and contains important opt-out provisions. The provinces have until 2004 if they wish to enact their own privacy legislation. Alberta, Saskatchewan, and Manitoba already have some legislation. For information on Bill C-6 see Industry Canada at e-com.ic.gc.ca.

Do you think that government regulation or self-regulation is the best way to deal with issues of privacy and security in the new marketspace?

When and Where Online Consumers Shop and Buy

Shopping and buying also happen at different times in marketspace than in the traditional marketplace.[39] About 80 percent of online retail sales occur Monday through Friday. The busiest shopping day is Wednesday. By comparison, 35 percent of retail store sales are registered on the weekend. Saturday is the most popular shopping day. Monday through Friday online shopping and buying often occurs during normal work hours—some 40 percent of online consumers say they visit Websites from their place of work, which partially accounts for the sales level during the workweek.[40] Favourite Websites for workday shopping and buying include those featuring event tickets, online periodical subscriptions, flowers and gifts, consumer electronics, and travel. Websites offering health and beauty items, apparel and accessories, and music and video tend to be browsed and bought from a consumer's home.

Consumers are more likely to browse than buy online. Although 9 in 10 online consumers regularly shop in the marketspace of Websites, over half (51 percent) confine their purchases to the traditional retail store marketplace.[41] Consumer marketspace browsing and buying in the traditional marketplace has popularized multichannel marketing, which is described next.

Concept Check

1. What is the eight-second rule?

2. Which online consumer lifestyle segment spends the most money online and which spends the most time online?

3. What are the six reasons consumers prefer to shop and buy online?

MULTICHANNEL MARKETING TO THE ONLINE CONSUMER

The fact that a large number of consumers browse and buy in two market environments means that it is commonplace for companies to maintain a presence in both market environments of some kind and measure. This dual presence is called multichannel marketing.

Integrating and Leveraging Multiple Channels with Multichannel Marketing

Companies often employ multiple marketing channels for their products and services. *Dual distribution* is the term used to describe this practice, which focuses on reaching different consumers through different marketing channels. The Avon example that introduced Chapter 15 highlighted this practice. Avon markets its health and beauty products directly through Avon sales representatives, a brochure, shops in department stores, and an Avon Website. The various communication (representatives and brochures) and delivery (shops) channels allow Avon to reach different consumers, feature different brands, and provide different shopping and buying experiences.

MULTICHANNEL MARKETING
The blending of different communication and delivery channels that are mutually reinforcing in attracting, retaining, and building relationships with consumers.

Multichannel marketing bears some resemblance to dual distribution. For example, different communication and delivery channels are used such as catalogues, kiosks, retail stores, and Websites. In fact, retailers that employ two or more of these channels are labelled *multichannel retailers*, as described in Chapter 17. However, the resemblance ends at this point. **Multichannel marketing** is the *blending* of different communication and delivery channels that are *mutually reinforcing* in attracting, retaining, and building relationships with consumers who shop and buy

Sears Canada makes every effort to integrate all aspects of the customer's shopping experience.

MARKETING NEWSNET   The Multichannel Marketing Multiplier

Multichannel marketing is the blending of different communication and delivery channels that are mutually reinforcing in attracting, retaining, and building relationships with consumers who shop and buy in the traditional marketplace and marketspace. Industry analysts refer to the complementary role of different communication and delivery channels as an "influence effect."

Retailers that integrate and leverage their stores, catalogues, and Websites have seen a sizeable "lift" in yearly sales recorded from individual customers. Canadian Tire is a case in point. Customers who shop in two channels spend more money annually.

To build its multichannel operations and expand its contact list, Canadian Tire launched an online component to the "Big Spender Giveaway" contest in the fall of 2001. A total of $350 000 in merchandise and Canadian Tire money™ was given away to those entering either online or in-store. The online entrants were able to participate in an

extra game: looking for the "Big Spender Briefcase" hidden in the site. This is considered one of the most popular online promotions in Canada, attracting 2.5 million visitors to Canadian Tire's Website.

in the traditional marketplace and marketspace. Multichannel marketing seeks to integrate a firm's communication and delivery channels, not differentiate them. In doing so, consumers can browse and buy "anytime, anywhere, anyway" expecting that the experience will be similar regardless of channel. At Sears Canada, every effort is made to integrate all aspects of the customer's shopping experience. The multichannel retailer has 118 retail stores, 37 furniture and appliance stores, 15 outlet stores, 66 auto centres, 38 floor-covering centres, 131 dealer stores, and 2110 pick-up locations to support its catalogue business. Sears Canada is the dominant catalogue retailer in Canada and used its expertise to create Sears.ca, one of the most visited Websites in Canada.[42]

Multichannel marketing also can leverage the value-adding capabilities of different channels.[43] For example, retail stores can leverage their physical presence by allowing customers to pick up their online orders at a nearby store or return or exchange nonstore purchases if they wish. Catalogues can serve as shopping tools for online purchasing, as they do for store purchasing. Websites can help consumers do their "homework" before visiting a store. Office Depot has leveraged its store, catalogue, and Website channels, with impressive results. The company, which is the world's largest office supply retail chain, is the second largest Internet retailer in the world (behind Amazon.com), doing about $1 billion in online retail sales annually.[44] The benefits of multichannel marketing are also apparent in the spending behaviour of consumers, as described in the accompanying Marketing NewsNet.[45]

Implementing Multichannel Marketing

Not all companies employ Websites for multichannel marketing the same way. Different companies apply the value-creation capabilities of Internet/Web technology differently depending on their overall marketing program.

Websites play a multifaceted role in multichannel marketing because they can serve as either a communication or delivery channel. Two general applications of Websites exist based on their intended purpose: (1) transactional Websites, and (2) promotional Websites.

Multichannel Marketing with Transactional Websites *Transactional Websites* are essentially electronic storefronts. They focus principally on converting an online browser into an online, catalogue, or in-store buyer using the Website design elements described earlier. Transactional Websites are most common among store and catalogue retailers and direct selling companies, such as Tupperware. The Gap, for instance, generates more sales volume from its Website (www.gap.com) than any one of its stores, save one.[46] Retailers and direct selling firms have found that their Websites, while cannibalizing sales volume from stores, catalogues, and sales representatives, attract new customers and influence sales. Consider Victoria's Secret, the well-known specialty retailer of intimate apparel for women ages 18 to 45. It reports that almost 60 percent of its Website customers are men, most of whom generate new sales volume for the company.[47]

Transactional Websites are used less frequently by manufacturers of consumer products. A recurring issue for manufacturers is the threat of *channel conflict*, described in Chapter 15, and the potential harm to trade relationships with their retailing intermediaries. Still, manufacturers do use transactional Websites, often cooperating with retailers. For example, Ethan Allen, the furniture manufacturer, markets its product line at www.ethanallen.com. Whenever feasible, Ethan Allen retailers fill online orders, and receive 25 percent of the sales price. For items shipped directly from the Ethan Allen factory, the store nearest the customer receives 10 percent of the sales price.[48] In addition, Ethan Allen, like other manufacturers, typically lists stores on their Website where their merchandise can be shopped and bought. More often than not, however, manufacturers engage multichannel channels, using Websites as advertising and promotion vehicles.

Multichannel Marketing with Promotional Websites *Promotional Websites* have a very different purpose than transactional sites. They advertise and promote a company's products and services and provide information on how items can be used and where they can be purchased. They often engage the visitor in an interactive experience involving games, contests, and quizzes with electronic coupons and other gifts as prizes. Procter & Gamble maintains separate Websites for dozens of its leading brands, including Pringles potato chips (www.pringles.com), Vidal Sassoon hair products (www.vidalsassoon.com), Scope mouthwash (www.scope-mouthwash.com), and Pampers diapers (www.pampers.com).[49] Promotional sites can be effective in generating interest in and trial of a company's products

FIGURE 21–6
Implementing multichannel marketing with promotional Websites.

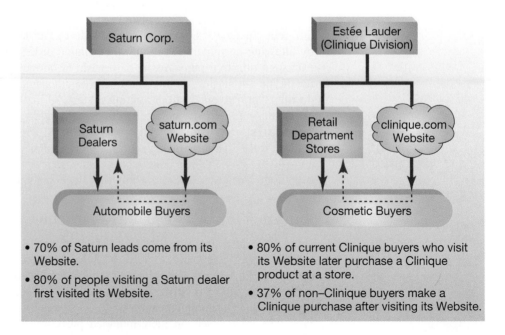

and services (see Figure 21–6).[50] General Motors reports that 80 percent of the people visiting a Saturn store first visited the brand's Website (www.saturn.com) and 70 percent of Saturn leads come from its Website.

Promotional Websites also can be used to support a company's traditional marketing channel and build customer relationships. This is the objective of the Clinique Division of Estée Lauder Companies, which markets cosmetics through department stores. Clinique reports that 80 percent of current customers who visit its Website (www.clinique.com) later purchase a Clinique product at a department store; 37 percent of non-Clinique buyers make a Clinique purchase after visiting the company's Website.

Concept Check

1. Multichannel marketing is _____.

2. Channel conflict between manufacturers and retailers is likely to arise when manufacturers use _____ Websites.

SUMMARY

1 Consumers and companies populate two market environments today—the traditional marketplace and the new marketspace. A company's marketspace success hinges largely on designing and executing a marketing program that capitalizes on the unique value-creation capabilities of Internet/Web technology.

2 Internet/Web technology creates time, place, form, and possession utility in novel ways, resulting in customer value.

3 Marketers benefit from two unique capabilities of Internet/Web-enabled technology that create customer relationships—interactivity and individuality—creating interactive marketing. Interactive marketing, in turn, is characterized by choiceboard and personalization systems transforming information supplied by customers into customized responses to their individual needs.

4 The quality of the customer experience creates meaningful marketspace presence measured by seven Website elements: context, content, community, customization, communication, connection, and commerce.

5 Online consumers, a segment of all Internet/Web users, differ demographically from the general population and exhibit distinct lifestyle and spending profiles. Six general product and service categories are bought by online consumers. However, banking services, computer hardware and software, books, music, and tickets to events account for the majority of consumer purchases.

6 Consumers refer to six reasons they shop and buy online: convenience, choice, customization, communication, cost, and control. Marketers capitalize on these reasons using a variety of approaches including electronic shopping agents (bots), Web communities, viral marketing, and dynamic pricing. However, consumers are concerned about electronic junk mail (spam) and online privacy and security.

7 Multichannel marketing is the blending of different communication and delivery channels that are mutually reinforcing in attracting, retaining, and building relationships with consumers who shop and buy in the traditional marketplace and marketspace.

8 Multichannel marketing can be approached with the use of transactional Websites and promotional Websites.

KEY TERMS AND CONCEPTS

bots p. 565
choiceboard p. 558
collaborative filtering p. 558
cookies p. 568
customer experience p. 560
customerization p. 566
dynamic pricing p. 567
eCRM p. 558
eight-second rule p. 566

interactive marketing p. 558
multichannel marketing p. 570
online consumers p. 562
permission marketing p. 559
personalization p. 559
portals p. 568
spam p. 567
viral marketing p. 567
Web communities p. 567

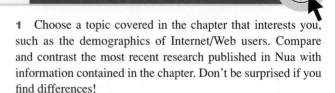

What are the most recent statistics and trends in interactive and multichannel marketing? Look no further than Nua Internet Surveys (Nua), an online service that abstracts up-to-date research on Internet/Web usage and applications from around the world. Nua conveniently organizes research by business, social, technical, demographic, and geographical categories for easy inspection.

Visit the Nua Website at www.nua.ic/surveys. Your assignment is as follows:

1 Choose a topic covered in the chapter that interests you, such as the demographics of Internet/Web users. Compare and contrast the most recent research published in Nua with information contained in the chapter. Don't be surprised if you find differences!

2 Choose two regions of the world, such as North America and Europe. How does Internet/Web usage and interactive marketing differ between the two regions based on the most recent research?

Want to get better grades, find tips on how to study more effectively, and stay up to date with happenings in the world of marketing? Visit the Online Learning Centre for practice tests, Study Smart software, and much more! www.mcgrawhill.ca/college/berkowitz
Interested in finding out what marketing looks like in the real world? *Marketing Magazine* is just a click away on your OLC! Visit www.mcgrawhill.ca/college/berkowitz

APPLYING MARKETING CONCEPTS AND PERSPECTIVES

1 By early 2002, about one-quarter of Internet/Web users had actually purchased something online. Have you made an online purchase? If so, why do you think so many people who have access to the Internet and the World Wide Web are not also online buyers? If not, why are you reluctant to do so? Do you think that electronic commerce benefits consumers even if they don't make a purchase?

2 Like the traditional marketplace, marketspace offers marketers opportunities to create greater time, place, form, and possession utility. How do you think Internet/Web-enabled technology rates in terms of creating these values? Take a shopping trip at a virtual retailer of your choice (don't buy anything unless you really want to). Then compare the time, place, form, and possession utility provided by the virtual retailer with that you enjoyed during a nonelectronic experience shopping for the same product category.

3 Visit Indigo Books & Music (www.indigo.ca). As you tour the company's Website, think about how shopping for books online compares with a trip to your university bookstore to buy books. Specifically, compare and contrast your shopping experiences with respect to convenience, choice, customization, communication, cost, and control.

4 Suppose you are planning to buy a new Ski Doo, so you decide to visit www.ski-doo.com. Based on your experience visiting that site, do you think you would enjoy more or less control in negotiating with the dealer when you actually purchase your vehicle?

5 Visit the Website for your university or college. Based on your visit, would you conclude that the site is a transactional site or a promotional site? Why? How would you rate the site in terms of the six Website design elements that affect customer experience?

6 One of the benefits that interactive marketing provides for companies is the ability to obtain consumer information that can be used to more effectively manage the marketing mix. Canadian Tire, for example, creates profiles of its online customers. Some consumers, however, worry about their privacy as companies like Canadian Tire create customer databases. Visit Canadian Tire's Website at www.CanadianTire.ca to determine what information you must provide. Is the added value of the Canadian Tire online money worth the price of the information you must reveal to participate? Why or why not?

VIDEO CASE 21–1 Connecting and Communicating without Wires

Consumers and businesses have embraced the Internet. Offering convenient and easy communication, the Internet continues to change our lives as new applications for its technology are developed. Internet use and applications have grown largely because manufacturers and software developers have continued to improve on the original concept and infrastructure. Now, wireless communication offers an opportunity to advance this process by stimulating new products, new processes, and new ways of communicating. Wireless opportunities and applications appear to be endless. An obvious benefit of wireless is the elimination of the nest of cables behind desks. From a manufacturing perspective, there are anticipated cost savings as well. Most promising, however, are the opportunities wireless offers for more interactive and instantaneous communication. The promise of wireless takes "anywhere, anytime" to a new level.

A variety of technologies can be used to create wireless products and services. There is long-range and short-range wireless. Wireless can be delivered via satellite or cellular, and now for short-range options there is Bluetooth and 802.11. Wireless technology development and adoption is where the Internet was more than five years ago. There is promise, there is excitement, and there is uncertainty.

CONSUMER ELECTRONICS PRODUCTS AND BLUETOOTH

What is Bluetooth and what could it possibly do for us? These were the questions on the minds of the attendees of the Consumer Electronics Show (CES) in Las Vegas, Nevada in 2001, where the buzz was "wireless." Just a few years ago Comdex, the largest computer trade show, attracted large audiences. However, with the slowdown in the computer and telecommunication industries, manufacturers are bringing new products to CES. The major players in the computer and telecommunications industries see the consumer electronics market as an opportunity to generate revenue by showcasing how they are using technology convergence to develop not just consumer gadgets, but new products and infrastructure formats to improve productivity and connectivity and to open new markets.

Bluetooth is a technology standard allowing electronic products, computers, and components to communicate with each other without the use of cables. It uses radio transmissions and the device looks like a tiny radio transmitter on a microchip. The range for Bluetooth transmission is about 10 metres, making it ideal for office and home use providing wireless connections between computers, keyboards, printers, and fax machines. "Cable spaghetti" from under the desk could be a thing of the past. In addition, the possibilities for wireless products include watches that can take pictures and watches that can help you if you are lost and need to know your location. There are attachments that can transform a personal digital assistant (PDA) into a phone. And, in case you don't have enough radio stations on your car radio, it is now possible to receive satellite radio in your car. Although this product is illegal in Canada, it is possible in other parts of the world to purchase a laser radio detector. Another benefit of Bluetooth comes from the ability to connect to the Internet from virtually anywhere using handheld devices.

A VIKING KING BRINGS TOGETHER MODERN MARKET COMBATANTS

Bluetooth is an appropriate name for this wireless technology standard that is undertaking to increase connectivity globally. Bluetooth was the nickname of a Danish king who was able to successfully bring together clans in Denmark to battle foreigners instead of each other. Like this Viking king, the Bluetooth Special Interest Group (SIG) is a consortium of major industry players in computing, telecommunications, and networking working with each other to develop and commercialize this particular wireless standard. Ericsson, a Swedish telecommunications company, was the founder, and has come together in a unique partnership with others such as IBM, Intel, Nokia, and Toshiba in an attempt to set the industry standard before the product battles in the marketplace happen. So, in contrast to the Beta and VHS battle for a video industry standard, a consortium of more than 2000 companies worldwide is jointly developing Bluetooth technology.

Skip Bryan from Ericsson is convinced that this big new idea will be successful where others have failed. To begin with, the large number of consortium members will assist in new-product development and adoption. Second, due to the large number of members, companies from a wide range of industries are developing wireless applications including such industries as health care, avionics, and oil and gas. Within these industries it is the large organizations such as Shell, Sony, Casio, and Boeing that are investing in and experimenting with this wireless standard. Unlike the competing wireless standard IEEE 802.11, Bluetooth adopters have access to it through a royalty-free licence. This removes a financial barrier for those companies wanting to experiment with wireless technology and product development. The access to this technology to use in product and service development is similar to the access of the Internet for new applications.

CANADIAN COMPANIES EMBRACE BLUETOOTH

Dr. Jeff Rabin, a technology analyst and leading expert on wireless technology from Dundee Securities in Toronto, believes Bluetooth has great potential to succeed. "There's so much momentum behind it and it's such a juggernaut moving forward." Dr. Rabin sees Canadian companies playing a role in the adoption of this technology. Canadian companies that are members of the consortium include Mitel and Research in Motion (RIM). Although RIM has yet to announce any Bluetooth products, Mitel is actively pursuing this opportunity.

The number of Canadian companies doing well with products and software applications to support Bluetooth continues to grow. Manufacturing companies like Mitel are developing wireless products; there are, however, more Canadian companies involved in the development of software and special applications rather than hardware. This, says Dr. Rabin, is due to the lower capital requirements necessary to start a software company compared with a manufacturing plant. Arkon Networks in Richmond, B.C. is a success story in providing design expertise in wireless technology. Other companies such as PsiNaptic in Calgary and Colligo Networks, Inc. in Vancouver are involved in developing applications for supporting wireless networks through unique offerings. There appears to be a wide range of applications for wireless technology in consumer electronics, computer and telecommunication hardware, and network services for both offices and home environments.

THE POSSIBILITIES OF A FUTURE WITH WIRELESS

An important factor to consider in the adoption of wireless products is the nature of the technology itself. Wireless benefits are obvious. The freedom to talk on the phone or use the computer without lines and cables is appreciated by anyone using electronic products. With cable-free access and lower costs, wireless success appears inevitable. However, it appears that these benefits are only the beginning. Applications for wireless are being explored in a wide range of industries for a multitude of purposes. Extending the access to connectivity is a reality. The C-pen scans text and sends it to a computer, eliminating that onerous task of rekeying information. Ericsson has introduced a wireless headset, for U.S.$299, to connect a cell phone in a purse, briefcase, or pocket. For those concerned about exposure to microwaves so near their head, this new headset provides hands-free access to a cell phone without fear of health issues. With new legislation in both Europe and the United States prohibiting the use of handheld phones while driving, wireless technology could play a role in making driving and talking safer. The wireless headset is one hands-free option, but DaimlerChrysler will soon introduce another option with a wireless docking station and entertainment unit.

There are many ways in which wireless technology will continue to provide new product development opportunities for companies and benefits for connecting everyone, everywhere. Wireless provides faster access to the Internet. In Europe, wireless data services such as text messaging are widely used. This is one of the most valuable benefits in the long term for this technology. Wireless means instantaneous information exchange, resulting in quicker decisions. Many believe that this is what will continue to drive demand and application development. Mike Walters, a Nokia marketing manager, says, "The single most valuable advertising space on the planet will be the display on your hand-set." Retailers need to be looking at the opportunities of "location-based advertising." This is where companies can provide local, timely messages to customers as they enter a store or restaurant. For example, McDonald's could use Bluetooth technology to transmit ads or discount coupons to any cell phone in one of its restaurants. Another possible use of the technology is within a bookstore, such as Indigo, where a customer could use his or her cell phone or PDA to receive book reviews of any book on the shelf. Location-based advertising has great potential to assist the customer in-store with specific information on products, services, discounts, coupons, and loyalty incentives. Marketers selling without wires will need to carefully implement their programs to meet the changing needs of their customers.

Cable replacement is not just for computers and peripherals. E-books could evolve into wireless books. Cars could be produced without wiring harnesses. Short-range wireless could make it easier for anyone in an office or plant to access important production or customer data—anywhere, anytime.

The possibilities with wireless appliances, electronics devices, PDAs, cell phones, computers and peripherals create almost endless opportunities to generate new products and markets. Changes in communication access and purchasing patterns began with the adoption of the Internet and e-mail. With the successful adoption and integration of wireless technology, the implications for marketing companies interested in interactive communication is wide ranging. Wireless technology enhances Internet access and broadens the scope of applications for a variety of industries to improve and increase communication with suppliers, customers, family, and friends.

The future of this technology lies in the ability of the computing, electronics, and telecommunication industries to continue working together in an effort to create products and applications useful to the market. The Bluetooth SIG has a vested interest in making technology convergence through wireless not just hype, but a reality.

Questions

1 Identify wireless products or applications that will enhance connecting a customer with a company. Discuss the implications of being able to connect with a customer everywhere.

2 In your opinion, will wireless technology support multichannel marketing? Yes or no. Discuss your position.

3 If you were a product manager at Maytag, a leading manufacturer of household appliances, would you be interested in exploring the possibilities of integrating wireless technology in any of your products? Why or why not? Discuss your position.

4 Location-based advertising is an interesting way to communicate with a customer. Discuss the pros and cons of this concept from the perspective of both the retailer and the customer.

PULLING IT ALL TOGETHER: THE STRATEGIC MARKETING PROCESS

AFTER READING THIS CHAPTER YOU SHOULD BE ABLE TO:

- Explain how marketing managers allocate their limited resources, both in theory and in practice.

- Describe three marketing planning frameworks: Porter's generic strategies, profit enhancement options, and market-product synergies.

- Describe what makes an effective marketing plan and some problems that often exist with them.

- Describe the alternatives for organizing a marketing department and the role of a product manager.

- Schedule a series of tasks to meet a deadline using a Gantt chart.

- Understand how sales and profitability analyses and marketing audits are used to evaluate and control marketing programs.

MARKETING STRATEGY AT GENERAL MILLS: SHARES, SEGMENTS, AND SYNERGIES

Assume you are a marketing manager at General Mills responsible for introducing successful new brands of ready-to-eat (RTE) cereal. Here are some facts to tell you how difficult your job is:

- Only one out of five new brands of RTE cereal succeed.[1]
- A new product launch typically costs millions of dollars.
- Busy consumers, who are on the run, are increasingly likely to eat a bagel, muffin, or yogurt for breakfast instead of cereal due to their inconvenience, causing cereal sales to plummet over the past several years. So new cereal offerings must steal or "cannibalize" sales from existing brands to be successful.
- Consumers are concerned about the healthiness of RTE cereals. Some contain sugar while others contain genetically modified grains.
- Small competitors have entered the RTE cereal market, introducing "bagged" or generic private-label versions of well-known brands, and selling them for much less than their branded counterparts.[2]

However, there is also some good news:

- Based on estimates for the period 1995 to 2010, the largest target markets for RTE cereal are consumers who are under 18 and consumers who are 45 and older, both which are growing segments.[3]
- General Mills is a RTE cereal market leader with two brands, Cheerios and Wheaties, ranked among the top five brands in terms of dollar and volume share.[4]
- To capitalize on changing and fast-growing consumer trends, General Mills introduced several new products targeted at specific market segments.[5]

  - Wheaties Energy Crunch, "The Breakfast of Everyday Champions," which combines added protein, carbohydrates, and B vitamins for people who engage in active, healthy lifestyles and want "all-day energy."
  - Harmony, a "nutraceutical" cereal that is fortified with soy, antioxidants, folic acid, and calcium targeted at women who want a healthier breakfast.
  - Chex Morning Mix in single-serve pouches, to "grab the nutrition and skip the bowl!"[6]
  - Yoplait Expresse, the adult version of Yoplait's Go-Gurt yogurt in a plastic, squeezable tube that can be eaten chilled or frozen without a spoon.
  - Big G Milk 'n' Cereal Bar, which combines cereal and a milk-based layer so that convenience-oriented consumers can "eat and go."

To make matters even a bit more complicated, General Mills acquired Pillsbury hoping to find important marketing, manufacturing, and supply-chain efficiencies and synergies. So in your position as a marketing manager at General Mills you'll face many tough challenges. But you can learn from past successes, such as the highly successful launch of Frosted Cheerios. Also, you can stretch your creative talents to find marketing synergies in merging General Mills and Pillsbury product lines.[7]

This chapter discusses issues and techniques related to planning, implementation, and control phases of the strategic marketing process, the kind of topics marketing strategists at General Mills face in achieving growth. The individual elements of the strategic marketing process were introduced in Chapter 2.

STRATEGIC MARKETING'S GOAL: EFFECTIVE RESOURCE ALLOCATION

As noted in Chapter 2, corporate and marketing executives search continuously to find a competitive advantage—a unique strength relative to competitors, often based on quality, time, cost, innovation, or customer intimacy. Having identified this competitive advantage, they must allocate their firm's resources to exploit it. The timing of product and market actions may also influence the magnitude and duration of a firm's competitive advantage.[8]

Allocating Marketing Resources Using Sales Response Functions

SALES RESPONSE FUNCTION

Relates the expense of marketing effort to the marketing results obtained. Measures of marketing results include sales revenue, profit, units sold, and level of awareness.

A **sales response function** relates the expense of marketing effort to the marketing results obtained.[9] For simplicity in the examples that follow, only the effects of annual marketing effort on annual sales revenue will be analyzed, but the concept applies to other measures of marketing success—such as profit, units sold, or level of awareness—as well.

Maximizing Incremental Revenue Minus Incremental Cost Economists give managers a specific guideline for optimal resource allocation: allocate the firm's marketing, production, and financial resources to the markets and products where the excess of incremental revenues over incremental costs is greatest. This parallels the marginal revenue–marginal cost analysis of Chapter 13.

Figure 22–1 illustrates this resource allocation principle, which is inherent in the sale response function. The firm's annual marketing effort, such as sales and advertising expenses, is plotted on the horizontal axis. As the annual marketing effort increases, so does the resulting annual sales revenue, which is plotted in the vertical axis. The relationship is assumed to be "S-shaped," showing that an additional $1 million of marketing effort from $3 million to $4 million results in far greater increases of sales revenue in the mid-range ($20 million) of the curve than at either end (an increase from $2 million to $3 million in spending yields an increase of $10 million in sales; an increase from $6 million to $7 million in spending yields an increase of $5 million in sales).

A Numerical Example of Resource Allocation   Suppose Figure 22–1 shows the situation for a General Mills product such as Count Chocula, a chocolate-flavoured cereal with vitamins and minerals targeted at kids. Also assume that the sales response function doesn't change through time as a result of changing consumer tastes and incomes. Point A shows the position of the firm in Year 1, whereas Point B shows it three years later, in Year 4. General Mills has decided to "re-characterize" Count Chocula with a series of playful new packages (shown here) plus advertising and sales promotion that, let's say, increases its marketing effort on the brand from $3 million to $6 million a year. If the relationship in Figure 22–1 holds true and is a good picture of consumer purchasing behaviour, the sales revenue of Count Chocula should increase from $30 million to $70 million a year.

Let's look at the major resource allocation question: What are the probable increases in sales revenue for Count Chocula in Year 1 and Year 4 if General Mills were to spend an additional $1 million in marketing effort? As Figure 22–1 reveals:

Year 1

Increase in marketing effort from $3 million to $4 million = $1 million
Increase in sales revenue from $30 million to $50 million = $20 million
Ration of incremental sales revenue to effort = $20 000 000; $1 000 000 = 20:1

Year 4

Increase in marketing effort from $6 million to $7 million = $1 million
Increase in sales revenue from $70 million to $73 million = $3 million
Ratio of incremental sales revenue to effort = $3 000 000:$1 000 000 = 3:1

Thus, in Year 1 a dollar of extra marketing effort returned $20 in sales revenue, whereas in year 4 it returned only $3. If no other expenses are incurred, it might

FIGURE 22–1
Sales response function showing the situation for two different years

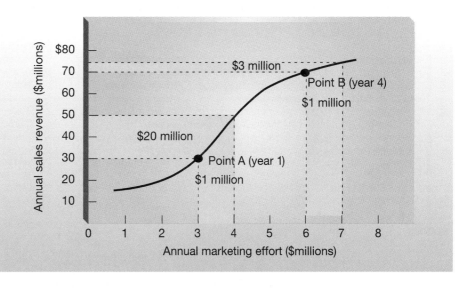

make sense to spend $1 million in Year 4 to gain $3 million in incremental sales revenue. However, it may be far wiser for General Mills to invest the money in products in one of its other products or brands, or even another business unit. The essence of resource allocation is simple: put incremental resources where the incremental returns are greatest over the foreseeable future.

Allocating Marketing Resources in Practice

General Mills, like many firms in these businesses, does extensive analysis using **share points**, or percentage points of market share, as the common basis of comparison to allocate marketing resources effectively. This allows it to seek answers to the question "How much is it worth to us to try to increase our market share by another 1 (or 2, or 5, or 10) percentage point?"

This also enables higher-level managers to make resource allocation trade-offs among different kinds of products or brands, or even other business units owned by the company. To make these resource allocation decisions, marketing managers must estimate (1) the market share for the product, (2) the revenues associated with each point of market share, (3) the contribution to overhead and profit (or gross margin) of each share point, and (4) possible cannibalization effects on other products in the line (for example, new Wheaties Energy Crunch might reduce Wheaties sales).[10]

The resource allocation process helps General Mills choose wisely from among the many opportunities that exist in its various products and markets.

FIGURE 22–2
The strategic marketing process; actions and information

Resource Allocation and the Strategic Marketing Process

Company resources are allocated effectively in the strategic marketing process by converting marketing information into marketing actions. Figure 22–2 summarizes

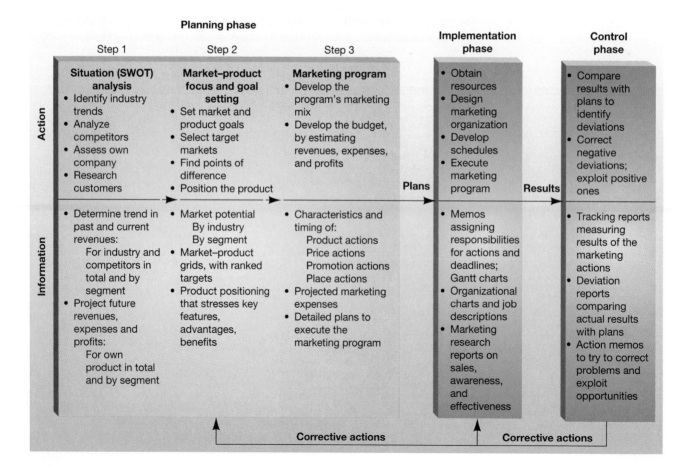

the strategic marketing process introduced in Chapter 2, along with some details of the marketing actions and information that compose it. Figure 22–2 is really a simplification of the actual strategic marketing process: while the three phases of the strategic marketing process have distinct separations in the figure and the marketing actions are separated from the marketing information, in practice these blend together and interact.

The upper half of each box in Figure 22–2 highlights the actions involved in that part of the strategic marketing process, and the lower half summarizes the information and reports used. Note that each phase has an output report:

PHASE	OUTPUT REPORT
Planning	Marketing plans (or programs) that define goals and the marketing mix strategies to achieve them
Implementation	Results (memos or computer outputs) that describe the outcomes of implementing the plans
Control	Corrective action memos, triggered by comparing results with plans, that (1) suggest solutions to problems and (2) take advantage of opportunities

The corrective action memos become "feedback loops" in Figure 22–2 that help improve decisions and actions in earlier phases of the strategic marketing process.

THE PLANNING PHASE OF THE STRATEGIC MARKETING PROCESS

Three aspects of the strategic marketing process deserve special mention: (1) the varieties of marketing plans, (2) marketing planning frameworks that have proven useful, and (3) some marketing planning and strategy lessons.

The Variety of Marketing Plans

The planning phase of the strategic marketing process usually results in a marketing plan that sets the direction for the marketing activities of an organization. As noted earlier in Appendix A, a marketing plan is the heart of a business plan. Like business plans, marketing plans aren't all from the same mould; they vary with the length of the planning period, the purpose, and the audience. Let's look briefly at two kinds: long-range and annual marketing plans.

Long-Range Marketing Plans   Typically, long-range marketing plans cover marketing activities from two to five years into the future. Except for firms in industries such as autos, steel, or forest products, marketing plans rarely go beyond five years into the future because the tremendous number of uncertainties present make the benefits of planning less than the effort expended. Such plans are often directed at top-level executives and the board of directors.

Annual Marketing Plans   Usually developed by a marketing or product manager (discussed later in the chapter) in a consumer products firm such as General Mills, annual marketing plans deal with marketing goals and strategies for a product, product line, or entire firm for a single year. Typical steps that firms such as Kellogg's, Coca-Cola, and Johnson & Johnson take in developing their annual marketing plans for their existing products are shown in Figure 22–3.[11] This annual planning cycle typically starts with a detailed marketing research study of current users and ends after 48 weeks

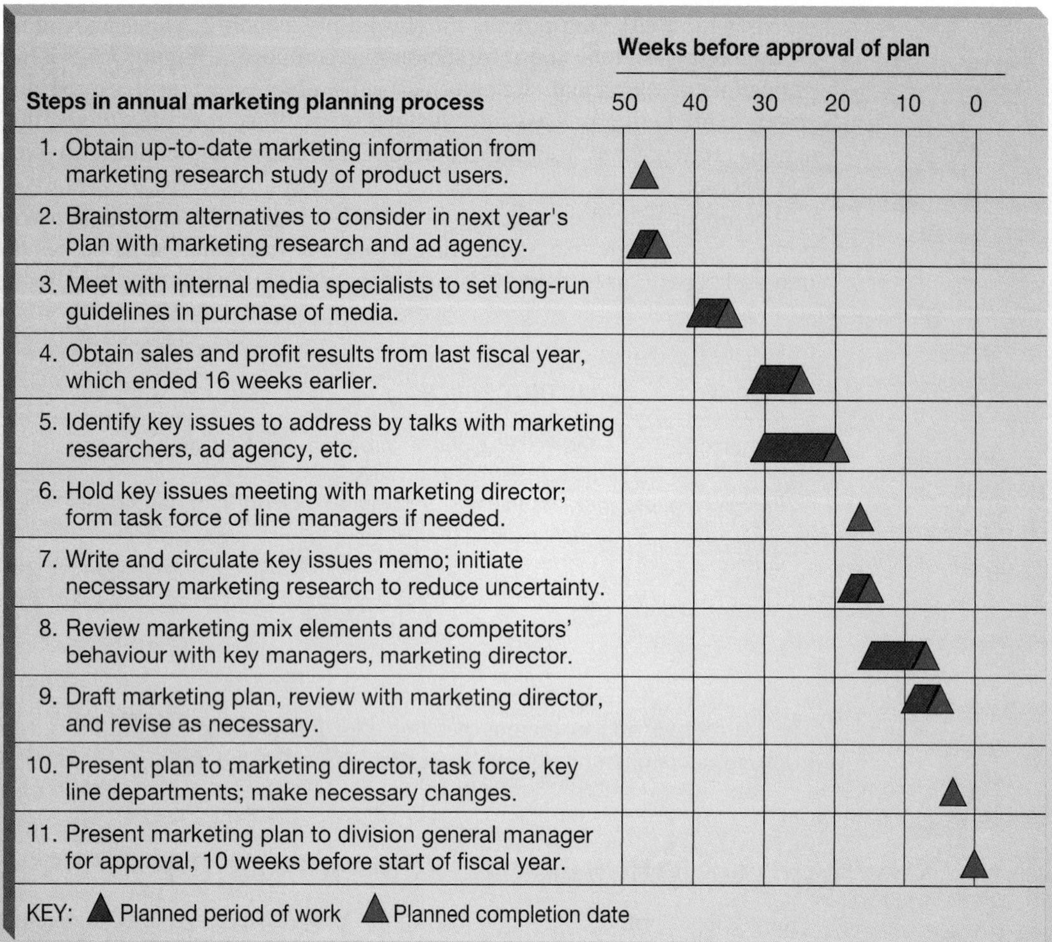

Steps in annual marketing planning process	Weeks before approval of plan					
	50	40	30	20	10	0
1. Obtain up-to-date marketing information from marketing research study of product users.	▲					
2. Brainstorm alternatives to consider in next year's plan with marketing research and ad agency.	◢▲					
3. Meet with internal media specialists to set long-run guidelines in purchase of media.		◢▲				
4. Obtain sales and profit results from last fiscal year, which ended 16 weeks earlier.			◢▲			
5. Identify key issues to address by talks with marketing researchers, ad agency, etc.			◢——▲			
6. Hold key issues meeting with marketing director; form task force of line managers if needed.				▲		
7. Write and circulate key issues memo; initiate necessary marketing research to reduce uncertainty.				◢▲		
8. Review marketing mix elements and competitors' behaviour with key managers, marketing director.					◢▲	
9. Draft marketing plan, review with marketing director, and revise as necessary.					◢▲	
10. Present plan to marketing director, task force, key line departments; make necessary changes.					▲	
11. Present marketing plan to division general manager for approval, 10 weeks before start of fiscal year.						▲

KEY: ▲ Planned period of work   ▲ Planned completion date

FIGURE 22–3

Steps a large consumer packaged goods firm takes in developing its annual marketing plan

with the approval of the plan by the division general manager—10 weeks before the fiscal year starts. Between these points there are continuing efforts to uncover new ideas through brainstorming and key-issues sessions with specialists both inside and outside the firm. The plan is fine-tuned through a series of often-excruciating reviews by several levels of management, which leaves few surprises and little to chance.

Concept Check

1. What is the significance of the S-shape of the sales response function in Figure 22–1?

2. What are the main output reports from each phase of the strategic marketing process?

3. What are two kinds of marketing plans?

Frameworks to Improve Marketing Planning

Marketing planning for a firm with many products competing in many markets—a multiproduct, multimarket firm—is a complex process. Three techniques that are useful in helping corporate and marketing executives in such a firm make important resource allocation decisions are (1) Porter's generic business strategies, (2) profit enhancement options, and (3) market–product synergies. All of these techniques are based on elements introduced in earlier chapters.

Which of Porter's generic strategies are Wal-Mart and Volkswagen using? For the answer and a discussion of the strategies, see the text.

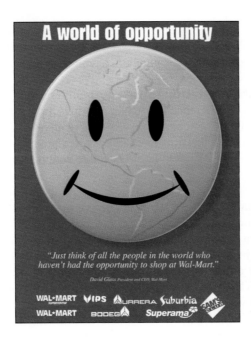

Porter's Generic Business Strategies   As shown in Figure 22–4, Michael E. Porter has developed a framework in which he identifies four basic, or "generic," strategies.[12] A **generic business strategy** is one that can be adopted by any firm, regardless of the product or industry involved, to achieve a competitive advantage. Some current research suggests that a firm needs several major competencies, not just one, to sustain its competitive advantage over longer periods;[13] other research suggests that the preferred strategy is to focus on a single discipline—such as operational excellence, product leadership, or customer intimacy.[14]

Although all of the techniques discussed here involve generic strategies, the phrase is most often associated with Porter's framework. In this framework the columns identify the two fundamental alternatives firms can use in seeking competitive advantage: (1) becoming the low-cost producer within the markets in which it competes or (2) differentiating itself from competitors through developing points of difference in its product offerings or marketing programs. In contrast, the rows identify the competitive scope: (1) a broad target by competing in many market segments or (2) a narrow target by competing in only a few segments or even a single segment. The columns and rows result in four generic business strategies, any one of which can provide a competitive advantage among similar business units in the same industry:

1. A **cost leadership strategy** (cell 1) requires a serious commitment to reducing expenses that, in turn, lowers the price or the items sold in a relatively broad array of market segments. One way is by securing raw materials from a lower-cost supplier. Also, significant investments in capital equipment may be necessary to improve the production or distribution process and achieve

GENERIC BUSINESS STRATEGY
Strategy that can be adopted by any firm, regardless of the product or industry involved, to achieve a competitive advantage.

COST LEADERSHIP STRATEGY
Using a serious commitment to reducing expenses that, in turn, lowers the price of the items sold in a relatively broad array of market segments.

FIGURE 22–4
Porter's four generic business strategies

Competitive scope	SOURCE OF COMPETITIVE ADVANTAGE	
	Lower cost	Differentiation
Broad target	1. Cost leadership	2. Differentiation
Narrow target	3. Cost focus	4. Differentiation focus

DIFFERENTIATION STRATEGY
Requires innovation and significant points of difference in product offerings, brand image, higher quality, advanced technology, or superior service in a relatively broad array of market segments.

COST-FOCUS STRATEGY
Involves controlling expenses and, in turn, lowering prices, in a narrow range of market segments.

DIFFERENTIATION FOCUS STRATEGY
Using significant points of difference in the firm's offerings to reach one or only a few market segments.

these lower unit costs. The cost leader still must have adequate quality levels. Wal-Mart's sophisticated systems of regional warehouses and electronic data interchange with its suppliers have led to huge cost savings and its cost leadership strategy.

2. A **differentiation strategy** (cell 2) requires innovation and significant points of difference in product offerings, brand image, higher quality, advanced technology, or superior service in a relatively broad array of market segments. This allows the firm to charge a price premium. Delphi Automobile Systems has used this strategy to use satellite communications to connect you and your car to 24-hour-a-day emergency services, directions to a destination, and the opportunity to order a movie while on the road.

3. A **cost-focus strategy** (cell 3) involves controlling expenses and, in turn, lowering prices, in a narrow range of market segments. Retail chains targeting only a few market segments in a restricted group of products—such as Office Max in office supplies—have used a cost-focus strategy successfully. Similarly, some airlines have been very successful in offering low fares between very restricted pairs of cities.

4. Finally, a **differentiation focus strategy** (cell 4) utilizes significant points of difference to one or only a few market segments. Volkswagen has achieved spectacular success by targeting the "nostalgia segment," 35- to 55-year-old baby boomers, with its technology-laden Beetle.[15]

These strategies also form the foundation for Michael Porter's theory about what makes a nation's industries successful, as discussed in Chapter 7.

Profit Enhancement Options   If a business wants to increase, or "enhance," its profits, it can (1) increase revenues, (2) decrease expenses, or (3) do both. Among these "profit enhancement options," let's look first at the strategy options of increasing revenues and then at those for decreasing expenses.

The strategy option of increasing revenues can be achieved only by using one or a combination of four ways to address present or new markets and products (Figure 22–5): (1) market penetration, (2) product development, (3) market development, and (4) diversification (which are described in Chapter 2).

FIGURE 22–5
Profit enhancement options for increasing a firm's profits

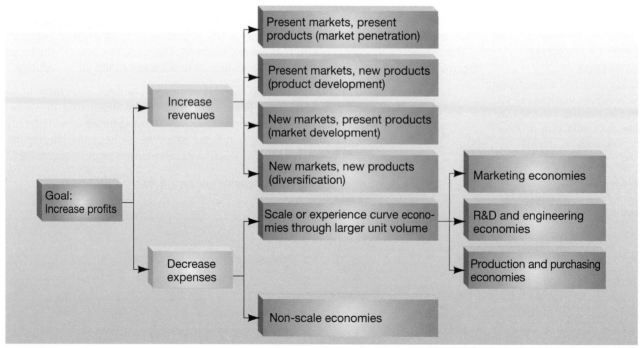

Procter & Gamble has followed a successful strategy of market penetration (present markets, present products) by concentrating its effort on becoming the market leader in each of its more than 30 product categories. It is currently first in market share in more than half these product categories. Recent research, however, suggests that while market share may be directly related to profitability in some industries, this is not true for all. Corporate goals such as increasing customer satisfaction may be more successful than simply maximizing market share.

In contrast, Johnson & Johnson has succeeded with a product development strategy—finding new products for its present markets—to complement popular brands such as Tylenol pain reliever and Accuvue contact lenses. To compete with Bristol-Meyers and other companies, Johnson & Johnson developed Tylenol PM—a combination pain killer and sleeping pill—and Surevue—a long-lasting disposable contact lens.

Walt Disney Co. pursued a market development strategy (new market, present product) following the success of the original Disneyland in Anaheim, California. The first market expansion, of course, was to Orlando, Florida, and more recently Disney built theme parks in Tokyo and Paris. Disney has also pursued a diversification strategy by entering into the motion picture business with the development of Touchstone Pictures, by buying and operating an NHL franchise, the Mighty Ducks, and by operating a cruise line.

Canadian Tire has pursued a multi-pronged strategy including increased market penetration in existing markets, market development (geographic expansion), introducing new products to expand its current product line, and diversification including the acquisition of Mark's Work Wearhouse, operating a car wash division, and participating in the financial services business. In fact, Canadian Tire Financial Services is the only non-bank institution in Canada that has a MasterCard licence.

Strategy options for decreasing expenses fall into two broad categories (Figure 22–5). One is relying on scale economies or experience curve benefits from an increased volume of production to drive unit costs down and gross margins up, the best-known examples being electronic devices such as fax or voice-mail machines whose prices fell by half in a few years. Scale economies may occur in marketing, as well as in R&D, engineering, production, and purchasing.

The other strategy option to decrease expenses is simply finding other ways to reduce costs, such as cutting the number of managers, increasing the effectiveness of the salesforce through more training, or reducing the product rejects by inspectors. In an effort to decrease costs, IBM Canada and Xerox Canada had both downsized in the past through layoffs. Procter & Gamble concluded the world didn't really need 31 varieties of Head & Shoulders shampoo, so it cut the number of packages, sizes, and formulas and thereby reduced expenses and increased profits.

Market–Product Synergies   Using the market–product grid framework introduced in Chapter 9, we can see two kinds of synergy that are critical in developing corporate and marketing strategies: (1) marketing synergy and (2) R&D–manufacturing synergy. While the following example involves external synergies through mergers and acquisitions, the concepts apply equally well to internal synergies sought in adding new products or seeking new markets.

A critical step in the external analysis is to assess how these merger and acquisition strategies provide the organization with synergy. As we saw in Chapter 9, synergy is the increased customer value achieved through performing organizational functions more efficiently. The "increased customer value" can take many forms: more products, improved quality on existing products, lower prices, improved distribution, and so on. But the ultimate criterion is that customers should be better off as a result of the increased synergy. The firm, in turn, should be better off by gaining more satisfied customers.

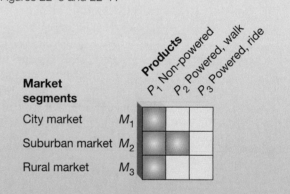
A market–product grid helps identify important trade-offs in the strategic marketing process. As noted in the Marketing NewsNet,[16] assume you are vice president of marketing for Great Lawns Corporation's line of non-powered lawnmowers and powered walking mowers sold to the consumer market. You are looking for new product and new market opportunities to increase your revenues and profits.

You conduct a market segmentation study and develop a market–product grid to analyze future opportunities. You identify three major segments in the consumer market based on geography: (1) city, (2) suburban, and (3) rural households. These market segments relate to the size of lawn a consumer must mow. The product clusters are (1) non-powered, (2) powered walking, and (3) powered riding mowers. Five alternative marketing strategies are shown in the market–product grids in Figure 22–6. As mentioned in Chapter 9, the important marketing efficiencies—or synergies—run horizontally across the rows in Figure 22–6. Conversely, the important R&D and production efficiencies—or synergies—run vertically down the columns. Let's look at the synergy effects for the five combinations in Figure 22–6:

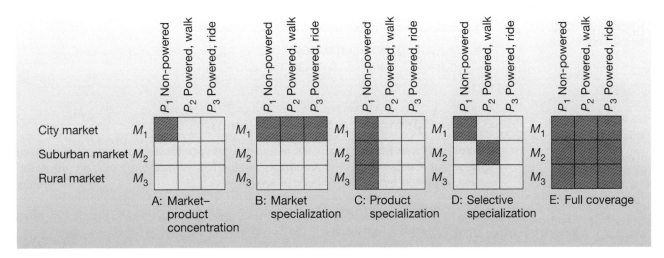

FIGURE 22–6

Market–product grid of alternative strategies for a lawnmower manufacturer

A. *Market-product concentration.* The firm benefits from "focus" on a single product line and market segment, but it loses opportunities for significant synergies in both marketing and R&D–manufacturing.

B. *Market specialization.* The firm gains marketing synergy through providing a complete product line, but R&D–manufacturing have the difficulty of developing and producing two new products.

C. *Product specialization.* The firm gains R&D–manufacturing synergy through production economies of scale, but gaining market distribution in the three different geographic areas will be costly.

D. *Selective specialization.* The firm doesn't get either marketing or R&D–manufacturing synergies because of the uniqueness of the market–product combinations.

E. *Full coverage.* The firm has the maximum potential synergies in both marketing and R&D–manufacturing. The question: Is it spread too thin due to the resource requirements needed to reach all market–product combinations?

The Marketing NewsNet posed the question of what the ideal partner for Great Lawns would be if it merged with another firm, given the market–product combinations shown in the box. If, as vice president of marketing, you want to follow a full-coverage strategy, then the ideal merger partner is shown in Figure 22–7. This would give the maximum potential synergies—if you are not spreading your merged companies too thin. Marketing gains by having a complete product line in all regions, and R&D–manufacturing gains by having access to new markets that can provide production economies of scale through producing larger volumes of its existing products.

FIGURE 22–7

An ideal merger for Great Lawns to obtain full market–product coverage

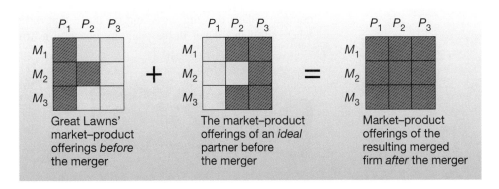

Great Lawns' market–product offerings *before* the merger

The market–product offerings of an *ideal* partner before the merger

Market–product offerings of the resulting merged firm *after* the merger

1. Describe Porter's four generic business strategies.

2. Where do (a) marketing synergies and (b) R&D–manufacturing synergies appear in a market–product grid framework?

Some Planning and Strategy Lessons

Applying these frameworks is not automatic but requires a great deal of managerial judgment. Common-sense requirements of an effective marketing plan are discussed next, followed by problems that can arise.

Guidelines for an Effective Marketing Plan   Dwight D. Eisenhower, when he commanded Allied armies in the Second World War, made his classic observation, "Plans are nothing; planning is everything." It is the process of careful planning that focuses an organization's efforts and leads to success. The plans themselves, which change with events, are often secondary. Effective planning and plans are inevitably characterized by identifiable objectives, specific strategies or courses of action, and the means to execute them. Here are some guidelines in developing effective marketing plans:

- *Set measurable, achievable goals.* Ideally, goals should be quantified and measurable in terms of what is to be accomplished and by when. So, "Increase market share from 18 percent to 22 percent by December 31, 2005" is preferable to "Maximize market share given our available resources." Also, to motivate people the goals must be achievable.
- *Use a base of facts and valid assumptions.* The more a marketing plan is based on facts and valid assumptions, rather than guesses, the less uncertainty and risk are associated with executing it. Good marketing research helps. For example, General Mills' research indicates a basic fact that busy consumers on the go want very convenient food products—ones they can eat with one hand. So when Steve Sanger, CEO of General Mills, receives plans for a new food product from his employees, he asks one question: Does it have the "one-handedness" feature that consumers want? Without that feature, the marketing plan for that product is not likely to be successful.
- *Utilize simple, but clear and specific, plans.* Effective execution of plans requires that people at all levels in the firm understand what, when, and how they are to accomplish their tasks.
- *Have complete and feasible plans.* Marketing plans must incorporate all the key marketing mix factors and be supported by adequate resources.
- *Make plans controllable and flexible.* Marketing plans must enable results to be compared with planned targets, which allows replanning—the flexibility to update the original plans.

Problems in Marketing Planning and Strategy   From postmortems on company plans that did work and on those that did not work, a picture emerges of where problems occur in the planning phase of a firm's strategic marketing process.

"Better ingredients, better pizza"—and better planning and attention to detail: Papa John's!

Papa John's International, Inc.

www.papajohns.com

The following list explores these problems:

1. Plans may be based on very poor assumptions about environmental factors, especially changing ecoomic conditions and competitors' actions. Canadians used to equate the name Listerine with mouthwash. But Scope started an anti-Listerine campaign and successfully convinced Canadians that mouthwash didn't have to taste bad to work. The result? Listerine lost its position as market leader.

2. Planners and their plans may have lost sight of their customers' needs. The "better ingredients, better pizza" slogan makes the hair stand up on the back of the necks of Pizza Hut executives. The reason is that this slogan of Papa John's International pizza chain reflects the firm's obsessive attention to detail, which is stealing market share from the five-times-bigger Pizza Hut! Sample detail: If the cheese on the pizza shows a single air bubble or the crust is not golden brown, the offending pizza is not served to the customer![17]

3. Too much time and effort may be spent on data collection and writing the plans. Westinghouse has cut its planning instructions for operating units "that looked like an auto repair manual" to five or six pages.

4. Line operating managers often feel no sense of ownership in implementing the plans. Andy Grove, when he was CEO of Intel, observed, "We had the very ridiculous system . . . of delegating strategic planning to strategic planners. The strategies these [planners] prepared had no bearing on anything we actually did."[18] The solution is to assign more planning activities to line operating managers—the people who actually carry them out.

Balancing Value and Values in Strategic Marketing Plans   Two important trends are likely to influence the strategic marketing process in the future. The first, value-based planning, combines marketing planning ideas and financial planning techniques to assess how much a division or strategic business unit (SBU) contributes to the price of a company's stock (or shareholder wealth). Value is created when the financial return of a strategic activity exceeds the cost of the resources allocated to the activity.

The second trend is the increasing interest in value-driven strategies, which incorporate concerns for ethics, integrity, employee health and safety, and environmental safeguards with more common corporate values such as growth, profitability, customer service, and quality. Some experts have observed that although many corporations cite broad corporate values in advertisements, press releases, and company newsletters, they have not yet changed their strategic plans to reflect the stated values.[19]

Finally, remember that it is easier to talk about planning than to do it well. Try your hand as a consultant to help Trevor's Toys make some strategic decisions, as described in the Web Link box.

THE IMPLEMENTATION PHASE OF THE STRATEGIC MARKETING PROCESS

The Monday-morning diagnosis of a losing football coach often runs something like "We had an excellent game plan: we just didn't execute it."

WEB LINK — Want to Be a BCG Consultant? Solve the Trevor's Toys Online Case

http://www.mcgrawhill.ca

The Boston Consulting Group, or BCG, is probably best known for its "growth-share" portfolio matrix discussed in Chapter 2. As a very active and respected management consulting organization, BCG maintains a Website to describe its services. Included in its Website is an interactive strategy case that asks potential employees to analyze typical strategic challenges faced by BCG clients.

Go to the BCG Website and assess the e-commerce strategy for Trevor's Toys. You can access the case by going to www.bcg.com/careers/interview_prep/interactive_case/interactive_case.asp. Read the case carefully, solve it within the time limits, and consider becoming a BCG consultant after graduation!

Is Planning or Implementation the Problem?

The planning-versus-execution issue applies to the strategic marketing process as well: a difficulty when a marketing plan fails is determining whether the failure is due to a poor plan or poor implementation. Figure 22–8 shows the outcomes of (1) good and bad marketing planning and (2) good and bad marketing implementation.[20] Good planning and good implementation in cell 1 spell success, as with General Electric's continuing leadership in lighting, which combines strong innovative products and the well-known GE brand with excellent advertising and distribution.

Most of the hundreds of failed dot-com firms fall into the "bad-bad" cell 4. The principal owner of the Expedia travel-booking Website says, "You have to deliver a better product to your customer, not just offer an Internet retail option for the sake of dabbling in some new technology." What often happened with the dot-coms was bad planning focused mainly on getting start-up money from investors—not providing value to customers—and bad implementation with large expenditures on traditional ads to try to promote their failing Websites. What is also clear is that while some Internet companies may have had good ideas for delivering physical products—like toys, books, and groceries—to their customer's door, they didn't understand inventories, warehouses, and physical distribution (cell 3 in Figure 22–8).[21]

Cells 2 and 3 indicate trouble because either the marketing planning *or* marketing implementation—not both—is bad. A firm or product does not stay permanently in cell 2 or 3. If the problem is solved, the result can be success (cell 1); if not, it is failure (cell 4).

Toyota used good implementation on a bad marketing strategy (cell 2) when it applied its superior automobile marketing skills to the introduction of its T100

FIGURE 22–8
Results of good and bad marketing planning and implementation

Marketing implementation	MARKETING PLANNING AND STRATEGY: Good (appropriate)	MARKETING PLANNING AND STRATEGY: Bad (inappropriate)
Good (effective)	1. *Success:* Marketing program achieves its objectives.	2. *Trouble:* Solution lies in recognizing that only the strategy is at fault and correcting it.
Bad (ineffective)	3. *Trouble:* Solution lies in recognizing that only implementation is at fault and correcting it.	4. *Failure:* Marketing program flounders and fails to achieve its objectives.

General Electric's army of innovative lights have benefited from having both good planning and implementation of their marketing programs—and by making it into one of Jack Welch's "three circles."

pickup truck. Consumer response was well below forecasts because the truck was too big to compete with smaller "compact" pickups and too small and underpowered to compete with full-size options. Goodyear Tire and Rubber Co. found itself in cell 3 after it successfully developed all-season radial tires but created problems with the 640-dealer distribution network by raising wholesale prices. The poor implementation led to a two-point decline in market share—a drop of 3 million tires.

Increasing Emphasis on Marketing Implementation

In the new millennium, the implementation phase of the strategic marketing process has emerged as a key factor to success by moving many planning activities away from the duties of planners to those of line managers.

As described in the Marketing NewsNet, General Electric's Jack Welch has become a legend in making GE far more efficient and far better at implementation. When Welch became CEO in 1981 he faced an organization mired in red tape, turf battles, and slow decision making. Further, Welch saw GE bogged down with 25 000 managers and close to a dozen layers between him and the factory floor. In his "delayering," he sought to cut GE's levels in half and to speed up decision making and implementation by building an atmosphere of trust and autonomy among his managers and employees. Although there are debates on some Welch strategies, businesses around the world are using his focus on implementation as a benchmark. One measure of GE's global impact: In 2000, *Fortune* magazine named General Electric "the world's most admired company."[22]

Improving Implementation of Marketing Programs

No magic formula exists to guarantee effective implementation of marketing plans. In fact, the answer seems to be equal parts of good management skills and practices, from which have come some guidelines for improving program implementation.

Communicate Goals and the Means of Achieving Them   Those called on to implement plans need to understand both the goals sought and how they are to be accomplished. Everyone in Papa John's—from founder John Schnatter to telephone order takers and make-line people—is clear on what the firm's goal is: to deliver

MARKETING NEWSNET

GE's Implementation Strategies: How Neutron Jack Became "One of the Most Acclaimed CEOs of the 20th Century"

Time magazine calls him "one of the most acclaimed CEOs (chief executive officers) of the 20th century." Yet employees at his company in the 1980s called him "Neutron Jack" because they said his corporate downsizings were alleged to leave the buildings standing with no people in them—like a neutron bomb would. However, his difficult strategy decisions and in-your-face leadership style probably assured the jobs of thousands of his firm's employees today.

He is Jack Welch, General Electric's CEO for two decades, up to mid-2001. Welch's implementation focus emerges in his five-box flowchart below:

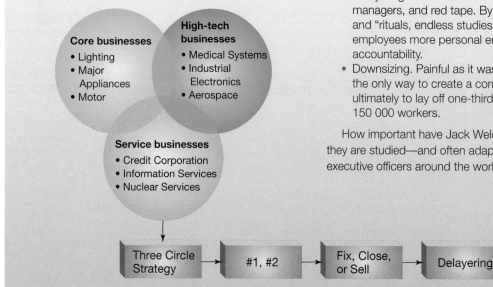

- Three Circle Strategy. In the early 1980s Welch looked at the 350 businesses in 43 strategic business units he inherited. By focusing GE's businesses in three key areas as shown in the illustration, he set the strategic direction for GE's future.
- #1, #2. Welch concluded that GE "winners" would be either #1 or #2 in their industry.
- Fix, close, or sell. This became GE's mantra. Coupled with "#1, #2," more than 100 businesses were closed or sold. An example is GE's housewares (small appliance) division that was sold to Black & Decker. The rest were fixed.
- Delayering. Welch felt GE was drowning in layers, managers, and red tape. By eliminating a lot of these and "rituals, endless studies, and briefings," he gave employees more personal empowerment and accountability.
- Downsizing. Painful as it was to him, Welch thought the only way to create a competitive organization was ultimately to lay off one-third of GE's employees: 150 000 workers.

How important have Jack Welch's ideas become? Today they are studied—and often adapted—by hundreds of chief executive officers around the world!

---

better pizzas using better ingredients. The firm's orientation packet for employees lists its six "core values," which executives are expected to memorize. Sample: Core value no. 4 is "PAPA," or "People Are Priority No. 1, Always."[23]

PRODUCT (OR PROGRAM) CHAMPION

A person who is able and willing to cut red tape and move the program forward.

Have a Responsible Program Champion Willing to Act   Successful programs almost always have a **product (or program) champion** who is able and willing to cut red tape and move the program forward. Such people often have the uncanny ability to move back and forth between big-picture strategy questions and specific details when the situation calls for it. Program champions are notoriously brash in overcoming organizational hurdles. In many cases, they adhere to the axiom "Better to ask forgiveness than permission." Using this strategy, 3M's Art Fry championed Post-it Notes to success, an idea he got when looking for a simple way to mark his hymnal while singing in his church choir.

Reward Successful Program Implementation   When an individual or a team is rewarded for achieving the organization's goal, they have maximum incentive to see a program implemented successfully because they have personal ownership and a stake in that success. At a General Electric surge protector plant, employees receive a bonus for each quarter that the facility meets plantwide performance goals.

Take Action and Avoid "Paralysis by Analysis" Management experts warn against paralysis by analysis, the tendency to excessively analyze a problem instead of taking action. To overcome this pitfall, they call for a "bias for action" and recommend a "do it, fix it, try it" approach.[24] Conclusion: Perfectionists finish last, so getting 90-percent perfection and letting the marketplace help in the fine tuning makes good sense in implementation.

Lockheed Martin's Skunk Works got its name from the comic strip *L'il Abner* and its legendary reputation from achieving superhuman technical feats with a low budget and ridiculously short deadlines by stressing teamwork. Under the leadership of Kelly Johnson, the Skunk Works turned out a series of world-class aircraft, from the world's fastest (the SR-71 Blackbird) to the nation's most untrackable aircraft (the F-117 Stealth fighter). Now on the drawing boards: the X-33 VentureStar, the planned replacement for the space shuttle. Two of Kelly Johnson's basic tenets: (1) make decisions promptly and (2) avoid paralysis by analysis. In fact, one study showed that Johnson's Skunk Works could carry out a program on schedule with 126 people, whereas a competitor in a comparable program was behind schedule with 3750 people.[25]

Foster Open Communication to Surface the Problems Success often lies in fostering a work environment that is open enough so employees are willing to speak out when they see problems without fear of recrimination. The focus is placed on trying to solve the problem as a group rather than finding someone to blame. Solutions are solicited from anyone who has a creative idea to suggest—from the caretaker to the president—without regard to status or rank in the organization.

Two more Kelly Johnson axioms from Lockheed Martin's Skunk Works apply here: (1) When trouble develops, surface the problem immediately, and (2) get help; don't keep the problem to yourself. This latter point is important even if it means getting ideas from competitors.

Saturn is General Motors' attempt to create a new company where participatory management and improved communications lead to a successful product. For example, to encourage discussion of possible cost reductions, each employee receives 100 to 750 hours of training, including balance sheet analysis. To avoid the "NIH syndrome"—the reluctance to accept ideas "not invented here" or not originated inside one's own firm—Saturn engineers bought 70 import cars to study for product design ideas and selected options that would most appeal to their target market.

For the unusual way General Motors avoided the "NIH syndrome" to help develop the Saturn, see the text.

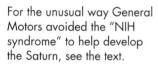

ACTION ITEM LIST
An aid to implementing a
market plan, consisting of
three columns: (1) the task,
(2) the name of the person
responsible for completing
that task, and (3) the date
by which the task is to be
finished.

Schedule Precise Tasks, Responsibilities, and Deadlines   Successful implementation requires that people know the tasks for which they are responsible and the deadline for completing them. To implement the tasks required to carry out its marketing plans, the Royal Canadian Mint prepares an **action item list** that has three columns: (1) the task, (2) the name of the person responsible for accomplishing that task, and (3) the date by which the task is to be finished. Action item lists are forward looking, clarify the targets, and put strong pressure on people to achieve their designated tasks by the deadline.

Related to the action item lists are formal *program schedules*, which show the relationships through time of the various program tasks. Scheduling an action program involves (1) identifying the main tasks, (2) determining the time required to complete each, (3) arranging the activities to meet the deadline, and (4) assigning responsibilities to complete each task.

Scheduling program activities can be done efficiently with *Gantt charts*. Developed by Henry L. Gantt, this method is the basis for the scheduling techniques used today, including elaborate computerized methods. The key to all scheduling techniques is to distinguish tasks that *must* be done sequentially from those that *can* be done concurrently. Scheduling tasks concurrently often reduces the total time required for a program. Software programs, such as Microsoft Project, simplify the task of developing a schedule or Gantt chart.

Concept Check

1. Why is it important to include line operating managers in the planning process?

2. What is the meaning and importance of a program champion?

3. Explain the difference between sequential and concurrent tasks in a Gantt chart.

LINE POSITIONS
People in line positions,
such as senior marketing
managers, have the authority
and responsibility to issue
orders to the people who
report to them, such as
product managers.

STAFF POSITIONS
People in staff positions
have the authority and
responsibility to advise
people in the line positions
but cannot issue direct
orders to them.

**PRODUCT LINE
GROUPINGS**
Organizational groupings in
which a unit is responsible
for specific product offerings.

FUNCTIONAL GROUPINGS
Organizational groupings
such as manufacturing,
marketing, and finance,
which are the different
business activities within
a firm.

Organizing for Marketing

A marketing organization is needed to implement the firm's marketing plans. Basic issues in today's marketing organizations include understanding (1) how line versus staff positions and divisional groupings interrelate to form a cohesive marketing organization, and (2) the role of the marketing or product manager.

Line versus Staff and Divisional Groupings   Although simplified, Figure 22–9 shows the organization of a Pillsbury business unit that was merged into General Mills. The similarity of marketing organizations in the two firms make the merger process easier. This business unit consists of the Breakfast Products, Refrigerated Baked Goods, and Desserts & Baking Mixes Groups. It highlights the distinction between **line** and **staff positions** in marketing. People in line positions, such as senior marketing manager for biscuits, have the authority and responsibility to issue orders to the people who report to them, such as the two product managers shown in Figure 22–9.

In this organizational chart, line positions are connected with solid lines. Those in staff positions (shown by dotted lines) have the authority and responsibility to advise people in line positions but cannot issue direct orders to them.

Most marketing organizations use divisional groupings—such as product line, functional, geographical, and market-based—to implement plans and achieve their organizational objectives. Some of these appear in some form in Pillsbury's organizational chart in Figure 22–9. At the top of the chart, Pillsbury organizes by **product line groupings**, in which a unit is responsible for specific product offerings such as breakfast products or refrigerated baked goods.

At levels higher than those shown in Figure 22–10, Pillsbury is organized by **functional groupings** such as manufacturing, marketing, and finance, which are the different business activities within a firm.

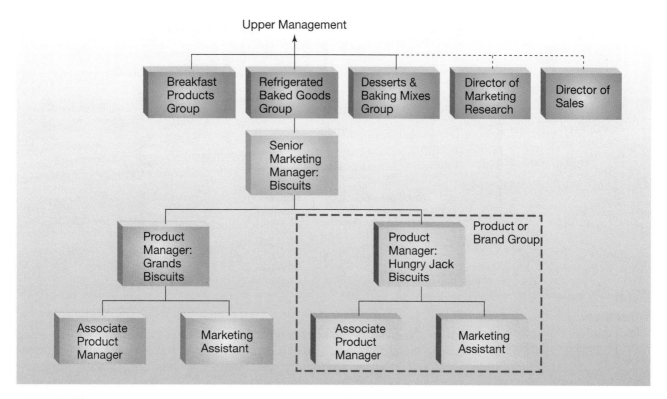

FIGURE 22-9
Organization of a Pillsbury
business unit, showing
product or brand groups

**GEOGRAPHICAL
GROUPINGS**
Organizational groupings in
which a unit is subdivided
according to geographical
location.

**MARKET-BASED
GROUPINGS**
Organizational groupings
that utilize specific customer
segments.

Pillsbury uses **geographical groupings** for its field sales representatives. Each director of sales has several regional sales managers reporting to him or her, such as Western, Eastern, and so on. These, in turn, have district managers reporting to them, with the field sales representatives at the lowest levels.

A fourth method of organizing a company is to use **market-based groupings**, which utilize specific customer segments, such as the banking, health care, or manufacturing segments. When this method of organizing is combined with product groupings, the result is a *matrix organization*.

A relatively new position in consumer products firms is the *category manager* (senior marketing manager in Figure 22–9). Category managers have profit-and-loss responsibility for an entire product line—all biscuit brands, for example. They attempt to reduce the possibility of one brand's actions hurting another brand in the same category. Procter & Gamble uses category managers to organize by "global business units" such as baby care and beauty care. Cutting across country boundaries, these global business units implement standardized worldwide pricing, marketing, and distribution.[26]

Role of the Product Manager   The key person in the product or brand group shown in Figure 22–9 is the manager who heads it. As mentioned in Chapter 10, this person is often called the *product manager* or *brand manager*, but in Pillsbury he or she carries the title *marketing manager*. This person and the assistants in the product group are the basic building blocks in the marketing department of most consumer and industrial product firms. The function of a product manager is to plan, implement, and control the annual and long-range plans for the products for which he or she is responsible.

There are both benefits and dangers to the product manager system. On the positive side, product managers become strong advocates for the assigned products, cut red tape to work with people in various functions both inside and outside the organization (Figure 22–10), and assume profit-and-loss responsibility for the performance of the product line. On the negative side, even though product managers have major responsibilities, they have relatively little direct authority, so most groups and functions shown in Figure 22–10 must be coordinated to meet the product's goals.[27] To coordinate the many units, product managers must use persuasion rather than orders.

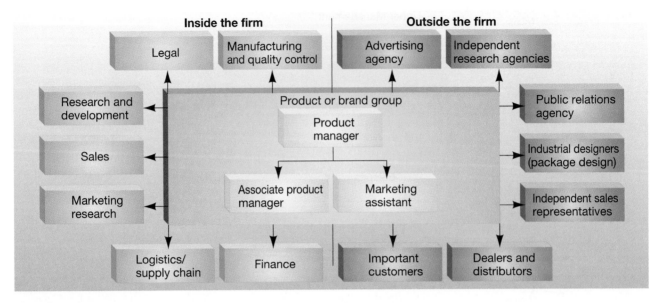

Inside the firm   **Outside the firm**

FIGURE 22–10
Units with which the product
manager and product group
work

But as Canadian firms move toward more customer-intimacy and relationship marketing strategies, product managers are no longer the only ones responsible for managing the product or customer base. Some Canadian firms have created new positions such as "manager of student segment" or "VP of financial services clients," which shadow the traditional product manager roles. These firms have divided their organizations into "customer-facing roles" (such as a segment manager). More and more often it is the segment managers, not the product managers, who make the final decisions on product, price, promotion, and place (distribution).

THE CONTROL PHASE OF THE STRATEGIC MARKETING PROCESS

The essence of control, the final phase of the strategic marketing process, is to compare results with planned goals for the marketing program in order to take necessary corrective actions.

The Marketing Control Process

Ideally, quantified goals from the marketing plans developed in the planning phase have been accomplished by the marketing actions taken in the implementation phase (Figure 22–11) and measured as results in the control phase. A marketing manager then uses *management by exception*, which means identifying results that deviate from plans to diagnose their causes and take new actions. Often results fall short of plans, and a corrective action is needed. For example, after 50 years of profits Caterpillar accumulated losses of $1.4 billion. To correct the problem, Caterpillar focused its marketing efforts on core products and reduced its manufacturing costs. At other times the comparison shows that performance is far better than anticipated, in which case the marketing manager tries to identify the reason and move quickly to exploit the unexpected opportunity.

Measuring Results   Without some quantitative goal, no benchmark exists with which to compare actual results. Manufacturers of both consumer and industrial products are increasingly trying to develop marketing programs that have not only specific action programs but also specific procedures for monitoring key measures of performance. Today marketing executives are measuring not only tangible financial targets such as sales revenues and profits, but also less tangible ones such as customer satisfaction, new-product development cycle time, and salesforce motivation.

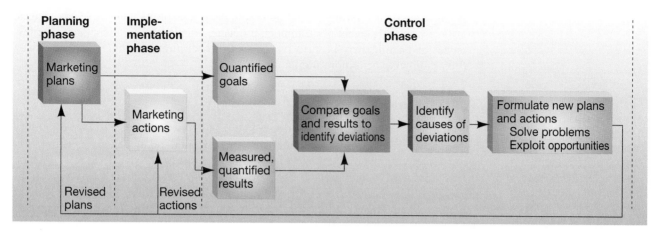

FIGURE 22–11

The control phase of the strategic marketing process

Taking Marketing Actions   When results deviate significantly from plans, some kind of action is essential. Deviations can be the result of the process used to specify goals or can be due to changes in the marketplace. Beaten badly for years in the Canadian toothpaste market by P&G's Crest, Colgate went on the offensive. It took aggressive marketing action to introduce its Total toothpaste. Not only does Total clean teeth, but it also helps heal gingivitis, one of the bleeding-gum diseases of increasing concern to aging baby boomers. For the first time in 30 years, Colgate usurped P&G's Crest to take the number-one spot.[28]

Sales Analysis

SALES ANALYSIS

A tool for controlling marketing programs using sales records to compare actual results with sales goals and to identify strengths and weaknesses.

SALES COMPONENT ANALYSIS

A tool for controlling marketing programs that traces sales revenues to their sources, such as specific products, sales territories, or customers. Also called *microsales analysis*.

For controlling marketing programs, **sales analysis**—using the firm's sales records to compare actual results with sales goals and identify areas of strength and weakness—is critical. All the variables that might be used in market segmentation may be used in **sales component analysis** (also called *microsales analysis*), which traces sales revenues to their sources, such as specific products, sales territories, or customers. Common breakdowns include the following:

- Customer characteristics: demographics, NAICS, size, reason for purchase, and type of reseller (retailer or wholesaler).
- Product characteristics: model, package size, and colour.
- Geographical region: sales territory, city, province, and region.
- Order size.
- Price or discount class.
- Commission to the sales representative.

Today's computers can easily produce these breakdowns, provided the input data contain these classifications. Therefore, it is critical that marketing managers specify the breakdowns they require from the accounting and information systems departments so that they get the needed information without information overload.

Profitability Analysis

PROFITABILITY ANALYSIS

A means of measuring the profitability of the firm's products, customer groups, sales territories, channels of distribution, and order sizes.

To their surprise, marketing managers often discover the 80/20 principle the hard way, on the job. **Profitability analysis** enables the manager to measure the profitability of the firm's products, customer groups, sales territories, channels of distribution, and even order sizes. This leads to decisions to expand, maintain, reduce, or eliminate specific products, customer groups, or channels.

For example, following the 80/20 principle, a marketing manager will try to find the common characteristics among the 20 percent of the customers (or products, brands, sales districts, salespeople, or kinds of orders) that generate 80 percent (or the bulk) of revenues and profits to find more like them to exploit competitive advantages. Conversely, the 80 percent of customers, products, brands, and so on that generate few revenues and profits may need to be reduced or even dropped entirely unless a way is found to make them more profitable.

The Marketing Audit

MARKETING AUDIT
A comprehensive, unbiased, periodic review of the strategic marketing process of a firm or a strategic business unit (SBU)

Often a broader marketing perspective is needed than is given by sales or profitability analyses, one that covers a longer time horizon and relates the marketing mix factors to environmental variables. This is the role of a **marketing audit**, which is a comprehensive, unbiased, periodic review of the strategic marketing process of a firm or SBU. The purpose of the marketing audit, which serves as both a planning and control technique, is to identify new problems and opportunities that warrant an action plan to improve performance.

Many firms undertaking a marketing audit use a checklist such as that shown in Figure 22–12 as a part of their situation analysis in their strategic marketing process. The checklist used covers factors ranging from the marketing mix factors and customer profiles to markets and competitors.

For a meaningful, comprehensive marketing audit, the individual or team conducting the audit must have a free rein to talk to managers, employees, salespeople, distributors, and customers, as well as have access to all pertinent internal and external reports and memoranda. They need to involve all levels of the organization in the process to ensure that resulting action recommendations have widespread support.

FIGURE 22–12
Marketing audit questions

PRODUCTS/SERVICES: THE REASON FOR EXISTENCE

1. Is the product/service free from deadwood?
2. What is the life-cycle stage?
3. How will user demands or trends affect you?
4. Are you a leader in new-product innovation?
5. Are inexpensive methods used to estimate new product potentials before considerable amounts are spent on R&D and market introduction?
6. Do you have different quality levels for different markets?
7. Are packages/brochures effective salespeople for the products/services they present?
8. Do you present products/services in the most appealing colours (formats) for markets being served?
9. Are there features or benefits to exploit?
10. Is the level of customer service adequate?
11. How are quality and reliability viewed by customers?

CUSTOMER: USER PROFILES

1. Who are the current and potential customers?
2. Are there geographic aspects of use: regional, rural, urban?
3. Why do people buy the product/service; what motivates their preferences?
4. Who makes buying decisions; when; where?
5. What is the frequency and quantity of use?

MARKETS: WHERE PRODUCTS/SERVICES ARE SOLD

1. Have you identified and measured major segments?
2. Are small potential market segments overlooked in trying to satisfy the majority?
3. Are the markets for the products/services expanding or declining?
4. Should different segments be developed; are there gaps in penetration?

COMPETITORS: THEIR INFLUENCE

1. Who are the principal competitors, how are they positioned, and where are they headed?
2. What are their market shares?
3. What features of competitors' products/services stand out?
4. Is the market easily entered or dominated?

PRICING: PROFITABILITY PLANNING

1. What are the objectives of current pricing policy: acquiring, defending, or expanding?
2. Are price policies set to produce volume or profit?
3. How does pricing compare with competition in similar levels of quality?
4. Does cost information show profitability of each item?
5. What is the history of price deals, discounts, and promotions?

Concept Check

1. What is the difference between a line and a staff position in a marketing organization?
2. What are four groupings used within a typical marketing organization?
3. What two components of the strategic marketing process are compared to control a marketing program?

SUMMARY

1 Marketing managers use the strategic marketing process to allocate their resources as effectively as possible. Sales response functions help them assess what the market's response to additional marketing effort will be.

2 The planning phase of the strategic marketing process usually results in a marketing plan that sets the direction for the marketing activities of an organization. Three kinds of marketing plans are long-range, annual, and new-product plans.

3 Three useful frameworks to improve marketing planning are (a) Porter's generic business strategies, (b) profit enhancement options, and (c) market–product synergies.

4 An effective marketing plan has measurable, achievable goals; uses facts and valid assumptions; is simple, clear, and specific; is complete and feasible; and is controllable and flexible.

5 The implementation phase of the strategic marketing process is concerned with executing the marketing program

developed in the planning phase and has achieved increased attention the past decade.

6 Essential to good scheduling is separating tasks that can be done concurrently from those that must be done sequentially. Gantt charts are a simple, effective means of scheduling.

7 Organizing marketing activities necessitates recognition of two different aspects of an organization: (a) line and staff positions and (b) product line, functional, geographical, and market-based groupings.

8 The product manager performs a vital marketing role in both consumer and industrial product firms, interacting with numerous people and groups both inside and outside the firm.

9 The control phase of the strategic marketing process involves measuring the results of the actions from the implementation phase and comparing them with goals set in the planning phase. Sales analyses, profitability analyses, and marketing audits are used to control marketing programs.

KEY TERMS AND CONCEPTS

action item list p. 596
cost leadership strategy p. 585
cost–focus strategy p. 586
differentiation focus strategy p. 586
differentiation strategy p. 586
functional groupings p. 596
generic business strategy p. 585
geographical groupings p. 597
line positions p. 596
market-based groupings p. 597

marketing audit p. 600
product line groupings p. 596
product or program champion p. 594
profitability analysis p. 599
sales analysis p. 599
sales component analysis p. 599
sales response function p. 580
share points p. 582
staff positions p. 596

INTERNET EXERCISE   www.mcgrawhill.ca/college/berkowitz

McKinsey & Company is a global management consulting firm with offices in more than 40 countries. As a leading firm in this competitive industry, McKinsey conducts "engagements" (consulting projects) for clients in a variety of industry sectors. Its distinctive competence is its "integrative thinking," which combines the knowledge gained from other industries and then applies the lessons learned to the specific problems faced by its clients.

The McKinsey Quarterly summarizes the knowledge obtained from serving its clients. Articles are organized by functional area and industry sector. To browse these

articles, go to www.mckinseyquarterly.com and click on their respective links.

1 Click on the "Marketing" link. Next, click on the "Organization" link located on the top menu bar. Scroll down until you find the article "A New Way to Market." Why do the authors say that the traditional organizational structure based on product, channels, customer groups and so on that focus on specific functional tasks, such as brand or segment management, hinders the strategic marketing process? What are the three principles that "new-style" marketing organizations must adhere to in order to seize market opportunities?

2 If you want to apply for a career at McKinsey, it, like the Boston Consulting Group, allows you to "try your hand" at solving a business problem. Go to www.mckinsey.com/careers/apply/solveacase/ and select one of the case options. To frame the problem, you need to learn how to ask the right questions; in other words, like a physician, you need to diagnose the problem before you can offer your client a recommended solution. As McKinsey says, "Finding the solution is not as important as how you arrived at it. We hope you'll enjoy the challenge."

Want to get better grades, find tips on how to study more effectively, and stay up to date with happenings in the world of marketing? Visit the Online Learning Centre for practice tests, Study Smart software, and much more! www.mcgrawhill.ca/college/berkowitz
Interested in finding out what marketing looks like in the real world? *Marketing Magazine* is just a click away on your OLC! Visit www.mcgrawhill.ca/college/berkowitz

APPLYING MARKETING CONCEPTS AND PERSPECTIVES

1 Assume a firm faces an S-shaped sales response function. What happens to the ratio of incremental sales revenue to incremental marketing effort at the (*a*) bottom, (*b*) middle, and (*c*) top of this curve?

2 What happens to the ratio of incremental sales revenue to incremental marketing effort when the sales response function is an upward-sloping straight line?

3 In 2002 General Mills invested millions of dollars in expanding its cereal and yogurt businesses. To allocate this money between these two businesses, what information would General Mills like to have?

4 Suppose your Great Lawns mower company has the market–product concentration situation shown in Figure 22–6A. What are both the synergies and potential pitfalls of following expansion strategies of (*a*) market specialization and (*b*) product specialization?

5 Are value-driven strategies inconsistent with value-based planning? Give an example that supports your position.

6 The first Domino's Pizza restaurant was near a university campus. What implementation problems are (*a*) similar and (*b*) different for restaurants near a university campus versus a military base?

7 A common theme among managers who succeed repeatedly in program implementation is fostering open communication. Why is this so important?

8 Why are quantified goals in the planning phase of the strategic marketing process important for the control phase?

VIDEO CASE 22–1   Clearly Canadian: How Marketing Strategies Lead to Growth

Clearly Canadian Beverage Corporation CEO Douglas L. Mason has a good understanding of the importance of linking marketing and corporate strategies. As he explains, the company's success requires that "our energy and resources must be concentrated in the areas where we can produce the greatest value." Mason describes the company's goal as "finding more ways to bring Clearly Canadian products to more people." To accomplish this goal Clearly Canadian's marketing efforts have focused on expanding current products, developing new innovative products, and meeting the needs of existing and new market segments.

THE COMPANY

Clearly Canadian Beverage Corporation started as small entrepreneurial venture in Vancouver in the late 1980s. Its first product, Clearly Canadian Sparkling Flavoured Water, was a huge success with consumers and led to extraordinary growth of the company. Today, Clearly Canadian is a leading producer of premium alternative beverages, the fastest growing category in the $10-billion beverage industry. The company markets and distributes its portfolio of beverages throughout Canada, the United States, and numerous countries around the world. Maintaining its position in the marketplace, however, has been a challenge!

When Clearly Canadian entered the beverage market it wanted to capitalize on the consumer trend toward innovative, good-tasting beverages. It carved out a niche using premium pricing and distinctive packaging to create a very sophisticated image. Premium pricing helped position Clearly Canadian as a high-quality product, and distinctive packaging allowed the product to stand out on crowded retail shelves. The company also achieved widespread distribution for its product in Canada and the United States, which was key to its early success. By 1992, Clearly Canadian was selling about 22 million cases of its beverage annually.

The following year, though, sales of Clearly Canadian dropped to 7 million cases. Experts observed that the beverage market had attracted many competitors. While many of the new brands were positioned to compete directly in the premium-priced niche with Clearly Canadian, others were using low-price strategies to attract customers. In addition, consumers' tastes were changing as new beverage types, such as ready-to-drink iced tea, became available. Clearly Canadian found itself losing market share in the market it had helped create!

THE STRATEGIC MARKETING PROCESS

Mason knew that if the company were to grow it needed a plan. A situation analysis revealed several strengths, weaknesses, opportunities, and threats. The company's strengths, for example, included a strong brand name that had pioneered the product category, distinct packaging, and a premium image. Its weaknesses were that it had been satisfied with its early success—reacting to market changes rather than being proactive—and it had limited resources compared to some of its competitors. Clearly Canadian's primary opportunity was that unlike the soft drink market, which was mature and dominated by a few brands, the alternative beverage market was growing and dynamic. Threats included competition from other sparkling waters, iced tea, natural sodas, and juice blends, and aggressive price discounting by many of its competitors.

The next step in Clearly Canadian's marketing plan was to consider growth opportunities in terms of its current products and markets and possible new products and markets. Six months of research, for example, led to a new package design for its flagship brand, and new flavours including Diet Cherry and Diet Blackberry. After the product's introduction in the United States and Canada, it was launched in international markets including the United Kingdom, Germany, the Netherlands, Denmark, and Kuwait. To better serve the variety of interests of its existing customers, Clearly Canadian introduced Tré Limone, a lemon-ginger drink inspired by European café sodas, and Cascade Clear, a non-carbonated pure drinking water. New products designed to attract new market segments were also introduced.

Orbitz, a fruit-flavoured beverage with gel spheres, was targeted at teenagers, and Clearly Canadian O+2 (a super-oxygenated water) and Reebok Fitness Water (a water beverage with vitamins, minerals, and electrolytes) were targeted at athletes.

Clearly Canadian designed its marketing programs to increase "consumer awareness and brand imagery" in each of the product–market combinations. National promotions, including joint sampling programs with Warner-Lambert Co. (Trident Gum) and Speedo and regional TV and radio campaigns were used to introduce products and to encourage consumers to try them. The marketing program for Reebok Fitness Water, for example, included sampling teams that drove vans to major sporting events, key grocery and retail outlets, and Reebok-sponsored events in major cities. The company also provided additional training for its salesforce and created stronger strategic partnerships with its distributors throughout the world.

While not all of the product and market initiatives were a success—Orbitz has been withdrawn from the market—the result of Clearly Canadian's overall plan was dramatic, reestablishing the company as a leading producer of premium alternative beverages. In fact, BevNet.com recently picked Clearly Canadian Sparkling Water as its Number 1 choice in the summer's Top Ten Hottest Beverages! John Craven, president of BevNET.com, observes that "with literally hundreds of new age products making their way to the shelves each year, it's difficult to pick a few . . .." Today's consumers are looking for beverages that provide a unique thirst-quenching experience and an image of health and style. Clearly Canadian believes it has a competitive advantage in its ability to identify and implement quick and effective changes to meet the changing demands of consumers.

THE FUTURE

Clearly Canadian has sold more than 2 billion bottles of its products since it started business. Now its efforts are focused on selling the next billion bottles. To achieve this goal, the company must continue to utilize the strategic marketing process to maintain its position in the

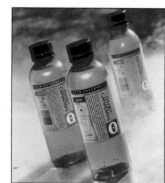

marketplace. New challenges include the expansion of the alternative beverage market to include sports beverages, ready-to-drink coffee, energy drinks, and vegetable/fruit blends. In addition, huge competitors such as Coke and Pepsi now offer water and sports drinks, and brands such as Snapple, AriZona, and SoBe have created new product attributes for consumers to consider. Finally, new potential uses of the company's limited resources—such as new products for restaurants and offices (e.g., larger sizes), new beverage types (e.g., coffee), and national advertising campaigns—continue to present themselves. So as long as the marketing environment continues to change, Doug Mason and Clearly Canadian will be asking Where are we now? Where do we want to go? and How do we get there?

Questions

1 Which phases and steps of the strategic marketing process does Clearly Canadian utilize to develop a plan that will lead to growth of the company?

2 Discuss the revenue-generation strategies (see Figure 22–5) that Clearly Canadian has pursued and continues to pursue today.

3 What recent changes in the marketing environment are likely to have an impact on Clearly Canadian? What new strategies would you recommend?

PART 5 CASE   **Coming of Age—From Pioneer to Profit**

In discussions of e-business or electronic retailing, Amazon.com is usually mentioned. Jeff Bezos, Amazon founder and chairman, has created a strong brand name for his Net-based company. June of 1999 was a milestone: Amazon.com made its 10-millionth online sale since opening its virtual door in 1995.[1] Unfortunately, high traffic and huge sales numbers did not translate into profits until the end of 2001.[2] Bezos launched his company with a vision of a cyberspace bookstore, but Amazon.com has become more than that. Bezos' company has grown from a one-product online store to an international multi-product virtual corporation. The objective to provide "Earth's Biggest Selection," as stated in its annual report, is audacious, but given the nature of the founder this goal may be achieveable.[3]

Amazon.com has supporters and it has critics. Those less supportive of the company believe the root of Amazon.com's struggle to make profits has to do with the fact that Amazon.com, like many other Internet companies, should not have gone public until profits were proven.[4] Jeff Bezos is not known for being conventional.

HIGH-SPEED GROWTH, SLOW-SPEED PROFITS

The birth and incredible growth of Amazon.com for the first five years of operation caused a ripple effect in more than one industry. Amazon.com's influence goes beyond electronic book retailing. In spite of the dot-com crash of 2000, there may be no stopping Jeff Bezos and his growth plans. There are many reasons why Amazon.com is considered a wonder in the e-commerce trade, but the most astounding fact is that even though the sales are staggeringly high with a growing customer base, the company struggled to make a profit. The pretax loss for

fiscal 1998 (the hottest dot-com year) was U.S.$124.5 million, with U.S.$605.0 million in net sales revenue.[5] Sales kept rising, as did the losses. Losses continued until the fourth quarter of 2001, showing a U.S.$5-million profit.[6] Operating profit for 2001 was U.S.$59 million. This is good news for Amazon.com, but doesn't necessarily create a happy ending for the Internet giant. There is still work to be done to prove that the virtual-company business model is sustainable in the long run. The net profit came from Amazon.com improving operating efficiencies, taking advantage of its fulfillment expertise, and selling its skills to other companies. A U.S.$16-million gain on foreign currency exchange resulting from a weakened euro also contributed to Amazon.com's profits.[7] This may never happen again. In addition, Amazon.com is carrying U.S.$2.2 billion in long-term debt accumulated since it first opened its virtual storefront.[8] This may make sustainable profit virtually unattainable.

The slow road to profitability has not stopped Amazon.com from charging ahead with plans to move beyond selling books and music to becoming the dominant global Website of online selling. Belief in the money-losing giant faltered by December 2000, from a high share price of U.S.$91.50 to a dramatic low of $6.01 a year later.[9] The stock price bounced back after the announcement of the 2001 profits, and in February 2002 it had moved up to U.S.$13.73. Not all is well, however, with Amazon.com's investors. A bondholders' class action suit against Amazon.com, although being played down, is a reality check for the company that it has not made investors happy.[10] Amazon.com executives are looking to settle out of court to keep the issue from blowing out of control.

Given all of this, Amazon.com is still pursuing an aggressive growth strategy. The strategy is a risky one, but Bezos is prepared to take the gamble. Amazon.com has adopted a much criticized "Wal-Mart–style" approach of increasing sales by continually adding product categories to its long list of offerings including electronics to tools to kitchen gear.[11] Amazon.com is moving into markets where established, branded companies will fight intensely to ward off the advances of this renegade.

AMAZON.COM—THE BEGINNING

Amazon.com was the brainchild of founder Jeff Bezos in 1994; after raising U.S.$1 million from family and friends for developing software and negotiating with suppliers, Bezos took the virtual bookstore online in 1995. Selling books began the saga of the company attributed as the pioneer in online selling. The story does not end on a bookshelf. Bezos expanded the product line to include music and other related entertainment products, such as videos. With each step expanding the product portfolio offered at Amazon.com, the company found itself competing in several mature industries, up against a number of established companies in the United States, in Canada, and around the world.

In book retailing, Amazon.com caught Barnes & Noble and Borders bookstore off guard. In Canada, the Internet company put pressure on Chapters Inc. and Indigo Books, Music & Café to create an online presence. After Amazon.com began selling books online, Barnes & Noble set up a new subsidiary to compete with Amazon.com head-to-head on the Net. The subsidiary, barnesandnoble.com, lost U.S.\$42 million for the parent company by the end of fiscal 1998, demonstrating that online business is an expensive undertaking, even for those experienced companies savvy in marketing and branding. Barnes & Noble is in a strong position to compete with Amazon.com due to the broad base of its business. In addition to its storefront and online bookstores, Barnes & Noble owns a direct-mail book selling business and a book publisher.[12] All of this has provided Barnes & Noble with the resources to defend its market from Amazon.com.

Another competitor in book retailing is Borders, which hasn't done well against Amazon.com. Borders, the second largest book chain in the United States, was slow to respond to the Amazon.com threat. Borders also has a presence in the United Kingdom, Australia, and Singapore. The chain has more than 1100 bookstores, including 250 book and music superstores and 900 Waldenbooks stores (found mostly in malls). The philosophy of Borders is similar to that of the two top Canadian book retailers. Borders, with its store layouts, encourages a laid-back approach to shopping for books—complete with snack bars and comfortable seating.[13] After losing money year after year with its own Website, in April 2001 Amazon.com took over the Web operations of Borders Group Inc.[14] Financial details were not released, but the deal included Borders paying Amazon.com a one-time fee for creating a new Borders.com Website. Amazon.com will take care of inventory, customer service, and shipping responsibilities. Amazon.com realizes all revenue from sales and pays Borders a commission on the sales. In time, it is believed that Borders.com and Borders Group will work together to provide the option of ordering online and picking up the book in store.

When Amazon.com added music to its product offering, CDNow took notice. Another online marketer, CDNow was started by twins Jason and Matthew Olim. Most of the items are CDs, but they also sell music videos, T-shirts, and movies. The interesting aspect of this Website is that there is a selection of obscure CDs catering to the eclectic audiophile. The value of the site is enhanced with music reviews and an option for a customer to create custom CDs through its superSonic BOOM unit.[15] CDNow was well on its way as the pioneer provider of music online when Amazon.com added CDs to its cyberspace shelves in June 1998.[16] CDNow has successfully survived Amazon.com even though market share declined when the online book seller also started selling music. In July 1999, Sony Corporation and Time Warner Inc. announced that their jointly owned Columbia House music and video would merge with CDNow.[17] This helped the struggling pioneer in digital music and also provided Columbia House with access to CDNow's database of over 16 million customers. CDNow is associated with two of the world's largest record companies, Warner Music and Sony Music, who together control 35 percent of recording sales in the United States. CDNow provides music downloads for a fee; free downloads are used on a time-limited basis to promote CDs. Selling CDs online is a marketspace segment ripe with lost potential. Napster created a challenge, but since its future is ambiguous, CDNow has a chance of surviving.

Amazon.com faces some powerful and determined competitors and yet maintains an optimistic perspective in attempting new ventures. Not every business venture Amazon.com tries works out. In 1999, Amazon.com struck a 10-year contract with Sotheby's auction house. The prestigious auction house formed the joint venture to develop and launch an online auction site for January 2000. Amazon.com invested U.S.\$45 million in the 255-year-old auction house. Plans were for Sotheby's to keep its own high-end Website; the jointly owned Website would focus on "lower end merchandise including coins, stamps, sports and Hollywood memorabilia."[18] By October 2000, however, Amazon.com and Sotheby's parted ways—leaving the auction house with the Website to manage and Amazon.com without much-needed cash. In January 2002, Sotheby's finally gave up and entered into a deal with eBay, giving the veteran e-auction site control of fine art auctions.[19]

THE AMAZON.COM MACHINE KEEPS MOVING

From its beginnings in online book retailing, Amazon.com has grown significantly since 1995. Not only is Amazon.com known as the number-one Internet company selling music, video, and books, but it also quickly moved into free electronic greeting cards and computer game titles. Gift wrapping is part of their service, as is the patented one-click shopping for regular customers, making the buying experience online as convenient and secure as possible. In addition to contacting previous buyers with personalized purchasing recommendations, in April 1999 Bid-Click was added to the Website to make it as interactive as possible.[20] Amazon.com continually looks for ways to improve the customer connection.

The year 2001 was good for Amazon.com, with revenue now coming from strategic alliances by leveraging the expertise it has developed in online technology, customer service, and fulfillment management. Amazon.com now manages the e-business of companies such as Toysrus.com, Borders, Circuit City, and Target.[21] Together with a number of strategic partners, Amazon.com now lists millions of items in a large range of categories including the core business of books, music, and DVDs as well as videos, electronics, computers, camera and photo items; computer software and video games; cell phones and service; tools and hardware; outdoor living items; kitchen and housewares; toys, baby items, and baby registry; travel services; and magazine subscriptions.[22] This is all done with three sales channels: online retail, marketplace (auctions and zShops), and third-party selling. Amazon.com is known for attempting unorthodox means to earn money. With the economy showing signs of slowing down and pressure to show a profit, Jeff Bezos and his team continue to forge into new territory in 2001.

Building a strong customer base has not been easy, but this is really what Amazon.com has done better than other Internet upstarts. Amazon.com's strength is knowing how to keep customers coming back. Adding unique services before anyone else does encourage customers to return. Amazon.com is working with a number of major publishers such as AOL Time Warner and Viacom Inc.'s Simon & Schuster to allow book shoppers to view pages of books on the Website before making a purchase.[23] The key to their approach is a customer who will return. Sixty-four per cent of all orders are from those online buyers who have already established a relationship with Amazon.com. Executives in the company believe that, "In cyberspace, branding is important, but it's not as important as building the right service. If you build something customers love, it creates the brand. Word-of-mouth experiences become your best advocate."[24]

Amazon.com now operates four international Websites. These are www.amazon.co.uk in the United Kingdom, www.amazon.de in Germany, www.amazon.fr in France, and www.amazon.co.jp in Japan. Amazon.com wants to own the Canadian market as well. In Summer 2002 Amazon.com is expected to make the move to launch a dedicated Canadian site.[25] Amazon.com prepared for this move by lowering prices, discounting shipping costs, and improving delivery times to Canadian customers.[26] However, for Amazon.com to move into Canada with a dedicated site, as they have in other countries, they have to adhere to strict federal legislation that protects the book industry.[27] Amazon.com currently relies on word of mouth in Canada, as it is not allowed to advertise here. Should the company decide to advertise, it is required to sell Canadian editions of Canadian books plus collect GST. They will not be able to sell U.S. editions of Canadian books, as they currently do. The Canadian investment law prevents Amazon.com from setting up a distribution centre without a majority Canadian partner.[28] These restrictions may only delay the inevitable, as Amazon.com has now made arrangements to use Canada Post's warehouse in Mississauga and also developed a relationship with BookExpress, a book wholesaler owned by Vancouver's Raincoast Book Distribution.[29] This is not good news for the Indigo/Chapters Web business because, according to Jupiter Media Metrix, Amazon.com is the number-one Website visited in Canada (as of October 31, 2001), with 9.4 million visits.[30] Drama and bookselling—it's unavoidable!

AND THE FUTURE IS...?

Amazon.com's strengths come from building relationships with customers, publishers, distributors, software companies, and now former competitors in the Internet realm. Forecasting for established companies in stable, mature industries is difficult. With Amazon.com and electronic retailing, it becomes even more challenging. Contrary to popular business practice, the company continues to expand. Before the end of 2001, Amazon.com announced it had purchased some assets from Egghead.com; by February 2002 Amazon had relaunched the site.[31] The company is not resting.

Sustainable profitability is still in the distance. In addition, Amazon.com continues to face risks in its operations due to the foreign investments, reliability on technology, and new relationships to test. Those watching Amazon.com are like spectators watching Wayne Gretzky on the ice: It's better to watch where the puck is going rather than where it is.

Discussion Questions

1 How would you define Amazon.com's business strategy and marketing strategy? How does the company leverage its strengths? Explain.

2 In your opinion, what does it mean for Amazon.com that they want to be "the Wal-Mart" of the Internet space? Discuss implications and risks associated with Amazon.com's international marketing strategy.

3 When looking at Amazon.com's product lines and new strategic alliances, can you identify any synergies? Do you think the new ventures support the company's overall objectives?

4 Discuss your views on Amazon.com's potential future success if it continues with the strategic approach it is now using.

GLOSSARY

above-, at-, or below-market pricing   Pricing based on market price. p. 374

account management policies   Policies that specify whom salespeople should contact, what kinds of selling and customer service activities should be engaged in, and how these activities should be carried out. p. 537

action item list   An aid to implementing a market plan, consisting of three columns: (1) the task, (2) the name of the person responsible for completing that task, and (3) the date by which the task is to be finished. p. 596

adaptive selling   A need-satisfaction sales presentation that involves adjusting the presentation to fit the selling situation. p. 531

advertising   Any paid form of nonpersonal communication about an organization, good, service, or idea by an identified sponsor. p. 471; p. 494

all-you-can-afford budgeting   Allocating funds to promotion only after all other budget items are covered. p. 481

attitude   A learned predisposition to respond to an object or class of objects in a consistently favourable or unfavourable way. p. 131

average revenue   The average amount of money received for selling one unit of a product. p. 353

baby boomers   The generation of children born between 1946 and 1964. p. 77

baby boomlet   Canadians born after 1977; also described as Generation Y or the Net Generation. p. 78

back translation   Retranslating a word or phrase into the original language by a different interpreter to catch errors. p. 182

balance of trade   The difference between the monetary value of a nation's exports and imports. p. 171

barriers to entry   Business practices or conditions that make it difficult for new firms to enter the market. p. 87

barter   The practice of exchanging goods and services for other goods and services rather than for money. p. 344

beliefs   A consumer's subjective perception of how well a product or brand performs on different attributes; these are based on personal experience, advertising, and discussions with other people. p. 131

benchmarking   Discovering how others do something better than your own firm so you can imitate or leapfrog competition. p. 35

bidders list   A list of firms believed to be qualified to supply a given item. p. 159

blended family   Formed by the merging into a single household of two previously separated units. p. 78

bots   Electronic shopping agents or robots that comb Websites to compare prices and product or service features. p. 565

brand equity   The added value a given brand name gives to a product beyond the functional benefits provided. p. 307

brand loyalty   A favourable attitude toward and consistent purchase of a single brand over time. p. 130

brand name   Any word, device (design, shape, sound, or colour), or combination of these used to distinguish a seller's goods or services. p. 306

brand personality   A set of human characteristics associated with a brand name. p. 307

branding   Activity in which an organization uses a name, phrase, design, or symbols, or combination of these, to identify its products and distinguish them from those of competitors. p. 306

breadth of product line   The variety of different items a store carries. p. 449

break-even analysis   A technique that analyzes the relationship between total revenue and total cost to determine profitability at various levels of output. p. 357

break-even chart   A graphic presentation of the break-even analysis. p. 358

break-even point (BEP)   Quantity at which total revenue and total cost are equal and beyond which profit occurs. p. 357

brokers   Independent firms or individuals whose principal function is to bring buyers and sellers together to make sales. p. 406

buildup forecast   Summing the sales forecasts of each of the components to arrive at the total forecast. p. 229

bundle pricing   The marketing of two or more products in a single "package" price. p. 369

business analysis   Involves specifying the features of the product and the marketing strategy needed to commercialize it and making necessary financial projections. p. 285

business goods   Products that assist directly or indirectly in providing products for resale (also known as *B2B goods*, *industrial goods*, or *organizational goods*). p. 271

business marketing   The marketing of goods and services to commercial enterprises, governments, and other profit and not-for-profit organizations for use in the creation of goods and services that they then produce and market to other business customers as well as individuals and ultimate consumers. p. 148

business unit   An organization that markets a set of related products to a clearly defined group of customers. p. 31

business unit level   Level at which business unit managers set the direction for their products and markets. p. 31

buy classes   Three types of organizational buying situations: new buy, straight rebuy, and modified rebuy. p. 156

buying centre   The group of people in an organization who participate in the buying process and share common goals, risks, and knowledge important to a purchase decision. p. 155

capacity management   Making service capacity as productive as possible without compromising service quality. p. 336

cause-related marketing   Occurs when the charitable contributions of a firm are tied directly to the customer revenues produced through the promotion of one of its products. p. 107

caveat emptor   The legal concept of "let the buyer beware" that was pervasive in Canadian business culture before the 1960s. p. 102

census metropolitan area (CMA)   Geographic labour market areas having a population of 100 000 persons or more. p. 78

central business district   The oldest retail setting, the community's downtown area. p. 458

channel captain   A marketing channel member that coordinates, directs, and supports other channel members; may be a producer, wholesaler, or retailer. p. 414

channel conflict Arises when one channel member believes another channel member is engaged in behaviour that prevents it from achieving its goals. p. 413

channel of communication The means of conveying a message to a receiver. p. 468

channel partnership Agreements and procedures among channel members for ordering and physically distributing a producer's product through the channel to the ultimate consumer. p. 409

choiceboard An interactive, Internet/Web-enabled system that allows individual customers to design their own products and services. p. 558

co-branding The pairing of two brand names of two manufacturers on a single product. p. 312

code of ethics A formal statement of ethical principles and rules of conduct. p. 103

cognitive dissonance The feeling of postpurchase psychological tension or anxiety a consumer often experiences. p. 123

collaborative filtering A process that automatically groups people with similar buying intentions, preferences, and behaviours and predicts future purchases. p. 558

commercial online services Companies that provide electronic information and marketing services to subscribers who are charged a monthly fee. p. 86

commercialization Positioning and launching a new product in full-scale production and sales. p. 288

communication The process of conveying a message to others, which requires six elements: a source, a message, a channel of communication, a receiver, and the processes of encoding and decoding. p. 468

community shopping centre A retail location that typically has one primary store (usually a department store branch) and 20 to 40 smaller outlets, serving a population of consumers who are within a 10- to 20-minute drive. p. 458

competencies An organization's special capabilities, including skills, technologies, and resources that distinguish it from other organizations. p. 35

competition The alternative firms that could provide a product to satisfy a specific market's needs. p. 86

Competition Act The key legislation designed to protect competition and consumers in Canada. p. 90

competitive advantage A unique strength relative to competitors, often based on quality, time, cost, innovation, or customer intimacy. p. 35

competitive parity budgeting Matching the competitors' absolute level of spending or the proportion per point of market share. p. 481

consultative selling Focuses on problem definition, where the salesperson serves as an expert on problem recognition and resolution. p. 531

consumer behaviour The actions a person takes in purchasing and using products and services, including the mental and social processes that precede and follow these actions. p. 120

consumer ethnocentrism The tendency to believe that it is inappropriate, indeed immoral, to purchase foreign-made products. p. 183

consumer goods Products purchased by the ultimate consumer. p. 271

consumer socialization The process by which people acquire the skills, knowledge, and attitudes necessary to function as consumers. p. 137

consumerism A grassroots movement started in the 1960s to increase the influence, power, and rights of consumers in dealing with institutions. p. 91

consumer-oriented sales promotions Sales tools used to support a company's advertising and personal selling efforts directed to ultimate consumers; examples include coupons, sweepstakes, and samples. p. 509

convenience goods Items that the consumer purchases frequently and with a minumum of shopping effort. p. 273

cookies Computer files that a marketer can download onto the computer of an online shopper who visits the marketer's Website. p. 568

cooperative advertising Advertising programs by which a manufacturer pays a percentage of the retailer's local advertising expense for advertising the manufacturer's products. p. 514

corporate level Level at which top management directs overall strategy for the entire organization. p. 31

cost leadership strategy Using a serious commitment to reducing expenses that, in turn, lowers the price of the items sold in a relatively broad array of market segments. p. 585

cost per thousand (CPM) The cost of reaching 1000 individuals or households with an advertising message in a given medium. (M is the Roman numeral for 1000.) p. 501

cost-focus strategy Involves controlling expenses and, in turn, lowering prices, in a narrow range of market segments. p. 586

cost-plus pricing The practice of summing the total unit cost of providing a product or service and adding a specific amount to the cost to arrive at a price. p. 370

countertrade The practice of using barter rather than money for making international sales. p. 171

cross-cultural analysis The study of similarities and differences among consumers in two or more nations or societies. p. 180

crossdocking The practice of unloading products from suppliers, sorting products for individual stores, and quickly reloading products onto trucks for a particular store. p. 426

cross-functional teams A small number of people from different departments in an organization who are mutually accountable to a common set of performance goals. p. 32

cross tabulation Method of presenting and relating data having two or more variables to analyze and discover relationships in the data. p. 255

cultural symbols Things that represent ideas and concepts. p. 181

culture The set of values, ideas, and attitudes of a homogeneous group of people that are transmitted from one generation to the next. p. 33; p. 79

currency exchange rate The price of one country's currency expressed in terms of another country's currency. p. 186

customary pricing A method of pricing based on tradition, a standardized channel of distribution, or other competitive factors. p. 373

customer contact audit A flowchart of the points of interaction between consumer and service provider. p. 330

customer experience The sum total of interactions that a customer has with a company's Website. p. 560

customer relationship management (CRM) The process of identifying prospective buyers, understanding them intimately, and developing favourable long-term perceptions of the organization and its offerings so that buyers will choose them in the marketplace. p. 21

customer service   The ability of logistics management to satisfy users in terms of time, dependability, communication, and convenience. p. 429

customer value   The unique combination of benefits received by targeted buyers that includes quality, price, convenience, on-time delivery, and both before-sale and after-sale service. p. 16

customerization   The growing practice of customizing not only a product or service but also personalizing the marketing and overall shopping and buying interaction for each customer. p. 566

customs   Norms and expectations about the way people do things in a specific country. p.181

data mining   The extraction of hidden predictive information from large databases. p. 227

decoding   The process of having the receiver take a set of symbols, the message, and transform them back to an abstract idea. p. 468

demand curve   The summation of points representing the maximum number of products consumers will buy at a given price. p. 352

demand factors   Factors that determine consumers' willingness and ability to pay for goods and services. p. 352

demographics   Describing the population according to selected characteristics such as their age, gender, ethnicity, income, and occupation. p. 75

depth interview   A detailed, individual interview with a person relevant to the research project. p. 214

depth of product line   The store carries a large assortment of each item. p. 449

derived demand   Demand for industrial products and services driven by, or derived from, demand for consumer products and services. p. 151

development   Turning the idea on paper into a prototype. p. 285

differentiation focus strategy   Using significant points of difference in the firm's offerings to reach one or only a few market segments. p. 586

differentiation strategy   Requires innovation and significant points of difference in product offerings, brand image, higher quality, advanced technology, or superior service in a relatively broad array of market segments. p. 586

direct channel   A marketing channel where a producer and ultimate consumer deal directly with each other. p. 401

direct forecast   Estimating the value to be forecast without any intervening steps. p. 230

direct investment   A domestic firm actually investing in and owning a foreign subsidiary or division. p. 190

direct marketing   Promotional element that uses direct communication with consumers to generate a response in the form of an order, a request for further information, or a visit to a retail outlet. p. 473

direct marketing channels   Allow consumers to buy products by interacting with various advertising media without a face-to-face meeting with a salesperson. p. 403

direct orders   The result of direct marketing offers that contain all the information necessary for a prospective buyer to make a decision to purchase and complete the transaction. p. 485

discretionary income   The money that remains after paying for taxes and necessities. p. 83

disintermediation   Channel conflict that arises when a channel member bypasses another member and sells or buys products direct. p. 413

disposable income   The money a consumer has left after paying taxes to use for necessities such as food, shelter, and clothing. p. 82

downsizing   Reducing the content of packages without changing package size and maintaining or increasing the package price. p. 318

dual distribution   An arrangement by which a firm reaches buyers by employing two or more different types of channels for the same basic product. p. 404

dumping   When a firm sells a product in a foreign country below its domestic price or below its actual cost. p. 193

dynamic pricing   The practice of changing prices for products and services in real time in response to supply and demand conditions. p. 567

economic espionage   The clandestine collection of trade secrets or proprietary information about a company's competitors. p. 102

economy   The income, expenditures, and resources that affect the cost of running an organization or a household. p. 81

eCRM   A Web-centric, personalized approach to managing customer relationships electronically. p. 558

eight-second rule   Customers will abandon their efforts to enter and navigate a Website if download time exceeds eight seconds. p. 566

80/20 rule   A concept that suggests 80 percent of a firm's sales are obtained from 20 percent of its customers. p. 247

electronic commerce   Any activity that uses some form of electronic communication in the inventory, exchange, advertisement, distribution, and payment of goods and services. p. 85

electronic data interchange (EDI)   Combines proprietary computer and telecommunication technologies to exchange electronic invoices, payments, and information among suppliers, manufacturers, and retailers. p. 427

electronic marketing channels   Employ the Internet to make goods and services available for consumption or use by consumers or business buyers. p. 402

e-marketplaces   Online trading communities that bring together buyers and supplier organizations. p. 161

emotional intelligence   The ability to understand one's own emotions and the emotions of people with whom one interacts on a daily basis. p. 539

encoding   The process of having the sender transform an abstract idea into a set of symbols. p. 468

environmental factors   The uncontrollable factors involving social, economic, technological, competitive, and regulatory forces. p. 25

environmental scanning   The process of continually acquiring information on events occurring outside the organization to identify and interpret potential trends. p. 74

ethics   The moral principles and values that govern the actions and decisions of an individual or group. p. 98

ethnographic research   Observational approach to discover subtle emotional reactions as consumers encounter products in their "natural use environment." p. 222

euro-branding   The strategy of using the same brand name for the same product across all countries in the European Union. p. 318

evaluative criteria   Factors that represent both the objective attributes of a brand and the subjective ones a consumer uses to compare different products and brands. p. 121

everyday low pricing   (1) The practice of replacing promotional allowances with lower manufacturer list prices. (2) Retailing strategy that emphasizes consistently low prices and eliminates most markdowns. p. 381

evoked set The group of brands that a consumer would consider acceptable from among all the brands in the product class of which he or she is aware. p. 122

exchange The trade of things of value between buyer and seller so that each is better off after the trade. p. 10

exclusive distribution Only one retail outlet in a specific geographical area carries the firm's products. p. 410

experience curve pricing A method of pricing based on the learning effect, which holds that the unit cost of many products and services declines by 10 percent to 30 percent each time a firm's experience at producing and selling them doubles. p. 370

experiment Obtaining data by manipulating factors under tightly controlled conditions to test cause and effect. p. 219

exporting Producing goods in one country and selling them in another country. p. 188

extranet A network that uses Internet-based technologies to permit communication between an organization and its suppliers, distributors, and other partners. p. 86; p. 428

failure fee A penalty payment made by a manufacturer to compensate the retailer for sales its valuable shelf space never made. p. 288

family life cycle The distinct phases that a family progresses through from formation to retirement, each phase bringing with it identifiable purchasing behaviours. p. 137

feedback The communication flow from receiver back to the sender that helps the sender know whether the message was decoded and understood as intended. p. 470

field of experience Similar understanding and knowledge; to communicate effectively, a sender and a receiver must have a mutually shared field of experience. p. 470

fixed cost The sum of expenses of the firm that are stable and do not change with the quantity of product that is produced and sold. p. 356

flexible-price policy Setting different prices for products and services depending on individual buyers and purchase situations. Also called *dynamic pricing*. p. 375

FOB origin pricing A method of pricing where the title of goods passes to the buyer at the point of loading. p. 381

focus group An informal session of 6 to 10 past, present, or prospective customers in which a discussion leader, or moderator, asks their opinions about the firm's and its competitors' products. p. 213

form of ownership Distinguishes retail outlets based on whether individuals, corporate chains, or contractual systems own the outlet. p. 447

formula selling presentation Providing information in an accurate, thorough, and step-by-step manner to inform the prospect. p. 530

four I's of service Four unique elements to services: intangibility, inconsistency, inseparability, and inventory. p. 325

franchising Contractual arrangement between a parent company (a franchisor) and an individual or firm (a franchisee) that allows the franchise to operate a certain type of business under an established name and according to specific rules. p. 408

freight forwarders Firms that accumulate small shipments into larger lots and then hire a carrier to move them, usually at reduced rates. p. 433

frequency The average number of times a person in the target audience is exposed to a message or advertisement. p. 501

full-service agency An advertising agency providing the most complete range of services, including market research, media selection, copy development, artwork, and production. p. 507

functional groupings Organizational groupings such as manufacturing, marketing, and finance, which are the different business activities within a firm. p. 596

functional level Level at which groups of specialists actually create value for the organization. p. 31

gap analysis An evaluation tool that compares expectations about a service offering to the actual experience a consumer has with the service. p. 331

Generation X The group of Canadians born between 1965 and 1976. p. 78

generic brand A no-name product with no identification other than a description of contents. p. 313

generic business strategy Strategy that can be adopted by any firm, regardless of the product or industry involved, to achieve a competitive advantage. p. 585

geographical groupings Organizational groupings in which a unit is subdivided according to geographical location. p. 597

global competition Exists when firms originate, produce, and market their products and services worldwide. p. 177

global consumers Customer groups living in many countries or regions of the world who have similar needs or seek similar features and benefits from products or services. p. 178

global marketing strategy The practice of standardizing marketing activities when there are cultural similarities and adapting them when cultures differ. p. 178

goals or **objectives** Convert the mission into targeted levels of performance to be achieved. p. 33

government units The federal, provincial, and local agencies that buy goods and services for the constituents they serve. p. 149

green marketing Marketing efforts to produce, promote, and reclaim environmentally sensitive products. p. 107

grey market A situation where products are sold through unauthorized channels of distribution; also called *parallel importing*. p. 193

gross domestic product The monetary value of all goods and services produced in a country during one year. p. 171

gross income The total amount of money made in one year by a person, household, or family unit. p. 82

gross rating points (GRPs) A reference number for advertisers, created by multiplying reach (expressed as a percentage of the total market) by frequency. p. 501

hierarchy of effects The sequence of stages a prospective buyer goes through from initial awareness of a product to eventual action (either trial or adoption of the product). The stages include awareness, interest, evaluation, trial, and adoption. p. 480

hypermarket A large store (more than 200 000 square feet) offering a mix of 40 percent food products and 60 percent general merchandise. p. 449

idea generation Developing a pool of concepts as candidates for new products. p. 282

idle production capacity When the service provider is available but there is no demand. p. 327

indirect channel A marketing channel where intermediaries are inserted between the producer and consumers and perform numerous channel functions. p. 401

industrial distributor   Performs a variety of marketing channel functions, including selling, stocking, delivering a full product assortment, and financing. p. 402

industrial firm   An organizational buyer that in some way reprocesses a good or service it buys before selling it again to the next buyer. p. 148

infomercials   Program-length (30-minute) advertisements that take an educational approach to communication with potential customers. p. 502

information technology   Designing and managing computer and communication networks to provide a system to satisfy an organization's needs for data storage, processing, and access. p. 226

in-house agency   A company's own advertising staff, which may provide full services or a limited range of services. p. 508

institutional advertisements   Advertisements designed to build goodwill or an image for an organization, rather than promote a specific good or service. p. 495

integrated marketing communications   The concept of designing marketing communications programs that coordinate all promotional activities—advertising, personal selling, sales promotion, public relations, and direct marketing—to provide a consistent message across all audiences and to maximize the promotional budget. p. 479

intensive distribution   A firm tries to place its products or services in as many outlets as possible. p. 410

interactive marketing   Two-way buyer–seller electronic communications in a computer-mediated environment in which the buyer controls the kind and amount of information received from the seller. p. 558

intermodal transportation   Combining different transportation modes to get the best features of each. p. 432

internal marketing   The notion that a service organization must focus on its employees, or internal market, before successful programs can be directed at customers. p. 335

Internet   An integrated global network of computers that gives users access to information and documents. p. 85

intertype competition   Competition between very dissimilar types of retail outlets. p. 450

intranet   An Internet/Web-based network used within the boundaries of an organization. p. 86

involvement   The personal, social, and economic significance of the purchase to the consumer. p. 124

ISO 14000   Worldwide standards for environmental quality and green marketing practices. p. 107

ISO 9000 standards   Registration and certification of a manufacturer's quality management and quality assurance system. p. 164

joint venture   An arrangement in which a foreign company and a local firm invest together to create a local business, sharing ownership, control, and profits of the new company. p. 190

jury of executive opinion forecast   Asking knowledgeable executives inside the firm about likely sales during a coming period. p. 231

just-in-time (JIT) concept   An inventory supply system that operates with very low inventories and requires fast, on-time delivery. p. 437

label   An integral part of the package that typically identifies the product or brand, who made it, where and when it was made, how it is to be used, and package contents and ingredients. p. 313

laws   Society's values and standards that are enforceable in the courts. p. 98

lead generation   The result of a direct marketing offer designed to generate interest in a product or a service, and a request for additional information. p. 485

lead time   Lag from ordering an item until it is received and ready for use or sale. Also called *order cycle time* or *replenishment time*. p. 429

learning   Those behaviours that result from (1) repeated experience and (2) thinking. p. 130

level of service   The degree of service provided to the customer by self-, limited-, and full-service retailers. p. 447

licensing   A contractual agreement whereby a company allows another firm to use its brand name, patent, trade secret, or other property for a royalty or fee. p. 309

lifestyle   A mode of living that is identified by how people spend their time and resources (activities), what they consider important in their environment (interests), and what they think of themselves and the world around them (opinions). p. 132

limited-service agency   Specializes in one aspect of the advertising process such as providing creative services to develop the advertising copy or buying previously unpurchased media space. p. 508

line positions   People in line positions, such as senior marketing managers, have the authority and responsibility to issue orders to the people who report to them, such as product managers. p. 596

logistics   Those activities that focus on getting the right amount of the right products to the right place at the right time at the lowest possible cost. p. 422

logistics management   The practice of organizing the cost-effective flow of raw materials, in-process inventory, finished goods, and related information from point of origin to point of consumption to satisfy customer requirements. p. 422

loss-leader pricing   Deliberately selling a product below its customary price to attract attention to it. p. 374

lost-horse forecast   Starting with the last known value of the item being forecast, listing the factors that could affect the forecast, assessing whether they have a positive or negative impact, and making the final forecast. p. 230

macromarketing   The study of the aggregate flow of a nation's goods and services to benefit society. p. 25

major account management   The practice of using team selling to focus on important customers so as to build mutually beneficial, long-term, cooperative relationships. Also called *key account management*. p. 535

make-buy decision   An evaluation of whether components and assemblies will be purchased from outside suppliers or built by the company itself. p. 159

manufacturer branding   The producer dictates the brand name using either a multiproduct or multibranding approach. p. 311

manufacturer's agents   Work for several producers and carry noncompetitive, complementary merchandise in an exclusive territory; also called *manufacturer's representatives*. p. 406

marginal analysis   A continuing, concise trade-off of incremental costs against incremental revenues. p. 357

marginal cost   The change in total cost that results from producing and marketing one additional unit. p. 356

marginal revenue   The change in total revenue obtained by selling one additional unit. p. 353

market modification   Strategy in which a company tries to find new customers, increase a product's use among existing customers, or create new-use situations. p. 304

market orientation   Focusing organizational efforts on (1) continuously collecting information about customers' needs and competitors' capabilities, (2) sharing this information across departments, and (3) using the information to create customer value. p. 25

market potential   Maximum total sales of a product by all firms to a segment during a specified time period under specified environmental conditions and marketing efforts of the firms (also called *industry potential*). p. 228

market segmentation   Aggregating prospective buyers into groups, or segments, that (1) have common needs and (2) will respond similarly to a marketing action. p. 43; p. 238

market segments   The groups that result from the process of market segmentation; these groups ideally (1) have common needs and (2) will respond similarly to a marketing action. p. 239

market share   The ratio of sales revenue of the firm to the total sales revenue of all firms in the industry, including the firm itself. p. 33

market testing   Exposing actual products to prospective consumers under realistic purchase conditions to see if they will buy. p. 287

market   People with the desire and with the ability to buy a specific product. p. 14

market-based groupings   Organizational groupings that utilize specific customer segments. p. 597

marketing   The process of planning and executing the conception, pricing, promotion, and distribution of ideas, goods, and services to create exchanges that satisfy individual and organizational objectives. p. 9

marketing audit   A comprehensive, unbiased, periodic review of the strategic marketing process of a firm or a strategic business unit (SBU). p. 600

marketing channel   Individuals and firms involved in the process of making a product or service available for use or consumption by consumers or industrial users. p. 398

marketing concept   The idea that an organization should (1) strive to satisfy the needs of consumers (2) while also trying to achieve the organization's goals. p. 21

marketing mix   The marketing manager's controllable factors; the marketing actions of product, price, promotion, and place that he or she can take to solve a marketing problem. p. 15

marketing plan   A road map for the marketing activities of an organization for a specified future period of time, such as one year or five years. p. 41

marketing program   A plan that integrates the marketing mix to provide a good, service, or idea to prospective buyers. p. 25

marketing research   The process of defining a marketing problem and opportunity, systematically collecting and analyzing information, and recommending actions to improve an organization's marketing activities. p. 207

marketing strategy   The means by which a marketing goal is to be achieved, usually characterized by a specified target market and a marketing program to reach it. p. 47

marketing tactics   The detailed day-to-day operational decisions essential to the overall success of marketing strategies. p. 47

market-product grid   Framework to relate the segment of a market to products offered or potential marketing actions by the firm. p. 241

marketspace   An information- and communication-based electronic exchange environment mostly occupied by sophisticated computer and telecommunication technologies and digitized offerings. p. 85

materials handling   Moving goods over short distances into, within, and out of warehouses and manufacturing plants. p. 434

mature households   Households headed by people over 50 years old. p. 76

merchandise line   How many different types of products a store carries and in what assortment. p. 447

merchant wholesalers   Independently owned firms that take title to the merchandise they handle. p. 405

message   The information sent by a source to a receiver in the communication process. p. 468

micromarketing   How an individual organization directs its marketing activities and allocates its resources to benefit its customers. p. 22

mission   A statement of the organization's scope. p. 32

missionary salespeople   Sales support personnel who do not directly solicit orders but rather concentrate on performing promotional activities and introducing new products. p. 526

mixed branding   A firm markets products under its own name and that of a reseller because the segment attracted by the reseller is different from its own market. p. 313

moral idealism   A personal moral philosophy that considers certain individual rights or duties as universal, regardless of the outcome. p. 104

motivation   The energizing force that causes behaviour that satisfies a need. p. 126

multibranding   A manufacturer's branding strategy giving each product a distinct name. p. 312

multichannel marketing   The blending of different communication and delivery channels that are mutually reinforcing in attracting, retaining, and building relationships with consumers. p. 570

multichannel retailers   Utilize and integrate a combination of traditional store formats and nonstore formats such as catalogues, television, and online retailing. p. 461

multidomestic marketing strategy   A multinational firm's offering as many different product variations, brand names, and advertising programs as countries in which it does business. p. 178

multiproduct branding   A company uses one name for all products; also called *blanket* or *family branding*. p. 311

national character   A distinct set of personality characteristics common among people of a country or society. p. 127

need-satisfaction presentation   A selling format that emphasizes probing and listening by the salesperson to identify needs and interests of prospective buyers. p. 531

new-product process   The sequence of activities a firm uses to identify business opportunities and convert them to a salable good or service. p. 281

new-product strategy development   Defining the role for a new product in terms of the firm's overall corporate objectives. p. 281

noise   Extraneous factors that can work against effective communication by distorting a message or the feedback received. p. 470

nonprobability sampling   Using arbitrary judgments to select the sample so that the chance of selecting a particular element may be unknown or zero. p. 224

North American Industry Classification System (NAICS)
Provides common industry definitions for Canada, Mexico, and the United States, which facilitate the measurement of economic activity in the three member countries of NAFTA. p. 149

objective and task budgeting   A budgeting approach whereby the company (1) determines its promotion objectives, (2) outlines the tasks to accomplish these objectives, and (3) determines the promotion cost of performing these tasks. p. 33; p. 482

observation   Watching, either mechanically or in person, how people behave. p. 221

odd–even pricing   Setting prices a few dollars or cents under an even number, such as $19.95. p. 369

off-peak pricing   Charging different prices during different times of the day or days of the week to reflect variations in demand for the service. p. 336

off-price retailing   Selling brand-name merchandise at lower than regular prices. p. 456

one-price policy   Setting one price for all buyers of a product or service. Also called *fixed pricing*. p. 374

online consumers   The subsegment of all Internet/Web users who employ this technology to research products and services and make purchases. p. 562

opinion leaders   Individuals who exert direct or indirect social influence over others. p. 133

order getter   A salesperson who sells in a conventional sense and identifies prospective customers, provides customers with information, persuades customers to buy, closes sales, and follows up on customers' use of a product or service. p. 535

order taker   Processes routine orders or reorders for products that were already sold by the company. p. 524

organizational buyers   Those manufacturers, wholesalers, retailers, and government agencies that buy goods and services for their own use or for resale. p. 24; p. 148

organizational buying behaviour   The decision-making process that organizations use to establish the need for products and services and identify, evaluate, and choose among alternative brands and suppliers. p. 151

organizational buying criteria   The objective attributes of the supplier's products and services and the capabilities of the supplier itself. p. 153

packaging   Any container in which a product is offered for sale and on which label information is communicated. p. 313

partnership selling   The practice whereby buyers and sellers combine their expertise and resources to create customized solutions; commit to joint planning; and share customer, competitive, and company information for their mutual benefit, and ultimately the customer. Sometimes called *enterprise selling*. p. 524

penetration pricing   Setting a low initial price on a new product to appeal immediately to the mass market. p. 367

perceived risk   The anxieties felt because the consumer cannot anticipate the outcomes of a purchase but believes that there may be negative consequences. p. 129

percentage of sales budgeting   Allocating funds to advertising as a percentage of past or anticipated sales, in terms of either dollars or units sold. p. 481

perception   The process by which an individual selects, organizes, and interprets information to create a meaningful picture of the world. p. 128

perceptual map   A means of displaying or graphing in two dimensions the location of products or brands in the minds of consumers. p. 257

permission marketing   The solicitation of a consumer's consent (called "opt-in") to receive e-mail and advertising based on personal data supplied by the consumer. p. 559

personal selling   The two-way flow of communication between a buyer and seller, often in a face-to-face encounter, designed to influence a person's or group's purchase decision. p. 472; p. 522

personal selling process   Sales activities occurring before and after the sale itself, consisting of six stages: (1) prospecting, (2) preapproach, (3) approach, (4) presentation, (5) close, and (6) follow-up. p. 527

personality   A person's consistent behaviours or responses to recurring situations. p. 127

personalization   The consumer-initiated practice of generating content on a marketer's Website that is custom tailored to an individual's specific needs and preferences. p. 559

points of difference   Those characteristics of a product that make it superior to competitive substitutes. p. 44

portals   Electronic gateways to the World Wide Web that supply a broad array of news and entertainment, information resources, and shopping services. p. 568

post-tests   Tests conducted after an advertisement has been shown to the target audience to determine whether it has accomplished its intended purpose. p. 508

power centre   A huge shopping strip with multiple anchor (or national) stores, a convenient location, and a supermarket. p. 458

prestige pricing   Setting a high price so that status-conscious consumers will be attracted to the product and buy it. p. 367

pretests   Tests conducted before an advertisement is placed to determine whether it communicates the intended message or to select among alternative versions of an advertisement. p. 507

price discrimination   The practice of charging different prices to different buyers for goods of like trade and quality. p. 382

price elasticity of demand   The percentage change in quantity demanded relative to a percentage change in price. p. 355

price   The money or other considerations (including other goods and services) exchanged for the ownership or use of a good or service. p. 344

price fixing   A conspiracy among firms to set prices for a product. p. 382

price lining   Setting the price of a line of products at a number of different specific pricing points. p. 368

price war   Successive price cutting by competitors to increase or maintain their unit sales or market share. p. 376

pricing constraints   Factors that limit the latitude of price a firm may set. p. 347

pricing objectives   Expectations that specify the role of price in an organization's marketing and strategic plans. p. 350

primary data   Facts and figures that are newly collected for the project. p. 212

private branding   When a company manufactures products but sells them under the brand name of a wholesaler or retailer (often called *private labelling* or *reseller branding*). p. 313

probability sampling   Using precise rules to select the sample such that each element of the population has a specific known chance of being selected. p. 224

product A good, service, or idea consisting of a bundle of tangible and intangible attributes that satisfies consumers and is received in exchange for money or some other unit of value. p. 270

product (or program) champion A person who is able and willing to cut red tape and move the program forward. p. 594

product advertisements Advertisements that focus on selling a good or service and take three forms: (1) pioneering (or informational), (2) competitive (or persuasive), and (3) reminder. p. 494

product class The entire product category or industry. p. 302

product differentiation (1) A firm's using different marketing mix activities, such as product features and advertising, to help consumers perceive the product as being different and better than competing products. (2) A firm's selling two or more products with different features targeted to different market segments. p. 239

product form Variations of a product within the product class. p. 302

product life cycle The stages a new product goes through in the marketplace: introduction, growth, maturity, and decline. p. 296

product line groupings Organizational groupings in which a unit is responsible for specific product offerings. p. 596

product line A group of products that are closely related because they satisfy a class of needs, are used together, are sold to the same customer group, are distributed through the same outlets, or fall within a given price range. p. 270

product mix The number of product lines offered by a company. p. 270

product modification Altering a product's characteristic, such as its quality, performance, or appearance, to try to increase and extend the product's sales. p. 304

product placement Using a brand-name product in a movie, television show, video, or a commercial for another product. p. 512

product positioning The place an offering occupies in consumers' minds on important attributes relative to competitive offerings. p. 256

production goods Items used in the manufacturing process that become part of the final product. p. 274

product-line pricing The setting of prices for all items in a product line. p. 375

profit The reward to a business firm for the risk it undertakes in offering a product for sale; the money left over after a firm's total expenses are subtracted from its total revenues. p. 30

profit equation Profit = Total revenue − Total cost, or Profit = (Unit price × Quantity sold) = Total cost. p. 346

profitability analysis A means of measuring the profitability of the firm's products, customer groups, sales territories, channels of distribution, and order sizes. p. 599

promotional allowance Cash payment or extra amount of "free goods" awarded sellers in the channel of distribution for undertaking certain advertising or selling activities to promote a product. p. 381

promotional mix The combination of one or more of the promotional elements a firm uses to communicate with consumers. The promotional elements include advertising, personal selling, sales promotion, public relations, and direct marketing. p. 474

protectionism The practice of shielding one or more sectors of a country's economy from foreign competition through the use of tariffs or quotas. p. 174

protocol A statement that, before product development begins, identifies (1) a well-defined target market; (2) specific customers' needs, wants, and preferences; and (3) what the product will be and do. p. 278

public relations A form of communication management that seeks to influence the feelings, opinions, or beliefs held by customers, prospective customers, shareholders, suppliers, employees, and other publics about a company and its products or services. p. 472

publicity A nonpersonal, indirectly paid presentation of an organization, good, or service. p. 472

pull strategy Directing the promotional mix at ultimate consumers to encourage them to ask the retailer for the product. p. 478

purchase decision process The stages a buyer passes through in making choices about which products and services to buy. p. 120

push strategy Directing the promotional mix to channel members to gain their cooperation in ordering and stocking a product. p. 478

quality Those features and characteristics of a product that influence its ability to satisfy customer needs. p. 35

quantity discounts Reductions in unit costs for a larger order. p. 378

quick response/efficient consumer response An inventory management system designed to reduce the retailer's lead time, thereby lowering its inventory investment, improving customer service levels, and reducing logistics expense. p. 429

quota A restriction placed on the amount of a product allowed to enter or leave a country. p. 174

rating The percentage of households in a market that are tuned to a particular TV show or radio station. p. 501

reach The number of different people or households exposed to an advertisement. p. 500

receivers Consumers who read, hear, or see the message sent by a source in the communication process. p. 468

reciprocity An industrial buying practice in which two organizations agree to purchase each other's products and services. p. 154

reference groups People to whom an individual looks as a basis for self-appraisal or as a source of personal standards. p. 136

regional marketing Developing marketing plans to reflect specific area differences in taste preferences, perceived needs, or interests. p. 78

regional shopping centres Consist of 50 to 150 stores that typically attract customers who live within an 8- to 16-km range, often containing two or three anchor stores. p. 458

regulation Restrictions the provincial and federal laws place on business with regard to the conduct of its activities. p. 89

relationship marketing Linking the organization to its individual customers, employees, suppliers, and other partners for their mutual long-term benefits. p. 16

relationship selling The practice of building ties to customers based on a salesperson's attention and commitment to customer needs over time. p. 524

repositioning Changing the place an offering occupies in a consumer's mind relative to competitive offerings. p. 257

reseller A wholesaler or retailer that buys physical products and resells them again without any processing. p. 148

response The impact the message had on the receiver's knowledge, attitudes, or behaviours. p. 470

restructuring Striving for more efficient corporations that can compete globally by reducing duplicate efforts in multiple company locations, closing or changing unprofitable plants and offices, and laying off employees. p. 88

retail life cycle   The process of growth and decline that retail outlets, like products, experience. p. 460

retail positioning matrix   Positions retail outlets on two dimensions: breadth of product line and value added. p. 455

retailing   All activities involved in selling, renting, and providing goods and services to ultimate consumers for personal, family, or household use. p. 444

retailing mix   In retailing strategy, the (1) goods and services, (2) physical distribution, and (3) communications tactics chosen by a store. p. 456

reverse auction   A buyer communicates a need for a product or service and would-be suppliers are invited to bid in competition with each other. p. 163

reverse logistics   A process of reclaiming recyclable and reusable materials, returns, and reworks from the point of consumption or use for repair, remanufacturing, redistribution, or disposal. p. 437

reverse marketing   The deliberate effort by organizational buyers to build relationships that shape suppliers' products, services, and capabilities to fit a buyer's needs and those of its customers. p. 154

sales analysis   A tool for controlling marketing programs using sales records to compare actual results with sales goals and to identify strengths and weaknesses. p. 599

sales component analysis   A tool for controlling marketing programs that traces sales revenues to their sources, such as specific products, sales territories, or customers. Also called *microsales analysis*. p. 599

sales engineer   A salesperson who specializes in identifying, analyzing, and solving customer problems and who brings know-how and technical expertise to the selling situations, but does not actually sell goods and services. p. 526

sales forecast   The maximum total sales of a product that a firm expects to sell during a specified time period under specified environmental conditions and its own marketing efforts (also called *company forecast*). p. 228

sales management   Planning the selling program and implementing and controlling the personal selling effort of the firm. p. 527

sales plan   A statement describing what is to be achieved and where and how the selling effort of salespeople is to be deployed. p. 533

sales promotion   A short-term inducement of value offered to arouse interest in buying a good or service. p. 473

sales response function   Relates the expense of marketing effort to the marketing results obtained. Measures of marketing results include sales revenue, profit, units sold, and level of awareness. p. 580

salesforce automation   The use of technology to make the sales function more effective and efficient. p. 541

salesforce survey forecast   Asking the firm's salespeople to estimate sales during a coming period. p. 231

sampling   The process of selecting subsets from a population. p. 223

scrambled merchandising   Offering several unrelated product lines in a single retail store. p. 449

screening and evaluation   The third stage of the new-product process, which involves internal and external evaluations of the new-product ideas to eliminate those that warrant no further effort. p. 284

secondary data   Facts and figures that have already been recorded before the project at hand. p. 212

selective distribution   A firm selects a few retail outlets in a specific geographical area to carry its products. p. 411

self-concept   The way people see themselves and the way they believe others see them. p. 127

self-regulation   An alternative to government control where an industry attempts to police itself. p. 91

selling agent   Represents a single producer and is responsible for the entire marketing function of that producer. p. 406

semiotics   The field of study that examines the correspondence between symbols and their role in the assignment of meaning for people. p. 181

service continuum   A range from the tangible to the intangible or goods-dominant to service-dominant offerings available in the marketplace. p. 328

services   Intangible activities, benefits, or satisfactions that an organization provides to consumers in exchange for money or something else of value. p. 324

share points   Percentage points of market share; often used as the common basis of comparison to allocate marketing resources effectively. p. 582

shopping goods   Items for which the consumer compares several alternatives on criteria such as price, quality, or style. p. 273

shrinkage   Breakage and theft of merchandise by customers and employees. p. 456

situation analysis   Taking stock of where the firm or product has been recently, where it is now, and where it is headed in terms of the organization's plans and the external factors and trends affecting it. p. 42

situational influences   The purchase situation affects the purchase decision process through five situational influences: (1) the purchase task, (2) social surroundings, (3) physical surroundings, (4) temporal effects, and (5) antecedent states. p. 125

Six Sigma   A means to "delight the customer" by achieving quality through a highly disciplined process to focus on developing and delivering near-perfect products and services. p. 282

skimming pricing   The highest initial price that customers really desiring the product are willing to pay. p. 366

slotting fee   The payment a manufacturer makes to place a new item on a retailer's shelf. p. 288

social audit   A systematic assessment of a firm's objectives, strategies, and performance in the domain of social responsibility. p. 108

social class   The relatively permanent, homogeneous divisions in a society into which people sharing similar values, lifestyles, interests, and behaviour can be grouped. p. 139

social forces   The demographic characteristics of the population and its values in the environment. p. 75

social responsibility   The idea that organizations are part of a larger society and are accountable to that society for their actions. p. 106

societal marketing concept   The view that an organization should discover and satisfy the needs of its consumers in a way that also provides for society's well-being. p. 22

source   A company or person who has information to convey. p. 468

spam   Electronic junk mail or unsolicited e-mail. p. 567

specialty goods   Items that a consumer makes a special effort to search out and buy. p. 273

staff positions People in staff positions have the authority and responsibility to advise people in the line positions but cannot issue direct orders to them. p. 596

stakeholders Individuals or groups, either within or outside an organization, that relate to it in what it does and how well it performs. p. 32

standard markup pricing Adding a fixed percentage to the cost of all items in a specific product class. p. 370

stimulus-response presentation A selling format that assumes the prospect will buy if given the appropriate stimulus by a sales-person. p. 530

strategic alliances Agreements among two or more independent firms to cooperate for the purpose of achieving common goals. p. 177

strategic channel alliances A practice whereby one firm's marketing channel is used to sell another firm's products. p. 404

strategic marketing process The approach whereby an organization allocates its marketing mix resources to reach its target markets. p. 41

strip location A cluster of stores serving people who live within a 5- to 10-minute drive. p. 458

subcultures Subgroups within the larger, or national, culture with unique values, ideas, and attitudes. p. 139

subliminal perception Means that you see or hear messages without being aware of them. p. 129

supply chain A sequence of firms that perform activities required to create and deliver a good or service to consumers or industrial users. p. 422

supply chain management The integration and organization of information and logistics activities across firms in a supply chain for the purpose of creating and delivering goods and services that provide value to customers. p. 422

supply partnership A relationship that exists when a buyer and its supplier adopt mutually beneficial objectives, policies, and procedures for the purpose of lowering the cost and/or increasing the value of products and services delivered to the ultimate consumer. p. 154

support goods Items used to assist in producing other goods and services. p. 274

survey A research technique used to generate data by asking people questions and recording their responses on a questionnaire. p. 216

survey of buyers' intentions forecast Asking prospective customers whether they are likely to buy the product during some future time period. p. 231

survey of experts forecast Asking experts on a topic to make a judgment about some future event. p. 231

sustainable development Conducting business in a way that protects the natural environment while making economic progress. p. 108

SWOT analysis An acronym describing an organization's appraisal of its internal strengths and weaknesses and its external opportunities and threats. p. 42

synergy The increased customer value achieved through performing organizational functions more efficiently. p. 243

target market One or more specific groups of potential consumers toward which an organization directs its marketing program. p. 15

target pricing Manufacturer deliberately adjusting the composition and features of a product to achieve the target price to consumers. p. 369

target profit pricing Setting an annual target of a specific dollar volume of profit. p. 371

target return-on-investment pricing Setting a price to achieve a return-on-investment (ROI) target. p. 372

target return-on-sales pricing Setting a price to achieve a profit that is a specified percentage of the sales volume. p. 372

tariff A government tax on goods or services entering a country primarily serving to raise prices on imports. p. 174

team selling Using an entire team of professionals in selling to and servicing major customers. p. 526

technology Inventions or innovations from applied science or engineering research. p. 84

telemarketing Using the telephone to interact with and sell directly to consumers. p. 453

third-party logistics providers Firms that perform most or all of the logistics functions that manufacturers, suppliers, and distributors would normally perform themselves. p. 431

top-down forecast Subdividing an aggregate forecast into its principal components. p. 229

total cost (1) The total expense incurred by a firm in producing and marketing a product. Total cost is the sum of fixed cost and variable cost. (2) In physical distribution decisions, the sum of all applicable costs for logistical activities. p. 356

total logistics cost Expenses associated with transportation, materials handling and warehousing, inventory, stockouts, order processing, and return goods handling. p. 428

total revenue The total money received from the sale of a product. p. 353

trade feedback effect A country's imports affect its exports and exports affect its imports. p. 171

trade name A commercial, legal name under which a company does business. p. 306

trademark Identifies that a firm has legally registered its brand name or trade name so the firm has its exclusive use. p. 306

trade-oriented sales promotions Sales tools used to support a company's advertising and personal selling efforts directed to wholesalers, distributors, or retailers. Three common approaches are allowances and discounts, cooperative advertising, and sales-force training. p. 513

trading down Reducing the number of features, quality, or price. p. 305

trading up Adding value to a product (or line) through additional features or higher-quality materials. p. 305

traditional auction A seller puts an item up for sale and would-be buyers are invited to bid in competition with each other. p. 161

traffic generation The outcome of a direct marketing offer designed to motivate people to visit a business. p. 485

trend extrapolation Extending a pattern observed in past data into the future. p. 231

ultimate consumers People—whether 80 years or 8 months old—who use the goods and services purchased for a household. p. 24

uniform delivered pricing The price the seller quotes includes all transportation costs. p. 381

unsought goods Items that the consumer either does not know about or knows about but does not initially want. p. 273

usage rate Quantity consumed or patronage—store visits—during a specific period; varies significantly among different customer groups. p. 247

utilitarianism   A personal moral philosophy that focuses on the "greatest good for the greatest number" by assessing the costs and benefits of the consequences of ethical behaviour. p. 104

utility   The benefits or customer value received by users of the product. p. 24

value analysis   A systematic appraisal of the design, quality, and performance of a product to reduce purchasing costs. p. 159

value consciousness   The concern for obtaining the best quality, features, and performance of a product or service for a given price. p. 81

value-pricing   The practice of simultaneously increasing service and product benefits and maintaining or decreasing price. p. 345

values   (1) Personally or socially preferable modes of conduct or states of existence that are enduring. (2) The ratio of perceived quality to price. p. 181; p. 345

variable cost   The sum of the expenses of the firm that vary directly with the quantity of product that is produced and sold. p. 356

vendor-managed inventory   An inventory management system whereby the supplier determines the product amount and assortment a customer (such as a retailer) needs and automatically delivers the appropriate items. p. 437

vertical marketing systems   Professionally managed and centrally coordinated marketing channels designed to achieve channel economies and maximum marketing impact. p. 407

viral marketing   An Internet/Web-enabled promotional strategy that encourages users to forward marketer-initiated messages to others via e-mail. p. 567

warranty   A statement indicating the liability of the manufacturer for product deficiencies. p. 317

Web communities   Websites that allow people to congregate online and exchange views on topics of common interest. p. 567

wheel of retailing   A concept that describes how new retail outlets enter the market as low-status, low-margin stores and gradually add embellishments that raise their prices, and status. They now face a new low-status, low-margin operator, and the cycle starts to repeat itself. p. 459

whistleblowers   Employees who report unethical or illegal actions of their employers. p. 104

word of mouth   People influencing each other during their face-to-face conversations. p. 135

workload method   A formula-based method for determining the size of a salesforce that integrates the number of customers served, call frequency, call length, and available selling time to arrive at a salesforce size. p. 537

World Trade Organization   A permanent institution that sets rules governing trade between its members through a panel of trade experts who (1) decide on trade disputes between members and (2) issue binding decisions. p. 175

World Wide Web   A part of the Internet that supports a retrieval system that formats information and documents into Web pages. p. 85

yield management pricing   The charging of different prices to maximize revenue for a set amount of capacity at any given time. p. 369

CHAPTER NOTES

CHAPTER 1

1. Data in Figure 1–1 are based on statistics published by the National Sporting Goods Association and the Sporting Goods Manufacturers Association.
2. Information supplied by Bauer Canada, July 2001.
3. Steven A. Meyerowitz, "Surviving Assaults on Trademarks," *Marketing Management*, No. 1 (1994), pp. 44–46; and Carrie Goerne, "Rollerblade Reminds Everyone That Its Success Is Not Generic," *Marketing News* (March 2, 1992), pp. 1–2.
4. "The Case for Brands," *The Economist* (September 8, 2001), p. 11; "Who's Wearing the Trousers?" *The Economist* (September 8, 2001), pp. 26–28; Gerry Khermouch, "The Best Global Brands," *Business Week* (August 6, 2001), pp. 50–64.
5. Peter D. Bennett, *Dictionary of Marketing Terms*, 2nd ed. (Lincolnwood, IL: NTC Publishing Group, 1995), p. 166.
6. Richard P. Bagozzi, "Marketing as Exchange," *Journal of Marketing* (October 1975), pp. 32–39; and Gregory T. Gundlach and Patrick E. Murphy, "Ethical and Legal Foundations of Relational Marketing Exchanges," *Journal of Marketing* (October 1993), pp. 35–46.
7. Robert M. McMath and Thom Forbes, *What Were They Thinking?* (New York: Times Business, 1998), pp. 3–22.
8. McMath and Forbes, pp. 181–82.
9. "And You Thought Atomic Fireballs Were Hot," *Time* (June 18, 2001), p. 20; "'Sweet Just Got Smart' as Pfizer Launches Body Smarts," *Pfizer Review* (Summer 2001), p. 5.
10. Peter Lewis, "Toro! Toro! Toro!" *Fortune* (July 9, 2001), p. 171.
11. Stephen H. Wildstrom, "Finally, Flat Is Better," *Business Week* (September 24, 2001), p. 20.
12. "Cereal and Junk Food Advertising," November 5, 2001; and "Watching for Weasel Words," November 27, 2001, www.media-awareness.ca, downloaded January 5, 2002.
13. E. Jerome McCarthy, *Basic Marketing: A Managerial Approach* (Homewood, IL: Richard D. Irwin, 1960); and Walter van Waterschoot and Christophe Van den Bulte. "The 4P Classification of the Marketing Mix Revisited," *Journal of Marketing* (October 1992), pp. 83–93.
14. James Surowiecki, "The Return of Michael Porter," *Fortune* (February, 1999), pp. 135–38; and Kathleen M. Eisenhardt and Shona L. Brown, "Time Pacing: Competing in Markets That Won't Stand Still," *Harvard Business Review* (March–April 1998), pp. 59–69.
15. Patti Summerfield, "Loyalty in the New Millennium," www.strategy.mag.com, April 22, 2002.
16. Michael Treacy and Fred D. Wiersema, *The Discipline of Market Leaders* (Reading, MA: Addison-Wesley, 1995); Michael Treacy and Fred Wiersema, "How Market Leaders Keep Their Edge," *Fortune* (February 6, 1995), pp. 88–89; and Michael Treacy, "You Need a Value Discipline—But Which One?" *Fortune* (April 17, 1995), p. 195.
17. Susan Fournier, Susan Dobseha, and David Glen Mick, "Preventing the Premature Death of Relationship Marketing," *Harvard Business Review* (January–February 1998), pp. 42–51.
18. The material on Rollerblade's current marketing strategy is based on a personal interview with David Samuels and with information from the Rollerblade Website and Rollerblade sales materials.
19. Leigh Muzlay, "Shoes that Morph from Sneakers to Skates Are Flying out of Stores," *The Wall Street Journal* (July 26, 2001), p. B1; The SGMA Report 2000, "The U.S. Athletic Footwear Market Today," published by the Sporting Goods Manufacturers Association.
20. Robert F. Keith, "The Marketing Revolution," *Journal of Marketing* (January 1960), pp. 35–38.
21. *Annual Report* (New York: General Electric Company, 1952), p. 21.
22. John C. Narver, Stanley F. Slater, and Brian Tietje, "Creating a Market Orientation," *Journal of Market Focused Management*, no. 2 (1998), pp. 241–55; Stanley F. Slater and John C. Narver, "Market Orientation and the Learning Organization," *Journal of Marketing* (July 1995), pp. 63–74; and George S. Day, "The Capabilities of Market-Driven Organizations," *Journal of Marketing* (October 1994), pp. 37–52.
23. The definition of customer relationship management is adapted from Rajendra K. Srivastava, Tasadduq A. Shervani, and Liam Fahey, "Marketing, Business Processes, and Shareholder Value: An Embedded View of Marketing Activities and the Discipline of Marketing," *Journal of Marketing* (special issue, 1999), pp. 168–79.
24. Jay Curry and Adam Curry, "The Customer Marketing Method: How to Implement and Profit from Customer Relationship Management." New York: The Free Press, 2000; Jim Berkowitz, "A Customer-Centric Philosophy," www.showcasecorp.com, April 25, 2002; www.crmguru.com, downloaded April 27, 2002.
25. Michael E. Porter and Claas van er Linde, "Green and Competitive Ending the Stalemate," *Harvard Business Review* (September–October 1995), pp. 120–34; Jacquelyn Ottman, "Edison Winners Show Smart Environmental Marketing," *Marketing News* (July 17, 1995), pp. 16, 19; and Jacquelyn Ottman, "Mandate for the '90s: Green Corporate Image," *Marketing News* (September 11, 1995), p. 8.
26. Shelby D. Hunt and John J. Burnett, "The Macromarketing/ Micromarketing Dichotomy: A Taxonomical Model," *Journal of Marketing* (Summer 1982), pp. 9–26.
27. Philip Kotler and Sidney J. Levy, "Broadening the Concept of Marketing," *Journal of Marketing* (January 1969), pp. 10–15.
28. www.modrobes.com, downloaded April 27, 2002.
29. John A. Byrne, "Caught in the Net," *Business Week* (August 27, 2001), pp. 114–16; Gary Gentile, "eToast," Star Tribune (March 3, 2001), pp. D1, D2.

Rollerblade: This case was written by William Rudelius and Giana Eckhardt.

CHAPTER 2

1. Information supplied by Bombardier Inc., May 1, 2002.
2. Roger A. Kerin, Vijay Mahajan, and P. Rajan Varadarajan, *Contemporary Perspectives on Strategic Marketing Planning* (Boston: Allyn & Bacon, 1990), chapter 1; and Orville C. Walker, Jr., Harper W. Boyd, Jr., and Jean-Claude Larreche, *Marketing Strategy* (Burr Ridge, IL: Richard D. Irwin, 1992), chapters 1 and 2.
3. Theodore Levitt, "Marketing Myopia," *Harvard Business Review* (July–August 1960), pp. 45–56.
4. Charles W. L. Hill and Gareth R. Jones, *Strategic Management: An Integrated Approach*, 4th ed. (Boston: Houghton Mifflin, 1998), pp. 37–38.
5. George Stalk, Phillip Evans, and Lawrence E. Shulman, "Competing on Capabilities: The New Rules of Corporate Strategy," *Harvard Business Review* (March–April 1992), pp. 57–69.
6. Roger A. Kerin and Robert A. Peterson, *Strategic Marketing Problems: Cases and Comments*, 8th ed. (Englewood Cliffs, NJ: Prentice Hall), pp. 2–3; and Derek F. Abell, *Defining the Business* (Englewood Cliffs, NJ: Prentice Hall, 1980), p. 18.
7. W. Edwards Deming, *Out of the Crisis* (Cambridge, MA: MIT Center for Advanced Engineering Study, 1986).
8. This material was gleaned from John Lorinc, "Attention Shoppers," www.robmagazine.com, Friday, March 29, 2002.

9. Adapted from "The Experience Curve Reviewed, IV. The Growth Share Matrix of the Product Portfolio" (Boston: The Boston Consulting Group, 1973).

10. Strengths and weaknesses of the BCG technique are based largely on Derek F. Abell and John S. Hammond, *Strategic Market Planning: Problem and Analytic Approaches* (Englewood Cliffs, NJ: Prentice Hall, 1979); and Yoram Wind, Vijay Mahajan, and Donald Swire, "An Empirical Comparison of Standardized Portfolio Models," *Journal of Marketing* (Spring 1983), pp. 89–99.

11. J. Scott Armstrong and Roderick J. Brodie, "Effects of Portfolio Planning Methods on Decision Making: Experimental Results," *International Journal of Research in Marketing* (Winter 1994), pp. 73–84.

12. H. Igor Ansoff, "Strategies for Diversification," *Harvard Business Review* (September–October 1957), pp. 113–24.

13. Hill and Jones, chapters 1–3.

14. Michael Totty, "Making the Sale," *The Wall Street Journal* (September 24, 2001), p. R6.

15. Peter Nulty, "Kodak Grabs for Growth Again," *Fortune* (May 16, 1994), pp. 76–78.

16. Mark Maremont, "Kodak's New Focus," *Business Week* (January 30, 1995), pp. 63–68.

17. Daniel Eisenberg, "Kodak's Photo Op," *Time* (April 30, 2001), pp. 46–47.

18. Michael Ryan, "Kodak's Big Moment," Smartbusinessmay.com (July 2001), pp. 79–84.

19. Mike Musgrove, "'Y' Factor: A Camera that Tapes and Plays," *Washington Post* (March 24, 2001), p. E1.

20. John R. Wilke and James Bandler, "New Digital Camera Deals Kodak a Lesson in Microsoft's Ways," *The Wall Street Journal* (July 2, 2001), pp. A1, A6.

Specialized Bicycle Components, Inc.: This case was written by Giana Eckhardt.

APPENDIX A

1. Personal interview with Authur R. Kydd, St. Croix Venture Partners.

2. Examples of guides to writing marketing plans include: William A. Cohen, *The Marketing Plan* (New York: Wiley, 1995); Mark Nolan, *The Instant Marketing Plan* (Santa Maria, CA: Puma Publishing Company, 1995); and Roman G. Hiebing, Jr., and Scott W. Cooper, *The Successful Marketing Plan*, 2nd ed. (Lincolnwood, IL: NTC Business Books, 1997).

3. Examples of guides to writing business plans include the following: Rhonda M. Abrams, *The Successful Business Plan: Secrets & Strategies*, 3rd ed. (Grants Pass, OR: The Oasis Press/PSI Research, 2000); Joseph A. Covello and Brian J. Hazelgren, *The Complete Book of Business Plans* (Naperville, IL: Sourcebooks, 1995); Joseph A. Covello and Brian J. Hazelgren, *Your First Business Plan*, 3rd ed. (Naperville, IL: Sourcebooks, 1998); and Angela Shupe, ed., *Business Plans Handbook*, vols. 1–4 (Detroit: Gale Research, 1997).

4. Abrams, *The Successful Business Plan*, p. 30.

5. Some of these points are adapted from Abrams, pp. 30–38; others are adapted from William Rudelius, *Guidelines for Technical Report Writing* (Minneapolis, MN: University of Minnesota, undated).

6. The authors are indebted to Randall F. Peters and Leah Peters for being allowed to adapt elements of a business plan for Paradise Kitchens, Inc., for the sample marketing plan and for their help and suggestions.

CHAPTER 3

1. David Kirkpatrick, "In Napster's Void: You've Got Misery!" *Fortune* (April 2, 2001), pp. 144–146; and Devin Leonard, "Don't Call Them Napster," *Fortune* (June 25, 2001), p. 44.

2. Patrick Brethour, "On-line music services seen flopping," *Technology Reporter*, February 9, 2002, p. B1; and Anita Castaldi, "Liquid Gold Retailing Tips," *Canadian-Grocer* (April 2001).

3. Patrick Brethour, "On-line music service coming," *Technology Reporter*, February 15, 2002, p. B6.

4. Chris Taylor, "More Pain for Napster," *Time* (April 16, 2001), p. 43; and Monica Roman, "Napster Gets Some Big Buddies," *Business Week* (June 18, 2001), p. 46.

5. "U.S. Consumption of Coffee Drops to Record Low," *Food and Drink Weekly* (April 20, 1998); and "Gourmet Coffee Craze Bucks National Decline in Coffee Consumption," *PR Newswire* (September 29, 1998); Shannon Dortch, "Coffee at Home," *American Demographics* (August 1995), pp. 4–6; and Marcia Mogelonsky, "Instant's Last Drop," *American Demographics* (August 1995), p. 10; and Anita Castaldi, "Liquid Gold Retailing Tips," *Canadian-Grocer* (April 2001).

6. Seanna Browder and Emily Thornton, "Reheating Starbucks," *Business Week* (September 28, 1998), pp. 66–70.

7. Anita Castaldi, "Liquid Gold Retailing Tips," *Canadian-Grocer* (April 2001).

8. "American Marketing Association Special Report on Trends and Forces Shaping the Future of Marketing," (Chicago: American Marketing Assocation), May 19, 1998; James Heckman, Maricris G. Briones, and Michelle Wirth Fellman, "Outlook 99: A Look at What the Year Ahead Will Bring," *Marketing News* (December 7, 1998), p. 1; Brent Schlendcr, "Peter Drucker Takes the Long View," *Fortune* (September 28, 1998, pp. 162–73; Michael I. Mandel, "The 21st Century Economy," *Business Week* (August 31, 1998), pp. 58–67; Statistics Canada, CANSIM Matrix 6231; and Goldfarb Consultants, Toronto, 1998; Nina Munk, "The New Organization Man," *Fortune* (March 16, 1998), pp. 63–74; and Harry S. Dent, Jr., *The Roaring 2000s* (New York: Simon and Schuster, 1998).

9. Statistics Canada, 2001 Census Analysis Series. A Profile of the Canadian Population: Where We Live. Catalogue: 96F 0030XIE01001-2001.

10. Statistics Canada. CANSIM matrix 6900.

11. Statistics Canada, www.statcan.ca/english/pgdb/people/population/demo23b.htm, downloaded March 10, 2002.

12. D. Allan Kerr, "Where There's Gray There's Green," *Marketing News* (June 22, 1998), p. 2.

13. Patricia Braus, "The Baby Boom at Mid-Decade," *American Demographics* (April 1995), pp. 40–45; and Cheryl Russell, "On the Baby Boom Bandwagon," *American Demographics* (May 1991), pp. 24–31.

14. Marcy Magiera and Pat Sloan, "Levis, Lee Loosen Up for Baby Boomers," *Advertising Age* (August 3, 1992), p. 9.

15. Todd Gutncr, "Generation X: To Be Young, Thrifty, and in the Black," *Business Week* (July 21, 1997), p. 76; Howard Gleckman, "Generation $ Is More Like It," *Business Week* (November 3, 1997), p. 44; Karen Ritchie, "Marketing to Generation X," *American Demographics* (April 1995), pp. 34–39; and Diane Crispell, "Generations to 2025," *American Demographics* (January 1995), p. 4.

16. Beck, "Generation Y: Next Population Bulge Shows Its Might"; and Susan Mitchell, "The Next Baby Boom," *American Demographics* (October 1995), pp. 22–31.

17. Statistics Canada, cat. 97-2I3-XPB (Ottawa, 1999).

18. Information supplied by Goldfarb Consultants, Toronto, 1998.

19. Statistics Canada, *Canada at a Glance*, 2002.

20. Statistics Canada, 2001 Census Analysis Series. A Profile of the Canadian Population: Where We Live. Catalogue: 96F 0030XIE01001-2001.

21. www.angusreid.ca.

22. Jo Marney, "Counting Ethnic Canadians In," *Marketing Magazine*, June 4, 2001.

23. Douglas Bell, "Immigration Trends Shape Demand," *Marketing* (May 21, 1993), p. 29; and Brandon Watson, "The New Frontiers:

packaged goods and retail are the latest sectors to launch ethnic campaigns," *Marketing Magazine*, June 21, 1999.

24. Fawzia Sheikh, "Lessons Learned: companies trip over cultural taboos and stereotypes," *Marketing Magazine*, June 4, 2001.

25. Sarah Smith, "Checking out the New Loblaws," www.marketingmag.ca, April 29, 2002; www.hbc.com, and www.imperialoil.com, April 26, 2002.

26. Information supplied by Clearly Canadian Beverage Corporation, January 3, 2002.

27. Lesley Young, "Super Supplements," www.marketingmag.ca, June 4, 2001.

28. Donalee Moulton, "Sobeys Takes Low Road in Food Pricing," *Marketing* (August 5, 1996), p. 2.

29. "Banks Poach Credit Card Business with Lower Rates," *Marketing* (August 5, 1996), p. 4.

30. David Dodge, "Current developments in the Canadian economy," *Bank of Canada Review*, Ottawa, Autumn 2001, pp. 39–40.

31. Statistics Canada Population "Estimates, by Age Groups and Sex, Canada, Provinces and Territories," *Market Research Handbook*, 2000 (catalogue No. 91–213–XPB and 91–213–XI–B).

32. Robert D. Hof, Gary McWilliams, and Gabrielle Saveri, "The 'Click Here' Economy," *Business Week* (June 22, 1998), pp. 122–28; Rochelle Garner, "The Ecommerce Connection,' *Sales and Marketing Management* (January 1999), pp. 40–46; Clint Willis, "25 Cool Things You Wish You Had and Will," *Forbes ASAP* (June 1, 1998), pp. 49–60; and Rebecca Piirto, "Cable TV," *American Demographics* (June 1995), pp. 40–43.

33. Elizabeth Corcoran, "The Next Small Think," *Forbes* (July 23, 2001), pp. 96–106; Michael J. Mandel and Robert D. Hof, "Rethinking the Internet," *Business Week* (March 26, 2001), pp. 117–122; Catherine Arnst, "The Birth of a Cancer Drug," *Business Week* (July 9, 2001), pp. 95–102; Clint Willis, "25 Cool Things You Wish You Had and Will," *Forbes ASAP* (June 1, 1998), pp. 49–60.

34. Neil Gross, Peter Coy, and Otis Post, "The Technology Paradox," *Business Week* (March 6, 1995), pp. 76–84.

35. Leon Jaroff, "Smart's the Word in Detroit," *Time* (February 6, 1995), pp. 50–52.

36. Clint Willis, "25 Cool Things You Wish You Had and Will," *Forbes ASAP* (June 1, 1998), pp. 49–60.

37. www.cpia.ca/staticcontent, Plastics Overview.

38. Nyla Matuk, "Green Roofing," *Canadian Architect*, vol. 46, issue 10, October 2001, p. 25.

39. Jim Carlton, "Recycling Redefined," *The Wall Street Journal* (March 6, 2001), pp. B1, B4; Stephanie Anderson, "There's Gold in Those Hills of Soda Bottles," *Business Week* (September 11, 1995), p. 48; Maxine Wilkie, "Asking Americans to Use Less Stuff," *American Demographics* (December 1994), pp. 11–12; and Jacquelyn Ottman, "New and Improved Won't Do," *Marketing News* (January 30, 1995), p. 9.

40. Marcie Sayner, Ipsos-Reid Survey Results, Spring 2001.

41. Michael J. Mandel and Robert D. Hof, "Rethinking the Internet," *Business Week* (March 26, 2001), pp. 117–122; Steve Hamm, David Welch, Wendy Zellner, Faith Keenan, and Peter Engardio, "E-biz: Down but Hardly Out," *Business Week* (March 26, 2001), pp. 126–130; and Spencer E. Ante, Amy Borrus, and Robert D. Hof, "In Search of the Net's Next Big Thing," *Business Week* (March 26, 2001), pp. 140–141.

42. Michael Porter, *Competitive Advantage*, (New York: Free Press, 1985); and Michael Porter, *Competitive Strategy*, (New York: Free Press, 1980).

43. Carey Hamel and Jeff Sampler, "The E-Corporation," *Fortune* (December 7, 1998), pp. 80–92; Shikhar Ghosh, "Making Business Sense of the Internet," *Harvard Business Review* (March–April 1998), pp. 127–35; Ramon J. Peypoch, "The Case for Electronic Business Communities," *Business Horizons* (September–October 1998), pp. 17–20; Harry S. Dent, Jr., *The Roaring 2000s*, p. 137; and

Erick Schonfeld, "Schwab Puts It All Online," *Fortune* December 7, 1998), pp. 94–100.

44. John Cooper, "Enhancing the competitive success of Candian SMEs," *CMA Management*, July/August 2001, pp. 16–21.

45. Peter Fitzpatrick, "CP splits to unlock value: five new divisions," *Financial Post-National Post*, February 14, 2001, pp. C1, C4.

46. Sinclair Stewart, "Cara vows to press bid for Second Cup: $43M all-cash offer," *Financial Post-National Post*, January 10, 2002, p. FP4; and Deirdre McMurdy, "Play for Second Cup leaves bitter aftertaste," *Financial Post-National Post*, January 14, 2002, p. FP1, FP7.

47. Canada Newswire, "Canada's Biggest Mergers and Acquisitions in 2001," December 20, 2001.

48. www.ic.gc.ca

Flyte Time Productions, Inc.: This case was written by William Rudelius based on personal interviews with Jimmy Jam and Terry Lewis, and the following sources: Jon Bream, "Flyte Tyme Is Still Ticking After 20 Years of Hits," Star Tribune (April 29, 2001), pp. F1, F7; "Jimmy Jam and Terry Lewis Make Flyte Tyme Studios No. 1," Business Wire (August 21, 2001).

CHAPTER 4

1. Information supplied by Molson Breweries, Public Affairs Department, Toronto, 2002.

2. Eugene R. Lazniak and Patrick E. Murphy, *Ethical Marketing Decisions: The Higher Road* (Boston: Allyn & Bacon, 1993), chapter 1.

3. Verne E. Henderson, "The Ethical Side of Enterprise," *Sloan Management Review* (Spring 1982), pp. 37–47. See also, Joseph L. Badaracco, Jr., *Defining Moments: When Managers Must Choose Between Right and Right* (Boston: Harvard Business School Press, 1997).

4. M. Bommer, C. Gratto, J. Grauander, and M. Tuttle, "A Behavioral Model of Ethical and Unethical Decision Making," *Journal of Business Ethics*, vol. 6 (1987), pp. 265–80.

5. F. G. Crane, "What's Ethical and What's Not with Canadian Business Students," Working Paper, 2001.

6. The Canadian Centre for Ethics and Corporate Policy, www.ethicscentre.com, downloaded August 29, 2001.

7. www.ethicscan.on.ca., downloaded August 15, 2001.

8. N. Craig Smith, "Marketing Strategies for the Ethics Era," *Sloan Management Review* (Summer 1995), pp. 85–97; Kenneth Labich, "The New Crisis in Business Ethics," *Fortune* (April 29, 1992), pp. 167ff.

9. Lawrence B. Chonko, *Ethical Decision Making in Marketing* (Thousand Oaks, CA: Sage, 1995).

10. William Beaver, "Levi's Is Leaving China," *Business Horizons* (March–April 1995), pp. 35–40.

11. Barry R. Shapiro, "Economic Espionage," *Marketing Management* (Spring 1998), pp. 56–58; and Dan T. Swartwood and Richard J. Hefferman, *Trends in Intellectual Property Loss, Survey Report* (Alexandria, VA: American Society for Industrial Security, 1998).

12. "Five years: $59.2 Billion Lost," *Software & Information Industry Association Press Release*, May 2000; Bryan W. Husted, "The Impact of National Culture on Software Piracy," *Journal of Business Ethics*, vol. 26 (2000), pp. 197–211.

13. Vern Terpstra and Kenneth David, *The Cultural Environment of International Business*, 3rd ed. (Cincinnati: South-Western Publishing, 1991), p. 12.

14. For an extended treatment of ethics in the exchange process, see Gregory T. Gundlach and Patrick E. Murphy, "Ethical and Legal Foundations in Relational Marketing Exchanges," *Journal of Marketing*, October 1993, pp. 35–46.

15. "Carnivore in the Cabbage Patch," *U.S. News & World Report* (January 20, 1997), p. 69.

16. "The Battle over Web Privacy," *The Wall Street Journal* (March 21, 2001), pp. B1, B4.

17. For an extensive examination on slotting fees, see Paul N. Bloom, Gregory T. Gundlach, and Joseph P. Cannon, "Slotting Allowances and Fees: Schools of Thought and Views of Practicing Managers," *Journal of Marketing* (April 2000), pp. 92–109. Also see, "FTC Pinpoints Slotting Fees," *Advertising Age* (February 26, 2001), p. 52.

18. This discussion contains statistics reported in Carolyn F. Siegel, "Introducing Marketing Students to Business Intelligence Using Project-Based Learning on the World Wide Web," *Journal of Marketing Education* (August 2000), pp. 90–98.

19. "P&G Expected to Get About $120 Million in Settlement of Chewy-Cookie Lawsuit," *The Wall Street Journal* (September 11, 1989), p. B10.

20. www.transparency.de, downloaded May 25, 2001.

21. *KPMG Business Ethics Survey*, KPMG Canada, 1999, www.kpmg.ca/ethics; and *Management Ethics*, The Canadian Centre for Ethics and Corporate Policy, www.ethicscentre.com, downloaded August 21, 2001.

22. "Simon Says, 'Behave'," *Success* (January 2000), p. 21; and Savior L.S. Nwachukwu and Scott J. Vitell, Jr., "The Influence of Corporate Culture on Managerial Ethical Judgments," *Journal of Business Ethics*, vol. 17 (1997), pp. 757–76.

23. "Workers Who Blow the Whistle on Bosses Often Pay a High Price," *The Wall Street Journal* (July 18, 1995), p. B1.

24. R. Eric Reidenbach and Donald P. Robin, *Ethics and Profits* (Englewood Cliffs, NJ: Prentice Hall, 1989); Chonko, *Ethical Decision Making*; Laziniak and Murphy, *Ethical Marketing Decisions*.

25. James Q. Wilson, "Adam Smith on Business Ethics," *California Management Review* (Fall 1989), pp. 59–72; and George M. Zinkham, Michael Bisesi, and Mary Jane Saxon, "MBAs: Changing Attitudes Toward Marketing Dilemmas," *Journal of Business Ethics*, vol. 8 (1989), pp. 963–74.

26. www.nestlecanada.ca, downloaded April 25, 2001.

27. Robert B. Reich, "The New Meaning of Corporate Social Responsibility," *California Management Review* (Winter 1998), pp. 8–17.

28. Harvey S. James and Farhad Rasseh, "Smith, Friedman, and Self-Interest in Ethical Society," *Business Ethics Quarterly* (July 2000), pp. 659–74.

29. "Beating the Odds in Biotech," *Newsweek* (October 12, 1992), p. 63.

30. For an extended description of the Perrier decision, see "Perrier—Overresponding to a Crisis," in Robert F. Hartley, *Marketing Mistakes and Successes*, 8th ed. (New York: Wiley, 2001), pp. 127–37.

31. Harvey Meyer, "The Greening of Corporate America," *Journal of Business Strategy* (January–February 2000), pp. 38–43; Irina Maslennikova and David Foley, "Xerox's Approach to Sustainability," *Interfaces* (May–June 2000), pp. 226–33. Also see Philemon Oyewale, "Social Costs of Environmental Justice Associated with the Practice of Green Marketing," *Journal of Business Ethics*, vol. 29 (2001), pp. 239–51; and Ajay Menon and Anil Menon, "Environpreneurial Marketing Strategy: The Emergence of Corporate Environmentalism as Market Strategy," *Journal of Marketing* (January 1997), pp. 51–67.

32. The ISO Survey of ISO 9000 and ISO 14000 Certificates (Geneva, Switzerland: International Organization for Standardization, 2000).

33. For an extended discussion on this topic, see P. Rajan Varadarajan and Anil Menon, "Causes-Related Marketing: A Coalignment of Marketing Strategy and Corporate Philanthropy," *Journal of Marketing* (July 1988), pp. 58–74. The examples given are found in "The Socially Correct Corporation," *Fortune* (July 24, 2000), special section; and "The Wider Benefits of Backing a Good Cause," *Marketing* (September 2, 1999), pp. 18–22.

34. "Reinventing Cause Marketing," *Brandweek* (October 27, 1997), p. 17.

35. These steps are adapted from J. J. Carson and G. A. Steiner, *Measuring Business Social Performance: The Corporate Social Audit* (New York: Committee for Economic Development, 1974). See also Sandra Waddock and Neil Smith, "Corporate Responsibility Audits:

Doing Well by Doing Good," *Sloan Management Review* (Winter 2000), pp. 75–84.

36. D.A. Rondinelli and G. Vastag, "International Standards and Corporate Policies: An Integrated Framework," *California Management Review* (November 9, 1998), p. 14.

37. "A World of Sweatshops," *Business Week* (November 6, 2000), pp. 84–86.

38. "Who's Responsible?" *American Demographics* (December 1999), p. 17; Meyer, "The Greening of Corporate America"; Waddock and Smith, "Corporate Responsibility Audits."

39. For a listing of unethical consumer practices, see Robert E. Wilkes, "Fraudulent Behavior by Consumers," *Journal of Marketing* (October 1978), pp. 67–75; and Catherine A. Cole, "Research Note: Determinants of Consumer Fraud," *Journal of Retailing* (Spring 1989), pp. 107–20.

40. "A Lighter Shade of Green," *American Demographics* (February 2000), p. 24

41. "Schism on the Green," *Brandweek* (February 26, 2001), p. 18.

42. Jason MacDonald, "Not So Easy Being Green," www.marketingmag.ca, June 4, 2001.

43. Dicter Bradbury, "Green Forest Products Gain Marketing Niche," *Maine Sunday Telegram* (May 11, 1997), pp. B1, B14.

PART 1 CASE

1. Tom Nicholson, "The Great Technology Race," *Managing Intellectual Property* (July/August, 1998), p. 24.

2. Melanie Warner, "Misadventures in the Me-First Economy," *Fortune* (March 20, 2000), p. 100

3. Paul Whitfield, "Dot.com shares crash threatens ad revenue," *Marketing* (London) (April 20, 2000), p. 3.

4. Colleen O'Connor, "B2C Dog-Eat-Dog-World Breeds Value for B&Ms," *The IPO Reporter*, (February 12, 2001).

5. Shawn Young, "Sprint sees net fall 60%, plans to cut 6,000 jobs or 7% of staff," *The Wall Street Journal* (October 18, 2001), p. B6; Sally Beatty, "Viacom to reduce MTV staff by 9%, restructure unit," *The Wall Street Journal* (October 30, 2001), p. B8; Nick Wingfield, "Yahoo restructuring to slash 400 jobs, help but its dependence on ad revenue," *The Wall Street Journal* (November 16, 2001), p. B10; and "2001 Winners & Losers—in a year most companies would rather forget, the bad eclipsed the good," *Internetweek* (December 17, 2001), p. 23.

6. John Rendleman, "Nortel to cut 20,000 jobs to regain focus," *Informationweek* (October 8, 2001), p. 32.

7. Brad Stone, "MP3.com gets ripped," *Newsweek* (September 2000), p. 72.

8. "Napster settles suits with music publishers," *The Wall Street Journal* (September 25, 2001), p. B4.

9. "2001 Winners & Losers—in a year most companies would rather forget, the bad eclipsed the good," *Internetweek* (December 17, 2001), p. 23.

10. Karin Halperin, "Differences in fee structures help drive Canadian online banking acceptance," *Bank Systems & Technology* (May 2001), p. 14.

11. Christian Bellavance, "A whole new game," *CA Magazine* (November 1999), p. 2.

12. "What happened to e-books," *The New York Times* (August 21, 2001) (ebusiness/28EBOO.html).

13. Michael Leventhal, "The golden age of wireless," *Intellectual Property & Technology Law Journal* (January 2002), p. 1.

14. Peter Verburg, "No wires, no limits," *Canadian Business* (May 14, 2001), p. 46.

15. Jamie Fenton, "Bluetooth brings era of cable-free networking," *Network World Canada* (December 2000), p. CT14.

16. Ibid.

17. David Atkin, "Bluetooth ready to bite into wide product use: Moves beyond mere hype," *Financial Post-National Post* (January 25, 2001), p. C8.

18. Heather Scoffield, "PM set to unveil Edmonton lab as Liberals try to woo Alberta," *Globe and Mail* (August 16, 2001), p. A1.

19. Fenella Saunders, "Big cures come in small packages," *Discover* (September 2001), vol. 22, no. 9, p. 16.

20. "GM, Partners notch first nanocomposite automotive application," *Canadian Plastics* (November 2001), p. 6.

21. Heather Scoffield; "Feds cough up $60 million for nanotechnology research facility in Edmonton," *Canadian Newswire Press* (August 17, 2001).

22. Mike Buetow, "The PCB market: A year of questions," *Printed Circuit Design* (July 2001), p. 34.

23. Robert Mundell, "One world currency: The biggest danger to the world economy is fluctuations in its three major currencies," *Financial Post-National Post* (April 10, 2000), p. C15.

24. "Foreign Exchange Rates," *Globe & Mail* (March 8, 2002), p. B14.

25. Sandra Cordon, "Exciting year saw economy slow, interest rates fall, rising jobless rate," *Canadian Press Newswire* (December 19, 2001); Sandra Cordon, "Slowing economy, low inflation suggest more rate cuts: economists," *Canadian Press Newswire* (November 25, 2001).

26. Mike Byfield, "Natural gas deregulation gets its first real test: Canadian consumers and producers face US-driven risks with a feeble dollar," *Report Newsmagazine* (June 25, 2001), p. 38.

27. Mike Byfield, "More leaping in the dark: lower prices ease the electricity deregulation crunch, but plenty of problems remain," *Report Newsmagazine* (July 3, 2001), p. 37; Astrid Van Den Broke, "Alberta to join energy deregulation club," *Marketing* (June 19, 2000), p. 11.

28. Linda McQuaig, "Shocking facts about deregulation," *Financial Post-National Post* (September 10, 2001), p. C14.

29. Wayne Lilley, "Tilting at Windmills," *National Post Business* (October 2001), p. 76.

CHAPTER 5

1. Elena Scotti, "Born to be Mild, or Wild?" *BRANDWEEK* (March 16, 1998), pp. 22–23; Jon Berry, "Consumers Keep the Upper Hand," *American Demographics* (September 1998), pp. 20–22; "GM Taps Harris to Help Lure Women," *Advertising Age* (February 17, 1997), pp. 1, 37; "Dealer Dilemma," *BRANDWEEK* (March 16, 1998), p. 22; and "Elle Launches Guide for Women Car Buyers," *Advertising Age* (April 6, 1998), p. 34.

2. James F. Engel, Roger D. Blackwell, and Paul Miniard, *Consumer Behavior*, 9th ed. (Fort Worth, TX: Dryden Press, 1998). See also Gordon C. Bruner III and Richard J. Pomazal, "Problem Recognition: The Crucial First Stage of the Consumer Decision Process," *Journal of Consumer Marketing* (Winter 1988), pp. 53–63.

3. For thorough descriptions of consumer experience and expertise, see Stephen J. Hoch and John Deighton, "Managing What Consumers Learn from Experience," *Journal of Marketing* (April 1989), pp. 1–20; and Joseph W. Alba and J. Wesley Hutchinson, "Dimensions of Consumer Expertise," *Journal of Consumer Research* (March 1987), pp. 411–54.

4. For in-depth studies on external information search patterns, see Sridhar Moorthy, Brian T. Ratchford, and Debabrata Tulukdar, "Consumer Information Search Revisited: Theory and Empirical Analysis," *Journal of Consumer Research* (March 1997), pp. 263–77.

5. "Portable CD Players," *Consumer Reports Buying Guide 2002*, p. 228.

6. For an extended discussion on evaluative criteria, see Del J. Hawkins, Roger J. Best, and Kenneth A. Coney, *Consumer Behavior*, 7th ed. (New York: Irwin/McGraw-Hill, 1998), pp. 550–67.

7. John A. Howard, *Buyer Behavior in Marketing Strategy*, 2nd ed. (Englewood Cliffs, NJ: Prentice Hall, 1994), pp. 101, 128–89, and F. G. Crane and T. K. Clarke, *Consumer Behaviour in Canada: Theory and Practice*, 2nd edition (Toronto: Dryden, 1994), pp. 26–28.

8. William J. McDonald, "Time Use in Shopping: The Role of Personal Characteristics," *Journal of Retailing* (Winter 1994), pp. 345–66;

Robert J. Donovan, John R. Rossiter, Gillian Marcoolyn, and Andrew Nesdale, "Store Atmosphere and Purchasing Behavior, "*Journal of Retailing* (Fall 1994), pp. 283–94; and Eric A. Greenleaf and Donald R. Lehman, "Reasons for Substantial Delay in Consumer Decision Making," *Journal of Consumer Research* (September 1995), pp. 186–99.

9. For a review of how computer-mediated buying can influence the consumer decision process, see Russell S. Winer et al., "Choice in Computer-Mediated Environments," *Marketing Letters*, vol. 8, no. 3 (1997), pp. 287–96.

10. Ruth N. Bolton and James H. Drew, "A Multistage Model of Customers' Assessment of Service Quality and Value," *Journal of Consumer Research* (March 1991), pp. 376–84.

11. Jagdish N. Sheth, Banwari Mitral, and Bruce Newman, *Consumer Behavior* (Fort Worth, TX: Dryden Press, 1999), p. 22.

12. Frederick F. Reicheld and Thomas Teal, "The Loyalty Effect," (Boston: Harvard Business School Press, 1996), "What's a Loyal Customer Worth?" *Fortune* (December 11, 1985); and Lisa A. Yorgey "Case Study: Sears Canada," *Target Marketing* (January 2002), p. 22.

13. Rahul Jacob, "The Struggle to Create an Organization for the 21st Century," *Fortune* (April 3, 1995), pp. 90–99.

14. John E. G. Bateson and K. Douglas Hoffman, *Managing Services Marketing*, Fourth Edition (Forth Worth: Dryden, 1998).

15. For an overview of research on involvement, see John C. Mowen and Michael Minor, *Consumer Behavior*, 5th ed. (Upper Saddle River, NJ: Prentice Hall, 1998), pp. 64–68; and Frank R. Kardes, *Consumer Behavior* (Reading, MA: Addison-Wesley, 1999), pp. 256–58.

16. For an overview on the three problem-solving variations, see Hawkins, Best, and Coney, *Consumer Behavior*, pp. 498–501; Howard, *Buyer Behavior*, pp. 69–162.

17. Russell Belk, "Situational Variables and Consumer Behavior," *Journal of Consumer Research* (December 1975), pp. 157–63. Representative recent studies on situational influences are discussed in Mowen and Minor, *Consumer Behavior*, pp. 451–75.

18. A. H. Maslow, *Motivation and Personality* (New York: Harper & Row, 1970). See also Richard Yalch and Frederic Brunel, "Need Hierarchies in Consumer Judgments of Product Designs: Is It Time to Reconsider Maslow's Hierarchy?" in Kim Corfman and John Lynch, eds., *Advances in Consumer Research* (Provo, UT: Association for Consumer Research, 1996), pp. 405–10.

19. Arthur Koponen, "The Personality Characteristics of Purchasers," *Journal of Advertising Research* (September 1960), pp. 89–92; Joel B. Cohen, "An Interpersonal Orientation to the Study of Consumer Behavior," *Journal of Marketing Research* (August 1967), pp. 270–78; and Rena Bartos, *Marketing to Women Around the World* (Cambridge, MA: Harvard Business School, 1989).

20. Terry Clark, "International Marketing and National Character: A Review and Proposal for an Integrative Theory," *Journal of Marketing* (October 1990), pp. 66–79.

21. Fawzia Sheikh, "Covering New Online Territory," *Sales and Marketing Management*, October 2000, p.143.

22. For an interesting analysis of self-concept, see Russell W. Belk, "Possessions and the Extended Self," *Journal of Consumer Research* (September 1988), pp. 139–68.

23. Myron Magnet, "Let's Go for Growth," *Fortune* (March 7, 1994), p. 70.

24. This example provided in Michael R. Solomon, *Consumer Behavior*, 4th ed. (Upper Saddle River, NJ: Prentice Hall, 1999), p. 59.

25. For further reading on subliminal perception, see Anthony G. Greenwald, Sean C. Draine, and Richard L. Abrams, "Three Cognitive Markers of Unconscious Semantic Activation," *Science* (September 1996), pp. 1699–1701; Joel Saegert, "Why Marketing Should Quit Giving Subliminal Advertising the Benefit of the Doubt," *Psychology & Marketing* (Summer 1987), pp. 107–20; Dennis L. Rosen and Surenda N. Singh, "An Investigation of Subliminal Embed Effect on

Multiple Measures of Advertising Effectiveness," *Psychology & Marketing* (March/April 1992), pp. 157–173; and Kathryn T. Theus, "Subliminal Advertising and the Psychology of Processing Unconscious Stimuli: A Review of Research," *Psychology & Marketing* (May/June 1994), pp. 271–90.

26. "I Will Love This Story," *U.S. News & World Report* (May 12, 1997), p. 12; "Dr. Feelgood Goes Subliminal," *Business Week* (November 6, 1995), p. 6; and "Firm Gets Message Out Subliminally," *Dallas Morning News* (February 2, 1997), pp. 1H, 6H.

27. "Customer Loyalty: Going, Going . . . ," *American Demographics* (September 1997), pp. 20–23; *Brand-Driven Marketers Are Beating Themselves in the War Against Price-Based and Private Label Competition* (New York: Bates USA, 1994), and Jo Marney, "Building Splurchases," *Marketing* (January 27, 1997); July 18, 1997.

28. Martin Fishbein and I. Aizen, *Belief, Attitude, Intention and Behavior: An Introduction to Theory and Research* (Reading, MA: Addison Wesley Publishing, 1975), p. 6.

29. Richard J. Lutz, "Changing Brand Attitudes through Modification of Cognitive Structure," *Journal of Consumer Research* (March 1975), pp. 49–59. See also Mowen and Minor, *Consumer Behavior*, pp. 287–88.

30. "Pepsi's Gamble Hits Freshness Dating Jackpot," *Advertising Age* (September 19, 1994), p. 50.

31. "The Marketing 100: Colgate Total," *Advertising Age* (June 29, 1998), p. 544.

32. "The Frontiers of Psychographics," *American Demographics* (July 1996), pp. 38–43; http://future.sri.com. See also "You Can Buy A Thrill: Chasing the Ultimate Rush," *American Demographics* (June 1997), pp. 47–51.

33. Michael Adams, *Better Happy Than Rich? Canadians, Money, and the Meaning of Life* (Toronto: Penguin Books Canada, Ltd. 2001), p. 33.

34. Michael Adams, *Better Happy Than Rich? Canadians, Money, and the Meaning of Life* (Toronto: Penguin Canada Ltd., 2000) pp. 189-204.

35. See, for example, Lawrence F. Feick and Linda Price, "The Market Maven: A Diffuser of Marketplace Information," *Journal of Marketing* (January 1987), pp. 83–97; and Peter H. Block, "The Product Enthusiast: Implications for Marketing Strategy," *Journal of Consumer Marketing* (Summer 1986), pp. 51–61.

36. "Survey: If You Must Know, Just Ask One of These Men," *Marketing News* (October 25, 1992), p. 13.

37. "Maximizing the Market with Influentials," *American Demographics* (July 1995), p. 42.

38. "Put People Behind the Wheel," *Advertising Age* (March 22, 1993), p. S-28.

39. F. G. Crane and T. K. Clarke, "The Identification of Evaluative Criteria and Cues Used in Selecting Services," *Journal of Services Marketing* (Spring 1988), pp. 53–59.

40. Representative recent work on positive and negative word of mouth can be found in Robert E. Smith and Christine A. Vogt, "The Effects of Integrating Advertising and Negative Word-of-Mouth Communications on Message Processing and Response," *Journal of Consumer Psychology*, 4 (1995), pp. 133–51; Paula Bone, "Word-of-Mouth Effects on Short-Term and Long-Term Product Judgments," *Journal of Business Research*, 32 (1995), pp. 213–23; Chip Walker, "Word of Mouth," *American Demographics* (July 1995), pp. 38–45; and Dale F. Duhan, Scott D. Johnson, James B. Wilcox, and Gilbert D. Harrell, "Influences on Consumer Use of Word-of-Mouth Recommendation Sources," *Journal of the Academy of Marketing Science* (Fall 1997), pp. 283–95.

41. "We Will Bury You . . . With a Snickers Bar," *U.S. News and World Report* (January 26, 1998), p. 50ff; "A Beer Tampering Scare in China Shows Peril of Global Marketing," *The Wall Street Journal* (November 3, 1995), p. B1; and "Pork Rumors Vex Indonesia," *Advertising Age* (February 16, 1989), p. 36.

42. David Serchay, "Urban Legends Reference Page," January 2002, p. 34.

43. For an extended discussion on reference groups, see Wayne D. Hoyer and Deborah J. MacInnis, *Consumer Behavior* (Boston: Houghton Mifflin Co., 1997), Chapter 15.

44. For an extended discussion on consumer socialization, see George P. Moschis, *Consumer Socialization* (Lexington, MA: Lexington Books, 1987).

45. "Get 'em While They're Young," *Marketing News* (November 10, 1997), p. 2.

46. This discussion is based on J. Paul Peter and Jerry C. Olson, *Consumer Behavior and Marketing Strategy*, 5th ed. (New York: Irwin/McGraw-Hill 1999), pp. 341–43; Robert E. Wilkes, "Household Life-Cycle Stages, Transitions, and Product Expenditures," *Journal of Consumer Research* (June 1995), pp. 27–42; and Jan Larson, "The New Face of Homemakers," *American Demographics* (September 1997), pp. 45–50.

47. Diane Crispell, "Dual-Earner Diversity," *American Demographics* (July 1995), pp. 32–37.

48. "Wearing the Pants," *BRANDWEEK* (October 20, 1997), pp. 20, 22; and "Look Who's Shopping," *Progressive Grocer* (January 1998), p. 18.

49. "Marketing," *BRANDWEEK* (May 18, 1998), pp. 46–52; and "Teen Green," *American Demographics* (February 1998), p. 39. See also James V. McNeal, "Tapping the Three Kids' Markets," *American Demographics* (April 1998), pp. 37–41; and "Hey Kid, Buy This," *Business Week* (June 30, 1997), pp. 62–69.

50. For a discussion of social class in Canada see Crane and Clarke, pp. 127–49.

51. Milton Yinger, "Ethnicity," *Annual Review of Sociology* (1985), pp. 151–80.

52. Francois Vary, "Quebec Consumer Has Unique Buying Habits," *Marketing* (March 23, 1992), p. 28; Louise Gagnon, "Metro Plays to Decline in Impulse Purchases," *Marketing* (May 12, 1997) www.marketingmag.ca, July 20, 1997; Louise Gagnon, "Eaton's Quebec Ads Target Hip Shoppers," *Marketing* (June 16, 1997) www.marketingmag.ca, July 18, 1997; Louise Gagnon, "Price Cuts Escalate Beer Battle," *Marketing* (June 30, 1997) www.marketingmag. ca, July 17, 1997.

53. Jo Marney, "Counting Ethnic Canadians In," *Marketing* (June 4, 2001), p. 32.

54. Ann Boden, "Aiming at the Right Target," *Marketing* (January 28, 1991), p. 6.

The Consumer on the Couch: This case was prepared by Barry Potyondi, Context Inc. Sources: Paco Underhill, *Why We Buy: The Science of Shopping* (New York: Simon and Schuster), 1999; "Retail Trade: Service Industries Overviews Series," *Industry Canada* (March 2001). p. 1 (sales figure from 2000 and employment statistic from 1999); Julie McCann, "Design that makes you buy: the tricks and techniques retailers use to separate you from your money," *National Post Business* (May 2001), pp. 62–68; "Canadian retail ripe for picking, Underhill says: Global competitors are coming, top consultant warns," *Financial Post-National Post* (March 9, 2002), p. FP5; Hollie Shaw, "Space: female shoppers' frontier: buying differences. Women more likely to spend time in an uncluttered store," *Financial Post-National Post* (October 23, 2000), p. C3; Hilary Davidson, "6 ways to sell more. Your one-stop shopping guide to today's best retail business opportunities," *Profit Magazine* (April 2002) (www.profitguide.com/magazine/issues_article.asp?ID=884); ABCNEWS.com, "Chat Transcript: Learning About The Science of Shopping with Paco Underhill." www.abcnews.go.com/onair/DailyNews/chat_990511underhill.html; Elizabeth Razzi, "Retailers' Siren Song. Merchants use psychology to entice you into spending more. Knowing what they know will make you a smarter shopper," *Kiplinger's Personal Finance* (November 2000); (www.kiplinger.com/magazine/archives/2000/November/spending/SHOPPING.html); "Retail anthropologist tracks time and money: Canadian malls 'frumpy'," *Canadian Press Newswire* (June 23, 2000); Scott S. Smith, "Attention, shoppers! Paco Underhill knows what they look at, what they buy and why, so get ready to put a huge dent in the concept of customers' free will," *Entrepreneur* (December 2001) (www.entrepreneur.com/Magazines/MA_SegArticle/0,1539,294668----1-,00.html)

CHAPTER 6

1. Interview with Gary Null, Honeywell, MICRO SWITCH Division, August 25, 1998.
2. Peter LaPlaca, "From the Editor," *Journal of Business and Industrial Marketing* (Summer 1992), p. 3.
3. Statistics Canada, www.statcan.ca, CANSIM II, 377-0002, September 3, 2001.
4. Statistics Canada, www.statcan.ca, CANSIM II, 385-0002, September 3, 2001.
5. www.statcan.ca/english/subjects/standard/index.htm; downloaded September 2, 2001.
6. An argument that consumer buying and organizational buying do not have important differences is found in Edward F. Fern and James R. Brown, "The Industrial/Consumer Marketing Dichotomy: A Case of Insufficient Justification," *Journal of Marketing* (Spring 1984), pp. 68–77. However, most writers on the subject do draw distinctions between the two types of buying. See, for example, Michael D. Hutt and Thomas W. Speh, *Business Marketing Management*, 7th ed. (Fort Worth, TX: Dryden Press, 2001); and H. Michael Hayes, Per V. Jenster, and Nils-Erik Aaby, *Business Marketing: A Global Perspective* (Chicago: Richard D. Irwin, 1996).
7. This listing and portions of the following discussion are based on F. Robert Dwyer and John F. Tanner, Jr., *Business Marketing*, 2nd ed. (Burr Ridge, IL: McGraw-Hill/Irwin, 2002; Edward G. Brierty, Robert W. Eckles, and Robert R. Reeder, *Business Marketing*, 3rd ed. (Upper Saddle River, NJ: Prentice Hall, 1998); Frank G. Bingham, Jr., *Business Marketing Management* (Lincolnwood, IL: NTC, 1998).
8. "Rumble Over Tokyo," *Business Week* (April 2, 2001), p. 80–82; "FedEx Chooses Airbus 380," www.airwise.com (January 16, 2001); "Qatar Opts for Super Jumbo," www.airwise.com (March 1, 2001); "Understanding the Next 20 Years," www.airwise.com/products/A380_Market (downloaded April 22, 2001).
9. "Latin Trade Connection," *Latin Trade* (June 1997), p. 72.
10. For a study of buying criteria used by industrial firms, see Daniel H. McQuiston and Rockney G. Walters, "The Evaluative Criteria of Industrial Buyers: Implications for Sales Training," *Journal of Business & Industrial Marketing* (Summer/Fall 1989), pp. 65–75. See also "What Buyers Look For," *Sales & Marketing Management* (August 1995), p. 31.
11. "Small Firms Flock to Quality System," *Nation's Business* (March 1998), pp. 66–67.
12. Michael R. Leenders and David L. Blenkhorn, *Reverse Marketing: The New Buyer-Supplier Relationship* (New York: Free Press, 1996).
13. "Chrysler's Neon," *Business Week* (May 3, 1993), p. 119.
14. For a discussion on JIT, see Douglas M. Lambert, James R. Stock, and Lisa M. Ellram, *Fundamentals of Logistics Management* (New York: Irwin/McGraw-Hill, 1998).
15. "$35 Million Machine: Wires Not Included," *Newsweek* (April 15, 1995), p. 25.
16. www.ibm.com/procurement/html/principles_practices, downloaded April 18, 2001; and Hayes, Jenster, and Aaby, *Business Marketing: A Global Perspective*.
17. Pratibha A. Dabholkar, Wesley J. Johnston, and Amy S. Cathey, "The Dynamics of Long-Term Business-to-Business Exchange Relationships," *Journal of Academy of Marketing Science*, vol. 22, 2 (1994), pp. 130–45.
18. www.internationaldelivers.com/news_room, April 26, 2002.
19. James C. Anderson and James A. Narus, *Business Market Management* (Upper Saddle River, NJ: Prentice Hall, 1999); and Neil Rackham, Lawrence Friedman and Richard Ruff, *Getting Partnering*

Right (New York: McGraw-Hill, 1996); and Joseph P. Cannon and Christian Homburg, "Buyer-Supplier Relationships and Customer Firm Costs, *Journal of Marketing* (January 2001), pp. 29–43.
20. Thomas V. Bonoma, "Major Sales: Who Really Does the Buying?" *Harvard Business Review* (May–June 1982), pp. 11–19. For recent research on buying centers, see Morry Ghinghold and David T. Wilson, "Buying Center Research and Business Marketing Practices: Meeting the Challenge of Dynamic Marketing," *Journal of Business & Industrial Marketing*, vol. 13, no. 2 (1998), pp. 96–108; and Philip L. Dawes, Don Y. Lee, and Grahame R. Dowling, "Information Control and Influence in Emerging Buying Centers," *Journal of Marketing* (July 1998), pp. 55–68.
21. Paul A. Herbig, *Handbook of Cross-Cultural Marketing* (New York: The Halworth Press, 1998).
22. Jule M. Bristor, "Influence Strategies in Organizational Buying: The Importance of Connections to the Right People in the Right Places," *Journal of Business-to-Business Marketing*, vol. 1 (1993), pp. 63–98.
23. These definitions are adapted from Frederick E. Webster, Jr., and Yoram Wind, *Organizational Buying Behavior* (Englewood Cliffs, NJ: Prentice Hall, 1972), p. 6.
24. "Can Corning Find Its Optic Nerve?" *Fortune* (March 19, 2001), pp. 148–50.
25. Representative studies on the buy-class framework that document its usefulness include Erin Anderson, Wujin Chu, and Barton Weitz, "Industrial Purchasing: An Empirical Exploration of the Buy-Class Framework," *Journal of Marketing* (July 1987), pp. 71–86; Morry Ghingold, "Testing the 'Buy-Grid' Buying Process Model," *Journal of Purchasing and Materials Management* (Winter 1986), pp. 30–36; P. Matthyssens and W. Faes, "OEM Buying Process for New Components: Purchasing and Marketing Implications," *Industrial Marketing Management* (August 1985), pp. 145–57; and Thomas W. Leigh and Arno J. Ethans, "A Script-Theoretic Analysis of Industrial Purchasing Behavior," *Journal of Marketing* (Fall 1984), pp. 22–32. Studies not supporting the buy-class framework include Joseph A. Bellizi and Philip McVey, "How Valid Is the Buy-Grid Model?" *Industrial Marketing Management* (February 1983), pp. 57–62; and Donald W. Jackson, Janet E. Keith, and Richard K. Burdick, "Purchasing Agents' Perceptions of Industrial Buying Center Influences: A Situational Approach," *Journal of Marketing* (Fall 1984), pp. 75–83.
26. See, for example, R. Vekatesh, Ajay Kohli, and Gerald Zaltman, "Influence Strategies in Buying Centers," *Journal of Marketing* (October 1995), pp. 61–72; Gary L. Lilien and Anthony Wong, "An Exploratory Investigation of the Structure of the Buying Center in the Metal Working Industry," *Journal of Marketing Research* (February 1984), pp. 1–11; and Wesley J. Johnston and Thomas V. Bonoma, "The Buying Center: Structure and Interaction Patterns," *Journal of Marketing* (Summer 1981), pp. 143–56. See also, Christopher P. Puto, Wesley E. Patton III, and Ronald H. King, "Risk Handling Strategies in Industrial Vendor Selection Decisions," *Journal of Marketing* (Winter 1985), pp. 89–98.
27. "Evolution, Not Revolution," *Forbes* (May 21, 2001), pp. 38–39; "Business Connections: The Wired Way We Work," *Newsweek* (April 30, 2001), p. 59; and "Behind the Crystal Ball," *The Industry Standard* (March 26, 2001), pp. 81–83.
28. This discussion is based on Mark Roberti, "General Electric's Spin Machine," *The Industry Standard* (January 22–29, 2001), pp. 74–83; "Smart Business 50," *Smart Business* (November 2000), pp. 121–50; and "Grainger Lightens Its Digital Load," *Industrial Distribution* (March 2001), pp. 77–79.
29. "Internet Trading Exchanges: E-Marketplaces Come of Age," *Fortune* (April 15, 2001), special section; and "Private Exchanges May Allow B-to-B Commerce to Thrive After All," *The Wall Street Journal* (March 16, 2001), pp. B1, B4.
30. This discussion is based on "B2B . . . to Be?" *Forbes* (August 21, 2000), pp. 125–30; "e-Marketmakers: How Digital Marketplaces are

Shaping the Future of B2B Commerce," Forrester Research, downloaded May 25, 2001; and Steven Kaplan and Mohanbir Sawhney, "E-Hubs: The New B2B Marketplaces," *Harvard Business Review* (May–June, 2000), pp. 97–103.

31. "A Little Guy's Marketplace," *Time* (November 27, 2000), pp. B15–B20; Eric Young, "Web Marketplaces that Really Work," Fortune/CNET Tech Review (Winter 2002), pp. 78–86.

32. This discussion is based on "Let's Build an Online Supply Network!" *The Wall Street Journal* (April 17, 2000), pp. B1, B4.

33. Robyn Meredith, "Harder Than the Hype," *Forbes* (April 16, 2001), pp. 188–94; "Some Assembly Required," *Business 2.0* (February 12, 2001), pp. 25–29.

34. A major portion of this discussion is based on Robert J. Dolan and Youngme Moon, "Pricing and Market Making on the Internet," *Journal of Interactive Marketing* (Spring 2000), pp. 56–73; and "Auctions Have Taken the Internet by Storm," *Dallas Morning News* (January 25, 2001), pp. 1F, 9F.

35. Bob Tedeschi, "GE Has a Bright Idea," *Smart Business* (June 2001), pp. 86–91.

36. Sandy Jap, "Going, Going, Going," *Harvard Business Review* (November–December, 2000), p. 30.

Lands' End: This case is based on information available on the company Website (www.landsend.com) and the following sources: Robert Berner, "A Hard Bargain at Lands' End?" *Business Week* (May 28, 2001), p. 14; Rebecca Quick, "Getting the Right Fit—Hips and All—Can a Machine Measure You Better Than Your Tailor?" *The Wall Street Journal* (October 18, 2000), p. B1; Stephanie Miles, "Apparel E-tailers Spruce Up for Holidays," *The Wall Street Journal* (November 6, 2001), p. B6; Dana James, "Custom Goods Nice Means for Lands' End," *Marketing News* (August 14, 2000), p. 5.

CHAPTER 7

1. Sarah Smith, "Sweet On Icewines," www.marketingmag.ca, downloaded August 20, 2002.

2. These estimates are based on data from *International Trade Statistics 2001* (Geneva: World Trade Organization) and trend projections by the authors. Trade statistics reported in this chapter also came from this source, unless otherwise indicated.

3. Masaaki Kotabe and Kristiaan Helsen, *Global Marketing Management*, 2nd ed. (New York: Wiley, 2001), p. 440.

4. "Bartering Gains Currency in Hard-Hit Southeast Asia," *The Wall Street Journal* (April 6, 1998), p. A10; and Beatrice B. Lund, "Corporate Barter as a Marketing Strategy," *Marketing News* (March 3, 1997), p. 8.

5. Statistics Canada, CANSIM matrix 6547, and cat.13-001XIB, www.statcan.ca., downloaded August 17, 2001.

6. Statistics Canada, CANSIM matrixes 3651 and 3685, www.statcan.ca, downloaded August 17, 2001.

7. Michael E. Porter, *The Competitive Advantage of Nations* (New York: The Free Press, 1990), pp. 577–615. For another view that emphasizes cultural differences, see David S. Landes, *The Wealth and Poverty of Nations* (New York: Norton, 1998).

8. Roger L. Martin and Michael E. Porter, "Canadian Competitiveness: Nine Years After the Crossroads," www.mgmt.utoronto.ca/research/competitive.htm, downloaded May 5, 2002.

9. "Trade Winds," *The Economist* (November 8, 1997), pp. 85–86.

10. "The Beef Over Bananas," *The Economist* (March 6, 1999), pp. 65–66; Gary C. Hufbauer and Kimberly A. Elliott, *Measuring the Cost of Protection in the United States* (Washington, D.C.: Institute for International Economics, 1994).

11. "It Ain't Just Peanuts," *Business Week* (December 18, 1995), p. 30.

12. This discussion is based on information provided by the World Trade Organization, at www.wto.org, downloaded April 20, 2001.

13. "Industrial Evolution," *Business Week* (April 27, 1998), pp. 100–01.

14. "Special Report: The Euro," *Business Week* (April 27, 1998), pp. 90–108.

15. "Betting on Free Trade," *Business Week* (April 23, 2001), pp. 60–62; and Gary S. Becker, "It's Time for NAFTA to Look Farther South," *Business Week* (January 8, 2001), p. 28.

16. "Special Report: East Asian Economies," The Economist (March 7, 1998), p. 88.

17. www.juniper.net/company, May 1, 2001; and General Mills, Inc., Annual Report, 2000.

18. For an excellent overview of different types of global companies and marketing strategies, see Warren J. Keegan, *Global Marketing Management*, 6th ed. (Upper Saddle River, NJ: Prentice Hall, 1999), pp. 43–54.

19. "Global Companies Don't Work; Multinationals Do," *Advertising Age* (April 18, 1994), p. 23; and David Benady, "Unilever in Global Ad Shake-Up," *Marketing Week* (February 11, 1999), p. 7.

20. For an extensive discussion on identifying global consumers, see Jean-Pierre Jeannet and H. David Hennessey, *Global Marketing Strategies*, 4th ed. (Boston: Houghton Mifflin, 1998).

21. Elissa Moses, *The $100 Billion Allowance: Accessing the Global Teen Market* (New York: Wiley, 2000); "Tracking Asia's Teens," *AdAge Global* (December 2001), pp. 26–27; "MTV Returns to Japan," *AdAge Global* (September 2000), p. 10; and "Bennetton Bounces Back," *Brandweek* (February 12, 2001), pp. 1, 8.

22. This discussion is based on "Behind the Crystal Ball," *The Industry Standard* (March 26, 2001), pp. 81–83; "The World's Online Populations," www.cyberatlas.com, downloaded April 15, 2001; "Fast Stats," *The Industry Standard* (November 27–December 4, 2000), p. 164; "Majority of Users will be Non-English Speakers," www.nua.ie, downloaded April 10, 2001; and "Global E-Commerce Approaches Hypergrowth," Forrester Research Press Release, April 25, 2000.

23. For comprehensive references on cross-cultural aspects of marketing, see Paul A. Herbig, *Handbook of Cross-Cultural Marketing* (New York: The Halworth Press, 1998); and Jean-Claude Usunier, *Marketing Across Cultures*, 2nd ed. (London: Prentice Hall Europe, 1996). Unless otherwise indicated, examples found in this section appear in these excellent sources.

24. "Clash of Cultures," *Brandweek* (May 4, 1998), p. 28. See also R. L. Tung, *Business Negotiations with the Japanese* (Lexington, MA: Lexington Books, 1993).

25. These examples appear in Del I. Hawkins, Roger J. Best, and Kenneth A. Coney, *Consumer Behavior*, 8th ed. (Burr Ridge, IL: McGraw-Hill/Irwin, 2001), chapter 2.

26. "Greeks Protest Coke's Use of Parthenon," *Dallas Morning News* (August 17, 1992), p. D4.

27. Saeed Saimee, "Customer Evaluation of Products in a Global Market," *Journal of International Business Studies*, third quarter, 1994, pp. 579–604.

28. "Geo Gaffes," *Brandweek* (February 23, 1998), p. 20.

29. "Global Thinking Paces Computer Biz," *Advertising Age* (March 6, 1995), p. 10.

30. Terrence A. Shimp and Subhash Sharma, "Consumer Ethnocentrism, Construction and Validation of the CETSCALE," *Journal of Marketing Research* (August 1987), pp. 280–89.

31. Jill Gabrielle Klein, Richard Ettenson, and Marlene D. Morris, "The Animosity Model of Foreign Product Purchase: An Empirical Test in the People's Republic of China," *Journal of Marketing* (January 1998), pp. 89–100.

32. This discussion is based on "So You Really Want To Do Business in China?" *Forbes* (July 24, 2000), pp. 92–96; "Coke Pours into Asia," *Business Week* (October 21, 1996), pp. 22–25.

33. "Selling in Russia: The March on Moscow," *The Economist* (March 18, 1995), pp. 65–66.

34. "Rubles? Who Needs Rubles?" *Business Week* (April 13, 1998), pp. 45–46.

35. "Betting on a New Label: Made in Russia," *Business Week* (April 12, 1999), p.122; "Russia and Central–Eastern Europe: Worlds Apart," *Brandweek* (May 4, 1998), pp. 30–31; "We Will Bury You . . . with a Snickers Bar," *U. S. News & World Report* (January 26, 1998), pp. 50–51.

36. Chip Walker, "The Global Middle Class," *American Demographics* (September 1995), pp. 40–47.

37. "Consumer Abroad: Developing Shopaholics," *U. S. News & World Report* (February 10, 1997), p. 55.

38. "Mattel Plans to Double Sales Abroad," *The Wall Street Journal* (February 11, 1998), pp. A3, A11.

39. Philip R. Cateora and John L. Graham, *International Marketing*, 11th ed. (Burr Ridge, IL: McGraw-Hill/Irwin, 2002), p. 560; and "Honda Takes Currency Hit in Europe," *The Wall Street Journal* (March 28, 2001), p. A16.

40. "EU Turning Into Battleground over More Curbs on Marketing," *Advertising Age* (September 18, 2000), p. 60; "Europe Forges Ahead with Web Innovations," *Marketing News* (August 14, 2000), p. 8; "Will East Asia Slam the Door?" *The Economist* (September 12, 1998), p. 88.

41. Sarah Smith, "Sweet on Icewines," www.marketingmag.ca, downloaded August 20, 2001.

42. The ISO Survey of ISO 9000 and ISO 14000 Certificates (Geneva, Switzerland: International Organization for Standardization, 2000).

43. For an extensive and recent examination of these market entry options, see, for example, Johny K. Johansson, *Global Marketing: Foreign Entry, Local Marketing, and Global Management*, 2nd ed. (Burr Ridge, IL: McGraw Hill/Irwin, 2000); Keegan, *Global Marketing Management*; Kotabe and Helson, *Global Marketing Management*; and Cateora and Graham, *International Marketing*.

44. Sarah Smith, "Sweet on Icewines," www.marketingmag.ca, downloaded August 20, 2001.

45. "McDonald's Reports Global Results," Corporate Press Release (January 24, 2001).

46. Avraham Shama, "Entry Strategies of U.S. Firms to the Newly Independent States, Baltic States, and Eastern European Countries," *California Management Review* (Spring 1995), pp. 90–109.

47. Michael Hirsch, "The New China: Tricks of the Trade," Newsweek (June 29, 1998), pp. 40–42.

48. "China's Coming Telecom Battle," *Fortune* (November 27, 2000), pp. 209–14; "Mercedes: Made in Alabama," *Fortune* (July 7, 1997), pp. 150ff.; and "Car Power," *Business Week* (October 23, 2000), pp. 72ff.

49. "Harley-Davidson Establishes Wholly-Owned Italian Subsidiary," Company News Release (October 13, 2000); and Shama, "Entry Strategies of U.S. Firms."

50. The examples in this section are found in "The Color of Beauty," *Forbes* (November 22, 2000), pp. 170–76; "It's Goo, Goo, Goo, Goo Vibrations at the Gerber Lab," *The Wall Street Journal* (December 4, 1996), pp. A1, A6; Donald R. Graber, "How to Manage a Global Product Development Process," *Industrial Marketing Management* (November 1996), pp. 483–98; and Herbig, *Handbook of Cross-Cultural Marketing*.

51. Jagdish N. Sheth and Atul Parvatiyar, "The Antecedents and Consequences of Integrated Global Marketing," *International Marketing Review*, vol. 18, no. 1 (2001), pp. 16–29. Also see, D. Szymanski, S. Bharadwaj, and R. Varadarajan, "Standardization versus Adaptation of International Marketing Strategy: An Empirical Investigation," *Journal of Marketing* (October 1993), pp. 1–17.

52. This discussion is based on John Fahy and Fuyuki Taguchi, "Reassessing the Japanese Distribution System," *Sloan Management Review* (Winter 1995), pp. 49–61; and Edward Tse, "The Right Way to Achieve Profitable Growth in the Chinese Consumer Market," *Strategy & Business* (Second Quarter, 1998), pp. 10–21.

53. "Parallel Imports: A Grey Area," *The Economist* (June 13, 1998), pp. 61–62; and "When Grey Is Good," *The Economist* (August 22, 1998), p. 17.

CNS Breathe Right Strips: This case was prepared by Giana Eckhardt. Sources: CNS, Inc. 1997 Annual Report (Minneapolis, MN: CNS, Inc., 1998); and personal interviews with Dr. Daniel E. Cohen and Kirk P. Hodgdon of CNS (June 1998).

PART 2 CASE

1. Andy Riga, "The Web Now Sells Toys to Vegetables," *The Financial Post-National Post* (December 10, 1998), p. C10; and www.nielsenratings.com (Top 25 Properties).

2. Angus Reid, "Your Net is ready: pollster Angus Reid puts his finger on the most important Internet trends and what you should do about them," *Profit: The Magazine for Canadian Entrepreneurs* (May 2001), p. 70.

3. Anne E. Scholosser, Sharon Shavitt, and Alaina Kanfer, "Survey of Internet users' attitudes toward Internet advertising," *Journal of Interactive Marketing* (1999), vol. 13, no. 3, pp. 34–54.

4. Marina Strauss, "U.S. Web sites Click with Canadian Shoppers," *Globe and Mail* (Tuesday, June 15, 1999), p. B1/B13.

5. Ipsos-Reid, "Canadians boost online spending," Public Release Date March 13, 2001 (www.angusreid.com).

6. Angus Reid, "Your Net is ready: pollster Angus Reid puts his finger on the most important Internet trends and what you should do about them," *Profit: The Magazine for Canadian Entrepreneurs* (May 2001), p. 70.

7. Andrea Z. Aster, "Portals cozy up to French market," *Marketing* (December 4, 2000), p. 3.

8. Ipsos-Reid, "Canadians boost online spending."

9. David Steinhart, "Canadians top Net bankers, US leads shopping stakes: Ipsos-Reid poll," *Financial Post-National Post* (August 22, 2001), p. C7.

10. Brent Lemanski and Kent S. Jamison, "Perceptions of Canadian financial planning needs," *LIMRA's Market Facts Quarterly* (Spring 2001), p. 22.

11. Don Tapscott, *Growing up Digital: the Rise of the Net Generation* (McGraw-Hill, 1998), p. 3.

12. Ibid, p. 36.

13. Julliet O'Neill, "Report refutes Web surfer stereotype," *Financial Post-National Post* (December 12, 2001), p. FP5.

14. Don Tapscott, p. 56.

15. Kortney Stringer, "E-commerce (a special report): Cover story–Young and restless: Teenagers spend a huge amount of time on the Web; but not buying," *Wall Street Journal* (September 24, 2001), p. R8.

16. Ipsos-Reid, "Young Americans first in line at virtual till," Media Release, February 23, 2001 (www.angusreid.com).

17. "Internet to play bigger role in distribution," *Purchasing* (April 22, 1999), pp. 47–50.

18. Marina Strauss, "U.S. Web sites Click with Canadian Shoppers," *The Globe and Mail* (June 15, 1999), p. B13.

19. "E-commerce: The bedrock beneath the shifting sands," *Canadian Business* (March 19, 2001), p. 81 (advertising supplement).

20. Ken Mark, "E-commerce confab," *Purchasing B2B* (April 2001), p. 10.

21. Jennifer Brown, "Airline B2B to help cut costs," *Computing Canada* (January 26, 2001), p. 9.

22. Robert Thompson, "Nothing like bills in that old electronic mailbox," *Financial Post-National Post* (May 29, 2001), p. C7.

23. Lesley Young, "Provincial privacy regs on the way," *Marketing* (August 27, 2001).

CHAPTER 8

1. John Horn, "Studios Play Name Game," *Star Tribune* (August 10, 1997), p. F11.

2. *2000 US Economic Review*, Worldwide Market Research Department, Motion Picture Association of America, pp. 14, 16.

3. Willow Bay, "Test Audiences Have Profound Effect on Movies," *CNN Newsstand & Entertainment Weekly* (September 28, 1998).

4. Thomas R. King, "How Big Will Disney's *Pocahontas* Be?" *The Wall Street Journal* (May 15, 1995), pp. B1, B8.

5. Richard Turner and John R. Emshwiller, "Movie-Research Czar Is Said by Some to Sell Manipulated Findings," *The Wall Street Journal* (December 26, 1993), p. A1.

6. Helene Diamond, "Lights, Camera . . . Research!" *Marketing News* (September 11, 1989), pp. 10–11; and "Killer!" *Time* (November 16, 1987), pp. 72–79.

7. Jeff Stickler, "*Titanic* Director Was Floating on Air after Local Test," *Star Tribune* (December 26, 1997), pp. D1, D2.

8. Carl Diorio, "Tracking Projectings: B. O. Calculations an Inexact Science," *Variety* (May 24, 2001).

9. For an expanded definition, consult the American Marketing Association's Website at www.ama.org/about/ama/markdef.asp; for a researcher's comments on this and other definitions of marketing research, see Lawrence D. Gibson, "Quo Vadis, Marketing Research?" *Marketing Research* (Spring 2000), pp. 36–41.

10. Joseph Pereira, "Unknown Fruit Takes on Unfamiliar Markets," *The Wall Street Journal* (September 9, 1995), pp. B1, B5.

11. Cyndee Miller, "Kiddi Just Fine in the U.K., But Here It's Binky," *Marketing News* (August 28, 1995). p. 8.

12. Michael J. McCarthy, "Ford Companies Hunt for a 'Next Big Thing' but Few Can Find One," *The Wall Street Journal* (May 6, 1997), pp. A1, A6.

13. "Focus on Consumers," *General Mills Midyear Report* (Minneapolis, MN: January 8, 1998), pp. 2–3.

14. Michael J. McCarthy, "Stalking the Elusive Teenage Trendsetter," The Wall Street Journal, (November 19, 1998), pp. B1, B10.

15. Roy Furchgott, "For Cool Hunters, Tomorrow's Trend is the Trophy," *The New York Times* (June 28, 1998), p. 10; and Emily Nelson, "The Hunt for Hip: A Trend Scout's Trail," *The Wall Street Journal* (December 9, 1998), pp. B1, B6.

16. Dale Burger, "Pushing Creativity to the Limit," *Computing Canada* (May 24, 1995), p. 37.

17. Joshua Grossnickle and Oliver Raskin, "What's Ahead on the Internet," *Marketing Research* (Summer 2001), pp. 9–13.

18. www.marketingmag.ca, downloaded August 20, 2001; and www.grogate.com and www.grocerygateway.com, downloaded May 5, 2002.

19. "Arbitron TV, Cable and Radio Audience Meter Passes Important U.S. Test Milestone," Arbitron news release (July 19, 2001), pp. 1–3. See www.arbitron.com/newsreleases/releases/2001/arbitron+PPM.htm.

20. Mark Maremont, "New Toothbrush Is Big-Ticket Item," *The Wall Street Journal* (October 27, 1998), pp. B1, B6; Emily Nelson, "P&G Checks Out Real Life," *The Wall Street Journal* (May 17, 2001), pp. B1, B4.

21. Gerry Khermouch, "Consumers in the Mist," *Business Week* (February 26, 2001), pp. 92, 94.

22. Dina Elboghdady, "Naked Truth," *Portland Press* (March 5, 2002), pp. C1, C5.

23. Patrick E. Murphy and Gene R. Laczniak, "Emerging Ethical Issues Facing Marketing Researchers," *Marketing Research* (June 1992), pp. 6–11.

24. Adapted from Donald S. Tul and Del I. Hawkins, *Marketing Research: Measurement and Method*, 5th ed. (New York: Macmillan Publishing, 1990), Chapter 23.

25. Mark A. Moon, John T. Mentzer, Carlo D. Smith, and Michael S. Garver, "Seven Keys to Better Forecasting," *Business Horizons* (September–October 1998), pp. 44–52.

26. Statistics Canada, CANSIM II 051-0001, 080-0001, 277-001, 02 and 63-005XIB, downloaded April 25, 2002; and www.retailcouncil.org, downloaded April 25, 2002.

27. Doug McCuaig and Christopher Holt, "Getting Intimate with Customers" Marketing (July 14, 1997), www.marketingmag.ca, downloaded July 17, 1997.

Bookworms, Inc.: This case was prepared by James E. Nelson.

CHAPTER 9

1. Material on sneakers is based on the SGMA Report 2000, "The U.S. Athletic Footwear Market Today," which is published annually by the Sporting Goods Manufacturers Association (www.sgma.com) based on a study by the NPD Group (www.npd.com). NPD polls 35 000 consumers and over 3 500 retailers to provide this information.

2. Ibid.

3. Ibid.

4. Ibid.

5. Matt Forney, "Harry Potter, Meet 'Ha-li Bo-te,'" *The Wall Street Journal* (September 21, 2000), p. B1; and Gerry Khermouch, "Buzzzz Marketing," *Business Week* (July 30, 2001), pp. 50–56.

6. David Leohnardt, "Two-Tier Marketing," *Business Week* (March 17, 1997), pp. 82–90.

7. "Special Report on Mass Customization: A Long March," *The Economist* (July 14, 2001), pp. 63–65.

8. Dana James, "Custom Goods Nice Means for Lands' End," *Marketing News* (August 14, 2001), pp. 5–6; Greg Morago, "Customizing for the Masses," *Star Tribune* (July 10, 2000), pp. E1, E3; Alex Witchel, "Custom Blend of Fragrance Is Most Personal," *Star Tribune* (July 10, 2000), pp. E1, E3; and Louise Lee, "Can Levi's Be Cool Again?" *Business Week* (March 13, 2000), pp. 144–48.

9. "Keeping the Customer Satisfied," *The Economist* (July 14, 2001), pp. 9–10.

10. Goldfarb Consultants, Toronto, February, 1999.

11. Example provided by Allison Scoleri, Goldfarb Consultants, Toronto, February 1, 1999.

12. Ibid.

13. Chris Daniels, "Wild for Wildless," www.marketingmag.ca, June 4, 2001.

14. Sanjoy S. Mehta and Gurinderjit B. Mehta, "Development and Growth of the Business Class: Strategic Implications for the Airline Industry," *Journal of Customer Service in Marketing and Management*, vol. 3, no. 1 (1997), pp. 59–78.

15. *National Consumer Survey Choices 3 Crosstabulation Report: Fast-Food Restaurants* (New York: Simmons Market Research Bureau, Spring, 2001).

16. Jennifer Ordonez, "Taco Bell Chef Has New Tactic: Be Like Wendy's," *The Wall Street Journal* (February 23, 2001), pp. B1, B4; and Jennifer Ordonez, "An Efficiency Drive: Fast-Food Lanes Are Getting Even Faster," *The Wall Street Journal* (May 18, 2000), pp. A1, A10.

17. The discussion of Apple's segmentation strategies through the years is based on information from its Website: www.apple-history.com/history.html.

18. Jim Carlton, "Apple to Post Profit Again on Sales Gains," *The Wall Street Journal* (January 6, 1999); pp. A3, A8.

19. Ibid.

20. Ibid.

21. Dennis Sellers, "Business Journal: Digital Hub Plan Just Might Work," *MacCentral* (January 16, 2001), Mac Publishing, LLC.

22. Wes George, "Opinion: Apple's Business Strategy," *MacCentral* (January 16, 2001), Mac Publishing LLC.

23. Kevin Lane Keller, "The Brand Report Card," *Harvard Business Review* (January–February 2000), pp. 147–57.

24. Rebecca Winters, "Chocolate Milk," *Time* (April 30, 2001), p. 20.

Nokia: This case was written by Michael Vessey and Steven Hartley based on information available on the company Website (www.nokia.com); correspondence with Keith Nowak; a personal interview with Paul Dittner of Gartner Dataquest; Ari Bensinger, "Weaker Signals for Mobile Phone Firms," *Business Week Online*, April 6, 2001; "The Cellular Telecommunications & Internet Association's Wireless Industry Survey," see www.wow-com.com; "Nokia's First Imaging Phone Marks Start of

Multimedia Messaging Era," Nokia press release, November 19, 2001; "New Nokia 6340 Handset to Enable Roaming Across TDMA, GSM Networks," Nokia press release, January 7, 2002; "Nokia Unveils a New Active Category for Mobile Phones," Nokia press release, November 19, 2001; "Users Say 'No Thanks' to Mobile Advertising Unless Vendors Take Right Approach," In-Stat Group press release, October 31, 2001, see www.instat.com.

PART 3 CASE

1. Dawne Shand, "Web is big news at media companies," *Informationweek* (September 21, 1999), p. 225.
2. Statistics Canada, "Service Indicators, 3rd Quarter 2001," cat. no. 63-016-XIB, p. 40.
3. Ibid, p. 46.
4. "The future of Canadian publishing: eleven industry leaders describe the road ahead," *Quill and Quire* (April 2000), p. 19.
5. Dawne Shand, "Web is big news at media companies."
6. Jim Milliot, "Industry sales float in 2001 at $25 billion," *Publishers Weekly* (March 4, 2002), p. 16.
7. Natalie Danford, "The paperback comeback," *Publishers Weekly* (July 30, 2001), p. 20.
8. James A. Matin, "Spinning a New Web," *Publishers Weekly* (April 26, 1999), p. 36.
9. www.nytimes.com/2000/11/29KING.html.
10. Judith Rosen, "And the sales keep climbing," *Publishers Weekly* (November 2000), p. 42.
11. Elena Cherney, "Harlequin Books ditch fairy tale to snag singles—Canadian Publisher is launching new series to target younger audience," *Wall Street Journal* (August 2, 2001), p. B4.
12. www.eharlequin.com.
13. Judith Rosen, "And the sales keep climbing."
14. Jana K. Riess, "New genres, emerging audiences," *Publishers Weekly* (August 21, 2001), p. S4.
15. Marc Aronson, "Coming of age," *Publishers Weekly* (February 11, 2002), p. 82.
16. Marc Aronson, "Coming of age."
17. Amanda Rogers, "Movie to fuel Potter mania: No shortage of all things boy wizard," *Calgary Herald* (March 18, 2001), p. C4.
18. Wayne Friedman, "Research shows who's just wild about 'Harry,'" *Advertising Age* (November 12, 2001), p. 34.
19. "Bookstores break sales records with release of new Harry Potter book," *Canadian Press Newswire* (July 10, 2000) (newswire article); and Harold Bloom, "Can 35 million book buyers be wrong? Yes," *Wall Street Journal* (July 11, 2000), p. A26.
20. Alan Cowell, "Bloomsbury believes in magic," *Financial Post-National Post* (October 20, 1999), p. C19.
21. "Fourth Harry Potter book arrives amid pajama party fanfare," *Canadian Press Newswire* (July 2, 2000) (newswire article).
22. Amanda Rogers, "Movie to fuel Potter mania."
23. Robert J. Wiersema, "Vancouver book camp gets children writing," *Quill and Quire* (September 2001), p. 10.
24. Daisy Maryles, "Behind the bestsellers," *Publishers Weekly* (December 17, 2001), p. 17.

CHAPTER 10

1. Personal interview with Kenneth M. Hart, Ph.D., 3M, 2001.
2. Ibid.
3. Terry Fiedler, "3M Innovation to Be Tested," *Star Tribune* (December 10, 2000), pp. D1, D11.
4. Definitions within this section are adapted from Peter D. Bennett, *Dictionary of Marketing Terms*, 2nd ed. (Lincolnwood, IL: NTC Publishing Group, 1995) and Committee on Definitions, *Marketing Definitions: A Glossary of Marketing Terms* (Chicago: American Marketing Association, 1985).

5. Julia Angwin, "Latest Dot-Com Fad Is a Bit Old-Fashioned: It's Called Profitability," *The Wall Street Journal* (August 14, 2001), pp. A1, A6.
6. Ronald Grover, Tom Lowry, and Larry Armstrong, "TV Guy Henry Yuen of Gemstar-TV Guide Wants to Take Control of Your Television," *Business Week* (March 12, 2000), pp. 66–76; and Steve Jarvis, "Interactive TV Now Pioneering Marketing Option," *Marketing News* (August 27, 2001), pp. 1, 19, 20.
7. Clayton M. Christenson, *The Innovator's Dilemma: When Technologies Cause Great Firms to Fail* (Cambridge, MA: Harvard Business School Press, 1997); and Stephen A. Butscher and Michael Laker, "Market-Driven Product Development," *Marketing Management* (Summer 2000), pp. 48–53.
8. Greg A. Stevens and James Burley, "3,000 Raw Ideas = 1 Commercial Success!" *Research-Technology Management* (May–June 1997), pp. 16–27.
9. R. G. Cooper and E. J. Kleinschmidt, "New Products—What Separates Winners from Losers?" *Journal of Product Innovation Management* (September 1987), pp. 169–84; and Robert G. Cooper, *Winning at New Products*, 2nd ed. (Reading, MA: Addison-Wesley, 1993), pp. 49–66; and Thomas D. Kuczmarski, "Measuring Your Return on Innovation," *Marketing Management* (Spring 2000), pp. 25–32.
10. Greg Burns, "Has General Mills Had Its Wheaties?" *Business Week* (May 8, 1995), pp. 68–69.
11. John Gilbert, "To Sell Cars in Japan, U.S. Needs to Offer More Right-Drive Models," *Star Tribune* (May 27, 1995), p. M1.
12. Marcia Mogelonsky, "Product Overload?" *American Demographics* (August 1998), pp. 5–12.
13. Amy Merrick, "As 3M Chief, McNerney Wastes No Time Starting Systems Favored by Ex-Boss Welch," *The Wall Street Journal* (June 5, 2001), pp. B1, B4; see General Electric's website (www.ge.com) for an in-depth explanation of Six Sigma that 3M and other Fortune 500 companies use to improve quality: "The Road to Customer Impact: What Is Six Sigma?"
14. Eric von Hippel, Stefan Thomke, and Mary Sonnock, "Creating Breakthroughs at 3M," *Harvard Business Review* (September–October 1999), pp. 47–57.
15. Morgan L. Swink and Vincent A. Mabert, "Product Development Partnerships: Balancing Needs of OEMs and Suppliers," *Business Horizons* (May–June 2000), pp. 59–68.
16. Alec Klein, "The Techies Grumbled, but Polaroid's Pocket Turned into a Huge Hit," *The Wall Street Journal* (May 2, 2000), pp. A1, A10.
17. www.sony.com
18. Otis Port, "Xerox Won't Duplicate Past Errors," *Business Week* (September 29, 1998), pp. 98–101.
19. Dennis Berman, "Now Tennis Balls Are Chasing Dogs," *Business Week* (July 23, 1998), p. 138.
20. Gary Hammel, "Innovation's New Math," *Fortune* (July 9, 2001), pp. 130–31.
21. Gardiner Harris, "With Big Drugs Dying, Merck Didn't Merge—It Found New Ones," *The Wall Street Journal* (January 10, 2001), pp. A1, A10.
22. Bill Vlasic, "When Air Bags Aren't Enough," *Business Week* (June 8, 1998) pp. 84–86; and Arthur J. Cummins, "Detroit Faces Crunch Time: Designing Gentler SUVs," *The Wall Street Journal* (February 25, 1998), pp. B1, B9.
23. Tom Molson and George Sproles, "Styling Strategy," *Business Horizons* (September–October 2000), pp. 45–52.
24. Jennifer Ordonez, "How Burger King Got Burned in Quest to Make the Perfect Fry," *The Wall Street Journal* (January 16, 2001), pp. A1, A8.

Palm Inc.: This case was written by Michael Vessey and Steven W. Hartley.

CHAPTER 11

1. Information supplied by Clearly Canadian Beverage Corporation, January 3, 2002.

2. For an extended discussion of the generalized product life-cycle curve, see David M. Gardner, "Product Life Cycle: A Critical Look at the Literature," in Michael Houston, ed., *Review of Marketing 1987* (Chicago: American Marketing Association, 1987), pp. 162–94; and Donald R. Lehmann and Russell S. Winer, *Product Management*, 3rd ed. (Burr Ridge, IL: McGraw-Hill/Irwin, 2002), pp. 261–65.

3. Glenn Rifkin, "Mach 3: Anatomy of Gillette's Latest Global Launch," *Strategy & Business* (Second Quarter 1999), pp. 34–41.

4. Orville C. Walker, Jr., Harper W. Boyd, Jr., and Jean-Claude Larréché, *Marketing Strategy*, 3rd ed. (New York: Irwin/McGraw Hill, 1999), p. 231.

5. Portions of the discussion on the fax machine industry are based on "The Technology That Won't Die," *Forbes* (April 5, 1999), p. 56; "Facsimile Is Still Preferred Method of Communication," *Purchasing Online* downloaded April 13, 2001; "Think Fax: The Technology, Not the Machine," *Purchasing Online* downloaded June 15, 2001; and "Atlas Electronic Corporation," in Roger A. Kerin and Robert A. Peterson, *Strategic Marketing Problems: Cases and Comments*, 8th ed. (Upper Saddle River, NJ: Prentice Hall, 1998), pp. 494–506.

6. "There's No Replacement—Not Even E-Mail," *Purchasing Online*, downloaded June 15, 2001; "Fax Is Still a Favorite, Despite the Alternatives," *Computing Canada* (June 25, 1999), pp. 62–65; and "We've All Got Mail," *Newsweek* (May 15, 2000), p. 73k.

7. "Why Coke Indulges (the Few) Fans of Tab," *The Wall Street Journal* (April 13, 2001), pp. B1, B4.

8. "Gillette's Edge," *Brandweek* (May 28, 2001), p. 5.

9. "How to Separate Trends from Fads," *Brandweek* (October 23, 2000), pp. 30, 32.

10. "Video-Game Sales Fell in 2000, Following Years of Record Growth," *The Wall Street Journal* (January 16, 2001), p. B6; "Video-Game Industry Is Seen Expanding at a Rapid Clip Next Five Years," *The Wall Street Journal* (May 25, 2001), p. B7; and "Video-Game Sales Surge More Than 30%," *The Wall Street Journal* (July 26, 2001), p. B10.

11. Everett M. Rogers, *Diffusion of Innovations*, 4th ed., (New York: Free Press, 1995).

12. Jagdish N. Sheth, Banwasi Mitral, and Bruce Newman, *Consumer Behavior* (Fort Worth, TX: Dryden Press, 1999).

13. www.marketingmag.ca, downloaded March 8, 1999.

14. For a historical perspective on the product/brand manager system, see George S. Low and Ronald A. Fullerton, "Brands, Brand Management, and the Brand Manager System: A Critical-Historical Evaluation," *Journal of Marketing Research* (May 1994), pp. 173–90.

15. "Haggar, Farah, Levi's Iron Out the Wrinkles," *Advertising Age* (March 6, 1995), p. 12; and John Heinzl, "Heinz squeezes out purple ketchup," *The Globe and Mail* (August 7, 2001), p. B8; and "Soda sales: Pepsi's going blue, Coke vanilla," *Portland Press*, May 8, 2002, p. 8C.

16. "Mass-Market Brands See More Upscale Heads," *Advertising Age* (September 25, 2000), p. S16.

17. "That's Dried Plums to You," *Dallas Morning News* (February 2, 2001), p. 2D; and Kenneth Li, "Power Player," *The Industry Standard* (September 2000), pp. 138–48.

18. "P&G's Soap Opera: New Ivory Bar Hits the Bottom of a Tub," *The Wall Street Journal* (October 23, 1992), p. B11.

19. Philip R. Cateora and John L. Graham, *International Marketing*, 11th ed. (Burr Ridge, IL: McGraw-Hill/Irwin, 2002), p. 359; and "Sneaker Company Tags Out-of-Breath Baby Boomers," *The Wall Street Journal* (January 16, 1998), pp. B1, B2.

20. "More People Are Eating for Health," *Research Alert* (October 20, 2000), pp. 5–6; "Calcium Craze Invading Two New Food Categories," *Advertising Age* (March 20, 2000), p. 28; and "Juice Marketers Boost Health Claims," *Advertising Age* (November 13, 2000), p. 46.

21. "It's Crunch Time," *Brandweek* (January 29, 2001), p. 3; Bag of Chips Not All That," *Dallas Morning News* (January 5, 2001), pp. 1D, 3D; "Don't Raise the Price, Lower the Water Award," *Brandweek* (January 8, 2001), p. 19.

22. This discussion is based on Kevin Lane Keller, *Strategic Brand Management* (Upper Saddle River, NJ: Prentice Hall, 1998); and Jennifer L. Aaker, "Dimensions of Brand Personality," *Journal of Marketing Research* (August 1997), pp. 347–56. See also Susan Fournier, "Consumers and Their Brands: Developing Relationship Theory in Consumer Research," *Journal of Consumer Research* (March 1998), pp. 343–73.

23. For an extended treatment of brand equity, see David A. Aaker, *Building Strong Brands* (New York: Free Press, 1996).

24. This discussion is based on Kevin Lane Keller, "Building Customer-Based Brand Equity," *Marketing Management* (July–August 2001), pp. 15–19.

25. Susan Heinrich, "The Leafs' Budding Brand," *National Post*, June 4, 2001, p. C4.

26. "Licensed to Thrive," *Advertising Age* (June 19, 2000), p. 16; and "Walt Disney Finalizes Licensing Deals with Rival Toy Makers Hasbro and Mattel," *The Wall Street Journal* (September 21, 2000), p. B16.

27. "Losing the Name Game," *Newsweek* (June 8, 1998), p. 44.

28. "A Good Name Should Live Forever," *Forbes* (November 16, 1998), p. 88.

29. Rob Osler, "The Name Game: Tips on How to Get It Right," *Marketing News* (September 14, 1998), p. 50; and Keller, *Strategic Brand Management*. See also Pamela W. Henderson and Joseph A. Cote, "Guidelines for Selecting or Modifying Logos," *Journal of Marketing* (April 1998), pp. 14–30; and Chiranjeev Kohli and Douglas W. LaBahn, "Creating Effective Brand Names: A Study of the Naming Process," *Journal of Advertising Research* (January–February 1997), pp. 67–75.

30. "Buying the Ranch on Brand Equity," *Brandweek* (October 25, 1992), p. 6; and "Kellogg Changes Name of Controversial Cereal," *Marketing News* (August 19, 1991), p. 22.

31. "A Survey of Multinationals," *The Economist* (June 24, 1995), p. 8.

32. John A. Quelch and David Kenny, "Extend Profits, Not Product Lines," *Harvard Business Review* (September–October 1994), pp. 153–60.

33. For an overview of brand equity and brand extensions, see Vicki R. Lane, "Brand Leverage Power: The Critical Role of Brand Balance," *Business Horizons* (January–February 1998), pp. 25–84; and David C. Court, Mark G. Leitter, and Mark A. Loch, "Brand Leverage," *The McKinsey Quarterly*, no. 2 (1999); pp. 100–10.

34. "When Brand Extension Becomes Brand Abuse," *Brandweek* (October 26, 1998), pp. 20, 22.

35. Stephanie Thompson, "Brand Buddies," *Brandweek* (February 23, 1998), pp. 22–23ff. For an in-depth discussion on co-branding, see Akshay R. Rao and Robert W. Ruekert, "Brand Alliances as Signals of Product Quality," *Sloan Management Review* (Fall 1994), pp. 87–97.

36. "Unilever Pares Down to Leading Brands," *Mergers and Acquisitions* (April 2001), pp. 18–22.

37. David Dunne and Chakravarthi Narasimhan, "The New Appeal of Private Labels," *Harvard Business Review* (May–June 1999), pp. 41–52.

38. "Kodak Pursues a Greater Market Share in Japan with New Private-Label Film," *The Wall Street Journal* (March 7, 1995), p. B11.

39. www.pez.com. downloaded August 30, 2001; "The National Peztime," *The Dallas Morning News* (October 9, 1995), pp. 1C, 2C; David Welch, Collecting Pez (Murphysboro, IL: Bubba Scrubba Publications, 1995); and "Pez Dispense with Idea It's Just for Kids," *Brandweek* (September 26, 1996), p. 10.

40. "Just the Facts," *Research Alert* (July 2001), p. 5.

41. "L'eggs Hatches a New Hosiery Package," *Brandweek* (January 1, 2001), p. 6.

42. "Coca-Cola Finds Success Trading New for the Old," *The Wall Street Journal* (March 24, 1995), p. B5.

43. Lawrence L. Garber, Jr., Raymond R. Burke, and Morgan Jones, "The Role of Package Color in Consumer Purchase Consideration and Choice," *Marketing Science Institute*, Report No. 00-104, 2000.

44. Cateora and Graham, *International Marketing*, pp. 369–72.

45. "Asian Brands Are Sprouting English Logos in Pursuit of Status, International Image," *The Wall Street Journal* (August 7, 2001), p. B7C.

46. This discussion is based, in part, on Barry N. Rosen and George B. Sloane, III, "Environmental Product Standards, Trade and European Consumer Goods Marketing," *Columbia Journal of World Business* (Spring 1995), pp. 74–86; "Life Ever After," *The Economist* (October 9, 1993), p. 77; and "How to Make Lots of Money, and Save the Planet Too," *The Economist* (June 3, 1995); pp. 57–58. See also Stuart L. Hart, "Beyond Greening: Strategies for a Sustainable World," *Harvard Business Review* (January–February 1997), pp. 66–77; and Ajay Menon and Anil Menon, "Enviropreneurial Marketing Strategy: The Emergence of Corporate Environmentalism as Market Strategy," *Journal of Marketing* (January 1997), pp. 51–67.

47. Paula Mergenbagen, "Product Liability: Who Sues?" *American Demographics* (June 1995), pp. 48–54; and "Bottled Up," *The Economist* (December 17, 1994), p. 69.

48. For representative research on warranties, see Joydeep Srivastava and Ansuuree Mitra, "Warranty as a Signal of Quality: The Moderating Effect of Consumer Knowledge on Quality Evaluations," *Marketing Letters* (November 1998), pp. 327–36; Melvyn A. Menezes and John A. Quelch, "Leverage Your Warranty Program, Sloan Management Review (Summer 1990), pp. 69–80; and "Broken? No Problem," *U.S. News & World Report* (January 11, 1999), pp. 68–69.

BMW: This case was written by Giana Eckhardt based on company interviews.

CHAPTER 12

1. "One-of-a-Kind Music and Dining Experience Ready to 'Rock' the Live Music Capital of the World," *PR Newswire* (June 25, 2001); "Hard Rock Café Reveals Its Own Treasures in New Book," *PR Newswire* (June 18, 2001); Stefani Eads, "A New Beat at the Hard Rock," *Business Week* (October 9, 2000), p. 166; Jeffrey A. Trachtenberg, "Ballad of a Mad Café," *Forbes* (November 19, 1984), pp. 288, 290.

2. B. Joseph Pine and James H. Gilmore, *The Experience Economy* (Boston: Harvard Business School Press); Rachel Brand, "Selling an Experience," *Denver Rocky Mountain News* (December 10, 2000), p. 1G; "The Personal Touch," *The Economist* (November 11, 2000); Jane E. Zarem, "Experience Marketing," *Folio* (October 2000); Scott MacStravic, "Make Impressions Last: Focus on Value," *Marketing News* (October 23, 2000), p. 44.

3. John E.G. Bateson and Douglas Hoffman, *Managing Services Marketing, Fifth Edition* (Fort Worth: Dryden 2001).

4. Herbert G. Grubel and Michael A. Walker, *Service Industry Growth* (Vancouver; The Fraser Institute, 1989).

5. Christopher H. Lovelock, *Services Marketing*, 4th edition (Upper Saddle River, NJ: Prentice-Hall, 2001).

6. Valarie A. Zeithhaml, 'How Consumer Evaluation Processes Differ Between Goods and Services," in James H. Donnelly and William R. Georges, eds., *Marketing of Services* (Chicago, IL; American Marketing Association, 1981).

7. Keith B. Murray, "A Test of Services Marketing Theory: Consumer Information Acquisition Activities," *Journal of Marketing* (January 1991), pp. 10–25; and F. G. Crane, *Professional Services Marketing: Strategy and Tactics* (New York: The Haworth Press, Inc., 1993).

8. Vicki Clift, "Everyone Needs Service Flow Charting," *Marketing News* (October 23, 1995), pp. 41, 43; Mary Jo Bitner, Bernard H. Booms, and Mary Stanfield Tetreault, "The Service Encounter: Diagnosing Favorable and Unfavorable Incidents," *Journal of Marketing*

(January 1990), pp. 71–84; Eberhard Scheuing, "Conducting Customer Service Audits," *Journal of Consumer Marketing* (Summer 1989), pp. 35–41; and W. Earl Susser, R. Paul Olsen, and D. Daryl Wyckoff, *Management of Service Operations* (Boston: Allyn & Bacon, 1978).

9. John Ozment and Edward Morash, "The Augmented Service Offering for Perceived and Actual Service Quality," *Journal of the Academy of Marketing Science* (Fall 1994), pp. 352–63.

10. A. Parasuraman, Valarie A. Zeithaml, and Leonard L. Berry, "Reassessment of Expectations as a Comparison Standard in Measuring Service Quality: Implications for Further Research," *Journal of Marketing* (January 1994), pp. 111–24; and Leonard L. Berry, *On Great Service* (New York: Free Press, 1995).

11. A. Parasuraman, Valarie A. Zeithaml, and Leonard L. Berry, "Reassessment of Expectations as a Comparison Standard in Measuring Service Quality."

12. Amy Ostrom and Dawn Iacobucci, "Consumer Trade-Offs and the Evaluation of Services," *Journal of Marketing* (January 1995), pp. 17–28; and J. Joseph Cronin, Jr., and Steven A. Taylor, "Measuring Service Quality: A Reexamination and Extension," *Journal of Marketing* (July 1992), pp. 55–68; A. H. Kizilbash, Nessim Y. Hanna, and John S. Wagle, "Is Gap Analysis a Useful Aid for Measuring Service Quality in Industrial Product Sales Organizations?" *Journal of Customer Service in Marketing and Management*, vol. 3, no. 4 (1997), pp. 75–80; Alain Genestre and Paul Herbig, "Service Quality: An Examination of Demographic Differences," *Journal of Customer Service in Marketing and Management*, vol. 3, no. 3 (1997), pp. 65–83; and Jack Dart, "Professional Service Quality: The Practice or the Professional?" *Journal of Customer Service in Marketing and Management*, vol. 3, no. 2 (1997), pp. 7–21.

13. Stephen S. Tax and Stephen W. Brown, "Recovering and Learning from Service Failure," *Sloan Management Review* (Fall 1998), pp. 75–88; Stephen S. Tax, Stephen W. Brown, and Murali Chandrashekaran, "Customer Evaluations of Service Complaint Experiences: Implications for Relationship Marketing," *Journal of Marketing* (April 1998), pp. 60–76; Stephen W. Brown, "Service Recovery Through IT," *Marketing Management* (Fall 1997), pp. 25–27; and Leonard L. Berry and A. Parasuraman, "Listening to the Customer—The Concept of a Service-Quality Information System," *Sloan Management Review* (Spring 1997), pp. 65–76.

14. Leonard L. Berry, "Relationship Marketing of Services—Growing Interest, Emerging Perspectives," *Journal of the Academy of Marketing Science* (Fall 1995), pp. 236–45; Mary Jo Bitner, "Building Service Relationships: It's All About Promises," *Journal of the Academy of Marketing Science* (Fall 1995), pp. 246–51; Kevin P. Gwinner, Dwayne D. Gremler, and Mary Jo Bitner, "Relational Benefits in Services Industries: The Customer's Perspective," *Journal of the Academy of Marketing Science* (Spring 1998), pp. 101–14; Susan Fournier, Susan Dobscha, and David Glen Mick, "Preventing the Premature Death of Relationship Marketing," *Harvard Business Review* (January–February 1998), pp. 42–51; and John V. Petrof, "Relationship Marketing: The Wheel Reinvented?" *Business Horizons* (November–December 1997), pp. 26–31.

15. Christopher Lovelock, *Services Marketing*; and Valarie A. Zeithaml and Mary Jo Bitner, *Services Marketing*, 2E (Burr Ridge, IL: McGraw-Hill, 2000)

16. Sundar G. Bharedwaj, P. Rajan Varadarajan and John Fahy, "Sustainable Competitive Advantage in Services Industries: A Conceptual Model and Research Propositions," *Journal of Marketing* (October 1993), pp. 83–99.

17. F. G. Crane, "The Relative Effect of Price and Personal Referral Cues on Consumers' Perceptions of Dental Services," *Health Marketing Quarterly*, vol. 13, no. 4 (1996), pp. 91–105.

18. Christopher Lovelock, *Services Marketing*, pp. 337–359.

19. Robert E. Hite, Cynthia Fraser, and Joseph A. Bellizzi, "Professional Service Advertising: The Effects of Price Inclusion, Justification, and Level of Risk," *Journal of Advertising Research* 30 (August/September 1990), pp. 23–31; and F. G. Crane, *Professional Services Marketing: Strategy and Tactics*.

20. F. G. Crane, *Professional Services Marketing: Strategy and Tactics*; and Kathleen Mortimer "Services Advertising: The Agency Viewpoint," Journal of Services Marketing No. 2 (2001) pp. 131–146.

21. Patriya Tansuhaj, Donna Randall, and Jim McCullough, "A Services Marketing Management Model: Integrating Internal and External Marketing Functions," *Journal of Services Marketing* (Winter 1988), pp. 31–38.

22. Christian Gronroos, "Internal Marketing Theory and Practice," in Tim Bloch, G. D. Upah, and V. A. Zeithaml, eds., *Services Marketing in a Changing Environment* (Chicago, IL: American Marketing Association, 1984); and Dennis J. Cahill, *Internal Marketing* (New York: The Haworth Press Inc., 1996).

23. Ibid.

24. Hong Lee and Robert Boissoneau, "Empowering People in Modern Organizations for Improved Customer Service," *Journal of Customer Service in Marketing and Management*, vol. 3, no. 2 (1997), pp. 55–69; and Scott W. Kelly, "Developing Customer Orientation among Service Employees," *Journal of the Academy of Marketing Science* (Winter 1992), pp. 27–36.

25. Frederick H. deB. Harris and Peter Peacock, "Hold My Place, Please," *Marketing Management* (Fall 1995), pp. 34–46, and Lovelock, p. 17.

26. Christopher Lovelock, *Services Marketing*

27. Thomas A. Stewart, "A New 500 for the New Economy," *Fortune* (May 15, 1995), pp. 166–78; Philip Elmer-Dewitt, "Mine, All Mine," *Time* (June 5, 1995), pp. 46–54; and James Brian Quinn and Penny C. Paquette, "Technology in Services: Creating Organizational Revolutions," *Sloan Management Review* (Winter 1990), pp. 67–78; and Joshua Quittner, "E-Book Report," *Time* (May 3, 1999), p. 84.

28. Timothy J. Mullaney, "Online Pics: A Sure Shot," *Business Week* (September 3, 2001), p. EB12; Adam Leitzes and Joshua Solan, "Use Napster Alternative LimeWire," *Forbes* (June 25, 2001), p. 56; Ginny Parker, "Looking for Prince Charming? In Japan, Check Your Cell Phone," *Time* (June 4, 2001), p. 88; Tim Larimer, "Internet I-mode," *Time* (March 5, 2001), pp. 54–56; Leyland Pitt, Pierre Berthon, and Richard T. Watson, "Cyberservice: Taming Service Marketing Problems with the World Wide Web," *Business Horizons* (January–February 1999), pp. 11–18; J. M. Stifle, "Best of the Web: Dating," *Forbes* (June 25, 2001), p. 109.

29. Pine and Gilmore, *The Experience Economy*.

30. Ibid.

NHL: This case was written by Frederick G. Crane. Source: National Hockey League.

CHAPTER 13

1. www.confederationbridge.com; and interview in CBSL, Aug. 2002.

2. www.lamborghini.itg.net and www.kbb.com.

3. Adapted from Kent B. Monroe, Pricing: *Making Profitable Decisions*, 2nd ed. (New York: McGraw-Hill, 1990), chapter 4. See also David J. Curry, "Measuring Price and Quality Competition," *Journal of Marketing* (Spring 1985), pp. 106–17.

4. Numerous studies have examined the price-quality-value relationship. See, for example, Jacob Jacoby and Jerry C. Olsen, eds., *Perceived Quality* (Lexington, MA: Lexington Books, 1985); William D. Dodds, Kent B. Monroe, and Dhruv Grewal, "Effects of Price, Brand, and Store Information on Buyers' Product Evaluations," *Journal of Marketing Research* (August 1991), pp. 307–19; and Roger A. Kerin, Ambuj Jain, and Daniel J. Howard, "Store Shopping Experience and Consumer Price-Quality-Value

Perceptions," *Journal of Retailing* (Winter 1992), pp. 235–45. For a thorough review of the price-quality-value relationship, see Valerie A. Ziethaml, "Consumer Perceptions of Price, Quality, and Value," *Journal of Marketing* (July 1998), pp. 2–22.

5. These examples are from Roger A. Kerin and Robert A. Peterson, "Throckmorten Furniture (A)," *Strategic Marketing Problems: Cases and Comments*, 9th ed. (Englewood Cliffs, NJ: Prentice Hall, 1998), pp. 235–45.

6. F. G. Crane, "The Relative Effect of Price and Personal Referral Cues on Consumers' Perceptions of Dental Services," *Health Marketing Quarterly*, vol 13, no. 4, 1996, pp. 91–105.

7. N. Craig Smith and John A. Quelch, *Ethics in Marketing* (Homewood, IL: Richard D. Irwin, 1993); and F. G. Crane, "What's Ethical and What's Not with Canadian Business Students," *Working Paper*, 1997.

8. Carol VinZant, "Electronic Books Are Coming at Last," *Fortune* (July 6, 1998), pp. 119–24.

9. Mike Dodd, "Cards Hold 50 Years of Memories," *USA Today* (March 27, 2001), pp. 1A, 2A; J. C. Conklin, "Don't Throw Out Those Old Sneakers, They're a Gold Mine," *The Wall Street Journal* (September 21, 1998) pp. A1, A20.

10. Daniel Levy, Mark Bergen, Shautanu Dutta, and Robert Venable, "The Magnitude of Menu Costs: Direct Evidence from Large U.S. Supermarket Chains," *The Quarterly Journal of Economics* (August 1997), pp. 791–825.

11. David Wessel, "The Price Is Wrong, and Economics Are in an Uproar," *The Wall Street Journal* (January 2, 1991), pp. B1, B6.

12. Ron Winslow, "How a Breakthrough Quickly Broke Down for Johnson & Johnson," *The Wall Street Journal* (September 18, 1998), pp. A1, A5.

13. Bruce Orwall, "Hollywood's Costs Rose 8% in 2000 to a Record High," *The Wall Street Journal* (March 7, 2001), p. B6; and Bruce Orwall, "Theater Consolidation Jolts Hollywood Power Structure," *The Wall Street Journal* (January 21, 1998), pp. B1, B2.

14. Jeff Lobb, "The Right (Pepsi) Stuff," *Marketing* (July 8, 1996), p. 15.

15. "Price War Is Raging in Europe," *Business Week* (July 6, 1992), pp. 44–45.

16. Michael Garry, "Dollar Strength: Publishers Confront the New Economic Realities," *Folio: The Magazine for Magazine Management* (February 1989), pp. 88–93; Cara S. Trager, "Right Price Reflects a Magazine's Health Goals," *Advertising Age* (March 9, 1987), pp. 5–8ff; and Frank Bruni, "Price of Newsweek? It Depends," *Dallas Times Herald* (August 14, 1986), pp. S1, S20.

17. Vanessa O'Connell, "How Campbell Saw a Breakthrough Menu Turn into Leftovers," *The Wall Street Journal* (October 6, 1998), pp. A1, A12.

18. Janice Revell, "The Price Is Not Always Right," *Fortune* (May 14, 2001), p. 240; Indrajit Sinha, "Cost Transparency: The Net's Real Threat to Prices and Brands," *Harvard Business Review* (March–April 2000), pp. 43–50; Walter Baker, Mike Marn, and Craig Zawada, "Price Smarter on the Net," *Harvard Business Review* (February 2001), pp. 122–27.

19. For an overview of price elasticity studies, see Ruth N. Bolton, "The Robustness of Retail-Level Elasticity Estimates," *Journal of Retailing* (Summer 1989), pp. 193–219; and Gerald J. Tellis, "The Price Elasticity of Selective Demand: A Meta-analysis of Econometric Models of Sales," *Journal of Marketing Research* (November 1988), pp. 331–41.

20. See, for example, Susan L. Holak and Srinivas K. Reddy, "Effects of a Television and Radio Advertising Ban: A Study of the Cigarette Industry," *Journal of Marketing* (October 1986), pp. 219–27; and Rick Andrews and George R. Franke, "Time-Varying Elasticities of U.S. Cigarette Demand, 1933–1987," *AMA Educators' Conference Proceedings* (Chicago: American Marketing Association, 1990), p. 393.

21. Linda Himelstein, "Webvan Left the Basics on the Shelf," *Business Week* (July 23, 2001), p. 43.
22. Kent B. Monroe, *Pricing: Making Profitable Decisions,* 2nd ed. (New York: McGraw-Hill, 1990), pp. 24–26.

Washburn International: The case is based on information and materials provided by the company.

CHAPTER 14

1. "Product News," gillette.com, downloaded June 15, 2001; "New Duracell Ultra with M3 Technology Is Now Available in North America; Breakthrough Design Makes Duracell Ultra the Most Powerful Battery in the World, Even More Powerful," The Gillette Company Press Release, September 26, 2000; "Duracell Makes Best Alkaline Battery Better with Duracell Ultra 3 Design," The Gillette Company Press Release, January 25, 2000.
2. "Nintendo Gamecube Set at Mass Market Price of $199.95"; "Dedicated Gameplay System Launches November 5, 2001, with Six First-Party Titles Priced at $49.95," Nintendo of America, Inc., Press Release, May 21, 2001.
3. For the classic description of skimming and penetration pricing, see Joel Dean, "Pricing Policies for New Products," *Harvard Business Review* (November–December 1976), pp. 141–53. See also, Reed K. Holden and Thomas T. Nagle, "Kamikaze Pricing," *Marketing Management* (Summer 1998), pp. 31–39.
4. Jean-Noel Kapferer, "Managing Luxury Brands," *The Journal of Brand Management* (July 1997), pp. 251–60.
5. "Time Is Money," *Forbes* (September 18, 2000), pp. 178–85.
6. "Premium AA Alkaline Batteries," *Consumer Reports* (March 21, 2001), p. 54; Kemp Powers, "Assault and Batteries," *Forbes* (September 4, 2000), pp. 54, 56; "Razor Burn at Gillette," *Business Week* (June 18, 2001), p. 37.
7. See, for example, V. Kumar and Robert P. Leone, "Measuring the Effects of Retail Store Promotions on Brand and Store Substitution," *Journal of Marketing Research* (May 1998), pp. 178–85; and "AT&T Simplifies Price Tiers," *Dallas Morning News* (November 5, 1997), p. 1D.
8. "Why That Deal Is Only $9.99," *Business Week* (January 10, 2000), p. 36. For further reading on odd–even pricing, see Robert M. Schindler and Thomas M. Kilbarian, "Increased Consumer Sales Response Through Use of 99-Ending Prices," *Journal of Retailing* (Summer 1996), pp. 187–99; Mark Stiving and Russell S. Winer, "An Empirical Analysis of Price Endings with Scanner Data," *Journal of Consumer Research* (June 1997), pp. 57–67; and Robert M. Schindler, "Patterns of Rightmost Digits Used in Advertised Prices: Implications for Nine-Ending Effects," *Journal of Consumer Research* (September 1997), pp. 192–201.
9. Thomas T. Nagle and Reed K. Holden, *The Strategy and Tactics of Pricing,* 3rd ed. (Englewood Cliffs, NJ: Prentice Hall, 2002), pp. 243–49.
10. www.rogers.com.
11. Kent B. Monroe, *Pricing: Making Profitable Decisions,* 2nd ed. (New York: McGraw-Hill, 1990), pp. 326–27. For a recent discussion of this topic, see Ramarao Desiraju and Steven M. Shugan, "Strategic Service Pricing and Yield Management," *Journal of Marketing* (January 1999), pp. 44–56.
12. Robert J. Dolan and Hermann Simon, *Power Pricing: How Managing Price Transforms the Bottom Line* (New York: Free Press, 1996), p. 249.
13. Peter M. Noble and Thomas S. Gruca, "Industrial Pricing: Theory and Managerial Practice," *Marketing Science,* vol. 18, no. 3 (1999), pp. 435–54.
14. George E. Belch and Michael A. Belch, *Introduction to Advertising and Promotion,* 5th ed. (New York: Irwin/McGraw-Hill, 2001), p. 93.
15. For a comprehensive discussion on the experience curve, see Roger A. Kerin, Vijay Mahajan, and P. Rajan Varadarajan, *Contemporary*

Perspectives on Strategic Market Planning (Boston: Allyn and Bacon, 1990), chapter 4.
16. "Hewlett-Packard Cuts Office-PC Prices in Wake of Moves by Compaq and IBM," *The Wall Street Journal* (August 22, 1995), p. B11.
17. "Retailers Using Cut-Rate Videos as Lures," *Dallas Morning News* (October 4, 1995), p. 5H.
18. "Cheap Thrills for Shoppers," *Newsweek* (April 16, 2001), p. 45.
19. This discussion is based on "How Technology Tailors Price Tags," *The Wall Street Journal* (June 21, 2001), p. A1; Robert D. Holf, "The Buyer Always Wins," *Business Week* (March 22, 1999), pp. EB26–EB28.
20. "How Dell Fine-Tunes Its PC Pricing to Gain Edge in a Slow Market," *The Wall Street Journal* (June 8, 2001), pp. A1, A8.
21. www.strategis.ic.gc.ca.
22. Monroe, *Pricing,* p. 34.
23. F.G. Crane, "The Relative Effect of Price and Personal Referral Cues on Consumers' Perceptions of Dental Services," *Health Marketing Quarterly,* vol. 13, no. 4 (1996), pp. 91–100.
24. For an extended discussion about price wars, see Akshay R. Rao, Mark E. Bergen, and Scott Davis, "How to Fight a Price War," *Harvard Business Review* (March–April 2000), pp. 107–16.
25. For an extensive discussion on discounts, see Monroe, *Pricing,* chapters 14 and 15.
26. Ian Ayres and Peter Sigelman, "Race and Gender Discrimination in Bargaining for a New Car," *The American Economic Review* (June 1995), pp. 304–21; and "Goodbye to Haggling," *US News & World Report,* October 20, 1997, p. 57.

My Own Meals: Sources: Personal interview with Mary Anne Jackson; Mike Duff, "New Children's Meals: Not Just Kids Stuff," *Supermarket Business* (May 1990), p. 93; Heidi Parson, "MOM, Incorporated," *Poultry Processing* (August–September 1989); Lisa R. Van Wagner, "Kids' Meals: The Market Grows Up," *Food Business* (May 20, 1991); Mary Ellen Kuhn, "Women to Watch in the 90's," *Food Business* (September 10, 1990); and Arlene Vigoda, "Small Fry Microwave Meals Become Big Business," *USA Today* (June 4, 1990); My Own Meals, Inc. Website (www.myownmeals.com); Tom Richman, "The New American Start-up," Inc. (September, 1998), p. 54; Jerry Stroud, "Kids Specially Targeted in New Prepared-Dinner Market Effort," *St. Louis Post-Dispatch* (May 29, 1989), p. 5.

CHAPTER 15

1. avoncompany.com, downloaded July 25, 2001; Rochelle Kass, "Experimental Beauty," *The Journal News* (July 21, 2001), pp. 1D, 2D; Nanette Byrnes, "Avon: The New Calling," *Fortune* (September 18, 2000), pp. 136–48; "Retail Makeover," *Dallas Morning News* (May 9, 2001), p. 2D; and "Cosmetic Firms Try Change of Face," *Dallas Morning News* (September 19, 2000), p. 4D.
2. See Peter D. Bennett, ed., *Dictionary of Marketing Terms,* 2nd ed. (Chicago: American Marketing Association, 1996).
3. PepsiCo, Inc., Annual Report, 1997.
4. Donald V. Fites, "Make Your Dealers Your Partners," *Harvard Business Review* (March–April 1996), pp. 84–95.
5. This discussion is based on Bert Rosenbloom, *Marketing Channels: A Management View,* 6th ed. (Fort Worth, TX: Dryden Press, 1999), pp. 452–58.
6. www.the-cma.org.
7. For a discussion on strategic channel alliances, see P. Rajan Vandarajan and Margaret H. Cunningham, "Strategic Alliances: A Synthesis of Conceptual Foundations," *Journal of the Academy of Marketing Science* (Fall 1995), pp. 282–96; and Johny K. Johansson, "International Alliances: Why Now?" *Journal of the Academy of Marketing Science* (Fall 1995), pp. 301–4. The examples appear in "Pepsi, Ocean Spray Renew Deal; Fruitworks Expands," *Brandweek* (April 6, 1998), p. 14; and "GM Pondering Consolidations in Field Marketing," *Advertising Age* (May 11, 1998), p. 4.

8. General Mills, Inc., Annual Report, 2000.

9. For an extensive discussion of wholesaling, see Louis W. Stern, Adel I. El-Ansary, and Anne T. Coughlan, *Marketing Channels*, 5th ed. (Upper Saddle River, NJ: Prentice Hall, 1996), chapter 3.

10. For an overview of vertical marketing systems, see Lou Peltson, David Strutton, and James R. Lumpkin, *Marketing Channels* (Chicago: Irwin, 1997), chapter 14.

11. For a review of channel partnering, see Robert D. Bussell and Gwen Ortmeyer, "Channel Partnerships Streamline Distribution," *Sloan Management Review* (Spring 1995), pp. 85–96. See also Jakki J. Mohr and Robert E. Spekman, "Perfecting Partnerships," *Marketing Management* (Winter/Spring 1996), pp. 35–43.

12. Edwin R. Rigsbee, *The Art of Partnering* (Dubuque, IA: Kendall/Hunt Publishing, 1994), pp. 82–83.

13. Joshua Levine and Matthew Swibel, "Dr. No," *Forbes* (May 28, 2001), pp. 72–76.

14. "Radio Shack Campaign Touts Its RCA Alliance," *Advertising Age* (June 5, 2000), p. 61; "Radio Shack, Compaq Pact Is Extended," *Dallas Morning News* (April 20, 2000), p. 2D.

15. "Apple to Open 25 Retail Stores This Year in a Bid to Reach Out to New Customers," *The Wall Street Journal* (May 16, 2001), p. B8; "Strip Malls Are Gateway Country," *The Industry Standard* (November 27–December 4, 2000), pp. 82–86.

16. Jonathan Mandell, "Speed It Up Webmaster, We're Losing Billions Every Second," *The New York Times* (September 22, 1999), p. 58D.

17. "5 down 95 to Go," apple.com, downloaded July 25, 2001; "Apple Retail Stores Welcome over 7700 People in First Two Days," Apple Computer, Inc., press release, (May 21, 2001); and Cliff Edwards, "Sorry, Steve: Here's Why It Won't Work," *Business Week* (May 21, 2001), pp. 44–45.

18. "Gillette Tries to Nick Schick in Japan," *The Wall Street Journal* (February 4, 1991), pp. B3, B4.

19. This discussion is based on "Foreign Firms Think Their Way into Japan," *Nikkei Weekly* (September 20, 1999), pp. 8–9; John Fahy and Fuyuki Taguchi, "Reassessing the Japanese Distribution System," *Sloan Management Review* (Winter 1995), pp. 49–61; Michael R. Czinkota and Jon Woronoff, *Unlocking Japanese Markets* (Chicago: Probus Publishing, 1991), pp. 92–97; and "Japan Keeping U.S. Products out of Asia; Intricate Network Known as 'Keiretsu' Excludes Outsiders," *The Baltimore Sun* (November 9, 1997), p. 6F.

20. For a managerial discussion on channel conflict, see Christine B. Bucklin, Pamela A. Thomas-Graham, and Elizabeth A. Webster, "Channel Conflict: When Is It Dangerous?" *The McKinsey Quarterly* (Number 3, 1997), pp. 36–43.

21. "Black Pearls Recast for Spring," *Advertising Age* (November 13, 1995), p. 49.

22. Studies that explore the dimensions and use of power and influence in marketing channels include the following: Gul Butaney and Lawrence H. Wortzel, "Distributor Power versus Manufacturer Power: The Customer Role," *Journal of Marketing* (January 1988), pp. 52–63; Kenneth A. Hunt, John T. Mentzer, and Jeffrey E. Danes, "The Effect of Power Sources on Compliance in a Channel of Distribution: A Causal Model," *Journal of Business Research* (October 1987), pp. 377–98; John F. Gaski, "Interrelations among a Channel Entity's Power Sources: Impact of the Exercise of Reward and Coercion on Expert, Referent, and Legitimate Power Sources," *Journal of Marketing Research* (February 1986), pp. 62–67; Gary Frazier and John O. Summers, "Interfirm Influence Strategies and Their Application within Distribution Channels," *Journal of Marketing* (Summer 1984), pp. 43–55; Sudhir Kale, "Dealer Perceptions of Manufacturer Power and Influence Strategies in a Developing Country," *Journal of Marketing Research* (November 1986), pp. 387–93; George H. Lucas and Larry G. Gresham, "Power, Conflict, Control, and the Application of Contingency Theory in Channels of Distribution," *Journal of the Academy of Marketing Science* (Summer 1985), pp. 27–37; and F. Robert Dwyer and Julie Gassenheimer, "Relational Roles and Triangle Dramas: Effects on Power Play and Sentiments in Industrial Channels," *Marketing Letters*, vol. 3 (1992), pp. 187–200.

23. "FTC Pinpoints Slotting Fees," *Advertising Age* (February 26, 2001), p. 52; "Ca-ching," *Forbes* (June 12, 2000), pp. 84–85. Also see Paul N. Bloom, Gregory T. Gundlach, and Joseph P. Cannon, "Slotting Allowances and Fees: Schools of Thought and Views of Practicing Managers," *Journal of Marketing* (April 2000), pp. 92–109.

CHAPTER 16

1. David Simchi-Levi, Philip Kaminsky, and Edith Simchi-Levi, *Designing and Managing the Supply Chain* (Burr Ridge, IL: Irwin/McGraw-Hill, 2000), pp. 82–95; and H. Lee, V. Padmanabhan, and S. Whang, "The Bullwhip Effect in Supply Chains," *Sloan Management Review* (Spring 1997), pp. 93–102.

2. These estimates are given in James R. Stock and Douglas M. Lambert, *Strategic Logistics Management*, 4th ed. (Burr Ridge, IL: McGraw-Hill/Irwin, 2001), p. 5; and "U.S. Logistics Closing on Trillion Dollar Mark," *Business Week* (December 28, 1998), p. 78.

3. *What's It All About?* (Oakbrook, IL: Council of Logistics Management, 1993).

4. This example described in Simchi-Levi et al., *Designing and Managing the Supply Chain*, p. 5.

5. This discussion is based on Robert B. Handfield and Earnest Z. Nichols, *Introduction to Supply Chain Management* (Upper Saddle River, NJ: Prentice Hall, 1998), chapter 1.

6. This discussion is based on Robyn Meredith, "Harder than the Hype," Forbes (April 16, 2001), pp. 188–94; Robert M. Monczka and Jim Morgan, "Supply Chain Management Strategies," *Purchasing* (January 15, 1998), pp. 78–85; and Handfield and Nichols, *Introduction to Supply Chain Management*.

7. Major portions of this discussion are based on Sunil Chopra and Peter Meindl, *Supply Chain Management: Strategy, Planning, and Operations* (Upper Saddle River, NJ: Prentice Hall, 2001), chapters 1–3; and Marshall L. Fisher, "What Is the Right Supply Chain for Your Product?" *Harvard Business Review* (March–April 1997), pp. 105–17.

8. Eric Young and Mark Roberti, "The Swoosh Stumbles," *The Industry Standard* (March 12, 2001), pp. 47–49.

9. Portions of this discussion are based on Chopra and Meindl, *Supply Chain Management: Strategy, Planning, and Operations*; Nick Wingfield, "In the Beginning . . . ," *The Wall Street Journal* (May 21, 2001), p. R18; "Putting the 'E' Back in E-Business," *Information Week* (January 31, 2000), pp. 19–22. See also Richard A. Lancioni, Michael F. Smith, and Terence A. Oliva, "The Role of the Internet in Supply Chain Management," *Industrial Marketing Management*, vol. 29 (2000), pp. 45–46; and Donald J. Bowersox, David J. Closs, and M. Bixby Cooper, *Supply Chain Logistics Management* (Burr Ridge, IL: McGraw-Hill/Irwin, 2002), Chapter 10.

10. For an extensive listing and description of total logistics costs, see Stock and Lambert, *Strategic Logistics Management*, pp. 28–31.

11. Simchi-Levi et al., *Designing and Managing the Supply Chain*, p. 6.

12. Toby B. Gooley, "How Logistics Drive Customer Service," *Traffic Management* (January 1996), p. 46.

13. Faith Keenan, "Logistics Gets a Little Respect," *Business Week e-biz* (November 20, 2000), pp. EB113–EB126.

14. Michael Levy and Barton A. Weitz, *Retailing Management*, 4th ed. (Burr Ridge, IL: McGraw-Hill/Irwin, 2001), pp. 335–36; "A&P Bets the Store," *The Industry Standard* (May 14, 2001), pp. 46–49; and Ursula Y. Alvarado and Herbert Kotzab, "Supply Chain Management: The Integration of Logistics in Marketing," *Industrial Marketing Management*, vol. 30 (2001), pp. 183–98.

15. Jon Bigness, "In Today's Economy, There Is Big Money to Be Made in Logistics," *The Wall Street Journal* (September 6, 1995), pp. A1, A9.

16. Robert C. Lieb and Arnold Maltz, "What's the Future for Third-Party Logistics?" *Supply Chain Management Review* (Spring 1998), pp. 71–79.

17. Erik Schonfeld, "The Total Package," *eCompany* (June 2001), pp. 91–97; and "Compaq, UPS Unit Sign Network Pact," *Dallas Morning News* (April 21, 2000), p. 2D.

18. For an extensive description of transportation modes, see Douglas M. Lambert, James R. Stock, and Lisa Ellram, *Fundamentals of Logistics Management* (New York: Irwin/McGraw-Hill, 1998).

19. "Supply News: The Virtual Organization in our Future," www-1.ibm.com/procurement/supplynews/febsupplynews, downloaded February 1, 2001; Sheree DeCovny, "Electronic Commerce Comes of Age," *Journal of Business Strategy* (November/December 1998), pp. 38–44.

20. Jeffrey Davis and Martha Baer, "Some Assembly Required," *Business 2.0* (February 12, 2001), pp. 78–87.

21. Ronald Henkoff, "Delivering the Goods," *Fortune* (November 28, 1994), pp. 64–78.

22. Ken Cottrill, "Reforging the Supply Chain," *Journal of Business Strategy* (November/December 1997), pp. 35–39.

23. Fisher, "What Is the Right Supply Chain for Your Product?"

24. For an excellent overview on reverse logistics, see Edward J. Marien, "Reverse Logistics as Competitive Strategy," *Supply Chain Management Review* (Spring 1998), pp. 43–53.

25. Bruce Caldwell, "Reverse Logistics," www.informationweek.com, downloaded May 25, 2001; and "Return to Sender," *Modern Material Handling* (May 15, 2000), pp. 10–11.

26. Scott McMurry, "Life after Death," *eCompany* (December 2000), pp. 167–78; and Harvey Meyer, "The Greening of Corporate America," *Journal of Business Strategy* (January/February 2000), pp. 38–43.

27. Doug Bartholomew, "IT Delivers for UPS," *Industry Week*

Amazon.com: This case is based on material available on the company Website, www.amazon.com, and the following sources: Robert D. Hof and Heather Green, "How Amazon Cleared That Hurdle," *Business Week* (February 4, 2002), p. 60; Heather Green, "How Hard Should Amazon Swing?" *Business Week* (January 14, 2002), p. 38: Robert D. Hof, "We've Never Said We Had To Do It All," *Business Week* (October 15, 2001), p. 53; "Amazon.com Selects Mercator E-Business Integration Brokers as Key Technology for Supply Chain Integration," *Business Wire* (November 28, 2000); Bob Walter, "Amazon Leases Distribution Center from Sacramento, Calif., Development Firm," *Sacramento Bee* (July 19, 2001).

CHAPTER 17

1. Information supplied by Tim Hortons, March 2002.

2. Kenneth Cline, "The Devil in the Details," *Banking Strategies* (November–December 1997), p. 24; and Roger Trap, "Design Your Own Jeans," *The Independent* (October 18, 1998), p. 22.

3. www.statcan.ca, CANSIM II—080-0001 and cat. no. 63=005X1B.

4. www.statcan.ca, CANSIM II—281-0001 and 281-0005 and cat. no. 72=002-KPB.

5. "Fortune Global 500 Ranked within Industries," *Fortune* (July 23, 2001), p. F15.

6. "Top Retailers Reinvent Themselves to Keep Pace," *PR Newswire* (July 5, 2001); William Echikson, Carol Matlack, and David Vannier, "American E-Tailers Take Europe by Storm," *Business Week* (August 7, 2000), pp. 54–55; "7-Eleven Wishes to Open 70 Stores in Denmark," *Borsen* (June 12, 2001), p. 12; "IKEA to Expand in the U.S.," *Dagens Nyheter* (June 13, 2001), p. 2; "The Sun Never Sets on Wal-Mart's Retail Empire," *MMR* (December 18, 2000), p. 110; Lorrie Grant, "Global Reach Rings Up Earnings Boost for U.S. Retailers," *USA Today* (March 23, 1998), p. 7B; "Retailers Rush to Capture New Markets," *Financial Times* (March 13, 1998), p. 2.

7. "Retail Trade—Establishments, Employees, and Payroll," *Statistical Abstract of the United States*, 120th ed. (Washington, DC: U.S. Department of Commerce, Bureau of the Census, October 2000);

Gene Koretz, "Those Plucky Corner Stores," *Business Week* (December 5, 1994), p. 26.

8. Christopher Palmeri, "Who's Afraid of Wal-Mart?" *Forbes* (July 31, 1995), p. 81.

9. Richard C. Hoffman and John F. Preble, "Franchising into the Twenty-First Century," *Business Horizons* (November–December 1993), pp. 35–43.

10. "How Widespread Is Franchising?" *International Franchise Association* (www.franchise.org), September 2001; John Ryans, Jr., Sherry Lotz, and Robert Krampf, "Do Master Franchisors Drive Global Franchising?" *Marketing Management* (Summer 1999), pp. 33–37.

11. "Franchise 500," *Entrepreneur* (January 2001); Scott Shane and Chester Spell, "Factors for New Franchise Success," *Sloan Management Review* (Spring 1998), pp. 43–50; and Canadian Franchise Association, www.cfa.org.

12. David Breitkopf, "From NCR, an Automated Checkout Line System," *The American Banker* (August 7, 2001), p. 10; "Food 4 Less Introduces U-Scan Self-Service Checkout at Hollywood Store," *PR Newswire* (February 13, 2001); Marc Rice, "Competition Fierce in Complex Business of Delivering Packages," *Marketing News* (May 22, 1995), p. 5.

13. "Can the Nordstroms Find the Right Style?" *Business Week* (July 30, 2001), p. 59; Cyndee Miller, "Nordstrom Is Tops in Survey," *Marketing News* (February 15, 1993), p. 12.

14. Aixa M. Pascual, "Can Office Depot Get Back On Track?" *Business Week* (September 18, 2000), p. 74.

15. Laurie M. Grossman, "Hypermarkets: A Sure-Fire Hit Bombs," *The Wall Street Journal* (June 25, 1992), p. B1.

16. Sarah Smith, "Checking Out the New Loblaws," www.marketingmag.ca, April 29, 2002, downloaded May 5, 2002.

17. Ginny Parker, "Vending the Rules," *Time* (May 7, 2001), p. 24.

18. Julie Mitchell, "Electronic Payment Services Move beyond Tollbooths," *Investor's Business Daily* (August 30, 2001), p. 10; and Steve Scrupski, "Tiny 'Brains' Seen for Vending Machines," *Electronic Design* (December 1, 1998), p. 64F.

19. www.the-cma.org; www.statcan.ca, CANSIM II-077-0001 and cat. no. 63-278-XPB, and 63-218, February 7, 2002.

20. Edward Nash, "The Roots of Direct Marketing," *Direct Marketing* (February 1995), pp. 38–40; and Edith Hipp Updike and Mary Kurtz, "Japan Is Dialing 1 800 BUYAMERICA," *Business Week* (June 12, 1995), pp. 61–64.

21. Monica Roman, "You Gotta Have a Catalog," *Business Week* (May 14, 2001), p. 56; Beth Viveiros, "Catalog and Internet Sales Grow More Quickly than Retail," *Direct* (July 2001); and Diane Brady and Julia Cosgrove, "A Big Break for Your Postman," *Business Week* (September 10, 2001), p. 16.

22. "Intimate Brands Reports August Sales," *PR Newswire* (September 6, 2001); Christopher Palmeri, "Victoria's Little Secret," *Forbes* (August 24, 1998), p. 58; and Dyan Machan, "Sharing Victoria's Secrets," *Forbes* (June 5, 1995), pp. 132–33.

23. "Joe Namath, Franco Harris, Boomer Esiason, and Tim Brown Appear On Home Shopping Network during Super Bowl Week," *PR Newswire* (January 23, 2001); "Cover Girls Queen Latifah and Molly Sims Brush Up on Youth Volunteerism," *PR Newswire* (August 22, 2001); Carole Nicksin, "QVC Opens Up in Mall Space," *HFN* (August 20, 2001), p. 6; Chris Wynn and Tim Adler, "Battle for UK Home-Shopping Viewers Heats Up as QVC Gets Heavyweight Rival," *New Media Markets* (May 11, 2001).

24. "Fast Forward: Accelerating Canada's Leadership in the Internet Economy," www.retailcouncil.org, downloaded, May 5, 2002.

25. "The Canadian Online Retailing Report," www.retailcouncil.org, downloaded February 6, 2002.

26. Ibid.

27. "My Virtual Model Inc. Acquires EZsize," *PR Newswire* (June 21, 2001); Steve Casimiro, "Shop Till You Crash," *Fortune* (December 21, 1998), pp. 267–70; and De'Ann Weimer, "Can I Try (Click) That Blouse (Drag) in Blue?" *Business Week* (November 9, 1998), p. 86.

28. "Usability Study of PC and TV-Based Web Platforms Reveals Online Shopping Tasks Confuse, Frustrate Users," *PR Newswire* (September 5, 2001); Chris O'Malley, "No Waiting on the Web," *Time* (November 16, 1998), p. 76; B. G. Yovovich, "Webbed Feat," *Marketing News* (January 19, 1998), p. 1, 18; and Joseph Alba, John Lynch, Barton Weitz, Chris Janiszewski, Richard Lutz, Alan Sawyer, and Stacy Wood, "Interactive Home Shopping: Consumer, Retailer, and Manufacturer Incentives to Participate in Electronic Marketplace," *Journal of Marketing* (July 1997), pp. 38–53.

29. See cybercafes.com; Michelle Megna, "Wireless at Starbucks," *Daily News* (August 16, 2001), p. 12; "Pinet and Softstar Cooperate in Online Game Market," *China Post* (November 2, 2000).

30. Donna Bursey, "Targeting Small Businesses for Telemarketing and Mail Order Sales," *Direct Marketing* (September 1995), pp. 18–20; "Inbound, Outbound Telemarketing Keeps Ryder Sales in Fast Lane," *Direct Marketing* (July 1995), pp. 34–36; "Despite Hangups, Telemarketing a Success," *Marketing News* (March 27, 1995), p. 19; Kelly Shermach, "Outsourcing Seen as a Way to Cut Costs, Retain Service," *Marketing News* (June 19, 1995), pp. 5, 8; and Greg Gattuso, "Marketing Vision," *Direct Marketing* (February 1994), pp. 24–26.

31. Brian P. Murphy, "Giving Cold Calls the Cold Shoulder," *Business Week* (July 2, 2001), p. 12; and "TeleWatch to Help Control Unethical Telemarketing," Telemarketing & Call Center Solutions (April 1998), p. 28.

32. Nanette Byrnes, "The New Calling," *Business Week* (September 18, 2000), pp. 137–48.

33. Bill Vlasic and Mary Beth Regan, "Amway II: The Kids Take Over," *Business Week* (February 1, 1998), pp. 60–70.

34. Mathew Schifrin, "Okay, Big Mouth," *Forbes* (October 9, 1995), pp. 47–48; Veronica Byrd and Wendy Zellner, "The Avon Lady of the Amazon," *Business Week* (October 24, 1994), pp. 93–96; and Ann Marsh "Avon Is Calling on Eastern Europe," *Advertising Age* (June 20, 1994), p. 116.

35. The following discussion is adapted from William T. Gregor and Eileen M. Friars, *Money Merchandizing: Retail Revolution in Consumer Financial Services* (Cambridge, MA: Management Analysis Center, Inc., 1982).

36. www.payless.com, downloaded May 7, 2002.

37. Gail Tom, Michelle Dragics, and Christi Holdregger, "Using Visual Presentation to Assess Store Positioning: A Case Study of JCPenney," *Marketing Research* (September 1991), pp. 48–52.

38. William Lazer and Eugene J. Keley, "The Retailing Mix: Planning and Management," *Journal of Retailing* (Spring 1961), pp. 34–41.

39. Francis J. Mulhern and Robert P. Leon, "Implicit Price Bundling of Retail Products: A Multiproduct Approach to Maximizing Store Profitability," *Journal of Marketing* (October 1991), pp. 63–76.

40. Gwen Ortmeyer, John A. Quelch, and Walter Salmon, "Restoring Credibility to Retail Pricing," *Sloan Management Review* (Fall 1991), pp. 55–66.

41. William B. Dodds, "In Search of Value: How Price and Store Name Information Influence Buyers' Product Perceptions," *Journal of Consumer Marketing* (Spring 1991), pp. 15–24.

42. Leonard L. Berry, "Old Pillars of New Retailing," *Harvard Business Review* (April 2001), pp. 131–37.

43. Neil Gross, "On beyond Shoplifting Prevention," *Business Week* (October 2, 2000), p. 170; and "A Time to Steal," *Brandweek* (February 16, 1999), p. 24.

44. Rita Koselka, "The Schottenstein Factor," *Forbes* (September 28, 1992), p. 104, 106.

45. Wendy Zellner, "Warehouse Clubs: When the Going Gets Tough . . ." *Business Week* (July 16, 2001), p. 60; "Warehouse Clubs Fine-tune Units," *Chain Drug Review* (June 29, 1998), p. 38; James M. Degen, "Warehouse Clubs Move from Revolution to Evolution," *Marketing News* (August 3, 1992), p. 8; Dori Jones Yang, "Bargains by the Forklift," *Business Week* (July 15, 1991), p. 152; and "Fewer Rings on the Cash Register," *Business Week* (January 14, 1991), p. 85.

46. Ira P. Schneiderman, "Value Keeps Factory Outlets Viable," *Daily News Record* (July 20, 1998), p. 10; Stephanie Anderson Forest, "I Can Get It for You Retail," *Business Week* (September 18, 1995), pp. 84–88; and Adrienne Ward, "New Breed of Mall Knows: Everybody Loves a Bargain," *Advertising Age* (January 27, 1992), p. 55.

47. Anne Faircloth, "Value Retailers Go Dollar For Dollar," *Fortune* (July 6, 1998), pp. 164–66.

48. Barry Brown, "Edmonton Makes Size Pay Off in Down Market," *Advertising Age* (January 27, 1992), pp. 4–5.

49. James R. Lowry, "The Life Cycle of Shopping Centers," *Business Horizons* (January–February 1997), pp. 77–86; Eric Peterson, "Power Centers! Now!" *Stores* (March 1989), pp. 61–66; and "Power Centers Flex Their Muscle," *Chain Store Age Executive* (February 1989), pp. 3A, 4A.

50. Pierre Martineau, "The Personality of the Retail Store," *Harvard Business Review* (January–February 1958), p. 47.

51. Julie Baker, Dhruv Grewal, and A. Parasuraman, "The Influence of Store Environment on Quality Inferences and Store Image," *Journal of the Academy of Marketing Science* (Fall 1994), pp. 328–39; Howard Barich and Philip Kotler, "A Framework for Marketing Image Management," *Sloan Management Review* (Winter 1991), pp. 94–104; Susan M. Keaveney and Kenneth A. Hunt, "Conceptualization and Operationalization of Retail Store Image: A Case of Rival Middle-Level Theories," *Journal of the Academy of Marketing Science* (Spring 1992), pp. 165–75; James C. Ward, Mary Jo Bitner, and John Barnes, "Measuring the Prototypicality and Meaning of Retail Environments," *Journal of Retailing* (Summer 1992), p. 194; and Dhruv Grewal, R. Krishnan, Julie Baker, and Norm Burin, "The Effect of Store Name, Brand Name and Price Discounts on Consumers' Evaluations and Purchase Intentions," *Journal of Retailing* (Fall 1998), pp. 331–52. For a review of the store image literature, see Mary R. Zimmer and Linda L. Golden, "Impressions of Retail Stores: A Content Analysis of Consumer Images," *Journal of Retailing* (Fall 1988), pp. 265–93.

52. Mary Jo Bitner, "Servicescapes: The Impact of Physical Surroundings on Customers and Employees," *Journal of Marketing* (April 1992), pp. 57–71.

53. Jans-Benedict Steenkamp and Michel Wedel, "Segmenting Retail Markets on Store Image Using a Consumer-Based Methodology," *Journal of Retailing* (Fall 1991), p. 300; and Philip Kotler, "Atmospherics as a Marketing Tool," *Journal of Retailing*, vol. 49 (Winter 1973–1974), p. 61.

54. Carole Nicksin, "Sears' New Ad Campaign to Stress Brand Image, Shopping Convenience," *HFN* (August 27, 2001), p. 4; and "Sears Buying Catalog Giant Lands' End," *Portland Press* (May 14, 2002), pp. 1A, 10A

55. The wheel of retailing theory was originally proposed by Malcolm P. McNair, "Significant Trends and Development in the Postwar Period," in A. B. Smith, ed., *Competitive Distribution in a Free, High-Level Economy and Its Implications for the University* (Pittsburgh: University of Pittsburgh Press, 1958), pp. 1–25; see also Stephen Brown, "The Wheel of Retailing—Past and Future," *Journal of Retailing* (Summer 1990), pp. 143–49; and Malcolm P. McNair and Eleanor May, "The Next Revolution of the Retailing Wheel," *Harvard Business Review* (September–October 1978), pp. 81–91.

56. Peter Kiekmeyer, "McDonald's Bet Heavily on McCafe," *The Montreal Gazette* (August 28, 2001), p. D2; "McDonald's Adds Sourdough Line and Cheesecake to Revolving Menu Offerings," *PR Newswire* (August 9, 2001); David Farkas, "Drive-Thru in the Fast Lane," *Chain Leader* (July 2001), p. 40.

57. Bill Saporito, "What's for Dinner?" *Fortune* (May 15, 1995), pp. 51–64.

58. William R. Davidson, Albert D. Bates, and Stephen J. Bass, "Retail Life Cycle," *Harvard Business Review* (November–December 1976), pp. 89–96.

59. Gretchen Morgenson, "Here Come the Cross-Shoppers," *Forbes* (December 7, 1992), pp. 90–101.

60. Ranjay Gulati and Janson Garino, "Getting the Right Mix of Bricks and Clicks," *Harvard Business Review* (May–June 2000), pp. 107–114; Marshall L Fisher, Ananth Raman, and Anna Sheen McClelland, "Rocket Science Retailing Is Almost Here: Are You Ready?" *Harvard Business Review* (July–August 2000), pp. 115–24; Charla Mathwick, Naresh Malhotra, and Edward Rigdon, "Experiential Value: Conceptualization, Measurement and Application in the Catalog and Internet Shopping Environment," *Journal of Retailing* (Spring 2001), pp. 39–56; Lawrence M. Bellman, "Bricks and Mortar: 21st Century Survival," *Business Horizons* (May–June 2001), pp. 21–28; Zhan G. Li and Nurit Gery, "E-Tailing—for All Products?" *Business Horizons* (November–December 2000), pp. 49–54; Bill Hanifin, "Go Forth and Multichannel: Loyalty Programs Need Knowledge Base," *Marketing News* (August 27, 2001), p. 23.

61. Mary Kuntz, Lori Bongiorno; Keith Naughton, Gail DeGeorge, and Stephanie Anderson Forest, "Reinventing the Store," *Business Week* (November 27, 1995), pp. 84–96; and David Fischer, "The New Meal Deals," *U.S. News & World Report* (October 30, 1995), p. 66.

IKEA: This case was prepared by Frederick G. Crane.

CHAPTER 18

1. "Best Promoted Brands of 2001," *PROMO* (September 2001), pp. 55–62; "Daring Disney," *Advertising Age* (March 26, 2001), p. 20; Wayne Friedman, "Disney's Twist on Film Promo," *Advertising Age* (March 19, 2001), p. 3; Wayne Friedman, "Disney Sets $250 Mil Birthday Bash," *Advertising Age* (July 2, 2001), p. 1; Bob Garfield, "Disney's Quest for Boomers Shows a Bit of Imagineering," *Advertising Age* (August 13, 2001), p. 29; Stephanie Thompson, "The Mouse in the Food Aisle," *Advertising Age* (September 10, 2001), p. 73; Lorraine Calvacca, "Mouse Trapping," *PROMO* (May 2001), p. 47; Stephanie Thompson, "A Disney Assist," *Advertising Age* (July 30, 2001), p. 39; Wayne Friedman, "Disney, Toys 'R' Us Sign Cross-Media Deal," *Advertising Age* (June 18, 2001), p. 3; Chester Dawson, "Will Tokyo Embrace Another Mouse?" *Business Week* (September 10, 2001), p. 65; and David Jackson, "How to Build a Better Mousetrap," *Time* (February 19, 2001), pp. 40–42.

2. Wilbur Schramm, "How Communication Works," in Wilbur Schramm, ed., *The Process and Effects of Mass Communication* (Urbana, IL: University of Illinois Press, 1955), pp. 3–26.

3. F. G. Crane and T. K. Clarke, *Consumer Behaviour in Canada: Theory and Practice*, 2nd ed. (Toronto: Dryden, 1994), pp. 287–98.

4. Cynthia L. Kemper, "Biting Wax Tadpole, Other Faux Pas," *The Denver Post* (August 3, 1997), p. G-04.

5. Adapted from *Dictionary of Marketing Terms*, 2nd ed., Peter D. Bennett, ed. (Chicago: American Marketing Association, 1995), p. 231.

6. Kusum L Ailawadi, Scott A. Neslin, and Karen Gedenk, "Pursuing the Value-Conscious Consumer: Store Brands versus National Brand Promotions," *Journal of Marketing* (January 2001), pp. 71–89;

7. B. C. Cotton and Emerson M. Babb, "Consumer Response to Promotional Deals," *Journal of Marketing*, vol. 42 (July 1978), pp. 109–13.

8. Robert George Brown, "Sales Response to Promotions and Advertising," *Journal of Advertising Research*, vol. 14 (August 1974), pp. 33–40.

9. Adapted from *Economic Impact: U.S. Direct Marketing Today* (New York: Direct Marketing Association, 1998), p. 25.

10. Siva K. Balasubramanian and V. Kumar, "Analyzing Variations in Advertising and Promotional Expenditures: Key Correlates in Consumer, Industrial, and Service Markets," *Journal of Marketing* (April 1990), pp. 57–68.

11. Don E. Schultz, "Consumer Marketing Changed by Advent of 29.8/7 Media Week," *Marketing News* (September 24, 2001), pp. 13, 15; Pamela Paul, "Getting Inside Gen Y," *American Demographics* (September 2001), pp. 43–49; Charles Pappas, "Ad Nauseam," *Advertising Age* (July 10, 2000), pp. 16–18; Dan Lippe, "It's All in Creative

Delivery," *Advertising Age* (June 25, 2001), pp. s8, s9; and Kate Fitzgerald, "Viral Marketing Breaks Through," *Advertising Age* (June 25, 2001), p. s10.

12. Dunn Sunnoo and Lynn Y. S. Lin, "Sales Effects of Promotion and Advertising," *Journal of Advertising Research*, vol. 18 (October 1978), pp. 37–42.

13. John Palmer, "Animal Instincts," *PROMO* (May 2001), pp. 25–33.

14. F. G. Crane and T. K. Clarke, pp. 237–38, 346.

15. James M. Olver and Paul W. Farris, "Push and Pull: A One-Two Punch for Packages Products," *Sloan Management Review* (Fall 1989), pp. 53–61.

16. Ken Riddell, "Advertising Sees Share of Pie Dwindling," *Marketing* (January 7, 1994), p. 2.

17. Fusun F. Gonul, Franklin Carter, Elina Petrova, and Kannan Srinivasan, "Promotion of Prescription Drugs and Its Impact on Physicians' Choice Behavior," *Journal of Marketing* (July 2001), pp. 79–90.

18. Joseph Weber, "Drug Ads: A Prescription for Controversy," *Business Week* (January 18, 1993), pp. 58–60.

19. Tom Duncan, "Is Your Marketing Communications Integrated?" *Advertising Age* (January 24, 1994), p. 26.

20. Kim Cleland, "Few Wed Marketing, Communications," *Advertising Age* (February 27, 1995), p. 10.

21. Don Schultz, "Objectives Drive Tactics in IMC Approach," *Marketing News* (May 9, 1994), pp. 14, 18; and Neil Brown, "Redefine Integrated Marketing Communications," *Marketing News* (March 29, 1993), pp. 4–5.

22. Richard Verrier, "Disney Seeks to Add China to Its World," *Los Angeles Times* (September 16, 2001), p. 3–1.

23. Robert J. Lavidge and Gary A. Steiner, "A Model for Predictive Measurement of Advertising Effectiveness," *Journal of Marketing* (October 1961), p. 61.

24. Brian Wansink and Michael Ray, "Advertising Strategies to Increase Usage Frequency," *Journal of Marketing* (January 1996), pp. 31–46.

25. www.marketingmag.ca/media-digest/html, downloaded March 1, 2002.

26. Don E. Schultz and Anders Gronstedt, "Making Marcom an Investment," *Marketing Management* (Fall 1997), pp. 41–49; and J. Enrique Bigne, "Advertising Budget Practices: A Review," *Journal of Current Issues and Research in Advertising* (Fall 1995), pp. 17–31.

27. John Philip Jones, "Ad Spending: Maintaining Market Share," *Harvard Business Review* (January–February 1990), pp. 38–42; and Charles H. Patti and Vincent Blanko, "Budgeting Practices of Big Advertisers," *Journal of Advertising Research*, vol. 21 (December 1981), pp. 23–30.

28. James A. Schroer, "Ad Spending: Growing Market Share," *Harvard Business Review* (January–February 1990), pp. 44–48.

29. Jeffrey A. Lowenhar and John L. Stanton, "Forecasting Competitive Advertising Expenditures," *Journal of Advertising Research*, vol. 16, no. 2 (April 1976), pp. 37–44.

30. Daniel Seligman, "How Much for Advertising?" *Fortune* (December 1956), p. 123.

31. James E. Lynch and Graham J. Hooley, "Increasing Sophistication in Advertising Budget Setting," *Journal of Advertising Research*, vol. 30 (February–March 1990), pp. 67–75.

32. Jimmy D. Barnes, Brenda J. Muscove, and Javad Rassouli, "An Objective and Task Media Selection Decision Model and Advertising Cost Formula to Determine International Advertising Budgets," *Journal of Advertising*, vol. 11, no. 4 (1982), pp. 68–75.

33. Don E. Schultz, "Olympics Get the Gold Medal in Integrating Marketing Event," *Marketing News* (April 27, 1998), pp. 5, 10.

34. "The Fellowship of the New Line," *PROMO* (September 2001), p. 84; and "Sneak Preview of Trailer for New Line Cinema's 'The Lord of the Rings: The Fellowship of the Ring'" *PR Newswire* (September 21, 2001).

35. Kate Fitzgerald, "Beyond Advertising," *Advertising Age* (August 3, 1998), pp. 1, 14; Curtis P. Johnson, "Follow the Money: Sell CFO on Integrated Marketing's Merits," *Marketing News* (May 11, 1998), p. 10; and Laura Schneider, "Agencies Show That IMC Can Be Good for Bottom Line," *Marketing News* (May 11, 1998), p. 11.

36. *Economic Impact: U.S. Direct Marketing Today* (New York: Direct Marketing Association, 2000), pp. 24–30; and www.the-cma.org, downloaded March 1, 2002.

37. "The Columbia House Company Selects Akamai EdgeSuite to Support Growing Online Business," *Business Wire* (September 5, 2001); "Back to College Market Fuels Growth in Internet Commerce and Traffic," *Business Wire* (September 10, 2001); and Carol Krol, "Columbia House Looks Down the Road for Gains from Play," *Advertising Age* (March 1, 1999), p. 20.

38. www.the-cma.org, www.retailcouncil.org, and www.strategis.ic.gc.ca.

39. Robert Berner, "Going that Extra Inch," *Business Week* (September 18, 2000), p. 84.

40. Adapted from *Economic Impact: U.S. Direct Marketing Today* (New York: Direct Marketing Association, 1998), pp. 25–26.

41. Carol Krol, "Club Med Uses E-Mail to Pitch Unsold, Discounted Packages," *Advertising Age* (December 14, 1998), p. 40.

42. "Rising to the Top," *PROMO* (September 2001), pp. 46–62.

43. Jean Halliday, "Taking Direct Route," *Advertising Age* (September 7, 1998), p. 17.

44. Julie Tilsner, "Lillian Vernon: Creating a Host of Spin-offs from Its Core Catalog," *Business Week* (December 19, 1994), p. 85; and Lisa Coleman, "I Went Out and Did It," *Forbes* (August 17, 1992), pp. 102–4.

45. Alan K. Gorenstein, "Direct Marketing's Growth Will Be Global," *Marketing News* (December 7, 1998), p. 15; Don E. Schultz, "Integrated Global Marketing Will Be the Name of the Game," *Marketing News* (October 26, 1998), p. 5; and Mary Sutter and Andrea Mandel-Campbell, "Customers Are Eager, Infrastructure Lags," *Advertising Age International* (October 5, 1998), p. 12.

46. Juliana Koranten, "European Privacy Rules Go into Effect in 15 EU States," *Advertising Age* (October 26, 1998), p. S31; and Rashi Glazer, "The Illusion of Privacy and Competition for Attention," *Journal of Interactive Marketing* (Summer 1998), pp. 2–4.

47. Douglas Wood and David Brosse, "Mulling E-Mail Options," *PROMO* (September 2001), p. 18; Kathleen Cholewka, "Making E-Mail Matter," *Sales and Marketing Management* (September 2001), pp. 21, 22; Arlene Weintraub, "When E-Mail Ads Aren't Spam," *Business Week* (October 16, 2000), p. 112; "Opting Out of E-Mail Ads Isn't So Easy to Do," *Business Week* (November 6, 2000), p. 20; "With E-Mail Marketing, Permission Is Key," *eStatNews* (on emarketer.com), September 2001; and www.the-cma.org, "New International Service to Reduce Unwanted Marketing E-mail," January 10, 2000.

CHAPTER 19

1. Daniel Eisenberg, "Making Brands Magically Appear," *Time* (July 23, 2001), p. 46; Christine Y. Chen, "TiVo Is Smart TV," *Fortune* (March 19, 2001), p. 124; Lee Gomes, "I Want My PC-TV—Two Products Take Baby Steps toward Ideal," *The Wall Street Journal* (August 16, 2001), p. B1; Khanh T. L. Tran, "TiVo, Sonicblue Still See the Bright Side," *The Wall Street Journal* (August 31, 2001), p. B3; Jennifer L. Schenker, "Death of a Salesman," *Time* (June 4, 2001), p. 54.

2. David A. Aaker and Donald Norris, "Characteristics of TV Commercials Perceived as Informative," *Journal of Advertising Research*, vol. 22, no. 2 (April–May 1982), pp. 61–70.

3. Larry D. Compeau and Dhruv Grewal, "Comparative Price Advertising: An Integrative Review," *Journal of Public Policy & Marketing* (Fall 1998), pp. 257–73; and William Wilkie and Paul W. Farris, "Comparison Advertising: Problems and Potentials," *Journal of Marketing* (October 1975), pp. 7–15.

4. Jennifer Lawrence, "P&G Ads Get Competitive," *Advertising Age* (February 1, 1993), p. 14; Jerry Gotlieb and Dan Sorel, "The Influence of Type of Advertisement, Price, and Source Credibility on Perceived Quality," *Journal of the Academy of Marketing Science* (Summer 1992), pp. 253–60; and Cornelia Pechman and David Stewart, "The Effects of Comparative Advertising on Attention, Memory, and Purchase Intentions," *Journal of Consumer Research* (September 1990), pp. 180–92.

5. Bruce Buchanan and Doron Goldman, "Us vs. Them: The Minefield of Comparative Ads," *Harvard Business Review* (May–June 1989), pp. 38–50; Dorothy Cohen, "The FTC's Advertising Substantiation Program," *Journal of Marketing* (Winter 1980), pp. 26–35; and Michael Etger and Stephen A. Goodwin, "Planning for Comparative Advertising Requires Special Attention," *Journal of Advertising*, vol. 8, no. 1 (Winter 1979), pp. 26–32.

6. Lewis C. Winters, "Does It Pay to Advertise to Hostile Audiences with Corporate Advertising?" *Journal of Advertising Research* (June/July 1988), pp. 11–18; and Robert Selwitz, "The Selling of an Image," *Madison Avenue* (February 1985), pp. 61–69.

7. Mary Lou Quinlan, "Women: We've Come a Long Way, Maybe," *Advertising Age* (February 22, 1999), p. 46.

8. Jean Halliday, "Of Hummers and Zen," *Advertising Age* (August 6, 2001), p. 29.

9. "Claritin Springs into Allergy Season with New Consumer Programs," *PR Newswire* (February 20, 2001).

10. Ira Teinowitz, "Self-regulation Urged to Prevent Bias in Ad Buying," *Advertising Age* (January 18, 1999), p. 4.

11. Bob Donath, "Match Your Media Choice and Ad Copy Objective," *Marketing News* (June 8, 1998), p. 6.

12. Michael S. LaTour and Herbert J. Rotfeld, "There Are Threats and (Maybe) Fear-Caused Arousal: Theory and Confusions of Appeals to Fear and Fear Arousal Itself," *Journal of Advertising* (Fall 1997), pp. 45–59.

13. Bob Garfield, "Allstate Ads Bring Home Point about Mortgage Insurance," *Advertising Age* (September 11, 1989), p. 120; and Judann Dagnoli, "'Buy or Die' Mentality Toned Down in Ads," *Advertising Age* (May 7, 1990), p. S-12.

14. Hank Kim and Scott Hume, "Positioning: Blue Cross, Kaiser Permanente Ads Play Big on HMO Trust Factor," *Brandweek* (September 14, 1998); Jeffrey D. Zbar, "Fear!" *Advertising Age* (November 14, 1994), pp. 18–19; John F. Tanner, Jr., James B. Hunt, and David R. Eppright, "The Protection Motivation Model: A Normative Model of Fear Appeals," *Journal of Marketing* (July 1991), pp. 36–45; Michael S. LaTour and Shaker A. Zahra, "Fear Appeals as Advertising Strategy: Should They Be Used?" *The Journal of Consumer Marketing* (Spring 1989), pp. 61–70; and Joshua Levine, "Don't Fry Your Brain," *Forbes* (February 4, 1991), pp. 116–17.

15. Patrick Allossery, "Make 'em Laugh: Advertising as Standup," *Financial Post*, April 23, 2001.

16. Anthony Vagnoni, "Best Awards," *Advertising Age* (May 28, 2001), pp. S1–18; Dana L. Alden, Wayne D. Hoyer, and Chol Lee, "Identifying Global and Culture-Specific Dimensions of Humor in Advertising: A Multinational Analysis," *Journal of Marketing* (April 1993), pp. 64–75; and Johny K. Johansson, "The Sense of 'Nonsense': Japanese TV Advertising," *Journal of Advertising* (March 1994), pp. 17–26.

17. Peter Brieger, "Cheers, Say Readers of Celtic Bar Pitchman," *Financial Post*, April 23, 2001, p. C4.

18. www.marketingmag.ca/media-digest/html, downloaded March 3, 2002.

19. Giles D'Souza and Ram C. Rao, "Can Repeating an Advertisement More Frequently than the Competition Affect Brand Preference in a Mature Market?" *Journal of Marketing* (April 1995), pp. 32–42.

20. Vicki R. Lane, "The Impact of Ad Repetition and Ad Content on Consumer Perceptions of Incongruent Extensions," *Journal of Marketing* (April 2000), pp. 80–91.

21. William F. Arens, *Contemporary Advertising*, 7th ed (New York: McGraw-Hill/Irwin, 1999), pp. 268; R20; and William G. Nickels, James M. McHugh, and Susan M. McHugh, *Understanding Business*, 5th ed. (Burr Ridge, IL: McGraw-Hill, 1999, p. 483).

22. www.marketingmag.ca/media-digest/html, downloaded March 3, 2002.

23. Ibid.

24. Surendra N. Singh, Denise Linville, and Ajay Sukhdial, "Enhancing the Efficacy of Split Thirty-Second Television Commercials: An Encoding Variability Application," *Journal of Advertising* (Fall 1995), pp. 13–23; Scott Ward, Terence A. Oliva, and David J. Reibstein, "Effectiveness of Brand-Related 15-Second Commercials," *Journal of Consumer Marketing*, no. 2 (1994). pp. 38–44; and Surendra N. Singh and Catherine Cole, "The Effects of Length, Content, and Repetition on Television Commercial Effectiveness," *Journal of Marketing Research* (February 1993), pp. 91–104.

25. www.marketingmag.ca/media-digest/html, downloaded March 3, 2002.

26. John Heinzl, "Silly Sells," *The Globe and Mail*, July 13, 2001, p. M1.

27. www.marketingmag.ca/media-digest/html, downloaded March 3, 2002.

28. www.marketingmag.ca, "The End of the Envelope," August 20, 2001.

29. Sandeep Krishnamurthy, "Deciphering the Internet Advertising Puzzle," *Marketing Management* (Fall 2000), pp. 35–39; Judy Strauss and Raymond Frost, *Marketing on the Internet: Principles of Online Marketing* (Englewood Cliffs, NJ: Prentice Hall, 1999), pp. 196–249; and Maricris G. Briones, "Rich Media May Be Too Rich for Your Blood," *Marketing News* (March 29, 1999), p. 4.

30. Heather Green and Ben Elgin, "Do e-Ads Have a Future?" *Business Week* (January 22, 2001), p. EB46; Ellen Neuborne, "For Kids on the Web, It's an Ad, Ad, Ad, Ad World," *Business Week* (August 13, 2001), p. 108; Ellen Neuborne, "Beyond the Banner Ad," *Business Week* (December 11, 2000), p. 16; Laurel Wentz, "Moo-It-Yourself," *Advertising Age* (July 9, 2001), p. 28.

31. Dana Blankenhorn, "Bigger, Richer Ads Go Online," *Advertising Age* (June 18, 2001), p. T10; Patricia Riedman, "Poor Rich Media," *Advertising Age* (February 5, 2001), p. 26; Heather Green, "Net Advertising: Still the 98-Pound Weakling," *Business Week* (September 1l, 2000), p. 36; Thom Weidlich, "Online Spots—A New Generation," *Advertising Age* (July 30, 2001), p. S10.

32. Arch G. Woodside, "Outdoor Advertising as Experiments," *Journal of the Academy of Marketing Science*, vol. 18 (Summer 1990), pp. 229–37.

33. Ed Brown, "Advertisers Skip to the Loo," *Fortune* (October 26, 1998), p. 64; John Cortex, "Growing Pains Can't Stop the New Kid on the Ad Block," *Advertising Age* (October 12, 1992), pp. 5–28; Allen Banks, "How to Assess New Place-Based Media," *Advertising Age* (November 30, 1992), p. 36; and John Cortex, "Media Pioneers Try to Corral On-the-Go Consumers," *Advertising Age* (August 17, 1992), p. 25.

34. Sehoon Park and Minhi Hahn, "Pulsing in a Discrete Model of Advertising Competition," *Journal of Marketing Research* (November 1991), pp. 397–405.

35. Peggy Masterson, "The Wearout Phenomenon," *Marketing Research* (Fall 1999), pp. 27–31; Lawrence D. Gibson, "What Can One TV Exposure Do?" *Journal of Advertising Research* (March–April 1996), pp. 9–18.

36. Rob Norton, "How Uninformative Advertising Tells Consumers Quite a Bit," *Fortune* (December 26, 1994), p. 37; and "Professor Claims Corporations Waste Billions on Advertising," *Marketing News* (July 6, 1992), p. 5.

37. Jack Neff, "Feeling the Squeeze," *Advertising Age* (June 4, 2001), pp. 1, 14–15; Laura Q. Hughes, "Measuring Up," *Advertising Age* (February 5, 2001), pp. 1, 34.

38. The discussion of post-testing is based on William F. Arens, *Contemporary Advertising*, 6th ed. (Burr Ridge, IL: Richard D. Irwin, 1996), pp. 181–82.

39. David A. Aaker and Douglas M. Stayman, "Measuring Audience Perceptions of Commercials and Relating Them to Ad Impact," *Journal of Advertising Research*, vol. 30 (August/September 1990), pp. 7–17; and Ernest Dichter, "A Psychological View of Advertising Effectiveness," *Marketing Management*, vol. 1, no. 3 (1992), pp. 60–62.

40. David Kruegel, "Television Advertising Effectiveness and Research Innovation," *Journal of Consumer Marketing* (Summer 1988), pp. 43–51; and Laurence N. Gold, "The Evolution of Television Advertising Sales Measurement: Past, Present, and Future," *Journal of Advertising Research* (June/July 1988), pp. 19–24.

41. Sinclair Stewart, "Advertising Complaints Hit New High," *Financial Post*, April 26, 2001, p. C3.

42. Keith McIntyre, "Sometimes Smaller Is Better," *Marketing* (November 28, 1994), p. 14.

43. *Couponing Trends* (Markham, ON: NCH Promotional Services, 2002).

44. Kapil Bawa and Robert W. Shoemaker, "Analyzing Incremental Sales from a Direct-Mail Coupon Promotion," Journal of Marketing (July 1998), pp. 66–78.

45. Roger A. Strang, "Sales Promotion—Fast Growth, Faulty Management," *Harvard Business Review*, vol. 54 (July–August 1976), pp. 115–24; and Ronald W. Ward and James E. Davis, "Coupon Redemption," *Journal of Advertising Research*, vol. 18 (August 1978), pp. 51–58. Similar results on favorable mail-distributed coupons were reported by Alvin Schwartz, "The Influence of Media Characteristics on Coupon Redemption," *Journal of Marketing*, vol. 30 (January 1966), pp. 41–46.

46. Hollie Shaw, "A Licence to Print Money," *Financial Post*, April 30, 2001.

47. Paula Lyon Andruss, "Survivor Packages Make Real-Life Money," *Marketing News* (March 26, 2001), p. 5; Wayne Friedman, "Eagle-Eye Marketers Find Right Spot, Right Time," *Advertising Age* (January 22, 2001), p. S2; David Goetzl, "TBS Tries Virtual Advertising," *Advertising Age* (May 21, 2001), p. 8; James Poniewozik, "This Plug's for You," *Time* (June 18, 2001) p. 76–77; "Never Say Never Again," *PROMO* (October 2001), p. 16.

48. Danon Darlin, "Junior Mints, I'm Going to Make You a Star," *Forbes* (November 6, 1995), pp. 90–94.

49. This discussion is drawn particularly from John A. Quelch, *Trade Promotions by Grocery Manufacturers: A Management Perspective* (Cambridge, MA: Marketing Science Institute, August 1982).

50. Michael Chevalier and Ronald C. Curhan, "Retail Promotions as a Function of Trade Promotions: A Descriptive Analysis," *Sloan Management Review*, vol. 18 (Fall 1976), pp. 19–32.

51. G. A. Marken, "Firms Can Maintain Control over Creative Co-op Programs," *Marketing News* (September 28, 1992), pp. 7, 9.

52. "Safetyforum.com and Public Citizen Report: NHTSA Forces Firestone to Recall Defective Tires, Expand Wilderness ATs Recall," *PR Newswire* (October 5, 2001); Cindy Skrzycki and Frank Swoboda, "Firestone Refuses Voluntary Recall," Safetyforum.com (July 20, 2001); Jim Suhr, "Tire Recall Response Time Defended," Safetyforum.com (August 10, 2000).

53. Scott Hue, "Free 'Plugs' Supply Ad Power," *Advertising Age* (January 29, 1990), p. 6.

54. Mike Harris, "Earnhardt's Lap Belt Was Broken," Safetyforum.com (February 23, 2001); and Marc Weinberger, Jean Romeo, and Azhar Piracha, "Negative Product Safety News: Coverage, Responses, and Effects," *Business Horizons* (May–June 1991), pp. 23–31.

55. www.tctrail.ca.

56. Martin O'Hanlon, "Meat Lovers Not Complete Lovers," *The Chronicle-Herald* (August 11, 1999), pp. A1, A2.

Lysol: This case was prepared by Frederick G. Crane.

CHAPTER 20

1. Kathleen Cholewka, "Xerox's Savior?" *Sales & Marketing Management* (April 2001), pp. 36–42; "Anne Mulcahy Named Xerox Chief Executive Officer," www.xerox.com, downloaded July 26, 2001; and "She's Here to Fix the Xerox," *Business Week* (August 6, 2001), pp. 47–48.

2. Statistics Canada, *Canada Year Book*, Cat. 11-402E (Ottawa, 2001).

3. "America's 25 Best Sales Forces," *Sales & Marketing Management* (July 2000), pp. 57–85.

4. For recent representative research on and commentary on relationship selling, see James Boles, Thomas Brashear, Danny Bellenger, and Hiram Barksdale, Jr., "Relationship Selling Behaviors: Antecedents and Relationship with Performance," *Journal of Business & Industrial Marketing*, vol. 15, no. 2/3 (2000), pp. 141–53; Neil Rackham, *Rethinking the Sales Force* (New York: McGraw-Hill, 1999); and Barton A. Weitz and Kevin D. Bradford, "Personal Selling and Sales Management: A Relationship Marketing Perspective," *Journal of the Academy of Marketing Science* (Spring 1999), pp. 241–54.

5. David W. Cravens, "The Changing Role of the Sales Force," *Marketing Management* (Fall 1995), pp. 49–57.

6. Douglas J. Dalrymple, William L. Cron, and Thomas E. DeCarlo, *Sales Management*, 7th ed. (New York: Wiley, 2001), pp. 55–57.

7. For a perspective on types of selling, see Thomas R. Wotruba, "The Evolution of Personal Selling," *Journal of Personal Selling & Sales Management* (Summer 1991), pp. 1–12. See also René Y. Darmon, "A Conceptual Scheme and Procedure for Classifying Sales Positions," *Journal of Personal Selling & Sales Management* (Summer 1998), pp. 31–46.

8. Christen Heide, *Dartnell's 31st Salesforce Compensation Survey 2000* (Chicago: Dartnell Corporation, 2000), p. 176.

9. "What a Sales Call Costs," *Sales & Marketing Management* (September 2000), p. 80.

10. "Keep Calling!" *Sales & Marketing Report* (May 2001), p. 3.

11. For representative research and commentary on team selling, see Keith A. Chrzanowski and Thomas W. Leigh, "Customer Relationship Strategy and Customer-Focused Teams," in Gerald J. Bauer et al., *Emerging Trends in Sales Thought and Practice* (Westport, CT: Quorum Books, 1998); and Mark A. Moon and Susan Forquer Gupta, "Examining the Formation of Selling Centers: A Conceptual Framework," *Journal of Personal Selling & Sales Management* (Spring 1997), pp. 31–41.

12. Neil Rackham, Lawrence Friedman, and Richard Ruff, *Getting Partnering Right* (New York: McGraw-Hill, 1996), pp. 47–48; and "The Selling Game," *The Wall Street Journal* (March 29, 1994), p. A1.

13. For a brief overview on prospecting, see "The Best Way to Prospect," *Sales & Marketing Management* (January 1998), p. 80.

14. Carol J. Loomis, "Have You Been Cold-Called?" *Fortune* (December 16, 1991), pp. 109–15.

15. "Corporate Cultures: Clearing Customs," *SKY Magazine* (July 1995), pp. 35–40.

16. "Don't Call Laws Raise False Hope for Peace, Quiet," *The Wall Street Journal* (December 22, 2000), pp. B1, B4.

17. James Pollock, "In Pursuit of Privacy," *Marketing* (June 4, 1993), pp. 1, 4.

18. Paul A. Herbing, *Handbook of Cross-Cultural Marketing* (New York: Holworth Press, 1998).

19. "What Do Customers Hate about Salespeople?" *Sales & Marketing Management* (June 2001), pp. 43–51.

20. "Japanese Business Etiquette," *Smart Business* (August 2000), p. 55.

21. For an extensive discussion on adaptive selling, see Barton Weitz, Stephen B. Castleberry, and John F. Tanner, Jr., *Selling: Building Partnerships*, 4th ed. (Burr Ridge, IL: McGraw-Hill/Irwin, 2001), chapter 6.

22. F. Robert Dwyer and John F. Tanner, *Business Marketing*, 2nd ed. (Burr Ridge, IL: McGraw-Hill/Irwin, 2002), p. 400.

23. "America's 25 Best Sales Forces," *Sales & Marketing Management*.

24. For an extensive discussion of objections, see Charles M. Futrell, *Fundamentals of Selling* (New York: Irwin/McGraw-Hill, 2002), chapter 10.

25. Philip R. Cateora and John L. Graham, *International Marketing*, 10th ed. (New York: Irwin/McGraw-Hill, 1999), pp. 128, 131; and Herbing, *Handbook of Cross-Cultural Marketing*, p. 60.

26. Theodore Levitt, *The Marketing Imagination* (New York: Free Press, 1983), p. 111.

27. "Leading Edge," *Sales & Marketing Management* (July 1995), p. 13. See also "Focus on the Customer," *Fortune* (September 7, 1998), special advertising section.

28. *Management Briefing: Sales and Marketing* (New York: Conference Board, October 1996), pp. 3–4.

29. "Why It Pays to Be Curious," *Sales & Marketing Management* (August 1998), p. 76.

30. Alan J. Dubinsky, Marvin A. Jolson, Ronald E. Michaels, Masaaki Katobe, and Chae Un Lim, "Ethical Perceptions of Field Sales Personnel: An Empirical Assessment," *Journal of Personal Selling & Sales Management* (Fall 1992), pp. 9–21; and Alan J. Dubinsky, Marvin A. Jolson, Masaaki Katobe, and Chae Un Lim, "A Cross-National Investigation of Industrial Salespeople's Ethical Perceptions," *Journal of International Business Studies* (Fourth Quarter 1991), pp. 651–70.

31. See Gilbert A. Churchill, Jr., Neil M. Ford, Orville C. Walker, Jr., Mark W. Johnson, and John F. Tanner, Jr., *Sales Force Management*, 6th ed. (Burr Ridge, IL: Irwin/McGraw-Hill, 2000), pp. 101–4.

32. Churchill et al., *Sales Force Management*, pp. 110–13. Also see Arun Sharma, "Who Prefers Key Account Management Programs? An Investigation of Business Buying Behavior and Buying Firm Characteristics," *Journal of Personal Selling & Sales Management* (Fall 1997), pp. 37–30; Dan C. Weilbaker and William A. Weeks, "The Evolution of National Account Management: A Literature Perspective," *Journal of Personal Selling & Management* (Fall 1997), pp. 49–50; and Paul Dishman and Philip S. Nitse, "National Accounts Revisited," *Industrial Marketing Management* (January 1998), pp. 1–9.

33. Several variations of the account management policy grid exist. See, for example, Dalrymple, Cron, and DeCarlo, *Sales Management*, pp. 173–74; Churchill et al., *Sales Force Management*, pp. 190–92.

34. Patricia Sellers, "How to Remake Your Sales Force," *Fortune* (May 4, 1992), p. 103. See also "Look Who's Calling," *Sales & Marketing Management* (May 1998), pp. 43–46.

35. This discussion is based on Dalrymple, Cron, and DeCarlo, *Sales Management*, pp. 325–31.

36. See, for example, "What Do Customers Hate about Salespeople?" *Sales & Marketing Management*; "What Buyers Look For," *Sales & Marketing Management* (August 1995), p. 31; and "The Best Sales Reps Will Take On Their Bosses for You," *Purchasing* (November 7, 1996), p. 81.

37. Weitz, Castleberry, and Tanner, *Selling*, p. 21. For further reading see Daniel Goleman, "What Makes a Leader?" *Harvard Business Review* (November–December 1998), pp. 93–102; A. Fisher, "Success Secret: A High Emotional IQ," *Fortune* (October 26, 1998), pp. 293–98; and Daniel Goleman, *Working with Emotional Intelligence* (New York: Bantam, 1999).

38. www.statcan.ca, downloaded September 5, 2001.

39. "America's 25 Best Sales Forces," *Sales & Marketing Management*.

40. See, for example, Nora Wood, "What Motivates Best?" *Sales & Marketing Management* (September 1998), pp. 71–78; Melanie Berger, "When Their Ship Comes In," *Sales & Marketing Management* (April 1997), pp. 60–65; William L. Cron, Alan J. Dubinsky, and Ronald E. Michaels, "The Influence of Career Stages on Components of Salesperson Motivation," *Journal of Marketing* (January 1988), pp. 78–82; Pradeep K. Tyagi, "Relative Importance of Key Job Dimensions and Leadership Behaviors in Motivating Salesperson Work

Performance," *Journal of Marketing* (Summer 1985), pp. 76–86; and Richard C. Beckerer, Fred Morgan, and Lawrence Richard, "The Job Characteristics of Industrial Salespersons: Relationship of Motivation and Satisfaction," *Journal of Marketing* (Fall 1982), pp. 125–35.

41. This breakdown is given in Dalrymple, Cron, and DeCarlo, *Sales Management*, p. 476.

42. "Mary Kay's Off-Road Bonus," *Business Week* (April 6, 1998), p. 8.

43. "Number Crunching," *Sales & Marketing Management* (September 2000), pp. 79–88.

44. For further reading, see Goutam N. Challagolla and Tasadduq A. Shervani, "A Measurement Model of the Dimensions and Types of Output and Behavior Control: An Empirical Test in the Salesforce Context," *Journal of Business Research* (July 1997), pp. 159–72; and Gregory A. Rich, William H. Bommer, Scott B. McKenzie, Philip M. Podsakoff, and Jonathan L. Johnson, "Apples and Apples or Apples and Oranges? A Meta-Analysis of Objective and Subjective Measures of Salesperson Performance," *Journal of Personal Selling & Sales Management* (Fall 1999), pp. 41–52.

45. "Measuring Sales Effectiveness," *Sales & Marketing Management* (October 2000), p. 136; "Quota Busters," *Sales & Marketing Management* (January 2001), pp. 59–63.

46. Melissa Campanelli, "Eastman Chemical: A Formula for Quality," *Sales & Marketing Management* (October 1994), p. 88; William Keenan, Jr., "What's Sales Got to Do with It?" *Sales & Marketing Management* (March 1994), pp. 66–70; and Cravens, "The Changing Role of the Sales Force," *Marketing Management*.

47. "Costly Lessons Abound with SFA Programs," *Marketing News* (April 9, 2001), pp. 5–6.

48. Cravens, "The Changing Role of the Sales Force," *Marketing Management*.

49. Robert L. Lindstrom, "Training Hits the Road," *Sales & Marketing Management*, part 2 (June 1995), pp. 10–14.

50. "Going Mobile, Part 2," *Sales & Marketing Management* (June 1994), p. 5.

51. "Supercharged Sell," *Inc. Tech* (November 1998), pp. 42–50.

52. "Intranets Grow Up," *Sales & Marketing Management* (December 2000), p. 105.

Reebok: This case was prepared by Giana Eckhardt.

PART 4 CASE

1. Jeet Heer, "Books for a song," *National Post* (August 30, 2001), p. B1.

2. Venkatesh Shankar, Gregory Carpenter, and Lakshman Krishnamurthi, "Late Mover Advantage: How Innovative Late Entrants Outsell Pioneers," *Journal of Marketing Research* (February 1998), p. 54.

3. Mark Tebbe, "Don't count out the brick-and-mortar companies yet," *InfoWorld* (June 29, 1999), p. 27.

4. Mark Evans, "Canadians trail U.S. in e-commerce," *The Globe and Mail*, (July 20, 1999), p. B5.

5. Chapters Inc, Fiscal 1998 Annual Report.

6. Paul Briggs, "A New Chapter," *Canadian Transportation and Logistics*, November/December 1998, p. 46.

7. Mikala Folb, "Digital Marketing–Online Book," *Marketing* (January 25, 1999), p. 15.

8. Ibid.

9. Sean Silcoff, "Secrets of a best seller," *Canadian Business* (June 26–July 10, 1999), p. 90.

10. John F. Baker, "Northern lights," *Publishers Weekly* (May 31, 1999), p. 52.

11. John F. Baker, "Canada: If you can make it here, you'll make it anywhere," *Publishers Weekly* (May 25, 1998), p. 41.

12. John F. Baker, "Northern lights," *Publishers Weekly* (May 31, 1999), p. 52.

13. "2001: What Odyssey? The Canadian book business faces challenges on all fronts," *Quill and Quire* (February 2001), p. 7.

14. Devin Crawley, "Chapters financials hobbled by Pegasus," *Quill and Quire* (August, 2001), p. 6; and John Lorinc, "Troubleshooting: To revitalize an overextended chain, Chapters' new executive team must get back to bookselling basics," *Quill and Quire* (September 2001), p. 17.

15. Canadian Press Newswire, "Major events in Canadian retailing during the past year," December 27, 2001 and Canadian News Facts, "Chapters capitulates to Trilogy," January 16–31, 2001.

16. Leah Eichler, "Publishers optimistic about new chain," *Publishers Weekly* (May 14, 2001), p. S5.

17. "Chapters-Indigo merger approved," *Canadian News Facts* (April 1–15, 2001), p. 6225.

18. Gary Norris, "Indigo books operating profit but $31.3 M net loss, expects "challenging" Xmas," *Canadian Press Newswire* (November 20, 2001).

19. Marina Strauss, "Chapters Indigo online traffic slows as rival Amazon lures Canadian readers," *Canadian Press Newswire* (November 16, 2001); and Hollie Shaw, "Indigo Web site executive stepping down," *Financial Post-National Post* (November 30, 2001), p. FP2.

20. "2001: What odyssey?"

21. Grant Buckler, "Don't put up a wall display screen yet: e-books may be convenient, but books still hold a lot of appeal," *Computer Dealer News* (November 3 2000), p. 18.

22. James Careless, "Publishing turns a new page," *eBusiness Journal* (July 1999), p. 11.

23. Issie Rabinovitch, "Tech novations," *CA Magazine* (May 2001), p. 16.

CHAPTER 21

1. Rafi A. Mohammed, Robert J. Fisher, Bernard J. Jaworski, and Aileen M. Cahill, *Internet Marketing: Building Advantage in a Networked Economy* (Burr Ridge, IL: McGraw-Hill/Irwin, 2002); and Yoram Wind, Vijay Mahajan with Robert E. Gunther, *Convergence Marketing* (Upper Saddle River, NJ: Prentice Hall, 2002).

2. "NPD e-Visory Report Shows Offline Sales Benefit from Online Browsing," *The NPD Group Press Release* (July 21, 2001).

3. Jupiter Media Matrix, "Industry Projections," www.jmm.com, downloaded September 22, 2001.

4. Retail Council of Canada, "The Canadian Online Retailing Report," prepared by The Boston Consulting Group, July 2000.

5. "Strip Malls Are Gateway Country," *The Industry Standard* (November 27–December 4, 2000), pp. 82–86.

6. "The Five-Year Forecast," *The Industry Standard* (March 26, 2001), pp. 82–83.

7. Michael Weiss, "Online America," *American Demographics* (March 21, 2001), pp. 53–60.

8. Mohammed et al., *Internet Marketing*.

9. Adrian J. Slywotzky, "The Age of the Choiceboard," *Harvard Business Review* (January–February 2000), pp. 40–41.

10. Christine Bittar, "Reflect: A Palatable Model," *Brandweek* (April 2, 2001), pp. 18–24; and "Reflect.com Shines Despite Downturn," *Silicon Valley Business iNK* (May 4, 2001), pp. 31–32.

11. For a description of collaborative filtering and similar types of systems, see Ward Hanson, *Principles of Internet Marketing* (Cincinnati, OH: South-Western College Publishing, 2000), pp. 207–19.

12. Michael Grebb, "Behavioral Science," *Business 2.0* (March 2000), p. 112.

13. Alan Rosenspan, "Participation Marketing," *Direct Marketing* (April 2001), pp. 54–66.

14. Ipsos-Reid, "Online Security and Privacy Concerns on the Increase in Canada," Press Release, November 28, 2001 (www.angusreid.com/media).

15. Chris Daniels, "E-mails with edge," *Marketing* (February 18, 2002), p. 8.

16. This discussion is drawn from Jeffrey F. Rayport and Bernard J. Jaworski, *e-Commerce* (Burr Ridge, IL: McGraw-Hill/Irwin MarketspaceU, 2001); and Mohammed et al., *Internet Marketing*.

17. The Canadian Internet Fact Page (www.angusreid.com/ca/data/dsp_little_cdn_fact_book.cfm); Canadian Netizens Report, CF Group, March 2002 (www.cfgroup.ca/services/syndicated-interactive-cn.html).

18. "Statistics: U.S. Online Shoppers," Shop.org. downloaded September 14, 2001.

19. "The Clicks-and-Bricks Way to Buy That Car," *Business Week* (May 7, 2001), pp. 128–30; and *The Next Chapter in Business-to-Consumer E-Commerce* (Boston: The Boston Consulting Group, March 2001).

20. "Statistics: U.S. Online Shoppers," Shop.org.

21. Weiss, "Online America," *American Demographics*.

22. "Future Shop," *Forbes ASAP* (April 6, 1998), pp. 37–45; and Foley and Sutton, "Boom Time for Electronic Commerce."

23. "The E-commerce Cometh," *Brandweek* (September 21, 1998), p. 10.

24. The breakdown shown in this figure consolidates several estimates, principally from Juniper Communications and Forrester Research. See, for example, "Online Shopping Revenues by Type: 1996–2002," *Advertising Age* (October 26, 1998), p. S14.

25. Marcie Sayiner, "Canadians boost online spending," Ipsos-Reid Press Release, March 13, 2001 (www.angusreid.com).

26. "How to Lose a Customer in a Matter of Seconds," *Fortune* (June 12, 2000), p. 326.

27. Jerry Wind and Arvind Rangaswamy, "Customerization: The Next Revolution in Mass Customization," *Journal of Interactive Marketing* (Winter 2001), pp. 13–32.

28. Mohammed et al., *Internet Marketing*.

29. "Global Babble," *Forbes* (October 15, 2001), p. 51.

30. "What's So New about the 'New Economy'? Glad You Asked . . ." *Business 2.0* (August/September 2001), p. 84.

31. For references on buzz and viral marketing, see "Buzz Marketing," *Business Week* (July 30, 2001), pp. 50–56; Renée Dye, "The Buzz on Buzz," *Harvard Business Review* (November–December 2000), pp. 139–46; "The Cool Kids Are Doing It. Should You?" *Business 2.0* (November 2001), pp. 140–41; "This Is One Virus You Want to Spread," *Fortune* (November 27, 2000), pp. 297–300; and "Why Are These CEOs Smiling?" *Time* (November 5, 2001), pp. Y1–Y4.

32. "Now Is the Price Right?" *Smart Business* (February 2001), pp. 36–38; and "Price Isn't Everything," *The Wall Street Journal* (July 12, 1999), p. R20.

33. Paul Hunt, "Pricing to Make a Net Profit," *Marketing*, January 29, 2001.

34. Weiss, "Online America," *American Demographics*.

35. "Branding on the Net," *Business Week*.

36. "Exposure in Cyberspace," *The Wall Street Journal* (March 21, 2001), p. B1; "Today's Privacy Policies Don't Protect e-Shoppers, Advocate Charges," *Computer World* (April 24, 2001), pp. 42–43; Pamela Paul, "Mixed Signals," *American Demographics* (July 2001), pp. 45–49; and "It's My Life," *The Wall Street Journal* (October 29, 2001), p. R9.

37. Clay Hathorn, "Online Business: Trying to Turn Cookies into Dough," Microsoft Internet Magazine Archive, www.microsoft.com, downloaded February 15, 1999.

38. This discussion is based on "By the Numbers: Buying Breakdown," *The Wall Street Journal* (September 24, 2001), p. R4; "Factoids," *Research Alert* (November 17, 2000), p. 4; and Weiss, "Online America," *American Demographics*.

39. Weiss, "Online America," *American Demographics*.

40. "NPD e-Visory Report Shows Offline Sales Benefit from Online Browsing," The NPD Group Press Release.

41. Lesley Young, "Provincial privacy regs on the way," *Marketing* (August 27, 2001).

42. For an extended discussion on leveraging multiple channels with multichannel marketing, see Ranjay Gulati and Jason Garino, "Get the Right Mix of Bricks and Clicks," *Harvard Business Review* (May–June 2000), pp. 107–14.

43. "Office Depot Finds an E-Business That Works," *Fortune* (March 25, 2001), p. 98.

44. *Multi-Channel Integration: The New Retail Battleground* (Columbus, OH: PricewaterhouseCoopers, March 2001); and Richard Last, "JCPenney Internet Commerce," presentation at Southern Methodist University (February 12, 2001).

45. Michael Krantz, "Click Till You Drop," *Time* (July 20, 1998), pp. 34–39.

46. *Multi-Channel Integration: The New Retail Battleground*.

47. *Fighting Fire with Water—from Channel Conflict to Confluence* (Cambridge, MA: Bain & Company, July 1, 2000).

48. "Can the Internet Hot-Wire P&G?" *Smart Business* (January 2001), pp. 69–79.

49. Tom Duncan, *IMC: Using Advertising and Promotion to Build Brands* (New York: McGraw-Hill, 2002); and Larry Chiagouris and Brandt Wansley, "Branding on the Internet," *Marketing Management* (Summer 2000), pp. 35–38.

Connecting and Communicating Without Wires: This case was written by Debi Andrus. Sources include an interview with Dr. Jeff Rabin, Technology Analyst, Dundee Securities, June 14, 2002 and information from David Hodgson and Jeff Rabin, "The Oncoming Bluetooth Juggernaut," *Investment Research Report*, Dundee Securities, November 9, 2000; David Atkin, "Bluetooth ready to bite into wide product use: Moves beyond mere hype," *Financial Post-National Post* (January 25, 2001), p. C8; www.arkon.bc.ca; www.psinaptic.com and www.synchropoint.com; "Bluetooth goes mass market in phone, car, fridge," www.globeandmail.com (June 14, 2002); Andrew Wahl, "The Great Wireless Hype," *Canadian Business* (February 18, 2002), p. 33; Gerry Blackwell, "Your future is wireless," *Profit–The Magazine for Canadian Entrepreneurs* (April, 2001), p. 27.

CHAPTER 22

1. Richard Gibson, "A Cereal Maker's Quest for the Next Grape-Nuts," *The Wall Street Journal* (January 23, 1997), pp. B1, B7.

2. David Leonhardt, "Cereal-Box Killers Are on the Loose," *Business Week* (October 12, 1998), pp. 74–77.

3. 1997 General Mills Annual Report (Minneapolis: General Mills, Inc., 1997), p. 5.

4. 2000 General Mills Annual Report (Minneapolis: General Mills, Inc., 2000), p. 2; 2000 Kellogg's Annual Report (Battle Creek: Kellogg Company, 2000), p. 7; Alejandro Bodipo-Memba, "Kellogg's Concedes Top Spot to Rival," *Detroit Free Press* (February 22, 2001) (see www.freep.com/newslibrary to access the article online).

5. H. D. Cantu, "Kellogg's Teaching Tony the Tiger Spanish," *Corvallis Gazette-Times* (February 25, 2000), p. C5; and 2000 General Mills Annual Report (Minneapolis: General Mills, Inc., 2000), pp. 2–3, 12–13.

6. Ellen Neuborne, "MMM! Cereal for Dinner," *Business Week* (November 24, 1997), pp. 105–6.

7. Ann Merrill, "Pillsbury Acquisition a Done Deal," *Star Tribune* (October 24, 2001), pp. A1, A10.

8. Roger A. Kerin, P. Rajan Varadarajan, and Robert A. Peterson, "First-Mover Advantage: A Synthesis, Conceptual Framework, and Research Proposition," *Journal of Marketing* (October 1992), pp. 33–52; and Pankaj Ghemawat, "Sustainable Advantage," *Harvard Business Review* (September–October 1986), pp. 53–58.

9. Murali K. Mantrala, Prabhakant Sirha, and Andris A. Zoltners, "Impact of Resource Allocation Rules on Marketing Investment-Level Decisions and Profitability," *Journal of Marketing Research* (May 1992), pp. 162–75.

10. Vanitha Swaminathan, Richard J. Fox, and Srinivas K. Reddy, "The Impact of Brand Extension Introduction on Choice," *Journal of Marketing* (October 2001), pp. 1–15; Deborah Roedder-John, Barbara Loken, and Christopher Joiner, "The Negative Impact of Extensions:

Can Flagship Products Be Diluted?" *Journal of Marketing* (January 1998), pp. 19–32; and Akshay R. Rao, Lu Qu, and Robert W. Ruekert, "Signalling Unobservable Product Quality through a Brand Ally," *Journal of Marketing Research* (May 1999), pp. 258–68.

11. This discussion and Figure 22–3 are adapted from Stanley F. Stasch and Patricia Longtree, "Can Your Marketing Planning Procedures Be Improved?" *Journal of Marketing* (Summer 1980), p. 82; by permission of the American Marketing Association.

12. Adapted with permission of The Free Press, a Division of Macmillan, Inc., from *Competitive Advantage: Creating and Sustaining Superior Performance* by Michael E. Porter. Copyright 1985 by Michael E. Porter.

13. William B. Wertner, and Jeffrey L. Kerr, "The Shifting Sands of Competitive Advantage," *Business Horizons* (May–June, 1995), pp. 11–17.

14. Michael Treacy and Fred Wiersoma, "How Market Leaders Keep Their Edge," *Fortune* (February 5, 1995), pp. 88–89.

15. Keith Naughton and Bill Viasie, "The Nostalgia Boom," *Business Week* (March 23, 1998), pp. 58–64; and David Woodruff and Keith Naughton, "Hard Driving Boss," *Business Week* (October 5, 1998), pp. 82–90.

16. Richard Siklos and Catherine Yang, "Welcome to the 21st Century," *Business Week* (January 24, 2000), pp. 36–47; and Carol J. Loomis, "AOL 1 TWX 5 ???" *Fortune* (February 7, 2000), pp. 81–84; and "Sears Buying Catalog Giant Lands' End," *Portland Press* (May 14, 2002), pp. 1A, 10A; and Carolyn Green, "Canadian Tire: Backing the Status Quo," *Canadian Retailer*, www.retailcouncil.org, downloaded May 5, 2002.

17. John Greenwald, "Slice, Dice, and Devour," *Time* (October 26, 1998), pp. 64–66.

18. Stratford Sherman, "How Intel Makes Spending Pay Off," *Fortune* (February 22, 1993), pp. 57–61.

19. Lee Ginsburg and Neil Miller, "Value-Driven Management," *Business Horizons* (May–June 1992), pp. 23–27; Richard L. Osborn, "Core Value Statement: The Corporate Compass," *Business Horizons* (September–October 1991), pp. 28–34; and Charles E. Watson, "Managing with Integrity: Social Responsibilities of Business as Seen by America's CEOs," *Business Horizons* (July–August 1991), pp. 99–109.

20. Reprinted by permission of the *Harvard Business Review*. An exhibit from "Making Your Marketing Strategy Work" by Thomas V. Bonoma (March/April 1984), Copyright ©1984 by the President and Fellows of Harvard College; all rights reserved; and Charles H. Noble and Michael P. Mokwa, "Implementing Marketing Strategies: Developing and Testing a Managerial Theory," *Journal of Marketing* (October 1999), pp. 57–74.

21. Julia Angwin, "Latest Dot-Com Fad Is a Bit Old-Fashioned: It's Called Profitability," *The Wall Street Journal* (August 14, 2001), pp. A1, A6; Jerry Useem, "Dot-Coms: What Have We Learned," *Fortune* (October 30, 2000), pp. 82–96.

22. Jeffrey A. Krames, *The Jack Welch Lexicon of Leadership* (New York: McGraw-Hill, 2002), pp. 54–56, 105–8, 187–88; Robert Slater, *Jack Welch and the GE Way* (New York: McGraw-Hill, 1999), pp. 59–68, 77–88, 279–86: Nicholas Stein, "The World's Most Admired Companies," *Fortune* (October 2, 2000), pp. 183–91; and Jim Rohwer, "GE Digs into Asia," *Fortune* (October 2, 2000), pp. 165–78.

23. Daniel Roth, "This Ain't No Pizza Party," *Fortune* (November 9, 1998), pp. 158–64.

24. Thomas J. Peters and Robert H. Waterman, Jr., *In Search of Excellence: Lessons from America's Best-Run Companies* (New York: Harper & Row, 1982).

25. Tom Peters, "Winners Do Hundreds of Percent over Norm," *Minneapolis Star Tribune* (January 8, 1985), p. 5B; and Ben Rich and Leo Janos, *Skunk Works* (Boston: Little Brown, 1994), pp. 51–53.

26. Peter Galuska, Ellen Neuborne, and Wendy Zeliner, "P&G's Hottest New Product: P&G," *Business Week* (October 5, 1998), pp. 92–96.

27. Robert W. Ruekert and Orville W. Walker, Jr., "Marketing's Interaction with Other Functional Units: A Conceptual Framework and Empirical Evidence," *Journal of Consumer Marketing* (Spring 1987), pp. 1–19. Shikhar Sarin and Vijay Mahajan, "The Effect of Reward Structures on the Performance of Cross-Functional Product Development Teams," *Journal of Marketing* (April 2001), pp. 35–53; and Amy Edmondson, Richard Bohmer, and Gary Pisano, "Speeding Up Team Learning," *Harvard Business Review* (October 2001), pp. 125–32.

28. Nelson D. Schwartz, "Colgate Cleans Up," *Fortune* (April 16, 2001), pp. 179–80.

Clearly Canadian: This case was prepared by Frederick G. Crane and Steven Hartley.

PART 5 CASE

1. Ann Saccomano, "Not the same old story," *Traffic World* (June 21, 1999), p. 19.
2. Robert D. Hof and Heather Green, "How Amazon cleared that hurdle," *Business Week* (February 4, 2002), p. 60.
3. Amazon.com, *Form 10K*, 2001.
4. Allan Sloan, "An Amazonian survival strategy," *Newsweek* (April 9, 2001), p. 40.
5. Amazon.com, *Form 10K*, 1998.
6. Jim Milliot, "Book group posts solid sales gains at Amazon," *Publishers Weekly* (January 28, 2002), p. 133.
7. Robert D. Hof and Heather Green.
8. Amazon.com, *Form 10K*, 2001.
9. Amazon.com, *Form 10K*, 2001, p. 20.
10. Mark Veverka, "Plugged in: New cot.com deal signals changing times," *Barron's* (January 14, 2002), p. T3.
11. Robert D. Hof and Heather Green.
12. Barnes & Noble Inc., *The Industry Standard*, www.thestandard.net, May 6, 1999.
13. Borders Group, Inc., *The Industry Standard*, www.thestandard.net, May 6, 1999.
14. Nick Wingfield and Erin White, "Borders deal bolsters Amazon's strategy," *Wall Street Journal* (April 12, 2001), p. B13.
15. CDNow, Inc., *The Industry Standard*, www.thestand.net, May 6, 1999.
16. "Amazon.world," Newsweek (April 12, 1999), p. 14.
17. "Sony and Time Warner make music deal," *Weekly Corporate Growth Report* (July 26, 1999), p. 10293.
18. "Amazon sells coin," *New Media Age* (June 24, 1999), p. 4.
19. Alexandra Peers and Nick Wingfield, "Sotheby's, eBay team up to sell fine art online," *Wall Street Journal* (January 31, 2002), p. B8.
20. "Amazon.com Names Joseph Galli President and Chief Operation Officer," *PR Newswire* (June 25, 1999), p. 6246.
21. Ted Kemp, "Partnerships R Us," *Internetweek* (October 15, 2001), p. PG14.
22. Amazon.com, *Form 10K*, 2001, p. 1.
23. "Amazon to offer book previews," *Wall Street Journal* (October 10, 2001), p. B4.
24. "Amazon.com Names Joseph Galli President and Chief Operation Officer," *PR Newswire* (June 25, 1999), p. 6246.
25. Marina Strauss, "Amazon.com plans Canadian site," www.globeandmail.com/newsletter, May 31, 2002.
26. Marina Strauss, "Booksellers want Amazon.com site reviewed," *Globe and Mail* (June 5, 2002), B2.
27. Charles Mandel, "Book value," *Canadian Business* (October 1, 2001), p. 30.
28. Devin Crawley, "Amazon's Canadian expansion a go, despite layoffs," *Quill and Quire* (March 2001), p. 5.

29. Marina Strauss, "Amazon.com plans Canadian site,"
    www.globeandmail.com/newsletter, May 31, 2002.
30. Hollie Shaw, "E-tailers may be singing silent night this Xmas,"
    Financial Post-National Post (December 1, 2001), p. FP1.
31. Marina Strauss, "Booksellers want Amazon.com site reviewed,"
    Globe and Mail (June 5, 2002), B2.
32. "Amazon buys Egghead assets," *Wall Street Journal* (December 5,
    2001), p. A6; and "Amazon revived Egghead.com," *Chain Store Age*
    (February 2002), p. 78.

CREDITS

CHAPTER 1

p. 4, Courtesy of Rollerblade, Inc.; p. 8, Courtesy of Rollerblade, Inc.; p. 12 (top left), Courtesy of New-Product Works, p. 12 (top right), Courtesy of New-Product Works, p. 12 (bottom left), © Brian Hagiwara, p. 12 (bottom right), © Brian Hagiwara; p. 15 (left), Courtesy Wal-Mart Stores, Inc., p. 15 (right), Reprinted with permission of Lands' End, Inc.; p. 18 (top), Courtesy of Rollerblade, Inc., p. 18 (bottom), Courtesy of Rollerblade, Inc.; p. 23 (left), Produced by the Registered Nurses Association of Ontario in consultation with the Registered Practical Nurses Association of Ontario, p. 23 (right), Developed for the Alberta HIV awareness campaign for young adults; p. 27, Courtesy of Rollerblade, Inc.

CHAPTER 2

p. 28, CP/ Ryan Remiorz; p. 38 (top), Courtesy of Microsoft Corporation, p. 38 (bottom), Duncan Hines ad: Courtesy of Aurora Foods; p. 41, Courtesy of Rick Armstrong; p. 44, © 1996 Paradise Kitchen, Inc. Reprinted with permission; p. 51, Courtesy of Specialized Bicycles.

APPENDIX A

p. 58, © 1996 Paradise Kitchens, Inc. All photos and ads reprinted with permission; p. 62, © 1996 Paradise Kitchens; p. 64, © 1996 Paradise Kitchens; p. 66, © 1996 Paradise Kitchens; p. 67 (left), © 1996 Paradise Kitchens, p. 67 (right), © 1996 Paradise Kitchens.

CHAPTER 3

p. 72, Courtesy Apple Computer; p. 77 (left), © The Procter & Gamble Company. Used by Permission, p. 77 (centre), Courtesy T. Rowe Price: Photo/Getty Images, p. 77 (right), Photograph by Michael Martin. Reproduced courtesy of Ask Jeeves, Inc. and Grey Worldwide San Francisco; p. 80 (left), Chinese advertising campaign for Ford of Canada - "Rational Choice", created by Can-Asian Advertising Ltd. Creative Director: Patrick Fong. Art Director: Pauline Lee, Copywriter: Winnie Ng, p. 80 (right), Courtesy of CIBC; p. 81, Courtesy of Sobeys Inc.; p. 83, Four Seasons Hotels and Resorts; p. 84 (left), Courtesy of Sony Electronics Inc., p. 84 (centre), Courtesy of Zenith Electronics Corporation, p. 84 (right), Courtesy EchoStar Communications Corporation; p. 85 (left), Courtesy Tomra North America, p. 85 (right), Courtesy of Lever Brothers Company; p. 94, Courtesy Lotus Development Corporation, an IBM company; p. 95, Courtesy of Flyte Time.

CHAPTER 4

p. 96, © Molson Canada; p. 101, Rex USA Ltd.; p. 103, Courtesy Transparency International; p. 107, Photograph by Sharon Hoogstraten; p. 108, Courtesy of McDonald's Corporation; p. 113 (left), CP/ Jonathan Hayward, p. 113 (right), Courtesy of Sierra Wireless.

CHAPTER 5

p. 118, Courtesy Jaguar Cars, Inc.: Agency: Young and Rubicam/Irvine; p. 122, © PhotoEdit; p. 123, Courtesy Kimberly-Clark Worldwide, Inc.; p. 125, © Tropicana Products, Inc.; p. 128, Courtesy Inscape for Time Warner Interactive; p. 129 (left), "FRESH STEP ® is a registered trademark of the Clorox Pet Products Company. Used with permission, p. 129 (right), © 2001 Mary Kay, Inc. Photos by Grace Huang/ For Sarah Laird; p. 131 (left), Courtesy of Colgate-Palmolive Company; p. 131 (right), The Bayer Company; p. 135 (left), Courtesy Omega SA, p. 135 (right), Courtesy Omega SA; p. 136, Courtesy of Snickers; p. 138, Courtesy of Haggar Clothing Co.

CHAPTER 6

p. 146, © 1999 Endacott Ltd.; p. 150, Reprinted with permission of the United States Census Bureau; p. 152, Courtesy Airbus; p. 153, Courtesy of Sylvania/GTE Products Corporation; p. 155, Dan Boslery/Tony Stone Images/Getty Images; p. 160, Courtesy of Allen-Bradley Company, Inc.; p. 162, Courtesy of Covisint, L.L.C.

CHAPTER 7

p. 168, Courtesy of Inniskillen, Agency: Gee Jeffery & Partners; p. 173 (left), Courtesy of Sony Electronics, Inc., p. 173 (right), Courtesy of Bruno Magli; p. 178, Courtesy of ALMAP/BBDO, Sao Paulo; p. 179, Photo: O.Toscani, Courtesy United Colors of Benetton; p. 180, Courtesy Nestle S.A.; p. 182, Antonio Rosario/The Image Bank/Getty Images; p. 183, Dennis Cook/AP World Wide Photos; p. 184, Courtesy of the Coca-Cola Company; p. 187, Courtesy of the PRS Group; p. 188, James Shneph; p. 189 (left), Courtesy of McDonald's Corporation, p. 189 (right), Courtesy of McDonald's Corporation; p. 192, Courtesy of the Gillette Company; p. 198, Courtesy of Don Tapscott.

CHAPTER 8

p. 204, "Lord of the Rings" Copyright 2001. New Line Productions, Inc. All rights reserved. Poster appears courtesy of New Line Productions, Inc.; p. 208, Dairy Farmers of Canada advertisement developed in conjunction with its advertising agency Allard-Johnson Communications; p. 212, Courtesy Ocean Spray; p. 215, Courtesy Teenage Research Unlimited; p. 220, Courtesy of Wendy's International; p. 221, Courtesy of Grocery Gateway; p. 222 (left), Courtesy the Gillette Company, p. 222 (right), Courtesy Sketchers.

CHAPTER 9

p. 236, © Brent Jones; p. 237, Courtesy Heelys™, Heeling Sports Limited; p. 238 (top), © M. Hruby, p. 238 (centre), © M. Hruby, p. 238 (bottom), Courtesy Heelys™. Heeling Sports Limited; p. 243, Courtesy of Customatix; p. 247, Courtesy of Bell Mobility; p. 248, Courtesy of Xerox Corporation; p. 249, DILBERT reprinted by permission of United Features Syndicate, Inc.; p. 251, Courtesy of Wendy's International Inc.; p. 253, Courtesy of Apple Computers; p. 259, Courtesy Nokia; p. 262, Photo provided courtesy of Harlequin Enterprises Limited; p. 263, CP/GNM/Fred Lum.

CHAPTER 10

p. 268, Courtesy 3M; p. 271, Nike; p. 272, Courtesy of Raymond Weil; p. 275 (left), © Laura Johansen, p. 275 (right), Courtesy of Microsoft Corporation, Agency: Edelman Worldwide/Seattle; p. 276a, Courtesy Canon U.S.A; Agency: DCA Advertising Inc., p. 276b, Courtesy Palm Inc., p. 276c, Courtesy QuickBooks ® 2002; Courtesy Intuit, p. 276d, Courtesy Swatch USA; p. 278 (left), New Product Showcase and Learning Center, Inc. / Photograph by Roger Haller, p. 278 (right), Courtesy of the Original Pet Drink Co., Inc.; p. 280, Dr. Robert McMath; p. 282, Polaroid Corporation; p. 284, Courtesy of Frito-Lay, Inc.; p. 286 (top), Courtesy Merck & Co. Inc., p. 286 (bottom), Jose Azel/Aurora; p. 289, Courtesy of the Hewlett-Packard Company.

CHAPTER 11

p. 295, Courtesy of Clearly Canadian; p. 296, Courtesy of Clearly Canadian; p. 299 (left), Courtesy American Honda Motor Co., Inc. Agency: Rubin Postaer & Associates; p. 299 (right), © Toshiba America Consumer Products, Inc.; p. 304, CP/AP/Keith Srakocic; p. 307 (left), Courtesy of Advance Research Labs, p. 307 (right), Courtesy of Liz Clairborne, Agency: Avrett Free & Ginsberg, Models: Roberto Sanches & Nadja Scantamburlo, Photographer: J.Westley Jones; p. 309 (top), CP; p. 309 (bottom), Courtesy of Elite Foods, Inc.; p. 312 (left), Courtesy of Black & Decker (US), Inc., p. 312 (right), Courtesy of DeWalt Industrial Tool Company; p. 314, Courtesy of Pez Candy, Inc.; p. 315, Courtesy of The Coca-Cola Company;

p. 316, © The Procter & Gamble Company. Used with permission; p. 319, © 2001 BMW of North America. Used with permission. The BMW name and logo are registered trademarks; p. 322.

CHAPTER 12

p. 322, Courtesy of the Hard Rock Café Montreal; p. 326, Courtesy of Fairmont Hotels & Resorts; p. 327, Courtesy of IBM: Agency: Ogilvy & Mather/New York; p. 333 (left), Courtesy of McDonald's Corporation, p. 333 (centre), Courtesy of Sprint, p. 333 (right), Courtesy of Canadian Red Cross; p. 334, Courtesy of Lasik; p. 335, Courtesy of the Legislative Assembly of Nunavut; p. 336, Courtesy of Mr. Lube; p. 338, Courtesy of Dr. Frederick G. Crane.

CHAPTER 13

p. 342, John Sylvester Photography; p. 345, Courtesy of Automobili Lamborghini S.p.A; p. 348 (left), Michael J. Hurby, p. 348 (right), Courtesy of Nike, Inc.; p. 351, Courtesy of Fiat USA, Inc.

CHAPTER 14

p. 364, Courtesy The Gillette Company; p. 368, © Terry McElroy; p. 370, CP/Frank Gunn; p. 371, Courtesy Panasonic Consumer Electronics Company; p. 375, © Ted Soqui; p. 376, Sharon Hoogstraten; p. 379, Courtesy of The Toro Company; p. 381, CP/HALC/Tim Krochak.

APPENDIX B

p. 394, Courtesy of the Caplow Company.

CHAPTER 15

p. 396, Courtesy of Avon Products; p. 404, Courtesy of Nestle S.A.; p. 408 (left), © M. Hruby, p. 408 (right), © M. Hruby; p. 409, Courtesy of Kensington Florist, Calgary Alberta. http://www.kensingtonflorist.com/; p. 411, Courtesy of Visa; p. 412, Courtesy Apple Computer; p. 413, Courtesy of Dai-Ichi Kikaku Co., Ltd. and Warner-Lambert.

CHAPTER 16

p. 420, Reprinted with permission of *Business Week*; illustration by David Cale; p. 424, Courtesy Saturn Corporation; p. 426 (left), Dell Computer Corporation; p. 426 (right), Courtesy Wal-Mart Store, Inc.; p. 427, Courtesy of J.D. Edwards World Solutions Company; p. 430, Mark Richards/Photo Edit; p. 432 (left), Courtesy of FedEx Corporation, p. 432 (right), Courtesy of Emery Worldwide; p. 434, Courtesy of Maersk, Inc.; p. 436, Courtesy of Rapistan Demag Corporation; p. 437 (left), Fritz Hoffman/Image works, p. 437 (right), Fritz Hoffman/Image Works; p. 438, © John B. Boykin/The Stock Market.

CHAPTER 17

p. 442, Cleo Photography, Whitby, Ontario; p. 444, Reprinted with permission of Tandy Corporation; p. 446 (top), Corbis/Bettmann, p. 446 (bottom), Courtesy Levi Strauss USA; p. 448, Reprinted with permission of Tandy Corporation; p. 451, Courtesy of Marconi Commerce Systems; p. 452a, Courtesy of L.L. Bean, Inc., p. 452b, Courtesy of QVC Network, Inc., p. 452c, Courtesy of Mysimon.com, p. 452d, Courtesy of Retail Canada; p. 453 (left), Courtesy Easy Everything the Internet Shop; p. 453 (right), Courtesy Easy Everything the Internet Shop; p. 454, Courtesy Public Technologies Multimedia Inc./Montreal; p. 460, Courtesy Taco Bell.

CHAPTER 18

p. 466, © Network Aspen; p. 469, Courtesy Mercedes-Benz U.S.A., Inc.; p. 474 (top), Courtesy Fence Magazine, p. 474 (bottom), Courtesy of Volkswagen of America, Inc.; p. 476 (top), Photography by Greg Wolff, p. 476 (bottom left), Courtesy Gulfstream Aircraft, Inc., p. 476 (bottom right), Courtesy H.J. Heinz Company. Used with permission; p. 478, Courtesy the Quantum Group.

CHAPTER 19

p. 492, Courtesy of Princeton Video Image; p. 494 (left), Reprinted with permission of the Jeep ® Brand, a Division of Daimler-Chrysler, p. 494 (centre), Courtesy of the Xerox Company, p. 494 (right), Courtesy FTD; p. 495, Courtesy of DDB Needham Worldwide and The Dial Corporation; p. 498, © 2002 Molson Canada; p. 500, Tom Sandler Photography; p. 503 (top), Courtesy of Ford Motor Company, p. 503 (bottom), Courtesy Teen People Magazine; A Division of Time, Inc.; p. 504 (left), Courtesy IBM; Agency; Ogilvy Interactive, p. 504 (right); p. 505, Federation des producteurs d'oeufs de consommation due Quebec; p. 506, Courtesy Captive Network; p. 508, Courtesy Starch™; p. 512 (top), Courtesy of Canadian Tire; p. 513 (top), © Shooting Star, p. 513 (bottom), Time Photo Illustration: Leave it to Beaver: Photofest.

CHAPTER 20

p. 520, Courtesy of Xerox Corporation; p. 523, © John Madere; p. 525, Mitch Kezar/Stone; p. 527, Courtesy Xerox Corporation; p. 529, Einzig Photography; p. 530, Steve Mason/Getty Images/Photodisc; p. 532, Ken Ross/FPG International; p. 539, Colour Day Production/ The Image Bank; p. 540, Courtesy of Mary Kay; p. 541 (left), Courtesy of Toshiba America Medical Systems and Interactive Media, p. 541 (right), Courtesy of Toshiba America Medical Systems and Interactive Media; p. 542, Jose Pelaez/The Stock Market; p. 545, Courtesy Reebok International Ltd.; p. 548, CP Picture Archive, Toronto Star.

CHAPTER 21

p. 554, © Tom White Images; p. 557 (left), Courtesy Orbitz, p. 557 (right), © 2001 Hertz System, Inc. Hertz is a registered service mark and trademark of Hertz System, Inc.; p. 560 (top), Weave Communications; p. 570, © Sears Canada Inc 2002; p. 571, Courtesy of Canadian Tire.

CHAPTER 22

p. 578, © M. Hruby; p. 581, © M. Hruby; p. 585 (left), Courtesy Wal-Mart, Inc., p. 585 (right), Courtesy Volkswagen of America, Inc.; p. 590, © M. Hruby; p. 591, Courtesy of Papa John's International; p. 593, GE Lighting Group; p. 595 (top), Courtesy Lockheed, p. 595 (bottom), 2002 General Motors Corporation. Used with permission GM Media Archives; p. 599, © M. Hruby; p. 603, Courtesy Clearly Canadian; p. 605, CP/Junji Kurokawa.

NAME INDEX

COMPANY/PRODUCT INDEX

SUBJECT INDEX

McGraw-Hill Ryerson
Online Learning Centre

McGraw-Hill Ryerson offers you an online resource that combines the best content with the flexibility and power of the Internet. Organized by chapter, the BERKOWITZ Online Learning Centre (OLC) offers the following features to enhance your learning and understanding of Health:

- Online Study Guide
- Microsoft® PowerPoint® Presentation
- Internet Application Questions
- Web Links

By connecting to the "real world" through the OLC, you will enjoy a dynamic and rich source of current information that will help you get more from your course and improve your chances for success, both in the course and in the future.

For the Instructor

Downloadable Supplements

All key supplements are available, password-protected for instant access!

PageOut   **PageOut**
Create a custom course Website with **PageOut**, free with every McGraw-Hill textbook.

To learn more, contact your McGraw-Hill publisher's representative.

Create your own course Web page for free, quickly and easily. Your professionally designed Web site links directly to OLC material, allows you to post a class syllabus, offers an online gradebook, and much more! Visit www.pageout.net

Primis Online   **Primis Online**

Primis Online gives you access to our resources in the best medium for your students: printed textbooks or electronic ebooks. There are over 350,000 pages of content available from which you can create customized learning tools from our online database at www.mhhe.com/primis

Marketing Magazine

Free online access to this leading magazine will help you bring current, Canadian examples into your classroom.